PAGE
44

ON THE ROAD

YOUR COMPLETE DESTINATION GUIDE
In-depth reviews, detailed listings
and insider tips

Langkawi, Kedah &
Perlis (p183)

Penang
(p149)

Perak
(p116)

East Coast Islands,
Kelantan & Terengganu
(p272)

Brunei
(p454)

Sabah
(p304)

Kuala Lumpur
(p46)

Pahang &
Tioman Island
(p242)

Selangor & Negeri
Sembilan (p97)

Johor
(p227)

Sarawak
(p379)

Melaka
(p207)

Singapore
(p473)

Directory A–Z 592
Transport 600
Health........................... 606
Language 611
Index............................. 621
Map Legend ....

Health

FORE YOU GO

* **Hepatitis A** Provides almost 100% protection for up to a year. A booster after 12 months provides at least another 20 years' protection.
* **Hepatitis B** Now considered routine for most travellers. Given as three shots over six months. A rapid schedule is also available, as is a combined vaccination with Hepatitis A.

D1166056

Cristian Bonetto, Celeste Brash, Joshua Samuel Brown,
Austin Bush, Adam Karlin, Daniel Robinson

welcome to Malaysia, Singapore & Brunei

Rainforests & Oceans

For many people this region is defined by its equatorial rainforest. Significant chunks of primary jungle – among the most ancient ecosystems on earth – remain intact, protected by national parks and conservation projects. Seemingly impenetrable foliage and muddy, snaking rivers conjure up the 'heart of darkness' – but join a ranger-led nature walk, for example, and you'll learn about the mind-boggling biodiversity all around, from the pitcher plants, lianas and orchids of the humid lowlands, to the conifers and rhododendrons of high-altitude forests. The icing on this verdant cake is the chance to encounter wildlife in its natural habitat.

The most common sightings will be of a host of insects or colourful birdlife, but you could get lucky and spot a foraging tapir, a silvered leaf monkey or an orangutan swinging through the jungle canopy. The oceans are just as bountiful with the chance to snorkel or dive among shoals of tropical fish, paint-box dipped corals, turtles, sharks and dolphins.

Urban Adventures

If urban exploration is more your scene, you won't be disappointed either. Singapore is the region's overachiever, a showstopper of a city combining a historical legacy of elegant colonial buildings with stunning contemporary architecture and world-class

Entwined by shared history, Southeast Asia's terrific trio offer steamy jungles packed with wildlife, beautiful beaches, idyllic islands, culinary sensations and multi-ethnic cultures.

(left) Sri Mariamman Temple (p484) in Singapore's Chinatown
(below) Turtles at Sipadan, Sabah, Malaysia (p359)

attractions such as its zoo, museums and amazing botanical gardens (two of them!). Malaysia's capital, Kuala Lumpur (KL), is less organised but perhaps more appealing because of that – a place where Malay *kampung* (village) life stands cheek by jowl with the 21st-century glitz of the Petronas Towers, and shoppers shuttle from traditional wet markets to air-conditioned megamalls. The historical cores of Melaka and George Town (Penang) are on the Unesco World Heritage list for their unique architectural and cultural townscapes, developed over half a millennium of Southeast Asian cultural and trade exchange. Both should be high on your to-visit list, but if you're looking for somewhere more under-the-radar then try Brunei's surprisingly unostentatious capital Bandar Seri Begawan: its picturesque water village, Kampung Ayer, is the largest stilt settlement in the world.

Cultural Riches

Mirroring the natural environment's diversity is the region's potpourri of cultures. Muslim Malays, religiously diverse Chinese, and Hindu and Muslim Indians muddle along with aboriginal groups (the Orang Asli) on Peninsular Malaysia and Borneo's indigenous people, scores of tribes known collectively as Dayaks. Each ethnic group has its own language and cultural practices, which you can best appreciate through a packed calendar of festivals and a delicious variety of cuisines.

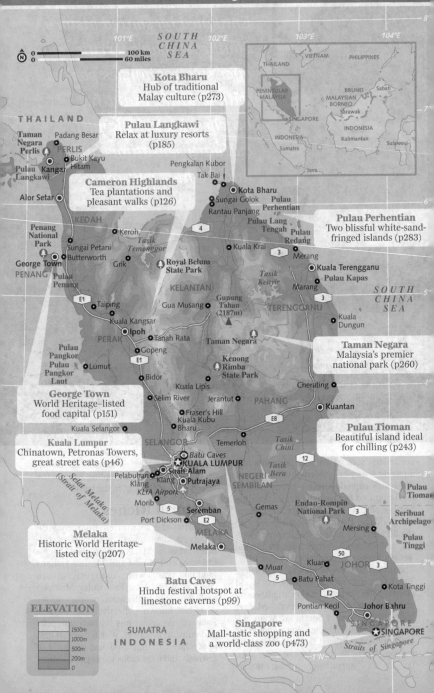

❯ Peninsular Malaysia & Singapore

Kota Bharu
Hub of traditional
Malay culture (p273)

Pulau Langkawi
Relax at luxury resorts
(p185)

Cameron Highlands
Tea plantations and
pleasant walks (p126)

Pulau Perhentian
Two blissful white-sand-
fringed islands (p283)

Taman Negara
Malaysia's premier
national park (p260)

George Town
World Heritage–listed
food capital (p151)

Pulau Tioman
Beautiful island ideal
for chilling (p243)

Kuala Lumpur
Chinatown, Petronas Towers,
great street eats (p46)

Melaka
Historic World Heritage–
listed city (p207)

Batu Caves
Hindu festival hotspot at
limestone caverns (p99)

Singapore
Mall-tastic shopping and
a world-class zoo (p473)

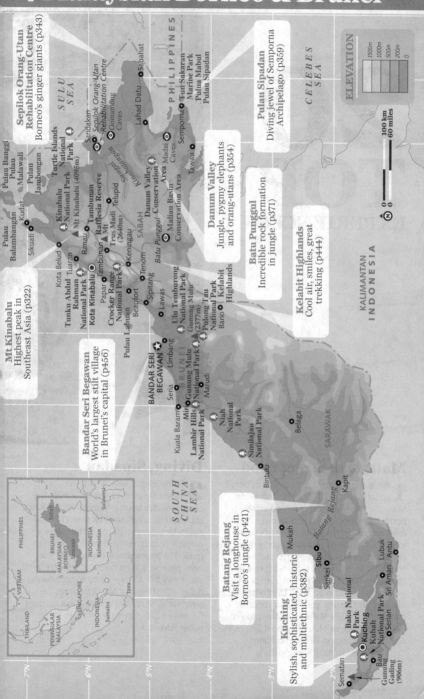

Malaysian Borneo & Brunei

Mt Kinabalu
Highest peak in Southeast Asia (p322)

Sepilok Orang-Utan Rehabilitation Centre (p343)
Borneo's ginger giants

Pulau Sipadan (p359)
Diving jewel of Semporna Archipelago

Danum Valley
Jungle, pygmy elephants and orang-utans (p354)

Batu Punggul
Incredible rock formation in jungle (p371)

Kelabit Highlands
Cool air, smiles, great trekking (p444)

Bandar Seri Begawan
World's largest stilt village in Brunei's capital (p456)

Batang Rejang
Visit a longhouse in Borneo's jungle (p421)

Kuching
Stylish, sophisticated, historic and multiethnic (p382)

ELEVATION
1500m
1000m
500m
200m
0

100 km
60 miles

20 TOP
EXPERIENCES

Malaysian Street Food

1 White tablecloth? Confounding cutlery? Snooty waiters? A roof? No thanks. In Malaysia, the best food is served in the humblest surroundings and involves the least amount of fuss. The country's seemingly countless vendors (p35) serve delicious dishes from mobile carts, stalls and shophouses, many still employing recipes and techniques handed down from previous generations. And in addition to informality, ubiquity and quality, you're also spoilt for choice; on a single Malaysian street you're likely to encounter Malay, regional Chinese, southern Indian and Western cuisines.
Central Market (p306), Kota Kinabalu

Diving, Sipadan

2 Sometimes it seems as if the world's most colourful marine life – from the commonplace to utterly alien fish, molluscs and reptiles, creatures that seem to have swum through every slice of the colour wheel – considers the seawall of Sipadan (p359) to be prime real estate. They live here, play here, hunt here and eat here, and you, lucky thing, may dance an underwater ballet with them. For any diver, from the amateur to seasoned veterans like Jacques Cousteau, Sipadan is the ultimate underwater adventure.

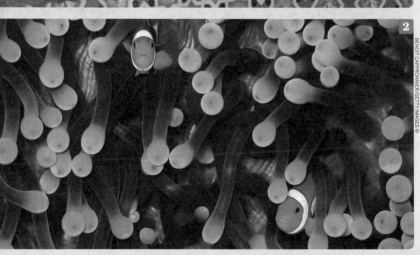

Kampung Ayer (Water Village), Brunei

3 Borneo is modernising quickly, but even the most tech-savvy entrepreneur is only a generation removed from the *kampung ayer*, or water village. Some only grow up in these waterbound communities, yet many live out their days in them. That's the case in the water village (p456) that hugs Brunei's capital, Bandar Seri Begawan, the largest of its kind in the world. Some residents live humbly, while others park sports cars before catching a water taxi home, a fascinating juxtaposition of nostalgia and development all set on stilts.

Jungle Treks, Danum Valley, Sabah

4 'Walk quickly', our guide tells us. 'Fire ants.' Once again we wonder: is this really fun? But it is. Trekking in the Danum Valley (p354) is one of the most stirring experiences in Borneo – walking through a forest that is older than humanity. And while this is no open African savannah, and spotting animals can be difficult in the brush, the wildlife we see is all the more amazing for that: iridescent flying lizards, curious frogs, emerald pit vipers and, peering out with its headlight eyes, an adorable slow loris.

Snorkelling, Pulau Perhentian, Terengganu

5 Though eastern Peninsular Malaysia has several islands offering unparalleled underwater activities, Pulau Perhentian (p283) wins when it comes to attracting snorkellers. Perhaps it's the water itself: clear and ethereally blue. Or the huge variety of marine life: sharks, tropical fish, turtles and nesting urchins. Living coral beds lie close to shore, and on most days you won't have to swim much further than the jetty at Long Beach before finding yourself inside a rainbow cloud of fish of all shapes and sizes.

ANDERS BLOMQVIST/GETTY IMAGES ©

George Town's Colonial District, Penang

6 Once abandoned by locals and seemingly forgotten by tourists, George Town (p151) has emerged as one of the region's hottest destinations in the last couple of years. The 2008 Unesco World Heritage declaration sparked a frenzy of cultural preservation, and the city's charismatic shophouses have been turned into house museums, boutique hotels and chic restaurants. Aggressive drivers aside, it's also one of the best cities in Southeast Asia to explore on foot. Pinang Peranakan Mansion (p155)

Sepilok Orang-Utan Rehabilitation Centre, Sabah

7 There is no primate quite like the orang-utan. These great apes are a stirring combination: brawn and grace; raw power and gentle restraint; cuteness. And behind their sparkling eyes lie deep reserves of what we can only call wisdom and, sometimes, sadness. All these complicated observations occur at the Sepilok Orang-Utan Rehabilitation Centre (p343), where visitors can see the apes from an often crowded viewing platform, the highlight of many a Sabah trip.

Indulgence, Pulau Langkawi, Kedah

8 Pulau Langkawi (p183) ain't called the Jewel of Kedah for nothin', and its white-sand beaches, isolated resorts, acclaimed diving and pristine jungles live up to the metaphor. Cheap booze (Langkawi is duty-free) and a decent restaurant and bar scene provide just the hint of a party vibe, while a glut of kid-friendly activities make it a great destination for families. But it's not just a holiday island; off-the-beaten-track-type exploration will reveal that Pulau Langkawi has managed to retain its endearing *kampung* soul. Tanjung Rhu beach (p189)

Kuching, Sarawak

9 Borneo's most sophisticated and stylish city, Kuching (p382) brings together an atmospheric old town, aromatic waterfront, fine cuisine and chic nightspots. But the city's biggest draw is what's nearby: some of Sarawak's finest natural sites, easy to visit on day trips. You can spot semiwild orang-utans or search out a giant Rafflesia flower in the morning, look for proboscis monkeys and wild crocs on a sundown cruise in the South China Sea, and then dine on superfresh seafood or crunchy midin fern tips. Sarawak State Assembly (p388)

Trekking, Kelabit Highlands, Sarawak

10 The air is clean and cool, the rice fields impossibly green, the local cuisine delicious and the trekking – from longhouse to longhouse – some of the best in Borneo, but the star attraction of the Kelabit Highlands (p444) is the people, justifiably famous for their ready smiles and easy way with visitors. Getting to Sarawak's remote northeastern corner is half the fun – you can either bust your butt on logging roads for 12 hours or take an exhilarating flight in a 19-seat Twin Otter turboprop. Indigenous Kelabit woman

Taman Negara, Pahang

11 To visit Taman Negara (p260) is to step back in time and experience the land as it was in primeval times. Inside this shadowy, nigh-impenetrable jungle, ancient trees with gargantuan buttressed root systems dwarf luminescent fungi, orchids, and flora rare and beautiful. Making their home within are elephants, tigers and leopards, as well as smaller wonders such as flying squirrels, lizards, monkeys, deer, tapirs and serpents of all sorts. Reticulated python

KARL LEHMANN/GETTY IMAGES ©

Mt Kinabalu, Sabah

12 It is the abode of the spirits, the highest mountain in Malaysia, one of the most dominant geographic features in North Borneo, the bone-shaking trek that has worn out countless challengers. Mt Kinabalu (p322) is all this as well as one of the most popular tourist attractions in Borneo. Don't worry – you will still have moments of utter freedom, breathing in the only alpine air in Sabah and, if you're lucky, enjoying a horizon that stretches to the Philippines. Or it will be cloudy. Whatever: the climb is still bloody exhilarating.

Cameron Highlands, Perak

13 Misty mountains, gumboots, Tudor-themed architecture, scones, strawberries and tea plantations all converge in this distinctly un-Southeast Asian destination. Activities such as self-guided hiking, nature trekking and agricultural tourism make the Cameron Highlands (p126) one of Malaysia's most worthwhile and approachable active destinations. It also represents a clever escape within a vacation, as the weather in the Cameron Highlands tends to stay cool year-round.
Boh Sungei Palas Tea Estate (p127)

Markets, Kota Bharu, Kelantan

14 A centre for Malaysian crafts, Kota Bharu (p273) offers traditional items such as batik, *kain songket* (fabric with gold thread), hand-crafted silverware, hand-carved puppets and locally made kites. Both the Central Market and the nearby Bazaar Buluh Kubuh (p279) are great places to buy spices, brassware and other local goods. For shoppers inclined to roam, the bikeable road from town to PCB beach is dotted with factories and workshops dedicated to the creation of crafts of all sorts.

Chillin', Pulau Tioman, Pahang

15 Welcome to paradise. What's your pleasure? Swimming off any of the dozens of beautiful beaches that run along Pulau Tioman's western shore? Challenging the surf that pounds the island's eastern beaches? Perhaps hiking is more your thing? If so, Tioman's myriad trails will challenge your legs, lungs and internal compass. Care to chill out by a waterfall? Swing in a hammock with a good book? Or simply do nothing? All of these goals (and others) are obtainable on Pulau Tioman (p243).

Visiting Longhouses, Sarawak

16 There's no better way to get a sense of indigenous tribal culture than to visit a longhouse (p404) – or, better yet, stay in one. Basically a whole village under one roof, these dwellings can be longer than two football fields and contain dozens of family units, each of which opens onto a covered common veran-dah used for economic activities, socialising and celebrations. All longhouses now feature at least some modern amenities, but many still have a few headhunted skulls on display. Longhouse at Sarawak Cultural Village (p404)

Jonker's Walk Night Market, Melaka

17 It starts by the river across from the pink Stadthuys building that glows in the street lights. Dr Ho Eng Hui is doing his nightly street show with a crowd in a circle around him; he makes kung-fu moves to the theme music of *Hawaii Five-O*. Edge through the crush along Jonker's Walk (p220, lined with stalls selling everything from cheap underwear to fresh sugarcane juice. Haggle, nibble and maybe stop by the Geographer cafe for a cold beer and some people-watching.

Chinatown, Kuala Lumpur

18 Plumes of smoke curl up from smouldering coils of incense, flower garlands hang like pearls from the necks of Hindu statues, and the call to prayer punctuates the honk of traffic. The temples and mosques of the city's Hindus, Muslims and Chinese Buddhists are shoulder-to-shoulder in this atmospheric neighbourhood (p51) that epitomises multicultural Malaysia. Don't miss the daytime Madras Lane hawker stalls and the bustle and fun of the night market along Jln Petaling (p72). Sze Ya Temple (p52)

Festivals, Batu Caves

19 It's always a very busy and colourful scene at this sacred Hindu shrine but, if you can, time your visit for a holy day. The biggest event is Thaipusam (p22), when around one million pilgrims converge on this giant limestone outcrop a few kilometres north of Kuala Lumpur. Guarding the 272 steps that lead up to the main Temple Cave is the 43m gilded statue of Lord Murugan, assisted by a platoon of lively macaques who show little fear in launching raids on tourists' belongings.

STUART DEE/GETTY IMAGES ©

20

HEATH HOLDEN/GETTY IMAGES ©

Singapore Zoo & Night Safari, Singapore

20 Cheeky orang-utans swinging metres above your head, a carefree sloth chomping inches away from your nose. It might sound like the depths of some primeval rainforest, but you're actually at Singapore Zoo (p493). Arguably the world's top urban animal sanctuary, its lush 28 hectares ditch soul-crunching cages for open-concept enclosures and faithfully recreated habitats. The result: happy, free-roaming animals and happy humans with unobstructed views. As the sun sinks, neighbouring Night Safari (p494) cranks up the atmosphere with its own cast of oh-so-close creatures, from swooping Malayan flying foxes to sneaky alligators.

White tigers, Singapore Zoo (p493)

need to know

Currency
» Malaysian ringgit (RM), Singapore dollar (S$), Brunei dollar (B$).

Language
» Bahasa Malaysia, English, Chinese dialects, Tamil.

When to Go

Kota Bharu
GO Mar–Nov

Penang
GO Mar–Nov

Kuala Lumpur
GO Mar–Nov

Singapore
GO Mar–Nov

Kuching
GO Mar–Nov

Tropical climate, rain year round
Tropical climate, wet & dry seasons

High Season
(Dec–Feb)

» End-of-year school holidays followed by Chinese New Year push up prices. Book transport and hotels in advance.

» Monsoon season for the east coast of Peninsula Malaysia and western Sarawak.

Shoulder
(Jul–Nov)

» July to August, vie with visitors escaping the heat of the Gulf States as the region enjoys what it calls Arab Season.

» The end of Ramadan (Hari Raya) also sees increased travel activity in the region.

Low Season
(Mar–Jun)

» Avoid the worst of the rains and humidity; there's also the chance to enjoy places without the crush of fellow tourists.

Your Daily Budget

Budget less than
RM100/ S$150/B$40

» Dorm bed; RM12–35/S$16–40/B$10.

» Hawker centres and food courts for meals.

» Use public transport; plan sightseeing around walking tours, free museums and galleries.

Midrange
RM100–400/ S$150–350/ B$40–100

» Double room in midrange hotel: RM100–400/S$100–250/B$70.

» Two-course meal in midrange restaurant RM40–60/S$50/B$10.

» Take taxis and guided tours of cities and nature sights.

Top End more than
RM400/ S$350/B$100

» Luxury double room RM450–1000/S$250–500/B$170.

» Meal in top restaurant RM200/ S$250/B$20.

Money

» ATMs widely available. Credit cards accepted by most businesses.

Visas

» Generally not required for stays of up to 60 (Malaysia), 90 (Singapore) and 30–90 days (Brunei).

Mobile Phones

» Local SIM cards can be used in most phones; if not, set your phone to roaming.

Transport

» Buses and trains run to many destinations on Peninsula Malaysia and Singapore; planes and boats go to major cities, islands and more remote destinations.

Websites

» **Tourism Malaysia** (www.tourismmalaysia. gov.my) Official national tourist-information site.

» **Visit Singapore** (www.visitsingapore. com) Official tourism board site.

» **Brunei Tourism** (www.bruneitourism. travel) Oodles of useful information.

» **Lonely Planet** (www. lonelyplanet.com) Information, bookings, forums and more.

» **Malaysiakini** (www. malaysiakini.com) Find out what's really going on in Malaysia.

Exchange Rates

Australia	A$1	RM3	S$1.28	B$1.28
Canada	C$1	RM3	S$1.23	B$1.23
Europe	€1	RM4	S$1.59	B$1.59
Japan	¥100	RM4	S$1.48	B$1.48
UK	UK£1	RM5	S$1.96	B$1.96
US	US$1	RM3	S$1.22	B$1.22

For current exchange rates see www.xe.com.

Important Numbers

	Mal	Sin	Bru
Country code	60	65	673
International access code	00	001	00
Police	999	999	993
Ambulance/Fire	994	995	991/995
Directory assistance	103	100	113

Arriving in Malaysia, Singapore & Brunei

» **Kuala Lumpur International Airport** Trains RM35; every 15 min from 5am-1am; 30 min to KL Sentral. Buses RM10; every hr from 5am to 1am; 1hr to KL Sentral. Taxis from RM75; 1hr to KL

» **Changi International Airport** MRT train, public and shuttle bus to town, 6am to midnight, S$1.80 to $9. Taxi $18-35

» **Brunei International Airport** Buses 23, 24, 36 and 38 to Bandar Seri Begawan. Taxi B$20-25

Responsible Travel

Cutting your carbon footprint by travelling overland to Peninsular Malaysia from Europe and most parts of Asia is possible as long as you're not in a hurry. The authoritative **Man in Seat 61** (www.seat61.com/Malaysia.htm) reckons it takes a minimum of 3 ½ weeks to reach KL from London by a combination of trains and buses.

Once in the region consider making your travels more sustainable by taking part in a homestay program, doing some volunteer work (p598), and supporting traditional craft industries when buying souvenirs. Check out recommendations by **Wild Asia** (www.wild asia.net), which seeks to up standards by handing out sustainable tourism awards. Also see our sustainable picks throughout the guide (indicated by ✏).

if you like...

Architecture

Vividly painted and handsomely proportioned wooden Malay houses pepper the region alongside a variety of interestingly decorated temples, mosques and churches. Adding to the rich architectural mix are colonial structures, and contemporary skyscrapers and civic complexes.

George Town Learn about the temples, shophouses, house museums and other unique structures of this Unesco World Heritage city via a guided tour. (p151)

Kampung Ayer The largest water village in the world, part of Brunei's capital, is a testament to Malay ingenuity and improvisation. (p456)

Petronas Towers The steel wrapped twin towers are the poster children of contemporary architecture in Malaysia. (p55)

Putrajaya See what a booming economy can buy in this showcase of modern urban planning and vaulting architectural ambition. (p104)

Melaka's Chinatown Malaysia's oldest functioning mosque, Catholic church and traditional Chinese temple are all with walking distance of each other. (p213)

Scenic Vistas

Bring your camera and sketch book because there's much visual beauty to capture in these three countries. As well as lush jungle scenery and idyllic palm-fringed beaches, sweeping panoramas of Southeast Asian metropolises and eye-poppingly colourful markets will be among your favourite scenic memories.

Tea plantations The Cameron Highlands' tea plantations comprise a landscape that is equal parts manicured and wild, not to mention breathtaking. (p126)

Gunung Stong State Park View one of the Peninsula's most spectacular waterfalls in this beautiful and relatively untrammeled park. (p282)

Southern Ridges Forest canopy, striking architecture and skyline views join forces on this urban nature trail along Singapore's southern coast. (p495)

Mt Kinabalu Assuming the weather is clear, you can't beat the view from the top of Malaysia's tallest mountain. (p322)

Atmosphere 360 Enjoy sweeping city views from the slowly revolving restaurant atop Menara KL. (p67)

Legendary Experiences

Malaysia, Singapore and Brunei are all steeped in legends and home to diverse cultures that have unique ways of doing things. So be prepared for lands where hungry ghosts are fed and fabled species can still be discovered in the region's dense jungles.

Cheong Fatt Tze Mansion More than just a collection of dusty antique furniture and old family photos, a visit to this refurbished George Town mansion is a fascinating crash course in feng shui and local legend. (p159)

Bukit Brown Cemetery In Singapore you'll find the largest Chinese cemetery outside of China, laced with ornate tombs and history-bearing jungle. (p496)

Endau-Rompin National Park Be alert on your jungle trek and you may just spot the Snaggle-toothed ghost – Malaysia's own yeti. (p239)

Melaka's themed trishaws Look for 'Becak Man' (with the Bat Man logo), or the Barbie mobile and turn up the sound system. (p225)

RICHARD I'ANSON/GETTY IMAGES ©

» George Town art (p162)

Museums

Learn about the region's history and salad bowl of cultures by exploring the many museums scattered across these three countries.

National Museum of Singapore Heritage architecture meets interactive ingenuity at this ode to Singaporean history, culture and food. (p476)

Asian Civilisations Museum, Singapore An epic, evocative journey through the history, beliefs and creativity of the world's largest continent. (p477)

Islamic Arts Museum, Kuala Lumpur Marvel at how craftspeople and artists have been inspired by the Muslim faith to produce gorgeous objects. (p53)

Sarawak Museum Displays one of the world's finest collections of indigenous Bornean art and artefacts. (p386)

Contemporary Art

The region's artists are a talented lot with their works on display in national institutions, commericial galleries, on the streets and in shopping malls.

Sekeping Tenggiri One of the best private collections of Malaysian contemporary art is in this KL guesthouse. (p65)

Singapore Art Museum An excellent showcase of Asian contemporary art. Also check out the new commercial galleries at Gillman Barracks. (p477)

Melaka's art galleries Browse an eclectic selection at the small galleries scattered around the World Heritage district. (p214)

George Town's street art Comical steel sculptures and quirky painted murals are a fun addition to the city's historic core. (p162)

Publika This innovative KL mall is decorated with eye-catching contemporary pieces and has several galleries. (p90)

Crafts & Shopping

Leave room in your suitcase for some beautiful traditional crafts including wood carvings, shadow puppets, fabrics and printings. All other consumer cravings are well tended to by a vast range of shopping complexes and megamalls.

Little Penang Street Market If you're a hopeless shopaholic, or are simply in need of a worthwhile souvenir, make sure your visit to George Town coincides with the last Sunday of the month and this popular open-air market. (p173)

Orchard Rd Megamalls, chic boutiques and retro gems fight for space on Singapore's legendary shopping strip. (p535)

Kuching's Main Bazaar Browse a wide selection of handmade Dayak crafts including textiles, baskets and masks as well as local foods and spices. (p396)

National Textiles Museum, Kuala Lumpur Admire skilful weaving, embroidery, knitting and batik printing. (p52).

month by month

Top Events

1. **Thaipusam**, January or February
2. **Chinese New Year**, January or February
3. **Hungry Ghosts Festival**, August
4. **Chingay**, February
5. **Rainforest World Music Festival**, July

Hindus, Muslims and Chinese all follow a lunar calendar, so the dates for many religious festivals vary each year. Muslim holidays typically move forward 11 days each year, while Hindu and Chinese festivals change dates but fall roughly within the same months. Dates have been given where they are known, but may be subject to slight changes.

January

New Year is a busy travel period. It's monsoon season on Malaysia's east coast and Sarawak.

 Thaipusam
Enormous crowds converge at the Batu Caves north of KL, the Nattukotai Chettiar Temple in Penang and in Singapore for this dramatic Hindu festival involving body piercing. Falls between mid-January and mid-February.

February

Chinese New Year is a big deal throughout the region and a busy travel period – book transport and hotels well ahead.

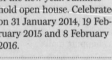 **Chinese New Year**
Dragon dances and pedestrian parades mark the start of the new year. Families hold open house. Celebrated on 31 January 2014, 19 February 2015 and 8 February 2016.

 Chingay
Singapore's biggest street parade (www.chingay.org.sg), a flamboyant, multicultural event, falls on the 22nd day after Chinese New Year.

April

The light monsoon season ends on Malaysia's west coast, but you should still always be prepared for rain.

 Petronas Malaysian Grand Prix
Formula 1's first big outing of the year (www.malaysiangp.com) in Southeast Asia is held at the Sepang International Circuit over three days, usually at the start of the month. Associated events and parties are held in KL.

May

This quiet month, prior to the busy school holidays, is a good time to visit the region.

Wesak (Vesak) Day
Buddha's birth, enlightenment and death are celebrated with various events, including the release of caged birds to symbolise the setting free of captive souls, and processions in KL, Singapore and other major cities. Celebrated on 24 May 2013, 13 May 2014 and 1 June 2015.

June

School holidays and one of the hottest months so get ready to sweat it out.

Gawai Dayak
Held on 1 and 2 June but beginning on the evening of 31 May, this Sarawak-wide Dayak festival celebrates the end of the rice-harvest season.

 Dragon Boat Festival
Commemorates the Malay legend of the fishermen

who paddled out to sea to prevent the drowning of a Chinese saint, beating drums to scare away any fish that might attack him. Celebrated from June to August, with boat races in Penang.

July

Busy travel month for Malaysian Borneo so book ahead for activities, tours and accommodation.

 George Town Festival

This arts and performance festival (www.georgetown festival.com) includes international artists, innovative street performances and new street art.

 Rainforest World Music Festival

A three-day musical extravaganza (www.rainforest music-borneo.com) held in the Sarawak Cultural Village near Kuching in the 2nd week of July.

 Singapore Food Festival

This month-long celebration of food (www.singapore foodfestival.com) includes events, cooking classes and food-themed tours.

 Sultan of Brunei's Birthday

Colourful official ceremonies (www.royalbirthday. org.bn) are held on 15 July to mark the Sultan's birthday and include an elaborate military ceremony presided over by the supremo himself.

August

Ramadan may fall in this month, so look out for night food markets.

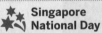 **Singapore National Day**

Held on 9 August (though dress rehearsals on the two prior weekends are almost as popular), Singapore National Day (www.ndp.org.sg) includes military parades, fly-overs and fireworks.

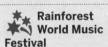 **Hungry Ghost Festival**

Chinese communities perform operas, host open-air concerts and lay out food for their ancestors. Celebrated towards the end of the month and in early September.

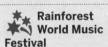 **Malaysia's National Day**

Join the crowds at midnight on 31 August to celebrate the anniversary of Malaysia's independence in 1957. Events are usually held in Dataran Merdeka in KL. There are parades and festivities the next morning across the country.

September

Haze from forest and field clearance fires in Indonesia create urban smog across the region.

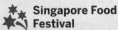 **Hari Raya Puasa**

The Muslim fasting month of Ramadan culminates in this major festival traditionally celebrated at home with big banquets; the Malaysian prime minister

opens his official home in Putrajaya to the public.

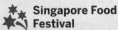 **Singtel Singapore Grand Prix**

It's Singapore's turn to host the Formula 1 crowd with a night race (www. singaporegp.sg) on a scenic city-centre circuit. Book well in advance for hotel rooms with a view.

October

Start of the monsoon season on Malaysia's west coast, but it's not so heavy or constant to affect most travel plans.

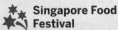 **Deepavali** Tiny oil lamps are lit outside Hindu homes to attract the auspicious gods Rama and Lakshmi. Indian businesses start the new financial year, with Little Indias across the region ablaze with lights.

December

A sense of festivity (and monsoon rains in Singapore and east coast Malaysia) permeates the air as the year winds down. Christmas is a big deal in Singapore, with impressive light displays on Orchard Rd.

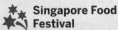 **Zoukout** Held on Siloso Beach, Sentosa, this annual outdoor dance party (www. zoukout.com) is one of the region's best such events with a 25,000-strong crowd bopping to international DJs.

itineraries

Whether you've got six days or 60, these intineraries provide a starting point for the trip of a lifetime. Want more inspiration? Head online to lonelyplanet. com/thorntree to chat with other travellers.

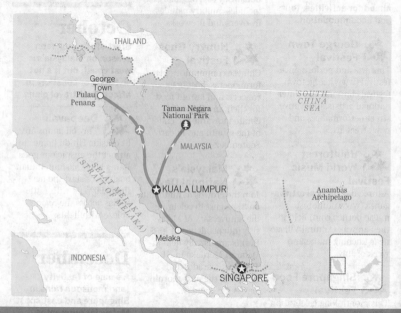

Two Weeks

Essential Malaysia & Singapore

> Ease yourself into Malaysian life by spending three days in **Kuala Lumpur (KL)**. On your to see and do list should be the **Petronas Towers**, **Chinatown** for shopping and eating, and the Lake Gardens for the **KL Bird Park** and **Islamic Arts Museum**. Head to the magnificent national park **Taman Negara** where even on a two-day visit you can clamber across the canopy walkway and make some short jungle treks. Return to KL and hop on a flight to **Penang** where three days will give you a good taste of the heritage district of **George Town** and other island highlights such as **Kek Lok Si Temple**.

Historic **Melaka**, another Unesco World Heritage Site, deserves a couple of nights but visit midweek to avoid the crowds. Then head across the causeway to **Singapore** where you can spend your final four days enjoying everything from maxing out your credit card at glitzy shopping malls and sampling delicious hawker food to the eye-boggling space age architecture of **Marina Bay**, the excellent **zoo and night safari**, and the vacation island of **Sentosa** for some beachside R & R.

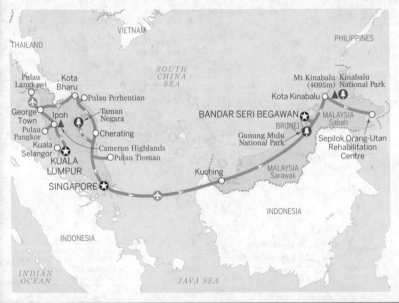

Six Weeks
The Grand Tour

> Schedule a week in **KL** and surrounds for sightseeing and acclimatisation. Day trips could include **Batu Caves**, **Forestry Research Institute of Malaysia (FRIM)** and **Putrajaya**, the nation's fast-evolving administrative capital and a showcase of modern Malaysian architecture. The sleepy old royal capital of **Kuala Selangor**, near to which you can observe the dazzling natural display of fireflies, is also only a couple of hours drive from KL.

After a pit stop in the happening foodie destination of **Ipoh**, which has some great accommodation options, your second week takes you up to the **Cameron Highlands** for a cooler climate and invigorating walks past verdant tea plantations. Return to the coast and hop across to **Pulau Pangkor** for a few days further relaxation on this off-the-beaten track island with white sand beaches and jungle interior.

Suitably refreshed you should be ready for the urban delights of **George Town** on **Penang**, particularly the Unesco World Heritage district packed with colourful, fascinating sights. Do plenty of walking to work up an appetite, as Penang is also Malaysia's number one food destination with oodles of tempting dishes to sample. A quick flight away are the resorts, gorgeous beaches and jungle hinterlands of **Pulau Langkawi**.

Into week four and it's time to cross the mountainous spine of the peninsula to **Kota Bharu**, a great place to encounter traditional Malay culture. Island- and beach-hop down the east coast, pausing at **Pulau Perhentian**, **Cherating** and **Pulau Tioman**. For jungle adventures head to **Taman Negara** or, to avoid the crowds, opt for nearby **Kenong Rimba State Park**.

Singapore can easily swallow up a week of shopping, museum viewing and world-class eating. From here you can fly to **Kuching** in Sarawak, a good base for a longhouse excursion or for arranging a trek in the **Gunung Mulu National Park**. Rack up the visa stamps by taking the overland and river route from Sarawak to Sabah via Brunei stopping in the capital **Bandar Seri Begawan (BSB)**.

Having made it to Sabah's capital **Kota Kinabalu**, your final challenge, should you choose to accept it, is to climb **Mt Kinabalu**. Alternatively, it's difficult to resist the chance to eyeball close up the supercute ginger apes at **Sepilok Orang-Utan Rehabilitation Centre**.

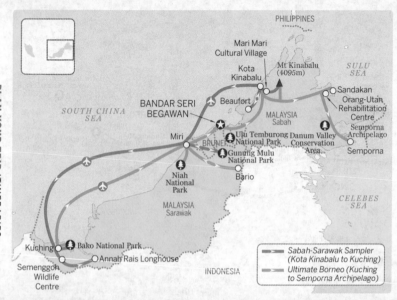

Sabah-Sarawak Sampler
(Kota Kinabalu to Kuching)

Ultimate Borneo (Kuching to Semporna Archipelago)

One Month
Ultimate Borneo

From **Kuching** explore the local **longhouses** and **Bako National Park**. Fly to **Miri**, which is the base for trips to the impressive **Niah Caves**; **Gunung Mulu National Park** for more caves (the world's biggest), the heart-pumping trek to the Pinnacles and a sweat-drenching trek along the Headhunters Trail; and **Bario**, a quiet farming community tucked away in the vine-draped **Kelabit Highlands**.

You'll need to pass through Miri again to make your way overland to **Bandar Seri Begawan**, Brunei's friendly microcapital. While here don't miss out on **Ulu Temburong National Park** in Temburong, Brunei's pristine sliver of primary rainforest.

Cross back into Malaysia and pause in **Kota Kinabalu** before setting your sights on **Mt Kinabalu**. Catch some ape love at **Sepilok Orang-Utan Rehabilitation Centre**, followed by a layover in **Sandakan** for a brief lesson in colonial history. The mighty **Sungai Kinabatangan** is next, offering wildlife enthusiasts plenty of photo fodder. If you've got the time (and the dime), head deep into Sabah's green interior for a trek through the **Danum Valley Conservation Area**. Explore the magnificent dive sites of the **Semporna Archipelago** accessed from **Semporna**.

Two Weeks
Sabah–Sarawak Sampler

Start with Sabah's star attraction, **Mt Kinabalu**. Assaults on Malaysia's highest peak can be launched from the state's government seat, **Kota Kinabalu (KK)**, which encapsulates Southeast Asian city life on a manageable scale. You'll be obliged to spend a day or two here sorting permits, during which you can stoke up on energy by indulging in the flavourful local cuisine. Consider a day-trip cruise (including buffet dinner) down one of the tea-brown rivers in the **Beaufort Division**, or learn a little about the local culture at the **Mari Mari Cultural Village**.

Leapfrog by plane from KK to Miri and then on to **Gunung Mulu National Park**, home to the world's largest caves, and several memorable jungle treks, including the notorious Headhunters Trail. Pass through Miri once more for a quick flight down to **Kuching**. Sarawak's capital is a real charmer and will easily keep you occupied for several days. Break up your time in town with a visit to **Semenggoh Wildlife Centre**, **Bako National Park** and, if you have time, to a longhouse such as **Annah Rais Longhouse**.

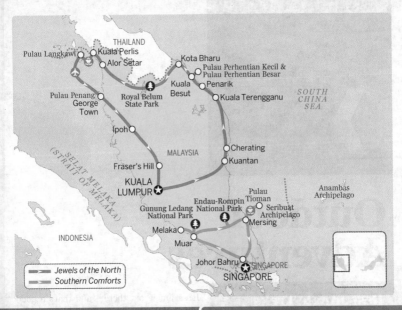

Legend:
- Jewels of the North
- Southern Comforts

Three Weeks
Jewels of the North

Explore **KL** for a few days then take a bus across the peninsula to **Kuantan**. Beach- and island-hop up the east coast pausing in laid-back **Cherating** and **Kuala Terengganu**, with its pretty Chinatown and the **Kompleks Muzium Negeri Terengganu**. At **Penarik** see fireflies and stay at the **Terrapuri Heritage Village**, a resort made up of 29 classically furnished antique houses.

Although other island idylls await further up the coast it's difficult to ignore the Perhentians, accessed from Kuala Besut. **Pulau Perhentian Besar** tends to be less crowded and just as gorgeous as its more popular twin, **Pulau Perhentian Kecil**. Back on the mainland, linger a day or two in **Kota Bharu**, for its museums, cultural events and night market, then head to northern Perak, making the **Royal Belum State Park** your base.

Dig into fish-head curry in **Alor Setar** before taking the ferry from **Kuala Perlis** to **Pulau Langkawi** where there's yet more opportunities for sunbathing, island hopping and jungle exploration. Fly to **George Town**, the essential stop on Penang. Connect to **Ipoh** from where you could cool off in **Fraser's Hill** (Bukit Fraser) before returning to KL.

Three Weeks
Southern Comforts

Singapore is the logical start and finish to this loop around the southern end of Peninsula Malaysia; leave yourself several days to soak up its multiple attractions. If you're strapped for cash then **Johor Bahru** just across the causeway is a cheaper base. Recently spruced up, it's become a decent hangout, not least for its street food and duty-free booze.

The lethargic riverside town of **Muar** has a graceful colonial district that's worth a look, and can be used as a base for assaults on 1276m Gunung Ledang, Johor's highest mountain, within the **Gunung Ledang National Park**. Recover in World Heritage–listed **Melaka** where you can spend several days soaking up the enduring Portuguese and Dutch influence.

Explore the last remaining stands of lowland forest on the peninsula in **Endau-Rompin National Park**, the last refuge of the Sumatran rhinoceros. Stunning **Pulau Tioman** has epitomised an island paradise since it doubled for Bali Hai in *South Pacific*. Alternatively, indulge in some island hopping and diving around the 64 comparatively little visited gems of the **Seribuat Archipelago**.

Outdoor Adventures

Best Jungle Treks
Taman Negara
Maliau Basin
Kelabit Highlands
Endau-Rompin National Park
Ulu Temburong National Park

Best Mountain Climbing
Mt Kinabalu
Gunung Ledang
Gunung Mulu
Gunung Tahan
Mt Trus Madi

Best Diving and Snorkelling
Semporna Archipelago
Pulau Perhentian
Pulau Redang
Pulau Tioman
Seribuat Archipelago

Best Caving
Gunung Mulu National Park
Niah National Park
Gomantong Caves
Wind Cave Nature Reserve

It's a jungle out there – and that's a good thing! Malaysia, Singapore and Brunei offer a broad range of treks through some of the world's oldest undisturbed areas of rainforest, from simple strolls along marked paths to multiday marathons practically hacking through virgin jungle. If that doesn't appeal to the adventurer in you, then there are mountains to climb, caves to explore and tropical seas teeming with marine life to dive as well as other aquatic-based activities such as surfing, yachting, kayaking and white-water rafting.

Trekking

Fancy seeing what life was possibly like 100 million years ago? Trekking into the deepest parts of the region's jungles will give you a clue as they were largely unaffected by the far-reaching climatic changes brought on elsewhere by the Ice Age. Significant chunks of these rainforests have been made into national parks, in which all commercial activities apart from tourism are banned.

The British established the first national park in Malaysia in 1938 and it is now included in Taman Negara, the crowning glory of Malaysia's network of national parks, which crosses the borders of Terengganu, Kelantan and Pahang. In addition to this and the 27 other national and state parks across the country (23 of them located in Malaysian

Borneo), there are various government-protected reserves and sanctuaries for forests, birds, mammals and marine life. Even in the heart of KL it's possible to stretch your legs in the Bukit Nanas Forest Reserve; alternatively head a little north of the city to find a fantastic network of forest trails and the suspended walkway at the Forestry Research Institute of Malaysia (FRIM, p100).

Only 1 sq km of Brunei's 500 sq km Ulu Temburong National Park is accessible to the public, but what a treat it presents being one of the most pristine slices of rainforest in the region. Even Singapore offers up trekking possibilities: the country's National Parks Board manages 10% of the island's total land area, which comprises over 50 major parks and four nature reserves, including Bukit Timah Nature Reserve.

When to Go

The region has wet months and less wet months. Global warming has also affected the monsoons so that year to year precipitation varies widely. In short, no matter where or when you go, you're likely to get wet – and if not from rain then certainly from sweating!

What is seasonal, however, is the number of other travellers you'll be competing with for experienced guides and lodgings. Northern hemisphere residents often come to the region during the summer holidays in their home countries, so if you plan to trek in July or August book a tour far in advance. Also watch out for regional travel highpoints such as Chinese New Year holidays and the so-called 'Golden Week' of holidays that Japanese people usually take late in April or early May.

Permits, Guides & Bookings

Many of the region's national parks and natural beauty spots charge a nominal entrance fee – around RM10. At a few, if you wish to trek or engage in other activities such as fishing or mountain climbing, then there may be additional permits to purchase and guides to hire. In particular, Mt Kinabalu has stringent visitor regulations, as does Gunung Mulu National Park.

Accommodation is generally not a problem when visiting most national parks. Various types are available, from hostel to luxury resorts. Transport and accommodation operations are increasingly being handled

TOP WILDLIFE SPOTS

Taman Negara (p260) Malaysia's oldest and most prestigious national park is home to everything from fireflies to elephants.

Royal Belum State Park (p147) Home to 10 varieties of hornbill and most of Malaysia's big mammals.

Sungai Kinabatangan (p348) Spot wild orang-utans and pygmy elephants along the banks of Sabah's longest river.

Bako National Park (p400) One of the region's best places to see proboscis monkeys.

Singapore Zoo (p493) One of the world's best, along with the Night Safari and the new River Safari experience.

Ulu Temburong National Park (p470) Breathtaking forest canopy views in Brunei's Temburong region.

by private tour companies, who require you to book in advance and pay a deposit.

Many national parks have well-marked day trails and can be walked unaccompanied. But for almost all overnights, only a fool would set out without a local guide. Remember, trail maps of any sort are completely unavailable and signage along remote trail networks is nonexistent. A good guide will be able to gauge your abilities and push you a little, rather than taking the easiest way as a matter of course. Try a shorter guided hike before setting off on an overnight adventure to get a sense of how you fare in tropical trekking conditions.

Especially in Sabah, Brunei and Sarawak, the national parks are very strict about allowing only licensed guides. We've heard stories of groups being turned back when they arrived with an uncertified leader. Before you fork over any cash, compare notes with other travellers and ask to see the guide's national-park certification.

Guides for day walks can sometimes be hired at national park HQ, but for overnights you'll need to contact either a freelance guide or a tour agency. Budget from RM50 to RM200 per day for a guide depending on the duration and difficulty of the trek you are planning.

RESPONSIBLE TREKKING

Jungle trekking can be one of the highlights of a trip to the region. However, to the uninitiated, it can be something of a shock – like marching all day in a sauna with a pile of bricks strapped to your back. To make the experience as painless as possible, it's necessary to make some preparations:

» On overnight trips, bring two sets of clothing, one for hiking and one to wear at the end of the day (always keep your night kit separate and dry in a plastic bag). Within minutes of starting, your hiking kit will be drenched and will stay that way throughout your trip.

» If you'll be travelling through dense vegetation, wear long trousers and a long-sleeved shirt. Otherwise, shorts and a T-shirt will suffice. Whatever you wear, make sure that it's loose fitting.

» Bring fast-drying synthetic clothes. Once cotton gets wet it won't dry until you bring it to the laundry back in town.

» It can be cool in the evening, so bring a fleece top to keep warm.

» Unless you like a lot of support, consider hiking in running shoes with good traction. You could also go local and buy a pair of 'kampung Adidas' – a Malaysian jungle version of a hiking shoe, shaped like an Adidas soccer cleat but made out of rubber (like a souped-up Croc). They're cheap (around RM5 a pair) and popular with porters and guides.

» Buy a pair of light-coloured leech socks – they're not easy to come by in the region so buy them online before coming.

» Drink plenty of water. If you're going long distances, you'll have to bring either a water filter or a water-purification agent like iodine (most people opt for the latter to keep weight down).

» Get in shape long before coming to the region and start slowly, with day hikes before longer treks.

» Always go with a guide unless you're on a well-marked, commonly travelled trail.

» Wear loose underwear to help prevent chafing. Bring talcum powder to cope with the chafing caused by wet undergarments.

» If you wear glasses, treat them with an antifog solution (ask at the shop where you buy your glasses).

» Consider putting something waterproof over the back padding to keep the sweat out of your pack, or consider a waterproof stuff sack.

» Keep your camera in a waterproof container, with a pouch of silica gel or other desiccant.

» Pack sunscreen, insect repellent, a water bottle and a torch (preferably a headlamp to keep your hands free).

The following points are also worth bearing in mind if you are planning a mountaineering or caving adventure:

» Hire a local guide – it's the best way to make sure you're in touch with local customs and concerns as you move through tribal lands.

» Follow the golden rule of rubbish: if you carried it in, carry it out. Never bury your rubbish – it may be out of sight, but it won't be out of reach of animals.

» Where there isn't a toilet, bury your waste in a small hole 15cm deep and at least 100m from any watercourse. Use toilet paper sparingly and cover everything with soil and a rock.

» Always stick to the marked trails, however indistinct they may be. Carving your own path through the jungle can disrupt local people, not to mention the plants and wildlife.

Mountain & Rock Climbing

Towering above the forests of Borneo are some brilliant mountains. Even nonclimbers know about 4095m Mt Kinabalu, the highest peak between the Himalayas and the island of New Guinea. This craggy monster simply begs to be climbed, and there is something magical about starting the ascent in humid tropical jungle and emerging into a bare, rocky alpine zone so cold that snow has been known to fall. But beyond the transition from hot to cold, it's the weird world of the summit plateau that makes Mt Kinabalu among the world's most interesting peaks. It's got a dash of Yosemite and a pinch of Torres del Paine, but at the end of the day, it's pure Borneo.

Sabah's second highest peak, Mt Trus Madi (2642m), is a far more difficult peak to ascend than Mt Kinabalu – and a more difficult trip to arrange.

Gunung Mulu (2376m) isn't quite as high but it's almost as famous, thanks in part to being a Unesco World Heritage Site. If you're a real glutton for punishment, you'll probably find the five-day return trek to the summit of this peak to your liking. Those who make the journey experience a variety of pristine natural environments, starting with lowland dipterocarp forest and ending with rhododendron and montane forest.

Pulau Berhala in the Sandakan Archipelago is also a prime destination for rock climbers; Fieldskills Adventures (p311) arranges rock climbing tours here.

On the peninsula, Gunung Ledang (1276m) is a good introduction to tropical mountaineering. There are also several good climbs in Taman Negara, including Gunung Tahan (2187m), an expedition that takes between seven to nine days.

Costs

Guide fees could be anything between RM100 and RM200 per day. There will also be national park entry fees (RM1 to RM15) and climbing permits (RM100 in the case of Mt Kinabalu) to consider.

Pre-Trip Preparations

Climbing one of Malaysia's mountains is like a jungle trek except more – more exhausting, more psychologically challenging and especially more vertical. Be prepared for ascents that turn your legs to rubber and much colder weather.

PLAN YOUR TRIP OUTDOOR ADVENTURES

MALAYSIA'S TOP 10 NATIONAL & STATE PARKS

PARK	FEATURES	ACTIVITIES	BEST TIME TO VISIT
Bako	beaches, proboscis monkeys	coastline walks, trekking	May-Sep
Batang Ai	primary forest crawling with wild orang-utan	trekking	year-round
Endau-Rompin	lowland forest, unique plants, Sumatran rhinos, waterfalls and rivers	trekking, wildlife-spotting	Apr-Sep
Gunung Mulu	caves, the Pinnacles, Headhunters Trail	caving, trekking, mountain climbing	May-Sep
Kinabalu	Mt Kinabalu	mountain climbing	May-Sep
Niah	caves	caving, trekking	May-Sep
Penang	meromictic lake, monkeys	trekking	Apr-Jul
Taman Negara Perlis	Gua Wang Burma cave, stump-tailed macaques, Malaysia's only semideciduous forest	caving, trekking	Jun-Aug
Taman Negara	canopy walkway, hides, jungle trails, rivers	trekking, wildlife-spotting, river trips	Apr-Sep
Tun Sakaran	sand-fringed islands, technicolour reefs	snorkelling, diving	year-round

» (above) Gunung Mulu National Park (p438), Sarawak, Borneo
» (left) White-water rafting in Kedah (p184), Malaysia

JOAKIM LEROY/AGE FOTOSTOCK/ROBERT HARDING ©

As with longer treks, book well ahead. Many of the agencies that handle trekking also offer mountain ascents. Some of the more experienced guides in Sarawak's Kelabit Highlands can take you to two rarely climbed peaks, Batu Lawi and Gunung Murud.

Keen mountain climbers should search out a copy of *Mountains of Malaysia – A Practical Guide and Manual* by John Briggs.

Caving

Slice one of Malaysia's limestone hills in half and chances are you'll find that inside it looks like Swiss cheese. Malaysians have been living, harvesting birds' nests, planning insurgencies and burying their dead in these caves *(gua)* for tens of thousands of years. These days, the country's subterranean spaces – including some of the largest caverns anywhere on earth – are quiet, except for the flow of underground streams, the drip of stalactites and the whoosh of the wings of swiftlets and bats.

Sarawak's Gunung Mulu National Park is a place of spelunking superlatives. It's got the world's second-largest cave passage (the Deer Cave, 2km in length and 174m in height), the world's largest cave chamber (the Sarawak Chamber, 700m long, 400m wide and 70m high) and Asia's longest cave (the Clearwater Cave, 107km in length). Several of the park's caves are – like their counterparts in Niah National Park – accessible to nonspelunkers: you can walk through them on well-maintained walkways.

Other caves open to the public include the Dark Cave at the Batu Caves; various caverns in and around Gunung Stong State Park; those in Taman Negara; and the Gomantong Caves in Sabah.

Pre-Trip Preparations

A pitch-black passageway deep in the bowels of the earth is not the ideal place to discover that you can't deal with narrow, confined spaces. Before heading underground, seriously consider your susceptibility to claustrophobia and fear of heights (some caves require scaling underground cliffs). If you have any concerns about a specific route, talk with your guide beforehand.

Be prepared to crawl through muck, including bat guano, and bring clothes you won't mind getting filthy (some guides and agencies supply these).

Aquatic Adventures
Diving & Snorkelling

Reasonable prices, an excellent variety of dive sites and easy access make Malaysia a great diving choice for both first-timers and old hands. Island-based boat dives are the most common, but a few areas, like Sabah's Pulau Sipadan, have some cracking sites right off the beach. You may also come across live-aboard boats to get you to more remote spots.

The standards of diving facilities in Malaysia are generally quite high and equipment rental is widely available. Most places offer the universally recognised Professional Association of Diving Instructors (PADI) certification.

When to Go

The northeast monsoon brings strong winds and rain to the east coast of Peninsular Malaysia from early November to late February, during which time most dive centres simply shut down. Visibility improves after

---

RESPONSIBLE DIVING

Consider the following tips when diving or snorkelling, and help preserve the ecology and beauty of the reefs:

» Do not use anchors on the reef, and take care not to ground boats on coral.

» Avoid touching living marine organisms with your body, or dragging equipment across the reef.

» Be conscious of your fins. Clouds of sand or even the surge from heavy fin strokes can damage delicate organisms.

» Major damage can be done by divers descending too fast and colliding with the reef, so practise buoyancy control across your trip.

» Resist the temptation to collect (or buy) coral or shells from reefs of dive sites. Some sites are even protected from looting by law.

» Ensure that you take home all your rubbish and any litter you may find.

» Don't feed the fish, as this can disturb their habits or be detrimental to their health.

the monsoon, peaking in August and September. On the west coast conditions are reversed and the best diving is from September to March. In Malaysian Borneo the monsoons are less pronounced and rain falls more evenly throughout the year, making diving a year-round activity.

Costs

Most dive centres charge around RM200 to RM300 for two dives, including equipment rental. A three-dive day trip at Sipadan costs around RM700. PADI open-water courses average around RM800. Many resorts and dive operators also offer all-inclusive dive packages, which vary widely in price.

Pre- & Post-Trip

While it is possible simply to show up and dive at some of the larger dive centres like Pulau Tioman, it's a good idea to make arrangements in advance, if only to avoid waiting a day or two before starting. Diving at Sipadan is capped at 120 divers per day.

Note that it is unsafe to dive directly after flying due to poorly pressurised cabins and dehydration. It's also a serious health risk to fly within 24 hours of your last dive.

Kayaking & White-Water Rafting

Malaysia's mountains and rainforests equal fast-flowing rivers, which result in ideal opportunities for rafting and kayaking enthusiasts.

On the peninsula, Kuala Kubu Bharu has become the white-water hot spot, with rafting and kayaking organised along the Sungai Selangor; **Pierose Swiftwater** (www.raftmalaysia.com) is a reputable company.

In Gopeng on Sungai Kampar, 20 minutes' drive north of Ipoh, rafting trips and other outdoor adventures are offered at the MY Gopeng Resort (p126).

White-water rafting has become quite the craze in Sabah, with Kota Kinabalu–based operators taking travellers south of the city to the Beaufort Division for some Grade 3–4 rapids on the Sungai Padas (Padas River). Calmer water at Sungai Kiulu near Mt Kinabalu is a tamer option for beginners.

Kayaking is offered by both **Kuching Kayak** (☑082-253 005; www.kuchingkayak.com; 269 Jln Padungan) and **Borneo Trek & Kayak Adventure** (www.rainforestkayaking.com) in Kuching.

BIRD-WATCHING

Malaysia's tropical jungles and islands are home to over 600 species of birds. The principal twitching destinations are:

» Cape Rachado Forest Reserve
» Endau-Rompin National Park
» Fraser's Hill (Bukit Fraser,
» Bako National Park
» Gunung Mulu National Park
» Kenong Rimba State Park
» Lambir Hills National Park
» Mt Kinabalu
» Royal Belum State Park
» Taman Negara

Boating

The following yachting clubs offer chances for those interested in a sailing trip around the region or learning how to sail:

Royal Langkawi Yacht Club (☑04-966 4078; www.langkawiyachtclub.com), Kuah

Royal Selangor Yacht Club (☑03-3168 6964; www.rsyc.com.my), Pelabuhan Klang

Avillion Admiral Cove (p113), Port Dickson.

Boating adventures can also be had on the region's lakes, rivers and mangrove-lined estuaries. Taking a sundown boat ride through the mangroves of Kuching Wetlands National Park to spot crocodiles and fireflies can be a magical experience. Firefly-spotting boat trips out of Kuala Selangor are also popular.

On larger rivers, transport is by 'flying coffin' – long, narrow passenger boats with about 70 seats, not including the people sitting on the roof. Thanks to their powerful engines, these craft can power upriver against very strong currents.

Surfing

Wannabe Layne Beachleys and Kelly Slaters should haul their boards to Cherating and Juara on Pulau Tioman, Malaysia's surfing hot spots. **Surfing in Malaysia** (http://surfingmalaysia.blogspot.com.au) is a useful blog with links to other sources of information for boarders.

Eat Like a Local

When to Go

As might be expected of a people consumed with food and its pleasures, Singaporeans, Malaysians and Bruneians mark every special occasion with celebratory edibles.

Chinese New Year (January/February)

In the weeks leading up to Chinese New Year, every table is graced with *yue sang* (*yee sang* or *yu sheng* – 'fresh fish'), a mound of grated raw vegetables, pickles, pomelo pieces and crispy, fried-dough pieces topped with sliced raw fish.

Ramadan (June/August)

During Ramadan special food markets swing into action in the late afternoons, offering a wide variety of Malay treats.

Deepavali (October/November)

During the Indian Festival of Lights, make your way to a Little India, where you'll find special sweets such as *jalebi* (deep-fried fritters soaked in sugar syrup) and savoury snacks like *muruku* (crispy fried coils of curry leaf–studded dough).

Eating like a local in Malaysia, Singapore and Brunei is a snap. The food is absolutely delicious and hygiene standards are among the highest in the region. Not only is it easy to make sense of restaurant menus and signs here, but most vendors also speak at least some English. And an almost perverse obsession with food among the locals means that visitors are often smothered in culinary companionship; the traveller who makes the effort to partake in the region's edible delights will undoubtedly make a few *makan kaki* (food friends) along the way. Simply put, in this part of the world it's not 'How are you?' but *'Sudah makan?'* (Have you eaten yet?).

Top Restaurants

» **Rebung** (p83, Kuala Lumpur) – The next best thing to Malay home cooking is the expansive buffet of Malay specialities at this rustically charming restaurant.

» **Xin Quan Fang** (p123, Ipoh) – A legendary hole-in-the-wall serving amazingly rich curry *mee*, a combination of rice and wheat noodles in a spicy, rich broth with chicken, pork and shrimp.

» **Teksen** (p167, George Town) – Shophouse-bound restaurant that does excellent Chinese and Chinese/Malay fare.

» **Muda Coffee Shop** (p203, Alor Setar) – Yes, we're recommending that you eat steamed fish head. Yes, we think you'll love it.

» **Pak Putra Restaurant** (p220, Melaka) – Fabulous Pakistani cuisine including tandoori dishes, seafood and mutton rogan josh.

FASTING & FEASTING

Don't be deterred from visiting Malaysia during Ramadan, the Muslim holy month of sunrise-to-sunset fasting. Indian and Chinese eateries remain open during the day to cater to the country's sizeable non-Muslim population and, come late afternoon, Ramadan bazaars pop up all over the country. These prepared-food markets offer a rare chance to sample Malay specialities from all over the country, some of which are specific to the festive season or rarely found outside private homes. One of the country's biggest Ramadan markets is held in KL's Malay enclave of Kampung Baru. Cruise the stalls and pick up provisions – but don't snack in public until the cry of the muezzin tells believers it's time to *buka puasa* (break the fast).

» **Roost Juice & Bar** (p231, Johor Bahru) – Hainese noodles, mutton chops and Nonya-style fish are on the menu at JB's most chilled eatery.

» **Ana Ikan Bakar Petai** (p256, Kuantan) – Freshly caught fish, crab and shrimp is priced by weight and cooked to your specifications.

» **Bubu Resort** (p289, Perhentian Kecil) – Serving the best seafood BBQ on Peninsula Malaysia's east coast.

» **The Dyak** (p392, Kuching) – Book ahead for this elegant restaurant, the first to treat Dayak home cooking as true cuisine.

» **Moon Bell** (p314, Kota Kinabalu) – Spicy Xinjiang cuisine from China's northwest frontier.

» **Iggy's** (p526, Singapore) – Top-end Japanese–European gastro fusion in a decadent setting.

» **Pondok Sari Wangi** (p462, Bandar Seri Begawan) – A beloved BSB institution serving Indonesian/Chinese dishes.

Cheap Eats

» **Madras Lane** (p72, Kuala Lumpur) – Hidden behind the wet market, these stalls serve noodles and *yong tau fu* (tofu stuffed with fish paste) in a fish broth.

» **Haji Shariff's Cendol** (p111, Seremban) – Sample the classic Malay dessert plus its own take on *rojak* (a type of fruit salad).

» **Kedai Kopi Prima** (p145, Taiping) – Busy, buzzy open-air hawker joint where you'll be hard-pressed to spend more than RM10.

» **Lorong Baru (New Lane) Hawker Stalls** (p170, George Town) – Everything that's tasty and cheap about Penang, all in one narrow lane.

» **Capitol Satay** (p221, Melaka)– Try *satay celup*, a Melaka adaptation of satay steamboat.

» **Medan Selera Meldrum Walk** (p232, Johor Bahru) – Alleyway stalls frying up *ikan bakar*, the local curry laksa and other such delights.

» **Akob Patin House** (p256, Kuantan) – Riverside operation serving the town's speciality *ikan patin* (silver catfish).

» **Night Market** (p278, Kota Bharu) – Specialties include *ayam percik* (marinated chicken on bamboo skewers) and *nasi kerabu* (rice with coconut, fish and spices).

» **Open-Air Market** (p393, Kuching) – The best spot for Sarawak laksa, the local version of the national classic.

» **Night Market** (p306, Kota Kinabalu) – Best, cheapest and most interesting spot in KK for dinner.

» **Chomp Chomp Food Centre** (p522, Singapore) – Arguably Singapore's best hawker centre, this option in Serangoon Gardens has a chilled vibe.

» **Noralizah & Iskandar House of Curry** (p463, Bandar Seri Begawan) – Dip a selection of Indian flatbreads into a variety of delicious curries.

Cooking Courses

A standard one-day course usually features a shopping trip to a local market to choose ingredients, followed by preparation of curry pastes, soups, curries, salads and desserts.

» **Rohani Jelani** (p59, Kuala Lumpur)

» **Nazlina's Spice Kitchen** (p159, George Town)

» **Roselan's Malay Cookery Workshop** (p273, Kota Bharu)

» **Nancy's Kitchen** (p215, Melaka)

» **Bumbu Cooking School** (p389, Kuching)

» **Equator Adventure Tours** (p312, Kota Kinabalu)

» **Cookery Magic** (p513, Singapore)

Culinary Highlights

Don't leave the region without trying:

» **Ambuyat** Think of Brunei's sago mash as a blank palette upon which to paint the vibrant flavours of accompanying dishes.

» (above) Hawker stall in George Town (p170)
» (left) Chicken curry with *roti canai* (flaky, flat bread)

» **Cendol** Shaved ice, fresh coconut milk, pandan 'pasta' and sweet, smoky palm sugar beat the heat deliciously.

» **Roti canai** Flaky, crispy, griddled bread dipped in curry and dhal served with a mug of frothy *teh tarik* ('pulled' tea) is one of the world's best breakfasts.

» **Char kway teow** Silky rice noodles, plump prawns, briny cockles, chewy Chinese sausage, crispy sprouts, fluffy egg, a hint of chilli – all kissed by the smoke of a red-hot wok. Need we say more?

» **Hainanese chicken-rice** Tender poached chicken accompanied by rice scented with stock and garlic and a trio of dipping sauces, plain and spicy.

Intrepid Eating

Adventurous diners should seek out these specialties:

» **Perut ikan** This Penang Nonya coconut-milk curry, made with fish innards, pineapple and fresh herbs, is spicy, sweet, sour and – yes – a little fishy.

» **Siat** When stir-fried, plump sago grubs turn golden and crispy and boast a savoury fattiness reminiscent of pork crackling.

» **Bak kut teh** Order this comforting stewed pork dish 'with everything' and be converted to porcine bits and bobs.

» **Sup torpedo** Malay bull's penis soup – like many 'challenging foods' – is said to enhance sexual drive.

» **Kerabu beromak** On Langkawi, coconut milk, chillies and lime juice dress this 'salad' of rubbery but appealingly briny sea-cucumber slices.

Where To Eat

Many locals would argue that the best (and best-value) food is found at hawker stalls, and who are we to argue? Most of these dishes can't be found in restaurants and

BRAIN FOOD *AUSTIN BUSH*

'Today fish head bigger,' said the waiter, as he slapped down the aluminium tray that contained an immense steaming fish head. He was aware of the discrepancy because on the previous night I'd eaten this very dish at this very restaurant.

When doing research for Lonely Planet guides I don't generally get the chance to eat at the same restaurant twice – there are simply too many places to investigate. And steamed fish head is an unlikely candidate to draw anyone, even someone as food-obsessed as me, back to the same restaurant on two consecutive nights. But the dish was easily one of the most delicious things I ate on my trip to Malaysia.

This encounter took place in Alor Setar, the capital and main city of tiny Kedah state, in northwestern Malaysia. It's a sleepy, predominately ethnic Malay place, and in contrast to just about everywhere I'd been previously in the country, it didn't appear to have many restaurants or food stalls. So in an effort to find something interesting I did some web research, which led me to a blog post and, ultimately, the fish head at Muda.

Muda has no sign, is distinctly aesthetically challenged, and is run by elderly Chinese Malaysians who can't be described as friendly or proficient in English. It also doesn't open until 8pm, but on the two nights I ate there customers would arrive from 7:45pm, place their orders and wait impatiently as the dining room gradually filled with oily smoke. Most of the cooking is done by one old man, so this can mean a long wait: on both visits I arrived at 8pm and ended up spending the next hour playing with my iPhone and nursing bottles of Malaysian Guinness until I was served.

But it was worth it.

Fish head may not seem like an especially meaty item, but the dish as served at Muda is really one of the meatiest, most *umami*-packed (savoury) dishes I've ever encountered. The fish head itself is actually more like a fish half and contains quite a bit of tender seabass flesh, both in the head and the body. This meatiness is boosted by a broth that includes soy sauce, tomatoes and mushrooms, countered by the tartness of salted plum, crunchy chunks of pickled vegetables and slivers of young ginger. With all this going on, the final garnish of thinly sliced leeks and deep-fried crispy garlic almost seems like a last-ditch, overzealous effort to include every ingredient in the kitchen.

Be the fish head big or small, I'm glad I ate at Muda twice, as it took the first visit for me to realise that steamed fish head served in a grotty restaurant with grumpy service is obviously not an ideal recommendation. And it took the second visit to realise that I didn't care – it's simply too good not to go in the book.

when they are, they're rarely as tasty, so hawker-stall dining is a must if you really want to appreciate the region's cuisines in all their glory. To partake, simply head to a stand-alone streetside kitchen-on-wheels, a coffee shop or a food court; place your order with one or a number of different vendors; find a seat (shared tables are common); and pay for each dish as it's delivered. After you're seated you'll be approached by someone taking orders for drinks, which are also paid for separately. Hawker food in Malaysia and Brunei is perfectly safe to eat, but the squeamish may want to start slowly, in one of Singapore's sanitised hawker centres.

Kopitiam generally refers to old-style, single-owner Chinese coffee shops. These simple, fan-cooled establishments serve noodle and rice dishes, strong coffee and other drinks, and all-day breakfast fare like soft-boiled eggs and toast to eat with *kaya* (coconut jam).

Restoran (restaurant) applies to eateries ranging from casual, decades-old Chinese establishments to upscale establishments boasting international fare, slick decor and a full bar. Between the two extremes lie Chinese seafood restaurants where the main course can be chosen live from a tank, as well as the numerous cafes found in Malaysia's many shopping malls.

Consider grazing at one or more *pasar* (markets). Morning markets usually have Chinese-owned stalls selling coffee and Indian-operated *teh tarik* stalls offering freshly griddled roti. Triangular *bungkus* (packages) piled in the middle of tables contain *nasi lemak* (rice boiled in coconut milk served with *ikan bilis* – small, dried sardines or anchovies – peanuts and a curry dish); help yourself and pay for what you eat. *Pasar malam* (night markets) are also good hunting grounds, where you'll find everything from laksa to fresh-fried sweet yeast donuts.

When to Eat

To those of us used to 'three square meals', it might seem as if the locals are always eating. In fact, five or six meals or snacks is more the order of the day than strict adherence to the breakfast-lunch-dinner trilogy. Breakfast is usually grabbed on the run: *nasi lemak* wrapped to go *(bungkus)* in a banana leaf or brown waxed paper, a quick bowl of noodles, toast and eggs, or griddled Indian bread.

Come late morning a snack might be in order, perhaps a *karipap* (deep-fried pastry filled with spiced meat or fish and potatoes).

Lunch generally starts from 12.30pm, something to keep in mind if you plan to eat at a popular establishment.

The British left behind a strong attachment to afternoon tea, consumed here in the form of tea or coffee and a sweet or savoury snack like *tong sui* (sweet soups), various Indian fritters, battered and fried slices of cassava, sweet potato, banana and, of course, local-style sweets, *kuih*.

Vegetarians & Vegans

Given the inclusion of shrimp paste and other seafood products in many dishes, vegetarians and vegans may find it difficult to negotiate their way around many menus. Chinese vegetarian restaurants and hawker stalls are a safe bet (signage will include the words *'sayur sayuran'*); they're especially busy on the 1st and 15th of the lunar month, when many Buddhists adopt a vegetarian diet for 24 hours. Look also for Chinese stalls and eateries displaying rows of stainless-steel pans and advertising 'economy rice'; this type of restaurant will have several pure vegetarian dishes. South Indian restaurants are another haven, for snacks like *idli* (savoury, soft, fermented rice-and-lentil cakes) to eat with dhal, *dosa* (crispy pancakes sometimes filled with potato curry) and *thali* (full meals consisting of rice or bread with numerous small servings of curries and vegetables). Some offer vegetarian banana leaf rice meals and economy rice–like displays of varied 'meat' and 'fish' dishes made with gluten and soy.

regions at a glance

Kuala Lumpur

Shopping ✓✓
Food ✓✓✓
Art Galleries ✓✓✓

Super Shopping
Kuala Lumpur (KL) sports a multiplicity of malls, classic Southeast Asian fresh-produce markets and atmospheric night markets; the most famous is along Chinatown's Jln Petaling. Don't miss souvenir treasure house Central Market, based in a lovely art-deco building.

Fantastic Food
Allow your stomach to lead the way around KL. Tuck in with locals at the fantastic hawker stalls along Jln Alor, Imbi Market or Madras Lane. Sample Indian food in Brickfields and Little India, and a brilliant array of international options in Bangsar Baru and along the party strip Changat Bukit Bintang.

Contemporary Art
Access Malaysia's vibrant contemporary art scene at the National Visual Art Gallery or at exhibitions held in smaller commercial galleries such as MAP and Valentine Willie Fine Arts.

p46

Selangor & Negeri Sembilan

Wildlife ✓✓
Food ✓✓
Architecture ✓✓✓

Wildlife Encounters
Orang-utans and tigers are at Zoo Negara and monkeys scamper around the Batu Caves. Spot birds at Fraser's Hill, Cape Rachado Forest Reserve near Port Dickson, and the coastal mangroves near Kuala Selangor, where there's also the firefly flicker-fest.

Eating Adventures
Klang's Little India is the place for pork stew *bak kut teh*. Seremban also has delights ranging from the dessert *cendol* to handmade beef-ball noodles.

Architectural Wonders
Putrajaya is stacked with contemporary architecture around an artificial lake. The Istana Lama is a black hardwood palace in Sri Menanti.

p97

Perak

Nature ✓✓✓
Food ✓✓✓
Architecture ✓✓

Jungles & Mangroves
Perak is home to the jungles of Royal Belum State Park and the forests of Matang Mangrove Forest Reserve. Gopeng, outside of Ipoh, also has a burgeoning adventure-travel scene.

Culinary Destination
Ipoh, Perak's largest city, is home to top regional Chinese cuisine, and some great Malay food. Ipoh is also allegedly where Malaysia's ubiquitous 'white coffee' was created.

Colonial Architecture
Ipoh and the surrounding Kinta Valley are virtual time warps into colonial-era Malaysia. Taiping also has its share of historical buildings, while Kuala Kangsar is a royal Disneyland of mosques and palaces.

p116

Penang

Architecture ✓✓✓
Food ✓✓✓
Museums ✓✓✓

World Heritage

There's a reason George Town was declared a Unesco World Heritage site: the city is home to countless protection-worthy antique shophouses, mansions, Chinese clan houses, markets and temples.

Food & Drink

George Town is home to quality hawker centres; street vendors selling Chinese, Indian and Malay dishes; and an increasingly sophisticated contemporary eating and drinking scene.

Museums & Galleries

The streets of George Town are already something of an open-air museum, but the city also features excellent state-run and private institutions and contemporary art galleries, ensuring you'll be entertained for days.

p149

Langkawi, Kedah & Perlis

Beaches ✓✓✓
Nature ✓✓
Eating ✓

Splendid Beaches

Pulau Langkawi's beaches are world famous for a reason: the sand is white and fine, the water is clear and there has been relatively less development than in other Southeast Asian destinations.

Mountainous Jungle

The ancient jungle on Pulau Langkawi can be explored from above, via the Panorama Langkawi cable car, or seen up close at one of the island's numerous waterfalls or on a guided jungle trek.

International Eating

Pulau Langkawi is home to many foreign restaurants, from Thai to Turkish. And the island is duty-free so the bar scene won't do as much damage to your wallet.

p183

Melaka

Heritage ✓✓✓
Food ✓✓✓
Shopping ✓✓

Walkable Heritage

Learn about history, culture and architecture at many museums. Or just experience it wandering past Chinese shophouses, Dutch colonial architecture, Chinese and Hindu temples, mosques and churches.

Sit-down Meals

Take a dim-sum breakfast, eat banana-leaf curry for lunch and dine on Nonya specialities for dinner. Melaka isn't swarming with hawker stalls like KL and Penang but it offers a fine choice of eateries.

Shopping Options

Shop Chinatown's hippy-ish clothing, beaded Nonya shoes, and trinkets. Or go modern in air-con malls for electronics. Don't miss Jonker's Walk Night Market.

p207

Johor

Trekking ✓✓
Diving ✓
Nightlife ✓

Malaysia's Wilds

Endau-Rompin National Park isn't as well known as Taman Negara in Pahang, but that's what makes it so magical. Trek through myriad green jungles and along clear rivers to several impressive waterfalls, or go deeper in hope of spotting one of the park's elephant herds.

Under-the-radar Islands

The Seribuat Archipelago is where all the in-the-know expats living in Singapore and southern Malaysia go. Here you'll find low-key beaches, spectacular diving and family-friendly lodgings.

Duty-free Booze

The Zon is Johor Bahru's duty-free port. Hop from one bar/nightclub to the next without spending all your ringgit.

p227

Pahang & Tioman Island

Beaches ✓✓✓
Jungles ✓✓✓
Food ✓✓

East Coast Islands, Kelantan & Terengganu

Beaches & Islands ✓✓✓
Jungles ✓✓
Culture ✓✓

Sabah

Wildlife ✓✓✓
Trekking ✓✓✓
Diving ✓✓✓

Sarawak

Hiking & Trekking ✓✓✓
Caves ✓✓✓
Wildlife ✓✓

Beach Life

Coastal Pahang offers the supremely chilled-out surf town of Cherating. Pulau Tioman's Juara Beach is paradise.

Jungle Adventures

The vast primeval jungle preserve of Taman Negara offers myriad trekking and wildlife-spotting opportunities. Pulau Tioman's many trails will make you glad you packed hiking boots along with your sandals.

Culinary Travel

Kuantan is a food-lover's city, from the cheap and delicious food stalls next to the bus station to the hard-to-find but oh-so-worth-it seafood paradise of Ana Ikan Bakar Petai restaurant. Perhaps you'll even make a pilgrimage to taste Raub's famous fish-head curry.

p242

Aquatic Adventures

Home to some of Southeast Asia's loveliest and most accessible islands, including the Perhentians, east-coast Malaysia is a magnet for those looking to dive, snorkel and swim.

Off the Beaten Track

Gunung Stong State Park offers mountain treks, swimming and caving, and a breathtakingly steep waterfall. Though accessible by train, your fellow travellers will be few here in Kelantan's wild interior.

Cultural Insights

Kelantan is amazingly rich in opportunities for cultural exploration. Further south, Terengganu offers visitors the chance to explore Malay culture – both modern and classical.

p272

Land & Underwater Wildlife

From the iconic orang-utan to pygmy elephants, Sabah is home to some of the world's rarest animal species. Land animals are tough to spot in the thick jungle, but it's easy to find all manner of marine life underwater.

Hiking & Trekking

The mountains and hills of Sabah are a trekker's paradise, taking travellers past raging rivers that flow out of and through some of the most primordial forests in the world. Remember: it gets hot here.

Diving & Snorkelling

Sabah is well known for its scuba scene. The diving in Layang Layang and the famous Sipidan is some of the best in the world.

p304

Hiking & Trekking

Trekking from Bario to Ba Kelalan or to the summit of Gunung Mulu will thrill hikers, but even a stroll through one of Kuching-area's national parks will envelope you in equatorial rainforest.

Cave Exploration

The Wind Cave, Fairy Cave and Niah National Park boast caverns with stalactites and bats, but for size and spectacle you can't beat Gunung Mulu National Park, famed for the Deer Cave and the 700m-long Sarawak Chamber.

Jungle Wildlife

See wild proboscis monkeys at Bako National Park, orang-utans at Semenggoh Nature Reserve and crocodiles in the waters of Kuching Wetlands National Park.

p379

Brunei

Food ✓✓✓
Architecture ✓
Nature ✓✓✓

Food Mad

Brunei's Muslim population frowns on alcohol as decadent, but the nation has no problem indulging in a little gastronomic debauchery. The sultanate is food mad, and the opening of a restaurant is usually a major social event.

Grand Architecture

Between the Sultan's palace, the opulent Empire Hotel, mosques and the largest water village in the world, this nation compensates for its small size with some huge construction projects.

Primary Jungle

The sultanate has done a fine job of preserving its tracts of primary jungle. They're protected within a tightly controlled national park, providing breathing space for Borneo's beasts.

p454

Singapore

Food ✓✓✓
Shopping ✓✓✓
Museums ✓✓✓

Food

Food in Singapore is both a passion and a unifier across ethnic divides, with Chinese, Indian, Indonesian and Nonya (a fusion of Chinese and Malay) specialities. Find legendary hawker centres and food courts, as well as experimental, fine-dining hotspots.

Shopping

All bases are covered, from lavish malls and boutiques, to heirloom handicraft studios, beautiful antiques stores and local galleries peddling contemporary local art.

Museums

While giants like the National Museum of Singapore and the Asian Civilisations Museum are a must, make time for lesser-known NUS Museums and the haunting Changi Museum & Chapel.

p473

Every listing is recommended by our authors, and their favourite places are listed first

Look out for these icons:

 TOP CHOICE Our author's top recommendation

 A green or sustainable option

 FREE No payment required

KUALA LUMPUR 46

SELANGOR & NEGERI SEMBILAN . . 97
SELANGOR 99
Batu Caves 99
Forestry Research Institute of Malaysia (FRIM) 100
Hulu Klang & Gombak. . . 100
Genting Highlands 101
Fraser's Hill (Bukit Fraser) 102
Putrajaya 104
Klang Valley. 105
Kuala Selangor 107
NEGERI SEMBILAN 109
Seremban 109
Sri Menanti 112
Kuala Pilah 112
Port Dickson 113

PERAK 116
Ipoh. 118
Gopeng & Around. 125
Cameron Highlands. 126
Pulau Pangkor 134
Kuala Kangsar. 140
Taiping 142
Around Taiping 146
Royal Belum State Park . . 147

PENANG. 149
George Town 151
Batu Ferringhi 176
Teluk Bahang & Around . . 179

Pulau Jerejak. 180
Snake Temple 181
Batu Maung. 181
Kampung Pulau Betong . . 181
Teluk Kumbar 182

LANGKAWI, KEDAH & PERLIS . . . 183
KEDAH 184
Pulau Langkawi 185
Alor Setar 200
Around Alor Setar 204
PERLIS 204
Kangar 204
Taman Negara Perlis 205

MELAKA. 207
MELAKA CITY 209
AROUND MELAKA CITY . . 225
Ayer Keroh. 225
Pulau Besar. 225
Alor Gajah 225
Tanjung Bidara 226

JOHOR 227
Johor Bahru 228
Muar 234
Mersing 234
Seribuat Archipelago. 237
Endau-Rompin National Park 239

PAHANG & TIOMAN ISLAND . . . 242
Pulau Tioman 243
Endau 252

Pekan 252
Kuantan 254
Around Kuantan 257
Cherating. 257
Taman Negara. 260
Jerantut 265
Kuala Lipis. 267
Kenong Rimba State Park 268
Raub 269
Temerloh 270
Around Temerloh 270

EAST COAST ISLANDS, KELANTAN & TERENGGANU. 272
KELANTAN 273
Kota Bharu 273
Around Kota Bharu 281
EAST COAST ISLANDS . . . 283
Pulau Perhentian 283
Pulau Lang Tengah. 291
Pulau Redang 292
Pulau Kapas 293
TERENGGANU 294
Kuala Terengganu. 295
Around Kuala Terengganu 299
North of Kuala Terengganu 299
South of Kuala Terengganu 300

SABAH 304
KOTA KINABALU 306
AROUND KOTA KINABALU 320

See the Index for a full list of destinations covered in this book.

On the Road

Tunku Abdul Rahman National Park 320

NORTHWESTERN SABAH 322

Mt Kinabalu & Kinabalu National Park .. 322
Around Mt Kinabalu..... 330
Northwest Coast 332
Offshore Islands........ 336

EASTERN SABAH 337
Sandakan................ 337
Sepilok 343
Sandakan Archipelago .. 347
Sungai Kinabatangan ... 348
Lahad Datu 353
Danum Valley Conservation Area 354
Tabin Wildlife Reserve ... 356
Semporna 357
Semporna Archipelago .. 359
Tawau 363
Tawau Hills Park 367
Maliau Basin Conservation Area 367

SOUTHWESTERN SABAH 369
The Interior 369
Beaufort Division 372
Pulau Tiga National Park .374
Pulau Labuan 375

SARAWAK 379
KUCHING 382
WESTERN SARAWAK..... 400
Bako National Park 400
Santubong Peninsula ... 404

Kuching Wetlands National Park 406
Semenggoh Nature Reserve 407
Kampung Benuk........ 408
Annah Rais Longhouse .. 408
Kubah National Park 409
Bau & Environs.......... 411
Lundu................. 413
Gunung Gading National Park 413
Sematan 414
Tanjung Datu National Park 415
Talang-Satang National Park 415

CENTRAL SARAWAK 417
Sibu 417
Batang Rejang 421
Bintulu 426
Similajau National Park . 427
Niah National Park...... 429
Lambir Hills National Park 431
Miri 432

NORTHEASTERN SARAWAK 438
Gunung Mulu National Park 438
Kelabit Highlands....... 444
Limbang Division 451

BRUNEI 454
BANDAR SERI BEGAWAN 456
TUTONG & BELAIT DISTRICTS............. 467

Tutong 467
Jalan Labi 467
Seria.................. 467
Kuala Belait............ 468

TEMBURONG DISTRICT ..468
Bangar 468
Pulau Selirong 470
Batang Duri........... 470
Peradayan Forest Reserve 470
Ulu Temburong National Park 470

SINGAPORE 473
SINGAPORE SURVIVAL GUIDE 537
Directory A–Z 537
Transport............... 541

Kuala Lumpur

📞03 / POP 1.38 MILLION / AREA 243 SQ KM

Includes »

Sights 47
Activities..................... 58
Courses 59
Tours............................. 60
Festivals & Events 60
Sleeping....................... 60
Eating 66
Drinking........................ 84
Entertainment............... 86
Shopping...................... 88

Best Places to Eat

» Kedai Makanan Dan Minuman TKS (p66)

» Rebung (p83)

» Robson Heights (p83)

» Frangipani (p66)

» Sri Nirwana Maju (p83)

Best Places to Stay

» Villa Samadhi (p62)

» The Courtyard (p62)

» YY38 Hotel (p62)

» BackHome (p61)

» Reggae Mansion (p61)

Why Go?

Less than two centuries since tin miners hacked a base out of the jungle, Kuala Lumpur (KL) has evolved into an affluent 21st-century metropolis remarkable for its cultural diversity. Ethnic Malays, Chinese prospectors, Indian migrants and British colonials all helped shape this city, and each group has left its indelible physical mark as well as a fascinating assortment of cultural traditions.

KL lacks much of an overall plan and has few obvious sights. Its quirky charm lies in historic temples and mosques rubbing shoulders with contemporary towers and shopping malls; traders' stalls piled high with pungent durians and counterfeit handbags; monorail cars zipping by lush jungle foliage; and locals sipping cappuccinos in wi-fi–enabled cafes or feasting on delicious streetside hawker food.

Eating and shopping are highlights, but when urban pressures begin to wear you down there are many easy day trips; see Selangor & Negeri Sembilan (p97) for details.

When to Go
Kuala Lumpur

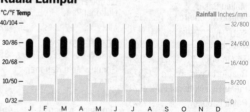

Jan & Feb Enjoy the Chinese New Year and the dramatic Hindu festival Thaipusam.

Mar & Apr Catch the first of the city's general sales and the Malaysian Grand Prix.

Aug & Sep Enjoy Ramadan night markets across the city; celebrate Independence and Malaysia Day.

History

In 1857 87 Chinese prospectors in search of tin landed at the apex of the Klang and Gombak Rivers and imaginatively named the place Kuala Lumpur, meaning 'muddy confluence'. Within a month all but 17 of the prospectors had died of malaria and other tropical diseases, but the tin they discovered in Ampang attracted more miners and KL quickly became a brawling, noisy, violent boomtown.

As in other parts of the Malay Peninsula, the local sultan appointed a proxy (known as Kapitan China) to bring the unruly Chinese fortune-seekers and their secret societies into line. The successful candidate Yap Ah Loy ('Kapitan China' from 1868 to 1885) took on the task with such ruthless relish that he's now credited as the founder of KL.

Yap had barely established control, however, when fighting broke out between local sultans for the throne of Perak. KL was swept up in the conflict and burnt to the ground in 1881. This allowed the British government representative Frank Swettenham to push through a radical new town plan that transferred the central government from Klang to KL. By 1886 a railway line linked KL to Klang; by 1887 several thousand brick buildings had been built; and in 1896 the city became the capital of the newly formed Federated Malay States.

After occupation by Japanese forces during WWII (when many Chinese were tortured and killed, and many Indians were sent to work on Burma's 'Death Railway'), the British temporarily returned, only to be ousted when Malaysia declared its independence in 1957.

KL's darkest hour came on 13 May 1969 when race riots – mainly between the Malays and Chinese communities – claimed hundreds, perhaps thousands, of lives. A year later local government elections were suspended – ever since, KL's mayor has been appointed by the Federal Territories Minister.

In 1974 the sultan of Selangor ceded the city's land to the state so it could officially become the Federal Territory of Kuala Lumpur. The city has prospered ever since as Malaysia's political and commercial capital.

⊙ Sights

Apart from KL's major sights, be sure to also explore some of the city's eye-boggling shopping malls – all part of the essential KL experience.

GOLDEN TRIANGLE

Menara KL   OBSERVATION TOWER
(KL Tower; Map p68; ☎2020 5448; www.kltower. com.my; 2 Jln Punchak; observation deck adult/ child RM47/27, shuttle bus every 15 min free; ⊙observation deck 9am-10pm, last tickets 9.30pm, shuttle bus 9am-9.30pm) The best view of KL is from atop this telecommunications tower, which sits amid the leafy surrounds of Bukit Nanas Forest Reserve. Avoid the touristy hoopla (including pony rides, an F1 race simulator and small aquarium) at the tower's base and head straight for the **observation deck** in the bulb at the top; its shape is inspired by a Malaysian spinning toy. One floor above is the revolving restaurant Atmosphere 360 (p67); having a meal here is likely the best deal. A **shuttle bus** runs up to the tower from the gate on Jln Punchak.

Aquaria KLCC   AQUARIUM
(Map p68; ☎2333 1888; www.klaquaria.com; concourse level, KL Convention Centre; adult/ child aquarium RM45/35, aquarium & aquazone RM80/52; ⊙11am-8pm) This impressive aquarium is in the basement of the KL Convention Centre. As well as tanks of colourful fish and touch-a-starfish–type activities, you can walk through a 90m-long underwater tunnel to view sinister-looking (but mostly harmless) sand tiger sharks and giant gropers.

🌳 **Bukit Nanas**
Forest Reserve   NATURE RESERVE
(Map p68; ⊙7am-6pm) Rather than taking the shuttle bus to the base of Menara KL, climb the short and well-labelled nature trails through this lowland dipterocarp forest reserve; it gained protection in 1906 making it the oldest protected piece of jungle in Malaysia. There are good displays and leaflets in the **Forest Information Centre** (☎2026 4741; www.forestry.gov.my; Jln Raja Chulan; ⊙9am-5pm) at the base of the hill.

FREE **Galeri Petronas**   ART GALLERY
(Map p56; ☎2051 7770; www.galeripetronas.com. my; 3rd fl, Suria KLCC; ⊙10am-8pm Tue-Sun) Swap consumerism for culture at this excellent art gallery showcasing contemporary photography and paintings. It's a bright, modern space with interesting, professionally curated shows that change every few months.

Kuala Lumpur Highlights

1 Admire the glittering exterior of the **Petronas Towers** (p55), then head up to the observation deck

2 Day or night, bustling **Chinatown** (p51) is a dynamic place to eat, shop and people watch

3 Stand at KL's colonial heart on **Merdeka Square** (p52) surrounded by a handsome ensemble of heritage buildings

4 Spot all kinds of feathered beauties in **KL Bird Park** (p53), showpiece of the lush Lake Gardens

5 Admire beautiful objects gathered from around the Islamic world in the **Islamic Arts Museum** (p53)

6 Pay respects to the heavenly mother at the riotously colourful **Thean Hou Temple** (p58)

7 Dive into the streetside dining adventure of **Jln Alor** (p72)

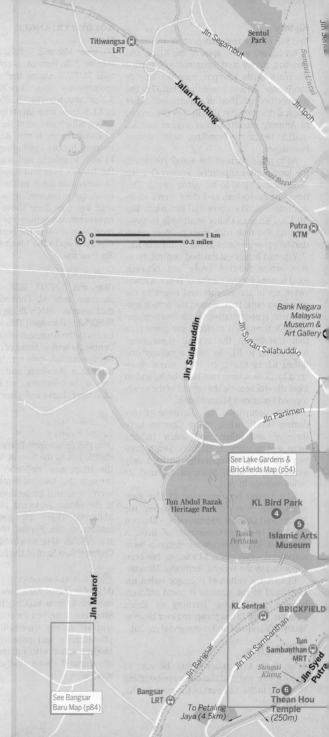

See Lake Gardens & Brickfields Map (p54)

See Bangsar Baru Map (p84)

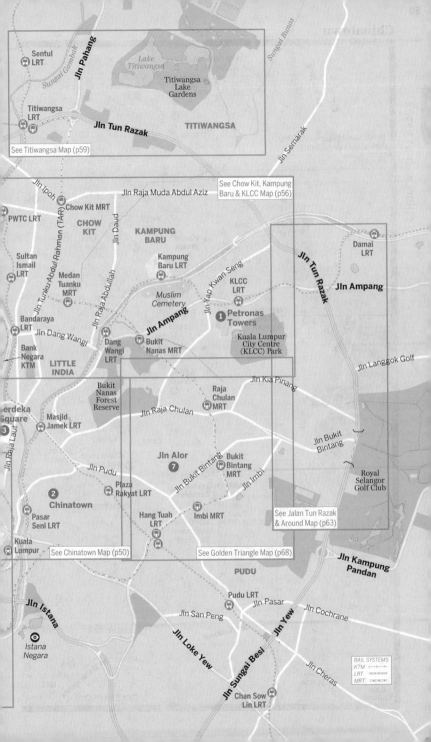

Chinatown

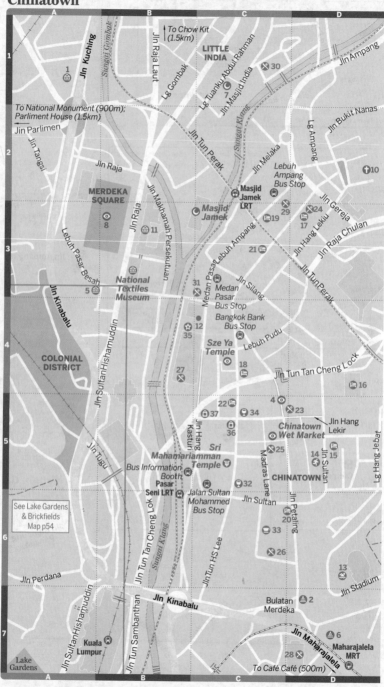

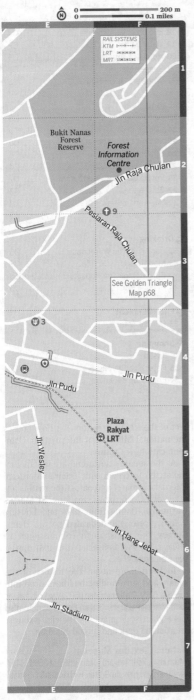

Badan Warisan Malaysia

NOTABLE BUILDING

(Heritage of Malaysia Trust; Map p63; ☎2144 9273; www.badanwarisan.org.my; 2 Jln Stonor; ☻9am-5pm Mon-Sat) Find out about the work of this built heritage preservation society at its head office located in a 1925 colonial bungalow in the shadow of the Petronas Towers. The property's grounds contain the **Rumah Penghulu** (Map p63; suggested donation RM10; ☻tours 11am & 3pm Mon-Sat), a handsome example of a restored Malay-style wooden house from Kedah. The trust also holds exhibitions in the bungalow, where there's a gift store stocking books, wooden antique furniture and local handcrafted items.

CHINATOWN, MERDEKA SQUARE & MASJID JAMEK

Jalan Petaling

MARKET

(Map p50; ☻10am-11pm) Chinatown's commercial heart is one of the most colourful and busiest shopping parades in KL, particularly at night when stalls cram the covered street. It offers everything from fresh fruit and cheap clothes and shoes to copies of brand-name watches and handbags, and pirated CDs and DVDs. Be prepared to bargain.

Sri Mahamariamman Temple

HINDU TEMPLE

(Map p50; 163 Jln Tun HS Lee; ☻6am-8.30pm) The oldest Hindu shrine in Malaysia was founded by migrant workers from the Indian state of Tamil Nadu in 1873. Flower-garland vendors crowd the entrance and the temple is crowned by a huge *gopuram* (temple tower) covered in riotously colourful statues of Hindu deities. Locals leave incense, flowers, coconuts and strings of limes as offerings to Mariamman, the south Indian mother goddess, an incarnation of Durga. An idol from the temple is paraded to Batu Caves in a silver chariot during Thaipusam (p571). Non-Hindus are welcome to visit, but leave your shoes at the entrance.

Masjid Jamek

MOSQUE

(Friday Mosque; Map p50; off Jln Tun Perak; ☻8.30am-12.30pm & 2.30-4pm Sat-Thu, 8.30-11am & 2.30-4pm Fri) Constructed in 1907 at the confluence of the Klang and Gombak Rivers, this beautiful onion-domed mosque is an island of serenity, with airy open pavilions shaded by palm trees. The designer was British architect AB Hubbock, who sought inspiration from the Mughal mosques of northern India. Visitors are welcome outside prayer times, but should dress appropriately.

Chinatown

⊙ Top Sights
Chinatown Wet Market C5
Masjid Jamek C3
National Textiles Museum B3
Sri Mahamariamman Temple C5
Sze Ya Temple C4

⊙ Sights
1 Bank Negara Malaysia Museum &
  Art Gallery A1
2 Chan She Shu Yuen Temple D7
3 Court Hill Ganesh Temple...................E4
4 Jalan Petaling......................................C5
5 KL City Gallery A3
6 Koon Yam (Guanyin) Temple D7
7 Masjid Little India C1
8 Merdeka Square B3
9 St Andrew's Presbyterian Church........F2
10 St John's Cathedral.............................D2
11 Sultan Abdul Samad Building..............B3

⊕ Activities, Courses & Tours
12 C Woks Design.....................................C4
13 Chin Woo Stadium...............................D6
14 Going Places Tours D5

⊜ Sleeping
15 5 Elements Hotel D5
16 AnCasa Hotel & Spa Kuala
  Lumpur...D4
17 BackHome...D3

18 Explorers Guesthouse C4
19 Hotel 1915 ....C3
20 Hotel Lok Ann D6
21 Reggae Mansion..................................C3
22 Wheelers Guest House C5

⊗ Eating
23 Ikan Panggang.....................................D5
24 LOKL..D3
25 Madras Lane Hawkers C5
26 Old China Café.....................................C6
27 Precious B4
28 Purple Cane Tea Restaurant................D7
29 Sangeetha..C3
30 Saravanaa Bhavan C1
31 Sing Seng Nam C3

⊙ Drinking
32 Bar Art @ The Warehouse....................C5
33 Moontree House...................................C6
  Purple Cane Tea House .... (see 33)
34 Reggae Bar C5

⊛ Entertainment
35 Doppel Kafe B4

⊜ Shopping
  Justin Yap .... (see 36)
36 Peter Hoe Beyond................................C5
37 Peter Hoe Evolution C5

Sze Ya Temple   CHINESE TEMPLE
(Map p50; Jln Tun HS Lee; ⊙7am-5pm) This atmospheric Taoist temple was constructed in 1864 on the instructions of 'Kapitan China' Yap Ah Loy. You can see a statue of Yap just left of the main altar. Its odd position, squished between rows of shophouses, was determined by feng shui.

Merdeka Square   SQUARE, PLAZA
(Map p50) The huge open square where Malaysian independence was declared in 1957 is ringed by heritage buildings and dominated by an enormous flagpole and fluttering Malaysian flag. In the British era, the square was used as a cricket pitch.

On the east side of the square is the fantasy-like **Sultan Abdul Samad Building** (Map p50; Jln Raja) with its distinctive copper-plated cupolas. This blend of Victorian, Moorish and Moghul architecture is typical of many of KL's colonial buildings. Designed by AC Norman (an associate of AB Hubbock, archi-

tect of the KL Train Station), it now houses the national Ministry of Information, Communications & Culture.

At the square's north end are low memorial arches inscribed with 'Dataran Merdeka' (Merdeka Square) and across the road is another of AC Norman's creations, **St Mary's Cathedral**, dating from 1894 and housing a fine pipe-organ dedicated to Sir Henry Gurney, the British high commissioner to Malaya. He was assassinated in 1951 during the Emergency.

To learn more about the history of the square and surrounding buildings drop into the **KL City Gallery** (Map p50; www.klcitygallery. com; Merdeka Square; ⊙8am-6pm), which also has a giant scale model of the city, a tourist information desk and a good gift shop.

National Textiles Museum   MUSEUM
(Muzium Tekstil Negara; Map p50; ☎2694 3457; www.jmm.gov.my; Jln Sultan Hishamuddin; ⊙daily 9am-6pm) Four darkened exhibition spaces

KUALA LUMPUR IN...

Two Days

Breakfast at **Imbi Market** then head to the Kuala Lumpur City Centre (KLCC) to secure tickets up the **Petronas Towers** and explore the **Suria KLCC** mall. Alternatively, ascend **Menara KL** and get your bearings of the city from the revolving restaurant **Atmosphere 360**. Spend the afternoon at the **National Museum**. Go souvenir shopping at the **Central Market**, then explore **Chinatown**, ending up at **Jln Petaling** for food and the night market.

On day two explore Tun Abdul Razak Heritage Park (formerly known as the Lake Gardens Park), dropping by the **KL Bird Park** and the **Islamic Arts Museum**. Have afternoon tea in **Starhill Gallery**, go shopping at **Pavilion KL**, then trawl the night food stalls of **Jln Alor**.

Three Days

There are great views of the city skyline from **Lake Titiwangsa**, where you can also visit the **National Visual Art Gallery**. Amble through the Malay area of Kampung Baru, then take a taxi to the splendid **Thean Hou Temple** close to where you can eat at **Robson Heights**. Check to see if there are concerts at the **Dewan Filharmonik Petronas** or **No Black Tie**. Grab a nightcap at **Palate Palette**.

---

help preserve the delicate textiles on display – there are some beautiful pieces and plenty of explanation of how they are made. The sad thing is that many of the time-consuming skills necessary for the production of such textiles are dying out, making these pieces increasingly rare. In the attached shop many batik pieces are sourced from Indonesia.

LAKE GARDENS & BRICKFIELDS

TOP CHOICE **Islamic Arts Museum**   MUSEUM
(Muzium Kesenian Islam Malaysia; Map p54; ☑2274 2020; www.iamm.org.my; Jln Lembah Perdana; adult/child RM12/6; ☺10am-6pm, restaurant closed Mon) This outstanding museum is home to one of best collections of Islamic decorative arts in the world. Aside from the quality of the exhibits, which include fabulous textiles, carpets, jewellery and calligraphy-inscribed pottery, the building itself is a stunner, with beautifully decorated domes and glazed tilework. The gift shop stocks beautiful products from around the Islamic world.

KL Bird Park   AVIARY
(Map p54; ☑2272 1010; www.klbirdpark.com; Jln Cenderawasih; adult/child RM48/38; ☺9am-6pm) This fabulous aviary brings together some 200 species of (mostly) Asian birds flying free beneath an enormous canopy. Star attractions include ostriches, hornbills, eagles, flamingos and parrots. It's worth getting to the park for feeding times (hornbills 11.30am, eagles 2.30pm) or the bird shows (12.30pm and 3.30pm), which feature plenty of parrot tricks to keep youngsters amused. The park's **Hornbill Restaurant** (Map p54; ☑2693 8086; mains RM40-60; ☺9am-8pm; ☏) is also recommended.

National Museum   MUSEUM
(Muzium Negara; Map p54; ☑2282 6255; www.muziumnegara.gov.my; Jln Damansara; adult/child RM5/2; ☺9am-6pm, tours 10am Mon-Thu & Sat in English, Tue & Thu in French, Thu in Japanese) A major renovation has resulted in four main galleries with interesting, well-organised displays: Early History, where you'll find the bones of Perak Man; Malay

---

ⓘ KUALA LUMPUR BY FOOT

Six-lane highways and flyovers slice up the city, and pavements are often cracked or nonexistent. Even so, the best way to get a feel for KL's vibrant atmosphere is to walk. The city centre is surprisingly compact – from Chinatown to Little India takes little more than 10 minutes on foot – and some sights are so close together that it's often quicker to walk than take public transport or grab a cab (which can easily become snarled in traffic and KL's tortuous one-way system).

Lake Gardens & Brickfields

Kingdoms, including the history of the Melaka; Colonial Era, from the Portuguese through to the Japanese occupation; and Malaysia Today, which charts the country's post-WWII development. There are more things to see outside, including a regularly changing exhibition (extra charge) and a couple of small free galleries: the Orang Asli Craft Museum and Malay World Ethnology Museum, which has good displays of batik and other fabrics.

Time your visit to coincide with one of the free tours given by enthusiastic volunteer guides. In the future you'll be able to access the museum from KL Sentral station, but for now the easiest way here is by taxi, the hop-on-hop-off bus or via the walkway over the highway south of the Lake Gardens.

🌿 **Tun Abdul Razak Heritage Park (Lake Gardens Park)**   PARK
(Map p54; Jln Tembusu; ☺daylight hours) This 70 hectare park, laid out during colonial times, is planted with a variety of native plants, trees and shrubs. In the middle is a good children's adventure playground and nearby is the sprawling lake for which the gardens are named. You can rent boats for RM6 per hour and watch t'ai chi practitioners in the early morning. At the northern end of the lake is the National Monument (Map p54; Jln Parlimen, Plaza Tugu Negara; ☺7am-6pm), a giant bronze sculpture created in 1966 by Felix de Weldon, the artist

Lake Gardens & Brickfields

◎ **Top Sights**
Islamic Arts Museum	B2
KL Bird Park	A2
Masjid Negara	B2
National Museum	A2

◎ **Sights**
1 Butterfly Park	A1
2 Deer Park	A1
3 KL Train Station	B2
4 Majestic Hotel	B2
5 Malayan Railway Administration Building	B2
6 National Planetarium	B2
7 Sam Kow Tong Temple	B3
8 Taman Bunga Raya	A1
Taman Orkid	(see 8)

9 Tun Abdul Razak Heritage Park (Lake Gardens Park)	A2
10 Wei-Ling Gallery	B3

🎫 **Activities, Courses & Tours**
11 Buddhist Maha Vihara	A4
12 Temple of Fine Arts	A4
YMCA	(see 14)

🛏 **Sleeping**
13 Hilton Kuala Lumpur	A3
14 YMCA	B3

🍴 **Eating**
Annalakshmi	(see 12)
15 Hornbill Restaurant	A2
16 Kompleks Makan Tanglin	B1
17 Vishalatchi	B3

responsible for Washington DC's Iwo Jima monument.

Other interesting sights in the park include the **Butterfly Park** (Taman Rama Rama; Map p54; ☏2693 4799; Jln Cenderawasih; adult/child RM18/9; ☺9am-6pm), opposite the KL Bird Park, the **National Planetarium** (Map p54; ☏2273 4303; www.angkasa.gov.my/planetarium; 53 Jln Perdana; gallery free, planetarium RM12/6; ☺9am-4.30pm Tue-Sun) and **Deer Park** (Taman Rusa & Kancil; Map p54; Jln Perdana; ☺10am-6pm, closed noon-2pm weekdays).

Masjid Negara   MOSQUE
(National Mosque; Map p54; Jln Lembah Perdana; ☺9am-noon, 3-4pm & 5.30-6.30pm, closed Fri morning) The main place of worship for KL's Malay Muslim population is this gigantic mosque, inspired by Mecca's Grand Mosque. Its umbrella-like blue-tile roof has 18 points symbolising the 13 states of Malaysia and the five pillars of Islam. Rising above the mosque, a 74m-high minaret issues the call to prayer, which can be heard across Chinatown. Non-Muslims are welcome to visit outside prayer times but dress appropriately and remove your shoes before entering.

Brickfields   NEIGHBOURHOOD
Major developments around KL Sentral station are transforming this traditionally Indian area. Finally, the monorail terminal has been connected to the train station via a new shopping and office complex. A ceremonial arch graces Jln Brickfields and a colourful fountain with sculpted elephants is at the junction with Jln Travers.

Dragons fly off the corners of the **Sam Kow Tong Temple** (Map p54; 16 Jln Thambapillai; ☺7am-5pm), just around the corner from the monorail terminus, making for a striking contrast with the soaring hotel towers above KL Sentral. Other interesting buildings to be seen include the Temple of Fine Arts (p60) and Wei-Ling Gallery (p90).

KL Train Station   HISTORIC BUILDING
(Map p54; Jln Sultan Hishamuddin) The British architect AB Hubbock's Moorish- and Moghul-inspired fantasy, Kuala Lumpur Station, dates from 1911. Sadly, the station is looking shabby and forlorn especially since KL Sentral took over most of its services. This said, it's still a visually handsome building and is best seen from the forecourt of the grand **Malayan Railway Administration Building** (Map p54; Jln Sultan Hishamuddin) opposite; step inside this building to admire the soaring central stairwell. An underpass

---

ⓘ GETTING TO THE LAKE GARDENS

The Lake Gardens can seem like an island of greenery cut off from the city by railway lines and highways. However, it is possible to walk here: take the pedestrian bridge across from the Central Market to Kompleks Dayabumi and then head south around the back of the post office to the underpass leading to the Masjid Negara. Another set of overhead pedestrian bridges lead into KL Station from where you can also walk up to the gardens.

Alternatively, the KL Hop-On Hop-Off Bus stops at Masjid Negara, KL Bird Park, the National Monument and the National Museum. Once in the Lake Gardens, taxi drivers will likely insist on charging RM15 to RM20 to cover the short distance back to the city and refuse to use the meter.

---

from here leads you across the busy highway to inside the station where KTM Komuter trains still stop.

🎨 Urban Village   ARTS CENTRE
(☏2201 0306; www.urbanvillage.my; 25 Jln Abdullah, Bangsar Utama) It's difficult to categorise this 'creative entrepreneur hub' that provides working space for local talents from the worlds of art, music and fashion. If you have musical skills, it's possible to help out with their program to get kids into music and start a band. Various performances and talks happen here too and there's a shop selling some of the artists' work, including t-shirts.

LITTLE INDIA, KAMPUNG BARU & CHOW KIT

Petronas Towers   NOTABLE BUILDING
(Map p56; www.petronastwintowers.com.my; Jln Ampang; adult/child RM80/30; ☺9am-9pm Tue-Sun) Headquarters of the national oil and gas company Petronas, the 88-storey steel clad twin towers, nearly 452m tall, epitomise contemporary KL. Resembling twin silver rockets plucked from an early episode of *Flash Gordon,* they are the perfect allegory for the meteoric rise of the city from tin miners' shanty town to space-age metropolis.

Designed by Argentinian architect Cesar Pelli, the twin towers' floor plan is based on

Chow Kit, Kampung Baru & KLCC

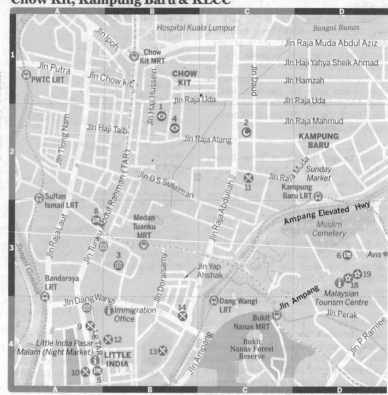

Chow Kit, Kampung Baru & KLCC

◎ Top Sights
Petronas Towers E3

◎ Sights
1 Bazaar Baru Chow Kit B2
Galeri Petronas ....(see 20)
2 Kampung Baru Mosque C2
3 Loke Mansion B3
Petrosains ....(see 20)
4 Tatt Khalsa Diwan Gurdwara B2

🛏 Sleeping
5 Frenz Hotel A4
6 Hotel Maya D3
7 Mandarin Oriental E4
8 Tune Hotel A3

☒ Eating
9 Capital Café A4

10 Coliseum Café A4
11 Ikan Bakar Berempah C2
Little Penang Kafé ....(see 20)
12 Sagar B4
13 Thai-la B4
14 Yut Kee B4

◎ Drinking
15 Apartment Downtown E3
16 Marketplace E2

✪ Entertainment
17 Dewan Filharmonik Petronas E3
18 Saloma D3
Tanjung Golden Village ....(see 20)
19 Zouk Club D3

🛍 Shopping
20 Suria KLCC E3

Loke Mansion

HISTORIC BUILDING

(Map p56; ☎2691 0803; 273A Jln Medan Tuanku) Rescued from the brink of dereliction by the law firm Cheang & Ariff, Loke Mansion was once the home of self-made tin tycoon Loke Yew, although the original part of the structure was built in the 1860s by another rich merchant, Cheow Ah Yeok. The Japanese high command also set up base here in 1942. Access to the interior is by appointment only; admiring the beautifully restored, whitewashed exterior is free to all passersby.

Kampung Baru

NEIGHBOURHOOD

Somehow this Malay area has managed to retain its sleepy village atmosphere in the midst of the city: traditional wooden houses stand amid leafy gardens and people go quietly about their daily lives – with the exception of Saturday night when a lively *pasar malam* (night market) takes over the area close to the Kampung Baru Light Rail Transit (LRT) station. Look out for the impressive **Tatt Khalsa Diwan Gurdwara** (Map p56; www.tattkhalsa.org; 24 Jln Raja Alang), the largest Sikh temple in Southeast Asia and the **Kampung Baru Mosque** (Map p56; Jln Raja Alang), built in 1924, with its gateway decorated in beautiful glazed tiles. Explore the streets around here at the junction with Jln Daud to find many old wooden houses.

Bank Negara Malaysia Museum & Art Gallery

MUSEUM, ART GALLERY

(Map p56; http://museum.bnm.gov.my; 2 Jln Dato Onn; ◷10am-6pm) The national bank's conservatively chosen, but attractive art collection is housed in a futuristic metal-clad complex (designed by top Malaysian architect Hijjas Kasturi) within walking distance of Bank Negara train station. Also here are exhibitions on the region's currency and Malaysia's economic history.

Petrosains

MUSEUM

(Map p56; ☎2331 8181; www.petrosains.com.my; Level 4, Suria KLCC; adult/youth/child RM25/20/15; ◷9.30am-4pm Tue-Fri, 9.30am-5pm Sat & Sun) Fill an educational few hours at this interactive science discovery centre in Suria KLCC with all sorts of buttons to press and levers to pull. Many of the activities and displays focus on the wonderful things that petrol has brought to Malaysia – no prizes for guessing who sponsors the museum.

an eight-sided star that echoes arabesque patterns. Islamic influences are also evident in each tower's five tiers – representing the five pillars of Islam – and in the 63m masts that crown them, calling to mind the minarets of a mosque and the Star of Islam.

Get in line before 8am to be sure of securing one of the 960 tickets issued daily (half of which are sold in advance) for a guided 45-minute tour up to the 86th floor, including a 15-minutes walk across the Skybridge connecting the towers on the 41st floor. The ticket office is in the tower basement at the KLCC.

KLCC Park

PARK

(Map p68; ◷24hr, playground & paddling pool 10am-7.30pm Tue-Sat) Here you'll find a soft-surface jogging track, synchronised fountains, a fantastic (under 12s only) playground and paddling pool and – of course – great views of the Petronas Towers.

THEAN HOU TEMPLE

The multilayered and highly ornate **Thean Hou Temple** (Map p54; ☎2274 7088; www. hainannet.com; off Jln Syed Putra; ☺9am-6pm) is one of the most visually impressive in Malaysia. It's dedicated to the heavenly mother, Thean Hou. Her statue takes centre stage in the main hall, with Kuan Yin (the Buddhist goddess of mercy) on her right and Shuiwei Shengniang (the goddess of the waterfront) to her left. Statues of Milefo (the laughing Buddha), Weituo and Guandi further contribute to this Taoist–Buddhist hodgepodge.

There are great views from the temple's upper decks while at its base are tourist restaurants and shops. To reach the temple, 3km south of the centre of town, take either a taxi or the monorail to Tun Sambanthan station, cross Jln Syed Putra using the overpass and walk up the hill.

TITIWANGSA

Lake Titiwangsa
LAKE

(Map p59) For a picture-postcard view of the city skyline head to Lake Titiwangsa and the relaxing park that surrounds it. If you're feeling energetic, hire row boats, pedal boats and canoes (per hour from RM3) to glide across the lake, or go for a jog. The park is a favourite spot for courting Malaysian couples – and strict police on the lookout for improper behaviour!

Lake Titiwangsa is an 800m walk east of the Titiwangsa monorail station.

National Visual Art Gallery
ART GALLERY

(Balai Seni Lukis Negara; Map p59; ☎4026 7000; www.artgallery.org.my; 2 Jln Temerloh; ☺10am-6pm) There are often interesting temporary shows of local and regional artists, as well as pieces from the gallery's permanent collection of 4000 works including paintings by Zulkifi Moh'd Dohalan, Wong Hoi Cheong, Ahad Osman and the renowned batik artist Chuah Than Teng. A new portrait gallery section was in the works during our latest visit. The interior is dominated by a swirly Guggenheim Museum–style staircase but overall you can't help feeling that so much more could be made of the place.

Next to the gallery is the theatre Istana Budaya (p88). Designed by Mohammed Kamar Ya'akub, the building's soaring roof is based on a traditional Malay floral decoration of betel leaves, while its footprint resembles a *wau bulan* (Malay moon kite).

🏃 Activities

Chin Woo Stadium
SWIMMING

(Map p50; ☎2072 4602; www.chinwoo.org.my; Jln Hang Jebat; adult/child RM4/1.50; ☺2-8pm Mon-Fri, 9am-8pm Sat & Sun) Great city views at this 50m outdoor pool. You must wear a proper swimsuit or swimming trunks.

Lightworks
YOGA

(Map p68; ☎2143 2966; www.lightworks.com.my; 19 Jln Mesui) New Age centre that offers relaxing hatha yoga classes with an expat instructor. Drop-in classes are RM40 per session and are held at noon on Tuesday, and 7pm on Monday and Thursday.

Kompleks Sukan Bangsar
SPORTS

(Map p84; Bangsar Sports Complex; ☎03-2284 6065; 3 Jln Terasek 3, Bangsar Baru; admission RM3; ☺9.30am-noon, 2-4.30pm, 6-8:30pm, closed Sun mornings) Home to a 25m pool, which can get crowded. Also has tennis courts, and squash and badminton facilities.

Spa Village
SPA

(Map p68; ☎2782 9090; www.spavillageresort. org; 168 Jln Imbi, Ritz Carlton; ☺9am-9pm) Indoor and outdoor beauty and massage treatments, a sensory room and a second outdoor pool with waterfalls. Health club facilities include 24-hour fitness centre, sauna, steam room and whirlpool.

Asianel Reflexology Spa
SPA

(Map p68; ☎2142 1397; www.asianel.com; ☺10am-8pm) Upmarket massage and reflexology spa, one of several classy operations on the 'Pamper Floor' of Starhill Gallery.

Reborn
MASSAGE, REFLEXOLOGY

(Map p68; ☎2144 1288; www.reborn.com.my; 18 Jln Bukit Bintang; ☺11am-3am) One of the more pleasantly designed massage and reflexology joints along Jln Bukit Bintang, offering spa treatments as well as a fish spa.

Titiwangsa

📖 Courses

Check directly with each provider for prices and exact course times and details. Malay cooking courses are also offered by Rebung (p83) and Reggae Mansion (p61).

TOP CHOICE Rohani Jelani   COOKING
(www.rohanijelani.com/intro.htm) Learn to cook traditional Malaysian dishes in hands-on group classes run by friendly cookbook author Rohani Jelani in a beautiful countryside retreat where you can also stay the night. Each class ends with a sit-down meal of the dishes prepared that day.

LaZat Malaysian Home Cooking Class   COOKING
(☎019-238 1198; www.malaysia-klcookingclass .com) The classes are held on Tuesday and Saturday mornings. Their location is a 25-minute drive from central KL. Check the website for the different menus on offer.

C Woks Design   BATIK
(Map p50; ☎012-257 2344; http://batikcwok .blogspot.com; Central Market Annexe; ⊙10am-9pm) Paint your own batik panel from RM20. Either choose a readily prepared design or create your own. The C Woks team also have an outlet at Kompleks Budaya Kraf (p89).

School of Hard Knocks   ARTS & CRAFTS
(☎4145 6122; http://visitorcentre.royalselangor. com/vc; 4 Jln Usahawan 6; classes RM50; ⊙9am-5pm) This famous pewter centre offers entertaining classes (30 minutes) where you make your own pewter bowl; advance booking required.

Titiwangsa

◎ Top Sights

Lake Titiwangsa C1
National Visual Art Gallery C2

🎯 Activities, Courses & Tours

1 Sutra Dance Theatre B1

🎭 Entertainment

2 Istana Budaya B2
Sutra Dance Theatre .... (see 1)

YMCA   LANGUAGE
(Map p54; ☎2274 1439; www.ymcakl.com; 95 Jln Padang Belia) Offers Bahasa Malaysia classes, as well as courses studying Thai, Mandarin, Cantonese and Japanese. You can also study martial arts and different types of dancing here.

Buddhist Maha Vihara   MEDITATION
(Map p54; ☎2274 1141; www.buddhistmahavihara. com; 123 Jln Berhala) Meditation and chanting classes plus dharma talks take place most days. Classes are run on a donation basis.

Kuala Lumpur Performing Arts Centre   MUSIC & DANCE
(klpac; ☎4047 9060; www.klpac.org; Jln Strachan, Sentul West) A variety of performing arts courses are offered here, including courses on traditional instruments, such as the gamelan (traditional Malay orchestra).

Sutra Dance Theatre   MUSIC & DANCE
(Map p59; ☎4021 1092; www.sutrafoundation.org .my; 12 Persiaran Titiwangsa 3) Courses in Odissi and other forms of classical Indian dance are offered at this cultural centre near Taman Tasik Titiwangsa.

FISH SPAS

Often combined with foot reflexology operations, fish spas bring a new meaning to feeding the fish. Immerse your feet in a tank filled with the small *Garra rufa* and *Cyprinion macrostomus*, also known as Doctor Fish, and allow the flapping podiatrists to gently nibble away at the dead skin. It's an initially ticklish, but not wholly unpleasant, experience lasting 30 minutes (or as long as you can stand it!).

Among the places you can sample this service, which costs around RM30:

Foot Master Dr Fish Spa (Map p68; ☎2144 1916; 6th fl, Berjaya Times Sq, 1 Jln Imbi; ☺10am-10pm)

Morino Kaze (Map p68; ☎2141 1916; www.morinokaze.com.my; 2nd fl, Piccolo Galleria, 101 Jln Bukit Bintang; ☺noon-midnight)

Kenko (Map p68; ☎2141 6651; www.kenko.com.sg; Level 5, Pavilion KL, 169 Jln Bukit Bintang; ☺10am-10pm)

Temple of Fine Arts   MUSIC & DANCE
(Map p54; ☎2274 3709; www.tfa.org.my; 114-116 Jln Berhala) This Indian cultural centre offers courses in classical Indian dance, song and music. Stage shows take place here throughout the year.

☞ Tours

Simply Enak   FOOD TOUR
(☎017-287 8929; www.simplyenak.com; tours RM150, minimum of two people) 'Food Experience Captain' Pauline Lee will guide you on an informative and tasty voyage of Chinatown and Bangsar. 'Eat a local' home-cooked dinners (RM200) and cooking classes (RM550) can also be arranged.

KL Hop-On Hop-Off   BUS TOUR
(☎2166 6162; www.myhoponhopoff.com; adult/child 24hr RM38/17, 48hr RM65/29; ☺8.30am-8.30pm) This double-decker wi-fi–enabled air-con bus makes a circuit of the main tourist sites half-hourly throughout the day. Stops include KLCC, Jln Bukit Bintang, Menara KL, Chinatown, Merdeka Square and the attractions of Lake Gardens. Tickets, which can be bought on the bus, last all day and you can get on and off as often as you like.

Going Places Tours   ADVENTURE TOUR
(Map p50; ☎2078 4008; www.goingplaces-kl.com; 60a Jln Sultan, Original Backpackers Inn) Offers tours tailored to the backpacker market, including more adventurous options such as rafting, caving and rock-climbing adventures.

✸ Festivals & Events

The capital puts on a show for Malaysia's major holidays and festivals, including Chinese New Year, National Day and Deepavali.

City Day   ARTS & CULTURE
KL commemorates becoming a federal territory on 1 February each year with celebrations at Tasik Perdana and Titiwangsa Lake Gardens.

Malaysian Grand Prix   CAR RACE
(www.malaysiangp.com.my) Special shopping promotions and events along Jln Bukit Bintang accompany the Formula 1 race at Sepang International Circuit. March/April.

KL International Film Festival   FILM
(www.kliff.my) Catch screenings and symposiums on local and international films in June.

KL Festival   ARTS & CULTURE
(www.klfestival.org.my) July is a month of events showcasing Malaysian art, dance, theatre and music.

KL Tower BASE Jump   ADVENTURE SPORTS
(www.kltowerjump.com) The only time you'll be able to see people legally flinging themselves off Menara KL is when the international BASE-jumping fraternity are in town, usually in September.

🛏 Sleeping

KL is awash with both luxury hotels and budget hotels, plus many grubby fleapits offering windowless boxy rooms, appealing only for their rock-bottom rates. Characterful midrange options are thin on the ground.

Always ask about special deals as practically all midrange and top-end places offer promotions that can substantially slash rack rates; booking online will almost always bring the price down. The only time you should book ahead to be sure of accommodation are public holidays, when room discounts will not apply.

Chinatown is crammed with budget places (most are pretty awful) and there's a backpacker scene in the Golden Triangle. The best places fill up quickly, so book ahead. If other locations are full, Little India and the seedy Chow Kit area further north also have plenty of low-priced accommodation.

In KL budget ($) means hotels and backpackers offering a dorm bed or a double room with an attached bathroom for under RM100 net; midrange ($$) properties have double rooms with attached bathrooms for RM100 to RM400 net; top-end ($$$) places charge over RM400. At all budget places prices will be net, but at many others 10% service and 6% tax (expressed as ++) will be added to the bill.

CHINATOWN & MASJID JAMEK

TOP CHOICE BackHome   BACKPACKERS $$

(Map p50; ☑2022 0788; www.backhome.com.my; 30 Jln Tun HS Lee; dm/d with breakfast from RM42/120; ✳@⊜) This chic pit stop for flashpackers offers polished concrete finishes, Zen simple decoration, fab rain showers and a blissful central courtyard sprouting spindly trees. It can be noisy on the street outside, but they've got that covered by offering earplugs for light sleepers. Also check out its cool cafe LOKL (p72).

TOP CHOICE Reggae Mansion   BACKPACKERS $$

(Map p50; ☑2072 6877; www.reggaehostels malaysia.com/mansion/; 49-59 Jln Tun H S Lee; dm/d from RM38/120) Grooving to a superior beat than most backpacker places, including its own guesthouses in the heart of Chinatown, this is one cool operation. The decor is white-washed faux colonial with contemporary touches including a flash cafe-bar on the groundfloor, a rooftop bar, and a mini cinema (RM7) where the ticket includes a drink and popcorn.

5 Elements Hotel   HOTEL $$

(Map p50; ☑2031 6888; www.the5elementshotel. com.my; Lot 243 Jln Sultan; s/d with breakfast from RM180/220; ✳@⊜) Offering a good range of rooms, some with views towards KL Tower, this hotel makes a credible stab at boutique stylings. We particularly liked the sensuous design motif snaking its way across the corridor and bedroom walls.

Hotel Lok Ann   HOTEL $

(Map p50; ☑2078 9544; www.birdnestguesthouse. com; 113 Jln Petaling; dm/d/tr RM30/80/100; ✳⊜) Rebranding itself a 'heritage' hotel, the retro Lok Ann offers sparklingly clean, freshly painted spacious rooms with windows, TV, phone and large shower rooms. Rates include breakfast and there's also a kitchen and pleasant common area.

Hotel 1915   HOTEL $$

(Map p50; ☑2026 0042; www.hotel1915kl.com; 49 Jln Leboh Ampang; r from RM118; ✳@⊜) It's worth paying an extra RM10 at this appealing new hotel to get a room with a window. Each floor is named after a curry ingredient, but the decor is monochrome rather than spicy.

AnCasa Hotel & Spa Kuala Lumpur   HOTEL $$

(Map p50; ☑2026 6060; www.ancasa-hotel.com; Jln Tun Tan Cheng Lock; d from RM360; ✳@) Promotions halve the rack rates at one of Chinatown's best midrange options, although

---

KUALA LUMPUR FOR CHILDREN

There are dozens of attractions around KL set up specifically to keep little ones entertained. A good starting point is the **Lake Gardens** area, particularly the **KL Bird Park** and the playground and boating pond in the **Tun Abdul Razak Heritage Park** (formerly known as the Lake Gardens Park). The waterfall splash pool in the **KLCC Park** is also great for waterbabies, as is the adjacent adventure playground and the **Aquaria KLCC**.

Kids will also enjoy KL's malls. Berjaya Times Square has shops for kids of all ages, plus an indoor theme park. For younger kids, try **Megakidz** (☑2282 9300; www.megakidz .com.my; 3rd fl, Mid Valley Megamall; under 2/2-16yr Mon-Fri RM11/22, Sat & Sun RM14/28, crèche service under/over 4yr RM30/35 for 2hr; ◷10am-9.30pm) in the Mid Valley Megamall – there are storytelling sessions, art activities and an indoor adventure playground, and the centre provides a crèche service for kids aged four and over.

There are more theme parks dotted around KL, including the indoor and outdoor parks at **Genting Highlands** and the wet and wild park at **Sunway Lagoon**. For nature activities, head to **Zoo Negara** or the canopy walkway at the **Forest Research Institute of Malaysia**.

there's a small surcharge for weekend stays and internet access is chargeable. The comfortable rooms are well equipped. The hotel also has a Balinese-style spa and can arrange homestays around the peninsula.

Explorers Guesthouse
BACKPACKERS $

(Map p50; ☑2022 2928; www.theexplorersguesthouse.com; 128-130 Jln Tun H S Lee; dm/s/d & tw from RM30/68/88; ❋@❧) Another of the new backpackers giving the Chinatown oldies a hiding. Explorers follows up a comfy, spacious lobby with clean, airy rooms, colourfully painted walls and a few arty touches.

Hotel Chinatown (2)
HOTEL $

(☑2072 9933; www.hotelchinatown2.com; 70-72 Jln Petaling; s/d from RM69/90; ❋@❧) The cheapest rooms have no windows but are also away from the noisy main street. The lobby offers a comfy lounge area, water feature, book exchange and piano.

Wheelers Guest House
HOSTEL $

(Map p50; ☑2070 1386; www.backpackerskl.com/wheelers.htm; 131-133 Jln Tun HS Lee, level 2; dm/r with shared bathroom from RM13/25, r with private bathroom RM50; ❋@) Prison-like rooms, but this hostel does have a mini-aquarium, gay-friendly staff, a great rooftop terrace where free Friday-night dinners are hosted, and homemade yoghurt and muesli for breakfast.

GOLDEN TRIANGLE, KLCC & JALAN TUN RAZAK

TOP CHOICE Villa Samadhi
BOUTIQUE HOTEL $$$

(☑2143 2300; www.villasamadhi.com.my; 8 Jln Madge; r from RM500; ❋@❧❅) It's hard to believe you're in the heart of KL while staying at this gorgeous 21-room boutique villa. The black polished concrete, bamboo and reclaimed timber rooms with luxurious light fixtures, idyllic central pool, lush foliage, rooftop bar (serving complimentary cocktails) and intimate modern Malay restaurant Mandi Mandi combine to conjure an antidote to urban stress.

TOP CHOICE The Courtyard
HOTEL $$

(Map p68; ☑2141 1017; www.courtyard.com.my; 623 (No 51D) Tengkat Tong Shin; d from RM192; ❋@❧) A former backstreet hostel has been transformed into this calm, stylish oasis steps away from both the eats of Jln Alor and the bars of Changkat Bukit Bintang. Contemporary design rooms are very comfy and great value for what they offer.

TOP CHOICE YY38 Hotel
HOTEL $$

(Map p68; ☑2148 8838; www.yy38hotel.com.my; 38 Tengkat Tong Shin; s/d/loft room from RM100/120/360; ❋❧) The bulk of the rooms here are fine but no-frills. However, the 7th floor offers 17 creatively designed duplexes, each sleeping three, with fun themes ranging from Marylin Monroe to circus; it features a sawn-in-half classic mini as part of the decor!

Sekeping Sin Chew Kee
APARTMENT $$$

(Map p68; www.sekeping.com; 3 Jln Sin Chew Kee; apt RM700; ❋❧) Architect Ng Seksan's pared-back, quirky style is in full evidence at his latest venture, tucked away on the edge of the Golden Triangle on a street of old houses. Raw and beautiful, the two apartments here sleep up to six and have full kitchens and outdoor relaxation spaces.

Hotel Maya
HOTEL $$$

(Map p56; ☑2711 8866; www.hotelmaya.com.my; 138 Jln Ampang; r/ste with breakfast from RM700/1000; @❧❅) Still one of KL's most stylish hotels, even if there's wear and tear to some of their sleek timber-floored studios and suites. Rack rates include airport transfers, as well as a host of other goodies, while promotional rates – nearly half the official ones – include only breakfast and wi-fi. Their hydrotherapy pool is a plus.

Mandarin Oriental
HOTEL $$$

(Map p56; ☑2380 8888; www.mandarinoriental.com/kualalumpur; Jln Pinang; r/ste from RM1080/3000; ❋@❧❅) Backing onto the greenery of KLCC Park, the Mandarin is one for sybarites. Silks and batiks lend an Asian feel to the rooms, which have every conceivable amenity. The Oriental Club rooms are the ones to pick, allowing access to a lounge with a great view of the Petronas Towers. There's a spa and an infinity pool that seems to merge into the parkland beyond.

Impiana
HOTEL $$$

(Map p68; ☑2141 1111; www.impiana.com; 13 Jln Pinang; d with breakfast from RM450; ❋@❧❅) This chic property offers spacious rooms with parquet floors and lots of seductive amenities including a spa and an infinity pool with a view across to the Petronas Towers (partly marred by the soon-to-open Grand Hyatt). Not to be outdone by the Hyatt, the Impiana is adding a second tower of rooms.

Jalan Tun Razak & Around

N 0 ___ 400 m
0 ___ 0.2 miles

A | B

See Chow Kit, Kampung Baru & KLCC Map p56

Damai LRT

Thai Embassy
Irish Embassy
French Embassy
Jln Ampang
British Embassy
German Embassy
Canadian Embassy
Kuala Lumpur City Centre (KLCC) Park
Brunei Embassy
Singapore Embassy
US Embassy
Jln Binjai
Jln Stonor
Persiaran Stonor
Jln U Thant
Jln Tun Razak
Jln Kia Peng
Jln Conlay
See Golden Triangle Map p68
Jln Bukit Bintang
Indonesian Embassy
Jln Jati
Jln Delima
Transtar Travel
Jln Kemuning
Jln Inai
Jln Utara
Jln Melati
Jln Rawa
Royal Selangor Golf Club
To Pudu Market (1km)

Jalan Tun Razak & Around

◎ Sights
1 Badan Warisan Malaysia....................A4
2 Rumah Penghulu A4

⊜ Sleeping
3 G Tower Hotel A2
4 MiCasa All Suite Hotel.......................B2

⊗ Eating
5 Acme Bar & Coffee.............................A2
   Cilantro.. (see 4)
6 Imbi Market A5
7 Top Hat..A3

⊜ Shopping
8 Kompleks Budaya Kraf A4

Traders Hotel Kuala Lumpur HOTEL $$$
(Map p68; ☎2332 9888; www.tradershotels.com; KLCC, off Jln Kia Peng; d/ste from RM719/963; ❄@🖥🏊) The views are good either way, but it's probably worth paying the small supplement for a room facing the Petronas Towers at this contemporary design addition to KL's portfolio of luxe hotels. Their rooftop pool and bar is a famous KL hangout.

Sahabat Guest House GUESTHOUSE $
(☎2142 0689; www.sahabatguesthouse.com; 41 Jln Sahabat; d with breakfast from RM96; ❄@🖥) Rush to book this adorable blue-painted eight-room guesthouse tucked away off Tengkat Tong Shin. Small but comfy bedrooms, with small en suite bathrooms, are brightened up with a feature wall plastered in vivid patterned wallpaper. There's a small kitchen and a grassy front garden in which to relax. Rates are slightly higher from Friday to Sunday.

Anggun Boutique Hotel BOUTIQUE HOTEL $$
(Map p68; ☎2145 8003; www.anggunkl.com; 7-9 Tengkat Tong Shin; d with breakfast from RM340; ❄🖥) Two 1920s shophouses have been combined to create this antique-style, boutique property that's a welcome addition to a busy strip. The rooftop restaurant and bar is a leafy oasis hung with twinkling lights. Avoid rooms facing the noisy street though – or bring earplugs.

Sarang Vacation Homes GUESTHOUSE $$
(Map p68; ☎012-210 0218; www.sarangvacation homes.com; 6 Jln Galloway; s/d from RM130/150; ❄🖥) Michael and Christina run this appealing bed-and-breakfast operation. They have houses, apartments and rooms for rent in

G Tower Hotel HOTEL $$$
(Map p63; ☎2168 1919; www.gtowerhotel.com; 199 Jln Tun Razak; s/d with breakfast from RM592/626; ❄@🖥🏊) There's an exclusive atmosphere at this slickly designed property atop an office complex. Only hotel guests and tenants can access the gym, infinity pools, and top-floor lounge, restaurant and bar. Arty black-and-white prints set a sophisticated tone in the bedrooms. Ask for one of the slightly bigger corner rooms, preferably with a view of Tabung Haji.

five nearby locations. The furnishings are a bit worn, but the vibe is relaxed and welcoming and the location is excellent. It's a skip away from Jln Alor in a lowrise residential enclave.

Rainforest Bed & Breakfast
HOSTEL $$

(Map p68; ☎2145 3525; www.rainforestbnbhotel.com; 27 Jln Mesui; dm/d/tw with breakfast RM35/105/130; ❋@☎) The lush foliage sprouting around and tumbling off the tiered balconies of this high-quality guesthouse is eye-catching and apt for its name. Inside, bright red walls and timber-lined rooms (some without windows) are visually distinctive, along with the collection of Chinese pottery figurines. Friendly staff also make it a very appealing option.

Classic Inn
HOSTEL $$

(Map p68; ☎2148 8648; www.classicinn.com.my; 52 Lg 1/77A, Changkat Thambi Dollah; dm/s/d RM35/88/118; ❋@) Occupying a smartly renovated, yellow-painted shophouse on the southern edge of the Golden Triangle, this is a retro-charming choice with dorms and private rooms, a small grassy garden and welcoming staff.

Lodge Paradize Hotel
HOTEL $$

(Map p68; ☎2142 0122; www.lodgeparadize.com; 2 Jln Tengah; d from RM125; ❋@) This nicely revamped hotel in a four-storey 1940s building offers good value budget rooms at the back, which are more sheltered from traffic noise than the better furnished rooms in the main building. Long-stay deals are also available.

Number Eight Guesthouse
GUESTHOUSE $$

(Map p68; ☎2144 2050; www.numbereight.com.my; 8-10 Jln Tengkat Tong Shin; r without/with private bathroom RM85/115; ❋@☎) A recent change of ownership has seen some transformations at the long-running Number Eight. The minimalist design is looking a little shabby, but remains appealing and its value-for-money rooms, some with TVs and DVD players, leave many budget competitors standing. Rates include breakfast.

Radius International Hotel
HOTEL $$

(Map p68; ☎2715 3888; www.radius-international.com; 51A Changkat Bukit Bintang; r from RM190; ❋@❈) At the foot of KL's most buzzing restaurant and bar strip, Radius has all the facilities of an international chain hotel, including a decent-sized swimming pool,

but at lower prices. Opt for the tasteful 'premier' rooms which start at RM300.

Hotel Capitol
HOTEL $$$

(Map p68; ☎2143 7000; www.fhihotels.com; Jln Bulan; r from RM450; ❋@❈) Bland but reliable and very central. The pricier loft-style and premium corner rooms sport hip furnishings and good views. Guests have access to the nearby Federal Hotel's swimming pool.

Royale Bintang Kuala Lumpur
HOTEL $$$

(Map p68; ☎2143 9898; www.royale-bintang-hotel.com.my; 17-21 Jln Bukit Bintang; r from RM534) No design diva but a well-run and pleasantly presented hotel; their outdoor pool is a plus.

Piccolo Hotel
HOTEL $$$

(Map p68; ☎2146 5000; www.thepiccolohotel.com; 101 Jln Bukit Bintang; r from RM480; ❋@☎) Although its boutique look is somewhat cheaply thrown together, we do like the striking marine life images decorating the walls at this hotel in the midst of the Bintang Walk shopping strip. Almost constant promotional rates via online bookings bring it down to a budget category.

Red Palm
HOSTEL $

(Map p68; ☎2143 1279; www.redpalm-kl.com; 5 Tengkat Tong Shin; dm/s/d/tr incl breakfast RM30/55/75/105; @☎) Cosy shophouse hostel offering small and thin-walled rooms with shared bathrooms. However, the communal areas are great and the owners charming.

LITTLE INDIA

Tune Hotel
HOTEL $

(Map p56; www.tunehotels.com; r from RM90; ❋@☎) Book online six months in advance and it's possible to snag a room with a bathroom for under RM50. The basic rate, however, just gets you the room – air-con, towel and toiletries, and wi-fi access is extra. Each floor is sponsored, which means you'll find yourself gazing at an ad for, say, Maggi or Nippon Paints, in your room and along the corridors.

Frenz Hotel
HOTEL $$

(Map p56; ☎2693 7878; www.frenzhotel.com.my; 135 Jln TAR; s/d from RM210/260; ❋☎) A step up from other midrange options in the area, with confortable, clean rooms. Promotional rates are usually on offer, and breakfast (RM12) is served in Zam Zam restaurant next door.

BRICKFIELDS, KL SENTRAL & BANGSAR BARU

TOP CHOICE **Sekeping Tenggiri** GUESTHOUSE **$$**
(☎017-207 5977; www.tenggiri.com; 48 Jln Tenggiri, Bangsar; r from RM200; ※🅿🛜🛏) Even if it didn't provide access to architect Ng Seksan's superlative private collection of contemporary Malaysian art (displayed in the rooms of the adjoining house) this would be a lovely place to stay. The rough luxe mix of concrete, wood and wire decor (with cleverly recycled materials making up lamp fixtures) is softened by abundant garden greenery and a cooling plunge pool. There's a basic kitchen, a housekeeper, and several great places to eat on nearby Lg Kurau. The owners also run the similar **Sekeping Terasek** (Map p84; ☎017-207 5977; www.sekeping.com/terasek; 42a Jln Terasek, Bangsar; r/house RM200/1000; ※🛜) nearby and **Sekeping Sin Chew Kee** (p62) in KL's centre.

Hilton Kuala Lumpur HOTEL **$$$**
(Map p54; ☎2264 2264; www.hilton.com; 3 Jln Stesen Sentral; d/ste from RM650/1300; ※@🛜🛏)

Sharing a fabulous landscaped pool and spa with the Meridien next door, the Hilton is a design diva's dream. Sliding doors open to join the bathroom to the bedroom, picture windows present soaring city views and rooms are decked out from floor to ceiling in eye-catching materials.

Majestic Hotel HISTORIC HOTEL **$$$**
(Map p54; ☎2785 8000; www.majestickl.com; 5 Jln Sultan Hishamuddin; r from RM500; ※🛜) Originally opened in 1932, and pre-WWII the KL equivalent of Raffles in Singapore, this long-shuttered hotel reopened at the end of 2012. The heritage building has been impeccably refurbished, although the bulk of the rooms are in the newly built Tower wing. The Charles Rennie Mackintosh–inspired decor of the spa adds extra elegance while the Colonial Cafe and Tea Lounge play up to the heritage experience.

YMCA HOTEL **$$**
(Map p54; ☎2274 1439; www.ymcakl.com; 95 Jln Padang Belia; d or tw RM118, tr without bathroom

---

SERVICED APARTMENTS

Some of the KL's best accommodation deals, particularly for longer stays, are offered by serviced apartments. Studios and suites tend to be far larger and better equipped than you'd get for a similar price at top-end hotels. There are quite a few of these complexes scattered across the city, some attached to hotels and sharing their facilities. For short stays breakfast is usually included. Our top picks:

Parkroyal Serviced Suites (Map p68; ☎2084 1000; www.parkroyalhotels.com; 1 Jln Nagansari; apt from RM424; ※@🛜🛏) New property in a great location with sophisticated design studios and one-/two-bedroom suites. Good facilities include two outdoor pools, one on the roof.

Fraser Place Kuala Lumpur (Map p68; ☎2118 6288; http://kualalumpur.frasershospitality.com; 10 Jln Perak, Lot 163; apt from RM638; ※@🛜🛏) Good workspaces and walk-in closets feature in these colourfully designed apartments. The facilities, including an outdoor infinity pool, gym, sauna and games room, are top notch.

Westin Kuala Lumpur (Map p68; ☎2731 8333; www.westin.com/kualalumpur; 199 Jln Bukit Bintang; d/apt from RM800/1300; ※@🛜🛏) It's easy to see why long-term residents love its spacious, modern rooms with their full kitchens and glassed-in balconies. It also has a good gym and stylish restaurants and bars.

MiCasa All Suite Hotel (Map p63; ☎2179 8000; www.micasahotel.com; 368B Jln Tun Razak; apt from RM420; ※@🛜🛏) A choice of one-, two- or three-bedroom suites – all reasonably priced, with wooden floors and kitchens. Relax beside the large, palm-tree-fringed pool, or enjoy their small spa and the gourmet restaurant **Cilantro** (Map p63; ☎2179 8082; www.cilantrokl.com; set lunch/dinner RM150/270; ⏱noon-2pm Fri, 6pm-1am Mon-Sat).

Pacific Regency Hotel Suites (Map p68; ☎2332 7777; www.pacific-regency.com; Jln Punchak, Menara Panglobal; apt from RM650; ※🛜🛏) Several new floors of rooms with an updated design were in the works during our latest visit. Head to the roof to enjoy the rooftop pool and the cocktail/DJ bar **Luna**.

RM138; ✳☎) Handy for KL Sentral, the Y has spic-and-span rooms with TVs, telephones and proper wardrobes (not just hangers on a wall hook). There's laundry facilities, a shop and a cafe with wi-fi access as well as tennis courts for hire if you become a member.

Eating

KL is a nonstop feast. You can dine in incredible elegance or mingle with locals at thousands of street stalls – it's all good and it's seldom heavy on the pocket.

Whether you're on a budget or not, most often the best food is from the hawker stalls, cheap cafes (called *kopitiam*) and inexpensive restaurants *(restoran)*. Hygiene standards at hawker stalls are generally good and you should have little to fear from eating at them. However, if this is not your thing – or you just want air-con with your meal – then KL's many food courts, usually located in shopping malls, offer an answer.

GOLDEN TRIANGLE & KLCC

TOP CHOICE Kedai Makanan Dan Minuman TKS   CHINESE $$

(Map p68; Jln Alor; mains RM15-30; ⊙5pm-4am) Our favourite place to eat on KL's busiest food street is this nontouristy Sichuan joint that has a menu only in Chinese (don't panic, there are pictures and the friendly staff speak English). Prepare for a taste explosion from the chilli-oil fried fish to the gunpowder chicken buried in a pile of mouth-numbing fried chillies.

TOP CHOICE Imbi Market   HAWKER $

(Map p63; Jln Kampung, Pasar Baru Bukit Bintang; meal RM10; ⊙6.30am-12.30pm Tue-Sun) The official name is Pasar Baru Bukit Bintang, but everyone knows it simply as Imbi Market. Breakfast is like a party here with all the friendly and curious locals happily recommending their favourite stalls. We like Sisters Crispy Popiah; Teluk Intan Chee Cheung Fun, where Amy Ong serves a lovely oyster-and-peanut *congee* (rice porridge), and egg puddings; and **Bunn Choon** for the creamy mini egg tarts. The market will be moving to a new building in the next few years as the area is slated for redevelopment.

TOP CHOICE Frangipani   FRENCH $$$

(Map p68; ☎2144 3001; www.frangipani.com.my; 25 Changkat Bukit Bintang; 3-course menu RM170; ⊙6.30pm-10.30pm Tue-Sun) Much feted for its innovative approach to European fusion

GOOD FOOD BLOG

KLlites have strong opinions about their favourite places to eat – and they're very happy to share them online. One site we highly recommend is **Fried Chillies** (www.friedchillies.com), which includes spot-on reviews by some of the most enthusiastic foodies we've met, as well as video clips.

cooking, Frangipani is leagues ahead of most of the competition. The decor is as slick as the menu, with a stunning dining room surrounding a reflecting pool, and there's an equally stylish bar upstairs.

Pinchos Tapas Bar   TAPAS $$

(Map p68; ☎2145 8482; www.pinchos.com.my; 18 Changat Bukit Bintang; tapas RM13-30; ⊙5-11pm food, until 3am bar) Serving delicious tapas, this real deal place is run by a Spaniard and packed with KL's approving Spanish-speaking community. Ideal either for a solo meal and drink, or fun with a group so you can munch your way through the wide-ranging menu.

Twenty One Kitchen & Bar   FUSION $$$

(Map p68; ☎2142 0021; www.drbar.asia; 20-1 Changkat Bukit Bintang; meals RM60-80; ⊙noon-3am; ☎) Lots of interesting choices on the menu here, several of which you can sample together on tasting plates. The bar upstairs, with a deck overlooking the street, gets cranking at weekends when a DJ spins chill and dance tunes.

Little Penang Kafé   MALAY, NONYA $$

(Map p56; ☎2163 0215; Level 4, Suria KLCC; mains from RM15; ⊙11.30am-9.30pm) At peak meal times expect a long line outside this mall joint serving authentic food from Penang, including specialities such as curry *mee* (spicy soup noodles with prawns) and spicy Siamese *lemak laksa* (curry laksa) available only from Friday to Sunday. There's also a branch at Mid Valley Megamall.

Ben's   INTERNATIONAL $$

(Map p68; ☎2141 5290; www.thebiggroup.co/bens; Level 6, Pavilion KL, 168 Bukit Bintang; mains RM10-40; ⊙11am-10pm Sun-Thu, until midnight Fri & Sat; ☎) The flagship brand of the BIG group of dining outlets (which include the classy Plan B cafes) delivers on both style and substance. There's a tempting range of eastern and western comfort foods, appealing, a relaxed resort-feel design, and nice touches such as a box of cards with recipes and talk topics on each table. Other branches are in Suria KLCC and Publika.

Bijan
MALAY $$$

(Map p68; ☎2031 3575; www.bijanrestaurant.com; 3 Jln Ceylon; mains RM30-70; ◉6.30-11pm Mon-Sat) Serves skilfully cooked traditional dishes in a sophisticated dining room that spills out into a tropical garden. Must-try dishes include *rendang daging* (dry beef curry with lemongrass), *masak lemak ikan* (Penang-style fish curry with turmeric) and *ikan panggang* (grilled skate with tamarind).

Top Hat
NONYA, BRITISH $$$

(Map p63; ☎2142 8611; www.top-hat-restaurants.com; 3 Jln Stonor; meals RM60-110; ◉noon-10.30pm) Set in a spacious bungalow surrounded by peaceful gardens and serving both traditional British – think oxtail stew and bread-and-butter pudding – as well as local dishes, such as Nonya laksa (RM28). All meals come with signature 'top hats' (pastry shells filled with sliced veggies) and choice of local dessert.

Cuisine Gourmet by Nathalie
FRENCH $$$

(Map p68; ☎2072 4452; www.cuisinegourmetbynathalie.com; Menara Taipan, Jln Punchak; mains RM45-90; ☎) Having made her mark with a smaller outlet in Publika (also worth visiting), Nathalie gets more creative in this fine dining space, elegantly decked out in mauve and grey. The bento style lunches are a bargain and the desserts sublime.

Enak
MALAY $$$

(Map p68; ☎2141 8973; www.enakkl.com; Feast fl, Starhill Gallery, 181 Jln Bukit Bintang; meals RM70-100; ◉noon-1am) One of many options on Starhill Gallery's 'Feast' floor, Enak is justly famous for finely presented Malay cuisine with a sophisticated twist.

Atmosphere 360
MALAY, INTERNATIONAL $$$

(Map p68; ☎2020 2020; www.atmosphere360.com.my; 2 Jln Puncak, Menara KL; buffet lunch/afternoon tea/dinner RM88/58/198; ◉noon-2.30pm & 6.30-11pm) It takes 90 minutes for you to see all of KL from your seat at this revolving restaurant atop KL Tower. The buffets feature a wide range of Malay and international dishes and are consistently good. Book at least a day ahead for a window seat or dinner, when there's also a live band and more dishes on offer.

Blue Boy Vegetarian Food Centre
CHINESE, MALAY $

(Map p68; ☎2144 9011; Jln Tong Shin; mains RM3-10; ◉7.30am-9.30pm; ☎) It's hard to believe that everything prepared at this spotless

---

TRADITIONAL WET & DRY FOOD MARKETS

The relocation of Imbi Market to make way for a new financial district is a sign of the times in KL: Western-style supermarkets have become far more common here than the semi-outdoor wet and dry food markets found across Asia. However, a few such traditional markets still exist and are worth searching out – arrive early in the morning to experience them at full throttle.

Pudu Market (Map p68; Jln Pasar Baru; ◉6am-2pm) KL's biggest wet and dry market is a frenetic place, full of squawking chickens, frantic shoppers and porters forcing their way through the crowds with outrageous loads. Stalls here sell everything from goldfish to pigs' heads, cows' tongues and durians in baskets. The market is five minutes' walk from Pudu LRT station; go south along Jln Pudu, right onto Jln Pasar, then right down Jln Pasar Baharu, passing the colourful Choon Wan Kong, a Chinese temple dating from 1879.

Bazaar Baru Chow Kit (Chow Kit Market; Map p56; 469-473 Jln TAR; ◉8am-9pm) Apart from freshly butchered meat and filleted fish, there's a staggering array of weird and wonderful tropical fruit and vegetables on sale here, as well as clothes, toys, buckets, stationery, noodles, spices and other commodities. Pushing through the narrow aisles is a heady, sensory experience.

Chinatown Wet Market (Map p50; ◉7am-3pm) Running west of the main market towards Jln Tun HS Lee is this covered market where locals shop for fresh fish, vegetables and gruesomely anatomical cuts of meat – those clucking chickens in cages don't stay alive for long!

Golden Triangle

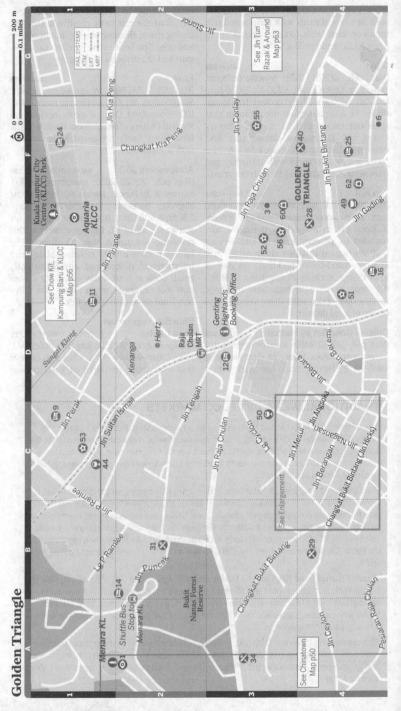

See Jln Tun Razak & Around Map p63

GOLDEN TRIANGLE

Jln Kia Peng

Changkat Kia Peng

Jln Conlay

Jln Stonor

Jln Raja Chulan

Jln Bukit Bintang

Jln Gading

Kuala Lumpur City Centre (KLCC) Park

Aquaria KLCC

See Chow Kit, Kampung Baru & KLCC Map p56

Jln Pinang

Genting Highlands Booking Office

Raja Chulan MRT

Hertz

Jln Tengah

Jln Raja Chulan

Jln Sultan Ismail

Kenanga

Jln Perak

Sungai Klang

Lg Ceylon

Lg P Ramlee

Jln P Ramlee

Jln Puncak

Jln Mesui

Jln Nagasari

Jln Berangan

Jln Angsoka

Jln Beremi

Jln Bedara

Changkat Bukit Bintang (Jln Hicks)

See Enlargement

Menara KL

Shuttle Bus Stop to Menara KL

Bukit Nanas Forest Reserve

Changkat Bukit Bintang

Jln Ceylon

Pesiaran Raja Chulan

See Chinatown Map p50

RAIL SYSTEMS
KTM ←——→
LRT
MRT

200 m
0.1 miles

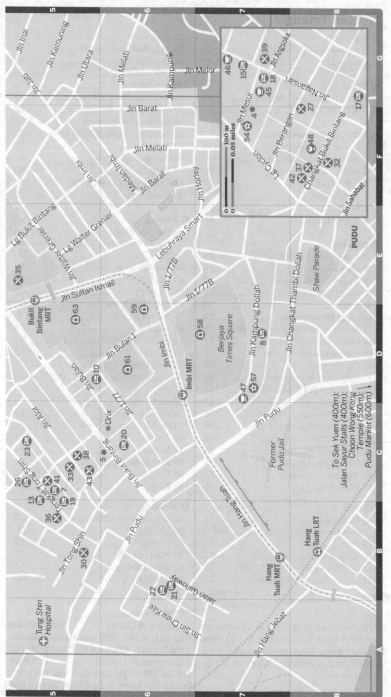

Golden Triangle

◎ Top Sights
Aquaria KLCC E1
Menara KL A1

◎ Sights
1 Bukit Nanas Forest Reserve A2
2 KLCC Park E1

✛ Activities, Courses & Tours
Asianel Reflexology Spa .... (see 62)
Foot Master Dr Fish Spa .... (see 58)
3 Kenko E3
4 Lightworks F7
Morino Kaze .... (see 16)
5 Reborn C6
6 Spa Village F4

◉ Sleeping
7 Anggun Boutique Hotel C5
8 Classic Inn D7
9 Fraser Place Kuala Lumpur C1
10 Hotel Capitol D5
11 Impiana E1
12 Lodge Paradize Hotel D3
13 Number Eight Guesthouse B5
14 Pacific Regency Hotel Suites B2
15 Parkroyal Serviced Suites G7
16 Piccolo Hotel E4
17 Radius International Hotel G8
18 Rainforest Bed & Breakfast G7
19 Red Palm B5
20 Royale Bintang Kuala Lumpur C6
21 Sarang Vacation Homes B6
22 Sekeping Sin Chew Kee B6
23 The Courtyard C5
24 Traders Hotel Kuala Lumpur F1
25 Westin Kuala Lumpur F4
26 YY38 Hotel C5

✴ Eating
27 Albion KL F8
Atmosphere 360 .... (see 1)
28 Ben's E4
29 Bijan B4
30 Blue Boy Vegetarian Food Centre B5
31 Cuisine Gourmet by Nathalie B2
Enak .... (see 62)

32 Frangipani F8
33 Kedai Makanan Dan Minuman TKS C5
34 La Vie En Rose A3
Loaf .... (see 60)
35 Lot 10 Hutong E5
36 Ngau Kee Beef Ball Noodles B5
37 Pinchos Tapas Bar F8
38 Restoran Beh Brothers C5
39 Restoran Nagansari Curry House G7
40 Santouka F4
41 Sao Nam C5
Sisters Noodle .... (see 38)
42 Twenty One Kitchen & Bar F8
43 Wong Ah Wah C5

◉ Drinking
Frangipani Bar .... (see 32)
Luk Yu Tea House .... (see 62)
Luna .... (see 14)
44 Neo Tamarind C1
45 Palate Palette G7
46 Paper + Toast G7
47 Sixty Nine Bistro D7
Sky Bar .... (see 24)
48 Social F8
49 Starhill Tea Salon E4
50 Taps Beer Bar C3
Teeq Brasserie .... (see 35)
Village Bar .... (see 62)

◉ Entertainment
51 Blue Boy E4
52 Golden Screen Cinemas E3
53 KL Live C1
54 No Black Tie F7
55 Seri Melayu F3
56 The Venue E3
57 Wings D7

◙ Shopping
58 Berjaya Times Square D7
59 Imbi Plaza D6
60 Pavilion KL E3
61 Plaza Low Yat D6
62 Starhill Gallery F4
63 Sungei Wang Plaza D5

hawker-style cafe at the base of a backstreet apartment block is vegetarian, but it's true. The *char kway teow* (broad noodles fried in chilli and blackbean sauce) is highly recommended.

Acme Bar & Coffee INTERNATIONAL $$
(Map p63; ☏2162 2288; www.acmebarcoffee.com; Troika, Ground Fl, 19 Persiaran KLCC; mains RM30-60; ⊙11am-midnight Mon-Thu, 11am-1am Fri, 9.30am-1am Sat, 9.30am-5pm Sun) Blink and you might be in a chic bistro in New York, Paris or Syd-

ney. Service can be slapdash, but it's good for weekend brunch or drinks and nibbles. In the works – and sure to be a showstopper, if only for its stunning skyline views – is **Troika Sky Dining** on the 23rd level of the same Norman Foster–designed building.

Loaf
BAKERY **$$**

(Map p68; ☑2145 3036; www.theloaf.net; Levels 3 & 4, 168 Jln Bukit Bintang, Pavilion KL; meals RM10-20; ⊙10am-10pm) This bakery cafe and bistro (which has ex-PM Dr Mahathir as an investor) is a Malaysian take on a Japanese baked goods shop. Its big range of baked goods is uniformly divine and we love the mini cheesecakes for a quick snack.

Restoran Nagansari Curry House
MALAY, INDIAN **$**

(Map p68; Jln Nagansari; meals RM5-10; ⊙7am-midnight) This simple hawker-style restaurant serves a good selection of Malay dishes – soup *mee*, tom yum and so on – with a few Indian favourites thrown in for good measure. Fans blow moist air around the dining hall to keep diners cool.

Sao Nam
VIETNAMESE **$$**

(Map p68; ☑2144 1225; www.saonam.com.my; 25 Tengkat Tong Shin; mains RM20-35; ⊙noon-2.30pm & 7.30-10.30pm) Stand by for huge plates of delicious Vietnamese food, garnished with basil, mint, lettuce and sweet dips. The starter *banh xeo* (a huge Vietnamese pancake with meat, seafood or vegetables) is a meal all by itself.

La Vie En Rose
FRENCH **$$$**

(Map p68; ☑2078 3883; http://www.cuisine-studio.net/; 39 Jln Raja Chulan; mains RM40-80; ⊙noon-2.30pm & 6.30-10.30pm Tue-Fri, 10am-10.30pm Sat & Sun; 🛜) The location, in an airy bungalow with a terrace overlooking Bukit Nanas and KL Tower, is unique, along with its canned fished served *in* the can. Best for weekend brunch (from RM50) when breads and pastries flow freely from its own bakery.

Ngau Kee Beef Ball Noodles
CHINESE **$**

(Map p68; Tengkat Tong Shin; noodles RM5; ⊙24hr) The dish at this venerable street stall comes in two parts: dry, steamed noodles topped with a thick soy-sauce mince, and the chunky beef balls in a clear soup – delicious! Refresh your palate with their salty-sweet lime drink.

Lot 10 Hutong
FOOD COURT **$$**

(Map p68; 50 Jln Sultan Ismail, Basement, Lot 10; mains RM3-20; ⊙10am-10pm) The concept is a collection of greatest hits from around Malaysia's culinary map made by experienced vendors. In the warren-like set-up you can dine on classic renditions of dishes such as pork stew *bak kut the*, chicken rice and Hokkien *mee*.

Santouka
JAPANESE **$$**

(Map p68; ☑2143 8878; www.santouka.co.jp; Level 6, Pavilion Kuala Lumpur, 168 Jln Bukit Bintang; mains RM30-40; ⊙11am-9.45pm) Slurp ramen noodles in a rich pork broth at this joint in Pavilion's Tokyo Street, an outlet of a famous stall originating from the Japanese island of Hokkaido.

DON'T MISS

JALAN ALOR

The great common denominator of KL's food scene – hauling in everyone from sequined society babes to penny-strapped backpackers – are the restaurants and stalls lining Jln Alor. From around 5pm till late every evening, the street transforms into a continuous open-air dining space with hundreds of plastic tables and chairs and rival caterers shouting out to passersby to drum up business (avoid the pushiest ones!). Most places serve alcohol and you can sample pretty much every Malay–Chinese dish imaginable, from grilled fish and satay to *kai-lan* (Chinese greens) in oyster sauce and fried noodles with frogs' legs. Thai food is also popular.

Recommended options include Kedai Makanan Dan Minuman TKS (p66) for amazing Sichuan dishes; the small complex **Restoran Beh Brothers** (Map p68; 21A Jln Alor; meals RM10-15; ⊙24hr), one of the few places open from 7am for breakfast, where the **Sisters Noodle** (Map p68) stall does delicious 'drunken' chicken *mee* (noodles) with rice wine, and there's also a good Hong Kong–style dim sum stall (24 hours); and **Wong Ah Wah** (Map p68; Jln Alor; ⊙4pm-4am), unbeatable for addictive spicy chicken wings, as well as grilled seafood, tofu and satay.

CHINATOWN & MASJID JAMEK

TOP CHOICE Madras Lane Hawkers   HAWKER $

(Map p50; Madras Lane; noodles RM5; ☺8am-4pm Tue-Sun) Weave your way through Chinatown's wet market to find this short alley of stalls tucked between Jln Tun HS Lee and Jln Petaling. Standout operators including the one offering 10 types of *yong tau fu* in a fish broth (9.30am to 3.30pm) and, at the far end of the strip, the one serving *asam* (tamarind) and curry laksa.

TOP CHOICE Old China Café   MALAY, NONYA $$

(Map p50; ☏2072 5915; www.oldchina.com.my; 11 Jln Balai Polis; mains RM40-50; ☺11.30am-10pm) Housed in the old guild hall of the Selangor & Federal Territory Laundry Association, this long-established, atmospheric cafe serves Nonya dishes from Melaka and Penang, including a fine beef rendang (coconut and lime-leaf curry) with coconut rice and fiery Nonya laksa soup with seafood. Their branch **Precious** (Map p50; ☏2273 7372; 1st fl, Central Market; mains RM40-60; ☺11.30am-10pm) in Central Market serves a similar menu and tends to be less busy.

Ikan Panggang   HAWKER $$

(Map p50; ☏019-315 9448; spicy seafood RM12; ☺5-11pm Tue-Sun) Tuck into spicy fish and seafood dishes and luscious chicken wings from this unsigned stall outside Hong Leong Bank, tucked behind the stalls on the corner of Jln Petaling and Jln Hang Lekir. It generally takes 20 minutes for your foil-wrapped pouch of seafood to cook, allowing time to explore the market. Wash the meal down with a glass of *mata kucing* (meaning 'cat's eye'), a refreshing Asian fruit drink, also bought from a stall on the same corner.

LOKL   INTERNATIONAL, MALAY $$

(Map p50; http://loklcoffee.com; 30 Jln Tun HS Lee; mains RM14-20; ☎) From its clever name (pronounced 'local') and slick design to its tasty twists on comfort foods, such as their cholesterol bomb deep-fried Hainanese meatloaf sandwich and dessert toasties, LOKL ticks all the right boxes. Their local coffee comes from Kluang, their Western-style brews are Illy.

Purple Cane Tea Restaurant   CHINESE $$

(Map p50; ☏2272 3090; www.purplecane.com.my; 1 Jln Maharajalela; mains RM10-20; ☺11am-10pm) Tucked behind the Chinese Assembly Hall, this laid-back place uses tea as an ingredient in most of its dishes. Intriguing specials include chicken soup with tea and ginseng, and beef simmered in lychee tea. There are also branches in Mid Valley Megamall and the Shaw Centre near Pudu.

Sing Seng Nam   CHINESE $

(Map p50; 2 Medan Pasar; mains RM5-10; ☺7am-5pm Mon-Sat) KL is fast filling up with new 'old-style' *kopitiam* (coffee shop), but this is the genuine object, busy with locals enjoying breakfast of *kaya* (coconut-cream jam) toast and runny boiled egg or a *kopi peng* (iced coffee with milk). Later in the day, tuck into inexpensive bowls of chicken rice and 'curry fish'.

Sangeetha   INDIAN, THALI $

(Map p50; ☏2032 3333; 65 Lebuh Ampang; meals RM10; ☺8am-11pm; ☛) This well-run vegetarian restaurant serves lots of South Indian delights such as *idli* (savoury, soft, fermented-rice-and-lentil cakes) and *masala dosa* (rice-and-lentil crepes stuffed with spiced potatoes).

LITTLE INDIA & KAMPUNG BARU

Saravanaa Bhavan   INDIAN $$

(Map p50; ☏2287 1228; www.saravanabhavan.com; 52 Jln Maarof, Bangsar; meals RM10-20; ☺8am-11pm; ☛) This global chain of restaurants offers some of the best quality Indian food you'll find in KL. Their banana-leaf and mini-tiffin feasts are supremely tasty and you can also sample southern Indian classics such as *masala dosa*.

Thai-la   THAI $$

(Map p56; ☏2698 4933; ground fl, Cap Square; meals RM20-30; ☺noon-10pm Mon-Sat) The food's tasty and made by Thai chefs, the decor has a chic charm and Zaki, the entertaining owner, can talk the hind legs off a donkey.

Sagar   INDIAN $

(Map p56; ☏2691 3088; Jln Masjid India, Semua House; meals RM10; ☺8am-8pm) Enjoy the good-value *thali* meals (rice or bread served with assorted vegetables and curries for under RM10) at this footpath cafe, and soak up the street life of Little India. There's also an air-con section inside.

Ikan Bakar Berempah   HAWKER $

(Map p56; Jln Raja Muda Musa, Gerak Pak Lang; meals RM5-10; ☺24hr) If you can't make it to Kampung Baru for its Saturday *pasar malam* (night market), head to this excellent barbecued-fish stall, within a hawker-stall market covered by a zinc roof. Once you've picked your fish off the grill there's a long buffet of great Malay *kampung*-style side dishes you can add to it.

Regional Specialities

Chillies at Bazaar Baru Chow Kit (p67), Kuala Lumpur

Malaysia, Singapore and Brunei are a hungry traveller's dream destination – a multiethnic region boasting a wide-ranging cuisine shaped over the centuries by the European, Indonesian, Indian and Chinese traders, colonisers and labourers who have landed on its shores. Fancy breakfasting on Chinese dim sum? How about an Indian *dosa* (savoury pancake) for lunch, followed by a selection of rich Malaysian curries for dinner?

If the region has any single culinary constant at all, it's undoubtedly noodles. But even these differ from country to country and coast to coast. *Laksam,* the Kelantanese take on laksssa, combines fantastically toothsome wide, flat rice noodles in *budu*-spiked coconut milk and topped with bean sprouts and herbs, while in Sarawak laksa is breakfast food: locals wake to a spicy, coconut-rich curry soup packed with rice vermicelli, omelette strips, chicken and prawns. In Penang, Hokkien mee is a spicy noodle soup with bean sprouts, pork and prawns, but elsewhere it's a mound of thick stir-fried noodles with pork and cabbage in a dark soy sauce.

Rice also features prominently across the region. *Nasi lemak,* an unofficial 'national dish' of Malaysia, is rice steamed with coconut milk and topped with *ikan bilis,* peanuts, cucumber, sweet-hot *sambal* paste and hard-boiled egg (curry optional); banana leaf rice – rice and curry served on a banana leaf 'plate' – is daily Indian fare.

Penang is generally regarded as the region's gastronomic ground zero; some KL residents make the four-hour drive for a single meal, and Singaporeans pack out hotels on weekends. Along with regional Chinese, southern Indian and Malay specialties, the island is a hotspot for Nonya cooking, born of intermarriage between Chinese immigrants and local women. In the former Portuguese outpost

Clockwise from top left
1 Food stalls in Chinatown (p72), Kuala Lumpur 2 Stall at Central Market (p279), Kota Bharu, Peninsular Malaysia 3 Penang Hokkien mee

of Melaka you'll find Cristang (a blend of Portuguese and local cooking styles) dishes like *debal*, a fiery Eurasian stew.

If it's all a bit too overwhelming, head to the peninsular east coast, the heartland of traditional Malay cooking. Kelantan and Terengganu, considerably isolated from the rest of the country, received few Chinese and Indian immigrants. Consequently, regional specialities have remained staunchly Malay. Graze the region long enough and you may develop a few cavities; local cooks excel at making all manner of *kuih* and even savoury dishes have a noticeably sweet edge.

If you'd like to diverge from the local cuisine entirely, then look no farther than Singapore; its high-end dining scene is second to none in Southeast Asia. Here you'll sate your craving for handmade papardelle, steak frites, fresh sashimi or a molecular gastronomic morsel snap-frozen in liquid nitrogen and bedecked with foam.

Given the endless choices, gastronomic malaise is unlikely to be a problem. It's a blessing, but also a curse – so many dishes, so little time.

Penang

Penang is known for its Nonya or Peranakan cuisine, a fusion of Chinese, Malay and Indian ingredients and cooking techniques. Examples include *kerabu beehoon*, rice vermicelli tossed with *sambal* and lime juice and garnished with fresh herbs, and *otak otak*, curried fish 'custard' steamed in a banana leaf.

This is also the home of *nasi kandar*, rice eaten with a variety of curries, a *mamak* (Indian Muslim) speciality named after the *kandar* (shoulder pole) from which ambulant vendors once suspended their pots of rice and curry.

Penang's hawker food is a must. Wide, flat *kway teow* noodles are stir-fried with prawns, cockles, egg and bean sprouts for the hawker speciality *char kway teow*. Other don't-miss dishes include the laksa twins: *asam* (round rice noodles in a hot and sour fish gravy topped with slivered pineapple, cucumber, mint leaves and slightly astringent torch ginger flower) and *lemak* (with a coconut milk-based broth).

Kedah, Perlis & Perak

Thai culinary influence extends to foods in Malaysia's west-coast states of Perlis and Kedah, where fish sauce is as common a seasoning as *belacan* (fermented prawn paste). Here, look for laksa *utara*, a lighter but still spicy and intensely fish-flavoured version of Penang's *asam* laksa.

Farther south is Ipoh, the mostly Chinese capital of Perak state and a town with a reputation for excellent eating. Pasta lovers rave over Ipoh's rice noodles, said to derive their exceptional silky smoothness from the town's water. Judge for yourself with the local version of Hainanese chicken – served with a side of barely blanched bean sprouts and noodles instead of rice – and *hor fun*, rice noodle soup with shredded chicken breast.

Clockwise from top left
1 Frying up noodles in George Town (p167), Penang 2 Red Garden Food Paradise & Night Market (p170), George Town, Penang 3 *Asam* laksa 4 Noodles on Gurney Drive (p170), George Town, Penang

Melaka

Melaka's specialities include *ayam pong teh* (chicken cooked with *taucu,* dark soy sauce and sugar), *ikan cili garam* (fish curry), *satay celup* (skewered meat, seafood, and vegetables cooked at the table in a tub of peanut-based sauce) and Hainanese chicken served with rice moulded into balls.

Often overlooked here is Cristang cuisine, the edible result of intermarriage between Portuguese colonisers and local women and an intriguing blend of Chinese/Peranakan, Indian, Malay and, of course, European ingredients.

Johor & Pahang

Johor state boasts two tasty Malay noodle specialties: *mee bandung,* yellow noodles topped with a zippy, tomatoey shrimp gravy; and *mee rebus,* the same type of noodles doused with a sweet-savoury sauce thickened with sweet potatoes. The state also has its own variation on the laksa theme, consisting of noodles in a thin spicy fish gravy topped with chopped fresh herbs.

Pahang's rivers are known for ikan patin, known in English as silver catfish, a freshwater fish that's a local delicacy.

Kelantan & Terengganu

Kelantan state's capital Kota Bharu boasts Malaysia's most beautiful wet market, as well as plenty of places to try specialties like *ayam percik* (chilli paste–marinated chicken, grilled and doused with coconut sauce) and visually arresting *nasi kerabu,* rice tinted blue with natural colouring obtained from dried pea flowers.

In Terengganu state, a vendor dishing up mounds of red rice signals *nasi dagang.* The slightly nut-flavoured grain is cooked with coconut water and eaten with fried chicken and *sambal.*

Clockwise from top left
1 A noodle maker **2** *Ayam percik* (marinated chicken on skewers) **3** Central Market (p279), Kota Bharu, Kelantan

GREG ELMS/GETTY IMAGES ©

Kuala Lumpur, Selangor & Negeri Sembilan

Almost all of Malaysia's specialties can be found in Kuala Lumpur, but two dishes in particular are more easily found here than elsewhere: *pan meen* (literally 'board noodles'), thick and chewy wheat noodles tossed with dark soy and garnished with chopped pork, *ikan bilis* and shredded cloud ear mushrooms; and *sang har meen* ('fresh sea noodles'), huge freshwater prawns in gravy flavoured with rice wine and prawn fat served over crispy noodles.

Farther south, in Negeri Sembilan state, descendents of Minangkabau who immigrated from the Indonesian island of Sumatra hundreds of years ago dish up a mean *nasi padang* – rice accompanied by a parade of fiery curries, *gulai* (fish and vegetables cooked in mild coconut milk gravy), soups and *sambal*.

Singapore

Singapore's culinary landscape is a near replica of Malaysia's, but in miniature. Still, Singaporeans do lay special claim to a few dishes, including crab stir-fried with black pepper, and fried carrot cake (squares of radish-flour cake stir-fried with bean sprouts, chilli sauce and salted radish). *Kari kepala ikan* (fish-head curry) was allegedly invented by a Singaporean-Indian cook playing to the Chinese love of fish cheeks. Hainanese chicken-rice, a plate of rice flavoured with garlic, broth, tender poached chicken, sliced cucumber and dipping sauces, assumes similarly iconic status here.

Singaporeans love their *roti prata* (the equivalent of Malaysia's *roti canai*) for breakfast, and have their own version of laksa – simply called 'laksa' – noodles in a prawn and coconut-milk-based, highly spiced soup.

RICHARD I'ANSON/GETTY IMAGES ©

Clockwise from top left
1 Street snacks, Chinatown (p72), Kuala Lumpur
2 Hawker stalls backed by the Petronas Towers, Kuala Lumpur 3 Hainanese chicken-rice 4 Laksa

Borneo (Sarawak & Sabah)

Sarawak's highlanders specialise in dishes cooked in bamboo, like the chicken dish *ayam pansoh* (a special occasion dish of chicken wrapped in tapioca leaves and cooked with water inside a length of bamboo).

If you're in Kota Kinabalu, consider splurging on a meal of bounty from the South China Sea, chosen by your own self from a fish tank and cooked to order at one of the city's many seafood restaurants. Two other piscine specialties that deserve a mention: *umai* (sometimes called *hinava*, and also found in Sarawak), raw fish seasoned simply with lime juice, coconut milk and chillies, served along with noodles made of fish paste in a magnificent seafood broth with fish balls and chunks of sea bass.

Brunei

If Brunei had a national dish it would be *ambuyat*, a glutinous mass made from the pith of the sago tree, ground to a powder and mixed with water. Served by twisting around chopsticks or long-twined forks, *ambuyat* is usually dipped into cacah, a *sambal belacan* and tamarind–based sweet-and-tart sauce, and accompanied by boiled or smoked seafood and salads. *Ambuyat* itself doesn't have a taste – it's the sauce that gives it its zing. Shrimp-and-chilli mixes are the most popular, although you can technically dip the dish in anything you'd like (we've heard of people using vanilla ice cream!).

If you are invited to a Bruneian home you'll probably be served *bualulu* with your tea. This simple dessert is made from eggs, flour and sugar. *Kuripit sagu*, a biscuit-like version of *buahulu*, is jazzed up with mild coconut flavours.

Clockwise from top left
1 *Pulut panggang* (glutinous-rice sweet wrapped in banana leaves) 2 Grilling chicken, Kota Kinabalu (p306). Sabah

LAKE GARDENS & BRICKFIELDS

TOP CHOICE Robson Heights CHINESE $$$

(2274 1633; www.robsonheights.com; 10B Jln Permai, off Jln Syed Putra; mains RM30-60; 10.30am-2.30pm & 5.30-11.30pm) Top-class food is served at this rickety hillside joint. While specialities such as stir-fried pig intestines with dried prawn and chilli or braised terrapin may not appeal to all, we can vouch for their delicious baked spare ribs in honey sauce and stir-fried udon noodles in black pepper sauce (RM8).

Annalakshmi INDIAN $

(Map p54; 2272 3799; 116 Jln Berhala, Temple of Fine Arts; lunch RM12; 11.30am-3pm & 6.30-10pm Tue-Sun;) The fancy main restaurant charges for its tasty vegetarian cuisine with a daily lunch buffet (a good deal for RM12). It's next to the car park beneath the building. It's still 'eat as you wish, give as you feel' at their simpler Annalakshmi Riverside operation.

Vishalatchi INDIAN $

(Map p54; 2274 4755; 18 Jln Scott; meals RM5; 7.30am-10.30pm;) Great banana-leaf meals of spicy southern Indian food are served up at this long-running Brickfields favourite. Good for tiffin snacks and a refreshing lassi, too.

Yogitree MALAY, WESTERN $$

(2282 6763; www.yogitree.com; 1st fl, Jln Syed Putra; meals RM20-70; 10am-10pm) We love anywhere that serves breakfast until 6pm. This 'real food' cafe and yoga clothing boutique, located in the Mid Valley Megamall, uses plenty of organic produce in its mix-and-match local and Western food menu.

Kompleks Makan Tanglin HAWKER $

(Map p54; Jln Cendarasari, Lake Gardens; meals RM10; 7am-4pm Mon-Sat) Yet another good reason for hanging out in the Lake Gardens is the chance to grab a meal at this hawker-stall complex – **Ikan Bakar Pak Din's stall** is a popular one.

BANGSAR BARU

TOP CHOICE Rebung MALAY $$

(2283 2119; www.rebung.com.my; 4-2 Lorong Maarof; buffet RM50; 11am-11pm;) The flamboyant celebrity chef Ismail runs the show at this excellent Malay restaurant, one of KL's best, respected for its authenticity and consistency. The buffet spread is splendid with all kinds of dishes that you'd typically

NIGHT MARKETS

The best time to visit Little India is during the Saturday *pasar malam* (night market) on Lg Tuanku Abdul Rahman, the alley between Jln TAR and Jln Masjid India. From midafternoon, this narrow lane becomes crammed with food stalls serving excellent Malaysian, Indian and Chinese food.

Kampung Baru's Saturday *pasar malam* – called the Sunday Market because it runs into the early hours of Sunday morning – is also worth attending. The main action here is focused at the end of Jln Raja Alang, not far from the LRT station.

Bangsar Baru's *pasar malam* is held each Sunday night in the car park off Jln Telawi 1. Sample wonderful spicy-sour *asam laksa*, freshly made *popiah* (spring rolls) and crepe-like *apam balik*.

only be served in a Malay home, such as *onde onde* (glutinous rice balls filled with jaggery) made freshly. Check their website for details of their cooking classes.

TOP CHOICE Sri Nirwana Maju INDIAN $$

(Map p84; 2287 8445; 43 Jln Telawi 2; meals RM10-20; 7am-2am) There are far flashier Indian restaurants in Bangsar, but who cares about the decor when you can tuck into food this good and cheap? This place serves it all from roti for breakfast to banana-leaf curries throughout the day.

Wondermama MALAY $$

(Map p84; 2284 9821; www.facebook.com/mywondermama; Bangsar Village I, 1 Jln Telawi 1, Bangsar Baru; mains RM14-24; 9am-10.30pm;) Traditional meets contemporary at this design savvy two-level space serving Malay comfort foods and burgers with a creative twist.

Delicious WESTERN $$

(Map p84; 2287 1554; www.delicious.com.my; ground fl, Jln Telawi 1, Bangsar Village II; mains from RM40; 11am-midnight Sun-Thu, to 1am Fri & Sat) Serving healthy salads, pasta, sandwiches and pies among many other things in a cool contemporary setting. Apart from this buzzing branch you'll find others near KLCC and in the Mid Valley Megamall.

Bangsar Baru

0 — 100 m
0 — 0.05 miles

Bangsar Baru

Eating
1 Alexis Bistro.............................B2
2 Bangsar Fish Head Corner.................A3
3 Chawan....................................B2
4 Chelo's Appam Stall......................A4
5 Delicious.................................B2
6 Les Deux Garcons.........................A2
7 Nam Chuan Coffee Shop..................A4
8 Restaurant Mahbub.......................A3
9 Sri Nirwana Maju........................B2
10 Wondermama.............................A3

Drinking
Upstairs @ Alexis Telawi.............(see 1)

Shopping
11 Bangsar Village I & II.................B2
12 Dude & the Duchess....................B2
13 Lasting Impressions...................B2
14 Never Follow Suit.....................B2
15 Silverfish Books......................A2
16 Valentine Willie Fine Art.............B1

the wasabi and jasmine flavours) and beautiful cakes are served along with coffee at this tiny, pristine patisserie.

Restaurant Mahbub INDIAN $$
(Map p84; ☑2095 5382; www.restoranmahbub.com; 17 Lg Ara Kiri 1; mains RM6-12; ☺7am-2am) Tables spill out onto the street from this long-running operation famous for its fragrant biryani rice and lucious honey chicken.

The Bee INTERNATIONAL $$
(☑673 6142; www.thebee.com.my; 36B, Level G2, Publika, Solaris Dutamas; mains RM15-20; ☺9am-midnight Mon-Thu, 9am-1am Fri, 10am-1am Sat, 10am-midnight Sun; ☒) Their burgers and sandwiches are the real deal and they have good salads, local gourmet ice creams and coffee brewed just right. A stage is well used for various free events including live gigs, film screenings and open mic nights.

Drinking

Do you want bubble tea, iced *kopi-o*, a frosty beer or a flaming Lamborghini? KL's cafes, teahouses and bars can deliver it all. Changkat Bukit Bintang in the Golden Triangle continues to sizzle, offering a nonstop party practically every night. Unless otherwise noted standard opening hours are 5pm to 2am.

Alexis Bistro MALAY, WESTERN $$
(Map p84; ☑2284 2880; www.alexis.com.my; Jln Telawi 3, Bangsar Baru; mains from RM30; ☺noon-midnight Sun-Thu, to 1am Fri & Sat) Consistently good food is delivered at this Bangsar stalwart where Asian favourites such as Sarawak laksa (the owner is originally from this Malaysian state) mix it up with European fare.

Chawan MALAY $
(Map p84; ☑2287 5507; 69-G Jln Telawi 3; mains RM5-10; ☺8am-midnight) A chic contemporary take on a *kopitiam,* offering megastrength coffees from all of the country's states to wash down dishes such as beef rendang and a brown-paper-wrapped *nasi lemak.*

Les Deux Garcons PATISSERIE $$
(Map p84; ☑2284 7833; www.lesdeuxgarcons.com.my; 36 Jln Telawi, Bangsar Baru; macarons & cakes RM5-20; ☺11am-8pm) Divine macarons (try

GOLDEN TRIANGLE & KLCC

TOP CHOICE Palate Palette CAFE
(Map p68; www.palatepalette.com; 21 Jln Mesui; ☺noon-midnight Tue-Thu, to 2am Fri & Sat; ☏) Colourful, creative, quirky and super cool, this cafe-bar is our favourite place to eat, drink, play board games, and mingle with KL's boho crowd. The menu (mains RM10 to RM30) features dishes as diverse as shepherd's pie and teriyaki salmon. Check the website for details of events.

TOP CHOICE Taps Beer Bar CRAFT BEER
(Map p68; www.tapsbeerbar.my/; One Residency, 1 Jln Nagansari; ☺5pm-1am; ☏) A very welcome addition to KL's drinking scene, Taps specialises in real ale from around the world with some 80 different microbrews on rotation, 14 of them on tap. Sample three for RM30. They have live acoustic music, too.

TOP CHOICE Village Bar BAR
(Map p68; Feast fl, Starhill Gallery, 181 Jln Bukit Bintang; ☺noon-1am) Columns of glasses and bottles and cascades of dangling lanterns lend an *Alice in Wonderland* quality to this basement bar.

Paper + Toast CAFE
(Map p68; ☏2141 6752; www.paperandtoast.com; One Residency, 1 Jln Nagansari; ☏) Decent coffee and snacks plus space for digital nomads to park their laptops, work and host meetings. We like that they encourage customers to bring their own containers for takeaway drinks and food.

Teeq Brasserie CAFE
(Map p68; ☏2782 3555; www.teeq.com.my; Level 8, 50 Jln Sultan Ismail, Lot 10; ☺6.30-10.30pm, bar open to 1am Tue-Sun) Beside the rooftop garden of Lot 10 is this contemporary-styled brasserie with a relaxed alfresco bar from which you can observe the commercial frenzy of Bintang Walk at a calm distance.

Neo Tamarind BAR
(Map p68; www.samadhiretreats.com; 19 Jln Sultan Ismail; ☺11.30am-2.30pm & 6.30-10.30pm) This sophisticated restaurant–bar feels like a slice of Bali smuggled into the heart of KL. Sip cocktails by flickering tealights under leafy trees.

Luna BAR
(Map p68; ☏2332 7777; Jln Punchak, Menara Pan-Global; ☺3pm-1am, to 3am Fri & Sat) You certainly get the twinkling view of KL's skyline right at this sophisticated rooftop bar surrounding

KUALA LUMPUR DRINKING

WORTH A TRIP

OLD-SCHOOL DINING

Each of these long-time survivors of KL's dining scene oozes retro charm as well as providing lip-smacking meals:

Coliseum Cafe (Map p56; ☏2692 6270; 100 Jln TAR; meals RM15-60; ☺10am-10pm) Little has changed here since Somerset Maugham tucked into sizzling steaks and downed a G'n'T in the wood-panelled bar next door. A KL classic, not to be missed, they also serve Chinese food.

Yut Kee (Map p56; ☏2698 8108; 35 Jln Dang Wangi; meals RM10-15; ☺7.30am-4.45pm)It can get very busy at this beloved Hainanese *kopitiam*, but the staff remain calm and polite. House specialities include toast with homemade *kaya (coconut-cream jam)*, *roti babi* (deep-fried bread filled with shredded pork and onions) or the fried Hokkien mee noodles. Their roast rolled pork with apple sauce, available from Friday to Sunday, usually sells out by 2.30pm.

Sek Yuen (Map p68; ☏9222 9457; 313-315 Pudu; mains RM20-40; ☺noon-3pm & 6-10pm Tue-Sun) Occupying the same time-worn, Art Deco building for the past 60 years, Sek Yuen serves up meals that offer an experience of KL food history. There's no written menu, but you can trust the aged chefs toiling in the wood-fired kitchen to make something delicious; try the *kau yoke* (belly pork), *char siew* (barbecued pork), fried rice and sweet-and-sour fish.

Capital Cafe (Map p56; 213 Jln TAR; dishes RM3.50-5; ☺7am-8.30pm Mon-Sat) Since it opened in 1956, this truly Malaysian cafe has had Chinese, Malays and Indians all working together. Try their excellent mee goreng, *rojak* or satay (only in the evening).

DON'T MISS

LUCKY GARDENS

South of Jln Ara, Bangsar's Lucky Gardens may not be as ritzy as the grid of Telawis, but locals love to hit the morning fruit and veg market here and it is blessed with some delicious and inexpensive dining options. Time your visit to the **Nam Chuan Coffee Shop** (Map p84; Lg Ara Kiri 2; ⊙7am-10pm), a busy, no-frills food court, so you can enjoy a bowl of Christina Jong's fantastic Sarawak laksa (RM5). There's also a fantastic strip of outdoor hawker stalls along Lg Ara Kiri: sample vegan Indian delights at **Chelo's Appam Stall** (Map p84; RM5; ⊙7am-10pm Mon-Sat; ✍) and the tastebud explosion of **Bangsar Fish Head Corner** (Map p84; meals from RM30; ⊙7am-4pm Mon-Sat).

a swimming pool. Also up here, inside and facing towards KL Tower, is the smoke-free **Cristallo**, a playboy-esque bar lined with silver velour sofas, and draped with strings of glittering crystals.

Apartment Downtown CAFE
(Map p56; 1st fl, Suria KLCC, Jln Ampang; ⊙11am-10pm) Imagine you actually live at KLCC at this convivial lounge-like cafe-bar with outdoor seating overlooking the park – a lovely spot to revive after a hard day's shopping at the mall.

Luk Yu Tea House TEAHOUSE
(Map p68; ☎2782 3850; Feast fl, Starhill Gallery, 181 Jln Bukit Bintang; ⊙10am-1am) Enjoy a premium brew inside a charming traditional Chinese teahouse along with dim sum and other dainty snacks.

Sixty Nine Bistro CAFE
(Map p68; 14 Jln Kampung Dollah; ⊙noon-1.30am, from 2pm Fri & Sat) A very funky youth venue that has a junk-shop chic vibe to its decor, a fun menu of bubble teas and the like, and resident fortune tellers.

Sky Bar BAR
(Map p68; ☎2332 9888; Level 33, Traders Hotel; ⊙7pm-1am, to 3am Fri & Sat) Head to the rooftop pool area of this hotel for a grand view across to the Petronas Towers – it's the perfect spot for sundowner cocktails or late-night flutes of bubbly.

Starhill Tea Salon TEAHOUSE
(Map p68; ☎2719 8550; Starhill Gallery, 181 Jln Bukit Bintang; ⊙10am-1am) Grand columns created from tea caddies and luxurious sofas set an elegant tone for this tea salon appropriately sited on Starhill Gallery's 'Indulge' floor. Afternoon tea (3pm to 5pm) is RM70 for two.

CHINATOWN
Bar Art @ The Warehouse BAR
(Map p50; www.thewarehouse.com.my; 198 Jln Tun HS Lee; ⊙10am-1am Tue-Sun; ☎) Showing potential is this newish operation that combines a so-so art gallery with a cafe-bar and steak restaurant (upstairs). Wednesday's open mic night and Thursday's mixology cocktail sessions provide a break from the usual Chinatown scene.

Reggae Bar BAR
(Map p50; www.reggaebarkl.com.my; 158 Jln Tun HS Lee; ⊙10.30am-3am) Travellers gather in droves at this pumping bar in the thick of Chinatown, which has outdoor seats if you'd like to catch the passing parade. There are beer promos, pool tables and pub grub served till late.

Moontree House CAFE
(Map p50; www.moontree-house.blogspot.com; 1st fl, 6 Jln Panggong; ⊙10am-8pm Wed-Mon; ☎) Quiet space for a coffee, also sells cute handicrafts and feminist literature.

Purple Cane Tea House TEAHOUSE
(Map p50; 3rd fl, 6 Jln Panggong; ⊙11am-8pm) Serves a broad range of Chinese green and jasmine teas; their tea shop is around the corner on Jln Sultan.

BANGSAR BARU
Upstairs @ Alexis Telawi BAR
(Map p84; ☎2284 2880; www.alexis.com.my; 29 Jln Telawi 3; ⊙6pm-1am, to 2am Fri & Sat) Bangsar's most chilled-out drinking spot. Sink into comfortable chairs and relax to the soothing sounds on the decks. Live jazz is free on the first Monday of the month.

Social BAR
(Map p68; ☎2282 2260; 57-59 Jln Telawi 3; ⊙10pm-2am) Classy sports bar offering pool tables and good food as well as drinks. There's also a branch on Changkat Bukit Bintang.

☆ Entertainment

KL's entertainment options include a wide range of live music, theatre and dance.

Mainstream movies are screened at the multiplexes in the malls. Tickets are around RM12. Cultural centres ocassionally screen art-house films. There's a lively but fluid clubbing scene; stay up to date by reading *Time Out* or *Juice*. Clubs are typically open Wednesday to Sunday and usually charge a cover (including one drink) of RM20 to RM50 Thursday to Saturday.

TOP CHOICE Dewan Filharmonik Petronas
CONCERT HALL

(Map p56; ☎2051 7007; www.mpo.com.my; Box Office, Tower 2, Petronas Towers; tickets RM10-210; ⊗box office 10am-6pm Mon-Sat) Don't miss the chance to attend a concert at this gorgeous concert hall at the base of the Petronas Towers. The polished Malaysian Philharmonic Orchestra plays here (usually Friday and Saturday evenings and Sunday matinees, but also other times) as well as other local and international ensembles. There is a dress code.

TOP CHOICE No Black Tie
LIVE MUSIC

(Map p68; ☎2142 3737; www.noblacktie.com.my; 17 Jln Mesui; cover RM20-50; ⊗5pm-2am Tue-Sun) Blink and you'd miss this small chic live-music venue, bar and Japanese bistro, as it's hidden behind a grove of bamboo. NBT, as it's known to its fans, is owned by Malaysian concert pianist Evelyn Hii who has a knack for finding talented singer-songwriters, jazz bands and classical-music ensembles who play here from around 9.30pm.

Zouk Club
CLUB

(Map p56; www.zoukclub.com; 113 Jln Ampang; ⊗Zouk 10pm-late Wed, Fri & Sat, Phuture 9pm-late Wed, Fri & Sat, Velvet Underground 9pm-late Wed-Sat, Wine Bar 6pm-2am Tue, to 3am Wed & Thu, to 4am Fri & Sat) KL's top club offers spaces to suit everyone and a great line-up of local and international DJs. As well as the two-level main venue, there's the more sophisticated Velvet Underground (which is also the venue for the popular monthly Time Out KL stand-up comedy nights), with a dance floor that's glitter-ball heaven, Phuture for hip-hop and the cutting-edge Bar Sonic.

Kuala Lumpur Performing Arts Centre
PERFORMING ARTS

(klpac; ☎4047 9000; www.klpac.com; Jln Strachan, Sentul Park; tickets RM20-300) Part of the Sentul West regeneration project, this modernist performing-arts complex puts on a wide range of progressive theatrical events. Combine a show with a stroll in peaceful Sentul Park and dinner at Yu Ri Tei, beside the Sentul Park Koi Centre.

Actors Studio@Lot 10
THEATRE

(☎2142 2009; www.theactorsstudio.com.my; 50 Jln Sultan Ismail, Lot 10) Apart from staging shows at klpac, the Actors Studio theatre and comedy group has its base at this splendid, state-of-the-art venue located on the roof of Lot 10. Other theatre and dance companies also get to put on shows here. Prices depend on the performance.

GAY & LESBIAN KUALA LUMPUR

Check out www.utopia-asia.com and www.fridae.com for the latest on KL's small but friendly gay scene.

Friday is the official gay night at **Frangipani Bar** (Map p68; ☎2144 3001; 25 Jln Changkat Bukit Bintang; cover Fri RM30; ⊗5pm-1am Tue-Thu & Sun, 5pm-3am Fri & Sat), above the restaurant of the same name. On other nights of the week, you'll find a very gay-friendly crowd here, too.

Friday and Saturday nights are when **Marketplace** (Map p56; ☎2166 0750; www.marketplacekl.com; 4A Lg Yap Kwan Seng; cover Sat RM35; ⊗Sat 10pm-3am) welcomes the rainbow crowd. There's a superb view of the Petronas Towers from the restaurant's spacious rooftop, which provides a respite from the body-to-body action on the cramped dancefloor.

Sip creative cocktails such as 'I Am Curious, Orange' and 'Crayons are Attractive' at the gay-owned modern British-themed restaurant and bar **Albion KL** (Map p68; ☎2141 9282; www.albionkl.com; 31 Jln Berangan; ⊗noon-3pm, 5-11pm Tue-Sat, noon-10.30pm Sun).

Still going after donkey's years is **Blue Boy** (Map p68; ☎2142 1067; 54 Jln Sultan Ismail; ⊗8.30pm-2am). Forget decor – it's all about karaoke with the winking lady boys, and the crowds of rent boys and their admirers.

DANCE & CULTURAL SHOWS

If you'd like to see and hear traditional Malaysian dances and music, there are good shows at the Malaysian Tourism Centre (p91) at 3pm Tuesday to Thursday and 8.30pm Saturday. There's also an evening dance show at 8.30pm daily in the attached restaurant **Saloma** (Map p56; ☑2161 0122; show only RM40, buffet & show RM75).

The tourist restaurant **Seri Melayu** (Map p68; ☑2145 1833; www.serimelayu.com; 1 Jln Conlay) also offers live performances of traditional music and dance. Drop by the information desk at Central Market as there are sometimes free cultural events staged here, too.

KL Live
LIVE MUSIC

(Map p68; www.kl-live.com.my; 1st fl, 20 Jln Sultan Ismail, Life Centre) One of the best things to happen to KL's live-music scene in a while has been the opening of this spacious venue, which has been packing in rock and pop fans with an impressive line-up of overseas and local big-name artists and DJs.

The Venue
LIVE MUSIC

(Map p68; ☑2143 3022; www.thevenue.com.my; Connection level 4, Pavilion KL, 168 Jln Bukit Bintang; ⊙6.30pm-12.30am) Specialising mainly in jazz, this new spot in the Pavilion provides a classy performance space for artists from around the region. The first set starts at 9.45pm.

Wings
CAFE-BAR

(Map p68; www.wingsmusicafe.com; 16 Jln Kampung Dollah; ⊙6.30am-1am, to 2am Fri & Sat) A few doors down from Sixty Nine Bistro, this cheerful student hangout has regular live music, though most drinkers prefer to chill out on the front terrace.

Doppel Kafe
LIVE MUSIC

(Map p50; ☑017-200 8631; www.facebook.com/DoppelKL; Central Market Annexe, Jln Hang Kastruri; ⊙noon-9pm Sun-Thu, noon-1am Fri & Sat; 🛜) Local bands and singers perform on an ad-hoc basis at this laid-back cafe-bar on the mezzanine floor. It also sells a small selection of CDs and occasionally hosts music swap-meets.

Golden Screen Cinemas
CINEMA

(Map p68; ☑8312 3456; www.gsc.com.my; Level 6, Pavilion KL, 168 Jln Bukit Bintang) Book a seat in Gold Class (RM40) for reclining chairs and drinks service.

Tanjung Golden Village
CINEMA

(Map p56; ☑7492 2929; www.tgv.com.my; Level 3, Suria KLCC) Tanjung Golden Village is Kuala Lumpur's most convenient multiscreen cinema located smack bang in the City Centre at Suria KLCC, a six-storey shopping extravaganza at the foot of the Petronas Towers.

Sutra Dance Theatre
DANCE

(Map p59; ☑4021 1092; www.sutrafoundation.org.my; 12 Persiaran Titiwangsa 3) The home of Malaysian dance legend Ramli Ibrahim has been turned into a showcase for Indian classical dance, as well as a dance studio, gallery and cultural centre near Lake Titiwangsa. See the website for upcoming shows.

Istana Budaya
PERFORMING ARTS

(National Theatre; Map p59; ☑4026 5555; www.istanabudaya.gov.my; Jln Tun Razak; tickets RM100-300) Big-scale drama and dance shows are staged here, as well as music performances by the National Symphony Orchestra and National Choir. There's a dress code: no shorts, and men must wear long-sleeved shirts.

Shopping

Take your pick from street markets proffering fake-label goods to glitzy shopping malls (all open 10am to 10pm) packed with the real deal. Clothing, camera gear, computers and electronic goods are all competitively priced. You'll also find original handicrafts from all over the country as well as contemporary art. The shops in the National Textiles Museum (p52) and Islamic Arts Museum (p53) are both packed with appealing items.

GOLDEN TRIANGLE & KLCC

TOP CHOICE **Pavilion KL**
MALL

(Map p68; www.pavilion-kl.com; 168 Jln Bukit Bintang) Pavilion sets the gold standard in KL's shopping scene. Amid the many familiar international luxury labels, there are some good local retail options, including branches of the fashion houses **British India**; **MS Read** for larger-sized gals; **Salabianca** and **Philosophy for Men** for fun casual wear. Their basement food court is excellent and for a quick trip to Japan head to **Tokyo Street** on the 6th floor.

Sungei Wang Plaza   MALL
(Map p68; www.sungeiwang.com; Jln Sultan Ismail) This ragbag of retail fun promises 'all kinds of everything' and you'd better believe it. Connected with **BB Plaza**, Sungei Wang is confusing to navigate but jam-packed with youth-oriented fashions and accessories. Teens and youthful fashionistas should hunt out **HK Station** on the 6th floor.

Suria KLCC   MALL
(Map p56; www.suriaklcc.com.my; Jln Ampang) Even if shopping bores you to tears, you're sure to find something to interest you at this fine shopping complex at the foot of the Petronas Towers. Amid the usual plethora of international lables, look out for the following local business: **Pucuk Rebung** (level 3) for upmarket arts, crafts and antiques; **iKAR-RTini** (level 2) for batik design fashions with separate men's and women's outlets; and **Aseana** (ground level) for fancy party frocks. There's also an excellent branch of the bookshop **Kinokuniya** (level 4), scores of restaurants and cafes, two food courts, a cinema, gallery and a kids' museum.

Starhill Gallery   MALL
(Map p68; www.starhillgallery.com; 181 Jln Bukit Bintang) Break out the platinum charge card – this glitzy mall is the domain of exclusive fashion brands including Louis Vuitton, Salvatore Ferragamo, Alfred Dunhill and – hmm – British department store Debenhams? The basement level is a virtual village of upmarket restaurants. Beautiful batik prints can be bought from **Jendela** ('Explore' floor).

Kompleks Budaya Kraf   ARTS & CRAFTS
(Map p63; ☎2162 7533; www.malaysiancraft.com; Jln Conlay; ☺9am-8pm Mon-Fri, to 7pm Sat & Sun) A government enterprise, this huge complex mainly caters to coach tours, but it's worth a visit to browse the shops and stalls selling batik, wood carvings, pewter, basketware, glassware and ceramics. You can see craftspeople and artists at work in the surrounding **Art Colony**. The complex also has a small museum and offers batik-making courses.

Plaza Low Yat   ELECTRONICS
(Map p68; www.plazalowyat.com; 7 Jln Bintang, off Jln Bukit Bintang) KL's best IT mall, packed with six floors of retailers big and small offering deals on laptops, digital cameras, mobile phones, computer peripherals and accessories. If you can't find what you need

here (in particular electronic parts) then scout around the stalls in nearby **Imbi Plaza** (Map p68; Jln Imbi; ☺11am-9pm).

Berjaya Times Square   MALL
(Map p68; ☎2117 3081; www.timesquarekl.com; 1 Jln Imbi) Teen fashions and toy stores abound at this mammoth mall. The **Metrojaya** department store has good deals on clothes and there's a big branch of **Borders** bookstore on level 2. The centre also has a bowling alley, karaoke, fish spa, cinema and an indoor theme park.

CHINATOWN

TOP CHOICE Peter Hoe Evolution   HOME DECOR
(Map p50; 2 Jln Hang Lekir; ☺10am-7pm) Both here and at the much bigger **Peter Hoe Beyond** (Map p50; 2nd fl, Lee Rubber Bldg, 145 Jln Tun HS Lee; ☺10am-7pm) around the corner you can satisfy practically all your gift-and-souvenir-buying needs, with selections from the KL-based designer's creative and affordable range of original batik designs on sarongs, shirts and dresses, and home furnishings. The Beyond branch has a cafe that's worth visiting in its own right and the atelier of **Justin Yap** (www.justinyap.com), one of Malaysia's rising fashion stars.

Central Market   MARKET
(www.centralmarket.com.my; Jln Hang Kasturi, Pasar Seni; ☺10am-9pm) It's easy to spend an hour or more wandering around this treasure house of souvenirs, batik, kites, clothes and jewellery. Asian artifacts and antiques are also available, but you'll need to bargain hard to get good deals; **Art House Gallery Museum of Ethnic Arts** in the annex has interesting pieces from Borneo and Tibet.

BANGSAR BARU & BRICKFIELDS

TOP CHOICE Never Follow Suit   FASHION
(Map p84; ☎2284 7316; 28-2, Jln Telawi 2, Bangsar Baru) You're guaranteed to find something special at this extraordinary boutique hidden away on the 2nd floor. New and upcycled clothes and accessories are displayed like art works in a hipster, shabby-chic gallery.

TOP CHOICE Bangsar Village I & II   MALL
(Map p84; www.bangsarvillage.com; cnr Jln Telawi 1 & Jln Telawi 2) These twin malls – linked by a covered bridge – offer upmarket fashions, including international brands and local Malaysian designers, such as Richard Tsen at **Dude & the Duchess** (Map p84; upper ground fl,

Bangsar Village II), which marries tailored fits and design to interesting fabric choices, or Shuenkee Chong at leathergoods shop **Thirtyfour** (http://thirtyfour.net). Asian interior-design shop **Lasting Impressions** (Map p84; www.lasting-impressions.com.my; 2nd fl Bangsar Village II) has great decorative pieces.

Mid Valley Megamall MALL
(www.midvalley.com.my; Lingkaran Syed Putra) Mega is the only way to describe this enormous mall where you could easily lose yourself for days in the 300 stores, two department stores, 18-screen cinema, bowling alley, huge food court and even the colourful Hindu temple. For more upmarket shopping, the luxe **Gardens Mall** (www.thegardens.com.my; Mid Valley City, Lingkaran Syed Putra) is also part of the development. The KL Komuter Mid Valley station makes getting here a cinch. There are also Rapid KL buses to Chinatown and a free shuttle bus to Bangsar LRT station.

Valentine Willie Fine Art ART GALLERY
(Map p84; ☑2284 2348; www.vwfa.net; 17 Jln Telawi 3; ☺noon-8pm Mon-Fri, noon-6pm Sat) One of KL's best galleries has frequent shows and represents some of the country's top artists.

Wei-Ling Gallery ART GALLERY
(Map p54; www.weiling-gallery.com; 8 Jln Scott; ☺noon-7pm Mon-Fri, 10am-5pm Sat) The top two floors of this old shophouse have been imaginatively turned into a contemporary gallery to showcase local artists.

Silverfish Books BOOKS
(Map p84; ☑2284 4837; www.silverfishbooks.com; 28-1 Jln Telawi; ☺10.30am-8.30pm Mon-Fri, to 6pm Sat) Good local bookshop and publisher of contemporary Malaysian literature and writing.

ELSEWHERE
Royal Selangor
Pewter Factory ARTS & CRAFTS
(☑4145 6122; www.visitorcentre.royalselangor.com; 4 Jln Usahawan Enam; ☺9am-5pm) Located 8km northeast of the city centre, the world's largest pewter manufacturer offers some very appealing souvenirs made from this malleable alloy of lead and silver. You can try your own hand at creating a pewter dish at the **School of Hard Knocks** (p59). The factory has an interesting visitor centre (to get here, take the LRT to Wangsa Maju station and then a taxi), or you can visit the retail outlets in KL's malls including **Suria KLCC**.

ℹ Information

Immigration Offices
Immigration Office (☑2095 5077; Block I, Pusat Bandar Damansara; ☺8.30am-5pm Mon-Fri, closed 12.15-2.45pm Fri) Handles visa extensions; 2km west of Lake Gardens.

Internet Access
Internet cafes are everywhere; the going rate per hour is RM3. If you're travelling with a wi-fi–enabled device, you can get online at hundreds of cafes, restaurants, bars and several hotels for free.

WORTH A TRIP

PUBLIKA

Not all KL malls are equal. A five-minute taxi ride northwest of the Lake Gardens and Bangsar is **Publika** (www.publika.com.my; 1 Jln Dutamas, Solaris Dutamas), where contemporary art, culture, shopping and dining are combined to create what the creative team behind the mall like to call 'Manhanttan'. The vibrant creativity and liberal vibe is certainly a striking contrast to the conservative Islamic high court and a giant mosque that are the complex's neighbours.

Low rents have encouraged new talents to open up shops, creative spaces and businesses in the mixed-use development. Dazzling murals in the food court, quirky themes for the toilets, a great kids' play space and inspirational quotes carved into the flagging of the public square all add to visual interest. Anchoring the basement space is the fabulous grocer **B.I.G.**, and there are plenty of great places to eat and drink including The Bee (p84).

Gallery spaces include **MAP**, where an interesting roster of events are held in the White and Black Box spaces. Free films are screened each Monday in the square, there's an interesting arts and crafts market on the last Sunday of the month, as well as other occasional events.

Media

Juice (www.juiceonline.com) Free clubbing-oriented monthly magazine available in top-end hotels, restaurants and bars.

Time Out (www.timeoutkl.com; RM5) Monthly magazine in a globally familiar format; sign up online for their weekly 'what's going on' digest.

Medical Services

Pharmacies are all over town; the most common is Guardian, located in most shopping malls.

Hospital Kuala Lumpur (✆2615 5555; www.hkl.gov.my; Jln Pahang) North of the city centre.

Tung Shin Hospital (✆2072 1655; http://tungshin.com.my; 102 Jln Pudu)

Twin Towers Medical Centre KLCC (✆2382 3500; www.ttmcklcc.com.my; Level 4, Suria KLCC, Jln Ampang; ⊙8.30am-6pm Mon-Sat)

Money

You'll seldom be far from a bank/ATM. Moneychangers offer better rates than banks for changing cash and (at times) travellers cheques; they're usually open during later hours and on weekends and are found in shopping malls.

Post

Main Post Office (Jln Raja Laut; ⊙8.30am-6pm Mon-Sat, closed 1st Sat of month) Across the river from the Central Market.

Tourist Information

Malaysian Tourism Centre (MaTiC; ✆9235 4900; http://matic.gov.my; 109 Jln Ampang; ⊙8am-10pm) Housed in a mansion built in 1935 for rubber and tin tycoon Eu Tong Seng, this is KL's most useful tourist office. Also hosts good cultural performances.

❶ Getting There & Away

Air

KL's main airport is **Kuala Lumpur International Airport** (KLIA; ✆8777 8888; www.klia.com.my), 75km south of the city centre at Sepang. AirAsia's flights are handled by the nearby **Low Cost Carrier Terminal** (LCCT; ✆8777 8888; http://lcct.klia.com.my), which will be replaced during 2013 by the new **KLIA2** (http://klia2.org) terminal.

Firefly and Berjaya Air flights go from **SkyPark Subang Terminal** (Sultan Abdul Aziz Shah Airport; ✆7845 1717; ww.subangskypark.com), around 20km west of the city centre.

Bus

KL has several bus stations, the main one being Pudu Sentral (formerly Puduraya), just east of Chinatown. From here services fan out all over Peninsular Malaysia, as well as to Singapore and Thailand. The only long-distance destinations that Pudu Sentral doesn't handle are Kuala Lipis and Jerantut (for access to Taman Negara) – buses to these places leave from Pekeliling bus station; and Kota Bharu and Kuala Terengganu, buses for which leave from Putra bus station.

Other long-distance bus services are operated by the following:

Aeroline (✆6258 8800; www.aeroline.com.my) Daily services to Singapore (from RM90) and Penang (RM60) leave from outside the Corus Hotel, Jln Ampang, just east of KLCC.

Nice (✆2272 1586; www.nice-coaches.com.my) Services run from outside the old KL Train Station on Jln Sultan Hishamuddin to Singapore (RM88, 10 daily), Penang (RM75, 7 daily), Butterworth (RM68, twice daily) and Melaka (RM27, twice daily) as well as other destinations.

Transtar Travel (✆2141 1771; www.transtar.com.sg) Services go to Singapore (RM28 to RM90, depending on size of bus) and Penang (RM45) from 138 Jln Imbi, opposite Overseas Restaurant.

PASIR SENI STATION

From beside Pasar Seni LRT station in Chinatown, frequent buses include U64, U65, U80 and U81 to Shah Alam (RM3), U91 to Klang (RM3), Cityliner bus 710 for Pelabuhan Klang (Port Klang; RM4), and U85, U87 and U88 to Petaling Jaya (RM3).

PEKELILING BUS STATION

Next to Titiwangsa LRT and monorail stations, just off Jln Tun Razak. Buses leave here for Kuala Lipis (RM14.70, four hours, eight daily) and Raub (RM10.90, 2½ hours, six daily). Several companies including **Plusliner** (www.plusliner.com) run services to Kuantan (RM22.10, four hours), which leave at two-hourly intervals between 8am and 8pm; many go via Temerloh (RM11.30). Buses to Jerantut (RM16.80, three hours) also go via Temerloh. Buses to Genting Highlands (RM6) leave every half-hour between 7am and 9.30pm.

PUDU SENTRAL BUS STATION

Recently given a major facelift, this crowded bus station remains the kind of place you want to get in and out of quickly. The crowds provide plenty of cover for pickpockets and bag snatchers, and agents for various bus companies will pounce on you as soon as you enter. Close to the main entrance is an information counter. At the rear is a **left-luggage counter** (per day per bag RM3; ⊙6am-midnight), as well as the tourist police.

Inside are dozens of bus company ticket-windows. Staff will shout out destinations, but check to be sure the departure time suits you as they sometimes try to sell tickets for buses that

INTERSTATE BUS FARES FROM PUDU SENTRAL

DESTINATION	FARE (RM)	DURATION (HRS)
Alor Setar	40.20	5
Butterworth	31.40	4½
Cameron Highlands	35	4
Ipoh	17.50	2½
Johor Bahru	31.30	4
Kuantan	22.10	4
Lumut	24.80	4
Melaka	22.50	2
Mersing	30	5½
Penang	35.20	5
Singapore	88.50	5½
Sungai Petani	36.50	5
Taiping	24.80	3½

aren't leaving for many hours. Buses leave from numbered platforms in the basement.

On the main runs, services are so numerous that you can sometimes just turn up and get a seat on the next bus. However, tickets should preferably be booked at least the day before, and a few days before during peak holiday periods, especially to the Cameron Highlands and east-coast destinations, which only have a few daily services.

Transnasional Express (☑1300-888 582; www.transnasional.com.my) is the largest operation here, with buses to almost all major destinations. Outside the terminal, on Jln Pudu, there are several private companies handling tickets for buses to Thailand, Singapore and some Malaysian destinations.

PUTRA BUS STATION
A number of mainly east-coast services leave from this quieter and less intimidating station opposite PWTC station (easily reached by taking the LRT to PWTC, or a KTM Komuter train to Putra station).

There are services to Kota Bharu (RM40.30, eight hours, 12 daily), Kuantan (RM22.10, four hours, four daily) and Kuala Terengganu (RM40.20, seven hours, five daily).

TERMINAL BERSEPADU SELATAN
Connected to the Bandar Tasik Selatan train station hub, about 15 minutes south of KL Sentral, is the new **Terminal Bersepadu Seletan** (☑9051 2000; www.tbsbts.com.my; Bandar Tasik Selatan) serving destinations south of KL.

Among other places, there are very frequent departures to Seremban, Melaka, Muar, Johor Bahru and Singapore.

Car
KL is the best place to hire a car for touring the peninsula. However, navigating the city's complex (and mostly one-way) traffic system is not for the timid.

All the major companies have offices at the airport. City offices, which are generally open 9am to 5.30pm Monday to Friday and 9am to 1pm Saturday, include the following companies:
Avis (☑2144 4487; www.avis.com.my; main lobby, Crowne Plaza Mutiara Kuala Lumpur, Jln Sultan Ismail)
Hertz (☑2148 6433; www5.hertz.com; ground fl, Kompleks Antarabangsa, Jln Sultan Ismail)
Orix (☑2142 3009; www.orixauto.com.my; 35 Jln Bukit Bintang, ground fl, Federal Hotel)

Taxi
Long-distance taxis – often no faster than taking a bus – depart from upstairs at Pudu Sentral bus station. It you're not prepared to wait to get a full complement of four passengers, you will have to charter a whole taxi. Prices should include toll charges.

Train
Kuala Lumpur is the hub of the **KTM** (Keretapi Tanah Melayu Berhad; ☑1300-885 862; www.ktmb.com.my; ⊙info office 9am-9pm, ticket office 7am-10pm) national railway system. All long-distance trains depart from KL Sentral; the information office in the main hall can advise on schedules and check seat availability.

There are daily departures for Butterworth, Wakaf Baharu (for Kota Bharu and Jerantut), Johor Bahru, Thailand and Singapore; fares are cheap, especially if you opt for a seat rather than a berth (for which there are extra charges), but

FIXED FARES FOR WHOLE TAXI

DESTINATION	FARE (RM)
Cameron Highlands (Tanah Rata)	350
Fraser's Hill	180
Genting Highlands	60
Ipoh	240
Johor Bahru	380
Lumut	350
Melaka	150
Penang	500

TRAIN FARES FROM KUALA LUMPUR

DESTINATION	PREMIER (RM)	SUPERIOR (RM)	ECONOMY (RM)
Butterworth		34	
Ipoh		22	12
Jerantut		29	17
Johor Bahru	64	33	
Kuala Lipis		33	20
Padang Besar		44	24
Seremban	58	13	9
Singapore	68	34	
Taiping		28	18
Tampin	50	17	11
Tapah Rd		19	10
Tumpat		43	31
Wakaf Baharu		42	30

journey times are slow. KTM Komuter trains also link KL with the Klang Valley and Seremban.

ℹ Getting Around

KL Sentral is the hub of a rail-based urban network consisting of the KTM Komuter, KLIA Ekspres, KLIA Transit, LRT and Monorail systems. Unfortunately the systems – all built separately – remain largely unintegrated. Different tickets generally apply for each service, and at stations where there's an interchange between the services they're rarely conveniently connected. This said, you can happily get around much of central KL on a combination of rail and monorail services, thus avoiding the traffic jams that plague the inner-city roads.

To/From the Airports

KLIA

The fastest way of reaching KL from KLIA is on the **KLIA Ekspres** (www.kliaekspres.com; adult/child one way RM35/15, return RM70/30, with departures every 15 minutes between 5am and 1am, 28 minutes). From KL Sentral you can continue to your destination by KTM Komuter, LRT, Monorail or taxi.

The **KL Transit train** (adult/child one way RM35/15) also connects KLIA with KL Sentral (35 minutes), but stops at three other stations en route (Salak Tinggi, Putrajaya and Cyberjaya, and Bandar Tasik Selatan).

If flying from KL on Malaysia Airlines, Cathay Pacific, Royal Brunei or Emirates you can check your baggage in at KL Sentral before making your way to KLIA.

The **Airport Coach** (www.airportcoach.com.my; one way/return RM10/18) takes an hour to KL Sentral; for RM18, however, it will also take you to any central KL hotel from KLIA and pick you up for the return journey for RM25. The bus stand is clearly signposted inside the terminal.

Taxis from KLIA operate on a fixed-fare coupon system. Standard taxis cost RM75 (up to three people), premier taxis for four people cost RM103, and family-sized minivans seating up to eight cost RM200. The journey will take around one hour. Buy your taxi coupon before you exit the arrivals hall to avoid the aggressive pirate taxis that hassle you to pay a few hundred ringgit for the same ride. Going to the airport by taxi, make sure that the agreed fare includes tolls; expect to pay at least RM65 from Chinatown or Jln Bukit Bintang.

If you're changing to a flight on AirAsia, there's a **shuttle bus** (RM3, every 20 minutes) between KLIA and the LCCT. Penny-pinchers can use this bus to get to Nilai (RM3.50) to connect with the KTM Komuter train to KL Sentral (RM4.70). A taxi between the two airports costs RM42.

LCCT

Skybus (www.skybus.com.my; one way RM9) and **Aerobus** (adult/child one way RM8/4) services depart at least every 15 minutes from 4.30am to 12.45am. Travelling from the LCCT, prepaid taxis charge RM70 to Chinatown or Jln Bukit Bintang (50% more from midnight to 6am). Buy your coupon at the desk near the arrival hall exit. A taxi from the city to LCCT will cost around RM65.

KLIA TRANSIT HOTELS

If all you need to do is freshen up before or after your flight, you might find the **Airside Transit Hotel** (☏8787 4848; www.klairporthotel.com/airside-transit -hotel; Gate 5, Satellite Bldg, KLIA; d per 6hr RM185; ✳@) useful. The hotel includes a fitness centre, business centre, spa and sauna, and all rooms come with attached bathroom and TV.

The budget **Tune Hotel** (www.tune hotels.com) has a branch next to the LCCT, while the luxurious **Pan Pacific KLIA** (☏8787 3333; www.panpacific.com; r from RM500; ✳@✱) is linked by a bridge to the main KLIA terminal.

SKYPARK SUBANG TERMINAL

As long as there's no traffic, a taxi from Subang to the city should take about 20 minutes and cost RM40.

Bus

Most buses are provided by either **Rapid KL** (☏7885 2585; www.rapidkl.com.my) or **Metrobus** (☏5635 3070). There's an **information booth** (⊙7am-9pm) near Pasir Seni station in Chinatown.

Rapid KL buses are the easiest to use as destinations are clearly displayed. They are divided into four classes, and tickets are valid all day on the same class of bus. Bas Bandar (routes starting with B, RM2) services run around the city centre. Bas Utama (routes starting with U, RM3) buses run from the centre to the suburbs. Bas Tempatan (routes starting with T, RM1) buses run around the suburbs. Bas Ekspres (routes starting with E, RM4) are express buses to distant suburbs.

Local buses leave from half a dozen small bus stands around the city – useful stops in Chinatown include Jln Sultan Mohamed (by Pasar Seni), Bangkok Bank (on Lebuh Pudu) and Medan Pasar (on Lebuh Ampang).

KL Monorail

The air-conditioned **monorail** (www.myrapid .com.my; RM1.20-2.50; ⊙6am-midnight) runs between KL Sentral in the south to Titiwangsa in the north, linking up many of the city's sightseeing areas.

KTM Komuter Trains

KTM Komuter (☏1300-885 862; http://ktm komuter.com.my; ⊙6am-11.45pm) train services run every 15 to 20 minutes and use KL Sentral as a hub. There are two lines: Tanjung Malim to Sungai Gadut and Batu Caves to Pelabuhan Klang. Useful stops include Batu Caves, Mid Valley (for the Mid Valley Megamall), Subang Jaya (for Sunway Lagoon), Nilai (for the cheap local bus to the airports), Klang, Pelabuhan Klang (for ferry services to Sumatra) and Seremban. Trains run every 15 to 20 minutes from approximately 6am to 11.45pm. Tickets start from RM1 for one stop.

Light Rail Transit (LRT)

In addition to the buses, **Rapid KL** (☏7885 2585; www.rapidkl.com.my) runs the Light Rail Transit (LRT) system. There are three lines: Ampang/Sentul Timur, Sri Petaling/Sentul Timur and Kelana Jaya/Terminal Putra. The network is poorly integrated because the lines were constructed by different companies. As a result, you sometimes have to buy a new ticket to change from one line to another, and you may also have to follow a series of walkways, stairs and elevators, or walk several blocks down the street.

An electronic control system checks tickets as you enter and exit via turnstiles. Single-journey fares range from RM1 to RM2.80. You can buy tickets from the cashier or electronic ticket

MYRAPID & TOUCH 'N GO CARDS

You may find one of these electronic credit storage cards useful if you plan to stay for an extended period in KL or Malaysia. The prepaid **MyRapid** (www.myrapid.com.my) card is valid on Rapid KL buses, the monorail and the Ampang and Kelana Jaya LRT lines. It costs RM10 (including RM8 in credit) and can be bought at monorail and LRT stations. Just tap at the ticket gates or when you get on the bus and the correct fare will be deducted. Rapid KL also offers the **Rapidpass Flexi Touch 'n Go**, valid from one to 30 days (RM10 to RM150).

The **Touch 'n Go card** (www.touchngo.com.my) can be used on all public transport in the Klang Valley, at highway toll booths across the country and at selected parking sites. The cards, which cost RM10 and can be reloaded with values from RM20 to RM500, can be purchased at KL Sentral and the central LRT stations KLCC, Masjid Jamek and Dang Wangi.

KLANG VALLEY RAIL TRANSIT MAP

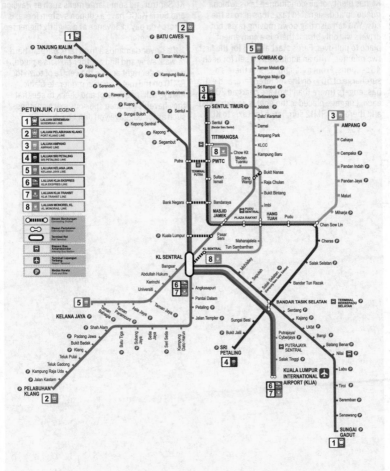

machines. Trains run every six to 10 minutes from 6am to 11.45pm. If you're going to be in KL for a while, consider getting one of the credit storage cards.

Taxi

KL has plenty of air-conditioned taxis, which queue up at designated taxi stops across the city. You can also flag down moving taxis, but drivers will only stop if there is a convenient place to pull over. Fares start at RM3 for the first two minutes, with an additional 20 sen for each 45 seconds. From midnight to 6am there's a surcharge of 50% on the metered fare, and extra passengers (more than two) are charged 20 sen each. Luggage placed in the boot is an extra RM1 and there's an RM12 surcharge for taxis to KLIA.

Some drivers have a limited geographical knowledge of the city and some also refuse to use the meter, even though this is a legal requirement. Taxi drivers lingering outside luxury hotels or tourist hot spots such as KL Bird Park are especially guilty of this behaviour. Note that KL Sentral and some large malls such as Pavilion and Suria KLCC have a coupon system for taxis where you pay in advance at a slightly higher fee than the meter.

If a driver demands a fixed fare, bargain hard, or walk away and find another taxi. As a guide, you can get right across the centre of town for RM10 on the meter even in moderate traffic. Always ask for a receipt and check to see that they haven't included spurious extra charges, such as for baggage you don't have.

Selangor & Negeri Sembilan

Includes »

Selangor 99
Batu Caves 99
Forestry Research Institute
of Malaysia (FRIM) 100
Genting Highlands 101
Fraser's Hill (Bukit
Fraser) 102
Putrajaya 104
Klang Valley 105
Kuala Selangor 107
Negeri Sembilan 109
Seremban 109
Port Dickson 113

Best Places to Eat

» Ye Olde Smokehouse
Fraser's Hill (p102)

» Mohana Bistro (p107)

» Haji Shariff's Cendol (p107)

» Sin Yee Kee (p107)

Best Places to Stay

» Ye Olde Smokehouse
Fraser's Hill (p102)

» Avillion Port Dickson
(p113)

» Thistle Port Dickson
Resort (p114)

» De Palma Hotel Kuala
Selangor (p108)

Why Go?

Selangor (www.tourismselangor.org), Malaysia's most urbanised and industrialised state, offers some top tourist attractions, such as the Batu Caves and the Forestry Research Institute of Malaysia (FRIM), both easy half-day trips from Kuala Lumpur (KL). Rewarding stopovers include lush Fraser's Hill (Bukit Fraser) and the old royal capital of Kuala Selangor, with its wildlife-watching and *kampung* (village) atmosphere.

South of KL, Malaysia's administrative capital of Putrajaya is packed with striking contemporary architecture. Further south, in Seremban, state capital of Negeri Sembilan (http://tourismnegerisembilan.com), you can learn about Minangkabau culture and feast on local cuisine.

Towns along the murky Strait of Melaka aren't the best in Malaysia for a beach holiday, but if that's what you want, then Port Dickson has pleasant beaches and resorts of every calibre. It's also near Cape Rachado Forest Reserve, the last remaining patch of native jungle on the west coast.

When to Go
Kuala Selangor

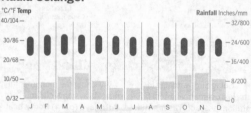

Jan–Feb During Thaipusam the Batu Caves are mobbed by one million pilgrims.

Mar–Apr At Cape Rachado Forest Reserve watch the raptors' annual northwards migration.

Jun Escape the lowland heat at Fraser Hill's International Bird Race.

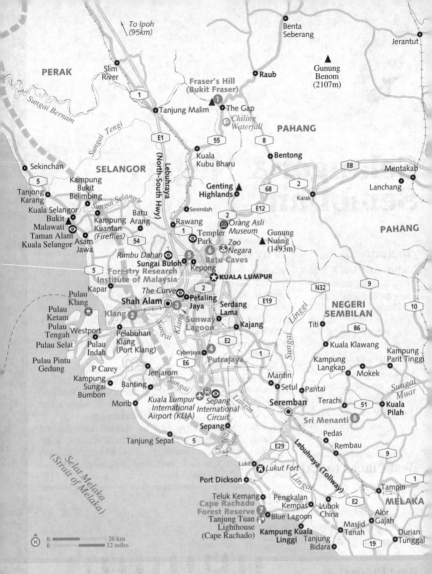

Selangor & Negeri Sembilan Highlights

① Going bird-watching in the lush, climatically cool hill station resort of **Fraser's Hill** (Bukit Fraser, p102)

② Tucking into delicious Indian and Chinese food in historic **Klang** (p104)

③ Cooling off on the water slides and in the tidal pool at **Sunway Lagoon** (p105)

④ Viewing the monumental new Malaysian architecture of **Putrajaya** (p104) from a boat on its central lake

⑤ Getting a treetop look at Kuala Lumpur (KL) from the canopy walkway at the **Forest Research Institute of Malaysia (FRIM,** p100)

⑥ Climbing the 272 steps to the psychedelic Hindu galleries of **Batu Caves** (p99)

⑦ Hiking through the verdant jungle and hidden beaches of the **Cape Rachado Forest Reserve** (p113)

⑧ Marvelling at the intricate woodwork of Sri Menanti's grand **Istana Lama** (p112)

History

In the 15th century, all of what is now Selangor and Negeri Sembilan was controlled by Melaka. With the rising power of the Bugis (a seafaring group of warrior-like Malay settlers from Sulawesi) in Selangor, Minangkabau settlers from Sumatra felt increasingly insecure, so they turned to their former homeland for protection. Raja Melewar, a Minangkabau prince from Sumatra, was appointed the first *yang di-pertuan besar* (head of state) of Negeri Sembilan in 1773. Out of this initial union emerged a loose confederation of nine *luak* (fiefdoms). The royal capital of Negeri Sembilan was established at Sri Menanti.

After Melaka fell to the Portuguese in the early 16th century, control of Selangor was also hotly contested, partly because of its rich tin reserves. By the middle of the 18th century, the Buginese had established a sultanate, based at Kuala Selangor. A century later the success of the tin trade and the growing wealth of the Chinese communities in the fledgling city of Kuala Lumpur led to conflicts both among and between the Selangor chiefs and the miners. The outcome was a prolonged civil war, which slashed tin production and destroyed KL. In 1874, with the civil war over, the British took control. The sultan was forced to accede to the installation of a British Resident at Klang, and for the next 25 years the state prospered, largely on the back of another boom in tin prices.

Negeri Sembilan was likewise rich in tin, so for much of the 19th century it also suffered from unrest and political instability motivated by greed. After Raja Melewar's death, the title of *yang di-pertuan besar* was taken by a succession of Sumatran chiefs, until a series of protracted tin-related wars in 1824–32 led to the severance of political ties with Sumatra.

British Resident Frank Swettenham cajoled the sultans of Selangor, Negeri Sembilan, Perak and Pahang into an alliance that eventually became the Federated Malay States in 1896. The federation was centrally administered from a phoenix-like KL, which had become a well-ordered and prosperous city by the turn of the 20th century. In 1974 Selangor's sultan ceded KL as a federal territory, and Shah Alam took over the role of state capital. In the late 1990s the federal administrative capital of Putrajaya was also cleaved off from Selangor.

SELANGOR

Batu Caves

Just 13km north of KL, a short distance off the Ipoh road, a towering limestone outcrop is home to these impressive caves, officially discovered around 120 years ago by American naturalist William Hornaday. A short time later a small Hindu shrine was built in the vast open space, later known as Temple Cave.

An enormous golden statue of Muruga, also known as Lord Subramaniam, to whom the caves are dedicated, stands at the foot of a flight of 272 steps leading up to Temple Cave. Beyond the towering main cavern, the space opens to an atrium-like cave at the rear. Monkeys scamper around the shrines, which are dwarfed by the scale of the cave.

◉ Sights

Dark Cave CAVE

(www.darkcavemalaysia.com/site; adult/child RM35/25; ⊙10am-5pm Tue-Fri, 10.30am-5.30pm Sat & Sun, tours every 20 min) At step 204, branch off to the Dark Cave to follow a 45-minute guided tour along around 800m of the 2km of surveyed passageways with seven different chambers. Dramatic limestone formations, two species of bats and hundreds of other life forms, including the rare trapdoor spider, make this a fascinating, excursion. See the website about organising a more challenging two- to three-hour tour that involves crawling through the cave's narrow tunnels.

Cave Villa CAVE

(☎012-910 8389; www.cavevilla.com.my; adult/child RM15/7; ⊙9am-6pm) At the base of the outcrop you have to pay to enter the Cave

---

ℹ THAIPUSAM AT BATU CAVES

Each year in late January or early February a million pilgrims converge on the Batu Caves during the three days of Thaipusam (p571). Lord Muruga's silver chariot takes pride of place as it makes its way from the Sri Mahamariamman Temple in KL's Chinatown to the caves. Get here by dawn if you want to see anything amid the crowds, and bring food and water with you.

ⓘ RIMBU DAHAN

Check the website of **Rimbun Dahan** (☏6038-3690; www.rimbundahan.org/home.html), a private property about 20 minutes' drive west of Kepong and one hour from KL, for the handful of times a year when it's open to the public. There's a gallery inside this centre for developing traditional and contemporary art, as well as buildings designed by Hijjas Kasturi, the architect of the striking Tabung Haji and Menara Maybank buildings in KL. The property also boasts a 19th-century traditional Malay house and an indigenous garden.

Villa, fronted by a pond packed with koi carp. Psychedelically painted sculptures of Hindu gods arranged to tell parables from the *Bhagavad Gita* and other Hindu scriptures decorate the caves. Outside there's a small bird sanctuary, an area containing over 100 different species of reptiles (including a 7.6m-long python) and classical Indian dance shows on the half hour.

ⓘ Getting There & Away

KTM Komuter trains terminate at Batu Caves station (RM1.30 from KL Sentral, 25 minutes, every 30 minutes). Bus U6 (RM2.50, 45 minutes, every 30 minutes) leaves from Medan Pasar in KL. A taxi from KL costs around RM20.

Forestry Research Institute of Malaysia (FRIM)

Birdsong and wall-to-wall greenery replaces the drone of traffic and air-conditioning at the **Forestry Research Institute of Malaysia** (FRIM; ☏6279 7575; www.frim.gov.my; Selangor Darul Ehsan; admission RM5; Canopy Walkway adult/child RM10/1; ☉information centre 8am-5pm Mon-Fri, 9am-4pm Sat & Sun; Canopy Walkway 9.30am-1.30pm Tue-Thu, Sat & Sun; museum 9am-4pm Tue-Sun; Malay Teahouse 9am-7pm). The highlight of this 600-hectare jungle park at Kepong, part of the Bukit Lagong Forest Reserve 16km northwest of KL, is its **Canopy Walkway**. The 200m walkway, hanging a vertigo-inducing 30m above the forest floor, is reached by a steep trail from FRIM's **information centre**, where you should go first to register and to pick up maps of the

other trails in the park. Heading down from the walkway, the trail picks its way through the jungle to a shady picnic area where you can cool off in a series of shallow waterfalls. The return hike, incorporating the walkway, takes around two hours. Bring water with you.

Elsewhere in the park there's a couple of handsome traditional wooden houses, relocated from Melaka and Terengganu, and a **museum**, which has some interesting displays explaining the rainforest habitat and the forest-related research carried out by FRIM. Several arboreta highlight different types of trees, there's a wetland area and a pond containing a giant araipama.

ⓘ Getting There & Away

Take a KTM Komuter train to Kepong (RM1.30) and then a taxi (RM5); arrange for the taxi to pick you up again later. Bring a picnic to enjoy in the park; alternatively the FRIM's canteen is open all day and serves decent home-cooked Malay food (around RM10 including a drink).

Hulu Klang & Gombak

Laid out over 62 hectares around a central lake, **Zoo Negara** (National Zoo; ☏03-4108 3422; www.zoonegaramalaysia.my; adult/child RM15/6, insect zoo and butterfly park adult/child RM5/3; ☉9am-5pm), 13km northeast of KL in **Hulu Klang**, is home to a wide variety of native wildlife, including tigers, as well as other animals from Asia and Africa. Although some of the enclosures could definitely be bigger, it is one of Asia's better zoos.

You can buy bags of carrot chips and bunches of green bamboo to feed the elephants, camels, deer and giraffes yourself – these foodstuffs are selected to complement the animals' natural diet. It's possible to spend a day as a volunteer here – the website has details for arranging this.

Taxis charge around RM30 from central KL or you can take Metrobus 16 or KL Rapid U23 (RM3) from Medan Pasar.

In the sleepy village of **Gombak**, 25km north of KL, the **Orang Asli Museum** (☏6189 2113; www.jheoa.gov.my/web/guest/25; ☉9am-5pm Sat-Thu) is a fine introduction to the customs and culture of Malaysia's indigenous people. The fascinating exhibits include clothes made from the bark of terap and ipoh trees, personal adornments, musical instruments and hunting implements, all accompanied by informative descriptions of the various Orang Asli cultures and ways of life. The helpful staff will play video documentaries on the Orang Asli, if you ask.

The museum's shop sells the striking wood carvings of the Hma' Meri people who live on Pulau Carey, as well as *tongkat ali*, a kind of ginseng that's marketed as Malaysian Viagra.

Bus U12 (RM3, 1½ hours) from Medan Pasar in KL runs here.

Genting Highlands

This hill station, 50km north of KL on the Pahang border, is in stark contrast to the old English style of other Malaysian upland resorts, its raison d'être being **Resort World Genting** (☏2718 1888; www.rwgenting.com); this glitzy casino is the only one in the country. In its slender favour is its cool weather; at 2000m above sea level there's no need for air-conditioning. The 3.4km-long **Genting Skyway** (one-way RM6; ☺7.30am-11pm Mon-Thu, 7.30am-midnight Fri-Sun) is a gentle 11-minute cable-car glide above the dense rainforest. Kids will also enjoy the **indoor and outdoor theme parks** (outdoor park adult/child from RM50/35; indoor park RM30/28, both parks RM66/45); they include water slides, thrill rides, a climbing wall and a fierce wind tunnel for a simulated skydive.

Sleeping & Eating

Genting is an easy day trip from KL, but if you do decide to stay, the resort has a choice of five hotels (sleeping a total of 10,000 people). Rates vary enormously, the most expensive nights generally being Saturday and all public holidays; check on the website or with the KL **booking office** (☏2718 1118; 28 Jln Sultan Ismail, Wisma Genting; ☺8.30am-6pm Mon-Fri, 8.30am-1pm Sat). There's no shortage of places to eat, including cheap fast-food outlets and noisy food courts.

First World Hotel HOTEL $$
(r from RM150; @☎) With 6500 beds, this is Malaysia's largest hotel, with plain but quite acceptable rooms.

Maxims Genting HOTEL $$$
(r from RM550; @☎☒) Genting's most luxurious digs, designed to pamper high rollers.

Getting There & Away

Buses leave at hourly (and sometimes half-hourly) intervals from 7.30am to 8.30pm from KL's Pudu Sentral bus station (adult/child RM8.50/6.80, 1½ hours), and on the hour from 8am to 7pm from KL Sentral (RM8.30/6.70); the price includes the Skyway cable car. A taxi from KL will cost around RM70.

The **Go Genting Golden Package** (RM58) includes return transport from KL, the Skyway transfer and either an Outdoor Theme Park ride pass or buffet lunch at the Coffee Terrace. Buy the pass from Genting's ticket office at KL Sentral or from its **main sales office** (☏2718 1118; www.rwgenting.com; 28 Jln Sultan Ismail, Wisma Genting; ☺8.30am-6pm Mon-Fri, 8.30am-1pm Sat), where you can also book resort accommodation.

WORTH A TRIP

KUALA KUBU BHARU

Most travellers zip through Kuala Kubu Bharu, 72km north of KL, en route to Fraser's Hill. However, the charming, stuck-in-time town known as KKB is the jumping off point for various adventurous outdoor activities such as rafting and kayaking on the Selangor Dam, Sungai Selangor and Sungai Chiling. A recommended outfitter is **Pierose Swiftwater** (www.raftmalaysia.com).

A popular jungle trek is to the 20m-tall **Chiling Waterfall** on Sungai Chiling. This is a 1½ hour walk from the so-called Rainbow Bridge on route 55 leading up to Fraser's Hill. The route is clearly marked, but it's a good idea to hire a guide since you have to cross the river five times and it's important to be aware of flash flooding. **Happy Yen** (☏017-369 7831; www.happyyen.com; tour R250 per person) organises tours to the falls from KL.

KKB is connected to KL by the KTM Komuter train (RM5.60); you'll need to change at Rawang. From the station a taxi to the town centre costs around RM5. Accommodation in KKB is limited to basic hotels. Better to use Fraser's Hill as a base, or the rough-luxe **Sekeping Serendah Retreat** (☏012-324 6552; www.serendah.com; cabins from RM500/650; ☒), self-catering cabins in the rainforest near Serendah, 35km south of KKB and also on the train line.

Fraser's Hill (Bukit Fraser)

🎧 09

Of all the hill stations, Fraser's Hill (Bukit Fraser), around 100km north of KL, retains the most colonial charm and attracts a fraction of the visitors of Genting or the Cameron Highlands. Situated across seven densely forested hills at a cool altitude of 1524m, this quiet and relatively undeveloped place is best visited for gentle hikes and bird-watching.

Fraser's Hill is named after Louis James Fraser, an adventurous Scotsman who migrated to Malaysia in the 1890s. Trying his luck in the country's booming tin-mining industry, Fraser set up a mule-train operation to transport the ore across the hills and is also rumoured to have run gambling and opium dens. These had vanished (along with Fraser himself) by 1917, when Bishop Ferguson-Davie of Singapore came looking for Fraser. Recognising the area's potential as a hill station, the bishop wrote a report to the High Commissioner on his return to Singapore. A couple of years later this 'little England' in the heart of the Malaysian jungle began to be developed.

Like the Genting Highlands, Fraser's Hill is on the Selangor–Pahang border, but almost all visitors come through Selangor, and the state border actually cuts right through the station. For more information see www.fraserhill.info.

⊙ Sights & Activities

Fraser's Hill's main attraction is its abundant flora and fauna, in particular its birdlife. Some 265 species of birds have been spotted here, including the Malaysian whistling thrush, the Kinabalu friendly warbler, the brilliantly coloured green magpie, and the long-tailed broadbill with its sky-blue chest. In June the hill station hosts its International Bird Race, in which teams of bird-watchers compete to record the highest number of species. In the sports centre opposite the Puncak Inn, there's a Bird Interpretation Centre at the **golf clubhouse** (Map p103); get the key from the staff at the Puncak Inn.

Pick up a leaflet from the Puncak Inn outlining various hikes, most pretty straightforward and signposted. You'll need to arrange a guide for the 5km-long Pine Tree Trail, which takes around six hours and crosses three mountain peaks, including 1505m Pine Tree Hill; a recommended guide is **Mr Durai** (📱013-983 1633; durefh@hotmail.com), who charges around RM30 per hour.

Opposite the Puncak Inn is the picturesque nine-hole **golf course** (Map p103; 📱362 2129; Jln Genting; green fees Mon-Fri/Sat & Sun RM30/40, hire of half/full set of clubs RM15/30); guests at the Puncak and Shahzan Inns receive a 20% discount. At the **paddock** (Map p103) to the east of the golf course, you can go horse riding (RM5 to RM8) or practise archery (RM8). Alternatively hire a paddleboat (RM6 per 15 minutes) to explore Allan's Waters, a small lake next to the flower nursery.

About 4km northwest of the town centre, along Jln Air Terjun, is **Jeriau Waterfall**, where you can also swim. It's a 20-minute climb up from the road to reach them.

🛏 Sleeping

There's plenty of accommodation but musty, damp rooms and cottages go with the territory. Many places charge 20% to 40% more on weekends and public holidays when you will need to book ahead. Rates typically include breakfast.

TOP CHOICE Ye Olde Smokehouse

Fraser's Hill HOTEL $$$

(Map p103; 📱362 2226; www.thesmokehouse. my; Jln Jeriau; d/ste from RM308/385) Exposed beams, log fires, four-poster beds and chintz – the Smokehouse goes for broke with its English-charm offensive. Even if you don't stay here, drop by for a well-made pie or roast at lunch or afternoon tea (from RM18) on the **garden terrace**.

Highland Resthouse

Holdings Bungalows BUNGALOW $$

(📱in KL 09-362 2645; www.hrhbungalows.com; 📶) Check the website of this company for details about the range of rooms and bungalows at Fraser's Hill, starting from RM180 per room at the eight-bedroom Pekan bungalow, a well-kept property overlooking the golf course, to RM2000 for full hire of the four-bedroom **Jerantut bungalow** (Map p103). Its other properties include the **Brinchang** (Map p103), **Jelai** (Map p103), **Raub** (Map p103), **Pekan** (Map p103) and **Temerloh** (Map p103) bungalows.

Puncak Inn HOTEL $$

(📱09-3622 007; puncakinn1@yahoo.com; r with breakfast RM100, apt/bungalow RM120/300) Newly renovated Puncak has the best-value rooms in Fraser's in a handy central location.

Fraser's Hill (Bukit Fraser)

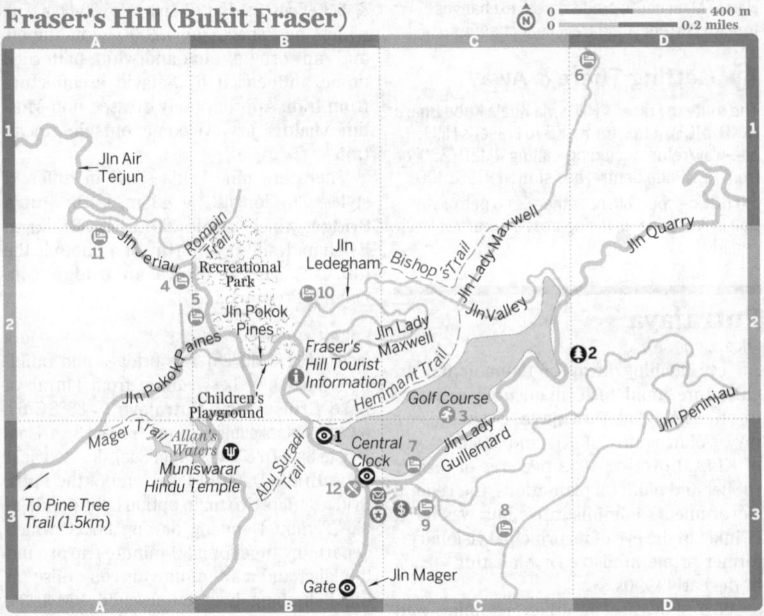

Fraser's Hill (Bukit Fraser)

Sights
1 Golf Clubhouse B3
2 Paddock (Horse Riding, Archery) D2

Activities, Courses & Tours
3 Golf Course C2

Sleeping
4 Brinchang Bungalow A2
5 Jelai Bungalow B2
6 Jerantut Bungalow D1
7 Pekan Bungalow C3
8 Raub Bungalow C3
9 Shahzan Inn Fraser's Hill C3
10 Temerloh Bungalow B2
11 Ye Olde Smokehouse Fraser's Hill A2

Eating
12 Hill View B3

It also rents out studio, two- and three-bed apartments in the Fraser's Silverpark Resort, and four cottages, sleeping between four and 15 people.

Shahzan Inn Fraser's Hill HOTEL $$
(Map p103; ☎362 3300; shahzan7@streamyx.com; Jln Lady Guillemard; garden/golf course view r incl breakfast from RM150/174; 📶) One of the most attractive places to stay. All rooms have balconies, a kettle and satellite TV; the ones overlooking the golf course are the nicest.

Eating

There a couple of small stores as you come into Fraser's Hill for self-catering supplies as well as a hawker stall complex beside the kids' playground. All the hotels have restaurants, Ye Olde Smokehouse's being the best.

Hill View WESTERN, CHINESE $
(Map p103; Hawker's Stalls, Pine Tree Rd; mains from RM10; ⏲9.30am-9pm) Simple dishes are cooked up by a family who have run this stall for a couple of generations.

Information

Fraser's Hill Tourist Information (FHDC; ☎362 2207; www.pkbf.org.my; Puncak Inn, Jln Genting; ⏲8am-5pm Mon-Fri) The front desk provides information, maps and brochures; staff can help arrange hiking guides.

Maybank (Shahzan Inn, Jln Lady Guillemard; ⏲9.15am-4.30pm Mon-Thu, 9.15am-4pm Fri)

Has ATM, accepts credit cards, exchanges foreign currency and travellers cheques.

ℹ Getting There & Away

The route to Fraser's Hill is via Kuala Kubu Bharu (KKB, p101). A taxi from KKB to Fraser's Hill is one-way/return including waiting RM80/200, or from KL's Pudu Sentral bus station R150/300.

If driving yourself, note there's no petrol station in Fraser's Hill; the nearest ones are at Raub and KKB.

Putrajaya

📞 03 / POP 68,000

An eye-catching array of monumental architecture amid lush, manicured greenery is on display in **Putrajaya** (www.ppj.gov.my), 25km south of KL and 20km north of KLIA. Covering 4932 hectares of former rubber and palm-oil plantations, the Federal Government's administrative hub was but a twinkle in the eye of its principal visionary – former prime minister Dr Mahathir – back in the early 1990s.

As a showcase of urban planning and vaulting architectural ambition, Putrajaya is impressive, but it can also be a strange place to visit. Its heart is a 600-hectare artificial lake fringed by landscaped parks and an eclectic mix of buildings and bridges, best viewed when illuminated at night. However, it's still a long way off its envisioned population of over 300,000 – this sprawling city is practically devoid of streetlife. Just over 97% of Putrajaya's population is Muslim.

◉ Sights & Activities

Urban Putrajaya   NEIGHBOURHOOD
(Putra Mosque for non-Muslims 9am-1.30pm & 3-6pm Sat-Thu, 3-6pm Fri) Monumental buildings, each a different design, line the main boulevard Persiaran Perdana, which runs from the elevated spaceship-like **Putrajaya Convention Centre** (📞8887 6000; Presint 5), worth visiting for the views, to the circular **Dataran Putra** (Putra Square). Look out for the Mughal-esque **Istana Kehakiman** (Palace of Justice), the modernist Islamic gateway fronting the **Kompleks Perdadanan Putrajaya** (Putrajaya Corporation Complex) and steel-clad **Tuanku Mizan Zainal Abidin Mosque**.

Framing Dataran Putra on two sides are **Perdana Putra**, housing the offices of the prime minister, and the handsome **Putra Mosque** (⊙for non-Muslims 9am-12.30pm, 2-4pm

& 5.30-6pm Sat-Thu, 3-4pm & 5.30-6pm Fri), which has space for 15,000 worshippers and an ornate pink-and-white-patterned dome, influenced by Safavid architecture from Iran. Appropriately dressed non-Muslim visitors are welcome outside prayer times.

There are nine bridges, all in different styles. The longest, at 435m, is the **Putra Bridge**, which mimics the Khaju Bridge in Esfahan, Iran. Also worthy of a photo is the futuristis sail-like **Wawasan Bridge** connecting Presint 2 and 8.

Lake Cruise   BOAT TOUR
(adult/child RM40/26) The bridges and buildings look their best viewed from Putrajaya Lake. **Cruise Tasik Putrajaya** (📞8888 3769; www.cruisetasikputrajaya.com; ⊙10am-6pm Mon-Thu, to 8pm Fri & Sat, to 7pm Sun), located just beneath the Dataran Putra end of the Putra Bridge, offers two main options: the gondola-like Perahu Dondang Sayang boats, which depart any time for a 30-minute trip around the lake; and a 45-minute air-con cruise on the Belimbing boat (adult/child RM50/35, leaves hourly).

Taman Botani   GARDENS
(Botanic Gardens; 📞8888 9090; Presint 1; admission free; ⊙9am-noon & 2pm-5pm Sat-Thu, 9am-11am & 3-5pm Fri) North of Perdana Putra, near the prime minister's official residence, this 93-hectare site features attractive tropical gardens, a visitors centre, a beautifully tiled Moroccan pavilion and lakeside restaurant. A tourist tram (RM4) trundles between the flower beds and trestles, and you can hire bicycles (RM2 per hour).

Taman Wetland   PARK
(Wetland Park; 📞8887 7773; admission free; ⊙park 7am-7pm, nature interpretation centre 9am-6pm) Further north is this serene, contemplative space with peaceful nature trails, aquatic animals and water birds, fluttering butterflies and picnic tables overlooking the lake. Canoeing and boating trips can be arranged here.

🛏 Sleeping & Eating

Putrajaya Shangri-la   HOTEL $$$
(📞8887 8888; www.shangri-la.com; Taman Putra Perdana, Presint 1; r from RM430; 🅿❄@🛜🏊) This elegant, contemporary styled hotel has large, calming rooms and a great hillside view across to the lake. Its **Azur** restaurant

serving nicely presented international food is one of Putrajaya's best.

Pullman Putrajaya Lakeside   RESORT $$$
(☎8890 0000; www.pullmanputrajaya.com; 2 Jln P5/5, Presint 5; r from RM417; ❉@🛜☲) Close to the Convention Centre, this massive resort complex offers four styles of room – Indian, Chinese, Malay and Borneo (overlooking the lake). The rooms and resort facilities are excellent and include an alfresco restaurant built over the lake.

Alamanda   MALL $
(www.alamanda.com.my; meals RM10; ⊙10am-10pm) Putrajaya's swish shopping mall is home to several restaurants as well as an excellent food court where you can join the local bureaucrats for a meal.

Selera Putra   FOOD COURT $
(meals RM10; ⊙9am-7pm Mon-Fri, 9am-9pm Sat & Sun) Head to this food court beneath Dataran Putra and enjoy the lakeside view while enjoying a wide range of inexpensive Malaysian dishes.

ⓘ Getting There & Away

KLIA transit trains from KL Sentral and KLIA stop at the Putrajaya-Cyberjaya station (from KL Sentral it costs RM9.50 one way and takes 20 minutes).

Buses 100, 101 and 300 run from the train station to close to Dataran Putra (50 sen); a taxi there is RM13, while hiring one for an hour to tour the sights (the recommended option) is RM40.

Bicycles (RM4 per hour) can be hired from the **tourist information booth** (⊙8am-1pm, 2-5.30pm Sat-Thu, 8am-12.15pm & 2.45-5.30pm Fri) on Dataran Putra. From here and Putrajaya station, the two-hour **Best of Putrajaya bus tour** (☎03-8887 7690; RM1; ⊙11.30am & 3pm Sat & Sun) runs on the weekends only.

Klang Valley

Heading southwest of KL along the Klang Hwy, the **Kota Darul Ehsan** ceremonial arch marks the transition between the city and Selangor. Just over the boundary, Petaling Jaya blends into Shah Alam, the state capital, which blends into Klang, the old royal capital – pretty much all in one seamless stretch of housing estates and industrial parks. Efficient public transport to and from KL makes for easy day trips.

PETALING JAYA
🖉03

Many of the people you'll meet in KL actually live in the neighbouring city of Petaling Jaya (PJ). This sprawling community is defined by its giant shopping malls. Apart from these, there's not a whole lot else to detain you here.

◉ Sights & Activities
Sunway Lagoon & Sunway
Pyramid Theme Park   AMUSEMENT PARK

There are few more fun ways to cool down than splashing around at **Sunway Lagoon** (☎5639 0000; www.sunwaylagoon.com; 3 Jln PJS, 11/11 Bandar Sunway; adult/child from RM80/65; ⊙11am-6pm Mon & Wed-Fri, 10am-6pm Sat & Sun). Built on the site of a former tin mine and quarry, the highlights of this multizone theme park are the water slides, and what's claimed to be the world's largest artificial surf beach. There's also a Wild West–themed section with all the regular thrill rides, an interactive wildlife zoo (ie you're allowed to stroke the giant tortoises and cuddle the hamsters) and an extreme park with all-terrain vehicles, a rock-climbing wall and paintball fights.

The park is behind the vast **Sunway Pyramid** (☎7494 3100; www.sunwaypyramid. com; skating rink admission incl skate hire Mon-Fri

---

SEPANG INTERNATIONAL CIRCUIT

The **Sepang Circuit** (☎03-8778 2222; www.sepangcircuit.com), 65km south of KL and a 10-minute drive east of KLIA, is where Formula One holds the Malaysian Grand Prix every March or April. Tickets go for as little as RM100. During the three days of the race, plenty of special train and bus transport to the circuit is on offer, from around RM80 return from KL city centre.

Other car and motorcycle races are held here throughout the year – check the website for details. On nonrace days call ahead to book a tour of the facilities including a run through **auto museum** (admission free; ⊙9am-6pm). Also check the website for track days when the circuit is open to wannabe Michael Schumachers to rev up their own cars (RM200) or motorbikes (below 250cc RM70, over 250cc RM100).

RM13, Sat & Sun RM16; ⊘skating rink 9am-8pm) mall, distinguished by its giant lion gateway, faux Egyptian walls and crowning pyramid. Inside is a skating rink as well as a bowling alley, a multiplex cinema and the usual plethora of shops and dining outlets.

The easiest way here is take the Putra LRT to Kelana Jaya (RM2.10), then feeder bus T623 (RM1) or a taxi (RM15) to the Sunway Pyramid. Buses U63, U67 and U76 (RM3) run here from Pasir Seni in KL. A taxi from central KL will cost around RM25.

SHAH ALAM
♪03

Selangor's state capital, which started to be buiit in the 1970s, has a well-developed infrastructure, huge public buildings and a rapidly growing population. It's a staunchly Muslim city, dominated by its mosque, one of the largest in Southeast Asia.

◉ Sights

Masjid Sultan Salahuddin
Abdul Aziz Shah MOSQUE
(☎5159 9988; ⊘10am-noon & 2-4pm Sat-Thu) Called the Blue Mosque for its azure dome (larger than that of London's St Paul's Cathedral), this mammoth complex is covered in a rosette of verses from the Quran and accommodates up to 24,000 worshippers. Its four minarets, looking like giant rockets, are the tallest in the world (over 140m). You'll need to be appropriately dressed if you want to look inside.

City of Digital Lights
at i-City TECHNOLOGY PARK
(www.i-city.my; per car RM10; ⊘6pm-3am) Some bright spark had the idea to jolly up this otherwise dull technology park with a million and one LED light displays. As well as forests of multicoloured trees, giant peacocks and cacti, there's Snowalk, a giant walk through a refrigerator housing ice sculptures. Kids and collectors of supremely kitsch experiences will love it.

❶ Getting There & Away

From Pasar Seni in KL, frequent buses include U80, U65, U64 and U81 to Shah Alam (RM3)

KLANG & PELABUHAN KLANG
♪03

About 10km west of Shah Alam is Klang, once Selangor's royal capital. This is where the British installed their first Resident in 1874. Its few sights should take no more than a couple of hours to see, leaving you plenty of time to enjoy the real reason for heading

here: satisfying your stomach in the restaurants of Klang's vibrant Little India.

Five stops futher down the line the KTM Komuter trains terminate at Pelabuhan Klang, once KL's main seaport until the establishment of the modern harbour on Pulau Indah, 17km to the southwest. The main reason for coming here is to either catch a ferry to Sumatra or Pulau Ketam.

◉ Sights

Klang is small enough to see on foot. Heading south from the train station, along Jalan Stesyn, you'll pass several attractive rows of Chinese shophouses (to the right).

Little India NEIGHBOURHOOD
Running parallel to Jln Stesyn to the right is Jln Tengku Kelana, heart of Klang's colourful Little India. Especially frenetic around the Hindu festival of Deepavali, this Little India is more vibrant than that of KL and includes several fortune tellers, who squat on the pavement and predict the future with the aid of green parrots trained to pick out auspicious cards.

FREE Galeri Diraja Sultan
Abdul Aziz MUSEUM
(☎3373 6500; www.galeridiraja.com; Jln Stesen; ⊘10am-5pm Tue-Sun) A grand whitewashed 1909 colonial building houses the royal gallery, devoted to the history of the Selangor Sultanate (dating back to 1766), contains a wide array of royal regalia, gifts and artifacts, including replicas of the crown jewels.

Istana Alam Shah PALACE
(Jln Istana) Heading uphill along Jln Istana will bring you to the sultan's palace before the capital was moved to Shah Alam. The park opposite gives a pleasant view of the city.

Masjid Di Raja Sultan Suleiman MOSQUE
(Jln Kota Raja) East of the palace, along Jln Kota Raja, this former state mosque, opened in 1934, is a striking blend of art deco and Middle Eastern influences. Several sultans are buried here. Step inside to admire its stained-glass dome.

✖ Eating

Indian food is Klang's highlight, but it's not the only thing on offer: the town's Chinese community is also famous for inventing *bak kut* (pork-rib soup with hints of garlic and Chinese five spice).

ISLAND ESCAPES

If you're looking to escape the Klang Valley's urban sprawl, two islands – one reached by ferry, the other by road – make for off-beat day trips.

Chill out on the 30-minute ferry trip (return R14) through the mangroves from Pelabuhan Klang to **Pulau Ketam** (Crab Island), where you'll find a charming fishing village built on stilts over the mudflats. There's little to do here other than wander around the wooden buildings of the village and enjoy a Chinese seafood lunch at one of several restaurants. Air-con ferries depart roughly every hour starting from 8.45am; the last ferry back from Pulau Ketam is at 5.30pm (6pm on weekends).

If you don't have your own wheels, hire a taxi to get you out to **Pulau Carey** (from Klang one way/return RM80/150), an island largely covered with palm-oil plantations. Tiny **Kampung Sungai Bumbon** is home to an Orang Asli tribe known as the Hma' Meri (also written as Mah Meri). Here you can see the woodcarvers who have put the Mah Meri's art on the cultural map. There's also a **community centre** (⊘9am-5pm), where you can pick up pretty woven baskets and other products made from dyed pandanus palm leaves as well as an interesting booklet in English about Hma' Meri culture.

TOP CHOICE **Mohana Bistro** INDIAN $$
(☑3372 7659; 119 Jln Tengku Kelana; meals RM10-16; ⊘7am-10.30pm; 🖉) Deservedly popular spot for banana-leaf curry spreads and spice-laden biryani rice. The waiters bring round trays of tempting veg and meat dishes to choose from.

Seng Huat Bak Kut Teh MALAY, CHINESE $
(☑012-309 8303; 9 Jln Besar; meal RM10; ⊘7.30am-1pm & 5.30-8.30pm; 🖉) Sample the fragrant, flavoursome pork stew at this unpretentious eatery, steps away from the train station, just beneath the Klang Bridge – get here early though as it's popular and they run out of meat towards the end of their opening sessions.

Asoka INDIAN $
(105 Jln Tengku Kelana; meals RM5-10; ⊘7am-11pm) Vividly orange-and-cream-painted parlour of Indian culinary goodness, including a great selection of sweets, juices and crispy *dosai* pancakes served with coconut chutney.

Sri Barathan Matha Vilas INDIAN, CHINESE $
(34-36 Jln Tengku Kelana; meals RM5-10; ⊘6.30am-10.30pm) It's hard to resist a bowl of this restaurant's signature dish of spicy mee goreng (fried noodles); the chef prepares them constantly in a giant wok beside the entrance.

❶ Getting There & Away

KLANG

It's best to come here by train from KL (RM3.60, 1 hour, every 30 minutes), as the KTM Komuter station is closer to the sights. Klang's bus station is opposite the My Din shopping complex, on the northern side of the river. There are several buses every hour to central KL (RM3) or Kuala Selangor (RM5).

PELABUHAN KLANG

KTM Komuter trains run to/from KL and Klang, and the station is just a stone's throw from the ferry terminal.

Ferries to Tanjung Balai (Asahan; one way including tax RM110, 4 hours, one to three daily) and Dumai (RM110, 3½ hours, one daily) in Sumatra depart from here. Citizens of Australia, America, Britain and several European nations can get a visa on arrival in Indonesia; otherwise you must have an Indonesian visa before boarding. To check on ferry times call the **terminal** (☑3167 7186, 3165 2545).

Kuala Selangor

☑03

Where the Sungai Selangor flows into the sea is the old royal capital of Kuala Selangor. The hilltop fort at this small sleepy town was briefly conquered by the Dutch when they invaded Selangor in 1784; Sultan Ibrahim took it back a year later. The town became embroiled in the Selangor Civil War (1867–73) when the fort was partly destroyed. Later the British built a lighthouse on the hill, which still stands.

Off the beaten tourist track, Kuala Selangor has a friendly *kampung* (village) atmosphere and a good wildlife park. It's possible to do as a day trip from KL, but an overnight stop is recommended so you can catch the nightly show put on by fireflies along the Sungai Selangor.

⊙ Sights & Activities

Kampung Kuantan
FIREFLY VIEWING

The best place from which to see the fireflies this region is famed for is the tiny village of Kampung Kuantan, 9km east of Kuala Selangor. Malay-style wooden boats row out on the river to the 'show trees' and their dazzling displays. Boats take four people at RM15 each for the 20-minute trip, and leave on demand throughout the evening from around 7pm until 10pm. The trips are not recommended on full-moon or rainy nights, when the fireflies are not at their luminous best. Take mosquito repellent.

To reach the village, take the turn-off to Batang Berjuntai, 2km south of Kuala Selangor. A taxi from Kuala Selangor costs RM40 return. You can also see the fireflies at the Firefly Park Resort (p108) at Kampung Bukit Belimbing.

Bukit Malawati
VIEWPOINT

It's a pleasant, short walk through landscaped parklands to the top of Bukit Malawati, featuring views across the mangrove coastline. The hill has long been an ideal site for monitoring shipping in the Selat Melaka (Strait of Melaka), first for the sultans of Selangor and then for the Dutch, who destroyed the sultan's fort during their invasion in 1784, then rebuilt it, naming it Fort Atlingsburg after their governor general.

All that remains today are some sections of the fort's wall and a few cannons. At the summit you'll find the British lighthouse (dating from 1909) and a podium for viewing the new moon. Tame silvered leaf monkeys hang out here, too.

The road up Bukit Malawati starts one block away from the old bus station in the town centre. It does a clockwise loop of the hill; you can walk up and around in less than an hour.

🌿 Taman Alam Kuala Selangor Nature Park
WILDLIFE RESERVE

(☑3289 2294; www.mns.org.my; Jln Klinik; adult/child RM4/1; ⊙8am-6pm) On the estuary of Sungai Selangor, at the foot of Bukit Malawati and reached by a flight of steps from the hill, is this 240-hectare park containing three ecosystems: secondary forest, a manmade lake and a mangrove forest with views out to sea. Explore them all on a 3km trail

that includes a raised walkway above the mangroves.

🛏 Sleeping

TOP CHOICE De Palma Hotel
Kuala Selangor
HOTEL $$

(☑3289 7070; www.depalmahotel.com; Jln Tanjung Keramat; r with breakfast from RM200; ❄@🛜🏊) Around 1.5km north of the old bus station (follow the signs) is this decent mini-resort offering a range of accommodation in nicely furnished and reasonably well-maintained wooden chalets. It rents bicycles (RM5 an hour) and can arrange a trip out to see the fireflies (RM66). The best deal is their two-day, one-night packages (RM140 per person), which include accommodation and the fireflies trip.

Firefly Park Resort
HOTEL $$

(☑3260 1208; www.fireflypark.com; Jln Haji Omar; chalets from RM130; ❄) This modern resort has plainly decorated, comfortable four-person chalets perched on stilts over the river, and pleasant landscaped grounds. Boat trips to watch the fireflies cost RM15/10 for adults/children, and fishing trips cost RM40 per hour.

Taman Alam Kuala Selangor Nature Park
HUTS, CHALETS $

(☑3289 2294; www.mns.org.my; Jln Klinik; r from RM30) Offers simple A-frame huts (RM30) or two-bed (one single, one queen) wooden chalets (RM60) with fan and attached bathroom.

🍴 Eating

If seafood is what you're after, head to Pasir Penambang, a fishing village on the north side of the river, where a number of atmospheric seafood restaurants are clustered; a taxi from Kuala Selangor costs around RM10.

Auntie Kopitiam
CHINESE, MALAY $

(No C3, Jln Sultan Ibrahim; meals RM5-10; ⊙6am-6pm; 🛜) Next to the bus station, this old-style coffee shop serves Malaysian favourites such as *nasi lemak* and chicken chop.

❶ Getting There & Away

Frequent buses from Klang head to Kuala Selangor (RM5, one hour, every 15 minutes) terminating at the old bus station beside Bukit Melawati. From the new bus station, 2km outside the town centre, bus 149 connects with KL (RM7.50, 2 hours, every hour).

Approximate fares for a taxi ride from Kuala Selangor: KL (RM100), Klang (RM60) and Teluk Intan (RM130) in Perak.

NEGERI SEMBILAN

Seremban

☎06 / POP 550,000

Like KL, Seremban's roots lay in the discovery of tin in the 19th century causing prospectors to flock to the village originally called Sungai Ujong. Today Negeri Sembilan's state capital, 64km southeast of KL, is a much more low key place, generally overlooked by international visitors but worth visiting for its lovely gardens, interesting mix of architecture and the chance to eat some tasty local specialities. It's also the transit point for other destinations in Negeri Sembilan, including the beachside resorts of Port Dickson.

The Muzium Negeri, a component of the Taman Seni Budaya Negeri on the outskirts of town, provides an access point to Minangkabau culture. The city itself is home mostly to Chinese and Indian populations.

⦿ Sights

**Lake Gardens &
Colonial District**   NEIGHBOURHOOD
(Map p110) The lake dominates this lush reserve that's a very pleasant stroll just east of the train station. To the south east is the **King George V School** (Map p110; Jln Za'aba), the premier colonial academic instiution for Seremban's elite; it still functions as a high school. To the north east is the striking **Masjid Negeri** (State Mosque; Map p110; Jln

Dato Hamzah); its nine external pillars represent the nine original fiefdoms of Negeri Sembilan.

A short walk north of the mosque is **Kompleks Kraf Negeri Sembilan** (Map p110; ☎767 1388; cnr Jln Bukit & Jln Sehala; ⊗9am-5pm), in a handsome 1912 mansion that was once home to British Resident Captain Murray. Inside is an exhibit on local crafts, including rattan weaving and ceramics, and a shop – you'll likely have the place to yourself. From the same colonial era is the even grander neoclassical **State Library** (Map p110; off Jln Dato Hamzah), designed by AB Hubback, the architect responsible for many of KL's historic buildings.

Across the road is the **Istana Besar** (Map p110; Jln Bukit; ⊗closed to the public), home of the sultan of Negeri Sembilan, and the **Wisma Negeri** (Map p110; btwn Jln Dato Abdul Kadir & Jln Dato Abdul Malek), part of the State Secretariat complex, its wonderful multiple roof-points a fine melding of modern and traditional architecture.

FREE **Muzium Negeri**   MUSEUM
(State Museum; Jln Sungai Ujong; admission free; ⊗10am-6pm Tue, Wed, Sat & Sun, 8.15am-1pm Thu, 10am-12.15pm & 2.45-6pm Fri) Built in the style of a Minangkabau palace, this mildly diverting museum displays handicrafts and historical exhibits. You'll find it inside the park **Taman Seni Budaya Negeri,** (Arts & Cultural Park; Jln Sungai Ujong; admission free) along with two orignial pieces of architecture transported and reconstructed here from elsewhere in the state: the timber **Ampang Tinggi Palace**, dating from 1870, and the **Rumah Negeri Sembilan**, a less ornate traditional house with a shingle roof showing

---

THE MINANGKABAU

Hailing originally from Western Sumatra, the **Minangkabau** people have lived in Peninsula Malaysia since at least the 15th century settling, primarily in the region now covered by Negeri Sembilan. Following Islam but also incorporating older animist beliefs and traditional customs (known as *adat*) into their daily lives, they have long since blended in with the Malay population. However, aspects of Minangkabau culture remain. The most noticeable feature is the distinct **traditional architecture** of the region: homes with sweeping curved roofs and pointed gables that are supposed to resemble buffalo horns. Good examples of this architectural style can been seen in Seremban's Taman Seni Budaya Negeri and the old royal town of Seri Menanti. The village of **Terachi**, 27km east of Seremban at the turn-off to Sri Menanti, also has some particularly fine traditional houses, although all have replaced the traditional thatch of the roofs with more durable corrugated iron.

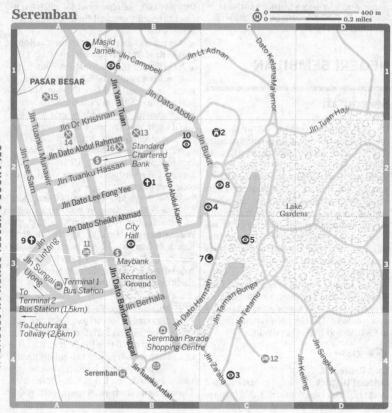

Seremban

Seremban

◎ Sights
1 Church of the Visitation	B2
2 Istana Besar	C2
3 King George V School	C4
4 Kompleks Kraf Negeri Sembilan	C2
5 Lake Gardens & Colonial District	C3
6 Liesheng Temple	B1
7 Masjid Negeri	C3
8 State Library	C2
9 Wesley Church	A3
10 Wisma Negeri	B2

🛏 Sleeping
11 Carlton Star Hotel	A3
12 Royale Bintang Resort & Spa Seremban	C4

✕ Eating
13 Haji Shariff's Cendol	B2
14 Kee Mei Siew Pao	A2
15 Sin Yee Kee	A1
16 Top Curry	B2

the hallmark curved-roof style based on the buffalo horn. The park is located 3km west of the city centre close to the E2 North–South expressway; a taxi here is around R5.

Liesheng Temple TEMPLE
(Map p110; Jln Dr Samuel; ⊙daylight hr) This small, attractive Taoist temple has a roof decorated with dragons, and a fine carving of a boat hanging above the door. The main altar is dedicated to three Taoist idols, chief

among which is Guandi (the God of War). The Chinese characters above the altar mean 'Your needs will be answered'.

Church of the Visitation
CHURCH

(Map p110; 85a Jln Yam Tuan) Flee from the heat into the cool, white interior of this Catholic church, dating from 1899 and so called because it was where French priests would break their journey between KL and Malaka to receive the locals' confession.

Wesley Church
CHURCH

(Map p110; Jln Dato Sheikh Ahmad) Founded in 1915 to cater to the Christian Chinese migrants who flooded into the area following the discovery of tin. The similar era Anglo-Chinese School (SMK Methodist) shares the church's compound.

🛏 Sleeping

Seremban lacks any truly distinctive accommodation. You're better off staying in KL and visiting for day; alternatively both Port Dickson and Melaka are only about an hour away by road.

Royale Bintang Resort &
Spa Seremban
HOTEL $$

(Map p110; ☎766 6666; www.royalebintang-seremban.com; Jln Dato AS Dawood; r from RM290; ❄️🛜🏊) Seremban's top hotel has comfortable, well-maintained rooms, a good range of restaurants and amenities (swimming pool with landscaped waterfalls, fitness centre, a jogging track to the nearby lake gardens and more) and helpful staff.

Carlton Star Hotel
HOTEL $

(Map p110; ☎762 5336; www.carltonstar.com; 47 Jln Dato Sheikh Ahmad; s or d/tr/q RM75/95/115; ❄️🛜) Within walking distance of Terminal 1 bus station and the train station, this hotel has boring but big business–style rooms. The staff are friendly.

🍴 Eating

The best reason for visiting Seremban is to eat. Apart from the famous *cendol* (a pandan-leaf flavoured desert served with shaved ice, red beans, jaggery syrup and coconut milk) and beef noodle stalls that we review, also search out Minangkabau-style dishes, such as *masak lemak* (fish, meat or vegetables cooked in coconut milk), rendang (a thick, dry meat curry usually served with rice cooked in coconut milk) and *dendeng*

balado (beef with chilli). Another thing to sample, courtesy of Seremban's Chinese community, are the local *siew pao*, delicious flaky pastry buns stuffed with either pork or chicken.

TOP CHOICE Haji Shariff's Cendol
MALAY $

(Map p110; 44 Jln Yam Tuan; cendol/rojak from RM1.30/3; ⏰10.30am-6pm, closed alternate Fridays) Three generations of the Shariff family have been dolling out refreshingly sweet bowls of *cendol* to appreciative locals. Now installed in a distinctively green-painted 1919 shophouse, they also serve a local verison of *rojak* with a spicy tomato rather than soy sauce.

TOP CHOICE Sin Yee Kee
CHINESE $

(Map p110; Stall 742, Upper floor, Pasar Besar Seremban, Jln Dato Bandar Tunggal; noodles RM6; ⏰Fri-Wed 7.30am-3pm) There's a good selection of hawker stalls at the day-time food court above Seremban's food market. This family-run beef noodle stall, that's been going since the 1960s, is the standout star for its friendly service and tasty product – they make their own fat Hainanese-style noodles from rice flour. Tell them whether you want tripe with your chunks of meat or not.

Top Curry
INDIAN $

(Map p110; ☎767 2294; btwn Jln Tuanku Hassan & Jln Dato Abdul Rahman; banana-leaf meals RM6.50) This cavernous cafe serves excellent southern Indian curries. We defy you to resist ordering the fried fish or chicken you can see being made in a wok on the footpath outside.

Kee Mei Siew Pao
MALAY $

(Map p110; cnr Jln Dr Krishnan & Jln Dato Bandar Tunggal; pao RM1.30; ⏰8am-6pm) This takeaway shop is the place to pick up some of Seremban's famous *pao* (steamed pork buns), as well as other tasty baked buns and tarts.

ℹ Getting There & Away

Seremban lies on the main north–south rail line from KL to Singapore. KTM Komuter trains (RM6, one hour 15 minutes, every 30 minutes) shuttle between KL Sentral and Seremban.

Long-distance buses leave from Terminal 1 bus station on Jln Sungai Ujong; departures include:

PLACE	PRICE	DURATION	FREQUENCY
KL	RM6	one hour	every 20 minutes
Singapore	RM45	five hours	one daily
Melaka	RM7	1½ hours	hourly
Kampung-Kuantan	RM22	six hours	one daily
Kuala Pilah	RM3.40	one hour	every 15 minutes
Kuala Terengganu	RM40	six hours	one daily
Port Dickson	RM4	one hour	every 20 minutes

Some long distance buses stop at Terminal 2 about 1.5km from town centre – free shuttle buses run from here to Terminal 1.

Long-distance taxis operate from outside both the train station and Terminal 1 bus station; one-way fares include Port Dickson (RM45), Kuala Pilah (RM45), Seri Menanti (RM40), KLIA (RM70), LCCT (RM60), KL (RM80).

To reach Seremban from KLIA, first take a bus from the airport to Nilai (RM3) and change to a KTM Komuter train to Seremban (RM2.50).

Sri Menanti

☑06

Tidy and placid Sri Menanti, 6km off the Seremban–Kuala Pilah road, is the old royal capital, first settled over 400 years ago by Minangkabau immigrants from Sumatra. Swathed in a silence only interrupted by bird song, this sleepy, disengaged hamlet nestles in a highland valley surrounded by green jungle hills, fringed with simple dwellings and scampering chickens.

Beside the Sri Menanti Resort is the magnificent **Istana Lama** (Old Palace; admission free; ☺10am-6pm). Designed by master craftsmen, the beautiful black hardwood palace is open to the public as a museum. Arranged over four floors, the palace was fashioned without the use of nails in 1908 as a temporary replacement for an even older palace that was razed by British soldiers during the Sungai Ujong wars. The structure is elevated on 99 pillars, many of them carved, each one representing the legendary 99 *luak* (clan) warriors. Inside you can see the king and queen's bedchambers, the children's playroom, a large dining room and huge dining table, as well as kris weaponry and royal regalia. Climb to the top floor for views over the gardens.

Back towards the main road in the compound next to the mosque is the **Makam Di Raja** (Royal Cemetery), which has a distinctive Victorian/Moorish pavilion. The prominent grave of Tuanku Abdul Rahman, the first king of independent Malaysia, is immediately inside the gates.

The attractive **Sri Menanti Resort** (☑ 497 0049; r/chalet including breakfast RM159/212), next to Istana Lama, has reasonably well-maintained and surprisingly stylish rooms, including concrete chalets over an ornamental lake where you can go fishing. Nonguests can use the small swimming pool for RM5.

To reach Sri Menanti from Seremban, take a bus to Kuala Pilah (RM3.40) and then a taxi (return trip around RM30); a direct taxi from Seremban is R80 round-trip.

Kuala Pilah

☑06

A pleasant valley town 40km east of Seremban, Kuala Pilah is colourfully decorated with brightly painted shophouses; the one on the corner of Jln Muar opposite the bus station is a stunner.

Its few temples of note include the **Kuil Sri Kanthaswamy** (Jln Melang; ☺main prayer hall 6.30am-7pm), overflowing with colour and arrayed with deities. The **Sansheng Gong** (Sansheng Temple; Jln Dato Undang Johol) has a skilfully carved boat, from the time of Qing emperor Guangxu, hanging just inside the door. The fierce-looking bearded idol in the centre is Guandi (God of War). There are marvellous carvings along the front of the temple and worn frescoes on the wall. Opposite the temple is an elaborate Chinese-style decorative archway dedicated to Martin Lister, the first British Resident (1889–97) of Negeri Sembilan.

There's no reason to get stranded here, but if you do, Kuala Pilah has several cheap Chinese hotels. The **Desa Inn** (☑481 8033; 745 Jln Dato Abdul Manap; d/f RM60/81; ☎) offers clean doubles with tiled floors, air-con, small TVs, kettle, coffee and small balcony (but you may get woken by the sonorous 6am call to prayer).

For dinner, the lively **night market** (Jln Yam Tuan), near Desa Inn, kicks off at around 6pm daily. At this time, the air becomes palpably heavy with the fragrance of satay (from 60 sen) and a medley of Malay and Indian aromas.

There are regular buses from Seremban (RM4.30, one hour, every 15 minutes). Buses from Kuala Pilah also connect to Johor Bahru (RM25.10, five daily), Kuantan (RM22.10, daily) and KL (RM9.40, eight daily).

Port Dickson

🎵06

When people talk about Port Dickson (PD) they're usually referring to the long coastline studded with beaches – the actual Port Dickson is a small, uninteresting town slightly inland. The beach area is a popular spot with vacationing Malaysians and Singaporeans, but outside of weekends and holidays it's nearly deserted and is a good place to find a bargain resort and relax poolside for a few days or more. When you feel the need for activity, Cape Rachado Forest Reserve has some fabulous treks. For futher information on the area see **Port Dickson's tourism website** (http://portdickson.info).

At the festival of **Navarathiri** (September or October), the goddess Sri Maha Mariamman is conveyed at night on a chariot procession around Port Dickson. The goddess performs a similar journey during the **Anniversary Prayers procession** (June or July).

⊙ Sights & Activities

The strip of white sand that extends for some 16km along the coast is more popular for it's proximity to KL than anything else, but it's pretty and a pleasant getaway. Unfortunately the water is fairly polluted from oil refineries in the vicinity.

📷 Cape Rachado
Forest Reserve   NATURE RESERVE

Port Dickson's highlight is the 80-hectare **Cape Rachado Forest Reserve** (also called the Tanjung Tuan Forest Reserve), the only remaining patch of coastal forest on the west coast of Peninsular Malaysia. This jungle of towering lowland trees has secluded beaches that are ideal turtle laying grounds and is also a stopover for over 300,000 migratory birds every year. The turn-off to the reserve is near the Km 16 marker (the local bus can let you off here); head down the road for 2km to the Ilham Resort and then through the forest reserve for another kilometre to the **Tanjung Tuan lighthouse** (Rumah Api). Unfortunately the lighthouse, which was first built in 1528 by the Portuguese and is the oldest in Malaysia, isn't open to the public. You can, however, walk around to the front of it for great views; on a clear day you can see Sumatra, 38km away across Selat Melaka. A simple network of trails heads into the forest from around the lighthouse and from the road towards the lighthouse to a handful of beaches (bring lots of water – it's a steep climb).

Avillion Admiral Cove   HOTEL, SPORTS
(🎵647 0888; www.avillionadmiralcove.com; Km 8, Jln Pantai; r from RM209) At this vaguely Mexican hacienda–style hotel, apartment and marina complex there's a wide range of activities on offer. **Yacht cruises** (RM157; 2 hours; minimum two people) leave at 9am or 5.30pm and there are various other ways of getting on the water from **jet skis** (RM200 for 30 minutes) to **kayaks** (RM20 for 1 hour). If you prefer to stay on land, **bicycles and tandems** (RM16 for 30 minutes) can be hired or you can take aim on the **archery range** (RM5 for 10 arrows). The hotel itself has large, reasonably designed rooms but isn't a patch on Avillion Port Dickson (p113), its sister property up the coast.

Port Dickson Ostrich Farm   FARM
(🎵06 662 7496; 13 Jln Kemang, Km 14.5; adult/child RM10/6; ☺9am-5.30pm) You can ride an ostrich or watch them race (1pm to 3pm on weekends only), where the birds reach speeds of up to 70kph. Small ones will get some fun from the mini-farm teeming with goats, peacocks, horses, donkeys, rabbits and chickens.

🛌 Sleeping

Unless mentioned all rates include breakfast. Also rates rise significantly on Friday, Saturday and public holidays.

TOP CHOICE Avillion Port Dickson   RESORT $$$
(🎵647 6688; www.avillionportdickson.com; Jln Pantai, Km 5; r from RM406; ❄🤖🏊) This is a beautifully designed and lushly landscaped resort. The accommodation highlight is the over-the-water chalets that have big terraces you can swim from at high tide. The cheapest rooms are classier than just about anywhere else, with their hardwood floors, elegant wood furnishings, flagstone bathrooms and loads of natural light. Also at hand are several good restaurants, a huge pool with slides, a tennis court and a gym.

DON'T MISS

IN RAPTURE OF RAPTORS

Around mid-February to mid-April, migrating raptors (birds of prey such as kestrels, falcons and eagles) make the crossing from Sumatra to the Asian continent via the Cape Rachado Forest Reserve. Some 25 species head north for the summer each year and, having used up most of their energy getting across the Straits of Melaka, are tired and fly so low that you can see them stunningly close-up. The birds that arrive late in the afternoon or evening often rest and recuperate at the reserve for the night before heading off again on their long journeys. Without this precious forested rest area, naturalists say that many of the birds would die of exhaustion or starvation.

Sightings are of course not guaranteed, and you'll have the best luck seeing the birds from around the Tanjung Tuan Lighthouse between 11am and 3pm when the heat of the day creates thermals for the birds to soar on.

The **Raptor Watch Festival** is held during the height of the migratory period, usually during the first week of March when the lighthouse opens to the public, jungle walks are led by naturalists, live bands come out to the cape to play and more. For more information and specific dates for the next festival go to http://mnsrw2012. wordpress.com.

TOP CHOICE Thistle Port
Dickson Resort
RESORT $$$

(☑648 2828; www.thistle.com/asia; Jln Pantai, Km 16; r from RM496; ❇❈@❋❅) Set in 90 acres of landscaped grounds with manicured lawns, a private 3km beach, a golf course, magnificent pool, beautiful views, a fitness centre and more, this resort is one of the most luxurious and classy in the region. Large rooms have an appealing contemporary design.

PNB Ilham Resort
RESORT $$

(☑662 6800; www.ilhamresort.com; Batu 10, Tanjung Biru, Km 16; r from RM278; ❇❋❅) Next to Cape Rachado Forest Reserve, this is a massive, elegant resort on a calm bay. The rooms are stylish with hardwood floors and muted light. There's a great pool and a quiet stretch of white-sand beach. It rents out mountain bikes and has plenty of other activities on offer.

Casa Rachado Beach Resort
RESORT $$

(☑662 5177; www.casarachadoresort.com; Batu 10, Tanjung Biru, Km 16; r from RM102; ❇❋❅) This brightly painted resort is near the Cape Rachado Forest Reserve entrance. Rooms are a little musty but upgrading to a suite gets you an apartment-sized place with a kitchen and views of the sea. There's a tiny mangrove-fringed beach out the front and an OK pool. You can also camp here for RM50 for two people – tent, floor mat and kerosene lantern included.

Eagle Ranch Resort
RESORT $$

(☑6610 495; www.eagleranch.com.my; Batu 14, Jln Pantai; r RM125-250; ❇❋❅) Around 23km south of Port Dickson and not near a good beach, this unique Wild West–styled resort is worth considering if only for the chance to stay in a tepee (RM125) or covered wagon (RM200). There's an obstacle course and a vast range of other activities too.

Corus Paradise Resort
RESORT $$

(☑647 7600; www.corusparadisepd.com; Jln Pantai, Km 3.5; r from RM238; ❇❋❅) This is a kitschy kid-friendly choice with a protected artificial lagoon and a big pool with water slides. Rooms are plain but comfortable and there is a handful of mediocre on-site restaurants.

Selesa Beach Resort
RESORT $$

(☑647 4090; www.selesabeachresort.com; Jln Pantai, Km 8; r from RM280; ❇❋❅) Minangkabau-style resort with sea-facing rooms, all with small balcony and rather old-style furniture. This is a particularly good stretch of beach.

Kong Ming Hotel
HOTEL $

(☑662 5683; Km 13; d from RM35) Seriously old and rundown but right on the beach, this place is clean, friendly and exudes a gritty, ancient charm.

Rotary Sunshine Camp
Holiday Hostel
HOSTEL $

(☑647 3798; Jln Pantai, Km 5; dm/r RM10/25) Despite its less than salubrious exterior – a cluster of blue barracks-style buildings behind a chain-link fence – this hostel is so well tended and the staff so friendly that it'll soon win you over. Shower and cooking facilities are shared and it's a short walk to a good beach and cheap food. On weekdays you'll probably have the place to yourself.

✖ Eating

There's a **night market** with yummy local food stalls every Saturday, but daily beachside food is limited to a few mediocre food courts, seafood *rumah makan* (stalls) selling crab by the kilo (around RM30) and restaurants at the resorts.

PD Eating Point MALAY, CHINESE **$**
(8 Taman Segahtera, Jln Seremban; mains RM4-5; ⊘7am-11pm; 🛜) About 1km north of PD town is this old-style coffee shop serving tasty hawker foods as well as all-day Western-style breakfasts. They also have free wi-fi.

El Cactus BAR **$$**
(📱012-646 3772; Km 4, Lot 2674, Jln Pantai; meals RM25; ⊘5.30pm-midnight) A relaxing spot for dinner or a nightcap or two, with outside seating, a music system creatively mounted atop half a Fiat, lounge area and pool table.

❶ Getting There & Around

Buses depart for Seremban (RM4, one hour, every 20 minutes) from where you can get connections to KL, Melaka and beyond. The taxi station is next to the bus station in the centre of town; taxi fares include Melaka (RM120), Seremban (RM50) and KL (RM130).

From Port Dickson town, local buses (RM1) run about every hour and will drop you off wherever you like along the beach. Ubiquitous share taxis are more reliable and convenient and cost RM2 for the first three or four kilometres – expect to pay RM5 to RM15 to get from Port Dickson town to your hotel (depending on the distance). You can flag share taxis down anywhere from the side of the road.

Perak

♫05 / POP 2,258,428 / AREA: 21,035 SQ KM

Includes »

Ipoh..............................118
Gopeng & Around..........125
Cameron Highlands.....126
Pulau Pangkor..............134
Kuala Kangsar..............140
Taiping..........................142
Around Taiping.............146
Royal Belum
State Park......................147

Best Places to Eat

» Xin Quan Fang (p123)
» Seri Ilhan (p139)
» Kedai Kopi Prima (p145)
» Nasi Lemak Ayam
Kampung (p122)
» Restoran Onn Kee (p123)

Best Places to Stay

» Sekeping Kong Heng
(p120)
» Tiger Rock Resort (p138)
» Sentosa Villa (p143)
» French Hotel (p120)
» Belum Eco Resort (p147)

Why Go?

The old saying 'What do you prefer, the mountains or the ocean?' is pretty well received in Perak, Peninsular Malaysia's second-largest state. 'Perak' means 'silver' in Malay, but historians debate whether the word references the state's tin mines or the fish off its sandy coast. For travellers, this ambiguity simply reinforces the variety of the region. If you're not in the Cameron Highlands (in Pahang state, but accessible from here), Malaysia's premier hill retreat, or looking for elephants in the upland jungles of Royal Belum State Park, you're probably lazing along the Straits of Melaka on Pulau Pangkor. And even if you're the type who tends to shy from the extremes, Perak's lowland cities – the royal seat of Kuala Kangsar; the garden metropolis of Taiping; and sprawling Ipoh, with its enviable eating scene and colonial architecture – are eminently worthwhile destinations.

When to Go
Ipoh

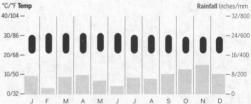

Nov–Jan Head to Perak's high country to forget you're in sweaty Southeast Asia.

Aug Even at summer's peak, temperatures in the Cameron Highlands rarely exceed 21°C.

Oct–Nov Tourist numbers are low during Perak's wettest months.

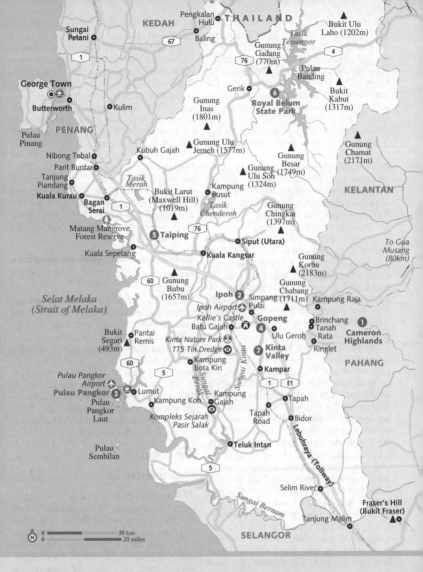

Perak Highlights

1 Visiting a tea plantation, hiking the hills or eating strawberries and scones in the **Cameron Highlands** (p126)

2 Snacking on cheap eats in **Ipoh** (p122) – arguably one of Malaysia's most underrated food destinations

3 Lazing on one of the fine beaches on little-visited **Pulau Pangkor** (p134)

4 Caving, hiking, bird-watching or just getting generally outdoorsy at **Gopeng** (p125)

5 Soaking up the colonial charm of **Taiping** (p142)

6 Getting your feet muddy in the jungles of **Royal Belum State Park** (p147)

7 Taking a guided tour of historical tin-mining country in the **Kinta Valley** (p126)

History

Today's sultanate of Perak dates back to the early 16th century, when the eldest son of the last sultan of Melaka, Sultan Muzaffar Shah, established his own dynasty on the banks of Sungai Perak (Perak River). The state's rich tin deposits quickly made it a target of both covetous neighbours and foreign forces.

Dutch efforts in the 17th century to monopolise the tin trade were unsuccessful, but remains of their forts can still be seen on Pulau Pangkor (Pangkor Island) and at the mouth of Sungai Perak. In the 18th century the Bugis from the south and the Siamese from the north made concerted attempts to dominate Perak, but British intervention in the 1820s trumped them both.

The British had remained reluctant to meddle in the peninsula's affairs, but growing investment in the strait settlements, along with the rich tin mines of Perak, encouraged their interest. The mines also attracted a great influx of Chinese immigrants, who soon formed rival clan groups allied with local Malay chiefs, all of whom battled to control the mines.

The Perak sultanate was in disarray, and fighting among successors to the throne gave the British their opportunity to step in, making the first real colonial incursion on the peninsula in 1874. The governor, Sir Andrew Clarke, convened a meeting at Pulau Pangkor at which Sultan Abdullah was installed on the throne in preference to Sultan Ismail, the other major contender. The resultant Pangkor Treaty required the sultan to accept a British Resident, who would be consulted on all issues other than those relating to religion or Malay custom. One year later, Sultan Abdullah was forced, under threat of deposition, to accept administration by British officials on his behalf.

Various Perak chiefs united against this state of affairs, and the Resident, James WW Birch, was assassinated at Pasir Salak in November 1875. Colonial troops were called in to fight a short war, Sultan Abdullah was exiled and a new British-sanctioned sultan was installed. The next British Resident, Sir Hugh Low, had administrative experience in Borneo, was fluent in Malay and was a noted botanist – he even had a pitcher plant named after him (*Nepenthes Lowii*). He assumed control of taxes from the tin mines and practised greater intervention in state affairs. In 1877

he introduced the first rubber trees to Malaysia, and experimented with planting tea and coffee as well. The sultans, meanwhile, maintained their status, but were increasingly effete figureheads, bought out with stipends.

The first railway in the state, from Taiping to Port Weld (now known as Kuala Sepetang), was built in 1885 to transport the wealth of tin; the result was rapid development in Taiping and Ipoh. In 1896 Perak, along with Selangor, Pahang and Negeri Sembilan, became part of the Federated Malay States. The Resident system persisted, however, even after the Japanese invasion and WWII, ending only when Perak became part of the Federation of Malaya in 1948. Perak joined the new independent state of Malaysia in 1957.

Ipoh

POP 704,572

Ipoh is one of Malaysia's more pleasant midsized cities, chock full of colonial architecture, faded tropical mansions, friendly folks and some of the country's best food. The elegant layout and design of the city's 'Old Town' speaks to the wealth once generated here from Kinta Valley tin mines; in its day, Ipoh was one of the wealthiest cities in Southeast Asia. Today, the city can be approached as a worthwhile urban interlude, or as a convenient gateway to Pulau Pangkor and the Cameron Highlands.

◉ Sights

NORTHERN IPOH

FREE **Muzium Darul Ridzuan**　　MUSEUM
(2020 Jln Panglima Bukit Gantang Wahab; ⊙9.30am-5pm) North of the *padang* (field or grassy area), this museum is housed in a 1926 villa built for a wealthy Chinese tin miner. Although being renovated when we were in town, previously the museum has featured less than inspiring displays that recount the history of tin mining (downstairs) and forestry (upstairs) in Perak. The occasional temporary exhibitions are more interesting.

OLD TOWN

Ipoh's grand colonial architecture, a mixture of gleaming whitewash and romantic dilapidation, is found in the Old Town, west of the Sungai Kinta.

IPOH'S TEMPLE CAVES

The hills that surround Ipoh are riddled with caves that are believed to be a great source of spiritual power, and over the years meditation grottoes became large-scale temples. The caves are relatively difficult to reach by public transport; Mr Raja (☏012-524 2357), a local guide, can take two or more people on a half-day trip to all three for around RM320.

Sam Poh Tong (⊘9am-4pm) A few kilometres south of Ipoh is the largest cave temple in Malaysia. The main attraction here is the turtle pond, where locals bring turtles to release in the hope of balancing their karma. Inside the temple is a huge cavern with a small reclining Buddha, and smaller vases set about it. The ornamental garden in front of the temple is quite scenic, and pomelo (a citrus fruit) stalls line the highway. The temple can be reached by any Kampar-bound bus from Ipoh's local bus station.

Perak Tong (⊘8am-5pm) Founded in 1926 by a Buddhist priest, this temple extends back into an impressive complex of caverns and grottoes with amazing murals on the interior walls, including some interesting juxtapositions of Theravada Buddhas from Southeast Asia and Chinese Buddhas and Buddhist saints. The cave is located 6km north of Ipoh. From the local bus station, buses bound for Kuala Kangsar can stop at Perak Tong.

Gua Kok Look Tong (⊘7am-7pm) To get off the beaten path, you can visit this smaller, more serene temple. At the cave temple's entrance, climb up to the Three Sages in the central cavern. At the back is a fat Chinese Buddha of Future Happiness sitting in the company of three other Bodhisattvas. Behind the cave is an ornamental garden with ponds and pagodas. Gua Kok Look Tong is a long walk from Sam Poh Tong; the easiest way to reach it is on a guided tour with Mr Raja.

PERAK IPOH

FREE **Train Station**　HISTORIC BUILDING
(Map p120; Jln Panglima Bukit Gantang Wahab) Known locally as the 'Taj Mahal', and dating from 1914, Ipoh's train station is a blend of Moorish and Victorian architecture designed in the 'Raj' style you see everywhere in India.

Town Hall　HISTORIC BUILDING
(Map p120; Jln Panglima Bukit Gantang Wahab, Dewan Bandaran; ⊘8am-5pm) Ipoh's Town Hall dates back to 1916. Not open to the public.

Court House　HISTORIC BUILDING
(Mahkanah Tinggi; Map p120; Jln Panglima Bukit Gantang Wahab) Ipoh's Court House was built in 1928 by government architect AB Hubbock – the same architect who designed the city's train station and Town Hall. Not open to the public.

FREE **Birch Memorial Clock Tower**　MONUMENT
(Map p120; Jln Dato' Sagor) The clock tower was erected in 1909 in memory of James WW Birch, Perak's first British Resident, who was murdered at Pasir Salak. The friezes on the clock tower are meant to illustrate the growth of civilisation, featuring figures such as Moses, Buddha, Shakespeare and Charles Darwin. A figure representing Mohammed has since been erased. The road on which this memorial stands has been renamed for one of Birch's killers, who are seen today as nationalists.

Royal Ipoh Club　HISTORIC BUILDING
(Map p120; Jln Panglima Bukit Gantang Wahab) A mock-Tudor building dating back to 1895, and overlooking the playing fields of the *padang*. Still a centre of exclusivity, and not open to the public.

St Michael's Institution　HISTORIC BUILDING
(Map p120; Jln SP Seenivasagam) On the *padang's* northern flank is this neo-Gothic, three-storey colonial school with arched verandahs, founded by the Catholic La Sallean brothers in 1927. Not open to the public.

FREE **Masjid India Muslim**　MOSQUE
(Map p120; Jln SP Seenivasagam; ⊘8am-5pm) Built in the Mogul style in 1908 for the local Indian population. Only Muslims are allowed inside.

Ipoh

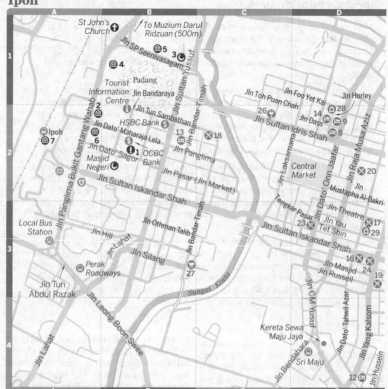

Activities

The best way to cover all of the colonial-era architecture in Ipoh's Old Town is via a walking tour. You can do a self-led tour, using the excellent *Ipoh Heritage Trail* maps 1 and 2, available at Ipoh's tourist information centre.

Ipoh Heritage Walk   WALKING TOUR
(RM20; ☺8am-noon Sat) If you're in town on a Saturday, consider doing the walking tour led by **Mr Raja** (☏012-524 2357) or **Roselyn Lim** (☏012-500 9400). The tour starts at Ipoh's train station at 8am, taking three hours.

Sleeping

Most of Ipoh's hotels are found in New Town on the eastern side of Sungai Kinta. There are some interesting midrange and top-end hotels in and around Ipoh, but the town's budget places are generally a sorry lot.

TOP
CHOICE **Sekeping Kong Heng**   HOTEL $$
(Map p120; ☏012-227 2745; www.sekeping.com/kongheng/home.html; Jln Bandar Timah; r RM200-800; ❉☀) Unless we told you, you'd probably never spot this sexy new hotel cleverly built over and around an ancient cafe. Fittingly, the eight standard rooms are designed to blend in with the structure's original elements – think peeling paint, worn wood floors and chipped plaster. The two huge family rooms up the ante, taking up an entire floor each and featuring elevated beds in glass air-conditioned cubes and walls made from metal screens and vines. Easily the quirkiest place to stay in Ipoh, if not all of northern Malaysia.

TOP
CHOICE **French Hotel**   HOTEL $$
(Map p120; ☏241 3030; 60-62 Jln Dato' Onn Jaafar; r RM138-168; ❉☀) No French maids here, but you will find an attractive and competent midrange hotel. The French actually goes

back several decades, but a recent renovation has left the rooms feeling modern and functional. The hotel's location in New Town is convenient and staff are friendly and know what they're doing.

Tune Hotel
HOTEL $$

(Map p120; ☎nationwide 03-962 5888; www.tune hotels.com; Jln Dass; r RM110; ✳🛜) AirAsia's hotel chain now has an Ipoh branch. It's definitely a budget hotel – the base price increases as you tack on everything from towels to air-con – but it's at least as comfortable and competent as most midrange places. The price quoted above was for a walk-in with most amenities.

D'Eastern Hotel
HOTEL $$

(Map p120; ☎254 3936; 118 Jln Sultan Idris Shah; r/ste RM98/268; ✳🍴🛜) D'Eastern is your typical, classic-feeling Southeast Asia midranger: huge rooms with dark woods (complemented by tacky paintings), carpet, big

functional bathrooms and capable staff. It's not new, but it's clean and it works.

Indulgence
BOUTIQUE HOTEL $$$

(☎255 7051; www.indulgencerestaurant.com; 14 Jln Raja Dihilir; r incl breakfast RM420, ste RM629-790; ✳🛜) The seven rooms in this 1930s-era mansion span a variety of styles – from Thai to Roccoco – all with a classically girly aesthetic. Yet even the most macho of travellers will find them huge and sumptuous-feeling, and the hotel and attached restaurant both get great reviews. Indulgence is located, somewhat inconveniently, just east of central Ipoh.

Impiana Hotel
HOTEL $$

(☎255 5555; www.impiana.com; 18 Jln Raja Dr Nazrin Shah; incl breakfast r RM250-500, ste RM1000-2500; ✳@🛜⛱) The Impiana is your best bet for a reputable four-star chain hotel relatively close to the city. Rooms are big and stylish, and you can expect the usual amenities and facilities. An impending renovation will hopefully erase the reminders of a previous life that appears to date back to the 1980s. The Impiana is located just east of central Ipoh; a taxi here will cost around RM10.

Banjaran Hotsprings Retreat
RESORT $$$

(☎210 7777; www.thebanjaran.com; 1 Persiaran Lagun Sunway 3; villas incl breakfast RM1360-2500; ✳@🛜⛱) This is an exclusive spa resort at the base of limestone cliffs, 8km northeast of Ipoh. The 26 villas have features such as private pools and Jacuzzi fed by the natural hot springs, and spa activities include a thermal steam cave and ice bath. Transport can be arranged by the resort.

New Caspian Hotel
HOTEL $

(Map p120; ☎242 3327; 6-10 Jln Jubilee; r RM72-92; ✳✳🛜) A fresh coat of paint has done wonders for this old-school hotel. Rooms remain emphatically budget-level, but are bright, clean, and have TV and air-con and free wi-fi. It's probably the best budget choice we came across in Ipoh, although it's worth mentioning that communicating in English may be a problem here.

YMCA
HOSTEL $

(☎254 0809; www.ymca-ipoh.com; 211 Jln Raja Musa Aziz; dm RM18, r RM60-80; ✳🛜) Ostensibly Ipoh's only real backpacker accommodation, the YMCA features cheap-n-tidy dorm beds and institutional-but-clean budget rooms. It's located about 1km north of the centre

Ipoh

Sights

1	Birch Memorial Clock Tower	B2
2	Court House	A2
3	Masjid India Muslim	B1
4	Royal Ipoh Club	B1
5	St Michael's Institution	B1
6	Town Hall	A2
7	Train Station	A2

Sleeping

8	D'Eastern Hotel	D2
9	French Hotel	D2
10	Hotel Robin	E3
11	New Caspian Hotel	E3
12	Ritz Garden Hotel	D4
	Ritz Kowloon Hotel	(see 12)
13	Sekeping Kong Heng	B2
14	Tune Hotel	D2

Eating

15	Evening Hawker Stalls	E2
16	Famous Mee Hakka	D3
17	Funny Mountain Soya Bean	D3
18	Lee Heng Fatt	C2
19	M. Salim	D3
20	Medan Selera Dato' Tawhil Azar	D2
21	Ming Court	E2
22	Nasi Lemak Ayam Kampung	E4
23	Restoran Onn Kee	D3
24	Xin Quan Fang	D3

Drinking

25	Bricks & Barrels	E1
26	Over Time	C2
27	Sin Yoon Loong	B3

Shopping

28	Flea Market	D2
29	Gerbang Malam	D3

of Ipoh; follow Jln Raja Musa Aziz until you reach the northern end of the large park.

Ritz Garden Hotel
HOTEL $$

(Map p120; ☎242 7777; www.ritzgardenhotel.com; 86 Jln Yang Kalsom; incl breakfast r/ste RM170-600/550-2300; ❄@🛜🏊) Formerly fancy, now staunchly midrange, this hotel has seen better days, but rooms are clean and functional. Facilities, from pool to cafe, are perks.

Ritz Kowloon Hotel
HOTEL $

(Map p120; ☎254 7778; 92-96 Jlan Yang Kalsom; incl breakfast r/ste RM78-89/118-148; ❄🛜) The rooms here won't inspire any postcards home, but all have windows (a luxury in this price range), and breakfast and free wi-fi make them a pretty good deal.

Hotel Robin
HOTEL $

(Map p120; ☎242 1888; 100-110 Jln Mustapha Al-Bakry; r/ste RM53-63/80-103; ❄) The better of Ipoh's Chinese-owned budget places. Zero character, but rooms are clean and the owner speaks English.

✗ Eating

Foodies rejoice, as Ipoh is home to one of Malaysia's more underrated street food scenes. The excellent range of options are predominantly Chinese and Malay; for Western food consider the hotel restaurant at Indulgence (p121) or the bar snacks at Over Time (p123) or Bricks & Barrels (p123).

TOP CHOICE Nasi Lemak Ayam Kampung
MALAY $

(Map p120; 43-45 Jln Ali Pitchay; mains RM5.50-30; ☽4.30pm-2.30am) This popular restaurant is the place to come for fancy-pants and delicious *nasi lemak* (rice boiled in coconut milk, served with fried *ikan bilis* – dried sardines or anchovies – peanuts and a curry dish). It serves a few variations on the dish, with sides ranging from the house fried chicken to cockles. Don't miss the deliciously tart and peppery eel soup.

M. Salim
MALAY $

(Map p120; cnr Jln Yang Kalsom & Jln Che Tak; mains RM3-20; ☽6.30am-12.30am Sat-Thurs, 6.30am-1pm & 2pm-12.30am Fri) This longstanding and tidy restaurant does tasty versions of Indian-Muslim (also known as Mamak) faves. Think rich *nasi beryani*, huge *murtabak* (roti filled with pieces of mutton, chicken or vegetables) and a dauntingly large fish-head curry – all of which should ideally be accompanied by the delicious house mango juice, here supplemented with lychee.

Indulgence
INTERNATIONAL $$

(www.indulgencerestaurant.com; 14 Jln Raja Dihilir; mains RM28-59; ☽9am-11.30pm Wed-Sun) Located in the hotel of the same name, Indulgence does progressive yet homey-feeling cuisine; think poached cucumber barrels with toppings of smoked salmon, lamb rashers, cottage cheese, and lined with chilli and olive oil tapenade. Intriguing, but if we're being honest, we never made it past the delicious pastries and the one-of-a-kind Earl Grey *teh tarik* (Malaysian-style sweet tea).

Lee Heng Fatt
CHINESE $

(Map p120; Jln Tun Sambathan; mains from RM2.60; ⊙dinner) Virtually the only restaurant open after dark in Old Town, Lee Heng Fatt serves *hor mee*, your choice of dumplings (fish, pork, tofu) in broth served with wheat noodles. It also has a huge and delicious selection of fresh fruit juices – try the cucumber and apple.

Funny Mountain Soya Bean
CHINESE $

(Map p120; 49 Jln Theatre; mains RM0.90-4.80; ⊙breakfast & lunch) Funny Mountain is immensely popular for two dishes: bean-curd pudding and soy-bean milk. The curd, served with a bit of syrup and/or grass jelly, is smooth and sweet, while the drink is rich and refreshing.

Medan Selera Dato' Tawhil Azar
MALAY $

(Map p120; Jln Raja Musa Aziz; mains RM2-8; ⊙dinner) Better-known as the Children's Playground, this large food centre has mostly Malay stalls arranged around a small square filled with slides and swings.

Evening Hawker Stalls
CHINESE, HAWKER $

(Map p120; Jln Sultan Idris Shah; mains RM3-10; ⊙dinner) This street is home to at least 30 vendors, mostly serving cheap and tasty Chinese dishes.

Drinking

Bricks & Barrels
BAR

(Map p120; 28-30 Jln Lau Ek Ching; ⊙4pm-1am) A surprisingly sophisticated place for Ipoh, Bricks & Barrels serve a good selection of beers – including imported draught beer – and a few single malts as well. It was the most popular place in town when we passed through, and there's live music from 9pm on weekends.

Over Time
BAR

(Map p120; www.overtime.asia; 59 Jln Sultan Idris Shah; ⊙11am-3am) A brew pub with an assertively clubby feel, Over Time serves three kinds of draught beer – aromatic, lager and *dunkel* (dark beer) – along with a menu of meaty Western and Asian dishes (RM14 to RM55).

PERAK IPOH

IPOH'S BEST EATS

They say it's the water: Ipoh has a glowing reputation as a food city, and locals believe that deposits from the rich karst formations around town seep into the groundwater, making the city's food unique. We tend to agree, and with this in mind, here's some of the city's best dishes and where to eat them:

Curry mee A combination of rice and wheat noodles in a spicy, rich and often oily broth, served with chicken, pork and shrimp. Arguably the best place to eat it is is at **Xin Quan Fang** (Map p120; 174 Jln Sultan Iskandar Shah; mains from RM3.80; ⊙breakfast & lunch), but be ready for a wait; the family here has been making the dish for decades, and didn't get their loyal following by rushing.

Ayam tauge Tender boiled chicken served with Ipoh's fat bean sprouts and rice (the latter cooked in chicken broth) or a bowl of rice noodles is probably the dish most closely associated with Ipoh. **Restoran Onn Kee** (Map p120; 51 Jln Yau Tet Shin; mains from RM3; ⊙1:30pm-3am) does a good version, or you could try any other of the several restaurants nearby that specialise in the dish.

Kopi putih The method of roasting beans with palm-oil margarine was allegedly invented at **Sin Yoon Loong** (Map p120; 15A, Jln Bandar Timah; coffee drinks from RM1.40; ⊙7am-6pm Mon-Sat). Kopi putih is known in English as Ipoh white coffee.

Hakka mee Flat wheat noodles topped with salty ground pork, and served with a side bowl of broth with fish and pork balls and tofu, is best at **Famous Mee Hakka** (Map p120; 163 Jln Sultan Iskandar Shah; mains RM3; ⊙7am-noon).

Dim Sum Ipoh's Chinese community is predominately of Cantonese origin, so it's not a surprise that dim sum is popular here. Although it's not as flashy as the other dim-sum palaces nearby, locals eat at **Ming Court** (Map p120; 32-36 Jln Leong Sin Nam; dim sum RM2.20-4.90; ⊙6am-noon Wed-Mon).

🛍 Shopping

Gerbang Malam
MARKET

(Night Market; Map p120; Jln Dato' Tahwil Azar; ⏰7pm-midnight) Ipoh's night market is expansive, but its offerings are mostly limited to sports-related clothing and a few snacks.

Flea Market
MARKET

(Map p120; Jln Horley; ⏰6am-noon Sun) A busy flea market virtually engulfs the streets surrounding Tune Hotel every Sunday morning.

ℹ Information

Ipoh Hospital
HOSPITAL

(☏253 2533; http://hipoh.moh.gov.my; Jln Hospital) Ipoh's main hospital is located about 1.5km northwest of the centre of town; a taxi here should cost about RM10.

Tourist Information Centre
TOURIST INFORMATION

(☏208 3155; Jln Bandaraya; ⏰8am-5pm Mon-Fri & 10am-3pm Sat)

ℹ Getting There & Away

Air

Ipoh's airport, **Sultan Azlan Shah Airport** (www.ipoh.airport-authority.com), is about 3km southeast of the city centre; a taxi here from central Ipoh costs RM20. At the time of research, **Firefly** (☏nationwide 03-7845 4543; www.firefly.com.my; Sultan Azlan Shah Airport) was the only operator, with twice-daily flights to Singapore (1½ hours, RM300).

Bus

Ipoh's long-distance bus station, known as **Medan Gopeng** (Jln Raja Dr Nazrin Shah), is 5km south of the city centre and is linked by shuttle buses to the local bus station (RM1.30, every 15 minutes from 6am to 6.15pm) and taxis (RM15). We were informed that the bus station is scheduled to move to a new location at Meru Raya, approximately 8km north of Ipoh, probably by the time you read this.

Destination	Duration (hr)	Fare (RM)	Frequency
Alor Setar	4	21.70-26	Frequent, 9am-4.50pm
Butterworth/ George Town	2	13.90-17.60	Frequent, 8.30am-8.30pm
Hat Yai (Thailand)	6-7	45	12.30pm & midnight
Johor Bahru	7	48.50	Frequent, 9am-11pm

Destination	Duration (hr)	Fare (RM)	Frequency
Kuala Lumpur (also KLIA/ LCCT)	2½-3	17.50-43	Hourly, 4.30am-9.30pm
Kota Bharu	6	33.30	9.30am, 10am, 11.30am & 10pm
Lumut (for Pulau Pangkor)	2	8	12.30pm, 1.30pm, 3pm, 4.30pm & 5.45pm
Melaka	5	33-34	Frequent, 9.30am-12.45am
Singapore	8	56-75	Frequent, 8.30am to 10.30am & 8.30pm to 11pm
Tanah Rata (for Cameron Highlands)	2	15	Frequent, 9.30am-5.30pm

Closer to town, **Sri Maju** (☏253 8898; Jln Bendahara) has its own station, from where it runs 'luxury' buses to many of the same destinations as Medan Gopeng.

Perak Roadways (☏254 4895; Jln Tun Abdul Razak), whose office is a short walk from the local bus station, runs regular buses to Lumut (for Pulau Pangkor; RM8.50, two hours) with frequent departures from 6.50am to 7.30pm, and Gerik (for Royal Belum State Park; two hours, RM13.10) with departures at noon, 2.30pm, 4.30pm and 6.30pm.

The local bus station is off a roundabout south of the train station.

Destination	Duration (hr)	Fare (RM)	Frequency
Kampar (for Sam Poh Tong temple cave)	20min	1.50	Every 15min, 6am-6.15pm
Gopeng	40min	2.70	Every 15min, 6am-6.15pm
Kuala Kangsar	80min	R6.20	Every 15min, 5.30am-8.45pm
Taiping	1½hr	8.40	Hourly, 6.15am-7pm
Tanah Rata (for Cameron Highlands)	2½hr	16.80	8am, 11am, 3pm & 6pm

Train

Ipoh's train station is on the main Singapore–Butterworth line. There are daily trains (including a very frequent intercity service) to Kuala Lumpur (RM22 to RM40, 4½ hours) and Butterworth (RM21 to RM36, 3½ hours), the latter continuing to Hat Yai in Thailand (RM34 to RM87, 10½ hours); check with www.ktmb.com.my for the latest info on fares and schedules.

ℹ Getting Around

Most of central Ipoh is accessible on foot, although transport – public or hired – is necessary to get to the attractions outside of town.

For a car with driver, contact **Mr Raja** (☏012-524 2357), a local guide who charges RM130 per day for destinations around Ipoh. Car hire is handled by **Kereta Sewa Maju Jaya** (☏255 5510; www.carrentalipoh.com; Jln C.M. Yusuff; ◷8am-8pm), who also has an office at Ipoh's airport.

Gopeng & Around

If city life isn't your thing, relish in the knowledge that less than 30km away from Ipoh lies a little-known and burgeoning outdoor destination. Gopeng, a relatively well-preserved former tin-mining outpost, has palpable and interesting remnants of the boom town it once was, but the real highlight is the hilly rural area approximately 6km east of the town – a base for rafting, caving, trekking and other outdoor activities.

◉ Sights

Gua Tempurung　　　　　　　CAVE
(www.guatempurung.com; tours RM6-22; ◷9am-3pm Sat-Thurs) The 'Coconut Cave', so-called for its domelike interior, is located about 7km from Gopeng. It's nearly 2km long, spanning five separate domed rooms; inside you'll find impressive cave formations, an underground river and the usual creepy cave animals. Gua Tempurung can only be explored by a guided tour, available at the cave entrance or, if you don't have transport, via a visit arranged with one of the three resorts outside Gopeng. There are four tours (between 45 minutes and four hours), which range from walking along easy marked paths to slogging through a river.

FREE **Kinta Nature Park**　　WILDLIFE RESERVE
Located 6km south of Batu Gajah, this is a yet to be gazetted nature area. Based around a lake that was formed as a result of tin mining, wetlands are home to an estimated 130 species of birds as well as other animals, including otters. Kinta Nature Park can be visited via **Mr Raja** (☏012-524 2357), an Ipoh-based tour guide, or via a guided tour organised at Gopeng Rainforest Resort.

Heritage House　　　　　　　MUSEUM
(Jln Pasar; admission by donation; ◷9am-3pm Sat-Sun) A restored shophouse decorated with original furniture and explored via an informal tour. Located off the main highway near Gopeng's monument roundabout.

Muzium Gopeng　　　　　　　MUSEUM
(Jln Eu Kong; admission by donation; ◷9am-5pm Fri-Tue) A somewhat random collection of old-fashioned housewares and vintage furniture supplemented with displays on local history. Located in an antique shophouse along the road that leads to Gopeng's bus station.

🏃 Activities

Any of the resorts can arrange guided activities including **rafting** (half-day per person RM150), **rafflesia spotting** (half-day per person from RM80), **wet abseiling** (half-day per person RM100) and **caving** in Gua Tempurung (half-day per person RM40). Rafting and some of the more advanced caving excursions are only for groups of eight or more; in general, prices are cheaper the larger your group is.

🛏 Sleeping & Eating

About 6km east of Gopeng is a secluded wooded area home to three mostly similar resorts, all located within walking distance of hiking, rafting and a range of other outdoor activities. With the exception of Clearwater Sanctuary, the fee includes one night of accommodation and three meals; transport from Gopeng's bus station can be arranged for about RM10.

Clearwater Sanctuary　　RESORT $$$
(☏366 7433; www.cwsgolf.com.my; Batu Gajah; r RM250-475; ❄🛜) This vast, rural-feeling retreat calls itself a golf resort, but it's really a lot more than that. Accommodation is more comfortable than it is luxurious, but the real highlight is its setting by a large lake and the host of activities, which include archery and fishing. Clearwater is located outside Batu Gajah, about 15km south of Ipoh, and the resort can provide transport for guests.

WORTH A TRIP

KINTA VALLEY HERITAGE LOOP

The area surrounding Ipoh was built on tin – literally and figuratively – and a fascinating half-day excursion can be made through the boom towns in the Kinta Valley that sprang up in the 1870s as a result of the ore. Unfortunately, infrequent public transport makes hiring a driver a necessity. **Mr Raja** (☏ 012 524 2357) is a native of Batu Gajah, the capital of Kinta District, and will drive visitors along the loop for RM20 per person, plus an additional RM130 for transport.

Leaving Ipoh, head south on Hwy 5, passing the present-day ghost towns of Lahat and Papan. After about 20km you'll reach **Batu Gajah**, an important settlement since the early 19th century. The town is a remarkably intact remnant of the colonial era, with a busy market and commercial area near the highway, and, on a hill *(changkat)* looking over the town, the British administrative zone, complete with mansions, churches, a hospital and – of course – a prison. The excellent *Batu Gajah Heritage Driving Trail*, available at Ipoh's tourist information office, provides a map of the town as well as details on the town's primary historical structures.

Continue 9km south to the **TT5 tin dredge** (admission adult/child RM5/3; ⊗ 8.30am-noon & 1-6pm). Today an open-air museum, the now-defunct dredge dates back to 1936 and is one of the earliest of its type in Malaysia.

Returning to Batu Gajah, head east along Hwy A8, where after about 6km you'll reach **Kellie's Castle** (admission adult/child RM5/3; ⊗ 9am-6pm). Also known as Kellie's Folly, it is one of those leftovers of British eccentricity you occasionally find scattered in some random corner of the old empire. Here's the story: in 1915 William Kellie Smith, a wealthy Scottish rubber plantation–owner and lover-of-all-things-India, commissioned the building to be the home of his son. Not only bricks, but artisans and labourers were sourced from India to build what would have been, if finished, one of the most magnificent residences in Malaysia. Poor Smith died in 1926 and the house was abandoned; today, the remaining six-storey structure is a well-tended tourist site.

About 500m from the castle is a **Hindu temple**, built for the artisans by Smith when a mysterious illness decimated the workforce and the remaining workers believed the gods needed to be appeased. To show their gratitude to Smith, the workers placed a figure of him, dressed in a white suit and pith helmet, among the Hindu deities on the temple roof. The temple is now semiderelict but still in use, and the resident priest will point out the statue of Smith.

After visiting Kellie's Castle, continue east until you reach Hwy 1, the former main north–south highway. Turn south to visit Gopeng – the town's historic centre is another remnant of the tin era – or turn north, where after 13km, you'll arrive back in Ipoh.

Adeline's Villa　　　　　RESORT $$
(☏ 359 1651; www.adelinevilla.com; per person RM188-238; ❈) The most sophisticated – and most expensive – accommodation in the area, Adeline's takes the form of 10 rooms in cutesy wooden villas that can sleep up to nine people.

My Gopeng Resort　　　　RESORT $$
(☏ 016-549 3777; www.mygopengresort.com; per person RM168) Resort with a campground-like feel. Rooms are basic but comfortable, and can sleep up to 24 people; bathrooms facilities are shared.

Gopeng Rainforest Resort　　RESORT $$
(☏ 012-516 8200; www.gopengrainforest.com; per person RM98-108) The location here is stunning,

but accommodation is very basic – think mattresses in fan-cooled structures with shared bathrooms. The food and activities get good reports.

❶ Getting There & Away

Gopeng's bus station is located about 300m east of Hwy 1. Frequent buses shuttle passengers the 13km between Gopeng and Ipoh from 6.30am to 10.30pm (RM2.70, 30 minutes).

Cameron Highlands

OK traveller, you've been sweating through the jungles, the beaches and the lowlands of Malaysia for weeks now. Another sticky day will make your clothes unwearable. Another sweaty night and you'll lose the ability to sleep. We grant you a reprieve. Come to the Cameron Highlands.

This is Malaysia's most extensive hill station, an alpinescape of blue peaks, green humps, fuzzy tea plantations, small towns and white waterfalls cutting throughout. Trekking, tea tasting and visiting local agro-tourism sites is the done thing here. And best of all, with an altitude of 1300m to 1829m, the temperature rarely drops below 10°C or climbs above 21°C; practically cool enough to make you forget you're in Malaysia.

Though the Cameron Highlands – the colloquial name for the area that roughly encompasses the towns of Kampung Raja, Brinchang, Tanah Rata, Ringlet and environs – lie in Pahang, they're accessed from Perak.

◉ Sights

Cameron Bharat
Tea Plantation TEA PLANTATION
(Map p128; bharattea.com.my; ⊗8.30am-7pm) Located at the side of the road around 4km south of Tanah Rata, the views over this plantation are breathtaking. There are no guided tours here, but you can wander around parts of the plantation, and there's an attractively set tea house overlooking the estate. A taxi here will cost RM10. There's another branch (⊗7.30am-6pm), likewise

equipped with a cafe, located 12km away on the main road heading northeast Brinchang, although the views aren't as impressive.

Sam Poh Temple TEMPLE
(Map p128; Brinchang) As unexpected sites in the hills go, a temple dedicated to a Chinese eunuch and naval officer just about tops the list. This temple, just below Brinchang about 1km off the main road, is a brilliant pastiche of imperial Chinese regalia, statuary dedicated to medieval admiral and eunuch Zheng Ho and, allegedly, the fourth-largest Buddha in Malaysia.

Kok Lim Strawberry Farm FARM
(Map p128; Brinchang; Time Tunnel admission adult/ child RM5/3; ⊗9am-5pm, Time Tunnel 8.30am-6.30pm) Just north of Brinchang, RM30 gets you the chance to be a labourer for the day and go home with 0.5kg of hand-picked strawberries. The attached Time Tunnel is a cheesy-but-fun underground passage stuffed full of 'antiques' and displays dedicated to local history.

FREE Ee Feng Gu Honey Bee Farm FARM
(Map p128; www.eefenggu.com; Brinchang; ⊗8am-7pm) A working apiary about 3km northeast of Brinchang, with pleasant, flower-filled gardens to walk around, and honey to buy. There's also an indoor maze (adult/child RM3/2) for the kids.

PERAK CAMERON HIGHLANDS

TEA COUNTRY

Even if you're a dedicated coffee drinker, don't miss the breathtakingly beautiful **Boh Sungei Palas Tea Estate** (www.boh.com.my; ⊗9am-4.30pm Tue-Sun), set in an almost otherworldly green patchwork of hills and tea plants.

The narrow approach road leads past worker housing and a Hindu temple (tea pickers are predominantly Indian) to the modern visitor centre, where you can witness tea production first-hand. There's also a gift shop selling every version of Boh tea you can imagine and a modern cafe (⊗9am-4:30pm Tue-Sun) where you can sip tea while looking out over the lush plantations below. Free 15-minute tours showing the tea-making process are conducted during opening hours. If you are in fact a tea drinker, we suggest doing one of the plantation's hour-long **Tea Appreciation Tours** (RM35; ⊗9am, 11am, 1pm & 3pm Tue-Sun), which include a guided walk through tea plantations, a factory tour and tea sampling.

The estate is located in the hills north of Brinchang, off the road to Gunung Brinchang. Public buses running between Tanah Rata and Kampung Raja pass the turn-off to Gunung Brinchang. From there it's 4km along the winding road, after which it's another 15 minutes' walk downhill to the visitor centre. Taxis in Tanah Rata will take you to the estate and back for RM50.

Boh has another almost equally impressive **estate** (www.boh.com.my; admission free; ⊗9am-4.30pm Tue-Sun) southeast of Tanah Rata and 8km off the main road. There's a small cafe and tours are given every 15 minutes from 9.30am to 4.15pm. Taxis in Tanah Rata will do a round-trip here for RM60.

Cameron Highlands

Cameron Highlands

⊙ Sights

1 Cameron Bharat Tea	
Plantation	A4
2 Cameron Highlands Butterfly	
Farm	D1
3 Ee Feng Gu Honey Bee Farm	D1
4 Kok Lim Strawberry Farm	C2
5 Raaju's Hill Strawberry Farm	C1
6 Sam Poh Temple	C2
7 Sri Tehndayuthapany Swamy	B2

🛏 Sleeping

8 Bala's Holiday Chalet	B3
9 Equatorial	C1
10 Hotel De'La Ferns	B3
11 Lakehouse	B5
12 Smokehouse	B3
13 Strawberry Park Resort	B2

✴ Eating

| Smokehouse | (see 12) |

JEK YAP: NATURE ENTHUSIAST

Jek Yap is a member of Kinta Heritage, a group of eight individuals seeking to promote Perak's rich natural heritage.

Is Perak a strong nature destination? What are some visit-worthy natural/protected areas? It is one of the richest states in Malaysia in terms of natural attractions. Royal Belum State Park possesses an immense wealth of flora and fauna, with much of the area still unexplored. Kinta Nature Park is the largest heronry in Malaysia; there are currently 180 species of birds found there. The nightly light show of the fireflies in the Matang Mangrove Forest Reserve is another excellent outing.

Is there any kind of flora or fauna found in Perak that isn't found anywhere else? There are at least two species of Rafflesia only found in Perak; the parent plant of the national flower of Singapore is an orchid species endemic to the Kinta Valley; not to mention seasonal sightings of 10 species of hornbills in Royal Belum State Park.

Are Perak's natural areas under threat? Like any other natural area in this region they are threatened by human development.

What kind of outdoor/adventure activities does Perak offer? What's a good destination for outdoor activities? Perak offers golf, bird-watching, white-water rafting, tubing, kayaking, abseiling, jungle trekking, cycling and caving. Visitors basing themselves at Gopeng have easy access to all of these activities.

PERAK CAMERON HIGHLANDS

Cameron Highlands Butterfly Farm FARM
(Map p128; Brinchang; adult/child RM5/2; ⊙9am-6pm Mon-Fri, 8.30am-7pm Sat-Sun) Home to a fluttering collection of tropical butterflies, including the majestic Raja Brooke.

FREE **Raaju's Hill Strawberry Farm** FARM
(Map p128; Brinchang; ⊙8.30am-6.30pm) It may hold the attention of anyone with a keen interest in hydroponic strawberry cultivation, but the main reason for visiting is for the strawberry jam and ice cream.

Sri Tehndayuthapany Swamy TEMPLE
(Map p128; Brinchang; ⊙7am-6pm) Located just south of Brinchang is this colourful Hindu place of worship – the Tamil Nadu–style sculptures were created by Indian aritists, and the temple primarily serves the local tea-picking population.

☞ Tours

The distance between sights plus infrequent public transport makes booking a guided tour a popular option in the Cameron Highlands. Most are half-day tours that focus on the tea plantation/strawberry picking/flower farm highlights of the area.

CS Travel & Tours TOUR
(Map p131; ☑491 1200; www.cstravel.com.my; 47 Jln Besar, Tanah Rata; ⊙7.30am-7.30pm) This agency leads popular half-day 'countryside tours' of the Highlands, leaving around 8.45am and 1.45pm (adult/child RM25/15). Longer tours such as the full-day 'adventure tour' (adult/child RM80/60) take in Gunung Brinchang and an Orang Asli village. Guides for the hiking trails can also be arranged.

Eco Cameron TOUR
(Map p131; ☑491 5388; www.ecocameron.com; 72A Psn Camellia 4, Tanah Rata; ⊙8am-9.30pm) This outfit specialises in nature-oriented tours of the area – think hiking, orchid walks, birdwatching, insect-spotting – ranging in price from RM45 per person (half-day tours close to town) to RM120 per person (full-day tours outside of town).

🛏 Sleeping

Tanah Rata has the greatest spread of hotels in the Cameron Highlands, including several decent budget places. Brinchang, 4km north, also has a fair spread of accommodation, but most places are targeted at domestic tourists, so it's an awkward place to stay if you're dependent on public transport. There are a few interesting places to stay outside of the main towns, but private transport is a must.

The Highlands are at their busiest during the school holidays in April, August and December. During these times you should book accommodation in advance. Air-con is not necessary in the Cameron Highlands, and few, if any, hotels have it.

HIKING IN THE CAMERON HIGHLANDS

Besides getting in touch with your inner Englishman via tea and strawberries, the main thing to do in the Cameron Highlands is hike. Trailheads are generally clearly marked with yellow-and-black signboards, but it's worth mentioning that many of the trails aren't well maintained, and can be slippery and/or unclear. Always carry water, some food and rain gear to guard against the unpredictable weather. The following is a short-list of a few of the more popular trails:

Trail 1 This trail officially starts at white stone marker 1/5 on the summit of Gunung Brinchang (2031m), but we don't advise making this descent – it's a steep, muddy, over-grown trail, often closed for repairs. Instead, start your walk at the end point of the trail, at white stone marker 1/48 just north of Cactus Valley. This section of the trail should take about two hours to complete. From the summit take the 7km-long sealed road back to Brinchang through the tea plantations – a pleasant walk of about two hours.

Trail 4 One of the more popular trails starts next to the river just past Century Pines Resort in Tanah Rata. It leads to Parit Falls, but garbage from the nearby village finds its way here, and it's not the most bucolic spot. The falls can also be reached from the road around the southern end of the golf course. Both hikes are about half a kilometre.

Trail 8 This trail splits off Trail 9 just before Robinson Falls and is another steep three-hour approach to Gunung Beremban. It can be a strenuous trail, especially if you're walking away from the mountain.

Trail 9A Trails 9 and 9A start together 1.5km from the main road in Tanah Rata – follow the sign that says Robinson Falls and look for the footbridge. From here, the trail leads downhill past Robinson Falls to a metal gate, about 15 minutes away. Trail 9, which is not recommended, goes through the gate and follows the water pipeline down a steep, slippery incline through the jungle to the power station. We suggest you take Trail 9A, which branches to the left at the metal gate and, after about an hour's walk, emerges at the road that leads to Robinson Power Station. Follow this south to the main road, where you can either head east for another 5km to Boh Tea Estate, or west to Habu Power Station for buses back to Tanah Rata.

Smokehouse BOUTIQUE HOTEL $$$
(Map p128; ☎491 1215; www.thesmokehouse.com.my; incl breakfast r/ste RM365/450-710; ☞) This characterful old house dating back to 1937 looks as if it's been lifted straight from deepest Surrey, complete with a red British phone box outside. Indoors, the exposed beams, open fireplaces and chintzy decor complete the picture. Rooms, which are decked out with heavy antique furniture, are more comfy than luxurious, although, like the rest of the house, they possess their own English charm.

Smokehouse is located about 2km north of Tanah Rata along the road to Brinchang.

Hillview Inn GUESTHOUSE $$
(Map p131; ☎491 2915; www.hillview-inn.com; 17 Jln Mentigi, Tanah Rata; r RM70-140; @☞) Located in a three-storey home at the edge of town, this midrange guesthouse has a variety of rooms, both with and without attached bathrooms, and supplemented with communal TV rooms and a ground-floor cafe. Rooms vary in size and amenities, so ask to see a few.

Eight Mentigi GUESTHOUSE $
(Map p131; ☎491 5988; www.eightmentigi.com; 8A Jln Mentigi, Tanah Rata; r RM50-150; @☞) Two linked houses with simple but exceedingly clean rooms. A homey feel is provided by Smith, your kind host. Located at the western edge of town, on the small road that leads behind an unsightly abandoned building.

Hotel De'La Ferns HOTEL $$$
(Map p128; ☎491 4888; www.hoteldelaferns.com.my; r/ste RM380-580/680-1800; @☞) Hotel De'La Ferns is the type of multistorey mock-Tudor monstrosity that has come to define accommodation in the Cameron Highlands. Fortunately, the theme is relegated to the exterior, and inside you'll find large rooms decked out in an attractively subtle, yet modern theme. It's located about 1.5km north of Tanah Rata along the road to Brinchang.

Tanah Rata

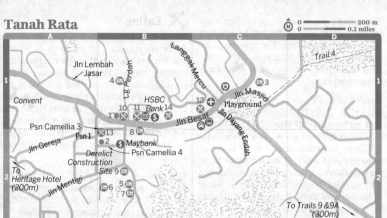

Tanah Rata

◎ Activities, Courses & Tours
1 CS Travel & Tours	B1
2 Eco Cameron	B2

◎ Sleeping
3 Century Pines Resort	C1
4 Daniel's Lodge	B1
5 Eight Mentigi	B2
6 Hillview Inn	B2
7 KRS Pines	B2
8 Planter's Hotel	B2
9 Twin Pines	B2

⊗ Eating
10 Jasmine Cafe	B1
11 KouGen	B1
12 Lord's Cafe	C1
May Flower	(see 2)
13 Restaurant Bunga Suria	B2
14 Restoran Sri Brinchang	B1
Rosedale Bistro	(see 11)
Vintage Café	(see 12)

Planter's Hotel HOTEL **$$**

(Map p131; ☎490 1001; www.plantershotel.com.my; 44A Jln Besar, Tanah Rata; r RM120-260; ☞) This is the place to stay if you don't need frills or atmosphere, and want to be in the middle of all the action in Tanah Rata. Premier rooms are vast, while standard rooms don't have windows. Rates increase by about 20% on Friday and Saturday.

KRS Pines GUESTHOUSE **$**

(Map p131; ☎491 2777; http://twinpines.cameron highlands.com; 7 Jln Mentigi, Tanah Rata; dm/r RM15/35-110; @☞) KRS offers a range of shared and private rooms in a squattish tower block. All accommodation is spic and span, making this a excellent border-line budget/midrange option. Prices rise by about 30% on weekends.

Heritage Hotel HOTEL **$$**

(☎491 3888; www.heritage.com.my; Jln Gereja, Tanah Rata; incl breakfast r/ste RM180-350/310-670; ☞)

This huge mock-Tudor hotel has 238 rooms at the western edge of town. If you can swing it, go for the larger, newer and more attractive rooms in the Deluxe Wing. All rooms have access to the hotel's facilities, which include a playroom for kids, washing machines, pool table and library. Rates are about 20% more on weekends.

Daniel's Lodge HOSTEL **$**

(Map p131; ☎491 5823; danielslodge@hotmail.com; 9 Lg Perdah, Tanah Rata; dm/r RM12-15/35-55; @) The backpacker force remains strong at this longstanding hostel, also known as Kang's. There's a dorm upstairs, the cheapest rooms share bathrooms, and there are on-site facilities ranging from internet terminals (per hour RM3) to a bar, not to mention lots of inviting communal areas.

Twin Pines HOSTEL **$**

(Map p131; ☎491 2169; http://twinpines.cameronhigh lands.com; 2 Jln Mentigi, Tanah Rata; r RM15-20; ☞)

Twin Pines is a good option for trekkers wanting backpacker rates with a less backpackery (read: party) atmosphere. The attic rooms are closetlike and feature little more than a mattress on the floor, but are a steal; other facilities are well kept.

Bala's Holiday Chalet   GUESTHOUSE $$
(Map p128; ☑491 1660; bala.reservation@gmail.com; incl breakfast r/ste RM140-250/280-380; @) The 25 rooms here are set in a mock-Tudor building, originally built as a boarding school in 1934. Many of the rooms are huge, making Bala's a good choice for families, but they can also feel a bit aged. Bala's is located 1.5km north of Tanah Rata – it's not the easiest place to get to if you don't have a car.

Century Pines Resort   HOTEL $$$
(Map p131; ☑491 5115; www.centurypinesresort.com; 42 Jln Masjid; incl breakfast r/ste RM350-490/638-988; ☎) It's set in landscaped gardens at the eastern edge of Tanah Rata, but this complex is more hotel than resort. The rooms have a somewhat dated 1990s-era feel, but they're clean and comfortable, and come stocked with the kind of amenities – huge beds, TV, minibar, safe – that you'd expect for price.

Lakehouse   BOUTIQUE HOTEL $$$
(Map p128; ☑495 6152; www.lakehouse-cameron.com; incl breakfast r RM720, ste RM850-1170; ❈@☎) Overlooking the lake 2km north of Ringlet is this English country house-style hotel with just 19 rooms. The relatively high room tariff is justified by classy touches like four-poster beds, antique furnishings and, in the Foster Suite, a real fireplace.

Strawberry Park Resort   RESORT $$$
(Map p128; ☑491 1166; www.strawberryparkresorts.com; Brinchang; r RM550, ste 700-2200; @☎❈) A sprawling 'neo-Tudor' resort in the hills west of Brinchang, popular with package-tour groups and anyone needing a bit of pampering up in the hills. The Studio Suites are generous in size, and everybody has access to the indoor pool, tennis courts, sauna and spa. The resort is 2km from the main road along an inclining, windy road; you'll need a car to get here.

Equatorial   HOTEL $$
(Map p128; ☑496 1777; www.equatorial.com; Brinchang; r/ste RM180-420/320-620; @☎❈) Ginormous modern hotel (290 rooms) located about 3km north of Brinchang. Rooms are large, albeit bland; deluxe rooms are located on higher floors and have bathtubs.

 Eating

Tanah Rata is home to the majority of the area's restaurants – many with a Malay/Muslim feel, along with a few international cuisines thrown in for good measure. While most travellers should find something to please their palate, it's probably safe to say that people come to the Cameron Highlands for the activities, scenery and cool weather, not the food. Brinchang's abundance of Chinese restaurants are for the most part indistinguishable.

Smokehouse   ENGLISH $$
(Map p128; www.thesmokehousehotel.com; ⊘breakfast, lunch & dinner) Located in the hotel of the same name, this restaurant specialises in English cuisine – think roasts, meat pies, fish and chips, and bangers and mash – much of it done quite well, and served in a setting that is as English as the food. It doesn't come cheap though, and a more economic alternative might be one of the afternoon tea sets (RM25 to RM33) available throughout the day. The Smokehouse is located about 2km north of Tanah Rata; a taxi here will cost RM8.

KouGen   JAPANESE, INTERNATIONAL $$
(Map p131; 35 Jln Besar, Tanah Rata; mains RM13.90-20.90; ⊘11am-9pm) Run by an apparent Japanophile from KL, this new restaurant does a mix of traditional Japanese (sushi, tempura) and the not-so-traditional (lamb stew, minced beef and pork steak). All main dishes are served with rice and soup; for something lighter go for the starters, including yakitori or Japanese-style croquettes. One of the most interesting places to eat in Tanah Rata.

Jasmine Cafe   INTERNATIONAL $$
(Map p131; 45 Jln Besar, Tanah Rata; mains RM7-33; ⊘noon-9pm; ☎) Get ready for some cultural confusion here: Jasmine Cafe is a Dutch-themed restaurant that serves mostly Western-style food prepared by an ethnic Chinese chef. Against all odds it works, and dishes such as the peppery chicken chop, particularly if accompanied by a glass of fresh strawberry juice, are some of the tastiest in town.

Lord's Cafe   CAFE $
(Map p131; Jln Besar, Tanah Rata; mains RM2.50-4.90; ⊘10am-9pm Mon-Fri, to 6pm Sat) This cosy cafe serves what are allegedly the Cameron Highlands' best scones – in addition to a variety of teas and no shortage of Christian scripture. Located above fast-food restaurant Marrybrown.

PARTHIPAN RAMADASS: TEA EXPERT

Parthipan Ramadass is a tour officer at Boh's Sungei Palas Estate, Cameron Highlands

What should one look for in a good cup of tea? It's for you to decide – do you like light or robust? If light, then look for light colour, texure and aroma. In terms of flavours, it should be soothing to the tongue. If you like something more robust, you should look for more colour, more tanginess and a robust taste that you can feel on your tongue.

The best way to prepare a cup of tea? Always use loose tea, not teabags – the leaves are supposed to open. The measurement is a teaspoon – one for yourself and one for the pot. Tea should be brewed with boiling water. Steep three minutes for light tea and for strong tea that you'll drink with milk, five minutes. Strain the tea as you pour.

May Flower CHINESE $$
(Map p131; 72A Psn Camellia 4, Tanah Rata; hotpot per person RM16, mains RM7-24; ⊙8.30am-10pm; 🖉) When in the Cameron Highlands, the locals eat hotpot (also referred to as steamboat) and so should you. This place does a few versions of the dish, including a vegetarian hotpot.

Restoran Sri Brinchang INDIAN $
(Map p131; 25 Jln Besar, Tanah Rata; mains RM4-20; 🖉) This bright place serves a range of simple Indian fare, including tandoori chicken set meals, fish-head curry and vegetarian dishes.

Vintage Café MALAY, INTERNATIONAL $$
(Map p131; 13 Jln Besar, Tanah Rata; mains RM6.50-40) There's not a lot that's terribly 'vintage' about this place per se, but it does serve a decent line-up of Western and Malay staples.

Restaurant Bunga Suria INDIAN $
(Map p131; 66A Persiaran Camellia 3, Tanah Rata; set meals RM6-10) Meat, veg, *dosa*, curry, whatever: it's all good, spicy and served in large portions on a banana leaf.

Rosedale Bistro INTERNATIONAL $$
(Map p131; 42A Jln Besar, Tanah Rata; mains RM7-20) The Rosedale's thick menu spans several cuisines (Chinese, Malay, European and Indian).

ⓘ Information

The **post office**, **hospital** and **police station** are all found on Jln Besar in Tanah Rata.

ⓘ Getting There & Away

Bus

Tanah Rata's **bus station**, known as Terminal Freesia, is located at the eastern end of Jln Besar.

Destination	Duration	Fare (RM)	Frequency
Brinchang	20 min	1.50	Hourly, 6.15am-6.30pm
Kampung Raja	30 min	4	Every 2 hr 8.30am-6.30pm
Ipoh	2hr	10-18	4 daily, 8am-6pm
Kuala Lumpur	4hr	22.50-35	4 daily, 8am-4.30pm
Penang	5hr	30-35	8am, 2.30pm
Singapore	10hr	125	10am

Taxi

Taxis also wait at Terminal Freesia. Full-taxi fares are RM80 to Tapah, RM140 to Ipoh, 300 to KL and RM350 to Penang.

ⓘ Getting Around

While we never recommend hitchhiking, many travellers do so to get between Tanah Rata and Brinchang and the tea plantations beyond.

Bus

Getting between Tanah Rata and Brinchang is not a problem between 6.30am and 6.30pm, as buses run every hour or so. There are also regular buses every hour from Tanah Rata heading east to Kampung Raja, but it's more like two or three hours until the next one happens by. These buses also pass the turn-off to Gunung Brinchang and the Sungai Palas Tea Estate.

Taxi

Taxi services from Tanah Rata include Brinchang (RM6) and Ringlet (RM20); for prices on additional destinations, including hiking trailheads and tea estates, see the price list posted at the taxi stop at Terminal Freesia. For touring around, a taxi costs RM25 per hour.

Pulau Pangkor

POP 25,000

Pulau Pangkor ('Beautiful Island') is a former pirate hideout and bit-player in the battle to control the Selat Melaka (Strait of Melaka). In the 17th century, the Dutch built a fort here in their bid to monopolise the Perak tin trade, but were driven out by a local ruler before returning briefly some 50 years later. In 1874 a contender for the Perak throne sought British backing and the Pangkor Treaty was signed, ushering in British Residents and the colonial period.

These days, the only people invading the island are Malaysian weekend warriors. Pangkor doesn't see many foreign tourists, probably because its beaches aren't among Malaysia's best. Instead, the real highlight here is the low-key, village feel. The jungly interior, in particular, is wild, unexplored and isolated. During the week you've got the sand to yourself, and when it's raining on other islands, it somehow stays sunny here.

◉ Sights

Pulau Pangkor lends itself well to exploration by motorcycle. The island's east coast is its workaday side, home to **Sungai Pinang Kecil** (SPK) and **Sungai Pinang Besar** (SPB) – two Chinese-feeling fishing villages. The road that runs along the east coast turns west at Pangkor Town and runs directly across the island to **Pasir Bogak**. The beach here is a lovely, if rather narrow, stretch of sand. It's fine for swimming, but during holidays it can get crowded. From there the road runs north to the village of **Teluk Nipah**, another busy beach, and a good destination if you want to participate in water sports or snorkelling. Moving north, **Coral Beach** is the best (public) beach on Pangkor. The water is a clear, emerald-green colour due to the presence of limestone, and the beach is usually quite clean and pretty. The road then goes to the northern end of the island, past the airport, to Pangkor's luxury resorts and private beaches.

The island's religious gathering places also function as tourist sights.

Kota Belanda
RUIN

(Map p135) At Teluk Gedong, 3km south of Pangkor Town, is the Dutch Fort, built in 1670 and sacked in 1690. The Dutch managed to rebuild the fort in 1743; only five years later they abandoned it for good after local warrior chiefs repeatedly attacked them. The old fort was totally swallowed by jungle until 1973, when it was reconstructed as far as the remaining bricks would allow, which wasn't much.

Batu Bersurat
HISTORIC SITE

(Map p135) On the waterfront at Teluk Gedong, 3km south of Pangkor Town, is this mammoth stone carved with the symbol of the Dutch East India Company (Vereenigde Oost-Indische Compagnie; VOC) and other graffiti, including a faint depiction of a tiger stealing a kid. Supposedly, the child of a local European dignitary disappeared while playing near the rock; the Dutch liked the idea of a tiger abduction, although she was more likely nabbed by disenchanted locals.

Pulau Pangkor

◉ **Sights**
1	Batu Bersurat	D6
2	Foo Ling Kong	C5
3	Galeri Pangkor	D5
4	Hindu Temple	D4
5	Kota Belanda	D6

◎ **Sleeping**
6	BestStay Hotel	C5
7	Coral Bay Resort	C5
8	Pangkor Island Beach Resort	B2
9	Pangkor Laut Resort	B6
10	Pangkor Sandy Beach Resort	C5
11	Pangkor Village Beach Resort	B5

12	Puteri Bayu Beach Resort	C5
13	Sea View Hotel	C5
14	Teluk Dalam Resort	C3
15	Tiger Rock Resort	D6
16	Vikri Beach Resort	B5

◉ **Eating**
17	Guan Guan Seafood	C5
18	Pangkor Kopitiam	D5
19	Restoran Pasir Bogak	C5
	Seri Ilhan	(see 7)
20	Sin Nam Huat Seafood Restaurant	D6

Pulau Pangkor

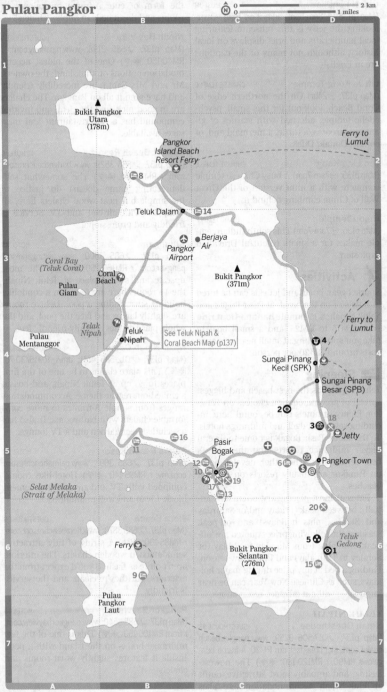

Galeri Pangkor
MUSEUM

(Map p135; ⊗8am-5pm; admission free) Overlooking the jetty is this museum featuring local handicrafts and brief displays on local history, although not many of the captions are in English.

Lin Je Kong Temple
CHINESE TEMPLE

(Map p137; ⊗24hr) On the northern edge of Coral Beach, look out for this small, psychedelic temple, adorned with statues of giant mushrooms, a turtle, a mermaid and, of course, Donald Duck.

Foo Ling Kong
CHINESE TEMPLE

(Map p135; ⊗7am-7pm) A busy Chinese temple complete with a mini version of the Great Wall of China climbing behind it.

Hindu Temple
HINDU TEMPLE

(Map p135; ⊗7am-7pm) This south Indian temple makes for a small, colourful Dravidian explosion.

Activities

Snorkel gear, boats and jet skis can be hired at hotels or on the beach at Pasir Bogak and Teluk Nipah; a 15-minute banana-boat ride costs RM15 to RM25, and a small boat to take you snorkelling at small nearby islands costs around RM20 per person.

Sleeping

Teluk Nipah has the best beach and biggest spread of accommodation choices on Pangkor. Plenty of hotels can be found here, including several budget and midrange hotels. To the south, Pasir Bogak is home to several bigger midrange resorts and the island's best restaurants. The other developments on Pangkor are luxury resorts on isolated beaches.

Rates at most places vary, often substantially, between peak (Friday and/or Saturday and Sunday, plus holidays) and off-peak seasons; the following prices quoted are 'off-peak', available from Monday to Friday (or Sunday to Thursday) and in the low season. Finding a bed at any price during major holidays, such as Chinese New Year, can be near impossible without advance reservations.

TELUK NIPAH

Nipah Guesthouse
GUESTHOUSE $$

(Map p137; ☎017-506 9259; www.pangkorbeachchalet.com; incl breakfast dm RM30, A-frame bungalows RM90, r RM120-180; ❋⊜) The newest-feeling, and arguably most attractive, outfit at Teluk Nipah. Accommodation here takes the form of cute A-frame bungalows, or rooms and dorm beds in duplex 'chalets'.

Nipah Bay Villa
GUESTHOUSE $

(Map p137; ☎685 2198; www.nipahbay.com; r RM40-150; ❋⊜) One of the oldest accommodation options on the island; the owners, Mr and Mrs Sabtu, are incredibly friendly and have seen it all on Pangkor. The chalets are in good nick, and the clean and inviting compound has a cafe/restaurant and massages available.

Budget Beach Resort
HOTEL $

(Map p137; ☎685 3529; www.budgetbeachresort.com; r RM75-120; ❋⊜) The somewhat self-deprecating name doesn't do justice to the simple but neat wood chalets here, all equipped with air-con and TV. Service is friendly and professional.

Anjungan
HOTEL $$

(Map p137; ☎685 1500; www.anjunganresortpangkor.com; r RM160-250; ❋⊜≋) The most upscale and stylish place at Teluk Nipah; the 44 rooms here are found in a condolike building surrounding a pool. Deluxe rooms are slightly larger and face the pool, and the whole place exudes a family-friendly feel.

Nazri Nipah Camp
GUESTHOUSE $

(Map p137; ☎012-585 4511; dm/r RM15/30-70; ❋⊜) This place claims to be one of the first places to go up at Teluk Nipah, and boasts a chilled-out reggae theme. Accommodation ranges from simple A-frames to more comfortable chalets with bathrooms. It also has a secluded beer garden and a TV lounge.

Palma Beach Resort
HOTEL $$

(Map p137; ☎685 3693; www.palmabeachresort.com.my; r RM95-140; ❋⊜) Hotel-like rooms, equipped with TV and air-con, in a cement block. Clean and well maintained.

Flora Beach
GUESTHOUSE $

(Map p137; ☎685 3878; www.florabeachresort.com; r RM85-100; ❋⊜) A string of tidy, attractive semidetached wooden chalets. The interiors aren't quite as flash as you'd expect from the exteriors, but they're clean, and the service is friendly.

Pangkor Bayview
HOTEL $$

(Map p137; ☎685 3540; www.pangkorbayview.com; r from RM105-150; ❋⊜) This is one of the few midrange hotels on the island with a pool. Inside it features slightly worn rooms and chalets.

Teluk Nipah & Coral Beach

N 0 ——————— 200 m
0 ——————— 0.1 miles

◎ **Sights**
1 Lin Je Kong Temple A1

🛏 **Sleeping**
2 Anjungan A2
3 Budget Beach Resort B3
4 Flora Beach...A3
   Horizon Inn .... (see 14)
5 Hornbill Resort A3
6 Nazri Nipah Camp B2
7 Nipah Bay Villa A2
8 Nipah Guesthouse B3
9 Palma Beach Resort A3
10 Pangkor Bayview A3
11 Pangkor Indah Beach Resort B3

🍴 **Eating**
12 Daddy's Café A1
13 Evening Seafood Stalls A2
14 Horizon Restaurant A2
15 Nasi Campur...A2

PERAK PULAU PANGKOR

Pangkor Indah Beach Resort GUESTHOUSE $
(Map p137; ☏685 2107; www.pangkorindah.com; r RM65; ❄🛜) They may not have much character, but the 48 rooms here are clean, good-value and equipped with air-con and TV.

Horizon Inn GUESTHOUSE $
(Map p137; ☏685 3398; r RM80-90; ❄🛜) Located above the restaurant of the same name, the 16 rooms here are plain but cosy.

Hornbill Resort GUESTHOUSE $$
(Map p137; ☏685 2005; www.pangkorhornbillresort.com; r RM100-250; ❄) Right across the street from the beach, this basic resort features rooms that are nicer than the rather plain exterior suggests.

PASIR BOGAK
Pangkor Sandy Beach Resort RESORT $$
(Map p135; ☏685 3027; www.pangkorsandybeach. com; incl breakfast r RM175-325, bungalows RM175; ❄🛜🏊) The youngest resort in a 'hood filled with old-timers. Rooms edge an inviting pool and there are three beachfront bungalows.

Vikri Beach Resort RESORT $$
(Map p135; ☏685 4258; http://vikribr.googlepages. com; r RM100-200; ❄🛜) Vikri has a dozen simple but cosy wooden and brick chalets located in scrappy gardens across the road from

the beach. More attractive are the newer 'hill view' bungalows out back. It's a peaceful, homely environment, with a kitchen serving up home-cooked Indian food (with advance notice, and for hotel guests only) and a very friendly, almost motherly staff.

Coral Bay Resort HOTEL $$
(Map p135; ☏685 5111; www.pangkorcoralbay.com. my; incl breakfast r/ste RM160-330/340; ❄🛜🎦) Ostensibly the tallest building on the island, this condo-feeling tower is filled with large and well-equipped, if dull, rooms that surround a pool.

Sea View Hotel RESORT $$
(Map p135; ☏685 1605; www.seaviewpangkor.com; incl breakfast r RM150-180, bungalows RM200-250; ❄🛜) This beachfront place has that old-school, seafront holiday vibe you may recall from family vacations (and indeed, most guests are Malaysian families). There's an inviting, palm-fringed pool, though the spartan brick bungalows have a somewhat institutional feel.

Puteri Bayu Beach Resort RESORT $$
(Map p135; ☏685 1929; www.puteribayu.com; incl breakfast RM120-175, bungalows RM200-450; ❄🛜) This vast compound, set in landscaped gardens on the beach, has a choice of adequate hotel rooms and more attractive wooden chalets.

Pangkor Village Beach Resort RESORT $$
(Map p135; ☑685 2227; www.pangkorvillageresort.
com; r RM100-180; ❀☎) Rather plain wood
and concrete bungalows at the northern end
of Pasir Bogak. The complex is located right
on the beach – a relative rarity on Pangkor –
although the proximity of water sports does
mean that noise can be an issue.

ELSEWHERE ON THE ISLAND

TOP CHOICE **Tiger Rock Resort** BOUTIQUE HOTEL $$$
(Map p135; ☑019-574 7183; www.tigerrock.info; full
board RM630-790; ❀@☎☒) For something
truly different, consider a stay in one of
these five cosy and stylish houses, each one
decked out in the individual design tastes
and assorted knick-knacks of the owners.
Whichever house you stay in, there's always
a feeling of jungly isolation thanks to the secluded location of the 5 acre grounds. Note
that the hotel doesn't accept walk-ins, and
reservations must be made at least a couple
of days in advance. Tiger Rock is found in
a somewhat concealed location behind Kota
Belanda, at Teluk Gedong; hotel staff can
provide transport or directions.

Pangkor Island Beach Resort RESORT $$$
(Map p135; ☑685 1091; www.pangkorislandbeach.
com; incl breakfast r RM452-742, bungalows RM905-
1020; ❀@☎☒) This large, secluded resort is
located on a private sandy bay at Teluk Be-
langa, at the northern end of the island, and
is the most luxurious spot on Pangkor. Some
of the rooms would benefit from a fresh coat
of paint, but the traditionally styled 'sea vil-
las' are superb. A highlight is the private
beach – probably Pangkor's best – and rec-
reational facilities include two pools, tennis
courts and a spa. There are organised activi-
ties for children.

Teluk Dalam Resort RESORT $$
(Map p135; ☑685 5000; www.pangkorresorts.com;
incl breakfast r RM230-360; ❀☎) Fronting a
wide bay at the northern end of the island
is this peaceful four-star resort. The rustic
wooden chalets and bungalows are set in
landscaped gardens overlooking the sea. It's
a little isolated and the beach isn't great, but
there's a tennis court and a children's pool as
well as organised trips and activities.

BestStay Hotel HOTEL $
(Map p135; ☑685 3111; www.beststay.com.my; r
RM70-130; ❀☎) A new-feeling hotel a brief
walk from Pangkor Town and the jetty.
Rooms are largely plain, but this is more

than made up for by the kind and outgoing
hosts, Simon and Rachel.

PANGKOR LAUT

Pangkor Laut Resort RESORT $$$
(Map p135; ☑699 1100; www.pangkorlautresort.
com; incl breakfast r RM960-1070, bungalow RM1680-
1990; ❀@☎☒) The tiny, private island of
Pangkor Laut, just opposite Pasir Bogak, is
occupied by one of Malaysia's most exclusive
tourist developments. This ridiculously luxu-
rious resort is speckled with hillside, seafront
and above-water villas stocked with king-
sized beds, balconies and huge bathrooms.
There are also private 'estates' – uniquely
designed houses, with two to four bedrooms,
private pools and gardens, on a secluded bay
away from the main resort. Every conceiv-
able amenity is at hand, and the resort boasts
seven dining outlets, a private beach and a
spa village.

✖ Eating & Drinking
TELUK NIPAH & CORAL BEACH

Daddy's Café INTERNATIONAL $$
(Map p137; mains RM14-48; ☺11am-11pm) Locat-
ed at Coral Beach, the 'Dinner Mega Entree'
at Daddy's features a decent spread of hearty
Indian set meals, as well as Western and local dishes. But the best reason to visit comes
at dinner, when Daddy's puts tables directly
on the beach.

Horizon Restaurant MALAYSIAN $$
(Map p137; mains RM9-28; ☺2-10pm) This long-
standing place has sunset views, alfresco
dining and a mix of consistently tasty Chi-
nese and Malaysian seafood and curries.
Prices are relatively high and opening times
can be unpredictable.

Evening Seafood Stalls MALAY $$
(Map p137; mains RM3-20; ☺dinner) Every night,
the strip of road that backs Teluk Nipah is
host to several informal restaurants selling
Malay-style seafood dishes.

Nasi Campur MALAY $
(Map p137; mains RM2-6; ☺breakfast, lunch & dinner) Locals stop here for cheap and tasty
Malay dishes. After dark, pickings tend to
be slim.

PASIR BOGAK
This is easily Pangkor's best eating 'hood.
Even if you're not staying here, it's worth
making the trip for at least one dinner.

TOP CHOICE **Seri Ilhan** MALAY $$

(Map p135; mains RM4-30; ⌚dinner) A roadside, Malay-style seafood shack, this place put together our most memorable meal on Pulau Pangkor. Try the rich *sup tulang* (bone soup) accompanied with a spicy grilled stingray. If you've got a serious sweet tooth, try the ABC – shaved ice drizzled with flavoured syrups and topped with ice cream.

Restoran Pasir Bogak CHINESE $$

(Map p135; mains RM8-44; ⌚dinner) This is where locals go for a Chinese-style seafood splurge and a beer – we suspect they carry every local brand of the latter. Make a point of ordering the dry chilly chicken, served with a rich, spicy paste and curry leaves – it's Chinese-Indian-Malay fusion that works a treat.

Guan Guan Seafood CHINESE, INTERNATIONAL $$

(Map p135; mains RM7-20; ⌚lunch & dinner) A simple Chinese-style seafood place doing solid versions of the usual beachy faves, as well as a few quasi-Western dishes.

PANGKOR TOWN

There are a few busy Chinese *kedai kopi* (coffee shops) in Pangkor Town, and if you've got your own wheels, the village of Sungai Pinang Besar is a great place for an old-school Chinese-style breakfast.

Sin Nam Huat Seafood Restaurant CHINESE $$

(Map p135; mains RM10-35; ⌚lunch & dinner) Longstanding place, good for crab, lobster and prawn dishes, and it serves beer late into the night. Sin Nam Huat is located at the southern end of Pangkor Town.

Pangkor Kopitiam MALAY $

(Map p135; mains RM4.50-18.90; ⌚8am-11pm) Local-style tea and coffee drinks in air-con comfort, looking over the jetty. It also does a brief menu of fried rice–type dishes.

ℹ Information

The island's **hospital** and **police station** are just west of Pangkor Town, on the road towards Pasir Bogak. There are a couple of banks and an internet cafe in Pangkor Town.

ℹ Getting There & Away

Lumut is the land gateway for Pulau Pangkor. The town is serviced by many buses, but if you get stuck, you could always crash at the **Hotel DJ Palace** (☎683 7888; www.dj.my; r RM80-130; ❄📶), located across the street from the bus station.

Air

Pangkor's tiny airport is serviced by **Berjaya Air** (☎685 1061; www.berjaya-air.com; Pangkor Airport; ⌚8am-6pm), which runs flights between Pulau Pangkor and Kuala Lumpur's Subang airport (40 minutes, RM224) every Sunday, Wednesday and Friday.

Boat

Mesra Feri and **Duta Pangkor Ferry** run boats every 30 minutes/45 minutes on an alternating basis from Lumut's jetty between 7am and 8.30pm (round-trip RM10). Many ferries from Lumut stop at SPK before reaching Pangkor Town, so don't hop off too soon. From Pangkor, boats run between 6.30am and 8.30pm. Tickets can be bought at either pier and outside of busy holidays, advance booking is not necessary.

Pangkor Island Beach Resort, Teluk Dalam Resort and Pangkor Laut Resort are all served by their own ferry service from Lumut.

Bus

Lumut's scruffy bus station is a brief walk from the jetty to Pulau Pangkor and is well connected to points elsewhere in Malaysia and abroad.

Destination	Duration (hr)	Fare (RM)	Frequency
Ipoh	2	7.20-8.50	Every 30 min, 7.30am-10.30pm
Butterworth	3½	16.30-19.60	Frequent, 8.30am-6.30pm
Kuala Lumpur	4	24.50	Frequent, 7.30am-10.30pm
Melaka	8	38	Frequent, 8.15am-8pm
Kota Bharu	8	40.30	9.45am & 9.45pm
Singapore	8-9	56	Frequent, 9-10am & 7-9pm
Hat Yai (Thailand)	9	58	8.30am & 10.30pm

ℹ Getting Around

There are no public buses available to tourists, so you will be obliged to use Pangkor's candy-pink minibus taxis, which operate between 6.30am and 9pm. Set-fare services for up to four people from the jetty in Pangkor Town include Pasir Bogak (RM10), Teluk Nipah (RM15),

Pangkor Island Beach Resort (RM20) and the airport (RM20). Travel between Teluk Nipah and Pasir Bogak will cost you RM10.

An ideal way to see the island is by motorcycle or bicycle. There are numerous places at Pangkor Town, Pasir Bogak and Teluk Nipah that rent motorcycles from around RM30 per day and bicycles for RM15.

Kuala Kangsar

POP 39,000

An easy-going town with a deep-seated sense of Malay ethnic identity, Kuala Kangsar, seat of the sultan of Perak, is one of the most pleasant royal capitals in Malaysia. It has also sat at the centre of many of the events of the past two centuries that defined modern Malaysia: first foothold of the British, who moved to control the peninsula by installing residents at the royal courts here in the 1870s; birthplace of Malaysia's rubber industry; and site of the first Durbar, or conference of Malay sultans in 1897. Yet by the 1890s, the rapid growth of Ipoh and Taiping had left Kuala Kangsar a quiet backwater steeped in Malay tradition.

The small town centre is something of a scruffy jumble, but to the southeast the royal district is spacious and quiet. The main sights are few, but they're impressive and can easily be explored on a day trip from Taiping or Ipoh.

⊙ Sights

Masjid Ubudiah   MOSQUE
(Ubudiah Mosque; Map p141; Jln Istana; admission by donation; ⊙7am-6pm) Heading out on Jln Istana beside the wide Sungai Perak, the first striking example of the wealth of the sultanate is this small but magnificent mosque, designed by AB Hubbock, the architect of many of Ipoh's colonial edifices. The mosque, with its huge golden onion-dome, was begun in 1913 but, due to wartime delays and the smashing of imported Italian marble by ram-

paging elephants, wasn't completed until 1917. The caretaker will show you around the outside of the building for a small donation, but non-Muslims are not allowed inside.

FREE **Istana Kenangan**   MUSEUM
(Map p141; Jln Istana; ⊙9.30am-5.30pm, 9.30am-12.15pm & 2.45-5.30pm Sat) Also known as the Palace of Memories, Istana Kenangan is made entirely of wood and woven bamboo, without the use of a single nail. It was built in 1931 and served as the temporary royal quarters until the nearby Istana Iskandariah, the current residence of the sultan of Perak, was completed. Today, the structure is home to a museum with displays on the state's history and the Perak royal family, although it was in the process of being renovated when we stopped by.

Istana Kota   MUSEUM
(Map p141; Jln Istana; admission adult/child RM4/2; ⊙10am-5pm Sat-Thu, 10am-noon & 2.45-5pm Fri) The Istana Kota is a beautifully restored former royal palace, incorporating Renaissance and neoclassical elements; it could put you in mind of a Mexican villa on a sunny day. Built in 1903, it now hosts an exhibition honouring the life of the current sultan of Perak, Sultan Azlan Shah: see his sunglasses, passport, shoes and a separate building that holds his five Rolls Royces, Louis Vuitton luggage and official state gifts. It's a tough life, clearly.

Istana Iskandariah   PALACE
(Map p141; Jln Istana) Overlooking the river is this palace, the official residence of the sultan of Perak and arguably the most attractive royal palace in Malaysia. Built in 1933, the building is an intriguing mix of Arab and art-deco architectural styles; if you could combine the hotels in Miami's South Beach with a mosque, it might end up looking something like this. The palace is not open to the public.

RUBBERY FACTS

In the late 1870s, a number of rubber trees were planted by British Resident Sir Hugh Low in his gardens in Kuala Kangsar from seed stock allegedly smuggled out of Brazil or taken from London's Kew Gardens. However, it was not until the invention of the pneumatic tyre in 1888, and then the popularity of the motorcar at the start of the 20th century, that rubber suddenly came into demand and rubber plantations sprang up across the country. Almost all of the trees in the new plantations were descended from Low's original rubber trees or from the Singapore Botanic Gardens. You can still see one of those first trees in Kuala Kangsar's **District Office** (Map p141; Jln Raja Chulan) compound.

Kuala Kangsar

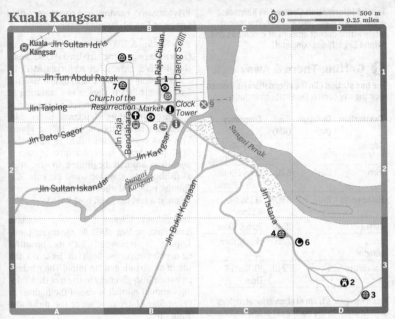

Kuala Kangsar

◎ Sights
1. District Office B1
2. Istana Iskandariah D3
3. Istana Kenangan D3
4. Istana Kota..C3
5. Malay College B1
6. Masjid Ubudiah D3
7. Pavillion Square Tower B1

⊜ Sleeping
8. Kangsar Hotel.....................................B2

⊗ Eating
9. Medan Cendol Dan Laksa C1

Malay College HISTORIC BUILDING
(Map p141; Jln Tun Abdul Razak) To the north of
town is the most impressive colonial building in Kuala Kangsar. Established in 1905, it
was the first Malay school to provide English education for the Malay elite destined
for the civil service. In the 1950s Anthony
Burgess wrote his first book while teaching
here. Not open to the public.

Pavillion Square Tower HISTORIC BUILDING
(Map p141; Jln Raja Bendahara) Opposite the Malay College is a delightful tower overlooking

the surrounding parkland and playing fields.
Built in 1930, this small three-storey sports
pavilion of Malay and colonial design allowed royalty and VIPs to view polo matches
in comfort. Not open to the public.

🛏 Sleeping & Eating

Kuala Kangsar is an easy day trip from either Ipoh or Taiping, and there's really no
reason to stay. In addition to the food hall
below, there are numerous coffee shops and
fast-food outlets around the town centre.

Kangsar Hotel BUDGET HOTEL $
(Map p141; ☎776 7301; www.kangsar-hotel.com; 32
Jln Kangsar; r RM69-128; ❄🐾) Basic but bright
and clean rooms in the centre of town.

Medan Cendol Dan Laksa MALAY $
(Map p141; Cnr Jln Temenggong & Psn Sungai Perak;
mains from RM2; ⊙lunch) As the name suggests, this open-air food hall is entirely devoted to various laksa dishes, *cendol* (shaved
ice, coconut milk and palm-sugar syrup) and
soft drinks.

ℹ Information

There are banks with ATMs along the main strip
Jln Kangsar.

Tourist Information Centre (Jln Kangsar; ⊘9am-6pm Tues-Sun) Privately run tourist office with a decent amount of brochures and helpful English-speaking staff.

① Getting There & Away

The **bus station** (Jln Raja Bendahara) is located near the city centre. Destinations include:

Destination	Duration (hr)	Cost (RM)	Frequency
Taiping	1	3.90	Every 30min, 6am-8.30pm
Ipoh	1½	6.20	Every 20min, 6am-7.35pm
Butterworth	2	9.90	11.15am & 4.15pm
Lumut	2	10.40	5pm & 10pm
Kuala Lumpur	3	22.20	Hourly, 9am-9pm
Kota Bharu	5	29.10	10.30am & 11pm

Kuala Kangsar's **train station** is located, less conveniently, to the northwest of town. All Kuala Lumpur–Butterworth trains stop here. There are four daily trains to KL (RM26 to RM49, 3½ hours) and three to Butterworth (RM17 to RM28, four hours); check with www.ktmb.com.my for the latest info on fares and schedules.

Taiping

POP 212,562

At first glance, Taiping may not appear to offer much, but scratch the surface and you'll find one of Malaysia's most well-preserved colonial towns. Not surprisingly, tourist brochures still boast of Taiping's '31 Firsts' for Malaysia, including the first museum; first railway; first newspapers in English, Malay and Tamil; and first zoo. Today, the town is a pleasing, quiet little place with a nice colonial district and great street food.

◎ Sights & Activities

FREE **Muzium Perak**   MUSEUM
(Jln Taming Sari; ⊘9am-5.30pm Sat-Thu, 9am-12.25pm & 2.45-5.30pm Fri) Perak's State Museum is housed in an impressive colonial building. Correspondingly, it's the oldest museum in Malaysia, having opened in 1883 – a fact evidenced by the rather motley collection of stuffed animals in the Natural Life section. There are several displays on the Orang Asli, and the cultural collection includes traditional kris (daggers), carvings and costumes, with a fair bit of English-language explanation.

Zoo Taiping & Night Safari   ZOO
(www.zootaiping.gov.my; Jln Taman Tasik; adult/child RM12/8, night safari adult/child RM16/10; ⊘8.30am-6pm daily, night safari 8-11pm Sun-Fri & 8pm-midnight Sat) If they're not snoozing in the midday heat, you can see all manner of creatures, including elephants, tigers, Malayan sun bears and tapirs, lolling about. The zoo's **night safari**, billed as Malaysia's first, provides a better chance of seeing nocturnal animals beginning to stir, such as fishing bats, slow loris and big cats. Zoo Taiping is located about 2km east of central Taiping; a taxi here will cost RM10.

Taman Tasik Taiping   GARDENS
(Lake Gardens; Map p143; Jln Kamunting Lama) Taiping is renowned for its beautiful 62-hectare gardens, built in 1880 on the site of an abandoned tin mine. The gardens owe their lush greenery to the fact that Taiping's annual rainfall is one of the highest in Peninsular Malaysia – hence the nickname 'Rain City'.

All Saints' Church   CHURCH
(Map p143; Jln Taming Sari; ⊘8-noon Sun) This church, dating back to 1886, is one of the oldest Anglican churches in Malaysia. The cemetery contains the graves of early colonial settlers, most of whom died of tropical diseases or failed to achieve the colonial pension needed to return home to Britain or Australia.

Commonwealth Allied War Cemetery   CEMETERY
(Jln Bukit Larut; ⊘24hr) This small cemetery has row upon row of headstones for the British, Australian and Indian troops killed during WWII. The cemetery is located about 2km east of central Taiping, along the way to Bukit Larut; a taxi here costs RM10.

Ling Nam Temple   TEMPLE
(Jln Taming Sari; ⊘7am-6pm) This colourful, gaudy temple is the oldest Chinese temple in Perak. There's sadly not much left apart from a boat figure dedicated to the emperor who built China's first canal.

Perak Prison   HISTORIC BUILDING
(Map p143; Jln Taming Sari) Opposite Muzium Perak, the prison, built in 1879 to house lawless miners, was used by the Japanese during WWII and later as a rehabilitation centre for captured communists during the

Taiping

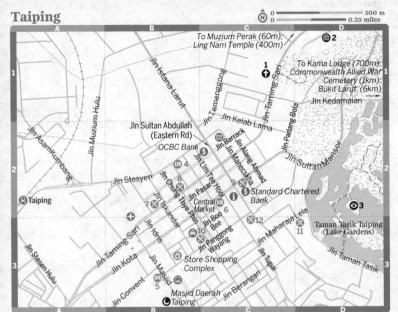

Emergency. It's still a functioning prison and is not open to the public.

Burmese Pools
RIVER

(Jln Bukit Larut; ⊙8am-7pm) A popular bathing spot in the river; a few vendors nearby sell snacks and toys. The Burmese Pools are located about 3km east of central Taiping, off the road that leads to Bukit Larut; a taxi here will cost RM10.

🛏 Sleeping

TOP CHOICE **Sentosa Villa**
HOTEL $$

(☑805 1000; www.sentosa-villa.com; Jln 8; r/villa RM148-458/258-628; ❄☎) Easily the most appealing place to stay in Taiping; the bad news is that you'll need private transport to get here. The attractive rooms are either in the main structure or in a handful of standalone and duplex wooden villas, all located at the foot of Bukit Larut (Maxwell Hill). Woods, walking paths and running water lend the place a rural, natural feel. Sentosa Villa is located about 3km outside of town, off the road that leads to Bukit Larut – follow the signs.

Panorama Hotel
HOTEL $$

(Map p143; ☑808 4111; www.panoramataiping.com; 61-79 Jln Kota; r/ste RM115-160/250; ❄☎) The

Taiping

◎ Sights
1 All Saints' Church C1
2 Perak Prison D1
3 Taman Tasik Taiping D2

🛏 Sleeping
4 Cherry Inn B2
5 Legend Inn B3
6 Panorama Hotel C2

✖ Eating
7 Annapoorana B2
8 Bismillah Restoran B2
9 Kedai Kopi Prima C2
10 Larut Matang Food Court C3
11 Pusat Makanan Taman Tasik D3
12 Pusat Penjaja Taiping C3

rooms are huge and clean in this 'downtown' Taiping hotel, if lacking in style. There's free wi-fi, and permanent discounts knock 15% off the prices shown here.

Legend Inn
HOTEL $$

(Map p143; ☑806 0000; www.legendinn.com; 2 Jln Long Jafaar; r/ste RM158-176/220-450; ❄☎) Located across a busy road from the bus station, this modern block has all the requisite

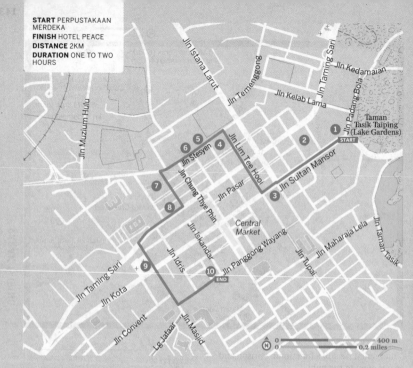

START PERPUSTAKAAN MERDEKA
FINISH HOTEL PEACE
DISTANCE 2KM
DURATION ONE TO TWO HOURS

Walking Tour
Colonial Taiping

❭ Taiping's former role as a prosperous and important colonial-era outpost is still palpable in the town's unique and well-preserved architecture. This walking tour takes in Taiping's most notable colonial-era buildings, from religious monuments to state institutions.

Start at ❶ **Perpustakaan Merdeka** (1882), the Independence Library. Nearby, the neoclassical ❷ **District Office** is on Jln Alang Ahmad. Continue south along Jln Kota until you reach ❸ **Jam Besar Lama** (1890), the Old Clock Tower, which once functioned as Taiping's fire station and now houses the tourist information centre.

Turn right at Jln Lim Tee Hooi. Upon reaching Jln Stesyen, on your left is the ❹ **Town Rest House** (1894), formerly the governor's residence (it was being renovated when we were in town). Across Jln Stesyen is the gracious, colonial ❺ **King Edward VII School** (1905), the classrooms of which were used as torture chambers by the Japanese during WWII. Taiping's original ❻ **train station** is a

few steps west; Taiping was the starting point for Malaysia's first railway line, now defunct. Opened in 1885, it ran 13.5km to Port Weld (Kuala Sepetang).

Further west on Jln Stesyen is ❼ **St George's School** (1915). Head south on Jln Iskandar then turn right onto Jln Taming Sari; here you'll find Taiping's tiny ❽ **Little India**. Follow the street west until Jln Masjid; opposite you'll see the ❾ **Old Kota Mosque** (1897), the oldest in Taiping, mainly of note for its hexagonal design.

Moving south along Jln Masjid, turn left on Jln Panggong Wayang, where you'll see the ❿ **Hotel Peace**; the Peranakan architecture of this building has stucco tiles, stained glass and beautifully carved bird and flower designs on the upper-wall dividers inside. The coffee shop downstairs is a good spot for a beer, but the scruffy hotel upstairs should be avoided.

midrange amenities, and rooms are large and brightly furnished. Expect a discount of up to 50% off the published rates.

Hotel Seri Malaysia · HOTEL $$

(☑806 9502; www.serimalaysia.com.my; 4 Jln Sultan Mansor; r incl breakfast RM140-160; ❄@🍸🏊) The large rooms (family rooms can accommodate three or four people) and pool make this a great choice for families, although the distance from the centre of town makes private transport necessary.

Cherry Inn · HOTEL $

(Map p143; ☑805 2223; 17 Jln Stesyen; r RM60-120; ❄🍸) The exterior speaks of comfy little inn, while the interior resembles a museum dedicated to Chinese kitsch. Confusing things even further, the rooms here are actually quite plain (but clean). A fully-equipped two-bedroom apartment is also available for RM250. Conveniently located.

Kama Lodge · HOTEL $$

(☑806 1777; 7 Jln Bukit Larut; r/ste RM160-200/300-320; ❄🏊) Wedding-cake duplex bungalows surround a child-friendly pool in a semirural setting. The rooms are somewhat drab and musty, but this is a good, quiet and affordable choice for families, although guests will need to have their own car – Kama is 1km east of town, along the way to Bukit Larut.

✗ Eating

Bismillah Restoran · MALAY $

(Map p143; 138 Jln Taming Sari; mains from RM3; ☉7am-5pm) Your typical *nasi kandar* (Indian/Malaysian-style dishes served over rice) restaurant found all over Malaysia; the biryani here is particularly tasty.

Annapoorana · INDIAN $

(Map p143; Jln Taming Sari; mains from RM3; ☉9am-9pm) This shophouse restaurant offers a mix of southern Indian and Nepali dishes; fresh chapattis and vegetarian rice sets define the latter.

ℹ Information

You'll find a few banks with ATMs along Jln Kota.

Tourist Information Centre (355 Jln Kota; ☉10am-5pm) Located in the former clock tower, this office offers a few brochures, but little information is available in English, and the same goes for the staff.

ℹ Getting There & Away

Taiping's long-distance bus station, Kemunting Raya, is 7km north of the town centre, at Kemunting – hop on bus 8 (RM1.20, 6am to 8.30pm) to get to/from the local bus station, or take a taxi (RM10) to the town centre. Destinations include:

Destination	Duration (hr)	Fare (RM)	Frequency
Ipoh	1½	8.40	Frequent, 7am-6.30pm
Butterworth	2	7	Hourly, 6.30am-8.40pm
Kuala Lumpur	4	23	Every 30min, 6.30am-10.30pm
Kota Bharu	8	31.90	10.45am
Singapore	9	55	11am, 9pm, 10.30pm & 11pm

PERAK TAIPING

STREET FOOD CITY

Despite being a heck of a lot smaller, Taiping just about rivals George Town in the street-food department.

Kedai Kopi Prima (Map p143; cnr Jln Kota & Jln Mancksha; mains from RM3; ☉10am-midnight) This big, busy Chinese coffee shop spills out onto the street in the evenings, with several vendors selling a mix of Chinese and Malay dishes. Big-screen TVs, music and endless crowds make for a lively atmosphere.

Pusat Makanan Taman Tasik (Map p143; Jln Maharaja Lela; mains from RM3; ☉24hr) A busy hawker court/coffee shop with a good selection of mostly Chinese stalls.

Pusat Penjaja Taiping (Map p143; Jln Tupai; mains from RM3; ☉9am-11pm) Open-air food court with a mix of vendors. Open at lunch but busier at night.

Larut Matang Food Court (Map p143; Jln Panggung Wayang; mains from RM3; ☉11am-7pm) Busiest at lunch, this gritty court is half Chinese and half Malay; the offerings at the latter generally get more takers, but you'll need to get there before 7pm.

Local buses leave from the local bus station across the street from Masjid Daerah Taiping; **taxis** depart from the Central Market. Destinations include Kuala Kangsar, with departures every half hour from 6am to 8.30pm (one hour, RM3.90), and Lumut (for Pulau Pangkor), with one daily departure at 7am (three hours, RM10).

Taiping's train station is 1km west of the town centre, on the Kuala Lumpur–Butterworth line. There are four daily trains to Kuala Lumpur (RM28 to RM53, four to 5½ hours) and three to Butterworth (RM15 to RM23, around two hours).

Around Taiping

BUKIT LARUT

Crouched in a wet and cool colonial atmosphere some 1019m above sea level is Bukit Larut (Maxwell Hill), the oldest hill station in Malaysia. It's not nearly as developed as the Cameron Highlands, and while the scenery is a little less dramatic, there's more of a sense of what hill stations were originally about: elegant bungalows, quiet lanes, sweet-smelling gardens and not much more noise than the wind in the leaves. There are no attractions other than the above, which suits some folks just fine.

Few people visit Bukit Larut, however – in fact, bungalows here only accommodate around 70 visitors. During the school holidays, all are full. Even if you don't stay, Bukit Larut can be an excellent day trip. Getting up to the hill station is half the fun, and once there, you've got excellent opportunities for walks and fine views over Taiping far below.

◎ Sights & Activities

Most visitors go up and back by Land Rover, though the hill is also a favourite with locals who walk up in the mornings. It's a very scenic path, but don't imagine this is some casual stroll – you need to be fit to complete the walk, which spans more than 10km and can take as long as four hours.

The Land Rovers take visitors as far as KM10.3, home to a few state-run bungalows and a sporadically manned visitor centre. Beyond this point, walking along the main road, with rich forest on either side, is pleasant enough, and at the summit of the mountain – an additional 30-minute walk – a rougher trail leads off the main road from between the two transmission towers. The trail follows a practically abandoned path to Gunung Hijau (1448m). You can usually only follow the leech-ridden path for about 15 minutes to an old pumping station (now functioning as a small Shiva shrine), but even on this short walk there's a good chance of seeing monkeys and numerous birds. Beyond the shrine the trail is periodically cleared but quickly becomes overgrown; it's advisable to take a guide with you. If you do make it to the summit, on clear days you can see clear out to the Selat Melaka (Strait of Melaka).

🛏 Sleeping & Eating

In addition to the below, there are quite a few more private bungalows for rent on Bukit Larut; details and reservations can be obtained at the Land Rover station.

Cendana Hut   HOTEL **$$**
(☑806 2777; r 110-170) This hilltop villa is the only accommodation on Bukit Larut that offers rooms, as opposed to entire bungalows. Cendana is also home to the only restaurant (serving simple Malaysian dishes; mains RM2.50 to RM7) on Bukit Larut. The downside is that the rooms – despite having names like Monte Carlo and Christmas Marvel – are past their prime and are rather musty, making them overpriced. Cendana is a short walk uphill from KM10.3. The views from here are great.

Government Bungalows   BUNGALOW **$$**
(☑807 7241; bungalow RM150-300) The government oversees three bungalows located around the Land Rover stop at KM10.3. The bungalows can accommodate up to 10 people and come complete with kitchens – a necessity, as there's only one restaurant on Bukit Larut. Call ahead or inquire at the Land Rover station.

❶ Getting There & Away

Prior to WWII, you had the choice of walking, riding a pony or being carried up in a sedan chair, as there was no road to the station. Today there's a road, but private cars are not allowed on it – it's only open to government Land Rovers, which run a regular service (round-trip RM6) from the station at the foot of the hill; a taxi here from Taiping should cost RM10. In theory, the Land Rovers operate roughly every hour on the hour from 8am to 3pm, but they usually only run when there's enough customers. The trip takes about 30 minutes.

MATANG MANGROVE FOREST RESERVE

Found outside Kuala Sepetang – still shown on some maps under its old name of Port

Weld – is this reserve (⊘8am-5pm Mon-Fri), a small part of the mangrove forest that stretches from here up the coast of Perak towards Seberang Perai (Penang). The greater area represents almost half of all Malaysia's gazetted mangrove cover, and is one of the country's most significant nature reserves. It is particularly known for its fireflies, which light up light Christmas trees every night.

The entrance to the reserve is about 500m outside the town; ask the bus driver to let you off when you see the big gateway and sign on your right reading 'Pejabat Hutan Kecil Paya Laut'. Here a raised wooden walkway winds its way through a small section of the reserve, allowing you to explore this fascinating ecosystem without getting your feet damp. There are several signs along the route explaining, in English, what plants you are looking at and how it all works. Smooth otters, leopard cats and macaques all inhabit this landscape, though you're unlikely to see much more than the odd bird and scampering lizard unless you're here in the early morning or evening.

You can explore the mangroves further by charter boat – which allows views of the reserve's famous fireflies if you book at night – although it can get quite expensive. The reserve office can set you up with a guide, but expect to pay around RM350 to RM500 for the day.

❶ Getting There & Away

Blue Omnibus 77 runs every 40 minutes from 6.05am to 7pm between Taiping's local bus station and Kuala Sepetang (30 minutes, RM1.90). Buses can drop you at the reserve on request.

Royal Belum State Park

This state park (☑522 5125; www.royalbelum. my) in the northernmost corner of Perak is one of Peninsular Malaysia's largest stretches of virgin jungle. This green dream of a wilderness, which constitutes the Belum-Temenggor Forest, fairly seethes with birdlife and some of the nation's most dramatic megafauna: tapirs, tigers, sun bears, panthers and the endangered Sumatran rhino, whose preservation was one of the motivating factors behind gazetting the park.

Visiting the state park requires advance permission, which can be arranged by just about any hotel in the area at least one week in advance. Otherwise, the resorts below all offer various excursions into the jungle south of the park. Because much of the area was inundated after Temenggor Dam was completed in 1972, all excursions are conducted by boat.

🍴 Sleeping & Eating

Although none of the below is located in the state park, each is well positioned for excursions in and around the protected area.

TOP CHOICE **Belum Eco Resort** RESORT $$
(☑012-524 9184; www.belumecoresort.com.my; all-inclusive 3-day/2-night package per person RM590) Be a guest of the Khong family on their own private island – previously a mountaintop before the Temenggor Dam was built. Accommodation here is in a houseboat, bungalow or villa, and the fee includes boat transport to and from the island, all meals and accommodation, and excursions including a visit to an Orang Asli village and jungle trekking to a waterfall and rafflesia flower. Although Steve Khong is a welcoming host, it's worth mentioning that accommodation here is on the basic end of the spectrum. Book ahead to ensure a bed and to arrange transport from the jetty to Pulau Banting.

Belum Rainforest Resort RESORT $$
(☑791 6800; www.belumresort.com; r incl breakfast RM288-388; ❈@🛜) A smallish resort of 76 rooms successfully combining industrial (textured concrete, brick) and natural (bamboo) elements. When we visited, a spa, a pool and additional rooms were being built. As with the other resorts in the area, visits to the protected area and other outdoor pursuits can be arranged here (per person RM70 to RM351).

Jemputree HOTEL $$
(☑791 2214; www.jemputreeresort.my; incl breakfast r/ste RM250-380/600; ❈🛜🏊) Looking over the lake, this huge complex (115 rooms) is clean and professional (if lacking a little character), with the Superior rooms offering great views over Temenggor Lake. Nature activities in the surrounding jungle can be arranged here.

Hotel Sun HOTEL $
(☑791 4797; 29 Jln Toh Shah Bandar, Gerik; r RM60-90; ❈🛜) If you get stuck in Gerik, the transit town to Belum, you can do much worse than this new hotel behind the bus station. There are a few similar places, and several restaurants, nearby.

PERAK ROYAL BELUM STATE PARK

ℹ Getting There & Away

There are two ways to get to Belum. The easiest is to hop on any bus bound for Kota Bharu from Butterworth, Ipoh, Kuala Kangsar or Taiping; ask the driver to drop you off at Jeti Pulau Banting for the boat to Belum Eco Resort, or at either of the other two resorts above. All are located near Hwy 76, which continues towards the Thai border and Kota Bharu; you'll be expected to pay the full fare to Kota Bharu.

Another option is to get yourself to Gerik (sometimes spelt Grik and pronounced 'Greek'), where taxis at the town's bus station will take you the remaining 40km to Jeti Pulau Banting or the resorts for RM50.

Leaving Belum, buses from Kota Bharu are unpredictable, so you'll probably have to take a taxi to Gerik (RM50), and continue by bus from there. Departures from Gerik's bus station include the following:

Destination	Duration (hr)	Fare (RM)	Frequency
Ipoh	2	13.10	8.30am, 11am, 2pm, 4pm & 7pm
Kota Bharu	4	29.10	11.45am
Kuala Lumpur	5	30.50	9am, 10.45am, 10pm & 2am

Penang

Includes »

George Town...................151
Batu Ferringhi 176
Teluk Bahang &
Around...........................179
Pulau Jerejak................180
Snake Temple.................181
Batu Maung....................181
Kampung Pulau
Betong...........................181
Teluk Kumbar 182

Best Places
to Stay

» 23 Love Lane (p164)

» Straits Collection (p164)

» Lone Pine Hotel (p177)

» China Tiger (p166)

» New Asia Heritage
Hotel (p163)

Best Places to Eat

» Lorong Baru (New Lane)
Hawker Stalls (p170)

» Teksen (p167)

» China House (p167)

» Sea Pearl Lagoon
Cafe (p169)

» Gurney Drive Hawker
Stalls (p170)

Why Go?

'Pearl of the Orient', Penang's nickname, conjures romantic images of trishaws pedalling past watermarked Chinese shophouses, blue joss smoke and a sting of chilli in the air; or maybe it's ornate temples, and gold-embroidered saris displayed in shop windows, next to mosques sending a call to the midday prayer. But really, whatever you're imagining, chances are that Penang *is* that reality. Add surprises like slick cafes, antiseptic shopping malls, jungles and white beaches and you'll have an even sharper image.

Historically, Penang was the waterway between Asia's two halves and the outlet to the markets of Europe and the Middle East. As such, the island sits on the juncture of Asia's great kingdoms and colonial empires. Today the culture of this region, forged over decades of colonialism, commercial activity and hosting tourists, is one of Malaysia's most tolerant, cosmopolitan and exciting, especially on the palate.

When to Go
George Town

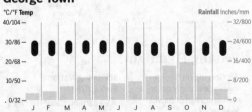

Jan–Feb Book accommodation in advance if visiting George Town during Chinese New Year.	**Jun–Jul** Penang's famous durian and other fruit are at their peak during summer.	**Jul** The George Town Festival lights up the entire month with theatre, dance and music.

History

Little is known of Penang's early history. Chinese seafarers were aware of the island, which they called Betelnut Island, as far back as the 15th century, but it appears to have been uninhabited. It wasn't until the early 1700s that colonists arrived from Sumatra and established settlements at Batu Uban and the area now covered by southern George Town. The island came under the control of the sultan of Kedah, but in 1771 the sultan signed the first agreement with the British East India Company, handing them trading rights in exchange for military assistance against Siam.

Fifteen years later Captain Francis Light, on behalf of the East India Company, took possession of Penang, which was formally

PENANG GEORGE TOWN

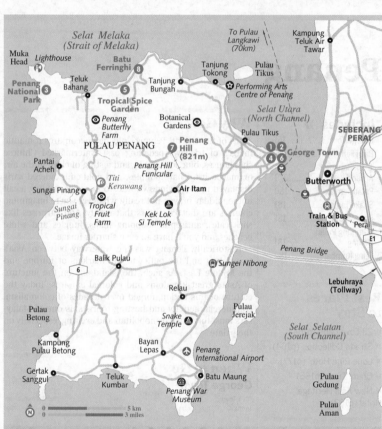

Penang Highlights

1 Gorging on George Town's seemingly never-ending spread of **hawker food** (p167)

2 Getting a virtual crash-course in feng shui at the **Cheong Fatt Tze Mansion** (p159)

3 Hiking through jungles to monkey beaches

at **Penang National Park** (p179)

4 Learning about the city's architectural heritage from street level on a **walking tour** (p161) of George Town

5 Becoming familiar with the contents of your spice rack at the **Tropical Spice Garden** (p177)

6 Indulging in a stay at one of George Town's unique **heritage hotels** (p162)

7 Enjoying the cool breezes and fantastic views of the island from atop **Penang Hill** (p157)

8 Sun-tanning and cocktail drinking at a resort in **Batu Ferringhi** (p176)

signed over in 1791. Light renamed it Prince of Wales Island, as the acquisition date fell on the prince's birthday. Light permitted new arrivals to claim as much land as they could clear and this, together with a duty-free port and an atmosphere of liberal tolerance, quickly attracted settlers from all over Asia. By the turn of the 18th century Penang was home to over 10,000 people.

Penang briefly became the capital of the Straits Settlements (which included Melaka and Singapore) in 1826, until it was superseded by the more thriving Singapore. By the middle of the 19th century, Penang had become a major player in the Chinese opium trade, which provided more than half of the colony's revenue. It was a dangerous, rough-edged place, notorious for its brothels and gambling dens, all run by Chinese secret societies.

There was little action in Penang during WWI but WWII was a different story. When it became evident that the Japanese would attack, Penang's Europeans were immediately evacuated, leaving behind a largely defenceless population. Japan took over the island on 19 December 1941, only 12 days after the attack on Pearl Harbour in the US. The following three and a half years were the darkest of Penang's history.

Things were not the same after the war. The local impression of the invincibility of the British had been irrevocably tainted and the end of British imperialism seemed imminent. The Straits Settlements were dissolved in 1946; Penang became a state of the Federation of Malaya in 1948 and one of independent Malaysia's 13 states in 1963.

With its free-port status withdrawn in 1969, Penang went through several years of decline and high unemployment. Over the next 20 years, the island was able to build itself up as one of the largest electronics manufacturing centres of Asia and is now sometimes dubbed the 'Silicon Valley of the East'. Today, Penang is the only state in Malaysia that has elected an ethnic Chinese chief minister since independence.

George Town

☑04 / POP 740,200

It's full of car exhaust fumes and has a marked lack of footpaths, but George Town is able to woo even the most acute cityphobe with its explosive cultural mishmash in a scene fit for a movie set.

Dodge traffic while strolling past Chinese shophouses where people might be roasting coffee over a fire or sculpting giant incense for a ceremony. Trishaws, sightseeing tourists and locals cruise around the maze of chaotic streets and narrow lanes, past British Raj–era architecture, strings of paper lanterns and retro-chic pubs, boutiques and cafes that wouldn't be out of place in a Western city. Arrive on an empty stomach and graze at will; between the city's outrageous hawker food and a handful of burgeoning modern restaurants this is the food capital of Malaysia.

Though each of the city's districts is distinct, they do overlap; you'll find Chinese temples in Little India and mosques in Chinatown. Along certain streets you'll have your pick of delicious Indian curries, spicy Malay specialities or local Chinese noodle creations all lined up one after the other. And just to confuse you even more, outside the historic centre, Western-style soaring skyscrapers and massive shopping complexes gleam high above.

◉ Sights

CHINATOWN

Khoo Kongsi HISTORIC BUILDING
(Map p152; www.khookongsi.com.my; 18 Cannon Sq; admission adult/child RM10/1; ◉9am-6pm) The *kongsi*, or clanhouse, is a major node of overseas Chinese communities, and the Khoo Kongsi is the most impressive one in Penang.

PENANG GEORGE TOWN

ISLAND OR STATE?

The strip of mainland coast known as Seberang Perai (or Province Wellesley) is the mainland portion of the state that many people don't even know is Penang. The state of Penang is divided both geographically and administratively into two sections: Pulau Penang (Penang Island), a 293 sq km island in the Strait of Melaka, and Seberang Perai, a narrow 760 sq km strip on the peninsular mainland. George Town, on Penang Island, is the state capital, while Butterworth is the largest town in Seberang Perai. Confusingly, the city of George Town is often referred to as just 'Penang' or 'Pinang'.

George Town

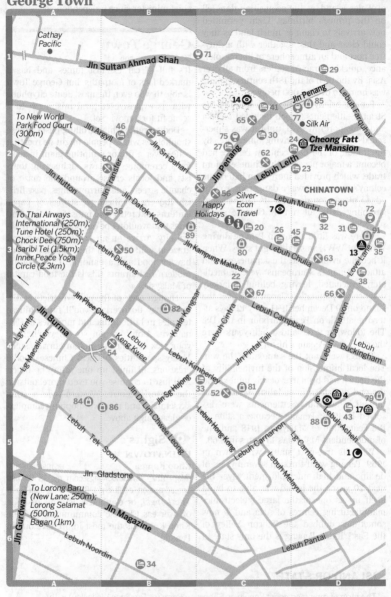

To New World
Park Food Court
(300m)

To Thai Airways
International (250m);
Tune Hotel (250m);
Chock Dee (750m);
Isaribi Tei (1.5km);
Inner Peace Yoga
Circle (2.3km)

To Lorong Baru
(New Lane; 250m);
Lorong Selamat
(500m),
Bagan (1km)

PENANG

Jln Sultan Ahmad Shah

Cathay
Pacific

Jln Penang

Lebuh Farquhar

Silk Air

**Cheong Fatt
Tze Mansion**

Lebuh Leith

CHINATOWN

Lebuh Muntri

Silver-
Econ
Travel

Happy
Holidays

Jln Argyll

Jln Sri Bahari

Jln Penang

Jln Transfer

Jln Hutton

Jln Datok Keya

Jln Kampung Malabar

Lebuh Dickens

Kuala Kangsar

Lebuh Chulia

Love Lane

Lebuh Campbell

Lebuh Cintra

Lebuh Carnarvon

Lebuh
Buckingham

Jln Phee Choon

Lebuh
Keng Kwee

Lebuh Kimberley

Jln Pintal Tali

Lg Kintra

Lg Macalister

Jln Burma

Jln Dr Lim Chwee Leong

Jln Sg Hujong

Lebuh Hong Kong

Lebuh Carnarvon

Lg Carnarvon

Lebuh Acheh

Lebuh Melayu

Jln Gladstone

Jln Gurdwara

Jln Magazine

Lebuh Noordin

Lebuh Pantai

Lebuh Tek Soon

The Khoo, who trace their lineage back 25 generations, are a successful clan, and they're letting the world know. Stone carvings dance across the entrance hall and pavilions, many of which symbolise or are meant to attract good luck and wealth.

Note the Sikh guardian watchman at the entrance. The interior is dominated by incredible murals depicting birthdays, weddings and, most impressively, the 36 celestial guardians (divided into two panels of 18 guardians each). The fiery overhead lighting

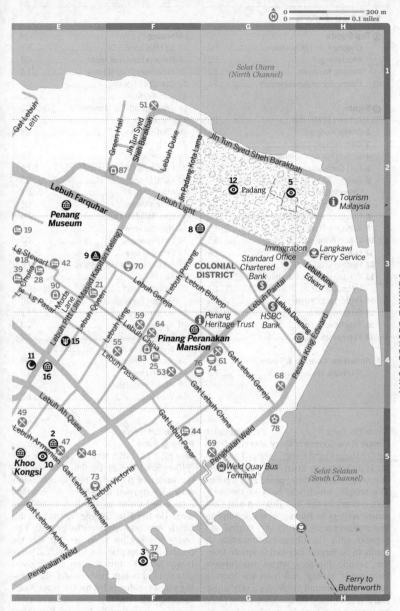

N
0 — 200 m
0 — 0.1 miles

Selat Utara
(North Channel)

Gat Lebuh Leith

Green Hall

Jln Tun Syed Sheh Barakbah

Lebuh Duke

Jln Padang Kota Lama

Jln Tun Syed Sheh Barakbah

51

87

Lebuh Farquhar

Penang Museum
19

Lebuh Light

12 Padang

5

Tourism Malaysia

8

Lg Stewart
18
39
28
90

9

70

Immigration Office
Standard Chartered Bank

Langkawi Ferry Service

Lebuh King Edward

Lg Chulia
Muda Lane
21

Lebuh Pitt (Jln Masjid Kapitan Keling)
Lebuh Queen

Lebuh Penang

Lebuh Gereja

Lebuh Bishop

COLONIAL DISTRICT

Lebuh Pantai

Lebuh Downing

Pesara King Edward

Lg Pasar
42

15

Lebuh King

Lebuh China

59
64

Penang Heritage Trust

Pinang Peranakan Mansion

HSBC Bank

11
16

55

Lebuh Pasar

83

25
53

76
74

61

Gat Lebuh Gereja

68

Lebuh Ah Quee

Gat Lebuh China

Gat Lebuh Pasar

49

Lebuh Armenian

2
47

48

78

Khoo Kongsi
10

73

Lebuh Victoria

44

69

Pangkalan Weld

Weld Quay Bus Terminal

Selat Selatan
(South Channel)

Gat Lebuh Armenian

Gat Lebuh Acheh

Pangkalan Weld

3
37

Ferry to Butterworth

E
F
G
H

1
2
3
4
5
6

PENANG GEORGE TOWN

comes courtesy of enormous paper lamps. Gorgeous ceramic sculptures of immortals, carp, dragons, and carp becoming dragons (a traditional Chinese motif symbolising success) dance across the roof ridges. As impressive as all of this is, Khoo Kongsi

was once more ostentatious; the structure caught fire on the night it was completed in 1901, an event put down to divine jealousy. The present *kongsi* dates from 1906. At research time, a hotel was being built on the premises.

George Town

◉ Top Sights

Cheong Fatt Tze Mansion.....................D2
Khoo Kongsi..................................E5
Penang Museum................................E2
Pinang Peranakan Mansion.................F4

◉ Sights

1 Acheen St Mosque D5
2 Cheah Kongsi.................................E5
3 Clan Jetties................................F6
4 Dr Sun Yat Sen's Penang Base.............D5
5 Fort Cornwallis................................G2
6 George Town World Heritage Inc.
    Headquarters............................. D5
7 Hainan Temple.................................C3
8 House of Yeap Chor Ee.........................F3
9 Kuan Yin Teng................................E3
10 Lebuh Armenia................................E5
11 Masjid Kapitan Keling........................E4
12 Padang................................G2
13 Penang Gelugpa Buddhist
    Association D3
14 Protestant Cemetery C1
15 Sri Mariamman Temple........................E4
16 Teochew Temple................................E4
17 Yap Kongsi................................D5

◉ Activities, Courses & Tours

18 Nazlina's Spice Station E3

◉ Sleeping

19 23 Love Lane................................E3
20 Banana Boutique Hotel C3
21 Broadway Budget Hotel E3
22 Campbell House C3
23 Cathay Hotel................................D2
24 Cheong Fatt Tze Mansion D2
25 China Tiger................................F4
26 Chulia Heritage..................................C3
27 Cititel Hotel................................C2
28 Coffee Atelier................................E3
29 Eastern & Oriental Hotel......................D1
30 Hotel Malaysia C2
31 Moon Tree 47................................D3
32 Muntri Mews................................D3
33 New Asia Heritage Hotel C4
34 Noordin Mews................................B6
35 Old Penang................................D3
36 Penaga Hotel................................B3
37 PG Chew Jetty Homestay F6
38 Red Inn................................D3
    Red Inn Court.............................(see 21)
    Reggae Penang............................(see 38)
39 Roommates................................E3
40 Ryokan................................D3
41 Segara Ninda C2
42 Seven Terraces E3
43 Straits Collection...................................D5
44 Victoria Inn................................F5
45 Yeng Keng Hotel................................D3
46 Yes Hotel B2

Kuan Yin Teng   BUDDHIST TEMPLE

(Temple of the Goddess of Mercy; Map p152; Lebuh Pitt (Jln Masjid Kapital Keling); ☺24hr) This temple is dedicated to Kuan Yin – the goddess of mercy, good fortune, peace and fertility. The temple, which was built in the early 19th century by the first Hokkien and Cantonese settlers in Penang, is not so impressive architecturally, but it's very central and popular with the Chinese community. It seems to be forever swathed in smoke from the outside furnaces where worshippers burn paper money, and from the incense sticks waved around inside. It's a very active place, and Chinese theatre shows take place on the goddess' birthday, celebrated on the 19th day of the second, sixth and ninth lunar months.

The temple was being renovated when we were in town, and there's talk of adding a visitor centre.

Dr Sun Yat Sen's Penang Base   MUSEUM

(Map p152; 120 Lebuh Armenian; admission RM3; ☺10am-5pm Mon-Sat) Dr Sun Yat Sen was the leader of the 1911 Chinese revolution, which overturned the Ching dynasty and established China as the first republic in Asia. He lived in George Town with his family for about six months in 1910. This house was not his residence but was the central meeting place for his political party. It was here the 1910 Canton uprising was planned – although unsuccessful, the uprising was a turning point for the revolution's success. Today the structure serves as a museum documenting Dr Sun Yat Sen's time in Penang, and even if you're not interested in history, it is worth a visit simply for a peek inside a stunningly restored antique shophouse.

⊗ Eating

	1885	(see 29)
47	Amelie	E5
48	China House	E5
49	Edelweiss	E5
50	Ee Beng Vegetarian Food	B3
51	Esplanade Food Centre	F1
52	Goh Huat Seng	C4
53	Hui Sin Vegetarian Restaurant	F4
54	Joo Hooi	B4
55	Karai Kudi	F4
56	Kashmir	C2
57	Kheng Pin	C2
58	La Bohème	B2
59	Madras New Woodlands Restaurant	F4
60	Nasi Padang Minang	B2
61	Quay Café	G4
62	Red Garden Food Paradise & Night Market	C2
63	Sky Hotel	D3
64	Sri Ananda Bahwan	F4
65	Sup Hameed	C2
66	Teksen	D3
67	Tho Yuen Restaurant	C3
68	Via Pre	G4
69	Weld Quay Seafood Restaurant	G5

⊙ Drinking

70	B@92	F3
71	Beach Blanket Babylon	C1
72	Behind 50 Love Lane	D3
73	Canteen	E5
	Farquhar's Bar	(see 29)
74	Jing-Si Books & Cafe	G4
75	Soho Free House	C2
76	Ten Yee Tea Trading	F4
77	Upper Jln Penang Bars	D2

⊙ Entertainment

78	QEII	G5

🔒 Shopping

79	88 Armenian Street	D5
80	Ban Hin	C3
81	Bee Chin Heong	C4
	China Joe's	(see 79)
82	Chowraster Bazaar	B4
83	Gallery 29	F4
84	Komtar	A5
85	Little Penang Street Market	D1
86	Prangin Mall	B5
87	Royal Selangor	F2
88	Rozanas Batik	D5
89	Sam's Batik House	B3
90	Springsfield	E3
91	Unique Penang	D3

PENANG GEORGE TOWN

Acheen St Mosque MOSQUE

(Map p152; Lebuh Acheh; ⊙7am-7pm) Built in 1808 by a wealthy Arab trader, the Acheen St Mosque was the focal point for the Malay and Arab traders in this quarter – the oldest Malay *kampung* (village) in George Town. It's unusual for its Egyptian-style minaret – most Malay mosques have Moorish minarets.

Hainan Temple CHINESE TEMPLE

(Map p152; Lebuh Muntri; ⊙9am-6pm) Dedicated to Mar Chor Poh, the patron saint of seafarers, this temple was founded in 1870 but not completed until 1895. A thorough remodelling for its centenary in 1995 refreshed its distinctive swirling dragon pillars and brightened up the ornate carvings.

COLONIAL DISTRICT & LITTLE INDIA

Pinang Peranakan Mansion MUSEUM

(Map p152; www.pinangperanakanmansion.com.my; 29 Lebuh Gereja; admission adult/child RM10/5; ⊙9.30am-5.30pm Mon-Sat) This building rivals the Cheong Fatt Tze Mansion as the most stunning restored residence in the city. Every door, wall and archway is carved and often painted in gold leaf; the grand rooms are furnished with majestic wood furniture with intricate mother-of-pearl inlay; and bright-coloured paintings and fascinating black and white photos of the family in regal Chinese dress grace the walls. The house belonged to Chung Keng Quee, a 19th-century merchant, secret society leader and community pillar as well as being one of the wealthiest Baba-Nonyas of that era.

After visiting the house, be sure to also check out Chung Keng Kwi Temple, the adjacent ancestral hall, which by comparison feels decidedly less flashy.

Penang Museum MUSEUM

(Map p152; www.penangmuseum.gov.my; Lebuh Farquhar; admission RM1; ⊙9am-5pm Sat-Thu) This is one of the best-presented state museums in Malaysia. There are engaging exhibits on the customs and traditions of Penang's various ethnic groups, with photos, documents, costumes, furniture and other well-labelled displays. Upstairs is the history

UNESCO & GEORGE TOWN

In 2008 the historic centre of George Town was declared a Unesco World Heritage Site for having 'a unique architectural and cultural townscape without parallel anywhere in East and Southeast Asia'. Property values skyrocketed and old buildings, once abandoned, were snatched up by developers hoping to cash in on the ensuing boom. Thankfully, Penang is full of heritage activists, and in general, the city has safeguarded its age-old feel while also reaping the benefits of a facelift.

For information on George Town's World Heritage status, stop by the **George Town World Heritage Inc. Headquarters** (Map p152; www.gtwhi.com.my; 116-118 Lebuh Acheh; ☉8am-1pm & 2-5pm Mon-Thurs, 8am-12.15pm & 2.45-5pm Fri), where you'll find displays and media about the city's architectural heritage. An excellent guide to the city's build-ings that also covers many of the main sights is the *George Town World Heritage Site Architectural Walkabout*, available at the Penang Heritage Trust (p174). *Value Your Built Heritage*, available at George Town World Heritage Inc., is an informative and entertain-ing pocket guide to George Town's shophouse styles.

gallery, with a collection of early 19th-centu-ry watercolours by Captain Robert Smith, an engineer with the East India Company, and prints showing landscapes of old Penang. You can also play videos of Penang's many cultural festivals.

House of Yeap Chor Ee   MUSEUM
(Map p152; www.houseeyce.com; 4 Lebuh Penang; admission adult/child RM8/free; ☉10am-6pm Tues-Sun) This museum, housed in an exquisitely restored three-storey shophouse mansion, is dedicated to a former resident, itinerant barber-turned-banker Yeap Chor Ee. In ad-dition to family photos and mementos, the museum has interesting exhibits on Chinese immigration to Penang. An audio tour is available for RM10, and admission is free if you dine at Sire, the attached restaurant.

Clan Jetties   NEIGHBOURHOOD
(Map p152; Pengkalan Weld) During the late 18th and early 19th centuries, Pengkalan Weld was the centre of one of the world's most thriving ports and provided plentiful work for the never-ending influx of immi-grants. Soon a community of Chinese grew up around the quay, with floating and stilt houses built along rickety docks; these dock-ing and home areas became known as the clan jetties.

Today the clan jetties are low-income areas with a jumble of dilapidated floating houses and planks, and are becoming popu-lar tour bus stops. If you get here sans tour bus, it's a fun place to wander around with docked fishing boats, folks cooking in their homes and kids running around. There is also a homestay option here (p166).

Fort Cornwallis   HISTORIC SITE
(Map p152; Lebuh Light; admission adult/child RM2/1; ☉9am-7pm) For all its size, this fort isn't particularly impressive; only the outer walls stand, enclosing a rather aged and spare park within. The fort is named for Charles Cornwallis, perhaps best known for surrendering at the Battle of Yorktown to George Washington, effectively ending the American Revolution. It was at the site of the fort that Captain Light first set foot on the virtually uninhabited island in 1786 and established the free port where trade would, he hoped, be lured from Britain's Dutch ri-vals. Between 1808 and 1810 convict labour replaced the then-wooden building materi-als with stone. The star-profile shape of the walls allowed for overlapping fields of fire against enemies.

Protestant Cemetery   CEMETERY
(Map p152; Jln Sultan Ahmad Shah; ☉24hr) Here you'll find the graves of Captain Francis Light and many others, including governors, merchants, sailors and Chinese Christians who fled the Boxer Rebellion in China (a movement opposing Western imperial-ism and evangelism) only to die of fever in Penang, all under a canopy of magnolia trees. Also here is the tomb of Thomas Le-onowens, the young officer who married Anna – the schoolmistress to the King of Siam made famous by *The King and I*.

Sri Mariamman Temple   HINDU TEMPLE
(Map p152; Lebuh Pitt (Jln Masjid Kaptian Keling); admission free; ☉7am-7pm) For local Tamils, this temple fulfils the purpose of a Chinese clanhouse; it's a reminder of the motherland and the community bonds forged within the

diaspora. Sri Mariamman was built in 1883 and is George Town's oldest Hindu house of worship. It is a typically south Indian temple, dominated by the *gopuram* (entrance tower).

Penang's Thaipusam (p160) procession begins here, and in October a wooden chariot takes the temple's deity for a spin around the neighbourhood during Vijayadasami festivities.

Masjid Kapitan Keling   MOSQUE
(Map p152; cnr Lebuh Buckingham & Lebuh Pitt (Jln Masjid Kapitan Keling); admission free; ☉7am-7pm) Penang's first Indian Muslim settlers (East India Company troops) built Masjid Kapitan Keling in 1801. The mosque's domes are yellow, in a typically Indian-influenced Islamic style, and it has a single minaret. It looks sublime at sunset. Mosque officials can grant permission to enter.

GURNEY DRIVE, JALAN BURMA & AROUND

Penang Hill   MOUNTAIN
(www.penanghill.gov.my; funicular adult/child RM30/15, museum admission free; ☉6.30am-7pm Mon-Fri, to 9pm Sat-Sun, funicular every 30 mins during opening hours) The top of Penang Hill, 821m above George Town, is generally about 5°C cooler than at sea level, and provides a cool retreat from the sticky heat below. From the summit there's a spectacular view over the island and across to the mainland. There are some gardens, a simple food court, an exuberantly decorated Hindu temple and a mosque as well as David Brown's (p172), a colonial-style British restaurant serving everything from beef Wellington to high tea.

On weekends and public holidays lines for the funicular can be horrendously long, with waits of up to 30 minutes, but on weekdays queues are minimal. From the trail near the upper funicular station you can walk the 5.5km to the Botanical Gardens (Moon Gate) in about three hours. The easier 5.1km tarred jeep track from the top also leads to the gardens, just beyond the Moon Gate. From Weld Quay, Komtar or Lebuh Chulia, you can catch the frequent bus 204 (RM2). A taxi here from the centre of George Town will set you back about RM25.

Kek Lok Si Temple   BUDDHIST TEMPLE
(☉9am-6pm) The 'Temple of Supreme Bliss' is also the largest Buddhist temple in Malaysia and one of the most recognisable buildings in the country. Built by an immigrant Chinese Buddhist in 1890, Kek Lok Si is a cornerstone of the Malay-Chinese community, who provided the funding for its two-decade-long building (and ongoing additions).

To reach the entrance, walk through a maze of souvenir stalls, past a tightly packed turtle pond and murky fish ponds, until you reach **Ban Po Thar** (Ten Thousand Buddhas Pagoda; admission RM2), a seven-tier, 30m-high tower. The design is said to be Burmese at the top, Chinese at the bottom and Thai in between. A **cable car** (one way/return RM4/2; ☉8.30am-5.30pm) whisks you to the highest

GEORGE TOWN STREET NAMES

Finding your way around George Town can be slightly complicated since many roads have both a Malay and an English name. While many street signs list both, it can still be confusing. In this book we use primarily the Malay name. Here are the two names of some of the main roads:

MALAY	ENGLISH
Lebuh Gereja	Church St
Jln Masjid Kapitan Keling	Pitt St
Jln Tun Syed Sheh Barakbah	The Esplanade
Lebuh Pantai	Beach St
Lebuh Pasar	Market St

To make matters worse, Jln Penang may also be referred to as Jln Pinang or as Penang Rd – but there's also a Penang St, which may also be called Lebuh Pinang! Similarly, Chulia St is Lebuh Chulia but there's also a Lorong Chulia, and this confuses even the taxi drivers.

CLANHOUSES

Between the mid-1800s and the mid-1900s Penang welcomed a huge influx of Chinese immigrants, primarily from China's Fujian province. To help introduce uncles, aunties, cousins, 10th cousins, old neighbourhood buddies and so on to their new home, the Chinese formed clan associations and built clanhouses to create a sense of community, provide lodging and help find employment for newcomers. In addition to functioning as 'embassies' of sorts, clanhouses also served as a deeper social, even spiritual, link between an extended clan, its ancestors and its social obligations.

As time went on, many clan associations became extremely prosperous and their buildings became more ornate. Clans – called 'secret societies' by the British – began to compete with each other over the decadence and number of their temples. Thanks to this rivalry, today's Penang has one of the densest concentrations of clan architecture found outside China. Arguably George Town's most impressive clanhouse is the Khoo Kongsi (p151), while other notable clanhouses include:

Cheah Kongsi (Map p152; 8 Lebuh Armenian; ⊘9am-5pm) Besides serving as a temple and assembly hall, this building has also been the registered headquarters of several secret societies. Each society occupied a different portion of the temple, which became a focal point during the 1867 riots. The fighting became so intense that a secret passage existed between here and Khoo Kongsi (p151) for a quick escape.

Teochew Temple (Han Jiang Ancestral Temple; Map p152; Lebuh Chulia; ⊘9am-5pm) This 1870 clanhouse was renovated in 2005 by Chinese artisans and features informative displays on the immigration of the eponymous Chinese group.

Yap Kongsi (Map p152; 71 Lebuh Armenian; ⊘9am-5pm) The main structure here, today painted a distinct shade of light green and originally built in 1924 in 'Straits Eclectic' style, is not always open to the public; instead, stop in at the adjacent temple, Choo Chay Keong.

level, which is presided over by an awesome 36.5m-high bronze statue of Kuan Yin, goddess of mercy.

There are several other temples in this complex, as well as shops and a **vegetarian restaurant** (mains from RM5; ⊘10am-7pm Tue-Sun; 🖉).

A taxi here from the centre of George Town starts at about RM25, or you can hop on bus 204 to Air Itam (RM2).

Botanical Gardens   GARDENS
(Waterfall Rd; ⊘5am-8pm) Don't join the throngs of Penang visitors who miss these 30-hectare gardens, which are also known as the Waterfall Gardens after the stream that cascades through from Penang Hill, or the Monkey Gardens for the many long-tailed macaques that scamper around. Don't be tempted to feed them: monkeys do bite, and there's a RM500 fine if you're caught. You'll also see dusky leaf monkeys, black giant squirrels and myriad giant bugs and velvety butterflies, which are all considerably more docile.

Once a granite quarry, the gardens were founded in 1884 by Charles Curtis, a tireless British plant lover who collected the original specimens and became the first curator. Today Penangites love their garden and you'll find groups practising t'ai chi, jogging, picnicking and even line-dancing here.

The Botanical Gardens are located about 8km outside of George Town. To get there, take bus 102 (RM2) from Komtar or Weld Quay; a taxi will cost at least RM25.

FREE **P Ramlee House**   MUSEUM
(4A Jln P Ramlee; ⊘10am-5.30pm Tue-Sun, 10am-noon & 3-5.30pm Fri) This centre consists of three sections dedicated to Malaysia's biggest megastar, P Ramlee. Ramlee was particularly known for his singing; he also acted in and directed 66 films in his lifetime. Opposite the large building that functions as a performing arts centre, a small museum contains artefacts and photos about P Ramlee's life. Adjacent to the museum is Ramlee's birthplace, a humble, thoroughly restored *kampung* house built in 1926.

P Ramlee's music plays as a constant soundtrack throughout the grounds. Although visitors may not be familiar with his work, the old photos and the house are interesting, and there are a few kitschy souvenirs in the museum's gift shop.

P Ramlee House is about 5km west of George Town; heading south on Jln Perak from Jln Dato Keramat, turn right on Jln P Ramlee – the house is about 300m down this road. A taxi here will cost RM15.

Suffolk House HISTORIC BUILDING
(www.suffolkhouse.com.my; 250 Jln Ayer Itam; admission tour/self-guided RM15/10; ⏰10am-6pm) This impressive Georgian-style mansion is built on the site of the original residence of Francis Light, founder of the colony and native of Suffolk, England. Situated on the banks of the Air Itam river, 6.5km west of George Town's centre, it's a grand square building with sweeping verandas, a massive ballroom and a breezy colonial plantation feel.

The renovation of the grounds and exterior were completed in 2007, but the interior has relatively little to see, and a visit is probably best combined with high tea at the attached restaurant. A taxi here will cost around RM15.

Courses

Nazlina's Spice Station COOKING COURSE
(Map p152; ☎012-453 8167; www.penang-cooking-class.com; 71 Lg Stewart; class RM135; ⏰9am-1pm Tue-Sat) The bubbly and enthusiastic Nazlina leads instruction in local dishes including assam laksa and prawn curry. Visit a morning market, grind your own supplies and have fun seeing how much work goes into Malaysian cuisine. Classes are held at the cooking school and, on Wednesdays, at the Eastern & Oriental Hotel (p163).

Inner Peace Yoga Circle YOGA
(☎229 2540; www.innerpeaceyogacircle.com; 293 Jln Burma, 2nd fl; drop-in class RM20) Offers all types of yoga plus retreats and teacher-training programs. Ten per cent of the company's proceeds go to charity. The class schedule is available on the website.

The studio is on Jln Burma about 2.3km northwest of Jln Transfer; a taxi here will cost around RM20.

Tours

There's a huge variety of self-guided tours of George Town, from food tours to traditional trades to architecture – pick up a pamphlet of the routes at the tourist office or at the Penang Heritage Trust (p174). This NGO

KIND OF BLUE

The magnificent 38-room, 220-window Cheong Fatt Tze Mansion (Map p152; www.cheongfatttzemansion.com; 14 Lebuh Leith; admission RM12; ⏰tours 11am, 1.30pm & 3pm Mon-Sat) was built in the 1880s, commissioned by Cheong Fatt Tze, a Hakka merchant-trader who left China as a penniless teenager and eventually established a vast financial empire throughout east Asia, earning himself the dual sobriquets 'Rockefeller of the East' and the 'Last Mandarin'.

The mansion, rescued from ruin in the 1990s, blends Eastern and Western designs with louvred windows, art nouveau stained glass and beautiful floor tiles, and is a rare surviving example of the eclectic architectural style preferred by wealthy Straits Chinese of the time. The best way to experience the house, now a boutique hotel, is to stay here; otherwise hour-long guided tours give you a glimpse of the beautiful interior.

conducts a variety of walking tours of central George Town, including the 'Little India Experience' and the 'Heritage Trail'. Both last around three hours and cost RM60 – be sure to book at least a day in advance. The office also has free brochures with details of self-guided walks.

Another option is presented by the Penang Global Ethic Project (www.globalethicpenang.net/webpages/act_02b.htm), whose World Religion Walk takes you past the iconography and houses of worship of Christians, Muslims, Hindus, Sikhs, Buddhists and Chinese traditional religion.

There's also a free tourist shuttle bus (⏰6am-midnight), which runs between the Weld Quay and Komtar, winding its way through the colonial core of George Town. It's a good way to get a quick overview of the town, and you can get on and off at one of 19 stops.

Heritage Walking Tour WALKING TOUR
(☎016-440 6823; jsk_27@hotmail.com; tours from RM60) Discover George Town by foot with Joann Khaw, a Penang native and heritage expert who also runs feng shui and food tours, among others. Highly recommended.

BUDDHISM IN PENANG

While Malaysia is officially and predominantly Muslim, the Chinese population has remained mostly Buddhist. As one of Malaysia's most Chinese states, Penang has an uncommonly diverse and burgeoning Buddhist community that embraces not only traditional Chinese Buddhism but also the Thai, Burmese, Sinhalese and Tibetan schools of Buddhist philosophy. In addition to the below, Penang's visit-worthy Buddhist temples include Kuan Yin Teng (p154), the oldest Chinese temple in Penang and the second oldest in the country, and Kek Lok Si Temple (p157) near Penang Hill, Malaysia's biggest Buddhist temple.

Wat Chayamangkalaram (Temple of the Reclining Buddha; Lorong Burma; ⊘7am-6pm) The Temple of the Reclining Buddha is a typically Thai temple with it sharp-eaved roofs and ceiling accents; inside it houses a 33m-long reclining Buddha draped in a gold-leafed saffron robe. The temple is located about 2.5km northwest of central George Town; a taxi here will cost RM15.

Dhammikarama Burmese Buddhist Temple (Lorong Burma; ⊘7am-6pm) This is a rare instance of a Burmese Buddhist temple outside Burma (now Myanmar). There's a series of panel paintings on the life of the Buddha lining the walkways, the characters dressed in typical Burmese costume, while inside typically round-eyed, serene-faced Burmese Buddha statues stare out at worshippers. This was Penang's first Buddhist temple, built in 1805; it has been significantly added to over the years. The temple is located about 2.5km northwest of central George Town; a taxi here will cost RM15.

Wat Buppharam (8 Perak Rd; ⊘8am-6pm) This Thai temple is home to the lifting Buddha, an allegedly 1000-year-old, gold-leaf-encrusted Buddha statue about the size of a well-fed house cat. As a seeker, kneel in front of the statue, pay respects to the figure with a clear mind and then ask, in your mind, the yes or no question you wish to have answered; ask also that you wish for the figure to become light for an affirmative answer. Try to lift the statue. To verify the answer, ask your question again, only this time ask that the statue become heavy. Lift again. When the statue is heavy it won't budge and when it's light it lifts off the platform like a butterfly. Heading northwest on Jln Burma, turn right on Jln Perak about 500m after Hotel 1926. The temple is about 150m down this road.

Penang Gelugpa Buddhist Association (Map p152; Love Lane; ⊘7am-6pm) This Buddhist temple next to Loo Pun Hong isn't particularly impressive compared with Penang's other religious buildings, but it is unique for being the major representative structure of the Gelugpa (Yellow Hat) school of Buddhism. The Yellow Hats are a Tibetan order, and as such there are some beautiful Tibetan wall hangings in this temple that you'd be hard pressed to find outside a museum.

Penang Private Tour　　　GUIDED TOUR
(☎019 529 5959; www.rasamalaysia.com/penang -private-tour-and-culinary-tour; tours from RM200) CK Low is a native of Penang who leads a variety of guided food-based tours, as well as more general sights based tours of the entire island.

Street Food Excursions & Photography Walks　　　GUIDED TOUR
(www.eatingasia.typepad.com; tours from US$120) The folks behind the food blog EatingAsia offer custom, private food- or photography- centric tours of George Town and beyond.

✦ Festivals & Events

A good resource for Penang festivals is the state's official tourism website, **Visit Penang** (www.visitpenang.gov.my).

January–April

Thaipusam　　　HINDU
This masochistic festival is celebrated as fervently as in Singapore and KL, but without quite the same crowds. Held in late January/ early February.

Chinese New Year　　　CHINESE
Celebrated with particular gusto in George Town. The Khoo Kongsi is done up for the

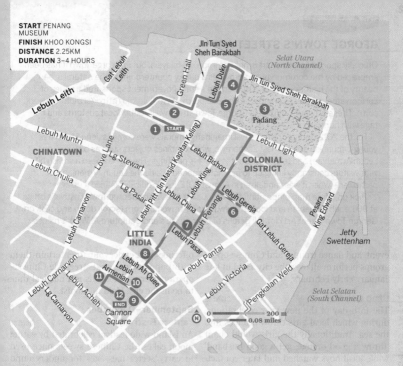

START PENANG MUSEUM
FINISH KHOO KONGSI
DISTANCE 2.25KM
DURATION 3–4 HOURS

Walking Tour
Five Cultures on Two Feet

❯ This walk will give you a glimpse of George Town's cultural grab bag: English, Indian, Malay, Baba-Nonya and Chinese.

Starting at **①** **Penang Museum**, head west and then north towards the waterfront, passing the **②** **Supreme Court**. Note the statue of James Richardson Logan, advocate for nonwhites during the colonial era. Walk up Lebuh Duke to the waterfront, then right and right again down Jln Padang Kota Lama past the green **③** **padang** (field) and grandiose architecture of the **④** **City Hall** and **⑤** **Town Hall.** Proceed left along Lebuh Light, then right on Lebuh Penang. A short detour finds the impressive **⑥** **Pinang Peranakan Mansion**, the old digs of one of George Town's great Baba-Nonya merchant barons.

Continue down Lebuh Penang into **⑦** **Little India** and take a deep breath of all that spice; if it's around lunchtime, refuel with a curry. At Lebuh Pasar, head right past shops selling milky Bengali sweets, then left at Lebuh King to the intersection of **⑧** **Lebuh King** and **Lebuh Ah Quee,** a literal example of Penang's cultural crossroads: to your south is a Chinese assembly hall and rows of fading Chinese shopfronts; to your north is a small Indian mosque; and across the street is a large Malaysian cafeteria.

Left onto Lebuh Ah Quee, right on Jln Pantai, then right on **⑨** **Lebuh Armenian** (if you want to go off-map to explore side lanes and alleyways, this is the time to do it). The street became a centre for Chinese secret societies and was one of the main fighting stages of the 1867 riots. Stroll past dusty shops till you reach **⑩** **Cheah Kongsi**, home to the oldest Straits Chinese clan association in Penang.

Cross the street to the corner of Lebuh Pitt and the small 1924 Hokkien clanhouse **⑪** **Yap Kongsi**, its outer altar decorated in symbols from the *Tao Teh Ching.* Left and left onto Cannon Sq brings you to the magnificently ornate **⑫** **Khoo Kongsi**, the most impressive *kongsi* in the city.

GEORGE TOWN'S STREET ART

Officially sponsored street art is not common in Malaysia, but in George Town it has been embraced by the community and provides a quirky counterpoint to the natural urban beauty of the historic core. In 2010 Penang's state government sponsored a series of cartoon steel art pieces created by the Sculpture At Work studio (http://sculptureatwork.com). These artworks, affixed to George Town street walls, detail local customs and heritage with humour.

For the 2012 George Town Festival imaginative murals were commissioned from the young Lithuanian artist Ernest Zacharevic, who combines objects such as bicycles (on Lebuh Armenian) and telephone booths with his paintings. The art has been a smash hit with visitors constantly lining up to be photographed beside the Lebuh Armenian piece in particular – when it was vandalised in August 2012, locals quickly cleaned it up again.

Pick up a free map pinpointing the various art sites from George Town Festival's office at 90 Lebuh Armenian and look at www.penang-traveltips.com (scroll down and click on George Town Street Art) for full details of Zacharevic's and Sculpture At Work's pieces.

event, and dance troupes and Chinese-opera groups perform all over the city. Held in late January/early February.

Chap Goh Meh
CHINESE

The 15th day of the new year celebrations, during which local girls throw oranges into the sea. Traditionally the girls would chant 'throw a good orange, get a good husband' while local boys watched and later contacted their dream girl through matchmakers. The new year is also one of the only times to see Baba-Nonya performances of *dondang sayang* (spontaneous and traditional love ballads). Held in February.

Penang World Music Festival
MUSIC

(www.penangworldmusic.com) Three-day festival featuring a lineup of international and local musicians. Held in March/April.

May–August

Penang International Dragon Boat Festival
REGATTA

(www.penangdragonboat.gov.my) A colourful and popular regatta held at Teluk Bahang, featuring traditional dragon boats. Held in late June/early July.

George Town Festival
PERFORMING ARTS

(www.georgetownfestival.com) An arts and performance festival celebrating the city's Unesco status. Held in July.

Hungry Ghosts Festival (Phor Thor)
CHINESE

The gates of hell are said to be opened every year on the 15th day of the seventh month of the Chinese lunar calendar. To appease the hungry ghosts, Penangites set out food offerings and endeavour to entertain them with puppet shows and streetside Chinese-opera performances. This is a magical time to be in the city. Held in August.

September–December

Lantern Festival
CHINESE

An island-wide festival celebrated by eating moon cakes, the Chinese sweets once used to carry secret messages for underground rebellions in ancient China. Held in mid-September.

Deepavali
HINDU

The Hindu Festival of Lights is celebrated with music and dancing at venues in Little India. Held in October.

Pesta Pulau Pinang
CARNIVAL

The annual Penang Island Festival features various cultural events, parades and a funfair in George Town. Held in November/December.

🛏 Sleeping

George Town has all the accommodation possibilities you would expect in a big, bustling tourist city, from the grungiest hostels to the swankiest hotels, although it's worth noting that there's not a whole lot to choose from in the midrange. Cacophonic Lebuh Chulia and quieter Love Lane make up the heart of Penang's backpacker land, crammed with cheap hostels and hotels – it pays to check a few out before parting with your cash. The Unesco-designated 'core zone' is home to several new boutique hotels in heritage buildings.

Be warned that during holidays, most notably Chinese New Year (January/February), hotels tend to fill up very quickly and prices can become ridiculously inflated; if you intend to stay at this time, book well in advance.

CHINATOWN

TOP CHOICE **New Asia Heritage Hotel**   HOTEL **$$**
(Map p152; ☑262 6171; www.newasiahotel.com; 71 Lebuh Kimberly; r RM88-158; ❋❒) As we were told by the gruff-but-friendly manager here, 'The most important thing about this hotel is that everything is the same in every room.' And he's right; the 24 rooms in this clean, well run, comfortable mid-ranger are similarly equipped with TV, air-con, and relatively attractive and functional furniture, although some rooms are slightly larger and have huge balconies. If you favour value rather style, this would be your best option in George Town.

TOP CHOICE **Moon Tree 47**   HOTEL **$$**
(Map p152; ☑264 4021; 47 Lebuh Muntri; r RM80-120; ❋❒) The main structure of this antique shophouse holds three rooms, all sharing a bathroom, while out back are three two-level suites (three additional family rooms were being built at research time). The place has a funky, retro vibe and friendly service, making it perfect for young couples or solo travellers; older travellers or families might be put off by some of the hotel's rather rustic amenities and features.

Roommates   HOSTEL **$**
(Map p152; ☑261 1567; www.roommatespenang.com; 178 Lg Chulia; dm incl breakfast RM28-30; ❋@❒) This new hostel – allegedly the island's smallest – boasts a young, communal, chummy vibe. There are 16 pod-like dorm beds and a living room–like communal area, but the real highlight is Yen, the friendly owner, who leads guests on free pub-crawls, eating tours and other activities.

Eastern & Oriental Hotel   LUXURY HOTEL **$$$**
(E&O; Map p152; ☑222 2000; www.eohotels.com; 10 Lebuh Farquhar; ste incl breakfast RM350-2480; ❋@❒❖) One of the rare hotels in the world where historic opulence has gracefully moved into the present day. Originally established by the Sarkies brothers in 1885, today the hotel comprises of the Heritage Wing, which includes the original domed lobby, and additional wings that date to the 1970s and 2001. A new wing was under construction at the time of research. The suites seamlessly blend European comfort with Malaysian style using hardwood antiques and sumptuous linens; those with a sea view are worth the extra outlay.

Ryokan   HOSTEL **$**
(Map p152; ☑250 0287; www.myryokan.com; 62 Lebuh Muntri; incl breakfast dm/r RM35-38/136; ❋@❒) As the name suggests, this new flashpackers has a minimalist – if not particularly Japanese – feel. The dorms, which range from four to six beds, are almost entirely white (except for the pink women's dorms, which also include a large mirror), and the bunk-style beds include a private light and power point. 'Chillax', TV and reading rooms are also stylish and inviting, and come equipped with iPads. The similarly white rooms with en suite bathrooms are comfortable yet overpriced, and lack windows.

Chulia Heritage   BOUTIQUE HOTEL **$$**
(Map p152; ☑263 3380; www.chuliaheritagehotel.com; 380 Lebuh Chulia; r RM90-280; ❋❒) The White House would probably be a more apt name for this recently opened hotel. It's housed in an all-white former mansion, with smallish rooms also decked out in virginal white, with of course, white furnishings and amenities. It's all very pure and clean looking, if somewhat lacking in atmosphere (and colour). The cheapest rooms lack windows and share bathrooms.

Reggae Penang   HOSTEL **$**
(Map p152; ☑262 6772; www.reggaehostelsmalaysia.com; 57 Love Lane; dm incl breakfast RM28-30; ❋@❒) Another brick in Malaysia's Reggae empire, this expansive heritage building has several four- to 12-bed dorm rooms. Beds are double-decker pod style, and have individual lights, power point and free wi-fi. The lobby, outfitted with pool table and coffee shop, feels more like a bar than a hostel. Perfect for the social traveller.

Yes Hotel   HOTEL **$**
(Map p152; ☑229 8880; yeshotel@ymail.com; 60-60A Jln Transfer; r RM69-109; ❋❒) One of the few midrange options in central George Town, this hotel provides the necessities in a new-feeling, tidy package, with little – actually no – fuss. Many rooms lack windows and all are RM10 to RM30 more expensive on weekends.

PENANG GEORGE TOWN

GEORGE TOWN'S HERITAGE HOTELS

The last couple years have seen a virtual explosion of boutique hotels in central George Town. Many have taken advantage of the city's antique buildings, with rustic interiors often supplemented with modern touches, making the accommodation have some of the more unique and atmospheric we've encountered in Southeast Asia. Here are some of our favourites:

23 Love Lane (Map p152; ☎ 262 1323; www.23lovelane.com; 23 Love Lane; r incl breakfast 800-1200; ❄@ 🛜) The 10 rooms here, which are found both in the main structure (a former mansion) or the surrounding buildings (former kitchen and stables), tastefully combine antique furniture and fixtures with modern design touches and artsy accents. There's lots of open spaces and high ceilings to catch the breezes, inviting communal areas, a peaceful aura, and service that complements the casual, homey vibe.

Straits Collection (Map p152; ☎ 262 7299; www.straitscollection.com; 89-95 Lebuh Armenia; ste RM450-490; ❄@ 🛜) If you've ever dreamed of living in a retro-chic restored Chinese shophouse, head here. Each residence is essentially a house (but with no cooking facilities), artfully decorated with regional antiques, bright-coloured cushions and attractive original art. Each is different but all have some sort of unforgettable detail such as wooden Japanese bathtubs or ancient sliding doors.

Coffee Atelier (Map p152; ☎ 261 2261; www.coffeeatelier.com; 47-55 Lg Stewart; ste incl breakfast 380-410; ❄🛜) Unlike the rather slick heritage hotels you'll find elsewhere in town, the renovation of these two shophouses dating back to 1927 has left them feeling wonderfully rustic, and the peeling paint and quirky original furnishings provide heaps of character. Each house is divided into two units, with a second child-sized bedroom on the first floor, and the ground floor rooms have huge courtyard-style bathrooms.

Clove Hall (☎ 229 0818; www.clovehall.com; 11 Jln Clove Hall; ste incl breakfast RM550-650; ❄🛜) A white Edwardian Anglo-Malay mansion restored to unpretentious hardwood and tiled elegance, this is the place to go if you want to feel and be treated like a mogul of the early 1900s. In fact, this is the site of the Sarkies brothers' first Penang home. Jln Clove Hall is located off Jln Burma, about 1km north of Jln Transfer; a long walk or a RM15 taxi ride from central George Town.

Noordin Mews (Map p152; ☎ 263 7125; www.noordinmews.com; 77 Lebuh Noordin; incl breakfast r/ste RM250/350-550; ❄@🛜💦) These two restored shophouses boast an attractive 1950s-era feel, down to the antique adverts and retro furniture. A pool and breakfast make the 14 standard rooms here a great deal.

Penaga Hotel (Map p152; ☎ 261 1891; www.hotelpenaga.com; cnr Lg Hutton & Jln Transfer; r/ste RM450-470/750-1080; ❄@🛜💦) This expansive hotel takes up most of a city block and has three sections: one with a row of two-storey family-friendly minihomes, another with apartment-sized suites and the last with generous but more simple rooms. All are decorated with a magical mix of antiques and some surprising touches like cow-hide rugs, mid-century bright-hued couches and modern art. The stack of amenities include a pool, central gardens and a coffee shop.

Campbell House (Map p152; ☎ 261 8290; www.campbellhousepenang.com; 106 Lebuh Campbell; r incl breakfast 270-550; ❄@🛜) This former hotel, dating back to 1903, is seeing a new life as a thoughtful, sumptuous boutique. The European owners have employed their extensive experience in the luxury world to include amenities such as locally sourced, organic toiletries, beautiful Peranakan tiles in the bathrooms, Nespresso machines and high-quality mattresses.

Cheong Fatt Tze Mansion (Map p152; ☎ 262 5289; www.cheongfatttzemansion.com; 14 Lebuh Leith; r RM420-800; ❄@🛜) If you were impressed with George Town's famous Blue Mansion, you don't necessarily have to leave. This house museum was one of Penang's first heritage boutique hotels, and although rooms remain large, atmospheric and comfortable, it's worth noting that they're starting to show signs of wear and tear.

Muntri Mews   HISTORIC HOTEL $$$

(Map p152; ☑263 5125; www.muntrimews.com; 77 Lebuh Muntri; r RM300-360; ❄@☎) This building's original owners would no doubt be shocked to learn that their former stablehouse (mews) is today an attractive boutique hotel. The nine rooms boast an elegant minimalist vibe, with each room boasting an inviting lounge area and a retro black-and-white tiled bathroom, but conspicuously at this price range, no wardrobe, minibar or safe.

Hotel Malaysia   HOTEL $$

(Map p152; ☑263 3311; www.hotelmalaysia.com. my; 7 Jln Penang; r incl breakfast RM130-230; ❄@☎) Crisp sheets, professional service and views over the Cheong Fatt Tze Mansion to the Penang Bridge make this place a winner in the bland category and a good deal for the price. A buffet breakfast is included and wi-fi costs RM11.60 per day.

Yeng Keng Hotel   HISTORIC HOTEL $$$

(Map p152; ☑262 2177; www.yengkenghotel.com. my; 362 Lebuh Chulia; incl breakfast r/ste RM380-440/440-600; ❄@☎☒) Smack in the heart of backpacker-land, the Yeng Keng is a revamp of a 150-year-old hotel. The 20 rooms are small and come stuffed with slightly cheesy Chinese faux-antique touches; plenty of breezy passageways connect them all. There's a tiny but inviting pool, and the front patio cafe has attracted an upscale local following.

Banana Boutique Hotel   BOUTIQUE HOTEL $$

(Map p152; ☑261 0718; 422 Lebuh Chulia; r incl breakfast RM168-469; ❄@☎) An imposing and recently refurbished mansion with 51 rooms. The lobby boasts a fountain and a rather brash Chinese theme, but the rooms border on the bland end of the interior design spectrum. A better reason to stay here is the convenient location and the popular restaurant/cafe next door serving Western and Malay dishes.

Segara Ninda   HISTORIC HOTEL $$

(Map p152; ☑262 8748; www.segaraninda.com; 20 Jln Penang; r RM70-150; ❄@☎) This elegant century-old villa was once the town residence of Ku Din Ku Meh, a wealthy timber merchant and colonial administrator. His home has been tastefully renovated, incorporating original features such as the carved wooden ventilation panels, staircase and tiled floors. The 16 rooms are simply but mostly elegantly furnished, and the place boasts a homey atmosphere.

Cititel Hotel   HOTEL $$

(Map p152; ☑370 1188; www.cititelpenang.com; 66 Jln Penang; incl breakfast r/ste RM243-301/649-904; ❄@☎) Cititel towers over Penang's old town; the views from its large modern rooms are particularly lovely, especially those overlooking the sea. It's brightly lit and always busy, and offers regulation business-traveller comforts, along with a few restaurants. Discounts are normally available.

Seven Terraces   LUXURY HOTEL $$$

(Map p152; ☑264 2333; www.7terraces.com; Lg Stewart; ste incl breakfast RM550-2200; ❄@☎☒) On the brink of opening during our last visit, this hotel – crafted from a row of seven shophouses by the people behind Muntri Mews and Noordin Mews – is set to be among the more luxurious places to stay in central George Town. The 18 two-storey suites (including three even larger multiroom 'apartments') have been decorated with an eclectic mix of original antiques, reproductions and contemporary pieces, and surround a central courtyard. A restaurant and bar open to the public face the main street.

Cathay Hotel   HOTEL $

(Map p152; ☑262 6271; 15 Lebuh Leith; r with fan/ air-con RM58/76-140; ❄☎) There's an unmistakable allure to the spacious colonial building with its light-infused courtyard, high ceilings, latticed windows and grand entrance. But the place is faded, decorated with shabby furniture and with tiles permanently stained from decades of who knows what.

Old Penang   HOSTEL $

(Map p152; ☑263-8805; www.oldpenang.com; 53 Love Lane; incl breakfast dm/r 23-25/45-90; ❄@☎) Hardwood floors, white walls, high ceilings and splashes of red paint add a solid-coloured hip vibe to this hostel, otherwise set in a restored pre-WWII house that could easily serve as a set piece in a Maugham or Theroux short story. Rooms are microscopic and offer little in the way of amenities or furniture.

Red Inn   HOSTEL $

(Map p152; ☑261 3931; www.redinnpenang.com; 55 Love Lane; incl breakfast dm RM30-34, r RM80-90; ❄☎) The heritage house and communal areas here – including elevated lounge area – are attractive and inviting, but the private rooms can feel like little more than beds in a closet. Dorms range from two to four beds and, although they're a little cramped, they're clean and have good mattresses.

COLONIAL DISTRICT & LITTLE INDIA

TOP CHOICE China Tiger
HOMESTAY $$$

(Map p152; ☎012-501 5360, 264 3580; www.china tiger.info; 25 & 29 Lebuh China; apt RM500, all-inclusive homestay RM950; ✳@📶) You have your choice of experiences here: be completely independent in either of two open-concept self-catering apartments above an art gallery, or live in Chinese heritage elegance in one of the two homestay-style apartments attached to the owner's restored shophouse home. If you can't decide, keep in mind that the latter option involves being pampered and taken around town by your hosts.

Red Inn Court
HOSTEL $

(Map p152; ☎261 1144; www.redinncourt.com; 35B & 35C Lebuh Pitt (Jln Masjid Kapitan Keling); incl breakfast dm/r RM28-35/88-108; ✳@📶) A low-key, newish backpackers with lots of services and communal amenities. Service is friendly and personal, although the lobby has a somewhat commercial 'Tourist Information' office feel.

Victoria Inn
HOTEL $$

(Map p152; ☎262 2278; www.victoriainn.com.my; 278 Lebuh Victoria; incl breakfast dm/r RM45/115-135; ✳📶) There is a hint of style here, from the faux wood floors, designer coloured paint and arty Penang photos on the walls, but other than that it's really just a standard hotel with good beds, TV, air-con and attached bathrooms.

Broadway Budget Hotel
HOTEL $

(Map p152; ☎262 8550; www.broadwaybudget hotel.com; 35F Lebuh Pitt (Jln Masjid Kapitan Keling); r RM50-90; ✳📶) The Broadway is a good deal if you want some comfort minus a heck of a lot of atmosphere. It's centrally located, rooms are large (if bland), have en suite bathrooms, and there's in-room wi-fi.

PG Chew Jetty Homestay
HOMESTAY $$

(Map p152; ☎019-554 4909; pgcjhomestay@gmail. com; Chew Jetty; r RM80-120; ✳📶) For the epitome of a local experience, book one of the basic rooms in this pier-bound home at the edge of George Town's biggest clan jetty. As the name implies, you'll be crashing with a local family. Bathrooms are shared and the noise from grandma's TV is free, although breakfast will set you back an extra RM5.

PERSERIAN GURNEY, JALAN BURMA & AROUND

Mango Tree Place
BOUTIQUE HOTEL $$$

(☎246 2132; www.mangotreeplace.com; 29 Jln Phuah Hin Leong; r incl breakfast RM380-600; ✳@📶) It takes stepping inside one of the three rather standard-looking shophouses dating back to 1934 to grasp the young, fun vibe of this hotel. Open spaces, primary colours, attractive subtle furniture and natural light establish the feel here. Ground floor rooms have a garden terrace while the upper floor rooms have two bedrooms; all share an expansive communal area equipped with a computer. By the time this has been printed, an additional four rooms will have been completed.

THE EASTERN & ORIENTAL HOTEL

Originally built in 1884, the stylish E&O (p163) was the archetypal 19th-century colonial grand hotel. It was established by two of the Armenian Sarkies brothers, Tigram and Martin, the most famous hoteliers in the East, who later founded Raffles Hotel in Singapore.

In the 1920s the Sarkies promoted the E&O as the 'Premier Hotel East of Suez'. High-ranking colonial officials and wealthy planters and merchants filed through its grand lobby, and the E&O was established as a centre for Penang's social elite. Rudyard Kipling, Noel Coward and Somerset Maugham were just some of the famous faces who passed through its doors.

The Sarkies almost closed the E&O when the rent was raised from £200 to £350 a month, but they kept it open largely at the insistence of Arshak Sarkies, the third brother (and a gambler by nature). Arshak's was legendary – some observers said he ran the E&O not to make money, but to entertain. Shortly before his death, Arshak began lavish renovations to the hotel. This expense, coupled with loans to friends that were conveniently forgotten, finally bankrupted the family business in 1931.

In the 1990s the E&O closed and fell into disrepair, but a huge renovation program came to its rescue. In 2001 it once again opened for business, as a luxury, all-suite grand hotel with elegant, spacious rooms decorated in the best of colonial style.

Jln Phuah Hin Leong is located off Jln Burma, about 1km north of Jln Transfer; a long walk or a RM15 taxi ride from central George Town.

Palanquinn — BOUTIQUE HOTEL $$

(227 1088; www.palanquinn.com; 39 Lorong Bangkok; r RM200-350; ❅@❧) Palanquinn comprises three houses dating back to 1927; its six rooms feel spacious and homey. We particularly liked the huge bathrooms – some with retractable roof – in most units. And you'd be hard-pressed to find a friendlier and more courteous host than Kelvyn.

Lorong Bangkok is located just off Jln Burma, about 2.5km north of Jln Transfer, a RM15 taxi ride from central George Town.

G Hotel — HOTEL $$$

(238 0000; www.ghotel.com.my; 168 Perserian Gurney; r incl breakfast RM450-1248; ❅@❧) The 303 rooms here are studies in minimalist, cubist cool, collections of geometric form set off by swatches of blocky colour. There's a good crowd of creative and simply successful professionals blowing through the doors, giving the G a vibe that's as Manhattan as it is Malaysia.

The hotel is about 3.5km northwest of central George Town; a taxi here will cost RM15.

Tune Hotel — HOTEL $$

(nationwide 03-7962 5888; www.tunehotels.com; 100 Jln Burma; r RM116.80; ❅@❧) Tune is part of a chain of budget hotels run by AirAsia; its rooms are very clean, decent sized and decorated with an IKEA look broken by multiple AirAsia posters (yet no TV). You'll save a lot by booking ahead, and it's worth noting that the base price here includes no amenities – you pay extra for everything from towels to air-con. The price quoted above is for a same-day booking with most amenities.

Tune Hotel is located on Jln Burma, 250m northwest of Jln Transfer.

✖ Eating

People come to George Town just to eat. Even if you thought you came here for another reason, your priorities might change dramatically once you start digging into the Indian, Chinese, Malay and various hybrid treats available. Days revolve around where and what to eat, and three meals a day starts to sounds depressingly scant. And it's the same for locals, for whom eating out is a daily event.

CHINATOWN

TOP CHOICE Teksen — CHINESE $$

(Map p152; 18 Lebuh Carnavon; mains from RM10; ❧noon-2.30pm & 6-9pm Wed-Mon) A recent 'branding and uplifting enterprise' has elevated this longstanding restaurant a couple steps up from Penang's typically gritty shophouse restaurants. There's a lengthy menu translated into English but we suggest you do as the locals do and ask the staff for the daily specials – this strategy rewarded us with some great soups, a tasty Malaysian-style stir-fry of morning glory and sambal, and a delicious dish of stir-fried roast pork. Highly recommended.

TOP CHOICE China House — INTERNATIONAL $$$

(Map p152; 263 7299; www.chinahouse.com.my; 153 & 155 Lebuh Pantai) Where do we start? This new complex of three co-joined three heritage buildings features two dining outlets; a cafe/bakery, Kopi C (p172); two galleries; and a bar, Canteen (p171).

BTB (mains RM-38-68; ❧dinner), the flagship dining venue, does a short but appetising menu of Middle Eastern- and Mediterranean-influenced dishes; think seared sea bass with Ras-el-Hanout spices, cauliflower puree and roasted pumpkin, pine nut and pomegranate dressing.

Courtyard Cafe (mains RM12-30; ❧5pm-midnight) does a more casual burger and tapas menu. Whew.

Kashmir — INDIAN $$

(Map p152; Oriental Hotel, 105 Jln Penang; mains RM6.90-54.90; ❧lunch & dinner) Don't be fooled by this hotel-basement restaurant's cheesy 1970s, den-like interior; Kashmir serves some super delicious tandoori. Attentive service, an assertive Indian soundtrack and yes, cocktails, complete the package.

Sup Hameed — MALAY $

(Map p152; 48 Jln Penang; mains from RM3; ❧24hr) On the surface, this is very much your typical *nasi kandar* shop found all over Malaysia, and we don't recommend eating here during the day. But come night, Hameed sets out tables on the street and serves his incredibly rich soups (try *sup kambing* – goat soup), served with slices of white bread.

Goh Huat Seng — CHINESE $$

(Map p152; 59A Lebuh Kimberley; hotpot RM40-80; ❧5-9.30pm) With five decades under its belt, Goh Huat Seng continues to serve Teo

PENANG GEORGE TOWN

Chew-style hotpot the old way: in charcoal-fired steamboats. Get some friends together and enjoy some communal dipping or, if you've got the language skills, order classic Teo Chew dishes from the restaurant's Chinese-language menu on the wall.

Tho Yuen Restaurant   CHINESE $
(Map p152; 92 Lebuh Campbell; dim sum RM1-5; ⏰6am-3pm Wed-Mon) Our favourite place for dim sum. It's packed with newspaper-reading loners and chattering groups of locals all morning long, but you can usually squeeze in somewhere – as long as you arrive early. Servers speak minimal English but do their best to explain the contents of their carts.

Sky Hotel   CHINESE $
(Map p152; Lebuh Chulia; mains from RM6; ⏰lunch) It's incredible that this gem sits in the middle of the greatest concentration of travellers in George Town, yet is somehow almost exclusively patronised (in enthusiastic numbers) by locals. It is incumbent on you to try the *char siew* (barbequed pork), *siew bak* (pork belly), *siew cheong* (honey-sweetened pork) and roast duck.

Joo Hooi   HAWKER $
(Map p152; Cnr Jln Penang & Lebuh Keng Kwee; mains from RM3; ⏰11am-6pm) The hawker centre equivalent of one-stop shopping, this cafe-style joint has all of Penang's best dishes in one location: laksa, *rojak*, *char kway teow*, *lor bak* (deep-fried meats served with dipping sauces), *cendol* (shaved ice with palm sugar, coconut milk and jellies) and fresh fruit juices.

La Bohème   FRENCH $
(Map p152; 42 Jln Sri Bahari; pastries & desserts RM3.5-10, mains RM12-21; ⏰10am-6pm Mon-Sat) If you're feeling like a retro-themed tea hall, this casual place serves French pastries and light meals courtesy of a French pastry chef and his Malaysian wife. Think quiches, croissants and crème brûlée.

Amelie   WESTERN $$
(Map p152; 6 Lebuh Armenian; mains RM16-23; ⏰9am-5pm Tues-Fri, to 7pm Sat-Sun) Pint-sized Amelie does a short but revolving menu of pasta standards – think spaghetti carbonara or gnocchi with sausage – supplemented with a few sandwiches and salads. It's all hearty, homey and tasty, if not entirely creative.

Kheng Pin   HAWKER $
(Map p152; 80 Jln Penang; mains from RM4; ⏰7am-3pm Tue-Sun) Locals swear by the specialities at this aged hawker joint, most famously *lor bak* (deep-fried meats dipped in sauce) and Hainan chicken rice (steamed chicken with broth and rice), one of the great fast foods of East Asia.

Nasi Padang Minang   INDONESIAN $
(Map p152; 92 Jln Transfer; mains from RM4; ⏰lunch) Buffet-style Indonesian curries, stir-fries, soups, salads and grilled dishes.

Edelweiss   SWISS $$
(Map p152; 38 Lebuh Armenian; mains RM18-39.50; ⏰11am-10pm Tues-Sun) Items like currywurst and bratwurst carry a distinct German accent, while fondue and rösti (Swiss-style potato pancakes) give Edelweiss its Swiss twang. The antique-filled dining room is a delight, and there's a small selection of pricey imported beers.

Ee Beng
Vegetarian Food   CHINESE, VEGETARIAN $
(Map p152; 20 Lebuh Dickens; meals around RM5; ⏰breakfast, lunch & dinner; 🅟) Popular self-service place for cheap, mostly vegetarian food of the tofu and green vegetables variety.

COLONIAL DISTRICT & LITTLE INDIA
Weld Quay Seafood Restaurant   CHINESE $$
(Tree Shade Seafood Restaurant; Map p152; Pengkalan Weld; mains RM10-50; ⏰lunch & dinner Thur-Tues) Named for its location under a giant tree, this is where locals head for cheap and tasty seafood. Pick your aquatic protein from the trays out front, and the staff will fry, steam, soup or grill it up for you. Located directly across from the Weld Quay bus terminal.

Madras New Woodlands
Restaurant   INDIAN, VEGETARIAN $
(Map p152; 60 Lebuh Penang; set lunch RM5.25, mains from RM1.50; ⏰8.30am-10pm; 🅟) It draws you in with its display of Indian sweets outside (try the *halwa*), but once you experience the food you might not have room for dessert. Tasty banana-leaf meals and north Indian specialities are the mainstays, as well as the thickest mango lassi in town. The daily set lunch for RM5.25 might be Penang's greatest food bargain.

Via Pre   ITALIAN $$
(Map p152; www.via-pre.com; 5 Pengkalan Weld; mains RM6.90-54.90; ⏰lunch & dinner) This KL-based Italian staple has imported a

BEE YINN LOW: FOOD WRITER

Bee is a native of Penang, a best-selling author, and the blogger behind popular cooking website **Rasa Malaysia** (www.rasamalaysia.com).

How is the food of Penang different than elsewhere in Malaysia? Penang is predominantly Chinese, so you will find myriad Chinese dishes. It's a Straits settlement, so one can find delicious Nonya food, much of which is influenced by Thai food. And the surrounding sea means that fresh seafood such as shrimp, cockles and fish are widely used.

What are a few dishes visitors to Penang should make a point of seeking out? *Char kway teow*, flat rice noodles fried with prawn, cockles and Chinese sausage; Hokkien mee, a noodle dish with a rich, shrimp-based broth, and topped with shrimp, pork, and fried shallots; *assam* laksa, rice noodles in a spicy and sour fish broth, garnished with herbs and vegetables; and curry mee, noodles in spicy and aromatic curry broth with fried tofu puffs and cockles.

Which hawker centre should visitors not miss? In the evening, head to New Lane (also known as Lorong Baru) and try the street food sold by the hawkers in the area.

And what's a good all-around restaurant? I love Hai Boey (p182), a modest seafood restaurant by the beach at Teluk Kumbar. The food is good and you can't beat the views, especially during sunset.

Any particular fruit or produce visitors shouldn't miss? Penang offers some of the best durian in the region; it's absolutely creamy, rich, and sweet.

Is there any sort of drink particularly associated with Penang? Nutmeg juice. You can get it at any coffee shop.

previously unknown level of sophistication to sleepy George Town. Expect traditional Italian dishes, tasty pizzas and superb desserts in a beautifully refurbished warehouse overlooking the mainland.

Quay Café ASIAN, VEGETARIAN $
(Map p152; 2 Gat Lebuh Gereja; mains RM5-15; ☺lunch Mon-Sat; ☑) Slick cafeteria serving Asian-style meat-free dishes. Expect set meals, an emphasis on noodle dishes, and fresh juices and herbal teas.

Sri Ananda Bahwan INDIAN $
(Map p152; 55 Lebuh Penang; mains from RM3; ☺breakfast, lunch & dinner; ☑) Busy and tidy *nasi kandar*-type restaurant, seemingly forever full of chatting locals, which serves up tandoori chicken, *roti canai* and *murtabak* (*roti canai* filled with meat or vegetables). There's also an air-con dining hall.

Karai Kudi INDIAN $
(Map p152; 20 Lebuh Pasar; set meals from RM6.50, mains RM4-20; ☺11am-11pm; ☑) This outrageously tasty air-con place specialises in southern Indian Tamil Chettinad cuisine but also serves tandoori at dinner. Banana-leaf meals are huge and some sets include ice cream for dessert.

Hui Sin
Vegetarian Restaurant CHINESE, VEGETARIAN $
(Map p152; 11 Lebuh China; meals around RM4; ☺8am-4pm Mon-Sat; ☑) This excellent-value buffet restaurant is the place to go for a filling meat-free lunch. Take what you want from the selection of vegetables, curries and beancurds on offer, and you'll be charged accordingly.

PERSIARAN GURNEY, JALAN BURMA & AROUND

TOP CHOICE **Sea Pearl Lagoon Cafe** CHINESE $$
(☎899 0375; off Jln Tanjong Tokong; dishes from RM8; ☺11am-10pm Thurs-Tue) On the surface, this somewhat gritty open-air place isn't much different than many of George Town's hawker cafes. But the view looking out over the North Channel and the food – salt roasted prawns, *ikan bakar* (fish grilled with sambal) and excellent satay – combine to make it one of our favourite places to eat outside the city centre.

Sea Pearl Lagoon is located 7km northwest of George Town, in Tanjong Toking next to Thai Pak Koong Temple; a taxi here from central George Town will set you back about RM25.

Nyonya Breeze NONYA $$
(50 Lorong Abu Siti; mains RM8.60-22; ☺lunch & dinner Wed-Mon) Considered by many local

HAWKER-STALL HEAVEN

Penang's reputation as a must-see destination hinges greatly on its food, and the best the city has to offer is served at hawker stalls and food courts. Not eating at a stall in George Town is like missing the Louvre in Paris – you simply have to do it.

Hawker stall vendors run flexible schedules, so don't be surprised if one isn't there during your visit. Most importantly, avoid Mondays and Thursdays when many vendors tend to stay at home. Dishes generally fall between RM3 and RM10.

Lorong Baru (New Lane) (New Lane, cnr Jln Macalister & Lg Baru; ⊙dinner) If you ask locals where their favourite hawker stalls are, after listing a few far-flung places, they'll always mention this night-time street extravaganza, not for a particular stall but because all the food is reliably good. There's an emphasis on Chinese-style noodle dishes, and we particularly liked the *char koay kak* stall, which in addition to spicy fried rice cakes with seafood, also does great *otak otak* (a steamed fish curry). Lorong Baru intersects with Jln Macalister, about 250m northwest of the intersection with Jln Penang.

Gurney Drive (Persiaran Gurney; ⊙dinner) Penang's most famous food area sits amidst modern high-rises bordered by the sea. It's posh for a hawker area so the food is a bit pricier than elsewhere, but you'll find absolutely everything from Malay to Western. It's particularly known for its laksa stalls (try stall 11). For the best *rojak* head to the famous Ah Chye. Gurney Drive is located about 3km west of George Town near Gurney Plaza mall; a taxi here will set you back RM15.

Esplanade Food Centre (Map p152; Jln Tun Syed Sheh Barakbah; ⊙dinner) You can't beat the seaside setting of this food centre, which is nestled right in the heart of George Town's colonial district. One side is called 'Islam' and serves halal Malay food, and the other is called 'Cina' and serves Chinese and Malay specialities, including the absolutely delicious *rojak* at Rojak Ho Wei Jeng. Esplanade is often very quiet on Monday and Wednesday.

Padang Brown Food Court (Jln Pantai; ⊙lunch & dinner Fri-Wed) Everyone in town knows that this is the spot for delectable *popiah* (spring rolls), although the *won ton mee* (egg noodles served with pork dumplings or sliced roast pork) and *bubur caca* (dessert porridge made with coconut milk and banana) is another good reason to try the food in this area. In the afternoons try the *yong tau foo* (clear Chinese soup with fish balls, lettuce, crab sticks, cuttlefish and more). Padang Brown is about 1.5km west of the centre of George Town, off Jln Dato Keramat; a taxi here will cost about RM15.

Lorong Selamat (cnr Jl Macalister & Lg Selamat; ⊙dinner Sat-Thurs) The south end of Lorong Selemat is the place to go for the city's most famous *char kway teow*, but you'll also find lip-smacking *won ton mee* and other Chinese Penang favourites. Lorong Baru intersects with Jln Macalister about 500m northwest of Jln Penang.

New World Park Food Court (cnr Jln Hutton & Lg Swatow; ⊙11am-7pm) Every stall serves something different at this ultramodern, covered food court with mist-blowing fans and shiny industrial decor. The *ais kacang* (shaved-ice dessert with syrup, jellies, beans and sometimes even corn on top) here gets particularly good reviews. There are also a number of fast-food-feeling restaurants in this complex including Nonya and Indian. New World is off Jln Hutton, about 400m northwest of Jln Transfer.

Red Garden Food Paradise & Night Market (Map p152; Lebuh Leith; ⊙lunch & dinner) This place has a convenient location in the heart of Chinatown and offers a wide selection of food, including most local specialities. It's a good choice for families looking for something easy and has lots of options for fussy eaters.

Peranakans to serve the best Nonya food, this cafeteria-like place makes you feel at home while you sample exquisite specialities like *kari kapitan* (chicken curry with coconut milk and kaffir lime) and *sambal goreng* (prawns, eggplant and cashews in chilli sauce). There's lots of daily specials and weekday lunchtime set meals (RM13.90).

Lorong Abu Siti intersects with Jln Burma, about 500m northwest of Jln Transfer.

Isaribi Tei
JAPANESE $$

(cnr Jln Burma & Jln Chow Thye; set menu RM22-40; ⊘lunch & dinner) Fresh, expertly prepared sushi is served in a vine-covered hardwood setting that looks more like the heart of the jungle than the middle of the city. Beyond sushi, Japanese-style grilled-fish set menus are the speciality with salmon, cod, trout and much more on offer.

Isaribi Tei is 1.5km northwest of Jln Transfer; a taxi here will set you back about RM15.

Chock Dee
THAI $$

(231D Jln Burma; mains RM13-50; ⊘lunch & dinner Sun-Tues) Chock Dee has garnered an impressive reputation among local eaters. Menu highlights include squid in lemon sauce and *hor mok*, Thai-style *otak otak* (steamed curry). Chock Dee is on Jln Burma about 750m northwest of Jln Transfer; a taxi here will cost around RM12.

🍷 Drinking & Entertainment

Between the largely hotel-based bars and some rather commercial-feeling pubs and clubs, Penang doesn't have much of a sophisticated bar scene. That said, there are a few fun places for a night out.

TOP CHOICE Canteen
BAR

(Map p152; www.chinahouse.com.my; 183B Lebuh Victoria, China House; ⊘5pm-midnight) This is about as close as George Town comes to a hipster bar – minus the pretension. Canteen has an inviting artsy/warehouse vibe, there's live music from Thursday to Sunday, and great bar snacks available every night. Canteen is also accessible via China House's entrance on Lebuh Pantai.

TOP CHOICE B@92
BAR

(Map p152; 92 Lebuh Gereja; ⊘noon-late) Need a drinking buddy while in town? Resident Serbian Aleksandar is more than happy to oblige. Food, an eclectic music selection and friendly regulars make B@92 the kind of bar you wish you could throw in your backpack and carry with you across Southeast Asia. Bring this guidebook, or ask about the origin of Aleks's skull ring, and you might just get a discount.

That Little Wine Bar
BAR

(www.thatlittlewinebar.com; 54 Jln Chow Thye; ⊘5pm-midnight Mon-Sat) A cosy yet chic bar and lounge run by a German chef and his wife. Enjoy a selection of wine – glasses start at RM20 – and champagne cocktails at this cosy yet chic bar and lounge. Accompany your drink with tapas (RM18 to RM60) and slightly heavier mains (RM28 to RM65).

Jln Chow Thye is located off Jln Burma, about 1.5km northwest of Jln Transfer; a taxi here will set you back about RM15.

Beach Blanket Babylon
BAR

(Map p152; 32 Jln Sultan Ahmad Shah; ⊘11am-1am Mon-Fri, to 2am Sat-Sun) The open-air setting and relaxed vibe contrast with the rather formal restaurant this bar is linked to. Saturday night is men's night at this gay-friendly spot, with half price on standard pours and a discount on beer for males.

Farquhar's Bar
BAR

(Map p152; Eastern & Oriental Hotel, 10 Lebuh Farquhar; ⊘11am-1am) Colonial British-style bar inside the E&O Hotel, serving beer, traditional pub food and cocktails; try its signature drink, the Eastern & Oriental sling (RM38) brought to you by a white-coated barman. There's live music Thursday to Saturday, and Happy Hour between 5pm and 8pm.

Behind 50 Love Lane
BAR

(Map p152; Lebuh Muntri; ⊘6pm-1am Wed-Mon) Pocket-sized, retro-themed bar that draws a largely local following, despite being close to the backpacker strip. There's a classic rock soundtrack and a short menu of Western-style comfort dishes (RM14.90 to RM18.90).

Bagan Bar
BAR

(Macalister Mansion, 228 Jln Macalister; ⊘5pm-1am) This sleek, dark, velvet-coated den is probably the most sophisticated bar in town – a fact seemingly verified by the rather strict dress code (no shorts, t-shirts or sandals). There's live music from 9pm.

Upper Jln Penang Bars
BAR

(Map p152; Jln Penang; ⊘8pm-2am) This strip of road at the far northern end of Jln Penang is George Town's rather commercial-feeling entertainment strip. There's a row of about 10 open-air and air-con bars, but most flock to the mega-clubs: **Slippery Senoritas** offers live music shows that are as corny as the bar's name suggests, although it's popular and all in good fun; while **Voodoo** offers much of the same in a slightly more sophisticated package.

Soho Free House
BAR

(Map p152; 50 Jln Penang; ⊘noon-midnight) This place starts rocking out early with cheesy '80s hits and a Chinese clientele who nosh bangers and mash and swill pints with the handful of expats.

QEII
BAR, CLUB

(Map p152; 8 Pengkalan Weld; ☉6pm-1am Mon-Tues, 1pm-2am Wed-Sat, 3pm-2am Sun) QEII, with 360-degree views of the Strait of Melaka, serves passable pizza and better ambience; on Friday and Saturday nights, QEII transforms into a dance club.

Golden Screen Cinemas
CINEMA

(www.gsc.com.my; Gurney Plaza, Persarian Gurney) Penang's biggest cinema complex with 12 screens and THX sound is in the Gurney Plaza shopping complex.

 Shopping

Unique Penang
ARTS & CRAFTS

(Map p152; www.uniquepenang.com; 62 Love Lane; ☉5pm-midnight Sun-Fri & 9pm-midnight Sat) This

shophouse gallery features the work of the friendly young owners, Clovis and Joey, as well as the colourful paintings of the latter's young art students. As the couple point out, paintings are notoriously hard to squeeze in a backpack, so nearly all of the gallery's art is available in postcard size.

Rozanas Batik
ARTS & CRAFTS

(Map p152; 81B Lebuh Acheh; ☉11.30am-6.30pm) Tiny shop featuring the owner's beautiful handmade batik items. If you want to learn more, take a walk-in two-hour class in the adjacent studio (RM50 to RM 75).

Springsfield
ARTS & CRAFTS

(Map p152; 8 Muda Lane; ☉9am-6pm) Pick up some hand-painted Peranakan tiles (made in Vietnam) at this boutique in a restored shophouse. There's a few other interesting local-style knick-knacks available, and the profits go to help stray animals.

HI, TEA!

Penang's English, Chinese and Indian legacies have left an appreciation for tea that remains strong today. More recent immigrants to George Town have imported an enviable Western-style cafe culture.

Suffolk House (www.suffolkhouse.com.my; 250 Jln Ayer Itam; high tea for two RM68; ☉2.30pm-6pm) For the ultimate English tea experience, head to this 200-year-old Georgian-style mansion, where high tea, featuring scones and cucumber sandwiches, can be taken inside or in the garden. Suffolk House is located about 6.5km west of George Town; a taxi here will cost around RM15.

Ten Yee Tea Trading (Map p152; 33 Lebuh Pantai; ☉9.30am-6.30pm Mon-Sat) Fine teas are on sale here but the fun part is deciding which to buy. For RM20 you choose a tea (which you can share with up to five people), then a specialist shows you how to prepare it the proper Chinese way. A full explanation of all the different brews is given alongside the tea drinking.

Jing-Si Books & Cafe (Map p152; 31 Lebuh Pantai; drinks RM5; ☉noon-8pm) A stylish oasis of spiritual calm, this outlet for a Taiwanese Buddhist group's teachings is a wonderful place to revive in hushed surroundings over a pot of interesting teas or coffees – all of which go for the reasonable price of RM5.

Kopi C (www.chinahouse.com.my; China House, 153 & 155 Lebuh Pantai; mains from RM10; ☉9am-midnight) Located in the rambling China House complex, this cafe/bakery does good coffee and some of the best pastries and ice creams (on a good day 16 of the latter – we like the salted caramel) we've encountered in Southeast Asia.

1885 (Map p152; ☎261 8333; Eastern & Oriental Hotel, 10 Lebuh Farquahar; English afternoon tea RM52; ☉2-5pm) The E&O Hotel's main restaurant offers a daily English afternoon tea with scones, smoked salmon and, of course, cucumber sandwiches.

Café 55 (www.coffeeatelier.com; Coffee Atelier, 47-55 Lorong Stewart; coffee drinks from RM8; ☉8.30am-5pm Tue-Sun) Located in what was formerly a coffee roaster (ask to see the former roasting oven out back), this sophisticated cafe, with attached gallery, does both new-school and old-school coffee drinks.

David Brown's (www.penanghillco.com.my; Penang Hill; afternoon tea RM34-78; ☉9am-6pm) Located at the top of Penang Hill, this is yet another atmospheric destination for colonial-style high tea.

China Joe's
ARTS & CRAFTS

(Map p152; 95 Lebuh Armenian; ⏰9am-7pm) Ladies will love the fabrics – both new and antique – boxes, stationery, bags and other classy Asian bric-a-brac. There's a gallery upstairs and an adjacent tea salon.

88 Armenian Street
ARTS & CRAFTS

(Map p152; 88 Lebuh Armenian; ⏰10am-6pm Mon-Sat) This address houses three floors of art: the ground floor showcases the exquisite fused-glass creations of Penang artist Wong Keng Fuan, the 1st floor is the showroom for Jonathan Yun's sculptural jewellery, and the 2nd floor houses Howard Tan's Penang-centric photos.

Gallery 29
ARTS & CRAFTS

(Map p152; www.rebeccaduckett.com; 29 Lebuh China; ⏰9am-6pm) Rebecca Duckett's gallery shows off her modern yet traditionally inspired art in colourful splashes. There is also a good selection of books on local topics, and vintage items and crafts on offer.

Straits Quay
MALL

(www.straitsquay.com; ⏰10.30am-10pm) This is Penang's newest, largest and flashiest mall, built on reclaimed land just outside of the city centre. In addition to the usual mall suspects, **Séntuhan** (www.sentuhan.com; ⏰10.30am-10pm) sells a unique selection of crafts and housewares made by disadvantaged Malaysian women, and **Royal Selangor** (Map p152; ⏰10.30am-10pm) has a visitor centre that offers a course in making pewter sculptures daily at 11am, 2.30pm and 4.30pm (per person RM60). If you're not into shopping, it's also home to the **Performing Arts Centre of Penang** (www.penangpac.org) and there are a couple decent restaurants and bars strategically positioned to soak up the sea breezes.

Straits Quay is located about 7km northwest of George Town; buses 101 and 104 pass the mall (RM4), and a taxi here will cost about RM20. At research time, there were plans underway to have a free shuttle boat from the Eastern & Oriental Hotel (p163) to the mall.

Ban Hin
ANTIQUES

(Map p152; Lebuh Chulia; ⏰9am-7pm) This old shophouse is literally stuffed full of old adverts, packages, tins, ceramics, toys and other quasi-antiques. Located roughly across from Banana Boutique Hotel.

Bee Chin Heong
ANTIQUES

(Map p152; 58 Lebuh Kimberley; ⏰10am-8.30pm) This interesting outlet sells a colourful, bewildering assortment of religious statues, furniture and temple supplies; if you're after a huge Chinese couch, a household shrine or have RM55,000 to spend on a 2m-tall carved-wood Buddha, this is the place to come. Even if you're not buying, it's still worth a look round.

Gurney Plaza
MALL

(Persiaran Gurney; ⏰10am-10pm) Penang's classiest mall, with international chain stores like the Body Shop and Esprit. Mac users will find an Apple store here, and there's a massive music store, bookstore and several electronics outlets. There's also a mini theme park, fitness centre and a health spa. Gurney Drive is located about 3km west of George Town; a taxi here will set you back RM15.

Chowraster Bazaar
MARKET

(Map p152; Jln Penang; ⏰8am-6pm) This sweaty old market hall is where to go for a frenetic, souk-like experience. It's full of food stalls and vendors selling headscarves, batik shirts, fabrics and *kebaya* (blouses worn over a sarong).

Komtar
MALL

(Map p152; Jln Penang; ⏰10am-10pm) Penang's oldest mall is housed in a 64-storey landmark tower (at one time the tallest building in Malaysia). There are hundreds of shops in a place with the feel of an ageing bazaar. Here you'll find everything from clothes, shoes and electronics to everyday goods, and you can take an elevator ride (RM5) from the ground floor to the 58th floor where there's a viewing area with views over the island. Adjacent **Prangin Mall** (Map p152; ⏰10am-10pm) has a cinema showing the odd Western blockbuster; **1st Avenue** (⏰10am-10pm) is another mall with similarly international shops.

Sam's Batik House CLOTHING
(Map p152; 159 Jln Penang; ⊙8am-7pm) Nicknamed 'Ali Baba's Cave', this deep shop of silky and cottony goodness is the best place in town to buy sarongs, batik shirts and Indian fashions. Girls can go nuts over hand-embroidered dresses while the guys try on Bollywood shirts.

Information

Immigration Offices

Immigration Office (☑261 5122; 29A Lebuh Pantai; ⊙7.30am-3.45pm Mon-Fri) Visa extensions are available here.

Internet Access

Most lodging options offer wi-fi and many also have a computer terminal for guest use. Wi-fi is also widely available at restaurants, cafes and in shopping malls. Internet cafes have lifespans slightly longer than a housefly, and loads of them can be found along Lebuh Chulia.

Medical Services

Hospital Pulau Pinang (☑229 3333; www. hpp.moh.gov.my; Jln Hospital)
Loh Guan Lye Specialist Centre (☑228 8501; www.lohguanlye.com; 19 Jln Logan)
Penang Adventist Hospital (☑222 7200; www.pah.com.my; 465 Jln Burma)

Money

Branches of major banks are on Lebuh Pantai and Lebuh Downing near the main post office, and most have 24-hour ATMs. At the northwestern end of Lebuh Chulia there are numerous moneychangers open longer hours than banks and with more competitive rates.

Post

Post Office (Lebuh Downing; ⊙8.30am-6pm Mon-Sat)

Tourist Information

Penang Heritage Trust (PHT; ☑264 2631; www.pht.org.my; 26 Lebuh Pantai; ⊙9am-5pm Mon-Fri, 9am-1pm Sat) Information on the history of Penang, conservation projects and heritage walking trails.
Penang Tourist Guide Association (☑261 4461; www.ptga.my) Call or check the website to find a local tour guide.
Tourism Malaysia (☑262 0066; www.tourism. gov.my; 10 Jln Tun Syed Sheh Barakbah; ⊙8am-5pm Mon-Fri) George Town's main tourist information office gives out maps and bus schedules.

Travel Agencies

Most, but not all, of the agencies in George Town are trustworthy. Reliable operators that many travellers use to purchase discounted airline tickets:

Happy Holidays (☑262 9222; 432 Lebuh Chulia; ⊙9am-6pm Mon-Fri, to 1pm Sat)
Silver-Econ Travel (☑262 9882; 436 Lebuh Chulia; ⊙9am-6pm Mon-Fri, to 3pm Sat)

Websites

www.visitpenang.gov.my Official website of state tourism entity; great for details on festivals and events.
www.igeorgetownpenang.com An excellent newsletter aimed at Penang residents; gives good under-the-skin information on George Town.
www.tourismpenang.gov.my Details of sights and restaurants in Penang.

GETTING TO & FROM BUTTERWORTH

Butterworth, the city on the mainland bit of Penang (known as Sebarang Perai), is home to Penang's main train station and is the departure point for ferries to Penang Island. Unless you're taking the train or your bus has pulled into Butterworth's busy bus station from elsewhere, you'll probably not need to spend any time here.

The cheapest way to get between Butterworth and George Town is via the **ferry** (per adult/car RM1.20/7.70; ⊙5.30am-1am); the terminal is linked by walkway to Butterworth's bus and train stations. Ferries take passengers and cars every 10 minutes from 5.30 to 9.30pm, every 20 minutes until 11.15pm, and hourly after that until 1am. The journey takes 10 minutes and fares are charged only for the journey from Butterworth to Penang; returning to the mainland is free.

If you choose to take a taxi to/from Butterworth (approximately RM50), you'll cross the 13.5km Penang Bridge, one of the longest bridges in the world. There's a RM7 toll payable at the toll plaza on the mainland, but no charge to return.

At research time, construction was well underway on a second bridge linking Batu Maung at the southeastern tip of the island to Batu Kawan on the mainland. It should be completed by the time you're reading this.

www.penangmonthly.com Webpage of the monthly news magazine.

www.what2seeonline.com Penang-based food blog.

www.penang.ws Fairly up-to-date clearing house of hotel and restaurant listings.

❶ Getting There & Away

AIR

Penang's **Bayan Lepas International Airport** (📞643 4411) is 18km south of George Town and was being renovated at the time of research. The airport has money exchange and car rental booths and a **Tourism Malaysia counter** (📞642 6981; ground floor; ⏰7am-10pm). The following airlines operate from Penang's airport:

AirAsia (📞nationwide 600-85 8888; www.airasia.com) Flights to Bandung (Indonesia), Bangkok, Hong Kong, Jakarta, Johor Bahru, Kota Kinabalu, Kuala Lumpur, Kuching, Langkawi, Medan (Indonesia), Singapore and Surabaya (Indonesia).

Cathay Pacific (www.cathaypacific.com) Daily flights to/from Hong Kong.

Firefly (📞nationwide 03-7845 4543; www.firefly.com.my) Flights to Banda Aceh (Indonesia), Kota Bharu, Kuala Lumpur, Kuantan, Langkawi, Medan (Indonesia), Melaka and Phuket (Thailand).

Jetstar (📞nationwide 1800-81 3090; www.jetstar.com; Bayan Lepas International Airport; ⏰7am-9pm) Flights to Adelaide (Australia), Bangkok, Gold Coast (Australia), Ho Chi Minh City (Saigon), Hong Kong, Jakarta, Launceston (Australia), Medan (Indonesia), Melbourne (Australia), Perth (Australia), Phuket (Thailand), Singapore, Surabaya (Indonesia) and Taipei.

Malaysia Airlines (📞nationwide 1300-88 3000; www.malaysiaairlines.com) Conducts daily flights to/from Kuala Lumpur.

Silk Air (📞263 3201; www.silkair.com; 12th fl, Plaza MWE, 8 Lebuh Farquhar; ⏰8.30am-5.30pm Mon-Fri) Daily flights to Singapore.

Thai Airways International (📞226 6000; www.thaiairways.co.th; 2nd fl, Burmah Place, 142-L Jln Burma; ⏰9am-5.30pm Mon-Fri) Conducts daily flights to/from Bangkok.

BOAT

Several ferry providers, including **Langkawi Ferry Service** (LFS; 📞264 3088; www.langkawi-ferry.com; PPC Bldg, Pesara King Edward; ⏰7am-5.30pm Mon-Sat, to 3pm Sun) have merged and operate a shared ferry service to Langkawi (adult/child one way RM60/45, return RM115/85; 1¾ to 2½ hours). Boats leave at 8.15am and 8.30am. Boats return from Langkawi at 2.30pm and 5.15pm. Book a few days in advance to ensure a seat.

BUS

All long-distance buses to George Town arrive at the Sungei Nibong Bus Station, just to the south of Penang Bridge, while buses bound for Butterworth arrive at the Butterworth Bus Station. A taxi from Sungei Nibong to George Town costs RM25; a taxi from Butterworth can cost as much as RM50.

Buses to destinations in Malaysia can be boarded at Sungai Nibong and more conveniently, the Komtar bus station; international destinations only at the latter. Note that transport to Thailand (except to Hat Yai) is via minivan; minivans are also an option in getting to the Cameron Highlands and the Perhentian Islands.

DESTINATION	DURA-TION (HR)	FARE (RM)	FREQUEN-CY
Ipoh	2½	20	Frequent departures, 7.15am-3pm & 7.30pm-8pm
Hat Yai (Thailand)	4	30	5am, 8.30am, noon, 3.30pm & 4pm
Kuala Lumpur	5	35	Every 30min, 7am-1am
Tanah Rata	5	35-38	Frequent departures, 7.15am-2pm
Perhentian Islands (includes boat transfer)	6	150	7.30am, 8am & 11.30am
Kota Bharu	7	40	9am & 9pm
Melaka	7	45	Frequent, 9-10.30am & 10.30-11pm
Kuala Terengganu	8	50	9am & 9pm
Johor Bahru	9	55	Hourly, 8am-11.30pm
Singapore	10	53	Hourly, 9am & 8.30-11.30pm
Ko Samui (Thailand; Surat Thani transfer)	12	80	5am, 8.30am & noon
Ko Phi Phi (Thailand; Hat Yai transfer)	12	90	5am
Bangkok (Thailand; Surat Thani transfer)	17	115	5am, 8.30am & noon

TRAIN

Penang's train station is next to the ferry terminal and bus and taxi station in Butterworth. There are three daily trains to Kuala Lumpur (six hours, RM34 to RM67) and one in the opposite direction to Hat Yai in Thailand (four hours, RM26 to RM108); check with www.ktmb.com.my for the latest info on fares and schedules.

❶ Getting Around

TO/FROM THE AIRPORT

Penang's Bayan Lepas International Airport is 18km south of George Town. The fixed taxi fare to most places in central George Town is RM44.70.

Taxis take about 30 minutes from the centre of town, while the bus takes at least an hour. Bus 401 runs to and from the airport (RM3) every half hour between 6am and 11pm daily and stops at Komtar and Weld Quay.

BUS

Buses around Penang are run by the government-owned **Rapid Penang** (www.rapidpg.com.my). Fares are between RM1.40 and RM4. Most routes originate at Weld Quay Bus Terminal and most do also stop at Komtar and along Jln Chulia.

DESTINATION	ROUTE NO	PICK-UP
Batu Ferringhi	101	Pengkalan Weld, Lebuh Chulia, Komtar
Bayan Lepas International Airport, Teluk Kumbar	401	Pengkalan Weld, Lebuh Chulia
Persiaran Gurney	103	Pengkalan Weld, Air Itam, Komtar
Penang Hill	204	Pengkalan Weld, Lebuh Chulia, Komtar
Sungei Nibong Bus Station	401	Pengkalan Weld, Lebuh Chulia, Komtar
Teluk Bahang	101, 102	Pengkalan Weld, Bayan Lepas International Airport

CAR

La Belle (☑262 7717; www.labelle.net.my; 48 Lebuh Leith) car rental operates out of George Town. The companies listed below are based at Bayan Lepas International Airport.

New Bob Rent-A-Car (☑644 1111; www.bobcar.com.my; Bayan Lepas International Airport; ◷8am-10pm Mon-Fri, to 8pm Sat-Sun)

Avis (☑643 9633; www.avis.com; Bayan Lepas International Airport; ◷8am-9pm Mon-Fri, to 5pm Sat-Sun)

Kasina (☑644 7893; www.kasina.com.my; Bayan Lepas International Airport; ◷7.30am-10pm Mon-Sat & 8.30am-5pm Sun)

Pacific Rent-A-Car (PRAC; ☑643 8891; www.iprac.com; Bayan Lepas International Airport; ◷7.30am-10pm Mon-Sat & 8am-6pm Sun)

MOTORCYCLE

You can hire motorcycles from many places, including guesthouses and shops along Lebuh Chulia or out at Batu Ferringhi. Manual bikes start at about RM20 and automatic about RM30, for 24 hours.

TAXI

Penang's taxis all have meters, which drivers flatly refuse to use, so negotiate the fare before you set off. Typical fares to places outside of the city centre start at around RM12. Taxis can be found on Jln Penang, near Cititel Hotel, at the Weld Quay Bus Terminal and near Komtar bus station.

TRISHAW

Bicycle rickshaws are a fun, if touristy, way to negotiate George Town's backstreets and cost around RM40 per hour – the same as with taxis, it's important to agree on the fare before departure. Drivers can be found waiting near Cititel Hotel.

Batu Ferringhi

For years, and no doubt aided by the tourism authorities, the lure of sun and sand at Batu Ferringhi was the main reason people came to Penang. In reality, the beach can't compare to Malaysia's best; the water isn't as clear as you might expect, swimming often means battling jellyfish, and the beach itself can be dirty, especially on weekends when hordes of day trippers visit. Still, it is the best easy-access beach stop on the island, and it does make a pleasant break from the city.

The vast majority of the area's accommodation and restaurants are located along Jln Batu Ferringhi, the main strip, a short walk from the beach.

🏃 Activities

You'll find plenty of **watersports** rental outfits along the beach; they tend to rent **wave runners** (RM120 for 30 minutes), as well as offer **water-skiing** (RM60 for 15 minutes) and **parasailing** (RM80 per ride) trips.

SPICE UP YOUR LIFE

Along the road to Teluk Bahang is the **Tropical Spice Garden** (881 1797; www.tropical spicegarden.com; Jln Teluk Bahang; adult/child RM14/10, incl tour RM22/15; 9am-6pm), an oasis of exotic, fragrant fecundity of more than 500 species of flora, with an emphasis on spices. Ferns, bamboo, ginger and heliconias are among the lush vegetation and you might spot a giant monitor lizard or two. The restaurant here, Tree Monkey, is also excellent, and the garden also offers **cooking courses** (RM200; lessons 9am-1pm Mon-Sat).

To get here, take bus 101 towards Teluk Bahang and ask to get off at the Spice Garden (RM2).

After which you might need a relaxing **massage**. All sorts of foot masseuses will offer you their services; expect to pay around RM40 for a 30-minute deep-tissue massage.

✦ Festivals

Penang Beach Carnival   CARNIVAL
This carnival in Batu Ferringhi is highlighted by traditional sporting events such as *gas uri* (top spinning) and *sepak takraw* (a ball game played over a net, much like badminton but with the players using their feet). Held in November.

Penang Island Jazz Festival   MUSIC
(www.penangjazz.com) This event features local and international artists at changing venues in Batu Ferringhi. Held in November/December.

🛏 Sleeping

Batu Ferringhi has lots of somewhat overpriced, chain-style resorts catering to families, and quite a few extremely overpriced, homestay-type budget places, but very little in between.

TOP CHOICE / Lone Pine Hotel   RESORT $$$
(886 8686; www.lonepinehotel.com; 97 Jln Batu Ferringhi; incl breakfast r/ste RM680-840/950-2940; ❄@🛜🏊) Dating back to the 1940s, the Lone Pine is one of Batu Ferringhi's oldest resorts. A 2010 remodel and expansion has given the hotel a new lease on life, while still preserving many of its classier original aspects. The 90 rooms all have some kind of perk, personal plunge pools, for example, or private gardens. They also feel quite large, and are decorated with splashes of colour and attractive furniture. The grounds have a stately, national park–like feel, with hammocks suspended between the pines (actually casuarina trees), and a huge saltwater pool as a centrepiece.

Rasa Sayang Resort   RESORT $$$
(881 1966; www.shangri-la.com; Jln Batu Ferringhi; incl breakfast r/ste RM1080-2130/1710-10,000; ❄@🛜🏊) Part of the Shangri-La chain, this is a vast and luxurious establishment – the island's only five-star resort – that feels like something out of a South Sea dream. Rooms are large and decorated with fine hardwood furniture, and cloud-like white duvets float on the beds; all have balconies and many have sea views. There's a yoga studio, tennis courts, a putting green and several restaurants. The hotel's Chi Spa is among the poshest on Penang.

EQ   HOTEL $$
(885 1533; www.eqferringhi.com; 17 Lorong Sungai Emas; r RM88-148; ❄🛜) If you need a midrange hotel and are OK with zero character and a short walk to the beach, this is your place. Rooms are spacious, and equipped with air-con, TV and large-feeling bathrooms with hot water – and that's about it.

EQ is located behind the Eden Parade shopping complex, near the petrol station intersection; there are a couple similar places nearby.

Hard Rock Hotel   RESORT $$$
(881 1711; www.penang.hardrockhotels.net; Jln Batu Ferringhi; incl breakfast r/ste RM700-1300/1350-4000; ❄@🛜🏊) If you can stomach the corny hyper-corporate vibe (and the unrelenting gaze of Beatles memorabilia), this resort – at research time, Batu Ferringhi's youngest – can be a fun place to stay. There's a particular emphasis on family friendliness, and child-friendly pools, kid-friendly suites and teen-themed play areas (complete with pool table and video games), making it an easy decision for anybody travelling with children.

Parkroyal   RESORT $$$
(881 1133; www.parkroyalhotels.com; Jln Batu Ferringhi; incl breakfast r/ste RM745-1245/1245-2745;

✳@🛜✖) The 1980s-era exterior here is a pretty good indicator of what's going on inside: 324 standard and comfortable, but non-flashy rooms. The grounds are more a reason to stay, with three pools, some with islands in them, lots of lawn to bask on and a great strip of beach out front.

Ferringhi Inn
HOTEL $$

(☎881 9999; www.feringghiinn.blogspot.com; 3A Lorong Sungai Emas; r RM80-160; ✖🛜) The flagship rooms at this budget hotel are located behind the Eden Parade shopping centre, a couple of blocks from the sea. A more appealing option is the duplex brick bungalow, right on the beach in the backpacker zone, that's been made into two large and comfy rooms equipped with TV, air-con, fridge and terrace.

D'Feringghi
HOTEL $$

(☎881 9000; www.dferingghihotel.com; 66 Jln Batu Ferringhi; r RM145-180; ✖🛜) This hotel won't inspire any postcards home, but it's a contender within its price bracket. Rooms are clean and – for Batu Ferringhi, at least – inexpensive.

Located roughly opposite Tarbush restaurant, a brief walk to the beach.

Holiday Inn Resort
RESORT $$

(☎881 1601; www.holidayinnresorts.com/penang; 72 Jln Batu Ferringhi; incl breakfast r/ste RM550-660/810; ✖@🛜✖) A big, family-friendly resort with accommodation blocks on either side of the main road – you can't miss this hotel. It's yet another place that's great for kids, with expansive pools and themed 'kidsuites', which come with TV, video and Playstation. There's also tennis courts and a gym for the adults.

Lazy Boys
GUESTHOUSE $

(☎881 2486; www.lazyboystravelodge.net; off Jln Batu Ferringhi; dm/r RM18/35-150; ✖) This is the type of budget place some travellers live for and others flee from. Think of your university dorm if it was run by a laid-back Malaysian rocker, and you begin to get the idea. Dorms and rooms are clean enough, and there's amenities ranging from a kitchen to free laundry, but the music room (complete with drum kit) and spotty service are bad signs for those who cherish convenience and/or quiet.

Lazy Boys is located just of the main strip, approximately across from Tarbush restaurant.

Baba Guest House
GUESTHOUSE $

(☎881 1686; babaguesthouse2000@yahoo.com; 52 Batu Ferringhi; r RM50-95; ✖) This is a wonderfully ramshackle, blue-painted house that shows off the heart and soul of its resident (and very active) Chinese family. Rooms are large and spotless – although bare – and most have shared bathrooms, while the dearer air-con rooms come with a fridge and shower.

Shalini's Guest House
GUESTHOUSE $

(☎012-407 3822; www.shanilisguesthouse.blogspot.co; 56 Batu Ferringhi; r RM40-250; ✖) This old, two-storey wooden house on the beach has a family atmosphere. Rooms are basic but neat and some have balconies. The priciest ones have private bathrooms.

ET Budget Guest House
GUESTHOUSE $

(☎881 1553; etguesthouse2006@yahoo.com; 47 Batu Ferringhi; fan/air-con RM50/85; ✖) In a bright and open double-storey Chinese home with polished wood floors. Only the air-con rooms have TVs and en suite bathrooms.

Ismail Beach Guest House
GUESTHOUSE $

(☎016-454 1953; cabinkdn@yahoo.com; Batu Ferringhi; r RM80-160; ✖) Right on the beach, the rooms here have air-con, attached bath as well as TV.

✖ Eating & Drinking

You can get a beer at most non-Halal places, but toes-in-the-sand type beach bars are few – Bora Bora (Jln Batu Ferringhi; ⊙noon-1am Sun-Thur, to 3am Fri-Sat) is an exception.

Tree Monkey
THAI $$

(Tropical Spice Garden, Teluk Bahang; mains RM12.80-48.80; ⊙9am-11pm) A Thai owner oversees a huge variety of tasty Southeast Asian and Thai dishes, including several 'tapas' sets (RM30 to RM98). This is alfresco at its best, under a thatched roof and surrounded by gorgeous gardens with a view of the sea. It's also an excellent place for a sunset cocktail.

Tree Monkey is located at the Tropical Spice Garden, about halfway between Batu Ferringhi and Teluk Bahang; hop on bus 101 (RM2) or take a taxi from Batu Ferringhi (around RM10).

Tarbush
MIDDLE EASTERN $$$

(www.tarbush.com.my; Jln Batu Ferringhi; mains RM12-55; ⊙10-1am; ✖) Middle Eastern tourists and residents have brought their food to Batu Ferringhi, and Lebanese restaurants line the town's main strip. The best of the lot is most likely this branch of a KL restaurant empire. There's lots to choose from, but we like the two 'mezze platters', which bring together everything from tabouli (a bulgur salad) to *kibbeh* (meatballs with bulgur).

Tarbush is located approximately in the middle of town – look for the large seaside building topped with a fez.

Long Beach
MALAYSIAN $$

(Jln Batu Ferringhi; mains from RM4; ⊘6.30-11.30pm) This buzzy hawker centre has the usual selection of Chinese noodle dishes, Indian breads and meat curries, and Malaysian seafood dishes.

Long Beach is located approximately in the centre of Batu Ferringhi's main strip, not far from the petrol station intersection.

Bungalow
INTERNATIONAL $$

(☑886 8686; www.lonepinehotel.com; 97 Jln Batu Ferringhi, Lone Pine Hotel; mains RM16-48; ❖) The eponymous bungalow dates back to the 1940s, and is where the Lone Pine hotel sprang from. Today, the restaurant maintains the historical link with dishes such as Chicken chop and Macaroni pie – remnants of the era when Hainanese chefs, former colonial-era domestic servants, dominated restaurant kitchens. Other Malaysian and international dishes are available.

Ferringhi Garden
INTERNATIONAL $$

(Jln Batu Ferringhi; mains RM20.80-95.80; ⊘dinner) Everyone falls in love with the outdoor setting here of terracotta tiles and hardwoods surrounded by bamboo, tall potted plants, hanging mosses and cut orchids in elegant vases. Unfortunately the menu, which emphasises steaks and prawns, isn't as inspiring. During the daytime hours, an adjacent café serves breakfast and real coffee – a relative rarity in Batu Ferringhi.

Ferringhi Garden is located a block or so west of the Holiday Inn.

🚹 Getting There & Away

Bus 101 runs from Weld Quay and from Komtar, in George Town, and takes around 30 minutes to reach Batu Ferringhi (RM4). A taxi to Batu Ferringhi from George Town will cost at least RM35.

Teluk Bahang & Around

If Batu Ferringhi is Penang's version of Cancun or Bali, Teluk Bahang is the quiet (sometimes deathly so) beach a few kilometres past the party.

◉ Sights

At research time, Escape (www.escape.my), an 'eco theme park', was under construction near the Butterfly Farm – it should be open by the time you're reading this.

There area couple worthwhile sights (a tropical fruit farm and a butterfly farm) south of Teluk Bahang; both can be reached on bus 501, which runs from Teluk Bahang four times a day (RM2).

Penang National Park
PARK

(Taman Negara Pulau Pinang; admission free, canopy walkway adult/child RM7/5; ⊘canopy walkway 10am-1pm & 2-4pm Sat-Thurs) At just 2300 hectares, Penang National Park is the smallest in Malaysia; it's also one of the newest, attaining national park status in 2003. It has some interesting and challenging trails through the jungle, as well as some of Penang's finest and quietest beaches.

The office (☑881 3500; ⊘8am-6pm) at the park entrance has a few maps and leaflets and can help you plan your day. Just across from the main park office is the Penang Nature Tourist Guide Association (PNTGA) (☑881 4788; www.pntga.org) office, which offers guide services with a slew of options, such as trekking (four hours for RM100) and many where you can hike one way then get a ride back in a boat (four hours including boat transport for two people RM200), and also specialist tours such as birdwatching, seasonal visits to a turtle hatchery and mangrove tours. It's best to reserve longer tours in advance with agencies around George Town or at your hotel.

The park entrance is a short walk from Teluk Bahang's main bus stop. From here it's an easy 20-minute walk to the 250m-long canopy walkway, suspended 15m up in the trees from where you can hear water flowing from the mountain and get a view over the broccoli-headed park. The walkway was being renovated when we stopped by, and closes if it's raining. From here, you have the choice of heading towards Teluk Tukun and Muka Head or to Pantai Kerachut. The easiest walk is the 20-minute stroll to Teluk Tukun beach where Sungai Tukun flows into the ocean. There are some little pools to swim in here. Following this trail along the coast about 25 minutes more brings you to the private University of Malaysia Marine Research Station, where there is a supply jetty, as well as **Tanjung Aling**, a nice beach to stop at for a rest. From here it's another 45 minutes or so down the beach to **Teluk Duyung**, also called Monkey Beach, after the numerous primates who scamper about here on the beach on **Muka Head**, the isolated rocky promontory at the extreme northwestern corner of the island. On the peak of the head, another 15 minutes along, is an off-limits 1883 lighthouse and an Achenese-style graveyard. The views of the surrounding islands from up here are worth the sweaty uphill jaunt.

A longer and more difficult trail heads left from the suspension bridge towards **Pantai Kerachut**, a beautiful white-sand beach that is a popular spot for picnics and is a green turtle nesting ground. Count on about two hours to walk to the beach on the well-used trail. On your way is the unusual meromictic lake, a rare natural feature composed of two separate layers of unmixed freshwater on top and seawater below, supporting a unique mini-ecosystem. From Pantai Kerachut beach you can walk about two hours onward to further-flung and isolated **Teluk Kampi**, which is the longest beach in the park; look for trenches along the coast that are remnants of the Japanese occupation in WWII.

Tropical Fruit Farm
FARM

(www.tropicalfruits.com.my; tour adult/child RM35/28; ⊙9am-5pm) About 2km south of Teluk Bahang is the 10-hectare hillside farm, which cultivates over 250 types of tropical and subtropical fruit trees, native and hybrid. Its one-hour **tours** include fruit tastings and a glass of fresh juice.

Penang Butterfly Farm
FARM

(www.butterfly-insect.com; 830 Jln Teluk Bahang; adult/child RM27/15; ⊙9am-5pm) Several thousand live butterflies representing over 150 species flap around here like buttery pastel clouds. There's also some fascinating beetles, lizards and spiders crawling about.

🛏 Sleeping & Eating

Teluk Bahang is only 4km from Batu Ferringhi so if the few sleeping options here don't suit you, there are plenty more over there.

The main shopping area along the road heading east to Batu Ferringhi has a few coffee shops where you'll find cheaper Chinese dishes and seafood, as well as a couple of South Indian places, such as **Restoran Khaleef** (Jln Teluk Bahang; mains from RM4; ⊙24hr), that sell *murtabak* and *dosa* (savoury Indian pancakes).

Chalet Sportfishing
HOTEL $$

(✆881 9190; Jln Teluk Bahang; r RM80-130; ❄🛜) Probably Teluk Bahang's most comfortable place to stay, the two floors of plain rooms are at the edge of the beach and look over the fishing pier. The more expensive rooms have up to five beds. The Malay owner doesn't speak a great deal of English.

Ali's Motel
HOTEL $$

(✆885 1937; Jln Teluk Bahang; d/r RM30/80-180; ❄) The rooms here are plain, but come equipped with TV, air-con and hot water showers. If the friendly, English-speaking owner isn't around, service is nonexistent and communication can be difficult. Ali's is located next door to Restoran Khaleel, near Teluk Bahang's main bus stop.

❶ Getting There & Away

Bus 101 runs from George Town every half-hour all the way along the north coast of the island as far as the roundabout in Teluk Bahang (RM4). A taxi here from the centre of George Town will cost at least RM40.

Pulau Jerejak

Lying 1.5 nautical miles off Penang's southeast coast, thickly forested Pulau Jerejak has been home to a leper colony and a prison in its time, and is today occupied by the **Jerejak Rainforest Resort** (✆658 7111; www.jerejakresort.com; r RM210-420; ❄@🛜☃). Packages available through the website, which usually include transport, breakfast and a massage, make staying here good value. **Camping** (RM80 to RM100) is also an option.

The resort has its own jetty, with boats leaving roughly every two hours (adult/child RM6/3). **Day-trip package tours** (adult/child RM50-60/30-35) allow access to pool and other activities including rock climbing.

No buses run past the jetty; a taxi from George Town will cost around RM50.

Snake Temple

The most misleadingly named destination in Penang is about 3km before the airport. Yes, there are snakes at the temple (Temple of the Azure Cloud; snake exhibition adult/child RM5/3; ⊗9:30am-6pm) but, c'mon, with a name like that you expect beating drums and mad monks wielding 20-foot vipers. It's heavily touted but is essentially just a temple with some snakes sleeping on sticks. There's a very depressing snake exhibition with tanks containing various snakes in a walled-off section, and a few bored-looking snake handlers who will charge RM30 for taking your photo holding a snake.

Bus 302 runs every 30 minutes from Weld Quay and Komtar and passes the temple (RM4).

Batu Maung

At the end of the Bayan Lepas Expressway you'll reach the turn-off to the Chinese fishing village of Batu Maung. Once home to a biodiverse mangrove swamp, encroaching development from the Bayan Lepas Industrial Zone has resulted in extensive clearing. Development here is expected to skyrocket with the building of the new bridge linking Penang to the mainland. It's Penang's deep-sea fishing port so there are plenty of dilapidated, brightly painted boats along the coast.

The renovated seaside temple here, **Sam Poh Temple** (admission free), has a shrine dedicated to the legendary Admiral Cheng Ho, who was also known as Sam Poh. The temple sanctifies a huge 'footprint' on the rock that's reputed to belong to the famous navigator.

Perched on top of the steep Bukit Batu Maung is the **Penang War Museum** (☎626 5142; Bukit Batu Maung; adult/child RM35/17; ⊗9am-6pm & 7-11pm). This former British fort, built in the 1930s, was used as a prison and torture camp by the Japanese during WWII. Today, the crumbling buildings have been restored as a memorial to those dark days. Barracks, ammunition stores, cookhouses, gun emplacements and other structures can be explored here, which also offers 'suspense & eerie' night visits and paintball (from RM75).

Also in town is the **Penang Aquarium** (admission adult/child RM5/2; ⊗10am-5pm Thur-Tue), which houses 25 tanks filled with colourful fish; there is a tactile tank with a young green turtle, and visitors can also feed koi.

Bus 307 leaves for Batu Maung every half hour from Weld Quay and Komtar (RM4); a taxi here will cost about RM50.

Kampung Pulau Betong

This is a fishing village utterly off the beaten track with delightful *kampung* houses, flowers and colourful docked boats. At around 5.30pm the fishing boats come in and sell their fish at the little market near the dock. Bus 403 runs from Balik Pulau as far as the market (RM1.40), but if you walk another 1.5km you'll come to **Pantai Pasir Panjang**, an empty, pristine beach with white sand the texture of raw sugar – one of the prettier spots on the island for the

ESCAPING THE WORLD

Every now and then a Lonely Planet writer comes across a place so special it makes all the days of tirelessly slogging through sweaty cheap hotels worth it. **Malihom** (☎226 4466; www.malihom.com; all-inclusive RM570-700; ✳@🛜✳) is one of those places. Nine 100-year-old rice barns were imported from Thailand and brought up to this 518m peak where they have been restored to a cramped but comfortable state in a Balinese style. But you won't want to stay inside; walk around the small complex to gawk at the 360-degree view over hills of jungle, the sea and several villages. The most serene infinity pool on the island is guarded by white Buddhas, the grounds are a perfect balance of shade, flowers and koi ponds, there's a conference room and yoga studio, and indoor hang-out areas perfect for sipping espresso or a glass of wine from the cellar, reading a book or watching movies. Basically you come here to completely relax because, aside from a few walks, mountain biking or fruit picking, there's blissfully little to do.

The retreat is located off winding Route 6 between Balik Pulau and Kampung Sungai Batu, and you'll need to be shuttled in their 4WD up the steep hill that leads to Malihom.

few who make the effort to get here. The beach is backed by a National Service Training Centre for young graduates entering the army. Be vigilant if you go into the water – there's a heavy undertow.

Teluk Kumbar

Penangites come to Teluk Kumbar with one thing in mind: seafood. While some housing estates have sprung up recently, the village is still a calm and beautiful stretch of sands. Stop at one of the Malay food stalls for some *mee udang* (spicy noodles with prawns) or visit Hai Boey Seafood (☎013-488 1114; 29 MK9 Pasir Belanda, Teluk Kumbar; mains RM8-50; ⊙lunch & dinner), one of Penang's most famous destinations for seafood; call ahead to reserve a table on weekends or holidays.

Buses 401 and 401E pass Teluk Kumbar (RM4); a taxi here will cost about RM60.

Langkawi, Kedah & Perlis

📖 04 / POP 2,117,123 / AREA 10,321 SQ KM

Includes »

Kedah	184
Pulau Langkawi	185
Alor Setar	200
Around Alor Setar	204
Perlis	204
Kangar	204
Taman Negara Perlis	205

Best Places to Eat

» Muda Coffee Shop (p203)

» Hungry Monkey (p197)

» Siti Fatimah (p198)

» Ashkim (p198)

» Langkawi's night market (p197)

Best Places to Stay

» Bon Ton & Temple Tree (p193)

» Ambong Ambong (p194)

» Tanjung Sanctuary (p195)

» Tanjung Rhu Resort (p196)

» Datai Langkawi (p196)

Why Go?

The Malays are known as *bumiputra* (sons of the soil). That soil, physical and cultural, is most fertile in Kedah and Perlis. Limestone pillars thrust up through this paddyscape, which makes for the harvest of over half of Malaysia's rice supply.

Not that many foreigners see this. While it may be one of the most touristed states in Malaysia, most travellers would draw a blank if you asked them anything about 'Kedah'. That's because almost everyone knows it by its biggest island and Malaysia's number-one holiday destination: Pulau Langkawi. And justifiably so; Langkawi's clear waters and wide beaches warrant the attention they receive, while corners of the island even seem to mimic the green, fecund terrain of the mainland.

Perlis, Malaysia's smallest state, has an even lower profile. It's also proximate to Thailand, and most travellers rush through here on their way to that kingdom. Their loss: this corner of the country is part of the Malay heartland, which makes it overwhelmingly friendly and culturally significant.

When to Go

Kuala Kedah

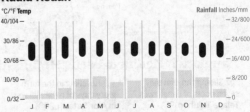

Feb Generally the region's driest month, although temperatures can be relatively high.

Apr–Oct The wettest time of year; the odd tropical storm is expected and tourist numbers are low.

Jul Typically Pulau Langkawi's coolest month.

KEDAH

For travellers' purposes there are essentially two Kedahs: the tropical island of Pulau Langkawi and its attached islets; and rural, little-visited mainland Kedah. The paddy field is the eternal horizon of the latter, also known as Malaysia's 'rice bowl'. Two blocks of colour constantly kiss at the edge of your eyesight: robin's-egg blue on top and deep, alive green on the bottom, with strips of bitumen webbing through. If you find inspiration in the rustic, clean-lined aesthetic of Asian agriculture, this state is the field of sunflowers to your inner van Gogh.

The other Kedah is the stuff of tourist brochures that don't skimp on descriptions such as 'sun-kissed' or 'paradise'. The good news is that Langkawi's beaches generally live up to the hype, and you'll even

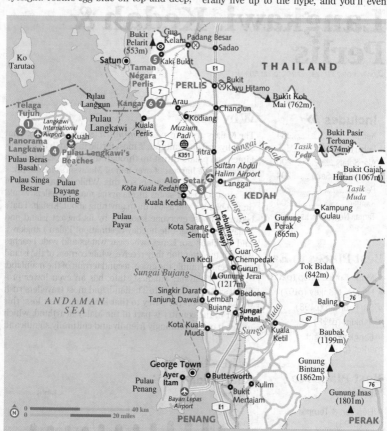

Langkawi, Kedah & Perlis Highlights

1 Sliding through the seven pools of Langkawi's **Telaga Tujuh** (p193)

2 Riding the **Panorama Langkawi** (p187) cable car all 708m to the top of Gunung Machinchang to enjoy the spectacular views

3 Revelling in the former glory days of royal Malaysia in **Alor Setar** (p200)

4 Relaxing on one of the stunning beaches of **Pulau Langkawi** (p185)

5 Exploring the limestone cliffs and remote border feel of **Taman Negara Perlis** (p205)

6 Visiting one of the country's better provincial museums at the **Muzium Kota Kayang** (p204)

7 Getting into the groove of small-town Malaysia in tiny **Kangar** (p204)

find pockets of the mainland's unique green landscape, in addition to an island destination that continues to maintain its Malay roots. If, like most, you've only included Pulau Langkawi on your itinerary, you can rest assured in the fact that you'll get the chance to witness both Kedahs.

History
Kedah is one of the most historically significant Malay states. Settlement goes back to the Stone Age, and some of the earliest excavated archaeological sites in the country are near Gunung Jerai. More recent finds in Lembah Bujang date back to the Hindu-Buddhist period in the 4th century AD, and the current royal family can trace its line directly to this time. Discoveries in Lembah Bujang show that it was the cradle of Hindu-Buddhist civilisation on the peninsula – the society that would become the foundation stone for Malay culture – and one of the first places to come into contact with Indian traders. The latter would eventually bring Islam to Malaysia, a religion whose cultural impact cannot be overstated here.

During the 7th and 8th centuries, Kedah paid tribute to the Srivijaya Empire of Sumatra, but later fell under the influence of the Siamese until the 15th century, when the rise of Melaka led to the Islamisation of the area. In the 17th century Kedah was attacked by the Portuguese, who had already conquered Melaka, and by the Acehnese, who saw Kedah as a threat to their own spice production.

In the hope that the British would help protect what remained of Kedah from Siam, the sultan handed over Penang to the British in the late 18th century. Nevertheless, in the early 19th century Kedah once again came under Siamese control, where it remained, either directly or as a vassal, until early in the 20th century when Siam passed control to the British. This history of changing hands between the Thai and the British manifests, in places, as a somewhat hybrid Malay-Thai culture.

After WWII, during which Kedah (along with Kelantan) was the first part of Malaya to be invaded by the Japanese, Kedah became part of the Federation of Malaya in 1948, albeit reluctantly.

During the 2008 elections, Kedah, which is traditionally a breeding ground for leaders of the Barisan National ruling party, came out strongly in favour of the opposition, particularly the Islamist Parti Islam se-Malaysia (PAS).

Pulau Langkawi
POP 64,792

Langkawi is synonymous with 'tropical paradise' – and with good reason. Since 2008 the archipelago's official title has been *Langkawi Permata Kedah* (Langkawi, the Jewel of Kedah), no doubt inspired by the island's clear waters, relatively pristine beaches and intact jungle. The district's been duty free since 1986 and roping in tourists well before that. Yet despite their immense drawing power, these 99 islands, dominated by 478.5-sq-km Pulau Langkawi, have not been overdeveloped beyond recognition. Get just a little way off the main beaches and this is idyllic rural Malaysia, all *kampungs* (villages) and oil lamps. It's the kind of tropical island where there's no lack of spas, seafood restaurants and beach bars, but where the locals continue to go about their ways just as they have for generations.

Sights & Activities
KUAH & AROUND
Kuah is Langkawi's main town, and the only reason to stop here is for banks, ferries or duty-free shopping.

FREE Lagenda Langkawi Dalam Taman THEME PARK
(Map p186; Jln Persiaran Putra; ⊙8am-7pm) A landscaped 'folklore theme park' that stretches along the waterfront. Bright statues dotted amid the lakes illustrate several Langkawi legends – with signboards in English – and there's a narrow, mediocre strip of beach. It's a popular spot for joggers.

Langkawi Bird Paradise ZOO
(Map p186; 1485 Jln Kisap, off Jln Air Hangat; admission adult/child RM28/18; ⊙8.30am-6pm) Langkawi Bird Paradise touts itself as Asia's first fully covered wildlife park. While there are plenty of animals around (with an emphasis on exotic birds), the fact that feeding is encouraged, coupled with the relatively poor state of the animals' environments, compels us to include this listing more as a discouragement than a recommendation. Langkawi Bird Paradise is located about 3km north of Kuah.

PANTAI CENANG
Underwater World AQUARIUM
(Map p190; www.underwaterworldlangkawi.com.my; Pantai Cenang; admission adult/child RM38/28; ⊙10am-6pm) Malaysia's largest aquarium,

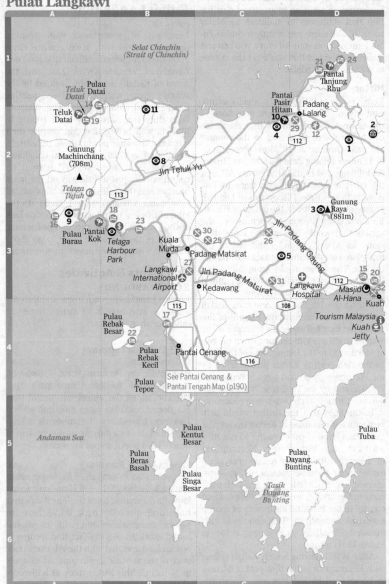

featuring 200 different species of marine and freshwater creatures. Some exhibits (especially the rainforest walk) are well executed; some feel like a tropical aquarium in need of a cleaning, but in general it's a great place for the kids.

FREE Laman Padi   MUSEUM
(Rice Garden; Map p190; ☺10am-6pm) Kids will love this somewhat abandoned-feeling 'eco-tourism' complex comprising rice paddies populated by water buffaloes and ducks. If you can locate the staff (we couldn't), you

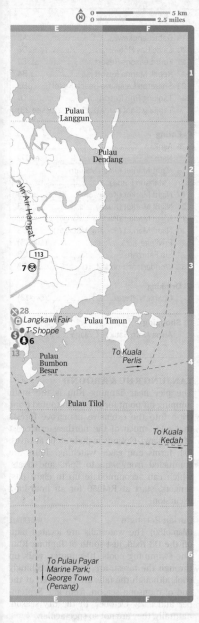

the breeze while you're pummelled and oiled by Thai masseurs (massages RM45 to RM100).

Nithi Ayurvedic Massage   SPA
(Map p190; ☎955 9078; www.langkawi-ayurvedic-massage.com; Pantai Cenang; ⊙10am-7pm) Customers rave about treatments like *shiro dhara*, where a continual flow of warm herbal oil is poured over your forehead as your head and shoulders are massaged. Treatments run from RM65 to RM195.

PANTAI TENGAH
The place to go for a massage or pedicure, the main strip along Pantai Tengah is home to the bulk of the island's spas. Massage treatments average about RM150 per hour, while facials and other treatments start at about RM60. Many of the below also offer complimentary transfer; call for details.

Alun-Alun Spa   SPA
(Map p190; ☎955 5570; www.alunalunspa.com; ⊙11am-11pm) With three branches across the island, Alun-Alun is accessible and gets good reviews. The spa's natural/organic products are also available for purchase.

Ishan Spa   SPA
(Map p190; ☎955 5585; www.ishanspa.com; ⊙10am-8pm) The six spa suites here offer some pretty posh pampering – air treatments, body scrubs and the like – in a space that screams traditional.

Ayer Spa   SPA
(Map p190; ☎955 6776; www.ayerspa.com.my; ⊙10am-11pm) Affordable Malay-style massage treatments in a cosy wood structure.

Sun Spa   SPA
(Map p190; ☎955 9287; ⊙1-10pm) Offers an interesting repertoire of affordable packages.

PANTAI KOK & AROUND
Oriental Village   AMUSEMENT PARK
(Map p186; www.orientalvillage.my; Pantai Kok; ⊙most outlets 10am-7pm) Even if you're not into shopping, this Disneyland-like open-air mall is home to one of the island's most worthwhile attractions. **Panorama Langkawi** (Map p186; www.panoramalangkawi.com; ⊙10am-8pm Mon-Tue, noon-8pm Wed, 10am-8pm Thu, 9.30am-8pm Fri-Sun) is a cable car that takes visitors on a vertiginous 20-minute trip to the top of the majestic Gunung Machinchang (708m). There are some incredible views along the way, and at the top, you can walk across the SkyBridge,

can learn about or even have a hand in planting rice. There's also a basic museum dedicated to rice cultivation, a restaurant and **Nawa Sari Spa** (Map p190; ☎955 4168; Laman Padi; ⊙10am-8pm), where you can contently watch rice paddies sway under

Pulau Langkawi

⊙ **Sights**
1 Durian Perangin D2
2 Galeria Perdana D2
3 Gunung Raya D3
4 Kompleks Kraf Langkawi C2
5 Kota Mahsuri C3
6 Lagenda Langkawi Dalam Taman E4
7 Langkawi Bird Paradise E3
8 Langkawi Crocodile Farm B2
9 Oriental Village A3
10 Pantai Pasir Hitam C2
11 Temurun Waterfall.................................B2

🚴 **Activities, Courses & Tours**
12 Air Hangat D2
13 East Marine..E4
    Langkawi Coral................................(see 6)
    Langkawi Elephant Adventures .....(see 9)
    Panorama Langkawi ....(see 9)
    Tiger! Tiger!.....................................(see 9)

🛏 **Sleeping**
14 Andaman Langkawi A1
15 Bayview Hotel...D3
16 Berjaya Langkawi...................................A3
17 Bon Ton & Temple Tree B4
18 Danna B3

19 Datai Langkawi A2
20 Eagle Bay Hotel......................................D3
21 Four Seasons Resort D1
22 Rebak Marina Resort B4
23 Sheraton Langkawi Beach Resort........B3
24 Tanjung Rhu Resort D1
    Tanjung Sanctuary ....(see 23)

🍽 **Eating**
25 Ashkim..C3
    Nam..(see 17)
26 Night Market (Jalan Makam
    Mahsuri Lama)...................................C3
27 Night Market (Kedawang)......................B3
28 Night Market (Kuah)..............................E3
29 Night Market (Padang Lalang) D2
30 Night Market (Padang Matsirat) C3
    Privilege...(see 18)
31 Siti Fatimah C3
32 Wonderland Food Store D3

🍷 **Drinking**
    Charlie's Place ....(see 13)

🛍 **Shopping**
    Atma Alam Batik Art Vilage ....(see 25)

a single-span suspension bridge located 100m above old-growth jungle canopy. Other attractions at Oriental Village include the overpriced **Langkawi Elephant Adventures** (Map p186; www.gajah.org; elephant rides for 2 adults & 1 child 5min RM80, 15min RM200; ☺10.30am-1pm & 2-5.45pm); **Tiger! Tiger!** (Map p186; admission free; ☺10am-7pm), a tiger exhibit and gallery; and a handful of restaurants and souvenir shops.

TELUK DATAI & AROUND
Temurun Waterfall WATERFALL
(Map p186) A brief walk from the main road, the falls here – the island's tallest – are worth a look; the turn-off is just east of a huge concrete archway spanning the road.

Langkawi Crocodile Farm FARM
(Map p186; admission adult/child RM20/15; ☺9am-6pm) If you're not a kid or sympathetic to reptiles you may enjoy the twice-daily 'stunt' shows and hourly feedings, but the small, dirty pools and the fact that many of the farm's residents are turned into meat is a turn-off for many.

TANJUNG RHU & AROUND
The pier near Tanjung Rhu is the main jumping-off point for the much-touted **boat trips** into the extensive mangrove forests that edge much of the northeastern coast of Langkawi. Options include stops at caves, fish farms and eagle watching. Tours are conducted from 9am to 5pm, and boats, which can accommodate up to eight passengers, start at RM250 for an hour-long excursion.

Durian Perangin WATERFALL
(Map p186) The waterfalls are located 3km off the 113 road, just south of Tanjung Rhu. The swimming pools, 10 minutes' walk up through the forest, are always refreshingly cool, although the falls are best seen at the end of monsoon season, from late September and early October. In the dry season, naturally, they are not so spectacular.

Air Hangat HOT SPRINGS
(Map p186; ☺8am-6pm) This village, located south of Tanjung Rhu, is known for its hot springs. Soak your feet for free or bathe in a private room for RM70 per hour. Massage is also available for RM80 per hour. The

modern complex also holds occasional 'cultural shows' – contact Langkawi's tourist office to see if anything is lined up. As with so many places on Langkawi, the springs are associated with an intriguing legend.

Pantai Pasir Hitam   BEACH

(Map p186) West of Tanjung Rhu and firmly on the tour-bus route is Langkawi's much touted but ultimately disappointing 'black-sand beach'. It isn't technically a black-sand beach, but mineral oxides have added their colour scheme to the coast. There's a small tourist market and, as a disturbing backdrop, the Kedah cement plant, which stands out like a post-apocalyptic, smoke-belching thumb amid the green.

ELSEWHERE ON THE ISLAND

Gunung Raya   MOUNTAIN

(Map p186) The tallest mountain on the island (881m) can be reached by a snaking, paved road through the jungle. It's a spectacular drive to the top with views across the island

and over to Thailand from a lookout point and a small teahouse (assuming there's no fog). Access to the mountain may occasionally be restricted by the government; the gate at the foot of the mountain will be lowered.

Kota Mahsuri   SHRINE

(Mahsuri's Fort; Map p186; admission adult/child RM15/5; ☺8am-6pm Mon-Thu, to 6.30pm Fri-Sun) Back around 1819 (the date is debated), the Malay princess Mahsuri was unjustly accused of adultery and executed by stabbing. With her dying breath she cursed Langkawi with seven generations of bad luck and expired, supposedly bleeding white blood, a sign of her innocence. Not long after, the Siamese invaded the island, and some 160 years later, in 1987 (that's about seven generations), Langkawi took off as a tourism destination. That's the story anyways, and its been commemorated by this historical complex that includes Mahsuri's Shrine as well as a re-creation of a traditional house, a

---

A CHEAT SHEET TO LANGKAWI'S BEACHES

Langkawi is big, folks, almost 500 sq km. Kuah, in the southeast corner of the island, is the main town and the arrival point for ferries, but the beaches are elsewhere.

The busiest and most developed beach is the 2km-long strip of sand at **Pantai Cenang**. The beach is gorgeous: white sand, teal water, green palms and all that good stuff. There are watersports activities at hand, and the water is good for swimming, but jellyfish are common, so you might feel a bit tingly when you go for a dip. A sandbar sometimes appears at low tide, allowing you to inspect local sea life. Between November and January you can walk across this sandbar to the nearby island of **Pulau Rebak Kecil**, but only for two hours around low tide. The island of **Pulau Tepor** can be reached by hired boat from Pantai Cenang. There are some very fine top-end resorts at Cenang, as well as the bulk of Langkawi's budget and midrange accommodation. Come night time, an odd mix of expats, domestic tourists, backpackers and package holidaymakers take to the main road to eat, drink, window shop and generally make merry.

Head south and Langkawi gets a little more polished; as the road loops around a rocky headland, you're in upscale **Pantai Tengah**. It's a slightly smaller, narrower beach, with less noisy watersports activity than on Pantai Cenang. There are a few big, all-inclusive resorts here, good restaurants and bars, and a few cheaper chalet clusters.

On the western part of the island, 12km north of Pantai Cenang, **Pantai Kok** fronts a beautiful bay surrounded by limestone mountains and jungle. Unfortunately an outdoor shopping centre and the nearby harbour have left it feeling somewhat overdeveloped. There are a handful of equidistantly located upscale resorts around here, many with their own small strips of beach.

On the far northwestern corner of the island, the beaches at **Teluk Datai** are arguably some of the island's most beautiful and secluded, but are really only accessible if you're staying in one of the area's two luxury resorts.

Also on the north coast, **Tanjung Rhu** is one of Langkawi's wider and better beaches, fronted by magnificent limestone stacks that bend the ocean into a pleasant bay. On clear days, the sunsets here give 'stunning' new meaning. The water is shallow, and at low tide you can walk across the sandbank to the neighbouring islands, except during the monsoon season. Accommodation is provided by two upscale resorts.

theatre, a 'diorama museum' and some simple food outlets.

A legacy of Mahsuri's curse can still sometimes be seen in the 'field of burnt rice' at nearby Padang Matsirat. There, villagers once burnt their rice fields rather than allow them to fall into the hands of Siamese invaders. It's said heavy rain still sometimes brings traces of burnt grains to the surface.

These sites are west of Kuah, a few kilometres off the road leading to the west-coast beaches and the airport.

Galeria Perdana   MUSEUM

(Map p186; Mukim Air Hangat; admission RM10; ⏰8.30am-5.30pm) Established by former Prime Minister Dr Mahathir Mohamad, this museum displays the sort of weird gifts that get passed between foreign nations and heads of state (F-1 racers, Ming vases painted with Mahathir's face – that sort of thing). Galeria Perdana is located about 8km north of Kuah.

🏃 Activities & Tours

The tours below can be booked at any of the numerous travel agents in Kuah and along Pantai Cenang, and at most upmarket resorts that organise tours. During the monsoon season from July to mid-September, the seas are often too rough and unpredictable for many of the boat trips.

Cruises

There are several cruise operators in Langkawi, nearly all of whom offer daily dinner, sunset and cocktail cruises. Boats depart from various piers across the island and bookings can be made by phone or online, or via travel agents.

Blue Water   CRUISE

(☎013-407 3166; www.bluewaterstarsailing.com) This outfit runs an infamously boozy dinner cruise every day from 2pm to 8pm (RM450). Boats depart from pier at Kuah; transport is not included.

Crystal Yacht Holidays   CRUISE

(☎955 6545; www.crystalyacht.com; Pantai Cenang) Operates popular sunset dinner cruises (RM250). Boats depart from the pier near the Awana Porto Malai, south of Pantai Tengah, and transport from most hotels is included.

Tropical Charters   CRUISE

(☎012-588 3274; www.tropicalcharters.com.my; Pantai Tengah) Offers a variety of cruises, starting from RM220. Boats depart from the pier

near the Awana Porto Malai, south of Pantai Tengah, and transport from most hotels is included.

Diving & Snorkelling

Strung out like several green jewels in the teal is the **Pulau Payar Marine Park**, the focus of Langkawi's dive and snorkelling expeditions. Most trips come to 2km-long Pulau Payar, but you probably won't see the interior of the island – all the action centres on a diving platform and horseshoe-bend of coast. Inquire about the water conditions beforehand, as it can be murky. But when it's clear you don't even have to snorkel to be treated to some wonderful views of tropical fish. Recommended diving outfits include:

East Marine   DIVING & SNORKELLING

(Map p186; ☎966 3966; www.eastmarine.com.my; Jln Pantai Dato Syed Omar, Royal Langkawi Yacht Club, Kuah; snorkelling/diving trips from RM230/250;

Pantai Cenang & Pantai Tengah

Pantai Cenang & Pantai Tengah

◎ Sights
1 Laman Padi A1
2 Underwater World B3

◑ Activities, Courses & Tours
3 Alun-Alun Spa.. B4
　Ayer Spa...(see 3)
　Helitours Langkawi ....(see 10)
4 Ishan Spa B4
　Nawa Sari Spa .... (see 1)
5 Nithi Ayurvedic Massage A1
　Sun Spa ....(see 3)

🛏 Sleeping
6 AB Motel.. A2
　Ambong Ambong...........................(see 4)
7 Beach Garden Resort A1
　Cabin Resort...................................(see 14)
8 Casa del Mar A1
9 Delta Motel... B3
10 Frangipani B3
11 Gecko Guesthouse A1
12 Green Village B4
13 Holiday Villa B4
14 Langkapuri Inn B3
15 Malibest Resort A1
16 Meritus Pelangi Beach Resort &
　　Spa A1
17 Palms Guest House A1

18 Rainbow Lodge A1
19 Sweet Inn A1
20 Tropical Resort B4
21 Villa Molek B3
　Zackry Guest House ....(see 22)

◐ Eating
　English Tea Room........................ (see 27)
22 Fat Mum...B4
23 Hungry Monkey B3
24 La Chocolatine B3
25 Night Market (Bohor Tempoyak).......... B1
　Orkid Ria ....(see 15)
　Osteria ....(see 21)
26 Putumayo B2
27 Red Tomato...B2
　Sheela's ....(see 22)
28 Tomato B2
29 Troppo Co..B4
　Unkaizan...(see 4)
30 USSR Restaurant B4

◉ Drinking
　Babylon...(see 15)
31 Cliff A3
　La Sal ....(see 8)
　Little Lylia's Chill Out Bar ....(see 14)
32 Sunba Retro Bar B4
　Yellow Café.......................................(see 14)

8am-6pm) Probably the most reputable diving outfit on the island. East Marine conduct full-day diving and snorkeling excursions to Pulau Payar, as well as PADI certification courses starting at RM1300.

Langkawi Coral　　　　DIVING & SNORKELLING
(Map p186; ☎899 8822; www.langkawicoral. com; 64 Jln Tanjung Tokong, Kuah; snorkelling/ diving from RM300/455) Diving and snorkelling trips to Pulau Payar include a buffet lunch along with some time for sunbathing and fish-feeding. Langkawi Coral operate a stall at Kuah's ferry pier, open approximately 7am to 9pm.

Coral Island　　　　DIVING & SNORKELLING
(www.coralisland.com.my; snorkelling/diving from RM120/200) Diving and snorkelling excursions to Pulau Payar. Booking is done online or by phone, and Coral Island offer transport from most parts of the island to the jumping-off point at Kuah.

Helicopter

Helitours Langkawi　　　　SCENIC FLIGHTS
(Map p190; ☎012-484 2270; Pantai Tengah; tours RM550-3750) This outfit offers helicopter tours of the area ranging in time from five to 45 minutes. The R44 helicopter can accommodate three guests.

Island Hopping

The most popular day trip is the island-hopping tour, offered by most tour and diving companies, and costing as little as RM25 per person; the operator **Coral Island** (www. coralisland.com.my) gets good reviews. Tours usually take in Dayang Bunting (Lake of the Pregnant Maiden), located on the island of the same name. It's a freshwater lake surrounded by craggy limestone cliffs and dense jungle, and it's good for swimming. Other destinations include Pulau Beras Basah, sea stacks, sea caves and a cruise around mangroves for a look at the local eagles. Pulau Singa Besar might also be visited, with its resident population of mouse deer and crotchety monkeys.

LEGENDARY LANGKAWI

The name Langkawi combines the old Malay words *helang* (eagle) and *kawi* (strong). Classical Malay literature claims the island as one of the resting places of Garuda, the mythological bird that became Vishnu's vehicle. The whole island is steeped in legends, and the favourite story is of Mahsuri, a maiden who was wrongly accused of infidelity. Before finally allowing herself to be executed, she put a curse on the island for seven generations. As proof of her innocence, white blood flowed from her veins, turning the sands of Langkawi's beaches white. Her mausoleum is known today as Kota Mahsuri.

Another legend concerns the naming of places around the island. Pulau Langkawi's two most powerful families became involved in a bitter argument over a marriage proposal. A fight broke out and all the kitchen utensils were used as missiles. The *kuah* (gravy) was spilt at Kuah and seeped into the ground at Kisap, which means 'to seep'. A pot landed at Belanga Perak (Broken Pot) and finally the saucepan of *air panas* (hot water) came to land where Air Hangat village is today. The fathers of these two families got their comeuppance for causing all this mayhem – they are now the island's two major mountain peaks. You can learn more at the intriguing Lagenda Langkawi Dalam Taman in Kuah.

Nature & Adventure Tours

Dev's Adventure Tours GUIDED TOUR
(494 9193; www.langkawi-nature.com; Pantai Cenang; tours RM100-220) Cycling, birdwatching, mangrove excursions, jungle walks, culture tours... This outfit offers a fat menu of options, and its guides and service get rave reviews. Booking is done online or by phone, and transport is provided from most hotels.

Langkawi Canopy Adventures GUIDED TOUR
(012-466 8027; www.langkawi.travel; tours RM180-220) The main highlight here is 'airtrekking' through the rainforest canopy, with excursions divided into two levels of difficulty. Booking can be done by phone or online, and needs to be done at least a day in advance. You'll need to arrange a taxi to take you to the site – a 30-minute ride from most parts of the island – at Lubuk Semilang, in the middle of Pulau Langkawi.

✴✴ Festivals & Events

April

Langkawi International Water Festival WATER SPORTS
Sandcastle-building, kayak racing, underwater treasure hunting and fishing are just some of the events held at this annual festival. Most competitions are held at Pantai Kok and Pantai Cenang.

Langkawi International Festival of Arts (LIFA) ARTS
Held every other year, this is a 10-day festival celebrating local and international art; the next one will take place in 2014.

October/November

Langkawi International Maritime and Aerospace Exhibition AIR SHOW
(www.lima.com.my) LIMA is considered one of the world's major air shows.

🛏 Sleeping

Despite the apparent variety, and perhaps due to the island's general isolation, accommodation on Langkawi doesn't have the same high standard as other beachy places in Southeast Asia. Sure, there are some amazing luxury resorts, but midrange places (and even many of the upscale ones) can feel lacklustre, and there are relatively few budget-oriented hostels and dorms.

During school holidays and the peak tourist season (approximately November to February), Pulau Langkawi can become crowded and advance bookings are generally necessary. At other times of the year supply far outstrips demand.

See our cheat sheet to the island's beaches to determine where to stay.

KUAH

There's really no reason to stay in Kuah unless you *seriously* have a thing for duty-free shopping. But if you've somehow managed to get stranded at the jetty, consider the following:

Bayview Hotel HOTEL $$$
(Map p186; 966 1818; www.bayviewhotels.com; 1 Jln Pandak Mayah; incl breakfast r/ste RM375-635/715-835; ❄@🔊🏊) This is your standard high-rise chain hotel. The rooms were slightly musty when we visited, but this was made

up for by great views from the higher floors. If you stay here, please let us know what goes on in the hotel's Woodpecker Lounge.

Eagle Bay Hotel
HOTEL $$

(Map p186; ☏966 8585; www.eaglebay.com.my; 33 Jln Persiaran Putra; r/ste RM270-390/440-500; ❄️🛜🏊) This hotel's eagle-themed exterior is a short walk from the jetty. Promotional rates are typically half of those listed here, making it one of the few budget/midrange places in Kuah.

PANTAI CENANG & AROUND

TOP CHOICE Bon Ton & Temple Tree
BOUTIQUE HOTEL $$$

(Map p186; ☏955 1688; ❄️@🛜🏊) These two quasilinked boutique hotels are our favourite places on Langkawi, if not in the region. **Bon Ton** (www.bontonresort.com.my; villas incl breakfast RM650-1270) takes the form of eight Malay stilt-houses perched over a grassy, coconut palm-studded plot of land, each one decked out with dark wood and positioned to catch the breeze. With its organic accents and traditional craftwork, it's somehow regal and rustic all at once. Next door, **Temple Tree** (www.templetree.com; r/villas incl breakfast RM670-1370) ups the stakes with a collection of antique structures relocated from various points in Malaysia. An imposing Chinese mansion, a wooden villa from Penang, colonial-style shophouses and other restored structures make up the stately, park-like compound. Linking both locations is a common thread of class, style, thoughtful service and – take this as a warning if you don't care to share your villa with Felix – cats.

Beach Garden Resort
HOTEL $$

(Map p190; ☏955 1363; www.beachgardenresort.com; r RM230-320; ❄️🛜🏊) An unabashedly old-school, yet clean 'n cheery, resort-style place right on a relatively quiet patch of Pantai Cenang. All 12 rooms are decked out with the same aged furniture, and share access to a tiny pool and the resort's rustically inviting restaurant.

Rebak Marina Resort
RESORT $$$

(Map p186; ☏966 5566; www.rebakmarina.com; incl breakfast r/ste RM1100-1450/1750-2050; ❄️@🛜🏊) Lying just off Pantai Cenang, the small island of Rebak Besar plays host to this exclusive resort, which offers spacious and elegant chalets in beautifully landscaped grounds. It has all the facilities you would expect, including a gym, spa, tennis courts and restaurants. Transfers from Langkawi airport are included in the price, and package deals strip a significant amount off the rates shown here.

Casa del Mar
BOUTIQUE HOTEL $$$

(Map p190; ☏955 2388; www.casadelmar-langkawi.com; ste incl breakfast RM1200-2100; ❄️@🛜🏊) This is a sumptuous, vaguely Spanish-themed place on the quieter northern end of Pantai Cenang. Rooms are decked out with thoughtful design touches and techie amenities, as well as a small private garden or balcony. Various package deals are available, and rates can vary dramatically according to occupancy.

Malibest Resort
HOTEL $$

(Map p190; ☏955 8222; www.malibestresort.com; r RM120-250; ❄️🛜) Malibest is a friendly, social-feeling place with rooms right on the busiest

LANGKAWI, KEDAH & PERLIS PULAU LANGKAWI

SLIPPIN' & SLIDIN'

If you've been splashing around the ocean, why not add some variety to your life and lounge in some freshwater rock pools? **Telaga Tujuh** (Seven Wells), located at the top of a waterfall inland from Pantai Kok, is a series of small pools connected by a thin trickle of refreshingly cool mountain water. The pools are surrounded by thick jungle that is home to a family of cheeky (and somewhat intimidating – keep any food out of sight) monkeys, and also offer brilliant views of the island. The smooth rut between the pools is slick enough to slide down, especially towards the bottom, but it's worth nothing that over the years, a few people have managed to slip past the partially gated edge of the falls, resulting in serious injury and even death.

You can get here by rented car, motorbike or taxi; follow the main road 1km past Pantai Kok, then turn right at the t-intersection, continuing until the road dead-ends at a car park. From here it's a steady 10-minute climb through the rainforest (stay to the right) to the wells at the top of the falls. You can make a 2.5km hike from here to the cable-car station in Oriental Village; this is a taxing route that requires sound shoes and a good level of physical fitness.

NARELLE MCMURTRIE: HOTELIER

Narelle has lived on Pulau Langkawi for 18 years and is the owner of Bon Ton & Temple Tree (p193).

How is Langkawi different from other beachy places in Southeast Asia? Langkawi has very few hotels. In the last eight years only one five-star hotel has opened. So development is slow and this is the pace of life. Tourists get to see a real island with people totally unaffected by tourism.

What's your favourite beach? One of the deserted beaches at Dayan Bunting island: beautiful little cove, clear water and a private beach.

Can you recommend a good place to eat? My favourite lunch place is Siti Fatimah. Normally 70 dishes are on offer, buffet style, for approximately RM7 with a drink. They are not after the tourist dollar and serve from the heart – very genuine people.

And a good bar? La Sal for sunset cocktails, surf and sand.

One must-do Langkawi activity? Hire a car to explore the island.

What's one interesting peek into local life? If you happen to be here for fasting month (Ramadan), you get to sample amazing home cooking from all the little stalls that appear from nowhere.

When's the best time to visit Langkawi? For the tan it's December, January and February; otherwise March when there is no rain.

stretch of Pantai Cenang. These range from relatively modern brick duplex bungalows to the undisputed king of the crop: 'treetop' chalets that sit atop tall wooden pylons and enjoy uninterrupted sea views.

Cabin Resort
HOTEL $$
(Map p190; ☑012-417 8499; www.thecabin.com.my; r RM150; 🕸🛜) With a vibe verging on caravan park, the Cabin features 10 cutesy duplex bungalows a short walk from the beach. Rooms are pleasantly cosy (read: small) but, decked out with colourful IKEA furniture, have more character than most places in this price range.

Meritus Pelangi Beach Resort & Spa
RESORT $$$
(Map p190; ☑952 8888; www.meritushotels.com; r/ste from RM1030; 🕸@🛜🛋) An expansive, family-oriented resort with a full roster of facilities, kids' activities, restaurants and a seemingly never-ending swimming pool. The rooms generally have a dark, slightly conservative feel, but this may change with the ongoing renovations.

Delta Motel
HOTEL $
(Map p190; ☑955 1307; www.facebook.com/del tamotel; r RM60-140, bungalows RM70-100; 🕸🛜) Tall trees and A-frame bungalows give this beachfront place a distinct campground vibe. The interiors of the A-frames don't live up to their recently renovated exteriors; you're better off staying in one of the newer rooms.

Langkapuri Inn
HOTEL $$
(Map p190; ☑955 1202; r incl breakfast RM140-220; 🕸🛜) A pleasant clutch of connected chalets at the southern end of the beach. The pricier ones have sea views and a pinch of character; the cheapest are in need of a renovation and should be avoided.

AB Motel
HOTEL $$
(Map p190; ☑955 1300; r RM60-150; 🕸) As the dull name essentially implies, this is a relatively basic complex of scrubbed-down rooms that gets good reviews from travellers for its cleanliness and extremely easy beach access.

PANTAI TENGAH & AROUND

TOP CHOICE Ambong Ambong
HOTEL $$$
(Map p190; ☑955 8428; www.ambong-among.com; ste incl breakfast RM685-1195; 🕸🛜🛋) This clutch of minimalist, contemporary structures on a jungly hillside results in a noteworthy and pleasing contrast. Choose between one of four inviting studio suites or one of the vast-feeling two-bedroom cottages; all are stylish and airy, have balconies overlooking the greenery, and a stay includes a complimentary massage. One of Langkawi's more sophisticated places to stay.

Villa Molek
HOTEL, APARTMENT $$$
(Map p190; ☑955 2995; www.villamolek.com; ste incl breakfast RM635; 🕸🛜🛋) Those looking for a quiet, homelike stay should head here. Accommodation takes the form of

12 apartment-style suites, each with living room and kitchenette. Rooms are situated in a small, secluded garden across the road from the beach and, as under 18s aren't welcome, draw a largely mature clientele.

Frangipani
RESORT $$$

(Map p190; ☎952 0000; www.frangipanilangkawi. com; incl breakfast r/ste RM700-1200/1500-1800; ❄@🛜🏊) Friendly service, genuine efforts towards ecologic conservation and a location right on a quiet stretch of beach are the reasons to stay at this vast resort, less so the slightly cramped rooms.

Zackry Guest House
GUESTHOUSE $

(Map p190; www.zackryguesthouse.langkawinetworks. com; r RM35-90; ❄@🛜) This messy, friendly, rambling, family-run guesthouse is the kind of place where you're likely to fall in with a local crowd. Rooms are basic, yet clean and cosy, and there are lots of ramshackle communal areas. Note that there's a two-night minimum, no phone bookings and only about half of the rooms have an attached bathroom.

Tropical Resort
HOTEL $$

(Map p190; ☎955 4075; www.tropicalresortlang kawi.com; r incl breakfast RM120-150; ❄@🛜) Located in this quiet spot at the back of the beach, just a few minutes' walk from the seashore, is this string of spotless and well-run chalets. A renovation at research time was injecting a bit of style in to the rooms, and there was talk of installing a swimming pool.

Green Village
HOTEL $$

(Map p190; ☎955 3117; www.greenvillagelang kawi.com; r incl breakfast RM140-230; ❄@🛜🏊) Green Village takes the form of several linked, low-rise villas surrounding a pool and gardens. Rooms are small and rather plain, but bikes, a treehouse and a pool table make this the clever choice for a family on a budget.

Holiday Villa
RESORT $$$

(Map p190; ☎952 9999; www.holidayvillahotellang kawi.com; incl breakfast r/ste RM460-520/1000-3600; ❄@🛜🏊) A vast resort complex retaining a palpable '80s feel, not to mention tennis courts, a gym, several restaurants and an indoor pool 'exclusively for ladies'. Rooms are airy and brightly furnished, and look out over the lawns and the soft white-sand beach.

Awana Porto Malai
RESORT $$$

(☎955 5111; www.awana.com.my; incl breakfast r/ ste RM358-531/849-4800; ❄@🛜🏊) A grand yet isolated-feeling resort just south of Pantai Tengah. Rooms are clean, if a little dated, and many look over an attractive harbour. The only beach is on an island just opposite the resort, a short boat ride away.

PANTAI KOK & AROUND

TOP CHOICE Tanjung Sanctuary
RESORT $$$

(Map p186; ☎952 0222; www.tanjungsanctuary. com.my; ste incl breakfast RM1000-1300; ❄@🛜🏊) Wind through thick jungle to emerge at a rocky headland and this subtle, classy resort.

BUDGET ACCOMMODATION

Pantai Cenang is home to the bulk of Langkawi's budget accommodation.

Sweet Inn (Map p190; ☎955 8864; r incl breakfast RM80-100; ❄🛜) Super Sweet, actually: a cute orange building dotted with umbrella-shaded tables, plain rooms that manage to keep cool in the heat and a friendly common area where meeting fellow congregants at the temple of backpacking is easy and breezy.

Palms Guest House (Map p190; ☎017-631 0121; r RM55-75; ❄🛜) Rooms here are basic and clean, and centred around a gravel-strewn courtyard shaded by (have a guess) palms. It's a good-value option, although we found service fluctuated between scarce and nonexistent.

Gecko Guesthouse (Map p190; ☎019-428 3801; rebeccafiott@hotmail.com; dm/r RM15/35-60; ❄🛜) Here you'll find a jungly collection of bungalows, chalets and dorms, and lotsa dreadlocked folk in the common area and very good chocolate milkshakes behind the bar.

Rainbow Lodge (Map p190; ☎955 8103; www.rainbowlangkawi.com; dm/r RM18/50-150; ❄@🛜) Set a little way back from the beach, this is a suitable option for those needing a cheap place to rest in between eating, drinking, hangover, and more drinking.

The 16 duplex villas are spacious and well appointed, but we liked the resort's remote, almost wild location, and the generous real estate between villas. Recommended.

Danna
LUXURY HOTEL $$$

(Map p186; ☑959 3288; www.thedanna.com; incl breakfast r/ste RM1400-1700/3000-20,000; ❄@🛜🏊) The imposing, colonial-themed Danna seems intent on setting a new standard for luxury on Langkawi. Rooms are huge and come decked out with attractive furniture and marble floors, and the hotel boasts its own man-made private island and Langkawi's biggest hotel pool. The Danna has several dining outlets of its own, but also has the benefit of being next door to the dining and nightlife options at Telaga Harbour Park.

Berjaya Langkawi
RESORT $$$

(Map p186; ☑959 1888; www.berjayahotel.com; incl breakfast r/ste RM820-1510/1770-2610; ❄@🛜) Past the headland at the northwestern end of the beach, the Berjaya seems to take up the entire northwest coast of the island. There's some 350 rooms spread over a vast area; guests are ferried between reception and their chalets in minibuses. The waterfront suites are the most attractive, while others look out onto the lush rainforest; a stay includes a complimentary tour of the latter.

Sheraton Langkawi Beach Resort
RESORT $$$

(Map p186; ☑952 8000; www.sheraton.com/langkawi; incl breakfast r/ste RM1380-1500/1700-6700; ❄@🛜🏊) To the southeast of the other resorts, the Sheraton Langkawi has all the usual five-star amenities in an attractively secluded setting on a forested headland by the sea. Yet despite an ongoing renovation, many of the rooms tend to feel somewhat dark and past their prime.

TELUK DATAI

Datai Langkawi
RESORT $$$

(Map p186; ☑959 2500; www.thedatai.com.my; incl breakfast r/ste RM2300-3200/3300-22,000; ❄@🛜🏊) Tucked into a jungly corner in the far northwest of the island, the Datai manages to feel both untamed and luxurious. Choose between the spacious and modern rainforest or seafront villas, all of which have access to a small city's worth of amenities (spas, gyms, yoga – the works), not to mention one of the island's best beaches. A unique luxury experience.

Andaman Langkawi
RESORT $$$

(Map p186; ☑959 1088; www.luxurycollection.com/andaman; incl breakfast r/ste RM1200-1900/2300-3000; ❄@🛜🏊) In a grand wooden Malay-style building seemingly dropped in the middle of the jungle is this luxurious retreat with the usual multistar amenities and dining outlets, as well as its own stunning semi-private beach. There are no villas or bungalows, but the rooms are large and inviting, many with great views.

TANJUNG RHU

TOP CHOICE Tanjung Rhu Resort
RESORT $$$

(Map p186; ☑959 1033; www.tanjungrhu.com.my; incl breakfast r/ste RM1400-1600/1800-2800; ❄@🛜🏊) This beautifully situated resort has large and comfy rooms with balconies and great views of the limestone and green water at Tanjung Rhu. Service is a pleasant blend of competent and friendly, and the resort has a family-friendly vibe. The only real downside is its distance from virtually all of Langkawi's attractions, restaurants and nightlife.

Four Seasons Resort
RESORT $$$

(Map p186; ☑950 8888; www.fourseasons.com/langkawi; incl breakfast r/ste RM2000-2700/5900-21,800; ❄@🛜🏊) Sporting a youthful (at least for a Four Seasons resort) vibe and a vaguely Moroccan theme, this is among Langkawi's most unique and luxurious resorts. Amenities are everything you'd expect at this level and service is impeccable. Bathrooms-so-big-you'll-get-lost-in-them aside, we loved the manicured jungle setting and the semi-private beach.

✗ Eating

AROUND KUAH

Wonderland Food Store
CHINESE $$

(Map p186; Lot 179-181, Pusat Perniagaan Kelana Mas, Kuah; mains from RM10; ☺dinner) Of the string of Chinese-style seafood restaurants just outside Kuah, Wonderland has been around longer than most and gets the best reviews. It's an informal, open-air place where the food is both cheap and tasty.

PANTAI CENANG & AROUND

Nam
INTERNATIONAL $$

(Map p186; ☑955 3643; mains RM30-74; ☺11am-11pm; 🌱) At Bon Ton Resort, Nam boasts a well-executed menu of fusion goodness, from chargrilled rack of lamb with roast pumpkin, mint salad hummus and tomato jam, to a nine-course sampler of Straits

LANGKAWI'S ROVING NIGHT MARKET

Local food can be a bit hard to find on Langkawi. Fortunately, for fans of Malay eats there's a rotating *pasar malam* (night market) held at various points across the island. It's a great chance to indulge in cheap, take-home meals and snacks, and is held from about 6pm to 10pm at the following locations:

Monday Jalan Makam Mahsuri Lama (Map p186), in the centre of the island, not far from the MARDI Agro Technology Park

Tuesday Kedawang (Map p186), just east of the airport

Wednesday & Saturday Kuah (Map p186), opposite the Masjid Al-Hana; this is the largest market

Thursday Bohor Tempoyak (Map p190), at the northern end of Pantai Cenang

Friday Padang Lalang (Map p186), at the roundabout near Pantai Pasir Hitam

Sunday Padang Matsirat (Map p186), near the roundabout just north of the airport

Chinese cuisine. There are lots of veggie options, and at night, amid Bon Ton's starry jungle grounds, the setting is superb. Reservations recommended during peak season (December/January).

Orkid Ria
CHINESE $$$
(Map p190; dishes from RM12; 11.30am-3pm & 6-11pm) The place to go on Pantai Cenang for Chinese-style seafood. Fat shrimp, fish and crabs are plucked straight from tanks out front, and there's the added benefit of air-con. It don't come cheap though.

English Tea Room
CAFE $
(Map p190; mains RM6-15; 8am-5pm) Come to this closet-sized cafe for good-quality sandwiches, sausage rolls, pies, scones and cakes. A great choice if you're growing weary of hotel breakfasts.

Tomato
MALAYSIAN $
(Map p190; mains from RM4; 24hr) This, your typical Malaysian *kandar* (Indian-influenced dishes served over rice) joint, serves excellent rotis and a standard curry-rice Indian/Malay menu at all hours – take note, nighthawks.

Red Tomato
INTERNATIONAL $$
(Map p190; mains RM20-40; 9am-11pm) The Red Tomato is run by expats who crank out some of the best pizza and pasta on the island. Of all the midrange places serving Western standards on the Cenang strip, this is probably your best bet.

Putumayo
ASIAN, INTERNATIONAL $$
(Map p190; mains RM18-48; 1-11pm) Excellent service (the waiter folds your napkin in your lap) amid a beautiful open-air courtyard. The

cuisine ranges from across Asia, looping from Malaysia through Thailand to China; we highly recommend the fish cooked Nonya style.

PANTAI TENGAH & AROUND

Hungry Monkey
TURKISH $$
(Map p190; mains RM29-139; 9.30am-11pm) Hungry Monkey features a cosy dining room, friendly service and a menu that extends far beyond döner kebab. We loved the Adana lamb kebab with eggplant dip, which, like most dishes, was filling and tasty, and came served with a loaf of yeasty, homemade bread.

Troppo Co.
INTERNATIONAL $
(Map p190; mains RM10-28; 9am-5pm Wed-Mon) A tiny cafe serving real coffee and fruit smoothies, supplemented with a menu of hearty breakfast dishes and creative sandwiches.

La Chocolatine
FRENCH $$
(Map p190; mains RM10-15; 9am-9pm) Excellent French desserts – croissants, tarts and éclairs – as well as light salads, sandwiches and quiches. Did we mention coffees, teas and real hot chocolate? A sophisticated, air-conditioned snack stop.

Osteria
ITALIAN $$
(Map p190; mains RM25-56; noon-11pm) Favoured by local residents, this breezy, quasi open-air dining room serves wood-fired pizzas, homemade pasta and other Italian specialties. Osteria is at its sexy best when it's dark out, so consider a dinner visit.

Unkaizan
JAPANESE $$$
(Map p190; 955 4118; www.unkaizan.com; mains RM40-60; dinner) Lauded Japanese food, served in a cosy bungalow, with seating

LANGKAWI, KEDAH & PERLIS PULAU LANGKAWI

either Japanese-style at low tables or on an open patio. The menu spans all that Japan is known for, but don't forget to ask for the specials board, which often includes dishes made with imported Japanese seafood. Reservations recommended.

Sheela's
INTERNATIONAL $$

(Map p190; mains RM11-45; ☺dinner Tue-Sun) A menu that's all over the map – Malay faves to lamb chops – served in an inviting garden setting.

Fat Mum
CHINESE $

(Map p190; mains RM7-16; ☺dinner Wed-Mon) A cheap and cheerful destination for Chinese that can get pretty boisterous.

USSR Restaurant
RUSSIAN $$

(Map p190; mains RM20-35; ☺lunch & dinner) Casual place serving an unexpected menu of borscht, *manti* (steamed dumplings) and other Russian staples.

PANTAI KOK & AROUND

Privilege
MALAY, INTERNATIONAL $$

(Map p186; 1st fl, Telaga Harbour Park; mains RM32-178; ☺noon-11pm Mon-Sat) We liked the intimate, jazzy dining room here and its views over the harbour, but weren't so crazy about the dulled-down 'modern Malaysian' dishes. Still, it's a good choice for those scared by spice or who favour style over flavour.

ELSEWHERE ON THE ISLAND

TOP CHOICE Siti Fatimah
MALAY $

(Map p186; Jln Kampung Tok Senik, Kawasan Mata Air; meals from RM5; ☺8am-5pm Thu-Tue) Quite possibly Langkawi's most famous destination for Malay food – and it lives up to the rep. Food here is served buffet style, and it's up to you to choose from among the tens of rich curries, grilled fish, dips, stir-fries and other Malay-style dishes. The flavours are strong and the prices low. Siti Fatimah is located on Jln Kampung Tok Senik, the road that leads to Kota Mahsuri; most taxi drivers are familiar with the place.

TOP CHOICE Ashkim
TURKISH $$

(Map p186; ☎012-687 0494; Jln Padang Matsirat, Padang Matsirat; mains RM22-150; ☺9.30am-11pm Mon-Sat, noon-11pm Sun) Run by an impossibly friendly Turkish-German couple, this is an unpretentious spot for homey Turkish and Mediterranean-style food. Expect kebabs, salads, mezze and fresh bread, much of which is made using imported ingredients.

Ashkim is located on Jln Padang Matsirat, next door to the Atma Alam Batik Gallery; call for directions.

 Drinking

As Langkawi is a duty-free island, it's arguably the best spot for booze in Malaysia. While you can get alcohol at many restaurants and hotels for half the price on the mainland, there are some decent beach-style bars here as well, most found along the southern end of Pantai Cenang.

Little Lylia's Chill Out Bar
BAR

(Map p190; Pantai Cenang; ☺9am-4am) This longstanding, chummy bar spills out on to Pantai Cenang until the late hours. The chairs and tables may be practically falling apart, but friendly service and a chilled-out vibe hold the place together.

Cliff
RESTAURANT, BAR

(Map p190; www.theclifflangkawi.com; Pantai Cenang; ☺11am-11pm) Perched on the rocky outcrop that divides Pantai Cenang and Pantai Tengah, Cliff is located for a sunset cocktail. Expect a full bar, a good wine selection and an eclectic menu that spans from Europe to Malaysia (mains RM38 to RM68).

Yellow Café
RESTAURANT, BAR

(Map p190; Pantai Cenang; ☺1pm-1am Tues-Sun) A fun, breezy place with tables right on the beach and a few imported beers. Come between 4pm and 6pm when beers are buy one get one free.

Babylon
BAR

(Map p190; Pantai Cenang; ☺4pm-1am) At a glance, this appears to be your typical beach reggae bar, but with a fat menu of cocktails, its own satay stall and two levels of seating, it emerges a bit more sophisticated than most.

La Sal
RESTAURANT, BAR

(Map p190; www.casadelmar-langkawi.com; Casa del Mar, Pantai Cenang) Open-air restaurant/cocktail bar with some creative drinks and a vaguely Euro vibe. Come evening, tables in the sand and torchlight make La Sal a sexy sunset drink destination.

Charlie's Place
RESTAURANT, BAR

(Map p186; Jln Pantai Dato Syed Omar, Langkawi Yacht Club, Kuah; ☺9am-midnight) About 500m uphill from the jetty is this glass cube looking over the harbour. Yes, it's located at the Langkawi Yacht Club, but it's a friendly, unpretentious place that functions equally well as a restaurant (mains RM22 to RM60) or bar.

Sunba Retro Bar
BAR

(Map p190; www.sungroup-langkawi.com; Pantai Tengah; ⊙7pm-late) A cover band, DJ, and yes, duty-free alcohol, form the fuel that propel parties late into the night here.

Shopping

If you haven't already noticed, Langkawi is a duty-free zone, and is a relatively cheap place to buy imported luxury goods, especially alcohol. The greatest conglomeration of duty-free shops is at the jetty in Kuah and at the southern end of Pantai Cenang, near Underwater World.

Atma Alam Batik Art Vilage
HANDICRAFTS

(Map p186; www.atmaalam.com; Padang Matsirat; ⊙9am-6pm) A huge handicraft complex – set to a funky karaoke-like soundtrack – with an emphasis on batik. Visitors can paint and take home their own swatch of batik for RM30. Atma Alam is located in Padang Matsirat, not far from the airport; most taxi drivers are familiar with it.

Kompleks Kraf Langkawi
HANDICRAFTS

(Map p186; www.malaysiacraft.com.my; Langkawi Craft Complex; Pantai Pasir Hitam; ⊙10am-6pm) An enormous handicrafts centre where you can watch demonstrations of traditional crafts and buy any traditional Malaysian product or craft you can imagine. There are also a couple of on-site exhibitions devoted to local legends and wedding ceremonies. The complex is located in the far north of the island, virtually across from Pantai Pasir Hitam.

ⓘ Information

Internet Access

The vast majority of hotels and many restaurants offer wi-fi, but internet cafes are few and far between.

Happy Sky Net Cafe (Pantai Cenang; per hr RM5; ⊙9am-11pm)

Medical Services

Langkawi Hospital (☑966 3333; Jln Bukit Tengah, Kuah)

Money

The only banks are at **Kuah** and **Telaga Harbour Park**, although there are also ATMs at the airport, the jetty and at **Underwater World**. There are a couple of **moneychangers** at Pantai Cenang, but elsewhere most travellers have to rely on the resort hotels, which a) give bad rates and b) might not change money if you are not a guest.

Tourist Information

Tourism Malaysia (☑966 7789; Jln Persiaran Putra, Kuah; ⊙9am-5pm) Located at the jetty in Kuah, this office offers comprehensive information on the whole island. At research time, an additional office was being opened at Langkawi's airport.

Websites

www.langkawigeopark.com.my Information on the island's natural areas.

www.langkawi-online.com A comprehensive source of island information.

www.mylangkawi.com Another source of island info.

ⓘ Getting There & Away

Air

Langkawi International Airport (☑955 1311) is located in the west of the island at Padang Matsirat. It's well stocked with ATMs, exchange booths, car-rental agencies, travel agencies, and by the time you read this, a Tourism Malaysia office.

The following airlines operate from Langkawi:

AirAsia (☑nationwide 600-85 8888; www.airasia.com) Langkawi International Airport (☑nationwide 600-85 8888; ground floor, Langkawi International Airport; ⊙7.30am-9pm) Daily flights to Kuala Lumpur, Penang and Singapore.

Firefly (☑nationwide 03-7845 4543; www.firefly.com.my) Langkawi International Airport (ground floor, Langkawi International Airport; ⊙9am-5pm) Daily flights to Kuala Lumpur (Subang Airport) and Penang.

Malaysia Airlines (☑nationwide 1300-88 3000; www.malaysiaairlines.com) Langkawi International Airport (☑955 6322, nationwide 1300-88 3000; www.malaysiaairlines.com; ground floor, Langkawi International Airport; ⊙8.30am-4.30pm & 5.30-7.30pm) Five daily flights to Kuala Lumpur.

TRAVEL AGENCIES

Both **FE Holidays** (☑955 3716; fe.holidays@gmail.com; Pantai Cenang; ⊙10am-10pm) and **Travel Shop** (☑955 8829; Pantai Cenang; ⊙10am-10pm) sell the usual gamut of tickets and car rentals, and can also sell seats and provide information on local snorkelling and boat tours.

LANGKAWI, KEDAH & PERLIS PULAU LANGKAWI

Silk Air (✆955 9771; www.silkair.com; 1st floor, Langkawi International Airport; ☺2-10pm Sun, 9am-5pm Mon, 2-10pm Tue, 9am-5pm Wed-Thu & 2-10pm Sat) Daily flights to Singapore.

Boat

All passenger ferries operate from Kuah's busy ferry terminal. Several ferry providers, including **Langkawi Ferry Service** (LFS; ✆966 9439; www.langkawi-ferry.com), have merged and operate a shared ferry service to George Town, Penang. Other destinations include:

DESTINATION	DURATION (HR)	FARE (RM, ADULT/ CHILD)	FREQUENCY
Kuala Perlis	1	18/13	Every 1½hr, 7.30am-6.30pm
Kuala Kedah	1½	23/17	Hourly, 7.30am-6.30pm
Satun (Thailand)	1½	30/23	9am, 1pm & 5.15pm
Ko Lipe (Thailand)	1½	118	9.15am (October-May only)
George Town	2½-3	60/45	2.30pm & 5.15pm

ⓘ Getting Around

To/From the Airport/Jetty

Fixed taxi fares from the airport include Kuah jetty, Pantai Cenang or Pantai Kok (RM24), Tanjung Rhu (RM30) and Teluk Datai (RM60). Fares to these destinations from the jetty in Kuah are nearly equivalent. Buy a coupon at the desk before leaving the airport terminal and use it to pay the driver.

FERRY WARNING

During the monsoon season, from July to mid-September, you may want to shelve any notions of taking the ferry to Langkawi. During this time of year the seas are typically very rough and the ferry ride (in reality a large speedboat) can be a terrifying and quite literally vomit-inducing experience. Our trip from Penang, in mid-July, was both of these; we flew back. Consider yourself warned.

Car

Cars can be rented cheaply, and touts from the travel agencies at the Kuah jetty will assail you upon arrival. Rates start at around RM60 per day, but drops with bargaining. Elsewhere, a convenient place to rent cars or motorcycles is **T-Shoppe**, with branches at **Kuah**, **Pantai Cenang** and **Pantai Tengah**.

Motorcycle & Bicycle

The easiest way to get around is to hire a motorbike for around RM35 per day. You can do a leisurely circuit of the island (70km) in a day. The roads are excellent, and outside Kuah it's very pleasant and easy riding. Motorbikes can be hired at stands all over the island starting at about RM20 for 24 hours. A few places also rent mountain bikes for RM15 per day.

Taxi

As there is no public transport available, taxis are the main way of getting around, but fares are relatively high and it may be worth your time to rent your own vehicle. There are taxi stalls at the airport, jetty and at **Pantai Cenang**, across from Mertius Pelangi Beach.

Alor Setar

POP 405,523

Most travellers use the capital of Kedah, also known as Alor Star, as a hopping-off point to Langkawi or southern Malaysia, but there's enough around to keep you exploring for a day. This is a very Malay city, culturally rooted in a conservative mindset that references a fairly strict interpretation of Islam and reverence for the local monarchy.

⊙ Sights

FREE **Muzium Negeri** MUSEUM
(Lebuhraya Darul Aman; ☺10am-5pm Sat-Thu) The State Museum is 2km north of the *padang* (grassy area that also functions as the town square). The small collection includes early Chinese porcelain, artefacts from archaeological excavations at Lembah Bujang and dioramas of royal and rural Malaysian life. A taxi from the town centre costs RM10.

FREE **Mahathir's Birthplace** MUSEUM
(Map p201; 18 Lg Kilang Ais; ☺10am-5pm Sat-Thu, 10am-noon & 3-5pm Fri) Dr Mahathir bin Mohamad, fourth prime minister of Malaysia and longtime keystone of national politics, was born the youngest of nine children in Alor Setar in 1925. His childhood home, Rumah Kelahiran Mahathir is now preserved

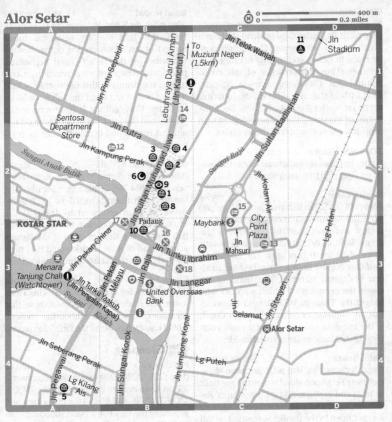

Alor Setar

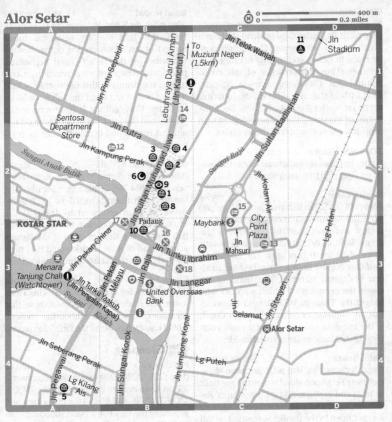

Alor Setar

◎ Sights

1 Balai Besar	B2
2 Balai Nobat	B2
3 Clock Tower	B2
4 Galeri Sultan Abdul Halim	B2
5 Mahathir's Birthplace	A4
6 Masjid Zahir	B2
7 Menara Alor Star	B1
8 Muzium Diraja	B2
9 Padang	B2
10 State Art Gallery	B3
11 Wat Siam Nikrodharam	D1

💤 Sleeping

12 Comfort Motel	B2
13 Holiday Villa	C3
14 Hotel Samila	B1
15 New Regent	C2

🍴 Eating

16 Kim Bee Chew	B3
17 Muda Coffee Shop	B3
18 Pekan Rabu	B3

as a small museum, containing family effects, photos and the politician's old bicycle.

Menara Alor Star　　　　　　　TOWER
(Telekom Tower; Map p201; www.menaraalorstar. com.my; Lebuhraya Darul Aman; admission adult/ child RM10/5; ⊙9am-10pm) If the Petronas

Towers weren't enough for you in KL, the second-tallest tower in the country is the Menara Alor Star, which at 165.5m high is by far the tallest structure in town. A glass-sided lift will take you to the observation deck for good views of Alor Setar and the surrounding countryside.

Wat Siam Nikrodharam
BUDDHIST TEMPLE

(Map p201; Jln Stadium; ⊙7am-4pm) Although Alor Setar has weathered Thai occupation, its main Buddhist community is Chinese in heritage. Thus the presence of this cross-cultural wat (Buddhist temple): typically Thai with its stupas and fire-in-the-lotus imagery, yet scattershot with Chinese Buddhist saints, of import to the Chinese donors who funded the construction of this complex.

TOWN SQUARE
Some impressive buildings front the padang (Map p201), or town square.

Masjid Zahir
MOSQUE

(Map p201; Jln Sultan Muhaman Jiwa; ⊙7am-7pm) This, the Kedah state mosque, is one of the largest and most beautiful mosques in Malaysia. Built in 1912, it has a classical beauty, more of an apparition from *The Thousand and One Nights* than a smoothed-out modern Malaysian mosque. The building encloses the cemetery of Kedah warriors who fought the Thais in 1821. Behind the structure, in contrast to the secular High Court, is the religious *syariah* (sharia) court complex. Only Muslims are allowed inside.

Balai Besar
HISTORIC BUILDING

(Royal Audience Hall; Map p201; Jln Sultan Muhaman Jiwa) This open-sided structure was built in 1898 and is still used by the sultan of Kedah for royal and state ceremonies, though it is not open to the public. Supported on tall pillars topped with Victorian iron lacework, the building also shows Thai influences in its decoration.

FREE Muzium Diraja
MUSEUM

(Royal Museum; Map p201; Jln Raja; ⊙9am-5pm Sat-Thu, 9am-12.30pm & 2.30-5pm Fri) Now a museum, these connected structures formerly served as the royal palace for the sultan and other members of the family from 1856. Besides housing paraphernalia of the royal family, it's quite enjoyable to wander round the courtyard and admire the buildings.

FREE State Art Gallery
ART GALLERY

(Map p201; Jln Sultan Muhaman Jiwa; ⊙9am-5pm) The elegant structure of this gallery, built in 1893 as a courthouse, is enough of a reason to visit, less so the rather uninspiring gallery of contemporary Malaysian art it holds.

Balai Nobat
HISTORIC BUILDING

(Map p201; Jln Sultan Muhaman Jiwa) Built in 1906, this is a striking octagonal tower topped by an onion-shaped dome. It's the repository of the *nobat* (royal orchestra), principally composed of percussion instruments; the drums in this orchestra are said to have been a gift from the sultan of Melaka in the 15th century. It isn't open to the public, and the instruments are brought out only on ceremonial occasions such as royal weddings.

Galeri Sultan Abdul Halim
MUSEUM

(Map p201; Jln Sultan Muhaman Jiwa; admission adult/child RM5/2; 10am-5pm Sat-Thu) The former High Court, erected in 1922, is today a museum dedicated to Abdul Halim Mu'adzam Shah, the current Sultan of Kedah and at the time of writing, Malaysia's acting Head of State. Inside you'll find photos and memorabilia from the sultan's life.

Clock Tower
HISTORIC BUILDING

(Map p201; Jln Sultan Muhaman Jiwa) This clock tower was erected in the early 1900s so that the muezzin at the neighbouring mosque would know when to call the faithful to prayer.

🛏 Sleeping

Holiday Villa
HOTEL $$

(Map p201; ☏734 9999; www.holidayvilla.com.my; 162 Jln Tunku Ibrahim; incl breakfast r/ste RM300-440/630-2800; ❉@🛜🏊) This towering hotel adjoining the City Point Plaza shopping mall is easily the best place in town. It has spacious, tastefully furnished rooms with all the amenities, and a range of facilities, including a gym, pool and spa.

New Regent
HOTEL $$

(Map p201; ☏731 5000; info.newregent@yahoo.com; 1536 Jln Sultanah Badlishah; incl breakfast r/ste RM140-200/280; ❉🛜) A 2012 makeover has the exterior and lobby of this longstanding hotel looking downright sexy. The rooms, however, although clean, functional and relatively attractive, still carry traces of the slightly more utilitarian hotel that it used to be.

Hotel Samila
HOTEL $

(Map p201; ☏731 8888; 27 Jln Kanchut; r/ste RM88-128/198-278; ❉🛜) The exterior and logo of this hotel remind us of something from 'The Jetsons'. Inside, the rooms are huge and feature the kind of furniture you'd expect in a Jetsons-style hotel, although we did find some of the amenities (stained sheets, ragged towels) disappointingly unfuturistic.

Comfort Motel HOTEL **$**
(Map p201; ☎734 4866; 2C Jln Kampung Perak; r RM28-50; ❄) This is a good-value, Chinese-style budget hotel, located in a renovated wooden house across from a mosque. The rooms are tidy and come equipped with TV and air-con, but are otherwise bare and share bathrooms.

✗ Eating

TOP CHOICE Muda Coffee Shop CHINESE **$**
(Map p201; 111 Jln Pekan China; mains RM3-20; ◷8pm-1am Sat-Thu) We should start by making it clear that this place is for adventurous eaters only: the grumpy/indifferent staff don't speak much English, and the highlight is a dish of steamed fish head. But oh what a fish head. Accompanied with *or mee* (noodles fried with dark soy sauce) and a beer, it was frankly one of the tastiest meals we had in Malaysia.

Kim Bee Chew MALAY **$**
(Map p201; Jln Tunku Ibrahim; mains from RM5; ◷breakfast & lunch) Chinese coffee shop that's also home to a popular *nasi kandar* vendor; expect fragrant yellow rice topped with a variety of rich curries.

Pekan Rabu MALAY **$**
(Wednesday Market; Map p201; Jln Langgar; ◷breakfast & lunch) The ground floor of this tidy market has a food court featuring Malay dishes.

❶ Information

Tourist Information Office (Jln Raja; ◷9am-5pm Sun-Wed, to 3.30pm Thu) South of the town centre.

❶ Getting There & Away

Air

Sultan Abdul Halim Airport is 11km north of town just off the Lebuhraya. **AirAsia** (☎nationwide 600 85 8888; www.airasia.com; Sultan Abdul Halim Airport; ◷9am-9pm), **Firefly** (☎nationwide 03-7845 4543; www.firefly.com. my; Sultan Abdul Halim Airport)and **Malaysia Airlines** (☎nationwide 1300-88 3000; www. malaysiaairlines.com; Sultan Abdul Halim Airport) all offer daily flights to Kuala Lumpur (one hour, from RM446).

Bus

The tiny **local bus station** (Jln Langgar) handles frequent departures to Kuala Kedah (one hour, RM3), from 7am to 10pm.

The main bus terminal, **Shahab Perdana**, is 4km north of the town centre. A taxi there costs RM10. Destinations include the following:

DESTINATION	DURATION (HR)	FARE (RM)	FREQUENCY
Kangar	1	5.30	Hourly, 6.45am-8.30pm
Kuala Kedah	1	11	Hourly, 7am-10pm
Butterworth	1½	9.90	Every 30min, 6.30am-7.30pm
Ipoh	4	24	10.30am & 4.30pm
Kota Bharu	6	35	9am & 9.30pm
Kuala Lumpur	7	40	Every 30min, 8am-midnight
Melaka	8	51	10.45am & 10pm
Singapore	12	70	9pm & 10pm

GETTING TO THAILAND: BUKIT KAYU HITAMO TO HAT YAI

Getting to the border The border at Bukit Kayu Hitamo, 48km north of Alor Setar, is the main crossing between Malaysia and Thailand. The Lebuhraya handles the vast majority of road traffic between the two countries, and as there are no taxis or local buses at this border, the only practical way to cross here is on a through bus from points elsewhere in Malaysia.

At the border The Malaysian border post is open every day from 6am to midnight. All passengers must disembark to clear customs and immigration (both Thai and Malaysian) before reboarding.

Moving on Again, lack of local transport means that you'll most likely pass this border on a bus already bound for Hat Yai.

Train

The **train station** (Jln Stesyen) is southeast of the town centre. There is one daily northbound train to Hat Yai in Thailand (RM9 to RM16, three hours), and one southbound to KL (RM22 to RM101, 9½ hours); check with www.ktmb.com.my for the latest info on fares and schedules.

ⓘ Getting Around

There is an informal **taxi stand** on Jln Tunku Ibrahim. A taxi to/from the airport costs RM20. The town centre is accessible on foot.

Around Alor Setar

MUZIUM PADI

The **Paddy Museum** (off Hwy K351; admission adult/child/camera RM3/1/2; ☺9am-5pm Sat-Thu, 9am-12.30pm & 2.30-5pm Sat) is all about Kedah's main crop: rice. It's located about 10km northwest of Alor Setar, amid, appropriately enough, green rice paddies. The complex, which has a distinctly socialist feel, and which resembles stacked brass flying saucers, is supposed to emulate the gunny sacks used by rice farmers. Inside...well, if you're *really* into rice, you'll love it. The main event is a top-floor rotating observation deck that looks out onto a mural of the surrounding rice fields (rather than the rather idyllic fields themselves); the gimmick pays homage to Gunung Keriang, a nearby limestone hill that, according to local folklore, is also supposed to rotate.

A taxi here from Alor Setar will cost around RM25.

KUALA KEDAH

The main attraction at this busy fishing village 11km from Alor Setar is **Kota Kuala Kedah** (☺9am-7pm), a fort built around 1770 opposite the town on the far bank of Sungai Kedah. In one of history's little twists, this Portuguese-built castle became a bastion of Malay independence against warring Siamese, finally falling to invaders in 1821. Try to find 'Meriam Badak Berendam' (the Wallowing Rhino), a cannon stuck in the debris of the collapsed sea wall, believed to be the abode of the fortress's guardian spirit.

Kuala Kedah also functions as a gateway to Pulau Langkawi. Ferries leave approximately every hour from 7am to 7pm (adult/child RM23/17).

A taxi to Kuala Kedah from Alor Setar will cost RM20; hourly buses also make the run from Alor Setar (one hour, RM3) between 7am and 10pm.

PERLIS

Perlis is Malaysia's smallest state and doesn't tend to register on most travellers' radar except as a transit point to Thailand or Langkawi (via Kuala Perlis). Even Malays tend to regard it as essentially a rice-producing pocket along the Thai border. This isn't an area that's particularly heavy on sites of interest to tourists, but at the risk of stereotyping, as in many rural backwaters the population here is quite friendly. It can be a kick just to hang out with the locals and improve your Bahasa Malaysia (because English definitely isn't widely spoken). Otherwise, small but beautiful Taman Negara Perlis state park is worth exploring.

History

Perlis was originally part of Kedah, though it variously fell under Thai and Acehnese sovereignty. After the Siamese conquered Kedah in 1821, the sultan of Kedah made unsuccessful attempts to regain his territory until, in 1842, he agreed to Siamese terms. The Siamese reinstalled the sultan, but made Perlis into a separate vassal principality with its own raja.

As with Kedah, power was transferred from the Thais to the British under the 1909 Anglo-Siamese Treaty, and a British Resident was installed at Arau. A formal treaty between Britain and Perlis wasn't signed until 1930. During the Japanese occupation in WWII, Perlis was 'returned' to Thailand, and then after the war it again returned to British rule until it became part of the Malayan Union, and then the Federation of Malaya in 1957.

Kangar

POP 48,898

Kangar, 45km northwest of Alor Setar, is the state capital of Perlis. As with the state it's the capital of, there's not a heck of a lot to do here besides relax, pray or chat, all of which are fine options for those awaiting an onwards bus.

⊙ Sights

FREE **Muzium Kota Kayang**   MUSEUM
(☺10am-5pm) Around 7km southwest of Kangar, the small but impressive Muzium Kota Kayang houses displays on local history, including Neolithic tools, royal regalia and ceramics. There are some real treasures here, and facilities are surprisingly modern, with clear English descriptions. The museum is attractively located on a plot of land

backed by limestone cliffs and shallow caves, as well as the modest mausoleums of two 16th-century sultans of Kedah. You'll need to catch a taxi from Kangar to get here (RM15).

FREE **Muzium Negeri Perlis** MUSEUM
(National Museum; Jln Kolam, Kompleks Warisan Negeri; ☺9am-4pm Sun-Thu, noon Sat) Kangar town's sole attraction is the Muzium Negeri Perlis, with dry exhibitions on the history of the state and the royal family.

🛏 Sleeping & Eating

There are many cheap restaurants and cafes sprinkled around the bus station.

Hotel Ban Cheong HOTEL **$**
(☎976 1184; 79 Jln Kangar; r RM60-160; ✻🐕) This long-standing Chinese hotel in the town centre has basic singles with fan and shared bathrooms and air-con doubles with private facilities. It's a reasonable budget option for an overnight stay.

Hotel Sri Garden HOTEL **$$**
(☎977 3188; www.hotelsrigarden.webs.com; 96 Persiaran Jubli Emas; r incl breakfast RM106-170; ✻🐕) Standard Malaysian midranger with clean and airy rooms.

❶ Getting There & Away

Bus

The **long-distance bus station** is on the southern edge of town, off Jln Jubli Perak. Departures include:

DESTINATION	DURATION (HR)	FARE (RM)	FREQUENCY
Alor Setar	1	5.30	Every 30min, 6.40am-7.30pm
Butterworth/ George Town	3	11.90-15.70	Every 30min, 8am-4pm
Ipoh	6	27.20	9am, 2.30pm & 8pm
Kota Bharu	8	38.70	9am & 9pm
Kuala Lumpur	9	45.70	Every 30min, 8.30pm-11pm
Melaka	10	48.50-55.20	Frequent, 9am-10pm
Singapore	12	75	6.30pm & 8pm

Infrequent buses to Padang Besar (RM4.20) leave from the chaotic **local bus station** on Jln Tun Abdul Razak. There's also a taxi stall here, and drivers can take you to Padang Besar (RM30) and Alor Setar (RM50).

Kuala Perlis, about 10km southwest of Kangar, is yet another jumping off point for Pulau Langkawi. From Kangar, the pier can be reached by bus (RM2) or taxi (RM14), and ferries to Langkawi leave approximately every hour from 7am to 7pm (adult/child RM23/17). From Kuala Perlis, there are frequent buses to a number of destinations across Malaysia.

Taman Negara Perlis

The small state park of Taman Negara Perlis in the northwest of the state runs for 36km along the Thai border, covering about 5000 hectares. It comprises the Nakawan Range – the longest continuous range of limestone hills in Malaysia – and the Mata Ayer and Wang Mu Forest Reserves.

The nearest town is Kaki Bukit, from which a winding mountain road leads to the tiny border village of Wang Kelian, 3km from the park visitor centre.

◉ Sights & Activities

Taman Negara Perlis has heavily forested slopes and numerous cave systems, such as **Gua Wang Burma**, which has intriguing limestone formations. The park is the country's only semideciduous forest and is rich in wildlife; this is the only habitat in Malaysia for the stump-tailed macaque. White-handed gibbons and a rich array of birds can also be found here.

Just outside Kaki Bukit, **Gua Kelam** (Cave of Darkness; ☺8am-5.30pm Sun-Fri to 6pm Sat) is a 370m-long cavern gouged out in tin-mining days, although it was closed when we stopped by. When open, a river runs through the cave and emerges in a cascade at a popular swimming spot and a landscaped park. The old tin mine is a short walk from the far end of the cavern. The cave is a long 1km walk from Kaki Bukit; a guide is obligatory and costs RM40 for up to 10 people.

The **Wang Kelian Sunday Market** straddles the Malaysia–Thailand border. Fruit, vegetables and clothes from both countries are for sale, and provided you stay in the market area no passport is needed. The Malaysian side of the market is open every day.

LANGKAWI, KEDAH & PERLIS TAMAN NEGARA PERLIS

GETTING TO THAILAND: PADANG BESAR TO HAT YAI

Getting to the border There are regular buses from Kangar (RM4.20), stopping at an unmarked bus stop near BSN bank, about 500m from the border. The taxi stand is on the left before you reach the bus stop, and fares are posted for destinations, including Kangar (RM36) and Alor Setar (RM80).

At the border The Malaysian border post is open every day from 6am to 10pm. All passengers must disembark to clear customs and immigration (both Thai and Malaysian) before reboarding. Very few people, if any, walk the more than 2km of no-man's land between the Thai and Malaysian sides of the border. Motorcyclists shuttle pedestrian travellers back and forth for about RM2 each way.

Moving on There is one daily train connection between Padang Besar and Hat Yai (RM6 to RM13, 50 minutes).

Sleeping & Eating

The modern wooden chalets in the **park visitor centre** (dm/chalets RM10/50-1100; ▣) are very comfortable. There's no restaurant, but staff can prepare food.

❶ Information

The **park visitor centre** (☎945 7898; admission RM2; ◷9am-noon & 2-5pm)is at Wang Kelian, 2km from the Thai border; guides (RM40

for four hours) can also be hired at the centre, and are obligatory for many areas.

❶ Getting There & Away

There is no public transport to the park. Buses to Kaki Bukit run from Kangar's local bus station every two hours from 8.45am to 6.45pm (RM4.20). A taxi to the park from Kangar will cost at least RM50.

Melaka

📷06 / POPULATION: 788,700 / AREA: 1652 SQ KM

Includes »

Melaka City....................209
Around Melaka City......225
Ayer Keroh....................225
Pulau Besar 225
Alor Gajah.....................225
Tanjung Bidara 226

Best Places to Eat

» Pak Putra (p220)

» Capitol Satay (p221)

» Nancy's Kitchen (p220)

» Selvam (p222)

» Hainan Food Street (p220)

Best Places to Stay

» 45 Lekiu & The Stable (p217)

» Majestic Malacca (p219)

» River View Guesthouse (p217)

» Hotel Puri (p217)

» Apa Kaba Home & Stay (p219)

Why Go?

Back when Kuala Lumpur was a malaria-ridden swamp and Penang was yet to become the 'Pearl of the Orient,' Melaka was already one of the greatejost trading ports in Southeast Asia. Over time it lost ground to Singapore and became a sleepy backwater compared with its high-rolling cousin. Ultimately this downturn preserved much of the ancient architecture as well as the old ways of life, and today Melaka is hugely back on the tourist radar thanks to its 2008 designation as a Unesco World Heritage Site.

More allure comes from the city's mixed Malay, Chinese, Indian and European heritage and the serene *kampung* (villages) scattered among the state's tropical forests, farmlands and beaches. Over generations, this cultural mix has developed variations on traditional cuisine, including the famed Malay-Chinese Nonya food, which is so delicious that just the food is reason enough to visit.

When to Go

Melaka

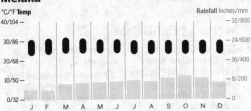

Jan–Feb Chinese New Year, high temperatures and little rainfall.	**Apr–Jul** The coolest temperatures and tons of festivals.	**Nov–Dec** Christmas and Deepavali are celebrated with great fanfare.

History

However the history of the city-state of Melaka is told, the story of the state is inseparable from that of the city for which it was named. Before the late 14th century, Melaka was a simple fishing village.

Founded by Parameswara, a Hindu prince from Sumatra, and located halfway between China and India, and with easy access to the spice islands of Indonesia, Melaka attracted merchants from all over the East and became a favoured port.

In 1405 the Chinese Muslim Admiral Cheng Ho arrived in Melaka bearing gifts from the Ming emperor and the promise of protection from Siamese enemies. Chinese settlers followed, who mixed with the local Malays to become known as the Baba and Nonya, the Peranakans or Straits Chinese. By the time of Parameswara's death in 1414,

Melaka was a powerful trading state. Its position was consolidated by the state's adoption of Islam in the mid-15th century.

In 1509 the Portuguese came seeking the wealth of the spice and in 1511 Alfonso de Albuquerque forcibly took the city. Under the Portuguese, the fortress of A'Famosa was constructed, and missionaries strove to implant Catholicism. While Portuguese cannons could easily conquer Melaka, they could not force Muslim merchants from Arabia and India to continue trading there, and other ports in the area, such as Islamic Demak on Java, grew to overshadow Melaka.

Suffering harrying attacks from neighbouring Johor and Negeri Sembilan, as well as from the Islamic power of Aceh in Sumatra, Melaka declined further. The city passed into Dutch hands after an eight-month siege in 1641 and the Dutch ruled Melaka for

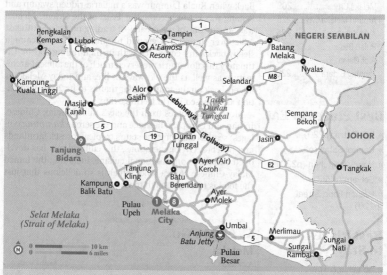

Melaka Highlights

❶ Eating Chinese dim sum for breakfast, Nonya food for lunch and Pakistani tandoori for dinner at Melaka's **fabulous restaurants** (p220)

❷ Catching glimpses of old-time Melaka while leisurely wandering through historic **Chinatown** (p213)

❸ Snacking and perusing trinket stands at the

Jonker's Walk Night Market (p223)

❹ Feeling like a happy fool while rocking out to '80s dance hits in a wacky Melaka **trishaw** (p209)

❺ Imagining the past and all its intricacies at the **Baba-Nonya Heritage Museum** (p214)

❻ Spending a day browsing Chinatown's varied **art**

galleries (p213) and chatting with the artists

❼ Getting lost in the tangle of the three downtown **shopping malls** (p223) and stumbling upon a local stage show

❽ Watching freighters move down the Strait of Melaka while lounging on the white sands of **Tanjung Bidara** (p226)

about 150 years. Melaka again became the centre for peninsular trade, but the Dutch directed more energy into their possessions in Indonesia.

When the French occupied Holland in 1795, the British (as allies of the Dutch) temporarily assumed administration of the Dutch colonies. In 1824 Melaka was permanently ceded to the British.

Melaka, together with Penang and Singapore, formed the Straits settlements, the three British territories that were the centres for later expansion into the peninsula. However, under British rule Melaka was eclipsed by other Straits settlements and then superseded by the rapidly growing commercial importance of Singapore. Apart from a brief upturn in the early 20th century when rubber was an important crop, Melaka returned again to being a quiet backwater, patiently awaiting its renaissance as a tourist drawcard.

MELAKA CITY

☑06

Melaka's Chinatown was granted Unesco World Heritage Site status in 2008, and this sealed the city's claim as one as Malaysia's hottest tourist destinations. The development that has ensued is mind-boggling. Unfortunately, 'preserving heritage' has often been translated into gaudy shop signs, night market street vendors selling cheap trinkets rather than authentic Melakan items and big-name businesses constructing new buildings on the historic riverfront. The charm in Chinatown still lingers however, and is best represented by its resident artists, cooks and creative trishaws. With the oldest functioning mosque, Catholic church and Buddhist temple in the country, the city today (as it has for centuries) exudes a tolerance that accepts visitors of every creed and always promises to show them a good time. And all the modern action still blends in with the gorgeous surrounding Peranakan, Portuguese and Dutch architecture.

Plus there's the food. From the distinct Peranakan dishes to Eurasian Portuguese cooking and Indian banana-leaf shops, the citywide restaurant aromas add further colour to the cultural mosaic that makes Melaka such an astonishing destination.

It's easy to feel the town's old magic (and get a seat at the more popular restaurants) on the quiet weekdays, but during the weekends there are so many photo-snapping tourists that the whole town can feel like front row at a rock concert.

◉ Sights

The following sights are listed in geographical order and could be used as a walking tour: start going northwest on Jln Tun Tan Cheng Lock, follow the map to head southeast down Jln Tokong, then finish by heading northwest again up Jln Hang Jebet.

HISTORIC TOWN CENTRE

This area has a ridiculous number of museums clustered along Jln Kota. The **Islamic Museum** (Map p210; admission RM1; ⊘9am-5.30pm Wed-Sun), the **Architecture Museum** (Map p210; admission RM2; ⊘9.30am-5pm Tue-Sun), which focuses on local housing design, and the **Muzium Rakyat** (People's Museum; Map p210; adult RM2; ⊘9am-5.30pm Wed-Mon), which covers everything from *gasing uri* (top-spinning) to mutilation for beauty, are all worth visiting if you have time on your hands. Most of the others use a bland diorama format where visitors walk through a maze of wordy displays.

Stadthuys   HISTORIC BUILDING

(Town Sq; Map p210; ☑282 6526; admission adult/child RM5/2; ⊘9am-5.30pm Sat-Thu, 9am-12.15pm & 2.45-5.30pm Fri, History & Ethnography Museum guided tours 10.30am & 2.30pm Sat & Sun) Melaka's most unmistakable landmark and favourite trishaw pick-up spot is the Stadthuys, the imposing salmon-pink town hall and governor's residence. It's believed to be the oldest Dutch building in the East, built shortly after Melaka was captured by the Dutch in 1641, and is a reproduction of the former Stadhuis (town hall) of the Frisian town of Hoorn in the Netherlands.

Housed inside the Stadthuys is the nicely presented **History & Ethnography Museum** (Map p210; ⊘guided tours 10.30am & 2.30pm Sat & Sun), and also part of the complex is the mildly interesting **Literature Museum** (Map p210), focusing on Malaysian writers. Admission to both museums (as well as the **Governor's House** (Map p210) and the **Democratic Government Museum** (Map p210)) is included in the admission price to Stadthuys.

Porta de Santiago   RUIN

(A'Famosa; Map p210; Jln Bandar Hilir) A quick photo stop at this fort is a must. Porta de Santiago was built by the Portuguese as a

Melaka City

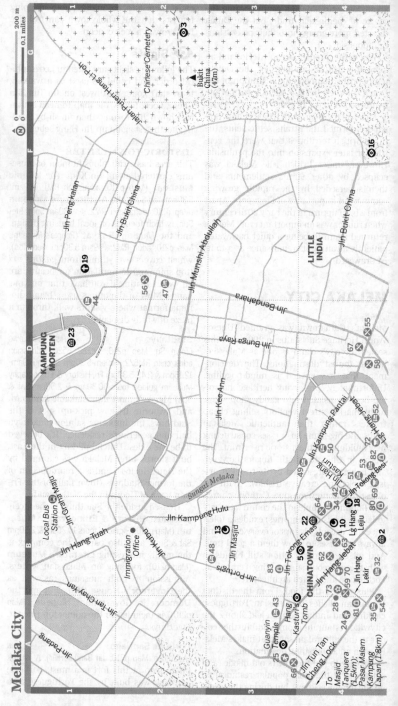

0 200 m
0 0.1 miles

G1
Chinese Cemetery
Bukit China (4/m)
Jalan Puteri Hang Li Poh
3

F
Jln Peng kalan
Jln Bukit China
16
LITTLE INDIA
Jln Bukit China

E
19
Jln Munshi Abdullah
56
47
Jln Bendahara
44

D
KAMPUNG MORTEN
23
Jln Bunga Raya
Jln Kee Ann
55
67
58

C
Local Bus Station Jln Graya Maju
Jln Graya Maju
Sungai Melaka
Jln Kampung Pantai
A9
50
Jln Hang Kasturi
51
53
42
34
64
52
82
69
80
18

B
Jln Hang Tuah
Immigration Office
Jln Kubu
Jln Kampung Hulu
13
Jln Masjid
Jln Portugis
48
83
Jln Tokong Emas
CHINATOWN
5
22
68
62
59
70
73
28
81
24
10
Lg Hang Lekiu
2
Jln Hang Jebat
Jln Hang Lekir
32
35
54

A
Jln Padang
Jln Tan Chay Yan
Guanyin Temple
43
Hang Kasturi's Tomb
25
66
Jln Tun Tan Cheng Lock
To Masjid Tanquera (1.5km); Pasar Malam Kampung Lapan (18km)

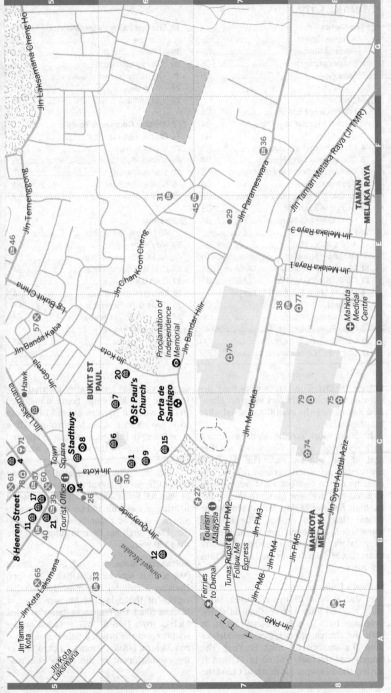

TAMAN
MELAKA RAYA

Jln Temenggong

Jln Laksamana Cheng Ho

Jln Parameswara

Jln Taman Melaka Raya (Jl TMR)

Jln Melaka Raya 3

Jln Melaka Raya 1

Jln Chan Koon Cheng

Ls Bukit China

Jln Banda Kaba

Jln Bandar Hilir

BUKIT ST
PAUL

Jln Kota

Proclamation of
Independence
Memorial

St Paul's
Church

Porta de
Santiago

Mahkota Medical
Centre

Mahkota
Medical
Centre

Jln Merdeka

Jln Syed Abdul Aziz

Stadthuys

Jln Gereja

Jln Laksamana

Town
Square

Tourist Office

8 Heeren Street

Jln Kota

Jln Kota Laksamana

Jln Taman
Kota

Jln Kota
Laksamana

Sungai Melaka

Jln Quayside

Tourism
Malaysia

Tunas Rupat
Follow Me
Express

Jln PM2

Jln PM3

Jln PM4

Jln PM5

Jln PM8

Jln PM9

MAHKOTA
MELAKA

Ferries
to Dumai

Melaka City

◎ **Top Sights**

8 Heeren Street...B5
Porta de Santiago C6
St Paul's Church C6
Stadthuys..C5

◎ **Sights**

1 Architecture Museum C6
2 Baba-Nonya Heritage Museum B4
3 Bukit China G2
4 Cheng Ho Cultural Museum C5
5 Cheng Hoon Teng Temple B4
6 Democratic Government Museum.......C6
7 Governor's House C6
8 History & Ethnography Museum C5
9 Islamic Museum.....................................C6
10 Kampung Kling Mosque........................B4
11 Kim Hai Gallery.......................................B5
King's Well ....(see 16)
Literature Museum ....(see 8)
12 Maritime Museum & Naval Museum B6
13 Masjid Kampung Hulu B3
14 Melaka Malay Sultanate Water
Wheel...C5
15 Muzium Rakyat C6
Paku Pakis Collection ....(see 4)
16 Poh San Teng Temple F4
17 Shih Wen Naphaporn Artist Studio B5

18 Sri Poyatha Venayagar Moorthi
Temple B4
19 St Peter's Church E1
20 Sultanate Palace....................................D6
21 Tham Siew Inn Artist Gallery B5
22 Titi Art Gallery B4
23 Villa Sentosa D1

◎ **Activities, Courses & Tours**

24 Biossentials Puri Spa A4
25 Massa Sūtra A3
26 Melaka River Cruise B5
27 Menara Taming Sari...............................B7
28 Nancy's Kitchen......................................A4
29 Wok & Walk E7

◎ **Sleeping**

45 Lekiu & The Stable ....(see 22)
30 Aldy Hotel..C6
31 Apa Kaba Home & Stay E6
32 Cafe 1511 Guesthouse...........................B4
33 Casa Del Rio B5
34 Chong Hoe Hotel B4
35 Courtyard@Heeren A4
36 Emily Travellers Home...........................F7
37 Hangout@Jonker....................................C5
38 Hatten Hotel..D7
39 Heeren House B5

fortress in 1511. The Dutch were busy destroying the bulk of the fort when Sir Stamford Raffles came by in 1810 and saved what remains today.

In 2006, work on the Menara Taming Sari revolving tower uncovered another part of the famous wall. The revolving tower was relocated further inland, the remains of the fortress walls were reconstructed and are now home to the 13-metre high **Melaka Malay Sultanate Water Wheel** (Map p210) replica. The original wheel would have been used to channel the river waters for the large number of traders swarming Melaka during the 15th and 16th centuries.

St Paul's Church   RUIN
(Map p210) St Paul's Church is a breezy sanctuary reached after a steep flight of stairs. Originally built by a Portuguese captain in 1521, the church offers views over Melaka from the summit of Bukit St Paul. The church was regularly visited by St Francis Xavier, and following his death in China the

saint's body was temporarily interred here for nine months before being transferred to Goa, where it remains today. Visitors can look into his ancient tomb (surrounded by a wire fence) in the centre of the church, and a marble statue of the saint gazes wistfully over the city.

When the Dutch completed their own Christ Church in 1590 at the base of the hill, St Paul fell into disuse. Under the British a lighthouse was built and the church eventually ended up as a storehouse for gunpowder. The church has been in ruins for more than 150 years.

Sultanate Palace   MUSEUM
(Map p210; Jln Kota; admission RM3; ☺9am-6pm) Housing a cultural museum, this wooden replica of the palace of Mansur Shah of Mansur Shah, the famous sultan who ruled Melaka from 1456 to 1477, is based on descriptions of the original palace from *Sejarah Melayu* (*Malay Annals*; a chronicle of the establishment of the Malay sultanate

40	Heeren Inn	B5
41	Holiday Inn	A8
	Hotel Equatorial	(see 29)
	Hotel Puri	(see 24)
42	Jalan Jalan Guesthouse	C4
43	Jonker Boutique Hotel	A3
44	Majestic Malacca	D1
45	Malacca Straits Hotel	E7
46	Old Town Family Guesthouse	E5
47	Renaissance Melaka Hotel	E2
48	Ringo's Foyer	B3
49	River View Guesthouse	C4
50	Rooftop Guesthouse	C4
51	Sama-Sama Guest House	C4
52	Tidur Tidur	C4
53	Voyage Guest House	C4

⊗ Eating

54	Baboon House	A4
55	Baker's Oven & Cafe	D4
56	Bulldog Cafe	E2
57	Capitol Satay	D5
58	Discovery Cafe	D4
59	Hainan Food Street	B4
60	Harper's Cafe	C5
61	Hoe Kee Chicken Rice	C5
62	Jonker 88 Heritage	B4
	Jonker's Walk Night Market	(see 43)

63	Limau-Limau Cafe	B4
64	Low Yong Mow	B4
	Nancy's Kitchen	(see 28)
65	Pak Putra Restaurant	B5
66	Poh Piah Lwee	A3
67	Selvam	D4
68	Vegetarian Restaurant	B4

⊘ Drinking

69	Cheng Ho Tea House	C4
70	Geographér Cafe	B4
71	Voyager Travellers Lounge	C5
72	Zheng Ho Tea House	C4

⊘ Entertainment

73	Eleven	B4
74	Golden Screen Cinemas	C8
75	Mixx	C8

⊜ Shopping

76	Dataran Pahlawan	D7
77	Hatten Square	D8
78	Jonker's Walk Night Market	C5
79	Mahkota Parade Shopping Complex	C8
80	Orangutan House	B4
81	Orangutan House	A4
82	Orangutan House	C4
83	Wah Aik Shoemaker	B3

and 600 years of Malay history), and is built entirely without nails.

Maritime Museum & Naval Museum
MUSEUM

(Map p210; Jln Quayside; admission RM5; ⊗9am-5.30pm Sun-Thu, 9am-9pm Fri & Sat) Housed in a huge recreation of the *Flor de la Mar*, a Portuguese ship that sank off the coast of Melaka, the Maritime Museum merits a visit. Clamber up for a detailed examination of Melaka's history, picked out by rather faded and dated props. The museum continues in the building next door with more absorbing exhibits featuring local vessels, including the striking *Kepala Burung* (a boat carved like a feathered bird) plus an assortment of nautical devices.

CHINATOWN

Chinatown is the heart of Melaka and is by far the most interesting area to wander around. Stroll along **Jln Tun Tan Cheng Lock**, formerly called Heeren St, which was the preferred address for wealthy Baba (Straits-born Chinese) traders who were

most active during the short-lived rubber boom of the early 20th century. The centre street of Chinatown is **Jln Hang Jebat**, formerly known as Jonker St (or Junk St Melaka), which was once famed for its antique shops but is now more of a collection of clothing and crafts outlets and restaurants. On Friday, Saturday and Sunday nights, the street is transformed into the Jonker's Walk Night Market (p223). Finally, the northern section of **Jln Tokong** (also known as Harmony St) houses a mosque, Chinese temple and a handful of authentic Chinese shops.

FREE **8 Heeren Street**
HISTORIC BUILDING

(Map p210; 8 Jln Tun Tan Cheng Lock; ⊗11am-4pm Tue-Sat) This 18th-century Dutch-period residential house was restored as a model conservation project. The project was partially chronicled in the beautifully designed coffee-table book *Voices from the Street*, which is for sale at the house along with other titles. You can also pick up an *Endangered Trades: A Walking Tour of Malacca's Living Heritage* (RM5) booklet

MELAKA'S ART GALLERIES

Almost hidden between the gaudy trinket shops and humble local businesses are an array of eclectic art galleries that make for a lovely day of browsing. Opening hours are erratic but many try to be open from 10am-6pm and most close on Wednesday. The following are some of our favourites listed by location so you could incorporate them into a walking tour:

Paku Pakis Collection (Map p210; 21 Jln Tukang Besi) Go here for Leong Hock Khoon's Baba-Nonya inspired art that ranges from realism to modern and stylised.

Shih Wen Naphaporn Artist Studio (Map p210; 14 Jln Tuna Tan Cheng Lock) A husband and wife duo. Chiang Shiwen is Melaka born and creates Cubo-futuristic works while Thai Naphapone Phanwiset uses fish, fruit and the female form as her muse in marvellous neutral-toned pieces.

Tham Siew Inn Artist Gallery (Map p210; 49 Jln Tun Tan Teng Lock) Than Siew works mostly with water colours while his son makes traditional stone Chinese stamps to order (from RM60).

Kim Hai Gallery (Map p210; 42 Jln Tun Tan Cheng Lock) Paints apples to create mosaics of colour.

Titi Art Gallery (Map p210; 4 Jln Tokong) Titi Kawok paints village and fishing landscapes as modern images.

and map for an excellent self-guided tour of the city centre.

Baba-Nonya Heritage Museum MUSEUM
(Map p210; ☑283 1273; 48-50 Jln Tun Tan Cheng Lock; adult/child RM10/5; ☺10am-12.30pm & 2-4.30pm Wed-Mon) Touring this traditional Peranakan townhouse takes you back to a time when women hid behind elaborate partitions when guests dropped by, and every social situation had its specific location within the house. The captivating museum is arranged to look like a typical 19th-century Baba-Nonya residence. The highlight is the tour guides, who tell tales of the past with a distinctly Peranakan sense of humour.

Cheng Hoon Teng Temple CHINESE TEMPLE
(Qing Yun Ting or Green Clouds Temple; Map p210; 25 Jln Tokong; ☺7am-7pm) Malaysia's oldest traditional Chinese temple (dating from 1646) remains a central place of worship for the Buddhist community in Melaka. Notable for its carved woodwork, the temple is dedicated to Kuan Yin, the Goddess of mercy. Across the street from the main temple is a traditional opera theatre.

Masjid Kampung Hulu MOSQUE
(Map p210; cnr Jln Masjid & Jln Kampung Hulu) This is the oldest functioning mosque in Malaysia and was, surprisingly, commissioned by the Dutch in 1728. The mosque is made up of predominantly Javanese architecture with a multitiered roof in place of the standard dome; at the time of construction, domes and minarets had not yet come into fashion.

Kampung Kling Mosque MOSQUE
(Map p210; Jln Tokong) This hoary mosque has a multitiered *meru* roof (a stacked form similar to that seen in Balinese Hindu architecture), which owes its inspiration to Hindu temples, and a Moorish watchtower minaret typical of early mosques in Sumatra.

Sri Poyatha Venayagar Moorthi Temple HINDU TEMPLE
(Map p210; Jln Tukang Emas) One of the first Hindu temples built in the country, this temple was constructed in 1781 on the plot given by the religiously tolerant Dutch and dedicated to the Hindu deity Venayagar.

Cheng Ho Cultural Museum MUSEUM
(Map p210; ☑283 1135; 51 Lg Hang Jebat; adult/child RM20/10; ☺9am-6pm Mon-Thu, 9am-7pm Fri-Sun) A lengthy paean to Ming Admiral Cheng Ho (Zheng He), this museum charts the tremendous voyages of the intrepid Chinese Muslim seafarer. It's your classic Malaysian museum with lots of dioramas and recreated scenes with dummies, but the subject is very interesting so you could spend a few hours in here.

AROUND THE CITY CENTRE

Bukit China · CEMETERY

(Map p210) More than 12,500 graves, including about 20 Muslim tombs, cover the 25 grassy hectares of this serene hill. Since the times of British rule there have been several attempts to acquire Bukit China for road widening, land reclamation or development purposes. Fortunately, Cheng Hoon Teng Temple (p214), with strong community support, has thwarted these attempts.

In the middle of the 15th century the sultan of Melaka imported the Ming emperor's daughter from China as his bride, in a move to seal relations between the two countries. She brought with her a vast retinue, including 500 handmaidens, to Bukit China and it has been a Chinese area ever since. **Poh San Teng Temple** (Map p210) sits at the base of the hill and was built in 1795. To the right of the temple is the **King's Well** (Map p210), a 15th-century well built by Sultan Mansur Shah.

Villa Sentosa · HISTORIC BUILDING

(Peaceful Villa; Map p210; ☏ 282 3988; entry by donation; ⊙ flexible but around 9am-6pm) A highlight of a visit to the area is viewing this 1920s Malay *kampung* house on Sungai Melaka. A member of the family will show you around the house and its collection of objects, including Ming dynasty ceramics and a 100-year-old copy of the Quran. Most of all, it's an opportunity to wander through a genuine *kampung* house and chat with your charming host.

St Peter's Church · CHURCH

(Map p210; Jln Bendahara) St Peter's Church is the oldest functioning Catholic church in Malaysia, built in 1710 by descendants of early Portuguese settlers. On Good Friday the church comes alive when Melakan Christians flock here, many of them making it the occasion for a trip home from far-flung parts of the country.

Kampung Chitty · NEIGHBOURHOOD

As well as the Baba-Nonya, Melaka also has a small community of Chitty – Straits-born Indians, offspring of the Indian traders who intermarried with Malay women. Having arrived in the 1400s, the Chitties are regarded as older than the Chinese-Malay Peranakan community. Their area of town, known as Kampung Chitty, lies west of Jln Gajah Berang, about 1km northwest of Chinatown; look for the archway with elephant sculptures beside the Mutamariman Temple. It's a pretty district in

which to wander and see traditional Malay-style houses. The tiny **Chitty Museum** (☏ 281 1289; ⊙ 9.30am-5pm Tue-Sun) is a community effort with a collection of colourful artefacts.

The best time to visit is in May, during the Mariamman Festival (Pesta Datuk Charchar), a Hindu celebration during which you might also be fortunate enough to witness a traditional Indian wedding ceremony.

Little India · NEIGHBOURHOOD

Heading east from Kampung Chitty, past Chinatown and across the river, is Melaka's surprisingly plain Little India. While it's not nearly as charming as the historic centre or Chinatown, this busy area along Jln Bendahara and Jln Temenggong is a worthwhile place for soaking up some Indian influence and grabbing an excellent banana-leaf meal. During Deepavali a section of Jln Temenggong closes to traffic to make way for Indian cultural performances and street-food vendors.

 ## Activities

Head to the fourth to sixth floors of the **Dataran Palawan mall** for a fun centre with ever-changing activities including carnival-style games, billiards and karaoke. The best at the time of research was **Super Roller** (6th floor Dataran Pahlawan mall; RM25 incl skate rental; ⊙ 11am-11pm Mon-Thu, 11am-12am Fri-Sat), a black-lit, neon-painted roller disco dubbed the 'biggest in Malaysia,' although it's actually about the size of lap pool.

Cookery Courses

Nancy's Kitchen · COOKERY

(Map p210; ☏ 283 6099; 15 Jln Hang Lekir; RM100 per person) Nancy of this near legendary Nonya restaurant (p220) teaches recommended cookery classes on request. Reserve well in advance.

Wok & Walk · COOKERY

(Map p210; ☏ Hotel Equatorial 282 8333; Hotel Equatorial; 2-day packages from RM340 per person) Nonya cooking workshops include six

---

NO SMOKING

In 2011 Melaka's Chinatown was declared a no-smoking zone. It's not heavily enforced but the air is noticeably more smoke-free than elsewhere in the city.

signature dishes and packages can include a stay at Hotel Equatorial and meals at the hotel restaurant.

Peranaken Culinary Journey COOKERY
(☎289 8000; www.majesticmalacca.com; Majestic Malacca Hotel, 188 Jln Bunga Raya; RM285 per person) Learn about each ingredient and the history of each dish in a gorgeous kitchen with a master Peranaken chef at the Majestic Malacca Hotel.

Massage & Reflexology

It seems that reflexology centres have opened up on every corner in Melaka. If you have specific ailments – anything from migraines to water retention – many will create a special treatment for you. There are also ear candles, fire cupping, body scrubs and more. A one-hour massage at these types of places is usually RM60 while a half-hour foot massage costs RM30.

Biossentials Puri Spa SPA
(Map p210; ☎282 5588; www.hotelpuri.com; Hotel Puri, 118 Jln Tun Tan Cheng Lock; spa services from RM80; ☺Thu-Mon) This international calibre spa in a sensual garden has a delicious menu of treatments including steams, body wraps, scrubs, facials and a variety of massages.

Massa Sūtra MASSAGE
(Map p210; ☎016-662 503; www.massasutra.com; 20 Jln Kubu; 1hr massage RM60) We can say with conviction that Chris Loh is a master masseur (using Thai or Zen techniques).

Other Activities

Menara Taming Sari OBSERVATION TOWER
(Map p210; Jln Merdeka; child/adult RM10/20; ☺10am-10pm) Take a ride upwards in this 80m revolving tower that's considered an eyesore by many. Waits can be long and it's all a bit tourist-tacky but it is a good way to get your bearings and enjoy great views.

☞ Tours

Historic walking tours are offered through several hotels. Particularly recommended are the ones led by Pek Choo Ho at the Majestic Malacca (p219) hotel.

Boat Trips

Melaka River Cruise BOAT TOUR
(Map p210; RM15) Frequent 40-minute riverboat trips (minimum eight people) along the Melaka River depart from two locations: the 'Spice Garden' on the corner of Jln Tun Mutahii and Jln Tun Sri Lanang in the north

of town, and the quay near the Maritime Museum. Cruises go 9km upriver past Kampung Morten and old godowns (river warehouses). There's also a hop-on, hop-off day pass for RM30.

Bike Tours

Eco Bike Tour BIKE TOUR
(☎019-652 5029; www.melakaonbike.com; RM100 per person, minimum 2 people) Explore the fascinating landscape around Melaka with Alias on his three-hour bike tour through 20km of oil-palm and rubber-tree plantations and delightful *kampung* communities surrounding town.

Malacca Night Cycling CYCLING
(☎016-668 8898; RM25-25) Touring Melaka at night takes the bite off the heat of the day and it's a pleasant time to cycle and see the city. Tours leave nightly at 8.30pm and last two to three hours.

★☆ Festivals & Events

Melaka celebrates all the major Malaysian holidays, including Chinese New Year and Thaipusam. The tourist department creates new festivals all the time but few become annual events.

Easter Good Friday and Easter Sunday processions are held outside St Peter's Church in March/April.

Festa San Pedro In late June, this festival honours the patron saint of the Portuguese fishing community. Celebrations take place at St Peter's Church and normally include a procession from the Porta de Santiago to Medan Portugis and carnival festivities.

Festa San Juan (Festival of St John) This festival is celebrated by Melaka's Eurasian community in late June by the lighting of candles in the Portuguese Settlement.

Dragon Boat Festival This June/July Chinese festival, marked by a dragon-boat race in the Strait of Melaka, commemorates the death, by drowning, of 3rd-century BC Chinese poet and statesman Qu Yuan.

Festa Santa Cruz In mid-September, this festival finishes with a candlelight procession of Melakan and Singaporean Catholics to Malim chapel.

🛏 Sleeping

So many new places are opening up in Melaka that accommodation options are particularly vulnerable to change. The good news is that quality is improving, but the bad news is that there's simply not enough tourism (except on weekends when everything books fast) to keep all these places open. Rooms have private showers and dorms have shared bathrooms, unless otherwise stated.

CHINATOWN

If you have the option of staying in Chinatown, do it. This is the vibrant historic centre of the city although it can get both busy and noisy.

🔺 TOP CHOICE 45 Lekiu & The Stable
HISTORIC GUESTHOUSE $$$

(Map p210; ☎012-623 4459; www.45lekiu.com; 45 Lg Hang Lekiu (45 Lekiu), No D Jln Hang Kasturi; 45 Lekiu weekdays/weekends RM999/1099, The Stable weekdays/weekends RM300/360; ❋🛜❄) These gorgeous restoration projects are in two different locations – when you stay at either, the whole house is yours and both have basic cooking facilitities. 45 Lekiu is the more upscale with four extremely comfortable storeys of big old beams and exposed original brick work all within a clean, modern decor.

Highlights include a bougainvillea-filled courtyard with an elongated dipping pool and upper terrace that overlooks Melaka's ancient rooftops.

The Stable is a smaller two-story home with louvered, heritage-style doors, wood floors, gorgeous period tiles and timber beams. Again the furnishings and finishing touches are artistically modern.

🔺 TOP CHOICE River View Guesthouse
GUESTHOUSE $

(Map p210; ☎012-327 7746; riverviewguesthouse@yahoo.com; 94 & 96 Jln Kampung Pantai; dm RM20, r RM45-70; ❋🛜) Bordering the ambient riverfront promenade, this immaculate guesthouse is housed in a large heritage building. There's a big shared kitchen and common area and the hosts begin your stay with a handy map of town and directions to all their favourite sights and restaurants.

Homemade cake is often on offer and you can choose to get through town via the serene riverside promenade at the back door rather than the busy streets of Chinatown at the front. The owner's overflow property,

Rooftop Guesthouse (Map p210; ☎327 7746; 39 Jln Kampong Pantai), is almost as nice but doesn't offer the riverfront perk.

🔺 TOP CHOICE Hotel Puri
HOTEL $$

(Map p210; ☎282 5588; www.hotelpuri.com; 118 Jln Tun Tan Cheng Lock; r RM164-564; ❋🛜) One of Chinatown's gems, Hotel Puri is an elegant creation in a superb old renovated Peranakan mansion. Its elaborate lobby, decked out with beautiful old cane and inlaid furniture, opens to a gorgeous courtyard garden. Standard rooms have butter-yellow walls, crisp sheets, satellite TV, wi-fi and shuttered windows. There's an on-site spa (Biossentials Puri Spa (p216), and breakfast, taken in the courtyard or air-conditioned dining area, is included.

Casa Del Rio
HOTEL $$$

(Map p210; ☎6289 6888; www.casadelrio-melaka.com; 88 Jln Kota Laksmana; r RM778-1008, ste RM1928-3858; ❋🛜❄) The biggest hotel in the Chinatown heritage area with a fabulous location right on the river. The palatial architecture blends Portuguese/Mediterranean with Malaysian for a result that's uniquely airy and grand. Rooms are massive with bathrooms fit for a Portuguese princess and riverview rooms capture the feel of Asia and Venice combined.

There's a rooftop infinity pool that overlooks the river and common areas are strewn with loungable couches and tons of cushions.

Heeren House
GUESTHOUSE $$

(Map p210; ☎281 4241; www.melaka.net/heerenhouse; 1 Jln Tun Tan Cheng Lock; all incl breakfast s RM119-139, d RM129-149, f RM259; ❋) Lodging here positions you right in the heart of Chinatown, on the waterfront and within range of top local restaurants and sights. The airy, clean and lovely rooms (six in all) in this former warehouse largely overlook the river, and have polished floorboards, traditional furniture (some with four-poster beds) and clean showers.

Cafe 1511 Guesthouse
GUESTHOUSE $

(Map p210; ☎286 0150; www.cafe1511.com; 52 Jln Tun Tan Cheng Lock; s/d incl breakfast RM60/90; @🛜) Set in a beautiful Peranakan mansion, the small, simple, spotless rooms here are jazzed up by tasteful international art on the walls. The place has an old-style feeling, set to the music of a water fountain in the lightwell that extends from the restaurant below.

Note that the guesthouse doesn't take guests under 30 years old. Because of demand the guesthouse recently opened an overflow property, Dlaksmana Guesthouse which isn't as heritage-y but is in a more quiet location a block out of Chinatown.

Courtyard@Heeren
HOTEL $$

(Map p210; ☎281 0088; www.courtyardatheeren. com; 91 Jln Tun Tan Cheng Lock; d RM200-250, f RM 250-300, ste RM300-800; ❄️🛜) Modern rooms here are each decorated uniquely with light and bright decor paired with antique wood furniture. Some have minimalist arty stained-glass details, modern takes on Chinese latticework or drapey canopies. Not many rooms have windows but there's plenty of light pouring in from the open central courtyard. It's very professionally run with great service.

Jonker Boutique Hotel
HOTEL $$

(Map p210; ☎282 5151; www.jonkerboutiquehotel. com; 52 Jln Tun Tan Cheng Lock; s/d incl breakfast RM198/288; ❄️🛜) Each of the large rooms here are different but decorated in a similar style using modern black-and-cream patterned wallpaper paired with neutral-coloured walls. Most rooms have windows, and bathrooms have retro black-and-white tiles. It's well run and centrally located, but be prepared for some street noise on Friday and Saturday nights when the night market's on. Room rates go up by about 30% on weekends and holidays.

Jalan Jalan Guesthouse
GUESTHOUSE $

(Map p210; ☎283 3937; www.jalanjalanguesthouse. com; 8 Jln Tukang Emas; dm/s/d RM15/30/50; @🛜) A lovely hostel in a restored old shophouse painted periwinkle blue. Fan-cooled rooms with one shared bathroom are spread out over a tranquil inner garden-courtyard. As with some other older places, though, noise from your neighbours might keep you awake at night. The hosts get great reviews and there's bike rental available.

Hangout@Jonker
HOTEL $$

(Map p210; ☎282 8318; www.hangouthotels.com; 19 & 21 Jln Hang Jebat; r incl light breakfast from RM147; ❄️@🛜) Opened as a second site by a popular hostel in Singapore, this location shares the same high standards of cleanliness and amenities (hang-out lounges, free movies and internet) but the spare modern style of concrete and tile is a little out of place in Melaka. Prices go up 20% on weekends and holidays.

Sama-Sama Guest House
GUESTHOUSE $

(Map p210; ☎305 1980; www.voyagetogether.com; 26 Jl Tukang Besi; dm RM15, r RM25-55) This place (the longest running hostel in Chinatown) has a great hippie-ish vibe, with a courtyard overflowing with potted plants, mini-ponds and wind chimes. The whole place, including the shared toilets, is kept relatively clean but when anyone walks down the hall it sounds like they are stomping in combat boots.

Ringo's Foyer
GUESTHOUSE $

(Map p210; ☎016-354 2223; 46A Jln Portugis; r RM60-90; ❄️🛜) Just far enough from central Chinatown to be quiet, but close enough to be convenient, Ringo's is plain and clean, and has friendly staff and a relaxing rooftop chill-out area that plays host to impromptu barbeques.

Chong Hoe Hotel
HOTEL $

(Map p210; ☎282 6102; 26 Jln Tukang Emas; s/d RM30/48; ❄️🛜) Chong Ho has stayed true to its no-frills functional personality and now, after all the years of staying exactly the same, it has an unpretentious charm that's lacking elsewhere. Except when Masjid Kampung Kling starts its call to prayer, it's a quiet and blissfully unexciting place to catch some Zs.

Aldy Hotel
HOTEL $$

(Map p210; ☎283 3232; www.aldyhotel.com.my; 27 Jln Kota; r incl breakfast RM160-450 ; ❄️🛜) At the foot of Bukit St Paul, this hotel has a location to die for and is a good choice for families. Small rooms are dark but modern and are equipped with satellite TV. A rooftop Jacuzzi adds to the package. There's no additional charge for children under 12 sharing a room with parents.

Tidur Tidur
GUESTHOUSE $

(Map p210; ☎014-9298 3817; tidurtidurgh@yahoo. com; 92 Lg Hang Jebat; weekdays/weekends per person RM15/20) Rooms with bunk beds are small and boxy and sleep four to five people, but the hip vibe (it's at the back of the owner's unique T-shirt shop) and riverside hangout area make this a great place to stay.

Voyage Guest House
GUESTHOUSE $

(Map p210; ☎281 5216; www.voyagetogether.com; Jln Tukang Besi; dm RM15) Clean, industrial-sized dorm rooms and common areas are decorated with a nouveau heritage Chinatown jazz-lounge look. It's run by Voyager

Travellers Lounge and you get free bike rental too.

JALAN TAMAN MELAKA RAYA & AROUND

This area is in the heart of Melaka's mall shopping zone and is only a short walk to the historic centre and Chinatown.

Hotel Equatorial
HOTEL $$$

(Map p210; ☎282 8333; www.equatorial.com; Jln Parameswara; r RM300-1000; ❄☏≋) While it's a bit frayed around the edges, somehow this adds to the old charm of this centrally located hotel. Good discounts online can cut prices nearly in half for excellent value. Service is well mannered and the overall presentation is crisp. There's a swimming pool, ladies-only pool, a quality fitness centre, tennis court and wi-fi access.

It's worth upgrading to one of the deluxe rooms (RM500), which have either balconies or heaps of extra room space. Special packages are available through the hotel, including tours and specials such as cookery courses.

Emily Travellers Home
GUESTHOUSE $

(Map p210; ☎012-301 8574; 71 Jln Parameswara; dm/s RM16/24, d RM32-48;; ☏) Enter the humble entrance off the busy road and step into another dimension filled with plants, koi ponds, a bunny hopping around (named Mr Playboy) and happy, mingling people. Every room is different, from funky cottages with semi-outdoor 'jungle showers' to simple wooden rooms in the house.

Note that this place is rustic and it's not for you if you need hot water or air-con.

Holiday Inn
HOTEL $$

(Map p210; ☎255 9000; www.melaka.holidayinn. com; Jln Sayed Abdul Aziz; r RM240-575; ❄@☏≋) Boldly facing historic Melaka like a gleaming white, middle finger, rooms here are comfy, new and carpeted, yet bland. Ask for a top-storey room for fantastic views over the Strait of Melaka.

Hatten Hotel
HOTEL $$

(Map p210; ☎286 9696; www.hattenhotel.com; Hatten Square, Jln Merdeka; r from RM370; ᴘ❄☏≋) Perched over Hatten Square mall and linked to both Dataran Palahwan and Parkinson malls (and steps from Mahkota Medical Centre), this modern place has sea views from the 13th floor upwards, a rooftop infinity pool plus excellent service and included breakfasts.

Malacca Straits Hotel
HOTEL $$

(Map p210; ☎286 1888; www.malaccastraitshotel. com; 27 Jln Chan Koon Cheng; r RM150, ste incl breakfast 220-315; ❄☏≋) Smack up against Hotel Equatorial, the spacious rooms are furnished with some exquisite teak furniture including four-poster beds in every room and batik fabrics everywhere. While standard rooms all have bathtubs, an upgrade to a suite adds a Jacuzzi. Prices go up about 25% on weekends and holidays.

LITTLE INDIA TO BUKIT CHINA

This is a varied area that will let you see a less touristed side of the city while still remaining close to the sights.

TOP CHOICE Majestic Malacca
HOTEL $$$

(Map p210; ☎289 8000; www.majesticmalacca. com; 188 Jln Bunga Raya; r RM410-2000; ❄@☏≋) Melaka's most elegant hotel is an interesting mix: the lobby is in a 1920s colonial Chinese mansion while the bulk of the hotel is in a tasteful modern building behind. Rooms continue with this old and new theme with hardwood floors, sheer ivory-coloured drapes and heritage-style wood furnishings – yet all are very modern in their level of comfort.

Of course the place is stacked with amenities including a small swimming pool, gym, a top-notch spa and stellar service.

TOP CHOICE Apa Kaba Home & Stay
GUESTHOUSE $

(Map p210; ☎283 8196; www.apakaba.hostel. com; 28 Kg Banda Kaba; r incl breakfast RM40-90; ❄☏) Nestled in a quiet and authentic Malay *kampung* that seems to magically float in a bubble in the heart of town, this homestay-style guesthouse is in a simple yet beautiful old Malay house complete with creaky wood floors, louvred shutters and bright paint.

You can chill out in the enormous garden (look for ripe mangos) or take a stroll out the back gate through tiny lanes that meander into Chinatown.

Renaissance Melaka Hotel
HOTEL $$$

(Map p210; ☎284 8888; www.marriott.com; Jln Bendahara; r RM350-900; ❄☏≋) The Renaissance offers good service and dated luxury. Large windows in the rooms take advantage of views that sweep over Melaka in all directions, while the spacious rooms are modern while incorporating classic Chinese touches. Suites aren't really worth the extra money unless you really need a windowless cave attached to your room.

Old Town

Family Guesthouse
GUESTHOUSE $

(Map p210; ☎286 0796; www.melakaguesthouse.com; 119 Jln Temenggong; dm RM15, r RM30-70; ❄️🛜) This basic French-Malay–run backpackers gets more points for its low-key ambience, cleanliness and friendly, helpful owners than for its plain but perfectly passable rooms. It's in the second storey of an apartment-type building but is quite spacious with plenty of tiled, open spaces for lounging. There's a kitchen for guests' use.

✴ Eating

Melaka's food mirrors the city's eclectic, multicultural DNA. Peranakan cuisine (Nonya; prepared here with a salty Indonesian influence) is the most famous type of cooking here, but there's also Portuguese Eurasian food, Indian, Chinese, Indonesian and more.

CHINATOWN

On Friday, Saturday and Sunday nights, Jln Hang Jebat turns into the not-to-be-missed **Jonker Walk Night Market** (Map p210; Jln Hang Jebat). Besides the official Hainan Food Street (p220), there are also hawker stalls along Jln Hang Jebat and on Jln Tokong where it meets Jln Portugis.

TOP CHOICE Pak Putra Restaurant
PAKISTANI $$

(Map p210; 56 Jln Taman Kota Laksmana; tandoori from RM8; ☉dinner, closed every other Mon) This fabulous Pakistani place cooks up a variety of meats and seafood in clay tandoori ovens perched on the footpath. Apart from the tandoori try the *taw* prawns (cooked with onion, yoghurt and coriander, RM11) or mutton rogan josh (in onion gravy with spices and chilli oil, RM9). Everything is so good that dinner conversation is often reduced to ohs and ahs of gustatory delight.

TOP CHOICE Nancy's Kitchen
NONYA $

(Map p210; 15 Jln Hang Lekir; meals RM10; ☉11am-5.30pm, closed Tue) In a town already known for its graciousness, this home-cooking Nonya restaurant is our favourite for friendly service. If you want an intimate meal, head elsewhere. The server is as chatty and full of suggestions as they come, and will have you making conversation with the other handful of customers in no time. It's like a happy dinner (or lunch) party with particularly good food. Try the house speciality, chicken with candlenut (a large white nut used to make a mild, creamy sauce). Still hungry? Nancy also offers cooking courses (p215).

Hainan Food Street
HAWKER $

(Map p210; Jln Hang Lekir; dishes from RM3; ☉6pm-12am Fri, Sat & Sun) About a dozen very good food stalls serving everything from Hainan chicken pie, Nonya laksa and Japanese BBQ open with the Jonker's Walk Night Market (p223) on weekends.

Low Yong Mow
CHINESE $

(Map p210; ☎282 1235; Jln Tokong; dim sum RM1-8; ☉5am-noon, closed Tue) Famous Malaysia-wide for large and delectably well-stuffed *pao* (steamed pork buns), this place is Chinatown's biggest breakfast treat. With high ceilings, plenty of fans running and a view of Masjid Kampung Kling, the atmosphere oozes all the charms of Chinatown. It's great for early-bus-departure breakfasts and is usually packed with talkative, newspaper-reading locals by around 7am.

Poh Piah Lwee
NONYA $

(Map p210; Jln Kibu; dishes from RM3; ☉9am-5pm) An authentic and lively hole in the wall with one specialist cook preparing delicious Hokkein-style *popiah* (lettuce, bean sprouts, egg and chilli paste in a soft sleeve; RM2), another making near-perfect *rojak* (fruit and vegetable salad in a shrimp

---

WORTH A TRIP

MEDAN PORTUGIS

There's really not much reason to head out to this nondescript neighbourhood other than to eat. On Friday and Saturday evenings, head to **Restoran de Lisbon**, where you can sample Malay-Portuguese dishes at outdoor tables. Try the delicious local specialities of chilli crabs (RM20) or the distinctly Eurasian devil curry (RM10). Any other time of the week, Medan Portugis has food stalls serving similar dishes to those found at restaurants at seaside tables.

DON'T LEAVE MELAKA WITHOUT TRYING...

laksa – a regional version distinguished by its coconut milk and lemongrass flavours

popiah – an uber-spring roll stuffed with shredded carrots, prawns, chilli, garlic, palm sugar and much, much more

cendol – a shaved-ice monstrosity with jellies, syrup and coconut milk

Nonya pineapple tarts – buttery pastries with a chewy pineapple jam filling

chicken rice ball – Hokkien-style chicken and balled-up rice dumplings

Assam fish heads – spicy tamarind fish-head stew.

satay celup – like fondue but better; you dunk tofu, prawns and more into bubbling soup and cook it to your liking

devil curry – a fiery Eurasian chicken curry

---

paste, lime juice, sugar and peanut dressing, RM3) while the third whips up a fantastic laksa (RM3).

Jonker 88 Heritage
DESSERT $

(Map p210; 88 Jln Hang Jebat; ⏰11am-10pm Tue-Thu, till 11pm Fri & Sat, till 9pm Sun) Many locals say this is Melaka's best *cendol* (a pandan-leaf flavoured desert served with shaved ice, red beans, jaggery syrup and coconut milk, from RM3). There are several variations on the theme, including a durian version, and the laksa here rocks as well. There's always a line on weekends.

Vegetarian Restaurant
VEGETARIAN $

(Map p210; 43 Jln Hang Lekui; mains around RM3; ⏰7.30am-2.30pm Mon-Sat; 🖉) Every Chinatown needs its basic vegetarian cafe and this is Melaka's. All the local specialties from laksa and wonton mee to 'fish balls' are here but, although they taste as good as the real thing, are completely meat-free.

Limau-Limau Cafe
WESTERN $

(Map p210; 9 Jln Hang Lekui; fruit juice from RM6, mains from RM7; ⏰Sun-Fri 9.30am-6.30pm, 9.30am-9.30pm Sat; 🖥🖉) Decorated with dark-coloured ceramics and an arty twist, this long-running quiet cafe serves the same predictably good salads, sandwiches, fruit juices and milk shakes. It's also a mellow stop for internet and wi-fi.

Hoe Kee Chicken Rice
MELAKAN $$

(Map p210; 4 Jln Hang Jebat; meals around RM20; ⏰8.30am-3pm, closed last Wed of month) Come here to try the local specialities, chicken rice ball and *asam* fish heads (fish heads in a spicy tamarind gravy). You'll need to arrive here off-hours or expect to wait, especially

on weekends. The restaurant's setting, with wood floors and ceiling fans, is lovely; the food can be hit or miss.

Harper's Cafe
FUSION $$

(Map p210; 2 & 4 Lg Hang Jebat; meals RM40; ⏰4pm-1am Mon & Wed-Sat, 11am-1am Sun) Perched elegantly over Sungai Melaka, breezy Harper's serves excellent (though small) Malay-European fusion dishes in a rather stark decor. It's worth visiting for the food, though the service can be slow.

Baboon House
BURGERS $$

(Map p210; 89 Jln Tun Tan Cheng Hok; burgers around RM14; ⏰10am-5pm Mon-Thu, till 7pm Fri-Sun; 🖥) This cafe is housed in a long Peranakan-style building with a light and plant-filled courtyard specialises in burgers on homemade buns.

LITTLE INDIA TO BUKIT CHINA
There's a whole string of local-style Chinese cafes around Jln Bunga Raya (ever-full of chattering locals) that serve chicken or duck rice as well as rice, noodle and soup dishes at very low prices.

TOP CHOICE Capitol Satay
MELAKAN $

(Map p210; ☎283 5508; 41 Lg Bukit China; meals around RM8) Famous for its *satay celup* (a Melaka adaptation of satay steamboat), this place is usually packed and is one of the cheapest outfits in town. Stainless-steel tables have bubbling vats of soup in the middle where you dunk skewers of okra stuffed with tofu, sausages, chicken, prawns and bok choy. Side dishes include pickled eggs and ginger.

COCONUT KUNG FU

While enjoying the Jonker's Walk Night Market, don't miss the performance by kung fu master **Dr Ho Eng Hui** (⏰around 6.30-9pm Fri & Sat) at the southern end of Jln Hang Jebat. He eats fire and throws knives, but the real reason to stick around is to see him pummel his finger into a coconut. Yes, he really appears to do this (his knarled finger adds evidence) and he's been entertaining folks with the trick for over 35 years. Dr Ho Eng Hui is in fact a doctor, and the purpose of his performance is to sell a 'miracle oil' (RM10) that cures aches and pains.

TOP CHOICE **Selvam** INDIAN $
(Map p210; ☎281 9223; 3 Jln Temenggong; meals around RM8; 🍴) This is a classic banana-leaf restaurant always busy with its loyal band of local patrons ordering tasty and cheap curries, roti and tandoori chicken sets. Even devout carnivores will second-guess their food preferences after trying the Friday-afternoon vegetarian special with 10 varieties of veg.

Restoran Ban Lee Siang Satay Celup MELAKAN $
(☎284 1935; 45E Jln Om Kim Wee; meals around RM8; ⏰5pm-midnight) This place is a little out of the way but locals claim the ingredients are the freshest. Go pick out your skewers from the fridge then cook them in the boiling vats of delectable satay sauce.

Bulldog Cafe NONYA, INTERNATIONAL $$
(Map p210; ☎292 1920; 145 Jln Bendahara; meals RM10) Nonya, Chinese, Thai and Western dishes are on offer at this local-feeling joint in a lovely Peranakan-style building. For cheap snacks, sample the Nonya *popiah* – lettuce, bean sprouts, egg and chilli paste in a soft wrapping or the *pai tee* (crispy cone-shaped morsels of rice flour, stuffed with vegetables).

Baker's Oven & Cafe BAKERY $
(Map p210; Jln Bendahara; continental breakfast set RM7.50; ⏰9am-5pm) Serves fresh European-style baked goods, coffee, tea, sandwiches and light meals.

🍷 Drinking

Unlike much of Malaysia, Melaka is studded with watering holes. The Friday-, Saturday- and Sunday-night Jonker's Walk Night Market (p223) in Chinatown closes down Jln Heng Lekir to traffic and the handful of bars along the lane become a mini street party with tables oozing beyond the sidewalks and live music.

Geographér Cafe BAR
(Map p210; ☎281 6813; www.geographer.com.my; 83 Jln Hang Jebat; ⏰10am-1am Wed-Sun) This ventilated, breezy bar with outside seating and late hours, in a prewar corner shophouse, is a godsend. Seat yourself with a beer amid the throng and applaud long-time resident artist and musician Mr Burns as he eases through gnarled classics. A tasty choice of local and Western dishes and laid-back but professional service rounds it all off.

TOP CHOICE **Cheng Ho Tea House** TEAHOUSE
(Map p210; Jln Tokong; ⏰10am-5pm) In an exquisite setting that resembles a Chinese temple garden courtyard, relax over a pot of fine Chinese tea (from RM15) or take a tea appreciation course with owner and tea connoisseur, Pak.

Zheng Ho Tea House TEAHOUSE
(Map p210; ☎016-764 0588; 3 Jln Kuli; tea ceremony for four people RM20) The best place in town for tea ceremony, this place is humble but the family are simply lovely and it just feels good to be here. There are also a few rooms for rent upstairs (from RM130 including one home cooked meal).

Voyager Travellers Lounge CAFE, BAR
(Map p210; ☎281 5216; 40 Lg Hang Jebat; 📶) Ease back into a wicker chair and order a cold beer (and/or an all-day Western-style breakfast) from the glowing bar built out of recycled bottles. There are often night-time activities on, from movies to mellow live music, and Yaksa, the young owner, can help arrange activities throughout Melaka.

⭐ Entertainment

Mixx CLUB
(Map p210; 2nd floor, Mahkota Arcade, Jln Syed Abdul Aziz; RM10; ⏰10pm-late Tue-Sat) Melaka's hottest new club has two parts: Paradox, a laser-lit warehouse-style venue where in-

ternational DJs spin techno and electronic beats; and Arris, which has a garden area and live bands. It ain't KL but for Melaka this place is very hip. Cover is charged on Friday and Saturday nights only (when the place gets VERY crowded) and includes one drink.

Eleven   CLUB
(Map p210; 11 Jln Hang Lekir) This is *the* place to go if you want to get your groove on in Chinatown. Yes there's hip heritage lounge-style seating and Eurasian food, but head here after around 11pm (weekends in particular) and resident DJs spin their best and the dance floor fills. It has been dubbed Melaka's only gay bar but it's a very relaxed scene and you'll find all sorts hanging out.

Wildlife Theatre   WILDLIFE SHOWS
(www.wildlifetheatre.com.my; Pulau Melaka; weekdays adult/child RM15/10, weekends adult/child RM20/15; ⊙shows at 3pm & 6pm; 🚸) This won't rival marine mammal shows in Europe or the Americas but the sea lions here do a good job of entertaining kids. There are also, birds, snakes and cultural shows from the Iban of Sarawak. While animal shows are always dubious in the treatment of their flock, this place is less depressing than you'd expect.

Golden Screen Cinemas   CINEMA
(Map p210; ☑281 0018; 2nd fl, Mahkota Pde & 3rd fl Dataran Pahlawan; tickets RM9) These silver screens show everything from Western blockbusters to Bollywood flicks.

🔒 Shopping

Taking time to browse Chinatown's eclectic mix of shops is an activity in itself. Melakan favourites include Nonya beaded shoes, Nonya 'clogs' (with a wooden base and a single plastic-strip upper), antiques (know your stuff and haggle aggressively), Southeast Asian and Indian clothing, handmade tiles, charms, crystals and more. Peek into the growing array of silent artists studios, where you might see a painter busy at work in a back room.

TOP CHOICE Jonker's Walk
Night Market   MARKET
(Map p210; Jln Hang Jebat; ⊙6-11pm Fri-Sun) Melaka's weekly shopping extravaganza keeps the shops along Jln Hang Jebat open late while trinket sellers, food hawkers and the occasional fortune teller close the street

to traffic. It has become far more commercial, attracting scores of Singaporean tourists over the years, but it is an undeniably colourful way to spend an evening shopping and grazing.

Orangutan House   CLOTHING
(Map p210; 59 Lg Hang Jebat; ⊙10am-6pm Thu-Tue) All shirts are the work of local artist Charles Cham and have themes ranging from Chinese astrology animals to rather edgy topics (at least for Malaysia) such as 'Use Malaysian Rubber' above a sketch of a condom. Other branches are at **96 Jln Tun Tan Cheng Lok** (Map p210; www.charlescham. com; 96 Jln Tun Tan Cheng Lok; ⊙closed Tue) and **12 Jln Hang Jebat** (Map p210; www.charles cham.com; 12 Jln Hang Jebat; ⊙closed Thu).

Wah Aik Shoemaker   NONYA SHOES
(Map p210; 56 Jln Tokong) Raymond Yeo continues the tradition begun by his grandfather in the same little shoemaker's shop that has been in his family for generations. The beaded Nonya shoes here are considered Melaka's finest and begin at a steep but merited RM300. Tiny silk bound-feet shoes (from RM90) are also available.

Dataran Pahlawan   MALL
(Map p210; Jln Merdeka) Melaka's largest mall, with a collection of upscale designer shops and restaurants in the western half and an odd, nearly underground-feeling craft-and-souvenir market in the eastern portion.

Mahkota Parade Shopping Complex   MALL
(Map p210; ☑282 6151; Lot B02, Jln Merdeka) For practical needs such as books, cameras, pharmacy goods or electronics, head to this shopping complex.

Hatten Square   MALL
(Map p210; Jln Merdeka) This new fashion-heavy mall – with Hatten Hotel (p219) on top – is linked by pedestrian bridge to Dataran Pahlawan and Mahkota Parade Malls so you could now theoretically spend days in these three massive complexes without ever going outside.

ℹ Information

Emergency
Melaka Police Hotline (☑285 1999; Jln Kota)

Immigration Offices
Immigration Office (☑282 4958; 2nd fl, Wisma Persekutuan, Jln Hang Tuah)

Internet Access

Most hotels and guesthouses have wi-fi and several cafes in Chinatown have a computer for clients and charge around RM3 per hour.

Medical Services

Mahkota Medical Centre (☑281 3333, 284 8222; Jln Merdeka) A private hospital offering a full range of services.

Money

Moneychangers are scattered throughout Chinatown and near the bus stations. The only ATM in Chinatown is at **Heeren Inn** (Map p210; ☑288 3600; heerenin@streamyx.com; 23 Jln Tun Tan Cheng Lock; d RM78-145; ❄@). There are more ATMs at the shopping malls.

Post

Post Office (Jln Laksmana; ☉8.30am-5pm Mon-Sat) Off Town Square.

Tourist Information

Tourism Malaysia (☑283 6220; Jln Mahkota; ☉9am-10pm) At the Menara Taming Sari tower; has very knowledgeable, helpful staff.

Tourist Office (☑281 4803; www.melak.gov. my; Jln Kota; ☉9am-1pm & 2-5.30pm) Diagonally across the square from Christ Church.

❶ Getting There & Away

Melaka is 144km from Kuala Lumpur, 224km from Johor Bahru and just 94km from Port Dickson.

Air

Melaka International Airport is 20km north of Melaka in Batu Berendam. **Firefly** (www.fireflyz. com.my) offers flights between Melaka and KL's Subang Airport (twice weekly) and Penang (one flight Wednesday). Wings Air (www.lionair.co.id) and Riau Airlines (www.riau-airlines.com) fly to/ from Pekanbaru in Indonesia twice a week.

Bus

Melaka Sentral, the huge, modern long-distance bus station, is inconveniently located opposite a huge branch of Tesco off Jln Tun Razak, in the north of town. Luggage deposit at Melaka Sentral is RM2 per bag. There is also an ATM and restaurants.

A taxi into town should cost RM20, or you can take bus 17 (RM1.40).

You can buy bus tickets in advance from downtown Melaka (not a bad idea on busy weekends or if you have a plane to catch) at **Discovery Cafe** (Map p210; 3 Jln Bunga Raya) – it charges RM5 for the service.

MELAKA BUSES

Destination	Fare	Frequency	Duration
Johor Bahru	RM24	hourly	3½ hours
KL	RM17.50-27.50	every half hour	two hours
KLIA/LCCT Airports	RM27.50	nine per day	three hours
Kota Bharu	RM51	one daily	10 hours
Mersing	RM28	three per day	4½hours
Muar	RM5	frequent	one hour
Penang	RM50	twice per day	7 hours
Singapore	RM27	four per day	4½ hour

Car

Car-hire prices begin at around RM150 per day. If driving, Melaka's one-way traffic system requires patience. Try **Hawk** (☑283 7878; 52 Jln Cempaka), north of town.

Taxi

Taxis leave from the long-distance bus station. Taxi rates: Johor Bahru (RM250), Mersing (RM300), KL (RM170) and KL airport (RM160).

Train

The nearest **train station** (☑441 1034) is 38km north of Melaka at Tampin on the main north–south line from KL to Singapore. Taxis from Melaka cost around RM60 or take the Tai Lye bus (RM5, 1½ hours), which leaves every half-hour from Melaka Sentral.

❶ Getting Around

Melaka is small enough to walk around or, for the traffic-fearless, you can rent a bike for around

---

GETTING TO INDONESIA: MELAKA CITY TO DUMAI

Getting to the border High-speed ferries make the trip from Melaka to Dumai, Sumatra, daily at 10am (one way/return RM119/170, 1¾ hours). The quay is walking distance or a short taxi ride from the town centre. Tickets are available at the **Tunas Rupat Follow Me Express** (☑283 2505; 310 Taman Melaka Raya) and other offices near the wharf.

At the border Citizens of most countries can obtain a 30-day visa on arrival (US$25).

Moving on Dumai is on Sumatra's east coast and is a 10-hour bus ride from Bukittinggi.

TRICKED OUT TRISHAWS

Nowhere else in Malaysia will you find such a wild and crazy collection of trishaws. Outrageously kitsch, the favourite decorations are plastic flowers, baby doll heads, religious paraphernalia, tinsel, Christmas lights and a sound system. While taking a ride in one of these things might be the most 'I'm a tourist' thing you do in Malaysia, it's good fun and supports an industry that is dying nearly everywhere else in the country. As a spectator, keep an eye out for Singaporean tourists hiring out trishaws en masse: the effect, with several '80s hits blaring at the same time, cameras snapping and all that glitzy decoration, turns the streets of Melaka into a circus-like parade.

RM3 per hour from guesthouses around Chinatown. A useful service is town bus 17, running every 15 minutes from Melaka Sentral to the centre of town, past the huge Mahkota Parade shopping complex, to Taman Melaka Raya and on to Medan Portugis.

Taking to Melaka's streets by trishaw is a must – by the hour they should cost about RM40, or RM15 for any one-way trip within the town, but you'll have to bargain.

Taxis should cost around RM15 for a trip anywhere around town with a 50% surcharge between 1am and 6am.

AROUND MELAKA CITY

Ayer Keroh
☑06

About 15km northeast of Melaka, Ayer Keroh (also spelled Air Keroh) has several contrived tourist attractions that are largely deserted on weekdays. Kids will like the lushly landscaped **Melaka Zoo** (adult/child RM7/4, night zoo adult/child RM10/5; ⊙9am-6pm daily, night zoo 8-11pm Fri & Sat), the second-largest zoo in the country (with 200 different species). The animals here are in good condition compared to many zoos in Asia.

But the main attraction in Ayer Keroh is the **Taman Mini Malaysia/Asean** (adult/child RM4/2; ⊙9am-6pm), a large theme park that has examples of traditional houses from all 13 Malaysian states, as well as neighbouring Asean countries. Also here is **Hutan Rekreasi Air Keroh** (Air Keroh Recreational Forest; admission free), part secondary jungle and part landscaped park with paved trails, a 250m canopy walk, picnic areas and a forestry museum.

Ayer Keroh can be reached on bus 19 from Melaka (RM2, 30 minutes), or a taxi will cost around RM45.

Pulau Besar
☑06

The small island of Pulau Besar, 5km off the coast southeast of Melaka, has some interesting graves and meditation caves that are popular pilgrimages for Indian Muslims, but the main reason to come here is for the white beaches and jungle walks. Unfortunately, in 2010 Besar will become the largest independent oil storage terminal in the country, which will surely make the already not-so-great water even more polluted.

A handful of basic *kedai kopi* (coffee shops) can be found near the boat dock.

Boats (return trip RM40, 30 minutes) depart from the jetty at Anjung Batu (☑261 0492) about every two hours from 8am (last boat returns at 10.30pm). The jetty is several kilometres past the old pier at Umbai, southeast of Melaka. Take an SKA bus from Melaka Sentral to Merlimau and ask to be let off at the jetty – it's about a 10-minute walk from the bus stop.

Alor Gajah

Just off the road to KL, 24km north of Melaka, is the countryside town of Alor Gajah. In the town centre is the peaceful and grassy Alor Gajah Square, which is bordered by an array of gaily painted shophouses. Most Melaka–KL buses stop in Alor Gajah so it's possible to stop here between the two cities if you're willing to change buses. A taxi to A'Famosa should cost around RM22.

◉ Sights

A'Famosa Resort THEME PARK
(www.afamosa.com; Water World adult/child RM35/25, Animal World Safari adult/child RM60/50; ⊙Water World 11am-7pm Mon & Wed-Fri, 9am-8pm Sat & Sun, Animal World Safari 9am-6pm) Half an

hour from Melaka and an hour from KL, the 520-hectare A'Famosa Resort is a cheesy, all-encompassing resort popular with Malay and Singaporean tourists. You'd be hard pressed not to have fun at the 8-hectare **Water World**, which has two seven-storey-high speed slides, a tube ride and a manufactured beach with a wave pool. **Animal World Safari** has animal shows, with an array of critters doing human activities and aren't something that animal lovers will enjoy. A special rate of adult/child RM75/61 gets you into both the Animal World Safari and Water World. Also within the resort is a 27-hole **golf course** that is rated in the country's top 10.

Tanjung Bidara
☑06

For an escape from the city, head to white-sand Tanjung Bidara, about 30km northwest of Melaka. It's well away from the main highway, requiring you to take back roads through rice paddies and farms to get to the shore. It's literally deserted

midweek, except for maybe one or two fishermen casting from the beach, and only one valiant stall at the beachfront food court is open outside of Saturday and Sunday. The water lapping on the fine sand is brown with sediment and pollution so it's not the best place for swimming, but it's fun to sit against the jungle and watch the massive freighters head down the famous Strait of Melaka.

The main beach area is at the recently refurbished **Tanjung Bidara Beach Resort** (☏384 2990; www.tanjungbidara.worldheritage.com.my; r from RM280 incl breakfast; ✳❄✳), an older resort with a small swimming pool and restaurant.

Further budget accommodation is strung out over several kilometres along the beach, broken only by a large military camp. There are several simple beachside chalet guest-houses in the friendly Malay village of Kampung Balik Batu.

Buses 42 and 47 from Melaka go to Masjid Tanah, from where a taxi to Tanjung Bidara Beach Resort or Kampung Balik Batu costs RM10.

Johor

☑ 06, 07 / POPULATION: 3.3 MILLION / AREA: 19,984 SQ KM

Includes »

Johor Bahru 228
Muar 234
Mersing 234
Seribuat Archipelago ... 237
Endau-Rompin
National Park 239

Best Outdoor Adventures

» Upeh Guling & Buaya Sangkut Falls (Endau-Rompin National Park, p239)

» Pulau Tinggi (p238)

» Takah Berangin & Takah Pandan Falls (Endau-Rompin National Park, p239)

» Pulau Sibu (p238)

» Gunung Ledang (p235)

Best Places to Stay

» Rimba Resort (p238)

» Thistle Johor Bahru (p231)

» Rawa Island Resort (p239)

» Mirage Island Resort (p237)

» Kampung Peta (p240)

Why Go?

Linked to Singapore at the tip of the Asian continent, Johor is the southern gateway to Malaysia. While it's the most populous state in the country, tourism has taken a back seat to economic development, leaving some great off-the-beaten-path destinations.

Some of Malaysia's most beautiful islands are found in the Seribuat Archipelago, off the state's east coast. These attract Singaporean weekenders but few others. It's prime dive territory, and you'll find similar corals and fish that you'll find at popular Tioman Island but without the crowds. You'll also find the low-key white-sand beaches which fringe gleaming turquoise waters and wild jungles.

For more adventure head to Endau-Rompin National Park. This jungle offers the same rich flora, (very elusive) fauna and swashbuckling action that visitors flock to experience at Taman Negara in Pahang, but in a much more pristine, un-touristed setting.

When to Go
Johor Bahru

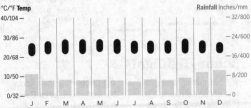

Nov–Feb Avoid the monsoon season – head to Rawa for the surfing season.

Mar–May The water's visibility is at its best for for diving.

Jun–Jul Pulau Besar closes for Expedition Robinson. Expect high temperatures everywhere.

Johor Bahru

07 / POP 1,371,000

After years of being criticised as a dirty, chaotic border town, Johor's capital Johor Bahru has been repaved and replanted and is suddenly a lively, appealing place to hang out. Even the sketchy watch salesmen and down-and-out sidewalk lurkers who congregated along Jln Tun Abdul Razak have been swept away by an increased police presence. Just off this main drag you'll find bustling food hawkers, interesting old architecture and wide, clean sidewalks. The city still has more crime compared with most Malaysian towns, but there's a real urban buzz and some surprisingly cosmopolitan corners to explore.

JB is connected to Singapore by road and rail across a 1038m-long causeway, across

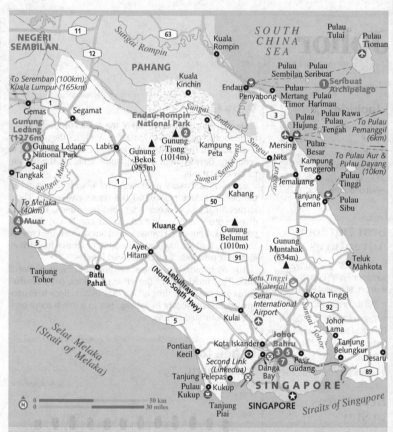

Johor Highlights

❶ Swimming, diving and beach bumming it to the max in the **Seribuat Archipelago** (p237)

❷ Cooling off in the sensational waterfalls of **Endau-Rompin National Park** (p239) after hiking through dense jungle

❸ Discovering the colonial backstreets of **Johor Bahru** (p228) and realising that the city is outgrowing its bad reputation

❹ Strolling the laid-back historic-architecture laden streets of **Muar** (p234)

❺ Admiring the sultans' treasures at the **Royal Abu Bakar Museum** (p229) in Johor Bahru

❻ Sweating your way up lofty **Gunung Ledang** (p235)

❼ Having a drink or four at one of Johor Bahru's hip **watering holes** (p232)

which Singaporeans flood for shopping and excitement on weekends and holidays. However, other than just for changing trains, planes or buses, few foreign travellers linger here even though it has great potential as a budget base for Singapore.

As one of the five 'economic zones' of the Iskandar development project that will radically change southern Malaysia over the next decade, JB is in for more than a makeover. Danga Bay, a 720-hectare area, 5km from the Causeway, is poised to be a financial and commercial centre with the lofty hopes of being as scenic and enticing as Sydney's Darling Harbour, although for now it's a bleak sprawl of construction.

Dangers & Annoyances

Although travelling in JB is generally safe, visitors should be alert to motorcycle-riding bag-snatchers and, as in any city, avoid walking alone down dark alleyways. If you have any troubles call the **police hotline** (☎225 6699).

◎ Sights

Heritage District   ARCHITECTURE
(Map p230) Wandering around the heritage area between Jln Ibrahim and Jln Ungku Puan is a real highlight of JB. Walk past colourful, old shophouses filled with sari shops, barbers, Ayurvedic salons, gorgeous temples, and old-style eateries.

Royal Abu Bakar Museum   MUSEUM
(Map p230; ☎223 0555; Jln Ibrahim; adult/child US$7/3; ⊙9am-5pm Sat-Thu, ticket counter closes 4pm) The marvellous Istana Besar, once the Johor royal family's principal palace, was built in Victorian style by Anglophile sultan Abu Bakar in 1866. It was opened as a museum to the public in 1990 and displays the incredible wealth of the sultans. It's now the finest museum of its kind in Malaysia, and the 53-hectare palace grounds (free entry) are beautifully manicured.

At the time of research the museum was getting an extensive, two-year remodel, but will no doubt have reopened by the time you're reading this, with the – possibly increased – entrance fee payable in ringgit.

**Sri Raja Mariamman
Devasthanam**   HINDU TEMPLE
(Map p230; 4 Jln Ungku Puan) This beautiful Hindu temple, with ornate carvings and devotional artwork, and a tall, brightly painted *gopuram* (tower) entrance way, is the heart of JB's Hindu community.

Sultan Abu Bakar Mosque   MOSQUE
(Jln Gertak Merah) The stunning whitewashed walls and blue-tiled roofing of the Sultan Abu Bakar features a mix of architectural influences, including Victorian. It was built between 1892 and 1900 and is quite rightly hailed as one of the most magnificent mosques in the area. Sadly, non-Muslims cannot enter the building itself.

Chinese Heritage Museum   MUSEUM
(Map p230; 42 Jln Ibrahim; RM10; ⊙9am-5pm Tue-Sun) Well laid-out exhibits chronicling the history of Chinese immigrants in this part of the Malay peninsula. Learn how the Cantonese brought their carpentry skills here, while the Hakkas traded in Chinese medicines and the Hainanese kick-started a trend in coffeeshops, which lasts to this day.

THE BRAVE NEW WORLD OF ISKANDAR

Started in 2006 and expected to be completed in 2025, the Iskandar Development Region stretches from Johor Bahru to Senai/Kulai in the north, Tanjung Pelepas at the west and Pasir Gudang at the east. The aim is for the region to become an international metropolis and liberal trade port not unlike China's Shenzhen and Hong Kong.

The administrative capital, Kota Iskandar, is literally being built from scratch (with a Moorish-Andalusian architectural theme) and was officially opened by the Sultan of Johor on April 16 2009.

The project has been harshly criticised by ex-PM Mahathir Mohamad, who has warned that the higher cost of living in the region, as well as the fact that most of the land is being sold to foreign investors (many Singaporean), will force out Malaysians. In the end, he prophesises, Iskandar will only be an extension of Singapore'.

The Iskandar project has been backed by more recent PM Najib Razak, who believes that growth and foreign investment can only be beneficial for Malaysia and its people. The hopes are that the wealth of Iskandar will spill over to the rest of the country and bring progress to the entire region.

Johor Bahru

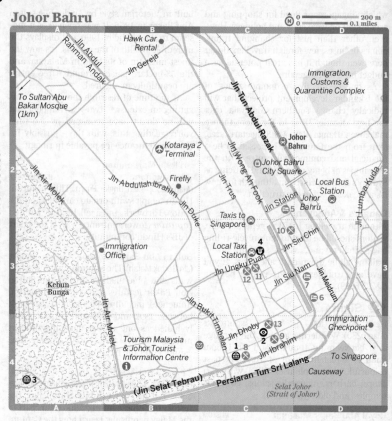

Johor Bahru

⊙ Sights
1 Chinese Heritage Museum C4
2 Heritage District C4
3 Royal Abu Bakar Museum A4
4 Sri Raja Mariamman Devasthanam C3

🛏 Sleeping
5 Citrus Hotel C2
6 JA Residence D3
7 Meldrum Hotel D3

⊗ Eating
8 Annalakshmi C4
9 Hiap Joo Bakery & Biscuit Factory C4
10 Medan Selera Meldrum Walk C3
11 Restoran Nilla C3
12 Restoran Nilla C3
13 Roost Juice & Bar C4
Roost Repurposed Recycled ....(see 13)

🛏 Sleeping

Hotel rooms mentioned here include private shower or bath, unless stated otherwise.

The main zone of cheap and low-bracket midrange hotels clusters on and around the relatively ambient Jln Meldrum, in the centre of town. Budget price tags are high for Malaysia, and most places ask for a room deposit of RM30 or more that's returned to you when you check out. More midrange business-oriented hotels hover in the lively area around KSL Mall, where you'll find tons of good eating options and shopping.

Many hotels inflate prices on Friday, Saturday and Sunday by about 10%.

LEGOLAND!

Got kids? Opened in September 2012, Southeast Asia's first **Legoland** (📞597 8888; www.legoland.com.my; Medini, Nusajaya; adult/child/senior RM140/110/110; ⊘10am-6pm) offers 31 hectares of fun with over 40 rides and attractions. Nearly everything is hands-on, and it's not just about the bricks. Expect to crawl around, pull yourself up a tower with ropes, ride a dragon-coaster and shoot lasers at mummies. The centrepiece is Minland where you'll find regional landmarks like the Petronas Towers and Singapore's Merlion built in miniature out of Lego.

TOP CHOICE Thistle Johor Bahru HOTEL $$

(📞222 9234; www.thistle.com.my; Jln Sungai Chat; r from RM240; ❄@🛜🏊) Overlooking the Straits of Johor, the hotel is the poshest city option this side of the Causeway. It's in a class above the rest with marble bathrooms, a lovely curving swimming pool and an airy, light ambience, although the location near Danga Bay is a little out of the way. Thistle is located about 4km from the town centre, just off the main road, Jln Lingkaran Dalam.

Meldrum Hotel HOTEL $

(Map p230; 📞227 8988; www.meldrumhotel.com; 1 Jln Siu Nam; dm RM40, s/d with shared bath RM70/80, r with bathroom from RM90; ❄🛜) All options here are air-conditioned, clean, spacious and freshly painted, and the rooms have TVs, free drinking water and kettles. It's worth upgrading to a RM100 superior room with attached bathrooms and free Wifi – these are downright plush. Dorms are air-conditioned but cramped, and filled largely with local men.

Grandeur Palm Resort RESORT $$$

(📞599 6000; www.palmresort.com; Jln Persiaran Golf; r from RM472; ❄@🛜🏊) Only a three-minute drive from Senai International Airport (28km from Central JB), this resort is a far cry from the city's hubbub. Alongside the elegant accommodation there are nearly unlimited activities available from golf to paintball, an Olympic-sized pool and ATV trails. Afterwards chill out at the on-site Le Spa.

Citrus Hotel HOTEL $$

(Map p230; 📞222 2888; www.citrushoteljb.com; 16 Jln Station; d/f from RM150/209; ❄🛜) Rooms are small but clean with white walls and bright coloured accents. Breakfasts are tasty, staff are helpful and the location just next to JB City Square couldn't be better.

KSL Hotel & Resort HOTEL $$$

(📞288 2999; www.kslresorts.com.my; 33 Jln Seladang; r from RM247; ❄@🛜🏊) This massive, lively family-friendly place, sitting atop one of JB's best shopping malls, puts you within steps of food courts, a cinema, mini golf and the resort's own giant swimming pool. Rooms are modern with black furniture and Japanese-style toilets in the bathrooms. The views over JB's sprawl get better the higher up you go.

JA Residence HOTEL $$

(Map p230; 📞221 3000; www.ja-residencehotel.com; 18 Jln Wong Ah Fook; r RM130-250; ❄@🛜) Right in the heart of JB, this is a comfortable, clean and modern high-rise hotel offering good value for money. Its cream coloured paint and polished wood interiors have some design flair and the staff are really friendly. Angle for a room on the upper floors, with views over the causeway.

✖ Eating

Whatever you think of JB, you can't complain about the food. The streets here (try the area around KSL City Mall) sizzle with some of the country's best seafood, as well as local specialities including a local, curry-heavy version of laksa.

Roost Juice & Bar INTERNATIONAL $$

(Map p230; Jln Dhoby; mains RM8-28, juice from RM7.90; ⊘12-4pm & 6pm-12am Mon-Sat, 6pm-12am Sun) JB's most chilled spot uses recycled wood, bottles and more to create a cafe/bar that feels like someone's (very hip) living room. And the food is great too. Try the Hainese noodles, fish n' chips, mutton ribs or Nyonya fish fillets and finish it off with fresh juice or a cold beer.

The same folks also run **Roost Repurposed Recycled** (Map p230), an excellent salad (from RM8.90) and frozen yogurt (from RM6.90) cafe just a few doors down.

Hiap Joo Bakery & Biscuit Factory
BAKERY **$**

(Map p230; 13 Jln Tan Hiok Nee; rolls & cakes RM1-4; ☉8am-6pm) For over 80 years this little bakery has baked delicious buns, cakes and biscuits in a charcoal oven just as the founder had done before in his native Hainan, China. The coconut buns and bread rolls are ready by 12.30pm, and sold out by 3pm. The banana cake is baked all day, with the last batch done by about 2.30pm.

Annalakshmi
INDIAN **$**

(Map p230; ☎227 7400; 39 Jln Ibraham; set meals by donation; ☉11am-3pm Mon-Fri; ☕) An authentic vegetarian Indian restaurant run by volunteers of the Temple of Fine Arts, with the motto of 'eat what you want and give as you feel'. Meals are a set and the ambience is classy.

Restoran Nilla
INDIAN **$**

(Map p230; Jln Ungku Puan & Jln Trus; mains from RM2; ☉7am-10pm; ☕) An excellent banana leaf place with two nearby outlets – the other is just around the corner, on **Jln Ungku Puan** (Map p230; Jln Ungku Puan). For some of the best chicken you've ever had, ask for the 'vegetarian chicken.' It is in fact tofu but it's so good you'll hardly believe it.

Medan Selera Meldrum Walk
HAWKER **$**

(Map p230; Medan Selera Meldrum; meals from RM3; ☉dinner) Every late afternoon, the little stalls crammed along this alley (parallel to Jln Meldrum) start frying up everything from *ikan bakar* to the local curry laksa. Wash down your meal with fresh sugar-cane juice or a Chinese herbal jelly drink. Nothing here is excellent but it's all good.

Drinking

The Zon
BAR, CLUBS

(☎221 9999; The Zon Ferry Terminal) Three words: duty free booze. About ten bars and clubs surround the courtyard of this happening spot. Hip Roost (p231) has an outlet here for drinking in funky recycled decor while Dolce and Cabana are probably the most fun places for dancing.

Shopping

JB promotes itself as a major shopping destination. Singaporeans do come across for shopping – petrol and groceries – but for most brand goods Singapore has better prices and a better range.

The best shopping centres are:

KSL City Mall
MALL

(www.kslcity.com.my; 33 Jln Seladang) Food and bars to a Tesco, clothing and home wares.

GETTING TO SINGAPORE: JOHOR BAHRU TO SINGAPORE

Getting to the border From JB Sentral you can clear immigration and take a bus or taxi across the Causeway to Singapore. From central JB, board your bus after clearing Malaysian immigration just before the Causeway – you can buy your tickets onboard. There are also frequent buses between JB's Larkin bus station, 5km north of the city, and Singapore's Queen St bus station. Most convenient is **Causeway Link** (www.causewaylink.com.my; from JB/Singapore RM2.50/S$2.40; ☉6.30am-midnight), running every 10 minutes. Registered taxis to Singapore depart from the Plaza Seni Taxi Terminal in the centre of town, with taxis to Orchard Rd or Queen St terminal costing around RM60. Local city taxis cannot cross the Causeway. Alternatively, **Trans Star Cross Border Coaches** (from JB/Singapore RM7/S$7; ☉ 5am-9pm) run hourly between the Kotaraya 2 Terminal in Johor Bahru and Singapore's Changi International Airport.

At the border All buses and taxis stop at Malaysian immigration. You'll need to disembark from your vehicle with your luggage (and ticket), clear immigration and reboard. Vehicles then stop at Singapore immigration; again, you'll clear immigration with your luggage, before getting back in your vehicle for the last leg to Queen St bus station. The next train stop south of JB Sentral is Woodlands CIQ in Singapore, which marks the end of Malaysia's railway network. If catching the train, you'll get out to clear customs on the Malaysia side before reaching Woodlands.

Moving on At Queen St there are buses, taxis and an MRT (light rail) system that can take you almost anywhere you need to go in the city. ATMs are handy at Singapore immigration and Queen St if you need to change your currency.

See p543 for details on doing the trip in the opposite direction.

Johor Premium Outlets   MALL

(www.premiumoutlets.com.my) Enjoy discounts of 25% to 65% at 80 big-name brand stores like Gap and Nike. The mall is in Kulai, about 25km from JB.

Tebrau City Shopping Centre   MALL

This is the biggest shopping centre in Johor. It's got a massive Jusco plus pretty much everything else you can think of. It's about 15 minutes drive from the Causeway.

Plaza Pelangi   MALL

(Jln Tebrau) A mishmash of everything and very popular.

ⓘ Information

ATMs and banks are everywhere in the central areas. Moneychangers infest Jln Wong Ah Fook, and have competitive rates

Immigration Office (📞223 8400; khidimat -johor@imi.gov.my; Jln Setia Tropika, Kempas) About 15km north of the Causeway.

KPJ Johor Specialist Hospital (📞Emergency 220 7505, 227 3000; www.kpjjohor.com; 39B Jln Abdul Samad) A squeaky clean, state-of-the-art, private hospital.

Tourism Malaysia & Johor Tourist Information Centre (📞223 4935; www.johortourism.com.my; CIQI Immigration Complex & 3rd fl, Jotic Bldg, 2 Jln Air Molek; ⊙9am-5pm Mon-Sat) Tourism Malaysia has two offices in JB, the most convenient being the one at the CIQ Complex, right after you pass immigration from Singapore.

ⓘ Getting There & Away

Air

JB is served by the **Senai International Airport** (📞599 4500; www.senaiairport.com) in Senai, 32km northwest of JB.

AIRLINE OFFICES

AirAsia (📞1300-889 933; www.airasia.com; Tune Hotel) Has low-cost flights to KL, Penang, Kuching, Kota Kinabalu, Sibu and Miri.

Firefly (📞603-7845 4543; mezzanine fl, Persada Johor International Convention Center, Jln Abdullah Ibrahim) Flies to Kuala Lumpur's Subang Airport and Kota Bahru.

Malaysia Airlines (📞334 1011, 331 0036; mezzanine fl, Persada Johor International Convention Center, Jln Abdullah Ibrahim) Flights to Kuching and Kuala Lumpur with easy connections to a variety of destinations. Prices are much lower than from Singapore.

Bus

Larkin bus station is a frantic sprawl of hawker stalls, restaurants, clothes shops and other outlets as well as numerous bus companies. There's also a left luggage counter (little/big bag RM3/4 per day; ⊙7am-10pm).

JOHOR BAHRU BUS FARES		
Destination	**Price**	**Duration**
Butterworth	RM62.60	9hr
Melaka	RM17	2½hr
KL	RM31	4hr
Mersing	RM12	2hr
Kuantan	RM20	5hr
Kuala Terengganu	RM33	8hr

Taxi

JB's main **long-distance taxi station** (📞223 4494) is at the Larkin bus station (5km north of town); there's a handier terminal on Jln Wong Ah Fook. Regular taxi destinations and costs (share taxi with four passengers) include Kukup (RM80), Senai Airport (RM50), Melaka (RM280), KL (RM460) and Mersing (RM160).

Train

Three daily express trains leave from the sparking JB Sentral train station in the CIQ complex, running to KL (6.30am, 2.56pm and 8.25pm). The line passes through Tampin (for Melaka), Seremban, KL Sentral, Tapah Rd (for Cameron Highlands), Ipoh, Taiping and Butterworth. The line bifurcates at Gemas so you can board the 'jungle train' for Jerantut (for Taman Negara), Kuala Lipis and Kota Bharu.

ⓘ Getting Around

To/From Senai International Airport

Senai International Airport, 32km northwest of town, is linked to the city centre by regular shuttle buses (RM8, 45 minutes) that run from the bus station at Kotaraya 2 Terminal.

A taxi between the airport and JB is RM60, taking 30 to 45 minutes, depending on traffic.

Bus

Local buses operate from several stops around town, the most convenient being the stop in front of Public Bank on Jln Ah Fook. From Larkin bus station bus 39 goes into Central JB (RM1.80).

Car

Car hire in JB is considerably cheaper than in Singapore, but check that the hire firm allows cars to enter Singapore. Car hire prices begin at around RM153 per day; prices are inclusive of insurance and tax. Many rental companies hire cars from Senai International Airport.

Hawk Car Rental (📞224 2849; Suite 221, 2nd fl, Pan Global Plaza, Jln Wong Ah Fook)

GETTING TO INDONESIA: JOHOR BAHRU TO PULAU BATAM & PULAU BINTAN (RIAU ISLANDS)

Getting to the border There are several daily departures to Batam (one way RM69, 1½ hours) and Tanjung Pinangon Bintan (one way RM86, 2½ hours), part of Indonesia's Riau Islands. Ferries depart from the ZON Ferry Terminal (for schedule details see www.zon.com.my/ferry.html), which is serviced by several buses from downtown Johor Bahru. Additional boats depart from Kukup, southwest of JB, to Tanjung Balai on Karimun (three times daily, RM130) and to Sekupang, Batam (twice daily, RM165); see www.ferrytuah.comoj.com for schedules and reservations. Buses travel to Kukup from Johor Bahru (RM7, 1½ hours) and KL (RM26, 3½hours). A taxi from Johor Bahru to Kukup is RM80.

At the border You'll be charged a RM10 seaport tax and stamped out of Malaysia before you board the boat in JB; from Kukup the fee is RM25 per person. From the Riau Islands there are ferry connections to Sumatra, Indonesia.

Taxi

Taxis in JB have meters, and drivers are legally required to use them. Flagfall is RM3, with an average trip costing RM10. Taxis can be hired at around RM35 per hour for sightseeing.

Muar

☑06

A lethargic riverside town, languorously Malaysian in mood and with the feel of a bustling Chinatown, Muar was historically an important commercial centre but today it's a very sleepy backwater. It makes for an off-the-beaten-path (though not very action-packed) stop between Melaka and Johor Bahru.

The graceful **colonial district** by the river turns up several buildings of note. Walk around the area and look out for the customs house, the courthouse, the high school (built in 1914) and Masjid Jamek, a Victorian fantasy in much the same style as JB's Sultan Abu Bakar Mosque.

⛏ Sleeping & Eating

Muar is known for its Nonya-style *otak-otak* (fish cakes) and satay breakfasts. You'll find hawker stalls on Jln Haji Abu just off Jln Ali.

Hotel Classic   HOTEL $$
(☑953 3888; 69 Jln Ali; r RM125-230; ⊗❋🛜🏊) Classy rooms here have complimentary newspaper, coffee- and tea-making facilities and satellite TV, and are the best in town. It's an amazing deal that would cost twice the price in a more touristy town.

Hotel Leewah   HOTEL $
(☑Jln Arab 951 5995, Jln Ali 952 1605; 44 Jln Ali & 75 Jln Arab; d without/with air-con & bathroom RM35/48; P❋🛜) Leewah comprises two separate yet nearby buildings: the Jalan Ali hotel is smaller and in an older building while the Jln Arab location is sprawling and has the friendliest reception you may find in Malaysia. The owners love children, and the hotel attracts a lot of families. All rooms are simple, ageing and clean.

ⓘ Getting There & Away

Regular buses to JB (RM16, 2½ hours) and KL (RM18, 2½ hours) depart from the Muar long-distance bus station by the river. Buses to/from Melaka (RM6, one hour), and Gunung Ledang/Segamat (RM5, one hour) operate from the local bus station. The taxi station is just to the right of the bus station.

Mersing

☑07

This busy, compact fishing town has everything that travellers passing through on their way to the islands might need: cheap internet, OK sleeping options, grocery stores, cold beer and a pharmacy. The river is clogged with colourful fishing boats, but beyond the riverfront there's not much to explore.

☞ Tours

Several places around the port work as booking offices for islands in the Seribuat Archipelago and Tioman Island, and can also arrange packages.

Omar's (Map p236; ☑799 5096, 019-774 4268; Jln Abu Bakar) at Omar's Backpacker's Hostel is the best option for backpackers, and offers day-long Seribuat island-hopping speedboat tours (RM100 per person; minimum four people) and a two-day, one-night Overland Tour (per person RM350 all inclusive; minimum four people) to Endau-Rompin National Park.

🛏 Sleeping

You may end up spending a night or two in Mersing waiting for ferries (due to weather or the tides).

Avoid arriving in Mersing during the Chinese New Year and other holiday periods, as midrange hotels can be booked solid.

Hotel Embassy   HOTEL $
(Map p236; ☑799 3545; 2 Jln Ismail; d/tr/q RM45/55/65; ❄🛜) This is a fabulous choice compared with the other cheapies in town, and is a great place to clean up and get back to reality after bumming it on island beaches. All rooms are huge, bright, have cable TV, air-con and attached bathrooms.

Teluk Iskandar Inn   B&B $$
(☑799 6037; www.iskandarinn.com; 1456 Jln Sekakap; r incl breakfast RM140-200; ☯❄🛜) With a lovely garden sloping all the way down to the beach, this well-groomed spot is quiet and secluded, 4.5km south of town. The two-person rooms are large and airy. The owners

can prepare Malay meals by arrangement. The hotel is on the left side of the road as you head east away from Mersing.

Omar's Backpackers' Hostel   HOSTEL $
(Map p236; ☑799 5096, 019-774 4268; Jln Abu Bakar; dm/d RM15/30; 🛜) At this tiny, social backpacker's pad very near the jetty, your experience will depend on Omar's variable mood. Reservations are recommended during the peak season.

Hotel Timotel   HOTEL $$
(Map p236; ☑799 5888; www.timotel.com.my; 839 Jln Endau; s & d incl breakfast from RM150; ❄@🛜) Just across the bridge over the river, this is a fading, business-style hotel with excellent service. Doubles are clean, spacious and have satellite TV.

🍴 Eating

Seafood stalls (Map p236) open up nightly near the bus station along the river.

Loke Tien Yuen Restaurant   CHINESE $
(Map p236; 55 Jln Abu Bakar; mains RM3.50-15; ☺lunch & dinner) Mersing's oldest Chinese restaurant is one of the friendliest, and busiest places in town. You may have to wait for a marble table to enjoy the deliciously prepared prawn and pork dishes. The specialty, whole steamed fish that you'll see all the locals eating, isn't on the English menu so ask your server.

JOHOR MERSING

GUNUNG LEDANG NATIONAL PARK

According to legend, the highest mountain in Johor, Gunung Ledang (also called Mt Ophir; 1276m), is the fabled home of Puteri Gunung Ledang, a mythical princess whose presence is said to still permeate the jungle slopes. This mountain is extremely popular with Malaysian and Singaporean groups but few foreigners visit the area. It's a very demanding – yet rewarding – two-day return trip from the National Park Office to the summit.

There are several camp sites (RM10 per night) along the way up the mountain. Also note that most camp sites and accomodation book out over the weekends – plan your trip on a weekday or reserve well in advance. Pre- and/or post-trek you can stay in one of the **park's accommodation options** (☑963 1030; www.johorparks.johordt.gov.my; Jln Muar; camp sites RM10, dorm RM25, chalets from RM75), or at the more comfortable **Gunung Ledang Resort** (☑06-977 2888; www.ledang.com; Jln Segamat, sales office BT 28, Sagil, Tangkak; cabins RM50, standard/deluxe tw RM150/250; ❄🛜🏊) a few kilometres down the road.

There's a park entrance fee of RM3 and an additional daily hiking fee of RM23. Mandatory guides bookable through the park's website cost RM140 per day. To get to the park take a bus or train to Segamat then hop on a local bus to Segil (RM5, 45 minutes), ask to get off at Gunung Ledang.

Mersing

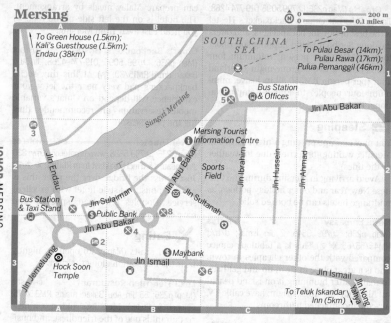

Mersing

⊙ Activities, Courses & Tours
1 Omar's...B2

🛏 Sleeping
2 Hotel Embassy A3
3 Hotel Timotel......................................A2
Omar's Backpackers' Hostel........(see 1)

🍴 Eating
4 Loke Tien Yuen Restaurant B3
5 Port Café & Bistro C1
6 Restoran Al-Arif C3
7 Seafood Stalls A2
8 Xiang Guo Bakery & Cake House B2

Restoran Al-Arif   INDIAN $

(Map p236; 44 Jln Ismail; mains around RM6;
⊙breakfast, lunch & dinner; 🖉) Serving up *roti
canai* (flaky, flat bread; 70 sen), *roti telur*
(roti with an egg; RM1.60), nasi goreng
(fried rice; RM3.50) and vegetarian options.

Xiang Guo Bakery & Cake House   BAKERY $

(Map p236; Jln Abu Bakar; cakes from RM1, pizzas
from RM22; ⊙breakfast, lunch & dinner; ❄🀄) A
lovely place to chill out in the air-con with
a meal (pizzas, Malay-style noodles, rice

dishes and more), a coffee and something
sinful like tiramisu or rich cheesecake.

Port Café & Bistro   WESTERN $$

(Map p236; Jln Abu Bakar; mains RM12-28;
⊙lunch & dinner) A little open-air bar and
eatery right at the jetty, with surprisingly
good Western grub like pizzas (from RM24)
and grilled chicken salads with balsamic
dressing (RM12). The bar serves beer, wine
and cocktails and there's live music some
nights.

ⓘ Information

Mersing Tourist Information Centre (Jln Abu
Bakar; ⊙Mon-Sat 8am-5pm) On the road to the
pier, stop in for helpful info, bus schedules and
pamphlets.

ⓘ Getting There & Away

Most buses as well as long-distance taxis depart
from the bus station near the bridge on the river,
although a few long-distance buses also leave
from bus company offices near the pier. Some
buses will also drop you off at the pier when you
arrive in Mersing if you ask nicely. For buses to
Cherating, travel first to Kuantan.

MERSING BUSES

Destination	Price	Duration	Frequency
Johor Bahru	RM13	2½hr	2 daily
Kahang	RM7	1hr	3 daily
KL	RM40	5½hr	5 daily
Kuala Terengganu	RM34	9hr	2 daily
Kuantan	RM17	5hr	2 daily
Melaka	RM25	4hr	3 daily
Singapore	RM16	3hr	2 daily

Taxi destinations and costs (per car) include Johor Bahru (RM160), Kuantan (RM220) and Pekan (RM150). Local buses run to Endau (RM5, 45 minutes). For boats to Sibu Island, take a taxi to Tanjung Leman (RM70).

Seribuat Archipelago
07

A cluster of 64 islands scattered off the east coast of Johor, the Seribuat Archipelago is a constellation of some of Malaysia's most beautiful islands. Most people only know of Pulau Tioman, the starlet and largest of the group, which is actually a part of Pahang. This leaves the rest of the archipelago as far less-visited dots of tranquillity.

Divers can expect to see excellent coral and an array of marine life: butterfly fish, parrot fish, barracudas, giant clams and more. The waters around the archipelago are frequently whipped into foam during the monsoon from November to February, so ferry services can be patchy, especially during the high monsoon (November and December)

Visitors to the Seribuat Archipelago (and Pulau Tioman) should purchase a **Marine Parks entry ticket** (adult/child RM5/2) at the jetty in Mersing.

PULAU BESAR
07

Easy to get to and perfect for a day or two of serious beach lounging, Pulau Besar's long white-sand beach is fronted by a veritable swimming pool when the sea is calm. If you tire of vegging out, there are trails to more hidden beaches and plenty of jungle to explore. That said, the coral isn't great here and there is no dive operator, so you'll have to spend your water time frolicking in the sandy-bottomed turquoise water or snorkelling along the scattered bits of reef.

You can visit Pulau Besar on a day trip by hopping on the resort's shuttle boats. At the time of research there were no public boats although there have been some in the past – inquire at the Mersing jetty for options.

Sleeping & Eating

The island's resorts are all situated along the beach on the west of the island. All have restaurants and provide transfers to/from Mersing for guests for around RM95 return.

Mirage Island Resort RESORT $$
(799 2334; www.mirageislandresort.com; chalets RM190-550) Cheaper digs are in stylish A-frames while the more expensive options are in huge, louvered wood chalets. All exude a tropical-colonial charm, the staff is young and fun and there's a bar and pool table in the restaurant area.

Aseania Resort RESORT $$$
(019-736 1277; www.pulaubesar.net; chalets incl breakfast from RM300; ✳✱) Rooms are big,

---

SURVIVING EXPEDITION ROBINSON

It will seem a little ironic while you're sipping your cocktail on a white sand beach, but other visitors to your island paradise might have munched on bugs and scrounged for water. This is because the Seribuat Archipelago is the location of *Expedition Robinson,* the original reality TV show that inspired *Survivor.* The program first aired in 1997 and the sets now host several groups (for different versions of the show) from countries such as Belgium, the Netherlands, Denmark and South Africa.

Base camp is on Pulau Besar, while many of the rougher 'survivor' locations are on the smaller, more remote islands. The Robinson TV crew begins setting up around April and filming takes place around June and July. During these two months Pulau Besar's hotels are shut to the public. You can however still make a daytrip to the island by hitching a ride with one of the many crew boats going back and forth to the mainland. Enquire at the Pulau Besar hotel offices at the Mersing jetty.

WORTH A TRIP

PULAU TINGGI

About 10 kilometres northeast from Pulau Sibu Besar, jungle-clad Tinggi is an impressive sight when seen from a distance – it's an extinct volcano (*tinggi* means 'tall') whose 600m-high cone creates a dreamy silhouette. Most resorts offer day trips around the island which involve excellent snorkeling and a trek to a beautiful waterfall.

The island supports three village populations: Kampung Tanjung Balang, Kampung Pasir Panjang and Kampung Sebirah Besar. The main place to stay on the island is the overpriced but beautifully located **Tad Marine Resort** (☎722 1777; www.tadmarineresort.com; two-night packages incl meals & transfers from RM690 per person; ✴✳) that caters mostly to Singaporean divers.

clean and have dark-wood interiors, while the service is stellar and the jungle pool, surrounded by a stylish wood deck, is a shady alternative to the beach.

PULAU SIBU
☑07

Apart from Tioman Island, this cluster of several islands (**Pulau Sibu Besar**, **Pulau Sibu Kukus**, **Pulau Sibu Tengah** and **Pulau Sibu Hujung**) is the most popular destination in the archipelago – particularly with expat families living in Singapore. The bulk of the accommodation is on Pulau Sibu Besar, a tiny island around 7km and 1km wide. Its main attractions are the good diving and even better beaches.

Tiny Pulau Sibu Tengah, which was once a Vietnamese refugee camp, is home to sea turtles that crawl ashore in July to lay their eggs. **Batu Batu** (www.batubatu.com.my; d incl breakfast & transfers from RM750; ✴@✦✳), a private, upscale resort was being completed here at the time of writing. The resort has partnered with Wild Asia (www.wildasia.org) to run turtle conservation projects.

Boats for Pulau Sibu do not depart from Mersing, but from the jetty at Tanjung Leman around 30km south of town. There are no public boats you'll have to organise transport with your resort (included in package prices).

🛏 Sleeping & Eating
All the following rates are per person and include full-board and boat transfers unless otherwise specified.

TOP CHOICE Rimba Resort RESORT $$
(☎012-710 6855; www.resortmalaysia.com; chalets from RM220 per person) Welcome to a super chilled-out beachy paradise on Sibu Besar, with comfy thatched huts all overlooking the island's best swimming and snorkelling beach. Spacious digs are quite stylish with

canopy mosquito nets, cushion-clad lounging spaces and sunken semi-open air bathrooms.

Guests from the other resorts are often lured here by the lovely white beach and loungable deck bar. There's a dive centre and massage hut, and the staff are delightful.

🌿 Sea Gypsy Village Resort RESORT $$
(☎799 3124; www.siburesort.com; A-frames RM180, chalets RM215, family chalets for 2 adults & 2 children RM680) This Sibu Besar resort is one of the best, most affordable places to relax with kids in Malaysia. Special children's meals are served throughout the day; there's a fun kids club, a mini playground and even an ingenious-worm composting system for ecological nappy disposal. The beach is better for playing in waves than for swimming.

Huts are dark but beds are comfortable and most units have a terrace, bathroom and fan. A-frames close to the jungle are the cheapest options. There's also a dive centre and plenty of activities on offer.

Sibu Island Resort RESORT $$
(☎222 5155; www.sibuislandresort.com.my; 1-night packages for 2 people incl breakfast from RM520; ✴@✳) On isolated Pulau Sibu Tengah, this relatively plush resort has all the mod-cons and good snorkelling. There's a full spa, dive centre, tennis courts and a ropes course for team-building corporate groups. The beaches are good but the restaurant and rooms are closed-in air-con-style and thus short on sea breezes. Expect karaoke on weekends.

PULAU RAWA
☑07

Edged by a fine white-sand beach, and luring bands of sunseekers, surfers and snorkellers, the tiny island of Rawa pokes out of the sea 16km from Mersing. Both resorts arrange transport for guests or you can try to hop on one of their boats for a day trip for RM60 per person.

🛏 Sleeping

Rawa's two resorts are right next to each other on one of the prettiest beaches in the Seribuat Archipelago. Think sugary white sand leading to a bowl of perfect blue.

Rawa Island Resort   RESORT $$$
(☏799 1204; www.rawaislandresort.com; 1-night packages incl full board & boat transfers per person RM380-1170; ❋@) The island's main resort has basic, ageing accommodation scattered over the hillsides and on the beachfront. But you won't be indoors. This is a lively, family-style heaven with peddle boats, a trampoline and a huge waterslide (not functioning when we passed). There's also a restaurant, dive centre and a wide range of facilities and activities.

Alang's Rawa Resort   RESORT $$
(☏012-715 5547; www.alangsrawa.com; two-night package per person incl meals & transfers from RM450) Cheerful white huts with sky-blue shutters line the best part of the beach for a perfect do-nothing escape. Service is non-existent and the cafe where meals are served is teeming with old drunk Chinese men – but in this setting, who cares?

PULAU AUR, PULAU DAYANG & PULAU PEMANGGIL
☏07
These three islands are so far from the mainland (four to six hours by boat) that you'll need to devote a few days here to make it worth the trip. In fact, you may not be able to get here at all outside weekends and holidays when the resorts run boats to pick up groups of Singaporean divers.

Eighty kilometres from the mainland, Pulau Aur has crystal-clear azure water, excellent coral and a few wrecks off the coast. **Diver's Lodge** (3-day/2-night dive packages from S$365), bookable through Singaporean dive tour opporators (try www.friendlywaters.com.sg) is where most folks go, although there's not much of a beach.

About 300 beds are available on Pulau Dayang, across the channel from Pulau Aur, at the scenic beach at **Dayang Blues Resort** (☏65-6536 6532; www.dayangnow.com; 1-night packages from S$380) in Kampung Pasir Putih.

Forty-five kilometres east of Mersing, beautiful Pulau Pemanggil supports a sparse population. Needless to say, the water is beautiful. **Lanting Resort** (☏799 3793; www.lantingresort.com.ny; 3-day/2-night package RM298) has a variety of chalet, longhouse and suite accommodation, and offers lots of fishing adventures in a rustic, family-run setting.

Endau-Rompin National Park

Endau-Rompin National Park is that pristine, waterfall-laden jungle teeming with animals which comes to mind when you hear the phrase 'deep Malaysian interior'. Straddling the Johor–Pahang border, the 260-million-year-old, 870-sq-km park is the second-largest one on the peninsula after the much more developed Taman Negara. In fact, there are few trails in Endau-Rompin so exploration is limited, but what you can see is spectacular. The park's lowland forests are among the last in Peninsular Malaysia and have been identified as harbouring unique varieties of plant life including enormous umbrella palms, with their characteristic fan-shaped leaves, and *Livinstona endanensis,* a species of palm with serrated circular leaves.

The park is also Malaysia's last refuge of Sumatran rhinoceros and tigers, although these roam only within the park's remote areas. Herds of elephants are sometimes spotted near Kampung Peta around sunset. The park's birds include red jungle fowl, the black hornbill and the grey wagtail. Monkeys cackle in the trees.

The majority of travellers arrive on tours arranged by private operators but it's just as easy (and less expensive) to organise a trip through the park itself. A good first stop is the **Johor National Parks Corporation** (www.johorparks.johordt.gov.my; Jln Sulaiman, Mersing; ☉8am-1pm & 2-5pm Mon-Sat) office in Mersing, who can help you get in touch with the appropriate park office.

There are two main entry ways to the park, the principal one at Kampung Peta accessed from Kahang and a less developed one at Selai which is about a 40-minute drive from the town of Bekok. No trails link the the two areas so you have to choose to base yourself at one or the other. A third, less used entry is in Pahang province 26km from Kuala Rompin and is not managed by the Johor Parks Corporation.

Endau-Rompin National Park

GUIDES

Officials of the Johor National Parks Corporation generally require that you hire a guide to explore the park. Guides can be hired for RM60 per day at the park headquarters at Kampung Peta, or at the Selai office, and are usually Orang Asli who come from the nearby villages and who have grown up in these jungles. A conservation fee (RM20) is also required.

KAMPUNG PETA ENTRANCE

The park office and lodging here is located right next to a charming Orang Asli village whose residents often give demostrations on local games (mostly puzzles – get ready to use your brain) and animal trapping techniques. It's a lush setting, a short walk from the river. To start walks you'll need to take a scenic boat trip about a half hour up river (RM140 for up to 10 people) – from here it's about a half-hour walk to **Kuala Jasin base camp** from where all the trails lead. To organise lodging and activities from this entrance, call the **Endau-Rompin Peta Office** (☑888 2812; 11 Jln Bawall, Kahang).

UPEH GULING & BUAYA SANGKUT FALLS

The main walk in the park follows the Sungai Jasin from Kuala Jasin base camp. On a one-day walk you'll go to multitiered **Upeh Guling Falls**, which is an easy, mostly flat walk with a few river crossings through pristine jungle. There's a nice leech-free picnic spot on a rock facing the falls.

For a two-day trek you'll continue for another 40 minutes to the flat rocks and camp site of **Batu Hampar**. It's about 4km of a challenging uphill slog over several ridges from Batu Hampar to the the top of the falls (a 40m drop) at Buaya Sangkut. Because the path is quite faint, only attempt this hike with a guide.

On the way back from one or two-day treks, most people stop for a swim at **Tasik Air Biru**, a bright blue, clear and refreshing swimming hole a few minutes walk from Kuala Jasin base camp.

SELAI ENTRANCE

Selai has far less facilities than Kampung Peta – most notably, there's no canteen so you have to bring your own food. Treks from Lubuk Tapah base camp in the west of the park follow the Sungai Selai to explore the many waterfalls along the river. To organise a trip from this entrance directly through the park, call the **Endau-Rompin Selai Office** (☑922 2875; 8 Jln Satrio 1, Bekok).

TAKAH BERANGIN & TAKAH PANDAN FALLS

About a 1.5 hour walk from base camp up a steep hill you'll reach the tall, single-drop Taka Beringin Falls where you can plop in for a dip and some body pummelling from the rapids. Thirty minutes on from here are the tall and slender Takah Pandan Falls where you can dive into a much calmer pool (around 2m deep).

TAKAH TINGGI FALLS

From base camp at the parks office, trek about 1.5 hours along a good trail to the roaring, low-slung Takah Tinggi Falls. Along the way you'll cross a few suspension bridges.

LOCAL KNOWLEDGE

ON THE TRAIL OF JOHOR'S SNAGGLE-TOOTHED GHOST

Johor's famed *hantu jarang gigi* (snaggle-toothed ghost) is a tall, hairy, camera-shy biped that's possibly stuck in the same evolutionary cul-de-sac as the yeti or sasquatch. The primate has been tracked unsuccessfully for decades, with regular Orang Asli sightings of the 3m-tall brown-haired 'missing link' – as well as discoveries of oversized footprints. A slew of sigtings were reported in 2005 near a river in the jungle around Kota Tinggi, when an entire family of primates was reportedly glimpsed by labourers. This instigated a giant and unsuccessful hunt for the beasts in 2006 and since then there have been no reports.

So note: if you encounter a fugitive yeti-like creature stumbling from the bushes, have your camera ready – and *no sudden movements*.

🛏 Sleeping & Eating

There are fan dorms and chalets, in good condition, available in Kampung Peta (dorm bed RM25, chalet RM80 to RM150) and simple A-frames at Kuala Jasin. At Selai, simple chalet accommodation (from RM60) is available at Lubuk Tapah base camp. Kampung Peta has a canteen where three good Malaysian-style meals per day (including a packed lunch if you're hiking) cost RM37. There's no canteen at Selai but there are simple cooking facilities.

You can camp at designated sites for RM5 per night per person.

❶ Getting There & Away

Unless you have your own 4WD getting to Endau Rompin will require you to either book a tour (Mersing is a good place for this) or make arrangements independently through the park itself.

Kampung Peta

Take a bus to Kahang and ask to be let off at the park office. Call the **Endau-Rompin Peta Office** (☎888 2812) in advance to charter one of the park's 4WDs with a driver (RM370) from here. It's 56km of rough road through palm-oil plantations to Kampung Peta. At the time of writing the last half of this road from Kampung Peta was being paved which may make the journey cheaper and shorter in future.

Selai

Take a train to Kampung Bekok station. Call the **Endau-Rompin Selai Office** (☎922 2875) in advance to arrange a 4WD (RM120) pick up from here for the 45-minute drive over rough road to base camp.

Pahang & Tioman Island

📍 09 / POP: 1.45 MILLION / 36,137 SQ KM

Includes »

Pulau Tioman 243
Endau 252
Pekan 252
Kuantan 254
Around Kuantan 257
Cherating 257
Taman Negara 260
Jerantut 265
Kuala Lipis 267
Kenong Rimba
State Park 268
Raub 269
Temerloh 270
Around Temerloh 270

Best Places to Eat

» Restoran Ratha Raub (p269)

» Ana Ikan Bakar Petai (p256)

» Bersatau Nipah Chalets (p251)

» ABC Restaurant (p248)

Best Places to Stay

» Swiss Cottage Resort (p246)

» Bushman (p249)

» Villa de Fedella (p258)

» Traveller's Home (p264)

Why Go?

Pahang, Peninsular Malaysia's largest state, is home to some of the county's most accessible outdoor action. It holds the region's grandest jungles and is bordered by 209km of surfable sandy beaches and the near-perfect tropical island of Tioman. A three hour drive from Kuala Lumpur brings you to the primordial national park of Taman Negara, with elusive elephants and tigers within its tracts of virgin jungle. If you're coming from Singapore, the green peaks and blue waters of Pulau Tioman are only four hours away. Those heading down the east coast from Terengganu shouldn't miss a stop at the super-laid-back surf-bum and artist haven of Cherating.

In between these tourism starlets, you will find off-the-beaten-path gems offering pristine jungles, wildlife and flora, Malaysian culture, colonial architecture and culinary delights, many as yet undiscovered by the tourist hordes.

When to Go

Endau

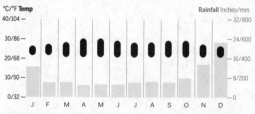

Jan–Apr The weather is at its warmest and driest and the crowds gather.

May–Dec Humidity exceeds 82% and there's intermittent rain.

Nov–Feb Monsoon season: some places close; others offer discounts for hardy travellers.

Pulau Tioman

☑09

Beautiful Tioman has a near-Polynesian feel to it, with its hibiscus flowers, steep green peaks and turquoise, coral-rich waters. At 20km long and 11km wide, the island is so spacious that your dream beach is surely here somewhere. But this is no secret: the island attracts around 190,000 visitors annually. Fortunately holidaymakers are ab-sorbed subtly and the island retains an unspoiled feel, with pristine wilderness and friendly, authentic village life.

A short stretch of road runs along the western side of the island from Berjaya Tioman Beach, Golf & Spa Resort to the northern end of Tekek, where it is inter-rupted by steps before continuing as a path to the end of Air Batang (known as ABC). A winding, newly paved road links Tekek with the dozy east coast idyll of Juara.

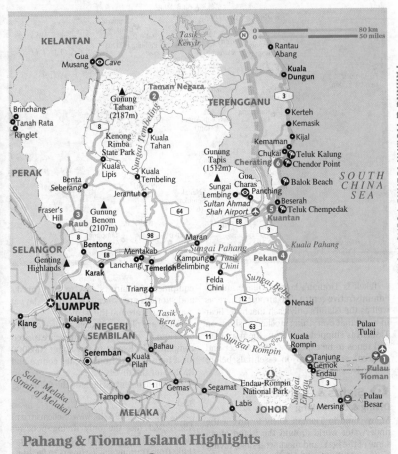

Pahang & Tioman Island Highlights

① Village hopping, diving, snorkelling and jungle trekking on **Pulau Tioman**

② Getting wet, muddy and covered in leeches in deep, dark and undeniably adventurous **Taman Negara** (p260)

③ Exploring and dining in the off-the-beaten-track colonial village of **Raub** (p269)

④ Being stared at by curious **Pekan** (p252) locals, who find visitors as interesting as we find their regal architecture

and charming *kampung* houses

⑤ Enjoying amazing food in **Kuantan** (p256)

⑥ Relaxing in the beach town of **Cherating** (p257)

Pulau Tioman

Tekek is Tioman's largest village and its administrative centre. The airport is here, as well as the island's only cash machine. Bear in mind that everything stocked in shops on Tioman is shipped over from the mainland and tends to be expensive (except beer and tobacco), so stock up on essentials before you arrive.

◉ Sights & Activities

Diving & Snorkelling

Many come to Tioman solely to dive – the underwater world around the island offers some of the best (and most accessible) diving and snorkelling in Malaysia. It's also one of the few places in the country where you have a good chance of seeing pods of dolphins.

There is good snorkelling off the rocky points on the west coast of the island, particularly those just north of ABC, but the best snorkelling is around nearby Pulau Tulai, better known as Coral Island. Snorkelling

equipment for hire is easy to find (masks and snorkels are typically RM10 per day) at many places around the island.

There are plenty of excellent dive centres on Tioman, and PADI courses are priced competitively. Expect to pay about RM1000 for a four-day PADI open-water course and RM100 for fun dives.

Established centres include the following:

B&J DIVING
(☏013-742 5063, 419 1218; www.divetioman.com) ABC's B&J has the only diving pool on Tioman and is equipped for doing everything from training novice divers to facilitating divers for experts.

DiveAsia DIVING
(☏419 1654; www.diveasia.com.my) DiveAsia has offices in Salang, Tekek and ABC; it offers excellent prices on open-water courses and fun dives.

Sunrise Dive Centre DIVING
(☎419 3102; www.sunrisedivecentre.com) Sunrise, in Juara, has the best access to the less-visited east coast sites.

Tioman Dive Centre DIVING
(www.tioman-dive-centre.com) Tekek-based Tioman Dive Centre has a stellar reputation with very responsible dive practices.

Ray's Dive Adventures DIVING
(☎019-3308062; www.raysdive.com) Ray's, which is based in ABC and run by local couple Ray & Chloe, offers a four-day open-water PADI course for RM1100 and has various dive packages as well.

Jungle Walks

Nautical pleasures aside, jungle filled Tioman also offers plenty of excellent hikes to keep the intrepid landlubber exhausted and happy. You'll see more wildlife here than in most of Malaysia's national parks, including black giant squirrels, long-tailed macaques, brush-tailed porcupines and – if you're out with a torch at dawn or dusk and incredibly lucky – the endangered, nocturnal binturong (bear cat).

The 7km Tekek to Juara Jungle Walk offers an excellent feel for the richness of the spectacular interior, not to mention the added bonus of bringing the hiker to beautiful

> ### WWII DIVE SITES
>
> Experienced divers won't want to miss two famous WWII era wreck sites 45 nautical miles north of Tioman, the final resting spots of the HMS *Repulse* and HMS *Prince of Wales*. Both sites are astounding for their historical significance and wide array of marine life, but they're challenging – best suited for those with more than a few dives under their belts.

Juara at hike's end. While the walk isn't too strenuous, parts of it are steep, and hiking in tropical heat can be taxing. Carry plenty of water; if you lose the trail, follow the power lines overhead. If you're setting out on foot, be wary of entering the jungle after around 4.30pm, as it's easy to get lost in the dark.

You'll find signs for the jungle walk just about 1km north of the main jetty in Tekek. You can also walk along the recently paved road to Juara, a longer and somewhat less satisfying hike. A car back from Juara will cost around RM90.

The 3.5km ABC to Salang Trail, which runs inland from the coast, is shorter but more difficult. The trail isn't well marked, but it does lead to some excellent empty

PAHANG & TIOMAN ISLAND PULAU TIOMAN

CHOOSING A SLICE OF PARADISE

The hardest part of your Tioman adventure may well be deciding where to go. We've broken the major options down for you, counter-clockwise from north to south:

Salang The most backpacker-esque of Tioman's *kampungs*. Come to snorkel off nearby Coral Island, stay for the beach parties.

ABC Slightly more upscale than Salang, ABC has a good choice of restaurants and accommodation, though the beach isn't all that spectacular.

Tekek Tioman's commercial hub is a good central location from which to explore the rest of the island, and the beach at the southern end of town is lovely.

Kampung Paya With two moderately priced resorts offering all inclusive packages, Paya is more popular with Singaporean students and the organised-tour set looking to snorkel off Paya beach.

Genting The beach here is fairly built up, but is surrounded by a local village with an appealing *kampung* atmosphere. A good spot for meeting local fisherman.

Nippah Beautiful, rugged and isolated, Nippah is an amazing choice for those wanting to bliss out on Tioman's serenest beach. The waters of Nippah are home to phosphorescent seaweed, and actually glow at night.

Mukut This traditional *kampung* may be one of the prettiest towns on the island, and the beach is lovely. If it's traditional Malaysian life your after, Mukut is your spot.

Juara It's the hardest to get to, but Juara has the best surfing beach in Tioman and enough restaurants and accommodation to make it well worth the trip.

TRAIL SAFETY

Don't let Tioman's laid-back vibe fool you into thinking you're not in the jungle.

» Carry enough water – many a day-tripper has learned too late the folly of heading out with insufficient fluids. On the subject of water, too much isn't always better than not enough.

» Rethink your hiking plans if it's been raining, especially during monsoon season, when nearly every trail becomes unpleasantly muddy at best and impossible to follow at worst.

» Take a headlamp if you think there's even the slightest chance you'll be out past sundown.

» The Old Testament only mentions one, but this Eden's got serpents to spare: 25 species, including the king cobra and reticulated pythons, have been recorded on the island.

beaches. Climb up to Bamboo Hill Chalets at the northern end of ABC bay for a 10-minute hike over the next headland to Panuba Bay. From here it's another 40 minutes through the rainforest to Monkey Beach, before the trail continues from the far end of the beach across the next headland to the white-sand beach at Monkey Bay. From here, it's a long, long, steep climb over the headland to Salang.

An easier 30-minute hike heads south from Tekek to Berjaya Tioman, either by the road or by rock-hopping around the headland at low tide. From there you can walk through the golf course; just before the telecommunications tower there is a trail to the deserted beach of Bunut. From the end of the beach, the occasionally faint trail continues over the headland to Paya. The trail from Paya to Genting is easy to follow and there are houses along the way where you can ask directions.

If you head north from Tekek, you can walk all the way to ABC. Boat transport for the return journey can be arranged at most of the guesthouses in ABC or Salang if you don't feel like walking.

Another beautiful but harder-to-reach trek can be found on Tioman's southern tip, Mukut, accessible by boat from Genting. The Asah Waterfall Trek leads to a stunning waterfall with a beautifully polished swimming hole.

🛏 Sleeping, Eating & Drinking

From Salung to Mukut, all towns and beaches with accommodation are serviced by regular ferries from Mersing. Ferries run to Juara run only when tidal conditions allow, and even then only when enough people are going to make it worth the captain's while.

Budget accommodation largely comprises small wooden chalets and longhouse rooms (all in poor condition), typically with a bathroom, fan and a mosquito net. More expensive rooms have air-con and hot showers. Most operations have larger family rooms for those with children, and many have restaurants.

TEKEK

While the central part of town, with its unsightly twin jetties, characterless marina and shabby duty-free shops isn't scenic, the village is getting gussied up a bit with a large paved waterfront promenade bordered with coconut palms.

All accommodation options lie close to each other on the excellent southern beach.

TOP CHOICE **Swiss Cottage Resort**   RESORT **$$**
(☏419 1642; www.swiss-cottage-tioman.com; long-house d fan/aiar-con RM100-120, garden-/sea-view chalets RM130-150, sea view bungalows RM180; ❊☎) This resort is clearly operated by creative folk. The rooms to nab here are the sea view chalets (RM180), which have breezy bamboo and wood interiors alongside colourfully painted walls and comfy deck furniture. Other options are nestled in a shady back garden, including the newly renovated beachside bungalow. The on-site chill-out spot is athe perfect place to hang out after diving with the folks at the also on-site Tioman Dive Centre (p245).

Coral Reef Holidays   LONGHOUSE **$$**
(☏419 1868; longhouse air-con standard/tw/tr RM130/160/160, dm RM25, d RM45 including breakfast; ❊☎) Adik and Hasnizah's lovely beachfront longhouse has rooms facing the sea, all with individually crafted stonework, raised platform beds, air-conditioning and colour televisions. The couple also offer air-conditioned and fan-cooled dorms, and operate an excellent restaurant serving Western and local food.

Babura Seaview Resort CHALET $
(📞419 1139; www.baburaseaview.com; r/chalets incl breakfast RM60-180; ❄️🛜) This family run place on the end of the beach offers long-house fan rooms and a selection of newer rooms and chalets with air-con and hot-water bathrooms. **Tioman Reef Divers** (www.tiomanreefdivers.com) has a shop here.

Chinese Sarang Seafood CHINESE $$
(📞013-706 6484; meals RM20; ⏲lunch & dinner) This spot does a particularly tasty sizzling hotplate bean curd (RM8) and serves beer.

AIR BATANG (ABC)

The beach here is usually best at the southern and northern ends, although the sands are constantly shifting so this is changeable. Most of the beachfront is rocky with little sand.

Internet in ABC is spotty; a few guest-houses have wireless, and **Mokhtar's Place** (per hr RM10; ⏲9am-10.30pm) has a small internet cafe that isn't always open during posted hours.

| TOP CHOICE | **ABC Chalet** | CHALET $ |

(📞419 1154; d chalets RM50-150; ❄️🛜) Swing on a hammock overlooking the sea at this lovely section of beach at the north end of ABC. Accommodation is spread over pleasant, well-tended grounds, with a couple of chalets almost on the beach. The large, pricier chalets come with hot water, air-con, sea views, hot showers, a freezer, and tea- and coffee-making facilities.

Bamboo Hill Chalets CHALET $$$
(📞419 1339; bamboosu@tm.net.my; chalets RM90-140; @🛜) These six well-kept chalets are in a stupendous location, perched on rocks on the northern end of the beach, surrounded by bougainvillea and humming cicadas alongside a waterfall and pool. They are almost always full, so call ahead.

TIOMAN'S RESORTS

Willing to pay for the privilege of not having to carve your own slice of paradise? Tioman has a number of resorts ranging from merely high-end to the downright extravagant. All have exclusive beaches and private jetties. Your best bet with most resorts is to book a package deal in advance, either through a travel agent or through their websites. Note that many of these resorts offer amazing deals (up to 50% off listed price) during the monsoon season (November to February).

Melina Beach Resort (📞419 7080; www.tioman-melinabeach.com; chalets for 4/5/6/8 people incl breakfast RM200-495) Melina is located on a remote beach of photogenic boulders and white sand. Each sleeping option is unique, creatively designed from wood, thatch and Plexiglas to create a certain Crusoe chic – the most interesting is a tree house that hovers right over the beach.Meals are served at the resort or you can walk for 20 minutes to Genting and try the restaurants there. The owners have set up a successful turtle hatchery, and plenty of activities are organised to keep folks entertained; there's also a beachside bar and BBQ. The relaxed atmosphere attracts lots of families.

Panuba Inn Resort (📞419 1424, 07-799 6348; www.panubainn.com; 3d/2n from RM355 per person) Peaceful Panuba Inn, over the headland from ABC, has a pier and restaurant and 30 chalets built on a hill overlooking the bay. Rooms all face the sea, ranging from simple fan affairs to chalets with hot shower, air-con and plenty of mod-cons.

Berjaya Tioman Beach, Golf & Spa Resort (📞419 1000; www.berjayaresorts.com/tioman; d RM407-1800) Berjaya is the biggest resort on Tioman. Its accommodation ranges from chalets and suites to entire villas, not to mention standout attractions including tennis, a football pitch, a kids' playground, donkey rides and an arcade. There's two swimming pools (one with great water slides), four restaurants and a beach bar. And – oh yes – there's golf.

Tunamaya Resort (📞238 8881; www.tunamayaresort.com; beach villas RM780, rainforest villas from RM680) New Tioman addition Tunamaya is operated by the same folks who run the highly regarded Tuna Bay (p286) on Perhentian. It was nearly completed at the time of research, and will be ready by the time you're reading this. The resort overlooks white sand beaches and promises high-quality amenities including spas and a bar with beers from around the world.

Nazri's Place
CHALET $$

(☑419 1329; www.nazrisplace.com; d incl breakfast RM60-180, f incl breakfast RM250; ✽@) Nazri's is at the far southern end of the beach, which has some of ABC's best sand. It has clean rooms and a wide range of accommodation, from budget rooms with air-con (cross a small river to the cheapies at the rear) to deluxe rooms and family rooms in the brick units. The restaurant is right on the water and serves an excellent seafood barbecue.

Johan's Resort
CHALET $

(☑419 1359; dm/chalets/f RM20/40/100) A friendly, welcoming place offering tons of information. The two four-bed dorms up the hillside are decent value; the chalets are pretty much the same as other cheapies on the beach.

SP Barakha
CHALET $

(☑419 1176; chalets RM50-150) Formerly known as South Pacific, this simple, family-run place just north of the jetty has a decent restaurant, laundry service, and a steadily growing library of secondhand books. Owner Tony is a wealth of information on Tioman.

B&J Dive Resort
HOTEL $$

(☑013-742 5063, 419 1218; www.divetioman.com; tw/tr/q RM250/300/360; ✽@) This is easily the most high-class spot in ABC. All rooms have flat screen TVs, air-con, safes, coffee makers and other mod-cons that'll make you think you're back in a three star hotel in KL.

Mokhtar's Place
CHALETS $

(d RM35-55; ✽@) There's a very mellow family vibe going on at this quiet spot on the south end of ABC. Cheaper bungalows are set back from the beach under pleasant shady trees and all rooms are spacious and clean. Internet is (sporadically) available for RM10 per hour.

Nazri's II
CHALET $$

(☑419 1375; d with fan/air-con RM80/140; ✽) Similar to Nazri's Place (p248), but on the north end of ABC and set in a particularly well-tended garden that spreads up the hillside.

Sri Nelayan Chalets
CHALET $

(☑019-732 6373; chalets RM40) This family-run place north of the jetty has four clean, fan-cooled chalets facing a well manicured lawn. The family also owns a small grocery store and arranges tours.

My Friend's Place
CHALET $

(☑419 1150; r RM35) My Friend's Place, south of the jetty, is busy, social, clean and priced a hair lower than the competition. Chalets all face a lovely garden.

Tioman House
HOTEL $

(☑019-704 5096; chalets RM50-150; ✽) Tioman House, at ABC's north end, offers rooms painted a happy yellow in a classic modern hotel decor.

oABC Restaurant
MALAY $$

(meals RM10-20; ⊙breakfast, lunch & dinner) This restaurant is packed most nights with travellers who flock to enjoy ABC's BBQ special (RM20), a tantalising array of freshly caught fish, prawn or squid. For less adventurous eaters, chicken will have to do. Beer is available.

Sunset Corner
RESTAURANT $

(pizzas from RM16; ⊙2pm-late) Last spot before the stairs leading south, Sunset serves beer, booze, milkshakes and pizza. Happy hour is from 5pm to 7pm.

The Deco Bar
BAR

(⊙2:30am till late) The Deco Bar is usually filled with divers in the evening playing guitar and swapping dive tales. Happy hour is from 5pm to 7pm.

SALANG

Salang has more of a party vibe than elsewhere on the island. A very wide and inviting white-sand beach is just south of the jetty and is good for swimming. For many, Salang's star attraction are the monstrous monitor lizards that lurk in the inky river than runs through the village centre.

Salang Indah Resort
RESORT $$

(☑419 5015; chalets from RM60-185; ✽@) An expanse of chalets seemingly sprawls forever at this resort complex. Most rooms aren't in tip-top condition, but if you look at several you'll probably find one to your liking. The most interesting are the Popeye-like chalets on stilts over the sea (RM120). The mosque-like restaurant acts as a hub of sorts and serves everything from cheeseburgers to cheap local-style seafood (dishes around RM8). There's also a bar, shop and internet access (RM10 per hour).

Ella's Place
CHALET $

(☑419 5004; chalets RM60-120; ✽) There's usually a lounge-able patch of sand at this cute-as-a-button family-run place at the quiet northern end of the beach. There are

10 clean chalets (some with air-con) and a small cafe.

Khalid's Place
CHALET $

(☎419 5317; salangpusaka@yahoo.com; d chalets with air-con RM80; ❋) Khalid's Place is south of the jetty, behind the Salang Complex and across a festering section of Sungai Salang. It has 47 cleanish chalets set in a large grassy area. Accommodation is set back from the beach; air-con chalets come with fridge and hot shower.

JUARA

Juara is a world of its own. It's the sole place to stay on the east coast of the island and hovers in a constant sleepy state of remote-hideaway bliss. There are two long stretches of wide white sandy beach here (separated by a small hill and boulder outcrop). The northern half of the beach (called Barok) is where most accommodation is found, while the southern strip (known as Menta-wak) is near-deserted and kicks up some of the country's best surfing waves during the monsoon.

Turtles nest on both beaches and the area has been proclaimed a 'green zone' by the Sultan of Johor. This means it is protected from development, including the building of any big new resorts. All the places to stay in Juara overlook the magnificent beach; a few places hire out kayaks (RM15 per hour), surfboards (RM20 per hour) and fishing rods (RM15 per hour).

TOP CHOICE Bushman
CHALET $

(☎419 3109; matbushman@hotmail.com; chalets fan/air-con RM50/80; ❋⬥) Nabbing one of Bushman's five new varnished wood chalets, with their inviting wicker-furnished terraces, is like winning the Juara lottery – reserve in advance! The location is right up against the boulder outcrop and a small river that marks the end of the northern beach. Bush-

man's little cafe serves breakfast, lunch and dinner, and is a wondrously languorous place to chill out.

TOP CHOICE Beach Hut
HOSTEL $

(☎012-696 1093; timstormsurf@yahoo.au; camp sites with tent for 2 RM15, dm/chalets RM15/45/55) By the time you read this, Tim & Izan's Beach Hut will have moved 100m north to a brand new location on Matawa beach. If the old spot (a long-time Lonely Planet favourite) is anything to go by, the new spot will incorporate the same colourful ecof-riendly building techniques, including shell mobiles, strategically placed driftwood and Bollywood fabrics run riot. Beachside tent and sleeping-bag accommodation will still be available, and of course, surf lessons (RM60 per hour) with surf legend Tim Brent are still available. The social, lounge-able Tube Café will also migrate to the new location.

Rainbow Chalets
CHALET $

(☎419 3140; rainbow.chalets@ymail.com; chalets fan/air-con RM40/80) Eight colourful chalets – three air-conditioned and five fan-cooled – await you at Rainbow, all with wooden porches decorated with shells and coral, and facing a particularly lovely stretch of beach. Owner Mohammad also runs a taxi service with better rates to Tekek than many other drivers.

Riverview
CHALET $$

(☎419 3168; chalet/beach chalet RM100/150; ⬥) Fairly chic A-frame huts have balconies directly over a lazy jungle river that winds its way to the sea. The large flat area of beach on the restaurant side has an inviting volleyball pitch and the rest of the grounds are covered in soft Japanese grass (go bare-foot!). They also rent kayaks (RM30) to guests.

PAHANG & TIOMAN ISLAND PULAU TIOMAN

GETTING TO JUARA

Juara is trickier to reach than other spots on Tioman, but oh so worth it. Though the paving of the Tekek–Juara road has technically made Juara more accessible, most taxi drivers still charge the same exorbitant (RM90 to RM120 per vehicle) pre-paved price for the 15-minute trip. A taxi boat from ABC will set you back RM150.

Though the town has a fine jetty, the east coast waves that attract surfers have thus far kept Juara from enjoying the same regular ferry service as towns on the west coast (though the Mersing Ferry sometimes stops here for four or more travellers).

Your best bet for getting here is to arrange transit with one of the hotels. If you're the hardy sort, hiking over from Tekek is definitely an option.

Juara Beach Resort RESORT $$

(☐013-771 1137; www.island.com.my/tioman; s/d/tr RM100-180; ❄🛜) Modern rooms at this resort face a grassy garden studded with coconut palms, and the friendly management has a wide variety of vacation packages to chose from, most of which involve meals, activities and transit from Tekek. The attached restaurant – open for breakfast, lunch and dinner – is one of the best on the island. The chef cooks up an excellent variety of Chinese and Malay (and even a few Western) dishes. They also serve cold beer.

Juara Lagoon CHALET $$

(☐419 3153; juaralagoon@yahoo.com; chalets & longhouse RM100) The Juara is situated at the very far end of the southern bay, and enjoys sensational views of the bay's entire sweep. The establishment runs its own turtle sanctuary and you can hang out with Jo, a deaf and blind green turtle cared for by the centre.

Mutiara Resort CHALET $$

(☐419 3159; www.juaramutiararesort.com; s/d/q chalets RM100/150/180; ❄) Mutiara, just south of the jetty, has lots of options with comparably high standards.

Mizani's Place CHALET $

(☐019-792 9640; chalets RM45) Mizani's is on the southern section of beach. Its simple, old but clean bungalows have fans, mosquito nets and attached bathrooms.

Paradise Point LONGHOUSE $

(☐419 3145; s/d/q RM40/60/100) Paradise Point, north of the jetty, offers simple, homey rooms in a longhouse.

Santai Bistro MALAY $$

(meals around RM12; ☺9am-11pm) This bar/restaurant right next to the jetty plays classic rock and serves up delights like sambal prawns (RM18), tom yum (RM12) and mixed vegetable salads (RM6). The beers are cold and the views hypnotising.

KAMPUNG PAYA

The short, wide, white-sand beach here is jam-packed with two resorts and a few restaurants and food shacks. The rocky seabed and shallow water make this a poor choice for swimming.

Paya Resort RESORT $$

(☐in Mersing 07-799 1432; www.payabeach.com; dm incl breakfast RM40, chalets incl breakfast RM200-480; ❄🛜📺) Spacious chalets are linked together by wooden bridges over a lily pond. There are also tidy, air-con four-bed dorm rooms and a restaurant, full spa, dive centre, lounge and a range of activities.

Sri Paya Tioman Chalet CHALET $$

(www.tiomanchalet.com; 3d/2n including all meals and activities RM360 p/p; ❄🛜📺) Sri Paya Tioman Chalet was opened in 2010 and has beautiful air-conditioned chalets, an on-site dive shop and a waterfront restaurant. Package deals include meals and organised snorkelling tours.

GENTING

Genting caters mostly to the weekend crowds from Singapore and KL, but its surrounding local village gives it a touch of authenticity.

Sun Beach Resort RESORT $$

(☐419 7027; www.sunbeachresort.com.my; tw RM58-98, tr RM78-108, f RM98-118, deluxe RM158-188, ocean-view suite RM358; ❄) Newly opened Sun Beach has beachfront chalets ranging from simple to deluxe (featuring minibars and televisions) and a great restaurant. Check the website for package deals.

📷 Golden Dish Café CHINESE $

(dishes from RM6; ☺10am-midnight; 🍴) This might be the only place on Tioman serving their own home-grown organic vegetables. There are also plenty of authentic Chinese seafood specialties and healing herbal drinks. If that isn't your thing, they also serve up beer for RM5.

Riverside Cafe MALAY $

(dishes from RM3.50; ☺breakfast, lunch & dinner) This very inexpensive place right next to the jetty serves up burgers from RM3.5, omelets from RM2.5, and Malay and Thai specialties like *kampung* noodles (RM4.5) and tom yum (RM6).

LEARN BATIK MAKING!

Genting is the home of Suhadi Mahadi, whose **Suzila Batik Arts & Crafts Centre** (☐013-751 4312; suzilabatik@gmail.com) is just south of the Jetty. Suhadi teaches batik making using traditional materials, Tuition varies from RM25-80; a simple batik might take an hour or two to make, while a more complex pattern might take the afternoon. Suhadi also sells ready-made Batik from RM30-1200.

NIPAH

Blissful, isolated Nipah Beach is a long strip of white with an unusual strip of black sand running through it. A river mouth at the southern end creates a deep blue swimming hole that's bordered on one side by a large, flat knuckle of sand with a volleyball pitch. This is the place to come to hang in a hammock, snorkel or hike in the jungle.

Both Nipah's hotels are open year round, and can arrange pick up from the ferry stop in Genting for RM30 each way.

Bersatu Nipah Chalets LONGHOUSE $
(☎07-797 0091, 012-655 7824; bersatunipah_tio man@yahoo.com; r with fan/air-con RM60/90; ❀) This clean beachfront longhouse has great service (the amiable Jalil and Amy) and an excellent riverside restaurant with dishes like freshly caught fish (priced by weight), calamari fritters (RM16) and a fried rice and chicken set (RM9). The mixed grill, containing a variety of poultry, fish and meat, with fruit and fries on the side, is especially popular (RM30). Jalil also runs a free river cruise for guests.

The Nipah Beach Tioman CHALET $
(☎019-735 7853; chalets from RM70) Young, friendly host Abbas runs these rustic chalets on stilts by the water's edge. They sit so close to the beach that the sound of waves lapping at the stairs will soothe you to sleep.

MUKUT

On the southern tip of Tioman, Mukut may be the loveliest – as well as most secluded – *kampung* on the island. The beach is a tad less amazing than the one in Juara, but this is made up for by the prettiness of the town itself, with its traditional homes and flower-lined paths.

Mukut Coral Resort CHALET $
(☎07-799 2612, 07-799 2535; r/chalets RM25/88; ❀) Traditional village-style chalets (all with air-con and hot water, some with TV) are set in a marvellous location beside Mukut's jetty. There's a sea-view restaurant serving Chinese and Western food.

Mukut Harmony Resort CHALET $
(☎07-799 2275; chalets RM50) Has a dozen fan-cooled chalets on a strip of grass next to the jetty.

❶ Information

Tioman's sole cash machine is in Tekek across from the airport and takes international cards.

It's been known to run dry, so consider getting cash in Mersing. Travellers cheques can be cashed at the Berjaya Tioman Beach, Golf & Spa Resort and there's a moneychanger at the airport. There's a small post office not far north of the Babura Seaview Resort in Tekek.

There are numerous public phones at Tekek, Air Batang (ABC) and Salang, but many are in disrepair. Only Telekom cards can be used for calls, on sale at shops around the island. The island's sole clinic is **Poliklinik Komuniti Tekek** (☎419 1880).

❶ Getting There & Away

Air
Berjaya Air (☎419 1309, in KL 03-7846 8228, in Singapore 02-6481 6302; www.berjaya-air.com) Has daily flights to/from KL and Singapore. Prices vary by day and season.

Boat
Mersing in Johor is the main access port for Tioman. **Island Connection Tours** (☎799 2535; return RM70) has an office in Mersing. Other operators sell tickets by the jetty for the same price. Boats run from early morning until late afternoon, stopping at Genting, Paya, Berjaya Tioman, Tekek, ABC and Salang, returning in the reverse order on the return trip. Decide where you want to get off and tell the ticket inspector. On weekends and holidays it's a good idea to buy your tickets in advance since the boats fill quickly.

Boat departures during the monsoon season (November to February) can be erratic, with trips becoming more regular during the low monsoon months (January and February).

Ferries also depart for Tioman from the **Tanjung Gemok ferry terminal** (☎413 1997; return RM70), 35km north of Mersing near Endau (p252). This route is useful if coming from the north. Call ahead and make sure the ferries are running before you arrive.

❶ Getting Around

Typical sea taxi fares from Telek are: Salang (RM30), ABC/Panuba (RM25), Paya Beach (RM30), Genting (RM30), Nipah (RM75) and Juara (RM105). Most chalets can arrange boat charter. Expect to pay around RM600 for a full day on a boat, and expect the sea to be far rougher on the Juara side of Tioman.

If you have the time, you can explore some of the island on foot. Bicycles can be hired at guesthouses on all the main beaches (RM5 per hour).

Though the road from Tekek to Juara is now paved, most operators are still trying to get the pre-paved price of RM90 to RM120 for the relatively short ride. Bargain hard!

Endau

☑09

There's little of interest in Endau, but fast boats speed to Pulau Tioman run from nearby **Tanjung Gemok**. If you get stuck here, you can spend the night at the **Hotel Seri Malaysia** (☑413 2723; smrom@serimalaysia.com.my; d incl breakfast RM150; ❇❇) in Tanjung Gemok, a few minute's walk from Endau.

Pekan

☑09

Pekan, the seat of the Pahang Sultanate, has a regal air and is uncommonly scenic with its wide clean streets, spacious *padang* (city square) and many grand buildings surrounded by expansive pristine lawns. There is also a collection of old Chinese shophouses along a shady river, excellent Malaysian street food and a cluster of beautiful mosques.

The blue-domed **Sultan Abdullah Mosque** (Map p253; Jln Sultan Ahmad) is a large, slightly mouldering creation dating back to 1932. Behind the mosque stands the old **Pekan Lama** (Map p253), a tower fashioned from wood and stone. The active **Abu Bakar Mosque** (Map p253; Jln Sultan Ahmad) is further west, crowned with gold domes.

Several examples of Pekan's non-Islamic houses of worship including the tiny **Mariamnan Hindu Temple** (Map p253) and the larger **Lei Shen Gong Buddhist Temple** (Map p253).

The focus of the Pekan's palm-lined royal quarter, Kampung Permatang Pauh, is the Regent of Pahang's palace, **Istana Permai** and further on, the sultan's palace, the **Istana Abu Bakar**, set in vast grounds of cow grass and adjacent to the verdant polo field of the **Royal Pahang Polo Club**.

TASIK CHINI

Beautiful Tasik Chini (Lake Chini) is a series of 12 lakes linked by vegetation-clogged channels. Environmentalists see increasing threat to the area, one of Pahang's natural flood retention basins, as a result of decades of uncontrolled mining and logging activities. But there is much to bring travellers to this magnificent landscape, and as elsewhere in Malaysia many hope that ecotourism will motivate the government to protect this fragile landscape. See p585 for more details.

Tasik Chini's shores are inhabited by the Jakun people, an Orang Asli tribe of Melayu Asli origin, and the surrounding jungle hills are some of the least-visited trekking areas in the country, still hiding tigers and elephants amidst glorious waterfalls and caves. Locals believe the lake is home to a serpent known as Naga Seri Gumum, sometimes translated as a 'Loch Ness Monster'. The best time to visit the lakes is from June to September when the lotuses are in bloom.

Tasik Chini offers two excellent all-inclusive options for travellers. **Rajan Jones Guest House** (☑017-913 5089; r per person incl breakfast & dinner RM35) lies nestled in flower-filled Kampung Gumum and acts as base camp for the titular Rajan Jones's excellent jungle and lake adventures. Rajan speaks perfect English, is close to the Orang Asli, has been leading treks for over 20 years and can arrange a spectrum of activities from jungle trekking (three-hour trips, RM50 per person), night hikes (RM30), longer treks (RM80 per day) waterfall trips (RM75) and lake trips (RM50 to RM100). All of Rajan's tours include transport and all meals.

A less rustic option is the magnificently landscaped **Lake Chini Resort** (☑0468 8088; tasikchiniresort@hotmail.com; r from RM150, dm RM25 incl breakfast), which has beautiful rooms facing the lake, an on-site restaurant and even karaoke. Eight-bed dorms are neat and often filled with student groups. Staff at the resort can arrange all activities for you.

The easiest way to get to Tasik Chini is to arrange transport from either Lake Chini Resort or Rajan Jones. The more complicated way involves taking a bus to Kampung Chini from either Kuantan (RM7, 2 hours) or Pekan (RM6, 11/2 hours) to Kampung Chini and then taking a private car the remaining 7.5km to Kampung Gunum for about RM20. You can a taxi from either Pekan or Kuantan for around RM80.

Pekan

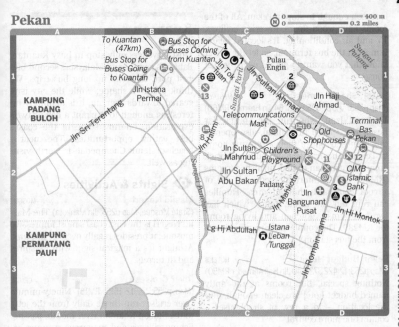

Sights

Museum Sultan Abu Bakar   MUSEUM

(Map p253; Jln Sultan Ahmad; admission RM1; ⊙9.30am-5pm Tue-Thu, Sat & Sun, 9am-12.15pm & 2.45-5pm Fri) The museum is housed in a wonderful building constructed by the British in 1929. Exhibits are largely about the Pahang royal family, with other displays featuring weapons, pottery (including Chinese porcelain and Arab ceramics unearthed on Pulau Tioman) and exhibits on wildlife in Pahang.

Galeri Pengangkutan Air   MUSEUM

(Map p253; admission RM1; ⊙9.30am-5pm Tue-Thu, Sat & Sun, 9am-12.15pm & 2.45-5pm Fri) Galeri Pengangkutan Air displays traditional Malaysian watercraft. Look out for the fabulously carved craft with the head of a mythical beast.

Sleeping & Eating

Staying a night in Pekan is a great way to shift into the low gear of small-town Malaysia. A few restaurants, **food stalls** (Map p253) and **fruit stalls** (Map p253) can be found in the grid of streets in between the Padang and Sungai Pahang and along the riverfront Jln Sultan Ahmad. Also, a handful of spicy Thai-style *ikan bakar* and tom

Pekan

⊙ Sights
1	Abu Bakar Mosque	C1
2	Galeri Pengangkutan Air	C1
3	Lei Shen Gong Buddhist Temple	D2
4	Mariamnan Hindu Temple	D2
5	Museum Sultan Abu Bakar	C1
6	Pekan Lama	C1
7	Sultan Abdullah Mosque	C1

⊜ Sleeping
8	Beach Shack Homestay	C2
9	Chief's Rest House	B1
10	Pekan Budget Hotel	D2

⊗ Eating
11	Food Stalls	D2
12	Fruit Stalls	D2
13	Ikan Bakar & Tom Yum Restaurants	C1
14	Umi Café	D2

yum **restaurants** (Map p253) open for dinner along Jln Sultan Abu Bakar.

Chief's Rest House   HISTORIC HOTEL $

(Map p253; ☎422 6941; Jln Istana Permai; d RM55-70; ❄) This circa-1929 colonial wooden building exudes atmosphere and style, and is reason enough to stop in Pekan. All of the rooms have wood floors, towering ceilings, TV and air-conditioning. It's located nearly 1km from the bus terminal, so let the driver know that you want to get off near the rest house.

Beach Shack Homestay HOMESTAY $
(Map p253; 012-696 1093; 64 Jln Halimi; r RM60) Tim and Izan, who run the spectacular Beach Hut (p249) in Tioman, also operate this homestay out of their *kampung* home in Pekan. The traditionally built red-brick home features fan-cooled furnished rooms (RM60) with comfortable beds and use of a cool courtyard chill-out area. Families can rent out the whole house, which has two bedrooms, a kitchen and living room, for RM230. The couple can arrange pickup from the bus station.

Pekan Budget Hotel HOTEL $
(Map p253; 422 3727; 40 Jln Haji Ahmad; r RM50) Nothing special, but rooms at the aptly named budget hotel are clean enough, and the location – in a row of shophouses – couldn't be more central.

Umi Café CHINESE, MALAY $
(Map p253; 22 Jln Bangunant Pusat; meals RM5-10; 7.30am-9pm) Right across from the shady *padang* this is the most airy and pleasant place to eat in town. There's a Chinese-Malay buffet at lunch and delicious curry *pao* (RM1; steamed bun filled with meat) all day.

ⓘ Information

There's internet access at **10 Net Cyber Café** (Jln Sultan Abu Bakar; per hr RM3; 10am-7pm).

CIMB Islamic Bank (Jln Rompin Lama) has an ATM that accepts foreign cards.

ⓘ Getting There & Away

Buses leave from **Terminal Bas Pekan** (Jln Engku Muda Mansor). **Utama Express** (422 8694) and **Cepat Express** (1300-8884 2538) both have offices here. Regular local buses run to/from Kuantan (RM7, one hour), Kuala Rompin (RM7, two hours) and to Chini Village (RM6, 1½ hours). Long-distance buses run to Kuala Terengganu (RM24) and to KL (RM30).

The taxi station is at the bus station. A taxi to/from Kuantan costs RM50; to Tasik Chini it's RM60.

Kuantan
09

Most travellers only stop in busy Kuantan, Pahang's capital and Malaysia's second biggest port, to break up long bus trips. We think this is a shame; while the city isn't geared towards tourism, it is definitely interesting enough to warrant a day or two's exploration, offering some of the coast's best eating opportunities. The nearby beach of Teluk Chempedak is worth visiting as well.

◉ Sights & Activities

Masjid Negeri MOSQUE
(State Mosque; Map p255; Jln Mahkota) The Masjid Negeri is the east coast's most impressive mosque; it presides regally over the *padang*. At night it's a magical sight with its spires and lit turrets.

River Cruises CRUISE
(Map p255; 512 1515; RM15) Ninety-minute river cruises run thrice daily from the jetty to the Sungai Kuantan river mouth, passing fishing villages and mangrove swamps before returning to town.

⏦ Sleeping

Kuantan has a host of new mid-priced hotels ranging from merely nice to charming, so unless you're on a serious budget it's worth splurging.

Classic Hotel BOUTIQUE HOTEL $
(Map p255; 516 4599; chotel@tm.net.my; 7 Jln Besar; d incl breakfast RM92-98; ❄☎) All rooms here (ask for a river view) are spacious and clean, with large bathrooms and all the mod-cons. Central location, ample Malay-style breakfast and considerate staff make this a great choice.

Seasons Boutique Hotel BOUTIQUE HOTEL $$
(Map p255; 516 3131; seasonsboutiquehotel@gmail.com; 2-8 Jln Beserah; r from RM100; ❄☎) Bright coloured walls and Zen-style furniture makes this a chic choice, though rooms are small and many are windowless. There's a spa offering reflexology and a big restaurant serving Malay and Western food.

Mega View Hotel BUSINESS HOTEL $$
(Map p255; 517 1888; Lot 567, Jln Besar; r RM150-350; ❄) More atmosphere than the other hotels in town thanks to its direct riverfront position and lots of natural light in the

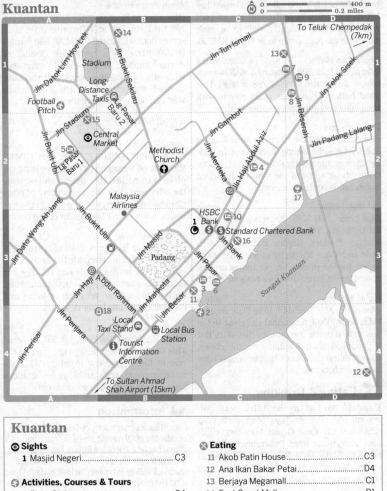

Kuantan

To Teluk Chempedak (7km)

To Sultan Ahmad Shah Airport (15km)

To Sungai Kuantan

PAHANG & TIOMAN ISLAND KUANTAN

Kuantan

⊚ Sights
1 Masjid Negeri.......................................C3

⊕ Activities, Courses & Tours
2 River Cruises......................................C4

⊜ Sleeping
3 Classic Hotel.......................................C3
4 Hotel Kosma.......................................C2
5 Hotel Makmur......................................A2
6 Mega View Hotel..................................C3
7 MS Garden Hotel..................................D1
8 Seasons Boutique Hotel......................D1
9 Signature Hotel....................................D1
10 Tai Wah Hotel.....................................C3

⊗ Eating
11 Akob Patin House...............................C3
12 Ana Ikan Bakar Petai..........................D4
13 Berjaya Megamall...............................C1
14 East Coast Mall..................................B1
15 Food Stalls...A2
16 Kohng Restoran..................................C3

⊙ Drinking
Alfresco Bar...................................(see 6)
17 O's Corner Cafe................................D2

⊜ Shopping
18 Kuantan Parade Mall..........................B4

lobby areas. Opt for a standard executive to get a balcony and uninterrupted river view. The RM165 family rooms are a great deal if you're travelling with kids.

MS Garden Hotel HOTEL $$
(Map p255; ☎555 5899; www.msgarden.com.my; Lot 5 & 10, Lg Gambut, off Jln Beserah; r incl breakfast from RM330; ❊@☏☎☈) Still Kuantan's poshest

hotel, the newly remodelled MS Garden has big rooms, a fitness centre and even a pool with waterslides. Regular walk-in specials can bring the price down to as low as RM250.

Signature Hotel
BOUTIQUE HOTEL **$**

(Map p255; ☎513 2919; signaturehotel2012@gmail.com; 41 Jln Beserah; s/d RM68/98; ❈@☎) This good budget choice has clean rooms with mod-cons and adorable counter staff.

Hotel Kosma
HOTEL **$**

(Map p255; ☎516 2214; 59 Jln Haji Abdul Aziz; s/d RM55/70; ❈@☎) Among the better of the budget choices, the ageing Kosma lacks the boutique vibe of some of the newer mid-priced hotels but is centrally located.

Tai Wah Hotel
HOTEL **$**

(Map p255; ☎517 8285; 29 Jln Haji Abdul Aziz; r RM30-48; ❈) This Chinese-run hotel has spartan doubles, singles and triples with beds and TVs – it's pretty much what you'd expect for the price. Cheaper rooms are fan cooled, more expensive ones have air-con.

Hotel Makmur
HOTEL **$**

(Map p255; ☎514 1363; 14 & 16 Lg Pasar Baru 1; r RM35-88; ❈) Dull, functional and close to the bus station pretty much sums this joint. But if you need central lodging on the cheap, Hotel Makmur will do. Cheaper rooms have shared bathrooms.

✕ Eating & Drinking

Kuantan's most distinctive dish is *patin* (silver catfish). The **Berjaya Megamall** (Map p255) and the **East Coast Mall** (Map p255) have everything from Délifrance and Starbucks to Malay-style food courts. The **food stalls** (Map p255) by the long-distance bus station are particularly excellent.

TOP CHOICE Ana Ikan Bakar Petai
SEAFOOD **$$**

(Map p255; Tanjong Lumpur; ⊙lunch and dinner) If it's authentic you're after, look no further than this huge open-air seafood restaurant across the river on the island of Tanjong Lumpur. On any given evening Malaysian families flock here to feast on a plethora of traditional Malay seafood dishes. An extraordinary selection of freshly caught fish, crab and shrimp is priced by weight and cooked to your specifications in small kitchens along the side of the dining area, while a larger kitchen in the back prepares traditional Malaysian rice and noodle dishes. No beer is needed here – an amazing assortment of fresh juices is available for whistle wetting.

Akob Patin House
MALAY **$**

(Map p255; Jln Besar; ⊙lunch) Fancy trying *patin*, the local delicacy? This riverfront place serves both wild caught (RM20) and farmed (RM8) *patin* in a *tempoyak* (fermented durian sambal) sauce served buffet-style with other Malay-style meat and vegetable dishes – the price is per fish. The friendly staff can help explain what's what.

Kohng Restoran
CHINESE **$**

(Map p255; 9 Jln Teluk Sisek; ⊙6pm-3am) This humble spot on the main drag serves some of the best Hainan chicken rice (RM10) this side of Singapore. On some nights the place is so packed that diners spill out into the alley next door, where a variety of other Chinese snacks are cooked well into the wee hours. Kohng can't be beat for cheap beer.

O's Corner Cafe
BAR

(Map p255; Jln Teluk Sisek; ⊙Mon-Sat 4pm-12am, Sun 2pm-12am) This riverside bar and restaurant swings with an in-house DJ. The bar has a wide variety of beers, both bottled and on tap, and a huge selection of juices and other nonalcoholic beverages.

Alfresco Bar
BAR

(Map p255; Mega View Hotel, Lot 567, Jln Besar) This venue sits right next to the river, at the rear of the Mega View Hotel (p254). It's a relaxing venue, with ambient music and a huge TV screen for live sports events.

ⓘ Information

Lots of banks (many with 24-hour ATMs) are on or near the aptly named Jln Bank. You'll find wi-fi in most hotels. There are internet cafes at the Berjaya Megamall (p256) and East Coast Mall (p256). **Espikey Internet** (Jln Haji; ⊙8am-11pm) is on the ground floor of a food court just north of **Kuantan Parade Mall** (Map p255).

Post Office (Jln Haji Abdul Aziz)

Tourist Information Centre (☎516 1007; Jln Mahkota; ⊙8am-1pm & 2-5pm Mon-Thu, 8am-12.45pm & 2.45-5pm Fri) Has particularly helpful staff and a range of useful leaflets.

ⓘ Getting There & Away

Air

Malaysia Airlines (☎1 300-88 3000; Jln Gambut, ground fl, Wisma Persatuan Bolasepak Pahang) has daily direct flights to KLIA with plenty of onward connections from there. **Firefly** (☎03-7845 4543) also has two daily flights to/from Subang Airport in KL and four weekly flights to Singapore. The airport is 15km away from the city; a taxi should cost RM20.

Bus

Long-distance buses leave from the station on Jln Stadium. The ticket offices, food court and left luggage centre (RM2 per piece) are on the 2nd floor of the building.

Buses for Pekan (RM5.30), Balok (RM3), Beserah (RM3) and Cherating (bus 27; RM5) depart from the local bus station on Jln Besar but sometimes let off next to the central market.

Destination	Price	Duration
Kuala Lumpur	RM24	4hr
Singapore	RM30	6hr
Jerantut	RM18	3.5hr
Mersing	RM16	3hr
Kuala Lipis	RM24	6hr
Melaka	RM27	6hr
Temerloh	RM12	2hr
Butterworth	RM51	8.5hr
Kuala Terengganu	RM17	4hr
Kota Bharu	RM31	6hr

Car

Hawk (☑538 5055; www.hawkrentacar.com. my; Sultan Ahmad Shah Airport, Kuantan)

Taxi

The **long-distance taxi stand** is in front of the long-distance bus station on Jln Stadium. Destinations and approximate cost (per car): Pekan (RM60), Mersing (RM200), Johor Bahru (RM380), Cherating (RM80), Kuala Terengganu (RM200), Jerantut (RM200) and KL (RM260). Prices may vary, and bargaining is possible.

Around Kuantan

Light waves crash on the shore of **Teluk Chempedak** while several **walking tracks** wind along the park jungle area at this strip of coast 6km east of Kuantan. There's also a small, strangely un-gated **zoo** about a kilometer out of town. From November to around February the beach break here becomes surfable; surfboards are rented for RM50/100 per hour/day from the Gandom Club next door to the Hyatt Regency.

The **Hyatt Regency Kuantan** (☑518 1234; www.kuantan.regency.hyatt.com; r from RM340; ❋@☎☀) is a spacious, breezy and effortlessly luxurious place, with amenable staff, lovely views and a solid list of amenities: two pools (one with a swim-up bar), two very good restaurants, two tennis courts, a spa, a children's play area and a water sports centre with catamarans and kayaks, and

a surfer's area, to name a few. Rooms are sumptuous and a whole bevy of activities are on offer, including walks along the cliffs to Methodist Bay. Discounts are available both online and on weekdays.

About 200m from the beach are a series of guesthouses, all of which are pretty decent and comparably priced. **The Pine Beach Hotel** (☑013-940 4458; s/d/f incl breakfast RM50/60/120; ❋☎) is clean and has newish rooms with air-con, TVs and hot-water showers. Ground floor rooms are windowless, but otherwise OK. Another good place is **Anjung Selesa** (☑568 4191; s/d/tr/f incl breakfast RM50/60/65/120; ❋☎). Prices rise by RM10 at weekends.

There is no public bus service between Kuantan and Teluk Chempedak. A taxi between the two towns costs RM15.

Cherating

☑09

A sweeping white beach bordered by coconut palms and a small village of guesthouses and shops with more monkeys, monitor lizards and cats walking around than humans, Cherating is a popular spot for surfing and general beachfront slacking.

⊙ Sights & Activities

Water Sports

Some of Malaysia's best surfing waves pound the beaches at Cherating and other spots to the north. Several places in town rent out surfboards for around RM20 per hour and you can get surf lessons at **Satu Saku** (Map p259; Main Rd; ☺November-March).

The Cherating beach isn't great for snorkelling but places all around town offer half-day **snorkelling tours** (RM50) to the aptly named Coral Island. There are also **fishing tours** (prices on demand) and you can rent **kayaks** (sea or river, per hr RM20) to cruise around on your own.

Wildlife Viewing

Night-time firefly boat tours along the mangroves upriver are a Cherating activity par excellence. The best tours are led by Hafiz, a long-time firefly enthusiast and self-made expert at **Cherating River Activities** (Map p259; ☑017-978 9256; http://hafizcheratingactivities.blogspot.com/; Main Rd; tours per person from RM20). Several places around town run river mangrove tours, turtle-watching (April to September), walks and other activities.

The **Turtle Sanctuary** (entry by donation; ⊙9am-5pm Tue-Sun) next to Club Med has a few basins with baby and rehabilitating sea turtles, and can offer information about the laying and hatching periods.

Other Sights & Activities

Batik-making is another Cherating specialty. **Matahari Chalets** (Map p259; ☎581 9835; small/large chalets RM25/35) and **Limbong Art** (Map p259; Main Rd) both offer courses (from RM25) where you can make your own batik handkerchief or sarong. You can also take riding lessons, either in the paddock or trotting along the beach, at the well-kept **Penn Equestrian Club** (Map p259; ☎012-282 9265; Main St, next to Holiday Villa; per hr RM100).

🛏 Sleeping

Budget digs tend to fill up with surfers during the monsoon surf season from November through January, and midrange places tend to fill up on the weekends; book in advance.

TOP CHOICE Villa de Fedella　　CHALET $$
(Tanjong Resort; Map p259; ☎010-2675 667; tan junginn@hotmail.com; d/f chalets with air-con RM170/250, d/tr chalets with fan RM70/85; ✱@⊚) This highly recommended place offers wooden chalets with decks set around a stunning lake surrounded by tall grass and fruit trees. All chalets have hot showers, and there's an excellent lending library in the reception area. Villa de Fedella is run by a lovely local family who'll make your visit to Cherating memorable.

TOP CHOICE Club Med　　RESORT $$$
(☎581 9133; www.clubmed.com.sg; all-incl package per night per person from RM550; ✱☱) Crafted to look like a particularly beautiful Malaysian *kampung* with wooden buildings on stilts, the resort comes fully equipped with its own stretch of beach, immaculate sprawling lawns, international restaurants, nightclub, kids' club, nearby turtle sanctuary and sports facilities. Contact the hotel for standard package deals.

Cherating Bayview Resort　　CHALET $$
(Map p259; ☎581 9248; http://cheratingbayviewre sort.blogspot.com; r with fan RM70, chalets with air-con RM135-260; ✱⊚☱) The Bayview, styled like a southern Californian apartment complex, is in the centre of town and has chalets that will fit up to four people; chalets are equipped with hot showers, TVs and living areas. There's also children's playground, swimming pool and restaurant.

Ruby's Resort　　RESORT $$
(☎016-938 1298; www.rubys-resort.com; d RM70; chalets incl breakfast from RM180; ✱⊚) Ruby's offers a series of colourful wooden cabins with panelled interiors, comfortable double beds, hot showers and TVs. All chalets have lovely balconies, and the 10-bed dorm is air-conditioned.

Maznah's Guest House　　CHALET $
(Map p259; ☎581 9072; chalets incl breakfast RM30-35) Spirited kids happily chase chickens around the collection of sturdy wooden bungalows here. The owners speak little English and *nasi lemak* is served for breakfast, making this a great, friendly place to go local.

Payung Guesthouse　　CHALET $
(Map p259; ☎581 9658; d/quad chalets RM50/70; ⊚) This excellent, friendly main-drag choice backs onto the river, with neat rows of ordinary chalets in the garden. The attached tour office offers everything from bike and

---

CAVE OF THE SLEEPING BUDDHA

Twenty-six kilometres north of Kuantan the limestone karst containing **Gua Charas** (Charas Caves; RM1) towers high above the surrounding palm plantations. The caves owe their fame to a Thai Buddhist monk who came to meditate here about 50 years ago. A steep climb up a stairway leads to the colossal **Sleeping Buddha Cave** (Wofo Dong), decorated with small altars to *Kuanyin Puxian*, other Bodhisattvas and Buddhist idols. The main attraction is the Sleeping Buddha in the rear of the cavern.

A taxi from Kuantan to the caves costs RM40, or you can take the Sungai Lembing–bound bus 48 (RM3, one hour) from the local bus station in Kuantan and get off at the small village of **Panching** just past the sign reading 'Gua Charas 4km'. You can walk or get someone in Panching to give you a lift on a motorcycle for RM2.

Cherating

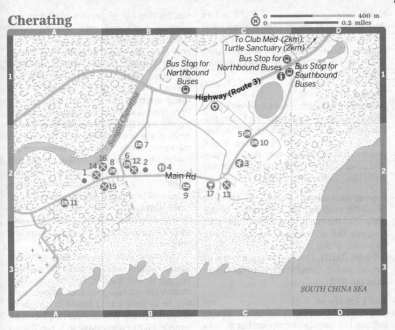

Cherating

⊕ Activities, Courses & Tours

1 Cherating River Activities	A2
2 Limbong Art	B2
3 Penn Equestrian Club	C2
4 Satu Saku	B2

🛏 Sleeping

5 Cherating Bayview Resort	C2
6 Matahari Chalets	B2
7 Maznah's Guest House	B2
8 Payung Guesthouse	B2
9 Ranting Beach Resort	B2
10 Residence Inn	C2
11 Villa de Fedella	A2

⊗ Eating

12 Cherating Cottage Café	B2
13 Duyong Restaurant	C2
14 Matahari Restaurant	A2
15 Nabill Café	B2
16 Payung Restaurant	B2

⊖ Drinking

17 Don't Tell Mama	C2

surfboard rentals to mangrove or snorkelling tours.

Ranting Beach Resort   CHALET **$$**
(Map p259; ☏581 9068; chalets RM120-180; ☀) The best chalets here are the wooden fan-cooled ones right on the busiest strip of the beach. More expensive chalets have air-con, and a four room house that sleeps ten can be rented out for RM600.

Residence Inn   HOTEL **$$**
(Map p259; ☏581 9333; http://ric.my/cherating/; r/chalet incl breakfast RM248/268; ☀🛜🏊) Surrounding a good swimming pool, the newly remodelled, crisp and modern rooms here are a a a decent choice. Service is great, there's a big restaurant and promotional rates from RM180 are often available.

✗ Eating & Drinking

Most guesthouses run their own restaurants, the best being **Matahari Restaurant** (Map p259; seafood barbecue from RM10; ⊘breakfast, lunch & dinner) at the west end of town. The **Cherating Cottage Café** (Map p259; breakfasts around RM5; ⊘breakfast, lunch & dinner) is the first to open in the mornings (around 8am) and serves good breakfasts.

Nabill Café
MALAY $

(Map p259; meals around RM6; ⊘dinner) Eat where the locals do and save a handful of ringgit. Choose your fresh seafood then watch it get grilled in a delicious spicy sambal.

Duyong Restaurant
MALAY $$

(Map p259; meals RM15; ⊘lunch & dinner) Raised on stilts at the western end of the beach, this place offers unbroken views around the bay. There's a large selection of seafood, steaks, poultry and vegetables, but it's the setting that is superlative. Try the tom yum (hot and spicy Thai seafood soup, RM8).

Payung Restaurant
WESTERN $$

(Map p259; meals from RM17; ⊘breakfast, lunch & dinner) Off the main road against the quiet riverside, this semi-outdoor hang-out serves thin-crust pizzas and a selection of pastas (all from RM17). There's often groovy music playing and a friendly extended family to hang out with.

Don't Tell Mama
BAR

(Map p259; ⊘till late) Don't Tell Mama, located right on the beach, is the hippest bar in town and is a great place to stop by day or night to make friends over a cold beer. Impromptu barbecues and parties are the norm.

ℹ Information

There are no banks in Cherating, so be sure and get cash in Kuantan or Pekan. **Yahya** (☑014-210 2973) dispenses information from the **Payung Guest House**.

ℹ Getting There & Away

From Kuantan's local bus station catch a bus marked 'Kemaman' and ask to be dropped at Cherating (look for a sign by the road that reads 'Pantai Cherating'). Buses leave every 30 minutes (RM5, one hour). When coming from the north, any bus heading for Kuantan will drop you on the main road. A taxi from Kuantan should cost about RM80.

From Cherating to Kuantan, wave down a Kuantan-bound bus from the bus stop on the highway (Route 3). For taxis from Cherating call the **Cherating Taxi Service** (☑581 9355). Expect to pay around RM55 for a ride to Kuantan and RM280 for a trip to Taman Negara.

Taman Negara

Taman Negara blankets 4343 sq km (from Pahang to Kelantan and Terengganu) in shadowy, damp, impenetrable jungle. Inside this buzzing tangle, ancient trees with gargantuan buttressed root systems dwarf luminescent fungi, orchids, two-tone ferns and even the giant rafflesia (the world's largest flower). Hidden within the flora are Asian elephants, tigers, leopards and rhinos, as well as smaller wonders such as flying squirrels, but these animals stay far from the park's trails and sightings are extremely rare. Even if they do come close, the chances are you'll never see them through the dense jungle. What you might see are snakes (dog-toothed cat snakes, reticulated pythons, temple pit vipers and red-headed kraits), lizards, monkeys, small deer, abundant birdlife and perhaps tapir. Nearly everyone who visits Taman Negara gets an upclose and personal meeting with leeches and an impressive array of flying and crawling insects.

The more time you put into a visit to Taman Negara, the more you'll get out of it. Though they're feasible, fleeting visits only scratch the surface. Consider an overnight trek or at least a long boat-trip up one of the park's rivers. Whether coming for an afternoon hike or a multiday trek, you'll need to buy a permit (park entrance/camera/fishing RM1/5/10) from either of the two operators at the Tourist Information Counter (p265).

At the time of research there was talk of raising the price of entry to Taman Negera substantially. Though nothing has been set, figures between 30RM and 90RM are being floated.

The park headquarters and the privately run Mutiara Taman Negara Resort (p263) are at Kuala Tahan at the edge of Taman Negara National Park; other accommodation and restaurants are across Sungai Tembing at Kampung Kuala Tahan. River taxis buzz between the two sides of the river (RM1 each way) throughout the day.

GUIDES & TOURS

Guides who are licensed by the Wildlife Department have completed coursework in forest flora, fauna and safety. Often the Kuala Tahan tour operators offer cheaper prices than those available at the Tourist Information Counter at Park Headquarters (whose guides are licensed), but talk with these guides first to find out what training they've had. Guides cost RM180 per day (one guide can lead up to 12 people), plus there is a RM100 fee for each night spent out on the trail.

Taman Negara

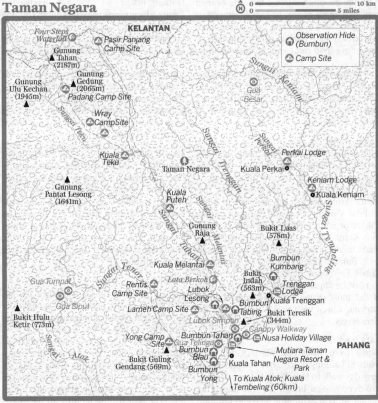

KELANTAN

0 —————— 10 km
0 —————— 5 miles

Observation Hide (Bumbun)
Camp Site

Four Steps Waterfall
Pasir Panjang Camp Site
Gunung Tahan (2187m)
Gunung Gedung (2065m)
Gunung Ulu Kechau (1945m)
Padang Camp Site
Sungai Teku
Wray Camp Site
Sungai Kenium
Guá Besar
Sungai Perkai
Kuala Teku
Taman Negara
Perkai Lodge
Kuala Perkai
Keniam Lodge
Kuala Keniam
Sungai Trenggan
Gunung Pantat Lesong (1641m)
Kuala Puteh
Sungai Tahan
Sungai Tembeling
Gua Tumpat
Sungai Tenois
Rentis Camp Site
Lata Berkoh
Lubok Lesong
Lameh Camp Site
Sungai Melantai
Gunung Raja
Kuala Melantai
Bukit Luas (578m)
Bumbun Kumbang
Bukit Indah (563m)
Trenggan Lodge
Bumbun Kuala Trenggan
Tabing
Bukit Teresik (344m)
Canopy Walkway
Nusa Holiday Village
Gua Siput
Bukit Hulu Ketir (773m)
Sungai Atok
Yong Camp Site
Bumbun Tahan
Gua Telinga
Bumbun Blau
Lubok Simpon
Kuala Tahan
Mutiara Taman Negara Resort & Park
Bukit Guling Gendang (569m)
Bumbun Yong
To Kuala Atok; Kuala Tembeling (60km)

PAHANG

PAHANG & TIOMAN ISLAND TAMAN NEGARA

Many travellers sign up for tours to an Orang Asli settlement. Tribal elders give a general overview and you'll learn how to use a long blowpipe and start a fire. While local guides insist that these tours provide essential income for the Orang Asli, most of your tour money will go to the tour company. A small handicraft purchase in the village will help spread the wealth.

🏃 Activities

Trekking brings folks here, a wide variety of possibilities – from an hour's stroll to nine arduous days up and down 2187m-high Gunung Tahan – exist. You can shorten your hiking time in most cases by taking river bus services or tours that include boat transport.

The trails around the park headquarters are convenient but heavily trafficked. Relatively few visitors venture far beyond the headquarters, and longer walks are much less trammelled.

Treks from Kuala Tahan

Easy-to-follow trails around park HQ are signposted and marked with approximate walking times; enquire at the information office for details on other routes.

Canopy Walkway & Around   SHORT HIKE
(adult/child RM5/3; ⏰10am-3.30pm Sat-Thu, 9am-noon Fri) This is easily the area's most popular hike. It begins past the park headquarters and leads along Sungai Tembeling to the canopy walkway, 30 minutes away. The walkway is suspended between huge trees and the entire circuit takes around 40 minutes.

From behind the canopy walkway a trail leads to Bukit Teresik (344m), from the top of which are fine views across the forest. The trail is steep and slippery in parts, but is easily negotiated and takes about an hour up and back. You can descend back along this trail to the Mutiara Taman Negara Resort or, near the canopy walkway, take the branch trail that leads across to Lubok Simpon, a swimming area on Sungai Tahan. From here it is an easy stroll back to park headquarters. The entire loop can easily be done in three hours.

Past the canopy walkway, a branch of the main trail leads to Bukit Indah (563m), another steep but rewarding hill-climb offering fine views across the forest and the rapids in Sungai Tembeling.

Kuala Trenggan   DAY HIKE

The well-marked main trail along the bank of Sungai Tembeling leads 9km to Kuala Trenggan, a popular trail for those heading to the Bumbun Kumbang hide. Allow five hours. From here, boats go back to Nusa Holiday Village (p264) and Kampung Kuala Tahan, or it's a further 2km walk to Bumbun Kumbang. An alternative longer trail leads inland, back across Sungai Trenggan from Bumbun Kumbang to the camp site at Lubok Lesong on Sungai Tahan, then back to park headquarters (six hours). This trail is flat most of the way and crosses small streams. Check with park headquarters for river levels.

Lata Berkoh   DAY HIKE

North from park headquarters, the trail leads to Gunung Tahan, but you can do an easy day walk to Lata Berkoh, the cascading rapids on Sungai Tahan. The trail passes the Lubok Simpon swimming hole and Bumbun Tabing, 1¼ hours from Kuala Tahan. There is one river crossing before you reach the falls, which can be treacherous if the water is high; do not attempt the river crossing in high water – you should hail one of the boatmen waiting on the opposite side to ferry you across.

Kuala Keniam   DAY HIKE, MULTIDAY HIKE

A popular walk is the trail from Kuala Trenggan to Kuala Keniam. It's normally done by chartering a boat to Kuala Keniam and then walking back to Kuala Trenggan (six hours). The trail is quite taxing and hilly in parts, and passes a series of limestone caves. This walk can be combined with one of the Kuala Tahan–Kuala Trenggan trails to form a two-day trip, staying overnight in the Trenggan Lodge or at Bumbun Kumbang. It is also possible to walk from Kuala Keniam to the lodge at Kuala Perkai, an easy two-hour walk.

Gunung Tahan   MULTIDAY HIKE

Really adventurous travellers climb Gunung Tahan (2187m), the highest peak in Peninsular Malaysia, 55km from park headquarters. It takes nine days at a steady pace, although it can be done in seven. A guide is compulsory (RM700 for seven days plus RM75 for each day thereafter). With no shelters along the way, you have to be fully equipped. Try to organise this trek in advance so you don't have to hang around park headquarters for a couple of days.

Rentis Tenor   MULTIDAY HIKE

From Kuala Tahan, this trek takes roughly three days. Day one: take the trail to Gua Telinga, and beyond, for about seven hours, to Yong camp site. Day two is a six-hour walk to the Rentis camp site. On day three cross Sungai Tahan (up to waist deep) to get back to Kuala Tahan. It's roughly a six hour walk, or you can stop over at the Lameh camp site, about halfway.

Fishing

Anglers will find the park a real paradise. Fish found in the park's rivers include the superb fighting fish known in India as the *mahseer,* but here as the *kelasa.*

Popular fishing rivers include Sungai Tahan, Sungai Keniam (north of Kuala Trenggan) and the remote Sungai Sepia. Simple fishing lodges are scattered through the park and can be booked at park headquarters. The best fishing months are February, March, July and August. Fishing permits are RM10; Rods can be hired across the river for between RM20 and RM30 per day.

GEAR HIRE

Leeches are everywhere inside the park (but are rarely found in Kampung Kuala Tahan). Wearing boots with gaiters or long socks tucked over your trousers and doused in DEET will make hiking more pleasant.

You can hire camping, hiking and fishing gear at the Mutiara Taman Negara Resort's shop or at several shops and guesthouses on the Kampung Kuala Tahan side. Asking prices per day are around RM8 for a sleeping bag, RM10 for a rucksack, RM25 for a tent, RM20 for a fishing rod, RM5 for a sleeping pad, RM8 for a stove and RM8 for boots.

River Bus & Boat Trips

The Mutiara Taman Negara Resort has daily boats that go upriver to Kuala Trenggan at 10am and 2.30pm. In the reverse direction, boats leave Kuala Trenggan at 11.15am and 3.15pm. These services are intended for guests only, but the trips into the park below are open to the public.

ROUND TRIP BOAT JOURNEYS FROM MUTIARA TAMAN NEGARA DOCK

Destination	Price	Trips	First Boat
Bunbun Yong	RM5	3 daily	8.30am
Canopy Walkway	RM15	2 daily	10.15am
Gua Telinga	RM15	4 daily	8.30am
Kuala Tembeling	RM30	1 daily	9am

🛏 Sleeping

KUALA TAHAN

Mutiara Taman Negara Resort RESORT $$

(☑266 3500, in KL 03-2145 5585; www.mutiarahotels.com; camp site RM5, dm/guesthouse/chalets/bungalows incl breakfast RM60/300/470/1800; ☕✸❄) Conveniently located right at park headquarters, there's a huge range of accommodation here from OK guesthouse rooms (all with garden terraces) to colonial-style family and honeymoon suites in wooden chalets and clean, eight-person dorms with air-con. Campers accepted in groups of 10 or more.

KAMPUNG KUALA TAHAN

Kampung Kuala Tahan, directly across the river from park headquarters, is where most of Taman Negara's lodging, restaurants and shops are found. Better places fill up quickly. Having spent decades as base camp for hordes of travellers has given Kuala Tahan something of an over-touristed 'banana pancake/backpacker trail' vibe, so if that isn't your style then consider entering the park through the less-travelled back entrance in Kelantan.

Yellow Guesthouse GUESTHOUSE $

(☑266 4243; dm/d RM70/80; ✸@❋) Up and over the top of the hill (behind the school) the Yellow Guesthouse consists of a single story house and a two- storey building cleaner and in better shape than most of the others. All rooms have hot showers; The building across from the main house has slightly larger rooms, but both have brightly painted walls and new mattresses and the owner is super-friendly and helpful.

Tahan Guesthouse GUESTHOUSE $

(☑266 7752; dm/d RM10/50) Far enough from 'town' to feel away from it all but close enough to be convenient, Tahan Guesthouse has excellent four-bed dorms and even better, colourfully painted bright rooms upstairs. The whole place feels like a happy preschool with giant murals of insects and flowers all over the place.

Mat Leon Village CHALET $$

(☑013-998 9517; dm/chalets RM50/120 incl breakfast) This boasts a supreme forest location with river views, a good restaurant and free boat pick-up from the Kampung Kuala Tahan jetty. On foot go past Durian Chalet for around 350m to the sign at the edge of the forest; follow the forest path for 200m and you will see the chalets on the far side of a small stream.

Tembeling Riverview Lodge LODGE $

(☑266 6766; www.trvtamannegara.blogspot.com; dm/d/tr RM10/50/60) Straddling the thoroughfare footpath, this place has fan cooled rooms with cold showers and mosquito netting and a pleasant communal areas overlooking the river. Staff is friendly, and there's a lovely restaurant serving roti John (RM6; a Malaysian sandwich made with local bread, meat, cheese and vegetables) as well.

Durian Chalet CHALET $

(☑266 8940; http://durian-chalet.blogspot.tw/; dm/d/f RM10/40/50) About 800m outside of the village (beyond the Teresek View Hotel) in a flowery garden between rubber and durian plantations, this family-run forest hideaway enjoys a good reputation, though we weren't able to review it during our last trip.

Dakilih House HOTEL $

(☑010-919 3658, 014-292 7069; camping RM5; d RM15, r RM50-80) Festive and colourful outside and in, Dakilih house sits on a hill overlooking the river a few minutes from the information center. Cheaper rooms have shared bathrooms. There's a cute little restaurant that serves breakfast, lunch and BBQ from RM25-40. Camping is also available for RM5.

Teresek View Motel MOTEL $

(☑019-970 6800; mr8seasons@gmail.com; chalets RM50-60, r RM70-90; ✸) You can't miss this eyesore of a cement building in the 'centre' of Kuala Tahan. The good rooms in the main building are tiled, clean and have hot-water bathrooms and terraces, but lack the homey feel of the family-run places elsewhere.

Agoh Chalets
CHALET $
(✆266 9570; d/f RM50/80; ❄@) Chalets here are made from concrete modelled to look like logs and all surround a shady garden in the middle of the village.

Rainforest Resort
HOTEL $$
(✆266 7888; www.rainforest-tamannegara.com; d/ ste incl breakfast from RM207/414; ❄@✇) Slightly behind town away from the river. The rooms are clean though somewhat generic.

Akih Chalet
CHALET $
(dm/d/chalet RM13/60/90; ❄) Nice looking chalets and decent dorm rooms surrounding a leafy garden. The staff don't speak any English.

SOUTH OF KAMPUNG KUALA TAHAN
Several peaceful places lie removed from the action west off the main Kampung Kuala Tahan–Jerantut road south of Kampung Kuala Tahan.

TOP CHOICE Traveller's Home
GUESTHOUSE $$
(✆266 7766; www.travellershome.com.my; d incl breakfast RM160, chalet incl breakfast & dinner RM185, family chalets RM300; ❄@✇) This bright and airy place, around 1km south of Kuala Tahan (look for the turn-off 2km south of Kuala Tahan (look for the signs), has impeccable, friendly service that will make you feel instantly at home. Rooms here are very new (with balcony) and there's a handy book and DVD library and internet access (per hour RM4), plus all-day free coffee, tea and soft drinks. Chalets are more private and luxurious, and are nestled in the garden's many fruit trees. Free shuttles to Kampung Kuala Tahan are available on demand. This is an excellent choice for families, offering three family rooms that will fit up to four.

TRV Motel & Lodge
MOTEL $$
(✆127-984 7043; www.trvtamannegara.blogspot. com; d RM150, fan-cooled q RM100; ❄) TRV is operated by the same people who run the Tembeling Riverview Lodge (p263), with more upscale lodgings than the Tembeling a bit further out of town. Free shuttles in and out of town are available.

Park Lodge
CHALET $
(✆017-983 2074; www.parklodge.nurnilam.com; fan d RM38, incl breakfast RM50) This quiet spot has eight chalets and a restaurant hidden away down a dirt track around 500m south of Kuala Tahan. Staff can drive guests to Kampung Kuala Tahan.

NUSA HOLIDAY VILLAGE
About a 15-minute boat ride upriver from park headquarters, Nusa Holiday Village (✆266 3043, in Jerantut 09-266 2369, in KL 03-4042 8369; www.tamannegara-nusaholiday.com. my; camp sites RM5, dm/A-frames/cottages/ houses RM15/55/90/110) is more of a 'jungle camp' than anything. The isolation paired with the staff's general lack of English skills makes this a difficult place to stay unless you're on a packaged itinerary (three-days and two-nights from RM295 per person). The double cottages are the best value, while the cheaper A-frames are literally falling in on themselves. The restaurant serves good but unexciting food. Camping costs RM15, tent included.

KUALA PERKAI & KUALA KENIAM
The Kuala Keniam Lodge (located about an hour's boatride upstream from Kuala Trenggan) and Kuala Perkai (a further two hours' walk past Kuala Keniam) are both officially closed and do not offer lodging; however, people still do camp there. If camping at either of these places, bring your own tent.

✖ Eating

Floating barge restaurants line the rocky shore of Kampung Kuala Tahan, all selling the same ol' cheap basic noodle and rice meals plus bland Western fare. All are open from morning until late, though most take rest breaks between two and four.

Mama Chop (meals around RM7), at the far northern end of the strip, serves Indian vegetarian banana-eaf meals at lunchtime and has very good clay-pot dishes for dinner.

At **Wan's Floating Restaurant** (meals around RM8) you'll find some of the best *kue teow* (flat noodles) in town; a large bowl of *hailam kue teow* (RM12), or noodles with chicken and gravy will hit the spot.

Family Restaurant serves a dish called *kerabu* (RM5), a finely diced meat and vegetable dish with a light lemongrass sauce that's got way more local cred than the standard banana pancakes. They also serve banana pancakes.

For something a bit more luxurious head to **Seri Mutiara Restaurant** (Mutiara Taman Negara Resort; ☺breakfast, lunch & dinner), which has salads (from RM16), sandwiches/burgers (from RM20), pizza (RM30), local dishes and a small kiddies' menu (from RM10). Breakfast (American/buffet RM30/40) is filling. This is also the only place in the area where you can get a beer.

ℹ Information

Daily **video shows** (☺9:30am, 3pm, 8:45pm) on Taman Negara are shown in the exhibition hall at the Mutiara Taman Negara Resort/park headquarters and at the NKS Restaurant in Kampung Kuala Tahan. The exhibition hall at the Mutiara also has informative displays on the park.

For health care, the **Poliklinik Komuniti** (Community Clinic) is adjacent to Agoh Chalets in Kampung Kuala Tahan, opposite the school.

Internet
Internet Cafe (per 10 min RM1; ☺8am-midnight) Just down from the Teresek View Motel.

Internet Cafe (per hr RM6) At Agoh Chalets. The internet wasn't working on our last visit.

Police
Police Station (☑266 6721) Located 300m up from the Teresek View Motel.

Tourist Information
Information Centre (☺9am-11pm) The centre is at the riverside end of the road in Kuala Tahan. It provides information on onward transport and tours, although some of the staff are more helpful than others.

Tourist Information Counter (permit: park entrance/camera/fishing RM1/5/10 ; ☺8am-10pm Sun-Thu, 8am-noon & 3-10pm Fri) Register here before heading off into the park. The counter, located in the building behind the Mutiara Taman Negara Resort's reception, also offers park information and guide services.

ℹ Getting There & Away

Most people reach Taman Negara by taking a bus from Jerantut (p265) to the jetty at Kuala Tambling, then a river boat from here to the park. However, there are also popular private minibus services that go directly to/from several tourist destinations around Malaysia directly to/from Kampung Kuala Tahan. **Han Travel** (☑012-674 9208; www.taman-negara. com), **NKS** (☑03-2072 0336) and **Banana Travel & Tours** (☑017-902 5952; Information Centre, Kampung Kuala Tahan) run several useful private services, including daily buses to KL (RM35), a bus/boat combination (RM70) and minibuses to Penang (RM120), the Perhentian Islands (RM165 including boat) and the Cameron Highlands (RM95). These minibuses can also drop you off en route anywhere in between.

You can also walk into or out of the park via Merapoh, at the Pahang–Kelantan border. The trail from Merapoh joins the Gunung Tahan trail, adding another two days to the Gunung Tahan trek. Guides are compulsory and can be hired in Merapoh to take you in. Popular and reputable travel guide **Zeck** (☑743 1613), from Zeck's Traveller's Inn (p277) in Kota Bharu, can arrange a trip into the park from Kelantan that will definitely take you well off the beaten path.

Boat
The 60km boat trip from Kuala Tembling (18km north of Jerantut) to Kuala Tahan takes two to three hours, depending on the level of the river. It's a beautiful journey and a highlight for many visitors.

Boats (one way, RM35) depart daily at 9am and 2pm (9am and 2.30pm Friday). Extra boats are laid on during the busy season, and service can be irregular from November to February. Boats are run by the Mutiara Taman Negara Resort (p263) and Nusa Holiday Village (p264). On the return journey, regular boats leave Kuala Tahan at 9am and 2pm (2.30pm on Friday).

Jerantut

☑09

This small town is the gateway to Taman Negara, and most travellers do little more than spend a night here before heading into the jungle (perhaps stocking up on booze at one of the Chinese owned liquor stores on Jln Diwangsa before heading to dry Kuala Tahan). However, the town is pleasant enough to spend an afternoon.

🛏 Sleeping

Most places offer luggage storage, are open 24 hours and can arrange transport to Taman Negara. Hotels can get very busy around July and August.

Sakura Castle Inn　　　　　　　HOTEL **$**
(Map p266; ☑266 5200; sakuracastleinn@yahoo. com; 51-52 Jln Bomba; d RM55-85, f RM95; ❇🛜) This is the classiest place in town (but maybe not for long – a new hotel was months away from completion at the time of research) and has clean, comfortable rooms all with TVs, hot water and air-con. There's also free wi-fi.

Greenleaf Traveller's Inn　　　　HOTEL **$**
(Map p266; ☑267 2131; 3 Jln Diwangsa; dm RM10, d RM20-30; ❇🛜) A quiet choice with simple,

Jerantut

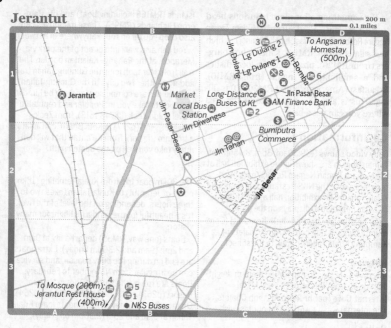

Jerantut

🛏 Sleeping

1 Chong Heng Hotel	B3
2 Greenleaf Traveller's Inn	C1
3 Hotel Chet Fatt	C1
4 Hotel Sri Emas	B3
5 NKS Hostel	B3
6 Sakura Castle Inn	D1
7 Town Inn Hotel	C1

🍴 Eating

8 Food Stalls	C1
NKS Café	(see 5)

clean rooms and dorms, owned by a sweet lady and her family, Ms Teh also runs a travel agency and can help you plan your trip to Taman Negara.

Chong Heng Hotel   HOTEL $

(Map p266; ☎2663 693; 24 Jln Besar; s/d/tr RM20/20/28; @) Run by an interesting fellow named Tan, this budget hotel is located in a lovely renovated shophouse on Jerantut's prettier east side. Fan cooled rooms are clean, comfortable and have shared bathrooms with hot-water showers. The ground floor is taken up by a small and colourful shop with brightly painted walls and antique birdcages.

Town Inn Hotel   HOTEL $

(Map p266; ☎266 6811; www.towninnhotel.com; Jln Tahan, Lot 3748; d/tr/q RM48/65/85; ❋@☎) Bright clean rooms here are a big step-up from the backpacker oriented places. Service is friendly.

Angsana Homestay   HOMESTAY $

(☎267 2131; Jln Sri Angsana 3B, Lot 85; r with bathroom RM60; ❋☎) A homestay in the newer area of town, about five minutes from the town centre, managed by the same nice family who run the more centrally located Greenleaf Traveller's Inn (p265). Rooms here are larger and airier than those at the inn, and there's a communal living room.

Hotel Chet Fatt   HOTEL $

(Map p266; ☎266 5805; 177 Jln Diwangsa; dm/d with shared bathroom RM10/20; @) If you arrive late at night you can stumble across the street from the bus station to this place with window-less rooms, internet terminals and free filtered water.

Hotel Sri Emas   HOTEL $

(Map p266; ☎266 4499; tamannegara@hotmail.com; 46 Jln Besar; dm/tr/f RM8/21/64, d without shower RM15-35, d with shower RM38; ❋@) Fan doubles with shared hot-water bathrooms have saggy mattresses, but are clean. Pricier rooms are bigger and have attached bathrooms and air-con. There's an internet terminal downstairs.

Eating

On Jln Pasar Besar there are excellent **food stalls** (Map p266) specialising in tom yum, while cheap *kedai kopi* (coffee shops) serving Chinese food and Malay favourites are scattered around town.

NKS Café   MALAY, WESTERN **$$**
(Map p266; NKS Hostel; 21-22 Jln Besar; meals RM10; ☺7.30am-9pm, closes 6pm low season) Serves mediocre Western breakfasts, Malay staples, *dou fu* (tofu) meals, sandwiches and beer. It's popular with backpackers, especially as it's the departure point for tours and buses.

ⓘ Information

Several banks in town can change cash and travellers cheques (change money before heading into Taman Negara). The ATMs do dry up sometimes so it's best to get money before reaching Jerantut.

AM Finance Bank (Jln Diwangsa; ☺9.30am-4pm Mon-Fri & 9.30am-noon Sat) Has an ATM that accepts most foreign cards, including Visa.

Bumiputra Commerce (Jln Tahan; ☺9.30am-4pm Mon-Fri & 9.30am-noon Sat) The ATM accepts MasterCard and Cirrus.

Internet (11 Jln Tahan, 1st fl; per hr RM3; ☺9am-5pm)

Internet Café (NKS Hostel; per hr RM5; ☺24hr)

Police (☎266 2222; Jln Besar)

ⓘ Getting There & Away

Bus

Long-distance buses leave from the ticket offices near the taxi stand. **Perwira Ekspres** (☎266 3919) and **SE Ekspres** (☎266 3188) both have offices here. Local buses depart from the station not far away on the same street.

Destination	Price	Duration
Kuala Lumpur	RM20	4hr
Kuantan	RM16	4hr
Kuala Lipis	RM5	1.5hr
Temerloh	RM6	1.5hr

NKS Hostel (Map p266; 21-22 Jln Besar; d with/without shower incl breakfast RM50/35) arranges minibuses and buses to a variety of destinations, including Tembeling jetty (RM5), KL (RM40), Perhentian Island jetty (RM65),

Kota Bharu (RM65) and the Cameron Highlands (RM65). Buses leave from the NKS Café (p267). NKS can also help you to arrange your ongoing river trip to the national park from the jetty in Kuala Tembeling. If you want to skip the riverboat, their minibuses goes directly from Kuala Tahan (RM25) at 8.30am and 1pm, returning 8am and 7.30pm.

Public buses go to the jetty at Kuala Tembeling (RM2, 45 minutes), for the boat to Taman Negara every hour from 7.45am to 5pm, although schedules are unreliable and don't necessarily coincide with boat departures.

Taxi

Taxi fares are as follows: Kuala Tembeling (RM20), Kampung Kuala Tahan (RM65), Temerloh (RM50), Cherating (RM240), Kuala Lipis (RM65), KL (RM200) and Kuantan (RM180). A surcharge of RM30 is enforced after 3pm.

Train

Jerantut train station (☎266 2219) is on the Tumpat–Gemas railway line (also known as the jungle railway). All northbound trains go via Kuala Lipis and Gua Musang.

Two express trains run daily to Singapore (2am, 12.30pm), via Johor Bahru. For KL Sentral, take the 12.30am express; there are four trains for Kuala Lipis.

For an up-to-date timetable and list of fares, consult **KTM** (www.ktmb.com.my).

Kuala Lipis

☑09

At the confluence of the Lipis and Jelai rivers, Kuala Lipis is a bustling little town with a charming colonial-era centre of Chinese shophouses. A large percentage of the population is Chinese or Indian, with the common language between them being English, so it's easy to chat with these particularly friendly locals and find your way around.

Lipis was a gold-mining centre long before the British arrived in 1887, but the town's heyday began in 1898 when it became the capital of Pahang. Grand colonial buildings date from this period, and trade increased when the railway came through in 1924. In 1957 the capital shifted to Kuantan and Kuala Lipis went into decline. The somewhat less charming 'New Town' is across the river from the old centre.

◉ Sights & Activities

It's a launching pad for visits to the nearby Kenong Rimba State Park, but Kuala Lipis also draws people for its lovely colonial-era architecture.

Maroon and white and decorated with arches, the noble **District Offices** are located off Jln Lipis on a hill 1km south of town centre. The offices overlook the exclusive **Clifford School**, a grand public building that began life as the Anglo-Chinese School in 1913. During the occupation, the school served as the headquarters of the Kempetai (the Japanese secret police).

The road next to the school leads up the hill to the black-and-white wooden **Pahang Club**, off Jln Lipis, a stately and dignified bungalow with wide, open verandahs.

A very pleasant walk starts on the road behind the Lipis Centrepoint Complex. Follow the road up the hill where the sign says 'Driving Range Lipis'. You will soon pass the **Istana Hinggap** on your right; keep going uphill and the road forks. Take either branch and you will be led to a series of colonial-era houses, some in the process of being reclaimed by jungle.

If you're in town on Friday evening, be sure to visit the excellent **night market** in the parking lot next to the bus station.

A taxi around town for an hour to see costs RM25.

🛏 Sleeping, Eating & Drinking

There are busy and popular food stalls on either side of the northern end of the overhead walkway crossing Jln Pekeliling.

Centrepoint Hotel & Apartments   HOTEL $
(☑312 2688; Jln Pekeliling, Lipis Centrepoint; economy s/d RM48/70, deluxe d from RM108; ❀🕸) One floor of this high-rise hotel is dedicated to mediocre economy rooms, while the rest of the place has more comfortable standard rooms. It's the busiest place in town and has a tour office (specialising in trips to Kenong Rimba), great service and a bustling food court down stairs. There's also free breakfast and wi-fi.

Residence Rest House   HISTORIC HOTEL $$
(☑312 2788; r RM60-150; ❀) This huge, homey colonial hilltop house once housed the British Resident; rooms here are massive with floral wallpaper, big windows and garden grounds. The restaurant is only open for dinner and a taxi to town costs RM7.

D'Valley Inn   HOTEL $
(☑312 5868; 44 Jln Bukit Bius; r RM78-98; ❀🕸) D'Valley, located behind the high-rise Centrepoint, has clean, newly refurbished

rooms. The management also offers bicycle rentals (RM5/25 per hour/day).

Appu's Guesthouse   GUESTHOUSE $
(☑013-945 9766, 312 3142; jungleappu@hotmail.com; 63 Jln Besar, Hotel Lipis; dm/q RM10/60, d RM20-35; ❀) Appu's is great for tourist info and guide services, but it's very rundown. Locks on the doors don't work well so lone women may not feel safe here.

Hotel London   HOTEL $
(☑312 1618; 82 Jln Besar; r RM38/43; ❀) Plain rooms in a refurbished Chinatown shophouse. Cheaper rooms have shared bathroom, and all have air-conditioning.

ℹ Information

Hand-drawn maps of Kuala Lipis are available at Appu's Guesthouse. There are a few banks with ATMs on Jln Besar and the post office is east of the train station.

Kiara Holidays (☑3122 777; www.kiaraholidays.com; 4th floor, Centrepoint Hotel) Kiara plans tours all over the area, including whitewater rafting and canoe trips down the Sungei Kesong and treks into Taman Negera and Kenong Rimba. Call or check their website for current trips and deals.

ℹ Getting There & Away

Buses run from the **bus station** (☑312 5055) in New Town to KL (RM15, 4.5 hours), Kuantan (RM26, six hours), Temerloh (RM16, one hour), Raub (RM5, 1.5 hours) and Gua Musang (RM16, 1.5 hours), from where you can catch onward buses to Kota Bharu.

Three trains run to Singapore (2.15am, 8.15am and noon) and one per day runs to KL (midnight). Trains bound for Singapore, KL or Gemas stop at Jerantut (for Taman Negara). Several local ('jungle') trains connect daily to Wakaf Baharu, the closest station to Kota Bharu.

Taxis leave from the bus station for KL (RM180), Jerantut (RM65), Kuala Tahan (RM50), Gua Musang (RM120), Temerloh (RM100) and Kuantan (RM200).

Kenong Rimba State Park
☑09

A sprawling area of lowland forest rising to the limestone foothills bordering Taman Negara, this 120-sq-km forest park can be explored on three- or four-day jungle treks organised from Kuala Lipis. It's a much less-visited alternative to Taman Negara. Sightings of big mammals are rare but expect to see monkeys, wild pigs, squirrels, civets and possibly nocturnal tapir; the park is also a prime destination for bird-watching. The park is also home to the Batek people, an Orang Asli tribe.

Visitors need to acquire a permit from the **Kuala Lipis District Forest Office** (☎312 1273). Guides are compulsory for entry to the park and can be arranged in Kuala Lipis. **Appu** (☎312 2619) of Appu's Guesthouse in Kuala Lipis does tours for RM80 per person per day plus RM200 (minimum three people) for the boat to and from Jeti Tanjung Kiara.

Tours include food, guide and all expenses in the park, but they are no-frills jungle experiences – you camp in the park, with all equipment and meals provided. Trips go when enough people are interested – it's best to get a group together yourself.

You can also book similarly priced trips through Kiara Holidays (p268) in Kuala Lipis.

ⓘ Getting There & Away

Access to Kenong Rimba is from Kuala Lipis on southbound local trains to Batu Sembilan (Mile 9). From Batu Sembilan, hire a boat (per person RM25) to Jeti Tanjung Kiara, just across the river from Kampung Kuala Kenong.

Raub
☎09

Raub is Malay for scoop, which makes sense as this colonial town was built around a gold mine in the waning days of British Malaya. It's a pretty little town, boasting colonial-era charm and architecture along with one of our favorite restaurants in Pahang.

◉ Sights & Activities

Like nearby Kuala Lipis, Raub also has both lovely colonial-era architecture and a more traditional *kampung* (village) feel on the outskirts. Raub is also a great base for exploring the nearby Sungai Pasu Recreation Centre, the Jeram Besu Rapids and the Bukit Telaga Waterfalls.

🛏 Sleeping & Eating

Rumah Rehat Raub HISTORIC GUESTHOUSE $$
(Raub Guesthouse; ☎355 9899; rumahrehat.ipsb@gmail.com; Jln Dato Abdullah; d/ste RM120/200; ❈🗐🗢) This historic guesthouse occupies the spacious grounds of a former colonial-era mansion. It features lovely rooms and a top-notch information centre.

Hotel Jelai HOTEL $
(☎013-983 1626; 35 Jln Tan Tiong; d RM88, deluxe RM108; ❈🗐🗢) The Raub branch of this chain hotel can be found easily by its candy-striped pink and red exterior. It's generic, but not in a bad way.

Hotel Seri Raub HOTEL $
(☎355 0888; Jln Dato Abdullah; r from RM80; ❈🗢) Rooms here are comfortable if a bit plain.

Hotel Tai Tong HOTEL $
(☎356 1053; Jln Dato Abdullah; r fan/air-con RM35/40; ❈🗢) This is one of the better of a few budget places across from the bus station. Rooms all have TV and hot shower.

TOP CHOICE Restoran Ratha Raub INDIAN, MALAY $$
(Jln Tun Razak; fish head curry for two RM36; ⊙Lunch & Dinner) Don't let the withered-looking fish head staring up from the buffet tray scare you – it's just for show. Though there are other dishes on the menu, what brings people here from as far away from KL is Ratha's kari kepala ikan Raub (Raub's famous fish head curry). All orders are prepared fresh and served in a metal tureen of fiery curry, green chilli, string beans, local eggplant and a special variant of light tofu that's been puffed with air and, of course, the split head of a large red snapper out of which tender bone-free cheek meat just spills. Ratha's also sells boxed 'curry in a hurry' home preparations.

Restoran Sentosa CHINESE SEAFOOD $$
(Jln Padang; dishes by weight; ⊙Dinner) Sentosa specialises in whole fish prepared in a more Chinese fashion, and served in a variety of ways – hot pot and grilled are quite popular. The building – a 100-year-old round pavilion with stained glass windows – is worth a visit alone. Expect to spend upwards of RM 50 for a meal here.

Sun Yen Cheong CAFE $
(Jln Tun Razak; ⊙breakfast and lunch) This traditional Chinese-Malaysian coffee shop is bursting with customers every morning.

ⓘ Information

Travel information is available from the friendly folks at Rumah Rehat Raub.There are several banks in town (some even sell gold), including an **HSBC** (Jln Tun Razak) with an ATM that accepts foreign cards.

ENVIRONMENTAL CONCERNS IN RAUB

Raub's Bukit Koman gold mine is a source of controversy, and multiple large-scale protests have been mounted by both Malaysian environmentalists and locals who claim to have been directly affected by cyanide used in a mining process called 'cyanide leach mining'. For the casual visitor, there should be no danger of cyanide poisoning from a short stay in Raub.

The negative impact of the area's other two major industries – palm oil and timber – are more noticable. Trucks carrying timber roll through town with noisy regularity, and much of what was once jungle outside of Raub has been transformed into palm-oil plantations. See p588 for more information on the environmental challenges facing Pahang.

❶ Getting There & Away

Raub's bus station is on Jln Dato Abdullh. A number of companies, including **Transnasional** (☑355 1342) and **MARA** (☑355 1622), run several buses daily between Raub and KL (RM10, four hours), Kuantan (RM21, four hours) and Bentong (RM4, 1 hour). A few buses also run to Kuala Lipis (RM5, 1 hour).

Taxi drivers tend to congregate at the bus station, offering rides to destinations all around Pahang.

Temerloh
☑09

An old town on the banks of the enormous Sungai Pahang, Temerloh has hints of colonial style and a colourful Sunday market. As the main city of central Pahang, it serves as a transport hub. The bus station is in the centre of the shop-and-restaurant filled new town (which is just a few minutes walk from the old) The train station is 12km away at Mentakab, a thriving satellite of Temerloh with a bustling nightly market.

Temerloh is a fairly satisfactory place to chill, especially if you're craving some modernity after a few days in the jungle. Budget lodgings seem limited, but there are a few mid-price options.

🛏 Sleeping & Eating

Hotel Green Park   HOTEL **$**
(☑296 3333; www.greenpark.com.my; Jln Terkukur, off Jln Merbah; r from RM83; ✴🖧) This tall hotel towers over the town and offers clean, pretty rooms with hot showers and coffee and tea making facilities.

Rumah Rehat Temerloh   GUESTHOUSE **$$**
(☑296 3218; Jln Hamzah; d RM100; ✴🖧) This government-run hotel is located in a colonial building east of the city centre. Carpeted rooms are well appointed, and there's

something of an old colonial garden party atmosphere.

E Station Cafe   JAPANESE **$**
(Jln Pak Sako 1; RM6-21) Come on, admit it – after weeks of *mee sup* and laksa, you're craving some sushi. Well, this is the place to get it, with fish brought in fresh from markets in KL and Kuantan. Best deal is the *chirashi* (RM21), three kinds of fresh fish over vinegar rice.

❶ Getting There & Away

Bus

Terminal Bas Utama Temerloh (Jln Sudirman) is where you'll find buses to various spots on the peninsula.

Destination	Price	Duration
Kuala Lumpur	RM10	3hr
Kuantan	RM12	2hr
Kuala Lipis	RM16	3hr
Jerantut	RM6	1.5hr
Melaka	RM17	4hr
Penang	RM55	6hr

Taxis from the bus station go to Mentakab (RM10), Jerantut (RM38), Kuantan (RM95) and KL (RM150).

Around Temerloh

◉ Sights

Kuala Gandah Elephant Conservation Centre   WILDLIFE RESERVE, THEME PARK
(☑279 0391; www.wildlife.gov.my/webpagev4_en/bhg _ekogandah.html; Kuala Gandah, Lanchang; entry by donation; ☺10am-4.45pm, video 1pm, 1.30pm & 3.45pm daily, also 12.30pm Sat & Sun) The Kuala Gandah Elephant Conservation Centre is the base for the Department of Wildlife and National Parks' Elephant Relocation Team,

which helps capture and relocate rogue elephants from across Southeast Asia to other suitable habitats throughout the peninsula, such as at Taman Negara. Most of the elephants at the centre are work elephants from Myanmar, India and Thailand.

Visitors to Kuala Gandah are first shown a video about the elephant's plight, then can watch and join in while the handlers wash down and feed the big guys fruit (2pm Saturday to Thursday, 2.45pm Friday). Next everyone is herded a central area where visitors can, for an additional fee, ride older elephants and bathe with bay elephants. While the mission of the park is noble, animal rights activists criticise the circus-like activities at the centre, which they claim are neither enjoyable for the animals nor in line with animal welfare principles. Our advice? Come and see the elephants, buy and distribute the various pachyderm treats on sale to your (and their) heart's content. But shun the rides and group bathing sessions.

Deerland ZOO
(☏013-967 6242; www.deerland.org; 67 Jln Zabidin; entry adult/child RM10/5; ☉10.30am-5.30pm Sat-Thu, medicinal herb jungle treks RM35 per person; reserve at a least day in advance) Deerland is a mini petting zoo in the forest with three species of deer that you can feed and pet. The deer are kept in reasonable sized enclosures, and don't seem all that unhappy with regular attention from travellers bearing carrots (sold by park management). There are also rabbits, peacocks, ostriches, and a fairly wide variety of birds living in the park, as well as a massive python that you can pose with for a memorable photos. The team here also leads 2½-hour medicinal herb jungle treks that include lunch and an adventurous river crossing along a network of swinging ropes. Similar treks lasting up to three days can also be arranged.

🛏 Sleeping & Eating

Buman Suri Biopurpose Resort HOMESTAY $
(☏013-377 3838; d RM50) Family-run Buman Suri Biopurpose Resort offers accommodation in a basic *kampung*-style house on the roadside.

Saudi's Cafe MALAY $
(meals RM4) Saudi's Cafe, on the grounds of the Kuala Gandah Elephant Conservation Centre (p270), serves simple Malay grub like nasi goreng and *mee sup* (noodle soup).

ⓘ Getting There & Away

These two sites are located about 150km east of KL near the town of Lanchang west of Mentakab. Most people visit on tours (including a visit to Kuala Gandah and Deerland), available from KL, Jerantut, Cherating and other tourist hubs on the peninsula. The most cost efficient way to visit the two is to combine a visit with your return trip to KL from Taman Negara with Han Travel (p265) in either their KL or Kuala Tembeling offices.

East Coast Islands, Kelantan & Terengganu

🔊09

Includes »

Kelantan	273
Kota Bharu	273
East Coast Islands	283
Pulau Perhentian	283
Pulau Lang Tengah	291
Pulau Redang	292
Pulau Kapas	293
Terengganu	294
Kuala Terengganu	295
Around Kuala Terengganu	299
North of Kuala Terengganu	299
South of Kuala Terengganu	300

Best Places to Eat

» Bubu Restaurant (p289)

» West Lake Eating House (p279)

» Four Seasons (p279)

Best Places to Stay

» Terrapuri Heritage Village (p301)

» D'Lagoon Chalets (p290)

» Pasir Belanda Homestay (p283)

» Shari-la Island Resort (p290)

Why Go?

Though Malaysia's east coast is beautiful, containing many a lovely beach and bucolic *kampung* (village) well worth visiting, what brings folks back to the region time and again are the tantalisingly beautiful islands offshore. 'Paradise' barely does these gems justice, though that'll likely be the word that comes to mind when you first lay eyes on the white sands and swaying palms of the Perhentians or Pulau Kapas. Snorkellers and scuba divers will find the coral and marine life beneath the azure waves second to none.

Cultural travellers, meanwhile, will find in cities like Kota Bharu and Kuala Terengganu a distinctively Malay vibe that's managed to remain fairly undiluted despite the nation's headlong rush to prosperity. And nature lovers will want to spend time exploring the vast and as yet largely untrammeled expanses of jungle that make up much of Kelantan's interior.

When to Go

Kuala Terrenganu

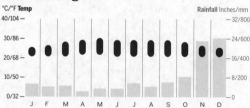

Apr–May Escape the heat in the higher mountainous regions.	Jun–Aug Drier weather and Kota Bharu's festivals make summer a great time to visit.	Nov–Feb Few options open, but discounts on offer for those braving monsoonal rains.

KELANTAN

Travellers often rush through Malaysia's northeastern-most state, seeing it as a way-point between Thailand and Pulau Perhentian. Those who don't linger are missing out on both a stronghold of Malay culture and one of Southeast Asia's great cultural blending zones, combining a distinctive blend of Chinese, Indian, Thai and Malay cultures.

Kota Bharu

POP 425,000

Kota Bharu has the energy of a mid-sized city, the compact feel and friendly vibe of a small town, superb food and a good spread of accommodation. A logical overnight stop between Thailand and the Perhentians, KB is a good base for exploring Kelantan. The state's villages are within day-tripping distance, and its crafts and culture are present in the city itself.

The centre of town is a busy area north-east of the clock tower, bounded by Jln Pintu Pong, Jln Kebun Sultan/Jln Mahmud, Jln Hospital and Jln Temenggong. The central bus station is just off Jln Padang Garong, opposite the 25-storey Kota Bharu Trade Centre.

◉ Sights

The real attraction of the Padang Merdeka area is the nearby cluster of museums (☏748 2266; www.kelantan.muzium.net), all contactable by the one phone number. You can hit them all in a day and come away a semi-expert in Malay history and culture.

Bank Kerapu　　　　　　　　MUSEUM
(WWII Memorial Museum; Map p276; Jln Sultan; adult/child RM2/1; ☺8.30am-4.45pm Sat-Thu)
Built in 1912 for the Mercantile Bank of India, the Bank Kerapu building is a gem of colonial architecture, the first stone structure in Kelantan and, during WWII, HQ of the *kempaitai*, Japan's feared secret police. Today it is also known as the 'War Museum', thanks to its focus on the Japanese invasion and occupation of Malaya and the 1948 Emergency. Exhibits mainly consist of old photography, rusty guns and other militaria.

FREE **Muzium Islam**　　　　　　MUSEUM
(Islamic Museum; Map p276; Jln Sultan; ☺8.30am-4.45pm Sat-Thu) Muzium Islam occupies an old villa once known as Serambi Mekah (Verandah to Mecca) – a reference to its days as

Kelantan's first school of Islamic instruction. Nowadays it displays a small collection of photographs and artifacts relating to the history of Islam in the state.

Istana Jahar　　　　　　　　MUSEUM
(Royal Ceremonies Museum; Map p276; Jln Istana; adult/child RM3/1.50; ☺8.30am-4.45pm Sat-Thu)
Kota Bharu's best museum, both in terms of exhibits and structure. It's an achingly beautiful chocolate-brown building that dates back to 1887, easily one of the most attractive traditional buildings in the city. The interior displays focus on Kelatanese ritual and crafts, from detailed descriptions of batik-weaving to the elaborate ceremonies that once marked the life of local youth, from circumcision to wedding nights to funerary rights.

Istana Batu　　　　　　　　MUSEUM
(Royal Museum; Map p276; Jln Istana; adult/child RM2/1; ☺8.30am-4.45pm Sat-Thu) The pale-yellow Istana Batu, also known as Muzium Diraja, was constructed in 1939 and was the crown prince's palace until donated to the state. The richly furnished rooms give a surprisingly intimate insight into royal life, with family photos and personal belongings scattered among the fine china and chintzy sofas, and the late sultan's collection of hats.

FREE **Kampung Kraftangan**　　ARTS CENTRE
(Handicraft Village; Map p276; Jln Hilir Kota; admission free, museum adult/child RM2/1; ☺museum 8.30am-4.45pm Sat-Thu) This handicraft village, a touristy affair opposite Istana Batu, has a one-room museum with displays of woodcarving, batik-making and other crafts.

Muzium Negeri Kelanta　　　MUSEUM
(State Museum; Map p276; ☏748 2266; Jln Hospital; adult/child RM2/1; ☺8.30am-4.45pm Sat-Thu)
This museum, next to the tourist information centre, is the official state museum. The exhibits on Kelantan's history and culture are interesting, but the signage is poor.

☛ Courses

**Roselan's Malay
Cookery Workshop**　　　　　COOKING
(☏call for address 017-933 7242) The ever-cheerful and civic-minded Roselan runs this popular Malay cookery workshop. Prices vary depending on the number of participants and ingredients used, but expect to pay around RM90 to RM125 per person for a group of four. Students are invited to a real, middle-class Malay home

East Coast Islands, Kelantan & Terengganu Highlights

1 Taking in sun, sand and sea on the amazingly varied beaches of the **Perhentian Islands** (Pulau Perhentian, p283)

2 Snorkelling and beach-combing in the less visited tropical paradise of **Pulau Kapas** (p293)

3 Taking a night-time boat tour through the ghostly mangrove swamps and being surrounded by fireflies blinking in synchronisation at the **Penarik Firefly Sanctuary** (p300)

4 Tempting your taste buds in the street stalls and restaurants of **Khota Bharu** (p278)

5 Checking out the Thai temples of **Tumpat** (p281)

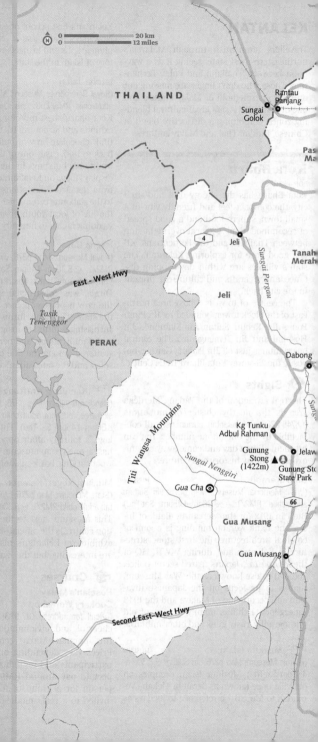

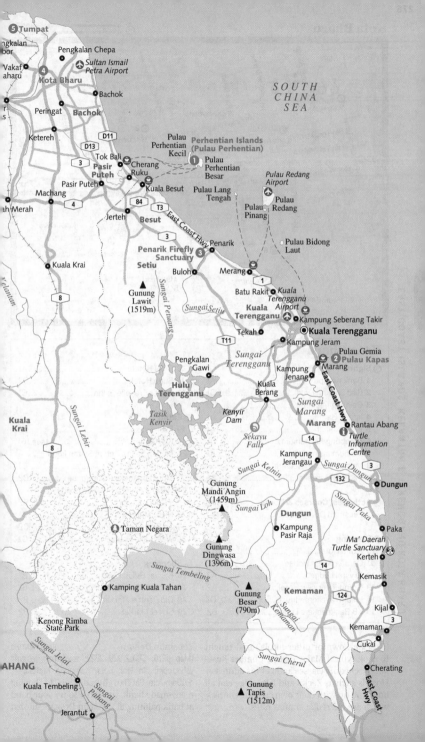

Kota Bharu

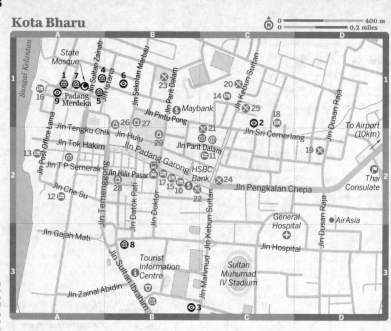

Kota Bharu

⊙ Sights

1 Bank Kerapu	A1
2 Bird Singing Field	C1
3 Gelanggang Seni	B3
4 Istana Batu	A1
5 Istana Jahar	A1
6 Kampung Kraftangan	B1
7 Muzium Islam	A1
8 Muzium Negeri Kelanta	B3
9 Padang Merdeka	A1

⊕ Activities, Courses & Tours

Zecsman Design	(see 6)

⊜ Sleeping

10 Azam Hotel	B2
11 Cerana Guest House	C2
12 Crystal Lodge	A2
13 Grand Riverview Hotel	A2
14 Ideal Travellers' House	C1
15 KB Backpackers Lodge	B2
16 Ridel Hotel	A1
17 Suria Hotel	B2
18 Zeck's Traveller's Inn	C1

⊗ Eating

19 Four Seasons	D2
K's Kitchen	(see 16)
20 Medan Selera Kebun Sultan Food Court	C1
21 Muhibah Aneka Cake House	C2
22 Nasi Air Hideng Pok Sen Food Court	B2
23 Night Market	B1
24 Sri Devi Restaurant	C2
25 West Lake Eating House	C1

⊜ Shopping

26 Bazaar Buluh Kubu	B1
27 Central Market	B1
28 Old Central Market	B2
29 Street Market	B2

(Roselan's own or other locals') and taught to cook typical Malay dishes. Contact Roselan to schedule classes and get his address. Hostels such as Zeck's and KB Lodge can all hook you up with their own cooking courses, which are offered at similar rates.

Zecsman Design BATIK PAINTING
(Map p276; ☑012-929 2822; zecs man_design@ yahoo.com; Jln Hilir Kota, Kampung Kraftangan; ☺10am-7pm Sat-Thu) In addition to buying ready-made batik, you can also try your hand at batik painting at Zecsman Design's tutored

four- to five-hour classes for between RM50 and RM70 (depending on size and fabric used in your work). A full-day course costs RM100.

Tours

Most hostels organise tours for their guests. Possible tours include two-day/three-night expeditions into the jungle around Gua Musang (RM250 to RM350), boat trips up small local rivers into sleepy fishing villages where silk kites are made by candlelight (RM60 to RM80), and short city tours (RM25 to RM35). Other tours include two-hour tours of the Tumpat temples (RM75) and half-day craft tours (RM90-115).

Pawi at KB Backpackers Lodge (p277), Zeck at Zeck's Traveller's Inn (p277), and freelance tour guide Roselan (017-933 7242) are all reputable and knowledgeable.

Festivals & Events

Kota Bharans love birdsong, to the point where they broadcast the chirping of birds in an abandoned building across loudspeakers set up through the city. Each year around August the city holds a bird-singing contest, during which you can see Malay songbirds perform; the ornate cages the birds are housed in are almost as pretty as their songs. Finally, every Friday and Saturday morning there's a bird-singing contest in a bird singing field (Map p276) near Zeck's Traveller's Inn, where locals hang decorative bird cages up on long poles, then sit back and listen. Travellers are often invited to watch and even provide a bit of amateur judging.

The spectacular kite festival (Pesta Wau) is held in June, and the cultural carnival (Karnival Kebudayaan Kelantan), featuring drumming and top-spinning contests, takes place in September. The Sultan's Birthday celebration (March/April) involves a week of cultural events. The dates vary, so check with the tourist information centre.

From March until September, a cultural show takes place at the Cultural Centre three days a week featuring dancing, kite-making, top-spinning and displays of both local games, dancing and singing. Shows are usually held in the evenings on Saturday (twice), Monday afternoon, Wednesday (afternoon and night). Performance times change, so ask Miriam at Zeck's guest house.

Sleeping

Kota Bharu is a popular stop on the backpacker trail, and there's plenty of cheap hostels around town, including several along Jln Padang Garong. Midrange and luxury options are aimed at business travellers.

TOP CHOICE Zeck's Traveller's Inn HOMESTAY $
(Map p276; 743 1613; 7088G Jln Sri Cemerlan; dm/s/d from RM10/15/25, air-con RM45-60; ✳@🛜) Zeck and Miriam ('call me mama') Zaki's home is located in a peaceful nook north of the city centre, with an attractive little garden to lounge about in and light meals and drinks always at hand. Friendly and social, this family-owned and -run place is a great way to get a feel for genuine Malaysian *kampung* (village) life in the heart of Kota Bharu. The Zaki family are a mine of information and travel hook-ups, and will be glad to help you with your ongoing travel plans throughout Malaysia. Zeck also helps to arrange tours into Taman Negara through the park's far-less travelled Kelantan entrance.

KB Backpackers Lodge HOTEL, HOSTEL $
(Map p276; 019-9445222,7488841; www.kb-backpackers.com.my; 1872D Jln Padang Garong; dm/r from RM8/20; ✳@) KB's rooms are only so-so (the bigger the better is the rule). But owner Pawi is so helpful and a wealth of information, and the vibe at his hostel is so internationally chill in the way that made us love backpacking in the first place, that it more than makes up for it. Pawi is also a mad bicycling enthusiast and organises bike trips (on and off road) and rents out high-quality bicycles to guests. Make sure you've got the right place – a somewhat dingy hostel calling itself 'KB Backpackers Inn' operates across the street.

GET CULTURED

A wide variety of local cultural events, including *gasing uri* (top-spinning), *silat* (a Malay form of martial arts), kite-making, drumming and shadow-puppet shows are held regularly at the Gelanggang Seni (Cultural Centre; Map p276; 744 3124; Jln Mahmud). The events are especially kid-friendly, and best of all they're totally free. Sessions are held Monday, Wednesday and Saturday from February to September, currently between 3.30pm and 5.30pm, and 9pm and 11pm, but check with the tourist information centre (p279), or your hotel's owners, who should have a full timetable of events.

Ridel Hotel
HOTEL **$$**

(Map p276; ☎747-7000; www.ridelhotel.com.my; Block A, Pelangi Mall, Jln Pasar Lama; s/d/tr from RM97/107/147; ❄@🤝) Sitting on the riverfront just up from the jetty, this new 85-room hotel is larger than it seems from the outside. Rooms are small but chic, with pastel painted walls and a minimalist design. Snag a room with a riverfront view if you can.

Grand Riverview Hotel
HOTEL **$$**

(Map p276; ☎743 9988; www.grh.com.my; 9 Jln Post Office Lama; r/ste from RM215/318; ❄❄) Perched on the river edge, this huge hotel offers high standards at reasonable prices; long-term 'promotions' will shave around 40% off the published rates. Rooms at the back have some fine views across the water, and all have king-sized beds and big bathrooms with both showers and baths.

Cerana Guest House
GUESTHOUSE **$**

(Map p276; ☎956 7141; www.ceranaguesthouse.com; 39521 Jln Padang Garong; dm/d/f RM12/35/35; ❄@🤝) This pleasant and colourful guesthouse is a block away from the main drag and offers clean, unpretentious rooms and a cool, pastel-painted communal chill-out spot. Cheaper rooms have shared bathrooms and fans, while pricier ones offer cool air and privacy. From the bus station hang a left at the Pizza Hut; the main entrance is in a quiet back alley just north of Jln Padang Garong.

Suria Hotel
HOTEL **$**

(Map p276; ☎743 2255; suria.kb@tm.net.my; Jln Padang Garong; s/d from RM75, tr RM90; ❄) Just up the street from the bus station, the Suria is a welcoming hotel with a friendly staff. The cheaper rooms are windowless but there are some more appealing choices boasting natural light. Rooms overlooking the street may be noisy.

Crystal Lodge
HOTEL **$$**

(Map p276; ☎747 0888; www.crystallodge.com.my; 124 Jln Che Su; s/d from RM150/299; ❄@🤝) This clean and airy place is decent value, with comfortable rooms, free in-house movies and daily newspapers. There's an attractive rooftop restaurant with a great view over the river.

Azam Hotel
HOTEL **$**

(Map p276; ☎747 0508; 1872A Jln Padang Garong; s/d from RM80, f from RM110; ❄) This cozy if boring hotel is set right in the heart of town above the photography shop of the same name. It has decent rooms; try to get one towards the back of the building to avoid street noise.

Ideal Travellers' House
GUESTHOUSE **$**

(Map p276; ☎744 2246; www.ugoideal.com; 3954F Jln Kebun Sultan; s/d/tr RM12/28/35; @🤝) This serious backpacker pad is located down an alley off Jln Kebun Sultan and has cramped, fan-cooled rooms. There's a pleasant garden for having a laze during the day, with drinks and snacks available.

✗ Eating

TOP
CHOICE **West Lake Eating House**
CHINESE **$**

(Map p276; Jln Kebun Sultan; mains from RM5; ☻10am-8pm; 🚗) Don't let the plain looking

---

QUICK EATS IN KOTA BHARU

One of the great things about KB is how well (and cheaply) you can eat without ever setting foot in a restaurant. The most popular spot is KB's **night market** (Map p276; Jln Pintu Pong), where stalls are set up in the evening around 5pm and stay open past midnight. Say 'Suka pedas' ('I like it hot') to eat as the locals do. Specialties include *ayam percik* (marinated chicken on bamboo skewers) and *nasi kerabu* (rice with coconut, fish and spices), blue rice, squid-on-a-stick and *murtabak* (pan-fried flat bread filled with everything from minced meat to bananas).

Food courts are an excellent option day or night. One good one is the **Nasi Air Hideng Pok Sen Food Court** (Map p276; Jln Padang Garong) on Jln Padang Garong (just across from the Pizza Hut), which has several stalls serving Malay specialties, a self-serve buffet, and a couple of stalls serving coffee and iced beverages in an open-air setting with two large flat screen TVs showing Hollywood films around the clock. The **Medan Selera Kebun Sultan Food Court** (Map p276; ☎746 1632; Jln Kebun Sultan; mains from RM3; ☻lunch & dinner) on Jln Kebun Sultan offers a variety of Chinese dishes like claypot chicken rice and *kway teow* (rice-flour noodles). They don't show Hollywood movies, but they do serve beer.

More food stalls can be found next to the river opposite the **Padang Merdeka** (Map p276) and by the Jln Hamzah bus station, and there's a modern **food court** (Jln Hamzah; ☻lunch & dinner) serving Western fast-food (burgers, fried chicken) inside KB Mall.

KELANTAN'S INFO NERVE CENTRE

Whether you're looking to find out the latest on Kelantan's festival scene, interested in spending some time in a traditional Malaysian Homestay, seeking a tour guide or are just after information in general, the friendly, multilingual staff at Kelantan's excellent **tourist information centre** (☎748 5534; Jln Sultan Ibrahim; ⊙8am-1pm & 2-4.30pm Sun-Thu) can help. While some tourist information centres in Malaysia are gussied-up souvenir shops, this place is the real deal and seems to exist solely to help travellers get the most out of their visit. Stop in for the air conditioning; stick around for the unbridled flow of local knowledge on tap.

decor and plastic chairs fool you. West Lake Eating House may well serve some of the tastiest Chinese fair in all of eastern Malaysia, thanks to a particularly talented chef who works ceaselessly in a tiny kitchen. Esoteric dishes like stewed bean curd stuffed with fish cakes and lightly sautéed purple eggplant with garlic sauce share the steam table with more common (but no less delicious) dishes like braised pork ribs, roast duck and stir-fried vegetables. Bravo, West Lake!

Four Seasons　　　　　　　CHINESE **$$**
(Map p276; www.fourseasonsrestaurant.com.my; 5670 Jln Sri Cemerlang; mains from RM15; ⊙lunch & dinner) The Four Seasons is packed nightly with locals enjoying seafood dishes like claypot prawn and dry cuttlefish with mango salad. Sold by weight, the house specialty, deep-fried soft-shell crab, should only set you back about RM40 for two people.

K's Kitchen　　　　　　　RESTAURANT **$**
(Map p276; Pelangi Mall, Jln Pasar Lama; mains from RM5.50; ⊙breakfast, lunch & dinner) Just below the Ridel Hotel, this cute restaurant serves Western and Malay food on rectangular tables with inset dioramas in which strange bits of flotsam are incorporated to create three-dimensional scenes of random artistry. If this doesn't float your boat, there's also a TV. Come for the decor alone – the food is standard rather than stand-out, and the juices are too sweet.

Muhibah Aneka Cake House　　CAFE **$**
(Map p276; Jln Pintu Pong; mains from RM4; ⊙8am-10pm) In addition to serving the best iced cappuccino in town (a good thing in a city where Nescafe is the rule), this lovely bakery has great cakes, iced desserts and even donuts!

Sri Devi Restaurant　　　　　MALAY **$**
(Map p276; 4213-F Jln Kebun Sultan; mains from RM4; ⊙lunch & dinner Sat-Thu) As popular with locals as it is with tourists, this is a great place for an authentic banana-leaf curry and a mango lassi.

🔒 Shopping

Kota Bharu is a centre for Malay crafts. Batik, *kain songket* (cloth brocaded with gold and silver), silverware, woodcarving and kite-making factories and shops are dotted around town.

One of the best places to see handicrafts is on the road north to Pantai Cahaya Bulan (PCB). There are a number of workshops, representing most crafts, stretched out along the road all the way to the beach. Your best bet in visiting these is to rent a bicycle from Pawi at KB's Backpackers Lodge.

Central Market　　　　　　MARKET
(Pasar Besar Siti Khadijah; Map p276; Jln Hulu; ⊙6am-6pm) One of the most colourful and active markets in Malaysia, the central market is at its busiest first thing in the morning, and has usually packed up by early afternoon. Downstairs is the produce section, while upstairs stalls selling spices, brassware, batik and other goods stay open longer.

Bazaar Buluh Kubu　　　　HANDICRAFTS
(Map p276; Jln Hulu; ⊙Sat-Thu) Near the central market, Bazaar Buluh Kubu is a good place to buy handicrafts such as batik, traditional Malay clothing and jewellery.

Old Central Market　　　　　MARKET
(Map p276; Jln Hilir Pasar; ⊙Sat-Thu) Kota Bharu's old central market consists of a block of food stalls on the ground floor, and a selection of batik, *songket* and clothing upstairs.

Street Market　　　　　　　MARKET
(Map p276; Jln Parit Dalam; ⊙6-10pm) A street market selling clothes, copy watches and DVDs takes over Jln Parit Dalam in the evenings.

EAST COAST ISLANDS, KELANTAN & TERENGGANU KOTA BHARU

GETTING TO THAILAND: RANTAU PANJANG TO SUNGAI KOLOK

Getting to the border The Thailand border is at Rantau Panjang; bus 29 departs on the hour from Kota Bharu's central bus station (RM4, 1½ hours). Share taxis from Kota Bharu to Rantau Panjang cost RM30 per car and take 45 minutes.

There's another border crossing at Pengkalan Kubor, on the coast, but transport links aren't as good and crossing here can be dodgy during periods of sectarian violence in southern Thailand. Inquire at the tourist information centre before using this crossing. During the day a large car ferry (RM1 for pedestrians) crosses the river to busy Tak Bai in Thailand. From Kota Bharu, take bus 27 or 43 (RM2.40) from the central bus station.

At the border From Rantau Panjang you can walk across the border to Sungai Kolok, where you can catch the train to Bangkok at the Sungai Kolok station.

❶ Information

Banks are open from 10am to 3pm Saturday to Wednesday, 9.30am to 11.30am Thursday, and are closed on Friday.

HSBC Bank (Jln Padang Garong)

Maybank (Jln Pintu Pong) Near the night market and usually open to 7pm.

Multimedia Internet (☎747 7735; 171 Jln Parit Dalam; per hr RM2)

❶ Getting There & Away

Air

Malaysia Airlines (☎771 4703; http://www.malaysiaairlines.com; Jln Gajah Mati), **AirAsia** (☎746 1671; www.airasia.com; airport) and **Firefly** (☎03-7845 4543; www.fireflyz.com.my; airport) all have direct flights to KL as well as other destinations. The latter two often offer specials that can make plane travel almost as cheap as taking a bus; check their websites for details.

Flights take off from Kota Bharu's Sultan Ismail Petra Airport , 8 km outside of the city centre. Bus 9 (RM2, 20 minutes) leaves hourly from the main bus station to the airport.

Bus

Most buses operate from the **central bus station** (☎747 5971, 747 4330; Jln Padang Garong). A few buses also leave from Lembah Sireh Bus Station near the Kota Bharu Tesco. Since these change from time to time it's best to ask your guesthouse or the tourist information centre where your bus leaves from.

Most regional buses leave from the central bus station. Destinations include Wakaf Baharu (buses 19 and 27, RM1.20), Rantau Panjang (bus 29, RM3), Tumpat (bus 19, RM1.50), Bachok (buses 2B, 23 and 29, RM3.30), Pasir Puteh (bus 3, RM5.10), Jerteh (bus 30, RM7.10) and Kuala Krai (bus 5, RM8.30). Note that some of these may be identified by destination rather than number.

LONG-DISTANCE BUSES

Destination	Price (RM)	Duration (hrs)
Alor Setar	35	8
Butterworth	35	8
Gua Musang	12	3
Ipoh	34	8
Kuala Lumpur	40	8
Kuala Terengganu	15	3
Kuantan	32	5
Lumut	45	9
Melaka	55	9
Singapore	80	11

Car

Travellers can hire cars from **Hawk** (☎773 3824; Sultan Ismail Petra Airport).

Taxi

The **taxi stand** is on the southern side of the central bus station. Avoid the unlicensed cab drivers who will pester you here and elsewhere around town, and take an official taxi as these are cheaper and safer.

Catching an early morning train? Arrange for the taxi to Wakaf Baharu the night before at your guesthouse.

Train

The nearest station is **Wakaf Baharu** (☎719 6986). There is a daily express train all the way to KL (economy seat /class-2 seat/class-2 bed RM30/42/54, 13 hours) leaving daily at 6:45pm stopping at Kuala Lipis, Jerantut and Gemas. Two daily local trains stop at almost every station to Kuala Lipis (RM19.20, 13 hours). There are also five local trains a day that go as far as Gua Musang (RM7.20, five to six hours).

KTM has a ticket office (counter 5) at Kota Bharu's Jln Hamzah bus station.

❶ Getting Around

The airport is 9km from town. You can take bus 8 or 9 from the old central market; a taxi costs RM20.

Trishaws can still be seen on the city streets, though they are not as common as they once were. Prices are negotiable but reckon on around RM5 and upwards for a short journey of up to 1km.

Around Kota Bharu

PANTAI CAHAYA BULAN (PCB)

Kota Bharu's main beach was once known as Pantai Cinta Berahi, or the Beach of Passionate Love. In keeping with Islamic sensibilities, it's now known as Pantai Cahaya Bulan, or Moonlight Beach, but most people call it PCB. The beach is nice, but is ruined somewhat by 25 nearly identical stall-type restaurants serving exactly the same deep-fried seafood stacked in greasy rows.

There are two places worth staying at PCB: the **Perdana Resort** (✆7774 4000; perdana resort.com.my; chalets from RM120-205 incl breakfast; ❋❄☎❋) is just off the main road (hang a right at the sign reading 'charmingly different') and offers lovely beachfront chalets with beautiful floor-to-ceiling windows in a bucolic garden setting, and an open-air restaurant. The sprawling 95-unit **PCB Resort** (✆774 4040, 796 4040; www.pcbresort.com.my; chalets from RM59-340; ❋❄☎) has chalets plus cheaper flats for travellers on a budget.

The road leading to PCB is quite pretty, especially by bicycle, and there are a number of small batik shops and workshops along the way.

TUMPAT'S TEMPLES

North of Kota Bharu, the Tumpat district is Malaysia's culturally porous hinterland, neither wholly Malay nor Thai, with a dash of Chinese culture thrown in for good measure. Numerous Buddhist temples are found all over the region, and **Wesak Day** (a celebration of Buddha's life, usually held in April or May) is a particularly good time to visit. The area is serviced by some local buses (details below); alternatively, you could hire a local tour guide.

Supposedly one of the largest Buddhist temples in Southeast Asia, **Wat Phothivihan** boasts a 40m-long reclining Buddha statue, erected in 1973. There are some smaller shrines within the grounds, as well as a canteen and a rest house for use by sincere devotees, for a donation. To get here, take bus 19 or 27 from Kota Bharu to Chabang Empat. Get off at the crossroads and turn left (southwest). Walk 3.5km along this road, through postcard villages and paddies, until you reach Kampung Jambu and the reclining Buddha (about one hour).

At Chabang Empat, if you take the turn to the right (north) at the light in front of the police station, you will come to **Wat Kok Seraya** after about 1km, which houses a modest standing female Buddha. While the temple's architecture is Thai, the female Buddha is more Chinese, which is probably attributable to most Buddhists here

Around Kota Bharu

being of Chinese origin. Continuing north about 4km towards Tumpat, you will come to **Wat Pikulthong**, housing an impressive gold mosaic standing Buddha. You can get to both on bus 19; continue past Chabang Empat and ask the driver to let you off.

Around 4km north of Chabang Empat near the village of Kampung Bukit Tanah is **Wat Maisuwankiri**. A richly decorated dragon boat surrounded by a channel of murky water constitutes the 'floating temple', but of more interest may be the preserved body of a former abbot kept on somewhat morbid

public display. The bus from Kota Bharu to Pengkalan Kubor stops outside the temple.

Also worth a look is **Wat Matchinmaram** with its magnificent 50m-high seated Buddha (more Chinese than Thai, but also decorated with an Indian-origin dharma wheel), allegedly the largest of its type in Asia. Just across the road from here is **Sala Pattivetaya**, a Thai temple and village complex dotted with colourful statues. They are located about 2km south of Tumpat.

KELANTAN'S WILD INTERIOR

To really understand Kelantan, you need to penetrate its wild and wooly southern jungle interior, accessible via the so-called Jungle Railway ('so-called' as much of the once-verdant jungle has been hacked down to make way for palm-oil plantations). Still, some jungle does remain, and bits and pieces of Peninsular Malaysia's mountainous backbone still evoke a feeling of tropical frontier adventure.

Lined with flowers, trees and a mixture of old and new style *kampung* (village) houses, the pretty jungle town of **Dabong** is an excellent exploration base. The town is about three hours by train from Tumpat and has a few restaurants, shops and guesthouses. Dabong village elder Abedin owns **Rumah Rehat Dabong** (☏019-960 6789; r from RM25; ✳☏), a 1980s longhouse with decent rooms and private showers. Abedin also rents rooms in a larger house just a few blocks away that has a more modern vibe to it.

Nearby village Jelawang is where you'll find **Homestay Kampung Jelawang** (☏010 9936 1152; RM50, includes meals), the immaculately clean four-bedroom home of the Kak-Dah family. Guests of the family are invited to eat meals and participate in a variety of activities, from caving and hiking to real-life stuff tapping rubber and making banana crackers. The price includes meals and a room with the family and their long haired cat Bingtang ('star').

There are several caves in the limestone outcrops a few kilometres southeast of Dabong; **Gua Ikan** (Fish Cave) is the most accessible, but the most impressive is **Stepping Stone Cave**, a narrow 30m corridor through a limestone wall that leads to a hidden grotto and on to **Kris Cave**. These latter two should not be attempted by claustrophobics.

About 15km from Dabong is **Gunung Stong State Park**. Named for the 1422m-high Gunung Stong mountain, the park offers amazing hiking, swimming and trekking opportunities. Next to the mountain, the park's star attractions are its waterfalls, located a 20-minute climb past the park's main resort; a further 45 minutes of climbing brings you to the top of the falls and a camp site, from which you can make longer excursions to the mountain's summit and the upper falls. Most tour companies divide the trek into three checkpoints. A combination of jungle mist and mountain fog can make for hazy conditions, but on good days you get the sense you're climbing over clouds humming with the screams of animals in the jungle below.

Should you decide to stay in the park, **Gunung Stong State Park Resort** (☏019-919 9898; d RM20, chalets from RM100, camping RM20; ✳) has some fine chalets. The best of these is the VIP Chalet (RM120), which offers a beautiful balcony hanging over the river, a comfortable queen-sized bed and a TV. Non-VIP chalets are equally nice, though lacking the TV and riverfront real estate. There's also camping available.

You can explore the area via a tour organised in Kota Bharu or just head down yourself by train and hire a taxi from Dabong station. With excellent English skills and boundless enthusiasm for the area, local guide **Bukhari 'Bob' Mat** (bobtg6084@gmail.com) leads caving, hiking and rafting tours all around the area.

PASIR BELANDA

The privately run **Pasir Belanda Homestay** (☎747 7046; www.kampungstay.com; Jln PCB; s/d/tr RM149/179/199; ✸☎) may well be one of the nicest accommodation options in Kelantan. Three sizes of traditional Malay homes have been decked out in smooth sheeting and with little luxuries such as coffee makers. You're close to the beach and can lose yourself there, or just watch the stars from under your *kampung* (village)–style awning.

To get here, take bus 10 (RM1.30) from behind Kampung Kraftangan (Handicraft Village) in Kota Bharu. A taxi costs RM30, and Pasir Belanda will arrange a pick-up from Kota Bharu with advanced notice.

EAST COAST ISLANDS

Pulau Perhentian

The Perhentians are a tropical paradise, boasting waters simultaneously electric teal and crystal clear; jungles thick and fecund, and beaches with sand so white from a distance it might pass for snow. At night bonfires and kerosene lamps on the beach and phosphorescence in the water make pin holes in the velvety black, the stars soar above you and the real world becomes something like a bad dream. Most people come to snorkel, dive or do nothing at all.

There are two main islands, Kecil ('Small'), popular with the younger backpacker crowd, and Besar ('Large'), with higher standards of accommodation and a quieter, more relaxed ambience. The quick hop between the two costs around RM20.

While you can usually find a beach party, the Perhentians are a long way from having a Thai-style party atmosphere. Alcohol is available at many restaurants.

Even paradise has its problems, though. The Perhentians are finding it increasingly difficult to deal with the by-product of increasing tourist traffic, and the sight (and smell) of burning piles of rubbish, especially plastic bottles, is unfortunately common.

The islands basically shut down during the monsoon (usually from mid-November to mid-February), although some hotels – especially in Coral Bay – remain open for hardier travellers. There are no banks or ATMs on the islands, so bring cash. Prices quoted here are for high season.

🏃 Activities

Diving & Snorkelling

There are coral reefs off both islands and around nearby uninhabited islands, Pulau Susu Dara in particular. The best bets for snorkelling off the coast are the northern end of Long Beach on Kecil, and the point in front of Coral View Island Resort on Besar. You can swim out to a living coral reef right in front of Tuna Bay Island Resort on Kecil. Most chalets organise snorkelling trips for around RM40 per person (more or less depending on the size of the group) and also rent out equipment.

For scuba divers there are several operations on both islands; prices are pretty uniform. At the time of research, open-water certification went from RM850 to RM1100, while dives cost around RM80 to RM125, with discounts for multiple dives. Many of the operators below also run dive excursions out to Pulau Redang. Reputable dive schools include the following:

Quiver Dive Team DIVING
(Map p284; ☎012-213 8885; www.quiver-perhentian .com) On Long Beach (Kecil), next to Bubu Resort; also operates from a **lot** (Map p284) next to Shari-la in Coral Bay.

Spice Divers DIVING
(Map p284; ☎096-911 555; www.spicedivers.net) On Kecil; offers two dives for RM140 and a full open-water course for RM950. Advanced courses, rescue courses and nitrox available.

Turtle Bay Divers DIVING
(Map p284; ☎019-913 6647, 019-333 6647; www. turtlebaydivers.com) With a main office in Long Beach on Kecil, Turtle Bay offers half-day discovery dives (RM200) and three- to four-day PADI courses (RM950). With a veritable UN of dive-masters, Turtle Bay has all linguistic bases covered. Also has an **office** (Map p284) at Mama's Chalet on Besar.

Watercolours DIVING
(Map p284; ☎691 1850; www.watercoloursworld. com) By Paradise Island Resort on Besar.

Pulau Perhentian

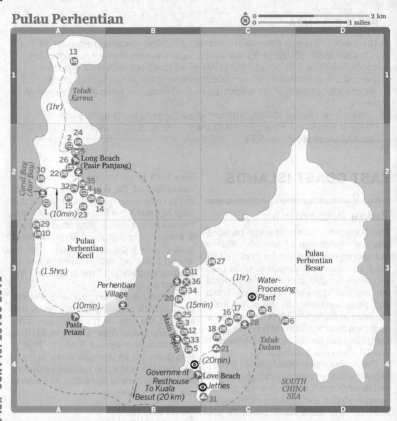

Divers with kids will be interested in their 'bubble making' course, a mini-dive course specifically for eight and nine year olds.

Panorama Divers DIVING
(Map p284; ☑019-648-5600; panoramadiver@gmail.com) This superfriendly Long Beach dive shop offers some of the best dive packages, including full PADI courses for RM1150 (includes accommodation) and three dives a day (and night dives upon request). Single dives are between RM70 and RM80. Check out their five-dive package for RM335.

Seahorse DIVING
(Map p284; ☑019-982 6667; facebook/seahorse) On Besar, just north of D'Ayumi House. As well as PADI courses, Seahorse offers discover scuba courses from RM150.

Pro Diver's World DIVING
(Map p284; ☑691 1705; www.prodiversworld.com) Connected to Coral View Resort on Besar;

offers regular 'free room for dive students' specials in conjunction with the resort, and free diving on birthdays. Tons of packages on its website.

Leisure World Divers DIVING
(Map p284; ☑019-987 5977; leisureworlddivers@gmail.com) Connected to Arwana Resort on Besar; offers underwater camera rental (RM50) and dive packages.

Angel Divers DIVING
(Map p284; ☑019-923 8840; angeldiversperhantian@live.com) Run from a two-storey, red wooden hut at Coral Bay on Kecil; offers fun dives from RM60 and PADI courses for around RM900.

Alu Alu Divers DIVING
(Map p284; ☑691 1650; www.alualudivers.com) At Bayu Dive Lodge on Besar.

Pulau Perhentian

Activities, Courses & Tours

	Alu Alu Divers	(see 7)
1	Angel Divers	A2
	Flora Bay Divers	(see 18)
	Leisure World Divers	(see 6)
	Panorama Divers	(see 26)
	Pro Diver's World	(see 11)
2	Quiver Dive Team	A2
	Quiver Dive Team	(see 29)
3	Seahorse	B4
4	Spice Divers	A2
	Turtle Bay Divers	(see 13)
	Turtle Bay Divers	(see 20)
	Watercolours	(see 34)

Sleeping

5	Abdul's Chalets	B4
6	Arwana Perhentian Resort	C4
	Aur Bay Chalet	(see 1)
7	Bayu Dive Lodge	C4
8	B'First Chalet	C3
9	Bubu Resort	A2
10	Butterfly Chalet	A3
11	Coral View Island Resort	B3
12	D'Ayumni House	B4
13	D'Lagoon Chalets	A1
14	D'Rock Garden Resort	A2
15	Ewan's Place	A2
16	Fauna Beach Chalet	C4
17	Flora 2	C4
18	Flora Bay Resort	C4
19	Lemon Grass	A2
20	Mama's Place	B3
21	Mandalica Beach Resort	C4
22	Matahari Chalets	A2
	Maya Guest House	(see 1)
23	Mohsin Chalet Bungalows	A2
24	Moonlight Beach Resort	A2
25	New Cocohut	B3
26	Panorama Diver & Chalet	A2
27	Perhentian Island Resort	C3
28	Samudra Beach Chalet	C3
29	Senja Bay Resort	A3
30	Shari-la Island Resort	A2
31	Teluk Ke Ke Camp Site	C4
32	Tropicana Backpacker Inn	A2
33	Tuna Bay Island Resort	B4
34	Watercolours Paradise Resort	B3
35	World Cafe & Chalets	A2

Eating

36	Reef Chalets	B3

Flora Bay Divers   DIVING
(Map p284; ☏691 1661; www.florabaydivers.com)
At Teluk Dalam on Besar.

Hiking

There's plenty of hiking on both islands. On Kecil, the jungle track between Long Beach and Coral Bay is an easy, signposted 15-minute walk. A longer track runs mostly along the shore between Coral Bay and Pasir Petani, and an even longer and more rugged path goes between Long Beach and Teluk Kerma.

Besar has excellent hiking, including a long and hilly track cutting from north to south from close to Perhentian Island Resort to Teluk Dalam at Fauna Beach Chalet. The hike from Love Beach to Teluk Dalam is also pretty rugged, though somewhat shorter.

More rugged tracks can get washed out in heavy rains, so use common sense. Hot and humid is the norm, so bring plenty of water, and don't hike at night without a flashlight.

Sleeping & Eating

BESAR

MAIN BEACH

Perhentian Besar's main beach stretches along the west coast of the island to the southern tip, interrupted by several rocky headlands – at low tide you can walk around them on the sand, otherwise you'll have to use a water taxi. A smaller beach taken up by Perhentian Island Resort is accessible via a footbridge on the northern end of the beach.

TOP CHOICE Reef Chalets   CHALET $$
(Map p284; ☏691 1762, 019-981 6762; chalets RM100-290; ❀☎) An absolute find, this family-owned chalet resort offers 12 beautiful chalets set along the beach and surrounding a beautifully maintained jungle garden featuring feather-soft grass and trees filled with lemurs, monkeys, birds and bats. The owners Rashida, Kamil and Kadir are extremely friendly and laid-back, and rent out canoes and snorkelling equipment, and will be happy to help you plan your stay. At the time of writing, Reef's was building

FINDING THE RIGHT BEACH

With a plethora of amazing beaches, your biggest dilemma on the Perhentians may well be choosing the right one. Knowing the lay of the land will help you decide. A narrow strait separates Perhentian Besar from Perhentian Kecil, so hopping between the two is just a matter of flagging down a boat.

Main Beach (Besar)

A good selection of accommodations and a long stretch of white sand that's almost as lovely (and less prone to currents) as Long Beach on Kecil. There's no shortage of good spots to explore by walking either north or south. There's more of a family vibe happening on the big island than elsewhere.

Teluk Dalam (Besar)

The big island's 'southern bite', this circular bay has white-sand beaches and excellent accommodation in all budget ranges. There are a few good restaurants, and good snorkelling spots on the bay's western edge.

Long Beach (Kecil)

Long Beach offers the best variety of budget accommodation and restaurants, from cookie-cutter BBQ beachfront joints to the excellent Bubu Restaurant. It also has the prettiest beach and the party-est vibe. This brings crowds, and Long Beach can sometimes feel a bit overtouristed. And the beautiful beach has some serious rip tides; there were two drowning deaths in early 2012 alone.

Coral Bay (Kecil)

A good variety of accommodation in all budget ranges makes Coral Bay the spot for those wanting to stay within walking distance of Long Beach's party vibe without being in it. Most of the resorts on the sheltered beach are open year-round. Coral Bay is more rocky than sandy, and an ongoing construction boom threatens to diminish the quaintness of this once-quiet spot.

Teluk Kerma (Kecil)

Home to a single accommodation option (D'Lagoon Chalets), this small bay has it going on when it comes to peace and quiet. There's great snorkelling, and a few equally isolated beaches within walking distance. But it's an hour's hike to your nearest neighbour (Long Beach), and if you stay out after dark your options for getting home will be limited and pricey (water taxis charge double after sundown).

an additional set of accommodation in the treetops. All chalets have sea views; some are fan-cooled, while more expensive ones have air-conditioning.

Abdul's Chalets CHALET $$
(Map p284; ☎019-912 7303; www.abdulchalet.com; s/d from RM80/260; ❄☎) Humble Abdul's has undergone a fairly substantial renovation since our last visit; Abdul's still has fan-cooled huts for RM80, but now there's a bevy of higher grade accommodation, from Garden View chalets with air-con for RM150 up to a full air-con, sea-view family room for RM240 and sea-view suites (with TV to compete with the sea view) for RM260. Many of the newer chalets have brand-new fur-

nishing, and smart-looking wood paneled walls. The newly redone dining area, serving freshly caught fish and a variety of Malay and Western dishes, is also pretty snazzy.

Tuna Bay Island Resort RESORT $$
(Map p284; ☎690 2902; www.tunabay.com.my; d/ tr/f from RM220/270/370; ❄@☎) This gathering of pristine chalets perches on a lovely stretch of white sand, with others set in the pretty gardens or facing the jungle behind. You can wade out to a living coral reef just offshore, and afterwards relax in the islands' best restaurant and only authentic cocktail bar with a Long Island ice tea or a cappuccino. Stick around for dinner, when Tuna Bay serves mulitcourse BBQ feasts

featuring prawn, squid, barracuda, snapper and more. Chicken and beef are also available. The resort is very popular with families.

D'Ayumni House
HUTS $

(Map p284; ☎019-436 4463, 691 1680; www.d-ayumnihouse.blogspot.com; dm RM55, r RM80-200; ❄@🛜) A pretty wooden house rises over a series of low-slung, teak-chic chalets and bungalows. Popular with divers and those seeking a bit of budget backpacker vibe in Besar. Owner Ms Lee is a font of information, and can arrange ongoing travel all over Southeast Asia. She also has a little shop and cafe with a moonlight deck.

Mama's Place
CHALET $$

(Map p284; ☎013-984 0232, 019-985 3359; www.mamaschalet.com.my; chalets fan RM65-85, air-con seaview RM160, family air-con seaview RM350) This sprawling property has 43 chalets on the beach. All are comfortable and clean, and the more expensive ones have sea views and air-conditioners. Mama's also has an alcohol-free restaurant serving local dishes.

Watercolours Paradise Resort
CHALET $

(Map p284; ☎691 1850; www.watercoloursworld.com; r RM70-130; ❄) This friendly resort has clean chalets operated under the same management as the attached Watercolours dive centre, and is about the best value on Besar. The 'Impiani' expansion is a little more upscale, but more in terms of price (RM150 to RM240) than actual quality of lodging.

Coral View Island Resort
RESORT $$

(Map p284; ☎697 4943; www.coralviewislandresort.com; r/ste from RM140/550; ❄@) Now boasting 101 chalets, the ever-expanding Coral View has a great location at the northern end of the beach. The accommodation is all lovely, from the simple fan-cooled two-bed chalets to the rather smart air-conditioned beachfront suites. At the time of research management was putting in another more backpacker-friendly guesthouse, with single and double rooms at budget rates. Coral View has good restaurants serving Asian and Western dishes (lunch RM30), and shops.

New Cocohut
CHALET $$

(Map p284; ☎691 1811; www.perhentianislandcocohut.com; r RM160-330; ❄🛜) Cocohut has a good choice of rooms including pleasant beachside chalets and a two-storey longhouse, which has some great views from the

---

LOCAL VOICE: BIRGIT WEBER

An instructor and assistant manager of the Turtle Bay Dive Shop, Birgit Weber has over a quarter of a century diving experience. Birgit chatted with us about different dive spots around the country.

What can I expect to see while diving around Perhentian?

Anything from turtles to black-tipped reef sharks, plus many varieties of stingrays and parrot fish. If it lives on the reef, you'll see it here.

What's the best spot for diving around the Perhentian Islands?

Sugar Wreck is a huge shipwreck, and every year there seem to be more and more fish around it. It's only 18m deep, so any diver who's taken the open-water course can go down there. It's also only 20 minutes from Long Beach. The Pinnacle is also great. You can see a huge variety of marine life in one place.

What's the best spot in Malaysia for the advanced diver?

Sipadan Island (p359), off the coast of Sabah in East Malaysia. It's an oceanic island as opposed to being on the continental shelf, so it drops down quite deep. You'll see dozens of turtles and sharks. The sheer number of marine animals you'll see is overwhelming. You need a permit to dive there, so book in advance.

How about for the beginner?

Definitely Perhentian. The dive sites are shallow and generally have lighter currents. They're also nearby, meaning less time on the boat. One of them you can even swim to!

What's your take on Tioman (p243) diving?

Tioman sites are a lot like those in Perhentian, but the dive sites are further from the shore, meaning more time in the boat. Plus, Tioman is closer to Singapore and KL, so the island tends to be more commercial and crowded. I prefer Perhentian myself.

VOLUNTOURISM IN THE PERHENTIANS

Interested in doing more than just sitting on the beach? Want to give back to the precious and varied marine life of the Perhentians? **Ecoteer** (www.ecoteerresponsibletravel. com) operates day-long to multiweek programs that incorporate snorkelling with data-gathering, beach-combing with beach-cleaning and homestays with local families. Expect to pay around RM664 for a week-long experience, which includes boat transfer, three meals a day, accommodation and all equipment. Prices drop during the low season. Check the website for details and testimonials.

upstairs balcony. The cheapest rooms are in the rear and closest to the generator. Coco-hut also manages another property called Cozy Chalet.

Perhentian Island Resort RESORT $$$
(Map p284; ☑ 691 1111; www.perhentianislandresort. net; 3-day/2-night packages RM378-1040; ❄❅❆) Offering a bewildering variety of set three-day/two-night packages, this luxurious option overlooks perhaps the best beach on the islands – a beautiful half-moon bay with good coral around the points on either side. There's a huddle of comfortable bungalows and a first-class restaurant serving Western and Malay dishes.

Teluk Ke Ke Camp Site CAMPGROUND $
(Map p284; camp site per person RM10) Camping is available at Teluk Ke Ke Camp Site, a 10-minute walk south of the government rest house. Its a beautiful slice of beach on the southern tip of the peninsula. Snorkelling equipment rental is available, and there's also a tiny restaurant on the beach.

TELUK DALAM

An easily missed track leads from behind the second jetty near Love Beach over the hill northeast to Teluk Dalam, a secluded bay with a shallow beach, but it's easier to hire a boat than to walk.

Mandalica Beach Resort CAMPING $
(Map p284; ☑ 019-983 7690; camping per camp site RM50) The extrafriendly Halim family lives on a lovely stretch of white sand on Te-luk Dalam's western end and offers covered camp sites with showers and toilets. There's a small cafe serving juices, amazing roti and barbecue, and the family rents all manner of aquatic toys from snorkels to kayaks to banana boats. The family arranges pick up from all over the Perhentians, fishing trips and just about anything else. Ida's banana chocolate roti is worth the walk across the island!

Flora Bay Resort CHALET $$
(Map p284; ☑ 691 1666; www.florabayresort.com; r RM60-210; ❄@❆) The aptly named Flora Bay (flowers abound!) has a variety of options at the back of the beach, ranging from hill-view fan huts for RM60 to 'deluxe' air-con beach chalets for RM210. **Flora 2** (Map p284), an extension of Flora Bay, is a little further along the beach, with a smaller range of pretty much identical chalets, but only Flora 1 has wireless. A restaurant was in the works at the time of our visit.

Bayu Dive Lodge CHALET $$
(Map p284; ☑ 691 1650; www.alualudivers.com; r RM68-213; ❄) A collection of smartly furnished, deep-brown chalets are situated around a beautifully manicured central garden courtyard. All rooms are lovely, with the more expensive ones having air-con and hot showers. Only open during the high season. Alu Alu Divers operates from here.

Arwana Perhentian Resort RESORT $$
(Map p284; ☑ 778 0888; www.arwanaperhentian. com.my; dm/d/ste from RM30/120/580; ❄❅) This huge, upmarket resort occupies the eastern flank of Teluk Dalam, although it has no beach frontage itself. The broad array of rooms includes, surprisingly, two dorm blocks at the very back. The cheaper 'standard' rooms are a bit pokey, but more expensive ones are decently furnished (some with balconies). Facilities include a snooker room, karaoke booths and a dive centre.

B'First Chalet CHALET $
(Map p284; ☑ 013-295 5138, 013-924 5946; r RM60-120) The Azman family runs this small resort and restaurant on the eastern edge of the beach. Fan-cooled chalets are comfortable and have two beds; air-con chalets have a double and a single bed. The restaurant serves genuine Malaysian food and barbecue every night.

Samudra Beach Chalet CHALET $
(Map p284; ☑691 1677; www.samudrabeachchalet.
com; r RM50-140) Samudra has traditional
Malaysian A-frame chalets. Slightly dark on
the inside, cheaper ones have fans; the air-
conditioned family room with two double
beds is a decent deal.

Fauna Beach Chalet CHALET $$
(Map p284; ☑691 7607; r RM50-140; ❄) Sitting
on an attractive stretch of sand, Fauna has a
choice of the usual creaky wooden huts and
more comfortable sea-view bungalows.

PULAU PERHENTIAN KECIL

LONG BEACH

TOP CHOICE Bubu Resort RESORT $$$
(Map p284; ☑03-2142 6688; www.buburesort.
com.my; Long Beach; r from RM415; ❄⦿) At
the northern end of the bay, this top-end
option offers 38 rooms in a modern, three-
storey setting overlooking Long Beach itself
and a gorgeous restaurant in *palapa* style
(open-sided, with a thatched roof made of
dried palm leaves). All rooms face the beach
and offer similar mod cons, including air-
con, hot showers and full wireless internet
access. Most rooms have balconies, and all
feature morning sun. The restaurant is the
highest-end eatery on Kecil, serving – in our
opinion – the best seafood BBQ in eastern
Malaysia. Even if you can't afford to stay
here, you owe it to yourself to stop by Bubu's
bar for a fruity beach drink.

TOP CHOICE D'Rock Garden Resort CHALET $$
(Map p284; ☑012-325 2162; Long Beach; d with/
without bathroom from RM120/45, deluxe r RM325)
Steep steps running up the southern end of
Long Beach will get you to this vertiginous
place on the rocks. Cheaper rooms are fan
cooled, and only the deluxe have hot show-
ers. The position of the huts (even the cheap-
er ones) overlooking the long sweep of Long
Beach is fabulous. D'Rock also has a little
restaurant offering the usual cuisine and the
same lovely view.

TOP CHOICE World Cafe & Chalets CHALET $$$
(Map p284; ☑016-260 3546; www.buburesort.
com.my; chalet d from RM450; ❄⦿) Managed
by the same people who run Bubu Resort,
this is another high-end option on otherwise
backpacker-y Long Beach. The six air-conditioned chalets have private terraces, hot-
water showers and huge, comfortable beds.
Even if you're not staying here, it's worth a

visit to the World Cafe, a *palapa* restaurant
sitting on the beach and serving coffee, cocktails and an eclectic mix of European foods.
Room prices include breakfast for two and
two evening cocktails per person at either
the World Cafe or Bubu. Low-season discounts available.

Panorama Diver & Chalet CHALET $
(Map p284; ☑691 1590; www.panormaperhentian.
com; r RM30-150; ❄@) A favourite with divers
and snorkellers, this ultrarelaxed chalet,
restaurant and dive shop (p285) is set back
a bit from Long Beach. Rooms range from
fan-cooled doubles to air-conditioned chalets. Nicest is the family room, which has
two queen-sized beds, near-wraparound
windows, a balcony and whimsical furniture. What makes Panorama so special
are the dive packages, with divers getting
sweet deals (up to 40% off) on all rooms.
Panorama's restaurant is especially good,
serving Asian and Western cuisine, not to
mention some of the best pizza in eastern
Malaysia.

Mohsin Chalet Bungalows BUNGALOW $$
(Map p284; ☑012-932 1929; facebook.com/mohsinchalet;
dm RM25 d with/without air-con RM100/130)
Mohsin's chalets are set on a steep hill on
the southern end of the beach (though the
path leading here is just behind the World
Cafe). The accommodation is fairly stand-
ard, but the ambience of the restaurant, the
views, and the surreal friendliness of the staff
– who'll greet you welcome drink in hand –
make this place well worth spending a few
days.

Matahari Chalets CHALET $
(Map p284; ☑019-914 2883; www.mataharichalet.
com; r RM25-120) Set back among the trees
with a walkway to the beach, Matahari is
one of the better chalet operations. It has a
good range of accommodation, from simple
huts with shared bathroom to spacious bun-
galows. There is also a restaurant, a shop
and a moneychanger.

Moonlight Beach Resort BUNGALOW $
(Map p284; ☑013-9827 457; dm RM20; r with
shared bathroom RM40; fan r RM60-70, air-con r
RM100; ❄) Located on the northern end of
the beach right by the jetty, Moonlight has
longhouse rooms, dorm rooms and small
chalets. Moonlight's staff are friendly, its A-
frame huts are fairly spruce and its regular
rooms are comfortable enough.

Lemon Grass
BUNGALOW $

(Map p284; ☏019-981 8393; chalets from RM40) At the southern tip of Long Beach, Lemon Grass has friendly management and 16 no-frills fan huts with shared bathrooms. There are great views from the verandah at reception and nice secluded spots to sit and gaze out to sea. All huts are the same price; try to get one with a sea view.

TELUK KERMA

TOP CHOICE D'Lagoon Chalets
HUT $

(Map p284; ☏019-985 7089; Teluk Kerma; camp site RM10, dm RM20, chalet RM60; tr RM150) Teluk Kerma is a pretty, isolated bay with fine coral and a location that can't be beat for tranquility. The folks at D'Lagoon have taken full advantage of their position as the bay's sole spot to create something right out of Peter Pan. Accommodation ranges from a longhouse with dorm beds to simple chalets on stilts to a honeymoon treehouse. Among the activities on offer are snorkelling, shark- and turtle-watching trips, jungle hikes to remote beaches, and the island's only zip line. Management will also arrange local music at night on request. Make sure you tell the boat captain to drop you here – otherwise it's an hour's hike from the Long Beach jetty. There's an on-site restaurant serving decent western and Malay food for breakfast, lunch and dinner.

CORAL BAY

A 15 minute walk west from the Long Beach Jetty takes you to Coral Bay.

TOP CHOICE Shari-la Island Resort
RESORT $$

(Map p284; ☏691 1500; www.shari-la.com; budget r RM60; r/ste from RM180/320; ✳@☎) Situated on the northern end of Coral Bay, and sprawling back into the jungle trail, this place offers a surprisingly posh package for the money. A-frame chalets are well furnished with wooden decks and comfy beds, the suites have satellite-equipped TVs and full bathrooms, and the budget rooms are some of the best on the island, with three beds each and air-conditioning (bathrooms are shared). Most chalets are equipped with solar hot-water showers, and Shari-la has its own secluded beach. One of the few places in Coral Bay that has 24-hour electricity. The onsite restaurant (Malay, Western and Thai dishes) is also quite good.

Butterfly Chalet
BUNGALOW $

(Map p284; r RM50) A series of basic wooden huts perched precariously on the headland, this place is reached by a steep clamber over the rocks next to Senja Bay Resort. It's all a bit tattered, but the setting, among blooming gardens and with superb views across the bay, is beautiful. There's no phone, electricity goes off during the day, and the sign reading 'don't be shy, check in by yourself' makes this one of the quirkier spots on the island.

Tropicana Backpacker Inn
BUNGALOW $

(Map p284; ☏6911 380; Coral Bay; dm/r RM15/40-80; ☎) Forty bungalows are spread out over a hillside here, equidistant between Coral Bay and Long Beach. The single rooms have double beds with mosquito netting and cold showers; higher priced rooms are fairly plain for the price. Dorms have eight beds, two bathrooms and screened-in windows that might keep the mosquitoes out. Management also makes cash advances on Visa and Mastercard, for those who have run out of cash mid visit.

Senja Bay Resort
RESORT $

(Map p284; ☏691 1799; www.senjabay.com; Coral Bay; fan/air-con/seaview & air-con r from RM100 /150/200; ✳@☎) The facilities at this cluster of bungalows and huts are a little more polished than many of the alternatives, and the family setting – a beachfront restaurant playing smooth jazz all day – may suit travellers wanting a little quiet.

Ewan's Place
HUT, CAFE $

(Map p284; ☏014-817 8303; Coral Bay; d RM50; ☎) Cookie-cutter pre-fab huts on the path leading from Coral Bay to Long Beach; rooms inside are clean and colourful, with comfortable double beds, mosquito netting and cold-water showers. The attached cafe serves the usual variety of everything.

Aur Bay Chalet
LONGHOUSE $

(Map p284; ☏013-9950817; Coral Bay; r RM30) Small but comfortable rooms with double beds, fans, cold showers and mosquito netting set in a longhouse structure just south of the Coral Bay Jetty.

Maya Guest House
GUESTHOUSE, CAFE $

(Map p284; ☏019-970 4426; Coral Bay; RM60/80 garden/seaview) Twelve fan-cooled rooms on Coral Bay. Leads ecofriendly snorkelling tours around the area and has an alcohol-free cafe.

ℹ️ Information

There is a RM5 conservation fee for everyone entering the marine park around the Perhentians; this fee will likely be tacked onto the price of your ticket at the jetty in Kuala Besut.

EMERGENCY The only medical facility on the islands is the very basic clinic. Dive operators and some of the bigger resorts can offer first aid if needed.

INTERNET ACCESS Wireless access is increasingly ubiquitous on Perhentian, and a few spots on Long Beach have internet service for between RM20 to RM24 per hour.

MONEY There are no banks or ATMs on the islands. If you run out money you can get a cash advance on your Visa or Mastercard at the Tropicana Backpacker Inn.

TELEPHONE There are no public telephones on the islands, but some hotels will allow you to make calls from their mobile phones for a fee. Mobile phone numbers for resorts given here may change from one season to the next, and some have no phones, but travel agents in Kuala Besut will have the latest contact details.

ℹ️ Getting There & Away

Speedboats (adult/child RM70/35 return, 30 to 40 minutes) run several times a day between Kuala Besut and the Perhentians from 8.30am to 5.30pm, although you can expect delays or cancellations if the weather is bad or if there aren't enough passengers. Tickets are sold by several travel agents around Kuala Besut. The boats will drop you off at any of the beaches.

In the other direction, speedboats depart from the islands daily at about 8am, noon and 4pm. It's a good idea to let the owner of your guesthouse know a day before you leave so they can arrange a pick-up. If the water is rough or tides are low you may be ferried from the beach on a small boat to your mainland-bound craft; you'll have to pay around RM3 for this.

ℹ️ Getting Around

While there are some trails around the islands, the easiest way to go from beach to beach or island to island is by boat. Chalet owners can arrange a taxi boat. From island to island, the trip costs RM20 per boat, and a jaunt from one beach to another on the same island usually costs about RM15. Prices double at night.

Pulau Lang Tengah

Tiny, idyllic Lang Tengah lies roughly halfway between Pulau Redang and Pulau Perhentian, and with only three resorts to choose from, it's a much quieter, less-developed place than its better known neighbours.

🛏️ Sleeping

The island's three resorts are spaced out on the west coast, and offer a bewildering variety of package deals; unless otherwise stated, those listed in this section are for three days and two nights.

Redang Lang Island Resort RESORT $$$ (☎623 9911; www.malaysiaislandresort.com; s/d from RM379/609; ✸) Offers basic but neat wooden chalets just a few steps from the beach, with a common TV lounge and karaoke bar. Cheaper rooms have no hot showers. Snorkelling and diving packages are available, and prices are slightly higher on weekends.

EAST COAST ISLANDS, KELANTAN & TERENGGANU PULAU LANG TENGAH

GATEWAY TO PARADISE

Poor Kuala Besut! Though a lovely seaside town, few indeed are the visitors who'll spend more than an hour or two here. Alas, such is the fate of the town whose claim to fame is being the gateway to Malaysia's best-known paradise.

Still, there are worse fates than getting stuck here overnight. The restaurants and coffee shops are all located on and around the jetty (where you can also rent snorkelling equipment – usually good quality – for use on the islands). The town's few hotels are also scattered around the jetty. The best of these is the **Samudera Hotel** (☎697 9326; www.kekal-samudera.com; Jln Pantai; r from RM65), which has large, simple rooms and private bathrooms.

There's no direct bus from Kota Bharu, so if you're coming from the north you'll need to switch at Jerteh or Pasir Puteh. A taxi from Kota Bharu is around RM80. The bus from Kuala Terengganu is RM8, and a taxi will set you back around RM100. There are also two daily buses from KL (RM40, nine hours). Many travel agents run minibus services to Kuala Besut from various tourist hotspots around Malaysia.

D'Coconut Lagoon
RESORT $$$

(☑03-4252 6686; www.dcoconutlagoon.com; r RM 465-888; ☀) The smallest of the resorts has fairly plain but comfy chalets with fridges, TVs and other mod cons, set around an attractive pool. These prices are per night, various package deals are also available.

Lang Sari Resort
RESORT $$$

(☑03-2166 1318; www.langsari.com; s/d from RM 348/478; ☀☀) Huge wooden chalets look over strings of lanterns, the beach and guests relaxing in hammocks. Activities include canoeing, turtle- or shark-watching, or just napping in the shade.

❶ Getting There & Away

Between April and August, ferries to Lang Tengah leave from the jetty in Merang at 10am and noon, and from the island at 8.30am and 2pm. From September to March they leave Merang at 12.30pm and depart the island at 2pm. If you're travelling independently, the one-way fare for adults/children is RM80/40.

Pulau Redang

Redang's position within a marine park lends itself to excellent diving and snorkelling, and you can easily lose yourself in between the golden sunlight, cackling jungle and lapping waves. Unfortunately, it's difficult to visit outside of package tours, which tend to be regimented affairs with arrival lectures and set times for meals, snorkelling and 'leisure'. It's popular with groups of young Malaysians and weekending Singaporeans.

Note that Pulau Redang basically shuts down from 1 November to 1 March; the best time to visit is from mid-March to late September. There is a RM5 conservation fee for entering the marine reserve, usually payable at your resort.

🛏 Sleeping & Eating

Accommodation on Pulau Redang needs to be arranged in advance. Tour companies sell packages for all the resorts, and several of the resorts have offices in Kuala Terengganu. Unless otherwise stated, all package prices in this section are for three days and two nights and are per person, based on two sharing, and include boat transfer from Merang, all meals and two snorkelling trips.

PASIR PANJANG

Most of the small resorts are built on a beautiful stretch of white-sand beach known as Pasir Panjang, on the east coast of the island.

Coral Redang Island Resort
RESORT $$

(☑630 7110; www.coralredang.com.my; s/d chalets per night from RM239/319; ☀) Towards the northern end of the beach, this resort has undergone a major renovation. There's a dive centre attached. A wide variety of snorkelling/diving packages starting at RM585/785 are on offer, including equipment but not boat transfer.

Redang Bay Resort
RESORT $$

(☑620 3200; www.redangbay.com.my; dm/d per person from RM338/418; ☀☎☀) At the southern end of the beach, this rather characterless resort has a mix of concrete block–style accommodation and chalets. Rooms are neat and clean, if a little Spartan. The karaoke lounge is open till all hours, and there's a 'beach disco' on weekends, so don't come looking for a quiet island retreat.

Redang Holiday Beach Villa
CHALET $$

(☑624 5500; www.redangholiday.com; r from RM 399, chalet RM499/549 garden/seaview; ☀☎) At the northern tip of the beach is this welcoming place, with a series of smart duplex chalets climbing the rocks (chalets S13 and S14 have the best outlooks). Larger chalets sleep up to eight.

Redang Pelangi Resort
RESORT $$

(☑624 2158; www.redangpelangi.com; r from RM 379; ☀☎) This is a casual, resort-style affair that offers fairly simple two- and four-bed wooden chalets. There's an on-site dive centre, a couple of shops and a beachfront bar.

SOUTH OF PASIR PANJANG

In the bay directly south of Pasir Panjang you will find several more places to stay, strung out along an excellent white-sand beach.

Ayu Mayang Resort
RESORT $$

(☑626 2020; www.redangkalong.com; r from RM 269; ☀) In seeming response to the highrise-type hotels that have taken over much of the seashore, Ayu Mayan consists of wooden chalets, more rustic than regal, that give a good Robinson Crusoe crossed with a *kampung* vibe. Room interiors are a bit plain for the price. Three-day snorkelling packages (RM439) include all meals, three snorkelling trips, karaoke and beach volleyball.

Redang Reef Resort RESORT $$
(☎622 6181; www.redangreefresort.com.my; r from RM399; ✱) On the headland, this small budget resort is in a great location, though you'll get your feet wet going to and fro at high tide. The two-storey wooden chalets are very basic but popular with student groups. The better chalets on the rocks are more secluded and have fantastic views of the bay. It also has a tiny private beach and a diving centre, and offers regular promotional packages.

Laguna Redang Island Resort RESORT $$
(☎630 7888; www.lagunaredang.com.my; r from RM560, ste RM1420; ✱@☒) Redang's biggest resort – a vast, 222-room complex – dominates this beach. It has luxurious sea-view suites with balconies, two restaurants, a diving centre and a full program of children's activities. Buildings are in traditional Malay style (designed by the same architect who built the state museum in Kuala Terengganu). Check the website for good-value diving/snorkelling package deals.

Redang Beach Resort RESORT $$
(☎623 8188; www.redang.com.my; r from RM409; ✱@) This place has an arrangement of modern double-storey chalets and boasts a five-star PADI diving centre, a few shops and a regular beach disco, which makes it a bit intense for a quiet escape. The resort's best three-day package is their snorkelling/diving package (RM529/769), which includes all meals, boat transfer equipment and activities.

Thetaraas Beach and Spa Resort RESORT $$$
(☎630 8866; www.berjayaresorts.com.my; chalets from RM1078; ✱@☒) Formerly known as Berjaya Redang Beach Resort, this is easily one of Redang's most luxurious resorts, offering a wide choice of sumptuous wooden chalets in delightful, landscaped gardens, and an excellent private beach. Personal pampering – spa and massage – are available. The two on-site restaurants (Asian All Day Dining and Beach Brasserie) serve meals all day, but only breakfast and boat transfer are included in the package price.

Redang Kalong Resort RESORT $$
(☎03-7960 7163; www.redangkalong.com; r from RM249; ✱) This quiet place is set among the palm trees in a private bay where turtles often come to lay their eggs. Standard rooms have three double beds while sea-view rooms have two. Various diving and snorkelling packages can be booked online; diving packages start at RM589 and include five dives.

❶ Getting There & Away

Nearly all visitors to Redang come on packages that include boat transfer to the island. Independent travellers can hitch a ride on one of the resort boats (adult/child RM100/50), but in the high season (April to September) room-only deals will be scarce. Ferries run from the string of jetties along the river in Merang. Ferries also run from Shahbandar jetty in downtown Kuala Terengganu, but are less frequent and must generally be arranged via your resort. A schedule for all resort ferries can be found at www.redang.org/transport.htm.

Redang's airport is near the Berjaya Redang Beach Resort; **Berjaya Air** (☎630 8866; www.berjaya-air.com) has daily flights to KL, Kuala Terengganu and Singapore.

It's also possible to visit Redang on a dive trip from Pulau Perhentian.

Pulau Kapas

An emerald coated in powder-white sand floating in a blue sea of tranquility, pretty Pulau Kapas has something for everybody. Serene on the weekdays, the island becomes overrun with day-trippers on holidays and long weekends, and actually shuts down during the east-coast monsoon season (November to March). If Kapas seems too large for you, tiny Pulau Gemia (home to the exclusive Gem Wellness Resort) sits just off the north coast. Aside from the Gem, all accommodation is concentrated on three small beaches on the west coast, but you can walk or kayak to quieter beaches if you're so inclined.

🏃 Activities

Kapas is a snorkelling paradise, with the best coral to be found on the less accessible beaches on the northern end of the island and around tiny Pulau Gemia. North of Gemia, a sunken WWII Japanese landing craft, now carpeted in coral, is a popular dive site.

All of the resorts listed here can arrange snorkeling and diving trips. The only dive shop on Kapas is **Aqua-Sport Divers** (☎019-983 5879; www.divekapas.com); they charge RM110/180 for one/two dives, including equipment. Trips out to the Japanese wreck are RM150, and snorkelling costs RM30 for a session.

🛏 Sleeping & Eating

Though most come to Kapas on all-inclusive package tours, it's possible to rock up and find a place to stay during the week. The aptly named Jetty Cafe, just off the jetty, sells basic staples and serves meals.

Kapas Turtle Valley
RESORT $$

(☑013-354 3650; www.kapasturtlevalley.com; bungalow incl breakfast RM170-360 ; ☎) Located in a nook on the Kapas' southern end, Sylvia and Peter's Turtle Valley Resort is a hidden gem. The couple's eight bungalows – all beautifully furnished and festooned with colourful local batiks – sit over a quiet, protected white-sand beach perfect for swimming, lounging and even snorkelling. There's an excellent on-site restaurant with an ever changing daily menu featuring an eclectic variety of dishes ranging from Irish beef stew (made with Guinness!) and Thai-style broiled fish to home-made deserts (the cheesecake is excellent) and cappuccino. Meal cost is extra – expect to pay around RM25 or so. The couple also offer free snorkeling equipment for guests. Please note that minimum stay is two nights.

Captain's Longhouse
LONGHOUSE $

(☑012-377-0214; d/tw/tr RM30/60/100) Formerly known as the Lighthouse, this superhip longhouse sits on the southernmost tip of the bay. Guest can enjoy art-covered walls, dorm beds bedecked in colourful batik blankets, and a divinely sociable front porch with hammocks, chairs and even an out-of-tune piano. Surrounded by trees, it's rustic but very comfortable.

Gem Wellness Spa
& Island Resort
RESORT $$$

(☑625 2505; information@gemisle.com; r RM260-450; ✳) Perched on tiny Pulau Gemia, 800m north of Pulau Kapas, this resort offers airy wooden chalets, a couple of small private beaches and a baby green turtle hatchery. The spa offers the usual pampering services, and all-inclusive package deals are available. The restaurant is pretty, but the food is highly disappointing.

Kapas Beach Chalet
CHALETS $

(☑019-343 5606; dm/r RM15-20/40-70; ☎) Also known simply as KBC, there's a choice of rooms here, ranging from very basic 'backpacker' rooms with outside (but private) toilets to more comfortable A-frame huts with TVs. The friendly Dutch owner can arrange fishing trips and barbecues. KBC also has a

restaurant that serves good food and fruit drinks in a chill setting.

Pak Ya Seaview Resort
CHALET $

(☑029-960 3130; r RM80) Just north of the jetty, Pak Ya offers eight charming, fan-cooled A-frame chalets with lovely sea-facing porches. They also rent kayaks and snorkelling gear, and have a little restaurant.

Kapas Island Resort
CHALET $

(☑631 6468; www.kapasislandresort.com; r RM140-220; ✳☎✳) Set among pretty landscaped gardens, the freestanding timber chalets here all have two single beds and a verandah. Cheaper ones, facing the jungle, are more secluded.

Mak Cik Gemuk Beach Resort
CHALET $

(☑624 5120; r RM40-120; ✳) This older place has a variety of basic rooms; take a look at a few before deciding. A few are in need of a good scrub, while a few have received a wash down.

Qimi Chalet
CHALET $

(☑019-951 8159; r RM80-120) A walkway leads to this small, northernmost collection of huts, on its own beach. Basic indeed, and isolated, but it has a certain castaway charm.

Kapas Coral Beach
CHALET $$

(☑618 1976; r RM80-120) North of the jetty, what this place lacks in character it makes up for in air conditioning and hot showers.

ℹ Getting There & Away

Boats (return RM40) leave from Marang's main jetty whenever four or more people show up. One good option is **MGH Boat Service** (☑013-915 9748), which offers discounted tickets for groups of six or more. Be sure to arrange a pick-up time when you purchase your ticket. You can usually count on morning departures at around 8am and 9am. The same boats will continue to Pulau Gemia if requested.

TERENGGANU

With so many amazing islands to chose from, Terengganu's coast is seen by many travellers as a mere pass-through to paradise. Travellers who take the time to explore between paradise-hops will fine the region rich in culture, cuisine and scenery that, on the islands, is simply unavailable.

Kuala Terengganu

POP 396,433

A microcosm of Malaysia's economic explosion: fishing village strikes oil, modernity ensues. Kuala Terengganu is surprisingly attractive despite the number of newly built (with petro-wealth), sterile-looking skyscrapers. There's a boardwalk, a couple of decent beaches, a few old *kampung*-style houses hidden among the high rises, and one of eastern Peninsular Malaysia's prettiest Chinatowns. With seafood-heavy local cuisine and good transport links, KT is worth a day or two in between the islands and jungles.

Sights

Chinatown   NEIGHBOURHOOD

(Map p296) Tiny (but more picturesque for its small size) Chinatown is the most interesting area to explore. There are atmospheric, watermarked buildings and faded alleyways clotting this small neighbourhood, which is centred on Jln Kampung Cina (also known as Jln Bandar). The oldest Chinese temple in the state, **Ho Ann Kiong** (Map p296), is a compact explosion of vibrant red and gold dating from the early 1800s.

Central Market   MARKET

(Map p296; Jln Sultan Zainal Abidin) For fish so fresh it's still in its death flop, look for the boats docking at the central market. Besides indulging your piscatorial fix, there's a good collection of batik and *kain songket*.

Bukit Puteri   FORT

(Princess Hill; Map p296; ⊘9am-5pm Sat-Thu) Across the road from the central market, look for a steep flight of steps leading up to Bukit Puteri, a 200m-high hill with good views of the city. On top are the scant remains of a mid-19th-century fort, some cannons and a bell.

Istana Maziah   PALACE

(Map p296; Jln Masjid Abidin) On the eastern flank of the hill near the central market is the sultan's palace. It's built in semi-tweedy colonial style, but renovations have given the structure a blocky, over-modernist feel. The palace is closed to the public, except for some ceremonial occasions.

Zainal Abidin Mosque   MOSQUE

(Map p296; Jln Masjid Abidin) The gleaming Zainal Abidin Mosque dominates the city centre.

Pantai Batu Buruk   BEACH

(Map p296) Pantai Batu Buruk is the city beach, popular with families and, unfortunately, litter bugs. It's not the best beach in Malaysia given the strong winds and rips, but it's pretty nonetheless. Across the road is the **Cultural Centre stage** (Map p296); check with the tourist office to see if any shows are lined up.

Pulau Duyung   HARBOUR, PORT

(Map p296) From the jetty near the Seri Malaysia Hotel you can take a 60-sen **ferry ride** to Pulau Duyung, the largest island in the estuary. Fishing boats are built here, for both local and international clients, using age-old techniques and tools, and visitors are welcome to look around.

Tours

Popular tours include day trips to Tasik Kenyir (from RM189), river cruises and packages to Pulau Redang. Going in groups reduces individual rates.

Heritage One Stop Travel & Tours (Map p296; ☑631 6468; www.heritageonestop.com.my; Blok Teratai, Jln Sultan Sulaiman) does tours to the islands, the jungles and around KT.

Kuala Terengganu

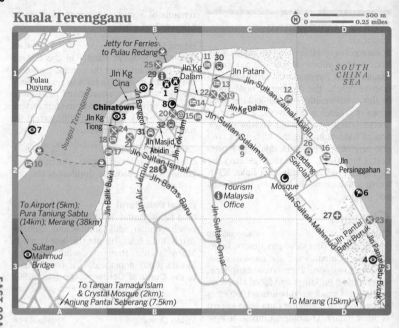

Kuala Terengganu

◎ Sights

1 Bukit Puteri	B1
2 Central Market	B1
3 Chinatown	B1
4 Cultural Centre Stage	D3
Ho Ann Kiong	(see 3)
5 Istana Maziah	B1
6 Pantai Batu Buruk	D2
7 Pulau Duyung	A2
8 Zainal Abidin Mosque	B1

◎ Activities, Courses & Tours

| 9 Heritage One Stop Travel & Tours | C2 |
| Ping Anchorage | (see 15) |

🛏 Sleeping

10 Awi's Yellow House	A2
11 Hotel Grand Continental	C1
12 Hotel Mini Indah	C1
13 Hotel Sri Tanjung	C1
14 Hotel YT Midtown	B1
15 Ping Anchorage Travellers' Inn	B1
16 Primula Beach Resort	D2
17 Seri Malaysia Hotel	B2
18 Yu Tian Fish Homestay	B2

✴ Eating

| 19 Billi Kopitiam | C1 |

20 Food Stalls	B1
21 Hawker Centre	B2
22 MD Curry House	C1
23 Night Market	D3
24 Restoran Golden Dragon	B2
T. Homemade Cafe	(see 18)
25 Terapung Puteri	B1

◉ Drinking

| Lounge Kuala Kopi | (see 16) |

⬤ Shopping

| Central Market | (see 2) |
| 26 Wanisma Craft & Trading | D2 |

ℹ Information

27 Hospital Kuala Terengganu	D2
28 HSBC	B2
29 Tourist Information Office	B1

ℹ Transport

30 Express Bus Station	C1
Local Bus Station	(see 20)
31 Long-Distance Taxi Stand	B2
32 Main Bus Station	B2

🛏 Sleeping

Primula Beach Resort
RESORT $$

(Map p296; ☎622 2100; www.primulahotels.com; Jln Persinggahan; s/d/ste RM280/280/650; ❄@☎) Kuala Terengganu's biggest option is this seafront hotel with spacious, attractively furnished rooms, including some outstanding suites with four-poster beds and multiple balconies. It's perched on a wide stretch of white sand, and is particularly popular with young families. It has a few very good restaurants and the best coffee bar in town.

Ping Anchorage Travellers' Inn
HOTEL $

(Map p296; ☎626 2020; www.pinganchorage.com.my; 77A Jln Sultan Sulaiman; r RM25-65; ☎) Spread over two floors above the travel agency of the same name, Ping's is a budget standby. Rooms are clean and tidy, with more expensive ones offering air-con and large windows. Self-service laundry facilities are a nice touch, and the central location can't be beat. Even if you aren't staying here, the inn's antique-filled rooftop cafe, which serves beer and food with a spectacular view of the city, is worth a visit.

Yu Tian Fish Homestay
HOSTEL $

(Map p296; ☎016-939 9393, 016-938 9888; 214 Jln Kg Cina; s/d/tr/q RM45/50/55/65; ❄☎) Run by the same folks who serve excellent eats downstairs at the T. Homemade Cafe, this homestay is right upstairs next to the Chinatown gate. There's a communal area with cable TV, and 14 clean and comfortable rooms with air-conditioning and single beds.

Awi's Yellow House
GUESTHOUSE $

(Map p296; ☎622 2080; r RM30) Awi's is (or sells itself as) what Terengganu was: a wooden stilt house, the smell of fish paste, salt and chilli, no air-con and nights that stick to you like a wet kiss. Built over the Sungai Terengganu on Pulau Duyung, don't come here if you don't like roughing it a little, but do if you want a taste of *kampung* life.

Wan Kay Homestay
HOMESTAY $$

(☎019-983 4360; www.wkhomestay.blogspot.com; 1 Taman Abadi, Jln Gong Badak; r/ste from RM100; ❄@) Wan Kay gives you the opportunity to stay with a friendly Malaysian family in their modest but spacious suburban home. The hosts, Beib and Wan, are happy to integrate you into their extended (and extensive) family, and get rave reviews for their hospitality from travellers. The homestay is tricky to reach independently – call Beib and Wan to arrange a pick-up.

Seri Malaysia Hotel
HOTEL $$

(Map p296; ☎623 6454; www.serimalaysia.com.my; 1640 Jln Balik Bukit; r RM140; ❄☎) Part of a popular chain with branches all over Peninsular Malaysia, this reliable place offers the standard, comfortable, could-be-anywhere set-up. Rooms are a bit faded and dated, but the lobby and riverside terrace restaurant are lovely.

Hotel Grand Continental
HOTEL $$

(Map p296; ☎625 1888; reservation_kt@ghihotels.com.my; Jln Sultan Zainal Abidin; tw/tr RM232/268; ❄☎❄) This reasonably swank high rise has comfortable though somewhat ordinary rooms. There's a swimming pool on the fourth floor, and a restaurant in the lobby.

Hotel Sri Tanjung
HOTEL $

(Map p296; ☎626 2636; Jln Sultan Zainal Abidin; s/d RM50/80; ❄) This little option is decked out in over-the-top shades of pink and white, but it is a well-kept place that's quite comfy and just within the budget bracket.

Hotel Mini Indah
HOTEL $

(Map p296; ☎622 9053; 60 Sultan Zainal Abidin; s/d RM50/65; ❄) The Mini Indah doesn't exactly drip with character, but it serves a very clean and functional purpose: getting you a pretty room within stumbling distance of the city beach.

Hotel YT Midtown
HOTEL $$

(Map p296; ☎623 5288; ythotel@streamyx.my; 30 Jln Tok Lam; r/ste from RM98/225; ❄@☎) The YT is a big, modern hotel in the centre of town with neat, good-value rooms that come with the regular mod cons such as TV, mini-fridge and kettle. There's a decent restaurant downstairs.

🍴 Eating & Drinking

Fish plays a big role in local cuisine, but the real local specialty is *kerepok*: a grey concoction of deep-fried fish paste and sago, usually moulded into sausages.

There are also cheap **food stalls** (Map p296) inside the main bus station; a beachfront **night market** (Map p296) nearby every Friday evening – a great place to sample *kerepok,* satay and sweets; and an outdoor

hawker centre (Map p296; off Jln Kampung Cina) in Chinatown, which is divided into Chinese and Malay sections and sizzles with cooking and socialising at night.

T. Homemade Cafe CHINESE, MALAY $
(Map p296; Jln Kampung Cina; mains from RM5; ◎lunch & dinner) Right next to the Chinatown gate, this place is actually a sort of cooperative conglomeration of a few food stalls in a shared space; you can get Chinese and Malay dishes here, as well as clay pots and refreshing, homemade juices.

Terapung Puteri MALAY $
(Map p296; Jln Sultan Zainal Abidin; mains from RM5; ◎lunch & dinner) This busy Malay restaurant is perched on stilts, *kampung*-style, on the seafront next to the jetty. There's a huge menu, with fish, prawns and crab featuring heavily, as well as local items, such as *kerepok*, and a few Western dishes.

Restoran Golden Dragon CHINESE $
(Map p296; 198 Jln Kampung Cina; mains from RM8; ◎lunch & dinner) The Golden Dragon seems constantly packed. There's beer aplenty and one of the finest Chinese seafood menus in town – anything steamed and off the fish list should serve you right.

Billi Kopitiam COFFEE SHOP $
(Map p296; No 5, Jln Kampung Dalam; mains from RM4; ◎lunch & dinner) This smooth little spot, decked out in Chinese vintage movie posters, brews a mean cup of Joe as well as serving up some interesting variations on standards like *nasi lemak* (rice boiled in coconut milk, served with fried *ikan bilis* – dried sardines or anchovies – peanuts and a curry dish) and anything *goreng* (fried).

MD Curry House MALAY $
(Map p296; Jln Kampung Dalam; mains from RM4; ◎lunch & dinner) Sometimes you need a curry and you need it served on a banana leaf by friendly locals. The MD pretty much has you covered in all regards.

Lounge Kuala Kopi CAFE
(Map p296; Jln Persinggahan; ◎3pm-late) If you need a bean fix, Lounge Kuala Kopi, inside the Primula Beach Resort, has an excellent range of coffees, including its unique house blend, *kopi de ganu*.

Shopping

Batik and *kain songket* are particularly good buys in Kuala Terengganu.

Kraftangan Malaysia HANDICRAFTS
(☎622 6458; ◎9am-5pm Sun-Thu) About 4.5km south of town, this outlet sells high-quality *kain songket* costing as much as RM12,000 for 2.5 sq m. There's also a tiny 'Songket Heritage Exhibition' showing varying designs. Minibus 13 will take you here from the bus station.

Wanisma Craft & Trading HANDICRAFTS
(Map p296; ☎622 3311; 32 Ladang Sekolah; ◎9.30am-6.30pm) This is a batik-dyeing and brass workshop (the largest brass workshop in the country, supposedly) where you can watch the skilled craftsmen at work. The results can be purchased in the shop.

Central Market MARKET
(Map p296; Jln Sultan Zainal Abidin) Handicrafts are sold upstairs at the central market. Bargaining is possible here – and necessary to get fair prices.

Information

You'll find plenty of banks on Jln Sultan Ismail (9.15am to 4.30pm, except Friday), most with 24-hour cash machines that accept international cards.

Golden Wood Internet (☎631 0128; 59 Jln Tok Lam; per hr RM5)
Hospital Kuala Terengganu (Map p296; ☎623 3333; Jln Sultan Mahmud)
Tourist Information Office (Map p296; ☎622 1553; www.tourism.terengganu.gov.my; Jln Sultan Zainal Abidin; ◎9am-5pm Sat-Thu)

❶ Getting There & Away

Air

Looking more like a Sultan's summer home than an airport, the newly built Kuala Terengganu airport is worth a trip for anyone burnt out on cookie-cutter airport design. **Malaysia Airlines** (☎662 6600; www.malaysiaairlines.com) and **AirAsia** (☎32-171 9333; www.airasia.com) both have direct flights to KL. **Firefly** (☎7845 4543; airport) offers flights to Singapore, and **Berjaya Air** (☎630 2228; www.berjaya-air.com) flies to Redang. All have offices inside the Kuala Terengganu airport.

Bus

The **local bus station** (Map p296; Jln Masjid Abidin) on Jln Masjid Abidin is a terminus for local buses while express buses leave from the **station** (Map p296; Jln Sultan Zainal Abidin) on Jln Sultan Zainal Abidin. Among the bus companies operating from this station are **Transnasional** (☎623 8384), **MARA** (☎622 2097), **Sani Express** (☎622 2717) and **Ekspres Sutera** (☎622 6299).

BUSES FROM KUALA TERENGGANU

Destination	Price (RM)	Duration
Dungun	8	2
Johor Bharu	45	8
Kota Bharu	15	3
Kuala Besut (Perhentians)	20	2
Kuala Lumpur	40	8
Kuantan	18	6
Melaka	45	8
Merang (Redang)	2	1
Penang	35	9
Rantau Abang	5	1.5
Singapore	60	11

Taxi

Kuala Terengganu's **main taxi stand** is near the local bus station, but taxis can be found throughout the city. Regular destinations include Marang (RM15), Kota Bharu (RM80), Kuala Besut (RM60), Rantau Abang (RM40), Merang (RM35) and Tasik Kenyir (RM120). Some long-distance taxis leave from a **stand** (Map p296) on Jln Masjid Abidin.

ⓘ Getting Around

A taxi to the airport costs around RM28. Local buses leave from the **main bus station** (Map p296; Jln Masjid Abidin) in the town centre.

The very pretty Heritage City Shuttle Town Bus goes to all of the major sites in and around town and runs through the main bus station on an hourly basis for RM1 per trip.

Taxis around town cost a minimum of RM5. There are also a few bicycle rickshaws plying their trade through town. Prices are highly negotiable.

Around Kuala Terengganu

Kuala Terengganu is the natural base for exploring Terengganu state. The museums are close in to the city, city, and Sekayu Falls and Tasik Kenyir are far to the southwest.

◉ Sights

Kompleks Muzium Negeri Terengganu   MUSEUM
(Terengganu State Museum; ☎622 1433; http://museum.terengganu.gov.my; adult/child RM15/10; ⊙9am-5pm Sat-Thu) Comprised of a series of interconnected buildings on 26 hectares of land, exhibits here range from the historically interesting (a Jawi – traditional Malay text – inscription that essentially dates the arrival of Islam to the nation) to the mildly bizarre (a wildlife exhibit featuring taxidermy that's seen better decades) to corporate propaganda (an exhibit touting the goodness of the oil industry). The complex of traditional houses that fronts the grounds is worth the price of admission. English signage is sparse, however. To get here, take minibus 10 (RM1), marked 'Muzium/Losong', from Kuala Terengganu's main bus station. A taxi from Kuala Terengganu will cost RM20.

Masjid Tengku Tengah Zaharah   MOSQUE
The most famous religious structure in the state is the 'Floating Mosque', located 4.5km southeast of Kuala Terengganu. It's not really floating, just set on a man-made island, but its white, traditional Moorish design is beautifully blinding in the strong daylight, and warmly enchanting as the sun sets. Bus 13 from Kuala Terengganu will drop you outside (RM1).

Taman Tamadu Islam   AMUSEMENT PARK
(☎627 8888; www.tti.com.my; admission RM15; ⊙10am-7pm Mon-Thu, 9am-7pm Fri-Sun) Touted as the world's first 'Islamic civilisation park', Taman Tamadu Islam, 2.5km west of Kuala Terengganu, is essentially a series of miniature models of famous Islamic landmarks from across the world including Jerusalem's Dome of the Rock and Mecca's Masjid al-Haram. The highlight of the park is the **Crystal Mosque**. Widely considered among the world's most beautiful mosques, it features a particularly striking steel, glass and crystal exterior. The Heritage Bus runs here, and a taxi will cost around RM15.

North of Kuala Terengganu

North of Kuala Terengganu the main road (Route 3) leaves the coast and runs inland to Kota Bharu, 165km north, via Jerteh. The quiet coastal back road (Route 1) from Kuala Terengganu to Kuala Besut runs along a beautiful stretch of coast and is popular with cyclists.

MERANG

Not to be confused with Marang (which it often is), the sleepy little fishing village of

Merang is the gateway to the island of Redang. The beach is attractive if you have to spend some time waiting for ferry connections to Redang, and worth a visit if you plan on checking out any of the resorts around town.

🛏 Sleeping

Aryani Resort
RESORT $$

(☎6532111;www.thearyani.com;Jln Rhu Tapai;r from RM369; ✳✷) One of Malaysia's most exclusive hotels lies on a secluded stretch of coast 4km south of Merang. The detached chalets are a mix of Malay and Javanese design, and are spread out in tranquil landscaped grounds just off the beach. All have private gardens and sunken outdoor baths. Best of all is the sumptuous Redang Suite (RM1055), a traditionally furnished 150-year-old Malay house on stilts. The restaurants serve Western and Malay cuisine, while the spa offers indulgent body treatments and massages.

Kembara Resort
BUNGALOW $

(☎6531770;http://kembararesort.tripod.com;dm/r RM10/35-60; ✳@) The Kembara is a cheap and friendly place whose plain but homely chalets are popular with the student crowd. There are organised activities and a common kitchen. Follow the signs from the main road from the village.

ⓘ Getting There & Away

Buses run from the main bus station in Kuala Terengganu to Merang (RM3). Taxis from Kuala Terengganu cost RM35 per car. Coming from the north is more difficult and it is easiest to go south as far as Kuala Terengganu and then backtrack. Otherwise, taxis from Kota Bharu cost RM70.

PENARIK

With its windswept beach and charmingly low-key population of farmers and fisher folk, the village of Penarik is as lovely a spot for a taste of coastal Malaysian culture as you could wish for. But for something truly magical, stick around until the sun goes down and charter a boat to take you down the Penarik river for a journey through the **Penarik Firefly Sanctuary**, where, on certain nights (the darker the better) you'll be treated to a most unusual sight: thousands of fireflies blinking in near-perfect synchronisation. This synchronised flashing pattern is unique to the area. Sex-crazed entomologists naturally suspect mating habits. The night-time boat trip through

the ghostly and ethereal mangrove forest is unforgettable.

A wide range of activities is offered at the Terrapuri Heritage Village (p301) resort, including excursions into local villages and and boat trips to the Firefly Sanctuary and outlying islands. Nonguests can book these same activities through Ping Anchorage (p295), who can also help arrange low-cost homestays with villagers in Penarik.

🛏 Sleeping

TOP CHOICE Terrapuri Heritage Village
RESORT $$$

(☎624 5020; www.terrapuri.com; house RM399-RM1099; ⊙minimum 2 nights; ✷✳) To step onto the beautifully manicured grounds of Terrapuri Heritage Village is like entering a set-piece for a film about the lives of the sultans of yore. Meaning 'Land Of Palaces', Terrapuri is equal parts conservation and restoration museum and resort. The resort features 29 classically furnished antique houses painstakingly restored and laid out to resemble Terengganu palace circa 1850 (though all fully equipped with modern amenities). The land on which Terrapuri sits is equally regal, flanked by the South China Sea (with stunning views of Pulau Perhentian, Lang Tengah and other islands) on one side and the Setiu Wetland mangrove river on the other. By night, the flashing of fireflies is reflected in Terrapuri's long swimming pool, and during the summer months visitors may see ocean-going green turtles laying their eggs on the sandy shore.

Terrapuri offers delicious traditional meals and a wide variety of activities. Full details are available on the website.

ⓘ Getting There & Away

Buses from Kuala Terengganu to Kuala Besut will let you off at the Penarik mosque for RM6. From the other direction, buses from Kota Bharu to Kuala Terengganu are RM15. Taxis from either city are also available.

South of Kuala Terengganu

MARANG

Marang is the jump-off point for ferries to Pulau Kapas. Once a quiet fishing town, much of Marang's seaside charm has disappeared beneath a recent flood of new buildings. It's still a nice place to hang out for an

LIVING HISTORY: BIDONG ISLAND

As the war in Vietnam ended, millions of Vietnamese citizens decided to take to the high seas rather than face communist rule in newly reunified Vietnam. Dubbed 'boat people' by the international community, many of these refugees wound up in Malaysia. In 1978, Bidong, a tiny island off the coast of Terengganu, was designated a refugee camp. For the next two decades, Bidong served as a temporary home and transit point for tens of thousands of refugees, who endured unsanitary living conditions in shelters made from salvaged materials. At one point, the tiny island held 40,000 people, making it the most densely populated place on the planet. The camp was closed in 1990, and Bidong has since returned to a pristine state. Small groups occasionally visit Bidong for day trips (there is no accommodation on the island); divers in particular are drawn to the fantastic coral lanscapes surrounding Bidong.

Trips to Bidong can be arranged through Ping Anchorage (p295).

evening on the way to or from Kapas, especially in summer, when numerous exotic fruit trees are in season.

If you are in town on Sunday be sure to check out the excellent **market**, which starts at 3pm near the jetty.

Ping Anchorage (p295) organises the Marang River Tour, a morning cruise (minimum two people) that brings visitors 6km down the Marrang river through a mangrove swamp filled with monkeys, monitor lizards, ergots and kingfishers. The tour stops at the traditional village of Jenang, where tropical drinks made from locally harvested coconut and sugarcane are available. Ping can also arrange meals and longer stays in Jenang.

🛏 Sleeping & Eating

There are a couple of basic *kedai kopi* (coffee shops) in the town centre, near the bus ticket office, and you can also find some **food stalls** (Jln Kampung Paya) near the jetties.

Marang Waterfront   HOTEL $$
(✆618 3999; 21600 Jln Kampung Paya; r with breakfast RM120-180; ❋❋🛜) Breezy and brand spanking new, the Marang Waterfront sits just north of the jetty and has clean, corporate hotel–type rooms with either two queen or three single beds. The bright, airy lobby is festooned with modern art, plants and a comfortable communal space and a restaurant facing the waterfront.

Marang Guesthouse   GUESTHOUSE $
(✆618 1976; www.marangguesthouse.com; Jln Kampung Paya Bukit; r from RM40; ❋) This guesthouse, connected by MGH Boat Service (p295), offers a series of dark, comfy,

if occasionally musty, chalets perched on a hill overlooking the main road down to the jetty. More expensive rooms have aircon. At night, the high-up location and surrounding jungle makes for an agreeably rustic escape.

ℹ Getting There & Away

There are regular local buses to Kuala Terengganu (RM3) and Dungun/Rantau Abang (RM6/4). Though there was once a ticket office in town it seems to have closed down; any of the travel agencies on the waterfront can help you get tickets for buses to Kuala Lumpur (RM35), Johor Bahru (RM35) or Kuantan-Cherating (RM15). You can catch buses at the bus stops on the main road in front of the mosque.

KEMASIK

Kemasik's palm-fringed beach has some of the clearest water on the east coast. The nearest accommodation is at the gargantuan, five-star **Awana Kijal Golf, Beach & Spa Resort** (✆864 1188; www.awana.com.my; r/ste from RM347/601; ❋❋@🛜❋) on the beach around 1km south, towards Kijal, stacked with the usual golf courses, tennis courts, spa etc. Discounts are often available, especially if you book over the internet. Take a local bus running between Kemaman/Cukai and Dungun, or if you're driving, turn off Route 3 (East Coast Highway) at the 'Pantai Kemasik' sign.

TASIK KENYIR

The construction of the Kenyir Dam in 1985 flooded some 2600 sq km of jungle, creating Southeast Asia's largest man-made lake, with clumps of wild overgrowth gasping over the water's surface. Today Tasik Kenyir (Lake Kenyir) and its 340 islands constitute Terengganu's most popular inland tourism

SEKAYU FALLS

Located 56km southwest of Kuala Terengganu, Sekayu Falls are part of the Sekayu Recreational Forest, a large park popular with locals on Fridays and public holidays. The falls extend down a mountainside; the main falls are 15 minutes in from the entrance. A further 20 minutes' walk brings you to the more attractive upper falls. There's also an orchard with a huge variety of seasonal tropical fruit. To get here, take one of three daily buses from Kuala Terengganu to the park entrance (RM5) and walk 2km to the falls. The first leaves at 9am, and the last bus comes back at 3pm. You can also arrange a trip through Ping Anchorage (p295), combining the falls with Kenyir Dam for RM99 per person, including lunch.

destination. If you're looking to spend a relatively luxurious night in the local jungle, which houses some 8000 species of flowers, this is the spot for you.

◉ Sights

Waterfalls and **caves** are high on the list of Kenyir's attractions, as are a number of fish farms. These can be reached by boat, as part of day trips from the lake's main access point, Pengkalan Gawi. Book trips from the kiosks surrounding Pengkalan Gawi's jetty, or from the resorts themselves. Perhaps more interesting are trips up the rivers that empty into the lake. Among these, a journey up **Sungai Petuang**, at the extreme northern end of the lake, is a highlight of a Kenyir visit. When the water is high, it's possible to travel several kilometres upriver into beautiful virgin jungle.

Fishing is a popular activity and the lake is surprisingly rich in species, including *toman* (snakehead), *buang* (catfish), *kelah* (a type of carp), *kelisa* (green arowana) and *kalui* (giant gouramy). You will need a permit (RM10) to fish here, which can be booked independently or through a fishing trip.

The water level varies considerably, peaking at the end of the rainy season in March or April and gradually decreasing until the start of the next rainy season in November. When the water is high the lake takes on an eerie atmosphere, with the tops of drowned trees poking through the surface; when low the lake is reduced to a series of canals through partially denuded jungle hills. The high water is undoubtedly more beautiful, so come in late spring or early summer if you can.

🛏 Sleeping & Eating

Most accommodation is in resort chalets or floating longhouse structures built over the lake. Resorts usually offer meals and boat transport from Pengkalan Gawi.

Another option is to explore Kenyir by houseboat, which allows you to reach remote regions of the lake, but you'll need a large group to make a trip economical. Ping Anchorage (p295) can help you arrange this.

Petang Island Resort   RESORT $$
(☎822 1276, 822 2176; www.pirkenyir.webs.com; dm/r/ste RM30/90/250; ❉❉) On its own little island in the middle of the lake, this is a quiet retreat with a choice of comfortably furnished single- or double-storey chalets and longhouse rooms. Chalets have kitchens if you want to cook for yourself, but there's a good restaurant here, too. Camp sites are available for RM5, and you can even rent a tent for RM25.

Lake Kenyir Resort   RESORT $$$
(☎666 8888; www.lakekenyir.com; r/villa/ste from RM380/440/1200; ❉❈❉) Formerly known as Kenyir Lakeview Resort, this peaceful resort – the most glamorous property on the lake – has spacious and well-equipped chalets with balconies overlooking the water or the rainforest. There's a restaurant serving a bountiful variety of Malay and Western dishes and very inviting lounge with a great view of the lake. The resort also has tennis courts, a gym, and plenty of organised activities.

Kenyir Sanctuary Resort   RESORT $$
(☎019-824 4360; fan-cooled d/tr RM100/120 deluxe r/q RM160/200; ❉) The Sanctuary has 40 rustic wooden chalets, and some of the cheapest rooms on the lake. Cheaper ones are fan cooled, while the pricier ones have air-con and TV.

Musang Kenyir Resort   RESORT $$
(☎623 1888; r from RM140; ❉) On the north shore of the lake, Musang consists of 15

rustic *kampung*-style houses plopped over the waters. Facilities are basic and somewhat rundown, but the setting is beautiful.

ℹ Information

There is a small **tourist information office** (☎626 7788; www.ketengah.gov.my/kenyir; ⊙9am-5pm) near the jetty in Pengkalan Gawi, the lake's main access point. Also at the jetty you'll find a cafe, a shop and a few kiosks where you can book boat trips. Trips start from RM600 for a jaunt to the nearest islands to significantly more for day trips and fishing expeditions across the lake.

ℹ Getting There & Away

The main access point is the jetty at Pengkalan Gawi on the lake's northern shore. A taxi from Kuala Terengganu should cost around RM120. Your best bet is to book an all-inclusive package from an agency in Kuala Terengganu.

Sabah

POP 3.39 MILLION / AREA 76,115 SQ KM

Includes »

Kota Kinabalu 306
Tunku Abdul Rahman
National Park 320
Mt Kinabalu & Kinabalu
National Park 322
Offshore Islands............336
Sandakan 337
Sungai Kinabatangan ...348
Danum Valley
Conservation Area........354
Semporna 357
Tawau 363
Maliau Basin
Conservation Area........367
Pulau Tiga
National Park 374
Pulau Labuan...............375

Best Places to Eat

» KK's Night Market (p306)
» Alu-Alu Cafe (p314)
» Moon Bell (p314)
» Sim Sim Seafood Restaurant (p342)

Best Places to Stay

» Mañana (p334)
» Lupa Masa (p331)
» Tampat Do Aman (p335)
» Orou Sapulot (p371)

Why Go?

Sabah's beauty is quite simply gut-wrenching. This is one of the most physically stunning places on Earth, a land of deep green jungle, craggy mountains and shockingly blue ocean that all seems to collide into one moving, magnificent vista.

It's a land for adventure enthusiasts and yet, we must stress, not only adventure enthusiasts. Many treks around Mt Kinabalu, for example, really consist of vigorous hikes, jaunts you want to be fit to attempt, but don't need to be in Olympic shape to finish. Similarly, the diving in East Sabah – some of the best in the world – is easily accessible to beginners. And anyone can sit on a boat and appreciate the majesty of spotting clever lizards, prowling civets, doe-eyed loris and great ginger orang-utans in the wild.

In addition, there is a thriving yet laid-back culture here. Sabah's citizens are wonderful: cosmopolitan, friendly, famously relaxed folks who are quick to laugh and slow to rile. Their good-humoured presence is the perfect accompaniment to the awe-inspiring scenery of their home.

When to Go

Kota Kinabalu

°C/°F Temp   Rainfall inches/mm

| **Jan–Apr** A dry, pleasant time, exploding with celebrations for Chinese New Year. | **Mar–Jul** The water calms; this is the best time for diving. | **Jun–Sep** Hot and often (but definitely not always) rainy. |

Sabah Highlights

1 Admiring the sea turtles among the **Semporna Archipelago's** (p359) reefs

2 Hoofing it over pitcher plants and granite moonscapes for the ultimate Bornean sunrise atop **Mt Kinabalu** (p325)

3 Breathing in the air of an actual virgin rainforest in the

Maliau Basin Conservation Area (p367)

4 Watching orang-utans in **Sepilok** (p343)

5 Discovering the hidden beaches of northern Borneo near **Kudat** (p335)

6 Floating down a river through primary jungle to the

Batu Punggul rock formation in **Sapulot** (p371)

7 Enjoying the nightlife and eating opportunities of **Kota Kinabalu** (p314)

8 Staying in a home stay and spotting primates from a boat on the **Sungai Kinabatangan** (p352)

KOTA KINABALU

POP 630,000

We realise you almost certainly didn't come to Sabah for the urban scene, but you have to book permits somewhere, you gotta sleep after climbing Mt Kinabalu/diving in Sipadan/exploring the jungle etc, and you need some place to connect to onward travel, and KK, as everyone calls it, is a good place (sometimes the only place) to do all of the above. The centre is walkable. The population is a spicy mix of expats, Chinese, indigenous Kadazan and of course, Malays. The food is good – surprisingly good, given you're in Malaysia's hinterlands. Nightlife is fun, a testament to Sabah's laid-back approach to life; there aren't a lot of bars. The downside is out of control construction; KK desperately seems to want to answer the question, 'How many empty malls can we build in one city?', but past this one demerit, it's hard not to love this town.

⊙ Sights & Activities

CITY CENTRE & WATERFRONT

Night Market   MARKET
(Map p308; Jln Tun Fuad Stephens; ⊙late afternoon-11pm) KK's main market is a place of delicious contrasts. Huddled beneath the imposing Le Meridien, the market is divided into two main sections: the southwest end is given over mostly to produce, while the northeast end (the area around the main entrance) is a huge hawker centre where you can eat your way right through the entire Malay gastronomy. A fish-and-food market extends to the waterfront; the closer you get to the ocean, the more the scent of salt water, death, blood and spices envelops you – an oddly intoxicating experience. If you've never seen a proper Southeast Asian market, this place will be a revelation.

Signal Hill   LANDMARK
(Map p308) There's a UFO-like observation pavilion on this hill at the eastern edge of the city centre. Come here to escape the traffic and get another take on the squatters' stilt village at Pulau Gaya . The view is best as the sun sets over the islands. From the top, it's also possible to hike down to the Wetland Centre on the other side, but it's a longer way than it looks – don't try this if it's getting dark, as the walk can take up to two hours. Near here are some shells of unfinished building sites that were rumored to

be haunted; the ghosts drove away the construction crews, presumably because they liked the idea of ugly concrete foundations overlooking KK.

Atkinson Clock Tower   LANDMARK
(Map p308) The modest timepiece at the foot of the hill is one of the only structures to survive the Allied bombing of Jesselton in 1945. It's a square, 15.7m-high wooden structure that was completed in 1905 and named after the first district officer of the town, FG Atkinson, who died of malaria aged 28.

Central Market   MARKET
(Map p308; Jln Tun Fuad Stephens; ⊙6.30am-6pm) The Central Market is fun to wander about, and a nice spot for people watching as locals transact their daily business. Nearby, the **Handicraft Market** (Filipino Market; Jln Tun Fuad Stephens; ⊙10am-6pm) is a good place to shop for inexpensive souvenirs. Offerings include pearls, textiles, seashell crafts, jewellery and bamboo goods, some from the Philippines, some from Malaysia and some from other parts of Asia. Needless to say, bargaining is a must.

KK Heritage Walk   WALKING TOUR
(www.kkheritagewalk.com; admission RM200; ⊙walks 9am Tue & Thu) This two-hour tour, which can be booked through any of KK's many tour operators (just ask at your hotel front desk), explores colonial KK and its hidden delights. Stops include Chinese herbal shops, bulk produce stalls, a *kopitiam* (coffee shop), and Jln Gaya (known as Bond St when the British were in charge). There's also a quirky treasure hunt at the end leading tourists to the Jesselton Hotel. Guides speak English, Chinese and Bahasa Malaysia.

Sunday Market MARKET

(Map p308; Jln Gaya; ⊙7am-3pm Sun) On Sundays, a lively Chinese street fair takes over the entire length of Jln Gaya. It's a pretty manic scene and a perfect spot for souvenir shopping, but animal lovers may want to avoid some sections.

BEYOND THE CITY CENTRE

Some of KK's best attractions are located beyond the city centre, and it's well worth putting in the effort to check them out.

Sabah Museum MUSEUM

(☑253199; www.museum.sabah.gov.my; Jln Muzium; admission RM20; ⊙9am-5pm Sat-Thu; ℗) Centred on a modern four-storey structure inspired by the longhouses of the Rungus and Murut tribes, this is the best place to go in KK for an introduction to Sabah's ethnicities and environments. It's slightly south of the city centre, on the hilly corner of Jln Tunku Abdul Rahman and Jln Penampang.

In the main building there are good permanent collections of tribal and historical artefacts including ceramics and exhibits of flora and fauna – some dusty, others well presented (including a centrepiece whale skeleton). The prehistory gallery has a replica limestone cave, in case you don't make it to any of the real ones. In the gardens, the **Heritage Village** offers the chance to wander round examples of traditional tribal dwellings, including Kadazan bamboo houses and a Chinese farmhouse, all nicely set on a lily-pad lake.

The adjoining **Science & Education Centre** has an informative exhibition on the petroleum industry, from drilling to refining and processing. The **Sabah Art Gallery** features regular shows and exhibitions by local artists. If you're heading east after KK, keep hold of

your admission ticket – it will also allow you entry to Agnes Keith House in Sandakan.

Mari Mari Cultural Village MUSEUM

(☑019-820 4921; www.traversetours.com/culturalvillage.php; Jln Kiansom; adult/child RM160/140; ℗) Mari Mari is an entertaining combination of semi-corny and semi-educational. It's supposed to offer insight into the living cultures of Sabah via a three-hour show-tour (beginning at 10am, 3pm and 7pm), which winds through the jungle passing various tribal dwellings along the way. At each stop, tourists learn about indigenous folkways and can try their hand at bamboo cooking, rice-wine making (and drinking!), fire starting, tattooing, blowpipe shooting etc. A short dance recital and meal are included in the visit – the centre must be notified of any dietary restrictions in advance. A trip to the cultural village can be combined with a white-water rafting tour; contact Riverbug for more information. The village is a 20-minute to 30-minute drive north of central KK, so most people visit it on a package tour, but if you come on your own the admission is RM80/70 for adults/children.

Rather than portraying living cultures, Mari Mari sort of freezes local ethnic groups into museum pieces. No one is dressing in

THE SOUTHSIDE CONNECTION

A paved road makes a frowning arc from KK to Tawau, passing Mt Kinabalu, Sepilok, Sandakan, Lahad Datu and Semporna (the gateway to Sipadan) along the way. It takes around 10 hours to complete the circuit.

Getting from KK to Tawau via the northern half of the island, via a big frown, is easy. Doing the smile side of the loop (going back to KK through the south from Tawau): not so much. The road here is not entirely paved, but there's at least finely crushed gravel the whole way through. A 2WD or even motorbike can make the drive, but drive carefully. An infrastructure of public buses does not yet exist here; minivans occasionally ran this stretch of road, but only when needed by logging camps. If you can get a lift to Keningau, the rest of the journey to KK is a breeze.

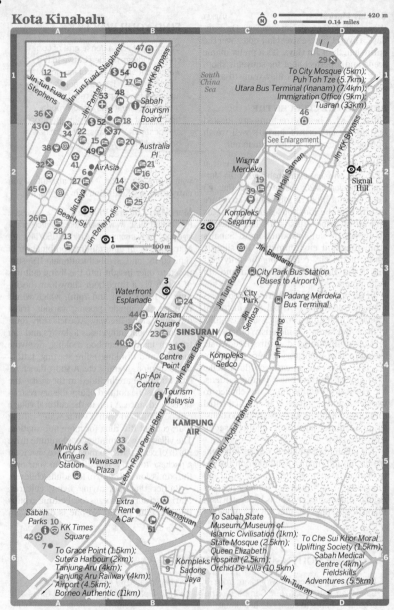

loincloths and feathers in Sabah, except maybe in the very deepest, remote interior. The Rungus and Murut may live in longhouses, but many of those longhouses have satellite television and air-con, and they hunt with guns, not blowpipes.

There is also a small waterfall – **Kiansom Waterfall** (admission RM1; ⊙ dawn-dusk) – about 400m beyond the cultural village, which is easily accessible by private transport or on foot. The area around the cascade lends itself well to swimming and

Kota Kinabalu

◎ **Sights**
1 Atkinson Clock Tower B3
2 Central Market C3
3 Night Market B3
4 Signal Hill D2
5 Sunday Market A2

◆ **Activities, Courses & Tours**
6 Adventure Alternative Borneo............. A2
7 Borneo Adventure A6
8 Borneo Divers B1
9 Borneo Nature Tours B6
10 Downbelow Marine & Wildlife
   Adventures... A6
11 GogoSabah A1
   Riverbug/Traverse Tours .... (see 12)
   Scuba Junkie/River Junkie..........(see 11)
12 Sutera Harbour...................................... A1

⬒ **Sleeping**
13 Akinabalu Youth Hostel...................... A3
14 Borneo Backpackers............................. B2
15 Borneo Gaya Lodge.............................. A2
16 Bunibon B2
17 Hotel Eden 54 .... B1
18 Hotel Sixty3.. B1
19 Hyatt Regency Kota Kinabalu............. C2
20 Jesselton Hotel..................................... B2
21 Kinabalu Backpackers B2
22 Kinabalu Daya A2
23 Klagan Hotel... B4
   Le Hotel ....(see 23)
24 Le Meridien Kota Kinabalu.................. B3
25 Lucy's Homestay B2
   Myne Hotel ....(see 23)
26 Rainforest Lodge A2
27 Sarangnova Hotel A2
28 Summer Lodge...................................... A3

✕ **Eating**
29 Alu-Alu Cafe D1
30 Borneo 1945 Museum Kopitiam.......... B2

31 Centre Point Basement Food
   Court B4
32 Chili Vanilla A2
   El Centro ....(see 38)
33 Grazie.. B5
34 Kedai Kopi Fatt Kee............................. A2
35 Kohinoor B4
   Nagisa ....(see 19)
36 Wisma Merdeka Food Court A1
37 Ya Kee Bah Kut Teh B2

🍸 **Drinking**
38 El Centro... A2
   Shamrock ....(see 35)
   Shenanigan's ....(see 35)
39 Upperstar.. C2

🎭 **Entertainment**
40 Bed.. B4
41 Black World.. A2
   Hunter's ....(see 22)
   Suria Sabah ....(see 46)
42 White Room.. A6

🛍 **Shopping**
   7-Eleven ....(see 32)
43 Borneo Books....................................... A2
44 Borneo Trading Post............................ B3
45 Milimewa Superstore........................... A2
46 Suria Sabah Shopping Mall D1
47 Tong Hing Supermarket....................... B1

ℹ **Information**
48 Australian Consulate B1
49 British Consul....................................... A2
50 HSBC... B1
51 Indonesian Consulate B6
52 Maybank A1
53 Permai Polyclinic................................. A1
54 Standard Chartered Bank B1

SABAH KOTA KINABALU

it's a great place to cool off after a visit to Mari Mari.

Lok Kawi Wildlife Park　　ZOO
(☎765710; www.lokkawiwildlifepark.com; Jln Penampang; adult/child RM20/10; ◷9.30am-5.30pm, last entry at 4:30pm; P) If you'd like to check out the orang-utans but won't make it out to Sepilok or the Kinabatangan, a visit to this wildlife park is highly recommended, especially for those with children in tow. There

are plenty of other animals as well, from tarsiers to Sumatran rhinos. Don't miss the giant aviary at the top of the hill, with its ominous warning sign 'beware of attacking birds'.

It's best to arrive by 9.50am at the latest – feedings take place throughout the park at 10am. After the various feedings, an interactive show takes place at the stage around 11.15am everyday. After feeding time, most of the animals take their daily siesta – only the humans are silly enough to stay out in the scorching midday sun.

The 17B minibus goes to Lok Kawi (RM2). Visitors with a private vehicle can access the park via the Papar–Penampang road or the Putatan–Papar road. Travel agents offer half-day tours, or you can hire a taxi, which will cost around RM150, including a two-hour wait.

Monsopiad Cultural Village   MUSEUM
(☎774337; www.monsopiad.com; admission adult/student/child RM75/50/free; ◷9am-5pm; P) On the banks of Sungai Moyog, Monsopiad is named after a legendary warrior and head-hunter, whose direct descendants established this private heritage centre in 1996. The highlight is the House of Skulls, which supposedly contains the ancient crania of Monsopiad's unfortunate enemies, as well as artefacts illustrating native rituals from the time when the *bobolian* (priest) was the most important figure in the community.

Many tour companies include Monsopiad on local itineraries. To get here independently, take a bus from central KK to Donggongon (RM1.50), where you can catch a minivan to the cultural village (RM1). You can also take a taxi or charter a minivan direct from KK for around RM40.

**🍃 Kota Kinabalu
Wetland Centre**   MUSEUM
(☎246955; www.sabahwetlands.org; Jln Bukit Bendera Upper; adult/child RM10/5; ◷8am-6pm Tue-Sun; P) This spot encompasses the last 24 hectares of a mangrove swamp that once stretched across what is now KK. A series of wooden walkways leads into a wetland rife with fiddler crabs, mangrove crabs, mud lobsters, mudskippers, skinks, turtles, water monitors and the adorably turd-like mangrove slug, among other swamp fauna (sadly, there are also plastic bottles). For many, the big attraction is a stunning variety of migratory birds, some from as far away as Siberia. The walkway ends at a spot that looks out over a flat marshscape that would feel virgin were it not for the high rise buildings behind it. Staff are cheerful but not always that helpful.

To get here, head north on Jln Fuad Stephens (the main road north out of town; in town it's also called Jln KK Bypass) and follow it as it curves around the coast. You'll then turn right at Jln Istidat and follow that for about 1km; signs for the Wetland Centre will be on your right.

Chinese Temples   CHINESE TEMPLE
(Jln Tuaran; P) The main road north to Tuaran runs past some impressive Chinese temples.

Che Sui Khor Moral Uplifting Society
About four minutes north of KK, this complex is anchored by an 11-storey pagoda that shimmers in orange and green. Tourists can't enter the actual pagoda, but the friendly members of the society don't mind you poking around the rest of their library. The Society espouses believing in the best Islam, Taoism, Buddhism and Christianity have to offer. You can get here via the bus terminal at Wawasan Plaza going north on the Jln Tuaran route (RM3). To get home, just stand outside the temple on the main road and a minibus or regular bus will pick you up. A return taxi should cost around RM20.

Puh Toh Tze Buddhist Temple
Also spelled 'Poh Toh Tse', this temple is 20 minutes north of KK, at Mile (Batu) 5.5. It's quite impressive: a stone staircase-pavilion flanked by 10 Chinese deities leads up to a main temple complex dominated by Kwan Yin, Goddess of Mercy. A Chinese-style reclining Buddha rests inside. You can to enter and wander around. The temple is on a small hill west of the main highway junction north; you can get here by taking the Jln Tuaran bus again or, more easily, hire a taxi; a round-trip shouldn't be more than RM36.

Museum of Islamic Civilisation   MUSEUM
(☎538234; admission incl in Sabah Museum ticket; ◷9am-5pm Sat-Thu; P) This museum consists of six galleries devoted to Muslim culture and history in Malaysia and beyond. The five domes represent the holy Five Pillars of Islam. It's in need of a facelift and an update, but can fill up an hour or two of a boring afternoon.

To get to the museum complex, catch a bus (RM1) along Jln Tunku Abdul Rahman and get off just before the mosque. Be warned: it's a short but steep walk uphill to the museum. Bus 13 also goes right round past the Queen Elizabeth Hospital and stops near Jln Muzium (look for the Sacred Heart Church). Taxi fare will run between RM10 and RM15.

City Mosque   MOSQUE
(off Jln Tun Fuad Stephens) Overlooking the South China Sea, this mosque is built in classical style, and is far more attractive than the State Mosque in terms of setting and design. Completed in 2000, it can hold up to 12,000 worshippers. It can be entered by

non-Muslims outside regular prayer times, but dress modestly (long trousers and arms covered is a good rule of thumb, although you may get away with just shoulders covered) and remove your shoes before entering. To get here, take bus 5A from Wawasan Plaza going toward UMS (RM1.50). Just ask the conductor to drop you off outside the City Mosque after the Tanjung Lipat roundabout.

State Mosque   MOSQUE
(Jln Tunku Abdul Rahman) Sabah's state mosque is a perfect example of contemporary Malay Muslim architecture: all modernist facade and geometric angles. The building is south of the city centre past the Kampung Air stilt village, not far from the Sabah Museum; you'll see the striped minaret and chevronned dome on your way to or from the airport. Non-Muslim visitors are allowed inside, but dress appropriately.

Tanjung Aru   BEACH
This pretty sweep of sand begins around the Shangri-La's Tanjung Aru Resort and stretches south to the airport. Tanjung Aru is a locals' beach, full of picnic spots, swoony-eyed couples and much familial goodwill. Food stalls are plentiful, most closing up a bit after dark, which reminds us: sunsets here are pretty perfect. We would advise against swimming here; the water may look nice, and some locals may tell you it's fine, but others claim it's tainted by run-off from KK and nearby water villages.

Orchid De Villa   FARM
(☏380611; www.orchid-de-villa.com.my; Jln Kiansom; ⊙8am-5pm; ℗) If you're just as crazy about flora as fauna, head to this farm, about 3 km from central KK, along the road to Penampang. The farm specialises in rare Bornean orchids, hybrid orchids, cacti and herbal plants.

👉 Tours

KK has a huge number of tour companies, enough to suit every taste and budget. Head to Wisma Sabah – this office building is full of agents and operators. We have highlighted three companies that specialise in off-the-beaten-track and/or ecotourism activities.

TOP CHOICE GogoSabah   SIGHTS
(Map p308; ☏316385, 317385; www.gogosabah.com; Lot G-4, ground fl, Wisma Sabah, Jln Tun Razak) Gogo is a fantastic tour company that does a great job of booking just about anything,

anywhere in Sabah. It's especially excellent for motorbike rentals – staff will help map out some of the choicest areas for exploration in Sabah. It also offers car rentals and a serviced apartment, too. It's a good go-to organisation for package tours, but can also help independent travellers out with logistics, itineraries and information.

TOP CHOICE Sticky Rice   TOURS
(☏250588; www.stickyricetravel.com) The Sticky Rice guys are extremely helpful, knowledgable about Borneo, and committed to natural immersion, community engagement and independent travel.

TOP CHOICE Adventure
Alternative Borneo   NATURE
(Map p308; ☏019-802 0549; www.adventurealternativeborneo.com; 97 Jln Gaya) Adventure Alternative specialises in getting Sabah visitors off the beaten/package tour path, and is an excellent resource for independent travellers, especially those who are interested in sustainable and responsible tourism.

Bike Borneo   BICYCLE RENTAL
(☏484734; www.bikeborneo.com; City Mall, Jln Lintas, Kota Kinabalu; 1-day tours from RM245) Our favourite means of getting around Sabah on two wheels (with no motor) is mountain biking, and the guys at Fieldskills Adventures, who run Bike Borneo, are the experts on the topic. They run their mountain biking activities largely out of Tuaran; packages include a day ride in the vicinity of town that crosses three (count 'em) swinging bridges and a four-day cycling adventure across the foothills of Mt Kinabalu.

Riverbug/Traverse Tours   SIGHTS
(Map p308; ☏260501; www.traversetours.com; Lot 227, Wisma Sabah, Jln Tun Fuad Stephens) An excellent and forward-thinking operator that has a wide variety of tours across Sabah. It makes admirable efforts to engage in sustainable travel practices.

Fieldskills Adventures   ADVENTURE TOUR
(☏484734; fieldskills.com.my; City Mall, Jln Lintas) If you're into outdoor activities and adventure, get in touch with these guys. This outfit leads well-regarded cycling, rock climbing, trekking and diving trips across Sabah.

Borneo Adventure   ADVENTURE TOUR
(Map p308; ☏486800; www.borneoadventure.com; Block E-27-3A, Signature Office, KK Times Square)

SABAH KOTA KINABALU

Award-winning Sarawak-based company with very professional staff, imaginative sightseeing and activity itineraries and a genuine interest in local people and the environment.

Borneo Authentic
BOAT TOUR

(☏773066; www.borneo-authentic.com; Lot 3, 1st fl, Putatan Point, Jln JKR) A friendly operation offering a variety of package tours including day-trip cruises on the Sungai Klias.

Equator Adventure Tours
CULTURAL TOUR

(☏766351, 013-889 9535; http://equator-adventure. com) Offers plenty of nature and adventure tours, as well as the Hajah Halimah Traditional cooking course (RM135), one of the few cooking courses currently offered in Sabah. Participants check out the local fresh and wet markets and prepare a meal in a Malaysian kitchen with an English-speaking guide. Its head office is in Putatan, 9km east of the city centre.

Borneo Divers
DIVING

(Map p308; ☏222226; www.borneodivers.net; 9th fl, Menara Jubili, 53 Jln Gaya) This is the longest-established Borneo dive outfit; it can arrange courses and dives just about anywhere and has its own dive shop. It's possible to get discounted rates as a walk-in.

Downbelow Marine & Wildlife Adventures
DIVING

(Map p308; ☏012-866 1935; www.divedownbelow. com; Lot 67 & 68, 5th fl, KK Time Square Block) A well-respected dive outfit with a PADI Centre on Pulau Gaya that can arrange all kinds of travel packages across Borneo.

Borneo Eco Tours
SIGHTS

(☏438300; www.borneoecotours.com; Pusat Perindustrian Kolombong Jaya, Mile 5.5 Jln Kolombong) This is a place with a good reputation, arranging tours throughout Malaysian Borneo, including travel to the Kinabatangan area.

Borneo Nature Tours
NATURE

(Map p308; ☏267637; www.borneonaturetours. com; Block D, Lot 10, Kompleks Sadong Jaya, Ikan Juara 4) A professional and knowledgeable operation that manages bookings for Danum Valley's Borneo Rainforest Lodge. Its office building is on the corner near a canal.

Scuba Junkie/River Junkie
DIVING, RAFTING

(Map p308; ☏255816; www.scuba-junkie.com; ground fl, Lot G7, Wisma Sabah, Jln Haji Saman) Runs diving trips in the Semporna Archipelago and white-water rafting trips in south-

west Sabah aimed at the Western backpacker (and flashpacker) crowd.

Sutera Harbour
CLIMBING

(Sutera Sanctuary Lodges; Map p308; ☏308914/5; www.suteraharbour.com; ground fl, Lot G15, Wisma Sabah, Jln Haji Saman) Sutera runs a lot of the tourism activities in Sabah, and has a monopoly on accommodation within the Mt Kinabalu ark. Make this your first stop in KK if you're planning to climb Kinabalu and didn't book your bed in advance.

🛏 Sleeping

Check out the **Sabah Backpacker Operators Association** (SBA; www.sabahbackpackers.com) which was set up in an effort to help shoestring travellers in the region. Check out its website for discount deals on accommodation and tours. KK's midrange options seem to be sliding towards either end of the budget spectrum. Although backpacker hangouts and top-end treats are in great proliferation, there are still several spots around town suiting those Goldilockses out there.

⭐ Sarangnova Hotel
HOTEL $$

(Map p308; ☏233750; www.sarangnova.com; 98 Jln Gaya; s/d from RM120/170) It's hard not to miss this fascinating hotel; there's a conceptual, woodsy slat fixture attached to the front. The rooms are just as distinctive as the exterior, seeing as they're themed after Borneo's birds. No, no feathers on the walls or anything, but the attractively minimalist decor is offset by gallery-style portraits of local avian life; this includes some picture compositions that are downright Warhol-ian. For being a little different, and still offering superlative service in all the ways that count (helpful staff, central location), we give the Sarangnova two beaks up.

Hotel Eden 54
BOUTIQUE HOTEL $$

(Map p308; ☏266054; www.eden54.com; 54 Jln Gaya; r RM119-179; ❄🅰🛜) This smart choice would likely cost five times what it does were it plopped in the West. Fortunately this Eden's contrasting solid dark and light colours, geometric design sensibility and immaculate furniture have turned up in Kota Kinabalu. A fine choice for flashpackers, couples, even families. One warning: the cheapest rooms are windowless and should be avoided.

Rainforest Lodge
HOTEL $$

(Map p308; ☏258228; www.rainforestlodgekk.com; Jln Pantai; dm/s/d/ste from RM40/115/135/165;

※@🛜) Located in the swinging centre of the 'Beach Street' complex, the Rainforest is all of a stairward stumble from some of KK's best nightlife. Rooms are refreshingly chic, a nice mix of modern and Sabah-tribal style, and many have cool balconies that look onto the Beach St parade below. Just be warned: it gets loud at night.

Hotel Sixty3 — HOTEL $$

(Map p308; 📞212663; www.hotelsixty3.com; Jln Gaya 63; r from RM190; ※🛜) This smart hotel offers business-class standard accommodation, with chilly air-con, flat-screen TVs and big soft beds, all in the heart of KK. The rooms, with their clean white lines and geometric accents, are popular with families and travellers needing a little pampering.

Le Meridien Kota Kinabalu — HOTEL $$$

(Map p308; 📞322222; www.starwoodhotels.com; Jln Tun Fuad Stephens; r from RM300; P※🛜🏊) 'If you can't undercut 'em, outclass 'em' seems to be the motto at KK's most central five-star venture, which just reeks of luxury, from the incredible views from the pool deck to the flat-screen TVs and DVD players. The eye-watering prices come down a little in low season, and may even get as low as RM200 if you catch the right discounts.

Klagan Hotel — HOTEL $$

(Map p308; 📞488908; www.theklagan.com/; Block D, Warisan Square, Jln Tun Fuad Stephens; r RM180-260; ※🛜) Funky molded recliners and bright yellows and reds in the superior rooms make this midrange option a cut above the competition.

Le Hotel — HOTEL $$

(Map p308; 📞319696; www.lehotel.com.my; Block B, 3rd fl, Warisan Sq, Jln Tun Fuad Stephens; r RM120-198; ※🛜) Rooms at the Le are a little smallish, but there's a cool blue colour scheme and midrange amenities, plus nice views of the waterfront at the higher end of the price scale.

Summer Lodge — HOSTEL $

(Map p308; 📞244499; www.summerlodge.com.my; Lot 120, Jln Gaya; dm/d RM28/70; ※🛜) Summer Lodge feels like a bed factory, but it's got that social vibe backpackers adore – 'How long have you been travelling? Where did you come from/where are you going? Isn't it funny when foreigners do that thing they do? Fancy a drink?' The answer to the last question is easily solved – the Beach St bar complex is just below.

Jesselton Hotel — HOTEL $$$

(Map p308; 📞223333; www.jesseltonhotel.com; 69 Jln Gaya; r/ste from RM180/450; ※🛜) The oldest hotel in KK doesn't need to manufacture character – it fairly drips it, in a dignified if dated way. Mock-colonial wood and marble make you want to don black-tie formal clothes, and the single suite even has its own fishpond. There's also a very good restaurant, coffee shop, business centre and red London cab to shuttle you to the airport.

Kinabalu Daya — HOTEL $$

(Map p308; 📞240000; www.kkdayahotel.com; Lot 3-4, Block 9, Jln Pantai; r/ste incl breakfast from RM140/270; ※🛜) Oddly angled hallways and strangely placed lifts give Kinabalu Daya a certain '10-year-old's-Lego-project' vibe. Nevertheless, tons of tourists swear by this midrange stalwart – and justifiably so – it's in the centre of the action, the Best Western branding ensures a certain amount of familiar comfort, and many rooms actually exude a stylish, boutique chic.

Akinabalu Youth Hostel — HOSTEL $

(Map p308; 📞272188; www.akinabaluyh.com/; Lot 133, Jln Gaya; dm/r incl breakfast from RM22/60; ※🛜) Friendly staff, fuchsia accent walls and trickling Zen fountains make this a solid option among KK's hostels, particularly if you find a quiet time to take advantage of the gratis internet and DVDs. Accommodation is mostly in basic four-bed rooms, with windows facing an interior hallway.

Lucy's Homestay — HOSTEL $

(Backpacker's Lodge; Map p308; 📞261495; lucyhomestay.go-2.net; Lot 25, Lg Dewan, Australia Pl; dm/s/d incl breakfast RM28/45/50; 🛜) Lucy's is one of the oldest of the old school hostels in Australia Pl. There's loads of charm, with wooden walls smothered in stickers, business cards and crinkled photographs. It may not suit if you're a party person or want cushy extras, and we get the sense Lucy is a bit more motherly to women than male guests.

Hyatt Regency Kota Kinabalu — HOTEL $$$

(Map p308; 📞221234; http://kinabalu.regency.hyatt.com; Jln Datuk Salleh Sulong; r from RM350; P※🛜) Located in the city centre, this branch of the Hyatt chain is all corporate glitz – a good spot to take a businessman for lunch while enjoying impressive views out of a top-storey suite. Rooms are done up in warm earth tones and packed with amenities, including quite possibly the best selection of cable-TV channels in the city.

SABAH KOTA KINABALU

Shangri-La's Tanjung Aru Resort & Spa
RESORT $$$

(STAR; ☎327888; www.shangri-la.com/kotakinaba lu/tanjungaruresort; Tanjung Aru; r from RM550; P✳❄🛜🏊) The Shangri-La is a good choice for those who want to combine the attractions of Kota Kinabalu with the features of a tropical resort. It's a sprawling complex, dotted with swaying palms and metal gongs, located in the Tanjung Aru area about 3km south of the city centre. Dozens of uniformed staff are constantly on hand to respond to your every whim.

Borneo Gaya Lodge
HOSTEL $

(Map p308; ☎242477; www.borneogayalodge.com; 78 Jln Gaya; dm/d from RM25/65; ✳🛜) A typical high-volume hostel. Staff are a peach, and will help organise nearly anything, and you're as centrally located in KK as can be.

Myne Hotel
HOTEL $$$

(Map p308; ☎448787; http://hotel.myne.com. my; Lot 21, Warisan Sq; r/ste from RM270/430; ✳🛜) It might be located within a mall, but the Myne, with its deep red and gold accents and brass fixtures, feels as gaudy as a chandelier. As high-end spots go, this is an executive-class kind of place, lacking the space of a resort but making up for it with a more central location.

Borneo Backpackers
HOSTEL $

(Map p308; ☎234009; www.borneobackpackers. com; 24 Lg Dewan, Australia Pl; dm/s/d incl breakfast from RM20/40/60; ✳🛜) This long-running backpackers is a bit cramped, but it's very popular, especially with younger travellers.

Bunibon
HOSTEL $

(Map p308; ☎210801; www.bunibonlodge.com/; Lot 21, Lorong Dewan; dm/s/d from RM25/50/68; ✳🛜) An attractive, friendly hostel with a social vibe and surprisingly nice private doubles.

Kinabalu Backpackers
HOSTEL $

(Map p308; ☎253385; www.kinabalubackpackers. com; Lot 4, Lorong Dewan; dm/s/d from RM25/55/68; ✳🛜) A bit bare, but cheap, cheerful and clean. It can organise onward travel and tours.

Eating

KK is one of the few cities in Borneo with an eating scene diverse enough to refresh the noodle-jaded palate. Besides the ubiquitous Chinese *kedai kopi* (coffee shops) and Malay halal restaurants, you'll find plenty of interesting options around the city centre – head to the suburbs if you're looking for some truly unique local fare.

CITY CENTRE

TOP CHOICE Alu-Alu Cafe
SEAFOOD $$

(Map p308; Jesselton Point; mains from RM10-30; ⏱10:30am-2:30pm & 6:30am-10pm; ✳) Technically part of the Gayana Eco Resort, Alu-Alu is a delicious restaurant that sources its ingredients from Borneo Eco-Fish, an organisation dedicated to harvesting and distributing seafood from sustainable sources – no shark fin here. Besides having a bit of a moral mission, Alu-Alu is legitimately delicious. It takes the Chinese seafood concept to new levels – lightly breading fish chunks and serving them drowned in a mouth-watering buttermilk sauce, or simmering amid diced chilies. Even the vegetables, simply steamed with a side of pungent garlic, are a main event as opposed to an afterthought.

Ya Kee Bah Kut Teh
CHINESE $

(Map p308; ☎221192; 74 Jln Gaya; mains from RM5; ⏱4pm-11pm) Kosher and halal readers need not apply because this spot is all about the pork. Pork, pork, pork, in herbal soup form (ie *Bah Kut The*). Fatty pork. Pork ribs. Pork belly. Pork with ginger and chillies. Pork offal. With all apologies to *Babe*, we gotta highly recommend this delicious option.

Grazie
ITALIAN $$

(Map p308; ☎019-821 6936; ground fl, Wawasan Plaza; mains from RM17; ⏱noon-3pm Fri-Sun, noon-6pm Mon-Thu; ✳) KK is chock-full of Italian places, but Grazie, run by Italian expat Salvatore Marcello, tops them all handily. Many ingredients are imported (including a fine shot of grappa we finished our meal with); the pizza is thin crust and divine; the pasta and other mains sent from on high. Grazie, *grazie* indeed.

Chili Vanilla
FUSION $$

(Map p308; 35 Jln Haji Sama; mains RM12-20; ⊙10am-10pm, closed Sun; ❉❢) KK is not the first city that springs to mind when we think 'Sure could use some goulash,' but then Chili Vanilla comes along. Run by a Hungarian chef and her local busines partner, this adorable spot dishes out some unexpected delights; besides the goulash there's Moroccan lamb stew, spicy duck tortillas and, just to bring it back to Asia, rich braised oxtail. Wash it all down with the incredible house lime juice, or order off the extensive wine menu.

El Centro
FUSION $

(Map p308; 32 Jln Haji Saman; RM9-16; ⊙5pm-midnight, closed Mon; ❢) El Centro serves up lovely Malaysian dishes, but honestly, we come here when we need a Western food fix (also: good music, nice atmosphere and tasteful decor). The burgers taste like real beef and the pasta dishes are comforting enough to make us long for home.

Borneo 1945 Museum Kopitiam
CAFE $

(Map p308; ☑272945; 24 Jln Dewan, Australia Pl; mains from RM3; ⊙7:30am-midnight; ❉) Odd name for a restaurant-cum-cafe? Yes, because this is a restaurant-cum-cafe-cum-museum, dedicated to the Allied fighting forces in Borneo during WWII. Perhaps the best iced coffee in KK is served here, alongside breakfast favourites like toast and *kaya* (coconut jam), indigenous fare like pandan chicken and rice, and (why not?) reproductions of Anzac biscuits. The on-site mini-museum is worth a visit by itself.

Kohinoor
INDIAN $$$

(Map p308; ☑235160; Lot 4, Waterfront Esplanade; dinner about RM50; ⊙11.30am-2.30pm & 5.30pm-11pm; ❉❢) There are several excellent restaurants along the Waterfront Esplanade, but this Indian place is an easy favourite. Take advantage of its authentic tandoori oven and don't forget to grab a side of pillowy garlic naan.

MAKAN: KOTA KINABALU–STYLE

Kota Kinabalu (KK) may be light on sights, and its urban core isn't a stunner, but the city comes up trumps in the food category. KK's veritable melting pot of cultures has fostered a lively dining scene that differentiates itself from the rest of Malaysia with a host of recipes fusing foreign recipes and local ingredients.

KK's four essential eats:

Sayur Manis – Also known as 'Sabah veggie', this bright-green jungle fern can be found at any Chinese restaurant worth its salt. It's best served fried with garlic, or mixed with fermented shrimp paste. The *sayur manis* plant is a perennial and can grow about 3m high. It is harvested year-round so it tends to be very fresh. Adventurous eaters might want to try other local produce like *tarap*, a fleshy fruit encased in a bristly skin, or *sukun*, a sweet-tasting tuber used to make fritters.

Filipino Barbecue – Located at the north end of the KK Night Market, the Filipino Barbecue Market is the best place in town for grilled seafood at unbeatable prices. Hunker down at one of the crowded tables and point to your prey. Once the waitress has sent your order off to the grill, she'll hand you a cup (for drinking), a basin (to wash your hands) and a small plate to prepare your dipping sauce (mix up the chilli sauce, soy sauce, salt and fresh lime for your own special concoction). No cutlery here! Just dig in with your bare hands and enjoy steaming piles of fresher-than-fresh seafood. Figure around RM15 for a gut-busting meal.

Hinava – Perhaps the most popular indigenous appetiser, colourful *hinava* is raw fish pickled with fresh lime juice, *chilli padi,* sliced shallots and grated ginger. The melange of tangy tastes masks the fishy smell quite well. The best place to try *hinava* is Grace Point, a posh local food court near Tanjung Aru. You'll find it at the 'Local Counter' for around RM2 per plate (the portions are small – the perfect size for a little nibble).

Roti Canai – The ubiquitous *roti canai*, a flaky flat bread fried on a skillet, is served from dawn till dusk at any Indian Muslim *kedai kopi* (coffee shop) around town. Although the dish may appear simple, there's actually a lot of skill that goes into preparing the perfect platter. The cook must carefully and continuously flip the dough (à la pizza chef) to create its signature flakiness. *Roti canai* is almost always served with sauce, usually dhal (lentil curry) or another curry made from either chicken or fish.

KOTA KINABALU'S HAWKER CENTRES & FOOD COURTS

As in any Southeast Asian city, the best food in KK is the street food and hawker stalls. If you're worried about sanitation, you really shouldn't be, but assuage your fears by looking for popular stalls, especially those frequented by families.

Night Market (p306) The night market is the best, cheapest and most interesting place in KK for dinner. Vegetarian options available.

Centre Point Basement Food Court (Map p308; Basement fl, Centre Point Shopping Centre, Jln Pasar Baru; mains RM3-10; ⊘11am-10pm) Your ringgit will go a long way at this popular and varied basement food court in the Centre Point Mall. There are Malay, Chinese and Indian options, as well as drink and dessert specialists.

Grace Point (Grace Point; mains RM2-8; ⊘11am-3pm) Take bus 15 out near Tanjung Aru for some local grub at this KK mainstay. The development is actually quite chic compared to the smoke-swathed food courts in the city centre. Go for the Sabahan food stall (located in the far right corner when facing the row of counters) and try *hinava* (raw fish pickled with fresh lime juice, chilli padi, sliced shallots and grated ginger).

Wisma Merdeka Food Court FOOD COURT $
(Map p308; Wisma Merdeka; mains from RM3; ⊘9am-5pm) For cheap, excellent eats, head to the top floor of the Wisma Merdeka mall and get stuck into the local food court. There's a nice diversity of stalls serving mainly Asian street food; the Chinese dumpling stand is delicious and cheap as chips. Note the above hours do not apply to each stall; some close shop earlier in the day and some stick around into the evening, but in general this is a breakfast and lunch food court.

Nagisa JAPANESE $$$
(Map p308; ☑221234; Jln Datuk Salleh Sulong; sushi from RM15; ⊘noon-10pm; ❋✎) For our money – and you'll spend a bit here – this is the best Japanese in KK. Why? Well, it's the sushi spot of choice for Japanese businessmen on return visits, which oughta tell you something. If they've got roe (caviar) on the menu, get it, and thank us later. Located in the Hyatt Regency.

Kedai Kopi Fatt Kee CHINESE $
(Map p308; 28 Jln Bakau; mains from RM5; ⊘noon-10pm Mon-Sat) The woks are always sizzlin' at this popular Chinese place next to Ang's Hotel. Its *sayur manis* cooked in *belacan* (shrimp paste) is a classic, and the salt-and-pepper prawns are tasty.

TANJUNG ARU

In the early evening, head to Tanjung Aru at the south end of town near the airport for sunset cocktails and light snacks along the ocean. The area has three beaches – First Beach offers up a few restaurants, Second Beach has steamy local stalls, and Third Beach is a great place to bring a picnic as there are no establishments along the sand. A taxi to Tanjung Aru costs RM20, or you can take public transport (RM1.80) – take bus 16, 16A or city bus 2.

Self-Catering

There are a variety of places to stock up on picnic items and hiking snacks, including the centrally located **Milimewa Superstore** (Map p308; Jln Haji Saman) and **Tong Hing Supermarket** (Map p308; Jln Gaya). **7-Eleven** (Map p308; Jln Haji Saman; ⊘24hr) is conveniently open throughout the evening.

🍷 Drinking & Entertainment

Get ready for loads of karaoke bars and big, booming nightclubs, clustered around the Waterfront Esplanade, KK Times Square – where the newest hot spots are congregating, and Beach St, in the centre of town, a semipedestrian street cluttered with bars and eateries.

TOP CHOICE **El Centro** BAR
(Map p308; 32 Jln Haji Saman; ⊘5pm-midnight, closed Mon) This fantastic spot, which doubles as a restaurant (p315), was sorely needed in KK. El Centro is the traveller's hangout you've been looking for: cool, Asian-mod decor, soft lighting, good music that isn't the same recycled pop every other Malaysian bar plays, and a general sense of chilled-out-ed-ness that makes it easy to meet other wanderers and form new friendships. Also: the drinks are strong. Stupid strong. And El Centro hosts impromptu quiz nights, costume parties and live music shows.

Bed
NIGHTCLUB

(Map p308; ✆251901; Waterfront Esplanade) It's big, it's crowded, it's cheesy – chances are you'll end up in Bed on one of your KK nights out. Yes, get those bed puns ready, as well as your dancing shoes and patience for a *lot* of hip Chinese and locals in outfits that are alternatively slinky/shiny/skimpy. Bands play from 9pm, followed by DJs till closing.

White Room
NIGHTCLUB

(Map p308; ✆017-836 7718; KK Times Sq) The hot thing with KK's young folks, the White Room is two levels of sweat, loud music, beautiful bodies and expensive drinks.

Shenanigan's
BAR

(Map p308; ✆221234; Hyatt Regency Hotel) Shenanigans is a hot mess, so we kinda love it, even though, honestly, it's just a hot mess. Live bands perform most nights from 9pm and the place is packed on weekends. Prices are horrendous (up to RM30 for a small beer) but get better during happy hour.

Shamrock
BAR

(Map p308; ✆249829; 6 Anjung Samudra, Waterfront Esplanade) This bar is as authentically Irish as, well, Borneo, but it is an authentic Irish Bar, Model 1.0: green, Guinness, meat stew, luck o' the lass o' the laddish behaviour. Still a nice place to shoot some stick and watch KK's monied elite get silly.

Hunter's
BAR

(Map p308; ✆016-825 7085; Kinabalu Daya Hotel) A favourite for local guides and expats, Hunter's offers up karaoke, sport on the plasma TV and balmy outdoor seating in the heart of the city.

Upperstar
BAR

(Map p308; Jln Datuk Saleh Sulong) Opposite the Hilton, this pleasant semi-outdoor bar offers cheap booze and decent pub grub.

Black World
KARAOKE

(Map p308; Jln Pantai; ⏱24hrs) We know. This is the only spot that stays open past 2am in central KK. But here's what to expect: cheap beer served in iced buckets, ear-shredding karaoke and dance music, sleazy male clientele, ladies of negotiable affection and bathrooms from the deepest pits of hell.

Suria Sabah
CINEMA

(Map p308; Suria Sabah Mall, Jn Haji Saman) The Suria Sabah mall houses a huge multiplex that shows all the Hollywood hits, usually in the original English with subtitles.

🛍 Shopping

Like any Malaysian metropolis, KK is all about shopping. Malls seem to pop up every year; at the time of research the big new complex was **Suria Sabah**, which is full of Western retail chains and very few people.

Borneo Trading Post
CRAFTS

(Map p308; ✆232655; Lot 16, Waterfront Esplanade, Jln Tun Fuad Stephens) Upmarket tribal art and souvenirs.

Borneo Books
BOOKSHOP

(Map p308; ✆538077/241050; www.borneobooks.com; ground fl, Phase 1, Wisma Merdeka; ⏱10am-7pm) A brilliant selection of Borneo-related books, maps and a small used-book section. Plenty of Lonely Planet guides, too.

ⓘ Information

Free maps of central KK and Sabah are available at almost every hostel or hotel.

Emergency
Ambulance (✆999, 218166)
Fire (✆994)
Police (✆241161, 999; Jln Dewan)

Internet Access
Every sleeping spot we list has some form of internet connection, be it dial-up or wi-fi.
Borneo Net (Jln Haji Saman; per hr RM3; ⏱9am-midnight) Twenty terminals, fast connections and loud headbanger music wafting through the air.
Net Access (Jln Pantai; per hr RM3; ⏱9-2am) Plenty of connections and less noise than other net places in KK. LAN connections are available for using your own laptop.

Immigration Office
Immigration office (✆488700; Kompleks Persekutuan Pentadbiran Kerajaan, Jln UMS; ⏱7am-1pm & 2-5:30pm Mon-Fri) In an office complex near the Universiti Malaysia Sabah (UMS), 9km north of town. Open on weekends, but only for Malaysian passport processing.

Medical Services
Permai Polyclinic (Map p308; ✆232100; 4 Jln Pantai) Excellent private outpatient clinic.
Sabah Medical Centre (✆211333; www.sabahmedicalcentre.com/; Lorong Bersatu, off Jalan Damai) Good private hospital care, located about 6km southeast of the city centre.

Money
Central KK is chock-a-block with 24-hour ATMs.
HSBC (Map p308; ✆212622; 56 Jln Gaya; ⏱9am-4.30pm Mon-Thu, 9am-4pm Fri)

Maybank (Map p308; 254295; 9 Jln Pantai; 9am-4.30pm Mon-Thu, 9am-4pm Fri) 24hr ATM.

Standard Chartered Bank (Map p308; 298111; 20 Jln Haji Saman; 9.15am-3.45pm Mon-Fri)

Post

Main Post Office (210855; Jln Tun Razak; 8am-5pm Mon-Fri) Western Union cheques and money orders can be cashed here.

Tourist Information

Sabah Parks (523500, 486430; www.sabah parks.org.my; 1st-5th fl, Lot 45 & 46, Block H, Signature Office; 8am-1pm & 2-4.30pm Mon-Thu, 8-11.30am & 2-4.30pm Fri, 8am-12.50pm Sat) Source of information on the state's parks.

Sabah Tourism Board (212121; www.sabah tourism.com; 51 Jln Gaya; 8am-5pm Mon-Fri, 8am-4pm Sat, 9am-4pm Sun) Housed in the historic post office building, KK's main tourist office has eager staff and a wide range of brochures. Fair warning, they're going to direct you towards package tours, so don't expect much in the way of independent travel advice.

Tourism Malaysia (248698; www.tourism. gov.my; ground fl, Api-Api Centre, Jln Pasar Baru; 8am-4.30pm Mon-Thu, 8am-noon &

1.30-4.30pm Fri) This office is of limited use for travellers, but does offer a few interesting brochures on sights in Peninsular Malaysia.

Getting There & Away

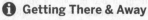

Air

KK is well served by **Malaysia Airlines** (1-300 883 000, 088-515555; www.malaysiaair lines.com; MAS; 1st fl, Departure Hall, KKIA; 5.30am-7.30pm) and **AirAsia** (03-2171 9333; www.airasia.com; ground fl, Wisma Sabah, Jln Gaya) offer the following international flights to/from KK: Brunei, Shenzhen, Jakarta, Manila, Singapore and Tapei. Within Malaysia, flights go to/from Johor Bahru, Kuala Lumpur and Penang in Peninsular Malaysia, and Kuching, Labuan, Miri, Sandakan, and Tawau in Borneo. **Jetstar** (www.jetstar.com) and **Tiger Airways** (www. tigerairways.com) both offer flights to Singapore.

Boat

All passengers must pay an adult/child RM3.60/1.80 terminal fee for ferries departing from KK. Passenger boats connect KK to Pulau Labuan twice daily at 8am and 1:30pm (adult first/economy class RM36/31, child first/ economy class RM23/18), with onward service to Brunei and to Tunku Abdul Rahman National

MAIN DESTINATIONS & FARES FROM KOTA KINABALU

The following bus and minivan transport information was provided to us by the Sabah Tourism Board and should be used as an estimate only: transport times can fluctuate due to weather, prices may change, and the transport authority has been known to alter departure points.

DESTINATION	DURATION (HR)	PRICE (RM)	TERMINAL	DEPARTURES
Beaufort	2	12	Padang Merdeka	7am-5pm (frequent)
Keningau	2½	17	Padang Merdeka	7am-5pm (8 daily)
Kota Belud	1	10	Padang Merdeka	7am-5pm (frequent)
Kuala Penyu	2	20	Segama Bridge	8-11am (hourly)
Kudat	3	22	Padang Merdeka	7am-4pm (frequent)
Lahad Datu	8	40	Inanam	7am, 8.30am, 9am, 8pm
Lawas (Sarawak)	4	25	Padang Merdeka	8.30am & 1.30pm
Mt Kinabalu NP	2	15-20	Inanam & Padang Merdeka	7am-8pm (very frequent)
Ranau	2	15	Padang Merdeka	7am-5pm
Sandakan	6	35-40	Inanam	7.30am-2pm (frequent) & 8pm
Semporna	9	50	Inanam	7am, 8.30am, 9am, 8pm
Tawau	9	55	Inanam	7.30am, 2pm, 8pm
Tenom	3½	25	Padang Merdeka	8am, noon, 4pm

RIDING THE BORNEO RAILS

Back in the late 19th-century, colonials used to swan around the western Sabah coast on the **North Borneo Railway**, which eventually fell into disuse and disrepair. Recently, the old rail line has been revived, not as a viable means of train travel but as a nostalgic attraction in its own right. The old iron horse has been restored, with natural wood interiors and the original exterior colour scheme of green and cream, set off with the railway's old brass emblem of a crown surmounting a tiger holding a rail wheel.

The train leaves KK at 9:30am and arrives in Papar at 11:45am, taking in mountains and rice paddies, with stops for a look at a Chinese temple and the Papar wet market. On the trip back to KK (12.20–1.40pm) a smashing colonially inspired tiffin lunch of cucumber sandwiches and satay (plus some other goodies) is served.

The railway is operated by Sutera Harbour (p312); adult/child tickets cost RM270/170. The train leaves the station in Tanjung Aru twice a week, on Wednesday and Saturday. For more information or to book tickets, contact Sutera Harbour at 308500 or nbrinfo@suteraharbour.com.my.

Park. Ferries depart from Jesselton Point, located a little way north of the **Suria Sabah shopping mall** (Map p308).

Bus & Minivan

Several different stations around KK serve a variety of out-of-town destinations. There is a bus to Brunei.

In general, land transport heading east departs from Inanam (Utara Terminal; 9km north of the city) while those heading north and south on the west coast leave from Padang Merdeka (Merdeka Field) Bus Station (also called Wawasan or 'old bus station'; at the south end of town). Local buses (RM1.80) from Wawasan can take tourists to Inanam if you don't want to splurge on the RM20 taxi. Have your hotel call ahead to the bus station to book your seat in advance. Same-day bookings are usually fine, although weekends are busier than weekdays. It's always good to ring ahead because sometimes transport will be halted due to flooding caused by heavy rains.

Taxi

Share taxis operate from the Padang Merdeka Bus Station. Several share taxis do a daily run between KK and Ranau, passing the entrance road to the Kinabalu National Park office. The fare to Ranau or Kinabalu National Park is RM25, or you can charter a taxi for RM100 per car (note that a normal city taxi will charge around RM200 for a charter).

ⓘ Getting Around

To/From the Airport

The international airport is in Tanjung Aru, 7km south of central KK. Please note that the two terminals of Kota Kinabalu International Airport (KKIA) are not connected – they feel like two different airports. Most airlines operate out of Terminal 1, but an increasing amount of carriers, including AirAsia, depart from Terminal 2. City bus 2 and bus 16A (RM1.50) service Terminal 2 and can be boarded at City Park station downtown. Minibuses (RM3) leave from City Park station for Terminal 1 (look for city bus 1 to access this terminal in the future). Public transport runs from 6am to 7pm daily. Taxis heading from terminals into town operate on a voucher system (RM38) sold at a taxi desk on the terminal's ground floor. Taxis heading to the airport should not charge over RM40 if you catch one in the city centre.

Car

Major car-rental agencies have counters on the first floor at KKIA and branch offices elsewhere in town. Manual cars start at around RM120 to RM140 per day and most agencies can arrange chauffeured vehicles as well.

Borneo Express (☎016-886 0793, In Sandakan 016-886 0789; http://borneocar.com/; Lot 1-L01 C4, Kota Kinabalu Airport)

Kinabalu Heritage Tours & Car Rental (☎318311; www.travelborneotours.com; Block F, Tanjung Aru Plaza)

Extra Rent A Car (☎251529, 218160; www.e-erac-online.com; 2nd fl, Beverly Hotel, Jln Kemajuan)

Minivans

Minivans operate from several stops, including Padang Merdeka Bus Station and the car park outside Milimewa Superstore. They circulate the town looking for passengers. Since most destinations in the city are within walking distance, it's unlikely that you'll need to catch a minivan, although they're handy for getting to the airport or to KK Times Square. Most destinations within the city cost RM1 to RM2.

Taxi

Expect to pay roughly between RM7 to RM10 for a ride in the city centre. Taxis can be found throughout the city and at all bus stations and shopping centres. There's a stand by Milimewa Supermarket (near the intersection of Jln Haji Saman and Beach St) and another 200m southwest of City Park.

AROUND KOTA KINABALU

Tunku Abdul Rahman National Park

Whenever one enjoys a sunset off KK, the view tends to be improved by the five jungly humps of Manukan, Gaya, Sapi, Mamutik and Sulug islands. These swaths of sand, plus the reefs and cerulean waters in between them, make up **Tunku Abdul Rahman National Park** (adult/child RM10/6), covering a total area of just over 49 sq km (two-thirds of which is water). Only a short boat ride from KK, the islands are individually quite pretty, but in an effort to accommodate the ever-increasing tourist flow (especially large numbers of Chinese), barbecue stalls and restaurants now crowd the beaches. On weekends the islands can get *very* crowded, but on weekdays you can find some serenity. Accommodation tends to be expensive, but most travellers come here for day trips anyway, and there are camping options.

Although it's no Sipadan, diving in the park is a popular activity, and the area is considered a good spot for getting open water certified. **Borneo Dream** (☎088-244064; www.borneodream.com; F-G-1 Plaza Tanjung Arum, Jalan Mat Salleh, Kota Kinabalu) and Downbelow (p312) both run diving programs on Pulau Gaya.

PULAU MANUKAN

Manukan is the most popular destination for KK residents and has plenty of facilities. It is the second-largest island in the group, its 20 hectares largely covered in dense vegetation. There's a good beach with coral reefs off the southern and eastern shores, a walking trail around the perimeter and a network of nature trails – if you want to thoroughly explore all of the above it shouldn't take more than two hours, and you don't need to be particularly fit. There's little clouds of tropical fish swimming around, many of which

can be seen simply by looking down from the jetty. When you depart the boat you'll likely be pointed towards a kiosk that hires equipment masks and snorkels (RM15), beach mats (RM5) and body boards (RM10).

Manukan Island Resort (☎017-833 5022; www.suterasanctuarylodges.com; villa from RM1120; ❄️⚡), managed by Sutera Sanctuary Lodges, has the only accommodation on the island. It comprises a restaurant, swimming pool and tennis courts, as well as 20 dark-wood villas, all overlooking the South China Sea and decked out in tasteful Bali-chic style; the cool stone showers hemmed in by flowering plants are a nice touch.

PULAU MANUKAN

Mamutik is the smallest island out here, a mere 300m from end to end. A nice beach runs up and down the east coast of the island, although it can get pretty kelp-y after bad weather. Snorkelling here is pretty good, but you may want to avoid the shallow area; the coral here will do a number on your bare feet. There's no resort, but camping (RM5 per person, pay on arrival) is possible. There's a small store-restaurant-snorkel-rental place, but it's a good idea to bring supplies.

PULAU SAPI

They should really rename Pulau Sapi (Cow Island) to Pulau Biawak (Monitor Lizard Island). This little speck also offers snorkelling and attractive beaches, but Sapi can also get very cramped with day-tripping families. The island is separated from Gaya by a very shallow 200m channel that you can swim across if you feel up to it, but be careful; there are definitely no life guards on duty. Otherwise, the main activities include wading, relaxing on the beach around the jetty or exploring the trails through the forest; it takes about 45 minutes to walk around the island. There are changing rooms, toilets, barbecue pits, and a small snack kiosk, plus an outfitted campsite (RM5 per person), but you'll need to bring most supplies from the mainland.

PULAU GAYA

With an area of about 15 sq km, Pulau Gaya is the Goliath of KK's offshore islands, rising to an elevation of 300m. It's also the closest to KK and covered in virtually undisturbed tropical forest. The bays on the east end are filled with bustling water villages, inhabited by Filipino immigrants (legal and otherwise) who live in cramped houses built on stilts in the shallow water, with mosques, schools and simple shops, also built on stilts. Residents of KK warn against exploring these water villages, saying that incidences of theft and other crimes have occurred. Three high-end resorts make up the accommodation options on Pulau Gaya.

Bunga Raya Island Resort RESORT $$$
(☎380390; http://bungarayaresort.com; villas from RM1715; ✳︎☎☂) Six stunning villas occupy a fertile patch of beachfront. The Plunge Pool has just that – its own deep body of water that looks over the beach and ocean – while the incredibly romantic Treehouse perches over a jacuzzi, lounge and its own private swimming hole. Operated by the owners of Gayana Eco Resort.

Gaya Island Resort RESORT $$$
(☎KL number 3 2783 1000; www.gayaislandresort.com; villas from RM1100; ✳︎☎☂) Six immaculate villas that blend modernity with open air accents, earth tones with cool whites, and a subtle integration of the ocean with green jungle perch over a half-moon bay. Attentive service makes for a property that drips with refined indulgence.

Gayana Eco Resort RESORT $$$
(☎380390; www.gayana-eco-resort.com; villas from RM1200; ✳︎☎☂) Five stunning villas stuffed with modern amenities and island chic touches make up posh Gayana. The Bakau (mangrove) Villa overlooks a series of tangled flooded forest, while the Palm Villa's deceptive simplicity masks steps that lead into the warm heart of Tunku Rahman's protected waters.

PULAU SULUG
Shaped like a cartoon speech bubble, Sulug has an area of 8.1 hectares and is the least visited of the group, probably because it's the furthest away from KK. It only has one beach, on a spit of land extending from its eastern shore. Unfortunately, the snorkelling is pretty poor. If you want a quiet getaway, Sulug is a decent choice, but you'll have to charter a boat to get here; the normal ferries don't stop here. If you want a secluded beach and don't want to lay out for a charter (at least RM240), you'll do better by heading to Manukan and walking down the beach to escape the crowds.

❶ Getting There & Away
Boat
Boats to the park leave from 8.30am to 4.15pm when full from KK's Jesselton Point Ferry Terminal (commonly known as 'The Jetty' by locals and taxi drivers); the last boats leave the islands for KK around 5pm. Service is every 30 minutes, but on slower days this can be every hour. Inquire at the counter for the next available boat, sign up for your chosen destination and take a seat until there are enough passengers to depart. Catch a boat in the morning, as it's much harder to make up boat numbers in the afternoon. Boats also run from Sutera Harbour – more convenient for those staying near Tanjung Aru (or for those wanting to reach Pulau Gaya). Return fares to Mamutik, Manukan and Sapi hover around RM30. You can also buy two-/three-island passes for RM40/48.

SABAH TUNKU ABDUL RAHMAN NATIONAL PARK

WATER MONITORING

If you look around the edge of the barbecue pits on Sapi, you may spot a fence cordoning off some of the jungle, and at said fence you'll usually find a hissing band of great, grey-green dragons: water monitor lizards, known locally as *biawak*. They're some of the largest reptiles in the world, with males averaging a length of 1.5m to 2m, sometimes growing as large as 3m, weighing anywhere from 19kg to 50kg. Within the lizard family they are only outstripped by Komodo Dragons.

These mini-Godzillas are found all over Malaysia, but on Pulau Sapi they are the king of the jungle – and the waves. It's amazing watching these lumbering beasts take to the water, where they instantly transform into graceful sea monsters reminiscent of aquatic dinosaurs (which, indeed, are believed to be the ancestors of monitor lizards). Despite their size, water monitors aren't apex predators in the vein of crocodiles or their Komodo Dragon cousins. Instead, they serve the purpose of coyotes in North America, or jackals in Africa: adaptable, clever scavengers that seem to thrive, rather than suffer, when humans are near, making use of our refuse dumps as their larders.

Water monitors are awesome creatures, but don't be an idiot like some tourists and try to pose next to them or hand feed them. Their mouths are filled with deadly bacteria and their claws can rip a gash in your flesh you won't soon forget.

The set fee for charter to one island is RM250, but this can be negotiated. Try to deal directly with a boatperson if you do this – don't talk to the touts who prowl the area. And don't consider paying until you return to the dock.

A RM3 terminal fee is added to all boat journeys, and a RM10 entrance fee to the marine park, paid when you purchase your ticket (if you are chartering a boat this should be included).

NORTHWESTERN SABAH

The northern edge of Sabah manages to compact, into a relatively small space, much of the geographic and cultural minutiae that makes Borneo so special. The ocean? Lapping at miles of sandy beach, sky blue to stormy grey, and concealing superlative dive sites. The people? Kadazan–Dusun, Rungus, rice farmers, mountain hunters, ship builders and deep-sea fishermen. And then, of course, 'the' mountain: Gunung Kinabalu, or Mt Kinabalu, the focal point of the island's altitude, trekkers, folklore and spiritual energy. For generations, the people of Sabah have been drawn to the mountain; don't be surprised when you fall under its spell too.

Mt Kinabalu & Kinabalu National Park

Gunung Kinabalu, as it is known in Malay, is more than the highest thing on the world's third largest island. And it is more than scenery. Mt Kinabalu is ubiquitous in Sabah to the point of being inextricable. It graces the state's flag and is a constant presence at the edge of your eyes, catching the clouds and shading the valleys. It is only when you give the mountain your full attention that you realise how special this peak, the region's biggest tourist attraction, truly is.

The 4095m peak of Mt Kinabalu may not be a Himalayan sky-poker, but Malaysia's first Unesco World Heritage Site is by no means an easy jaunt. The main trail up is essentially a very long walk up a very steep hill, past alpine jungle and sunlit moonscapes, with a little scrabbling thrown in for good measure. If you don't feel up to reaching the mountain top, its base has some worthy attractions, including a large network of nature trails.

That said, the main detriment to climbing is not the physical challenge, but the cost. Things are expensive within Mt Kinabalu

National Park. Bottled water costs four or five times what it goes for in KK and Sutera Sanctuary Lodges has a monopoly on accomodation. You'll have to decide if you want to accept these fees because they are basically the cost of climbing the mountain.

Amazingly, the mountain is still growing: researchers have found it increases in height by about 5mm a year. On a clear day you can see the Philippines from the summit; usually, though, the mountain is thoroughly wreathed in fog by midmorning.

History

Although it is commonly believed that local tribesmen climbed Kinabalu many years earlier, it was Sir Hugh Low, the British colonial secretary on Pulau Labuan, who recorded the first official ascent of Mt Kinabalu in 1851. Today Kinabalu's tallest peak is named after him, thus Borneo's highest point is ironically known as Low's Peak.

In those days the difficulty of climbing Mt Kinabalu lay not in the ascent, but in getting through the jungle to the mountain's base. Finding willing local porters was another tricky matter – the tribesmen who accompanied Low believed the spirits of the dead inhabited the mountain. Low was therefore obliged to protect the party by supplying a large basket of quartz crystals and teeth, as was the custom back then. During the subsequent years, the spirit-appeasement ceremonies became more and more elaborate, so that by the 1920s they had come to include loud prayers, gunshots, and the sacrifice of seven eggs and seven white chickens. You have to wonder at what point explorers started thinking the locals might be taking the mickey...

These days, the elaborate chicken dances are no more, although climbing the mountain can still feel like a rite of passage.

Check out Mountain Torq's website (www.mountaintorq.com) for more fun facts about Kinabalu's history.

Geology

Many visitors to Borneo assume Mt Kinabalu is a volcano, but the mountain is actually a huge granite dome that rose from the depths below some nine million years ago. In geological terms, Mt Kinabalu is still young. Little erosion has occurred on the exposed granite rock faces around the summit, though the effects of glaciers that used to cover much of the mountain can be detected by striations on the rock. There's no longer a

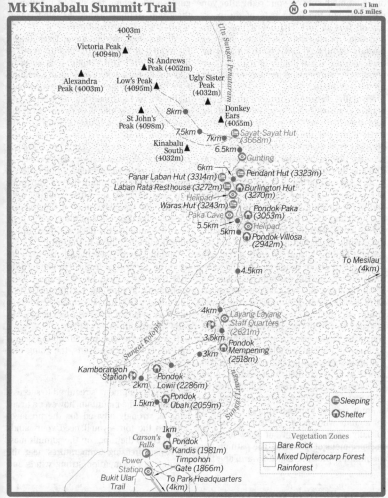

N
0 — 1 km
0 — 0.5 miles

4003m
Victoria Peak
(4094m) ▲

St Andrews
Peak (4052m) ▲

Alexandra
Peak (4003m) ▲

Low's Peak
(4095m) ▲

Ugly Sister
Peak
(4032m) ▲

St John's
Peak (4098m) ▲

8km

Donkey
Ears
(4055m) ▲

Sayat-Sayat Hut
(3668m)

7.5km
7km

Kinabalu
South
(4032m) ▲

6.5km

Gunting

6km

Pendant Hut (3323m)

Panar Laban Hut (3314m)

Burlington Hut
(3270m)

Laban Rata Resthouse (3272m)

Helipad

Pondok Paka
(3053m)

Waras Hut (3243m)

Paka Cave

5.5km

Helipad

5km

Pondok Villosa
(2942m)

To Mesilau
(4km)

4.5km

4km

Layang Layang
Staff Quarters
(2621m)

3.5km

Pondok
Mempening
(2518m)

3km

Kamborangoh
Station

2km

Pondok
Lowii (2286m)

1.5km

Pondok
Ubah (2059m)

1km

Carson's
Falls

Pondok
Kandis (1981m)

Power
Station

Timpohon
Gate (1866m)

Bukit Ular
Trail

To Park Headquarters
(4km)

Sungai Kolopis

Sungai Liwagu

Ulu Sungai Penataran

Sleeping
Shelter

Vegetation Zones
Bare Rock
Mixed Dipterocarp Forest
Rainforest

snowline and the glaciers have disappeared, but at times ice forms in the rock pools near the summit.

Orientation & Information

Kinabalu National Park HQ is 88km by road northeast of KK and set in gardens with a magnificent view of the mountain. At 1588m the climate is refreshingly cool compared to the coast; the average temperatures are 20°C in the day and 13°C at night. The hike to the summit is difficult.

On the morning of your arrival, pay your park entry fee, present your lodging reservation slip to the Sutera Sanctuary Lodges office to receive your official room assignment, and check in with the Sabah Parks office to pay your registration and guide fees. Advance accommodation bookings are *essential* if you plan on climbing the mountain.

PERMITS, FEES & GUIDES

A park fee, climbing permit, insurance and a guide fee are *mandatory* if you intend to climb Mt Kinabalu. All permits and guides must be arranged at the **Sabah Parks office** (⊙7am-7pm), which is directly next door to the Sutera Sanctuary Lodges office, immediately on your right after you pass through the main gate of the park. Pay all fees at park HQ before you climb and don't ponder an 'unofficial' climb as permits (laminated cards worn on a string necklace) are scrupulously checked at two points you cannot avoid passing on the way up the mountain.

Virtually every tour operator in KK can hook you up with a trip to the mountain; solo travellers are often charged around RM1400. It's possible, and a little cheaper, to do it on your own – but plan ahead. Packages are obviously easier if pricey, so if you find one that sounds enticing, go for it.

All visitors entering the park are required to pay a park entrance fee: RM15 for adults and RM10 for children under 18 (Malaysians pay RM3 and RM1, respectively). A climbing permit costs RM100/RM40 for adults/children, while Malaysian nationals pay RM30/RM12. Climbing insurance costs a flat rate of RM7 per person. Guide fees for the summit trek cost RM100. Climbers ascending Kinabalu along the Mesilau Trail will pay an extra RM10 (small group) or RM20 (large group) for their guide. Your guide will be assigned to you on the morning you begin your hike. If you ask, the park staff will try to attach individual travellers to a group so that guide fees can be shared. Couples can expect to be given their own guide. Guides are mostly Kadazan from a village nearby and many of them have travelled to the summit several hundred times. Try to ask for a guide who speaks English – he or she (usually he) might point out a few interesting specimens of plant life. The path up the mountain is pretty straightforward, and the guides walk behind the slowest member of the group, so think of them as safety supervisors rather than trailblazers.

All this does not include at least RM415 for room-and-board on the mountain at Laban Rata. With said lodging, plus buses or taxis to the park, you're looking at spending over RM800 for the common two-day, one-night trip to the mountain. That said, you *can* do a one-day hike if you show up at the park entrance when it opens (7am) and are judged physically fit by a ranger. This allows you to cut the cost of lodging, but there are two catches. First, when we say you need to be fit, we mean *fit*. A friend – one of those annoyingly healthy mountaineers who probably sleepwalks up the Alps – couldn't walk upstairs for two days after managing the one-day hike. Second, and more worryingly, there are rumours the park will discontinue allowing one-day hikes in the future.

Optional extra fees include a taxi ride from the park office to the Timpohon Gate (RM16.50 per vehicle, one-way, four-person maximum), a climbing certificate (RM10) and a porter (RM102 per trip to the summit or RM84 to Laban Rata) who can be hired to carry a maximum load of 10kg.

If you need a helicopter lift off the mountain for emergency reasons, the going rate is RM2500.

EQUIPMENT & CLOTHING

No special equipment is required to successfully summit the mountain, however a headlamp is strongly advised for the predawn jaunt to the top – you'll need your hands free to climb the ropes on the summit massif. Expect freezing temperatures near the summit, not to mention strong winds and

---

CAN I AVOID PLAYING MONOPOLY?

One of the most common questions travellers in Sabah ask is: is there any way to go up Mt Kinabalu that is less expensive? The best way to do so is the one-day climb, but that prospect is tough unless you're fit, and even then it is discouraged by park officials, and may be discontinued in the future.

Many travellers hate that Sutera has a monopoly on accomodation, or that they are encouraged to book their climb months in advance, which discourages just showing up and walking. If you feel this way, it may be best to walk the trails at the base of Mt Kinabalu or attempt the Mesilau Trail up to the first park checkpoint, which offers much of the full climb's scenery.

Sabah Parks won't allow a night climb, and permits are carefully checked at several points on the mountain. We did meet hikers who wanted to try the above, but this would involve a lot of sneaking around and tempting fate, be it a trekking accident or arrest, and we don't recommend this. If you're set against giving Sabah Parks or Sutera your money, trust us, there are plenty of other things to see and do here.

KINABALU PACKING LIST

» Headlamp (with spare batteries)
» Comfortable running shoes
» Wool socks and athletic socks
» Hiking shorts or breathable pants
» Three T-shirts (one made of lightweight synthetic material)
» Fleece jacket
» Lightweight shell jacket or rain jacket
» Fleece or wool hat
» Fleece gloves
» Long johns
» Hand towel
» Water bottle
» Sunscreen
» Insect repellent
» Light, high-energy snacks
» Camera
» Money
» Earplugs for dorms

The above items should easily fit into a small waterproof backpack. Apply a dab of sunscreen and insect repellent before you depart.

the occasional rainstorm. Don't forget a water bottle, which can be refilled at unfiltered (but potable) tanks en route.

THE CLIMB TO THE SUMMIT

This schedule assumes you're doing a two-day/one-night ascent of the mountain. You'll want to check in at park headquarters at around 9am (8.45am at the latest for *via ferrata* participants) to pay your park fees, grab your guide and start the ascent (four to six hours) to Laban Rata (3272m) where you'll spend the night before finishing the climb. On the following day you'll finish scrambling to the top at about 2.30am in order to reach the summit for a breathtaking sunrise over Borneo.

A climb up Kinabalu is only advised for those in adequate physical condition. The trek is tough, and *every step you take* will be uphill. You will negotiate several obstacles along the way, including slippery stones, blinding humidity, frigid winds and slow-paced trekkers. Mountain Torq compares the experience to squeezing five days of hiking into a 38-hour (or less, if you do the one-day climb) trek.

There are two trail options leading up the mountain – the Timpohon Trail and the Mesilau Trail. If this is your first time climbing Kinabalu, we advise taking the Timpohon Trail – it's shorter, easier (but by no means easy!) and more convenient from the park headquarters (an hour's walk or short park shuttle ride; RM16.50 one-way per vehicle, four-person maximum). If you are participating in Mountain Torq's *via ferrata,* you are required to take the Timpohon Trail in order to reach Laban Rata in time for your safety briefing at 4pm. The Mesilau Trail offers second-time climbers (or fit hikers) the opportunity to really enjoy some of the park's natural wonders. This trail is less trodden so the chances of seeing unique flora and fauna are higher.

As you journey up to the summit, you'll happen upon signboards showing your progress – there's a marker every 500m. There are also rest shelters *(pondok)* at regular intervals, with basic toilets and tanks of unfiltered (but potable) drinking water. The walking times that follow are conservative estimates – don't be surprised if you move at a slightly speedier pace, and certainly don't be discouraged if you take longer – everyone's quest for the summit is different.

ADDING INSULT TO INJURY

As your two-day Kinabalu adventure comes to an end and you limp across the Timpohon Gate a shrivelled bundle of aching muscles and bones, don't forget to glance at the climbing records chart. Every year the **Kinabalu International Climbathon** (http://climbathon.sabahtourism.com) attracts the fittest athletes from around the world for a competitive climb-off as dozens of hikers zoom up the mountain a la the Road Runner. The oldest person to reach the summit was a Japanese lady who battled her way to the top at the grand old age of 90. So just remember, when you're smugly slinking by slower hikers, there are pensioners out there who would leave you for dead...

TIMPOHON GATE TO LAYANG LAYANG

'Why am I sweating this much *already?*'

The trip to the summit officially starts at the Timpohon Gate (1866m) and from there it's an 8.72km march to the summit. There is a small bathroom outhouse located 700m before the Timpohon Gate, and a convenience shop at the gate itself for impulse snack and beverage purchases.

After a short, deceptive descent, the trail leads up steep stairs through the dense forest and continues winding up and up for the rest of the trip. There's a charming waterfall, **Carson's Falls**, beside the track shortly after the start, and the forest can be alive with birds and squirrels in the morning. Five *pondok* (shelters) are spaced at intervals of 15 to 35 minutes between Timpohon Gate and Layang Layang and it's about three hours to the Layang Layang (2621m) rest stop. Near **Pondok Lowii** (2286m) the trail follows an open ridge giving great views over the valleys and up to the peaks.

LAYANG LAYANG TO PONDOK PAKA

'Why did I put all that extra crap in my rucksack?'

This part of the climb can be the most difficult for some – especially around the 4.5km marker. You've definitely made some headway but there's still a long trek to go – no light at the end of the jungly tunnel quite yet. It takes about 1¾ hours to reach **Pondok Paka** (3053m), the seventh shelter on the trail, 5.5km from the start.

PONDOK PAKA TO LABAN RATA

'Why did I pay all that money just to climb a freakin' mountain?!'

Also known as the 'can't I pay someone to finish this for me?' phase, this part of the climb is where beleaguered hikers get a second wind as the treeline ends and the summit starts to feel closer. At the end of this leg you'll reach **Laban Rata** (3272m), your 'home sweet home' on the mountain. Take a

good look at the slender signpost announcing your arrival – it's the propeller of the helicopter once used to hoist the construction materials to build the elaborate rest station. This leg takes around 45 minutes.

LABAN RATA TO SAYAT-SAYAT HUT

'Why am I waking up at the time I usually go to bed back home?'

It's 2am and your alarm just went off. Is this a dream? Nope. You're about to climb the last part of the mountain in order to reach the summit before sunrise.

Most people set off at around 2.45am, and it's worth heading out at this time even if you're in great shape (don't forget your torch). The one-hour climb to **Sayat-Sayat** hut (3668m) involves a lot of hiker traffic and the crossing of the sheer Panar Laban rock face. There is little vegetation, except where overhangs provide some respite from the wind. It is one of the toughest parts of the climb, especially in the cold and dark of the predawn hours.

SAYAT-SAYAT HUT TO SUMMIT

'Why is it so darn cold out?! I'm standing near the equator!'

After checking in at Sayat-Sayat, the crowd of hikers begins to thin as stronger walkers forge ahead and slower adventurers pause for sips from their water bottle. Despite the stunning surroundings, the last stretch of the summit ascent is, of course, the steepest and hardest part of the climb.

From just beyond Sayat-Sayat, the summit looks deceptively close and, though it's just over 1km, the last burst will take between one to three hours depending on your stamina. You might even see shattered climbers crawling on hands and knees as they reach out for the top of Borneo.

THE SUMMIT

[Speechless...]

This is it – the million-dollar moment (or the RM800+ moment for those who are keeping score...). Don't forget the sunrise can be glimpsed from anywhere on the mountain. The summit warms up quickly as the sun starts its own ascent between 5.45am and 6.20am, and the weary suddenly smile; the climb up a distant memory, the trek down an afterthought.

Consider signing up with Mountain Torq to climb back to Laban Rata along the world's highest *via ferrata*.

THE JOURNEY BACK TO THE BOTTOM

'Why didn't I believe anyone when they said that going down was just as hard as going up?!'

You'll probably leave the summit at around 7.30am and you should aim to leave Laban Rata no later than 12.30pm. The gruelling descent back down to Timpohon Gate from Laban Rata takes between three and four hours (if you're returning to the bottom along the Mesilau Trail it will take more time than descending to the Timpohon Gate). The weather can close in very quickly and the granite is slippery even when dry. During rainstorms the downward trek feels like walking through a river. Slower walkers often find that their legs hurt more the day after – quicker paces lighten the constant pounding as legs negotiate each descending step. If you participated in the *via ferrata* you will be absolutely knackered during your descent and will stumble into Timpohon Gate just before sunset (around 6pm to 6.30pm).

A 1st-class certificate can be purchased for RM10 by those who complete the climb; 2nd-class certificates are issued for making it to Laban Rata. These can be collected at the park office.

WALKS AROUND THE BASE

It's well worth spending a day exploring the marked trails around park headquarters; if you have time, it may be better to do it before you climb the mountain, as chances are you won't really feel like it afterwards. There are various trails and lookouts.

The base trails interconnect with one another like a tied shoelace, so you can spend the day, or indeed days, walking at a leisurely pace through the beautiful forest. Some interesting plants, plenty of birds and, if you're lucky, the occasional mammal can be seen along the **Liwagu Trail** (6km), which follows the river of the same name. When it rains, watch out for slippery paths and legions of leeches.

At 11am each day a **guided walk** (per person RM3) starts from the Sabah Parks office and lasts for one to two hours. The knowledgeable guide points out flowers, plants, birds and insects along the way. If you set

VIA FERRATA

Mountain Torq has dramatically changed the Kinabalu climbing experience by creating an intricate system of rungs and rails crowning the mountain's summit. Known as *via ferrata* (literally 'iron road' in Italian), this alternative style of mountaineering has been a big hit in Europe for the last century and is just starting to take Asia by storm. In fact, Mountain Torq is Asia's first *via ferrata* system, and, according to the Guinness Book of World Records, it's the highest 'iron road' in the world.

After ascending Kinabalu in the traditional fashion, participants use the network of levers to return to the Laban Rata rest camp along the mountain's dramatic granite walls. Mountain Torq's star attraction, the **Low's Peak Circuit** (RM550; minimum age 17), is a four-to-five-hour scramble down metres upon metres of sheer rock face. This route starts at 3800m, passing a variety of obstacles before linking up to the Walk the Torq path for the last part of the journey. The route's threadlike tightrope walks and swinging planks will have you convinced that the course designers are sadistic, but that's what makes it so darn fun – testing your limits without putting your safety in jeopardy. Those who don't want to see their heart leaping out of their chest should try the **Walk the Torq** (RM400; minimum age 10) route. This two-to-three-hour escapade is an exciting initiation into the world of *via ferrata*, offering dramatic mountain vistas with a few less knee-shaking moments. No matter which course you tackle, you'll undoubtedly think that the dramatic vertical drops are nothing short of exhilarating.

Via ferrata may be an Italian import, but Mountain Torq is pure Bornean fun. For more information about Mountain Torq, check out www.mountaintorq.com.

FLORA & FAUNA OF MT KINABALU

Mt Kinabalu is a botanical paradise, designated a Centre of Plant Diversity as well as a Unesco-listed World Heritage Site. The wide range of habitats supports an even wider range of natural history, and over half the species growing above 900m are unique to the area.

Among the more spectacular flowers are orchids, rhododendrons and the *Insectivorous nepenthes* (pitcher plant). Around park HQ, there's dipterocarp forest (rainforest); creepers, ferns and orchids festoon the canopy, while fungi grow on the forest floor. Between 900m and 1800m, there are oaks, laurels and chestnuts, while higher up there's dense rhododendron forest. On the windswept slopes above Laban Rata vegetation is stunted, with *sayat-sayat* a common shrub. The mountain's uppermost slopes are bare of plant life.

Deer and monkeys are no longer common around park HQ, but you can see squirrels, including the handsome Prevost's squirrel and the mountain ground squirrel. Tree shrews can sometimes be seen raiding rubbish bins. Common birds are Bornean treepies, fantails, bulbuls, sunbirds and laughing-thrushes, while birds seen only at higher altitudes are the Kinabalu friendly warbler, the mountain blackeye and the mountain blackbird. Other wildlife includes colourful butterflies and the huge green moon moth.

out from KK early enough, it's possible to arrive at the park in time for the guided walk.

Many of the plants found on the mountain are cultivated in the **Mountain Garden** (Map p329; admission RM5; ⊙9am-1pm, 2:30am-4pm) behind the visitors centre. Guided tours of the garden depart at 9am, noon and 3pm and cost RM5.

🛏 Sleeping

Laban Rata (On The Mountain)

Camping is not allowed on the mountain, and thus access to the summit is limited by access to the huts on the mountain at Laban Rata (3272m). This *must* be booked in advance, the earlier the better. In order to have any hope of clear weather when you reach the summit, you must arrive around dawn, and the only way to do this is by spending a night at Laban Rata. If you attempt a one-day ascent starting around 7am, by the time you get to the summit it will almost certainly be clouded over or raining.

Sutera Sanctuary Lodges (☎088-308470, 088-318888, info 243 629; suterasanctuary lodges.com.my; Jln Haji Saman, Lot G15, ground fl, Wisma Sabah; ⊙8:30am-4:30pm Mon-Sat, 8:30am-12:30pm Sun) in Kota Kinabalu operates almost all of the accommodation here, but space is limited. Be mindful that travellers often report frustration with booking huts on the mountain – claiming the booking system is disorganised and inefficient, the huts are often full, or aren't full when they're told they are. Bookings can be made

online (but only if you book at least two nights), in person or over the phone – our experience was that it was best to book at Sutera's offices in KK if you haven't done so in advance.

The most common sleeping option is the heated dormitory (bedding included) in the Laban Rata Resthouse, which sells for RM485 per person. If you need privacy, twin shares are available for RM920. Three meals are included in the price. Non-heated facilities surrounding the Laban Rata building are also available for RM415 per person (meals included).

The other option at Laban Rata is to stay at **Pendant Hut**, which is owned and operated by **Mountain Torq** (pricing is on par with Sutera). All guests sleeping at Pendant Hut take two of three meals at Sutera's cafeteria, and are required to participate in (or at least pay for) the *via ferrata* circuit. Pendant Hut is slightly more basic (there's no heat, although climbers sleep in uberwarm sleeping bags). However, there's a bit of a summer-camp vibe here while Laban Rata feels more like a Himalayan orphanage. Prices for Pendant Hut are comparable to Sutera.

Park Headquarters (At the Base)

The following sleeping options are located at the base of the mountain and are operated by Sutera Sanctuary Lodges. They're overpriced compared to sleeping spots just outside the park.

SABAH MT KINABALU & KINABALU NATIONAL PARK

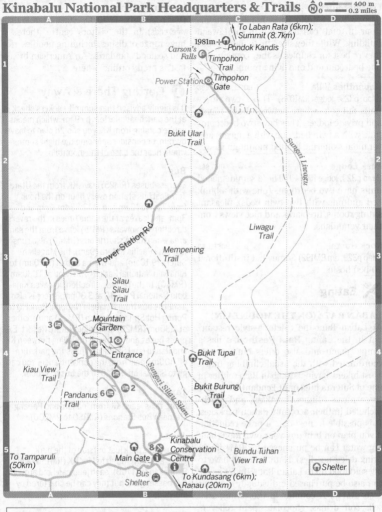

Map legend / labels: To Laban Rata (6km); Summit (8.7km); 1981m; Carson's Falls; Pondok Kandis; Timpohon Trail; Timpohon Gate; Power Station; Sungai Liwagu; Bukit Ular Trail; Power Station Rd; Liwagu Trail; Mempening Trail; Silau Silau Trail; Mountain Garden; Entrance; Bukit Tupai Trail; Kiau View Trail; Bukit Burung Trail; Pandanus Trail; Sungai Silau Silau; Kinabalu Conservation Centre; Bundu Tuhan View Trail; Main Gate; Bus Shelter; To Tamparuli (50km); To Kundasang (6km); Ranau (20km); Shelter

Kinabalu National Park Headquarters & Trails

◉ Sights
1 Mountain Garden	B4

⬛ Sleeping
2 Grace Hostel	B4
3 Hill Lodge	A4
4 Liwagu Suites	A4
5 Nepenthes Villa	A4
6 Peak Lodge	B4
7 Rock Hostel	B4

✖ Eating
Liwagu Restaurant	(see 4)
8 Restoran Kinabalu Balsam	B5

SABAH MT KINABALU & KINABALU NATIONAL PARK

Grace Hostel HOSTEL $$
(Map p329; dm RM192) Clean, comfortable 20-bed dorm with fireplace and drink-making area.

Hill Lodge CABIN $$$
(Map p329; cabin RM580) These semidetached cabins are a good option for those who can't face a night in the hostels. They're clean and comfortable, with private bathrooms.

SABAH AROUND MT KINABALU

Liwagu Suites
HOTEL $$$

(Map p329; ste RM700) These hotel-like rooms (four in total) can be found in the Liwagu Building. While they sleep up to four people, they're best for couples as they contain only one bedroom and one living room.

Nepenthes Villa
HOTEL, LODGE $$$

(Map p329; lodge RM1078) These two-storey units fall somewhere between hotel rooms and private lodges. They have two bedrooms (one with a twin bed, one with a queen) and verandahs offering limited mountain views.

Peak Lodge
UNIT $$$

(Map p329; lodge RM940) These semidetached units have two bedrooms (one with a bunk bed and one with two twin beds), pleasant sitting rooms, fireplaces and nice views from their verandahs.

Rock Hostel
HOSTEL $$

(Map p329; dm RM192) Somewhat institutional 20-bed hostel.

Eating

LABAN RATA (ON THE MOUNTAIN)

At Laban Rata the cafeteria-style restaurant in the **Laban Rata Resthouse** has a simple menu and also offers buffet meals coordinated with the usual climbing times. Most hikers staying at Laban Rata (either in one of Sutera's huts or at Pendant Hut) have three meals (dinner, breakfast and lunch) included in their accommodation packages. It is possible to negotiate a price reduction if you plan on bringing your own food (boiling water can be purchased for RM1 if you bring dried noodles). Note: you will have to lug said food up to Laban Rata. Buffet meals can also be purchased individually – dinner costs RM45. A counter in the dining area sells soft drinks, chocolate, pain relievers and postcards.

PARK HEADQUARTERS (AT THE BASE)

Restoran Kinabalu Balsam
CAFETERIA $$

(Map p329; dishes RM5-15; ⊙6am-10pm, to 11pm weekends) The cheaper and more popular of the two options in the park is this canteen-style spot directly below the park HQ. It offers basic but decent Malaysian, Chinese and Western dishes at reasonable prices. There is also a small but well-stocked shop in Balsam selling tinned and dried foods, chocolate, beer, spirits, cigarettes, T-shirts, bread, eggs and margarine.

Liwagu Restaurant
CAFETERIA $$

(Map p329; dishes RM10-30; ⊙6am-10pm, to 11pm weekends) In the visitors centre, there's a huge range of dishes, including noodles, rice and seafood standards. An 'American breakfast' is pretty ordinary here.

❶ Getting There & Away

It is highly advised that summit-seekers check in at the park headquarters by 9am, which means if you're coming from KK, you should plan to leave by 7am, or consider spending the night somewhere near the base of the mountain.

Bus

Express buses (RM25) leave KK from the Utara Terminal bus station every hour on the hour from 7am to 10am and at 12:30pm, 2pm and 3pm, and leaves at the same times in the reverse directions; minivans (RM15) leave from the same area when full. A shuttle bus (RM40) also runs from the Pacific Sutera (9am), the Magellan Sutera (9.10am) and Wisma Sabah (9.20am) to Kinabalu National Park HQ, arriving at 11.30am (RM40). In the reverse direction, it leaves Kinabalu National Park HQ at 3.30pm. There is also a shuttle bus from Kinabalu National Park HQ to Poring Hot Springs at noon (RM25) and another at 3.30pm (RM25) to Mesilau Nature Resort. Express buses and minivans travelling between KK and Ranau (and Sandakan) pass the park turn-off, 100m uphill from the park entrance. You can go to Sandakan (RM40) if the bus has room.

Taxi

Share taxis leave KK from Inanam and Padang Merdeka Bus Stations (RM150 to RM200).

Jeep

Share jeeps park just outside of the park gates and leave when full for KK (RM150) and Sandakan (RM400); each jeep can hold around five passengers, but they can be chartered by individuals.

Around Mt Kinabalu

Kinabalu National Park is home to Borneo's highest mountain and some of the island's best-preserved forest. Most travellers make a beeline for the mountain and the main park headquarters area, but the following spots are also worth exploring:

MESILAU NATURE RESORT

This lovely slice of country is the trailhead for an alternative approach up Mt Kinabalu, often favoured by trekkers as it's more challenging than the main route and much less crowded than park headquarters. The

Mesilau route wanders up the mountain and links up with the Timpohon route to continue the ascent to Laban Rata. Arrange your trip with (who else?) Sutera Sanctuary Lodges and your guide will meet you at Mesilau.

KUNDASANG MEMORIAL

The junction for the Mesilau Nature Resort on the KK–Ranau Hwy is the site of the **Kundasang War Memorial** (admission RM10; ⊙8am-5.30pm), which commemorates the Australian and British prisoners who died on the infamous Sandakan Death Marches. Four gardens, manicured in that bucolic yet tame fashion that is so very English, are separated by a series of marbled pavilions. In the Anzac Garden you can see a full list of the dead and at the back of the gardens is a viewpoint that offers a stunning view of Mt Kinabalu.

The memorial is in Kundasang, 6km east of Kinabalu National Park headquarters. You'll know you're in Kundasang when you see the market stalls on either side of the road. Take the turn on the left for Mesilau Nature Resort. The memorial is on the right 150m after the turn-off. Look for the flags and the stone fort-like structure above the road.

RANAU

Ranau is a collection of concrete shop blocks on the road between KK and Sandakan. There's a busy Saturday **night market**, but otherwise this a good town for passing through: rampant construction is scarring the lovely valley it sits in. That said, there is a podiatry experience here you don't want to miss (we don't often use those words). After your epic Kinabalu climb, head to **Tagal Sungai Moroli** (admission RM10) in Kampung Luanti for a truly unique massage experience. The term *tagal* means 'no fishing' in the local Kadazan-Dusun language, as the fish in the river (a species known locally as *ikan pelian*) are not to be captured – they are special massage fish. The townsfolk claim that they've trained the little swimmers to gently nibble at weary feet.

◉ Sights

Sabah Tea Garden   TEA PLANTATION
(☏440882; www.sabahtea.net; factory tour RM12, with set lunch RM34, 2-day, 1-night package from RM190) A pretty tea plantation that looks like a cluster of giant mossy tussocks huddles in the mountains near Ranau. Contact the tea garden to arrange tours of both the plantation and surrounding rainforests and river valleys. Overnight packages are available; you get to sleep in an on-site property in a tarted-up version of a traditional longhouse. Also offers tours of the facilities coupled with a trip to the fish foot massage (RM110).

PORING HOT SPRINGS

One of the few positive contributions the Japanese made to Borneo during WWII, **Poring Hot Springs** (adult/child RM15/10) has become a popular weekend retreat for locals. The complex is actually part of the Kinabalu National Park, but it's 43km away from the park headquarters, on the other side of Ranau.

The hot springs are located in a well-maintained forest park that does a fine job of giving casual visitors a small slice of the jungle – there's various nature paths and the like that the elderly and children can enjoy. But the springs themselves are not natural puddles. Steaming (seriously, it's hot), sulphurous water is channelled into man-made pools and tubs, some of which feel a little rundown. For some, it's a huge anticlimax, but others enjoy it. Don't forget a towel and your swimming trunks.

For our ringgit, the highlight of the place is actually way above the springs: a **Canopy Walkway** (admission RM15; ⊙9am-4pm) that consists of a series of walkways suspended from trees, up to 40m above the jungle floor, providing unique views of the surrounding forest. Get there early if you want to see birds or other wildlife. A **tropical garden** (adult/child RM3/1.50; ⊙9am-4pm), **butterfly farm** (adult/child RM4/2; ⊙9am-4pm Tue-Sun) and **orchid garden** (adult/child RM10/5; ⊙9am-4pm) are also part of the Poring complex. Rafflesia sometimes bloom in the area; look out for signs in the visitors centre and along the road.

TOP **Lupa Masa**   ECO-CAMP $
CHOICE
(☏019-802 0549, SMS advised 016-8068194; www.facebook.com/lupa.masa; dm (stretcher hammock) RM50) About a 10-minute drive from Poring you'll find this incredible ecolodge; the name comes from the Malay for 'forget time', which is pretty easy to do here. The green friendly spot contributes money to local communities and very much caters to independent travellers, which is a bit of a rarity in Sabah. That said, Lupa Masa isn't for everyone. It's rustic here. There are bugs

in the camp and leeches just outside. You get three good meals a day (vegetarian on demand), but there's no TV, no air-con and you're using squat toilets. Accommodation is in raised tents and traditional lodging made from local bamboo, roofed with palm leaves and kitted with stretcher hammocks and mosquito nets. You are in the jungle, folks. On the other hand: *what a jungle*. There are a few 'pools' on the property – incredible natural pools fed by mountain streams and waterfalls where you feel like you're in true, wild Borneo.

The owners offer guided treks and there's a great chance you'll run into local wildlife, especially on night walks. The trekking options include night, day and overnight treks (starting at RM20), as well as jungle survival courses. You can also opt for rooms in a traditional-style longhouse if you want a bit more privacy.

🛏 Sleeping outside Kinabalu Park

It's worth spending a night around the base of Kinabalu before your ascent, and there are plenty of accommodation options suiting everyone's budget. All of the following have attached restaurants:

The accommodation at Mesilau and Poring is run by Sutera Sanctuary Lodges with a notable exception. At forested Mesilau, the lodging (dm from RM428 per person) is in functional dorms and doubles, but if you want to splurge there are some oddly shaped chalets (they look like they were designed by Frank Gehry on a bad day) that start at RM1285 for a three-bed property. Mesilau Nature Resort is 30 minutes beyond the entrance to Kinabalu (when driving towards Ranau from KK). The Sutera lodging in Poring is located within the hot-springs complex and is same-same in terms of the room experience and prices.

There are privately owned sleeping options looping around Kinabalu's base. Most of these are located along the road between the park headquarters and Kundasang (east of the park's entrance). Two home stays in Kundasang, **Walai Tokou** (📞088-888166, 019-860 2270; koch_homestay@yahoo.com; Ranau; Packages from RM240) and **Mesilou Atamis** (📞017-832 5578, 019-580 2474; http://www. mesilau-homestay.com/; 2-day/1-night packages from RM350; ℗) are another option.

Wind Paradise YURT **$$**

(📞714563, 012-820 3360; http://windparadise2011. blogspot.com/; Jln Mesilau, Cinta Mata, Kundasang; d from RM170, yurt (4-person) RM300; ℗) There are elements of Wind Paradise that resemble just another (albeit well-executed) Mt Kinabalu resort: lodge-y rooms with attractive hardwood floors and an odd mix of modern, minimalist furniture and rather garish bedsheets. Then there are the yurts. If you're scratching your head, a yurt is the traditional tent used by Mongolian nomads. While these ones aren't really suitable for those wanting to pillage Eurasia from Korea to Poland, they are attractive, white-and-blue structures that also come with hardwood floors and cosy beds (one queen and two twins). Almost all lodging, rooms and yurts, comes with great views over the alpine jungle that surrounds Mt Kinabalu.

Mountain Guest House GUESTHOUSE **$**

(📞888632, 016-837 4040; dm/s/d incl breakfast from RM30/60/70) The closest non-Sutera accommodation to Mt Kinabalu park is about 4km from the trailhead that leads up the mountain. This guesthouse consists of bare but clean rooms plopped into huts and chalets that seem to precariously lean out from the side of Mt Kinabalu. Free breakfast and vegetarian dinners (RM8) are available.

D'Villa Rina Ria Lodge LODGE **$$**

(📞889282; www.dvillalodge.com.my; dm/r RM30/ 120; @) This charming lodge is run by friendly staff that maintains cute, cosy rooms and a dining area that overlooks a lovely view over the mountain ranges/thick clouds of afternoon fog, depending on the mercy of the weather gods.

❶ Getting There & Around

Bus & Van

KK round-trip buses stop in front of park headquarters and in Ranau (RM15 to RM20, two hours) from 7am to 8pm. Minivans operate from a blue-roofed shelter in Ranau servicing the nearby attractions (park HQ, Poring etc) for RM5. The national park operates a van service between the headquarters and Poring for RM25 – it leaves the park HQ at noon.

Northwest Coast

The northwest coast of Sabah is criminally underexplored. The A1 runs north from KK to Kudat and the tip of Borneo past wide headlands, rice paddies and hidden beaches.

This is a good area for renting a car or motorbike – the roads are pretty level, and public transport links aren't reliable for getting off the main road.

TUARAN

Tuaran, 33km from KK, is a bustling little town with tree-lined boulevard-style streets and the distinctive nine-storey **Ling Sang Pagoda**, whose approaches are dominated by vividly painted guardian deities. There's little point stopping in the town itself unless you happen to pass through on a market day (Tuaran is likely named for the Malay word *tawaran*, or 'sale', reflecting its history as a trading post), but the surrounding area conceals a few cool sights. You'll see signs for **Mengkabong Water Village**, a Bajau stilt village built over an estuary, but development and pollution has diminished this spot's charms.

◉ Sights & Activities

Rumah Terbalik HOUSE
(The Upside Down House; ☏088-260263; www.upsidedownhouse.com.my/; Kg. Telibong, Batu 21, Jln Telibong Tamparuli; adult/child RM18/5; ☻8am-10pm Mon-Sun; Ⓟ♿) Sabah has many great sights of the natural beauty sort, but very few that we'd call 'quirky'. And then there's Rumah Terbalik: the Upside Down House. Which is like a modern, tastefully designed and decorated house, but...wait for it...upside down! Crazy. Even the furniture and the car parked in the *garage sticks to the ceiling*. This is an amusing spot to visit, as much for the reaction of local Malaysians (who seem to find this place the funniest thing under the sun) as the actual novelty of the place.

⌖ Sleeping & Eating

Given the town's proximity to KK (with its heaps of accommodation options), you probably won't need to stay in town. However, if for some reason you need a room, try **Orchid Hotel** (☏012-820 8894, 088-793789; http://www.orchidhotel.netmyne.com/; 4 Jln Teo Teck Ong; r from RM80; ☀). It's somewhat overpriced but it'll do the trick for a night. Just a few doors away is **Tai Fatt** (Jln Teo Teck Ong; meals RM4; ☻7am-10pm), which has the best *kedai kopi* in Tuaran. It excels at *char mien/mee goreng*, the local, mouth-watering take on Chinese fried noodles, overflowing with vegetables, pork, oil, pork, egg, pork, wheat noodles, and yes, pork.

Shangri La Rasa Ria Resort RESORT $$
(☏088-792888; www.shangri-la.com; Pantai Dalit; r from RM450; Ⓟ☀@☎☲) This sister resort of the Shangri La Tanjung Aru Resort in Kota Kinabalu occupies a fine stretch of peach-hued dunes about 45 minutes north of the KK airport. It's a sprawling resort complete with its own 18-hole golf course, several fine restaurants, an amoeba-esque pool and a relaxing spa. The resort's best feature is the small nature sanctuary.

❶ Getting There & Away

All buses north pass through Tuaran, and minivans shuttle regularly to and from KK (RM5 to RM10, 30 minutes). Minivans to Mengkabong are less frequent and cost RM1. Regular minivans go from Tuaran to Kota Belud (around RM15, 30 minutes).

KOTA BELUD

You might think Kota Belud isn't much to look at, and frankly, you'd be right, but the town's Sunday **tamu**, or market, is definitely worth your time. It's a congested, colourful and dusty melee of vendors, hagglers, browsers, gawpers and hawkers, all brought together by a slew of everyday goods in a bustle that consumes the whole town every

---

DON'T MISS

THE ORANG-UTANS OF SHANGRI-LA

Sounds like a movie starring adorable primates in Tibet, right? No, we're just referring to the Sanctuary at Shangri-La's Rasa Ria Resort, sister resort of the Shangri La Tanjung Aru Resort in Kota Kinabalu, located near Tuaran.

The Sanctuary is a makeshift wildlife reserve owned and managed by the resort. There's all kinds of daily activities, from bird-watching trips to night walks (there are civets and loris on the reserve) to viewing the Sanctuary's orang-utans from a canopy walkway. Honestly, the red apes here are just as cute as the ones at Sepilok (p343), and it's way less crowded as well. Plus, your money is still going towards a preservation organisation. There's different rates for all of the above activities depending on whether or not you're a guest at the hotel; for more information, email rrr@shangri-la.com or call 88-797888. The two-hour orang-utan viewing occurs daily at 10am.

A DETACHED SENSE OF FEAR

If you're out at night in Kota Belud and hear a strange noise, or happen to be either pregnant or a newborn infant, get inside. Because you may become the next victim of the *penanggalan,* Kota Belud's resident phantasm. The *penanggalan* ("detach"), known locally as the *balan-balan,* to Westerners is an odd monster: a mix of banshee, vampire and biology experiment. By day it appears to be a beautiful young woman; at night it is also a beautiful young woman, or at least the head of one. The rest of the 'body' is a trailing mass of intenstines and other internal organs. The *balan-balan* is said to seek the scent of newborn flesh and the blood (and placentas) of pregnant women. There's a pretty great 2011 Malaysian horror movie on the subject called *Penanggal,* complete with flying heads, lots of screaming and folks getting eaten.

week (and a smaller version takes place on Wednesdays!). The most impressive site in Kota Belud is sadly an uncommon one these days: a procession of fully caparisoned Bajau horsemen from the nearby villages, decked out, along with their steeds, in vivid, multi-coloured satin 'armour'.

A *tamu* is not simply a market where villagers gather to sell their farm produce and to buy manufactured goods from traders; it's also a social occasion where news and stories are exchanged. These days tourists now often outnumber buffalo, and the horsemen have mostly moved away from the car park, though some do put on a show for visitors.

Visitors looking for tribal handicrafts and traditional clothing may find a prize here, but it's cheaply made stuff for tourists. Ironically, the best way to experience this commercial event is to come not expecting to buy anything – soak up the convivial, occasionally manic atmosphere, enjoy a good meal at the lovely food stalls and just potter about like Grandma at a Sunday flea market.

🛏 Sleeping & Eating

Most people visit Kota Belud as a day trip from KK, since you can make it there and back with plenty of time for the market.

Kota Belud is hardly a gastronome's delight, but tasty snacks can be picked up at the Sunday market. There are plenty of Chinese and halal coffee shops around the municipal offices.

TOP CHOICE **Mañana** GUESTHOUSE **$$**
(☎014-679 2679, 014-679 3679; www.manana-borneo.com; hammock/r/ste from RM50/70/150) This fantastic property is in the little village of Kampung Pituru Laut, way out on the coast. The name comes from a Canadian guest, who was so enchanted with the resort he kept putting off leaving till mañana...then mañana...then mañana... Owners Yan and Nani have situated the property on a private, boat-only-accesible beach that is basically a slice of heaven buttered with paradise. Simple, cleverly designed chalets look out onto clear water, hammocks sway in the ocean breeze, an on-site restaurant-bar serves hot food and cold beer, and the sunsets will blow your mind. Ask about diving trips to see what may be the world's largest brain coral. The owners prefer you book ahead so transport can be arranged; their suggested agent in KK is the excellent GogoSabah (p311).

Kota Belud Travelers' Lodge LODGE **$**
(☎088-977228; http://mykbtl.com; 6 Plaza Kong Guan; r without bathroom RM65, en suite RM85-115; ❋) A simple affair in the centre of town, it's about 200m southwest of the mosque in a shopping block (it's well marked, so finding it shouldn't be a problem). It's got the whole concrete-block-with-cosy-rooms vibe going that is oddly typical of interior Sabah hotels.

❶ Getting There & Away

MINIBUS & TAXI

Minivans and share taxis gather in front of Pasar Besar, the old market. Most of these serve the Kota Belud–KK route, (RM7 to RM10, two hours) or Kudat (RM10 to RM15, two hours), departing from 7am to 5pm. To get to Kinabalu National Park, take any minibus going to KK and get off at Tamparuli, about halfway (RM5, 30 minutes). There are several minivans from Tamparuli to Ranau every day until about 2pm; all pass the park entrance (RM5, one hour). To go all the way to Ranau costs RM13 (the trip takes just over an hour).

KUDAT

Despite being only a few hours from Kota Kinabalu, there's a dreamy, end-of-the-world feeling in Kudat. Maybe it's the drowsy quality of the air; Malaysian towns don't get much more laid-back and friendly than this. You can thank the local Rungus people. Filipinos too – there's loads of them around.

Kudat is a quiet port that rewards a bit of initiative. The town itself is fairly unremarkable; there is a large Chinese temple (admission free) by the main square and a fish market near the docks, but mainly this is a quiet place where it's nice to potter about, smile at people and be smiled at. It's the country that leads up to the tip of Borneo that you want to explore. There are miles and miles of beautiful beaches about, some of which are excellent for surfing, while others are good for watching lonely cattle and blood-red sunsets. The trick is finding these spots, as there's very little tourism infrastructure to speak of.

You can disappear down side roads that lead to the ocean and see what you find – we did and had a grand time, but we had our own wheels. We're purposely suggesting you do it yourself as there is such unreliable road signage here, yet not too many roads. Trust us when we say that with a little exploratory gusto you might find that mythical traveller pot of gold: the hidden, untouched beach. Swing by New Way Car Rental & Souvenir Centre (☑088-625868; 40 Jln Lo Thien Chok) if you want to explore the area under your own steam. Staff can also book your accommodation on Pulau Banggi.

🛏 Sleeping & Eating

TOP CHOICE **Tampat Do Aman** ECO-CAMP $
(☑013-880 8395; http://tampatdoaman.com/; r from RM30; 🖘) Tampat Do Aman means 'place of friends' in the local Rungus language. It's a fitting title; you'll be made to feel welcome as hell here by Howard Stanton and his Rungus wife. The couple are committed to creating sustainable tourism in the area, and work with the local Rungus community to preserve some of Kudat's lovely beaches and stretches of jungle. Howard will hook you up with bicycles and car rides out to some of the most isolated, lovely beaches in Sabah – ask to see the honeymooners' point, or for tips on snorkeling spots. Tampat Do Aman itself is a very rustic eco-camp, with fan-cooled basic thatch huts and longhouse, set in a supremely

romantic spot between the jungle and the ocean. The staff provides nice home-cooked meals (and plenty of beer) on demand.

🏄 Tip of Borneo Resort RESORT $$
(Tommy's Place; ☑013-811 2315, 088-493468; http://tipofborneoresort.com/; r RM130-160; ❄🖘) If you're not into the rustic camp atmoshere, head to Tommy's Place, the Tip of Borneo Resort. This is an excellent property of wonderful villas and chalets set up with sweeping views of the Kudat headlands. Staff are committed to preserving natural beauty and have engaged in projects to help sea turtles lay their eggs. You can look into diving, windsurfing and other activities here, and management is happy to direct you to awesome beaches.

TOP CHOICE **Hibiscus Riviera** VILLA $$$
(☑019-895 074; www.hibiscusvillaborneo.com; villas from US$800; ❄🖘⊠) The Hibiscus looks like the place where Jay-Z and *GQ* magazine would throw the mother of all Southeast Asian parties. It's tasteful – dark-wood floors, indigenous art, scrubbed pebbles and an incredible infinity pool – yet unmistakably, impeccably upper class. In short, this is one of the finest top-end accomodation options in Sabah. From late December to early January the rate climbs to US$1100 a night (US$1030 without breakfast) and there is a minimum 3-night stay rule.

Ria Hotel HOTEL $$
(☑088-622794; http://riahotel.blogspot.com/; 3 Jln Marudu; r RM120-275; ❄@) If you have to stay in Kudat town, the Ria has clean, spacious, well-appointed rooms, nice bathrooms with hot showers, and little balconies. It's a short walk southwest of the bus station.

❶ Getting There & Away

The bus station is in Kudat Plaza in the western part of town, very close to the Ria Hotel. Bus destinations include KK (RM25, three hours) and Kota Belud (RM15, 1½ hours). Minivans and jeeps also operate from here; a ride to KK in a full van will cost around RM45.

AROUND KUDAT

The area around Kudat includes many hidden coves, beaches and hill trails that are almost all tucked away down hidden or unmarked roads. You'll want to get in touch with the folks at Tampat Do Aman or Tip of Borneo Resort to find the best spots. You can attempt some of the side roads in a 2WD or motorbike, but be careful, especially if it's been raining (which doesn't happen often; this is the driest part of Sabah). Either way, make sure you take in one of the lovely tropical sunsets – Sabah's west coast is famous for 'em! The **Rungus longhouses** (Bavanggazo Rungus Longhouses/Maranjak Longhouse; ☑088-621673, 612846; per person per night from RM70) of Kampung Bavanggazo, 44km south of Kudat, are highly touted by Sabah Tourism, but were in a bit of a neglected state when we visited them.

TIP OF BORNEO

Sabah's northernmost headland, at the end of a wide bay some 40km from Kudat, is known as Tanjung Simpang Mengayu, or the Tip of Borneo. Magellan reputedly landed here for 42 days during his famous round-the-world voyage. Once a wild promontory, this windswept stretch where the cliffs meet the sea has been co-opted as a tourist attraction – there's a large, truncated globe monument dominating the viewpoint. A sign warns visitors not to climb down onto the rocks that form the mainland's actual tip, effectively guaranteeing that tourists will do exactly that. Seriously, please don't attempt to swim here; a Korean tourist drowned during our research.

There's no public transport, so you'll need to negotiate a taxi from Kudat (around RM90, including waiting time upon arrival) or drive yourself.

Offshore Islands

The real highlights of northwestern Sabah lie offshore. The first gem is Pulau Mantanani, perfect tropical islands lying about 40km northwest of Kota Belud. The second is Layang Layang, a diving mecca about 300km northwest of KK – it's basically just an airstrip built on a reef way out in the middle of the South China Sea. Famous for great visibility, seemingly endless wall dives and the occasional school of hammerheads, it's second only to Sipadan on Malaysia's list of top dive spots.

PULAU MANTANANI

Pulau Mantanani Besar (Big Mantanani Island) and **Pulau Mantanani Kecil** (Little Mantanani Island) are two little flecks of land fringed by bleach-blond sand and ringed by a halo of colourful coral, about 25km off the coast of northwest Sabah (about 40km northwest of Kota Belud).

Those on a budget – well, actually, anyone – should opt for the excellent **Mari Mari Backpackers Lodge** (☑088-260501; www.riverbug.asia; dm RM60, r RM80-175), operated by Riverbug. Guests are placed in raised stilt chalets pocketed around a white-sand beach. The huts are a modern take on the thatch-longhouse theme, and a well executed one at that. Diving and snorkelling activities feature high on the itinerary list, but this is also a lovely tropical escape if you just want to chill.

PULAU BANGGI

If you want to fall off the map, get out to Pulau Banggi, which lies some 40km northeast of Kudat. The Banggi people, known locally for their unusual tribal treehouses, are Sabah's smallest indigenous group, and speak a unique non-Bornean dialect. The island is a postcard-esque slice of sand, tropical trees and clear water, and is actually one of the largest offshore islands in all of Malaysia.

Accommodation is provided by a small government **resthouse** (r RM40) and the modest **Banggi Resort** (☑019-587 8078; r fan/air-con RM50/65, huts RM70; ❄), which can arrange boat trips and other activities. The small huts have kitchens and twin beds – make sure you request the charming treehouse hut. This place can get fully booked on weekends, so reserve in advance. At either location, ask staff about the trails that lead into the small jungle interior of the island.

Kudat Express (☑088-328118; one-way RM15) runs a ferry between Kudat and the main settlement on Pulau Banggi. It departs the pier (near the Shell station) at 9am and 2pm daily. In the reverse direction, it leaves Pulau Banggi daily at around 3pm.

LAYANG LAYANG

Some 300km northwest of Kota Kinabalu, Layang Layang is a tiny island that is surrounded by a coral atoll. It's an exclusive **dive location**, and is well known among scubaholics as part of the famous Borneo Banks. Thanks to its utter isolation, the reef here is healthy and diverse. Although it may not be quite as colourful as the reef at Sipadan, it's quite likely to be one of the most unspoilt bits of coral most divers have seen. There are plenty of reef fish and reef sharks, as well as a with a healthy population of rays.

Please note: there is *no decompression chamber* at Layang Layang, so don't press your luck while underwater. The resort only provides air – no nitrox. Trivia buffs may be pleased to know Layang Layang is the only one of the remote Spratly Islands that receives regular flights.

Layang Layang Island Resort (☏ in Kuala Lumpur 03-2170 2185; www.avillionlayanglayang. com; 6-day, 5-night all-inclusive package twin-share per person from US$1490; ✻ ☒) is the only game in town here and it's all about the diving. The five daily meals are scheduled around the dive times. The standard rooms are very comfortable, with air-con, TV, private verandahs and hot-water showers. The all-inclusive packages include accommodation, food, 12 boat dives and tank usage. Package rates for nondivers start at US$850. An extra night costs diver/nondiver $180/$125. Be warned, nondivers: besides a little snorkelling, there's nothing for you to do here but sunbathe.

The resort operates its own Antonov 26 aircraft, which flies every Tuesday, Thursday, Friday and Sunday between KK and Layang Layang. The flight over from KK in this bare-bones Russian prop plane is a big part of the adventure: it feels more like a military transport than a commercial airliner. The return flight costs US$285, which is not included in the accommodation-food-dive package.

EASTERN SABAH

Eastern Sabah takes nearly everything that is wonderful about the rest of Borneo and condenses it into one hard-hitting brew of an outdoor shot consisting of equal parts adventure, wildlife, undersea exploration and flat-out fun. Let's tick off some of the natural wonders that are packed into this relatively tiny corner of the island: the great ginger men – ie the orang-utans – of Sepilok; pot-bellied, flop-nosed proboscis monkeys in Labuk Bay; the looming vine tunnels and muddy crocodile highway of the Sungai Kinabatangan; pygmy elephants and tree-top canopies that scratch in the sky in the Danum Valley and Tabin; plunging seawalls rainbow-spattered with tropical marine life in the Semporna Archipelago; a forest as old as human civilisation in the Maliau Basin.

Did we just pique your travel appetite? Yeah, we thought so. With easier transport links and improved infrastructure, it's easier than ever to hit up the east side of Sabah.

You'll be told, when you're here, that the only way around is via package tours, but trust us – with a little prior planning and a bit of heart, you can explore this area independently and in-depth.

Sandakan

POP 480,000

Sabah's second city lacks the small cosmopolitan pulse that keeps KK throbbing; in contrast, Sandakan feels like a provincial city with provincial horizons, not to mention a grubby city centre. But Sandakan was once a major port of call, and as such it has played an important role in Borneo's past, as attested by religious relics, haunting cemeteries and stunning colonial mansions.

⊙ Sights

Central Sandakan is light on 'must-see' attractions, although history buffs will appreciate the *Sandakan Heritage Trail* brochure available at the tourist office. The centre, where you'll find most hotels, banks and local transport, consists of a few blocks squashed between the waterfront and a steep escarpment from where you can look out over the bay (Teluk Sandakan). Warning: don't go to Sandakan Crocodile Park unless you like watching sadly neglected reptiles.

Chinese Cemetery   CEMETERY
Sandakan's massive Chinese Cemetery essentially takes up all of a valley that runs into the hills east of Sandakan. Gravesites are studded into the slopes, many shaped by *feng shui* principles so that the back of the grave backs into the solid angle of the earth, while the front often features a small artificial pool, reflecting the traditional Chinese belief that an ideal home has a mountain behind it and running water in front. As you wander further along the cemetery, the graves become older and more decrepit – many have been claimed by the jungle. You will also see some charnel houses that accommodate the important members of Sandakan's major Chinese clans. Across the road from the cemetery is a cremation ground for Hindus and Sikhs.

Japanese Cemetery   CEMETERY
Located beyond the Chinese cemetery grounds, this is a poignant piece of Sandakan's ethnic puzzle. The gravesite was founded in the 1890s by Kinoshita Kuni, known to the English as Okuni of South Seas

Sandakan

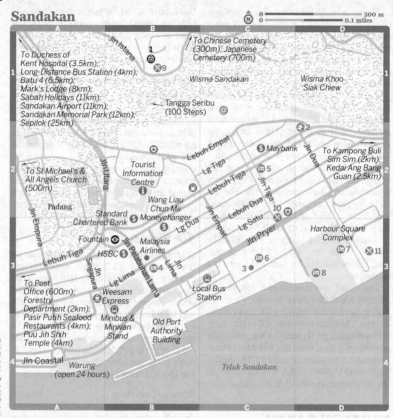

| | 0 | 200 m |
| N | 0 | 0.1 miles |

Sandakan

◎ Sights
1 Agnes Keith House B1

✪ Activities, Courses & Tours
2 Sepilok Tropical Wildlife
   Adventure.. D2
3 SI Tours C3
   Wildlife Expeditions .... (see 3)

⌂ Sleeping
4 Nak Hotel... B3
5 Rose Guesthouse C2

6 Sandakan Backpackers.........................C3
7 Sea View Sandakan Budget &
   Backpackers Hotel.............................D3
8 Swiss-Inn Waterfront Sandakan...........D3

✖ Eating
9 English Tea House & Restaurant B1
10 Habeeb Restaurant C2
11 New Market D3

☕ Drinking
Balin .... (see 4)

and to greater Sandakan as the successful madam-manager of the lucrative 'Brothel 8', once located on Lebuh Tiga. Today the cemetery is quite small, but at one time there were hundreds of buried dead, most of them prostitutes. A monument to the fallen Japa-

nese soldiers of WWII was erected in the cemetery in 1989. To get here and to the Chinese cemetery, climb the shady Tangga Seribu to Jln Residensi Dr and turn right; there will be signs pointing the rest of the way to the cemetery.

Agnes Keith House
MUSEUM

(Map p338; ☎089-221140; Jln Istana; admission RM15; ⏰9am-5pm) On the hill above town, overlooking Teluk Sandakan and the city itself, is Agnes Keith House, an old two-storey wooden villa now renovated as a museum. Keith was an American who came to Sandakan in the 1930s with her husband, then Conservator of Forests, and ended up writing several books about her experiences, including the famous *Land Below the Wind*. The house fell into disrepair during the 1990s, but Sabah Museum has since restored it as a faithful recreation of Keith's original abode.

The villa documents Sandakan in all its colonial splendour, with detailed displays on the lives of the Keiths. Most poignant are mementos of Agnes' imprisonment by the Japanese during WWII, when she had to try to care for her young son under gruelling conditions. There's some great vintage photographs, including a shot of Keith's husband standing with a dead elephant in full *Heart of Darkness* safari gear. The admission price includes entry to the various branches of the Sabah Museum in KK – now didn't we tell you to keep hold of your ticket? Also on the grounds is the English Tea House & Restaurant, conveniently ignoring Keith's American background and the fact that she found Sandakan to be 'too British' when she first arrived.

To reach the museum, follow Jln Singapura from the city centre and turn right up the hill, or head up the Tangga Seribu (100 Steps) to Jln Istana and turn left. Just below the museum gardens is an **observation pavilion** built by the local Rotary Club, which offers more fine views.

Sandakan Memorial Park
HISTORIC SITE

(⏰9am-5pm) This park marks the site of a Japanese POW camp and starting point for the infamous WWII 'death marches' to Ranau. Of the 1800 Australian and 600 British troops imprisoned here, the only survivors by July 1945 were six Australian escapees. Today the site of the POW camp has been converted into a quiet forest orchard and series of gardens.

Large, rusting machines testify to the camp's forced-labour program, and a pavilion at the park's centre includes accounts from survivors and photographs from personnel, inmates and liberators. In 2006 the original march route was officially reopened as a memorial trail – see www.sandakan-deathmarch.com for details.

To reach the park, take any Batu 8 (or higher-numbered) bus from the local bus station in the city centre (RM1.80); get off at the 'Taman Rimba' signpost and walk down Jln Rimba. A taxi from downtown costs about RM25 one way.

Puu Jih Shih Temple
TEMPLE

(Off Jln Leila) Architecturally, the Puu Jih Shih is one of the finer Chinese temples in Sabah: wrapped in the usual firework-colour display of reds, golds and twining dragons, festooned with lanterns that illuminate the grounds like a swarm of fat fireflies. As an added bonus, this large Buddhist temple is perched on a steep hill overlooking Teluk Sandakan, offering an extremely impressive view of the city. Take a bus to Tanah Merah and ask for directions; from where you depart the bus it's not a far walk, but it's a steep uphill one. A taxi here shouldn't cost more than RM6 one way, but don't be surprised if cabbies try to charge RM20 for a round-trip plus waiting at the temple.

St Michael's & All Angels Church
CHURCH

(Off Jln Puncak) This incongruous slice of the Home Counties is one of the few all-stone buildings in Malaysian Borneo and the former locus of colonial worship. In 1893, prison labourers lugged said stones across the jungle during the church's construction. Today, despite a little mouldering, the church very much looks like a displaced bit of the Cotswolds transplanted into the heart of Borneo. Although the church is officially off Jln Puncak, many people call the street 'Church Rd'.

Sam Sing Kung
TEMPLE

(Jln Padang) The Sam Sing Kung temple (also pronounced 'Sam Sing Gong') dates from 1887, making it the oldest building in Sandakan. The name means 'three saints' temple – in this case saints for general righteousness, fishermen and students (easy to see how the latter two would be important to Sandakan's education-oriented, dependent-on-the-sea Chinese community). The temple itself is a smallish, if attractive affair – a lovely example of a house of worship dedicated to the traditional Chinese Taoist pantheon.

Kampong Buli Sim Sim
VILLAGE

This traditional stilt village, located about 4km east of the town centre, is the original settlement Sandakan grew from. You'll likely be grinned at as you wander around

THE SANDAKAN DEATH MARCHES

Sandakan was the site of a Japanese prisoner-of-war camp during WWII, and in September 1944 there were 1800 Australian and 600 British troops interned here. What is not widely known is that more Australians died here than during the building of the infamous Burma Railway.

Early in the war, food and conditions were bearable and the death rate stood at around three per month. However, as the Allies closed in, it became clear to the officers in command that they didn't have enough staff to guard against a rebellion in the camps. They decided to cut the prisoners' rations to weaken them, causing disease to spread and the death rate to rise.

It was also decided to move the prisoners inland – 250km through the jungle to Ranau, on a route originally cut by locals to hamper the Japanese invaders, passing mainly through uninhabited, inhospitable terrain. On 28 January 1945, 470 prisoners set off; 313 made it to Ranau. On the second march, 570 started from Sandakan; just 118 reached Ranau. The 537 prisoners on the third march were the last men in the camp.

Conditions on the marches were deplorable: most men had no boots, rations were less than minimal and many men fell by the wayside. The Japanese brutally disposed of any prisoners who couldn't walk. Once in Ranau, the surviving prisoners were put to work carrying 20kg sacks of rice over hilly country to Paginatan, 40km away. Disease, starvation and executions took a horrendous toll, and by the end of July 1945 there were no prisoners left in Ranau. The only survivors from the 2400 at Sandakan were six Australians who escaped, either from Ranau or during the marches.

As a final bitter irony, it emerged postwar that a rescue attempt had been planned for early 1945, but intelligence at the time had suggested there were no prisoners left at the camp.

the wooden boards built over the water, as much an oddity to locals as their water village is to you. Have a stroll, be on the lookout for those budding entrepreneurs who have turned their homes into ad hoc souvenir shops, but please don't take pictures of people without asking permission. You can take a taxi here for no more than RM15.

☞ Tours

It is possible to visit many of the attractions around Sandakan independently, but if you want to stay at the river lodges on the Kinabatangan, you'll need to prebook accommodation. It's advisable to do so in Sandakan or in KK (p322). Sandakan also has plenty of general tour operators offering packages to Sepilok and the Gomantong Caves. Hotels in Sandakan and Sepilok are all capable of booking tours as well, as are many of the tour companies we list in KK. Borneo Express (p319), in KK, has an office in Sandakan, as does **Sandakan Car Rental** (☎019-823 7050, 016-815 0029; sandakancarrental.com; Bandar Maju Batu 1, Jln Utara).

Sabah Holidays
SIGHTS
(☎089-225718; www.sabahholidays.com; ground fl, Sandakan Airport) Rents cars and minivans,

and can arrange tours and accommodation in Kota Belud, the Danum Valley and Maliau Basin.

Sepilok Tropical Wildlife Adventure
NATURE
(Map p338; ☎089-271077; www.stwadventure.com; 13 Jln Tiga) This midpriced tour specialist is connected to Sepilok Jungle Resort and Bilit Adventure Lodge on the Sungai Kinabatangan.

SI Tours
NATURE
(Map p338; ☎089-213502; www.sitoursborneo.com; Lot 59, Block HS-5, Sandakan Harbour Square Phase 2) This full-service agency operates Abai Jungle Lodge and Kinabatangan Riverside Lodge.

Uncle Tan
NATURE
(Map p344; ☎089-535784; www.uncletan.com; Batu 14) Tour menu includes its Sukau River Lodge on the Kinabatangan. Located in Sepilok.

Wildlife Expeditions
NATURE
(Map p338; ☎089-219616; www.wildlife-expeditions.com; 9th fl, Wisma Khoo Siak Chiew, Lebuh Empat) Also has accommodation in Sukau. There's also a **KK office** (☎246000; Wisma Merdeka).

🛏 Sleeping

Sandakan doesn't bowl folk over in the lodging department, and budget options are sparse. That said, if you can shell out into RM80-and-above territory, there's some decent deals. If you're only passing through Sandakan to see the orang-utans, it's better to stay at Sepilok itself, since the rehabilitation centre is only 25km from town.

Nak Hotel   HOTEL $$
(Map p338; 📞089-272988; www.nakhotel.com; Jln Pelabuhan Lama; s/d incl breakfast from RM85/118; ❄🛜) The Nak is a solid midrange hotel that's a fair steal if you're travelling as a couple or with friends, and nice value even if you're by yourself. The oldest dedicated hotel in town has a somewhat Soviet-chic exterior, but once you get inside rooms are quite attractive: nice monochromatic colour schemes with hints of East Asian and Borneo-inspired design flairs. This is a well put-together spot, which is no surprise given the hotel's kick-ass roof lounge, Balin (p342) – a must even if you aren't staying here.

Sea View Sandakan Budget & Backpackers Hotel   HOSTEL $
(Map p338; 📞089-221221; Lot 126, 1st fl, Jln Dua, Harbour Square 14; dm from RM30, r from RM50; ❄🛜) The name of this place is a little deceptive; you won't be getting many sea views per se (especially because it seems a new building is going up right on the waterfront). That said, this is an excellent little hostel, with clean, good value rooms, helpful staff and a friendly vibe.

Mark's Lodge   HOTEL $$
(📞089-210055; www.markslodge.com; Lot 1-7, Block 36, Bandar Indah; r from RM154; ❄🛜) The word 'boutique' is written in fogged glass across the front entrance – just in case you didn't get the memo. This business-class hotel, located at Batu 4 (Bandar Indah) is a solid option for a comfortable sleep. The rooms are all about the 'dark tropical wood floors plus white sheets' look, and it comes off quite well. It's a RM15 taxi ride into town.

Rose Guesthouse   GUESTHOUSE $
(Map p338; 📞089-223582; www.shsbnb.com; HS10, Harbour Square Complex; dm/d RM20/40, d with bathroom RM47; ❄@) This is no delicate rose with lacy table settings and Devonshire teas. Think more of a modern, unnamed cookie-cutter Sabah budget spot for crashing out. Service is friendly and personable,

and fan dorms are dirt cheap (but not dirty). Near the Alliance Bank.

Sandakan Backpackers   HOSTEL $
(Map p338; 📞089-221104; www.sandakanback packers.com; Lot 108, Block SH-11, Harbour Square Complex; dm/s/d/tr RM25/40/60/90; ❄@) This place is one of the most popular budget deals in town and a firm fixture on the Borneo backpacker trail. Clean, well-lit, affordable and a decent place to meet other citizens of Backpackistan.

Swiss-Inn Waterfront Sandakan   HOTEL $$
(Map p338; 📞089-240888; www.swissgarden.com; Harbour Square Complex; r from RM161; ❄🛜🏊) If you're in the mood for an essentially Western style waterfront resort, the Swiss Garden is where you want to be. Big rooms, standard chain-style upper-class hotel decor, big windows that look out onto the water – there's no surprises here, and we mean that in a good way. A lovely pool, spa and workout facilities are all on-site at this business-class option.

🍴 Eating

For an authentic Malay meal, head to the KFC in the waterfront Harbour Square Complex (but don't eat there!) – the restaurants surrounding it are cheap and flavourful. Most are standard Malay *kedai kopi*, with prices that rarely top RM6 per mains; all are open from roughly 9am to 9pm. **Habeeb Restaurant** (Map p338; Jln Tiga) is good for a cheap curry; it's actually part of a chain that serves good Indian Muslim food, so if you see other branches around town, consider them a solid bet.

New Market   FOOD STALLS $
(Map p338; Jln Pryor; dishes RM3-10; ⊙7am-2pm) Despite being located in what looks like a multistorey car park, this is the best spot in town for cheap eats and stall food. On the bottom floor you'll find the usual 'wet' and 'dry' markets, selling fish, sea cucumber, herbs, vegetables, meat and such. Farmers and fishermen rock up here from their fields and boats throughout the day, bringing fresh produce, bloody butchered meat and flopping denizens of the ocean. Upstairs you'll find strictly halal food stalls, with a mix of Chinese, Malay, Indonesian and Filipino stalls. Hours given for the food stalls above are a bit flexible, but by 3pm most are empty.

Sim Sim Seafood Restaurant   SEAFOOD $
(Sim Sim 8; dishes RM5; ⊘8am-2pm) Located
in the heart of the Sim Sim stilt village, this
'restaurant' is more of a dockside fishery,
where the daily catch is unloaded and sorted
and prepared for the immediate consumption of travellers like you (and a lot of locals). A cluster of red plastic patio furniture
huddles in the corner – just grab a seat and
point to your prey! Or ask a friendly regular
for help ordering; there are lots of off-menu
specialities determined by what's caught
that day. Ask a cab to drop you off at 'Sim
Sim Bridge 8' (they'll very likely know where
you're going).

English Tea House
& Restaurant   TEA HOUSE $$$
(Map p338; ☑089-222544; www.englishteahouse.
org; 2002 Jln Istana; mains RM24-40, cocktails
RM26.50; ⊘breakfast, lunch & dinner) It seems
every place that suffered under colonialism
likes to recreate the atmosphere of being a
rich colonialist, the English Tea House being
Sabah's contribution to the genre. Don your
safari suit, wax that moustache and butter
that scone, *sahib*. The manicured gardens
are a particular joy, with wicker furniture
and a small croquet lawn overlooking the
bay, perfect for afternoon tea (RM17.25), a
round of sunset Pimms or some ice coffee.

 Drinking

Bandar Indah, commonly known as Mile
4 or Batu 4, is a buzzing grid of two-storey
shophouses and the playground of choice
for locals and expats alike, packed with res-
taurants, bars, karaoke lounges and night-
clubs. It comes alive at night in a way that
makes central Sandakan seem deader than
the morgue in a ghost town. Bars gener-
ally close around 1am or 2am, music venues
slightly later.

☐TOP
CHOICE ☐ **Balin**   BAR
(Map p338; ☑089-272988; www.nakhotel.com; Nak
Hotel, Jln Pelabuhan Lama; drinks from RM9, mains
from RM15; ⊘lunch & dinner) Bringing a certain
LA rooftop sexiness to Sandakan, Balin is
your best bet for nightlife in the city centre.
The three tiers of uberchill lounge space are
accented by a factory's worth of pillows and
some genuinely classy cocktails that any
boutique 'mixologist' bar in London or New
York would be justifiably jealous of.

 Information

Internet
Cyber Café (3rd fl, Wisma Sandakan, Lebuh
Empat; per hr RM3; ⊘9am-9pm)

Medical Services
Duchess of Kent Hospital (☑089-212111;
http://hdok.moh.gov.my/; Mile 2, Jln Utara)
Best private care in the area.

Money
HSBC (Lebuh Tiga)

Maybank (Lebuh Tiga) In addition to a full-
service bank and ATM, a sidewalk currency-
exchange window is open 9am to 5pm daily for
changing cash and travellers cheques.

Standard Chartered Bank (Lebuh Tiga)

Wang Liau Chun Mii Moneychanger (23 Lebuh
Tiga; ⊘8.30am-4.30pm) Cash only.

Post
Main post office (☑089-210594; Jln Leila)

Tourist Information
Tourist Information Centre (☑089-229751;
Wisma Warisan; ⊘8am-12.30pm & 1.30-
4.30pm Mon-Thu, 8-11.30am & 2-4.30pm
Friday) Located opposite the municipal offices
(known as MPS) and up the stairs from Lebuh
Tiga. The staff dispenses advice on everything
from regional attractions to local restaurants
and can link travellers together for group excur-
sions. One of the more helpful TICs in Sabah.

ℹ Getting There & Away
Air
Malaysia Airlines (☑1300-883 000; cnr Jln
Pelabuhan Lama & Lebuh Dua & 1st fl, airport)
has daily flights to/from KK and KL; its subsidi-
ary, **MASwings**, located in the same office, of-
fers one daily flight to/from Tawau and two to/
from KK. **AirAsia** (☑089-222737; 1st & 2nd fl,
Airport) operates two daily direct flights to/from
KL and KK.

Bus & Minivan
Buses and minibuses to KK, Lahad Datu, Sem-
porna and Tawau leave from the long-distance
bus station in a large car park at Batu 2.5, 4km
north of town (ie not particularly convenient).
Most express buses to KK (RM33 to RM40, six
hours) leave between 7am and 2pm, plus one
evening departure around 8pm. All pass the
turn-off to Kinabalu National Park headquarters.

Buses depart regularly for Lahad Datu
(RM20, 2½ hours) and Tawau (RM40, 5½ hours)
between 7am and 8am. There's also a bus to
Semporna (RM33, 5½ hours) at 8am. If you miss
it, head to Lahad Datu, then catch a frequent
minivan to Semporna.

Minivans depart throughout the morning from Batu 2.5 for Ranau (RM26, four hours) and Lahad Datu (some of those continuing to Tawau). Minivans for Sukau (RM15) leave from a lot behind Centre Point Mall in town.

Getting Around

To/From the Airport
The airport is 11km from the city centre. Batu 7 Airport bus (RM1.80) stops on the main road about 500m from the terminal. A coupon taxi to the town centre costs RM35; going the other way, around RM28.

Bus & Minivan
Buses run from 6am to 6pm on the main road to the north, Jln Utara, designated by how far from town they go, ie Batu 8. Fares range from RM1 to RM4.

Local minivans wait behind Centre Point Mall; fares cost from RM2. Use for the harbour area.

To reach the long-distance bus station, catch a local bus (RM1.50) from the stand at the waterfront; it takes about 20 minutes. The same bus leaves when full from the bus station for the city centre.

Taxi
Short journeys around town should cost RM10; it's about RM15 to Bandar Indah and RM40 to RM50 to Sepilok depending on your bargaining skills. A taxi from the long-distance bus station to town (or vice versa) will probably run RM20; you may be able to argue drivers down to the local fare of RM10.

Sepilok

The orang-utan is the associative species of Sabah, despite the fact that the living space of the beast shrinks annually. The most reliable place to see this primate is the little hamlet of Sepilok, which sees almost as many visitors as the granite spires of Mt Kinabalu. Sepilok's Orang-Utan Rehabilitation Centre (SORC) is the most popular place on earth to see Asia's great ginger ape in its native habitat. Those who have time to stick around will also uncover several scenic nature walks, sanctuaries for the adorable sun bear and elusive proboscis monkey, and a couple of great places to call home for a night or two.

Sights & Activities

Sepilok Orang-Utan Rehabilitation Centre (SORC)
ANIMAL SANCTUARY
(Map p344; ☏089-531180; soutan@po.jaring.my; Jln Sepilok; admission RM30, camera fee RM10; ⊙9-11am & 2-3.30pm, walking trails 9am-4.15pm) One of only four orang-utan sanctuaries in the world, this place occupies a corner of the Kabili-Sepilok Forest Reserve about 25km north of Sandakan. The centre was established in 1964; it now covers 40 sq km and has become one of Sabah's top tourist attractions, second only to Mt Kinabalu.

Orphaned and injured orang-utans are brought to Sepilok to be rehabilitated to return to forest life. We have to stress: while thousands of people see orang-utans during feeding time at Sepilok, there is a chance you won't. These are, after all, wild animals. On the bright side, there are two major feeding times a day, so if you miss them in the morning, you can always try again in the afternoon (or the next day).

Feedings are at 10am and 3pm and last 30 to 50 minutes. Schedules are posted at the visitor reception centre. Tickets are

Sepilok

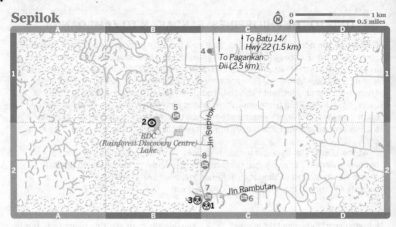

To Batu 14/ Hwy 22 (1.5 km)

To Pagankan Dii (2.5 km)

RDC (Rainforest Discovery Centre) Lake

Jln Sepilok

Jln Rambutan

Sepilok

◎ Sights

1 Borneo Sun Bear Conservation
   Centre..C2
2 Rainforest Discovery Centre
   (RDC)..B2
3 Sepilok Orang-Utan
   Rehabilitation Centre
   (SORC)...B2

➕ Activities, Courses & Tours

4 Uncle Tan......................................C1

🛏 Sleeping

5 Sepilok B&B...................................B1
6 Sepilok Forest Edge Resort...............C2
7 Sepilok Jungle Resort.....................C2
8 Sepilok Nature Resort.....................C2

valid for one day, although you can see two feedings in the same day. The morning feeding tends to be more tour-group heavy, so if you want a quieter experience, try the afternoon. Use the lockers for your valuables – orang-utans and macaques have been known to relieve tourists of hats, bags, sunglasses, cameras, even clothing. It's especially important that you don't bring any containers of insect repellent into the reserve, as these are highly toxic to the apes and other wildlife. Spray yourself before entering.

Nature Education Centre

A worthwhile 20-minute video about Sepilok's work is shown five times daily (9am, 11am, noon, 2.10pm and 3.30pm) opposite reception in the auditorium here.

Walking Trails

If you want to explore the sanctuary further, several walking trails lead into the forest; register at the visitor reception centre to use them. Trails range in length from 250m to 4km, and different paths are open at different times of year. Guided night walks can be arranged through the centre or at the various lodges. There's also a 10km trail through mangrove forest to **Sepilok Bay**; this is quite a rewarding walk, and if you're especially fit you may be able to complete it between feeding times. A permit from the **Forestry Department** (☎089-660811, 089-213966; Jln Leila) is required in advance for this route. The department can also arrange basic overnight accommodation at the bay (RM100) or a boat back to Sandakan. Some travel or tour agencies can assist with the permit and other arrangements.

🌿 **Borneo Sun Bear Conservation Centre** ANIMAL SANCTUARY
(BSBCC; Map p344; ☎089-534491; www.bsbcc.org. my; Jln Sepilok; RM30; ◎9am-4pm) The sun bear is the smallest of the world's bear species, as well as one of the most threatened. Named for the splotch of yellow fur that spreads like a bright Rorschach across their chests, sun bears, while adorable, also have razor claws that they use to build their nests (which very much resemble orang-utan nests). They are endangered thanks to the usual culprits of habitat loss and Chinese traditional medicine; the latter institution values the bears' bile. In China and Vietnam the beasts are strapped in tiny cages and hooked to IVs that pump bile from their gallbladders.

Thankfully this does not happen in Sabah, although the bears are still under enormous threat from habitat loss.

Set to open to the public in 2013, the BSBCC, at the time of research, cared for some 27 rescued sun bears. The pretty little beasts lumbered and played in open-air forest enclosures; visitors will be able to peek in on their activity from an expertly crafted walkway system. The BSBCC does good work, and is another activity option for tourists to consider when visiting Sepilok. Please note the centre's admissions and opening times may change, as it was not officially open at the time of writing.

Rainforest Discovery Centre (RDC)
NATURE RESERVE

(Map p344; ☑089-533780; www.forest.sabah.gov. my/rdc; adult/child RM10/5; ⊙8am-5pm) The RDC offers an engaging graduate-level education in tropical flora and fauna. Outside the exhibit hall – itself filled with displays that are easily accessible to children – a botanical garden presents varying samples of tropical plant life, the accompanying descriptions every bit as vibrant as the foliage. There's a gentle 1km lakeside walking trail, studded along the way with environmental education signage. A series of eight canopy towers connected by walkways give you a birds-eye view of the green rooftops of the trees, by far the most rewarding element of a trip here. Paddleboats (RM5) are available to ride around the inviting lake near the centre's entrance. You can also book night walks, which afford the chance to spot nocturnal animals like tarsiers and wild cats.

It's best to get there either at 8am or 4pm, as wildlife tends to hibernate during the sweltering hours in the middle of the day. A proper visit along the trails and towers takes around 1½ hours.

Labuk Bay Proboscis Monkey Sanctuary
SANCTURUARY

(☑089-672133; www.proboscis.cc; admission RM 60, camera/video RM10/20) Proboscis monkeys *(Nasalis larvatus)* are an even more exclusive attraction than orang-utans. After all, you can see orang-utans in Sumatra but the proboscis is found only on Borneo, although if you take a close look at them, you'd swear you've spotted one in the corner at a dodgy bar. Named for their long bulbous noses, proboscis monkeys are potbellied and red-faced, and males are constantly, unmistakably...aroused. With the arrival of Europeans, Malays nicknamed the proboscis *monyet belanda* (Dutch monkey). Because of their diets, proboscis monkeys tend to have severe flatulence, another attractive element of this already most graceful of species. Jokes aside, the proboscis are oddly compelling, and one of nine totally protected species in Sabah.

SABAH SEPILOK

THE WILD MAN OF BORNEO & HOW TO HELP HIM

The term 'orang-utan' literally means 'man of the wild', or 'jungle man' – a testament to the local reverence for these great ginger apes. Traditionally orang-utans were never hunted like other creatures in the rainforest; in fact, Borneo's indigenous people used to worship their skulls in the same fashion as they did the heads taken from enemy tribesmen. Orang-utans are the only species of great ape found outside Africa. A mature male is an impressive, not to mention hairy, creature with an arm span of 2.25m, and can weigh up to 144kg. Dominant males also have distinctive wide cheek pads to reinforce their alpha status. It was once said that an orang-utan could swing from tree to tree from one side of Borneo to the other without touching the ground. Sadly this is no longer the case, and hunting and habitat destruction continue to take their toll; it's estimated fewer than 15,000 specimens now exist in the wild.

If you'd like to get involved with the work of the Sepilok Orang-utan Rehabilitation Centre, contact **Sepilok Orang-Utan Appeal UK** (www.orangutan-appeal.org.uk) a UK-based charity. The Appeal's orang-utan adoption scheme is a particular hit with visitors: for UK£30 a year you can sponsor a ginger bundle of fun and receive updates on its progress; see the Appeal's website for details. If you're really taken with the place, Sepilok has one of the most popular overseas volunteer programs in Malaysia. Apply through **Travellers Worldwide** (www.travellersworldwide.com); as of recently, the cost of an eight-week volunteer package, including accommodation, meals and a number of excursions, was UK£3345.

A local palm-plantation owner has created a private proboscis monkey sanctuary, attracting the floppy-conked locals with sugar-free pancakes at 11.40am and 4.30pm feedings. A third feeding at 2.30pm often occurs during a ranger-led hike deeper into the sanctuary. An estimated 300 wild monkeys live in the 6-sq-km reserve. Animals in the reserve generally steer clear of human contact, except for those mischievous macaques, who just love snacks and sunhats. This is clearly more of a commercial affair than the feedings at the SORC; the proboscis monkeys are enticed onto the main viewing platform so tourists can get better pictures, which may put you off if you're looking for a more ecologically minded experience.

The sanctuary offers package trips. A half-day visit costs RM160, including transfers from Sandakan (RM150 from Sepilok). Overnight trips with meals and a night walk start at RM250. Food and accommodation are provided at the **Nipah Lodge**, on the edge of the oil-palm plantations that surround the sanctuary; the lodge is quite comfortable, a collection of chalets that are simply adorned, airy and inviting in a tropical-chic way. Guests can also venture out on mangrove treks into the surrounding jungle, night treks with guides, and are often invited to give basic English lessons at a nearby village schoolhouse.

Independent travel here is difficult unless you have your own vehicle, as Teluk Labuk (Labuk Bay) sits 15km down a rough dirt track off the main highway. If you're staying here, Nipah Lodge will handle all transfers; otherwise your lodging in Sepilok will be able to arrange transport for around RM120. You can also look for minivans and taxis in the car park of SORC; travellers who want to go to Teluk Labuk should be able to negotiate shared taxis and vans to the proboscis feeding for around RM150 (round-trip from Teluk Labuk back to your Sepilok lodging).

🛏 Sleeping & Eating

If you came to Sandakan for the orang-utans of Sepilok, do yourself a favour and stay near the apes. The lodging here tends to have more character than Sandakan spots. Most accommodation options are scattered along Jln Sepilok, the 2.5km-long access road to the rehabilitation centre.

TOP CHOICE Paganakan Dii   BOUTIQUE HOTEL $$

(☎089-532005; www.paganakandii.com; dm/chalet RM30/150; ✱) There are some places that reinvent what budget-to-midrange accommodation is capable of, and Paganakan Dii falls firmly into this vaunted category of hotel. This welcoming and quiet retreat sits deep within a deer preserve, just past a public park. Chic design details made from recycled materials, crisp white linens, smooth wooden chalets, views into a jungle seemingly sliced out of Eden and friendly staff will have you thinking the owners surely left a zero off the price tag. Overall, staying here is a great reason to get stuck in Sepilok. Transfers to the Sepilok Rehabilitation Centre are included in the price. The ridge chalets are some of the best value for money chalets in Sabah, especially seeing as they can be split between three to four people. Book early.

Sepilok Forest Edge Resort   RESORT $$

(Map p344; ☎089-533190, 089-533245; www.sepilokforestedge.com; Jln Rambutan, Sepilok Mile 14; dm/d/chalets from RM40/80/220; ✱❄) This fine resort grew out of the excellent Labuk B&B, which is still technically part of the Forest Edge property. Serviceable dorm and double rooms are located in a pretty longhouse, but it's the chalets that are the property's pièce de résistance. The comfortable cabins are peppered across an obsessively maintained acreage (think golf course). There's a relaxing tropical pool/jacuzzi on the grounds as well, which is reserved for chalet guests (or backpackers willing to drop an extra RM8).

Sepilok Nature Resort   RESORT $$$

(Map p344; ☎089-674999, 089-673999; http://sepilok.com; r from RM280; ✱@) This is as luxurious as Sepilok gets – the full five-star tropical treatment. Run by the very exclusive Pulau Sipadan Resort & Tours, these rattan-accented chalets are exquisitely decked out and have private verandahs overlooking scrumptious gardens and a shaded lagoon. The on-site restaurant cooks the best Western food in Sepilok (not that there's a lot of competition).

Sepilok B&B   B&B $

(Map p344; ☎089-532288, 019-833 0901; www.sepilokbednbreakfast.com; Jln Arboretum; dm/r RM45/60) This unpretentious option has a palpable summer-camp vibe. That goes for the large crowds who stay here and the decor of the place, which runs towards stark, simple yet cosy. Crooked picnic tables and varnished lounge chairs offer backpackers plenty of room to chill out after a sweaty day of orang-utanning under the equatorial sun. Located opposite the Rainforest Discovery Centre (RDC).

Uncle Tan GUESTHOUSE $
(☎016-824 4749, 089-535784; www.uncletan.com; dm/tw incl all meals RM48/100, plus RM50 per extra sharing; ❄@) The Uncle Tan empire is one of the oldest backpacker/adventure travel outfits in Sabah. Now they've set up shop in the heart of Sepilok with a couple of decent thatch-roofed gazebos and a stack of backpacker shacks.

Sepilok Jungle Resort RESORT $$
(Map p344; ☎089-533031; www.sepilokjungleresort.com; dm RM28, r RM105-220; ❄@≋) Everyone seems to stay here but it's hard to see why. Well, no, it's not – this is a big stop on the package-tour path. Some rooms are a bit drab: cheap carpeting and bedspreads and musty windows. Renovated rooms are a better deal – the sort of clean, if institutional hotel room you'd expect at home (but in a jungle).

Most accommodation in the area serves breakfast, and some offer guests three-meal packages. The **SORC cafeteria** (meals from RM5; ☺7am-4pm) vends sandwiches, noodle bowls, rice plates, snacks and beverages, though they are known for running out of items during the tourist rush. **Mah Fung Enterprise** (☺Mon-Sat), across from the turn-off to the RDC, sells cold drinks, snacks, sunscreen and insect repellent. There's also a small hut with a blue fence at Batu 14 serving snacks and cold drinks.

ℹ️ Information

Sepilok is located at 'Batu 14' – 14 miles (23km) from Sandakan. The street connecting the highway to the centre is lined with various accommodation (except Paganakan Dii, which is located on the other side of the road).

It's best to get **money** in Sandakan, but an ATM had been installed in a Petronas station on the road between Sandakan and Sepilok. The next-closest **ATM** is in Sandakan Airport. Money can be changed at upmarket sleeping spots for a hefty change fee.

ℹ️ Getting There & Away

Bus

Bus 14 from Sandakan (RM3) departs hourly from the city centre. If coming from KK, board a Sandakan-bound bus and ask the driver to let you off at 'Batu 14'. You will pay the full fare, even though Sandakan is 23km away.

Taxi

If you are coming directly from Sandakan, a taxi should cost no more than RM45 (either from the airport or the city centre). Taxi 'pirates', as they're known, wait at Batu 14 to give tourists a ride into Sepilok. It's RM3 per person for a lift. Travellers spending the night can arrange a lift with their accommodation if they book ahead of time. Walking to the SORC is also an option – it's only 2.5km down the road.

Minivan

You can usually organise a pick-up (in a shared minivan from the Kinabatangan operators) from Sepilok after the morning feeding if you are planning to head to Sungai Kinabatangan in the afternoon.

Sandakan Archipelago

While everyone knows about the Semporna Archipelago, it seems hardly anyone wants to visit the Sandakan Archipelago, off the coast of its namesake port. What gives? Don't like fluffy specks of emerald sprouting like orchids out of the Sulu Sea, or seabound rock walls, or tales of POW derring-do?

Although it's highly promoted by Sabah Tourism, we cannot recommend Turtle Islands National Park at this time. The trip to watch green sea turtles lay eggs is, at best, ill-managed, and at worst a circus. On any one night dozens of gawping tourists cluster round a single laying turtle; this seems to have the effect of scaring some of the reptiles off. Allowing visitors to handle baby turtles before releasing them is highly dubious. The illegal turtle egg trade is certainly alive in Sandakan: we have personally seen turtle eggs for sale within the city's markets, and while this activity is technically illegal, vendors weren't shy about approaching us. That's the sort of adventure on offer in the Sandakan Archipelago.

PULAU LANKAYAN

Pulau Lankayan isn't just photogenic; it's your desktop screen saver. Water isn't supposed to get this clear, nor sand this squeaky clean. A spattering of jungle, a few swaying palms...sigh. No wonder so many lovers come here for their honeymoons, which are often (but not necessarily) accompanied by dive expeditions at **Lankayan Island Resort** (☎088-238113, 089-673999; lankayan-island.com;

Batu 6; r RM3350/RM2728), the one accommodation option on Lankayan. There are a couple dozen cabins dotted along the sand where the jungle meets the sea, decked out in flowing light linens and deep tropical hardwood accents. Transfers from Sandakan are included in your accommodation.

Sungai Kinabatangan

The Kinabatangan River is Sabah's longest: 560km of water so chocolatey brown it would pose a serious safety risk to Augustus Gloop. It coils like the serpents that swim its length far into the Borneo interior. Riverine forest creeps alongside the water, swarming with wildlife that flee ever-encroaching palm-oil plantations. Lodges are set up all along the banks, while home stay programs pop up with the frequency of local monkeys. Dozens of tin boats putter along the shores offering tourists the opportunity to have a close encounter with a rhinoceros hornbill or perhaps a doe-eyed orang-utan.

◉ Sights

Gomantong Caves   CAVES
(☑089-230189; www.sabah.gov.my/jhl; adult/child RM30/15, camera/video RM30/50; ☺8am-noon & 2-4.30pm) Sarawak's Mulu and Niah caverns may be more famous, but for our ringgit, we think the Gomantong Caves give them a run for their money: a massive crack in a mountain, a cathedral-like grand inner chamber formed of limestone, spot-speckled with tubes of golden sunlight and a veritable small hill of bat shit, cockroaches and scorpions. The Gomantong Caves are disgusting, yes, but they're also magnificent.

The forested area around the caves conceals plenty of wildlife and a few good walks – we spotted a wild orang-utan out here, which local staff said was rare but not unheard of (sadly, that's because increased logging is pushing the primates into protected areas like this). The most accessible of the caves is a 10-minute walk along the main trail near the information centre. Head past the living quarters of the nest collectors to get to the main cave, **Simud Hitam** (Black Cave). Venture into the main chamber and keep walking counter-clockwise on the raised platform, which hovers over a steaming soup of bat crap and a chittering, chitinous army of roaches, centipedes and scorpions. The same lovely mix coats the walkway's handrails, so try not to grip

them when you (inevitably) slip on the river o' guano. A 45-minute uphill trek beyond the park office leads to **Simud Putih** (White Cave), containing a greater abundance of prized white swiftlets nests. Both trails are steep and require some sweaty rock climbing.

The majority of visitors to Gomantong come as part of an add-on to their Kinabatangan tour package. It is possible to visit the caves under one's own steam, though, usually by private vehicle. The turn-off is located along the road connecting Sukau to the main highway and is quite well signposted. Minivans plying the route between Sandakan and Sukau (RM17) can drop you off at the junction, but you'll have to walk the additional 5km to the park office.

Bukit Belanda   HILL
Bukit Belanda – Dutch Hill – is a 420m hill located behind the village of Bilit. The land is owned by the citizens of Bilit, who, despite pressures from logging companies, have not opened the hill to the timber industry, preferring to maintain it as a haven for wildlife. You can hike to the top in an hour if you're fit, where you'll be rewarded by lovely views of Sungai Kinabatangan and, if you're lucky, glimpses of local wildlife (at the very least, you're sure to hear the shrieks of local primates.) It's best to make this trek early in the morning for purposes of both catching the sunrise and avoiding the heat of the day. There's no official infrastructure when it comes to visiting the hill; just ask someone in your lodge or Bilit itself to guide you to the beginning of the ascent path.

Batu Tulug   CAVES
(☑089-565145; http://museum.sabah.gov.my; admission RM15; ☺9am-5pm, closed Fri) On the road from Sandakan to Lahad Datu you can catch a glimpse of Agop Batu Tulug, a jutting knife of white limestone slicing out of the jungle. This hill, located above the village of Batu Putih, is studded with caves that house the ancestors of both local Chinese and the Orang Sungai (People of the River). Because the Kinabatangan has a habit of frequently flooding, the final resting place of the dead has traditionally been located in cave complexes (a practice that has eroded thanks to Christianity and Islam). Heavy wooden coffins – it must have been an awful effort lugging them up the sheer rocks – are interred in the Batu Tulug caves with spears, knives, gongs, bells and Chinese curios. Some coffins

PULAU BERHALA

Berhala is supremely serene, an exemplar of a rare genre: a lovely tropical island hardly touched by tourists. Sandstone cliffs rise above the Sulu Sea, hemming in quiet patches of dusty, sandy prettiness. The vibe is so sleepy it's narcoleptic, an atmosphere accentuated by a quiet water village inhabited by fishing families, loads of migrating birds (their presence is heaviest in October and November) and...well, OK. There's not a lot else, except some very big rocks.

But oh what rocks. Rock climbers grade the formations here F5a – F6b, which is jargon for a mix of slow sloping walls and vertical cliff faces. Fieldskills Adventures (p311) in Kota Kinabalu runs 2-day/1-night rock-climbing trips out here for RM500 per person.

Berhala was a leper colony during the colonial period, and the Japanese used the island as a civilian internment centre and POW camp during WWII. Agnes Newton Keith was kept here awhile, as was a group of Australian POWs who managed to escape the island by boat and sail to Tawi-Tawi in the Philippines.

are carved with relatively simple geometric patterns, others in beautiful animal designs. This trove of artefacts makes the hill one of the most important archaeological sites in Sabah. **Sabah Museums** runs the site and has built wooden staircases that snake up the 40m hill. There are two main caves to explore, but if you climb the stairs to the top, you'll be rewarded with a nice view of the surrounding jungle and the Kinabatangan River. An interpretive information centre is also located on the site.

The easiest way to get here is to include the caves in your package tour of the Kinabatangan. If you've got your own vehicle, look for signs indicating the turn-off to Batuh Putih or Muzium Batu Tulug on the Sandakan–Lahad Datu road. The village is south of Sukau Junction, about 1½ hours from Sandakan and 45 minutes from Lahad Datu. GPS coordinates are N5024.935' E117056.548'.

Kinabatangan Orang-utan Conservation Project (KOCP)   RESEARCH CENTRE

(☎088-413293; www.hutan.org.my) Inside Sukau village is this conservation camp dedicated to studying and protecting Sabah's most iconic animal ambassador. The project is run in partnership with HUTAN, a French NGO, which also works with villagers to establish environmental-education programs, reforestation initiatives and an elephant-conservation project in the Sukau-Bilit area. This is not a tourist-oriented outfit like the Sepilok sanctuary, and as such is not open to casual visitors, but it may be worth contacting it as staff may be willing to hire out guides should you want to go searching for wild orang-utans.

Activities

Wildlife River Boat Cruises   BOAT TOUR

Wildlife is the number-one reason to visit Sabah, and a cruise down the Kinabatangan is often a highlight for visitors to the state. In the late afternoon and early morning, binocular-toting enthusiasts have a chance of spotting nest-building orang-utans, nosy proboscis monkeys, basking monitor lizards and hyper long-tailed macaques. That said, there is such a preponderance of operators out here that boats tend to cluster around the wildlife, which kind of ruins the sense of wild exposure. Also, the reason so many animals are here is depressing: the expansion of palm oil plantations has driven local wildlife to the riverbank. They simply have nowhere else to live.

Mammals can be seen all year, moving around in small groups while travelling through plantations. Colourful birds are a huge draw: all eight varieties of Borneo's hornbills, plus brightly coloured pittas, kingfishers and, if you're lucky, a Storm's stork or the bizarre Oriental darter all nest in the forests hugging the Kinabatangan. Avian wildlife is more numerous and varied during rainier months (usually October to late March), which coincides with northern-hemisphere migrations. Though friendly for birds, the rainy season isn't accommodating for humans. Flooding has been a problem of late and a couple of lodges will sometimes shut their doors when conditions are severe.

The success rate of animal-spotting largely depends on luck and the local knowledge of your guide – don't be afraid to ask hard questions about the specifics of your trip before you sign up. Elephants and other larger

THE BUSINESS OF BIRD NESTS

The Gomantong Caves are Sabah's most famous source of swiftlet nests, used for the most revered, rare, luck-and-'strength'-inducing dish of the traditional Chinese culinary oeuvre: the eponymous birds-nest soup. Wait, you ask, people *want* to eat bird nest? Well, it's not twigs and stones folk want to devour: swiftlets make their nests out of their own dried spit, which is the main ingredient in the soup. When added to soup broth, the swiftlet spit dissolves and becomes gelatinous. Wait, you ask, people *want* to eat bird vomit? Well, yes. Very much so.

There are two types of soupworthy bird nests: black and white. Black are a mix of twigs and spit, while the white nests are purely made from the birds' saliva. The white nests are significantly more valuable and Gomantong's got a relatively large amount of them. A kilogram of white swiftlet spit can bring in over US$4000, making nest-grabbing a popular profession despite the perilous task of shimmying up bamboo poles.

In the last few years visiting has been restricted due to dwindling bird populations (cash-hungry locals were taking the nests before the newborn birds had enough time to mature). Today, the caves operate on a four-month cycle, with closings at the beginning of the term to discourage nest hunters. It's worth asking around before planning your visit – often the caves are empty or off-limits to visitors. The four-month cycles are strictly enforced to encourage a more sustainable practice of harvesting.

animals come and go, as herds often break up to get through the palm plantations.

River tours should always be included in lodge package rates. If you prefer to explore independently, contact local home stay programs, which will be able to hook you up with a boat operator. Or ask about renting a boat in Sukau – everyone in the village is connected to the tourism industry either directly or through family and friends, and someone will be able to find you a captain. Another option: just before the entrance to Sukau village is a yellow sign that says 'Di sini ada boat servis' (Boat service here); different river pilots hang out here throughout the day. Whatever way you choose to find a boat and a guide, expect to pay at least RM100 for a two-hour river cruise on a boat that can hold up to six people (ie you can split the cost with friends).

Some of the villages you see along the river are inhabited by Filipino migrants who are stateless citizens, unrecognised by both Malaysia and the Philippines.

Trekking

Depending on the location of your lodge, some companies offer short treks (one to three hours) through the jungle. Night hikes are some of the best fun to be had on the Kinabatangan – there's something magical about being plunged into the intense, cavernlike darkness of the jungle at night. Headlamps should be carried in your hand, rather than worn on your head – bats tend to be attracted to light sources and may fly into them; they also secrete an enzyme causing localised paralysis (it's temporary but can muck up your typinghshshenfnvnwurj – just kidding. Seriously, it's temporary).

🛏 Sleeping & Eating

You'll need to book at river lodges in advance. In Kinabatangan lingo, a 'three-day, two-night' stint usually involves the following: arrive in the afternoon on day one for a cruise at dusk, two boat rides (or a boat-hike combo) on day two, and an early morning departure on day three after breakfast and a sunrise cruise. When booking a trip, ask about pick-up and drop-off prices – this is usually extra.

SUKAU

Sukau means 'tall tree' in the local dialect, and the name is quite fitting. The tiny town sits on the river among the skyscraping branches of a shaded thicket, across from massive stone cliffs that are quite attractive, seemingly lifted from a Chinese silk-scroll painting.

Last Frontier Resort　　RESORT $$$
(☎016-676 5922; www.thelastfrontierresort.com; 3-day, 2-night package RM550; ❋@☎) Getting to the Last Frontier is a good first step towards better cardiac health: the only hilltop lodge in the Kinabatangan region sits high, high up (538 steps!) on a hill overlooking the flood plains. Sadly, a Sherpa is not included

in the rates. What you do get is excellent fusion cuisine in the on-site **Monkey Cup Cafe** (this place is owned by a Belgian-Malaysian couple – anyone want *frites mit/avec nasi lemak?*), gorgeous views of the river, well-crafted, simple chalets and a host of trekking options.

Sukau Rainforest Lodge   LODGE $$$

(☎088-438300; www.sukau.com; 3-day, 2-night package RM1750; ✴🛜) The Rainforest Lodge participates in tree-planting projects aimed at reviving degraded portions of riverine forest, aims to reduce use of plastics and is pioneering the use of quiet electric motors on its river cruises (which utilise boats made of recycled materials). All this is well and good, but the sleeping experience is lovely as well: swish but unpretentious longhouses dotted into the jungle, situated around a lovely common space stuffed with gongs, tiki torches and *bubu* (local fish traps), welcome guests after their riverine adventures. Don't miss the 440m annotated boardwalk in the back that winds through the canopy.

Kinabatangan Riverside Lodge   LODGE $$$

(☎089-213502; www.sitours.com; 2-day, 1-night package per two people US$315; ✴🛜) Come here to fall gently asleep in a series of luxury chalets, adrift in simple white sheets and polished wood floors, all connected by a series of shady raised walkways through the jungle. A looping nature trail is out the back and an adorable dining area abounds with stuffed monkeys, faux foliage and traditional instruments. It's managed by SI Tours, which charges in US$.

Barefoot Sukau Lodge   LODGE $

(☎089-237525; www.barefootsukau.com; r RM250; 🛜) Smiling staff direct you to rooms that are small but covered with thick coats of white paint. Just outside Barefoot's cute waterfront cafe is a series of slate-grey cliffs mottled with jungle, creeper and vines.

Sukau Greenview B&B   B&B $

(☎013-869 6922, 089-565266; http://sukaugreenviewbnb.zxq.net/; 2-day, 1-night package from RM330) This pleasant option offers rooms with twin-size beds in a small cottage-style lodge. It's basic (the floors are made from particleboard) for the price.

BILIT

Bilit is a teeny-weeny village that is primarily full of friendly locals and home stays. River lodges are located on both the Bilit side of the Kinabatangan River and the opposite bank. There's a jetty from which boats depart to lodges on the other side of the river, and across the street is a small yard where you can park a car if you drove; the family that owns the house charges RM20 a day for the privilege. A small banana orchard acts as a magnet for pygmy elephants, which a) are popular with tourists and b) have a bad habit of trampling and eating local crops.

Nature Lodge Kinabatangan   LODGE $$

(☎088-230534, 013-863 6263; www.naturelodgekinabatangan.com; 3-day, 2-night package dm/chalet RM380/415) Located just around the river bend from Bilit, this charming jungle retreat is a decent choice for backpacker budgets. The campus of bungalows is divided into two sections: the Civet Wing caters to penny-pinchers with dorm-style huts, while the spiffed-up Agamid Wing offers higher-end twin-bed chalets. Neither sleeping experience will blow you away: mattresses are thin and the rooms get dank after the rains, so don't expect luxury. The activity schedule, on the other hand, is fantastic: the three-day, two-night packages include three boat tours, three guided hikes *and* all meals, which is good value as you'll find in these parts.

Bilit Rainforest Lodge   LODGE $$$

(☎088-448409; http://bilitrainforestlodge.com; 2-day, 1-night accommodation only RM420; ✴🛜) One of the more luxurious sleeping spots along the Kinabatangan, this snazzy option caters to an international clientele with huge bungalows, modern bathrooms and generous amounts of gushing air-con. Common areas are plucked from luxury travel magazine pictorial spreads, and the outdoor bar is especially lovely for nighttime drinks. Unlike many lodges we mention, Bilit charges based off the activites you chose; the above rate is for rooms only. Adding two boat tours and three meals a day increases the rate by RM310 a day. A huge array of package tours is available; see the website for more details.

Bilit Adventure Lodge   LODGE $$$

(☎089-271077; www.stwadventure.com; 2-day, 1-night package from RM665, with air-con RM740; ✴) This lodge allows you to adventure in (overpriced) style, or at least sleep as such, in a collection of 24 chalets, some fan-cooled and some with air-con, all decorated in safari style with wooden accents and big fluffy beds.

SABAH SUNGAI KINABATANGAN

Myne Resort RESORT $$$
(☎089-216093; www.myne.com.my; 2-day, 1-night package from RM1055; 🅿🅰) The newest up-market option on the river consists of over a dozen dark-toned chalets wedged into a dual ridgeline that overlooks a sweeping bend of the Kinabatangan. With fresh smooth sheets, comfy air-con and an enormous deck area for snacking and drinking, this is a solid upper-tier choice that tends to be popular with tour groups from Europe and China.

Kinabatangan Jungle Camp LODGE $$
(☎013-540 5333, 019-843 5017, 089-533190; www.kinabatangan-jungle-camp.com; 2-day, 1-night package RM550) This earth-friendly retreat caters to a niche market of birders and serious nature junkies; facilities are functional, with the focus emphasising quality wildlife-spotting over soft, comfortable digs. Packages include three meals, two boat rides, guiding and transfers. The owners also run the Labuk B&B in Sepilok, and four out of five travellers opt for a Kinabatangan-Sepilok combo tour.

DON'T MISS

HOME STAYS ON THE KINABATANGAN

Home stay programs are popping up with increasing frequency in Sukau, Bilit and other villages, giving tourists a chance to stay with local Orang Sungai – 'people of the river' – and inject money almost directly into local economies. Please note the contacts we provide are for local home stay program coordinators who will place you with individual families.

Our favourite home stay in the region is in the village of Abai. The villagers love hosting guests and, to the degree they can, chatting with you and generally forming cross-cultural bonds (the levels of English are admittedly not great). Expect to be asked to participate in the local village volleyball matches! This home stay is best arranged through Adventure Alternative Borneo (p311) in Kota Kinabalu, which maintains direct contact with the villagers.

In Sukau, **Bali Kito Homestay** (☎089-568472, 013-869 9026; http://sukauhomestay. com; 3-day, 2-night package for four RM650, one night with two meals RM50) can connect you with several different families and, for additional fees, hook you up with cultural programs, fishing trips, opportunities to work on traditional farms, treks, wildlife cruises and other fun. A special walk-in rate of RM30 is also available if you just rock up to the village (meals are RM10 each). A four-person three-day, two-night package that includes meals, four river cruises, transport to and from Sandakan and a visit to the Gomantong Caves runs to RM650 per person, but different packages can be arranged for smaller groups.

In tiny Bilit, we often wondered which houses *weren't* home stays. Contact the exceptionally helpful **Bilit Village Homestay** (☎013-891 3078, 019-537 0843, 019-853 4997; http://bilithomestay.wordpress.com; r from RM55). This outfit offers package deals that are much the same experience as what you would find in Sukau. Three-day, two-night rates, which include river cruises and trekking, run RM360 per person.

Near Batu Pulih (the village adjacent to the Batu Tulug caves), **Mescot/Miso Walai Homestay** (☎012-889 5379, 019-582 5214, 089-551070; www.mescot.org; r RM70) is one of the oldest, best-run community ecotourism initiatives in the area. By dint of its location, this home stay also happens to be outside the tourist crush in Sukau and Bilit, so your chances of spotting wildlife are a bit better.

When staying in a home stay, it is important to act as a guest in someone's home as opposed to a tourist on holiday. Privacy will be reduced, and you may be expected to help with chores, cooking, cleaning etc (this depends on the family you stay with). Men and women should dress modestly and couples will want to avoid overt displays of affection, which locals tend to frown on. English may not be widely spoken, especially at newer home stays, although you'll be impressed at the multilingual abilities of kids who have grown accustomed to meeting travellers from around the world! The experience is a different one, one which many visitors absolutely love, but it's certainly not everyone's cup of tea. That said, we strongly encourage giving home stays a shot if you haven't done so before.

Proboscis Lodge Bukit Melapi   LODGE $$

(✆088-240584; http://www.sdclodges.com; 2-day, 1-night package tw share per person RM330; ❄) The Proboscis is a study in subdued, simple luxury. The management has created a sociable ambience with its large bar area and comfy tree-stump seating. Wooden bungalows, strewn along a shrubby hill, have oxidised copper-top roofs that clink when it rains. The two-day, one-night packages include three meals, one river cruise and a pick-up from the Lapit jetty.

UPRIVER

Abai Jungle Lodge   LODGE $$$

(✆089-213502, 013-883 5841; www.sitoursborneo. com; 2-day, 1-night packages from US$290) Managed by SI Tours (p340) (the same company that runs Kinabatangan Riverside Lodge), Abai Jungle Lodge sits 37km upstream from Sukau just as the river emerges from the secondary forest. This is a great option for the adventurous – isolated and ecologically minded, Abai also manages to feel quite comfortably luxurious. The woodsy exterior pavilions are good for strolling after crashing in your cosy private room. Eco-conscious attempts are being made to increase sustainability: rainwater is collected in cisterns above the chalets, which run on low-emitting diesel engine generators.

Uncle Tan's Jungle Camp   LODGE $$

(✆016-824 4749, 089-535784; www.uncletan.com; 2-day, 1-night packages from RM320, 3-day, 2-night packages from RM420) Uncle Tan was one of the earliest guides and environmentalists working along the Kinabatangan. Although he died in 2002, his legacy lives on in the form of this lodge, a descendant of his original backpacker mecca. This camp isn't for everyone; some travellers may be put out by the spartan conditions, which are basic (running water is the concession to luxury). Others may embrace the roughing-it attitude, especially as the drop in creature comforts is offset by experienced staff members who are skilled at finding wildlife.

ⓘ Getting There & Away

Transfers are usually arranged with your lodging as part of your package, but you can save by arriving independently. Arrange transport from any of the drop-off points with your tour operator or with a local minivan. Don't get on Birantihanti buses – they stop anytime someone wants to get on or off, which could quadruple travelling time.

Bus & Minivan

From KK, board a Tawau- or Lahad Datu–bound bus and ask the driver to let you off at 'Sukau Junction', also known as 'Meeting Point' – the turn-off road to reach Sukau. If you are on a Sandakan-bound bus, make sure your driver remembers to stop at the Tawau-Sandakan junction – it's called 'Batu 32' or 'Checkpoint' (sometimes it's known as Sandakan Mile 32).

From Sepilok or Sandakan, expect to pay around RM20 to reach 'Batu 32', and around RM30 if you're on a Sandakan–Tawau bus and want to alight at 'Meeting Point'.

A minivan ride to 'Meeting Point' from Lahad Datu costs RM20. When buying your bus tickets remember to tell the vendor where you want to get off so you don't get overcharged.

Car

If you are driving, note that the Shell petrol station on the highway at Sukau Junction (at the turn-off to Sukau) is the last place to fill up before arriving at the river. The road to Sukau is pretty smooth, but as you get closer to Bilit you'll start running into some dirt patches. It is possible to get to Bilit via 2WD – just drive carefully, especially if it's been raining.

Lahad Datu

POP 220,000

Lahad Datu is where a lot of Eastern Sabah is heading: a company town where the company is palm oil plantations.

The locals are lovely and as proud of their home as folks are anywhere else in the world, but there's no real reason to stop here except to arrange a visit to the Danum Valley or Tabin Wildlife Reserve. **Borneo Nature Tours** (✆089-880207; www.borneonaturetours. com; Lot 20, Block 3, Fajar Centre), which runs the Borneo Rainforest Lodge (BRL), and the **Danum Valley Field Centre** (✆088-326300, 089-881092; rmilzah@gmail.com; Block 3, Fajar Centre) have offices next to each other in the upper part of town – known as Taman Fajr, or Fajar Centre. There is a difference between the two Danum options (and yes, these are your only two options). Most people are here to book a stay in the Danum Valley Field Centre, as those who can afford to stay with Borneo Nature Tours aren't likely to book at the last minute and will probably arrange lodging earlier (either in KK or overseas). Because the Field Centre is exactly that – a research centre that doesn't cater to tourists – its office can be slow about responding to emails or phone calls asking for lodging. Sometimes it is best to show up in person and politely request to speak with someone about sleeping arrangements. Otherwise, contact Rose John Kidi at rmilzah@gmail.com, or ☑088-326300, or else contact Patricia Mobilik or Mahdah Aripin (☑089-881688, 089-0881092; danum@care2.com).

Around the block, you'll find the booking office of Tabin Wildlife Holidays (p356), a secondary forest sanctuary on the other side of Lahad Datu. As this office is a tourism outfit, it is much better about responding to emails; nonetheless, you'll likely pass through Lahad Datu on your way to Tabin.

🛏 Sleeping & Eating

Hotel De Leon
HOTEL **$$**

(☑089-881222; www.hoteldeleon.com.my; Darvel Bay Commercial Centre; s/d from RM168/178; ❋@ ⬤) A good midrange option with business-class standard, fresh, air-conditioned rooms. Perfect for those needing a night of comfort after the bush. Wi-fi is only available in common areas.

Full Wah
HOTEL **$**

(☑089-884100; Jln Anggerik; s/d from RM40/60; ❋) If you're on a tight budget, we recommend Full Wah. While located in a *very* dowdy building, the interior rooms are exceedingly mediocre, in a good way – clean, characterless carpets and bedding. This is as opposed to mildew ceilings and mouldy bathrooms, which seem the unfortunate norm in Lahad Datu's cheaper accommodation.

MultiBake
BAKERY **$**

(cakes from RM1.80; ⊗8am-10pm; @) Malaysia's franchised patisserie is located in Fajar Centre (it has free wi-fi too).

Dovist
RESTAURANT **$**

(mains from RM5; ⊗lunch & dinner) Around the corner from the Danum booking offices; a respectable spot for a more substantial meal. It's worth stopping by one of the convenience stores in Fajar Centre to stock up on a couple of snacks before your trip into the Danum Valley.

❶ Getting There & Away

Air

MASwings (☑1800-883000, outside Malaysia 03-7843 3000) currently operates four daily flights to Lahad Datu from KK. The airport is in the upper part of town near Fajar Centre. You must take the first flight of the day (departing KK at 6:25am) if you don't want a one-day layover in town before heading to the Danum Valley.

Bus

Express buses on the KK–Tawau route stop at the Shell station (Taman Fajr) near the Danum Valley office in the upper part of town. Other buses and minivans leave from a vacant lot near Tabin Lodge in the lower part of town. There are frequent departures for Sandakan (RM35, 2½ hours), Sukau (RM23, two hours), Semporna (RM25 to RM30, two hours) and Tawau (RM25 to RM35, 2½ hours). Charter vehicles and 4WDs wait in an adjacent lot; these guys are difficult to hire after sunset.

Danum Valley Conservation Area

Flowing like a series of dark, mossy ripples over some 440 sq km of central Sabah, the Danum Valley is a humid, cackling, cawing mass of lowland dipterocarp arboreal amazement. The forest here is thick – so thick that it has never been (to the best knowledge of anyone living) settled permanently. By humans, that is. Oh, there's life here of another sort in abundance: orangutans, tarsiers, sambar deer, bearded pigs, flying squirrels, proboscis monkeys, gibbons and the pygmy elephant (to name a few), watered by Sungai Segama and shaded by 70m-high old-growth canopy and 1093m-high Mt Danum.

This pristine rainforest is currently under the protection of Yayasan Sabah (Sabah Foundation; www.ysnet.org.my), a semigovernmental organisation tasked with both protecting and utilising the forest resources of Sabah. They say that at any given time, there are over a hundred scientists doing research in the Danum Valley. Tourists are less frequent visitors, but they are here, and you should count yourself lucky if you join their ranks. That said, to come here you either need a lot of cash or persistence, as the only two places to stay are a very luxurious resort or a budget-priced research centre where the main priority is accommodating scientists as opposed to, well, you. See the website of the South East Asia Rainforest Research (www.searrp.org) for more information on research occurring in the valley.

◉ Sights & Activities

Both the Borneo Rainforest Lodge (BRL) and the Danum Valley Field Centre offer a variety of jungle-related activities. Only the BRL has official nature guides, whereas the Field Centre offers park rangers.

Trekking

The main activities at the BRL and the Danum Valley Field Centre are walking on more than 50km of marked, meandering trails.

At the BRL, take advantage of the well-trained guides who can point out things you would have never seen on your own. The Coffincliff Trail is a good way to start your exploration and get your bearings. It climbs 3km to a cliff where the remains of some Kadazan–Dusun coffins can be seen (although the provenance of the coffins is unclear). After reaching an eye-popping panoramic viewpoint 100m up the way, you can either return the way you've come or detour around the back of the peak to descend via scenic Fairy Falls and Serpent Falls, a pair of 15m falls that are good for a quick dip.

The Danum Trail, Elephant Trail and Segama Trails all follow various sections of Danum Valley and are mostly flat trails offering good chances for wildlife spotting. All can be done in an hour or two. The Hornbill Trail and East Trail have a few hills, but are still relatively easy, with similarly good chances for wildlife sightings. Finally, if you just need a quick breath of fresh air after a meal, the Nature Trail is a short plankwalk near the lodge that allows you to walk into the forest unmolested by leeches.

There are heaps of fantastic trails weaving around the Field Centre – you must bring a ranger along if you aren't a scientist (note that a guide is better than a ranger though, as rangers are not trained to work with tourists). About a two-hour hike away are the Tembaling Falls, a cool slice of tropical Edenic beauty. A more strenuous, four-hour trek gets you to the immensely rewarding Sungai Purut falls, a series of seven-tiered pools that are fed by waters that drop down 20m from the nearby mountains.

Birdwatching

Danum Valley is very popular with birdwatchers from around the world, who come here to see a whole variety of Southeast Asian rainforest species, including the great argus pheasant, the crested fireback pheasant, the blue-headed pitta, the Bornean bristlehead and several species of hornbill, among many others. If you're serious about birding, it may be best to stay at the Borneo Rainforest Lodge. The canopy walkway here is ideal for birdwatching, and some of the guides are particularly knowledgeable about birds; attempts are made to match birders up with these pros. The access road to BRL is also a good spot for birding, as is, frankly, your porch.

Canopy Walkway

As you'll probably know, most of the action in a tropical rainforest happens up in the forest canopy, which can be frustrating for earthbound humans. The BRL's 107m-long, 27m-high canopy walkway gives mere mortals a means of transcending the surly bonds of earth. The swinging bridges traverse a nice section of forest, with several fine *mengaris* and *majau* trees on either side. Birdwatchers often come here at dawn in hopes of checking a few species off their master list. Even if you're not a keen birder, it's worth rolling out of bed early to see the sun come up over the forest from the canopy walkway – when there's a bit of mist around, the effect is quite magical. It's located on the access road, a 10-minute walk from the lodge. You need to be a guest at the BRL to access the walkway.

Night Drives

This is one of the surest ways to see some of the valley's 'night shift', but driving in the forest hardly gets a gold star for eco-friendliness; sensitive souls might empathise with that 'caught-in-the-headlights' feeling. Expect to see one or two species of giant flying squirrels, sambar deer, civets, porcupines and possibly even leopard cats; lucky sightings could include elephants, slow loris and clouded leopards (if you spot those, boy are you ever lucky).

Night drives leave the BRL most evenings; the best trips are the extended night drives, which depart at about 8.30pm and return at 1am or 2am. Things you'll be glad you brought: light waterproof jacket, camera with flash, binoculars and a powerful torch. Drives can be arranged at the Field Centre as well, although you'll probably have to arrange the vehicle one day in advance.

🛏 Sleeping & Eating

There are two lodging options in the Danum Valley, and you absolutely must have accommodation arranged with one of them before you visit – no dropping in. If price is paramount go for the Field Centre. Wildlife fanatics who value professionally trained guides should pick the BRL. The people at Sabah Tourism will try to point you towards the BRL and are reluctant to recommend the Field Centre. Bear in mind: Danum is a jungle, and you may spend your entire time without spotting wildlife, which is one of the main complaints readers have sent us after staying in the following spots.

Borneo Rainforest Lodge RESORT $$$
(BRL; ☎088-267637, 089-880207; www.borneo naturetours.com; d standard/deluxe 3-day, 2-night package RM2390/2690 per person) Borneo Rainforest Lodge is a class act deep within the buzzing haze of Sabah's remaining old-growth forest. Want the experience of staying in an uber-luxurious chalet while keeping an eye peeled for an adorable tarsier? You're in luck. Go for the deluxe if you can; they have private jacuzzis on the wooden verandahs that overlook the quiet ravine – romantic as hell. Honeymooners should go for Kempas D11 – this room has a secluded jacuzzi in its own wooden pagoda. Meals are taken on a beautiful terrace also fronting the river. We were pretty impressed with the assortment of dishes at the buffet – especially since it all had to be lugged in by 4WD. The BRL's only downfall is its marketing strategy. Yes, the lodge is lovely and the outdoor jacuzzis in the superior rooms are undoubtedly lavish, but this isn't a five-star resort. And how could it be, surrounded by relentlessly encroaching jungle? We're impressed, though, that this much luxury exists so deep in the rainforest. Guests who temper their expectations will adore the ambience and find plenty of creature comforts at their fingertips (no air-con though). It's best to book online or in KK.

Danum Valley Field Centre LODGE $$
(DVFC; ☎088-326300, 088-881688; rmilzah@ gmail.com; resthouse r & board from RM180, camping RM30; ❄) An outpost for scientists and researchers, the field centre also welcomes tourists. Accommodation at the centre is organised into four categories: hostel, resthouse, VIP and camping. We recommend the resthouse rooms, which are located at arm's length from the canteen (the only place to eat). These rooms are basic but clean, sporting ceiling fans and twin beds. Towels are provided for the cold-water showers. The simple hostel is about a seven-minute walk from the canteen, and the barracks-style rooms are separated by gender. If you want to camp, you can lay your sleeping kit (no tent needed) out on the walkways – bug spray recommended! All buildings at the field centre run on generated power, which shuts off between midnight and 7am. There

are no professionally trained guides at the centre – only rangers who can show you the trails. You might luck out and find a friendly researcher who will point you in the direction of a few cool things, but some of the scientists (especially the birders) value their privacy (and can you blame them?). There is a kitchen on the campus, however it is reserved for the research assistants. Tourists take their meals in the cafeteria-style canteen (veggie-friendly).

❶ Getting There & Away
Bus & Car

The Danum Valley is only accessible by authorised private vehicle. Borneo Rainforest Lodge guests depart from the lodge office in Lahad Datu at 9am, arriving by lunchtime. If you do not want to spend the night in Lahad Datu, it is recommended you take the 6:25am MASwings flight from KK. If you've prebooked, the driver will wait should your flight be delayed.

Tourists staying at the Danum Valley Field Centre must board one of two jungle-bound vans that leave the booking office in Lahad Datu at 3.30pm on Mondays, Wednesdays and Fridays. Transport is RM100 per person each way (this may increase by the time you read this). Vans return to Lahad Datu from the Field Centre at 8.30am on the same days.

Tabin Wildlife Reserve

Tabin's patch of jungle is essentially the downmarket alternative to the Danum Valley. The 1205-sq-km reserve consists mainly of lowland dipterocarp forest with mangrove areas – most of it is technically secondary forest, but that doesn't seem to trouble the wildlife or visitors. The stars here are the elephants and primates – gibbons, red-leaf monkeys and macaques, plus a lot of orangutans. Rescued orangs from Sepilok are actually released here, so you've got a pretty good chance of spotting some hairy red primates in the wild. Birdlife is abundant, and there's a herd of the endangered Sumatran rhino, though you're unlikely to see them.

The park is managed by Tabin Wildlife Holidays (☎088-267266; www.tabinwildlife. my; Lot 11-1, Block A, Damai Point; 2-day, 1-night package from RM1150), which runs the on-site Tabin Wildlife Resort, a pretty retreat with a clutch of upscale chalets. Fair warning: the chalets are attractive, but they're overpriced for what you get. Five trails snake out into the jungle from in front of the resort. Try the Elephant Trail (800m) if you're interested in belching mud pits. **The Gibbon Trail** (2.8km) leads to the pretty **Lipa Waterfall**.

Tabin can be accessed with a rental vehicle (4WD is a must), but most folks arrange transport with Tabin Wildlife. There are several entrances to the reserve; the easiest one to navigate to is near the junction of Ladan Tungju and Ladang Premai (it's 15km from Lahad Datu Airport to Ladang Kajai).

Semporna

POP 142,000

Most travellers, upon reaching Semporna, turn into little kids on a long car trip: 'But how much *longer* till we get there', with 'there' being Sipadan. Semporna-the-town is the mainland stopping point before Semporna-the-archipelago and all your diving/snorkelling fantasies. Unless you're lucky enough to get here early in the morning, there's a good chance you'll be sticking around overnight. Semporna's fine for an evening of carousing at a bar before donning your fins or checking out the *pasar ikan* (fish markets) and water villages; past that, enjoy your sleep. Not much longer, kids.

◉ Sights & Activities

'Diving' or (rarer) 'snorkelling' is the answer every tourist gives when someone asks them why they're in Semporna. Scuba is the town's lifeline, and there's no shortage of places to sign up for it. Operators are clustered around the 'Semporna Seafront', while other companies have offices in KK. Due to the high volume of interest, it is best to do your homework and book ahead – diving at Sipadan is limited to 120 persons per day.

⛱ Sleeping

If you have to overnight in Semporna, your options are limited – but not dire. If you've already signed up with a scuba operator ask them about sleeping discounts (and don't be shy about trying to finagle a good deal, especially if you're sticking around for a while).

Sipadan Inn HOTEL $
(Map p358; ☑089-781766; www.sipadaninn-hotel. com; Block D, Lot No. 19-24, Semporna Seafront; s/d from RM84/95) If you're on a budget, this is one of the better spots in Semporna. The bright white rooms are military clean, without a speck of dust, and it's a stone's throw from most of the dive centres.

Seafest Hotel HOTEL $$
(Map p358; ☑089-782333; www.seafesthotel. com; Jln Kastam; r RM90-260; ✳) The jauntily dubbed Seafest is six storeys of bay-view, business-class comfort at the far end of the 'Semporna Seafront' neighbourhood. It's affiliated with Seafest fishery, so check the restaurant's catch of the day. Don't be shy about asking for discounts, and note suites aren't really worth the extra ringgit.

Dragon Inn HOTEL $
(Rumah Rehat Naga; Map p358; ☑089-781099; www.dragoninnfloating.com.my; 1 Jln Kastam; dm RM20, r incl breakfast from RM80; ✳@) The owners of Dragon figured 'Tourists want stilt houses built over the water and tiki tropical decor' and ran with that theme for several miles. It's a bit tacky, but in an endearing way, and the more upmarket rooms are actually attractive, with dark flooring and island chic decour. The water the Inn stands over is green slop, but the staff is so friendly and eager to please, we forgive this minor trespass.

Scuba Junkie Dive Lodge HOSTEL $
(Map p358; ☑089-785372; www.scuba-junkie. com; Lot 36, Block B, Semporna Seafront; dm/r RM50/120; ✳@) A sociable, clean and basic spot offering 50% discounts for divers who book through Scuba Junkie. There's an adjacent bar (open from 4pm till the last guest passes out) that gets kicking with the dive instructor set come night.

**Borneo Global
Sipadan BackPackers** HOSTEL $
(Map p358; ☑089-785088; www.borneotourstravel. com; Jln Causeway; dm/tr/f incl breakfast RM20/70/100; ✳) Near the Seafest (on the seafront – say that three times fast), this dullish spot is cheap and cheerful. There are posters of fish, to remind you of why you came to Semporna, we guess.

✗ Eating

Various *kedai kopi* line the 'Semporna Seafront', while restaurants at the Seafest Hotel complex offer Chinese seafood. If you wanna go native, sample the *nasi lemak* or *korchung* (rice dumplings) – Semporna is well known for these two dishes.

Anjung Paghalian Café SEAFOOD $
(Map p358; Jln Kastam; mains RM3-5; ⊙5pm-10pm) Beside the Tun Sakaran Marine Park entrance sign, this indoor-outdoor place on a pier features fish, prawn, chicken, squid and venison sold by portions (for two or

Semporna

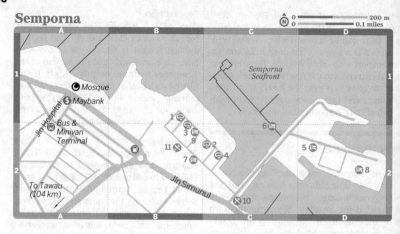

Semporna

⊕ Activities, Courses & Tours
Big John Scuba...........................(see 6)
1 Billabong Scuba.................................B1
Blue Sea Divers.........................(see 4)
2 Scuba Junkie..C2
3 Sipadan Scuba....................................B2
Sipadan Water Village................(see 3)
4 Uncle Chang's......................................C2

⊖ Sleeping
5 Borneo Global Sipadan
    BackPackers...................................D2
6 Dragon Inn..C2
7 Scuba Junkie Dive Lodge.................B2
8 Seafest Hotel.....................................D2
9 Sipadan Inn...B2

⊗ Eating
10 Anjung Paghalian Café......................C2
11 Mabul Steak House...........................B2

more people) and cooked in your choice of up to 12 different styles. It also has standard Malay hawker stalls and even one which serves burgers.

Mabul Steak House   STEAKHOUSE **$$**
(Map p358; ☎089-781785; Semporna Seafront; mains from RM11; ☉noon-11pm) This easygoing balcony restaurant's large and glacial 'ice-blended juices' are a soothing antidote for sucking bottled air. For further chilling, there's a leather couch and overstuffed chairs around a huge TV showing movies or sport. Malaysian standards are done well, and the signature steaks are a surprisingly mouthwatering treat after long days of diving.

ⓘ Information

If you're arriving in Semporna under your own steam, leave the bus and minivan drop-off area and head towards the mosque's spiking minaret. This is the way to the waterfront. Follow the grid of concrete streets to the right until you reach 'Semporna Seafront' – a collection of buildings decked out in primary colours that starkly contrast with the charmless pastels throughout the rest of town. This neighbourhood is home to the diving outfitters, each stacked one next to the other in a competitive clump. Sleeping and eating options crowd around here, too.

Decompression Chamber (☎089-783100) The closest **decompression chamber** is at the naval base in Semporna.

Maybank (☎089-784852; Jln Jakarullah) Expect small lines and the occasional beggar, especially in the evening.

ⓘ Getting There & Away
Air

Flights to Tawau from KK and KL land at Tawau Airport, roughly 28km from town. A private taxi from Tawau Airport to Semporna costs RM90, while Tawau–Semporna buses (RM15) will stop at the airport if you ask the driver nicely. Buses that do not stop at the airport will let you off at Mile 28, where you will have to walk a few (unshaded) kilometres to the terminal. Remember that flying less than 24 hours after diving can cause serious health issues, even death.

Bus

The 'terminal' hovers around the Milimewa supermarket not too far from the mosque's looming minaret. All buses run from early morning until 4pm (except Kota Kinabalu) and leave when full.

Kota Kinabalu	(RM65, nine hours) leaves at around 7am or 7pm.
Lahad Datu	(RM25 to RM30, 2½ hours)
Sandakan	(RM35 to RM40, 5½ hours)
Tawau	(RM15, 1½ hours)

Semporna Archipelago

Take the word 'blue' and mentally turn it over through all of its possibilities. From the deepest, richest shades to the light robin's egg shade of the sky to kelp-like aqua. This is the rippled waterscape of the Semporna Archipelago, broken up with pebbles of white sand and swaying palms and the rainbow-coloured boats of copper-skinned Sea Gypsies. But no one comes this way for islands, such as it were – rather it is the blue, the ocean and everything beneath it, that appeals, because this is first and foremost a diving destination, one of the best in the world.

◉ Sights & Activities

Maybe the name Semporna doesn't ring a bell – that's because the key word here is 'Sipadan'. Located 36km off Sabah's southeast coast, Sipadan (also called 'Pulau Sipadan') is the shining star in the archipelago's constellation of shimmering islands. The elliptical islet sits atop a stunning submerged pinnacle and world famous near-vertical walls. This underwater beacon is a veritable way station for virtually all types of sea life, from fluttering coral to school-bus-sized whale sharks. Sea turtles and reef sharks are a given during any dive, and luckier scubaholics

may spot mantas, eagle rays, octopus, scalloped hammerheads and monitor lizards that could double as Godzilla.

Roughly a dozen delineated dive sites orbit the island – the most famous being the aptly named Barracuda Point, where streamers of barracuda collide to form impenetrable walls of undulating fish. Reef sharks seem attracted to the strong current here and almost always swing by to say hello. South Point sits at exactly the opposite end of the island from Barracuda Point and usually hosts the large pelagics (manta magnet!). The west side of the island features technicolour walls that tumble down to an impossibly deep 2000m – words can't do the sight of this justice. The walls are best appreciated from out in the blue on a clear afternoon. The east coast tends to be slightly less popular, but that's a relative statement – turtles and sharks are still inevitable.

Although Sipadan outshines the neighbouring sites, there are other reefs in the marine park that are well worth exploring. The macro-diving around Mabul (or 'Pulau Mabul') is world-famous. In fact, the term 'muck diving' was invented here. The submerged sites around Kapalai, Mataking and Sibuan are also of note.

While it is possible to rock up and chance upon an operator willing to take you to Sipadan the following day, we strongly suggest that you book in advance. There are travellers and operators who say we are being too cautious with this advice, but your holiday is likely limited, and frankly, better safe than sorry. The downside to prebooking, of course, is that you can't visit each dive centre's storefront to suss out which one you like best, but Johnny-come-latelies might be forced to wait a few weeks before something opens up.

SABAH SEMPORNA ARCHIPELAGO

SNORKELLING IN SEMPORNA

Many nondivers wonder if they should visit Semporna. We give a qualified 'yes'. The diving here is obviously the main draw, as there are no real beaches to speak of (besides some small patches of sand). But if you like snorkelling, there's some incentive to come out this way. Snorkelling is not the obsessive hobby that diving is – people don't plan their holidays around it the way they do with diving. But if you're travelling in a group or as a couple where some dive and some don't, the Semporna islands are a lot of fun; dive and snorkelling trips are timed so groups leave and come back at similar times, so you won't feel isolated from each other. If you're on your own and only want to snorkel, it's still pretty great, but not as world class as the diving experience, and a bit pricey relative to the rest of Malaysia – snorkel trips cost around RM150, and you also have to factor in the relatively high cost of accommodation here and the price of getting out to the islands. Then again, you still have a good chance of seeing sting rays, sea turtles and all sorts of other macromarine wildlife while in the midst of a tropical archipelago, so really, who's complaining?

DON'T MISS

REGATTA LEPA

The big annual festival of local Bajau Sea Gypsies is the Regatta Lepa. (A *lepa* is a type of small boat, so the title somewhat redundantly means 'Boat regatta'.) Traditionally, the Bajau only set foot on mainland Borneo once a year; for the rest of the time they live on small islets or their boats. Today the Bajau go to Semporna and other towns more frequently for supplies, but the old cycle of annual return is still celebrated and marked by the regatta *lepa*. For visitors, the highlight of the festival is the *lepa*-decorating contest held between Bajau families. Their already rainbow-coloured boats are further decked out in streamers, flags (known as *tapi*), bunting, ceremonial umbrellas (which symbolise protection from the omnipresent sun and rain that beats down on the ocean) and *sambulayang*, gorgeously decorated sails passed down within Bajau clans. On each boat you can see a smaller, rectangular *lamak kapis* sail and the larger *lamak bua'an* sail, shaped to resemble the maw of a fish. Violin, cymbal and drum music, plus 'sea sports' competitions like duck catching and boat tug-of-war, punctuate the entire affair. It's a hell of a show. The regatta occurs in mid-April; check etawau.com for details, and don't miss the show if you're in town at this time of year.

The government issues 120 passes (RM40) to Sipadan each day (this number includes divers, snorkellers and day trippers). Bizarre rules and red tape, like having certain gender ratios, make the permit process even more frustrating. Each dive company is issued a predetermined number of passes per day depending on the size of its operation and the general demand for permits. Each operator has a unique way of 'awarding' tickets – some companies place their divers in a permit lottery, others promise a day at Sipadan after a day (or two) of diving at Mabul and Kapalai. No matter which operator you choose, you will likely be required to do a non-Sipadan intro dive unless you are a Divemaster who has logged a dive in the last six months. Permits to Sipadan are issued by day (and not by dive) so make sure you are getting at least three dives in your package.

A three-dive day trip costs between RM250 and RM500 (some operators include park fees, others do not – make sure to ask), and equipment rental (full gear) comes to about RM50 or RM60 per day. Cameras (around RM100 per day) and dive computers (around RM80 per day) are also available for rent at most dive centres. Top-end resorts on Mabul and Kapalai offer all-inclusive package holidays (plus a fee for equipment rental).

Although most of the diving in the area is 'fun diving', Open Water certifications are available, and advanced coursework is popular for those wanting to take things to the next level. The only problem with getting your Open Water certification here is that all other dive sites may pale in comparison! Diving at Sipadan is geared towards divers with an Advanced Open Water certificate (currents and thermoclines can be strong), but Open Water divers should not have any problems (they just can't go as deep as advanced divers). A three-day Open Water course will set you back at least RM950. Advanced Open Water courses (two days) cost the same, and Divemaster certification runs for around RM2500.

Several dive operators are based at their respective resorts, while others have shopfronts and offices in Semporna and/or KK. Please note we have listed the following alphabetically, not in order of preference – we simply didn't have the time to go diving with every outfitter in the islands. No matter where your desired operator is located, it is *highly* recommended you contact them in advance. The following dive operators are among the growing list of companies in the area:

Big John Scuba   DIVING
(Map p358; www.smiffystravels.com/BJSUBA2.htm) 'Big John' is a local guy who loves Sabah, Semporna and diving. He specialises in macro photography and muck diving and while he is an instructor, he separates his students from his diving groups. Has an office by the Dragon Inn.

Billabong Scuba   DIVING
(Map p358; 089-781866; www.billabongscuba.com; Lot 28, Block E, Semporna Seafront) Accommodation can be arranged at a rickety 'home stay' on Mabul.

Blue Sea Divers   DIVING
(Map p358; ☑781 322; www.blueseadivers-sabah.
com; Semporna Seafront) Reputable day-trip
operator in Semporna.

Borneo Divers   DIVING
(☑088-222226; www.borneodivers.info; 9th fl, Menara Jubili, 53 Jalan Gaya, Kota Kinabalu) The original operators in the area, Borneo Divers un-
veiled Sipadan to an awestruck Jacques Cousteau. It has maintained its high standards
throughout the years, offering knowledgeable
guides and comfy quarters. The office is located in Kota Kinabalu. There is a comely resort
on Mabul. Recommended.

Scuba Junkie   DIVING
(Map p358; ☑089-785372; www.scuba-junkie.com;
Lot 36, Block B, Semporna Seafront) Popular with
the young backpacker crowd.

Scuba Jeff   DIVING
(☑019-5855125, 017-8690218; www.scubajeffsip
adan.com) Jeff, a friendly local bloke, runs his
adventures out of the local fishing village in
Mabul. Good option for the budget crowd.

Seahorse Sipadan   DIVING
(☑012-279 7657, 016-835 5388, 089-782289;
www.seahorse-sipadanscuba.com) Backpacker-
oriented outfit that runs a hostel on Mabul.

Seaventures   DIVING
(☑088-261669; www.seaventuresdive.com; 4th fl,
Wisma Sabah) Highly regarded outfit that will
put you up in an ocean platform off the coast
of Mabul. Offices in KK.

Sipadan Scuba   DIVING
(Map p358; ☑089-784788, 089-919128; www.
sipadanscuba.com; Lot 23, Block D, Semporna Seafront) Twenty years of Borneo experience and
an international staff makes Sipadan Scuba
a reliable, recommended choice.

Sipadan Water Village   DIVING
(Map p358; ☑089-784227, 010-932 5783, 089-
751777, 089-950023; www.swvresort.com; Jln Kastam) A private operator based at the Mabul
resort with the same name.

SMART   DIVING
(☑088-486389; www.sipadan-mabul.com.my)
The dive centre operating at Sipadan-Mabul
Resort and Mabul Water Bungalow; both
are located on Mabul. Also has offices in KK.

Uncle Chang's   DIVING
(Borneo Jungle River Island Tours; Map p358;
☑089-786988, 017-895 0002, 089-781002; www.
ucsipadan.com/; 36 Semporna Seafront) Offers

diving and snorkelling day trips, plus stays
at its lodge on Mabul (RM90 per person).

🛌 Sleeping & Eating

From opulent bungalows to ragtag sea shan-
ties, the marine park offers a wide variety
of accommodation catering to all budgets.
Sleeping spots are sprinkled across the
archipelago with the majority of options
clustered on Mabul (Sipadan's closest neighbour). No one is allowed to stay on Sipadan.
Note that prices rise in August and September. Nondivers are charged at different rates
than divers.

At almost all of the places listed below,
you are tied to a set schedule of three to
five meals broken up by roughly three diving (or snorkelling) trips per day. Meals are
included; drinks are always extra, although
tea and coffee are often gratis. If you feel the
need to let loose at night, there are occasional parties at Uncle Tan's or Scuba Junkie
on Mabul. High-end resorts have their own
bars and restaurants; you may be able to eat
and drink here if you're staying in a budget
spot and the man at the gate is in a good
mood, but you'll pay for it.

Divers and snorkellers can also opt to
stay in the town of Semporna. That means
slightly better bang for your buck, but no
fiery equatorial sunsets. Perhaps more per-
tinently, it takes at least 30 minutes, and
usually a bit longer, to get to dive sites from
Semporna town.

Every one of the accommodation options listed below can arrange diving trips,
including certification courses and trips to
Sipadan.

SINGAMATA
Not an island at all, but rather a floating village built onto a sandbar about 30 minutes
from Semporna, Singamata (☑089-784828;
www.singamata.com; 3-day, 2-night diving/non-
diving RM720/500) is a pretty assemblage of
stilt chalets and decks with its own pool full
of giant fish (which you can snorkel amid). If
you feel like dipping into the water, you can
literally just step out of your room (annoyingly, rubbish from Semporna sometimes
still floats into the vicinity). Rooms are basic
but pretty and breezy. You may feel isolated
out here, but if you need an escape, this is a
lovely option.

MABUL
Mabul is the main accommodation centre
in the islands. This little speck is blessed

with one very small white-sand beach, fantastically blue waters and two small settlements: a camp of Bajau Sea Gypsies and a Malaysian water village of stilt houses built over the seashore, where most of the island's budget accommodation is clustered.

It's worth having a walk around the island, which should take you all of an hour or two. Behind the resorts are generators and barracks-style housing for resort staff. The locals are eager for your business; there's little shops in the villages that sell candy, crisps, cigarettes and other little incidentals. Plus watching the sunset bleed over stilt houses, as the Bajau set cooking fires in their houseboats, is mind-blowingly romantic, and a bit unexpected in a place that's so marketed towards diving.

Mabul Beach Resort   RESORT $$
(☎089-785372; www.scuba-junkie.com; dm RM95, r RM225-375; ✴️🛜) Owned and operated by Scuba Junkie, this spot is all the rage with the flashpacker crowd. Chalets with en suite bathrooms, porches and polished wood floors make for some posh digs priced (relatively) within the top of the budget range. Note the room prices are for single occupancy – rooms all have two beds, and are cheaper if rented out by two people.

Mabul Water Bungalow   RESORT $$$
(☎088-486389; www.mabulwaterbungalows.com; 3-day, 2-night dive package from US$1016, nondivers US$606; ✴️🛜) Travellers in Asia tend to love crystal-clear water and temples. These two concepts come together with a heaping dash of amazing at Mabul Water Bungalows, a gorgeously executed series of chalets-cum-Balinese shrines built over the Celebes Sea. This is easily the best upmarket option on Mabul. Rooms are effortlessly opulent, and the resort's only suite, the Bougain Villa (ha!), features a trickling waterfall in the bathroom, its own private dock and glass floors revealing the starfish-strewn sea floor.

Borneo Divers Mabul Resort   RESORT $$$
(☎088-222226; www.borneodivers.net; per person twin/single RM1148/765; ✴️@🛜) The oldest dive centre in the region offers lodging in a horseshoe of semidetached mahogany bungalows with bright-yellow window frames. Open-air pavilions with gauzy netting punctuate the perfectly manicured grounds. Wi-fi is available in the dining room.

Scuba Jeff   LODGE $
(☎019-5855125, 017-8690218; www.scubajeff sipadan.com; r RM80; 🛜) Jeff is a very friendly dude who maintains this large stilt house in the Malay fishing village. While his place is a little tatty, it reminds us of the fun of backpacking – staying in a flophouse and meeting random folk on a budget (including quite a few backpacking Malays).

Sipadan Adventures   HOME STAY $
(☎012-822 9984; www.sipadanadventures.com; dm/r per person RM70/90) Clean, remodeled rooms and a focus on budget travel make for a fun diving joint. Staff will help arrange dive trips for you and the owners cook up some mean fish.

Uncle Chang's   GUESTHOUSE $
(☎089-781002, 017-895 002, 089-786988; www. ucsipadan.com; per person dm/d RM70/90, per person d with air-con & bathroom RM100; ✴️) A Sipadan backpacking stalwart catering to the like-named dive operator, Chang's is a fun, sociable spot that periodically throws kicking little parties. The air-con rooms, clocking in at RM90, are good value for money.

Seaventures Dive Resort   RESORT $$$
(☎088-261669; www.seaventuresdive.com; 4-day, 3-night dive package from RM2160; ✴️) This oil rig (no, really) sits just off Mabul's silky shoreline. There are two schools of thought on Seaventures' aesthetic impressions: 'A worthy attempt at giving tourists a unique accommodation option, and 'That thing? Forget it.' Honestly, we're not sure where we fall in this debate, but its diving staff comes very highly recommended.

Billabong   GUESTHOUSE $
(☎089-781866; www.billabongscuba.com; per person r with fan/air-con RM70/120) Chill with fishermen, watch the sunset over the plankboards and set out for some diving adventures with associated Billabong Scuba at this home stay.

Sipadan-Mabul Resort   RESORT $$$
(SMART; ☎088-486389; www.sipadan-mabul. my; 7-day, 6-night dive package from US$1570, nondivers US$1186; ✴️🛜🏊) Even though the summer-camp styling suits the tropical landscape, the prices here are out of whack. Long-stays get the hard sell. If you feel like splurging why not go all the way and snag a room at SMART's sister property, Mabul Water Bungalow (p362)? Wi-fi is available in the dining area.

Sipadan Water Village Resort   RESORT $$$

(☎089-751777; www.swvresort.com; 4-day, 3-night package from RM4100; ✳@) Outmoded design details (although when were wooden tarantula ornaments ever in style?) quickly set the tone here – this resort-on-stilts doesn't pull off 'graceful elegance' quite like Mabul Water Bungalow next door, despite the idyllic location. If you decide that this is the spot for you, then go for the 'grand deluxe' bungalows.

Seahorse Sipadan   GUESTHOUSE $

(☎016-8355388, 089-782289; www.seahorse-sipadanscuba.com; dm/r from RM80/90) Basic digs for budget backpackers.

KAPALAI

Although commonly referred to as an island, Kapalai is more like a large sandbar sitting slightly under the ocean surface. From afar, the one hotel, Kapalai Resort (☎088-316011/3; http://sipadan-kapalai.com/; 63 Gaya Street, Kota Kinabalu; 4-day, 3-night package from RM2790; ✳@) looks like it's sitting on palm trunks in the middle of the sea. The resort designers went for a Sea Gypsy theme and tacked on an opulent twist, making the sea cabins out of shiny lacquered wood.

MATAKING

Mataking is also essentially a sandbar, two little patches of green bookending a dusty tadpole tail of white sand. Mataking Island Resort (☎089-786045, 089-770022; www.mataking.com; Jln Kastam; 3-day, 2-night package for divers/nondivers from RM2470/2110; ✳@) is the only accommodation here. This is an impeccably luxurious escape full of dark-wood chalets and gossamer sheets. This sandy getaway has some really beautiful diving – an artificial reef and sunken boats provide a haven for plenty of sea life – and has set up a novel 'underwater post office' at a local shipwreck site.

POM POM

Pom Pom needs no cheerleading – this stunning, secluded haven sits deep within the Tun Sakaran Marine Park, about one hour by boat from Semporna. Sipadan Pom Pom Island Resort (☎089-781918; pompomisland.com; 3-day, 2-night package RM1600-2000; ✳@) runs the only operation on the island. The poshest rooms are built over the water, while reed-and-thatch bungalows offer sea views from spacious balconies. The cheapest rooms are set back in a 'garden' area, but are still basically a hop from the ocean.

ROACH REEFS

This network of artificial reefs was once the private underwater playground for a wealthy businessman, but today Roach Reefs Resort (☎089-779332; www.roachreefsresort.com; 2-day, 1-night package for divers/nondivers per person US$185/148; ✳@) has opened its doors to tourists. You'll stay in simple shacks (a little *too* simple, frankly; we wouldn't mind a little more flash at these prices) plunked in a man-made spit of sand, shaded under coconut trees. Keep in mind boat transfers here come from Tawau, as opposed to Semporna.

❶ Information

The Semporna Islands are loosely divided into two geographical sections: the northern islands (protected as **Tun Sakaran Marine Park**) and the southern islands. Both areas have desirable diving – Sipadan is located in the southern region, as is Mabul and Kapalai. Mataking and Sibuan belong to the northern area. If you are based in Semporna you'll have a greater chance of diving both areas, although most people are happy to stick with Sipadan and its neighbours.

Consider stocking up on supplies (sunscreen, mozzie repellent etc) before making your way into the archipelago. Top-end resorts have small convenience stores with inflated prices. ATMs are nonexistent, but high-end resorts accept credit cards (Visa and MasterCard). Mabul has a small police station near the village mosque, as well as shack shops selling basic foodstuffs and a small pharmacy. Internet is of the wi-fi variety; most resorts now offer it, but service tends to be spotty.

The closest decompression chamber (p358) is at the Semporna Naval Base.

❶ Getting There & Around

Boat

With the exception of Roach Reefs, all transport to the marine park goes through Semporna. Your accommodation will arrange any transport needs from Semporna or Tawau Airport (sometimes included, sometimes for an extra fee - ask!), which will most likely depart in the morning. That means if you arrive in Semporna in the afternoon, you will be required to spend the night in town.

Tawau

POP 380,200

Ever been to an after-work happy hour and met a co-worker who is nice, courteous, polite, pleasant and agonisingly boring? Then you've met Tawau. There's nothing

Tawau

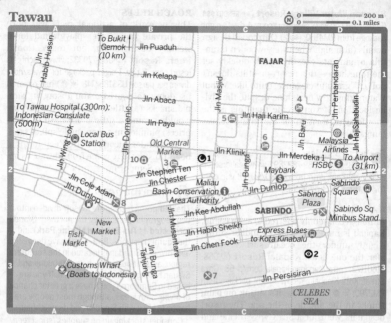

SABAH TAWAU

Tawau

⊙ Sights
1 Mosque...C2
2 Public Library.....................................D3

🛏 Sleeping
3 Hotel Soon Yee....................................B2
4 Kingston Executive Hotel...................D1
5 Monaco Hotel.......................................C1
6 Shervinton Executive Hotel...............C2

✗ Eating
7 Hawker Seafood...................................C3
8 Restoran Azura....................................B2
   Restoran Azura............................(see 9)
9 Sabindo Hawker Centre......................D2

🛍 Shopping
10 Servay Department Store..................B2

particularly *bad* we can write about this town, but (forgive us the pun) there's not a lot of 'wow' in Tawau either. This may be one of Sabah's larger cities, and it's the state's major border crossing to Indonesia – Kalimantan is just to the south. Apart from that? Not much. But if you're heading to Semporna or the Maliau Basin, there's a good chance you'll be passing through. And hey – the people *are* friendly, the food is decent and the lodging is a pretty good deal. Just don't expect much past this and you'll likely leave satisfied after eating the great scoop of vanilla ice cream that is Tawau.

Tawau is the only crossing point with Kalimantan where foreigners can get a visa to enter Indonesia.

⊙ Sights

Bukit Gemok Forest Reserve NATURE RESERVE
(adult/child RM5/1) Located 10km from Tawau town centre, this reserve is a gem, and the best option for those who need to while away a day here. Developed in the early 1990s, the jungle is filled with chattering monkeys, and has become popular with trekkers, Hash House Harriers runners and tour groups – many consider it to be far better than the trails around Poring Hot Springs. The most popular trail is a demanding one-hour (if you're fit!) jaunt up **Lim Man Kui Quarry Hill**, a slate-grey knife of rock. It's a huff to make it to the top, but the stunning views from the top are worth it, as is your casual disbelief at the middle-aged Chinese fitness nuts who *jog* up this track on a regular basis.

Within the reserve, a 231m **canopy walkway** offers lovely views of the surrounding countryside and Tawau itself.

Be on the lookout for the relatively enormous (15cm) seeds of the gourd *Alsomitra macrocarpa*; the seeds are flattened into aerodynamic pancakes and regularly glide hundreds of metres through the forest; they're fairly breathtaking to watch in flight. A taxi to the park costs RM30 – make sure your driver either waits for you or is willing to come back and pick you up, as there's little public transport out this way.

🛏 Sleeping

Splurge for a midrange option if you're stopping through. They cater to local businessmen and are excellent value – miles beyond anything you can get in KK. Jalan Bunga and Haji Karim are packed with options. Budget digs tend to be pretty dire.

Shervinton Executive Hotel   HOTEL $$
(Map p364; ☎770000; www.shervintonhotel.com; Jln Bunga; r/ste from RM98/200; ❈🛜) The Shervinton is the brightest, most well-lit and freshest option in the city centre. An on-site spa, salon and gym facility (there's even a bakery!) make this a surprisingly luxurious option.

Monaco Hotel   HOTEL $
(Map p364; ☎769911/2/3; Jln Haji Karim; r from RM80; ❈) It's not the Riviera – there's no oversized sunglasses or suave men in tuxedos playing baccarat in this version of Monaco. Instead: an exterior painted a shade of yellow that may make your eyes bleed, offset by quite lovely interior rooms done up like the Holiday Inn, Malaysia-style.

Kingston Executive Hotel   HOTEL $$
(Map p364; ☎702288; 4581-4590 Jln Haji Karim; d RM80-100; ❈@) The title of this hotel may seem ambitious, but this 'executive' is nonetheless quite excellent value-for-money. It's a cheering attempt at emulating boutique quirk, an odd experience in sedate Tawau. Some rooms have duvets made from *kain songket* (traditional Malay handwoven fabric with gold threads).

Hotel Soon Yee   HOTEL $
(Map p364; ☎772447; 1362 Jln Stephen Tan; r RM30-35; ❈) Soon Yee is a backpacker standard. There are no phones, no hot water, but there is lots of camaraderie and character. Cheaper fan-cooled rooms have shared bathrooms.

🍴 Eating

Locals love splurging on the buffet lunch at the **Belmont Marco Polo** which, for RM18 (RM33 on weekends), is a steal considering the variety of tasty bites. The interior courtyard around the Kingston Hotel has a few local haunts serving up tasty dishes, and there's cheap Chinese *kedai kopi* along Jalan Bunga; most open around 7am and close

TAWAU TREATS

Thanks to Tawau's proximity to Indonesia and large population of Indonesians, Filipinos, Bajau and Hakka Chinese, the town has developed some worthwhile culinary specialities. All of the following can be found in almost any of Tawau's *kedai kopi* (coffee shops) and in the Sabindo Hawker Centre:

Mee Jawa – Javanese-style noodles, the Javanese take on Asia's ubiquitous noodle soup. This version comes with a yellowish broth swimming with bean sprouts, groundnuts, bean curd, fish balls, the occasional prawn and sometimes (interestingly), sweet potato, plus the usual garlic, shallots, chillies and shrimp paste.

Gado gado – A deliciously simple Indonesian speciality: vegetable salad with prawn crackers and peanut sauce. The glory of *gado* is the variations of the standard recipe – every cook and hawker puts a different spin on it.

Nasi Kuning – Rice cooked with coconut milk and turmeric, hence the English translation of the name: 'yellow rice'. In Tawau, it is often wrapped and served in a banana leaf with deep-fried fish and eaten on special occasions.

Soto Makassar – Oh yes! Soto (also spelled 'coto' and pronounced 'cho-to') Makassar is buffalo/beef soup from Southern Sulawesi, Indonesia. The dark broth is made incredibly rich by the addition of buffalo/cow blood, and enriched by a plethora of some 40 spices, plus beef heart, liver, tripe and brain. If you have a weak stomach, ignore those ingredients and trust us: this stuff is *delicious*, like liquid essence of beef spiced with all the wonderful herbs and spices of Southeast Asia.

around 10pm. You may notice severe posters around town with pictures of mutilated fish that say *Bom ikan*. *Bom ikan* means 'bomb(ed) fish,' a reference to fish that have been harvested from dynamited coral reefs. The posters warn of the illegality of possessing or selling 'bombed fish'.

Self-caterers should try the **Servay Department Store** (Map p364; Jln Musantara) across from the Old Central Market, for everything from picnic lunches to DVDs of dubious authenticity.

Sabindo Hawker Centre
HAWKER $

(Map p364; Jln Waterfront; dishes from RM5; ⊙11am-10pm) Located along the Tawau waterfront, Sabindo is the place to come for impeccably fresh street stall food, which, as is often the case in Asia, is the tastiest stuff around. Prices run the gamut from cheap-as-chips soup stalls to Chinese seafood emporiums.

Restoran Azura
INDIAN $

(Map p364; ☑012-863 9934; Jln Dunlop; dishes RM3-6; ⊙8am-9pm) Recommended for its tasty South Indian food and snicker-worthy menu, Azura serves up a killer fish-head curry and sundry 'tits-bits'. The noodles are pretty good too. There's another branch at the Sabindo Hawker Centre (Map p364).

ℹ Information

Internet Access
City Internet Zone (☑760016; 37 Kompleks Fajar, Jln Perbandaran; per hr RM2-3; ⊙9am-midnight)

Banks
HSBC (Jln Perbandaran) ATM.
Maybank (☑762333; Jln Dunlop)

Tourist Information
Maliau Basin Conservation Area Authority (☑759214; maliaubasin@gmail.com; 2nd fl, UMNO Building; Jln Dunlop) Can provide information on and help arrange visits to the Maliau Basin.

ℹ Getting There & Away

Air
Malaysia Airlines (☑089-761293; Jln Haji Sahabudin) and **AirAsia** (☑089-761946; Jln Bunga) have daily direct flights to KK and KL. **MASwings** (☑1300-883 000) flies to Sandakan twice daily, the afternoon flight continuing to KK.

Bus & Minivan
Kota Kinabalu Daily express buses for KK (RM65, nine hours) leave from behind the Sabindo area in a large dusty lot at 8am and 8pm (not in between).
Sandakan Departs hourly from Sabindo Sq (RM35 to RM40, five hours, 7am to 2pm), one block on a diagonal from the KK terminus, behind the purple Yassin Curry House sign.

GETTING TO INDONESIA: TAWAU TO TARAKAN

Getting to the border Tawau is the only crossing point with Kalimantan where foreigners can get a visa to enter Indonesia. The local Indonesian consulate is known for being fast and efficient – many travellers are in and out in an hour. The consulate is in Wisma Fuji, on Jln Sinn Onn. You can flag down a taxi (RM10) or take a bus from the central bus station (RM0.80). These buses leave every 30 minutes – as the touts swarm around you, say 'Indonesia consulate' and they'll point you to the right vehicle. Ask the driver to drop you off in front of the consulate; to get back, just stand by the road and flag a bus or minibus down to return to the city centre for a similar fare.

Visa applications are processed between 9:30am to 2pm Monday to Friday. You technically need to either provide proof of onward travel or a credit card, which consulate staff will make a copy of. A 60-day tourist visa will run RM170 and require two passport photos. Bank on spending at least one night in town before shipping off to Indonesia, given the ferry departure schedule, and bring extra cash to the consulate, as there are no ATMs nearby.

Ferry companies Tawindo Express and Indomaya Express make the three- to four-hour trip to Tarakan (RM140; 11.30am Monday, Wednesday and Friday, 10.30am Tuesday, Thursday and Saturday) and the one-hour trip to Nunukan (RM65; 10am and 3pm daily except Sunday). We recommend showing up at least 60 minutes before departure to get a ticket; less than that is cutting it fine. A taxi ride to the ferry terminal costs RM5.

At the border Blue minivans in Tarakan can get you around the city for Rp3000; expect to pay around Rp20,000 to get to the airport.

That's also the spot for frequent minivans to the following:

Semporna (RM15, two hours)
Lahad Datu (RM15, three hours)

ℹ️ Getting Around

TO/FROM THE AIRPORT

The airport is 28km from town along the main highway to Semporna and Sandakan. A shuttle bus (RM15) to the local bus station in Tawau's centre leaves six times daily. A taxi costs RM45.

Tawau Hills Park

Hemmed in by agriculture and human habitation, this small reserve has forested hills rising dramatically from the surrounding plain. The park (admission RM10) is intended to protect the water catchment for settlements in the area, but not before most of the accessible rainforest had been logged. Much of the remaining forest clings to steep-sided ridges that rise to 1310m Gunung Magdalena.

If getting into the Maliau Basin or Danum Valley feels like too much of an effort, consider Tawau Hills a user-friendly alternative. The forest here may not be as primevally awesome, but it's still impressively thick jungle, and the trails are quite easy on your feet. On a clear day the Tawau Hills Park's peaks make a fine sight.

The first trail leads along the Sungai Tawau (chattering with birds like a Disney movie when we attempted it) for 2.5km to Bukit Gelas Falls that, when not swarmed with school groups and tourists, is perfectly picturesque. Another track leads 3.2km to a group of 11 hot springs that are frankly as impressive as anything you'll see in Poring; locals believe the *ubat kulit* (skin medication) water has medicinal properties. If the above doesn't appeal, you can always take a quick 30-minute walk to Bombalai Hill (530m) to the south – the views from here are also quite rewarding.

There's accommodation at Tawau Hills Park (Taman Bukit Tawau; ☏089-918827/768719, 019-800 9607; camping/dm/chalet RM5/20/200). Rates are lower on weekdays. Both dorms and chalets are utilitarian, and there's not much reason to stay here unless you can't stomach a night somewhere else. If you want to camp, you'll need to bring all of your own equipment.

Tawau Hills is 28km northwest of Tawau. A taxi will cost about RM30 to RM40.

Maliau Basin Conservation Area

In the minds of most travellers, and certainly the entire marketing division of Malaysia's tourism board, Sabah is associated with wild adventure. But while there are many wild stretches of Sabah, this state has also been heavily impacted by logging, oil palm and, on a smaller scale, suburban sprawl.

This pocket of truly untouched, Eden-as-God-made-it wilderness remains. Hemmed in by mountains, separated by distance and altitude and expanse, the Maliau Basin Conservation Area (MBCA), known very appropriately as 'Sabah's Lost World', is...well, something special.

The basin is exactly that – a bowl-shaped depression of rainforest that was unnoticed by the world until a pilot almost crashed into the walls that hem it off in 1947. Run by the Sabah Foundation, this is the single best place in Borneo to experience old-growth tropical rainforest. More than that, it is one of the world's great reserves of biodiversity, a dense knot of almost unbelievable genetic richness. A visit to the basin is always a poignant affair, as you'll share the road with a parade of logging trucks hauling trees out of the forest at an astonishing rate.

Unbelievably, there is no known record of human beings entering the basin until the early 1980s (although it is possible that indigenous peoples entered the basin before that time). It is only recently that the area has been opened up to a limited number of adventurous travellers. Getting here requires time and resources, and officially a lot of money, although there may be ways around the latter.

💿 Sights & Activities

Trekking

The trek through the Maliau Basin will likely be the most memorable hike of your Borneo experience. The density of the old-growth forest is striking, and as it is more remote than the Danum Valley, the preserved wildlife is even better. That said: you are in the jungle, and wildlife is not easy to spot. You may walk away without seeing anything but some of Borneo's most ancient trees, which isn't so bad, really.

Several treks are possible in the basin, ranging from short nature walks around Agathis Camp to the multiday slog to the rim of the basin via Strike Ridge Camp. The

INDEPENDENT EXPEDITIONS TO THE MALIAU BASIN

Private tour operators or employees of Sabah Tourism will tell you it is not possible to visit the Maliau basin without a prior tour arrangement, but we have found this is not necessarily true. With that said, you'll probably need at least RM1000 (and a fair bit of elbow grease) to make the following plan work, so this isn't an entirely budget proposal:

It's best to first contact the **Maliau Basin Conservation Area Authority** (☎089-759214; maliaubasin@gmail.com; 2nd fl, UMNO Building, Jln Dunlop) in Tawau. You may need to show up to the office in person, as this is not a tourism office accustomed to dealing with visitors. You can also try driving to the park entrance from Tawau (2½ hours) or KK (at least five hours); a 2WD Proton can make the trip with cautious driving, while a motorbike would be dodgy but doable.

To get into the park you need to pay an administration fee (RM60), a vehicle entry fee (RM5 per vehicle), and if you stay overnight, a conservation fee (RM50). If you plan to hike (and what else are you going to do?) you *must* hire a guide, which costs RM200 per day. The different camps in the basin cost RM180 to RM205 per person per night for a room; some offer dorm beds for RM70, and you can camp in your own tent for RM30. Meals can be taken in the guesthouses for RM40/50/60 per person for breakfast/lunch/dinner. You can also arrange meals while trekking; this requires a porter and costs RM70/100/130 for breakfast/lunch/dinner.

We have talked with travellers who were able to arrange all of the above at the park entrance without even stopping by the Tawau office. Our sense is this scenario will not be possible if a flood of travellers starts pounding on the basin's gates, so you may still want to check with the Tawau office before coming all the way out here. Ideally, if you're not buying the package tour, we advise prearranging your tour with the office in Tawau.

vast majority of visitors to the basin undertake a three-day, two-night loop through the southern section of the basin that we'll call the Maliau Loop. This brilliant route takes in wide swaths of diverse rainforest and four of the basin's waterfalls: **Takob Falls**, **Giluk Falls**, **Maliau Falls** and **Ginseng Falls**. Do not attempt the trek unless you are in excellent shape (in fact, Borneo Nature Tours will require a letter from a doctor testifying to your ability to undertake the trek). Your tour operator will supply a guide and porters to carry your food. You'll be in charge of your day pack, camera, leech socks, walking clothes and dry kit for the evening.

A **canopy walkway** stretches near the Basin study centre, and it is pretty astounding to walk its length amid rainforest canopy that has never felt a human cut.

🛏 Sleeping

Accommodation in the Maliau is in the form of simple camps, which range from basic bunkhouses to wood-frame two-storey huts with private bedrooms. None of the camps are luxurious, but after a day on the trail fighting leeches, they'll seem like paradise.

There are two ways to get here. **Borneo Nature Tours** (☎088-267637; www.borneonaturetours.com; Lot 10, ground fl, Block D, Kompleks Sadong Jaya) and affiliated agents offer a five-day, four-night all-inclusive tour of the Maliau for RM5220 per person for two to three people (this can go as low as RM4360 per person for a group of 10 to 15). The package is purposefully cost prohibitive to eliminate those who aren't the most diehard nature fans.

The other way is via your own steam and initiative. This method is not anywhere as easy as booking a tour, and it's not dirt cheap either, but it's a bit more affordable.

❶ Information

The Maliau Basin is located in the southern part of central Sabah, just north of the logging road that connects Tawau with Keningau. The basin is part of the Yayasan Sabah Forest Management Area, a vast swath of forest in southeastern Sabah under the management of **Yayasan Sabah** (www.ysnet.org.my), a semigovernmental body tasked with both developing and protecting the natural resources of Sabah.

The **MBCA security gate** is just off the Tawau–Keningau Rd. From the gate, it's a very rough 25km journey to the **Maliau Basin Studies Centre**, for researchers, and about 20km to **Agathis Camp**, the base camp for most visitors to the basin.

ℹ️ Getting There & Away

There is no reliable public transport to the park, so you either need to drive yourself or arrange transport. Borneo Nature Tours will handle all transport if you book through them.

Minibus

Minibuses occasionally ply the route bringing loggers to their camps, but this isn't a regular service and cannot be relied upon.

Self-drive

Although the road here is not paved, there is gravel all along the route, and the basin can even be reached by motorbike. Drive carefully and take some jerry cans of petrol. A small shop at Batu 41, 15km from the park entrance, sells expensive petrol, but we can't guarantee its hours. Once at the security gate to the park, you'll have to take a dirt track to Agathis Camp. Rangers may transfer you if you're worried about driving your car.

Van

If you've prearranged with the Maliau Basin Conservation Area Authority in Tawau, that office may get a minivan to take you to the park entrance for RM650. In the park, rangers can arrange vans to take you back to Tawau or Keningau (closer to KK) for a similar price.

SOUTHWESTERN SABAH

The Crocker Range is the backbone of southwestern Sabah, separating coastal lowlands from the wild tracts of jungle in the east. Honey-tinged beaches scallop the shores from KK down to the border, passing the turbid rivers of the Beaufort Division. Offshore you'll find Pulau Tiga, forever etched in the collective consciousness as the genesis site for the eponymous reality show *Survivor*, and Pulau Labuan, centre of the region's oil industry and the transfer point for ferries heading onto Sarawak and Brunei.

The Interior

Sabah's interior constitutes some of the wildest territory in the state, and the best place for accessing this largely unexplored hinterland is via the southwest part of the state.

The landscape is dominated by the Crocker Range, which rises near Tenom in the south and runs north to Mt Kinabalu. The range forms a formidable barrier to the interior of the state and dominates the eastern skyline from Kota Kinabalu down to Sipitang. Once across the Crocker Range, you descend into the green valley of the Sungai Pegalan that runs from Keningau in the south and to Ranau in the north. The heart of the Pegalan Valley is the small town of Tambunan, around which you'll find a few low-key attractions.

CROCKER RANGE NATIONAL PARK

Much of the Crocker Range has been gazetted as Crocker Range National Park. The main means of accessing this landscape by foot is via the Salt Trail (Salt Trails; ☎088-553500; www.sabahparks.org.my/eng/crocker_range_park/salt_trail.asp), a series of four treks that trace the path of traditional trade routes across the mountains. At their shortest the trails can be completed in half a day; the longest route, the Inobong-Terian-Buayan-Kionop-Tikolod trail, takes three days to finish (if you're fit!). At the time of writing the tourism infrastructure around the salt trails was quite minimal, making this an excellent adventure for DIY trekkers who want to get off Sabah's package tourism trail. You'll need to get in touch with Crocker Range National Park to organise guides.

Even if you're not trekking, the Crocker Range and Pegalan Valley make a nice jaunt into rural Sabah for those with rental vehicles. As you make your way over the range between KK and Tambunan, you'll be treated to brilliant views back to the South China Sea and onward to Mt Trus Madi.

TAMBUNAN

Nestled among the green curves of the Crocker Hills, Tambunan, a small agricultural service town about 81km from KK, is the first settlement you'll come to in the range. The region was the last stronghold of Mat Salleh, who became a folk hero for rebelling against the British in the late 19th century. Sadly, Salleh later blew his reputation by negotiating a truce, which so outraged his own people that he was forced to flee to the Tambunan plain, where he was eventually killed.

⊙ Sights

Tambunan Rafflesia Reserve NATURE RESERVE
(☎088-898500; admission RM5; ⊙8am-3pm)
Near the top of the Crocker Range, next to the main highway 20km from Tambunan, is this park devoted to the world's largest flower. The Rafflesia is a parasitic plant that grows hidden within the stems of jungle vines until it bursts into bloom, at which

point it eerily resembles the monster plant from *Little Shop of Horrors*. The large bulbous flowers can be up to 1m in diameter. The 12 or so species of Rafflesia here are found only in Borneo and Sumatra; several species are unique to Sabah, but as they only bloom for a few days it's hard to predict when you'll be able to see one. Rangers can guide you into the jungle reserve for the day for RM100. Keningau-bound buses will stop here if you ask the driver to let you off, but getting back to Tambunan will require hitching on the highway. A round-trip taxi from Tambunan costs RM100, which includes waiting time.

🛏 Sleeping

Tambunan Village Resort Centre   RESORT $$
(TVRC; ☏087-774076; http://tvrc.tripod.com; 24 Jln TVRC; r & chalets RM60-110; ❄) The main accommodation game is this quirky resort, located some 2km from the tiny town centre. The staff at the centre can help arrange trips up Mt Trus Madi. If you're driving here from KK, the centre is just south of the Shell station on the main road.

❶ Getting There & Away

BUS & MINIVAN

Regular minivans ply the roads between Tambunan and KK (RM15, 1½ hours), Ranau (RM15, two hours), Keningau (RM10, one hour) and Tenom (RM15, two hours). KK–Tenom express buses also pass through, though you may have to ask them to stop. The minivan shelter is in the middle of Tambunan town. Minivans to KK pass the entrance to the Rafflesia reserve; you'll usually be charged for the whole trip to KK.

MT TRUS MADI

About 20km southeast of Tambunan town is the dramatic **Mt Trus Madi**, Sabah's second-highest peak, rising to 2642m. Although logging concessions encircle the mount, the upper slopes and peak are wild and jungle-clad and classified as forest reserve. Ascents are possible, however it's more challenging than Mt Kinabalu, and more difficult to arrange. Independent trekkers must be well equipped and bring their own provisions up the mountain. It is possible to go by 4WD (RM500) up to about 1500m, from where it is a five- to seven-hour climb to the top. There are places to camp halfway up the mountain and on the summit. Before setting off, you are strongly advised to hire a guide (RM200) or at least get maps and assistance from the Tambunan Village Resort Centre or **Forestry Department** (Jabatan Perhutanan; ☏089-660811,

087-774691) in Tambunan. Bring winter clothes, as it gets cold towards the peak, and be prepared for a long, muddy slog.

You can get here on your own, but it's far easier to organise with a tour company. **Tropical Mountain Holidays** (☏013-545 7643, 013-549 2730; http://www.tropicalmountainholidaysmalaysia.com), based in KK, specializes in Trus Madi ascents. Their 2-day, 1-night climb up the mountain, which includes transfer from KK, runs US$300 per person, which is close to what you'll pay if you hire guides and your own vehicle to get out here.

KENINGAU

If you have a bent for the bucolic, you'll probably want to skip Keningau – this busy service town has a touch of urban sprawl about it, and most visitors only pass through to pick up transport, use an ATM or stock up on supplies. As far as attractions go, you might check out **Taipaek-gung**, a colourful Chinese temple in the middle of town, or the large **tamu** (market) held every Thursday.

For a sleepover, try **Hotel Juta** (☏087-337888; www.sabah.com.my/juta; Lg Milimewa 2; standard/superior d from RM175; ❄), which towers over the busy town centre. It's convenient to transport, banking and shopping needs, and rooms are nicely appointed in the Western-businessman style. There is a restaurant on the premises. Shabbier options include the nearby **Crown Hotel** (☏087-338555; Lg Milimewa; standard/superior d from RM40).

There are eight daily express buses to/from KK (RM15, 2½ hours) and four to/from Tenom (RM8, one hour). These buses stop at the Bumiputra Express stop on the main road across from the Shell station. Minivans and share taxis operate from several places in town, including a stop just north of the express bus stop; they all leave when full. There are services to/from KK (RM44, 2½ hours), Ranau (RM25, three hours) and Tenom (RM10, one hour).

TENOM

This sleepy little town at the southern end of the Crocker Range has seen better days but still manages to be more attractive than traffic-choked Keningau. Tenom was closely involved in uprisings against the British in 1915, led by the famous Murut chief Ontoros Antonom, and there's a **memorial** to the tribe's fallen warriors off the main road. Most people pass through Tenom on their way to the nearby Sabah Agricultural Park.

If you somehow get stuck in town, spend the night at Orchid Hotel (☏087-737600; Jln Tun Mustapha; s/d RM40/50; ✸) Rooms are clean and well kept and good value for money. There are cheaper hotels in the vicinity, but they're all a bit musty.

Minivans operate from the *padang* (field) in front of the Hotel Sri Perdana. Destinations include Keningau (RM10, one hour) and KK (RM42, two to four hours depending on stops). There are also regular services to Tambunan (RM15, two hours). Taxis congregate at a rank on the west side of the *padang*.

SABAH AGRICULTURAL PARK

Heaven on earth for horticulturalists: the vast Sabah Agricultural Park (Taman Pertanian Sabah; ☏087-737952; www.sabah.net.my/agripark; adult/child RM25/10; ☺9am-4.30pm Tue-Sun), about 15km northeast of Tenom, is run by the Department of Agriculture and covers about 6 sq km. Originally set up as an orchid centre, the park has expanded to become a major research facility, tourist attraction and offbeat camp site (RM10), building up superb collections of rare plants such as hoyas, and developing new techniques for use in agriculture, agroforestry and domestic cultivation.

Flower gardens and nature paths abound and a minizoo lets you get up close and personal with some farm animals and deer. Exploring by bicycle would be a good idea, but the fleet of rental bikes here has just about rusted to the point of immobility; if they've replaced them by the time you arrive, rentals cost RM3. There is a free 'train' (it's actually more like a bus) that does a 1½-hour loop of the park, leaving from outside the reception hourly from 9.30am to 3.30pm. If you're truly taken with the park, there's a bare bones on-site hostel (dm RM25), which is sometimes taken up by visiting school groups.

Take a minivan from Tenom heading to Lagud Seberang (RM5). Services run throughout the morning, but dry up in the late afternoon. Tell the driver you're going to Taman Pertanian. The park entrance is about 1km off the main road. A taxi from Tenom will cost around RM90.

SAPULOT & BATU PUNGGUL

Perhaps even more so than the Maliau Basin, this is as remote as it gets in Sabah. Not far from the Kalimantan border, Batu Punggul is a jungle-topped limestone outcrop riddled with caves, towering nearly 200m above Sungai Sapulot. This is deep in Murut country and the stone formation was one of several sites sacred to these people. Batu Punggul and the adjacent Batu Tinahas are traditionally believed to be longhouses that gradually transformed into stone. The view from the upper reaches of Batu Punggul may be the best in Sabah – in every direction is deep jungle, knifelike limestone outcrops and, if you are lucky, swinging orang-utans. It can be difficult and expensive to get here, but this is a beautiful part of Sabah that few tourists visit, and it offers a chance to rub shoulders with the jungle Murut. It is almost impossible to get out here on your own, as there is virtually no tourism infrastructure and English is almost non-existent, but even the most independent traveller will likely enjoy booking through Orou Sapulot.

TOP CHOICE Orou Sapulot   CULTURAL
(☏016-311 0056; www.orousapulot.com/; 3-day/2-night around per person RM750) Orou ('sun' in Murut) Sapulot is an excellent means of accessing the deepest areas of Sabah's interior. Run by Silas Gunting, a descendant of the local Murut who is now a succesful KK businessman, Orou is one of the more innovative eco-tourism projects in the state, and offers what may be the best package tour in Sabah.

The trip encompasses the Romol Eco Village, a modern longhouse home stay where visitors live with the Murut; the Pungiton ('bat' in Murut) Caves, an extensive cavern system that resembles a bat-shit-laced cheese wheel, complete with rushing underground rivers and enormous underground chambers plucked from a cathedral; an eco-camp by Pungiton located on the banks of a heavenly river; a trip to the crystalline Kabulungou waterfalls, and finally, a river trip to Batu Pungull, along a chocolate-brown river hemmed in by primary rainforest. You will get the chance to swim in this river, and let us tell you: swimming through virgin jungle is as Edenic as life gets.

All the while, Orou is doing good work. It is common in Sabah for poorer indigenous communities to sell their lands to palm oil and timber companies; the liquid assets they gain are usually spent within a few years. By employing local Murut and encouraging their families to keep their lands

SABAH THE INTERIOR

and preserve them for eco-tourism purposes, Orou is trying to stave off the worst ecological and economic impacts of this trend while providing a sustainable income for the communities of Sabah's interior.

The above prices are estimated rates that take in all of the activities mentioned above. To offset costs, Orou prefers groups of travellers, but single travellers or small groups are encouraged as well; you will likely be folded into a larger group. In KK, Sticky Rice and Adventure Alternative Borneo (p311) are Orou Sapulot's preferred booking agencies.

Beaufort Division

This shield-shaped peninsula, popping out from Sabah's southwestern coast, is a marshy plain marked with curling rivers and fringed by golden dunes. Tourists with tight travel schedules should consider doing a wildlife river cruise at Klias or Garama if they don't have time to reach Sungai Kinabatangan. Yes, the Kinabatangan is better, but packs of proboscis monkeys can still be spotted here and it's only a day trip from KK. You can book trips to Beaufort, Weston and the Klias and Garama rivers in any KK travel agency.

BEAUFORT

Born as a timber town, Beaufort has reinvented itself with the proliferation of palm-oil plantations. A suitable pit stop for tourists travelling between Sabah and Sarawak, this sleepy township is the gateway to white-water rapids on the Sungai Padas and the monkey-filled Klias and Garama areas. The Sungai Padas divides Beaufort into two sections: the aptly named Old Town with its weathered structures, and New Town, a collection of modern shophouses on flood-phobic stilts.

◉ Sights & Activities

Memorial Stone   MEMORIAL
(Jln Tugu) There's a small monument to Private Thomas Leslie Starcevich, an Australian WWII veteran. In 1945, Starcevich single-handedly overwhelmed a Japanese machine-gun position, for which he received the Victoria Cross, the British military's highest decoration. The stone is at the bottom of a small embankment and is marked by brown signs and an arch.

RAFTING

White-water rafting enthusiasts can book a river trip with **Riverbug** (☏088-260501; www.riverbug.asia; Wisma Sabah, Jln Fuad Stephen), the premier operator in the area. Scuba Junkie, which runs a very popular dive centre in Semporna has an affiliated river-rafting outfit here called, appropriately, **River Junkie** (☏019-6012145; www.river-junkie.com; Wisma Sabah, Jln Fuad Stephen), which comes highly recommended by travellers. Day trips organised out of KK cost around RM200 to RM400 per person, depending on what package you choose. The cheapest options involve leisurely boat tours and proboscis monkey spotting; more expensive tours include white-water rafting expeditions and side trips to sites like the Mari Mari Cultural Village (Riverbug also offers a combo paintball day!). All trips include transfers by van, and normally require 24 hours' advance notice. Tourists who seek more serene waters can ride the rapids of Sungai Kiulu (bookable through the aforementioned operators), which is located near Mt Kinabalu and calm enough to be popular with families.

🛏 Sleeping

There's really no need to spend the night in Beaufort, but if you must, then try the **MelDe Hotel** (☏087-222266; 9-20 Lo Chung Park, Jln Lo Chung; s/d/ste from RM70/80/90; ❄) The rooms are a bit crusty in the corners, but it's passable for a night's sleep while in transit. Go for a room on one of the upper floors – they have windows. The Chinese restaurant under the inn is very popular with locals. MelDe is located in Old Town. If you're stopping in town for a bite, make sure you try a pomelo (football-sized citrus fruit) and local *mee Beaufort* (Beaufort noodles) – both are locally famous.

❶ Getting There & Away

BUS

Express buses operate from near the old train station at the south end of Jln Masjid (the ticket booth is opposite the station). There are departures at 9am, 1pm, 2.15pm and 5pm for KK (RM10, 1½ hours). There are departures at 9.10am, 10.30am, 1.45pm and 6.20pm for Sipitang (RM5, 1½ hours). The KK to Lawas express bus passes through Beaufort at around 3pm; the trip from Beaufort to Lawas costs RM15 and takes 1¾ hours.

MINIVANS

Minivans operate from a stop across from the mosque, at the north end of Jln Masjid. There are frequent departures for KK (RM10, two hours), and less-frequent departures for Sipitang (RM12, 1½ hours), Lawas (RM15, 1¾ hours) and Kuala Penyu (RM8, until around 2.30pm, one hour). To Menumbok (for Labuan) there are plenty of minivans until early afternoon (RM10, one hour).

TAXIS

Taxis depart from the stand outside the old train station, at the south end of Jln Masjid. Charter rates include: KK (RM70), Kuala Penyu (RM55), Sipitang (RM35), Menumbok (RM50) and Lawas (RM100).

KUALA PENYU

Tiny Kuala Penyu, at the northern tip of the peninsula, is the jumping-off point for Pulau Tiga if you are not accessing 'Survivor Island' via the new boat service from KK. From KK, minivans leave from behind Wawasan Plaza (RM10 to RM15, two hours). From Beaufort minivans to Kuala Penyu (RM10) leave throughout the morning, but return services tail off very early in the afternoon, so you may have to negotiate a taxi or local lift back. A minivan to/from Menumbok costs RM65 per vehicle.

TEMPURUNG

Tempurung Seaside Lodge (☎088-773066; http://www.borneotempurung.com/; 3 Putatan Point; 2-day, 1-night package from RM310), set along the quiet coastal waters of the South China Sea, is a good spot for hermits who seek a pinch of style. The main lodge was originally built as a vacation home, but friends convinced the owners that it would be a crime not to share the lovely property with the world. Rooms are scattered between several chalet-style bungalows accented with patches of jungle thatch. The packages include fantastic meals. Nightly rates are also available.

Borneo Express (☎in KK 012-830 7722, in Limbang 085-211 384, in Miri 012-823 7722) runs buses from KK (departing from Wawasan) at 6.45am, 10am and 12.30pm daily. Ask the driver to let you off at the junction with the large Kuala Penyu sign. The bus will turn left (south) to head towards Menumbok; you want to go right (north) in the direction of Kuala Penyu. If you arranged accommodation in advance, the lodge van can pick you up here (it's too far to walk). Buses pass the junction at 9.30am and 3.30pm heading back to KK. If you're driving, take a right at the junction and keep an eye out for the turn-off on the left side of the road just before Kuala Penyu. We suggest calling the lodge for directions. A charter taxi from Beaufort will cost about RM50.

KLIAS

The tea-brown Sungai Klias looks somewhat similar to the mighty Kinabatangan, offering short-stay visitors a chance to spend an evening in the jungle cavorting with saucy primates. There are several companies offering two-hour river cruises. We recommend Borneo Authentic (p312), the first operator to set up shop in the region. Trips include a large buffet dinner and a short night walk to view the swarms of fireflies that light up the evening sky like Christmas lights. Cruises start at dusk (around 5pm), when the sweltering heat starts to burn off and animals emerge for some post-siesta prowling.

There is no accommodation in Klias, although Borneo Authentic can set you up with one of its comfy rooms at the Tempurung Seaside Lodge nearby. Tourists can make their own way to the row of private jetties 20km west of Beaufort, however, most trip-takers usually sign-up for a hassle-free day trip from KK (which ends up being cheaper since you're sharing transport).

GARAMA

Narrower than the river in Klias, the Sungai Garama is another popular spot for the popular river-cruise day trips from KK. Chances of seeing fireflies are slim, but Garama is just as good as Klias (if not better) when it comes to primate life. Gangs of proboscis monkeys and long-tailed macaques scurry around the surrounding floodplain offering eager tourists plenty of photo fodder.

Like Klias, the tours here start at around 5pm (with KK departures at 2pm), and after a couple of hours along the river, guests chat about the evening's sightings over a buffet dinner before returning to KK. There are several operators offering Garama river tours; we prefer **Only in Borneo** (☎088-260506; www.oibtours.com; package tour RM190), an offshoot of Traverse Tours. It has a facility along the shores of Sungai Garama and offers an overnight option in prim dorms or double rooms.

It is technically possible to reach Garama with one's own vehicle, but the network of unmarked roads can be tricky and frustrating. We recommend leaving early in the morning from KK if you want to get here on your own steam.

WESTON

The little village of Weston – a couple of shacks clustered around a gold-domed mosque – is the jumping-off point for a gentle yet jungly patch of wetlands that is equal parts serene and overgrown. The area was bombed beyond recognition during WWII, but recent conservation efforts have welcomed groups of curious proboscis monkeys into the tidal marshlands, which are shaded by towering nipa palms and copses of spiderlike mangroves. As the tide rolls in and out, entire swaths of jungle are submerged and revealed. Monkeys, monitor lizards, otters and mud skippers flash through the aquatic undergrowth, and as the sun sets, clouds of flying foxes (ie *big* bats) flap in with the darkness.

◉ Sights

Weston Wetland (☑016-813 4300, 013-881 3233; http://westonwetland.blogspot.com/) operates a variety of package tours including river-cruise day trips and sleepovers at its swamp-side longhouse (all-inclusive two-day, one-night package RM250). The dorm facilities are rustic at best, but the quality of the firefly show here is extremely high. Note that the folk at Weston Wetland insist you prebook before visiting.

While you're here, you can ask folk at the lodge to take you to **Che Hwa Schoolhouse**, the oldest wooden school building in Borneo and a fine example of antiquarian Chinese architecture.

MENUMBOK

The tiny hamlet of Menumbok is where you can catch car ferries to the Serasa Ferry Terminal in Muara, 25km northeast of Bandar Seri Begawan (Brunei), and to Pulau Labuan (adult/car RM5/40, departures every hour from 10.30am-3.30pm).

On land, a charter taxi from Beaufort costs RM60, minivans from Kuala Penyu cost RM50 per vehicle. There is a direct bus service connecting Menumbok to KK.

Pulau Tiga National Park

Outwit, outplay and outlast your fellow travellers on what is known throughout the world as 'Survivor Island'. The name Pulau Tiga actually means 'three islands' – the scrubby islet is part of a small chain created during an eruption of mud volcanoes in the late 1890s. Over 100 years later, in 2001, the island had its 15 minutes of fame when it played host to the smash-hit reality TV series *Survivor*. TV junkies still stop by for a look-see, although the 'tribal council' was destroyed in a storm and the debris was cleared after it turned into a home for venomous snakes. Whatever your viewing preferences, it's still a great place for relaxing on the beach, hiking in the forest and taking a cooling dip in burping mud pits at the centre of the island.

◉ Sights & Activities

Pulau Kalampunian Damit ('day-mit,' not 'dammit, I'm on snake island') is little more than a large rock covered in dense vegetation but is famous for the sea snakes that come ashore to mate, hence the island's nickname, **Snake Island**. Sounds like the tourism destination of the 21st century, right? On any one day up to 150 snakes can be present, curled up under boulders, among roots and in tree hollows. It's a fascinating phenomenon, made doubly enigmatic by the fact that the snakes are never seen on nearby Pulau Tiga. Pulau Tiga Resort runs boat trips to the island (RM40 per person), with a stop en route for snorkelling for RM30 extra. You can also dive off the island for RM100 per dive, or RM150 for a fun dive for those with no scuba experience; it's not the best diving in Borneo, but then again, you're in Borneo, so there's plenty of rainbow-coloured fish to peep at.

⊨ Sleeping & Eating

Pulau Tiga Resort   RESORT **$$**
(☑088-240584; www.pulau-tiga.com; 2-day, 1-night package from Kuala Penyu per person RM305-360, from KK RM455-510; ❀) Built to house the production crew for the *Survivor* series (Jeff Probst stayed in cabin E), this compound has been turned into a lovely seaside resort. Accommodation is available in dorm-style 'longhouse' rooms (three beds in each), while more luxurious private cabins have double beds and plenty of air-con. The beach-facing grounds offer amazing views of the sunset, while a detailed map is available for those that want to track down the beach where the Pagong Tribe lived (called Pagong Pagong Beach). There's currently only one staff member who was working here when *Survivor* was being filmed, but the most unpopular guest at the resort is still sent to Snake Island after dinner (joke!).

Sabah Parks CAMPING $
(☎088-211881; www.sabahparks.org.my; Lot 1-3, Block K, Kompleks Sinsuran, Jln Tun Fuad Stephens; r from RM75) Sabah Parks runs more basic lodging (ie block houses) on the island for less affluent survivalists. It's right next door to Pulau Tiga Resort, about 10m from where 'Tribal Council' was once held (sadly, tiki torches no longer line the way). Facilities here are limited and there's no restaurant, though a cooking area is provided.

🛈 Getting There & Away

Boat

From Kuala Penyu the boat ride takes about 20 minutes. Boats leave at 10am and 3pm. Most visitors to Pulau Tiga come as part of a package, in which case transport is included in the price. You can try showing up in Kuala Penyu and asking if you can board one of the day's boats out to the island (we don't recommend this option as priority is given to resort guests with bookings). For Sabah Parks' lodgings try to hop a ride with the Pulau Tiga Resort boat – chartering your own craft costs RM600 at least.

Pulau Labuan

POP 95,500

If you've ever wondered what a cross between a duty-free airport mall and a tropical island would look like, may we recommend the federal district of Pulau Labuan. Some call this Sabah's version of Vegas, and in the sense that Labuan offers both duty-free sin and tacky family fun, we kinda agree. By the way, everything here *is* duty free, because politically, Labuan is governed directly from KL. As such, a lot of the booze you consume and cigarettes you smoke in Sabah and Sarawak is illegally smuggled from Labuan.

The sultan of Brunei ceded Labuan to the British in 1846 and it remained part of the Empire for 115 years. The only interruption came during WWII, when the Japanese held the island for three years. Significantly, it was on Labuan that the Japanese forces in North Borneo surrendered at the end of the war, and the officers responsible for the death marches from Sandakan were tried here.

Bandar Labuan is the main town and the transit point for ferries linking Kota Kinabalu and Brunei.

⊙ Sights & Activities

BANDAR LABUAN
Labuan's main settlement is light on character but has a couple of passable attractions.

FREE **Labuan Museum** MUSEUM
(Map p376; ☎414135; 364 Jln Dewan; admission free; ◷9am-5pm) This museum on Jln Dewan takes a glossy, if slightly superficial, look at the island's history and culture, from colonial days, through WWII, to the establishment of Labuan as an independent federal territory. The most interesting displays are those on the different ethnic groups here, including a diorama of a traditional Chinese tea ceremony (the participants, however, look strangely Western).

FREE **Labuan Marine Museum** MUSEUM
(Map p376; ☎425927/414462; Jln Tanjung Purun; admission free; ◷9am-6pm) On the coast just east of the centre, the Labuan International Sea Sports Complex houses a decent little museum with a good shell collection and displays of marine life found in the area. Don't forget to head upstairs where you'll find a 42ft-long skeleton of an Indian fin whale. The real highlight, however, and a guaranteed hit with the kids, is the 'touch pool' opposite reception. This has to be the only shark-petting zoo we've ever seen (fret not: the sharks are less than a metre long).

SABAH PULAU LABUAN

DIVING

Labuan is famous for its **wreck diving**, with no fewer than four major shipwrecks off the coast (two from WWII and two from the 1980s). The only dive outfit operating here is **Borneo Star Dives** (☎087-429278; stardivers2005@yahoo.com; International Seasports Complex; dive packages from RM438), which does island-hopping tours and can take you out to all four sites. Note that only the 'Cement Wreck' is suitable for novice divers; the 'Blue Water Wreck' (in our opinion, the most impressive of the bunch) requires advanced open-water certification, and the 'American' and 'Australian' wrecks are only recommended for certified wreck divers.

Bandar Labuan

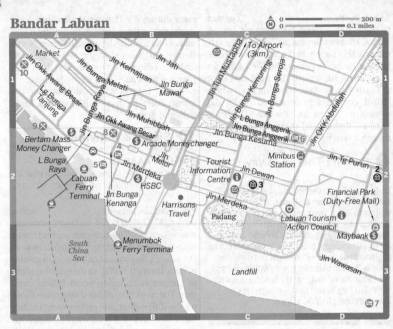

Bandar Labuan

◎ Sights
1 Chinese Temple	A1
2 Labuan Marine Museum	D2
3 Labuan Museum	C2

▣ Sleeping
4 ASV Backpackers	B2
5 Grand Dorsett Labuan	A2
6 Mariner Hotel	D2
7 Waterfront Labuan Financial Hotel	D3

⊗ Eating
8 Choice Restaurant	B2
9 Port View Restaurant	A1
10 Restoran Selera Farizah	A1

AROUND PULAU LABUAN
WWII Memorial
(Labuan War Cemetery) CEMETERY
A dignified expanse of lawn with row upon row of headstones dedicated to the nearly 4000 Commonwealth servicemen, mostly Australian and British, who lost their lives in Borneo during WWII. The cemetery is near the golf course, about 2km east of town along Jln OKK Abdullah. A **Peace Park** on the west of the island at Layang Layangan commemorates the place of Japanese surrender and has a Japanese war memorial.

Labuan Bird Park WILDLIFE RESERVE
(☑463544; adult/child/under 5 RM3/1/free; ☉10am-5pm, closed Fri) This pretty park offers refuge to a wide range of species in three geodesic domes, and a swath of rainforest – the birds look a little bored, but healthy. The park is located at the north end of the island on Jln Tanjung Kubong.

Chimney LANDMARK
Believed to be part of an old coal-mining station, this is the only historical monument of its kind in Malaysia, and has good views along the coast. It's at the northeast tip of the island, best accessed by minibus or taxi.

Labuan Marine Park PARK
Pulau Kuraman, Pulau Rusukan Kecil and Pulau Rusukan Besar are uninhabited islands lying southwest of Labuan that are now protected by the federal government. The beaches are pristine, but dynamite fishing has destroyed much of the coral. You can hire boats from the jetty at the Labuan International Sea Sports Complex to explore the marine park. A day's charter costs around RM600 per group of six people.

Thanks to financial deregulation Labuan is now the home of some major offshore bank accounts, so you may also want to be on the lookout for men in sunglasses with big briefcases, although we suggest not taking pictures of them.

If you want to dive here, enquire at Borneo Star Dives (p375).

🛏 Sleeping

TOP CHOICE Labuan Homestay Programme
HOMESTAY $

(✆422622; www.labuantourism.com; 1/2 days incl full board RM65/140) This excellent service matches visitors with a friendly local in one of three villages around the island: Patau Patau 2, Kampong Sungai Labu and Kampong Bukit Kuda. Some of the homes are just as grand as one of the international-class hotels on the waterfront! If you want to be near Bandar Labuan, ask for accommodation at Patau Patau 2 – it's a charming stilt village out on the bay. Stay a bit longer and learn how to make *ambuyat*, also known as 'gluey sago porridge' and Brunei's favourite dish.

If you want to enroll in the program, book online at least a few days in advance.

Grand Dorsett Labuan
HOTEL $$$

(Map p376; ✆422000; www.granddorsett.com/labuan; 462 Jln Merdeka; r from RM475; ✱@🤖🏊) The Grand Dorsett (once a link in the Sheraton chain) has everything you would expect from an international hotel, with five-star rooms, good restaurants and a pub hosting live bands. Weekend rates go down to as low as RM230.

Waterfront Labuan Financial Hotel
HOTEL $$

(Map p376; ✆418111; leslbn@tm.net.my; 1 Jln Wawasan; r RM250-580, ste RM580-2150; ✱🏊) Not just for merchant bankers – this is a large, luxurious leisure hotel which practically feels like a mall, with full facilities and a small marina attached. The rooms are spacious and have a corporate appeal, and some have great sea views. There's a huge outdoor pool and a restaurant.

Mariner Hotel
HOTEL $$

(Map p376; ✆418822; mhlabuan@streamyx.com; 468 Jln Tanjung Purun; r from RM110; ✱@) Pitched at the low-end business-class market, this smart block offers good facilities for the price. Rooms come with fridges, laminate floors and neat, spacious bathrooms.

ASV Backpackers
HOSTEL $

(Map p376; ✆413728; asvjau@yahoo.com; Lot U0101, Jln Merdeka; r with shared bathroom RM35; ✱) As backpacker spots go, ASV is in a respectable league – it manages to be cheap while more functionally clean and comfortable than most of the dingy midrangers around town. Shame there's not more, y'know, backpackers in Labuan.

🍴 Eating

Choice Restaurant
INDIAN $$

(Map p376; ✆418086; 104 Jln OKK Awang Besar; dishes RM3-10; ⊗8am-10pm) Forget false modesty, the Choice simply proclaims 'We are the best', and this seems to be corroborated by the popularity of the authentic Indian meals with the authentic Indian residents who turn out for *roti*, fish-head curry and *sambal*.

Port View Restaurant
SEAFOOD $$

(Map p376; ✆422999; Jln Merdeka; dishes RM15-30; ⊗lunch & dinner) An outpost of the successful Chinese seafood franchise in KK, this waterfront restaurant has air-con indoor seating and outdoor seating that affords a nice view, over Labuan's busy harbour.

Restoran Selera Farizah
COFFEE SHOP $

(Map p376; Lg Bunga Tanjung; meals from RM3; ⊗8am-10pm) If you prefer a Muslim *kedai kopi*, you could try this place, which serves *roti*, curries and *nasi campur*, accompanied by pro-wrestling videos.

ℹ Information

Banks
HSBC (✆087-422610; 189 Jln Merdeka)
Maybank (✆087-443888; Financial Park) ATM.

Tourist Information
Labuan Tourism Action Council (✆087-422622; ground fl, Labuan International Sea Sports Complex; ⊗8am-1pm & 2-5pm Mon-Fri) Located about 1km east of the town centre, this is the most useful information office in town. It stocks the excellent *Fly Drive Labuan Island & Town Map of Labuan*.

Tourist Information Centre (✆087-423445; www.labuantourism.com.my; cnr Jln Dewan & Jln Berjaya; ⊗8am-5pm Mon-Fri, 9am-3pm Sat) Tourism Malaysia office. Less useful than Labuan Tourism Action Council.

Harrisons Travel (✆087-408096; www.harrisonstravel.com.my; 1 Jln Merdeka) Handy and reputable travel agency.

SABAH PULAU LABUAN

GETTING TO BRUNEI: BANDAR LABUAN TO BANDAR SERI BEGAWAN

Getting to the border Ferries to Brunei depart Bandar Labuan daily at 1:30pm, arriving in Brunei's Serasa Ferry Terminal about an hour later. The entire trip for an adult/child costs RM60/38. Aim to show up at the ferry terminal around 12.30pm.

   At the border Most visitors are granted a visa on arrival for free, although Australians must pay a fee (see p471 for more information).

   Moving on The Serasa Ferry Terminal is 20km northeast of BSB. From here, shuttles can take you to central Bandar Seri Begawan for B$2 (40 minutes). The terminal is linked by ferry with Pulau Labuan, from where boats go to Menumbok in Sabah.

   See p465 for details on doing the trip in the opposite direction.

ⓘ Getting There & Away

Air

Malaysia Airlines (☏1300-883000; www.malaysiaairlines.com.my) has flights to/from KK (45 minutes) and KL (2½ hours), which are usually booked full of oil prospectors. **AirAsia** (☏480401; www.airasia.com) currently flies to KL only.

Boat

Kota Kinabalu Passenger ferries (1st/economy class RM41/31, 3¼ hours) depart Labuan from Monday to Saturday at 8am, and 1:30pm (3pm Sundays). In the opposite direction, they depart Labuan for KK from Monday to Saturday at 8am and 1pm, and 10:30am and 3pm on Sundays.

Sarawak There are daily speedboats to Limbang (2 hours, RM31) and Lawas (2 hours, 15 minutes, RM34) in Sarawak's Limbang Division.

ⓘ Getting Around

Minibus

Labuan has a good minibus network. Minibuses leave regularly, albeit more frequently before sunset, from the parking lot off Jln Tun Mustapha. Fares range from 50 sen for a short trip to RM2.50 for a trip to the top of the island.

Taxi

Taxis are plentiful and there's a stand opposite the local ferry terminal. The base rate is RM10 for short journeys, with most destinations costing around RM15.

Sarawak

Includes »

Kuching 382
Bako National Park 400
Kubah National Park 409
Gunung Gading
National Park 413
Sibu 417
Batang Rejang 421
Bintulu 426
Similajau
National Park 427
Niah National Park 429
Lambir Hills
National Park 431
Miri 432
Gunung Mulu
National Park 438
Kelabit Highlands 444

Best Places to Eat

» Dyak (p392)
» Top Spot Food Court (p392)
» Jambu (p392)
» Summit Cafe (p435)

Best Places to Stay

» Batik Boutique Hotel (p390)
» Dillenia Guesthouse (p433)
» Threehouse B&B (p390)
» Retreat (p413)

Why Go?

Sarawak makes access to Borneo's natural wonders and cultural riches a breeze. From Kuching, the island's most sophisticated and dynamic city, pristine rainforests – where you can spot orang-utans, proboscis monkeys, killer crocodiles and the world's largest flower, the Rafflesia – can be visited on day trips, with plenty of time in the evening for a delicious meal and a drink in a chic bar. More adventurous travellers can take a 'flying coffin' riverboat up the Batang Rejang, 'the Amazon of Borneo', to seek out remote longhouses, or fly to the spectacular bat caves and extraordinary rock formations of Gunung Mulu National Park, a Unesco World Heritage Site. Everywhere you go, you'll encounter the warmth, unforced friendliness and sense of humour that make the people of Malaysia's most culturally diverse state such delightful hosts.

When to Go
Kuching

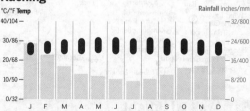

Jul Dayak bands and international artists jam at Kuching's Rainforest World Music Festival.

Jul–Sep It's tourist high season so book flights and treks early.

Nov–Jan Rough seas can make coastal boat travel difficult or impossible.

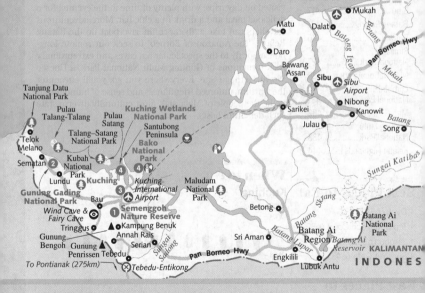

Sarawak Highlights

1 Watching semi-wild orang-utans swing through the canopy at **Semenggoh Nature Reserve** (p407)

2 Seeing the elusive Rafflesia, the world's largest

flower, at **Gunung Gading National Park** (p413)

3 Strolling the Waterfront Promenade in **Kuching** (p382)

4 Spotting endangered proboscis monkeys in **Bako**

National Park (p400) or **Kuching Wetlands National Park** (p406)

5 Watching the jungle glide by as you make your way into the very heart of Borneo along

To Pulau Labuan

Bandar Seri Begawan

Merapok

Lawas

Limbang

Pan Borneo Hwy

Kuala Belait

Kuala Baram

Seria

BRUNEI

Bangar

Medamit

Sungai Limbang

Miri

Miri Airport

Marudi

Lambir Hills National Park

Beluru

Long Terawan

Gunung Mulu National Park

Long Seridan

Batu Lawi

Pulong Tau National Park

Gunung Murud (2423m)

SABAH

Long Semado

Long Bawan

Ba Kelalan

Headhunter's Trail

Limbang Division

Gunung Mulu (2377m)

7

Niah National Park

8

Batu Niah

Long Teru

Batu Niah Junction

Long Miri

Long Lama

6 **Kelabit Highlands**

Bario

Ramudu

Long Lellang

Sungai Baram

Similajau onal Park

ntulu port

ulu

Simpang Bakun (Bakun Junction)

Tubau

Dulit Range

Sungai Tinjar

Long Akah

Bukit Seludong (1371m)

Tama Abu Range

Lio Matoh

Long Banga

Batang Kemena

Lumut Range

Sungai Asap Longhouses

Belaga

Batang Belaga

Bukit Semalong (1281m)

Bakun Dam

Murum Dam

Bukit Robertson (1710m)

KALIMANTAN

INDONESIA

gan

Batang Tatau

Sungai Linau

5 **Batang Rejang**

Batang Rejang

agus ipids

apit

Sungai Mujong

Batang Balui

Long Jawi

Hose Range

Interwau

Batang Baleh

Sungai Mengiong

Batang Baleh

the **Batang Rejang** (p421), 'Borneo's Amazon'

6 Experiencing longhouse life and Kelabit hospitality in the **Kelabit Highlands** (p444)

7 Ascending to the summit of Gunung Mulu, the highest peak in Borneo's best nature park, or going spelunking in **Gunung Mulu National Park** (p441)

8 Entering a netherworld of stalactites and bats in the caves of **Niah National Park** (p429)

History

After a century of rule by the White Rajahs and four years of Japanese occupation, Sarawak became a British Crown colony in 1946. At Westminster's urging, the territory joined the Malay Peninsula, Sabah and Singapore to form Malaysia in 1963 (Singapore withdrew two years later). At about the same time, neighbouring Indonesia, under the leftist leadership of President Soekarno, laid claim to all of Borneo, including Sarawak, launching a military campaign known as the Konfrontasi (1962–66). Tens of thousands of troops from the UK, Australia and New Zealand were deployed to secure Sarawak's border with Kalimantan.

Since 1981 Sarawak's chief minister has been Abdul Taib Mahmud, who has frequently been accused of corruption, most recently in a 2012 report by the Bruno Manser Fund (www.bmf.ch/en), a Swiss NGO. Entitled 'The Taib Timber Mafia', the dossier identifies Taib as Malaysia's richest man, with a personal fortune estimated at US$15 billion, and accuses him of abusing his office to award timber and other resource concessions to family and friends. In the state assembly elections of 2011, Taib's political coalition, the Barisan Nasional (BN), retained its two thirds majority but is under pressure in the run-up to Malaysia's 2013 federal elections.

KUCHING

POP 600,000

Borneo's most stylish and sophisticated city brings together a kaleidoscope of cultures, crafts and cuisines. The bustling streets – some very modern, others with a colonial vibe – amply reward visitors with a penchant for aimless ambling. Chinese temples decorated with dragons abut shophouses from the time of the White Rajahs, a South Indian mosque is a five-minute walk from stalls selling half-a-dozen Asian cuisines, and a landscaped riverfront park attracts families out for a stroll and a quick bite.

Kuching's other huge asset is its day trip proximity to a dozen first-rate nature sites.

◎ Sights

The main attraction here is the city itself. Leave plenty of time to wander aimlessly and soak up the relaxed vibe and charming cityscapes of areas such as Jln Carpenter (Old Chinatown), Jln India, Jln Padungan (New Chinatown) and the Waterfront Promenade.

Sarawak's excellent museums are free.

WATERFRONT PROMENADE

The **south bank** (Map p384; along Main Bazaar & Jln Gambier; river cruises RM20) of Sungai Sarawak, from the Indian Mosque east to the Hotel Grand Margherita Kuching, has been turned into a watery promenade, with paved walkways, lawns, flowerbeds, a children's playground, cafes and food stalls. It's a fine place for a stroll any time a cool breeze blows off the river, especially at sunset. In the evening the waterfront is ablaze with colourful fairy lights and full of couples and families eating snacks as trans-river *tambang* (small passenger ferries) glide past with their glowing lanterns. The loveliest panoramas are from the bend in the river across from the Hilton. Several companies offer **river cruises** (RM20). The water level is kept constant by a downstream barrage.

The promenade affords great views across the river to the white, crenellated towers and manicured gardens of the Astana; hilltop Fort Margherita, also white and crenellated; and, between the two, the Sarawak State Assembly, with its dramatic, golden pointy roof.

Chinese History Museum　　　MUSEUM
(Map p384; cnr Main Bazaar & Jln Wayang; ⊙9am-4.45pm Mon-Fri, 10am-4pm Sat, Sun & holidays) Housed in the century-old Chinese Court building, the Chinese History Museum provides an excellent introduction to the nine Chinese communities – each with its own dialect, cuisine and temples – who began settling in Sarawak around 1830. Highlights of the evocative new exhibits, inaugurated in 2011, include ceramics, musical instruments, historic photos and some fearsome dragon and lion dance costumes. The entrance is on the river side of the building.

Square Tower　　　HISTORIC BUILDING
(Map p384) Along with Fort Margherita, the Square Tower, built in 1879, once guarded the lazy river against marauders. Over the past century, the structure – still emblazoned with Sarawak's Brooke-era coat-of-arms – has served as a prison, a mess and a dance hall; it now houses an art gallery. Nearby Jln Gambier is named after a vine used for tanning and dyeing.

Old Court House Complex　　　HISTORIC BUILDING
(Map p384; btwn Jln Tun Abang Haji Openg & Jln Barrack) The Old Court House, now officially

called the Sarawak Tourism Complex, was built in the late 1800s to serve as the city's administrative centre. Today, this ensemble of airy, colonnaded structures – well worth a wander – is home to the very helpful Visitors Information Centre and the National Park Booking Office. Out front, across the street from the Square Tower, stands the Brooke Memorial, erected in 1924 to honour Charles Brooke.

OLD CHINATOWN

Jalan Carpenter   STREET

(Map p384) Lined with evocative, colonial-era shophouses and home to several vibrantly coloured Chinese temples, Jln Carpenter – the heart of Kuching's Old Chinatown – stretches from ornamental Harmony Arch (Map p384; cnr Jln Tun Abang Haji Openg & Jln Carpenter) eastward to Hong San Si Temple (Map p384; cnr Jln Wayang & Jln Carpenter; ⊗6am-6pm), with its roofline of tiled dragons. Established sometime before 1848 (and extensively restored in 2004), it is also known by its Hokkien name, Say Ong Kong.

There is a big celebration here in April, with a long procession of floats, lion and dragon dancers, and other groups winding their way through town following the altar of Kong Teck Choon Ong (the deity at the temple).

Hiang Thian Siang Temple   TEMPLE

(Sang Ti Miao Temple; Map p384; btwn 12 & 14 Jln Carpenter) Near the Harmony Arch end of the street, this temple, rebuilt shortly after the fire of 1884, serves the Teochew congregation as a shrine to Shang Di (the Emperor of Heaven).

The temple's most interesting celebration is the Hungry Ghost Festival, held on the 15th day of the seventh lunar month (mid-August or early September). The Chinese believe that the gates of hell swing open for the entirety of the month and the spirits of the dead are free to roam the earth. On the 15th day, offerings of food, prayer, incense and paper money are made to appease the spirits. A priest blesses the offerings and promptly burns an enormous effigy of the Hell King in a dramatic bonfire.

Directly across Jln Carpenter from the temple, you can dine on excellent Teochew Chinese dishes at Yang Choon Tai Hawker Centre (p393).

Hin Ho Bio   TEMPLE

(Map p384; 36 Jln Carpenter; ⊗6am-5pm) One of Kuching's hidden gems is tucked away on the roof of the Kuching Hainan Association.

Mount the staircase to the top floor (there are clean bathrooms on the 1st floor) and you soon get to a vivid little Chinese shrine, Hin Ho Bio (Temple of the Queen of Heaven), with rooftop views of the area.

Sarawak Textile Museum   MUSEUM

(Muzium Tekstil Sarawak; Map p384; Jln Tun Abang Haji Openg; ⊗9am-4.45pm Mon-Fri, 10am-4pm Sat, Sun & holidays) Housed in a 'colonial Baroque'-style building constructed in 1909, this museum displays some superb examples of traditional Sarawakian textiles, including Malay *songket* (gold brocade cloth), as well as the hats, mats, belts, basketwork, beadwork, silverwork, barkwork, bangles and ceremonial headdresses created by the Iban, Bidayuh, Penan and other Dayak groups. Dioramas recreate the sartorial exuberance of Orang Ulu, Malay, Chinese and Indian weddings. Explanatory panels shed light on materials and techniques.

The historic old General Post Office, an impressive, Corinthian-colonnaded structure built in 1931, is across the street.

JALAN INDIA AREA

Indian Mosque   MOSQUE

(Map p384; Indian Mosque Lane; ⊗6am-8.30pm except during prayers) Turn off Jln India (between Nos 37 and 39A) or waterfront Jln Gambier (between Nos 24 and 25A) onto tiny Indian Mosque Lane (Lg Sempit) and you enter another world. At the Jln Gambier end, shops sell spices in bulk (orange-yellow turmeric, greenish-yellow coriander, reddish-orange chilli powder) – the aromas are overwhelming and exhilarating! Further along, hole-in-the-wall hat shops sell the white crocheted caps (RM10) worn by men who have performed the hajj to Mecca; *songkok* (RM25), the black velvet hats worn by Malay men for formal occasions; and colourful headscarves for Muslim women.

About midway between the two thoroughfares, entirely surrounded by houses and shops, stands Kuching's oldest mosque, a modest structure built of *belian* (ironwood) in 1863 by Muslim traders from Tamil Nadu. Painted turquoise and notable for its simplicity, it is an island of peace and cooling shade in the middle of Kuching's commercial hullabaloo.

Jalan India   STREET

(Map p384; Jln India) Once Kuching's main shopping area for imported textiles, brassware and household goods, pedestrianised Jln India – essentially the western continuation

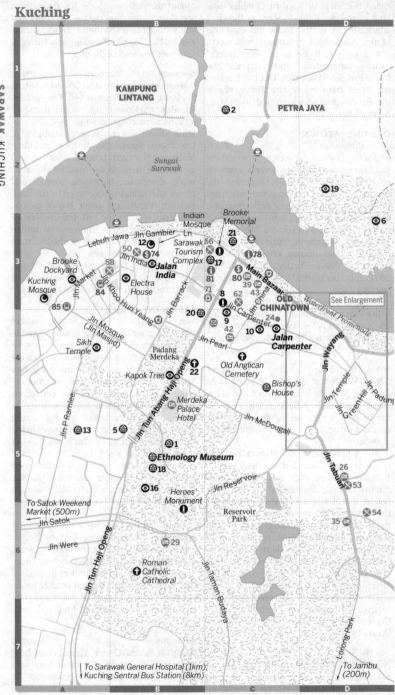

KAMPUNG LINTANG

PETRA JAYA

Sungai Sarawak

Brooke Dockyard

Kuching Mosque

Jln Market

Jln Khoo Hun Yeang

Jln Mosque (Jln Masjid)

Lebuh Jawa
Jln Gambier
Jln India

Jalan India

Electra House

Jln Barrack

Indian Mosque Ln

Brooke Memorial

Sarawak Tourism Complex

Main Bazaar

Jln China

OLD CHINATOWN

Waterfront Promenade

See Enlargement

Jln Carpenter

Jalan Carpenter

Jln Pearl

Jln Wayang

Sikh Temple

Padang Merdeka

Kapok Tree

Old Anglican Cemetery

Bishop's House

Jln Temple

Jln Green Hill

Jln Padung

Merdeka Palace Hotel

Jln McDougall

Jln P Ramlee

Ethnology Museum

Jln Tun Abang Haji Openg

Jln Tabuan

To Satok Weekend Market (500m)
Jln Satok

Heroes' Monument

Jln Reservoir

Reservoir Park

Jln Were

Jln Tun Haji Openg

Roman Catholic Cathedral

Jln Taman Budaya

Lorong Park

To Sarawak General Hospital (1km);
Kuching Sentral Bus Station (8km)

To Jambu (200m)

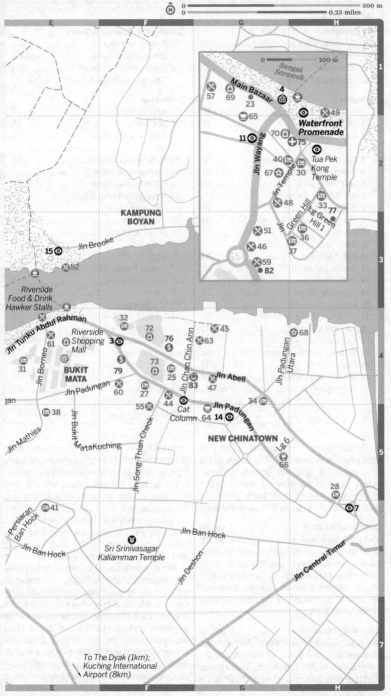

0 — 500 m
0 — 0.25 miles

Sungai Sarawak

0 — 100 m

57 69 Main Bazaar 4
23
65
Waterfront Promenade 49
70
11 Jln Wayang 75
40 Tua Pek Kong Temple
67 30
Jln Temple
48 33 77
Lg Green Hill 1
51 Green Hill
36
46 37
59
82

KAMPUNG BOYAN

Jln Brooke
15 52

Riverside Food & Drink Hawker Stalls

Jln Tunku Abdul Rahman
32
Riverside Shopping Mall 3
72 45
61 76 63 68
31 @ Jln Padungan Utara
BUKIT MATA 73 25
Jln Borneo 79 Jln Abell
Jln Padungan 60 27 83 47
38 55 44 34
Cat Column 64 14
Jln Padungan
Jln Song Thian Cheok Jln Bukit MataKuching NEW CHINATOWN Lg 6
66
Jln Mathies
28
41 7
Persiaran Ban Hock

Jln Ban Hock Jln Ban Hock
Sri Srinivasagar Kaliamman Temple
Jln Deshon
Jln Central Timur

To The Dyak (1km);
Kuching International
Airport (8km)

Kuching

◎ Top Sights

Ethnology Museum	B5
Jalan Carpenter	C4
Jalan India	B3
Waterfront Promenade	H1

◎ Sights

	Akuarium	(see 18)
1	Art Museum	B5
2	Astana	C1
3	Cat Fountain	F4
4	Chinese History Museum	G1
5	Dewan Tun Abdul Razak	B5
6	Fort Margherita	D3
7	Great Cat of Kuching	H6
8	Harmony Arch	C3
9	Hiang Thian Siang Temple	C4
10	Hin Ho Bio	C4
11	Hong San Si Temple	G2
12	Indian Mosque	B3
13	Islamic Museum	A5
14	Jalan Padungan	G5
15	Kampung Boyan	E3
16	Museum Garden	B5
17	Old Court House Complex	C3
18	Sarawak Museum	B5
19	Sarawak State Assembly	D2
20	Sarawak Textile Museum	B4
21	Square Tower	C3
22	St Thomas's Cathedral	B4
	Tun Jugah Foundation	(see 73)

◎ Activities, Courses & Tours

23	Borneo Adventure	G1
	Borneo Experiences	(see 40)
24	Bumbu Cooking School	C4
	Telang Usan Travel & Tours	(see 41)

◎ Sleeping

25	Abell Hotel	F4
26	B&B Inn	D5
27	Batik Boutique Hotel	F4
28	Beds	H5
29	Fairview Guesthouse	B6
30	Harbour View Hotel	H2
31	Hilton Kuching Hotel	E4
32	Hotel Grand Margherita Kuching	F4
33	John's Place	H2
34	Lime Tree Hotel	G4
35	Lodge 121	D6
36	Mandarin Hotel	H3
37	Nomad Borneo B&B	H3
38	Pullman Kuching	E5
39	Ranee	C3
40	Singgahsana Lodge	G2
41	Telang Usan Hotel	E6
42	Threehouse B&B	C4
	Tracks B&B	(see 37)
43	Wo Jia Lodge	C3

◎ Eating

44	21 Bistro	F4
45	Benson Seafood	G4
46	Bla Bla Bla	G3

of Jln Carpenter – remains an exuberant commercial thoroughfare. The shops along the eastern section are mostly Chinese-owned; those to the west are run by Indian Muslims with roots in Tamil Nadu. This is *the* place in Kuching to come for cheap textiles.

Sarawak Museum   MUSEUM

(Map p384; www.museum.sarawak.gov.my; Jln Tun Abang Haji Openg; ⊘9am-4.45pm Mon-Fri, 10am-4pm Sat, Sun & holidays) Established in 1891, this excellent museum has a first-rate collection of cultural artefacts and is a must-visit for anyone interested in Borneo's peoples, cultures and habitats.

Ethnology Museum   MUSEUM

(Map p384; ⊘9am-4.45pm Mon-Fri, 10am-4pm Sat, Sun & holidays) At the top of the hill, on the western side of Jln Tun Abang Haji Openg, the Ethnology Museum (the Old Building) – guarded by two colonial cannons – spotlights Borneo's incredibly rich indigenous cultures. Upstairs, it has superb exhibits on indigenous crafts, including masks, spears, basketry, musical instruments and a Bidayuh door charm for keeping evil spirits at bay; information on native customs such as tattooing and the infamous *palang* penis piercing; and long-houses, including a full-size Iban longhouse and scale models for other groups.

Downstairs is an old-fashioned natural-history museum whose highlight – remembered with horror by generations of Kuching children – is a hairball taken from the stomach of a man-eating crocodile, accompanied by the following explanation: 'human dental plate found attached to the hairball'. And if this isn't enough to put you off taking a dip in a muddy estuary, the 'watch found inside stomach' (the croc's stomach, of course) surely will – unless

47 Chong Choon Cafe...................................G4
   Everrise Supermarket ....(see 72)
48 Green Hill Corner G2
49 James Brooke Bistro & Cafe H1
50 Jubilee Restaurant..................................B3
51 Junk G3
52 Kampung Boyan Hawker
   Centres...E3
53 Kok Boon Café...D5
54 Lok Lok D6
55 Lyn's Thandoori Restaurant F5
   Magenta ....(see 56)
56 Magna Carta C3
57 Maria Kek Lapis.......................................G1
58 Open-Air Market B3
   Sin Wei Tong Café....................... (see 48)
59 Ting & Ting G3
60 Top Spot Food Court F4
61 Tribal Scoops E4
62 Yang Choon Tai Hawker Centre C3
63 Zhun San Yen Vegetarian Food
   Centre...G4

🍷 **Drinking**
64 Bing..G5
65 Black Bean Coffee & Tea
   Company...G2
   Junk ....(see 51)
   Ruai..(see 54)
66 Zeus Sports Bar G5

🎭 **Entertainment**
67 Star Cineplex G2

68 Terminal One Lounge H4

🛍 **Shopping**
   Fabriko...(see 69)
   Fantasy Sarawak ....(see 69)
69 Main Bazaar G1
   Mohamed Yahia & Sons .... (see 72)
70 Nelson's Gallery.......................................G2
   Popular Book Co...........................(see 73)
71 Sarawak Craft Council C3
72 Sarawak Plaza..F4
73 Tun Jugah Shopping Centre F4
   UD Siburan Jaya ....(see 69)
   Yusan Padan Gallery ....(see 21)

ℹ **Information**
74 KK Abdul Majid & Sons...........................B3
75 Klinik Chan H2
76 Maybank F4
   Medical Centre............................... (see 75)
   Mohamed Yahia & Sons .... (see 72)
77 Mr Clean H3
   National Park Booking Office........(see 81)
78 Sarawak Tourism Federation C3
79 Standard Chartered Bank F4
80 United Overseas Bank C3
81 Visitors Information Centre C3

ℹ **Transport**
82 An Hui Motor..G3
83 Bus Asia F4
84 Bus to Bako National Park A3
85 Saujana Bus Station................................A3

you'd like your smartphone to feature in a future exhibit!

Museum Garden GARDENS
(Map p384; ⏱9am-4.45pm Mon-Fri, 10am-4pm Sat, Sun & holidays) The landscaped Museum Garden stretches south from the Ethnology Museum, leading past flowers and fountains to a white-and-gold column called the **Heroes' Monument**.

The cast-iron, open-air pavilion behind the museum houses the **Akuarium** (Aquarium; Map p384; ⏱9am-6pm), run by the city, on a shoestring budget, for educational purposes. It houses fish tanks (it's nice to see local fish that aren't laid out on ice, ready to be grilled, fried or baked) as well as turtles.

Art Museum MUSEUM
(Map p384; ⏱9am-4.45pm Mon-Fri, 10am-4pm Sat, Sun & holidays) Down the driveway from the Ethnology Museum, the Art Museum (Muzium Seni) features sculpture and paintings inspired by Dayak motifs and traditions and by Borneo's flora, fauna and landscapes. May be closed at lunchtime.

Dewan Tun Abdul Razak MUSEUM
(Map p384; ⏱9am-4.45pm Mon-Fri, 10am-4pm Sat, Sun & holidays) Linked to the Ethnology Museum by a footbridge decorated with Orang Ulu motifs, Dewan Tun Abdul Razak (the New Building) has fine permanent exhibits on Sarawak's fascinating history, from the Brunei sultanate through to the Brooke era; prehistoric archaeology, including important finds from the Niah Caves; Chinese ceramics; and colourful Dayak crafts and costumes.

Islamic Museum MUSEUM
(Map p384; Jln P Ramlee; ⏱9am-4.45pm Mon-Fri, 10am-4pm Sat, Sun & holidays) Directly behind

Dewan Tun Abdul Razak, this museum offers a pretty good introduction to Malay-Muslim culture and its long ties with the Muslim heartland far to the west. Displays range from Bornean-Malay architecture, musical instruments and wood carvings to Arabic calligraphy and astrolabes of the sort that helped Arab mariners travel this far east.

NEW CHINATOWN
Jalan Padungan   STREET
(Map p384; Jln Padungan) Built starting in the 1920s, initially with money from the rubber boom, Kuching's liveliest commercial thoroughfare – pronounced pah-*doong*-ahn – is lined with Chinese-owned businesses and noodle shops. In recent years, the area has attracted a growing number of trendy cafes, bars and restaurants. Covered arcades make it a fine place for a rainy-day stroll. It stretches for 1.5km from Jln Tunku Abdul Rahman to the Great Cat of Kuching.

Tun Jugah Foundation   MUSEUM
(Map p384; 4th fl, Tun Jugah Tower, 18 Jln Tunku Abdul Rahman; ⊙9am-noon & 1-4.30pm Mon-Fri) Has excellent exhibits on Iban *ikat* and *sungkit* weaving, as well as beadwork. Iban woman come here to make traditional textiles using handlooms.

NORTH BANK OF THE RIVER
To get to Sungai Sarawak's northern bank, take a *tambang* (river ferry; 50 sen) from one of the docks along the Waterfront Promenade.

Kampung Boyan   NEIGHBOURHOOD
(Map p384) This sedate, old-time Malay *kampung* (village), filled with joyously colourful houses and a profusion of flowering plants, is a world away from the glitz and bustle of downtown Kuching, to which it's connected by boat (there's talk of building a pedestrian bridge). The waterfront area has two roofed hawker centres as well as other Malay-style eateries.

Fort Margherita   HISTORIC SITE
(Map p384; Kampung Boyan; ⊙9am-4.30pm) Built by Charles Brooke in 1879 and named after his wife, Ranee Margaret, this hilltop fortress long protected Kuching against surprise attacks by pirates. It did so exclusively as a remarkably successful deterrent: troops stationed here never fired a shot in anger.

Inspired by an English Renaissance castle, whitewashed Fort Margherita manages to feel both medieval-European and tropical. A steep spiral staircase leads up three flights of stairs to the crenellated roof, a great place to take in panoramic views of the river and get a feel for the lie of the city.

To get there from Kampung Boyan, follow the signs up the hill for 500m.

Astana   HISTORIC BUILDING
(Map p384; Petra Jaya; ⊙closed to public) Built by Charles Brooke in 1869, the Astana (Bahasa Sarawak for 'palace') – conveniently labelled in giant white letters – and its manicured gardens still serve as the home of the governor of Sarawak. The best views are actually from the south (city centre) bank of the river, so it's not really worth taking a *tambang* across.

To walk from the Astana to Fort Margherita, you have to circle a long way north, around the Sarawak State Assembly.

Sarawak State Assembly   NOTABLE BUILDING
(Map p384; Dewan Undangan Negeri, north bank of Sungai Sarawak, Petra Jaya; ⊙closed to public) Inaugurated in 2009, the iconic home of Sarawak's State Assembly is an imposing structure whose soaring golden roof is said to resemble either a *payung* (umbrella) or a *terendak* (Melanau sunhat). The best views are from Jln Bishopsgate and the Waterfront Promenade.

ELSEWHERE IN KUCHING
St Thomas's Cathedral   CHURCH
(Map p384; http://kuching.anglican.org; ⊙6am-6pm Mon-Sat, to 7pm Sun) Facing Padang Merdeka (Independence Sq), with its huge and ancient **kapok tree**, Kuching's Anglican cathedral (1954) has a mid-20th-century look and, inside, a bright red barrel-vaulted ceiling. The main gate is usually closed, so enter from Jln McDougall, named after Kuching's first Anglican bishop, who arrived here in 1848.

At the top of the hill, on the other side of the new Parish Centre (opened in 2012) from the cathedral, stands the **Bishop's House**. Kuching's oldest building, it was constructed in 1849 - with admirable solidness - by a German shipwright.

Tucked away in a corner of the Anglican compound, behind the Verger's Quarters, is the **Old Anglican Cemetery**, a number of whose tombs – there are just a few dozen – go back to the 1840s. Some are finely carved in granite while others are just weathered wooden planks; several belong to infants.

Cat Statues KITSCH

It's just a coincidence that in Bahasa Malaysia, Kuching means 'cat' (spelled 'kucing'), but the city fathers have milked the homonym for everything it's worth, branding Sarawak's capital as the 'Cat City' and erecting a number of marvellously kitschy cat statues to beautify the urban landscape.

The **Cat Fountain** (Map p384; Jln Tunku Abdul Rahman) is an ensemble of polychrome cats who pose and preen opposite the Hotel Grand Margherita Kuching. On the roundabout at the corner of Jln Padungan and Jln Chan Chin Ann, the **Cat Column** features four cats around the bottom and four Rafflesia flowers near the top – the latter are just below the cat-adorned shield of the South Kuching municipality. And the **Great Cat of Kuching** (Map p384; Jln Padungan), a 2½m-high white pussycat with blue eyes and wire whiskers, is perched at the eastern end of Jln Padungan, on a traffic island just outside the Chinese ceremonial gate.

FREE Cat Museum MUSEUM

(www.dbku.sarawak.gov.my; Jln Semariang, Bukit Siol; admission free, camera/video RM3/5; ⊙9am-5pm) A veritable shrine to feline kitsch, this homage to the city's name features hundreds of entertaining, surprising and bizarre *kucing* (cat) figurines – some the size of a cow, others tiny, ubercute and very Japanese – alongside learned presentations on 'Cats in Malay Society' and 'Cats in Chinese Art'. The cafeteria, used by council workers, is quite good.

Kuching North City Hall NOTABLE BUILDING

Situated 8km (by road) north of the city centre is the hilltop Kuching North City Hall (known by its Malay abbreviation, DBKU, a landmark prestige project – some say it looks like a UFO – inaugurated in 1993. Buses K5 and K15 (RM1.50, about hourly) link the Saujana Bus Station with the bottom of the hill. A taxi from the centre costs RM20 to RM25. If you're going to the Santubong Peninsula by car, you can stop here on the way.

🏃 Activities

Satok Weekend Market MARKET

(Pasar Minggu; Jln Satok; ⊙about noon-10pm Sat & 6am-1pm or 2pm Sun) Kuching's biggest and liveliest market begins around midday on Saturday, when rural folk, some from area longhouses, arrive with their fruits, veggies, fish and spices. The air is heady with the aromas of fresh coriander, ginger, herbs and jungle ferns, which are displayed among piles of bananas (10 kinds!), mangoes, custard apples and obscure jungle fruits. If you smell something overpoweringly sweet and sickly from November to February, chances are it's durian. Vendors are friendly and many are happy to tell you about their wares, which are often divided into quantities worth RM1 or RM2.

At research time, the market was situated on Jln Satok about 1km west of the Sarawak Museum – from the centre, walk south on Jln Tun Abang Haji Openg and turn east at Jln Satok (under the flyover). But there were plans – bitterly opposed by vendors – to move (some would say exile) it across the river to a complex about 2km further west.

Hash House Harriers FUN RUNS

Kuching's various Hash House Harriers (HHH) chapters hold about half-a-dozen one- to two-hour runs, over meadow and dale (and through thick jungle), each week. For details, ask around or visit www.kuchingcityhash.com, the website of the Saturday afternoon run. Visitors are welcome to join the fun.

Kuching Bike Hash CYCLING

(www.kbh.doturf.com) Bashers (bicycle hashes) gather every second Sunday afternoon to ride 17km to 25km. Visitors are welcome. Cycling has become hugely popular with outdoorsy Sarawakians in recent years.

Courses

Bumbu Cooking School DAYAK COOKING

(Map p384; ☎012-897 2297, 019-879 1050; http://bumbucookingclass.weebly.com; 57 Jln Carpenter; per person RM150, without market visit RM120; ⊙approx 8am or 9am-1pm & 2-6.30pm daily) Raised in a Bidayuh village, Joseph teaches the secrets of cooking with fresh, organic ingredients from the rainforest. At the market you'll learn how to spot top-quality, jungle ferns; back in the kitchen you'll prepare this crunchy delicacy, along with a main dish and a dessert that's served in a *pandan*-leaf basket you weave yourself. A bit pricey but gets great reviews. Maximum 10 participants.

☞ Tours

Telang Usan Travel & Tours TOUR

(Map p384; ☎082-236945; www.telangusan.com; Telang Usan Hotel, Persiaran Ban Hock) A well-regarded, veteran agency based in the Telang Usan Hotel. Audry, currently president of the Sarawak Tourism Federation, speaks English and French.

Rainforest Kayaking TOUR

(Borneo Trek & Kayak Adventure; ☑082-240571, 013-804 8338; www.rainforestkayaking.com) Specialises in river trips.

Borneo à la Carte TOUR

(☑082-236857; www.borneoalacarte.com) A Kuching-based agency offering innovative, tailor-made trips, mainly for a French-speaking clientele, to indigenous communities other agencies don't cover. Amélie, the owner, is known for having very reasonable prices and sharing receipts equitably with local communities.

Borneo Experiences TOUR

(Map p384; ☑082-421346; www.borneoexperiences. com; ground fl, Jln Temple; ⊙10am-7pm Mon-Sat, may also open Sun) Singgahsana Lodge's (p390) new travel agency. Destinations include a remote Bidayuh 'village in the clouds' and an Iban longhouse in the Batang Ai area (one/two nights per person RM688/888). Also offers cycling tours. Gets excellent reviews.

Borneo Adventure TOUR

(Map p384; ☑082-245175; www.borneoadventure. com; 55 Main Bazaar) Award-winning company that sets the standard for high-end Borneo tours and is the leader in cooperative projects benefiting Sarawak's indigenous peoples. Known for its outstanding guides.

Adventure Alternative Borneo TOUR

(☑Danny Voon 016-810 5614; borneo@adventure alternative.com) Offers sustainable trips that combine 'culture, nature and adventure'. Can help you design and coordinate an itinerary for independent travel to remote areas.

✦✦ Festivals & Events

Rainforest World Music Festival MUSIC

(www.rwmf.net; 1-/3-day pass RM110/300, child RM55/150; ⊙2nd weekend in Jul) This three-day musical extravaganza brings together Dayak bands with international artists. Held in the Sarawak Cultural Village. Accommodation gets booked out well in advance.

Kuching Festival Fair FOOD

(Jln Padungan; ⊙5-11pm for 2 or 3 weeks late Jul-Aug) Scores of food stalls serve the specialities of the various Chinese dialect groups, Nyonya desserts and beer. Held next to Kuching South City Hall (MBKS Building), about 2km southeast of the Hilton.

Chinese New Year CELEBRATION

(⊙late Jan or early Feb) The main festivities are along Jln Padungan.

Mooncake Festival STREET FAIR

(⊙Sep or early Oct) Musical performances and food stalls selling Chinese food, drink and, of course, mooncakes take over Jln Carpenter.

🛏 Sleeping

Kuching's accommodation options range from international-standard suites with high-rise views to windowless, musty cells deep inside converted Chinese shophouses. Many of the guesthouses – a great place to meet other travellers – are on or near Jln Carpenter (Old Chinatown), while the top-end spots are clustered a bit to the east in Kuching's high-rise district, on or near Jln Tunku Abdul Rahman. Cheap Chinse hotels can be found on or just off Jln Padungan and on the *lorong* (alleys) coming off L-shaped Jln Green Hill.

The majority of guesthouse rooms under RM50 have shared bathrooms; prices almost always include a very simple breakfast of the toast-and-jam variety. Rates at some guesthouses rise in July (especially during the Rainforest World Music Festival), or from June to September.

⬥TOP CHOICE Batik Boutique Hotel BOUTIQUE HOTEL $$

(Map p384; ☑082-422845; www.batikboutiqueho tel.com; 38 Jln Padungan; d incl breakfast RM250; ❋🛁) A superb location, classy design and a super-friendly staff make this a top mid-range choice. The 15 spacious rooms, six with balconies, are sleek and elegant, and even come with iPod docks.

⬥TOP CHOICE Threehouse B&B GUESTHOUSE $

(Map p384; ☑082-423499; www.threehousebnb. com; 51 Upper China St; dm/d RM20/60; @🛁) A spotless, family-friendly guesthouse in a great Old Chinatown location, with a warm and hugely welcoming vibe – everything a guesthouse should be! All nine rooms have shared bathrooms. Amenities include a common room with TV, DVDs and books, and a kitchen. Laundry costs RM8 per load, including drying.

⬥TOP CHOICE Singgahsana Lodge GUESTHOUSE $

(Map p384; ☑082-429277; www.singgahsana.com; 1 Jln Temple; dm RM30, d with shared/private bathroom RM88/98; ❋@🛁) Setting the Kuching standard for backpacker digs, this hugely popular guesthouse, decked out with stylish Dayak crafts, has an unbeatable location and a great chill-out lobby. Prices aren't low and the rooms, though colourful, are far from luxurious, but breakfast at the rooftop bar is included. The shared bathrooms are spotless. Laundry costs RM6.50 per kilo.

Telang Usan Hotel
HOTEL **$$**

(Map p384; 082-415588; www.telangusan.com; Persiaran Ban Hock; s/d from RM100/120) A famously welcoming hotel with gleaming tile hallways and 66 very clean rooms that come with freshly plumped pillows and crisply turned-back sheets. The decor is Kenyah and Kayan. Situated down the hill behind the Pullman Hotel, to which it's linked via an often-muddy track. Has an excellent restaurant. Outstanding value.

Lime Tree Hotel
HOTEL **$$**

(Map p384; 082-414600; www.limetreehotel. com.my; Lot 317, Jln Abell; d/family ste RM160/390; ❄@⎙) Dashes of lime green – a pillow, a bar of soap, a staff member's tie, the lobby's Cafe Sublime – accent every room of this well-run semi-boutique hotel. The 55 rooms are sleek and minimalist and offer good value. The rooftop lounge has lovely river views. Situated just a block from lively Jln Padungan.

Ranee
BOUTIQUE HOTEL **$$$**

(Map p384; 082-258833; www.theranee.com; 6 & 7 Main Bazaar; d RM380-650, ste RM1000; ❄⎙) Opened in 2012, this chic riverfront property – in an old shophouse that was completely rebuilt after a fire – has an urban resort feel. The 24 rooms are graced by high ceilings, floors made of rare merbau hardwood, and huge bathrooms with cool, indirect lighting.

Hilton Kuching Hotel
HOTEL **$$**

(Map p384; 082-233888; www.hilton.com; cnr Jln Tunku Abdul Rahman & Jln Borneo; s/d RM348/371; ❄@⎙⛲) The landmark Hilton has 315 spacious, international-standard rooms, in shades of cream, beige and maroon, with flat-screen consoles, LED reading lights and glass-topped work desks. Amenities include two business centres, a spa and a 24hr fitness centre. Wi-fi costs an outrageous RM55 for 24 hours.

Hotel Grand Margherita Kuching
HOTEL **$$**

(Map p384; 082-423111; www.grandmargherita.com; Jln Tunku Abdul Rahman; d incl breakfast RM275; ❄@⎙⛲) On a fine piece of riverfront real estate, this place will spoil you with a bright, modern lobby, 288 very comfortable rooms and amenities such as a fitness centre, a river-view swimming pool and a new spa. Wi-fi costs just RM5 for 24 hours.

Pullman Kuching
HOTEL **$$**

(Map p384; 082-222888; www.pullmankuching. com; 1A Jln Mathies, Bukit Mata; d from RM273; ❄@⎙⛲) Opened in 2010, the Accor-affiliated Pullman has a soaring white lobby and 389 rooms – in subdued tones of aquamarine, brown, white and green – spread over 23 floors. The focus is on business travellers.

Lodge 121
GUESTHOUSE **$**

(Map p384; 082-428121; www.lodge121.com; Lot 121, 1st fl, Jln Tabuan; d/tr RM99/129, dm/s/d/ tr/q with shared bathroom RM24/49/69/89/119; ❄@⎙) Polished concrete abounds at this mod charmer, whose owners have transformed a commercial space into a sleek, spotless and low-key hang-out for flashpackers. The carpeted, 10-bed dorm room, with mattresses on the floor, is in the garret. All 22 rooms – five with attached bath – either have windows to the outside or wood-slat openings to a hallway.

Nomad Borneo B&B
GUESTHOUSE **$$**

(Map p384; 082-237831; www.borneobnb.com; 3 Jln Green Hill; dm/s/d/f RM20/50/75/100; ❄@⎙) There's a buzzing backpacker vibe at this Iban-run favourite – guests often hang out in the lounge area with the friendly management. Of the 17 rooms, 10 have windows (the others make do with exhaust fans). Dorm rooms have either four or eight beds. Laundry costs RM8 per load.

Fairview Guesthouse
GUESTHOUSE **$**

(Map p384; 013-816 4560, 082-240017; www. thefairview.com.my; 6 Jln Taman Budaya; s/d/f incl breakfast RM50/70/150; ❄@) An oldie but a goodie, this nine-room garden villa, a bit out of the city centre, scores big points with visiting researchers for its unpretentious atmosphere and friendly owners, who run great tailor-made tours.

B&B Inn
GUESTHOUSE **$**

(Map p384; 082-237366; bnbswk@streamyx. com; 30-I Jln Tabuan; dm RM16, s/d/tr with shared bathroom RM25/35/45, d RM70; ❄@⎙) Clean and low-key, this establishment has a lived-in, old-fashioned feel and a dozen of the cheapest decent rooms in town. Air-con costs RM5 extra a day. Women and men have separate dorm rooms. A few rooms lack windows. If the street door is padlocked, ring the bell.

Beds
GUESTHOUSE **$**

(Map p384; 082-424229; www.bedsguesthouse. com; 229 Jln Padungan; dm/s/d RM30/50/70;

✳@☞) In the heart of Kuching's New Chinatown, this spotless guesthouse has attracted a loyal following thanks to comfy couches in the lobby, a kitchen you can cook in and 12 clean rooms with shared bathrooms, nine with windows. Dorm rooms have metal-framed bunks of generous proportions. A load of laundry, including drying, costs just RM5.

Harbour View Hotel   HOTEL $$
(Map p384; ☑082-274666; www.harbourview.com.my; Jln Temple; s/d/f RM130/155/200; ✳@☞) If it's modern comforts you're after, this 243-room tower, 13 storeys high, is one of Kuching's best bargains, offering full Western facilities for a thoroughly Southeast Asian price.

Wo Jia Lodge   GUESTHOUSE $
(Map p384; ☑082-251776; www.wojialodge.com; 17 Main Bazaar; dm/s/d/tr with air-con RM20/40/52/75, s/d with fan RM38/48; ✳@☞) A friendly, central spot to lay your head. The 18 gleaming rooms (five with windows, the rest with exhaust fans to the hallway) contain beds and nothing else. In an old Chinese shophouse – the lobby still has the original hardwood floors.

John's Place   GUESTHOUSE $
(Map p384; ☑082-258329; 5 Jln Green Hill; d RM55-60, tr RM80; ✳@☞) Hidden away in a commercial building, John's is a neat but rather unexciting spot to grab some Zs. Has 13 simple, practical rooms of medium size with spring mattresses – and without musty odours. The cheaper doubles look out onto the hallway.

Mandarin Hotel   HOTEL $
(Map p384; ☑082-418269; Lorong Green Hill 3; d/tr from RM55/75; ✳☞) This old-time Chinese hotel is head and shoulders above half-a-dozen similarly priced joints nearby. The 20 decent, no-frills rooms come with windows (no mustiness!), snow-white walls, 1960s Linoleum desks, 1970s-style window-unit air-con and a time-warp vibe.

Abell Hotel   HOTEL $$
(Map p384; ☑082-239449; www.abellhotel.com; 22 Jln Tunku Abdul Rahman; s/d from RM111/175; ✳@☞) Opened in 2011, this non-smoking hotel helps solve Kuching's shortage of good tourist-class hotels. The 80 rooms are stylish but not luxurious; the cheapest look out on an ersatz airwell. The name – like that of the street outside – is pronounced like the word 'able'.

Eating

Kuching is the best place in Malaysian Borneo to work your way through the entire range of Sarawak-style cooking. At hawker centres, you can pick and choose from a variety of Chinese and Malay stalls, each specialising in a particular culinary tradition or dish. Jln Padungan, home to some of the city's best noodle houses, is undergoing something of a restaurant, cafe and bar boom.

If you'd like to start a good-natured argument, ask a group of locals where Kuching's best Sarawak laksa (a deliciously spicy, tangy noodle soup) is served.

TOP CHOICE Dyak   DAYAK $$$
(☑082-234068; Jln Mendu & Jln Simpang Tiga; mains RM18-30; ☺noon-11pm, last order 9.30pm) Kuching's most important culinary event of the last few years was the opening of this elegant restaurant, the first to treat Dayak home cooking as true cuisine. The chef, classically trained in the Western tradition, takes traditional recipes, many of them Iban (a few are Kelabit, Kayan or Bidayuh), and fresh, organic jungle veggies to create mouth-watering dishes unlike anything else you've ever tasted. Vegetarian dishes, made without lard, are available upon request. Staff are happy to explain the origin of each dish. It's a good idea to reserve ahead on Thursday, Friday and Saturday nights. Dyak is situated 2km southeast of Old Chinatown. A taxi from the city centre – worth every cent – costs RM12.

TOP CHOICE Top Spot Food Court   SEAFOOD $$
(Map p384; Jln Padungan; fish per kg RM35-70, vegetable dishes RM8-12; ☺noon-11pm) A perennial favourite among local foodies, this neon-lit courtyard and its half-a-dozen humming seafooderies sits, rather improbably, on the roof of a concrete parking garage – look for the giant backlit lobster sign. Grilled white pomfret is a particular delicacy. Ling Loong Seafood and the Bukit Mata Seafood Centre are particularly good.

TOP CHOICE Jambu   MEDITERRANEAN $$$
(☑082-235292; www.jamburestaurant.com; 32 Jln Crookshank; mains RM28-55; ☺6-10.30pm, closed Mon) Once the venue for elegant colonial parties (check out the photos on the way to the bar), this 1920s mansion – with teak floors and soaring ceilings – is the best place in town for a romantic meal. Some of the tastiest

dishes are Mediterranean-inflected. It has a stylish lounge-bar that serves tapas. Named for the *jambu air* (water apple) tree in the yard. Situated 1.5km south of the centre.

Junk
ITALIAN $$$

(Map p384; ☎082-259450; 80 Jln Wayang; mains RM20-50; ⏱6-11pm, closed Tue; 🖥) Filled to the brim with antiques, this complex of chic dining rooms (three) and bars (two) – housed in three 1920s shophouses – is a favourite among Malaysian celebs. The Red Room is amply supplied with pillows and provocatively decorated with risque pop art. Pasta and lasagne cost RM24 to RM45, pizzas are RM25 to RM39.

Chong Choon Cafe
LAKSA $

(Map p384; Lot 121, Section 3, Jln Abell; mains RM4-5; ⏱7am-11.30am or noon, closed Tue) You'd never guess it from the picnic tables cooled by a fleet of overhead helicopter fans, but this unassuming, tile-floored cafe serves some of Kuching's most famously excellent Sarawak laksa.

Lyn's Thandoori Restaurant
INDIAN $$

(Map p384; Lot 267, Jln Song Thian Cheok; mains RM16-25; ⏱9am-10pm Mon-Sat, 5-10pm Sun; 🖥🖊) This North Indian place, a Kuching fixture since 1994, sports a huge menu featuring tandoori chicken (of course!) as well as delicious mutton, fish and veggie options (almost 50 of them, including 22 types of *paneer*), all made with top-quality ingredients. Situated 300m due north of one of Kuching's three Hindu temples.

Tribal Scoops
DAYAK $

(Map p384; Block H, Jln Borneo; mains RM4.50-10; ⏱10.30am-9.30pm Mon-Sat; 🖥) A convivial little slice of the Kelabit Highlands in downtown Kuching, this unpretentious restaurant is a huge hit with Kelabit students with a hankering for some home cooking. Specialities include *labo senutuq* (shredded beef cooked with wild ginger and dried chilli) and *ab'eng* (shredded river fish). Dishes are prepared without MSG or – because it didn't exist in the highlands in the old days – shrimp paste. A buffet lunch (RM16.50) is available from 11.30am to 2.30pm except Sunday. Situated across the street from the main entrance to the Hilton.

Open-Air Market
LAKSA $

(Map p384; Jln Khoo Hun Yeang; mains from RM3-4.50; ⏱6am or 7am-5pm, some stalls to midnight) Cheap, tasty dishes to look for include

superb laksa (available from about 7am to 4pm), Chinese-style *mee sapi* (beef noodle soup), red *kolo mee* (noodles with sweet barbecue sauce), tomato *kueh tiaw* (another fried rice-noodle dish) and shaved ice desserts (ask for 'ABC' at stall 17). An ideal spot for breakfast before boarding the bus to Bako National Park. Has two sections separated by a minivan parking area. The yellow tower was once used as a fire lookout.

Bla Bla Bla
FUSION $$

(Map p384; ☎082-233944; 27 Jln Tabuan; most mains RM24-45; ⏱6-11.30pm, closed Tue) Innovative, chic and stylish, Bla Bla Bla serves Chinese-inspired fusion dishes that – like the decor, the koi ponds and the Balinese Buddha – range from traditional to far-out. Specialities include *midin* (jungle fern) salad, cashew-nut prawns, ostrich meat stuffed with mozzarella, 'coffee chicken' and homemade cheesecake. The generous portions are designed to be shared.

Kok Boon Café
LAKSA $

(Map p384; 30J Jln Tabuan; mains RM3.50-5; ⏱laksa served 6.30am-1.30pm or 2pm) The three noodle stalls at this ordinary-looking, open-air corner eatery serve the usual Foochow and Hokkien noodle dishes, but it's the scrumptious *Sarawak laksa* that makes this place special for breakfast or an early lunch.

James Brooke Bistro & Cafe
WESTERN $$

(Map p384; Waterfront Promenade opposite Jln Temple; mains RM10-39; ⏱10am-11pm) Gets consistently good reviews both for the cuisine and the lovely river views. Local dishes such as *Sarawak laksa* and their own invention, wild Borneo laksa, are quite reasonably priced. The beef stroganoff has a following.

Yang Choon Tai Hawker Centre
CHINESE $

(Map p384; 23 Jln Carpenter; mains RM4-8; ⏱24hr) Six food stalls, run by members of the Teochew Chinese community, serve up an eclectic assortment of native bites, including rice porridge with pork (3am to 9am), *kolo mee* (flash-boiled egg noodles; available from 6am to 2pm) and super fish soup (3pm to 10pm).

Green Hill Corner
LAKSA $

(Map p384; cnr Jln Temple & Jln Green Hill; meals RM3-6; ⏱7am-11pm) Hugely popular with locals. Half-a-dozen stalls here crank out porridge, laksa, chicken rice and noodle dishes. The stall run by twin brothers serves superb beef noodle soup (RM4).

Benson Seafood
SEAFOOD $$

(Map p384; Jln Chan Chin Ann; 'small' mains RM10-20; ⏱11am-11pm Tue-Sun, 4-11pm Mon) In a gritty riverfront area that may become chic in five or 10 years, this open-air pavilion, its big round tables covered with red tablecloths and surrounded by red plastic chairs, serves fresh Chinese-style fish and seafood and Sarawak classics such as *midin* stir-fried with *belacan* (shrimp paste). From the northern end of Jln Chan Chin Ann, turn right along the riverfront for half a block.

Sin Wei Tong Café
VEGETARIAN $

(Map p384; 9 Jln Temple; mains RM3-4.50; ⏱6am-3.30pm; 🖉) Does cheap, tasty veggie versions of Chinese favourites such as *kueh chap* and chicken rice.

Zhun San Yen Vegetarian Food Centre
VEGETARIAN $

(Map p384; Jln Chan Chin Ann; mains per 100gr RM1.70; ⏱8am-2pm & 5-8pm Mon-Fri, from 9am Sat; 🖉) Serves Taiwanese- and Malaysian Chinese-style veggie meals (eg curries), made with soy or gluten, that are as healthy as they are delicious. Buffet style. Remarkably inexpensive.

21 Bistro
FUSION $$

(Map p384; 64 Jln Padungan; mains RM10-48; ⏱4pm-2am or later Mon-Sat, food until 11pm) This chic, sophisticated restaurant-cum-bar, popular with young professionals, made quite a splash when it opened in 2012. Serves excellent Western, Asian & fusion dishes, including pasta, grilled meats and fish (snapper is a speciality). As for the soundtrack, early evening jazz makes way for chill-out music later on.

Magna Carta
ITALIAN $$

(Map p384; Sarawak Tourism Complex, Jln Tun Abang Haji Openg; mains RM15-28; ⏱10.30am-midnight) For great Brooke-era atmosphere, you can choose between the breezy verandah, with garden views, and the interior, whose decor is a mash-up of medieval England and 19th-century Straits Chinese. Good options include pasta, pizza with exquisitely thin crust (RM22), homemade bread and freshly squeezed orange juice. Across the patio, **Magenta** (Map p384; mains RM26-58; ⏱5-11pm), under the same management, has a larger selection of meat and seafood dishes.

Lok Lok
MALAY $

(Map p384; 7D Jln Ban Hock; mains RM5; ⏱6pm-3am) This hugely popular nocturnal eatery specialises in *lok lok*, skewers (eg of fish, prawn, cuttlefish or bean curd; RM1.50 to RM2 each) that are either boiled or deep fried and eaten with sweet, sweet-and-sour, *belacan* or satay sauce. Also serves *rojak* and traditional mains such as curry chicken. Ideal for a late – or late-late – meal.

Kampung Boyan Hawker Centres
MALAY $

(Map p384; Jln Tunku Abdul Rahman; meals RM4.80-16, hawker centres mains RM3-4; ⏱evening, hawker centres 11am-midnight) What could be better than a romantic evening stroll along the river accompanied by a bite to eat? Or you can take a ferry across the river to Kampung Boyan, whose new promenade has two tent-roofed hawker centres.

Jubilee Restaurant
INDIAN $$

(Map p384; 49 Jln India; ⏱6.30am-5.30pm or 6pm) A fixture in the heart of Kuching's Indian Muslim district since 1974. Halal specialities include *nasi briyani* [sic] (rice with chicken, beef or lamb; RM6 to RM7) and *roti canai* (flatbread with egg and/or cheese; RM1 to RM2.60). The cook hails from Madras.

Self-Catering

Ting & Ting
SUPERMARKET $

(Map p384; 30A Jln Tabuan; ⏱9am-9pm, closed Sun & holidays) An impressive selection of wine (from Australia, California, Chile and France), Western-style snack food, chocolate, toiletries and nappies (diapers).

Everrise Supermarket
SUPERMARKET $

(Map p384; Jln Tunku Abdul Rahman; ⏱9.30am-9.30pm) On the lower floor of the Sarawak Plaza shopping mall.

Drinking

Cosmopolitan Kuching has a clutch of spirited drinking spots. Just for the record, Fort Margherita does not serve cocktails.

Jln Padungan hosts a growing selection of cool places to drink – many would not be out of place in Melbourne, London or San Francisco.

LAKSA LUCK

Borneo's luckiest visitors start the day with a breakfast of *Sarawak laksa*, a tangy noodle soup made with coconut milk, lemon grass, sour tamarind and fiery *sambal belacan* (shrimp-paste sauce), with fresh calamansi lime juice squeezed on top. Unbelievably *lazat* ('delicious' in Bahasa Malaysia)!

KEK LAPIS - COLOURFUL LAYER CAKES

The people of Kuching – from all communities – love to add a dash of colour to festivities, so it comes as no surprise to see stalls selling *kek lapis* (striped layer cakes) sprouting up around town (eg along Main Bazaar and the Waterfront Promenade) during festivals, including Hari Raya (Ramadan).

Kek lapis is made with wheat flour, egg, prodigious quantities of either butter or margarine, and flavourings such as melon, blueberry or – a local favourite – *pandan* leaves. Since *kek lapis* are prepared one layer at a time and each layer – there can be 30 or more – takes five or six minutes to bake, a single cake can take up to five hours from start to finish.

Over 40 flavours of *kek lapis* (with butter RM20, with margarine RM10) are available year-round – to satisfy demand from Peninsular Malaysians – at **Maria Kek Lapis** (Map p384; ☑252734; http://22.com.my/mariakeklapissarawak; ☺8am-5pm). Free tastes are on offer. Cakes stay fresh for one or two weeks at room temperature and up to a month in the fridge.

Junk
BAR

(Map p384; 80 Jln Wayang; ☺4pm-1.30am, closed Tue) Kuching's most stylish hang-out is more than a restaurant – it also has two bars: Junk Bar, tucked away on the side, and the Backstage Bar, lit by red Chinese lanterns and chock full of old radios and musical instruments.

Ruai
BAR

(Map p384; 7F Jln An Hock; ☺5pm-1am or 2am) This Iban-owned bar has a laid-back cool and welcoming spirit all its own. Decorated with old photos and Orang Ulu art (and, inexplicably, several Mexican sombreros), it serves as an urban *ruai* (the covered verandah of an Iban longhouse) for aficionados – local and expat – of vigorous outdoor activities such as caving, trekking and Hash House Harriers social runs. A great place to meet people. Starts to pick up after about 9pm.

Black Bean Coffee & Tea Company
CAFE

(Map p384; Jln Carpenter; drinks RM3-4.80; ☺9am-6pm Mon-Sat; ☏) The aroma of freshly ground coffee assaults the senses at this tiny shop, believed by many to purvey Kuching's finest brews. Specialities, roasted daily, include Arabica, Liberica and Robusta coffees grown in Java, Sumatra and, of course, Sarawak. Also serves oolong and green teas from Taiwan. Has just three tables. Decaf not available.

Zeus Sports Bar
BAR

(Map p384; cnr Jln Padungan & Lorong 6; ☺4pm-2am, closed Tue) Local rock bands strut their stuff from 9pm to 1am on Friday and 6.30pm to 10.30pm on Saturday (after that there's footy on the telly). The upstairs lounge is popular with the golfers. Owned by a personable golf aficionado – and, yes, although he's Iban, his first name is Polish.

Bing
CAFE

(Map p384; 84 Jln Padungan; coffee RM5.50-14; ☺10am-midnight, to 1am Fri & Sat; ☏) Kuching's tropical-chic answer to Starbucks, this uber-stylish, dimly lit coffee shop serves a dozen varieties of hot and iced Illy coffee.

☆ Entertainment

Kuching's after-dark charms range from the sedate (eating well) to the romantic (strolling along the Waterfront Promenade) to the loud and thumping (dancing the night away at a disco).

Terminal One Lounge
CLUB

(Map p384; http://t1lounge.com; Jln Padungan Utara, River end; admission free for women and Sun-Tue for men, men Wed-Sat RM35; ☺4pm-2am or 3am) Kuching's most popular dance club and a magnet for celebrities both local and Peninsular, T1 is a genuine, pumping disco, complete with batteries of flashing, spinning coloured lights. Attracts a well-off crowd, mainly over 25 or 30, often in couples or groups. Things really get going at 10.30pm or 11pm and hit their peak after midnight. The dress code for men bans short pants, singlets (tank tops), flip-flops and sandals. Serves finger food.

Star Cineplex
CINEMA

(Map p384; www.starcineplex.com.my; 9th fl, multi-coloured parking garage, Jln Temple; tickets RM5-9; ☺1st/last screenings at about noon/midnight) For a couple of hours of escapism – ideal on a rainy day – courtesy of Hollywood or the cinema industries of eastern Asia. Most films are English; the rest have English subtitles. The elevator/lift is directly across Jln Temple from the Wong Eye Clinic & Surgery.

🔒 Shopping

If it's traditional Borneo arts and crafts you're after, then you've come to the right place – Kuching is the best shopping spot on the island for collectors and cultural enthusiasts. Don't expect many bargains, but don't be afraid to negotiate either – there's plenty to choose from, and the quality varies as much as the price. Dubiously 'aged' items are common, so be sure to spend some time browsing to familiarise yourself with prices and range.

For insights into Sarawak's varied and rich handicrafts traditions, stop by the Sarawak Museum, the Textile Museum and the Tun Jugah Foundation and check out the website of the Kuching-based NGO **Crafthub** (www.crafthub.com.my), where you can download copies of *Crafts*, a quarterly magazine published for the Sarawak Craft Council.

Most of Kuching's shops are closed on Sunday.

Main Bazaar   HANDICRAFTS
(Map p384; Main Bazaar; ☺some shops closed Sun) The row of old shophouses facing the Waterfront Promenade is chock full of handicrafts shops, some outfitted like art galleries, others with more of a 'garage sale' appeal, yet others (especially along the Main Bazaar's western section) stocking little more than kitschy-cute cat souvenirs. Handmade items worth seeing (if not purchasing), many from the highlands of Kalimantan, include hand-woven textiles and baskets, masks, drums, brass gongs, statues (up to 2m high!), beaded headdresses, swords, spears, painted shields and cannons from Brunei. At many places, staff enjoy explaining the origin and use of each item.

UD Siburan Jaya   FOOD
(Map p384; 66 Main Bazaar; ☺8.30am-9pm Mon-Sat, 9.30-5pm Sun) Has an excellent selection of Sarawakian specialities such as pepper (black and white), laksa paste, sambal, Bario rice and even tax-paid *tuak* (Dayak rice wine).

Fabriko   CLOTHING
(Map p384; 56 Main Bazaar; ☺9am-5pm Mon-Sat) This fine little boutique has a well-chosen selection of made-in-Sarawak fabrics and clothing in both traditional and modern Orang Ulu-inspired designs, including silk sarongs and men's batik shirts.

Nelson's Gallery   ART
(Map p384; 54 Main Bazaar; ☺9am-5pm) Upstairs, artist Narong Daun patiently creates vibrant, jungle-themed batik paintings on silk.

Fantasy Sarawak   CLOTHING
(Map p384; 70 Main Bazaar; ☺10am-7pm) Has Sarawak's classiest collection of T-shirts.

Sarawak Craft Council   HANDICRAFTS
(Map p384; cnr Jln Tun Abang Haji Openg & Jln India; ☺9am-4.30pm Mon-Fri) Run by a non-profit government agency, this two-storey shop has a pretty good selection of Malay, Bidayuh, Iban and Orang Ulu handicrafts – check out the cowboy hats made entirely of bark and the conical *terendak* (Melanau hats). Housed in the Round Tower, constructed in 1886 and used by the dreaded Kempeitai (Japanese military police) during the occupation, which is why some locals believe it's haunted.

Tanoti   WEAVING
(56 Jln Tabuan; ☺8am-6pm, closed public holidays) Using the supplementary weft technique (in which designs are woven into the fabric as it's made), a dozen women hand-weave silk shawls (RM400 to RM2000), wedding veils and the like. Designs at this not-for-profit studio are both Bornean-traditional and modern.

Yusan Padan Gallery   ART
(Map p384; Sarakraf, Waterfront Promenade; ☺9.30am-4.30pm Mon-Sat) Sells crafts and fine art by Dayak artisans and artists. Occupies the historic Square Tower.

Mohamed Yahia & Sons   BOOKS
(Map p384; ☑082-416928; Basement, Sarawak Plaza, Jln Tunku Abdul Rahman; ☺10am-9pm) Specialises in English-language books on Borneo, including the four-volume *Encyclopaedia of Iban Studies*. Also carries Sarawak maps and guidebooks.

Popular Book Co   BOOKS
(Map p384; Level 3, Tun Jugah Shopping Centre, 18 Jln Tunku Abdul Rahman; ☺10am-9.30pm) A capacious modern bookshop with a big selection of English titles, including works by local authors, and guidebooks.

ℹ️ Information

Kuching has Indonesian and Bruneian consulates and honorary consuls representing Australia and the UK.

Dangers & Annoyances

There have recently been incidents of bag snatching from tourists (mainly women) by motorbike-mounted miscreants. Exercise reasonable caution when walking along deserted stretches of road (eg Jln Reservoir and Jln Tabuan), especially after dark.

Emergency

Police, Ambulance & Fire (☎999)

Internet Access

Cyber City (Ground fl, Block D, Taman Sri Sarawak; 1st/2nd hr RM4/3; ⊙10am-11pm Mon-Sat, 11am-11pm Sun & holidays) Hidden away behind the Riverside Complex shopping mall on Jln Tunku Abdul Rahman – to get there, exit the mall on the '2nd floor' and walk up the hill.

Laundry

Most hotels have pricey laundry services with per-piece rates, but some guesthouses let you do your washing for just RM5 to RM8 per load, including drying.

Mr Clean (Map p384; ☎082-246424; Lorong Green Hill 1; per kg RM8, 4hr service RM12; ⊙8am-6pm Mon-Sat, to 3pm Sun & holidays) A central, reliable place to have your clothes washed.

Medical Services

Kuching has some first-rate but affordable medical facilities – some of the doctors are UK- and US-certified – so it's no surprise that 'medical tourism', especially from Indonesia, is on the rise. For minor ailments, guesthouses and hotels can refer you to a general practitioner, who may be willing to make a house call.

Klinik Chan (Map p384; ☎082-240307; 98 Main Bazaar; ⊙8am-noon & 2-5pm Mon-Fri, 9am-noon Sat, Sun & holidays) Conveniently central. A consultation for a minor ailment costs RM30 to RM35.

Normah Medical Specialist Centre (☎082-440055, emergency 311 999; www.normah. com.my; Jln Tunku Abdul Rahman, Petra Jaya; ⊙emergency 24hr, clinics 8.30am-4.30pm Mon-Fri, to 1pm Sat) Considered Kuching's best private hospital by many expats. Has a 24-hour ambulance. Situated north of the river, about 6km by road from the centre. Served by the same buses as Bako National Park.

Sarawak General Hospital (Hospital Umum Sarawak; ☎082-276666; http://hus.moh. gov.my/v3; Jln Hospital; ⊙24hr) Kuching's large public hospital has modern facilities and remarkably reasonable rates but is often overcrowded. Situated about 2km south of the centre along Jln Tun Abang Haji Openg. To get there, take bus 2, K6, K8, K9 or K18.

Timberland Medical Centre (☎082-234466, emergency 234 991; www.timberlandmedical. com; Jln Rock, Mile 2-1/2; ⊙emergency 24hr) A private hospital with highly qualified staff. Has a 24-hour ambulance. Situated 5km south of the centre along Jln Tun Abang Haji Openg and Jln Rock.

Money

The majority of Kuching's banks and ATMs are on or near the Cat Fountain on Jln Tunku Abdul Rahman. If you need to change cash or travellers cheques, money changers are a better bet than banks, which often aren't keen on handling cash (especially banknotes with certain serial numbers – go figure!) – and US$100 bills.

KK Abdul Majid & Sons (Map p384; 45 Jln India; ⊙9am-6pm Mon-Sat, 9am-3pm Sun) A licensed money changer dealing in cash only.

Maybank (Map p384; Jln Tunku Abdul Rahman; ⊙9.15am-4.30pm Mon-Thu, to 4pm Fri) Has an ATM. Situated on the corner near KFC.

Mohamed Yahia & Sons (Map p384; Basement, Sarawak Plaza, Jln Tunku Abdul Rahman; ⊙10am-9pm) No commission, good rates and accepts over 30 currencies (including US$100 bills), as well as travellers cheques in US dollars, euros, Australian dollars and pounds sterling. Situated inside the bookshop.

United Overseas Bank (Map p384; 2 Main Bazaar; ⊙9.30am-4.30pm Mon-Fri) Has a 24-hour ATM around the corner on Jln Tun Abang Haji Obeng.

Police

Central Police Station (Balai Polis Sentral; ☎082-244444; 2 Jln Khoo Hun Yeang; ⊙24hr) In a blue-and-white building constructed in 1931.

Tourist Police (☎082-250522; Waterfront Promenade; ⊙8am-midnight) Most of the officers speak English. The pavilion is across the street from 96 Main Bazaar.

Post

Main Post Office (Jln Tun Abang Haji Openg; ⊙8am-4.30pm Mon-Sat, closed 1st Sat of month)

Tourist Information

National Park Booking Office (Map p384; ☎082-248088; www.sarawakforestry.com; Sarawak Tourism Complex, Jln Tun Abang Haji Openg; ⊙8am-5pm Mon-Fri) Sells brochures on each of Sarawak's national parks and can supply the latest news flash on Rafflesia sightings. Telephone enquiries are not only welcomed but patiently answered. Bookings for accommodation at Bako, Gunung Gading and Kubah National Parks and the Matang Wildlife Centre can be made in person, by phone or via http://ebooking.com.my. Situated next door to the Visitors Information Centre.

Visa Department (Bahagian Visa; ☑082-245661; www.imi.gov.my; 2nd fl, Bangunan Sultan Iskandar, Kompleks Pejabat Persekutuan, cnr Jln Tun Razak & Jln Simpang Tiga; ☺8am-5pm Mon-Thu, 8-11.45am & 2.15-5pm Fri) Situated in a 17-storey federal office building about 3km south of the centre (along Jln Tabuan). Served by City Public Link buses K8 or K11, which run every half-hour or so. A taxi from the centre costs RM15.

Visitors Information Centre (Map p384; ☑082-410942, 082-410944; www.sarawaktour ism.com; Jln Tun Abang Haji Openg, Sarawak Tourism Complex; ☺8am-5pm Mon-Fri) Located in the atmospheric old courthouse complex, this office has helpful and well-informed staff, lots of brochures (including the useful *Kuching Visitors Guide*) and oodles of practical information (eg bus schedules), much of it on bulletin boards.

Sarawak Tourism Federation (Map p384; ☑082-240620; www.stf.org.my; Waterfront Promenade; ☺8am-5pm Mon-Fri, closed public holidays) This is mainly an administrative office for local tourism professionals but Priscilla is happy to help travellers with questions.

ℹ Getting There & Away

As more and more Sarawakians have acquired their own wheels, public bus networks – especially short-haul routes in the Kuching area – have withered. For complicated political reasons, some services have been 'replaced' by unregulated and chaotic minibuses, which have irregular times, lack fixed stops and are basically useless for tourists.

The only way to get to many nature sites in Western Sarawak is to hire a taxi or join a tour. The exceptions are Bako National Park, Semenggoh Nature Reserve, Kubah National Park, Matang Wildlife Centre and, somewhat less conveniently, the Wind Cave and the Fairy Cave.

Air

Kuching International Airport, 12km south of the city centre, has direct air links with Singapore, Johor Bahru (the Malaysian city across the causeway from Singapore), Kuala Lumpur (KL), Penang, Kota Kinabalu (KK), Bandar Seri Begawan (BSB) and Pontianak.

MASwings, a subsidiary of Malaysia Airlines, is basically Malaysian Borneo's very own domestic airline. Flights link its hubs in Miri and Kuching with 14 destinations around Sarawak, including the lowland cities of Sibu, Bintulu, Limbang and Lawas and the upland destinations of Gunung Mulu National Park, Bario and Ba Kelalan.

The airport has three departure halls: 'Domestic Departures' for flights within Sarawak; 'Domestic Departures (Outside Sarawak)' for travel to other parts of Malaysia; and 'International Departures'.

Inside the terminal, there's a **Tourist Information Centre** (Arrival level, Kuching International Airport; ☺9am-10pm) next to the luggage carrousels and customs. Foreign currency can be exchanged at the **CIMB Bank counter** (Arrival level, Kuching International Airport; ☺7.30am-7.30pm) but rates are poor. Places with **free wi-fi** include Starbucks and McDonald's. Among the **ATMs** there is one in front of McDonald's. To buy a Celcom SIM Card, head to the **Blue Cube kiosk** (Departure level). For ticketing issues, drop by the **Malaysian Airlines & MASwings office** (Departure level, Kuching International Airport; ☺5am-8pm).

Those overweight kilos can be shipped to airports around Malaysia at the **Excess Baggage counter** (☑014-287 3330; Next to Departure Hall B, Kuching International Airport; ☺7.30am-8.30pm). One kilo costs RM3.50 to Sibu, Bintulu and Miri and RM6.50 to RM8.50 to KL (minimum weight: 10kg).

Boat

Ekspress Bahagia (☑in Kuching 016-889 3013, 082-412246, in Sibu 016-800 5891, 319-228) runs a daily express ferry from Kuching's Express Wharf, 6km east of the centre, to Sibu. Departures are at 8.30am from Kuching and at 11.30am from Sibu (RM45, five hours). It's a good idea to book a day ahead. A taxi from town to the wharf costs RM25.

Bus

Every half-hour or so from about 6am to 6.30pm, various buses run by City Public Link (eg K9) and STC (eg 3A, 4B, 6 and 2) link central Kuching's Saujana Bus Station with the Regional Express Bus Terminal. Saujana's ticket windows can point you to the next departure. A taxi from the city centre costs RM28 to RM30.

KUCHING SENTRAL This massive **bus terminal-cum-shopping mall** (cnr Jln Penrissen & Jln Airport), opened in 2012, handles almost all of Kuching's medium- and all long-haul routes. Situated about 10km south of the centre, it's also known as Six-and-a-Half-Mile Bus Station. Amenities include electronic departure boards and cafes offering wi-fi. Book your ticket at a company counter, then pay at counter 2 or 3 (marked 'Cashier/Boarding Pass'). Before boarding, show your tickets to the staff at the Check-In desk.

TO CENTRAL SARAWAK From 6.30am to 10.30pm, a dozen different companies send buses at least hourly along Sarawak's northern coast to Miri (RM80, 14½ hours), with stops at Sibu (RM50, 7½ hours), Bintulu (RM70, 11½ hours), Batu Niah Junction (jumping-off point for Niah National Park) and Lambir Hills National Park. Bus Asia, for instance, has nine departures a day, the first at 7.30am, the last at 10pm; unlike its competitors, the company has a **city centre office** (Map p384; ☑082-411111; cnr Jln Abell & Jln Chan Chin Ann; ☺6am to 10pm) and, from Monday to Saturday, runs shuttle buses out to Kuching Sentral. Luxurious 'VIP buses', eg those run by **Asia Star** (☏1300-888 287; http://asiastar.my), have just three seats across (28 in total), and some come with on-board toilets, and yet cost a mere RM10 to RM20 more than regular coaches. To get to Brunei, Limbang or Sabah, you have to change buses in Miri.

TO WESTERN SARAWAK Buses to the Semenggoh Wildlife Centre, Bako National Park, Kubah National Park and the Matang Wildlife Sanctuary stop at or near Saujana Bus Station. Buses to Lundu (including the Wind Cave and Fairy Cave) use Kuching Sentral.

Taxi

For some destinations, the only transport option – other than taking a tour – is chartering a taxi through your hotel or guesthouse or via a company such as Kuching City Radio Taxi (p400). Hiring a red-and-yellow cab for an eight-hour day should cost about RM250, with the price depending in part on distance; unofficial taxis may charge less. If you'd like your driver to wait at your destination and then take you back to town, count on paying about RM20 per hour of wait time.

Listed below is a sample of one-way taxi fares from Kuching (prices are 50% higher at night):

Destination	Fare
Annah Rais Longhouse	at least RM80
Bako Bazaar (Bako National Park)	RM40
Express Wharf (ferry to Sibu)	RM25
Fairy Cave	RM40 (including Wind Cave and three hours wait time: RM170)
Kubah National Park	RM50
Matang Wildlife Centre	RM60
Santubong Peninsula Resorts	RM50
Sarawak Cultural Village	RM50
Semenggoh Nature Reserve	RM40 (round-trip including one hour wait time RM90 to RM100)
Wind Cave	RM40

ⓘ Getting Around

Almost all of Kuching's attractions are within easy walking distance of each other so taxis or buses are only really needed to reach the airport, Kuching Sentral (the long-haul bus terminal), the Express Wharf for the ferry to Sibu and the Cat Museum.

To/From the Airport

The price of a red-and-yellow taxi into Kuching is fixed at RM26, including luggage; a larger *teksi eksekutif* (executive taxi), painted blue, costs RM35. Coupons are sold inside the terminal next to the car-rental counters.

Boat

Bow-steered wooden boats known as *tambang*, powered by an outboard motor, shuttle passengers back and forth across Sungai Sarawak, linking jetties along the Waterfront Promenade with destinations such as Kampung Boyan (for Fort Margherita) and the Astana. The fare for Sarawak's cheapest cruise is 50 sen (more from 10pm to 6am); pay as you disembark. If a *tambang* isn't tied up when you arrive at a dock, just wait and one will usually materialise fairly soon.

Bus

Saujana Bus Station (Map p384; Jln Masjid) handles local and short-haul routes. Situated in the city centre on the dead-end street that links Jln Market with the Kuching Mosque. Three companies use the Saujana Bus Station:

City Public Link (☏082-239178) Has a proper ticket counter with posted schedules. Line numbers start with K. Urban services run from 6.30am or 7am to about 5.30pm. Buses K3 and K10 go to Kuching Sentral (the long-distance bus station) several times an hour.

Sarawak Transport Company (STC; ☏082-233579) The ticket window is in an old shipping container. Buses 2 and 3A go to Kuching Sentral (2A) about three times an hour. Bus 2 to Kuching's Sarawak General Hospital and Bau is run in conjunction with **Bau Transport Company**.

Bicycle

On Jln Carpenter, basic bicycle shops can be found at Nos 83, 88 and 96. Borneo Experiences (p390) can rent out bicycles for RM30 per day.

Car

Not many tourists rent cars in Sarawak. The reasons: road signage is not great; even the best road maps are a useless 1:900,000 scale; and picking up a vehicle in one city and dropping it off in another incurs hefty fees. That said, having your own car can be unbelievably convenient.

Before driving off, make sure the car you've been assigned – some companies rent out vehicles that have seen better days – is in good shape mechanically and has all the requisite safety equipment (eg seat belts).

Half-a-dozen car-rental agencies have desks in the arrivals hall of Kuching Airport, including:

Ami Car Rental (☏082-427441, 082-579679; www.amicarrental.com)

Flexi Car Rental (☏082-452200, 082-335282, emergency 24hr 019-886 5282; www.flexicarrental.com)

Golden System (☎082-333609, 082-611359; www.goldencar.com.my) We've had good reports on this outfit.

Hertz (☎082-450740; www.hertz.com) Backed by an international reputation.

Motorbike

Renting a motorbike can be a great way to visit Kuching-area sights – provided you know how to ride, your rain gear is up to scratch and you manage to find your way despite the poor signage. Borneo Experiences (p390) have motorbikes for daily rent: RM40 for 100cc and RM50 for 125cc.

An Hui Motor (Map p384; ☎016-886 3328, 082-412419; 29 Jln Tabuan; ⊙8am-6pm Mon-Sat, 8am-noon Sun) A motorbike repair shop that charges RM30 per day for a Vespa-like Suzuki RG (110cc) or RGV (120cc) and RM40 for a 125cc scooter (including helmet), plus a deposit of RM100. Insurance covers the bike but not the driver and may be valid only within a 60km radius of Kuching, so check before you head to Sematan, Lundu or Annah Rais. Situated next to Ting & Ting supermarket.

Taxi

Kuching now has two kinds of taxis: the traditional red-and-yellow kind; and the larger, more comfortable – and pricier – executive taxis (*teksi eksekutiv*), which are painted blue.

Taxis can be hailed on the street, found at taxi ranks (of which the city centre has quite a few, eg at larger hotels) or ordered by phone 24 hours a day from:

ABC Radio Call Service (☎016-861 1611, 082-611611)

Kuching City Radio Taxi (☎082-348898, 082-480000)

T&T Radio Call Taxi (☎016-888 2255, 082-343343)

All Kuching taxis - except those on the flat-fare run to/from the airport (RM26) – are required to use meters; overcharging is not common so taking a taxi is only rarely an unpleasant experience. Flag fall is RM10; after the first 3km (or, in traffic, nine minutes of stop-and-go) the price is RM1.20 per km or for each three minutes. There's a RM2 charge to summon a cab by phone. Fares go up by 50% from midnight to 6am. One-way taxi fares from central Kuching:

Cat Museum (North Kuching)	RM20 to RM25
Indonesian consulate	RM25 to RM30
Kuching Sentral	(long-distance bus terminal) RM28 to RM30
Visa Department	RM15

WESTERN SARAWAK

From Tanjung Datu National Park at Sarawak's far western tip to Bako National Park northeast of Kuching, and inland to Annah Rais Longhouse and the Batang Ai Region, western Sarawak offers a dazzling array of natural sights and indigenous cultures. Most places listed below are within day trip or overnight distance of Kuching.

Bako National Park

Occupying a jagged peninsula jutting into the South China Sea, Sarawak's oldest **national park** (☎at Bako Bazaar 082-431336, at park HQ 082-478011; www.sarawakforestry.com; adult RM20; ⊙park office 8am-5pm) is just 37km northeast of downtown Kuching but feels like it's worlds away. It's one of the best places in Sarawak to see rainforest animals in their native habitats.

The coast of the 27-sq-km peninsula has lovely pocket beaches tucked into secret bays interspersed with wind-sculpted cliffs, forested bluffs and stretches of brilliant mangrove swamp. The interior of the park is home to streams, waterfalls and a range of distinct ecosystems, including classic lowland rainforest (mixed dipterocarp forest) and *kerangas* (heath forest). Hiking trails cross the sandstone plateau that forms the peninsula's backbone and connect with some of the main beaches, all of which can be reached by boat from park HQ.

Bako is notable for its incredible biodiversity, which includes almost every vegetation type in Borneo and encompasses everything from terrestrial orchids and pitcher plants to long-tailed macaques and bearded pigs. The stars of the show are the proboscis monkeys – this is one of the best places in Borneo to observe these endemics up close.

Bako is an easy day trip from Kuching, but it would be a shame to rush it – we recommend staying a night or two to really enjoy the wild beauty of the place. Getting to Bako by public transport is easy.

◉ Sights & Activities

Interpretation Centre   MUSEUM

Offers an old-fashioned introduction to the park's seven distinct ecosystems and an exposé of the co-dependent relationship between nepenthes (pitcher plants) and ants. There are plans to move the centre to the new HQ building.

Around Kuching

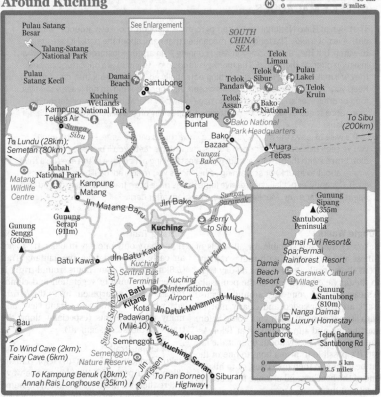

Wildlife Watching

Scientists estimate that Bako is home to 37 species of mammal, including silver-leaf monkeys, palm squirrels and nocturnal creatures such as the mouse deer, civet and colugo (flying lemur); 24 reptile species, among them the common water monitor, which can reach a length of over 1m; and about 190 kinds of bird, some of them migratory.

Jungle creatures are easiest to spot shortly after sunrise and right before sunset, so for any real wildlife watching you'll have to stay over. Surprisingly, the area around park HQ is a particularly good place to see animals, including reddish-brown proboscis monkeys, whose pot-bellied stomachs are filled with bacteria that help them derive nutrients from almost-indigestible vegetation. You often hear them as they crash through the branches long before seeing a flash of fur – or a male's pendulous nose flopping as he munches on tender young leaves.

Proboscis monkeys, who show little fear of, or interest in, humans, can often be found: on branches above the park's visitors chalets; around the mangrove boardwalk between the jetty and park HQ; in the trees along the Telok Assam Beach near park HQ; along the Telok Paku Trail, where they forage in the trees lining the cliff; and along the Telok Delima Trail.

The muddy floors of mangrove forests are home to an assortment of peculiar creatures, including hermit crabs, fiddler crabs and mudskippers (fish that spend much of their time skipping around atop the tidal mud under mangrove trees).

The Bornean bearded pigs that hang around near the cafeteria and chalets with their piglets are a big hit with kids. Not long ago a tourist guide was overheard commenting, 'at the longhouse they would be on the grill already!'

CHEEKY MACAQUES

That sign at Bako National Park's campground – 'Naughty monkeys around – watch out!' – is not a joke. The long-tailed macaques that hang about the park HQ are great to watch, but they are mischievous and cunning – an attitude fostered by tourists who insist on offering them food. The monkeys (and some tourists) are opportunists, and they will make running leaps at anything potentially edible they think they can carry off. Keep your room's doors and windows closed, zip your bags and do not leave valuables, food or drink – or anything in a plastic bag (known by macaques as the preferred human repositories for edibles) – unattended, especially on the beaches or on the chalet verandahs.

It's wise to leave the monkeys in peace – the males can be aggressive, and once you've seen a macaque tear open a drink can with his teeth you'll be happy that you didn't mess with them. Rangers advise against looking a macaque in the eye (he'll think you're about to attack) or screaming (if he knows you're scared, he'll be more aggressive). Recently, especially aggressive large males have been tranquilised, captured and released far, far away. Monkeys are not a problem after dark.

Jungle Walks

Bako's 17 trails are suitable for all levels of fitness and motivation, with routes ranging from short strolls to strenuous all-day treks to the far (ie eastern) end of the peninsula. It's easy to find your way around because trails are colour-coded and clearly marked with stripes of paint. Plan your route before starting out and aim to be back at Telok Assam before dark, ie by about 6pm at the latest. It's possible to hire a boat to one of the far beaches and then hike back, or to hike to one of the beaches and arrange for a boat to meet you there.

Park staff are happy to help you plan your visit, provide updates on trail conditions and tides, help with boat hire and provision you with a B&W map that has details on each of the park's hiking options. A billboard near the Education Centre lists conservative time estimates for each trail. Even if you know your route, let staff know where you'll be going so that they can inscribe you in the Guest Movement Register Book; sign back in when you return.

Take adequate water and be prepared for intense sun (with a sun hat and sunscreen) as the *kerangas* (distinctive vegetation zone of Borneo), has precious little shade for long stretches. Sun-sensitive folks might consider lightweight long-sleeve shirts and trousers. Mozzie repellent is a good idea as well.

A note on trail names: *bukit* means hill, *tanjung* means point, *telok* means bay, *pantai* means beach and *ulu* means upriver or interior.

Lintang Trail   HIKING

If you have only one day in Bako, try to get an early start and take the Lintang Trail (5.8km, 3½ to four hours round-trip). It traverses a range of vegetation and climbs the sandstone escarpment up to the *kerangas,* where you'll find some grand views and many pitcher plants (especially along the trail's northeastern segment).

Telok Limau Trail   HIKING

Bako's longest trail goes to Telok Limau, 13km from park HQ (8½ hours one-way), where there's a nice beach and a designated camping area. Consider hoofing it one way and taking a boat the other (RM164 for up to five people). Cellphone coverage is often available from the slopes above the beach but don't count on being able to coordinate with your boatman by mobile.

Swimming

At Bako, it's easy to combine rainforest tramping, which quickly gets hot and sweaty, with a refreshing dip in the South China Sea.

Stinging jellyfish can sometimes be a nuisance, especially in April and May. Also to be avoided, especially around Telok Paku: stingrays, whose stabs can be quite painful. To keep away the sandflies on the beach, use mozzie repellent.

The muddy, tannin-stained waters of Bako's rivers shelter crocodiles, so forget about taking a dip. A few years ago a schoolboy was eaten by a croc a bit upriver from Bako Bazaar; his body was never found.

Telok Assam Beach — BEACH
Swimming is allowed at the beach near park HQ but the water can be muddy. In the distance (to the west) you can see the wild east coast of the Santubong Peninsula.

Telok Pandan Beaches — BEACH
The gorgeous beach at **Telok Pandan Kecil**, a 2.6km walk from park HQ, is surrounded by spectacularly colourful sandstone formations. Pitcher plants can be seen on the trail down to the beach. Around the point (to the northwest) is the famous **Bako Sea Stack**, an islet that looks like a cobra rearing its head. To get close enough for a photo, though, you'll have to hire a boat.

As you move east, the next beach you come to is **Telok Pandan Besar**, a quiet, attractive stretch of sand accessible only by boat. Hiring a boat at park HQ costs RM40/80 one-way/return.

Telok Sibur Beach — BEACH
The rarely visited beach at Telok Sibur is accessible on foot (it's 5.5km from park HQ) but hard to reach as the descent is steep and you have to make your way through a mangrove swamp. Before heading out, check the tidal schedule with park staff to make sure the river won't be too deep to cross, either going or returning. A boat from park HQ costs RM105/210 one-way/return.

Telok Limau Beach — BEACH
At the park's northeastern tip, Telok Limau is 13km on foot from park HQ. A boat to/from Telok Limau and the nearby island of **Pulau Lakei**, which has a white-sand beach and the grave of a Malay warrior, costs RM164 one-way.

Telok Kruin Beach — BEACH
At the peninsula's far eastern tip, this bay is 12km on foot from park HQ; a boat ride all the way around Telok Limau costs RM250 one-way.

Nightwalk — WILDLIFE WATCHING
(per person RM10; ☺8pm) The best way to see creatures that are out and about at night – we're talking spiders, fireflies, cicadas, frogs, anemones, owls and the like – is to take a night-time walk led by a park ranger trained in spotting creatures that city slickers would walk right by. Reviewed by one traveller as 'awesome', Bako's 1½- to two-hour night treks, when available, are not to be missed. Bring a torch (flashlight).

 Tours
Park HQ does not have enough permanent staff to accompany individual visitors, so if you'd like to hike with a guide, enquire at the boat terminal in Bako Bazaar or, better yet, ask the National Park Booking Office in Kuching for the phone numbers of approved guides. The park is very strict about allowing only certified guides (unlicensed guides and the groups they're with are forced to leave). Kuching travel agencies charge about RM230 per person for a tour, including the boat ride.

🛏 Sleeping
Bako has developed a reputation for less-than-adequate accommodation but by the time you read this, the new hostel should be open and at least some of the chalets upgraded. There's a RM10 key deposit. Unlocked storage is available at park reception free of charge.

In-park accommodation often fills up, especially from June to October, so if you'd like to stay over book ahead:
» Online via http://ebooking.com.my
» By email (npbooking@sarawaknet.gov.my)
» By phone or in person through the National Park Booking Office in Kuching
» By phoning the park (only after 5pm Monday to Friday and on weekends and holidays)

Some travel agencies reserve blocks of rooms that they release a week ahead if their packages remain unsold, and individual travellers also sometimes cancel, so week-before and last-minute vacancies are far from unknown.

Forest Hostel — HOSTEL $
(dm RM15.90, 4-bed r RM42) The new hostel, made of concrete, will have a private bathroom in each simply-furnished, three-bed room. Bring your own towel and a top sheet (bottom sheets are provided).

Forest Lodge Type 5 — CHALET $$
(3-bed r RM106, 2-room chalet RM159) Each two-room (six-bed) chalet, two of which are being upgraded, has one bathroom and one fridge. Fan-equipped.

Forest Lodge Type 6 — CHALET $
(d RM53, 2-room chalet RM79.50) Each rustic, two-bed room has a wood-plank floor, private bathroom, fridge and fan.

Camping

CAMPGROUND $

(per person RM5) Because of 'naughty monkeys', tents can be set up at park HQ's fenced-in camping zone only after 6pm and must be taken down during the day. You can also pitch your tent in the park's far eastern reaches at Sibur, Kruin and Limau Beaches and on Pulau Lakei.

✖ Eating

Cooking is not allowed in park accommodation. The canteen charges RM0.50 for boiling water to prepare instant noodles. The nearest grocery is in Bako Bazaar.

Canteen

CAFETERIA $

(3-dish buffet meal approx RM8.50; ⊙7.30am-10pm) The new cafeteria, designed to be macaque-proof, serves a varied and tasty selection of fried rice, chicken, fish, hot dogs and cooked veggies. Buffet meals are available from 11.30am to 2pm and 6.30pm to 8pm.

❶ Getting There & Away

Getting to the park by public transport is a cinch. First take one of the hourly buses from Kuching to Bako Bazaar, then hop on a motorboat to Telok Assam jetty, about 400m along a wooden boardwalk from park HQ.

Park HQ and some other parts of the park have (low-power) mobile-phone coverage, ideal for coordinating your boat ride back to Bako Bazaar. At HQ, Celcom customers may have to head to the beach to get reception.

Boat

Motorboat hire (Bako Bazaar dock; ⊙8am-4pm) from Bako Bazaar dock, where visitors pay their park entry fee, to park HQ costs RM94 return; the journey takes about 20 minutes. Each vessel can carry up to five people; assemble a quintet to optimise cost-sharing. If you don't plan to return at the same time as your boat-mates, the fee for the return leg (RM47) may have to be split among a smaller number of passengers. If you link up with other travellers at the park and share a boat back to Bako Bazaar, your return voucher – valid whether you come back the same day or overnight at the park – is theoretically reimbursable. Changing your return time is easy: just phone your boatman's mobile phone (it's a good idea to note his boat number as well).

Most day trippers try to get back to Bako Bazaar by 4.15pm to catch the 4.30pm bus to Kuching (the 5.30pm bus is not 100% reliable). Note: buses have been known to leave a few minutes before their scheduled departure times.

When the tide is low, boats may not be able to approach the jetty at Telok Assam so you may have to wade ashore. Boatmen may insist on an early afternoon return time to beat a late afternoon low tide – but bold outboard jockeys have been known to make the trip back to Bako Bazaar even at the lowest of tides.

From late November to February or March, the sea is often rough.

Bus

Bright red bus 1 (RM3.50) leaves from 6 Jln Khoo Hun Yeang in Kuching (in front of Toko Minuman Jumbo buffet restaurant), right across the street from the food stalls of the Open-Air Market. Departures from Kuching are every hour on the hour 7am to 5pm, and from Bako Bazaar every hour on the half-hour from 6.30am to (usually) 5.30pm. If you miss the last bus, ask around the village for a minibus or private car (RM40) to Kuching.

In Kuching, bus 1 also picks up passengers at stops along the waterfront, on the river side of the street; motion to the driver to stop. These include bus shelters on Jln Gambier across the street from the Brooke Memorial; across the street from 15 Main Bazaar, next to the Chinese Museum; on Jln Tunku Abdul Rahman next to the 7-Eleven in the Riverside Suites; and on Jln Abell in front of Alliance Bank, a block northwest of the Lime Tree Hotel.

Taxi

A cab from Kuching to Bako Bazaar (45 minutes) costs RM40.

Santubong Peninsula

Like Bako National Park 8km to the east, the Santubong Peninsula (also known as Damai) is a 10km-long finger of land jutting out into the South China Sea. The main drawcards are the longhouses of the Sarawak Cultural Village, some beaches, jungle walks, a golf course and a great seafood restaurant in the fishing village of Kampung Buntal. Santubong is the best place in Sarawak for a lazy, pampered beach holiday.

◉ Sights & Activities

Sarawak Cultural Village　ECO-MUSEUM

(SCV; ☑082-846411; www.scv.com.my; adult/child 6-12yr RM60/30, cultural show 45 minutes; 11.30am & 4pm; ⊙9am-5.15pm, last entry 4pm) This living museum is centred on seven traditional dwellings: three Dayak longhouses (including a Bidayuh headhouse with skulls and the only Melanau tallhouse left in Sarawak), a Penan hut, a Malay townhouse (the only place you have to remove your shoes) and a

Chinese farmhouse. It may sound contrived and even hokey but the SCV is held in high esteem by locals for its role in keeping their cultures and traditions alive.

The dwellings are (supposed to be) staffed by members of the ethnic group they represent – except the Penan dwelling, that is, whose emissaries, true to their nomadic tradition, went walkabout. Signage, however, is poor, so if you don't ask questions of the 'locals' – who demonstrate crafts and cookie-making – the subtle differences in architecture, cuisine, dress and music between the various groups may not be apparent. At the Penan hut you can try a blowpipe (RM1 for three darts), while the Malay townhouse offers top spinning (three spins for RM1).

Twice a day, the **cultural show** showcases traditional music and dance. The lively Melanau entry involves whirling women and clacking bamboo poles, while the Orang Ulu dance (spoiler alert!) includes four women, several balloons and a blowpipe hunter.

It may be possible to book workshops (RM5 per person per hour) in handicrafts (eg bead-making), music and dance – contact the SCV in advance. If you're planning to get married, you can choose to tie the knot here with a colourful Iban, Bidayuh, Orang Ulu or Malay ceremony.

Hotels and tour agencies in Kuching offer packages (per person RM125), but it's easy enough to get out here by shuttle bus. The SCV is a short walk from both the Damai Beach Resort and the Permai Rainforest Resort.

Permai Rainforest Resort　　　BEACH
(☑082-846490; www.permairainforest.com; Damai Beach; adult/child RM5/2) The day rate at this bungalow complex is a real bargain. In addition to a safe, fine-sand beach with changing facilities, a variety of leisure and adventure activities are on offer, including a high-ropes course (per person RM60), a perfectly vertical climbing wall (RM48), sea kayaking (RM80 for three hours) and mountain biking (RM10 per hour). Great for tweens and teens.

Damai Beach Resort　　　BEACH
(www.damaibeachresort.com; Teluk Bandung, Santubong) Access to the hotel's lovely beach costs just RM2. For RM119 two adults and two children can have daytime (10am to 6pm) room access and can use the resort's wealth of facilities, including the pool.

Damai Central Beach　　　BEACH
A free beach with places to eat, situated across the parking lot from the Sarawak Cultural Village. From 10am to 7pm, amenities include showers (RM2), towel rental (RM5) and lockers (RM3).

Jungle Walks　　　HIKING
Several trails take you into the jungle interior of the peninsula, declared a national park in 2007. One, a challenging route with red trail markings, ascends towering **Gunung Santubong** (880m); the last bit is pretty steep, with steps and rope ladders, so it takes about three hours up and two hours down. A few recent climbers have gotten lost and stranded after dark so whatever happens start heading down by about 2pm. The peak – which some people want to make accessible by cable car – features in a variety of local ghost stories related to a princess captured by a prince.

Another trail, an easy-to-moderate circular walk (3km, two hours) with blue markings, passes by a pretty **waterfall**.

These trails can be picked up at two points along the main road to the beach resorts: at Bukit Puteri and, about 2km north, at Green Paradise Seafood, which tries to charge entry fees, a procedure currently being investigated by the government.

The east side of the peninsula – the coast you can see from Bako National Park – is wild and undeveloped, with a profusion of wildlife. Ask locals about how to get there on foot from the Permai Rainforest Resort and the main road to Kuching, or you can hire a boat in Kampung Buntal.

☞ Tours

Coastal areas west and east of the Santubong Peninsula are home to a wide variety of wildlife. Oft-spotted species include endangered Irrawaddy dolphins (known locally as *pesut*), proboscis monkeys, estuarine crocodiles and all manner of birds.

Resorts on the peninsula, and guesthouses and tour agencies in Kuching, can make arrangements, or you can contact:

CPH Travel　　　BOAT
(☑in Kuching 082-243708; www.cphtravel.com.my; Damai Puri Resort & Spa) Offers boat trips, including cruises through the Kuching Wetlands National Park.

Mr Ehwan bin Ibrahim BOAT
(☎019-878 5088; Kampung Buntal) A local boatman who offers three-hour dolphin-and-mangrove tours (per person for two/four people RM180/155) and four- or five-hour fishing trips that include a swimming stop at remote Polycarp Beach (RM500 for two people).

🛏 Sleeping

Many resorts allow children to stay in parents' rooms for no extra charge. Kampung Santubong has about 15 homestays. It's possible to camp at the Permai Rainforest Resort.

Permai Rainforest Resort BUNGALOW $$
(☎082-846490, 082-846487; www.permairainforest.com; Damai Beach; 6-bed longhouse RM260, 6-bed cabin RM305, 2-bed tree house RM300, camping per person RM15; @🖢) This lushly forested bungalow complex, on a beach-adjacent hillside, hosts macaques and silver-leaf monkeys in addition to paying guests. Accommodation ranges from rustic, simply furnished cabins to air-con wooden bungalows towering 6m off the ground. Offers plenty of outdoor activities. Prices drop from Sunday to Thursday.

Damai Beach Resort RESORT $$$
(☎082-846999; www.damaibeachresort.com; Teluk Bandung, Santubong; d incl breakfast from RM440; ❋@🖢🏊) A great getaway for families, this 252-room beach resort has enough activities and amenities to make you feel like you're on a cruise ship (in a good way), including boat excursions, sea kayaking (RM15 to RM20 per hour) and even an 18-hole **golf course** (www.damaigolf.com) designed by Arnold Palmer.

Nanga Damai Luxury Homestay B&B $$
(☎019-887 1017; www.nangadamai.com; Jln Sultan Tengah, Santubong; d incl breakfast RM100-160; ❋@🏊) The lovely living room, cosy chill-out verandah, 8m kidney-shaped pool and bright, comfortable rooms (six in total) make it easy to meet the two-night minimum stay. Not suitable for children under 16. The Kuching-Santubong shuttles pass by here.

Santubong Homestay HOMESTAY $
(☎013-895 1245, 082-846773; niesa0619@gmail.com; House 207, Kampung Santubong; per person RM30, with lunch RM40, with lunch & dinner RM40) Sauji and Mariah rent out three rooms in their home, one with attached bath. Homey and tranquil. Great value.

🍴 Eating

All the resorts have restaurants. At the Sarawak Cultural Village, the **restaurant** (meal RM7-10) serves a buffet of Sarawakian dishes.

TOP
CHOICE **Lim Hock Ann Seafood** SEAFOOD $$
(Kampung Buntal; mains RM8-20, fish per kg RM39-85; ⊙11am-2pm & 5-10pm, closed Mon lunch) A sprawling, open-air shed on stilts with a wide-plank floor and a tin roof, this classic Chinese-style seafood restaurant is in Kampung Buntal, a fishers' village 11km southeast of the SCV (on the east coast of the base of the peninsula). The fresh, locally landed fish is superb.

Damai Central HAWKER $
Across the parking lot from the Sarawak Cultural Village, this attractive new complex has several restaurants, a 7-Eleven and a food court (mains RM5 to RM8).

ℹ Getting There & Away

Minibus

Kuching is linked to the Santubong Peninsula (45 minutes) by the slow K15 bus (RM4) from Saujana Bus Station and minibuses operated by two companies:

Setia Kawan (☎019-825 1619; adult/child under 12yr RM10/5) Has departures from Kuching's waterfront every two hours from 7.15am to 10pm; stops include the Singgahsana Lodge (p390), which can take bookings; the Harbour View Hotel; and the Hilton, whose concierge is the go-to guy. Minibuses set off from the peninsula's Permai Rainforest Resort depart between 9am and 9pm.

Damai Beach Resort (☎082-380970, 082-846999) Has departures from Kuching's Grand Margherita Hotel and Riverside Majestic Hotel four times a day between 10.15am and 6.15pm; if possible, book a day ahead. The last run back to Kuching leaves the Damai Beach Resort at 5.15pm.

Taxi

A cab from Kuching to the SCV or the resorts costs RM50 to RM60 (RM70 from the airport).

Kuching Wetlands National Park

The only way to see the majestic mangroves of 66-sq-km Kuching Wetlands National Park is – as you would expect – by boat. Situated about 15km northwest of Kuching (as the crow flies), the park doesn't have a HQ complex, just low-lying islands and saline waterways lined with salt-resistant trees that provide food and shelter to proboscis monkeys, silver-leaf monkeys and fireflies (above the water line); estuarine crocodiles and amphibious fish called mudskippers (at the water line); and countless varieties of fish and prawns (below the water line). Nearby open water is one of the finest places in Sarawak to spot snub-nosed Irrawaddy dolphins.

The morning (about 9am) is the best time to see the dolphins, while late-afternoon cruises are optimal for sighting a flash of reddish-brown fur as proboscis monkeys leap from tree to tree in search of the tenderest, tastiest young leaves. Sunset on the water is magical – and unbelievably romantic, especially if your guide points out an *api-api* tree (a 'firefly tree', surrounded by swirling green points of light). After dark, by holding a torch up at eye level, you can often spot the reflections of animalian eyes, including – if you're lucky – a crocodile, its reptilian brain wholly focused on biting, drowning and then devouring its next warm-blooded victim.

Tours

Packages include transfers from and to your hotel. Boats usually set sail from the Sarawak Boat Club or Telaga Air.

CPH Travel Boat   BOAT
(☑in Kuching 082-243708; www.cphtravel.com. my) Has a near-monopoly on boats heading to the wetlands. Offers a mangrove and Irrawaddy dolphin sighting cruise (RM140 per person) at 8.30am and a wildlife cruise (RM160) at 4.30pm.

Semenggoh Nature Reserve

One of the best places in the world to see semi-wild orang-utans in their natural jungle habitat, swinging from trees and scurrying up vines, the **Semenggoh Wildlife Centre** (☑082-618325; www.sarawakforestry.com; ⊗8am-5pm), can be visited on a half-day trip from Kuching or combined with visit to Annah Rais Longhouse and/or Kampung Benuk.

Situated within the 6.8-sq-km Semenggoh Nature Reserve, the centre is home to 25 orang-utans: 11 who were rescued from captivity or orphaned and their 14 Semenggoh-born offspring, some mere babes-in-arms who spend their days hanging onto their mother's shaggy chests. Four of the tree-dwelling creatures are completely wild (ie find all their own food), but the rest often swing by (literally) park HQ to dine on bananas, coconuts, eggs and – though they don't know it – medications. There's no guarantee that any orang-utans, the world's largest tree-dwelling animal, will show up, but even in fruiting season (late November or December to February or March) the chances are excellent. Semenggoh is noticeably less touristy (and much cheaper) than Sepilok Orang-utan Rehabilitation Centre in Sabah.

Hour-long feedings, in the rainforest a few hundred metres from park HQ, run from 9am to 10am and from 3pm to 4pm. When the feeding session looks like it's over, rangers sometimes try to shoo away visitors (especially groups, whose guides are in any case eager to get back to Kuching), but orang-utans often turn up at park HQ, so don't rush off straightaway if everything seems quiet.

For safety reasons, visitors are asked to stay at least 5m from the orang-utans – the animals can be unpredictable – and are advised to keep a tight grip on their backpacks, water bottles and cameras because orang-utans have been known to snatch things in search of something yummy. To avoid annoying – or even angering – the orang-utans, do not point at them with anything that looks like a gun (eg a walking stick); do not scream or make sudden movements; and, when you take pictures, do not use flash.

Semenggoh Nature Reserve has two beautiful trails that pass through primary rainforest: the **Masing Trail** (Main Trail; red trail markings; 30 minutes), which links the HQ with the highway; and the **Brooke's Pool Trail** (yellow and red trail markings), a 2km loop from HQ. At research time both were closed because of attacks on staff and visitors by two particularly aggressive orang-utans, Ritchie and Delima ('Hot Mama'), whom rangers guess were mistreated in captivity. When the trails reopen, it should be possible to hire a guide at the Information Centre for RM30 per hour (for up to 10 people). Tickets are valid for the whole day so it's possible to come for the morning feeding, visit a longhouse, and then see the afternoon feeding as well. Note: there's nowhere in the park to buy food.

ℹ️ Getting There & Away

Two bus companies provide reliable public transport from Kuching's Saujana Bus Station to the park gate, which is 1.3km down the hill from park HQ (RM3, 45 minutes):

City Public Link – bus K6 departs from Kuching at 7.15am, 10.15am, 1pm and 3.30pm, and from Semenggoh (spelled 'Semenggok' on bus schedules) at about 8.30am, 11.15am, 2.15pm and 4.30pm.

Sarawak Transport Company – bus 6 has Kuching departures at 7am and 1pm; buses back pass by Semenggoh at about 9.45am and 3.45pm.

A taxi from Kuching costs RM45 one-way or RM90 to RM100 return, including one hour of wait time. Tours are organised by Kuching guesthouses and tour agencies.

Kampung Benuk

This quiet, flowery **Bidayuh village** (adult RM6), where the loudest sound is often the crowing of a cock, attracted lots of tourist back when the road ended here. These days, it gets relatively few visitors, despite being a pleasant place to spend a few hours.

The traditional, 32-door **longhouse** (Lg 5), with bouncy bamboo common areas, is still home to a few families, though most of the villagers now live in attractive modern houses. In the **barok** (ritual hall), you can see about a dozen head-hunted skulls, bone-white but tinged with green, hanging from the rafters; pick up the key at the reception office. And at the end of the lane, about 100m beyond the *barok*, the widow of the village shaman runs a **mini-museum** (donation requested; ⊙9am-5pm Mon-Sat) filled with all sorts of interesting bric-a-brac, including ceramic rice jars, monkey skulls, blow-dart pipes and two WWII helmets, one British, the other Japanese.

🛏️ Sleeping

Kurakura Homestay   HOMESTAY $$
(☎012-892 0051; www.kurakura.asia; per person incl meals RM160) Run by Norwegian-born Lars and his Bidayuh wife Liza, this superfriendly, sustainable jungle homestay occupies a wooden house built in 2008 on land that once belonged to her grandfather. Activities include kayaking and trekking (RM165 for an all-day outing). Situated 20 minutes to 40 minutes by boat from the village of Kampung Semadang. Rates include transport to and from Kuching or the Kuching Airport.

Annah Rais Longhouse

Although this Bidayuh longhouse has been on the tourist circuit for decades, it's still an excellent place to get a sense of what a longhouse is and what longhouse life is like.

The 500 residents of **Annah Rais** (adult/student RM8/4) are as keen as the rest of us to enjoy the comforts of modern life – they do love their mobile phones and 3G internet access – but they've made a conscious decision to preserve their traditional architecture and the social interaction it engenders. They've also decided that welcoming modern tourists is a good way to earn a living without moving to the city, something most young people end up doing.

◉ Sights & Activities

Longhouse Veranda   NOTABLE BUILDING
Once you pay your entry fee (in an eight-sided wooden pavilion next to the parking lot), you're free to explore Annah Rais' three longhouses (Kupo Saba, Kupo Terekan and, across the river, Kupo Sijo) with a guide or on your own.

The most important feature of a Bidayuh longhouse is the *awah*, a long, covered common verandah – with a springy bamboo floor – that's used for economic activities, socialising and celebrations. Along one side, a long row of doors – Annah Rais has a total of 97 – leads to each family's private *bilik* (apartment). Paralleling the *awah*, opposite the long row of doors, is the *tanju*, an open-air verandah.

Headhouse   NOTABLE BUILDING
Whereas the Iban traditionally hung hunted heads outside each family's *bilik*, the Bidayuh grouped theirs together in the community's *panggah* or *baruk* (communal meeting hall). The heads are no longer believed to protect the village – these days the people of Annah Rais are almost all Anglican (the Bidayuh of Kalimantan are mainly Catholic) – but about a dozen smoke-blackened human skulls still have pride of place in the headhouse, suspended over an 18th-century Dutch cannon. It is said that in some longhouses, a few old people still remember the name of each of the heads.

🛏️ Sleeping

Annah Rais is a peaceful, verdant spot to chill out. Half-a-dozen families run homestays with shared bathrooms, either in one of the three longhouses or in an adjacent detached house. Standard rates, agreed upon by the community, are RM98 per person for accommodation and delicious Bidayuh board, and RM298 per person – a bit much, perhaps – for a package that includes activities such as trekking, rafting, fishing, (mock) blowgun hunting, soaking in a natural hot spring and a dance performance.

Emily & John Ahwang　　　HOMESTAY $$
(☑Emily 010-977 8114, John 016-855 2195; http://22.
com.my/homestay) Emily and John, both of whom speak fluent English, love to welcome guests to their spotless, modern, two-storey home, built right into the longhouse.

Akam Ganja　　　HOMESTAY $$
(☑010-984 3821; winniejagig@gmail.com) It's a pleasure to be hosted by Akam, a retired forestry official, and his wife Winnie, an English teacher, at their comfortable detached house on the riverbank.

❶ Getting There & Away

Annah Rais is about 40km south of Kuching. A taxi from Kuching costs RM80 one-way.

A variety of Kuching guesthouses and tour agencies offer four-hour tours to Annah Rais (per person RM115, including Semenggoh Nature Reserve RM140).

Kubah National Park

Mixed dipterocarp forest, among the lushest and most threatened habitats in Borneo, is front and centre at this 22-sq-km national park (☑082-845033; www.sarawakforestry.com; admission incl Matang Wildlife Centre RM20; ☺8am-5pm), which more than lives up to its clunky motto, 'the home of palms and frogs'. Scientists have found here an amazing 98 species of palm, out of 213 species known to live in Sarawak; and they have identified 61 species of frog and toad

(www.frogsofborneo.org), out of Borneo's more than 190 species. In 2012 researchers identified what they believe to be a new species of frog, adding it to a list that includes the aptly-named (but oddly shaped) horned frog and a flying frog that can glide from tree to tree thanks to the webbing between its toes. Kubah's jungles are also home to a wide variety of orchids – and seven semi-wild orang-utans.

Kubah's trails are much more shaded than those at Bako National Park, making the park ideal for the sun-averse. And when you're hot and sweaty from walking, you can cool off under a crystal-clear waterfall.

❂ Sights & Activities

Rainforest Trails　　　HIKING
When you pay your entry fee, you'll receive a hand-coloured schematic map of the park's four interconnected trails (two other trails were closed as of mid-2012). They're well-marked so a guide isn't necessary. The park has about half-a-dozen rain shelters – keep an eye out for them so you'll know where to run in case of a downpour.

The **Selang Trail** (40 minutes to 60 minutes; trail-marked in yellow), linking the **Main Trail** (trail-marked in white) with the short segment of the **Rayu Trail** that's still open, passes by the **Selang Viewpoint**. Offshore you can see the turtle sanctuary of Pulau Satang.

The concrete-paved **Summit Road** (closed to non-official traffic), also known as the **Gunung Serapi Summit Trail**, runs along the park's southeastern edge from park HQ right up to the top of Kubah's highest peak, **Gunung Serapi** (911m), which holds aloft a TV and telecom tower; on foot, it's 3½ hours up and a bit less coming down. As you ascend, notice that the mix of trees and plants (including pitcher plants and ferns) changes with the elevation. The summit is often

SARAWAK KUBAH NATIONAL PARK

GETTING TO INDONESIA: KUCHING TO PONTIANAK

Getting to the border A variety of bus companies ply the route between Kuching's Kuching Sentral bus terminal (and other cities along the Sarawak coast) and the west Kalimantan city of Pontianak (economy RM60, 1st class RM80, seven/10 hours via the new/old road), passing through the Tebedu-Entikong crossing 80km south of Kuching.

At the border Travellers from 64 countries can get a one-month Indonesian visa on arrival at the road crossing between Tededu (Malaysia) and Entikong (Indonesia), the only official land border between Sarawak and Kalimantan.

Moving on Pontianak is linked to other parts of Indonesia and to Singapore by airlines such as Batavia Air (www.batavia-air.com).

shrouded in mist but near the top there's a viewing platform. When it's clear, there are stupendous views all the way from Tanjung Datu National Park on the Indonesian border (to the northwest) to Gunung Santubong and Kuching (to the east).

The **Waterfall Trail** (3km or 1½ hours from HQ one-way; trail-marked from the Summit Road in blue) passes by wild durian trees and *belian* trees, otherwise known as 'ironwood' (*Eusideroxylon zwageri*). This incredibly durable – and valuable, and thus endangered – tropical hardwood was traditionally used in longhouse construction. As you would expect, this trail ends at a waterfall and a natural swimming pool.

Some visitors combine the Selang Trail and the Waterfall Trail to create a circuit that takes four to six hours. It is no longer possible to walk to the Matang Wildlife Centre because of the risks posed by semi-wild orang-utans.

Natural Frog Pond　　　　WILDLIFE RESERVE
Situated 300m above sea level and about a half-hour's walk from park HQ, this artificial pool provides a breeding ground for numerous frog species. The delicate amphibians are especially active an hour or so after sunset (from about 8pm to 11pm), particularly when it's raining hard (during the day most prefer to hide in a hole in a tree), so the only way to see them is to overnight at the park. Bring a good flashlight. It may be possible to hire a ranger as a guide.

Palmetum　　　　GARDENS
A labelled palm garden near park HQ, on the Main Trail.

🛏 Sleeping

Kubah is a lovely spot to kick back and relax. The attractive chalets, which have a total of 74 beds, can be booked online through http://ebooking.com.my, by email (npbooking@sarawaknet.gov.my), through the National Park Booking Office in Kuching, or by calling the park office. There's usually space, even on weekends, except on public and school holidays. A **camping ground** (per person RM5) is being constructed.

Forest Lodge Type 4　　　　CHALET **$$**
(6-bed chalet RM225; ❄) These bi-level, all-wood chalets come with a balcony, a sitting room, a shower with enough room for two, a two-bed room and a four-bed room.

Forest Lodge Type 5　　　　CHALET **$**
(10-bed chalet RM150) Has a living room with couch and chairs, a dining table with a lazy Susan, and three bedrooms with a total of 10 beds. Fan-cooled.

Forest Hostel　　　　HOSTEL **$**
(dm RM15) Has 12 beds. Fan-cooled.

🍴 Eating

All accommodation options come with fully equipped kitchens, including a fridge, toaster and burners. There are plans to open a canteen (cafeteria) in the new HQ building but as of press time there was nowhere to buy food so bring all you'll need.

ℹ Getting There & Away

Kubah National Park is 25km northwest of Kuching. A taxi from Kuching costs RM50.

From Kuching's Saujana Bus Station, bus K21 to the Politeknik stops on the main road 400m from park HQ, next to the Kubah Family Park (RM4, one hour). Departures from Kuching are at 8am, 11am, 2pm and 4.30pm, and from the Politeknik, situated 2km beyond (ie north) of Kubah, at 6.30am, 9.30am, 12.30pm and 3.30pm.

MATANG WILDLIFE CENTRE

Situated at the western edge of Kubah National Park, the **Matang Wildlife Centre** (📞082-374869; www.sarawakforestry.com; admission incl Kubah National Park RM20; ⏱8am-5pm, last entry 3.30pm) has had remarkable success rehabilitating rainforest animals rescued from captivity, especially orang-utans and sun bears. The highly professional staff do their best to provide their abused charges with natural living conditions on a limited budget, but there's no denying that the centre looks like a low-budget zoo plopped down in the jungle. Because of the centre's unique role, it's home to endangered animals that you're unlikely to see anywhere else in Sarawak.

⊙ Sights & Activities

Interpretation Centre　　　　VISITORS CENTRE
Most of the display panels illustrate orang-utan rehabilitation. Inside the new HQ building.

Rescued Animals　　　　WILDLIFE RESERVE
Some of the creatures here were orphaned, some were confiscated and others were surrendered by the public. Unless they're needed as evidence in court, all are released as soon as possible – unless they lack survival skills, in which case returning them to the

wild would be a death sentence, either because they'll starve or because, having lost their fear of humans, they're liable to wander into a village and get eaten. (Unless it's a Malay village, that is – Malays, as Muslims, do not consume most rainforest animals).

Among the most celebrated residents of Matang is Aman, one of the largest male orang-utans in the world. Known for his absolutely massive cheek pads, he hit the headlines in 2007 when he became the first of his species to undergo phacoemulsification (cataract surgery). The procedure ended 10 years of blindness, though it did nothing to restore his tongue, removed after he chomped into an electric cable, or his index finger, bitten off by a rival dominant male.

Matang is home to three bearcats (binturongs), two of them females, that are too old to be releases. This extraordinary tree-dwelling carnivore, whose closest genetic relative is the seal or walrus, can tuck away a fertilised egg for months and perhaps years, delaying pregnancy until sufficient fruit is available (the trick is called embryonic diapause).

Other animals that live here include two clouded leopards and nine of the happiest captive sun bears in the world. In horrific condition when brought here, they are undergoing a rehabilitation program that's the first of its kind anywhere.

One of Matang's rarest creatures is the false (Malayan) gharial, the most endangered of the 16 species of crocodile. Easily identifiable thanks to its long, thin snout, scientists estimate that only about 2500 are left in the wild.

Rare birds that live here include a buffy (Malay) fish owl, a changeable (crested) hawk-eagle, a white-bellied sea eagle and a confiscated mallard duck (an exotic in these parts!) who's taken to following around a lesser adjutant stork, thinking perhaps that it's his mother.

Many of the centre's caged animals are fed from 9am to 10am.

Trails
HIKING

The **Animal Enclosure Trail** (8.30am-3.30pm) takes visitors through the jungle past animals' enclosures and cages. The 15-minute **Special Trail**, where you can see pitcher plants, is wheelchair accessible. If they've got time, rangers are happy to guide visitors around.

The Pitcher Nature Trail and the Rayu Trail to Kubah National Park are closed because of the risk of attacks by semi-wild orang-utans.

Volunteering
VOLUNTEERING

(2/4 weeks incl food & lodging US$2048/2984) For details on paid volunteering – nothing glamorous: we're talking hard physical labour – contact the **Great Orangutan Project** (www. orangutanproject.com) or, at the park, **Leo Biddle** (☑013-845 6531). In keeping with best practice, volunteers have zero direct contact with orang-utans because proximity to people (except a handful of trained staff) will set back their rehabilitation by habituating them to humans.

🛏 Sleeping

You can stay in a longhouse-style **Forest Hostel** (4-bed room RM40) with fan and attached bathroom, a spacious, two-room **Type 5 Forest Lodge** (chalet RM150; ❄) that sleeps eight, or a **campground** (per person RM5) equipped with open-air rain shelters (no need to bring a tent, just a mossie net and sheets or a sleeping bag). Book accommodation by phone, online via http://ebooking.com.my or at the National Park Booking Office in Kuching.

🍴 Eating

At research time there was no place to buy food, so bring your own. Cooking is forbidden in park accommodation but an electric kettle, great for making instant noodles, is available on request.

❶ Getting There & Away

Matang is about 33km northwest of Kuching. By the new road, it is 8km from Kubah National Park HQ. A taxi from Kuching costs RM60 one-way.

Bus K21 from Kuching's Saujana Bus Station to the Politeknik stops near the park entrance. Departures from Kuching are at 8am, 11am, 2pm and 4.30pm.

Bau & Environs

About 26km southwest of Kuching, the one-time gold-mining town of Bau is a good access point to two interesting cave systems and some Bidayuh villages.

WIND CAVE NATURE RESERVE

Situated 5km southwest of Bau, the **Wind Cave** (Gua Angin; ☑082-765472; admission RM5; ◷8.30am-4.30pm) is essentially a network of underground streams. Unlit boardwalks in the form of a figure eight run through the caves, allowing you to wander along the three main passages (total length: 560m) with chittering bats (both fruit- and insect-eating) swooping overhead.

Near HQ, 300m from the cave entrance, you can cool off with a refreshing swim in the waters of Sungai Sarawak Kanan; changing rooms are available.

Flashlights/torches are available for rent (RM3) – if you get a feeble one, ask to exchange it. No food is sold at the reserve itself, though there is a drinks stand.

ⓘ Getting There & Away

To get from Bau to the Wind Cave turn-off (a 1km walk from the cave), take Bus Transport Company (BTC) bus 3 or 3A – they depart about hourly from 7.40am to 5pm except from 1pm to 3pm.

A taxi from Kuching costs RM40 one-way, or RM170 return including the Fairy Cave and three hours of wait time. A tour from Kuching to both caves costs about RM125 per person.

FAIRY CAVE

About 9km southwest of Bau, the **Fairy Cave** (Gua Pari Pari; admission free; ⊙24hr) – almost the size of a football pitch and as high as it is wide – is an extraordinary chamber whose entrance is 30m above the ground in the side of a cliff; access is by staircase. Outside, trees grow out of the sheer rock face at impossible angles. Inside, fanciful rock formations, covered with moss, give the cavern an otherworldly aspect, as do the thickets of ferns straining to suck in every photon they can.

Cliff faces near the Fairy Cave, many rated 6a to 7a according to the UK technical grading system, are popular with members of Kuching's friendly rock climbing community, especially on Saturday and Sunday. The sheer white cliff 300m back along the access road from the cave has three easy routes and about 15 wall routes with bolts. Nearest the cave is the Tiger Wall; nearby routes include the Orchid Wall and the Batman Wall. For information on guided rock climbing, contact **Outdoor Treks** (http://bikcloud.com/rock ropes.htm).

ⓘ Getting There & Away

To get from Bau to the Fairy Cave turn-off (a 1.5km walk from the cave), take BTC bus 3A, which runs five times a day.

From Kuching, a taxi to the Fairy Cave costs RM40 one-way, or RM170 return including the Wind Cave and three hours of wait time. A tour from Kuching to both caves costs about RM125 per person.

TRINGGUS & GUNUNG BENGOH

Inland from Bau, most of the population is Bidayuh. Unlike their distant relations on the eastern side of the Bengoh (Bungo) Range – that is, in the area around Padawan and Annah Rais – the Bau Bidayuh have never lived in longhouses. The area's Bidayuh speak a number of distinct dialects.

Tour agencies in Kuching can arrange treks into the valleys around **Gunung Bengoh** (966m) – including the fabled **Hidden Valley** (aka Lost World) – either from the Bau side or the Padawan side. Kuching's Borneo Experiences (p390), for instance, runs treks to the remote and very traditional Bidayuh longhouse community of **Semban**, where a few old ladies still sport brass ankle bracelets. A three-day, two-night trip, including transport, food and a guide, costs RM700/600 per person in a group of two/five.

Tringgus Bong, the furthest-inland of the three Bidayuh hamlets known collectively as Tringgus, has a delightful **homestay** (per person incl food RM60) in House 392; for details, call **Baon** (☎012-882 9489). At the confluence of two burbling streams, facing a hillside pineapple patch and reached by a traditional wood-and-bamboo bridge, this paradisiacal corner of Borneo is a great place to get away from it all. The nearest Indonesian village, across the border in Kalimantan, is just two or three hours away on foot.

Two vans link Bau with Tringgus (RM4) four times a day until the early afternoon – for details, call **Baon** (☎012-882 9489) or **Bayin** (☎014-579 7814).

SEEING MOUNTAINS FROM THE INSIDE

Many of Sarawak's limestone hills are as filled with holes as a Swiss cheese. Boardwalks let you stroll around inside the Wind Cave, the Fairy Cave and the caverns of Niah National Park and Gunung Mulu National Park, but to get off the beaten track you need an experienced guide – someone like UK-born James, who runs **Kuching Caving** (☎012-886 2347; www.kuchingcaving.com). He knows more than almost anyone about the 467 cave entrances that have been found within two hours of Kuching, the longest of which is 11km. For an all-day caving trip, prices start at RM200 per person (minimum four).

Getting There & Away

Bau is 43km southwest of Kuching. The town is linked to Kuching's Saujana Bus Station (RM4.50, 1½ hours) by City Public Link bus B2 (hourly) and also by bus 2 (every 40 minutes), run jointly by Bau Transport Company (BTC) and Sarawak Transport Company (STC).

Lundu

The quiet town of Lundu, an overgrown fishing village about 55km west of Kuching, is the gateway to Gunung Gading National Park.

The road north out of town leads not only to Gunung Gading National Park but also to two beaches that are popular with Kuchingites on weekends and holidays. Romantic, coconut palm-fringed **Pantai Pandan**, 11km north of Lundu, is one of Sarawak's nicest beaches (despite the sandflies), with a gentle gradient that's perfect for kids. A few beachfront huts sell eats and drinks. Camping is possible. **Pantai Siar**, 8km north of Lundu, is home to several small resorts that appeal mainly to the domestic market.

Otto Steinmayer, an American-born literature professor who lives in – and loves – Lundu, has an interesting website, www. ikanlundu.com.

Sleeping

Retreat TOP CHOICE RESORT $$
(082-453027; www.sbeu.org.my; Pantai Siar; Sun-Fri/Sat chalet from RM158/248; ❄️📶🏊) Owned by the Sarawak Bank Employees Union, this is the ideal place to mix chilling on the beach with workers' solidarity. The grassy, family-friendly campus has 38 comfortable rooms, including 21 chalets, and gets enthusiastic reviews from travellers. Day use of the pool costs RM15/5 for adults/children; the beach itself is free. Situated 8km from Lundu.

Lundu Gading Hotel HOTEL $
(082-735199; 174 Lundu Bazaar; d RM60; ❄️) Few hotels have less style sense than Lundu's only hostelry, whose 10 rooms sport blue-tile floors, brightly coloured towels, big windows and peeling ceilings. Situated diagonally across the street from the RHB Bank.

Eating

Happy Seafood Centre SEAFOOD $
(mains from RM4.50; 7am-8pm) A very informal, open-air eatery with surprisingly good fish. Facing the bus station.

Fruit & Vegie Market HAWKER CENTRE $
(mains RM4; 8am-5pm) Chinese and Malay dishes are available upstairs. Situated across the grassy triangular square from the bus station.

Malay Night Market FOOD STALLS $
(5-10pm) Supposed to move from the Fruit & Vegie Market to the riverfront.

Getting There & Away

Buses run by the Sarawak Transport Company (STC) link Kuching Sentral long-haul bus station (counter 20) with Lundu (RM12, 1½ hours); departures in both directions are at 8am, 11am, 2pm and 4pm.

At the Lundu bus station, it's possible to hire a private car (RM5 per person) to take you to Gunung Gading National Park or Sematan.

Gunung Gading National Park

The best place in Sarawak to see the world's largest flower, the renowned rafflesia, **Gunung Gading National Park** (082-735144; www.sarawakforestry.com; adult RM20; 8am-5pm) makes a fine day trip from Kuching. Its old-growth rainforest covers the slopes of four mountains (*gunung*) – Gading, Lundu, Perigi and Sebuloh – traversed by well-marked walking trails that are great for day hikes. The park is an excellent spot to experience the incredible biodiversity of lowland mixed dipterocarp forest, so named because it is dominated by a family of trees, the Dipterocarpaceae, whose members are particularly valuable for timber and thus especially vulnerable to clear-cutting.

The star attraction at 41-sq-km Gunung Gading is the *Rafflesia tuan-mudae*, a species that's endemic to Sarawak. Up to 75cm in diameter, they flower pretty much year-round but unpredictably, so to see one you'll need some luck. To find out if a Rafflesia is in bloom – something that happens here with human knowledge only about 25 times a year – and how long it will stay that way (never more than five days), contact the park or call or visit the National Park Booking Office in Kuching.

Sights & Activities

A variety of well-marked, often steep trails lead through the lush jungle. Park signs give *one-way* hike times. Except when instructed otherwise by a ranger, keep to the trails to avoid crushing Rafflesia buds underfoot.

Don't count on seeing many animals as most species found here are nocturnal and wisely prefer the park's upper reaches, safely away from nearby villages.

Since these hikes must be done in one day (camping is permitted only at park HQ), you might want to arrive the day before to facilitate an early morning start.

Rafflesia Loop Trail
WALKING
(RM30 per hour for a group of up to 10) This 620m-long trail, which begins 50m down the slope from park HQ, goes through a stretch of forest that Rafflesias find especially convivial. Since most of the blooms are off the path, finding them requires hiring a ranger.

Hiking Circuit
HIKING
For views of the South China Sea, you can follow a circuit that incorporates the **Viewpoint Trail** (follow the red-and-yellow stripes painted on trees), the **Lintang Trail** (red stripes) and the **Reservoir Trail** (a cement stairway).

Gunung Gading
HIKING
Trekking up Gunung Gading (906m; trail-marked in red and yellow after Waterfall 7) takes seven to eight hours return, but don't expect panoramic views – the summit is thickly forested so you'll see mainly the bottom of the rainforest canopy. Somewhere atop the mountain are the ruins of a British army camp used during the Konfrontasi. At **Batu Berkubu** (10 to 12 hours return; trail-marked in red and blue), you can see a communist hideout from the same period.

Waterfalls
SWIMMING
Three lovely cascades are easily accessible along the **Main Trail** (market in red and white). You can take a dip at **Waterfall 1**, **Waterfall 7** (1.5km from park HQ) and the **swimming hole**, fed by a crystal-clear mountain stream, at the beginning of the Rafflesia Loop Trail.

🛏 Sleeping & Eating

The busiest times are weekends, school holidays and when a Rafflesia is blooming. Bookings can be made online via http://ebooking.com.my, or by phone or in person through the National Park Booking Office in Kuching. Nearby Lundu has one hotel.

The **hostel** (dm/r RM15/40) has four fan rooms, each with four beds, and shared bathroom facilities. Each of the two three-

bedroom **Forest Lodges** (RM150; ❄) sleeps up to six people. **Camping** (per person RM5) is possible at the park HQ, a bathroom-equipped site.

A canteen (cafeteria) is supposed to open soon inside the new park HQ building. Cooking is permitted in the chalets and the hostel. Another culinary option: driving or strolling about 2.5km to Lundu.

ℹ Getting There & Away

Gunung Gading National Park is 85km northwest of Kuching.

Four public buses a day link Kuching Sentral long-distance bus station with Lundu, but from there you'll either have to walk north 2.5km to the park, or hire an unofficial taxi (about RM5 per person).

A tour from Kuching costs about RM230 per person including lunch (minimum two people) – for a group, that's much more than chartering a taxi for the day (about RM250).

Sematan

The quiet fishing town of Sematan, Sarawak's westernmost town, serves as the gateway to Tanjung Datu National Park. The nearby Indonesian border – yes, those forested mountains are in Kalimantan – is not (yet) open to tourists.

◉ Sights & Activities

A grassy north-south **promenade** lines the waterfront, where a concrete **pier** affords wonderful views of the mouth of the river, its sand banks and the very blue, very clear South China Sea. The deserted beaches of **Telok Pugu**, a narrow spit of land across the mouth of the Sematan River from Sematan's jetty, can be reached by boat (RM30 return).

At the northern end of the row of stores facing the waterfront, check out the shop called **Teck Huat** (shops 1, 2 & 3), which hasn't changed in over a century. Built of *belian*, it still has wooden shutters instead of windows.

The sands of shallow **Pantai Sematan**, clean and lined with coconut palms, stretch along the coast northwest of town. It is home to several resorts that fill up with Kuchingites on the weekends.

🛏 Sleeping

Sematan Hotel
HOTEL $
(☑ 013-828 1068, 082-711162; 162 Sematan Bazaar; d RM50; ❄) The nine very basic rooms, all upstairs, have tile floors and rudimentary

furnishings. Bathrooms are attached but lack hot water. Situated 150m inland from the six columns on the waterfront. If no one's around, look for the owner in the Seaview Cafe across the street.

ⓘ Getting There & Away

Sematan is 107km northwest of Kuching, 25km northwest of Lundu and 30km (by sea) from Tanjung Datu National Park.

Buses link Kuching's Regional Express Bus Terminal but from there you'll have to catch a ride with locals or hire an unofficial taxi (about RM30 one-way) at the bus station.

Tanjung Datu National Park

Occupying a remote, rugged peninsula at Sarawak's far northwestern tip, this 14-sq-km national park (www.sarawakforestry.com; adult RM20) features endangered mixed dipterocarp rainforest, jungle trails that hear few footfalls, crystal-clear seas, unspoilt coral reefs and near-pristine white-sand beaches on which endangered turtles occasionally lay their eggs. Few visitors make the effort and brave the expense to travel out here, but those who do often come away absolutely enchanted.

The park has four trails, including the Telok Melano Trail from the Malay fishing village of Telok Melano (a demanding 2.7km), linked to Sematan by boat; and the Belian Trail, which goes to the summit of 542m-high Gunung Melano (2km, one hour) and affords breathtaking views of the coastlines of Indonesia and Malaysia. To spot nocturnal animals, you can take a night walk on your own or with a ranger (it's good form to tip him RM20).

Snorkelling (but not scuba diving) is allowed in certain areas; details are available at park HQ. Bring your own equipment, including water shoes (the coral can be sharp).

Celcom and Digi (but not Maxis) cellphone signals can be picked up about 15 minutes' walk from park HQ, along the beach.

Recent travellers report encountering giant stinging bees.

🛏 Sleeping & Eating

Park HQ offers four basic guest rooms (d/tr RM40/55) with electricity from 6pm to midnight and four open-sided, electricity-less shelters (per person RM15), each with space for three people. Blankets, sheets and mozzie nets are available for RM15. There's no way to book ahead – just show up.

For details on homestays (per person incl board RM70 to RM80) in Telok Melano, a steep, 2½-hour walk from park HQ, contact the National Park Booking Office in Kuching or ask around at the Sematan jetty.

Visitors must bring their own food. Cooking equipment can be rented for RM10 a day; cooking gas costs RM5.

ⓘ Getting There & Away

The only way to get to Tanjung Datu National Park or the nearby village of Telok Melano, both about 30km northwest of Sematan, is by boat (one to 1½ hours). Weather and waves permitting, locals often (but not necessarily every day) pile into a motorboat and head from Telok Melano to Sematan early in the morning, returning in the early afternoon (around 2pm or 3pm). If you join them, expect to pay RM30 to RM40 per person one-way. Sea conditions are generally good from February or March or October. The rest of the year (especially December), the sea can be rough, so much so that on some days boats don't run. Walking to Telok Melano – the only other way to get there – takes a full day.

Motorboats with room for five to eight people, either for a day trip (RM450 return) or an overnight (RM500 return), can be hired at the Sematan jetty for travel either to the park or to Telok Melano. To find a boatman, ask around the jetty or call or email Eric Yap at the Fairview Guesthouse (☑013-801 1561; www.thefairview.com.my; Kuching).

You can also arrange trips through the Fisheries Development Authority (Persatuan Nelayan Kawasan Sematan/Lundu; ☑082-711152; for Rosdin Mawi deenazy@yahoo.com.my; Jln Bauxite, Sematan; ⊙8am-5pm Mon-Fri). From the jetty, walk 100m south and a bit inland; the office is upstairs.

Talang-Satang National Park

Sarawak's first marine park (www.sarawakforestry.com), established in 1999 to protect four species of marine turtle, consists of the coastline and waters around four islands: the two Pulau Satang, known as *besar* (big) and *kecil* (small), which are 16km west of the Santubong Peninsula; and, 45km to the northwest, the two Pulau Talang-Talang, also *besar* and *kecil*, situated 8km due north of Sematan Beach.

Once every four or five years, female marine turtles swim vast distances – sometimes thousands of kilometres – to lay their eggs on the exact same beach where they themselves hatched. Of every 20 turtles that come ashore in Sarawak to lay eggs, 19 do so on a beach in 19.4-sq-km Talang-Satang National Park. But of the 10,000 eggs a female turtle may lay over the course of her life, which can last 100 years, only one in a thousand is likely to survive into adulthood. To increase these odds, park staff patrol the beaches every night during the egg-laying season (mainly June and July, with fewer in August and a handful in April, May and September) and either transfer the eggs to guarded hatcheries or post guards to watch over them *in situ*.

Snorkelling and diving are permitted but only within certain designated areas, and divers must be accompanied by an approved guide.

PULAU SATANG

While the national park's conservation area is managed by Sarawak Forestry, the islands themselves are the property of a family from Telaga Air – their 999-year lease, granted by the last White Rajah, Charles Vyner Brooke, expires in the year 2945. About 100 cousins now share ownership, but day-to-day management has devolved to Abol Hassan Johari, a retired accountant who lives in Telaga Air and is much more interested in conservation and research than in tourists. His family retains customary rights to the turtles' eggs but these are 'sold' to the state government and the money donated to an orphanage.

The larger of the two islands, 1-sq-km **Pulau Satang Besar**, has a fine beach and a small wooden shelter. Lucky overnight visitors can sometimes watch fragile eggs being moved from the beach to a hatchery and, possibly, witness baby turtles being released into the wild.

Abol's resolutely non-commercial approach to the island, and the exigencies of conservation, mean that while you can theoretically overnight on Pulau Satang Besar, which is 14km northwest of Telaga Air, you probably can't as green turtles, hawksbill turtles, olive ridley turtles, leatherback turtles, researchers and students (in that order) are given priority.

PULAU TALANG-TALANG

The two Pulau Talang-Talang, accessible from Sematan or as a stop on the boat trip from Sematan to Tanjung Datu National Park, can be visited only during the day. You're allowed to land but swimming is forbidden within the core protected zone (anywhere within a 2km radius of the islands' highest point).

ı With the park's **Sea Turtle Volunteer Programme** (4 days & 3 nights RM2850; ☉Jun-Sep), paying volunteers can stay on Pulau Talang-Talang Besar and help the staff of the Turtle Conservation Station patrol beaches, transfer eggs to the hatchery and even release hatchlings. For details, contact the National Park Booking Office in Kuching; booking is through Kuching-based tour agents such as Borneo Adventure (p390).

ⓘ Getting There & Away

The easiest way to visit the islands is to book a tour with a Kuching-based agency or to contact Eric Yap at Kuching's **Fairview Guesthouse** (✆082-240017; www.fairview.my), who has connections up and down the coast.

Day-trip charters (RM400 per person) to Pulau Satang can be arranged through tour agencies. Boats usually set out from the coastal villages of Telaga Air, 10km northeast (as the crow flies) from Kubah National Park.

If you hire a boat to get from Sematan to Telok Melano or Tanjung Datu National Park (RM450 return), you can arrange with the boatman to stop at Pulau Talang-Talang for an additional fee of RM10 per person. Hiring a boat for a day trip from Sematan costs RM250.

BATANG AI REGION

Ask anyone in Kuching where to find old-time longhouses – that is, those least impacted by modern life – and the answer is almost always the same: Batang Ai, many of whose settlements can only be reached by boat. This remote region, about 250km (4½ hours by road) southeast of Kuching, is not really visitable without a guide, but if you're genuinely interested in encountering Iban culture, the money and effort to get out here will be richly rewarded.

Managed with the help of an Iban community cooperative, the 240-sq-km **Batang Ai National Park** (www.sarawakforestry.com) is part of a vast contiguous area of protected rainforest that includes the Batang Ai Reservoir (24 sq km), Sarawak's Lanjak Entimau Wildlife Sanctuary (1688 sq km) and, across the border in West Kalimantan, Betung Kerihun National Park (8000 sq km). The park's dipterocarp rainforests have the highest density of wild orang-utans in central

Borneo (sightings are not guaranteed but are not rare either), and are also home to gibbons (more often heard than seen), langurs and hornbills.

Trips to the Batang Ai region can be booked in Kuching, either through a tour operator or with a freelance guide.

CENTRAL SARAWAK

Stretching from Sibu, on the lower Batang Rejang, upriver to Kapit and Bintulu and northeastward along the coast to Bintulu and Miri, Sarawak's midsection offers some great river journeys, fine national parks and modern urban conveniences.

Sibu

POP 255,000

Gateway to the Batang Rejang, Sibu has grown rich from trade with Sarawak's interior since the time of James Brooke. These days, although the 'swan city' does not rival Kuching in terms of charm, it's not a bad place to spend a day or two before or after a boat trip to the wild interior.

Situated 60km upriver from the open sea, Sibu is Sarawak's most Chinese city. Many of the two-thirds of locals who trace their roots to China are descendents of migrants who came from Foochow (Fujian or Fuzhou) province in the early years of the 20th century. The city was twice destroyed by fire, in 1889 and 1928. Much of Sibu's modern-day wealth can be traced to the timber trade.

◎ Sights

Strolling around the city centre (roughly, the area bounded by Tua Pek Kong Temple, Wisma Sanyan, Sibu Gateway and the Li Hua Hotel) is a good way to get a feel for Sibu's fast-beating commercial pulse. Drop by the tourist office for a brochure covering the new **Sibu Heritage Trail**.

Features of architectural interest include the old **shophouses** around the Visitors Information Centre, eg along Jln Tukang Besi, and the old **Rex Cinema** (Map p418; Jln Ramin), where art deco meets shophouse functionality.

Tua Pek Kong Temple　　　　　TEMPLE
(Map p418; Jln Temple; ◎6.30am-8pm) Established sometime before 1871 and damaged by Allied bombs in 1945, this colourful riverfront temple incorporates both a Taoist hall

on the ground floor, and a Chinese Buddhist sanctuary on the 1st floor. For a brilliant view over the town and up and down the muddy Batang Rejang, climb the seven-storey **Kuan Yin Pagoda**, built in 1987; the best time is sunset when a wheeling swirl of swiftlets buzzes the tower at eye level. Ask English-speaking Mrs Lee, at the ground-floor desk, for the key; as you ascend, don't forget to lock the gate behind you.

Sibu Heritage Centre　　　　　MUSEUM
(Map p418; Jln Central; ◎9am-5pm, closed Mon & public holidays) Housed in a gorgeously airy municipal complex built in 1960, this excellent museum explores the captivating history of Sarawak and Sibu. Panels, rich in evocative photographs, take a look at the various Chinese dialect groups, Sarawak's communist insurgency (1965-90), Sibu's Christian (including Methodist) traditions, and even local opposition to Sarawak's incorporation into Malaysia in 1963. Don't miss the photo of a 1940s street dentist – it's painful just to look at.

Rejang Esplanade　　　　　PARK
(Map p418; Jln Maju; ◎24hr) One of Sibu's 22 community parks – most donated by Chinese clan associations – this pleasant strip of riverfront grass affords views of the wide, muddy river and its motley procession of fishing boats, tugs, timber-laden barges and 'flying coffin' express boats.

Lau King Howe Memorial Museum MUSEUM
(Jln Pulau; ◎9am-5pm, closed Mon) One glance at this medical museum's exhibits and you'll be glad saving your life never required the application of early-20th-century drills, saws and stainless-steel clamps – or the use of a ferocious gadget called a 'urological retractor'. Another highlight: an exhibit on the evolution of local nurses' uniforms that some visitors may find kinky. Situated about 500m northwest of Wisma Sanyan.

Bawang Assan Longhouse Village　　　　　LONGHOUSE
An Iban village one hour downstream from Sibu (by road the trip takes just 40 minutes), Bawang Assan has nine 'hybrid' longhouses (ie longhouses that combine traditional and 21st-century elements). To stay here without going through a Sibu-based tour company, contact the **Bawang Assan Homestay Programme** (☑014-582 8105; http://ibanlonghouse stay.blogspot.com; per person incl 3 meals RM110); ask for Marcathy Gindau, who can often be

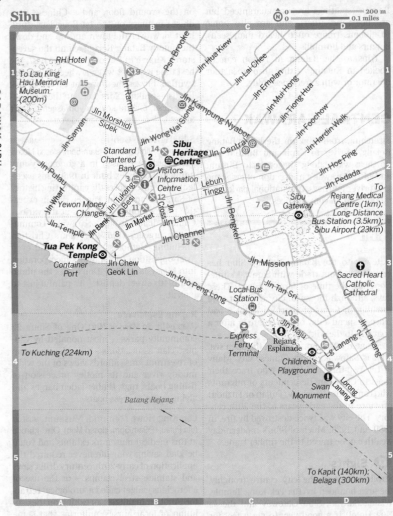

found in Sibu at the **Lehdo Inn** (Map p418; ☎084-331894; 21 Jln Tukang Besi). To arrange transport by van, call **Mr Broken** (☎019-836 1134).

☞ Tours

Two well-regarded Sibu-based travel agencies offer tours of the city and visits to sights both upriver and down.

Greatown Travel TOUR
(☎084-211243, 084-219243; www.greatowntravel.com; No 6, 1st fl, Lg Chew Siik Hiong 1A) Offers longhouse stays (eg at Bawang Assan and in the

Kapit area), visits to the 'Melanau heartland' around Mukah, and various other trips lasting three to six days. Staff are happy to tailor-make bespoke itineraries. Its office is about 1km northeast of the centre along Jln Pedada.

Great Holiday Travel TOUR
(☎084-348196; www.ghtborneo.com; No 23, 1st fl, Pusat Pedada, Jln Pedada) Based out near the long-distance bus station, this outfit can organise half-day walking tours of Sibu, a day trip or overnight to Bawang Assan Longhouse Village, and two-day trips up to the Kapit area. Reasonably priced.

Sibu

⊙ Top Sights
Sibu Heritage Centre	B2
Tua Pek Kong Temple	A3

⊙ Sights
1	Rejang Esplanade	C4
2	Rex Cinema	B2

🛏 Sleeping
3	Lehdo Inn	B2
4	Li Hua Hotel	D4
5	Premier Hotel	C2
6	River Park Hotel	D4
7	Tanahmas Hotel	C2

⊗ Eating
8	Café Café	B3
9	Islamic Nyonya Kafé	B1
10	Kopitiam	C4
	New Capitol Restaurant	(see 5)
11	Night Market (Chinese Stalls)	B2
12	Night Market (Malay Stalls)	B2
13	Sibu Central Market	B3
14	Vegetarian Food Stall	B2

⊙ Drinking
Queen	(see 8)

⊙ Shopping
	Public Book Store	(see 15)
15	Wisma Sanyan	A1

🎎 Festivals

Borneo Cultural Festival　　　CULTURE
(⊙10 days in early Jul) Brings to town music, dance, cultural performances and food representing Central Sarawak's Chinese, Malay-Melanau and Dayak traditions.

🛏 Sleeping

Sibu has dozens of hotels. Some of the ultra-budget places (ie those charging less than RM35 a room) are of a very low standard and double as brothels. Not long ago some Japanese tourists were bitten by rats while staying in one local dive!

TOP CHOICE Li Hua Hotel　　　HOTEL $$
(Map p418; ☏084-324000; www.lihua.com.my; cnr Jln Maju & Lg Lanang 2; s/d/ste from RM50/65/150; ❄@☎) Sibu's best-value hotel has 68 spotless, tile-floor rooms spread out over nine storeys and staff that are both highly professional and friendly. Lift-equipped. Especially convenient if you're arriving or leaving by boat. Book by phone or email.

Tanahmas Hotel　　　HOTEL $$
(Map p418; ☏084-333188; www.tanahmas.com.my; Jln Kampung Nyabor; s/d RM250/270; ❄@☎☀) As comfortable as it is central, with 114 spacious rooms. Amenities include a small fitness centre and an open-air pool, both on the 3rd floor.

Premier Hotel　　　HOTEL $$
(Map p418; ☏084-323222; www.premierh.com.my; Jln Kampung Nyabor; s/d from RM209/244; ❄☎) Offers 189 really nice, comfortable rooms in prime downtown location. About what you'd expect for this price – think 3½ stars. Four of the 10 floors are non-smoking.

River Park Hotel　　　HOTEL $
(Map p418; ☏016-578 2820; siewling1983@hotmail.com; 51-53 Jln Maju; d/tr/q from RM68/95/110; ❄☎) A well-run, 30-room hotel in a convenient riverside location. A decent option if the Li Hua Hotel is full.

🍴 Eating

Sibu is famous for Foochow-style Chinese dishes such as *kam pua mee* (thin noodle strands soaked in pork fat and served with a side of roast pork), the city's signature dish, and *kompia* (sesame-flecked mini-bagels filled with pork).

TOP CHOICE Sibu Central Market　　　MARKET $
(Pasar Sentral Sibu; Map p418; RM2.50-5; ⊙food stalls 3am-midnight) Malaysia's largest fruit and veggie market has more than 1000 stalls. Upstairs, Chinese-, Malay- and a few Iban-owned food stalls serve up local specialities, including porridge (available early in the morning and at night), *kam pua mee* (available at most of the noodle shops, but some of the best is on offer at evening-only Stall 102) and *kompia* (check out Stall 17 and Stall FL12, which faces Stall 91; both are open from 7am to 5pm). Most of the noodle stalls close around noon. Got questions? Head to Stall 98 and ask for Noriza.

SWANS

While Kuching's mascot is, famously, the cat, Sibu's is the swan, an 'ancient Chinese symbol of good fortune and health, an auspicious omen for a community living in harmony, peace and goodwill'. Keep an eye out for swan statues as you wander around town.

Café Café

FUSION $$

(Map p418; 10 Jln Chew Geok Lin; mains RM10-38, set weekday lunch RM10-15; ◷noon-4pm & 6-11.30pm, closed Mon;) Chic enough to create a buzz in Kuching (or Melbourne), Café Café serves outstanding fusion fare, including Nyonya-style chicken, amid decor that mixes Balinese, Chinese and Western elements. Vegetarian dishes are available upon request.

Islamic Nyonya Kafé

PERANAKAN $$

(Map p418; 141 Jln Kampung Nyabor; mains RM8-18; ◷10am-11pm;) Serves the deliciously spicy dishes of the Straits Chinese, including *ayam halia* (ginger chicken) and *kari kambing* (mutton curry). 'Islamic' means it's halal. Has great lunch deals (RM5.90 to RM9.90) from 11am to 2pm.

New Capitol Restaurant

CHINESE $$

(Map p418; 46 Jln Kampung Nyabor; mains RM10-30; ◷11am-2pm & 5-9pm) A classy, old-school Chinese restaurant. Among foochow specialities are sea cucumber soup (RM15), bean curd oyster soup (RM8) and duck with red fermented rice (RM30).

Night Market

FOOD STALLS $

(Pasar Malam; Jln Market; ◷5pm-midnight) **Chinese stalls** (Map p418), selling pork and rice, steamed buns etc, are at the western end of the lot, while **Malay stalls** (Map p418) (with superb satay and scrumptious BBQ chicken) are to the northeast. Also has a few Iban-run places.

Kopitiam

CAFE $

(Map p418; mains RM3.30-6; ◷6am-4pm) Several old-time *kopitiam* (coffee shops) can be found along Jln Maju, between the Express Ferry Terminal and the Li Hua Hotel. In the morning, locals gather to dine on Foochow specialities, read Chinese newspapers and chat – a typical Sarawakian scene.

Vegetarian Food Stall

VEGETARIAN $

(Map p418; Jln Central; mains RM3.50; ◷7.30am-2.30pm Mon-Sat;) In the small hawker centre on the ground floor of the Sibu Heritage Centre.

Drinking

Much of what passes for nightlife in Sibu involves cover versions of Western hits and scantily clad young women.

Queen

BAR

(Map p418; 12 Jln Chew Geok Lin; beer from RM10, cocktails RM22-38; ◷4pm-12.30am, closed Mon) Decked out like a Victorian sitting room, this chic, dimly lit bar features plush couches and overstuffed wing chairs in black and burgundy velvet. Stop by from 9pm to 11.30pm for live guitar and/or keyboard music. Food can be ordered from Café Café next door.

Shopping

Public Book Store

BOOKS

(Map p418; Level 4, Wisma Sanyan, 1 Jln Sanyan; ◷9am-9pm) The best bookstore in town, with a decent selection of English books. The mall, Wisma Sanyan, is owned by the Sanyan Group, a vast and politically well-connected timber company.

ⓘ Information

Email Centre (ground fl, Sarawak House Complex, cnr Jln Central & Jln Kampung Nyabor; per hr RM4; ◷9.30am-9pm Mon-Sat, to 3pm Sun) Internet access. The entrance is on the building's northern side.

ibrowse Netcafé (Shop 4.21, Level 4, Wisma Sanyan, 1 Jln Sanyan; per hr RM3; ◷9.30am-9.30pm) Internet access.

Main Post Office (Jln Kampung Nyabor; ◷8am-4pm Mon-Fri, to 3.30pm Sat) Changes cash.

Rejang Medical Centre (☏084-330733; www.rejang.com.my; 29 Jln Pedada) Used by most expats and tourists. Has 24-hour emergency services, including an ambulance. Situated about 1km northeast of the Sibu Gateway.

Sibu General Hospital (☏084-343333; http://hsibu.moh.gov.my; Jln Ulu Oya, Km 5-1/2) Situated 8km east of the centre, towards the airport.

Visitors Information Centre (☏084-340980; www.sarawaktourism.com; 32 Jln Tukang Besi; ◷8am-5pm Mon-Fri, closed public holidays) Well worth a stop. Has a friendly and informative staff (ask for Jessie), plenty of maps, bus and ferry schedules, and brochures on travel around Sarawak.

Yewon Money Changer (8 Jln Tukang Besi; ◷8.30am or 9am-5pm Mon-Sat) Changes cash. Look for the gold-on-red sign.

ⓘ Getting There & Away

Air

MASwings (www.maswings.com.my) has inexpensive services to Kuching, Bintulu, Miri and Kota Kinabalu (KK). **Malaysia Airlines** (www.malaysiaairlines.com) flies to Kuala Lumpur (KL), and **AirAsia** (www.airasia.com) flies to Kuching (40 minutes), KL and Johor Bahru (across the causeway from Singapore).

Boat

At the entrance to the **Express Ferry Terminal** (Jln Kho Peng Long, Terminal Penumpang Sibu; 🕿), ferry company booths indicate departure times using large clocks. Be on board 15 minutes before departure time – boats have been known to set sail early.

TO KAPIT & BELAGA

'Flying coffin' express boats head up the Batang Rejang to Kapit (RM20 to RM30, 140km, 2½ to three hours) once or twice an hour from 5.45am to 2.30pm. Water levels at the Pelagus Rapids permitting (for details, call Mr Wong at 013-806 1333), one boat a day, departing at 5.45am, goes all the way to Belaga, 155km upriver from Kapit (RM55, 11 hours).

TO KUCHING

Unless you fly, the quickest way to get from Sibu to Kuching is by boat. **Ekspress Bahagia** (☑ in Kuching 016-889 3013, 082-412246, in Sibu 016-800 5891, 084-319228) runs a daily express ferry to/from Kuching's Express Wharf (RM45, five hours) that passes through an Amazonian dystopia of abandoned sawmills and rust-bucket tramp steamers. Departures are 11.30am from Sibu and at 8.30am from Kuching. It's a good idea to book a day ahead.

Bus

Sibu's **long-distance bus station** (Jln Pahlawan) is about 3.5km northeast of the centre along Jln Pedada. A variety of companies send buses to Kuching (RM50 to RM60, seven to eight hours, regular departures between 6.15am and 4am), Miri (RM50, 6½ hours, roughly hourly from 6am to 3.30am) and Bintulu (RM25, 3¼ hours, roughly hourly from 6am to 3.30am).

ℹ Getting Around

To/From the Airport

Sibu Airport is 23km east of the city centre; a taxi costs RM35.

From the local bus station, the Panduan Hemat bus to Sibu Jaya passes by the airport junction (RM2.70, every hour or two from 6am to 7.15pm), which is five minutes on foot from the terminal.

Bus

To get from the local bus station (in front of the Express Ferry Terminal) to the long-distance bus station, take Lanang Bus 20 or 21 (RM1.20, 15 minutes, once or twice an hour 6.30am to 5.15pm).

Taxi

Taxis can be ordered 24 hours a day at 084-320773 or 084-311286. Taking a taxi from the city centre to the long-distance bus station costs RM13.

Batang Rejang

A trip up the tan, churning waters of 640km-long Batang Rejang (Rejang River) – the 'Amazon of Borneo' – is one of Southeast Asia's great river journeys. Express ferries barrel through the currents, eddies and whirlpools, the pilots expertly dodging angular black boulders half-hidden in the roiling waters. Though the area is no longer the jungle-lined wilderness it was in the days before Malaysian independence, it retains a frontier, *ulu-ulu* (upriver, ie back-of-the-beyond) vibe, especially in towns and longhouses accessible only by boat.

To get a sense of the extent of logging and oil palm monoculture, check out Google Earth.

LONGHOUSE VISITS

Many of the indigenous people of the Batang Rejang basin, both Iban and members of Orang Ulu groups such as the Kenyah, Kayan, Lahanan, Punan and Sekapan, still live in longhouses. While most aren't as traditional as travellers may envision, visiting one can be a great way to interact with some of Borneo's indigenous people.

Based on geography, Kapit and Belaga *should* be good bases from which to set out to explore longhouses along the upper Batang Rejang and its tributaries. Unfortunately, we've been hearing about two sorts of difficulties faced by some recent travellers:

Visiting longhouses without an invitation or a guide is becoming more complicated as traditional Dayak norms, according to which visitors are always welcome, are giving way to more 'modern' (ie commercial) ideas.

Some area tour guides and van drivers demand inflated prices and/or provide services that aren't up to standard. For instance, visitors may be dropped off at a longhouse with nothing to do and no way to communicate with the residents until they're picked up the next day.

In short, it can sometimes be difficult to find a guide who has good local knowledge and contacts, speaks English and charges reasonable prices. Some travellers report being invited by locals to their longhouses – but that's not something you can count on. One good option is to make arrangements through one of the tour agencies based in Sibu. For up-to-date feedback from other travellers, check out Lonely Planet's Thorn Tree forum (www.lonelyplanet.com).

ℹ Getting Around

Pretty much the only transport arteries into and around the Batang Rejang region are rivers. A road from Kapit to Kanowit (already connected to Sarawak's highway network) is being built and a rough logging road already connects Bintulu with Belaga, so come before easy land access changes this part of Borneo forever.

Boats can navigate the perilous Pelagus Rapids, between Kapit and Belaga, only when the water level is high enough – these days, determined mainly by how much water is released from the Bakun Dam. In an attempt to make navigation safer and less subject to fluctuating water levels, the government has recently been attaching explosive charges to some of the boulders that create the Pelagus Rapids and blowing them to smithereens.

Express river boats – nicknamed 'flying coffins' because of their shape, not their safety record – run by half-a-dozen companies head up the broad, muddy Batang Rejang from Sibu with goods and luggage strapped precariously to the roof. If you opt to ride up top for the view (not that we recommend it...), hang on tight! The passenger cabins tend to be air-conditioned to near-arctic frigidity.

From Sibu, boats to Kapit (140km, 2½ to three hours) leave once or twice an hour from 5.45am to 2.30pm; from Kapit, boats heading down to Sibu depart between 6.40am and 3.15pm. If you travel 2nd or 3rd class (RM20), boarding is likely to involve inching your way along a narrow, railless exterior gangway; 1st- (RM30) and business-class (RM25) passengers board near the prow.

If the water level at the Pelagus Rapids (32km upriver from Kapit) is high enough (for the latest low-water information, call Mr Wong in Sibu at 013-806 1333 or Daniel Levoh in Belaga at 013-848 6351), one 77-seat **express boat** (📞013-806 1333) a day goes all the way to Belaga, 155km upriver from Kapit, stopping at various longhouses along the way. Heading upriver, departures are at 5.45am from Sibu (RM55, 11 hours) and 9.30am from Kapit (RM35, 4½ hours). Coming downriver, the boat leaves Belaga at about 7.30am. When the river is too low, the only way to get to Belaga is overland via Bintulu!

KAPIT
POP 14,000

The main upriver settlement on the Batang Rejang, Kapit is a bustling trading and transport centre dating back to the days of the White Rajahs. A number of nearby longhouses can be visited by road or river but the pickings are thin when it comes to finding a good local guide.

Fans of Redmond O'Hanlon's *Into the Heart of Borneo* may remember Kapit as the starting point of the author's jungle adventures.

◉ Sights & Activities

Fort Sylvia   MUSEUM

(Map p424; Jln Kubu; ⊙10am-noon & 2-5pm, closed Mon & public holidays) Built by Charles Brooke in 1880 to take control of the Upper Rejang and to keep the peace, this wooden fort – built of *belian* – was renamed in 1925 to honour Ranee Sylvia, wife of Charles Vyner Brooke. On the facade, lines mark the high-water marks of historic floods, one of which crested at an incredible 19m above normal. Inside, the exhibits offer a pretty good intro to the traditional lifestyles of the Batang Rejang Dayaks and include evocative photos of the colonial era. A worthwhile stop before you head to a longhouse.

UPPER REJANG TRAVEL PERMITS

Theoretically, a free, two-week permit is required for all travel:

» Along the Batang Rejang to points upriver from the Pelagus Rapids (32km upstream from Kapit).

» Up the Batang Baleh, which flows into the Batang Rejang 9km upriver from Kapit.

In fact, we've never heard of anyone having their permit checked, and the whole arrangement seems to be a bureaucratic holdover from the time when the government sought to limit foreign activists' access to Dayak communities threatened by logging or the controversial Bakun Dam. Permits are not required, even in theory, if you travel to Belaga overland from Bintulu.

Permits are issued in Kapit at the **Resident's Office** (📞084-796230; www.kapitro. sarawak.gov.my; 9th fl, Kompleks Kerajaan Negeri Bahagian Kapit, Jln Bleteh; ⊙8am-1pm & 2-5pm Mon-Thu, 8-11.45am & 2.15-5pm Fri), in a nine-storey building 2km west of the centre. To get there, take a van (RM1.50) from the southeast corner of Pasar Teresang. To get back to town, ask the lobby guards for help catching a ride (offer to pay the driver).

Waterfront

PORT

(Map p424) Kapit's waterfront is lined with ferries, barges, longboats and floating docks, all swarming with people. Porters carry impossibly heavy or unwieldy loads – we've seen 15 egg crates stacked in a swaying pile – up the steep steps from the wharfs.

Pasar Teresang

MARKET

(Map p424; ⊙5.30am-6pm) Some of the goods unloaded at the waterfront end up in this colourful covered market. It's a chatty, noisy hive of grass-roots commerce, with a galaxy of unfamiliar edibles that grow in the jungle, as well as handicrafts. Orang Ulu people sell fried treats and steamed buns.

☞ Tours

LONGHOUSE TOURS

Longhouses, many of them quite modern and some accessible by road (river travel is both slower and pricier than going by minibus), can be found along the Batang Baleh, which conflows with the Batang Rejang 9km upstream from Kapit, and the Sungai Sut, a tributary of the Batang Baleh. Longhouses along these rivers tend to be more traditional (ie still have hunted heads on display) than their counterparts along the mainline Batang Rejang.

The problem is finding a good guide. Tours run by Alice Chua (☎019-859 3126; atta_kpt@yahoo.com), Kapit's only licensed guide, are pricey and, frankly, do not get rave reviews. You could also ask at your hotel for recommendations. A few lucky travellers get invitations from locals!

According to the Kapit Resident's Office, the license of one local guide has been revoked for cause. Despite this, he continues to approach visitors, some of whom have made complaints. Because licensed guides are rare in Kapit, and quite a few of Sarawak's unlicensed guides are competent and knowledgeable, it can be difficult to gauge a guide's suitability at first encounter. We advise that you talk to other travellers and local hotel owners as to which operators are recommended or best avoided.

VISITING LONGHOUSES ON YOUR OWN

A few communities around Kapit are accustomed to independent travellers, charging RM10 or RM15 for a day visit or RM50 per person if you overnight, including the preparation of food that you bring along. The headman may also expect a tip. Some people recommend bringing sweets or school supplies for the children. There may not be much to do at a longhouse, especially if there aren't any English speakers around.

Longhouses you may consider visiting:

» **Rumah Bundong** One of the area's few remaining traditional Iban longhouses. Situated on Sungai Kapit a 45-minute (10km) drive from Kapit.

» **Rumah Jandok** A traditional longhouse on Sungai Yong with quite a few English speakers, situated down the Batang Rejang from Kapit.

» **Nanga Mujong** This Iban longhouse, site of a school and a clinic, is served by a road that ends on the opposite bank of the Batang Baleh, from where boats ferry residents across.

» **Rumah Penghulu Jampi** An Iban longhouse at the final express-boat stop on the Batang Baleh.

» **Rumah Lulut Tisa** This longhouse has an official homestay. To get there, take the road to Rumah Masam, whence it's another 1½ hours by boat.

We've heard reports that a local minibus cooperative is charging outrageous rates (RM180 one-way!) for land transport to nearby longhouses. A better bet might be to join the locals on one of the service-taxi minivans that hang out around Kapit Town Square (at the corner of Jln Teo Chow Beng and Jln Chua Leong Kee) and at Pasar Teresang (on Jln Teo Chow Beng).

To get to longhouses accessible only by river, head to Jeti RC Kubu (Jln Temenggong Koh), the jetty facing Fort Sylvia, and negotiate for a longboat. These can be expensive – imagine how much fuel the outboard slurps as the boat powers its way upstream.

☆☆ Festivals & Events

Baleh-Kapit Raft Safari

RAFT RACE

A challenging, two-day race recreating the experience of Iban and Orang Ulu people rafting downstream to bring their jungle produce to Kapit. Often held in April. For details, check with the Resident's Office in Kapit or Sibu's Visitors Information Centre.

🛏 Sleeping

New Rejang Inn

HOTEL $

(Map p424; ☎084-796600; 104 Jln Teo Chow Beng; d RM68; ❈🛜) A welcoming and well-run hotel whose 15 immaculate, good-sized rooms come with comfortable mattresses, hot water, TV, phone and mini-fridge. The best-value accommodation in town.

Kapit

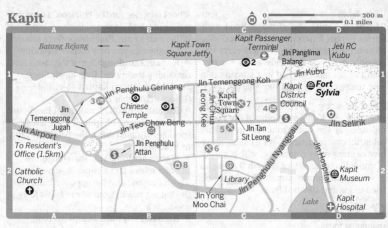

Kapit

⊙ Top Sights
Fort Sylvia D1

⊙ Sights
1 Pasar Teresang B1
2 Waterfront C1

🛏 Sleeping
3 Hiap Chiong Hotel A1
4 New Rejang Inn C1

🍴 Eating
5 Famous Bakery C2
Gelanggang Kenyalang .... (see 8)
6 Night Market C2
7 Soon Kit Café C1

🛍 Shopping
8 Sula Perengka Kapit B2

Hiap Chiong Hotel HOTEL $
(Map p424; ☎084-796314; 33 Jln Temenggong Jugah; d RM45-50; 🛜) The 15 rooms have dinged-up, outdated furniture but are clean and have tiny flat-screen TVs.

✕ Eating & Drinking

Soon Kit Café CHINESE $
(Map p424; 13 Jln Tan Sit Liong; mains RM2.70-6; ⊘5.30am-5pm) An old-time *kopitiam* with laksa (RM4) in the morning and delicious chicken rice (RM5).

Gelanggang Kenyalang FOOD COURT $
(Map p424; off Jln Penghulu Nyanggau; mains from RM3.20; ⊘6am-btwn 4pm & 7pm) A food court with Malay and Chinese favourites,

including breakfast yummies like laksa and *roti canai*.

Night Market FOOD STALLS $
(Map p424; Taman Selera Empurau; mains RM2.50-5; ⊘5pm-11pm or midnight) An excellent place for satay or BBQ chicken. Situated a block up the slope from Kapit Town Square.

Famous Bakery BAKERY $
(Map p424; 22 Jln Teo Chow Beng; pastries RM1-3.40; ⊘6am-6pm) Fresh Chinese and (approximately) Western-style pastries, cakes, mini-pizzas and other easy-to-pack day trip picnic fare.

🛍 Shopping

Sula Perengka Kapit HANDICRAFTS
(Map p424; off Jln Penghulu Nyanggau; ⊘8am-4pm Mon-Sat, 8am-noon Sun) A tiny, Iban-owned handicrafts place (Shop 21) upstairs at the Gelanggang Kenyalang food court.

ℹ Information

Kapit Hospital (☎084-796333; Jln Hospital; ⊘24hr) Three ambulances and half-a-dozen doctors.

ℹ Getting There & Away

BOAT
Express boats to Sibu (RM20 to RM30, 2½ to three hours, once or twice an hour) depart between 6.40am and 3.15pm from the **Kapit Passenger Terminal** (Jln Panglima Balang; 🛜), which has wi-fi that attracts whatever the river equivalent of road warriors is, and a nice verandah cafe with breezy river views.

Water levels permitting (for details, call Daniel Levoh in Belaga at 013-848 6351), an express boat heads upriver to Belaga (RM35, 4½ hours) from the **Kapit Town Square jetty** (two blocks downriver from the Kapit Passenger Terminal) once a day at about 9.30am.

One express boat a day heads up the Batang Baleh, going as far as the Iban longhouse of Rumah Penghulu Jampi. It departs from Kapit at about 10am and from Rumah Penghulu Jampi at 12.30pm.

VAN

A small road network around Kapit, unconnected to the outside world, links the town to a number of longhouses. Vans that ply these byways congregate at Kapit Town Square.

BELAGA
POP 2500

By the time you pull into Belaga after the long cruise up the Batang Rejang, you may feel like you've arrived in the very heart of Borneo – in reality, you're only about 100km (as the crow flies) from the coast. There's not much to do here except soak up the frontier vibe, but nearby rivers are home to quite a few Kayan/Kenyah and Orang Ulu longhouses.

⊙ Sights

To get a feel for the pace of local life, wander among the two-storey shophouses of the compact, mostly Chinese **town centre**, or stroll through the manicured **park** – outfitted with basketball and tennis courts – between Main Bazaar and the river. Along the riverfront, a wooden bridge leads downstream to **Kampung Melayu Belaga**, Belaga's Malay quarter, whose wooden homes are built on stilts. Although there's 24-hour electricity (provided by a generator – Belaga is not yet connected to the Bakun Dam grid), pretty much everything closes by 7pm.

🏃 Activities
LONGHOUSE VISITS

The main reason travellers visit Belaga is to venture up a jungle stream in search of hidden longhouses and secret waterfalls. Possible destinations include (listed alphabetically):

» **Dong Daah** – a Kayan longhouse 10 minutes upriver by boat from Belaga

» **Lirong Amo** – a Kayan longhouse about half-an-hour's walk from Belaga

» **Long Liten** – a huge, old Kejaman longhouse a ways upriver

» **Long Segaham** – a Kejaman longhouse situated upriver

» **Sekapan Panjang** – a traditional, all-wood Sekapan longhouse half-an-hour downstream by boat from Belaga

» **Sihan** – a Penan settlement a two-hour walk from the other bank of the Batang Rejang

Before you can share shots of *tuak* with smiling locals, however, you need to find a guide. A good package should include a boat ride, jungle trekking, a waterfall swim, a night walk and activities such as cooking and fruit harvesting.

Daniel Levoh TOUR
(☏013-848 6351, 086-461997; daniellevoh@hotmail.com; Jln Teh Ah Kiong) A Kayan former teacher and school headmaster, Daniel is friendly and knowledgeable. A daytrip costs RM150 to RM200 for two or three people, a three-day, two-night longhouse visit costs RM600 to RM750 for a group of three. Daniel can also arrange private transport around Belaga and Bintulu.

Hamdani TOUR
(☏019-886 5770) For a group of four, Hamdani charges RM75 per person for a day trip and RM115 per person for an overnight stay.

Hasbi Awang TOUR
(☏013-842 9767; freeland_blg@yahoo.com; 4 Main Bazaar, Belaga B&B) A day trip to two longhouses costs RM80 per person, an overnight trip is RM200 per person.

🎊 Events
Belaga Rainforest Challenge TRIBAL EVENT
(⊙Jul or Aug of even-numbered years) The three- or four-day event combines a 12km jungle run with boat races and traditional music and dance performances. Intended for area tribes but tourists are welcome.

🛏 Sleeping

Belaga's accommodation is of the cheap and shabby variety.

Daniel Levoh's Guesthouse GUESTHOUSE $
(☏013-848 6351, 086-461997; daniellevoh@hotmail.com; Jln Teh Ah Kiong; dm RM15, d/tr RM30/35; 🛜) The four simple rooms, each named after one of the owners' children, the chill-out balcony and the bathrooms are all on the 2nd floor. Owner Daniel Levoh, a retired teacher and one-time guide, is happy to share stories of Kayan longhouse life. Situated two blocks behind Main Bazaar.

Belaga Hotel HOTEL $
(☏086-461244; 14 Main Bazaar; d RM30-35; ❄) A convenient location makes up for the less-than-perfect standards at this veteran doss

house. The air-con – available in all but two of the 15 beat-up rooms – works, which is more than can be said for some of the plumbing.

Belaga B&B HOTEL $

(☎ 013-842 9767; Main Bazaar; r RM20-25; ❄) Has seven very basic rooms, some with air-con, and shared bathroom facilities. Owned by Hasbi, a long-time longhouse guide.

✕ Eating

Simple cafes serving Chinese and Malay dishes are sprinkled around the town centre, including Main Bazaar.

Kafeteria Mesra Murni MALAY $

(Jln Temenggong Matu; dishes RM3.50-6; ⊙7am-7pm) This family-run Malay restaurant has the only riverfront dining in town. Almost adjacent Crystal Cafe, owned by an Iban-Kenyah family, is also good for a simple meal.

❶ Information

The new BSM Bank branch has an ATM but it's often (or should we say usually) on the fritz. The medical clinic has one doctor. Several places to stay offer wi-fi.

❶ Getting There & Away

When the express boat is running, it's possible to visit Belaga without backtracking, cruising the Batang Rejang in one direction and taking the logging road to/from Bintulu in the other.

BOAT

If the water levels at the Pelagus Rapids (32km upriver from Kapit) are high enough, you can take an express boat to Kapit (RM35, 4½ hours) departing at about 7.30am. To find out if the boat is running, call tour guide Daniel Levoh (p425). When the river is too low, the only way to get out of Belaga is by 4WD to Bintulu.

LAND

A bone-jarring (and, in the rain, fiendishly slippery) logging road connects Belaga with Bintulu (160km). Part of the way the route follows the 125km-long paved road to the Bakun Dam.

4WD Toyota Land Cruisers link Belaga with Bintulu (RM50 per person, RM400 for the whole vehicle, four hours) on most days, with departures from Belaga at about 7.30am and from Bintulu in the early afternoon (between noon and 2pm). In Belaga, vehicles to Bintulu congregate in front of Belaga B&B at about 7am. To arrange a vehicle from Bintulu, call Daniel Levoh (p425).

If you're coming from Miri or Batu Niah Junction or heading up that way (ie northeast), you can arrange to be picked up or dropped off at Simpang Bakun (Bakun Junction), which is on the inland (old) highway 53km northeast of Bintulu and 159km southwest of Miri.

UPRIVER FROM BELAGA

About 40km upstream from Belaga, the Batang Rejang divides into several rivers, including the mighty Batang Balui, which wends and winds almost all the way up to the Kalimantan border. Just below this junction, the controversial Bakun Dam generates electricity and provides locals with a place to fish. Belaga-based guides can arrange visits to area longhouses.

One express boat a day links Belaga with Long Bangu (RM20, one hour), 2km downstream from the Bakun Dam. Departures are at about 3pm from Belaga and 6.15am from Rumah Apan.

Bintulu

POP 120,000

Thanks to huge offshore natural gas fields, Bintulu is Sarawak's most important centre for the production of LNG (liquefied natural gas) and fertiliser. The town, roughly midway between Sibu and Miri (about 200km from each), makes a good staging post for visits to Similajau National Park and for overland travel to Belaga.

◉ Sights & Activities

Tua Pek Kong TEMPLE

(Map p428; Main Bazaar; ⊙dawn-dusk) This classic Chinese temple adds vibrant colours to the rather drab city centre. Follow the cock-a-doodle-doos to the park around back, where young, impressively plumed **fighting cocks** (Map p428) – kept tethered to avoid strife – strut and crow.

Taman Tumbina GARDENS, ZOO

(www.tumbina.com.my; Jln Tun Abdul Razak; adult RM2; ⊙8am-5pm) This 57-hectare park includes an orchid garden, a butterfly house and lots of flamingos. The name is a contraction of the first syllables of two Malay words, *tumbuhan* (plant) and *binatang* (animal). Situated about 5km north of Bintulu Town (RM15 by taxi).

✻ Festivals

Borneo International Kite Festival KITES

(www.borneokite.com) An annual event, usually held over four or five days in September, that brings fanciful and extravagant kites from around the world to the old airport.

🛏 Sleeping

There are quite a few hotels, some on the dodgy side, on and near Jln Keppel, its

southern continuation, Jln Abang Galau, and parallel on Jln Masjid.

Kintown Inn
HOTEL $

(Map p428; ☑086-333666; 93 Jln Keppel; s/d RM80/86; ✳🛜) The 50 carpeted rooms are smallish but bright, with good views from the upper floors. Delivers the best value for your buck in town.

Riverfront Inn
HOTEL $$

(Map p428; ☑086-333111; riverfrontinn@hotmail.com; 256 Taman Sri Dagang; d with window RM104; ✳🛜) A long-standing favourite with business and leisure visitors alike, the Riverfront is low-key but has a touch of class. Try to get a deluxe room (RM110) overlooking the river – the view is pure Borneo.

✗ Eating & Drinking

Local nightlife, such as it is, consists mainly of single men hanging out along Jln Masjid.

Ban Kee Café
SEAFOOD $$

(Map p428; off Jln Abang Galau; mains RM6-15; ⊙6am-midnight; ☑) An indoor-outdoor Chinese seafood specialist with fresh fish (per kg RM40 to RM80) and seafood and, for breakfast, noodles and laksa (RM3.50).

Popular Corner Food Centre
HAWKER $

(Map p428; 50 BDA Shahida Commercial Centre; mains RM3-8; ⊙6am-10pm) Eight stalls sell laksa (morning only), rice porridge, dim sum and fresh Hong Kong-style seafood.

Night Market
FOOD STALLS $

(Map p428; off Jln Abang Galau; mains RM2.50-5; ⊙4-10pm or 11pm) A good place to snack track for fresh fruit and Malay favourites such as satay.

Pasar Utama
FOOD STALLS $

(Map p428; New Market; Main Bazaar; mains RM3-5; ⊙7am-5pm) Malay and Chinese food stalls fill the upper floor of this blue-coloured, figure-eight-shaped fruit and veggie market.

Chef
BAKERY $

(Map p428; 92 Jln Abang Galau; cakes from RM1; ⊙8.30am-9pm) Makes Chinese-inflected halal baked goods, including buns with hot dogs baked inside (RM1.70) and surprisingly tasty Belgian chocolate cake (RM6.80). Ideal fare for a picnic lunch.

❶ Information

Fi Wee Internet Centre (1st fl, 133 Jln Masjid; per hr RM2; ⊙9am-midnight) Has 27 internet computers at the top of a filthy staircase.

❶ Getting There & Away

To arrange transport by 4WD Toyota Land Cruiser from Bintulu to Belaga (per person RM50, four hours) on some pretty rough logging roads, call Daniel Levoh (p425). Departures are generally in the early afternoon (between noon and 2pm).

Air

AirAsia (www.airasia.com) and **Malaysia Airlines** (www.malaysiaairlines.com) have direct flights to Kuching and Kuala Lumpur (KL). MASwings (www.maswings.com.my) can whisk you to Kota Kinabalu (KK), Miri, Sibu and Kuching.

Bus

The long-distance bus station is at Medan Jaya, 5km northeast of the centre (aka Bintulu Town); a taxi costs RM15. About a dozen companies have buses approximately hourly:

Kuching (RM60 to RM65, 10 hours) Via Sibu (RM20 to RM25, four hours), from 6.45am to midnight.

Miri (RM20 to RM25, four hours) Via Niah Junction (RM12 to RM15, 2-3/4 hours), from 6am to 11.15pm.

❶ Getting Around
To/From the Airport

There is no public transport to/from the airport, which is 23km from the centre by road. A taxi costs RM35.

Similajau National Park

An easy 30km northeast of Bintulu, Similajau National Park (☑by satellite phone 086-489003, office in Bintulu 086-313726; www.sarawakforestry.com; admission RM20; ⊙park office 8am-1pm & 2-5pm Sat-Thu, 8-11.45am & 2.15-5pm Fri) is a fine little coastal park with golden-sand beaches, good walking trails and simple accommodation. Occupying a narrow, 30km-long strip along the South China Sea, its 90 sq km encompasses littoral habitats such as mangroves, *kerangas* (heath forest) and mixed dipterocarp forest, (classic lowland tropical rainforest). Four species of dolphin, including Irrawaddy, can sometimes be spotted out at sea, and green turtles occasionally trundle ashore to lay their eggs along Turtle Beach II and Golden Beach.

Bintuluans flock to Similajau (especially the beaches) on weekends and public holidays, but the park is gloriously deserted on weekdays.

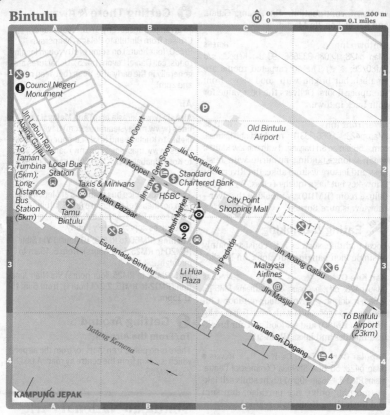

SARAWAK SIMILAJAU NATIONAL PARK

Bintulu

⊙ **Sights**
| 1 Fighting Cocks | C2 |
| 2 Tua Pek Kong | B3 |

⊜ **Sleeping**
| 3 Kintown Inn | B2 |
| 4 Riverfront Inn | D4 |

⊗ **Eating**
5 Ban Kee Café	D3
6 Chef	D3
7 Night Market	D3
8 Pasar Utama	B3
9 Popular Corner Food Centre	A1

DANGERS & ANNOYANCES

Similajau's waterways are prime crocodile habitat so do not swim or wade in the rivers or near river mouths, and be careful when walking near riverbanks, especially early or late in the day.

Because of dangerous undertows, swimming is forbidden at the two Turtle Beaches and at Golden Beach.

⊙ Sights & Activities

The casuarina-lined beach at park HQ, strewn with driftwood but clean, is a great place to chill out and swim – but watch out for jellyfish (if you get stung, rangers can provide vinegar to alleviate the pain).

Similajau's gently undulating **Main Trail** (Coastal Trail) parallels the coast, starting across Sungai Likau from park HQ and ending at **Golden Beach** (10km, four hours oneway). En route it passes by rocky headlands, small bays, **Turtle Beach I** (6km, three hours) and Turtle Beach II (7.5km, 3½ hours). For a view back along the coast towards Bintulu and its natural gas installations, head to the **View Point** (1.3km from HQ, 40 minutes).

Right after you cross the suspension bridge next to park HQ, a plankwalk to your right follows the river upstream. Both the 600m **Education Trail** and its continuation, the 1.7km **Circular Trail** (which takes you back to a point near the bridge), pass through brilliant estuarine mangroves and mixed dipterocarp forest.

Similajau's trails are easy to follow and are clearly marked (in the case of the Main Trail, in red) so a guide isn't necessary, though it's possible to hire one for RM30 per hour (RM40 per hour for a **night walk**). A simple but useful trail map is available at park HQ. Bring plenty of drinking water.

HQ staff are happy to arrange travel in a national park-owned boat with space for up to five passengers. Sea conditions sometimes get rough after about noon. Among your cruising options:

Night River Cruise (RM150; ☉7-9pm) A great way to see crocs. Reserve during office hours.

Batu Mandi Tide Pools (RM150) The tidal pools around this low, rocky island can only be visited at low tide and when the sea is calm.

Turtle Beaches I and II (one-way/return RM180/230) Take the boat out there (it's a half-hour ride) and you can walk back.

Golden Beach (one-way/return RM220/280) Another option for a one-way walk.

Sleeping

Similajau's rustic overnight options, just 100m from the beach, are booked out months ahead on public holidays and sometimes fill up on weekends. To reserve, contact the park by phone, fax (086-489 002) or email (norhider@sarawakforestry.com). Bookings *cannot* be made through the national park offices in Kuching or Miri.

Renting a towel costs RM6.

Chalets CHALET $$
(1/2 rooms RM106/159) Each of the six new chalets has two rooms, each of which has one queen bed, one twin bed and one fan.

Rest House CHALET $$
(per night RM318; ❄) Sleeps four in air-con comfort.

Hostel HOSTEL $
(per room RM42) Each room has four beds (bunks in the case of Hostel 3) and a wall fan. Hostels 1 and 2, built in 2011, have attached bathrooms. Dorm beds are not available individually.

Campground CAMPGROUND $
(per person RM5) Camping is only permitted next to park HQ. Showers are provided.

Eating

The park's **cafeteria** (Canteen; mains RM5-13; ☉7.30am-9pm; 🖋) serves noodle and rice dishes and can prepare packed lunches. Cooking is not allowed in the chalets or the hostel but there are designated sites for barbecuing. To prepare packaged noodles, you can borrow an electric kettle at the park office.

❶ Getting There & Away

The HQ of Similajau National Park is about 30km northeast of Bintulu, 9km off the coastal road to Miri. Count on paying RM50 one-way to hire a **taxi** (☎086-332009) – or a 10-seat minibus – from Bintulu's Pasar Utama (Main Bazaar) (p427); from the airport, the cab ride costs about RM75.

To get back to Bintulu, you can pre-arrange a pick-up time or ask HQ staff to help you call for a taxi.

Niah National Park

The vast limestone caverns of 31-sq-km **Niah National Park** (☎085-737450, 085-737454; www.sarawakforestry.com; admission RM20; ☉park office 8am-5pm) are among Borneo's most famous and impressive natural attractions. At the heart of the park is the Great Cave, one of the largest caverns in the world.

Niah's caves have provided groundbreaking insights into human life on Borneo way back when the island was still connected to mainland Southeast Asia. In 1958 archaeologists led by Tom Harrisson discovered the 40,000-year-old skull of an anatomically modern human, the oldest remains of a *Homo sapiens* discovered anywhere in Southeast Asia.

Rock paintings and several small canoe-like coffins ('death ships') indicate that the site was used as a burial ground much more recently. Some of the artefacts found at Niah are on display at the Sarawak Museum in Kuching; others (a handful) are in the park's own museum.

Niah's caves accommodate a staggering number of bats and are an important nesting site for swiftlets, some of whose species supply the vital ingredient for bird's-nest soup. Traditionally, the Penan are custodians and collectors of the nests, while the Iban have the rights to the caves' other commodity, bat and bird guano, which is highly valued as fertiliser (no prizes for guessing who got first pick). During the harvesting season (August to March), nest collectors can be seen on towering bamboo structures wedged against the cave roof.

We've heard travellers say that if you've been (or will be going) to Gunung Mulu National Park, going to Niah might not be worth the effort – unless you're fascinated by human prehistory, of course.

◉ Sights & Activities

Niah Archaeology Museum   MUSEUM
(motor launch per person 7.30am-5.30pm RM1, 5.30-7.30pm RM1.50, after 7.30pm RM3 by pre-arrangement; ⊘9am-4.30pm, closed Mon) Across the river from park HQ, this museum has rather old-fashioned displays on Niah's geology, ecology and prehistoric archaeology, including an original burial canoe that's at least 1200 years old, a reproduction of the Painted Cave, a case featuring swiftlets' nests, and a replica of the 40,000-year-old 'Deep Skull'.

To get to the museum from HQ, cross the Sungai Niah by motor launch.

If you don't have your own, torches/flashlights (RM5; make sure the one you get is working) – extremely useful if you want to go any distance into the caves – can be rented at the ferry terminal and the museum.

Great Cave & Painted Cave   CAVE
From the museum, a raised boardwalk leads 3.1km (3½ to four hours return) through swampy, old-growth rainforest to the mouth of the Great Cave, a vast cavern approximately 2km long, up to 250m across and up to 60m high. To make it back by nightfall, start your stroll by about 2pm.

As you walk, stop and stand silently every once in a while – you'll hear lots of birds and, if you're lucky, may hear or even see macaques, especially early in the morning or in the evening.

Just before the cave entrance, the boardwalk forks. The right fork leads to the cave, while the left fork goes to Rumah Patrick Libau, an Iban longhouse hamlet. Villagers usually sit at the junction selling cold drinks and souvenirs.

Inside the Great Cave, the trail splits to go around a massive central pillar, but both branches finish at the same point so

it's impossible to get lost if you stick to the boardwalk. The stairs and handrails are usually covered with dirt or guano, and can get very slippery in places. The rock formations are spectacular and ominous by turns, and as you slip in and out of the gloom you may find yourself thinking of Jules Verne's *Journey to the Centre of the Earth.* When the sun hits certain overhead vents, the cave is penetrated by dramatic rays of other-worldly light. When you're halfway through the dark passage known as **Gan Kira** (Moon Cave), try turning off your flashlight to enjoy the experience of pure, soupy blackness.

The **Painted Cave** is famed for its ancient drawings, in red hematite, depicting jungle animals, human figures and the souls of the dead being taken to the afterlife by boat. At research time it was closed for maintenance until further notice.

Bats & Swiftlets   FLYING CREATURES
At one time, some 470,000 bats and four million swiftlets called Niah home. There are no current figures, but the walls of the caves are no longer thick with bats and there are fewer bird's nests to harvest.

Several species of swiftlet nest on the cave walls. The most common by far is the glossy swiftlet, whose nest is made of vegetation and is therefore of no use in making soup. For obvious reasons, the species whose nests are edible (ie made of delicious salivary excretions) are far less abundant and can only be seen in the remotest corners of the cavern. Several types of bat also roost in the cave, but not in dense colonies, as at Gunung Mulu National Park.

The best time to see the cave's winged wildlife is at dusk (5.30pm to 6.45pm) during the 'changeover', when the swiftlets stream back to their nests and the bats come swirling out for the night's feeding. If you decide to stick around, let staff at the park HQ's Registration Counter know and make sure you either get back to the ferry by 7.30pm or coordinate a later pick-up time with the boatman.

Bukit Kasut   TRAIL
This 45-minute trail, part of it a boardwalk through freshwater swamp forest, goes from near the museum southward up to the summit of Bukit Kasut (205m). In the wet season, it can get muddy and treacherously slippery.

🛏 Sleeping & Eating

Park HQ has a decent **canteen** (Cafeteria; mains RM5-10; ⊗8am-10pm; 🖊). Cooking is prohibited in park accommodation but, except at the hostel, you can boil water to make instant noodles.

Batu Niah town, 4km from park HQ (3km if you walk), has a couple of basic hotels.

Niah National Park

Bookings for park-run accommodation can be made at park HQ (in person or by phone) or through one of the **National Park Booking Offices** (🖊in Kuching 082-248088, in Miri 085-434184) – but *not* through Sarawak Forestry's website. Lodges and rooms often fill up on Chinese, Malay and public holidays.

Forest Lodges   CHALET **$$**
(1/2 rooms with fan RM106/159, with air-con RM159/239) The park has six rustic two-room chalets with attached bath; each room can sleep up to four.

Hostel   HOSTEL **$**
(r RM42) Each basic hostel room has space for up to four people.

Homestay   HOMESTAY **$**
(🖊019-805 2415; per person incl dinner & breakfast RM70) The Iban longhouse village of Rumah Patrick Libau, near the Great Cave, has an informal homestay program.

Campground   CAMPGROUND **$**
(per person RM5) Camping is permitted near park HQ.

Batu Niah Junction

If your bus arrives late or is leaving early, you might consider overnighting at Batu Niah Junction, a major transport hub 15km south of park HQ.

Hangarlike **Batu Niah Food Court Centre** (⊗24hr) has lots of Chinese and Malay food stalls and, in the little grocery to the left as you enter the hall, **internet access** (per hour RM3; ⊗24hr). Bathrooms are way in back, beyond the terrariums holding reptiles believed to bring good luck – people leave cash offerings for the ancient river turtle, on loan from a Chinese temple, and the albino snake. There are more food stalls and a fruit and veggie market across the highway.

TTL Motel   HOTEL **$$**
(🖊086-738377; d from RM80-118; ⊗reception 24hr; ❄) This newish, 39-room low-rise complex is pricey for what you get, which is mostly convenience. All rooms have windows but some of the more expensive ones are a bit musty. To get there from Batu Niah Food Court Centre, go out the back door and hang a diagonal left.

ⓘ Getting There & Away

Niah National Park is about 115km southwest of Miri and 122km northeast of Bintulu. If you're pressed for time, it can be visited as a day trip from either city.

Park HQ is 15km north of Batu Niah Junction, a major transport hub on the inland (old) Miri–Bintulu highway. This makes getting to the park by public transport a wee bit tricky (but it's much harder to get to from the new coastal highway).

All long-haul buses linking Miri's Pujut Bus Terminal with Bintulu, Sibu and Kuching stop at Batu Niah Junction, but the only way to get from the junction to the park is to hire an unofficial taxi. The price should be RM30 (RM40 for a group of four) but you'll have to nose around the junction to find one. A good place to check: the bench in front of Shen Yang Trading, at the corner of Ngu's Garden Food Court. National park staff (or, after hours, park security personnel) can help arrange a car back to the junction.

From Batu Niah Junction, buses head to Miri (RM10 to RM12) from about 8am to 1am and to Bintulu (RM15, two hours) from about 8am to 10.30pm. Other well-served destinations include Sibu (RM30 to RM40, five to six hours) and Kuching (RM70 to RM80, 12 hours). Kiosks representing various companies can be found at both ends of the building directly across the highway from the Batu Niah Food Court Centre.

From Miri, a taxi to Niah costs RM150 one-way or RM300 return, including three hours of wait time.

Lambir Hills National Park

The 69-sq-km **Lambir Hills National Park** (🖊085-471609; www.sarawakforestry.com; admission RM10; ⊗park office 8am-5pm) shelters dozens of jungle waterfalls, plenty of cool pools where you can take a dip, and a bunch of great walking trails through mixed dipterocarp and *kerangas* forests. A perennial favourite among locals and an important centre of scientific research, Lambir Hills makes a great day or overnight trip out of the city.

The park encompasses a range of low sandstone hills with an extraordinary range of plants and animals – perhaps even, as noted in Sarawak Forestry's publications, 'the greatest level of plant biodiversity on the planet'. Studies of a 52-hectare research plot (closed to visitors) have found an amazing 1200 tree species! Fauna include clouded leopards, barking deer, pangolins, tarsiers, five varieties of civet, 10 bat species and 50 other kinds of mammals, though you are unlikely to see many of them around park HQ. Lambir Hills is also home to an unbelievable 237 species of bird, among them eight kinds of hornbill, and 24 species of frog – and more are being found all the time.

Activities

Lambir Hills' colour-coded trails branch off four primary routes and lead to 14 destinations – rangers, based in an ugly new HQ building opened in 2012, can supply you with a map and are happy to make suggestions. Make sure you get back to park HQ before 5pm – unless you're heading out for a night walk, that is, in which case you need to coordinate with park staff. Hiring a guide (optional) costs RM20 per hour for up to five people.

From HQ, the **Main Trail** follows a small river, Sungai Liam, past two attractive waterfalls to the 25m-high **Latak Waterfall** (1km, 15 minutes to 20 minutes one-way), which has a picnic area, changing rooms and a refreshing, sandy pool suitable for swimming. It can get pretty crowded on weekends and holidays.

You're likely to enjoy more natural tranquility along the path to **Tengkorong Waterfall**, a somewhat strenuous 6km walk (one-way) from park HQ.

Another trail, steep in places, goes to the summit of **Bukit Lambir** (465m; 7km one-way from HQ), which affords fine views. Keep an eye out for changes in the vegetation, including wild orchids, as the elevation rises.

Sleeping & Eating

The park has 13 reasonably comfortable, two-room **chalets** (1/2 rooms with fan RM50/75, with air-con RM100/150); the old ones are wooden, the four new ones are made of concrete. Fan rooms have two beds, while air-con rooms have three. If you get in before 2pm (check-in time), bags can be left at the camp office. **Camping** (per person RM5) is permitted near the park HQ. Individual dorm beds are not available.

Book by calling the park or through Miri's National Park Booking Office; on-line booking is not yet possible. Chalets are sometimes booked out on weekends and during school holidays.

A small **canteen** (Cafeteria; mains RM4-6; ⊘8am or 8.30am-5pm or later) serves fried rice and noodles. Cooking facilities are not available but you can rent an electric kettle (RM5) to boil water for instant noodles.

⊙ Getting There & Away

Park HQ is 32km south of Miri on the inland (old) highway to Bintulu. All the buses that link Miri's Pujut Bus Terminal with Bintulu, Sibu and Kuching pass by here (RM10 from Miri) – just ask the driver to stop. Local buses from Miri to 'Lambir' go to the village of Lambir on the coast, not to the park.

A taxi from Miri costs RM60 one-way (RM120 return, including two hours of wait time).

Miri

POP 295,000

The dynamic oil town of Miri is busy and modern – not much about it is Borneo – but there's plenty of money sloshing around so the eating is good, the broad avenues are brightly lit and there's plenty to do when it's raining. The city's friendly guesthouses are a good place to meet other travellers. The population is about 40% Dayak (mainly Iban), 30% Chinese and 18% Malay.

Miri serves as a major transport hub, so if you're travelling to/from Brunei, Sabah, the Kelabit Highlands or the national parks of Gunung Mulu, Niah or Lambir Hills, chances are you'll pass this way.

⊙ Sights

Miri is not big on historical sites – it was pretty much destroyed during WWII – but it's not an unattractive city. A walk around the centre is a good way to get a feel for the local vibe – streets worth a wander include (from north to south) Jln North Yu Seng, Jln South Yu Seng, Jln Maju and Jln High Street.

Miri City Fan   PARK

(Jln Kipas; ⊘24hr) Decked out in coloured lights at night, this 10.4-hectare park's Chinese- and Malay-style gardens and ponds are great for a stroll. Also boasts a beautiful, new library, an indoor stadium and an Olympic-sized swimming pool (RM1).

Canada Hill   HILL, MUSEUM

(Bukit Kanada, Bukit Tenaga) The low ridge 2km southeast of the town centre was the site of Malaysia's first oil well, the **Grand Old Lady**, drilled in 1910. Appropriately, the old derrick stands right outside the **Petroleum Museum** (Jln Canada Hill; ⊙9am-4.30pm, closed Fri), whose interactive exhibits, some designed for kids, are a good, pro-Big Oil introduction to the hugely lucrative industry that has so enriched Miri (and Malaysia's federal government).

The hill itself is a popular exercise spot, and it's worth driving up here at sunset (it's a bit far to walk) for the views across town to the South China Sea.

Saberkas Weekend Market   MARKET
(⊙3pm Fri-evening Saturday, daily during Ramadan) One of the most colourful and friendly markets in Sarawak. Vendors are more than happy to answer questions about their colourful products, which include tropical fruits and veggies, BBQ chicken, satay, grilled stingray and handicrafts. Situated about 3km northeast of the centre near the Boulevard Commercial Centre, Miri's newest shopping mall. Served by buses 1, 1A, 31, 42, 62, 63, 66 and 68.

San Ching Tian Temple   TEMPLE
(Jln Krokop 9) Said to be the largest Taoist temple in Southeast Asia. Built in 2000, the design features intricate dragon reliefs brought over from China. A huge new Chinese temple is being built right nearby. Situated about 1km northwest of the Saberkas Weekend Market. Served by bus 44.

🏃 Activities

Sandflies can be a pesky problem at Miri-area beaches.

Scuba Diving   SCUBA DIVING
Although the waters off Miri are better known for drilling than diving, the area – much of it part of the **Miri-Sibuti Coral Reef Marine Park** (www.fri.gov.my/friswak/epro coral.htm) – has some excellent 7m- to 30m-deep scuba sites, including old oil platforms teeming with fish and assorted trawler and freighter wrecks. Water visibility is at its best from March to September.

Red Monkey Divers (☎014-699 8296; www. redmonkeydivers.com; Jln Dato Abang Indeh, Gymkhana Club; ⊙10am-5pm Mon-Sat, closed Dec-Feb), based about 2km south of the Mega Hotel, is a professional outfit that offers PADI and BSAC diving courses.

Hash House Harriers   RUNNING
(www.mirihhh.com) Visitors are welcome to join friendly locals and expats for runs, which begin at 5.15pm every Tuesday and at 4.30pm on the first Saturday of the month. For details, ask the owners of the Ming Café (p436), who are enthusiastic hashers.

Megalanes East Bowling Alley   BOWLING
(Map p434; 3rd fl, Bintang Plaza, Jln Miri Pujut; per game RM3.80-5.90, shoes RM2; ⊙10am-midnight) The 24 lanes are a great escape on a rainy day.

☞ Tours

Miri-based companies offering trekking in northeastern Sarawak include:

Borneo Jungle Safari   TREKKING
(☎085-422595; www.borneojunglesafari.com; Lot 1396, 1st fl, Centre Point Commercial Centre II, Jln Kubu) Runs the Ba Kelalan Apple Lodge Homestay up in Ba Kelalan.

Borneo Tropical Adventure   TREKKING
(Map p434; ☎085-419337; www.borneotropicalad ventures.com; Lot 906, Shop 12, ground fl, Soon Hup Tower, Jln Merbau) Runs the Benarat Inn at Gunung Mulu National Park.

🎉 Festivals

Borneo Jazz Festival   JAZZ
(www.jazzborneo.com; Jln Temenggong Datuk Oyong Lawai; ⊙weekend in mid-May) Features an eclectic assemblage of international talent. Formerly known as the Miri International Jazz Festival.

🛏 Sleeping

Miri has some of Sarawak's best backpackers' guesthouses.

If you're on a tight budget, choose your bed carefully – at the cheapie dives catering to oil-rig roustabouts (eg on and east of Jln South Yu Seng), many of the dreary rooms are windowless and musty, and Miri's brothel business booms at some of the shadier bottom-end digs.

TOP CHOICE Dillenia Guesthouse   GUESTHOUSE $$
(Map p434; ☎085-434204; https://sites.google. com/site/dilleniaguesthouse; 1st fl, 846 Jln Sida; dm/s/d/q incl breakfast RM30/50/80/110; ❄@⊜) This super-welcoming guesthouse, with 11 rooms and lots of nice little touches (eg plants in the bathrooms), lives up to its motto, 'a home away from home'. Incredibly helpful Mrs Lee is an artesian well of useful travel information and tips – and leech socks. All rooms have shared bathrooms. Served by local bus 42.

Miri

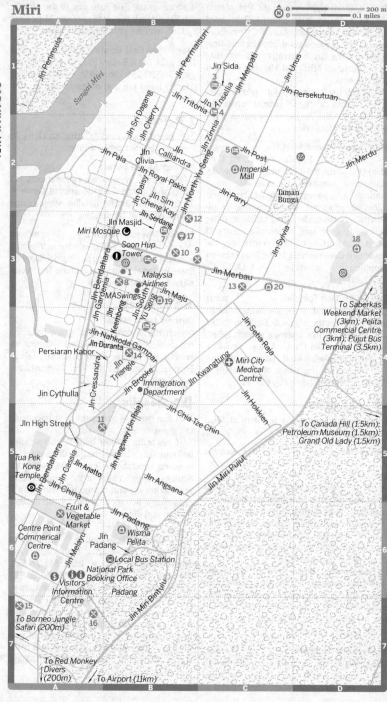

Miri

⊕ **Activities, Courses & Tours**
1 Borneo Tropical Adventure B3
Megalanes East Bowling Alley ..... (see 18)

⊜ **Sleeping**
2 Apollo Hotel B4
3 Dillenia Guesthouse C1
4 Highlands Backpackers C1
5 Imperial Hotel C2
6 Mega Hotel B3
7 Minda Guesthouse B3

⊗ **Eating**
8 Khan's Restaurant Islamic B3
9 Meng Chai Seafood B3
10 Ming Café B3

11 Miri Central Market A5
12 Muara Restoran B3
13 Rainforest Cafe C3
14 Sin Liang Supermarket B4
15 Summit Cafe A7
16 Tamu Muhibbah A7

⊖ **Drinking**
17 Barcelona B3

⊜ **Shopping**
18 Bintang Plaza D3
19 Borneo Arts B3
20 Miri Handicraft Centre C3
Popular Book Store .... (see 18)

Minda Guesthouse   GUESTHOUSE $
(Map p434; ☑085-411422; www.mindaguesthouse.
com; 1st & 2nd fl, Lot 637, Jln North Yu Seng; dm per
person incl breakfast RM20, d RM50-60; ❋@☎)
In the heart of Miri's dining and drinking
district, this comfy establishment offers
13 clean rooms with colourful bedclothes,
a small kitchen, a DVD lounge, unlimited
tea and coffee and a great rooftop sundeck.
Dorm rooms are pretty packed, with eight or
12 beds. Two rooms come with private bath.
Light sleepers be warned: the nightclub
across the street pumps out music until 2am.

Highlands Backpackers   GUESTHOUSE $
(Map p434; ☑085-422327; www.highlandsmiri.
com; 2nd fl, Lot 839, Jln Merpati; dm/d RM22/50;
❋@☎) Miri's original guesthouse, in new
digs since mid-2012, offers 15 rooms (52
beds), two-thirds of them with windows; a
lounge with satellite TV; and inexpensive
laundry (RM8 per load, including drying).
The dorm rooms have six to 14 beds. The
affable owner, a Twin Otter pilot from New
Zealand everyone calls Captain David, sometimes drops by. Served by local bus 42.

Imperial Hotel   HOTEL $$
(Map p434; ☑085-431133; www.imperialhotel.
my; Jln Post; d from RM200; ❋☎☎) The city
centre's poshest hotel boasts 23 floors, 266
rooms, business and fitness centres, a sauna
and a swimming pool.

Mega Hotel   HOTEL $$
(Map p434; ☑085-432432; www.megahotel.com.
my; 907 Jln Merbau; r from RM195; ❋@☎☎) Don't
judge a hotel by its tasteless exterior or tacky
lobby – the 288 rooms here, spread over 16

storeys, are comfortable and very spacious,
if a bit old-fashioned. Amenities include a fitness centre (7th floor) and a 30m pool with
town views and a jacuzzi (4th floor).

Apollo Hotel   HOTEL $
(Map p434; ☑085-433077; fax 085-419 964; 4 Jln
South Yu Seng; s/d/tr from RM65/75/85; ❋) An
old-fashioned but well-maintained Chinese
cheapie. Very central. The 18 rooms are simple and spotless. Reception is around behind
the Apollo Seafood Centre.

Miri Trail Guesthouse   AIRPORT HOTEL $
(☑012-8040806, 017-850 3666; www.miritrail
guesthouse.com; Airport Commercial Centre, Jln
Airport; dm/d incl breakfast RM25/55, day use
RM15/30; ❋@☎) A basic crash pad with six
rooms, most without windows. Bathrooms
are shared. Situated across the road from
the airport (above the MASwings office), so
if you're transiting through Miri you can rest
here overnight or during the day.

✗ Eating

TOP
CHOICE **Summit Cafe**   DAYAK $
(Map p434; Centre Point Commercial Centre, Jln
Melayu; mains from RM3; ⊙6am-early afternoon
Mon-Sat) If you've never tried Kelabit cuisine, this place will open up whole new
worlds for your tastebuds. Try the colourful
array of 'jungle food' – *canko manis* (forest
ferns), *dure'* (fried jungle leaf), minced tapioca leaves, and (sometimes) wild boar. The
best selection is available before 11.30am –
once the food runs out they close! Gets rave
reviews.

Meng Chai Seafood
SEAFOOD $$

(Map p434; 11a Jln Merbau; fish per kg RM25-80; ⊗4.30pm-midnight) Discerning locals crowd this first-rate eatery, housed in two and very unassuming adjacent buildings. Specialities include barbequed garlic fish, *kampung*-raised chicken and *midin* fern. Seawater tanks hold live clams and prawns. Does not serve pork.

Rainforest Cafe
CHINESE $$

(Map p434; 49 Jln Brooke; mains from RM10; ⊗10am-2pm & 5-11.30pm) Often packed with local families, this breezy, open-air eatery specialises in Chinese-style dishes such as 'braised rainforest bean curd', 'crispy roasted chicken' and 'pork leg Philippine style'.

Muara Restoran
INDONESIAN $$

(Map p434; Jln North Yu Seng; mains RM7-15; ⊗11am-4am) Expat Indonesian oil workers in bright yellow overalls flock to this tin-roofed shed for *lalapan* (tofu, tempeh, meat, spinach-like greens, raw cucumber and rice, eaten with spicy *sambal belacan*). Great for a late-late meal.

Ming Café
ASIAN, WESTERN $$

(Map p434; www.mingcafe.com.my; cnr Jln North Yu Seng & Jln Merbau; mains RM5-25; ⊗10am-2am) Take your pick of Chinese, Malay, buffet-style Indian (from RM5) and Western food at this ever-busy corner eatery. Fresh fruit juice and shakes cost RM6 to RM8.50. The bar stocks two dozen bottled beers and has six beers on tap, including Guinness. Happy hangout of the Hash House Harriers.

Khan's Restaurant Islamic
INDIAN $

(Map p434; 229 Jln Maju; mains RM4-8; ⊗6.30am-8.30pm;) This simple canteen is one of Miri's best North Indian eateries, whipping up tasty treats like mouth-watering chicken vindaloo (RM12) and seven veggie mains (RM4).

Miri Central Market
HAWKER $

(Map p434; Jln Brooke, Pasar Pusat Miri; mains RM2.50-4; ⊗7am-midnight) Especially popular Chinese food purveyors here include Stall 5, which serves up chicken curry rice in the morning, and Stall 6, known for its chicken porridge (available in the evening).

Tamu Muhibbah
MARKET

(Map p434; Jln Padang; ⊗2am-6pm or 7pm) Fruits and veggies, some straight from the jungle, are sold at stalls owned by Chinese, Malay, Iban and Orang Ulu.

Sin Liang Supermarket
SUPERMARKET $

(Map p434; Jln Duranta; ⊗8.30am-9pm) Well stocked with munchies, toiletries and Aussie wines.

🍺 Drinking

Barcelona
BAR

(Map p434; Jln North Yu Seng; draught beer RM8-12; ⊗4pm-2am, happy hour 4-9pm) More equatorial than Iberian, this place has a relaxed, upscale vibe and a big screen for footy. Seating is open-air at wooden tables. Liquid specialities range from Spanish and Australian wines to mojitos (RM15) and sex on the beach (RM20), not something you often find in Malaysia. Serves tapas and some Western dishes. The bar next door, World-Club Station, hosts a rockin' Filipino band from 10pm to 2am daily except Monday.

Pelita Commercial Centre
BAR DISTRICT

(cnr Jln Miri Pujut & Jln Sehati) If you're keen on a pub crawl, consider catching a cab to this warren of small streets lined with pubs, cafes, restaurants and dodgy karaoke places

---

ECO-LODGE

Looking for great place to hang out and be mellow, surrounded by tropical fruit trees? **TreeTops Lodge** (☎085-472172; www.treetops-borneo.com; Kampung Siwa Jaya; d/q incl breakfast RM120/180, with fan & shared bathroom RM80; ❄️🐭), run by Mike (a retired British pilot) and his Sarawakian wife Esther, has eight, beautifully maintained rooms – four of them quite basic – set in a lovely, calming garden. When you're not lounging on the beach (2km away), you can fish for tilapia in the pond or go hiking. A light lunch costs RM7, and dinner is RM22.

TreeTops is 15km southwest of Miri along the coastal (new) road to Bintulu. From Miri's local bus terminal, take bus 13 (RM4, every 1½ to two hours from 5.50am to 6.30pm) to the end of the line, whence it's a 2km walk. From the airport, a blue taxi costs about RM75. TreeTops is not far from the western reaches of Lambir Hills National Park but getting to park HQ involves a 40km drive (transport available).

3km north of the centre. Don't mess with the local toughs.

Shopping

Miri Handicraft Centre HANDICRAFTS
(Map p434; cnr Jln Brooke & Jln Merbau; ⊘8am-5.30pm) Thirteen stalls, rented from the city, sell colourful bags, baskets, sarongs, textiles etc made by Iban, Kelabit, Kenyah/Kayan, Lun Bawang, Chinese and Malay artisans. Stall No 7 has some fine Kelabit beadwork from Bario.

Borneo Arts HANDICRAFTS
(Map p434; Jln South Yu Seng; ⊘9am-9pm) Dayak handicrafts and souvenirs.

Popular Book Store BOOKS
(Map p434; 2nd fl, Bintang Plaza, Jln Miri Pujut; ⊘10am-10pm) A mega-bookshop with a huge selection of English books, and Lonely Planet titles in English and Chinese.

Bintang Plaza SHOPPING CENTRE
(Map p434; Jln Miri Pujut; ⊘10am-10pm) A modern, multi-storey, air-con mall that could *almost* be in Singapore. The 3rd floor is full of shops specialising in computers and cameras.

Information

For local low-down, some great tips and an outline of local history, see Miri's unofficial website, www.miriresortcity.com.

ATMs can be found at the airport and are sprinkled all over the city centre.

It's a good idea to stock up on medicines and first-aid supplies before heading inland to Gunung Mulu National Park or the Kelabit Highlands.

Internet Access
Internet Shop (1st fl, Shop 1-04, Soon Hup Tower, cnr Jln Bendahara & Jln Merbau; per hr RM2; ⊘8am-8pm) Popular with zombified teenage gamers.

IT Cyber Station (3rd fl, western end, Bintang Plaza, Jln Miri Pujut; per hr RM2.50; ⊘10am-10pm) Has 72 computers.

Laundry
If you drop off your clothes at **EcoLaundry** (☑016-878 9908, 085-414266; 638 Jln North Yu Seng; per kg RM5; ⊘7am-7pm Mon-Sat, to 5pm Sun) before flying up to Gunung Mulu National Park or the Kelabit Highlands, you'll save luggage weight and have clean undies when you return! Offers free pickup at guesthouses and hotels.

Medical Services
Colombia Asia Hospital (☑085-437755; http://columbiaasia.com/miri; Jln Bulan Sabit; ⊘24hr) A 35-bed private hospital, used by many expats, with a 24-hour accident and emergency ward and a 24-hour ambulance. Situated 4km northeast of the Mega Hotel.

Miri City Medical Centre (☑085-426622; www.mcmcmiri.com; 916-920 Jln Hokkien) Has an ambulance, a 24-hour accident and emergency department and various private clinics. Accepts direct payment for in-patient care from certain insurance companies. Conveniently located in the city centre.

Post
Main Post Office (Jln Post; ⊘8am-4pm Mon-Fri, to 2.30pm Sat)

Tourist Information
National Park Booking Office (☑085-434184; www.sarawakforestry.com; 452 Jln Melayu; ⊘8am-5pm Mon-Fri) Inside the Visitors Information Centre. Has details on Sarawak's national parks and can book beds and rooms at Niah and Lambir Hills (but not at Gunung Mulu or Similajau).

Visitors Information Centre (☑085-434181; www.sarawaktourism.com; 452 Jln Melayu; ⊘8am-5pm Mon-Fri, 9am-3pm Sat, Sun & public holidays) The helpful staff can provide city maps, information on accommodation and a list of licensed guides. Situated in a little park.

Visas
Immigration Department (Jabatan Imigresen; ☑085-442117; www.imi.gov.my; 2nd fl, Yulan Plaza, cnr Jln Kingsway & Jln Brooke; ⊘8am-5pm Mon-Thu, 8-11.45am & 2.15-5pm Fri) For visa extensions.

Getting There & Away

Miri is 212km northeast of Bintulu and 36km southwest of the Brunei border.

Air
AirAsia (www.airasia.com) can get you to Kuching, Kota Kinabalu (KK), Kuala Lumpur (KL), Johor Bahru (across the causeway from Singapore) and Singapore, while **Malaysia Airlines** (www.malaysiaairlines.com) flies to KL.

Miri is the main hub of the Malaysia Airlines subsidiary **MASwings** (www.maswings.com.my), whose inexpensive flights serve destinations such as Gunung Mulu National Park, Bario and Ba Kelalan (in the Kelabit Highlands), Kuching, Sibu, Bintulu, Marudi, Limbang, Lawas, Pulau Labuan and KK.

Miri's **airport** (Jln Airport) has a separate check-in area for MASwings' 'Rural Air Service' routes, eg to Gunung Mulu National Park and Bario. If you're flying on a Twin Otter, you'll be asked to weigh yourself on a giant scale while holding your carry-on.

Free wi-fi is available at Starbuck's, on the check-in level. In the departure area (beyond security), the Coffee Bean & Tea Leaf also has wi-fi; the password is posted next to the cash register.

Bus & Van

Long-distance buses use the Pujut Bus Terminal, about 4km northeast of the centre.

Once or twice an hour, buses head to Kuching (RM80, 12 to 14 hours, departures from 6am to 10pm) via the inland (old) Miri–Bintulu highway, with stops at Lambir Hills National Park, Batu Niah Junction (access point for Niah National Park; RM10 to RM12, 1½ hours), Bintulu (RM20 to RM27, 3½ hours) and Sibu (RM40 to RM50, seven to eight hours). This route is highly competitive so it pays to shop around. Taking a spacious 'VIP bus', with just three seats across, is like flying 1st class! Companies include **Bintang Jaya** (☑085-432178, 085-438301), **Bus Asia** (Biaramas; ☑414999, hotline 082-411111; http://mybus.com.my) and **Miri Transport Company** (MTC; ☑085-438161; www.mtcmiri.com).

Bintang Jaya also has services northeast to Limbang (RM45, four hours), Lawas (RM75, six hours) and KK (RM90, 10 hours). Buses leave Miri at 8.30am; departures from KK are at 7am. **Borneo Bus** (☑010-967 6648) serves the same destinations, except on Wednesday, at 7.45am; departures from KK are also at 7.45am. Bus Asia has a bus to Limbang at 2pm. Be aware that with all these companies, getting off in Brunei is not allowed.

ℹ️ Getting Around

To/From the Airport

A red-and-yellow **taxi** (☑013-838 1000; ⊙24hr) from the airport to the city centre (15 minutes, in traffic 25 minutes) costs RM22 (RM33 from 11.45pm to 6am); a *kupon teksi* (taxi coupon) can be purchased at the **taxi desk** (⊙7am-11pm) just outside the baggage-claim area (next to the car-rental desks). If you're heading from town to the airport, the fare is RM20. Spacious blue 'executive taxis' charge RM30.

Bus 28 links the local bus station with the airport (RM2.60) every 1½ hours or so; last departures are at 5.20pm (from the airport) and 6.30pm (from the local bus station). At the airport, the stop is on the Arrivals Island in front of the terminal (look for an upright reading 'Bas').

Bus

Local bus transport is handled by three companies: Miri City Bus, Miri Transport Company (MTC) and Miri Belait Transport. The **local bus station** (Jln Padang), next to the Visitors Information Centre, has schedules posted. Fares start at RM1; most lines run from 7am to 6pm.

MTC buses 20 and 33A link the local bus station with Pujut Bus Terminal (RM1.60 to RM2.60, hourly until 6.30pm).

Car

Most of Miri's guesthouses are happy to organise private transport to area destinations such as Lambir Hills National Park (RM85 return) and Niah National Park (RM180 return).

The half-dozen car rental companies with desks at Miri Airport, just outside of baggage claim, include:

FT Car Rental (☑085-438415; www.ftcarrental.com)

Golden System Car Rental (☑085-613359; www.gocar.com.my)

Hertz (☑012-879 2979, 085-614740; www.hertz.com; ⊙8am-5pm, closed Sun & public holidays)

Kong Teck Car Rental (☑085-617767; www.kongteck.com.my)

Taxi

Taxi stations are sprinkled around the city centre. A short cab ride around downtown is RM10, while a ride from the centre to the Pujut Bus Terminal costs RM15. Taxis run by the **Miri Taxi Association** (☑085-432 277; ⊙24hr) can be summoned by phone 24 hours a day.

NORTHEASTERN SARAWAK

Gunung Mulu National Park

Also known as the **Gunung Mulu World Heritage Area** (☑085-792300; www.mulupark.com; adult/child for 5-day pass RM30/10; ⊙HQ office 8am-5pm), this park is one of the most majestic and thrilling nature destinations anywhere in Southeast Asia. No surprise, then, that Unesco declared it a World Heritage Site in 2005.

Few national parks anywhere in the world pack so many natural marvels into such a small area. Home to caves (www.mulucaves.org) of mind-boggling proportions, otherworldly geological phenomena such as the Pinnacles, and brilliant old-growth tropical rainforest (the park has 17 different vegetation zones), this is truly one of the world's wonders.

Among the remarkable features in this 529-sq-km park are its two highest peaks, Gunung Mulu (2376m) and Gunung Api (1710m). In between are rugged karst

GETTING TO BRUNEI: MIRI TO BANDAR SERI BEGAWAN

Getting to the border The only company that's allowed to take passengers from Miri's Pujut Bus Terminal to destinations inside Brunei is **PHLS** (Jesselton Express; in Brunei +673-718-3838, +673-719-3835, +673-717-7755, in Miri 085-438301), which sends buses to Bandar Seri Begawan (BSB; RM40) via Kuala Belait (RM25) and Seria (RM25) at 8.15am and 3.45pm. Tickets are sold at the Bintang Jaya counter. Another option to BSB (RM50, 2¾ hours) is to take a **private van** (☑ in BSB +673-887 7642, in Miri 016-873 2742) from Pujut Bus Terminal; hotel pickup can be arranged. For details, contact the Dillenia (p433) (Mrs Lee), Minda (p435) or Highlands (p435) guesthouses in Miri or Miri's Visitors Information Centre (p437).

At the border Border formalities are usually quick and for most nationalities Bruniean visas are free (see p471 for more details), but the process can slow down buses.

Moving on Brunei's Serasa Ferry Terminal, 20km northeast of BSB, is linked by ferry with Pulau Labuan, from where boats go to Menumbok in Sabah. Several buses a day go from BSB to Sarawak's Limbang Division and destinations in Sabah. If you're eventually headed overland to Sabah, make sure you have enough pages in your passport for 10 new chops (stamps).

See p466 for details on doing the trip in the opposite direction.

mountains, deep gorges with crystal-clear rivers, and a unique mosaic of habitats supporting fascinating and incredibly diverse wildlife. Mulu's most famous trekking attractions are the Pinnacles, a forest of razor-sharp limestone spires, and the so-called Headhunters' Trail, which follows an old tribal war path down to Limbang.

Some cave tours (especially the more difficult ones) and treks (especially the longer ones) are booked out well in advance.

The park's facilities are managed by Borsarmulu, a controversial private company partly owned by the sister of Sarawak's chief minister.

◉ Sights & Activities

When you register, park staff will give you a placemat-sized schematic map of the park on which you can plan out your daily activities. HQ staff are generally very helpful in planning itineraries and are happy to (try to) accommodate special needs and interests (eg for family-friendly activities).

All the plankwalks (eg to the entrance to the Deer Cave) are wheelchair-accessible but cave interiors are not.

The park's excellent website (www.mulupark.com) and the brochures available at park HQ have details on walks and boat trips not covered here.

🏃 Activities Without Guides

Visitors are not allowed to go inside any of the caves without a qualified guide, but you

can take a number of **jungle walks** unaccompanied so long as you inform the park office (or, when it's closed, someone across the path in the Park Security building). For instance, you can walk to the **Bat Observatory** near the entrance to the Deer Cave and to **Paku Waterfall** (3km one-way), where it's possible to swim.

Mulu Discovery Centre   MUSEUM
(⏰7.30am-9pm) Offers a fine introduction to the park as a 'biodiversity hotspot' and to its extraordinary geology. Situated in the new HQ building, between the park office and Café Mulu.

FREE **Tree Top Tower**   BIRDWATCHING
(admission free, key deposit RM50) Basically a 30m-high bird hide. The best time to spot our feathered friends is early in the morning (5am to 9am) or in the late afternoon and early evening (4pm to 8pm). Reserve a time slot and pick up the key at park HQ or, after 4.30pm, from Park Security (across the boardwalk from the park office). Situated about 500m from park HQ.

Guided Forest Walks

Nightwalk   WALKING
(Night Shift; per person RM15; ⏰7pm except if raining) The ideal first-night introduction to the park's nocturnal fauna, this 1½- to two-hour walk (the route varies) wends its way through alluvial forest. Creatures you're very likely to see – but only after the guide points them out – include tree frogs just

1cm long, enormous spiders, vine snakes that are a dead ringer for a vine wrapped around a branch, and stick insects (phasmids), extraordinary creatures up to 30cm long that look like they've been assembled from pencils and toothpicks. If you put your torch (bring one!) up to eye level and shine it into the foliage, the eyes of spiders and other creatures will reflect brightly back.

Don't wear insect repellent or you risk repelling some of the insects you're trying to see. Mozzies are not a problem.

If you order dinner at the Wild Mulu Café before heading out, you can pick it up when you return (make sure you're back before 9.30pm). Eateries outside the park stay open later.

You can take the nightwalk trail on your own, without a guide, either before 5pm (so that your scent, which scares away the wildlife, dissipates before the guided group comes through) or after 8pm. Make sure you inform either the park office or, when it's closed, someone in the Park Security pavilion. Between 5pm and 8pm, you can design your own nightwalk by taking trails the guided group isn't using.

Mulu Canopy Skywalk   WALKING
(per person RM35; ⊙departures every 1 or 2 hrs 7am-2pm) Climbing up into the rainforest canopy is the only way to see what a tropical rainforest is all about because most of the flora and fauna do their thing high up in the trees, not down on the ground, where less than 2% of the forest's total sunlight is available. Mulu's 480m-long skywalk, unforgettably anchored to a series of huge trees, has handy signage and is one of the best in Southeast Asia. Often gets booked out early – for a specific time slot, reserve as soon as you've got your flight.

Show Caves
Mulu's 'show caves' (the park's name for caves that can be visited without specialised training or equipment) are its most popular attraction and for good reason: they are, quite simply, awesome. All are accessible on guided walks from park HQ. Bring a powerful torch.

Deer Cave & Lang's Cave   CAVE
(per person RM20; ⊙departures at 2pm & 2.30pm) A lovely 3km walk (40 minutes to 60 minutes) through the rainforest along a plankwalk takes you to these adjacent caverns. The highlight here is not so much what's in the caves as what comes out of them

every evening around dusk (unless it's raining): millions of bats in spiralling, twirling clouds that look a bit like swarms of cartoon bees. It's an awe-inspiring sight. The bats' corkscrew trajectory is designed to foil the dinner plans of bat hawks perched on the surrounding cliffs. Count on getting back to park HQ at around 7pm.

The **Mulu Bat-Cam** (www.muluparkbat cams.com) – in fact, five infrared webcams – follows the lives of bats inside the Deer Cave. It's not internet live-streamed yet but you can see the feed at the **Bat Observatory**, next to the cave's grassy bat-viewing amphitheatre, as well as back at HQ in the park office.

The Deer Cave – over 2km in length and 174m high – is the world's largest cave passage open to the public. (It was considered the world's largest cave passage, full stop, until what may be an even larger one was discovered in Vietnam in 2009.) It is home to two million to three million bats belonging to 12 species (more than in any other single cave in the world) who cling to the roof in a seething black mass as they gear up for their evening prowl.

We're not sure who did the calculations or how, but it's said that the Deer Cave's bats devour 30 tonnes of mosquitoes every night. That's one reason why mosquito bites are almost unknown at Mulu.

If it's raining, the bats usually (but not always) stay home because echolocation (the way they find prey) is not very good at honing in on flying insects amid an onslaught of raindrops.

Wind Cave & Clearwater Cave   CAVE
(per person incl boat ride RM55; ⊙departures at 8.45am & 9.15am) Zipping along an upland jungle river in a flat-bottomed longboat is not a bad way to start the day! This tour takes about four hours, leaving time for another cave visit in the afternoon – or the afternoon flight to Miri.

The Wind Cave, named for the deliciously cool breezes that flow through it, has several chambers – including the cathedral-like King's Chamber – filled with phantasmagorical forests of stalactites and stalagmites. Clearwater Cave is vast – as of 2012, 225km of passages had been surveyed – of which only a tiny segment is open to casual visitors. As the name suggests, the highlight here is an underground clearwater river.

After visiting the caves, you can take a dip in the refreshingly cool waters of a sandy

GUIDES, RESERVATIONS & FEES

For almost all caves, walks and treks in **Gunung Mulu National Park** (☎085-792300; www.mulupark.com), visitors must be accompanied by a guide licensed by Sarawak Forestry, generally supplied either by the park or by an adventure tour agency (eg those based in Kuching, Miri or Limbang). Prices in this chapter are for tours booked directly through the park, as are the time frames for making reservations; agencies charge considerably more but also supply extras, such as meals, and can often offer more flexibility when it comes to advance booking.

If you've got your heart set on adventure caving, or on trekking to the Pinnacles or up to the summit of Gunung Mulu, advance reservations – by phone or email (enquiries@ mulupark.com) – are a must. They're doubly important if you'll be coming in July, August or September, when some routes are booked out several months ahead, and are absolutely crucial if your travel dates are not flexible. If this is your situation, don't buy your air tickets until your trek or caving dates are confirmed.

Bookings are not a zero sum game: if the park has sufficient advance notice of your plans, they may be able to reassign guides to accommodate you. And if you can spend a week or two hanging out at the park (this usually means staying in a basic guesthouse outside the park's boundaries as in-park accommodation is in very short supply), trekking and caving slots do sometimes open up.

The park's own trekking and caving guides are well trained and speak good English but there are only about 15 of them. Park administrators have been working to improve the quality of the guides but this process has excluded – and thus angered – some locals who used to earn a living as (semi-qualified) park guides.

Some travellers hire freelance guides unattached to a tour agency, eg from a nearby village. Despite being licensed by Sarawak Forestry (they wouldn't be allowed to operate in the park if they weren't), such guides' nature knowledge and English skills vary widely, from excellent to barely sufficient. In addition, they may lack state-of-the-art safety training and equipment (eg two-way radios, which the park supplies to all of its own guides) and, perhaps most importantly, are unlikely to have proper insurance, a factor that could be crucial if a helicopter evacuation is necessary.

A caving group must consist of at least four participants (including the guide) so that if someone is injured, one person can stay with them and the other two can head out of the cave together to seek help.

Park prices for caving and treks are now on a straight per-person basis (minimum three people).

swimming hole so don't forget your swimsuit; changing facilities are available. It's no longer possible to walk back to park HQ.

Tours begin with a stop at the riverside village of Batu Bungan, set up by the government as part of a campaign to discourage the nomadic lifestyle of the Penan. Locals sell trinkets and handicrafts.

Fast Lane   CAVE
(per person incl boat RM55; ☺1.30pm) This route through Lagang Cave has gotten rave reviews since it opened in 2010 thanks to its extraordinary stalactites and stalagmites. Keep an eye out for 'moonmilk', a fibrous mineral formation – known to scientists as Lublinite – created when bacteria break down calcite, the main component of limestone. Don't touch it – it's very fragile!

Getting to the cave requires a one-hour walk; the entire visit takes three or four hours. Groups are limited to eight people.

Adventure Caves

Cave routes that require special equipment and a degree of caving (spelunking) experience are known here as 'adventure caves'. Rosters for the eight half- or all-day options fill up early so reserve well ahead. Groups are limited to eight participants. Heavy rains can cause caves to flood.

Caving routes are graded beginner, intermediate and advanced; guides determine each visitors' suitability based on their previous caving experience. If you have no background in spelunking, you will be required to do an intermediate route (Racer Cave) before moving on to an advanced one.

Minimum ages are 12 for intermediate and 16 for advanced. The park office has details on 'family adventure caving', ie a section of Lagang Cave that's suitable for the entire family. Fees include a helmet and a headlamp; bring closed shoes, a first-aid kit and clothes you won't mind getting dirty in.

Keep in mind that adventure caving is not for everyone, and halfway into a cave passage is not the best time to discover that you suffer from claustrophobia, fear the dark or simply don't like slithering in the mud with all sorts of unknown creepy crawlies.

Sarawak Chamber ADVANCED CAVING

(per person RM225; ⊙departure at 7am) Measuring an incredible 700m long, 400m wide and 70m high, this chamber – discovered in 1981 – has been called the world's largest enclosed space. Don't count on seeing much, though – ordinary lights are no match for the ocean of black emptiness, big enough to park 10 A380s lined up nose to tail. This circuit is very demanding – getting to the cave and back involves six hours of trekking (three hours each way) and moving around inside the cave requires some use of fixed ropes. The whole route takes 10 to 15 hours.

Clearwater Connection ADVANCED CAVING

(per person RM170) This 4.8km, four- to eight-hour circuit starts at Wind Cave and heads into the wilds of the vast Clearwater Cave system. There's a good bit of scrambling and the route includes a 1.5km river section.

Lagang Cave INTERMEDIATE CAVING

(per person RM95) Lots of stalagmites, stalactites and boulders, plus an ancient river bed. No climbing. Takes two to four hours.

Racer Cave INTERMEDIATE CAVING

(per person RM95; ⊙departure at 9am) Has some rope-assisted sections that require a bit of upper-body strength. Named after the non-dangerous cave racer snake, which dines mainly on bats. Takes two to four hours.

Trekking & Climbing

Mulu offers some of the best and most accessible jungle trekking in Borneo. The forest here is in excellent condition and there are routes for every level of fitness and skill.

Expect rain, leeches, slippery and treacherous conditions, and a very hot workout – carry lots of water. Guides are required for overnights, except for the Headhunters' Trail. Book well ahead. Don't even think of taking one of these treks if you've got asthma, or heart or knee problems.

Bring a first-aid kit and a torch/flashlight.

The Pinnacles TREKKING

(per person RM325) The Pinnacles are an incredible formation of 45m-high stone spires protruding from the forested flanks of Gunung Api. Getting there involves a boat ride (you can stop off at Wind Cave and Clearwater Cave for a fee of RM20) and, between two overnights at Camp 5, an unrelentingly steep 2.4km ascent; the final section – much more gruelling than anything on Mt Kinabalu – involves some serious clambering and some rope and ladder work. Coming down is just as taxing so when you stagger into Camp 5, a swim in the cool, clear river may look pretty enticing. The trail passes through some gorgeous jungle.

Bring shoes that will give you traction on sharp and slippery rocks, bedding (many people find that a sarong is warm enough at Camp 5) and enough food (eg instant noodles) for six meals. Cooking equipment and gas stoves are available at Camp 5, home – recent climbers report – to lots of stinging bees.

Gunung Mulu Summit TREKKING

(per person RM385, with a porter RM475) The climb to the summit of Gunung Mulu (2376m) – described recently by one satisfied ascendee as 'gruelling' and, near the top, 'treacherous' – is a classic Borneo adventure. If you're very fit and looking for real adventure, this 24km trek may be for you.

Bring proper hiking shoes, a sleeping bag (Camp 4 can get quite chilly), a sleeping pad (unless you don't mind sleeping on wooden boards), rain gear (some groups end up having rain the whole way) and enough food for four days. The camps along the way have very basic cooking equipment, including a gas stove. Bring water-purification tablets if you're leery of drinking the rainwater collected at shelters en route. Near the summit you may spend much of your time inside clouds; a fleece jacket is the best way to ward off the damp and cold. Recent trekkers report having been visited by rats at Camp 3 and by squirrels who were 'keen on noodles' at Camp 4. The trip takes four days and three nights.

Headhunters' Trail TREKKING

The physically undemanding Headhunters' Trail is a backdoor route from Mulu to Limbang and can be done in either direction, although most people start at the park. The route is named after the Kayan war parties that used to make their way up the Sungai Melinau from the Baram area to the Melinau Gorge, then dragged their canoes overland to the Sungai Terikan to raid the peoples of the Limbang region.

Starting in Limbang, it's possible travel up to the park without a guide, hiring transport (a vehicle and then a boat) as you go. The journey takes two days and one night. If you're on your own, don't forget to contact the park to reserve sleeping space at Camp 5.

Heading down to Limbang, getting from Kuala Terikan (11km on foot from park HQ) or nearby Lubang Cina, both uninhabited, to Medamit (linked by road with Limbang) is possible only if you arrange in advance to be met by a boatman or a guide. Mr Lim of Limbang-based **Borneo Touch Ecotour** (☏013-844 3861; www.walk2mulu.com) can organise a boat and a van in either direction for RM500 for up to five people, and also offers well-reviewed tour packages.

🛏 Sleeping

Accommodation options range from longhouse-style luxury to extremely basic digs. MASwings uses 68-seat turboprops for the Miri–Mulu route, so depending on how long people stay, there may end up being more seats on the planes than there are places to stay inside the park.

Camping is no longer permitted at park HQ but you can pitch a tent at some of the guesthouses just outside the park (across the bridge from HQ). Elsewhere in the park, the only places you can sleep out – and then only if you have reservations (space is limited) – are Camp 5 (tents prohibited) and several huts along the Gunung Mulu Summit trail.

Inside the National Park

Park HQ, a lovely spot set amid semi-wild jungle, has 24-hour electricity, tap water that's safe to drink and a total of 88 beds. All private rooms have attached bathrooms. Prices (except for Camp 5) include a delicious breakfast.

If you'll be travelling from July to September, staff recommend booking in-park beds before purchasing plane tickets – just call (☏085-792300) or email (enquiries@mulupark.com). Reservations cannot be made through Sarawak Forestry.

Rooms can be cancelled up to 48 hours ahead without penalty, which is why space sometimes opens up late in the game; phone for last-minute availability.

Garden Bungalows BUNGALOW $$
(s/d/tr incl breakfast RM200/230/250; ❄) Opened in 2011, these eight spacious units come with verandahs.

Chalets CHALET $$
(s/d/tr/q incl breakfast RM170/180/215/250; ❄) Each of the two chalets has two rooms and a huge living room.

Longhouse Rooms GUESTHOUSE $$
(s/d/tr/q incl breakfast RM170/180/215/250; ❄) There are eight of these, four in each of two wooden buildings.

Hostel HOSTEL $
(dm incl breakfast RM40) All 20 beds are in a clean, spacious dormitory-style room with ceiling fans. Lockers are available for a RM20 deposit.

Camp 5 CAMPGROUND $
(per person including boat ride RM160) An open-air sleeping platform with mats, cooking facilities (including cooking gas) and bathrooms. Space is limited (to 50 people) so only hikers who are heading up to the Pinnacles or down the Headhunters' Trail can stay here. Reserve ahead and pay at the park office. It's warm enough here without a sleeping bag (a sarong will do).

Outside the National Park

Several ultra-budget places, unaffiliated with the park, are located just across the bridge from park HQ, along the banks of the Melinau River. Reservations are not necessary so if you don't mind very basic digs, you can fly up without worrying about room availability.

For those on a generous budget, the Mulu Marriott Resort & Spa is also almost never full.

Contact Miri-based **Borneo Tropical Adventure** (☏085-419337; www.borneotropical adventures.com) for details on staying at the mid-range Benarat Inn.

Mulu Marriott Resort & Spa RESORT $$$
(☏085-792388; www.marriott.com; ❄@🖥🏊) Situated 3km from park HQ, this 100-room, all-wood complex is finally getting the major make-over it's badly needed for years.

Mulu River Lodge HOSTEL $
(Edward Nyipa Homestay; ☏012-852 7471; dm incl breakfast RM35) Has 30 beds, most in a giant,

non-bunk dorm room equipped with clean showers and toilets at one end. Electricity flows from 5pm to 11.30pm. This is the only guesthouse outside the park with a proper septic system.

Mulu Homestay
GUESTHOUSE $

(☑for Betty 012-875 3517; beds RM15, campsites per person RM5) Has 30 beds (more are being added), electricity from 6pm to 9pm and very personable owners.

Melinau Homestay
GUESTHOUSE $

(MC; ☑for Diang 012-871 1372; dm RM20) Has seven extremely basic rooms, river-water bucket showers and flickering electricity from 6pm to 10pm. This is the third guesthouse along the river from the bridge.

Eating

A handful of tiny shops sell a very limited selection of food items, eg instant noodles. Most food is flown in, which partly explains why prices are significantly higher than on the coast (eg RM6 for a large bottle of water).

Inexpensive curries, fried rice and noodle dishes are available at several places across the bridge from park HQ.

Cooking is not allowed at any park accommodation except Camps 1, 3, 4 and 5.

Café Mulu
ASIAN, WESTERN $$

(mains RM7.40-17; ⏰7.30am-9.30pm, last orders 9pm) The Berawan women who work here make great breakfasts (free if you're staying in the park, RM15.90 otherwise) and a few Western items, but the standouts are local dishes such as the spectacular *Mulu laksa*. A beer or a glass of wine, supremely relaxing after a day's hiking, costs RM9.60. Staff are happy to prepare packed lunches (RM18).

❶ Information

For sums over RM100, the park accepts Visa and MasterCard (but not American Express). Cash and travellers cheques can be exchanged at the Mulu Marriott Resort & Spa. There are no ATMs at the park.

The shop at park HQ has an excruciatingly slow **internet computer** (RM5 per hour; RM10 per hour if you're staying outside the park) but it's usually out-of-service. There's another **internet-enabled computer** (RM35 per hour) at the Mulu Marriott Resort & Spa, which is supposed to have wi-fi in the lobby.

The **clinic** in the nearby village of Batu Bungan is now staffed by a doctor and has a dispensary (small pharmacy).

❶ Getting There & Away

Air

MASwings (www.maswings.com.my) flies 68-seat ATR 72-500 turboprops from/to Miri and Kuching. Departures from Miri are at 9.20am and 1.50pm and from Mulu at 10.10am and 2.40pm, with onward flights to Kota Kinabalu (KK) and other destinations.

❶ Getting Around

Park HQ is a walkable 1.5km from the airport and 3km from Mulu Marriott Resort & Spa. Vans run by **Melinau Transportation** (☑for Diang 012-871 1372) and other companies meets incoming flights at the airport; transport to park HQ and the adjacent guesthouses costs RM5 per person. Oversized tuk-tuks shuttle guests between park HQ and Mulu Marriott Resort & Spa (RM6 per person one-way).

It's possible to hire local longboats for excursions to destinations such as the government-built Penan longhouse village of Long Iman (RM60 per person return, minimum three people), 40 minutes away by river.

Kelabit Highlands

Nestled in Sarawak's northeastern corner, the upland rainforests of the Kelabit (keh-*lah*-bit) Highlands are sandwiched between Gunung Mulu National Park and the Indonesian state of East Kalimantan. The main activity here, other than enjoying the clean, cool air, is trekking from longhouse to longhouse on mountain trails. Unfortunately, logging roads – ostensibly for 'selective' logging – are encroaching and some of the Highlands' primary forests have already succumbed to the chainsaw.

The area is home to the Kelabits, an Orang Ulu (inland Dayak) group who number only about 6500 worldwide and who inspire awe throughout Sarawak for their unparalleled ability to wrangle government investments and subsidies. For an excellent 'profile' of the Kelabits by Dr Poline Bala, a Bario-born anthropologist, see www.unimas.my/ebario/community.html. There's more information on Bario and the Kelabits, some of it out-of-date, at www.kelabit.net and on Facebook – see www.kelabit.org.

BARIO
POP 800

The 'capital' of the Highlands, Bario consists of about a dozen 'villages' – each with its own church – spread over a beautiful valley, much (though less and less) of it given over to growing the renowned local rice. Some of the appeal lies in the mountain climate (the valley is 1500m above sea level) and splendid isolation (the only access is by air and torturous 4WD track), but above all it's the unforced hospitality of the Kelabit people that will quickly win you over. An amazing number of travellers find themselves extending their stays in Bario by days, weeks or even years. Do yourself a favour and get stuck here for a while!

Before the Konfrontasi, Bario consisted of only one small longhouse, but in 1963 residents of longhouses near the frontier fled raids by Indonesian troops and settled here for safety.

Except for a few places powered by a small hydroelectric dam and by photovoltaic cells (a large solar farm is planned), Bario has electricity – provided by private generators – only in the evening. It's hard to imagine life in hyper-social Bario without the mobile phone, a technology unknown in these parts until 2009.

☉ Sights & Activities

The Bario area offers plenty of opportunities for jungle exploration even if you're not a hardcore trekker. Guides can arrange activities such as **fishing**, **bird-watching** and **kayaking** (☑for Stu 019-807 1640; per boat RM60).

The forests around Bario are a great place to spot pitcher plants, butterflies and even hornbills – and are an exceptional venue for tiger leeches to spot you. Most guesthouses are happy to pack picnic lunches.

Bario Asal Longhouse   LONGHOUSE

This all-wood, 22-door longhouse has the traditional Kelabit layout. On the *dapur* (enclosed front verandah) each family has a hearth, while on the other side of the family units is the *tawa'*, a wide back verandah – essentially an enclosed hall over 100m long – used for weddings, funerals and celebrations and decorated with historic family photos.

A few of the older residents still have earlobes that hang almost down to their shoulders, created by a lifetime of wearing heavy brass earrings. If you'd like a picture, it's good form to chat with them a bit (they may offer you something to drink) and only then to ask if they'd be willing to be photographed. Afterwards you might want to leave a small tip (RM5 or RM10).

Bario Asal has 24-hour electricity (evenings only during dry spells) thanks to a micro-hydro project salvaged from a larger government-funded project that functioned for just 45 minutes after it was switched on in 1999 (it had been designed to operate on a much larger river).

Tom Harrisson Monument   MEMORIAL

Shaped like a *sapé* (a traditional stringed instrument), this stainless-steel monument, dedicated in 2010, commemorates the March 1945 parachute drop into Bario by British and Australian commandos under the command of British Major Tom Harrisson. Their goal – achieved with great success – was to enlist the help of locals to fight the Japanese, whose cruelty had made them hugely unpopular. For the life story of this colourful and controversial character, see *The Most Offending Soul Alive*, a biography by Judith M Heimann. Harrisson's widow lived in Bario until her death in 2011.

The monument is a short walk up the slope from the Bario Asal Longhouse, on the site of Tom's one-time garden (his post-war house was about 100m from here, where the local cemetery now is).

Junglebluesdream Art Gallery   ART GALLERY

(http://junglebluesdream.weebly.com; ☉daylight hours) Many of artist Stephen Baya's paintings have traditional Kelabit motifs. In April 2013 his colourful illustrations of the Kelabit legend of Tuked Rini were to feature at the Museum of Archaeology and Anthropology in Cambridge, England (and in a children's book).

Prayer Mountain   TREKKING

From the Bario Asal Longhouse, it's a steep, slippery ascent (two hours) up to the summit of Prayer Mountain, which has a cross that was erected in 1973, thickets of pitcher plants and amazing views of the Bario Valley and of the mixed Penan and Kelabit hamlet of Arur Dalan, with its three defunct wind turbines. Two-thirds of the way up is what may be the world's least pretentious church.

⛏ Sleeping

Bario's various component villages are home to lots of guesthouses where you can meet English-speaking locals and dine on delicious Kelabit cuisine (accommodation prices almost always include board). Some of the most relaxing establishments are a bit out of town (up to 5km). Air-con is not necessary up in Bario but hot water – alas, not yet an option – will some day be a nice treat. Almost all rooms have shared bathroom facilities. If you're on a very tight budget, enquire about renting a bed without board.

No need to book ahead – available rooms outstrip the space available on flights, and guesthouse owners meet incoming flights at the airport. The places below are listed alphabetically.

Bario Airport Homestay GUESTHOUSE $

(☑013-835 9009; barioairporthomestay@gmail. com; beds RM20, per person incl board RM80; ☞) Five rooms right across the road from the airport terminal. Run by Joanna, the airport's personable dynamo of an operations manager.

Bario Asal Lembaa Longhouse HOMESTAY $

(☑for Jenette 014-590 7500, for Peter 014-893 1139; jenetteulun@yahoo.com; beds RM20, per person incl 3 meals RM60; ☞) Run as a cooperative by the entire longhouse. Some local families let out rooms, while others do the cooking. A great way to experience longhouse living. Transport from the airport costs RM10 per person each way.

De Plateau Lodge HOMESTAY $

(☑019-855 9458; deplateau@gmail.com; per person incl meals RM80; ☞) Situated about 2km east of the centre (bear left at the fork), this two-storey wooden chalet has seven rooms (including one triple) and a homey living room. It is owned by Douglas, a former guide. Recent visitors have missed flights due to transport confusion so make sure your needs are clear.

Gem's Lodge GUESTHOUSE $

(☑013-828 0507; gems_lodge@yahoo.com; per person incl meals RM70) Situated 5km southeast of town (bear right at the fork) five minutes from the longhouse village of Pa' Umor. Managed by Jaman, one of Bario's nicest and most experienced guides, this place is tranquillity incarnate, with eight pleasant rooms, a cosy common area, river swimming and solar power. Transport to/ from the airport by 4WD costs RM25 per person.

Junglebluesdream GUESTHOUSE $

(☑019-884 9892; http://junglebluesdream.weebly. com; per person incl board RM80; ☞) Owned by artist and one-time guide Stephen Baya, a Bario native, and his friendly Danish wife Tine, this super-welcoming lodge (and art gallery) has four mural-decorated rooms, good-quality beds and quilts, and fantastic Kelabit food. Guests can consult Stephen's extraordinary hand-drawn town and trekking maps. Organises kayaking excursions.

Libal Paradise GUESTHOUSE $

(☑019-807 1640; per person RM65, dm without board RM25; ☞) Surrounded by a verdant fruit and veggie garden where you can pick your own pineapples, this sustainably-run farm – an idyllic spot to chill – is run by a local woman, Dorkas Parir, and her Canadian husband Stu, who runs kayaking trips. Solar collectors power 24-hour LED lighting. Kitchen facilities are available. To get there from the airport terminal, walk eastward along the road that parallels the runway.

Nancy & Harriss GUESTHOUSE $

(Hill View Lodge; ☑013-850 5850, 019-858 5850; nancyharriss@yahoo.com; dm RM30; per person incl board RM70) Run by a former guide whose grandmother was once married to Tom Harrisson, this rambling place has seven guest rooms, a lovely verandah, a library-equipped lounge and endearingly tacky floor coverings. Situated 250m along a dirt track south of the main road; the turn-off is just east of Kaludai. Prices include airport transfer.

THE 'EBARIO MODEL'

Bario has produced some remarkable leaders, including local councillor John Tarawe, CEO of the award-winning internet initiative **eBario** (www.unimas.my/ebario and www. ebario.org), who is much sought after around the world by groups (eg the UNDP) that are interested in 'community mobilisation' among indigenous groups. His efforts to plug the Highlands into the internet (even in remote villages he'd like the children to grow up 'IT savvy') and establish a hugely popular community radio station, **Radio Tauh** (94MHz FM; ☉7.30-9am or 10am & 7-9pm or 10pm Mon-Sat), have been so groundbreaking that NGOs on distant continents are adopting the 'eBario model'.

THE PENAN

The Kelabit Highlands are home not only to the Kelabits but also the Penan, an indigenous group that was nomadic – surviving almost exclusively on hunting and gathering – until quite recently and has fared much less well than other indigenous groups in modern Malaysia. The Penan are often looked down upon, and discriminated against, by other Orang Ulu groups. Around Bario, if you see barefoot people wearing ragged clothes who drop their gaze when you approach, you can be sure they're Penan. Kelabits have intermarried with Chinese, Westerners, Malays and other Orang Ulu groups for several generations but the first Kelabit-Penan marriage took place only recently.

Since independence, the Sarawak state government has often sold off rainforest lands to well-connected logging companies and then evicted the Penan and other Dayak groups with minimal or no compensation. The Swiss rainforest and human-rights advocate **Bruno Manser** (www.bmf.ch) spent years living with the Penan and agitating to protect their human and civil rights. He disappeared near Bario in May 2000 and is presumed dead – many people, in the Kelabit Highlands and abroad, suspect he was murdered.

Ngimat Ayu's House   GUESTHOUSE $

(☏013-840 6187; engimat_scott@yahoo.com; per person incl board RM95) This brown, two-storey place, run by the impressive but personable son of the Kelabits' former *pemancha* (paramount chief), has seven rooms and a chill-out verandah with rice-field views. Situated on a slope 200m east of the yellow public library. Rates include transport from and to the airport.

✖ Eating

Most guesthouses offer full board – almost always delicious Kelabit cuisine – but Bario also has several modest eateries. **Pasar Bario**, the town's yellow-painted commercial centre, is home to half-a-dozen basic **cafes** (mains RM4; ☺7am-10pm, closed Sun morning) selling mainly generic fried noodle and rice dishes, though Kelabit food can sometimes be special-ordered.

🍷 Drinking

Finding a beer in Bario can be a bit of a challenge. This is a very Evangelical town – you're as likely to hear Christian country as the sound of the *sapé* – so most establishments do not serve alcohol, and some of those that do keep it hidden. But what was it that Matthew once said? 'Ask, and it shall be given you; seek, and ye shall find'.

At Pasar Bario, don't go through the swinging doors of the Bario Saloon looking for a stiff drink – it's a unisex beauty salon!

Y2K   BAR

(☺7am-midnight or later) Local men quaff beer (RM4 to RM6) and play pool. Has karaoke in the evening (until 10pm).

Keludai   BAR

(mains RM4; ☺noon-1am or 2am) An all-wood saloon with beer (RM4), instant noodles, satellite TV and a pool table.

🛍 Shopping

Sinah Rang   HANDICRAFTS

(Bario Asal Longhouse; ☺daily) Sinah sells lovely Kelabit beadwork, all locally made, from her living room. This is a good place to pick up a *kabo'* (RM50 to RM100, depending on the quality of the beads), a beadwork pendant shaped like a little beer barrel that's worn around the neck by Kelabit men.

Y2K   GENERAL STORE

(☺7am-midnight or later) An old-fashioned, Old West-style general store that sells everything from SIM cards to something called Zam-Zam Hair Oil.

ℹ Information

There are no banks, ATMs or credit-card facilities anywhere in the Kelabit Highlands so bring plenty of small-denomination banknotes for accommodation, food and guides, plus some extra in case you get stranded. Commerce is limited to a few basic shops, some of them in Pasar Bario, Bario's bright yellow commercial centre.

The best Malaysian cell-phone company to have up here is Celcom (Maxis works at the airport and in parts of Bario; Digi is useless). The airport has wi-fi, as do several guesthouses.

Bario Telecentre (www.unimas.my/ebario; Gatuman Bario; per hr RM4; ☺9.30-11.30am & 2-4pm, closed Sat afternoon & Sunday) Solar-powered internet access.

Klinik Kesihatan Bariio (☏085-796404; Airport Rd intersection; ☺8am-1pm & 2-5pm Mon-Thu, 8-11.45am & 2.15-5pm Fri, emergency 24hr) Bario's innovative, ecologically sustainable rural health clinic, powered by solar energy, has one doctor, two paramedics, a dispensary (small pharmacy) and a helicopter on standby.

❶ Getting There & Around

AIR

Bario Airport (☎for Joanna 013-835 9009, for Norman Peter 013-824 8006) is linked with Miri twice a day by Twin Otters operated by **MASwings** (www.maswings.com.my). Weather (especially high winds) not infrequently causes delays and cancellations. For flight updates or if you're having a problem making a flight out of Bario, just ring the friendly staff at the airport.

Twin Otters have strict weight limits, so much so that checked baggage is limited to 10kg, carry-ons to 5kg and passengers themselves are weighed on a giant scale when they check in. Enforcement is particularly strict on the way up because planes have to carry enough fuel to get back to Miri, and more cargo is flown into Bario than out. For the same reason, it's easier to find a seat from Bario to Miri than the other way around. Consider leaving some of your belongings in Miri at your hotel or guesthouse.

When you land in Bario, the first thing you should do is register for your flight out at the counter – your name will be inscribed in a crumpled old ledger. A schematic map of the Bario area is posted on a nearby wall.

The airport is about a 30-minute walk south of the shophouses but you're bound to be offered a lift on arrival. As you'll notice, the people of Bario treat the air link to Miri almost like their own private airline and absolutely love dropping by the wi-fi-equipped airport terminal to meet flights, hang out with arriving or departing friends, and surf the net.

CAR

The overland trip between Bario and Miri, possible only by 4WD (per person RM150), takes 12 hours at the very least and sometimes a lot more, the determining factors being the weather and the condition of the rough logging roads and their old wooden bridges. When things get ugly, vehicles travel in convoys so when one gets

stuck the others can push or winch it out. At press time, some sectors were being upgraded to make the route safer and more reliable.

A new road from Bario via Pa' Lungan to Ba Kelalan (already connected by road with Lawas) is under construction.

In Bario, 4WD vehicles can be hired for RM250 or RM300 a day including a driver and petrol; guesthouses can make arrangements.

BA KELALAN

Known for its rice, organic vegetables, apples and annual apple festival – and the general vibrancy of its farming sector – the Lun Bawang town of Ba Kelalan is a popular destination for treks from Bario.

Guesthouse options include the nice **Ba Kelalan Apple Lodge Homestay** (per person about RM70), run by **Borneo Jungle Safari** (☎013-286 5656, in Miri 085-422595; www.borneojunglesafari.com); the **Ba Kelalan Inn**, the only place in town that serves beer; and the **Green Valley Guesthouse** (per bed RM20).

❶ Getting There & Away

The only way to get from Ba Kelalan to Bario is on foot (a road via Pa' Lungan is in the works). A rough, 125km logging road links Ba Kelalan with Lawas (per person RM70 to RM80 by 4WD, seven hours, daily).

It's possible to get from Ba Kelalan to Long Bawan in Kalimantan by motorbike.

MASwings (www.maswings.com.my) flies Twin Otters from Ba Kelalan to Lawas and Miri three times a week.

TREKKING IN THE KELABIT HIGHLANDS

The temperate highlands up along Sarawak's far eastern border with Indonesia offer some of the best jungle trekking in Borneo, taking in farming villages, rugged peaks and supremely remote Kenyah, Penan and Kelabit settlements. Most trails traverse a variety of primary and secondary forests, as well as an increasing number of logged areas. Treks from Bario range from easy overnight

BARIO SALT

If you're interested in the Kelabit's culinary traditions, you might want to walk out to Bario's **main tudtu** (literally 'salty sweet'; natural salt lick; overnight facilities planned), under an hour's walk from Pa' Umor, where mineral-rich saline water is put in giant vats over a roaring fire until all that's left is high-iodine salt that goes perfectly with local specialities such as deer and wild boar. This traditional production technique is beginning to die out, but in Bario you can still purchase salt made the old way – look for something that resembles a 20cm-long green Tootsie roll wrapped in a leaf (RM17 to RM20).

RICE & PINEAPPLES

Bario is famous throughout Malaysia for two things: Bario rice, whose grains are smaller and more aromatic than lowland varieties; and sweeter-than-sweet pineapples (RM2.50 in Bario) that are free of the pucker-inducing acidity of their coastal cousins. Outside of the Kelabit Highlands, 1kg of Bario rice can cost a whopping RM16 and Bario pineapples are usually unavailable at any price.

excursions to nearby longhouses to one-week slogs over the border into the wilds of Kalimantan.

While the Highlands are certainly cooler than Borneo's coastal regions, it's still hard work trekking up here (don't forget the altitude) and you should be in fairly good shape to consider a multi-day trek. Be prepared to encounter leeches – many trails are literally crawling with them. Bring extra cell-phone and camera batteries as charging may not be possible.

The routes we list are intended to serve as a starting point. With so many trails in the area, there is ample scope for custom routes and creative planning.

MEGALITHS NEAR BARIO

Hidden deep in the jungle around Bario are scores of mysterious megaliths and other 'cultural sites'. For more information, ask your guide for a copy of the booklet *Stone Culture of the Northern Highlands of Sarawak, Malaysia* (RM20).

At research time, trails equipped with overnight shelters for megalith circuits lasting two to five days were being constructed. Overnight options include:

Pa' Umor Route
TREKKING

From Bario it's a 1½-hour walk – notorious for its legions of lecherous leeches – to **Pa' Umor**, where there's **longhouse accommodation** (☑for Jaman 013-828 0507, for Rian 013-812 8851). Continue on for 2km (50 minutes) and you come to a salt spring.

About 15 minutes from Pa' Umor is Arur Bilit Farm, home to **Batu Narit**, an impressive stone carving featuring a human in the spread-eagled position among its designs.

From the farm, use the log bridge to cross a small river (25 minutes) in order to reach **Batu Ipak**. According to local legend, this stone formation was created when an angry warrior named Upai Semering pulled out his parang (machete) and took a wrathful swing at the rock, cutting it in two. This circuit should take four or five hours – maybe a tad longer if your guide is a good storyteller.

Pa' Lungan Route
TREKKING

(homestays per person incl board RM70, boat ride up to 4 people RM250) A wide, muddy forest trail – used by water buffalos to pull sleighs carrying goods and, on occasion, medical evacuees – heads from Bario to **Pa' Lungan** (four hours). Unlike almost all the other Highland trails, this one is walkable without a guide as long as you have clear instructions. About halfway along you can stop at **Batu Arit**, a large stone featuring bird carvings and humanoid figures with heart-shaped faces.

From Pa' Lungan it's a two-minute walk to **Batu Ritung**, a 2m stone table (probably a burial site), although no one is quite sure as the site was created outside of living memory. Also near Pa' Lungan (15 minutes away) is **Perupun**, a huge pile of stones of a type assembled to bury the valuables of the dead who had no descendants to receive their belongings.

If you've got a bit more time, you could consider basing yourself for a day or two in Pa' Lungan, believed by many to produce the very best Bario rice. Longhouse homestays, including **Batu Ritung Lodge** (☑019-805 2119; baturitunglodge@yahoo.com), serve Kelabit-style dishes such as *pa'u* (fern) and *puluh* (bamboo shoots).

A scenic boat ride can be arranged to take you on the **Pa' Debpur** from a spot an hour's hike from Pa' Lungan back to Pa' Umur (in Kelabit, *pa'* means 'river').

BARIO TO BA KELALAN

The three- to four-day trek from Bario to Ba Kelalan covers a variety of mostly gentle terrain – some of it on the Indonesian side of the frontier – and gives a good overview of the Kelabit Highlands. An alternative route, the Kalimantan Loop, which takes five to seven days, goes deeper into Kalimantan, passing by Lembudud.

To avoid doubling back, you can trek from Bario to Ba Kelalan and then fly or take a 4WD down to the coast. Remember, though that you'll have to pay the guide for the two days it will take him to walk back to Bario.

HIRING A GUIDE: THE PRACTICALITIES

With very few exceptions, the only way to explore the Kelabit Highlands is to hire a local guide. Fortunately, this could hardly be easier. Any of the guesthouses in Bario can organise a wide variety of short walks and longer treks led by guides they know and rely on. Some of the best guides for longer treks live in Pa' Lungan, an easy walk from Bario. If you link up with other travellers in Bario or Miri, the cost of a guide can be shared.

Although there's a growing shortage of guides, in general it's no problem to just turn up in Bario and make arrangements after you arrive, especially if you don't mind hanging out for day or two in Bario. If you're in a hurry, though, or your trip coincides with the prime tourism months of July and August, consider making arrangements with your guesthouse in advance by email or phone.

The going rate for guides is RM100 per day for either a Bario-based day trip or a longer trek. Some itineraries involve either river trips (highly recommended if the water is high enough) or travel by 4WD – naturally, these significantly increase the cost. The going rate for a porter is RM80 to RM100 a day.

If you are connecting the dots between rural longhouses, expect to pay RM70 for a night's sleep plus three meals (you can opt out of lunch and save RM10 or RM15). Gifts are not obligatory but the people who live in remote longhouses are appreciative if, after you drink tea or coffee with them, you offer RM10 'to cover the costs' or 'to buy pens and paper for the children'.

If your route requires that you camp in the forest, expect to pay approximately RM120 per night; in addition, you may be asked to supply food, which is provided for both you and your guide when you stay in a longhouse. Equipment for jungle camping (eg a sleeping bag, hammock, mozzie net and bed roll) cannot be purchased in Bario so it's a good idea to bring your own, though Bario Asal Longhouse may be able to rent it out.

If you're trekking in one direction only (eg Bario to Ba Kelalan), you will be asked to continue paying the guiding fee while your guide returns home through the jungle (in this scenario, it would take them two days to trek from Ba Kelalan back to Bario).

Detailed topographical maps of Sarawak exist but it's nearly impossible to get hold of them. According to in-the-know locals, the government's calculation seems to be that activists will find it harder to fight for native land rights if they lack proper maps.

BATU LAWI

If you were sitting on the left side of the plane from Miri to Bario, you probably caught a glimpse of the two massive limestone spires known as Batu Lawi, the taller of which soars to 2040m. During WWII they were used as a landmark for parachute drops.

While an ascent of the higher of the two rock formations, known as the 'male peak', is only for expert technical rock climbers, ascending the lower 'female peak' – described by one veteran trekker as 'awe-inspiring' – is possible for fit trekkers without special skills. It's a tough, four- or five-day return trip from Bario. Be prepared to spend the second day passing through areas that have been impacted by logging. Only a handful of guides are experienced enough to tackle Batu Lawi – perhaps the best is Richard from Pa' Ukat.

GUNUNG MURUD

Sarawak's highest mountain (2442m), part of 598-sq-km Pulong Tau National Park, is just begging to be climbed, but very few visitors make the effort to put the trip together. This adventure is only for the fittest of the fit. Borneo Touch Ecotour (☏013-8443861; www.walk2mulu.com) offers four-day, three-night ascents for RM1500 per person (minimum four).

The mountain is linked by trails with both Ba Kelalan and Bario. From Bario, the more common starting point, a typical return trip takes six or seven days. You can also walk from Bario via Gunung Murud to Ba Kelalan (five days one-way), but as you approach Ba Kelalan you'll have to walk along a depressing logging road.

A rough logging road links the base of Gunung Murud with the lowland town of Lawas (five to eight hours by 4WD).

Limbang Division

Shaped like a crab claw, the Limbang Division slices Brunei in two and separates the diminutive sultanate from Sabah. Tourism is underdeveloped in these parts, but Bruneians love popping across the border to find shopping bargains, including cheap beer smuggled in from duty-free Pulau Labuan. As one local put it with just a hint of exaggeration, 'Los Angeles has Tijuana, BSB has Limbang'.

The area, snatched from the sultan of Brunei by Charles Brooke in 1890, is still claimed by Brunei.

LIMBANG

The bustling river port of Limbang (pronounced *lim*-bahng) is something of a backwater, but you may find yourself here before or after taking the Headhunters' Trail to/from Gunung Mulu National Park.

⦿ Sights & Activities

Limbang's old town stretches inland from riverfront Jln Wong Tsap En (formerly Main Bazaar) and southward from 12-storey Purnama Hotel, a useful landmark.

Limbang Regional Museum   MUSEUM
(www.museum.sarawak.gov.my; Jln Kubu; ⊙9am-4.30pm Tue-Sun) Features well-presented exhibits on the Limbang Division's archaeology, culture and crafts. Situated on the riverbank about 1km south of the Purnama Hotel, on the upper floor of a Charles Brooke fort built in 1897 and rebuilt (after a fire) in 1991.

Limbang Raid Memorial   MEMORIAL
(Jln Wong Tsap En) Commemorates four members of the Sarawak Constabulary and five members of the UK's 42 Commando Royal Marines killed before and during the famous Limbang Raid on 12 December 1962, which retook the town from rebels of the pro-Indonesian North Kalimantan National Army. As one local put it, 'if the rebels win, we will be Indonesian, not Malaysian'. A trailer for a TV documentary about the raid, *Return to Limbang*, can be found on www.vimeo.com. The memorial is 400m south of the Purnama Hotel, on the riverfront across the street from the police station.

Public Library   LIBRARY
(Perpustakaan Awam; 4th fl, Limbang Plaza Shopping Mall; ⊙9am-5pm Mon-Sat, closed public holidays) The library has an excellent collection of English-language books on Sarawak (on a shelf labelled 'Sarawakiana'). This is a great place to do air-conditioned research before an upcountry trek, especially on a rainy day. Free internet for up to an hour. Situated next to the Purnama Hotel.

⌖ Tours

The following outfits run canoe trips in the Limpaki Wetlands, where you can often see proboscis monkeys, and can take you to the crash site of a B-34 Liberator shot down by the Japanese in 1944, and to the salty Maritam Mud Spring (aka the 'Mud Volcano'), 34km towards BSB.

Chua Eng Hin   SIGHTSEEING, CANOEING
(☑019-8145355; chualbg@streamyx.com) A well-known local personality with a passion for Limbang District's largely unknown charms.

Borneo Touch Ecotour   CANOEING, TREKKING
(☑013-844 3861; www.walk2mulu.com; 1st fl, 2061 Rickett Commercial Bldg) Run by the dynamic Mr Lim (no, Limbang is not named for him), this local company offers highly recommended treks up or down the Headhunters'

CROSSING INTO INDONESIA

Thanks to long-standing cultural and personal ties across the Sarawak–Kalimantan frontier, drawn in colonial times by the British and the Dutch, a local trans-border initiative has made it possible for both Highland residents and tourists to cross from Ba Kelalan into Kalimantan to visit nearby settlements such as Long Bawan, Lembudud and Long Layu. All you need is a *pas lintas batas* (transboundary pass), issued locally according to an agreement signed between the Malaysian and Indonesian foreign ministries. Passports are not stamped and you must return to Sarawak within 14 days. To make arrangements, ask your guide or contact John Tarawe in Bario.

Malaysian ringgits are very popular in this remote part of Kalimantan but US dollars are not.

TREKKING IN THE PENAN HIGHLANDS

Community-based and sustainably managed, **Picnic with the Penan** (www.picnicwith thepenan.org) is a pioneering, non-profit tourism initiative that offers intrepid trekkers a rare chance to visit remote Penan villages in the *ulu-ulu* (back-of-the-beyond) Upper Baram area between the Highland airports of Long Lellang and Long Banga. Itineraries take at least five days and four nights. Booking is by email or through Highlands Backpackers (p435) in Miri.

Trail to/from Gunung Mulu National Park (RM950 per person for three days and two nights, including the Pinnacles; minimum four people).

🛏 Sleeping

East Asia Hotel   HOTEL $
(☎085-215 600; cnr Jln Wong Tsap En & Jln Wayang; d old/new RM45/78; ❄🔞) A waterfront hostelry with 33 clean and comfy rooms, eleven of them nicely remodelled; some have river views. Situated four short blocks south of the Purnama Hotel. Room deposit: RM100.

Purnama Hotel   HOTEL $$
(☎085-216700; www.purnamalimbang.com; Jln Buangsiol; s/d from RM105/115; ❄🔞) Ensconced in Limbang's tallest building (12 storeys), this uninspiring hotel – ornamented with rainbow-hued balconies – has 218 spacious but aesthetically challenged rooms that come with big views and small bathrooms.

🍴 Eating

Pusat Penjaja Medan Bangkita   MARKET $
(Jln Bangkita; ⊙6am or 7am-5pm or 6pm) Bisayah, Lun Bawang and Iban women sell jungle edibles, sausage-shaped Ba Kelalan salt and a dozen kinds of upland rice. The larger weekly *tamu* (market) takes place all-day Thursday and until noon on Friday. From the Purnama Hotel, go one long block inland.

Thien Hsing Vegetarian   CHINESE $
(mains RM3-4; ⊙6.30am-2pm; ☑) A very basic eatery serving veggie Chinese dishes. Situated on a back alley 3½ short blocks south of the Purnama Hotel, right behind Ling Brother Enterprise bike shop at 46 Jln Wayang.

Bangunan Tamu Limbang   HAWKER $
(Jln Wong Tsap En; mains RM3.50-5; ⊙6.30am-5.30pm) Houses Limbang's main Malay market, with an upstairs hawker centre. Diagonally opposite the Purnama Hotel.

Night Markets   FOOD STALLS $
In the afternoon and evening, food-stall action shifts to the **Malay night market** (⊙5pm-midnight), on the riverfront 300m northwest of the Purnama Hotel; and to the **Chinese night market** (Jln Bangkita; ⊙2-10pm), a block northeast of the Purnama Hotel.

ℹ Information

Limbang has several international ATMs.
Sun City Cybercafe (Jln Bangkita, 1st fl; per hr RM2.50; ⊙8.30am-midnight) A haven for gamers. One long block east of the Purnama Hotel, above the Cahaya Delima Cafe.

ℹ Getting There & Around

The Sungai Pandaruan ferry between Limbang and Bangar (Brunei), a major bottleneck, should be replaced by a bridge in 2013.

AIR
MASwings (www.maswings.com.my) links Limbang's airport, 7km south of the centre, with Miri. A taxi into town costs RM18.

BOAT
Express ferries from Limbang's immigration hall to Pulau Labuan (RM30, two hours, 8am daily) are run by two companies on alternate days, **Lim Pertama** (☎012-865 3753) and **Royal Limbang** (☎013-882 3736). Departures from Pulau Labuan are at 1.30pm. Bookings can be made by SMS/text message.

BUS
There's a tiny bus station at the eastern end of Jln Wayang, two blocks inland from the river. **Biaramas/Bus Asia** (☎012-828 2042) sends a bus to Miri's Pujut Bus Terminal (RM45, four hours) every day at 9am. A spot in a seven-person van to Miri costs RM50, with departures at around 8.30am and 1pm. The cheapest way to Bandar Seri Begawan (BSB) is to take Syarikat Bus Limbang's 1pm bus to Kualah Lurah (RM5) and then a local Bruneian bus (B$1).

The only company that can drop you off inside Brunei is **Jesselton Express** (PHLS; ☎in Brunei +673-718-3838, +673-717-7755, +673-719-3835, in KK 016-836 0009, in Limbang

016-855 0222, 085-212990), which has daily buses to BSB (RM20 or B$10) at 2pm or 3pm; and to Bangar, Lawas (RM30, 2 hours) and Kota Kimabalu (KK; RM50) at 9.30am. Heading *to* Limbang, a bus departs from BSB every day at 8am. Tickets are sold at **Wan Wan Cafe & Restaurant** (Jln Bangkita).

Bintang Jaya (016-859 4532) sends daily buses to Miri (RM45) at 1.45pm, and to Lawas (RM30) and KK (RM50) at 12.30pm. Tickets are sold at **Hock Chuong Hin Cafe** (Jln Bangkita).

TAXI & MINIBUS

Minibuses and red-and-yellow taxis hang out at the **Stesyen Teksi** (085-213781; Jln Wong Tsap En; 5am-6pm or later), on the waterfront a block south of the Purnama Hotel. If you're heading towards BSB, one-way travel to the Kuala Lurah crossing costs about RM60 (more after 7pm); cheap, frequent local buses can take you from there to BSB. If you're coming from BSB, taxis wait on the Malaysian side of the Kuala Lurah crossing.

Brunei

POP 410,000 / AREA 5765 SQ KM

Includes »

Bandar Seri Begawan ... 456
Tutong & Belait
Districts 467
Tutong 467
Jalan Labi 467
Seria 467
Kuala Belait 468
Temburong District 468
Bangar 468
Pulau Selirong 470
Batang Duri 470
Peradayan Forest
Reserve 470
Ulu Temburong
National Park 470

Best Places to Eat

» Taman Selera (p463)
» Lim Ah Siaw Pork Market (p462)
» Pondok Sari Wangi (p462)

Best Places to Stay

» Ulu-Ulu Resort (p472)
» Brunei Hotel (p461)
» Pusat Belia (p461)

Why Go?

The small sultanate of Brunei almost looks like a geographic comma plunked between Sarawak and Sabah. It certainly forms a conceptual one, because unless you're a petroleum engineer, when folks ask 'Why go to Brunei?' the answer is usually the travelling equivalent of a pause: transfer or stopover.

But there's more here than passport queues. This quiet *darussalam* (Arabic for 'abode of peace') has the largest oilfields in Southeast Asia, and because oil generates money, Brunei hasn't turned its rainforests into palm plantations. Old-growth greenery abounds, especially in verdant Ulu Temburong National Park. Because booze is banned, the citizens of the capital, Bandar Seri Begawan (BSB), are mad for food and shopping.

This tranquil (sometimes somnolent) nation is the realisation of a particular vision: a strict, socially controlled religious state where happiness is found in pious worship and mass consumption. Visit and judge the results for yourself.

When to Go
Bandar Seri Begawan

°C/°F Temp | Rainfall inches/mm

(climate chart showing temperature dots around 30/86 and rainfall bars across months J F M A M J J A S O N D, rising toward the end of the year)

Oct–Dec The rainiest, if coolest, months of the year.

Jan–May February and March are the driest months. National Day is celebrated on 23 February.

Jun–Aug It's *hot*. The sultan's birthday (15 July) is marked with festivities around the country.

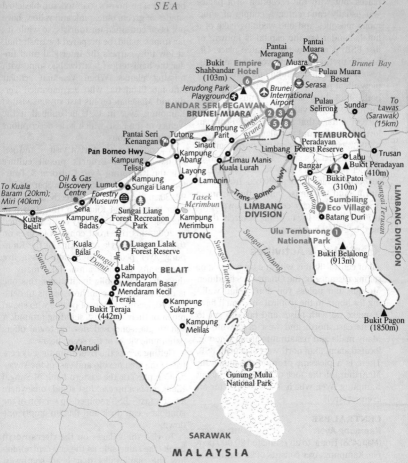

Brunei Highlights

1 Climbing high into the rainforest canopy and swimming in a cool jungle river at **Ulu Temburong National Park** (p470)

2 Tearing along mangrove-lined waterways on a **speedboat** (p466) from BSB to Bangar

3 Taking a water taxi to the water village of **Kampung**

Ayer (p456) and then indulging in a boardwalk stroll

4 Walking along BSB's newly refurbished **waterfront promenade** (p456)

5 Visiting BSB's opulent **mosques** (p456)

6 Marvelling at the **Empire Hotel & Country Club** (p461),

a sparkling monument to world-class profligacy

7 Relaxing amid rural greenery at **Sumbiling Eco Village** (p470) in Temburong District

8 Gorging yourself on the culinary delights of the many restaurants of **BSB** (p462)

BANDAR SERI BEGAWAN

POP 100,000

Cities built on oil money tend to be flashy places, but with the exception of a palace you usually can't enter, a couple of enormous mosques and one wedding cake of a hotel, Bandar (as the capital is known, or just BSB) is a pretty understated place. Urban life pretty much revolves around malls, restaurants and, depending on your level of piety, illicit parties or Islam (and sometimes both). BSB does have a few museums and the biggest water village in the world, a little slice of vintage that speaks to the Bruneian love of cosiness and nostalgia.

BSB's city centre is on the north bank of Sungai Brunei at a spot – 12km upriver from Brunei Bay – that's easy to defend against seaborne attack and sheltered from both storms and tsunamis. During the Japanese occupation, the city centre – known until 1970 as Brunei Town – was severely damaged by Allied bombing.

◉ Sights & Activities

All of central BSB is within easy walking or sailing distance of the Omar Ali Saifuddien Mosque, but unless you don't mind walking for hours in the tropical sun, you'll have to make do with buses and taxis to get to sights east, north and west of downtown. Many malls and restaurants are in Gadong, located about 5km northwest of central BSB. There is a pleasant promenade along Jln McArthur, at the foot of Jln Sultan facing Kampung Ayer, which is a nice spot for an evening stroll.

CENTRAL BSB

Kampung Ayer   WATER VILLAGES

(Map p458) Home to an estimated 20,000 people, Kampung Ayer consists of 28 contiguous stilt villages – named after the crafts and occupations traditionally practiced there – built along both (but especially the southern) banks of Sungai Brunei. A century ago, half of Brunei's population lived here, and even today many Bruneians – despite government inducements – still prefer the lifestyle of the water village to residency on dry land. If you look to the main roads on the opposite banks of the village you'll see luxury cars lined up on the shoulder of the road; many of these cars belong to water village residents. That said, Kampung Ayer is also home to a sizable population of undocumented immigrants that constitute Brunei's underclass.

Founded at least a thousand years ago, the village is considered the largest stilt settlement in the world and has its own schools, mosques, police stations and fire brigade. The houses, painted sun-bleached shades of green, blue, pink and yellow, have not been cutesified for tourists, so while it's far from squalid, be prepared for trash that, at low tide, carpets the intertidal mud under the banisterless boardwalks, some with missing planks. When Venetian scholar Antonio Pigafetta, who accompanied Ferdinand Magellan on his last voyage, visited Kampung Ayer in 1521, he dubbed it the 'Venice of the East', which is, as descriptions go, a bit ambitious.

A good place to start a visit – and get acquainted with Brunei's pre-oil culture – is the **Kampung Ayer Cultural & Tourism Gallery** (Map p458; ◷9am-5pm Sat-Thu, 9-11.30am & 2.30-5pm Fri), directly across the river from Sungai Kianggeh (the stream at the eastern edge of the city centre). Opened in 2009, this riverfront complex focuses on the history, lifestyle and crafts of the Kampung Ayer people and usually has a live handicrafts demonstration. Like many of the sultanate's public institutions, this one is overstaffed, yet somehow seems underserviced, leading to lots of people who spend much of their time just standing around. A square, glass-enclosed **viewing tower** offers panoramic views of the scene below.

Getting across the river from the city centre (ie the area next to and east of the Yayasan Complex) or the eastern bank of Sungai Kianggeh is a breeze. Just stand somewhere a water taxi – BSB's souped-up version of the gondola – can dock and flag an empty one down.

To visit the villages on the river's **north bank** (the same side as the city centre), follow the plankwalks that head southwest from Omar Ali Saifuddien Mosque, or those leading west (parallel to the river) from the Yayasan Complex, itself built on the site of a one-time water village.

Omar Ali Saifuddien Mosque   MOSQUE

(Map p458; Jln Stoney; ◷interior 8.30am-noon, 1.30-3pm & 4.30-5.30pm Sat-Wed, 4.30-5pm Fri, closed Thu, exterior compound 8am-8.30pm daily except prayer times) Built from 1954 to 1958, Masjid Omar Ali Saifuddien – named after the 28th sultan of Brunei (the late father of the current sultan) – is surrounded by an artificial lagoon that serves as a reflecting pool. The mosque is basically the happening

RAMADAN ROAD RULES

Brunei is an extremely religious, majority-Muslim nation that takes Ramadan seriously. If you're visiting during the holiest month of the Islamic year, keep in mind that by around 3pm, most people – especially drivers – are tired or stressed or both thanks to the daily fast. It's a documented fact that many car accidents occur at this time, and it's an anecdotal observation that normally polite Bruneians can get downright testy around this time. Just be mindful when interacting with locals and careful if you're out on the roads during late afternoon at this time.

centre of city life in Bandar come evenings; folks come for prayer, then leave to eat or shop, which is sort of Brunei in a nutshell. The 44m minaret makes it the tallest building in central BSB, and woe betide anyone who tries to outdo it – apparently the nearby Islamic Bank of Brunei building originally exceeded this height and so had its top storey removed by order of the sultan.

This being Brunei, the interior is pretty lavish. The floor and walls are made from the finest Italian marble, the stained-glass windows and chandeliers were crafted in England, and the luxurious carpets were flown in from Saudi Arabia and Belgium. Jigsaw enthusiasts can admire the 3.5-million-piece Venetian mosaic inside the main dome.

The ceremonial stone boat sitting in the lagoon is a replica of a 16th-century *mahligai* (royal barge).

FREE **Royal Regalia Museum** MUSEUM
(Map p458; Jln Sultan; ⊙9am-5pm Sun-Thu, 9-11.30am & 2.30-5pm Fri, 9.45am-5pm Sat, last entry 4.30pm) When called upon to present a gift to the sultan of Brunei, you must inevitably confront the question: what do you give a man who has everything? Here you'll see how various heads of state and royalty have solved this conundrum (hint: you'll never go wrong with priceless gold and jewels). We particularly like the mother of all beer mugs, given by Queen Elizabeth II.

Water-Taxi Cruise BOAT TOUR
The best way to see BSB's water villages and the sultan's fabled palace, Istana Nurul

Iman, is from a water taxi, which can be chartered along the waterfront for about B$30 to B$40 (a bit of negotiating will occur, but at least you know the locals can't claim the petrol is expensive!). Finding a boat won't be a problem, as the boatmen will have spotted you before you spot them.

After you admire the palace's backyard, your boatman can take you further upriver to **Pulau Ranggu**, an island that's home to a large colony of proboscis monkeys. The best time to head out is late afternoon, as the monkeys are easiest to spot around sunset.

EAST OF CENTRAL BSB

Brunei Museum MUSEUM
(✍224 4545; Jln Kota Batu; ⊙9am-5pm Sat-Thu, 9-11.30am & 2.30-5pm Fri, last entry 30 min before closing; P) Brunei's national museum, officially opened by Queen Elizabeth II in 1972, is a decent place to blow an hour of your time. It definitely feels a little dated.

The oldest pieces are in the newest, most well-kept section of the museum: the **Islamic Art Gallery**, which displays ceramics from Iran and Central Asia and blown glass from Egypt and the Levant dating from the 9th and 10th centuries. Other highlights include illuminated manuscripts of the Koran, tiny Korans the size of a matchbox and gold jewellery.

The **Brunei Traditional Culture Gallery** spotlights Brunei's role in Southeast Asia's history, cultures and commerce, and has a section on Western trade and intervention in Brunei, starting with the arrival of the Spanish and Portuguese in the 1500s. There's some frankly creepy, life-sized depictions of Malay rituals like weddings, child-rearing and (ouch) circumcision, and a collection of Brunei's famous ceremonial cannons, known as *bedil*, some with barrels shaped like dragon heads.

The **Natural History Gallery** is a decent introduction to Borneo's extraordinary biodiversity. Quite a few of the stuffed animals look to be on their last, moulding legs.

At the time of our visit there was an entire wing devoted to oil and gas extraction, the technology behind it, the good it has done for Brunei and an extensive exhibit on the kingdom's long-term plan for its economy after the oil runs out. Just kidding about that last bit.

The Brunei Museum is 4.5km east of central BSB along the coastal road, on a bluff overlooking Sungai Brunei. To get here, take the Central Bus line or a taxi (around B$10 from the bus station).

Bandar Seri Begawan

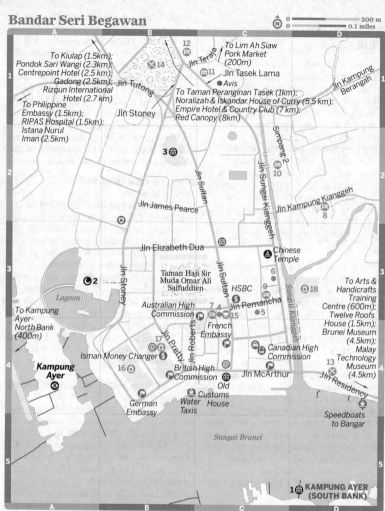

Malay Technology Museum   MUSEUM
(Jln Kota Batu; ⊙9am-5pm Sun-Thu, 9-11.30am & 2.30-5pm Fri, 9.45am-5pm Sat, last entry 30 min before closing) Linked to the Brunei Museum by a short path down the hill, this museum has somewhat outdated displays on life in a Malay water village (stilt architecture, boat making, fishing techniques, handicrafts) and a Murut (Lun Bawang) longhouse.

Twelve Roofs House   MUSEUM
(Bubungan Dua Belas; ☏224 4545; Jln Residency; ⊙9am-4.30pm Mon-Thu, 2:30am-4:30pm Fri, Sat 9am -11.30am; ℙ) The one-time residence

of Britain's colonial-era high commissioners, said to be the sultanate's oldest extant building, is now a museum dedicated to the longstanding 'special relationship' between Brunei and the UK. The evocative photos include views of Brunei as it looked a century ago and many fine shots of Queen Elizabeth II. The swimming pool out the back is rumoured to be haunted – during WWII the Japanese executed people there. It was unaccountably closed when we visited, so you may want to call ahead.

The building is 1.5km southeast of Sungai Kianggeh, towards the Brunei Museum, on

Bandar Seri Begawan

◎ **Top Sights**
Kampung Ayer A4

◎ **Sights**
1 Kampung Ayer Cultural &
Tourism Gallery D5
2 Omar Ali Saifuddien Mosque A3
3 Royal Regalia Museum B2

◎ **Activities, Courses & Tours**
4 Borneo Guide C3
5 Freme Travel Services C3
6 Intrepid Tours C3
Mona Florafauna Tours .... (see 9)

◎ **Sleeping**
7 Brunei Hotel C3
8 Jubilee Hotel D2

9 KH Soon Resthouse C3
10 Pusat Belia C2
11 Radisson Hotel C1
12 Terrace Hotel B1

◎ **Eating**
13 Gerai Makan Jalan Residency D4
14 Taman Selera B1
Tamu Kianggeh .... (see 18)

◎ **Drinking**
15 Coffee Bean & Tea Leaf C3

◎ **Shopping**
16 Hua Ho Department Store B4
17 Paul & Elizabeth Book Services B4
18 Tamu Kianggeh D3

a hilltop dominating the river. To get here from the city centre, take the Central Bus line, a taxi or a water taxi.

NORTH & WEST OF CENTRAL BSB

**Jame'Asr Hassanil
Bolkiah Mosque** MOSQUE
(Sultan Hassanal Bolkiah Hwy, Kampung Kiarong; ◎8am-noon, 2-3pm & 5-6pm Mon-Wed & Sat, 5-6pm Fri, 10.30am-noon, 2-3pm & 5-6pm Sun, closed Thu; P) Built in 1992 to celebrate the 25th year of the current sultan's reign, Brunei's largest mosque and its four terrazzo-tiled minarets dominate the 'suburbs' of BSB. It's certainly a...noticable building; because the sultan is his dynasty's 29th ruler, the complex is adorned with 29 golden domes. At night the mosque is lit up like a gold flame.

The interior is best described as jaw-droppingly over-the-top. The sheer volume in itself is amazing, not to mention the myriad woven rugs scattered across the men's prayer hall.

The mosque is about 3km northwest of the city centre towards Gadong. To get here, take buses 1 or 22 from the main bus terminal.

Istana Nurul Iman PALACE
(Jln Tutong) If you drink too much water before visiting Istana Nurul Iman (Palace of the Light of the Faith), the official residence of the sultan, never fear: the palace has 257 bathrooms. The 200,000-sq-m behemoth

boasts 1531 more rooms (that's 1788 in total) and is one of the largest habitations of any sort in the world – more than four times the size of the Palace of Versailles and three times larger than Buckingham Palace.

Designed by Filipino architect Leandro Locsin, the palace – 3km southwest of the centre of town – mixes Malay and Islamic elements with the sweep and oversized grandeur of an airport terminal. Nonetheless, it's relatively attractive from a distance or when illuminated in the evening.

Istana Nurul Iman is open to the public only during the three-day Hari Raya Aidil Fitri festivities at the end of Ramadan. The best way to check it out the other 362 days of the year, is to take a water-taxi cruise or to stop by the riverside pavilion at **Taman Persiaran Damuan**, a landscaped park 1.2km beyond the palace (when travelling from the city centre).

Taman Peranginan Tasek PARK
(Tasek Recreational Park; Jln Tasek Lama; P) BSB's tinier, dustier version of Central Park has greenery, picnic areas and peaceful walks to a small waterfall and a large reservoir. Locals come here to do t'ai chi (6am to 9am), jog (in the evening), use the exercise apparatus and admire the view. It's situated about 2km north of the city centre; to walk here turn east 400m north of the Terrace Hotel in the north of the city centre, otherwise catch a Northern Line bus.

JERUDONG

Jerudong Park Playground   AMUSEMENT PARK

(Jerudong; admission free, under 5/over 5 rides B\$8/10; ⏱4-10.30pm Wed, Thu & Sun, 2-10pm Fri & Sat, closed Mon & Tue except during school holidays) In its heyday, this B\$1 billion amusement park, a Prince Jefri project opened in 1994, was the pride of Brunei, and the only major modern amusement park in Southeast Asia. The concert hall hosted free shows by the likes of Whitney Houston and Michael Jackson, the latter to celebrate the sultan's 50th birthday, and the many rides included a giant roller coaster.

That attraction, along with most of the others, was sold off to repay debts, and today Jerudong is mostly a depressing lesson in hubris and economics: don't build something people don't want. Ostensibly 10 rides, including a merry-go-round and junior bumper cars, still operate. In our experience, this is not a sound assumption to make, so ask the person in front if any rides work before you buy a ride ticket. The park seems pretty busy on weekends, which is probably the best time to visit. The rumour is some party out there wants to convert the park into a smaller children's play area with basic rides and attractions, which sounds like a lovely idea.

There is no bus service to the park, which is near the coast about 20km northwest of BSB, so the only way to get here is by taxi (about B\$35 from the centre) or private car.

MUARA'S BEACHES

Pantai Muara (Muara Beach), near the tip of the peninsula, is a popular weekend retreat. It's pretty, but like many beaches in Borneo it's littered with driftwood and other flotsam that comes in with the tide. Quiet during the week, it has food stalls, picnic tables and a children's playground.

About 4km west of Muara along the Muara–Tutong Hwy, **Pantai Meragang** (Crocodile Beach) is another stretch of pleasant seaside sand that's not quite as crowded as the others on weekends. There are a couple of food stalls that make this a good place for a picnic. We've never heard of crocodiles here, by the way.

The beaches are about 25km northeast of BSB around the cargo, ferry and naval port of Muara, the site of an Australian amphibious landing in April 1945. Muara's town centre is served by buses 37, 38 and 39 (B\$1) from BSB city centre; bus 33 will take you from Muara town to Pantai Muara. Pantai Meragang is difficult to get to without your own transport.

☞ Tours

A number of local agencies offer tours of BSB and trips to nature sites around the sultanate, including Ulu Temburong National Park and the mangroves of Pulau Selirong, 45 minutes by boat from the city. Some also offer night safaris where you can spot proboscis monkeys, crocs and fireflies.

Borneo Guide   TOUR

(Map p458; ☎718 7138, 876 6796, 242 6923; www.borneoguide.com; Unit 204, Kiaw Lian Building, Jln Pemancha; ⏱9am-5pm Mon-Fri, 9am-1pm Sat) Excellent service, good prices and a variety of eco-programs around Brunei and Borneo. A day trip to Ulu Temburong National Park costs B\$120 from BSB (7.30am to 4.30pm or 5pm). Two days and one night at the park, including food and activities, costs B\$245 from BSB. The office also serves as a useful tourism information centre.

Intrepid Tours   TOURS

(Map p458; ☎222 1685, 222 1686; www.bruneibay.net/intrepidtours/index.html; 1st fl (Unit 105), PGGMB Building, Jln Sungai Kianggeh) Has its

---

BLASTED, BLASTING BEDIL

One of the more interesting exhibits in the **Brunei Museum** – partly because it's one of the few pieces of displayed culture that is native solely to Brunei, as opposed to the surrounding Malay culturesphere – is a series of *bedil*, or cannons. It was not oil but these bronze-cast weapons that were once the source of the sultanate's wealth and power. The cannons of Brunei subjugated many of the smaller kingdoms of Borneo and extended the sultanate's power all the way to the Philippines. They were so common they became an expected dowry gift; perhaps rightly so – *bedil* are beautiful. All are decorated in a baroque fashion, and some are carved to resemble dragons and crocodiles, because let's face it: what's more terrifying than a cannon ball erupting from a crocodile's mouth?

DON'T MISS

MONKEY BUSINESS

Long-tailed macaques and their adorable offspring often frolic in the trees along the road that heads up the hill (towards the radio tower) from the intersection between the Terrace and Radisson Hotels – listen for the tell-tale rustle of branches as they prance from tree to tree. As ever, don't approach the monkeys, no matter how beguiling they are. The primates are somewhere nearby all day long – sneaking into someone's kitchen through an open window, perhaps – but are easiest to spot very early in the morning, in the late afternoon and around dusk.

own lodge near Batang Duri (on the way to Ulu Temburong National Park). Main office located about 9km northeast of central BSB.

Mona Florafauna Tours　　　OUTDOORS, TOUR
(Map p458; ☏24hr 884 9110; jungle-dave.blogspot.
com.au; 209 1st fl, Kiaw Lian Bldg, 140 Jln Peman-
cha; ⊙8.30am-5pm) Specialises in outdoor and wildlife tours, with friendly and person-able service. Email or call in advance.

Freme Travel Services　　　　　TOUR
(Map p458; ☏223 4277; www.freme.com; 4th fl, office 4.03B, Wisma Jaya, Jln Pemancha) A bit cor-
porate, but has plenty of options, as befits one of Brunei's largest travel agencies.

🛏 Sleeping

Budget options are thin on the ground. Up-scale places often offer big discounts online.

Brunei Hotel　　　　TOP CHOICE　　HOTEL **$$**
(Map p458; ☏224 4828; thebruneihotel.com; 95 Jln Pemancha; incl breakfast r B$91-220, ste B$242-
440; ❄@⊚) The best bang for your Brunei dollar in town, the Brunei is...hip. OK, it's not the W or anything, but there are clean lines, monochromatic colour schemes, geo-metric patterns and a general sense of ul-tramodern cool, which is pretty unexpected in the sultanate. There's a decent breakfast buffet thrown into the deal served in the downstairs **Choices Cafe**, and the staff are friendly, helpful, competent and eager; the latter quality was frankly unexpected and greatly appreciated.

Pusat Belia　　　　　　　HOSTEL **$**
(Youth Centre; Map p458; ☏887 3066, 222 2900; Jln Sungai Kianggeh; dm B$10; ❄⊛) Gets rave reviews from backpackers despite the fact that couples can't stay together. The 28 spa-cious, strictly sex-segregated rooms, with four or 10 beds (all bunks), have functional furnishings, big windows, red cement floors and passable bathrooms. Situated at the

southern end of the Youth Centre complex (behind the cylindrical staircase). Recep-tion is supposed to be open from 7.45am to 4.30pm Monday to Thursday, and on call til 10pm otherwise, but staffing can be inter-mittent. If the office is locked, hang around and someone should find you. The adjacent swimming pool costs B$1. May fill up with government guests on holidays and for sports events.

Terrace Hotel　　　　　　　HOTEL **$$**
(Map p458; ☏224 3554, 224 3555, 224 3556, 224 3557; www.terracebrunei.com; Jln Tasek Lama; d B$65-75; ❄@⊚⊛) A classic tourist-class ho-tel whose 84 rooms are dowdy (think 1980s) but clean, and come with marble bathrooms. It also has a great little swimming pool. In a good location just 800m north of the water-front, near a hawker centre.

Empire Hotel & Country Club　RESORT **$$$**
(☏241 8888; www.theempirehotel.com; Muara-Tutong Hwy, Kampung Jerudong; r incl breakfast from B$400, villas B$1300-2900; ❄@⊚⊛) Pharaonic (or perhaps Dubaian) in its proportions and opulence, this 523-room extravaganza was commissioned by Prince Jefri as lodging for guests of the royal fam-ily. To recoup some of the US$1.1 billion investment, the property was quickly trans-formed into an upscale resort. So what's it like inside? To paraphrase Dolly Parton, it takes a lot of money to look this cheap. Sor-ry, we're just not ones for yards of marble and column-ed everything. Anyways, now anyone with a thing for Las Vegas–style bling can hang out in the lobby and enjoy one of the US$500,000 lamps made of gold and Baccarat crystal (the other one in the Emperor Suite can be appreciated privately for around B$17,000 per night). Even the cheapest rooms (except the recently opened Ocean rooms) have remote-control eve-rything, hand-woven carpets, gold-plated power points and enormous bathrooms

with marble floors, but the decor still somehow feels stodgy and unimaginative. But hey, worth a visit for the gilded spectacle; tea in the Lobby Lounge costs a mere B$5 a pot and the enormous pool complex outside is popular with expats and the wealthy. To get here, take bus 57 from the city centre or Gadong (runs two or three times a day; on the way back, book at the Transport desk), or a taxi (B$30 to B$35).

Radisson Hotel
HOTEL $$$

(Map p458; ☎224 4272; www.radisson.com/brunei; Jln Tasek Lama; r from B$170; ❉@🖥🌐⛱) This Radisson chain hotel, plopped on the edge of the town centre, flies the flag for international standards. The sparkling lobby exudes comfort and wealth, as do the business-class rooms. Amenities include two pools (one for kids), a fitness centre, a spa and two restaurants. Free shuttle service to Gadong and downtown three times a day.

Jubilee Hotel
HOTEL $$

(Map p458; ☎222 8070; www.jubileehotelbrunei.com; Jln Kampung Kianggeh; d B$70-95; f B$145; ❉@) The Jubilee's rooms aren't flash – they may remind you of your old aunt's seldom-used guest bedroom – but are liveable and clean. 'Superior' rooms come with kitchenettes.

Centrepoint Hotel
HOTEL $$$

(☎243 0430; www.thecentrepointhotel.com; Abdul Razak Complex; r B$280-380, ste from B$550; P❉🌐) The Centrepoint is a flash business-class hotel located in trendy Gadong. The rooms are plush and decently luxurious in an executive kind of way. To get to Gadong, either hop in a taxi or you can take the Circle Line bus.

KH Soon Resthouse
GUESTHOUSE $

(Map p458; ☎222 2052; khsoon-resthouse.tripod.com; 2nd fl, 140 Jln Pemancha; s/d B$35/39, with shared bathroom B$30/35; ❉) This rather matter-of-fact guesthouse, in a converted commercial space with floors the colour of a man-o-war's decks, offers budget rates, huge but spartan rooms, and a supercentral location. An extra bed costs around B$17.

Rizqun International Hotel
HOTEL $$$

(☎243 3000; www.rizquninternational.com; Abdul Razak Complex; r from B$320; ❉) Another tourist hotel in the Gadong district, the Rizqun is much more sophisticated than you'd expect for something growing out of a shopping mall. Plenty of restaurants, friendly staff and business-class amenities on hand. To get here, take a taxi or Circle Line bus.

Eating

BSB is not exactly a city that screams sex, drugs and rock 'n' roll – the second part of that equation is illegal, the other two are definitely happening behind closed doors. So how do people have fun? *Makan* (eat). *Makan, makan, makan.* "Food and instagraming our food is Brunei's national pastime," says Thanis Lim, a food blogger who's website (cookiemonzters.blogspot.com) is the go-to spot for those into the Brunei food scene.

In the city centre, restaurants can be found along the waterfront and on Jln Sultan (south of Jln Pemancha). The big shopping malls, including those out in Gadong, have **food courts** everywhere. Find a spot that looks busy and chow down. All restaurants listed have air-conditioning except outdoor food stalls.

⬛TOP CHOICE Pondok Sari Wangi
INDONESIAN, CHINESE $$

(☎244 5403; Block A, No.12-13, Abdul Razak Complex, Jln Gadong; mains B$5-$18; ⊙10am-10pm; 🍴) Located in Gadong, Pondok Sari Wangi is a beloved Bandar institution. The cuisine is Indonesian/Chinese, which means lots of gloriously rich, decadent, colourful grub like marinated 'smashed chicken', a fried fish with fiery sambal, sweet sauteed local greens and vegetables, mouth-watering satay with a heavily textured peanut sauce and the signature short ribs, braised to something like perfection. If you want to have some culinary indulgence on your trip, we recommend coming out here and ordering one of everything.

⬛TOP CHOICE Lim Ah Siaw Pork Market
HAWKER $$

(☎222 3963; Jln Teraja; mains B$3.50-9; ⊙6:30am-10pm) Lim Ah Siaw has great food, sure. Crispy braised pork knuckle, pork belly, pork buns, pork dumplings; it's seriously *Babe*'s hell. More so, because it is actually forbidden to raise pigs in Brunei, Lim Ah Siaw is the closest thing we found in Brunei to a speakeasy. Seriously. You kinda feel like a smuggler sneaking into this Chinese market-turned-restaurant. It also has the atmosphere of a Hong Kong gambling hall, which might take away from the food but certainly spices up the illicit zeitgeist.

Aminah Arif
AMBUYAT $$

(☏265 3036; Unit 2-3, Block B, Rahman Bldg, Spg 88, Kiulap; ambuyat for 2 B$16; ☺9am-10pm; ☝) Aminah Arif is synonymous with *ambuyat* (thick, starchy porridge), Brunei's signature dish. If you're up for trying a generous serving of wiggly white goo, this is a good spot to do so. Also serves rice and noodle dishes. Meals can be washed down with iced *kasturi ping* (calamansi lime juice; B$1.80). There are nine branches of Aminah Arif in town, but this one seems the most popular.

Tamu Kianggeh
HAWKER $

(Map p458; Jln Sungai Kianggeh; mains from B$1; ☺5am-5pm) The food stalls here serve Brunei's cheapest meals, including *nasi katok* (plain rice, a piece of fried or curried chicken and sambal; B$1) and *nasi lemak* (rice cooked in coconut milk and served with chicken, beef or prawn, egg and cucumber slices; also B$1). In the market's northeast corner, a vegetarian-Chinese stall called **Tamu Chakoi** (stalls 49-51; ☺8.30am-noon, closed Mon; ☝) serves a variety of inexpensive fried pastries and noodle dishes. We like the stalls for their food; we love them because this is one of the few places in Brunei that feels a little chaotic and messy, which is a little refreshing.

Taman Selera
HAWKER $

(Map p458; cnr Jln Tasek Lama & Jln Stoney; mains B$1-3.50; ☺4pm-midnight) At this old-fashioned hawker centre, set in a shady park, diners eat excellent, cheap Malaysian dishes under colourful tarps and ceiling fans. Options include satay (four skewers for B$1), fried chicken, seafood, rice and noodle dishes, and iced drinks (B$1). Situated 1km north of the waterfront, across from the Terrace Hotel.

Pasar Malam Gadong
NIGHT MARKET $

(Jln Pasar Gadong; ☺4-10pm) Thanks to its authentic Brunei-style snacks and dishes, this is Brunei's most popular and beloved night market. Unfortunately, it's geared to car-driving locals who take the food away so there are almost no places to sit. Situated 3km northwest of the city centre and 200m across the river from The Mall shopping centre. Served by buses 1 and 22, but after about 7pm the only way back to town is by taxi (B$15, more after 8pm).

Noralizah & Iskandar House of Curry
INDIAN $

(☏867 5781; Kompleks Awang Hj Ibrahim, Jln Berakas; mains B$3-7; ☺7am-8pm; ☝) It's all about the roti flatbreads at this spot, from flaky roti to deliciously oily paratha, stuffed with ground lamb and onions in a *murtabak*, or bananas and a dusting of sugar for a breakfast treat. Dip that deliciousness in one of several bowls of warming curry. Very popular with students looking for a cheap meal.

The restaurant is located near the airport. To get here you'll need to take a taxi ($B8-10 from the city centre) or a bus (Northern Lines 1 and 2 or the Central Line).

Kimchi
KOREAN $

(☏222 2233; Unit 19, Block B, Regent Sq; B$3-11; ☺11am-2:30pm & 6pm-10pm) Korean restaurants are pretty ubiquitous in BSB, and Kimchi, in Regent Sq west of the centre, is the best of the bunch. The titular *kimchi* (fermented cabbage) is delightfully smelly and spicy, rice cakes are drowned in a hot, rich sauce and the chicken wings...well, when are chicken wings a bad idea? The *bulgogi* (barbeque) is a lovely indulgence. Take a taxi or bus here (Central Line or the Northern Lines 1 and 2).

AMBUYAT – GUMMY, GLUEY & GLUTINOUS

Remember that kid in kindergarten who used to eat paste? Well, *ambuyat*, Brunei's unofficial national dish, comes pretty darn close. It's a gelatinous porridge-like goo made from the ground pith of the sago tree, which is ground to a powder and mixed with water, and eaten with a variety of flavourful sauces.

To eat *ambuyat*, you'll be given a special pair of chopsticks that's attached at the top (don't snap them in two!) to make it easier to twirl up the tenacious mucous. Once you've scooped up a bite-sized quantity, dunk it into the sauce. After your *ambuyat* is sufficiently drenched, place the glob of dripping, quivering, translucent mucilage in your mouth and swallow – don't chew, just let it glide down your throat.

The easiest way to try *ambuyat* is to stop by one of the nine branches of Aminah Arif in BSB.

Gerai Makan Jalan Residency HAWKER $
(Jalan Residency Food Court; Map p458; Jln Residency; mains B$2-5.50; ⊘4pm-midnight) Along the riverbank facing Kampung Ayer, this grouping of food stalls features satay (B$1 for four chicken or three lamb skewers), dozens of kinds of mee goreng and nasi goreng, and soups such as *soto* (noodle soup). The hours we give are not set in stone, and sometimes, some stalls are open 24 hours.

Red Canopy INTERNATIONAL $
(☑245 3879; Unit 11 Hassain Complex, Jln Delima; B$4-9; ⊘7am-11pm) Plunked by the airport, the Red Canopy serves up a tasty combination of Malay, Thai, Chinese and Western cuisine (not all at once, obviously). A Malay lunch buffet keeps customers satisfied by day; at night daily specials rotate in and out, from buttermilk chicken on Tuesdays to quail egg soup on Thursdays.

 Drinking

The sale and public consumption of alcohol is officially banned in Brunei, but locals and expats may know of places (often Chinese restaurants) that discreetly serve beer to regulars, or establishments that let you bring your own.

Locals are fond of *air batu campur* ('ice mix'), usually called ABC, which brings together ice, little green noodles, grass jelly, sago pearls and red beans.

Coffee Bean & Tea Leaf CAFE
(Map p458; Mayapuri Bldg, 36 Jln Sultan; ⊘8am-midnight Sun-Wed, to 1.30am Thu-Sat; 🛜) The hangout of choice for folks who need to bang out some work on their laptops or just relax in air-conditioned frigidity. Serves hot and 'ice blended' beverages, hearty breakfasts, pastries (muffins, cakes, scones), gourmet sandwiches (B$6 to B$8) and pasta (B$4.80 to B$7.50).

De Royalle Café CAFE
(Mayapuri Bldg, 38 Jln Sultan; ⊘24hr; 🛜) Organised into two mini living rooms plus sidewalk tables, this always-open establishment has a supply of perusable English-language newspapers and serves up pastries, sandwiches (B$4 to B$11 – lox is the priciest) and, of course, fresh-brewed coffee. A fine place for a relaxed rendezvous with friends.

☆ **Entertainment**

Locals often head to Gadong for a night out, which in Brunei usually amounts to nothing more than dinner and perhaps a movie. Based on what you hear, you might conclude that the area is a seething nightlife zone or at least a fine collection of smart restaurants. Unfortunately, it's neither – just some air-con shopping malls and commercial streets.

 Shopping

Shopping is Brunei's national sport. Locals bop through the shopping malls scouting out the best deals while bemoaning the fact that their micro-nation doesn't have as much variety as Singapore.

The country's only traffic jam occurs nightly in Gadong, about 3km northwest of the centre. The area features several air-conditioned bastions of commerce, including two huge malls, Centrepoint and The Mall.

Arts & Handicrafts Training Centre CRAFT
(☑224-0676; Jln Kota Batu; ⊘8am-5pm Sat-Thu, 8-11.30am & 2-5pm Fri) Sells silverwork, carved wood items, ornamental brass cannons (from B$500) and ceremonial swords (about B$500), made by the centre's students and graduates, for much, much more than you'd pay in Sarawak or Kalimantan. Not bad for window-shopping, though – check out the *jong sarat* (hand-woven cloth made from gold and silver threads; B$400 to B$4000 for a 2m-long bolt). If you're serious about Bruneian artisanship, pick up the sultanate's *Directory of Handicraft Entrepreneurs* (B$4.80). The centre is on the river 600m east of Sungai Kianggeh.

Paul & Elizabeth Book Services BOOKS
(Map p458; ☑222-0958; 2nd fl, eastern bldg, Yayasan Complex, Jln Pretty; ⊘9.30am-9pm) This place stocks a few books on Brunei, a street map of the entire sultanate and a small range of English-language paperbacks, including some ancient LP guides! There's also an internet cafe (p465).

Hua Ho Department Store DEPARTMENT STORE
(Map p458; ⊘10am-10pm) Don't miss four-level Hua Ho with its cache of traditional Bruneian sweets in the basement.

Tamu Kianggeh CRAFT
(Map p458; Jln Sungai Kianggeh) Woven crafts are sold along the river here, but prices are higher than in Malaysia.

❶ Information

Emergency

Ambulance (☏991)
Fire Brigade (☏995)
Police (☏993)

Internet Access

Amin & Sayeed Cyber Cafe (1st fl, cnr Jln Sultan & Jln McArthur; per hr B$1; ◷9am-midnight)
Paul & Elizabeth Cyber Cafe (2nd fl, eastern bldg, Yayasan Complex, Jln Pretty; per hr B$1; ◷9am-9pm) Overlooks the central atrium in the eastern building of the Yayasan complex. Decent connections, bad soundtrack.

Medical Services

RIPAS Hospital (☏224 2424; www.moh.gov. bn/medhealthservices/ripas.htm; Jln Tutong; ◷24hr) Brunei's main hospital, with fully equipped, modern facilities. Most of the senior staff are Western trained. Situated about 2km west of the centre (across the Edinburgh Bridge).
Jerudong Park Medical Centre (☏emergency 261 2461, 261 1433; www.jpmc.com.bn; Tutong-Muara Hwy; ◷24hr) Private medical facility; high standards of care. Located about 27km northwest of the BSB centre, accessible by bus 55.

Money

Banks and international ATMs are sprinkled around the city centre, especially along Jln McArthur and Jln Sultan. The airport has ATMs, and you can change travellers cheques at larger hotels.

HSBC (cnr Jln Sultan & Jln Pemancha; ◷8.45am-4pm Mon-Fri, to 11.30am Sat) Has a 24-hour ATM. You must have an HSBC account to change travellers cheques.

Isman Money Changer (ground fl, eastern bldg, Yayasan Complex, Jln Pretty; ◷9.30am-7.30pm) Changes cash but not travellers cheques. Just off the central atrium.

Post

Main Post Office (cnr Jln Sultan & Jln Elizabeth Dua; ◷8am-4.30pm Mon-Thu & Sat, 8-11am & 2-4pm Fri) Has a free internet computer. The Stamp Gallery displays some historic first-day covers and blow-ups of colonial-era stamps.

Tourist Information

Keep an eye out for the free **Borneo Insider's Guide** (BIG; www.borneoinsidersguide.com), a glossy magazine published four times a year.

For a mix of fresh news, business information and visitor tips about Brunei, check out www. brudirect.com.

Brunei Tourism (www.bruneitourism.travel), whose wonderful website has oodles of useful information, runs three tourist-information counters that can supply the only decent maps of the sultanate. One is at **Old Customs House**; one is in the arrival hall at the BSB Airport; and one at the Kampung Ayer Cultural & Tourism Gallery (p465), across the river from the city centre.

Airport (arrival hall; ◷8am-noon & 1.30-5pm)
Brunei Tourism (◷9am-5pm Sat-Thu, 9-11am & 2.30-5pm Fri) Across the river from the city centre.

❶ Getting There & Away

Air

Brunei International Airport (☏233 1747, flight enquiries 233 6767; www.civil-aviation. gov.bn) By the time you read this, flash new

---

GETTING TO SABAH: BANDAR SERI BEGAWAN TO BANDAR LABUAN

Getting to the border Travel by sea to Sabah is the easiest option, avoiding the hassles and delays of land borders – traffic at the Kuala Lurah crossing has been known to cause three-hour delays. Car ferries from Serasa Ferry Terminal in Muara, about 20km northeast of BSB, to the Malaysian federal territory of Pulau Labuan (1½ hours) are run by PKL Jaya Sendirian. If you've got a car, get there at least an hour before sailing.

PKL Jaya Sendirian also operates a car-ferry service from the Serasa Ferry Terminal to the Sabah port of Menumbok (2½ hours), which is 152km by road from Kota Kinabalu. Adult/car B$35/90 from Muara, RM80/210 from Menumbok; departures at 10.30am from Muara, 4pm from Menumbok. A new ferry service on the Kimanis-1 boat was scheduled to begin three round-trip services between BSB and Menumbok via Labuan as of press time.

Three express buses a day (B$3, 40 minutes) link BSB direct with the ferry; departures from BSB's bus terminal (from the berth for bus 39) are at 6.30am, 11.30am and 2.15pm. To go by public transport, you can take a more convoluted trip via bus 37, 38 or 39 to Muara town (B$1 at least twice an hour); from there it's a short ride on bus 33 to the ferry.

At the border Most travellers to Malaysia are granted a 30 or 60 day visa on arrival.

Moving on From Bandar Labuan, daily ferries go to Kota Kinabalu (115km by sea). See p378 for details on doing the trip in the opposite direction.

GETTING TO SARAWAK: BANDAR SERI BEGAWAN TO MIRI

Getting to the border PHLS Express (☎771 668) links BSB with Miri (B$18 from BSB, RM40 from Miri, 3½ hours) via Seria and Kuala Belait (two hours) twice a day. Departures from BSB's PGGMB building (on Jln Sungai Kianggeh just south of the Chinese Temple) are at approximately 7am and 1pm and from Miri's Pujut Bus Terminal at about 8am and 4pm. Tickets are sold on board. Travel between Miri and Seria or Kuala Belait costs B$12 or RM25.

Another option for travel between BSB and Miri is a 'private transfer' (RM60 per person) in a seven-seater van (☎016-807 2893, in Malaysia 013-833 2331) run by a father-son team. Departures from BSB are usually at 1pm or 2pm; departures from Miri are generally at 9am or 10am but may be earlier. It may also be possible to hitch a ride (RM50 per person, 3½ hours) with a newspaper-delivery van (☎in BSB 876 0136, in Miri before 4pm 012-878 0136). Departure from Miri is at 5.30am; be prepared for an hour's delay at customs.

At the border Most travellers to Malaysia are granted a 30 or 60 day visa on arrival.

Moving on The bus will leave you at Miri's Pujut Bus Terminal, a 4km taxi ride from the city centre.

See p439 for details on doing the trip in the opposite direction.

---

renovations are supposed to turn this small airport into a modern international hub.

TEMBURONG DISTRICT

The fastest way to get to Bangar is by speedboat (adult/senior B$6/5, 45 minutes, at least hourly from 6am to at least 4.30pm, until as late as 6pm on Sunday and holidays). The dock is on Jln Residency about 200m east of Sungai Kianggeh.

Bus & Van

BSB's carbon monoxide–choked bus terminal is on the ground floor of a multistorey parking complex two blocks north of the waterfront. It is used by domestic lines, including those to Muara, Seria, Tutong and Kuala Lurah, and services to Pontianak in Kalimantan, but not to Sabah or Sarawak. Schematic signs next to each numbered berth show the route of each line.

For details on various bus and van options to Malaysia, contact KH Soon Resthouse (p462) in BSB or Miri's Visitors Information Centre (p438).

ℹ Getting Around

To/From the Airport

The airport, about 8km north of central BSB, is linked to the city centre, including the bus terminal on Jln Cator, by buses 23, 24, 36 and 38.

A cab to/from the airport costs B$25-35; taxis are unmetered, so agree on a price before you get in. Some hotels offer airport pick-up.

Bus

Brunei's public bus system, run by a variety of companies, is rather chaotic, at least to the uninitiated, so getting around by public transport takes effort. Buses (B$1) operate daily from 6.30am to about 6.30pm (7pm on some lines); after that, your options are taking a cab or hoofing it. If you're heading out of town and will need to catch a bus back, ask the driver if and when they're coming back and when the last bus back is.

Finding stops can be a challenge – some are marked by black-and-white-striped uprights or a shelter, others by a yellow triangle painted on the pavement, and yet others by no discernible symbol. Fortunately, numbers are prominently displayed on each 20- or 40-passenger bus.

The bus station lacks an information office or a ticket counter, and while the schematic wall map may make sense to BSB natives, it's a bit of a cipher to the uninitiated. Some tourist brochures include a schematic route map.

Jesselton Express (☎012-622 9722, 717 7755, 719 3835, in BSB 718 3838, in KK 016-836 0009) sends a bus to KK (B$45, eight to nine hours) via Limbang, Bangar, Lawas and various towns in Sabah daily at 8am. Make sure you have your passport ready if you're travelling overland to Sabah because you'll be stopping at a whopping eight checkpoints (thanks mainly to the outgrowth of Temburong District). As long as your ID is in order you'll be fine; the trip is tedious rather than dodgy.

Car

Brunei has Southeast Asia's cheapest petrol – gasoline is just B$0.53 a litre and diesel goes for only B$0.30! If you're driving a car (eg a rental) with Malaysian plates and are not a Brunei resident, you'll be taken to a special pump to pay more (this is to prevent smuggling).

Hiring a car is a good way to explore Brunei's hinterland. Prices start at about B$80 a day. Surcharges may apply if the car is taken into Sarawak. Most agencies will bring the car to your hotel and pick it up when you've finished, and drivers can also be arranged, though this could add B$100 to the daily cost. The main roads are in good condition, but some back roads require a 4WD.

The following are among the rental companies (most of them local) with offices at the airport:

Avis (☑242- 6345, 876 0642; www.avis.com)

Hertz (☑245 2244, 872 6000; www.hertz.com)

Taxi

Taxis are a convenient way of exploring BSB – if you can find one, that is. There is no centralised taxi dispatcher and it's difficult or impossible to flag down a cab on the street. Hotels can provide drivers' cell-phone numbers. Most taxis have yellow tops; a few serving the airport are all white.

BSB's only proper taxi rank is two blocks north of the waterfront at the bus terminal on Jln Cator.

Some taxis use meters ($B3 for the first kilometre, and $B1 for every kilometre thereafter), although many drivers will just try to negotiate a fare with you. Fares go up by 50% after 10pm; the charge for an hour of wait time is B$30 to B$35. Sample day-time taxi fares from the city centre include the Brunei Museum (B$10), Gadong (B$15), the airport (B$30), the Serasa Ferry Terminal in Muara (B$35), the Empire Hotel & Country Club (B$35) and the Jerudong Park Playground (B$35 to B$40).

Water Taxi

If your destination is near the river, water taxis – the same little motorboats that ferry people to and from Kampung Ayer – are a good way of getting there. You can hail a water taxi anywhere on the waterfront a boat can dock, as well as along Venice-themed Sungai Kianggeh. Crossing straight across the river is supposed to cost B$0.50 per person; diagonal crossings cost more.

TUTONG & BELAIT DISTRICTS

Most travellers merely pass through the districts of Tutong and Belait, west of BSB, en route to Miri in Sarawak, but there are a few worthwhile attractions. Frequent buses link Kuala Belait, Seria and Tutong with BSB, but if you want to really see the sights the best way is to take a tour or rent a car.

Tutong

POP 20,000

About halfway between Seria and BSB, Tutong is the main town in central Brunei. The town itself is neat but unremarkable, but

the area is famous in Brunei for two things: pitcher plants and sand. Tutong has six species of pitcher plants and the locals cook a variety of dishes in their insect-catching sacs. Some of the sand near Tutong is so white that Bruneians will often take pictures with it while pretending it's snow (did we mention there's no booze here? Have your fun any way you can, Brunei). You can see *pasir putih* (white sand) in patches along the side of the Pan Borneo Hwy.

There's a great beach, **Pantai Seri Kenangan**, also known as Pantai Tutong, a couple of kilometres west of town, on Jln Kuala Tutong. Set on a spit of land, with the ocean on one side and the Sungai Tutong on the other, the casuarina-lined beach is arguably the best in Brunei. The royal family clearly agrees, as they have a surprisingly modest palace here for discreet getaways.

❶ Getting There & Away

The buses that link BSB with Seria stop in Tutong (B$3, one hour, every 30 to 60 minutes until 5pm).

Jalan Labi

A few kilometres after you enter Belait District (coming from Tutong and BSB), a road branches inland (south) to Labi and beyond, taking you through some prime forest areas. The easiest way into the interior of western Brunei, Jln Labi offers a chance to stop by Brunei's **Forestry Museum** (◷8am-12:15pm & 1:30am-4:30pm, closed Fri & Sun) and see a number of Iban longhouses, which in these parts come complete with mod cons and parking lots.

About 40km south of the coastal road, Labi is a small Iban settlement with some fruit arbours. Further south, you come to the Iban longhouses of **Rampayoh**, **Mendaram Besar**, **Mendaram Kecil** and finally, at the end of the track, **Teraja**, where a local guide may be able to take you to a nearby waterfall.

Seria

POP 34,000

Spread out along the coast between Tutong and Kuala Belait, low-density Seria is home to many of Brunei Shell's major onshore installations. A Ghurkha infantry battalion of the British Army is stationed here, the UK's last remaining military base in eastern Asia. A big market is held on Friday until about 3pm.

⊙ Sights

Oil & Gas Discovery Centre MUSEUM
(☑337 7200; www.bsp.com.bn/ogdc; off Jln Tengah; adult/teenager/senior B$5/2/3; ⊙8:30am-5pm Mon-Sat, 9:30am-6pm Sun) Puts an 'edutainment' spin on the oil industry. Likely to appeal to young science buffs and Shell employees. About 700m northwest of the bus station.

Billionth Barrel Monument MONUMENT
Commemorates (you guessed it) the billionth barrel of crude oil produced at the Seria field, a landmark reached in 1991. We really were hoping this monument would look like an actual oil barrel because, well, that'd be hilarious, but it's more like a bunch of blue noodles topped by the emblem of the sultanate. Which, come to think of it, is cool too. Out to sea, oil rigs producing the sultanate's second billion dot the horizon. Situated on the beach about 1km west of the Oil & Gas Discovery Centre.

🛏 Sleeping

Hotel Koperasi HOTEL $$
(☑322 7586, 322 7589, 322 7592; hotel_seria@brunet.bn; Jln Sharif Ali; s/d B$72/88; ❀🅰) Seria's only proper hotel, with 24 neat, if boring, rooms. Situated 150m northwest of the bus station.

ⓘ Getting There & Away

Frequent buses go southwest to Kuala Belait (B$1, three times an hour from 6.30am to 6.15pm) and northeast to BSB (B$6, 2½ hours, every 30 to 60 minutes until about 5pm) via Tutong.

Kuala Belait

POP 35,500

Almost on the Sarawak frontier, coastal Kuala Belait (KB) is a modern, sprawling company town – the company being Brunei Shell – of one-storey suburban villas interspersed with grasshopper-like pump jacks. Although there's a reasonable beach, most travellers just hustle through on their way to or from Miri.

🛏 Sleeping & Eating

In the town centre, restaurants can be found along Jln McKerron and, two short blocks east, on parallel Jln Pretty, KB's main commercial avenue. Locals recommend the roast duck.

Hotel Sentosa HOTEL $$
(☑333 1345; www.bruneisentosahotel.com; 92-93 Jln McKerron; s/d B$98/103; ❀@🅰) Clean, well-run, tourist-class accommodation right in the centre of town. Situated one block south of the bus station.

ⓘ Information

HSBC Bank (cnr Jln McKerron & Jln Dato Shahbandar) Has an international ATM. Situated diagonally opposite the bus station.

ⓘ Getting There & Away

The **bus station** (cnr Jlns McKerron & Dato Shahbandar) is smack in the town centre. **Miri Belait** (☑419 129) runs five daily buses to Miri (B$8/RM8), and PHLS Express (p466) (☑771 668) runs two more comfortable daily trips for similar prices. Purple minibuses go to Seria (B$1) three times an hour from 6.30am to 6.15pm.

TEMBURONG DISTRICT

This odd little exclave (that means a part of a country physically separated from the rest of the nation; feel free to take that to the next pub quiz night) is barely larger than Penang, but happens to contain one of the best preserved tracts of primary rainforest in all of Borneo. The main draw is the brilliant Ulu Temburong National Park, accessible only by longboat.

The speedboat ride from BSB out to Bangar, the district capital, is the most fun you can possibly have for B$6. You roar down Sungai Brunei, slap through the nipah-lined waterways and then tilt and weave through mangroves into the mouth of Sungai Temburong.

Want to get depressed? Go to Google Earth and look at the outline of Temburong District. It's easy to spot: at the Brunei frontier, Malaysia's logging roads – irregular gashes of eroded earth – and trashed hillsides give way to a smooth carpet of trackless, uninhabited virgin rainforest. Until not long ago, almost all of Borneo looked like this.

Bangar

Little Bangar, perched on the banks of Sungai Temburong, is the gateway to, and administrative centre of, Temburong District. It can be visited as a day trip from BSB if you catch an early speedboat, but you'll get more out of the town's easygoing pace if you stay over and explore the area, which has some fine primary rainforest and nine longhouses, not all of them very long.

Sleeping

Temburong District has a number of home stays used mainly by tour operators and locals with cars. In addition to the options listed below, there are also five or six guesthouses scattered around town. They're all acceptably clean and comfortable and otherwise nondescript.

Lukat Intan Guesthouse GUESTHOUSE $$
(☎864 3766, 522 1078; lukutintan@hotmail.com; B$30-50; P🏚) Run by a friendly older couple, Lukat offers spic and span rooms and personable service; you get breakfast and your stay and they're happy to give you free rides to the Bangar jetty.

Rumah Persinggahan Kerajaan Daerah Temburong GUESTHOUSE $
(☎522 1239; Jln Batang Duri; s/d/tr/q B$25/30/40/50, 4-person chalets B$80; 🏚🛜) Set around a grassy, L-shaped courtyard, this government-run guesthouse has friendly, helpful staff and six spacious but slightly fraying rooms with rather more bathtub rust and somewhat cooler hot water than many would deem ideal. Situated a few hundred metres west of the town centre, across the highway from the two mosques.

Youth Hostel HOSTEL $
(Pusat Belia; ☎522 1694; www.bruneiyouth.org.bn; dm B$10; ⏰office staffed 7.30am-4.30pm, closed Fri & Sat) Part of a youth centre, this basic hostel sits in a fenced compound across the street from (west of) the Tourist Information Centre. Rooms, each with six beds (bunks), are clean and fan-cooled. If no one's around try phoning or looking helplessly at passers by – worked for us.

Eating

The **fruit and veggie market**, behind the row of shops next to the Tourist Information Centre, has an upstairs **food court** (⏰7am-10pm).

A handful of restaurants serving passable Malay and Chinese food can be found around the market, along and just in from the riverfront.

Information

3 in 1 Services (per hr B$1; ⏰7.45am-9.30pm, closed Sun) Internet access on the first floor of the building next to the market (across the pedestrian bridge from the hawker centre). The shop number is A1-3.

Bank Islam Brunei Darussalam (⏰8.45am-3.45pm Mon-Thu, 8.45-11am & 2.30-4pm Fri, 8.45-11.15am Sat) The only bank in town. Changes US dollars and pounds sterling but not Malaysian ringgits. The ATM did not take international cards at time of research, but staff said this may change soon. On the river 150m north of the bridge.

Hock Guan Minimarket Exchanges Malaysian ringgits for Brunei dollars. In the second row of shops from the Tourist Information Centre.

Jayamuhibah Shopping Mart Carries some over-the-counter medicines (Temburong District does not have a proper pharmacy). In the second row of shops from the Tourist Information Centre.

Getting There & Away

Boat
By far the fastest way to/from BSB is by speedboat (adult/senior B$6/5, 45 minutes, at least hourly from 6am to at least 4.30pm, until as late as 6pm on Sunday and holidays). Bangar's **ferry terminal**, Terminal Perahu Dan Penumpang, is on the western bank of the river just south of the red bridge.

Boats depart at a scheduled time or when they're full, whichever comes first. When you get to the ticket counters, check which company's boat will be the next to leave and then pay and add your name to the passenger manifest. Peak-hour departures can be as frequent as every 15 minutes.

Bus
Buses run by **Jesselton** (☎719 3835, 717 7755, in BSB 718 3838) pick up passengers heading towards Limbang and BSB in the early afternoon; its bus to KK (B$25) and Lawas (B$10) passes through town at about 10am.

Taxi
Bangar doesn't have official taxis, but it's usually not too difficult to hire a car if you ask around under the rain awning in front of the ferry terminal. Drivers may not speak much English. Possible destinations include the Malaysian border towards Limbang (B$6), a distance of 4km; the town of Limbang (about B$40) and the Peradayan Forest Reserve (Bukit Patoi; about B$25 return).

Taxis do not wait on the Malaysian side of the border towards Limbang.

Pulau Selirong

At the northern tip of Temburong District, this 25-sq-km island is a sanctuary for mangroves and the fauna that live in them, including proboscis monkeys. The only way to visit is with a boat tour, which BSB tour operators can organise for around B$75. The trip across the open water of Brunei Bay takes about 45 minutes.

Batang Duri

Batang Duri, about 16km south of Bangar, is the jumping-off point for longboat rides to Ulu Temburong National Park. As you head south, the sealed road passes Malay settlements, then Murut (Lun Bawang) hamlets and finally a few partly modern Iban longhouses.

🛏 Sleeping

TOP CHOICE Sumbiling Eco
Village   GUESTHOUSE $$
(📞242 6923, 876 6796; borneoguide.com/eco village; per person incl meals B$50; 🅿@) If you're looking for Brunei's version of a jungle camp with basic amenities and a chilled-out atmosphere that encourages slipping into a green state of utterly relaxed Zen, come to Sumbiling. This ecofriendly rustic camp offers great Iban cuisine (served on simpur leaves) and plenty of outdoor activities, including visits to nearby Ulu Temburong National Park, jungle overnights, inner-tubing and a forest trek. The basic rooms have glassless windows and a fan attached to the ceiling to make sure air circulates inside the mozzie nets (nice touch). Also has a rain-protected camping area, organic composting and importantly, no handouts of single-use plastic bottles. Nearby is a five-door Iban longhouse with fierce, beautiful fighting cocks – each family's prized possessions – tethered outside. Prices do not include transport. Run by Borneo Guide (p460) in cooperation with the local community. Situated a few minutes downstream from Batang Duri.

Peradayan Forest Reserve

If you can't be bothered with the logistics or expense of a trip up to Ulu Temburong National Park, the Peradayan Forest Reserve is a good day-trip alternative. There's a 5km (one-way) trek up to the jungle-cloaked peak of **Bukit Patoi** (310m); it may also be possible to continue on to **Bukit Peradayan** (410m). The trail, through pristine jungle, begins at the picnic tables and toilet block of **Taman Rekreasi Bukit Patoi** (Bukit Patoi Recreational Park), about 15km southeast of Bangar (towards Lawas). Bring lots of water and be prepared to turn back if the path, not always properly maintained along its entire length, becomes too overgrown to follow.

If you don't have your own transport, you can get here from Bangar by unofficial taxi (about B$30 return).

Ulu Temburong National Park

It's odd that in a country as manicured and regulated as Brunei, there's still a sizable chunk of true untamed wilderness. Therein lays the appeal of **Ulu Temburong National Park** (admission B$5), located in the heart of a 500-sq-km area of pristine rainforest covering most of southern Temburong. It's so untouched that only about 1 sq km of the park is accessible to tourists, who are only admitted as part of guided tour packages. To protect it for future generations, the rest is off-limits to everyone except scientists, who flock here from around the world. Permitted activities include a canopy walk, some short jungle walks, and swimming in the cool mountain waters of Sungai Temburong – so don't forget your swimsuit.

The forests of Ulu Temburong are teeming with life, including as many as 400 kinds of butterfly, but don't count on seeing many vertebrates. The best times to spot birds and animals, in the rainforest and along river banks, are around sunrise and sunset, but you're much more likely to hear hornbills and Bornean gibbons than to see them.

🏃 Activities

Longboat Trip   BOAT TOUR
One of the charms of Ulu Temburong National Park is that the only way to get there is by *temuai* (shallow-draft Iban longboat). The exhilarating trip, which takes 25 to 40 minutes from Batang Duri, is tough on the boats, which last just a few years, and challenging even for experienced skippers, who need a variety of skills to shoot the rapids – going upstream – in a manner reminiscent of a salmon: submerged boulders and logs

DIRECTORY A–Z

» **Currency** Brunei dollar (B$)

» **Eating price categories**

$ less than B$6
$$ B$6–16
$$$ more than B$16

» **Emergency phone numbers**

Ambulance ☎991
Police ☎993
Fire ☎995
Search & Rescue ☎998
Directory enquiries ☎113

» **Public holidays** Brunei shares major public holidays with Malaysia. Holidays specific to Brunei include Brunei National Day (23 February), Royal Brunei Armed Forces Day (31 May) and the Sultan of Brunei's Birthday (15 July).

» **Tourist information** Brunei Tourism (www.bruneitourism.travel) is a very useful website, containing information on transport, business hours, accommodation, tour agencies and more.

» **Sleeping price categories**

$ less than B$60
$$ B$60–150
$$$ more than B$150

» **Visas** US travellers are granted a free 90 day visa on arrival; travellers from Western Europe, New Zealand, Singapore, Malaysia, among others, receive a free 30 day visa; Swiss, Japanese and Canadians get 14 free days. Australians can apply for a visa upon arrival: a three-day transit visa (B$5), a two-week single-entry visa (B$20) or a month-long multiple-entry visa (B$30). Israeli travellers are banned from entering Brunei.

For more information about your own country's visa policy see Immigration Brunei (www.immigration.gov.bn/002/html/melawat.html).

» **Cultural & legal matters** Brunei is a strictly Islamic country, with more restrictions and regulations than Malaysia and Singapore. Travellers would do well to keep the following cultural elements in mind:

» **Drugs & alcohol** The sale and public consumption of alcohol is forbidden in Brunei. That said, people do drink, but it tends to occur either in private residences or the back rooms of Chinese restaurants. Drug trafficking is punishable by the death penalty.

» **Homosexuality** According to www.smartraveller.gov.au, 'consensual homosexual acts between adults (of either sex) are illegal and penalties include prison sentences'.

» **Smoking** Brunei's tough anti-smoking laws ban puffing not only inside shops and malls but also in outdoor markets and around food stalls.

» **Women travellers** Discreet clothing is appropriate here – you certainly don't have to cover your hair, but walking around in a tank top or bikini top is a bad idea. Be mindful, too, that some women have reported being the object of catcalls and come-ons, especially from passing motorists.

have to be dodged, hanging vines must be evaded and the outboard must be taken out of the water at exactly the right moment. When it rains, the water level can quickly rise by up to 2m, but if the river is low you might have to get out and push.

Aluminium Walkway   CANOPY WALK

The park's main attraction is a delicate aluminium walkway, secured by guy-wires, that takes you through (or, more accurately, near) the jungle canopy, up to 60m above the forest floor. In primary rainforests, only limited vegetation can grow on the ground because so little light penetrates, but up in the canopy all manner of life proliferates. Unfortunately, there are no explanatory signs here and some guides don't have the background to explain the importance of the canopy ecosystem and point out the huge variety of organisms that can live on a single tree: orchids, bird's-nest ferns and other epiphytes; ants and myriad other insects; amphibians and snakes; and a huge selection of birds.

The views of nearby hills and valleys from the walkway are breathtaking, if you can get over the vertigo – the tower, built by Shell using oil-rig scaffolding technology, wobbles in the wind. Whatever you do, don't think of metal fatigue or lightning. If you'd like to share the experience with friends or loved ones back home and have a Malaysian cell phone, the tops of the towers are a good place to catch a cross-border signal.

The trail up to the canopy walk begins near the confluence of Sungais Belalong and Temburong. It's a short, steep, sweaty walk. If you stay overnight at the resort, you can do the canopy walk at sunrise, when birds and animals are most likely to be around.

Rivers & Waterfalls
SWIMMING
Places to take a refreshing dip in the park's pure mountain waters include several rivers and waterfalls – your guide can point out the best spots.

At one small waterfall, just outside the boundaries of the national park, you can stand in a pool, and 2cm- to 4cm-long fish that look like tiny sharks will come up and nibble your feet, giving you a gentle, ticklish pedicure as they feast on the dry skin between your toes. To get there, head downriver from the Ulu-Ulu resort for about 500m – your guide can help find the creek you need to follow upstream for a few hundred metres.

🛏 Sleeping

TOP CHOICE Ulu-Ulu Resort
LODGE $$$
(www.uluuluresort.com; per person from B$290; ❄) In Malay, *ulu* (as in Ulu Temburong) means 'upriver' and *ulu-ulu* means, essentially, 'back of beyond'. The park's only accommodation is an upscale riverside lodge, built entirely of hardwood, with some rooms thoughtfully built in the style of 1920s Malaysian-style chalets. It has a cinema for rainy evenings – after the canopy walk, Hitchcock's *Vertigo* might be an excellent choice. Prices include transport from BSB and board; activities tend to be expensive.

ℹ Getting There & Away

For all intents and purposes, the only way to visit the park is by booking a tour; several BSB-based agencies (p460) organise tour groups and guides.

Singapore

POP 5.3 MILLION / 710 SQ KM

Includes »

History...........................476
Sights...........................476
Activities.......................500
Courses.........................513
Tours.............................513
Festivals & Events.........514
Sleeping........................515
Eating...........................519
Drinking........................527
Entertainment..............531
Shopping.......................533
Directory A–Z...............537
Transport......................541

Best Places to Eat

» Jaan (p519)
» Chomp Chomp Food Centre (p522)
» Iggy's (p526)
» Blue Ginger (p520)
» Jumbo Seafood (p520)

Best Places to Sleep

» Capella Singapore (p518)
» Raffles Hotel (p515)
» Naumi (p515)
» Wangz (p516)
» Wanderlust (p517)

Why Go?

Love it or loathe it, Singapore is hard to ignore. It's a long-haul stopover staple and Southeast Asia's overachiever. It's also the perfect antidote to the region's trademark grit. But if you think Singapore is little more than endless malls and regulations, get set for a rethink. In recent years, the city-state has been revamping itself as Asia's new 'it kid', subverting staid stereotypes with cutting-edge architecture, dynamic museums and hip boutiques. Some of the world's hottest creatives have set up shop on these steamy streets, from celebrity New York chefs to fashion-forward local designers. Beyond the new and the hyped is a well-worn brew of Chinese, Malay, Indian and Western traditions, of hypnotic temples, gut-rumbling food markets and pockets of steamy jungle. Admit it: Asia's uptight geek is just a little cooler than you ever gave it credit for.

When to Go
Singapore

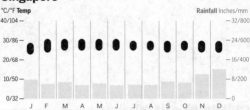

Feb Singapore celebrates Chinese New Year with fireworks, dragon parades and buzzing night markets.

May Bag some grin-worthy bargains at the Great Singapore Sale, launched annually in late May.

Sep Hotels are scarce and pricey, but speed demons will love the after-dark Formula One.

Singapore Highlights

① Bollyjamming your way through thumping **Little India** (p485)

② Exploring Straits Chinese culture at the **Peranakan**
Museum (p477) or the **Asian Civilisations Museum** (p477)

③ Cold beer and street food feasting at a local **hawker centre** (p519)

④ Hanging out with the wild ones at **Singapore Zoo** (p493), **Night Safari** (p494) and the brand-new **River Safari** (p495)

MALAYSIA

Pulau Seletar

Pulau Punggol Barat
Pulau Punggol Timor
Seletar Airport

YISHUN

Punggol Point
Punggol Rd

Pulau Ubin
Noordin Beach
Mamam Beach

Pulau Tekong Kechil

Pulau Tekong

Seletar Reservoir

JL KAYU
Punggol
PUNGGOL

Palau Serangoon
Pulau Ketam

8 **Pulau Ubin**

Changi Point
Changi Point Ferry Terminal

Setar Expwy
Central Expwy

Yio Chu Kang

Sengkang
Buangkok
HOUGANG
Hougang

Tampines Expwy

PASIR RIS

Pulau Ubin Ferry Terminal

Changi Golf Club

Changi
CHANGI

Changi Beach Park

Mo Kio

Ang Mo Kio Ave 3

Tampines Rd

Pasir Ris Park

Pasir Ris
LOYANG

Loyang Rd

Singapore Changi Airport

o Kio Ave 1
SERANGOON
Lorong Chuan

Kovan

TAMPINES

Changi Airport

nount
Bishan
Serangoon

Tampines

Upper Changi East Rd

ell
TOA PAYOH
PAYA LEBAR

Bedok Reservoir

Simei
SIMEI

Changi Coast Rd

Potong Pasir
KIM CHUAN

Simei Ave
Expo

e Little India & Kampong Glam Map (p486)

Aljunied
BEDOK
Bedok
Tanah Merah

Xilin Ave

on
Little India
1 **Little India**
Paya Lebar
Eunos
Kembangan
KATONG

rchard Rd
Lavender
GEYLANG

See Eastern Singapore Map (p492)

Bahru
2 **Peranakan Museum & Asian Civilisations Museum**

See Colonial District & the Quays Map (p478)

g
Marina Bay

e Chinatown & the CBD Map (p482)

Strait of Singapore

Lazarus Island (Pulau Sakijang Pelepah)

Kusu Island (Pulau Tembakul)

St John's Island (Pulau Sakijang Bendera)

5 Mall-hopping along fabled shopping strip **Orchard Rd** (p535)

6 Rampaging through greenery at **Bukit Timah Nature Reserve** (p494)

7 Losing your breath on the world's tallest duelling roller coasters at **Universal Studios** (p498)

8 Catching a bumboat to time-warped **Pulau Ubin** (p494)

History

Singapore has hardly looked back since Sir Thomas Stamford Raffles stepped into the mud in 1819 hell-bent on making the island a bastion of the British Empire. Despite a few ups and downs – invasion by the Japanese in WWII and getting booted out of the nascent federation of Malaysia in 1965 – the island has prospered in its role as a free-trade hub for Southeast Asia.

Yet despite a GDP growth rate of 14.9% in 2010 (number three in the world), the general election of 2011 delivered the highest proportion of contested seats (94.3%) since Singapore's independence in 1965. The election outcome saw the ruling People's Action Party (PAP) lose 6.46% of the electorate; in 2006, the party lost 8.69% of votes. The biggest gains went to the rival Worker's Party (WP), whose agenda better reflected concerns on the street, from housing affordability to an increasingly strained healthcare and transport system.

The strain is hardly surprising: Singapore's population has more than doubled from 2.4 million in 1980 to 5.1 million in 2011, mostly due to immigration. At 9.5 births per 1000 people, Singapore itself has one of the world's lowest birthrates. It's a fact not lost on Singapore's anxious government, which has offered everything from baby bonus tax breaks to government-subsidised speed dating events and salsa dance classes for singles. In the lead up to National Day in 2012, even mint-maker Mentos got in on the act, releasing a cheeky, viral tune with lyrics including: 'It's National Night and I want a baby, boo, I know you want it, so does the SDU (Social Development Unit)'. In typical Singaporean style, the video came with an important disclaimer, stating that only 'financially secure adults in stable, committed, long-term relationships should participate'.

Sights

Singapore's main city area is located on the southern part of the island. Here you'll find the Singapore River, flanked by Boat Quay, Clarke Quay and Robertson Quay. South of the river lie the CBD (Central Business District) and Chinatown, while immediately north of the river is the Colonial (also referred to as the Civic) District. Further north is Little India and Kampong Glam, while east of Kampong Glam you'll find Geylang, Katong (Joo Chiat), East Coast Park and Changi. Northwest of the Colonial

District is Orchard Road, while further west still lie the Singapore Botanic Gardens, and expat enclaves Dempsey Hill and Holland Village. At the river's mouth is Marina Bay, while further southwest lies Sentosa Island. Central-north Singapore is where you'll find Singapore Zoo and Night Safari.

COLONIAL DISTRICT, THE QUAYS & MARINA BAY

The Colonial District is Singapore's showcase district, adorned with elegant heritage architecture, trademark vistas and many of the city-state's top museums. On the river you'll find Boat Quay, Clarke Quay and Robertson Quay, three once-gritty trading areas revamped as buzzing eating, drinking and nightlife hubs. East of the Quays, the river spills into Marina Bay, an ambitious new precinct where bold architectural statements meet a Jetsons-esque casino resort and Singapore's striking new Gardens by the Bay.

TOP CHOICE National Museum of Singapore   MUSEUM

(Map p478; www.nationalmuseum.sg; 93 Stamford Rd; adult/child S$10/5; ⊙history gallery 10am-6pm, living galleries 10am-8pm; ⓂDhoby Ghaut) Imaginative, prodigiously stocked and brilliantly designed, Singapore's National Museum is good enough to warrant two visits. Staid exhibitions are ditched for lively, multimedia galleries that bring Singapore's action-packed bio to vivid life. It's a colourful, intimate journey, peppered with historical artefacts, personal accounts, and evocative reconstructions that span everything from Singapore's ancient Malay royals to colonial-era backstabbing, 20th-century rioting and reinvention, hawker food, fashion and film.

Part of the museum is housed in a superb 19th-century neoclassical building. Capped by a breathtaking, stained-glass rotunda, the building was home to the former Raffles Museum and Library.

TOP CHOICE Asian Civilisations Museum
MUSEUM

(Map p478; www.acm.org.sg; 1 Empress Pl; adult/child S$8/4, half price after 7pm Fri; ☺1-7pm Mon, 9am-7pm Tue-Thu, Sat & Sun, 9am-9pm Fri; MRaffles Place) The remarkable Asian Civilisations Museum houses Southeast Asia's most comprehensive collection of pan-Asian treasures. Its 11 beautifully curated galleries explore the history, cultures and religions of Southeast Asia, China, the Asian subcontinent and Islamic West Asia, with a multitude of ancient carvings, weaponry, glittering jewels and textiles. Add to this top-notch temporary exhibitions, and you have yourself one seriously satisfying cultural date.

TOP CHOICE Peranakan Museum
MUSEUM

(Map p478; www.peranakanmuseum.sg; 39 Armenian St; adult/child S$6/3, free admission 7-9pm Fri; ☺1-7pm Mon, 9.30am-7pm Tue-Sun, to 9pm Fri; MCity Hall) Stylish, interactive and thoroughly engrossing, Singapore's newest museum stands as a testament to the Peranakan (Straits-born locals) cultural revival in the Lion City. Explore 10 thematic galleries for an insight into both traditional and contemporary Peranakan culture, from marriage and folklore, to fashion and food. Artefacts include exquisite textiles, furniture and engaging multimedia displays.

Singapore Art Museum
MUSEUM

(Map p478; ☎6332 3222; www.singaporeartmuseum.sg; 71 Bras Basah Rd; adult/student & senior S$10/5, admission free 6-9pm Fri; ☺10am-7pm Sat-Thu, 10am-9pm Fri; MBras Basah) SAM showcases mostly modern and contemporary Southeast Asian art, from painting and sculpture, to site-specific installations and video art. The Wu Guanzhong gallery features a rotating exhibition of S$70 million worth of art donated by the father of modern Chinese painting. Round the corner from SAM, the art museum's newer extension, 8Q SAM (Map p478; www.singart.com/8qsam; 8 Queen St; admission free with SAM ticket; ☺10am-7pm Sat-Thur, 10am-9pm Fri; MCity Hall or Bras Basah), delivers quirky installations, interactivity and (more) contemporary creations.

Gardens by the Bay
PARK

(www.gardensbythebay.org.sg; 18 Marina Gardens Drive; admission free, conservatories adult/child S$28/15, skyway S$5/3; ☺5am-2am, conservatories & skyway 9am-9pm; last ticket sales conservatories 8pm, skyway 8pm Mon-Fri, 7pm Sat & Sun;

QUAYS OF THE CITY

The stretch of the riverfront that separates the Colonial District from the CBD is known as the Quays. The Singapore River, once a thriving gateway for bumboats bearing cargo into the *godown* (warehouses) that lined the riverside, now connects the three quays together. A walk through the Quays offers a revealing view to the changes that have impacted Singapore's trade through the years: from the dirt and grit of the once-filthy waterways to the gleaming steal and glass of today's financial district. To get a rundown on the area's history, visit the Asian Civilisations Museum.

Boat Quay (Map p478; MRaffles Place) Closest to the former harbour, Boat Quay was once Singapore's centre of commerce, remaining an important economic area into the 1960s. By the mid-1980s, many of the shophouses were in ruins, businesses having shifted to hi-tech cargo centres elsewhere on the island. Declared a conservation zone by the government, the area has reinvented itself as a major entertainment district packed with restaurants, bars, and thirsty suits.

Clarke Quay (Map p478; MClarke Quay) Named after Singapore's second colonial governor, Sir Andrew Clarke, pastel-hued Clarke Quay has become one of Singapore's most popular after-dark haunts, packed with restaurants, bars and clubs (those with the longest queues are usually the best). It's a love-it-or-loathe-it affair, pimped with gumdrop railings done out in kids' paintbox colours, lilypad umbrellas straight out of a Dr Seuss book, and many once-dignified shophouses now painted in ultrabright shades.

Robertson Quay (🚌64, 123, 143, Clarke Quay) At the furthest reach of the river, low-key Robertson Quay was once used for the storage of goods. Now some of the old godown have been sexed-up into bars and glitzy members-only party places. You'll also find several good restaurants and hotels clustered around here.

Colonial District & the Quays

Orchard Rd

Penang Rd

Eber Rd

Killiney Rd

Oxley Rise

Oxley Rd

Oxley Walk

Jln Rumbia

Clemenceau Ave

Penang La

Fort Canning Rd

Canning Walk

Ⓜ Dhoby Ghaut

Bras Basah Park

Lloyd Rd

National Museum of Singapore

Fort Canning Tunnel

×33

See Orchard Road Map (p490)

🏛25

3

Canning Rise

Kim Yam Rd

Mohamed Sultan Rd

Tank Rd

Merbau Rd

Unity St

10

Fort Canning Park

Fort Canning Reservoir

Cox Tce

Peranakan Museum

54

River Valley Rd

60

Martin Rd

Rodyk St

Nanson Rd

50

61

32

Liang Court

Clarke Quay

Read St

×36

Saiboo St

28

Robertson Quay

Clemenceau Ave

22

7

58

20

21

65

Hill St

High Street Centre

Magazine Rd

34

51

49

Read Bridge

38

Coleman Bridge

Clarke Quay Ⓜ

59

Riverwalk Galleria

Circular Rd

Jln Minyak

Cumming St

Merchant Rd

Havelock Rd

Carpenter St

Hongkong St

24

Chin Swee Rd

Pearl's Hill Tce

Havelock Square

People's Park Complex

Small Claims Tribunal

Hong Lim Park

North Canal Rd

George St

Synagogue St

14

See Chinatown & the CBD Map (p482)

Park Cres

New Bridge Rd

Upper Pickering St

Upper Hokien St

Hokien St

China St

Pekin St

OCBC Centre

Pearl's Hill Reservoir

Eu Tong Sen St

Chinatown Point

Hong Lim Complex

Nankin St

Chin Chew St

Outram Park

Upper Cross St

Mosque St

Chinatown Ⓜ

Pagoda St

South Bridge Rd

Club St

Amoy St

Telok Ayer St

Cross St

Pearl's Hill City Park

Pearl Bank

Chinatown Complex

Trengganu St

Smith St

Sago St

Pearl's Centre

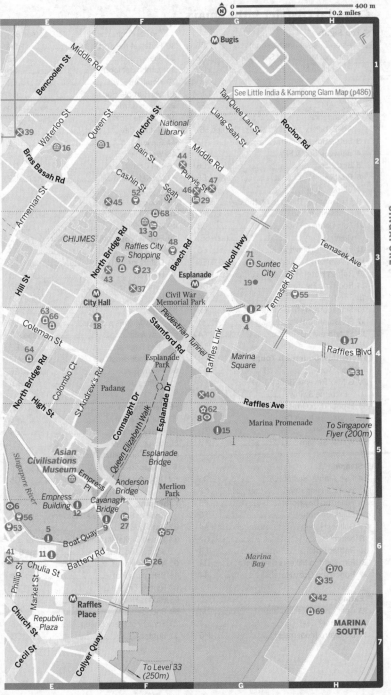

Colonial District & the Quays

◉ **Top Sights**

Asian Civilisations Museum E5
National Museum of Singapore D2
Peranakan Museum D3

◉ **Sights**

1 8Q SAM F2
2 Abundance..G4
Art-2 Gallery ....(see 65)
3 Battle Box Museum C2
4 Between Sea & Sky G4
5 Bird E6
6 Boat Quay E6
7 Clarke Quay C4
8 Esplanade – Theatres on the Bay........G5
9 First Generation F6
10 Fort Canning Park C3
Gajah Gallery ....(see 65)
11 Homage to Newton E6
12 Millennium E6
13 Raffles Hotel F3
14 Reclining Figures................................D6
15 Seed..G5
16 Singapore Art Museum E2
17 Six Brushstrokes................................H4
18 St Andrew's Cathedral F4

⊕ **Activities, Courses & Tours**

19 Duck Tour G3
20 G-Max Reverse Bungy & GX-5
   Extreme Swing D4
21 Hippo River Cruise D4
22 Singapore River Cruise C4
True Fitness.....................................(see 71)
23 Willow Stream F3

🛏 **Sleeping**

24 Five Stones Hostel D5
25 Fort Canning Hotel C2
26 Fullerton Bay Hotel F6
27 Fullerton Hotel....................................F6
28 Gallery Hotel A4
29 Naumi G2
30 Raffles Hotel F3
31 Ritz-Carlton Millenia Singapore...........H4
32 Robertson Quay Hotel........................B4

✖ **Eating**

33 Chef Chan's Restaurant D2
34 Coriander Leaf C4
35 DB Bistro Moderne H6

Din Tai Fung ....(see 69)
36 Flutes at the Fort D4
37 Jaan..F3
38 Jumbo Seafood C5
39 Kopitiam E2
40 My Humble House...............................G4
41 Peach Garden E6
42 Pizzeria Mozza....................................H7
43 Raffles City F3
44 Saveur...F2
45 Wah Lok F2
46 Yet Con G2
47 YY Kafei Dian.......................................G2

🍷 **Drinking**

48 Bar & Billiard Room.............................F3
49 Brewerkz C5
50 Brussels Sprouts Belgian Beer
   & Mussels A4
51 Cuba Libre C5
Harry's ....(see 56)
Lantern Bar ....(see 26)
Long Bar ....(see 68)
52 Loof F2
53 Molly Malone's E6
New Asia ....(see 37)
54 Next Page B3
55 Paulaner Bräuhaus..............................H3
56 Penny Black...E6
Raffles Hotel....................................(see 30)

🎭 **Entertainment**

57 Butter Factory.....................................F6
58 Crazy Elephant D4
59 Home Club...D5
60 Singapore Dance Theatre D3
61 Singapore Repertory Theatre..............B4
62 Singapore Symphony Orchestra G5

🛍 **Shopping**

Cape of Good Hope Art Gallery ...(see 65)
63 Cathay Photo E4
64 Funan DigitaLife Mall E4
John 3:16 ....(see 64)
65 MICA Building D4
66 Peninsula Plaza...................................E4
67 Raffles City F3
68 Raffles Hotel Arcade F3
69 Shoppes at Marina Bay Sands H7
70 Society of Black Sheep H6
71 Suntec City..G3

(M Bayfront) Catapulting nature into the future, Gardens by the Bay is the latest blockbuster attraction at Marina Bay and Singapore's newest botanic gardens. At present, only the Bay Garden South section is open. Highlights here include soaring, sci-fi 'supertrees' and futuristic conservatories housing plants from endangered habitats. The Heritage Gardens are inspired by Singapore's multicultural DNA. Check the website for project updates.

Raffles Hotel
HISTORIC BUILDING

(Map p478; www.raffleshotel.com; 1 Beach Rd; M City Hall) Birthplace of the Singapore Sling, and featured in novels by Joseph Conrad and Somerset Maugham, the grand old Raffles started life in 1887 as a 10-room bungalow fronted by the (since land-filled) beach. On the third floor of the Raffles Hotel Arcade, the Raffles Hotel Museum holds a fascinating collection of memorabilia documenting the hotel's gilded age.

Fort Canning Park
PARK

(Map p478; M Dhoby Ghaut) When Raffles rolled into Singapore in 1819, locals steered clear of Fort Canning Hill, then called Bukit Larangan (Forbidden Hill), out of respect for the sacred shrine of Sultan Iskandar Shah, ancient Singapura's last ruler. Today, you can glimpse 14th-century Javanese artefacts at the park's archaeological dig, get a natural high in the park's spice garden, and snoop around WWII bunkers at the Battle Box Museum (Map p478; www.legendsfortcanning.com/fortcanning/battlebox.htm; 2 Cox Terrace; adult/child S$8/5; ⊙10am-6pm, last entry 5pm).

Esplanade – Theatres on the Bay
ARTS CENTRE

(Map p478; ☎6828 8377; www.esplanade.com; 1 Esplanade Dr; ⊙10am-6pm, box office noon-8.30pm; M Esplanade) Poster-boy for contemporary Singapore, this S$600-million arts complex has been compared to flies' eyes, melting honeycomb and two upturned durians. The controversial aluminium shades reference Asian reed-weaving geometries and maximise natural light. There's a nonstop program of international and local performances, some great restaurants and free outdoor performances.

Singapore Flyer
OBSERVATION WHEEL

(www.singaporeflyer.com.sg; 30 Raffles Ave; adult/senior/child S$29.50/23.60/20.65; ⊙8.30am-10.15pm; M Promenade) Following the lead of other world cities, Singapore has pimped its skyline with a giant Ferris wheel. And in typical Singaporean style, its version is currently the world's largest. The pricey 30-minute ride offers dizzying views towards the Colonial District, CBD, Marina Bay, the high-rise housing landscape to the east and out to the boat-heavy South China Sea.

Kuan Im Thong Hood Cho Temple
BUDDHIST TEMPLE

(Map p486; 178 Waterloo St; ⊙6am-6.15pm; M Bugis) Dedicated to the goddess of mercy Kuan Yin (Guanyin), this is one of Singapore's busiest temples. Flower sellers, fortune tellers and incense-wielding devotees swarm around the entrance, the latter also rubbing the belly of

SINGAPORE IN...

Two Days

Start your Singapore fling with some cultural insight at the Asian Civilisations Museum, National Museum of Singapore or Peranakan Museum. Posh nosh at Flutes at the Fort, then check out Chinatown's Sri Mariamman Temple and Buddha Tooth Relic Temple. Treat your feet at Mr Lim Foot Reflexology, dine at Blue Ginger and slurp mojitos at rooftop La Terrazza. Start day two in Little India – breakfast at Ananda Bhavan and shop at Tekka Centre and Mustafa Centre. If you're on a roll, mall-hop Orchard Rd or browse boutiques on Haji Lane. Alternatively, escape to Singapore Zoo before 'going wild' at the Night Safari.

Four Days

Take an early morning stroll along the Southern Ridges before catching the cable car to Sentosa. Chow at Malaysian Food Street, then hit the rides at Universal Studios. On day four, catch a bumboat to Pulau Ubin for a jungle cycle. On the way back, pay your respects at the Changi Memorial & Chapel before chilli crab feasting at Jumbo. End the night at rooftop Lantern or party at Clarke Quay.

SINGAPORE SIGHTS

Chinatown & the CBD

0   200 m
0   0.1 miles

G

Raffles Place M

Ocean Building

Republic Plaza

Singapore International Chamber of Commerce

To Level 33 (250m)

1

Market St

Robinson Rd

Market St

F

Phillip St

Church St

China Square Food Court

Cross St

Pekin St

Hokien St

China St

Far East Square

Nankin St

Chin Chew St

Telok Ayer St

Boon Tat St

Cecil St

Robinson Rd

Maxwell Link

Raffles Quay

MARINA SOUTH

Marina Station Rd

2

24

E

Hong Lim Complex

Upper Cross St

Mosque St

South Bridge Rd

Ann Siang Hill Park

Amoy St

Stanley St

Telok Ayer St

McCallum St

3

34

38   13

2

6

37

8

27

URA Centre

36   33

5

14

15   39

4   18

Pagoda St

Temple St

20   9   32

Sago St   Sago Ln

Banda St

Kadayanallur St

Erskine Rd

23

Maxwell Rd

Peck Seah St

Choon Wallich St

Tanjong Pagar M

Guan St

D

Chinatown M

7

Smith St

Trengganu St

26

17

1

30   31

Murray St   Murray Tce

Duxton Hill

35

16

19

Tanjong Pagar Rd

Craig Rd

28

C

New Tong Sen St   New Bridge Rd

Eu Tong Sen St

Pearl's Centre

Kreta Ayer Rd

Keong Saik Rd

Teck Lim Rd

10   29

21   22

Jiak Chuan Rd

Duxton Rd

B

Pearl's Hill City Park

Pearl Bank

See Colonial District & the Quays Map (p478)

Outram Park

Bukit Pasoh Rd

12

Cantonment Rd

Neil Rd

A

Outram Park

To Wangz (270m); Tiong Bahru (1.8km)

Third Hospital Ave

Outram Park M   Outram Rd

Outram Park M

Eu Tong Sen St   New Bridge Rd

Second Hospital Ave

Asia Gardens

Baba House

Everton Rd

1

2

3

4

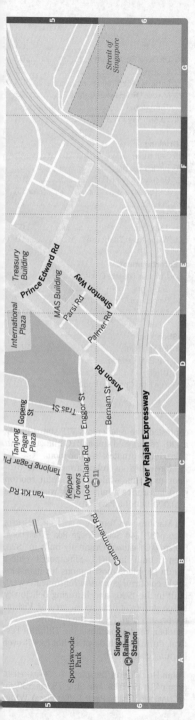

the large bronze Buddha Maitreya nearby for good luck.

Next door is the even more polychromatic Sri Krishnan Temple. It too attracts worshippers from the Kuan Yin temple, who show a great deal of religious pragmatism by also burning joss sticks and offering prayers at what is actually a Hindu temple.

St Andrew's Cathedral
CHURCH

(Map p478; www.livingstreams.org.sg; 11 St Andrew's Rd; ⊗9am-5pm Mon-Sat; MCity Hall) Singapore's sugar-white, wedding-cake cathedral stands in stark contrast against the buzzing cityscape. Completed in 1838 but torn down and rebuilt in its present form in 1862 after lightning damaged the original building (twice!), the cathedral has a 63.1m-tall tower, huge naves and lovely stained glass above the west doors. The grounds make a nice place for a picnic or siesta on the grass.

CHINATOWN & THE CBD
More about the vibe than must-see sites, historic Chinatown is a restless cacophony of scented temples, wet markets and hawker centres, antique shops, and retro malls peddling cheap reflexology. Restored shophouses belie the area's rough 'n' ready past, evocatively documented at the Chinatown Heritage Centre. Trendy night owls sip and sup on Ann Siang Hill, or south of Maxwell Rd in the equally gentrified Duxton Hill area.

Wedged between Chinatown and the Singapore River, the Central Business District (CBD) serves up some fantastic sculptures, especially around Raffles Place and the river. The area also harbours a few surviving colonial relics, the finest of which is the mighty Fullerton Hotel, housed in the former general post office.

TOP CHOICE Baba House
MUSEUM

(Map p482; ☎6227 5731; www.nus.edu.sg/cfa/museum/; 157 Neil Rd; admission free; ⊗1hr tours 2pm Mon, 6.30pm Tue, 10am Thu, 11am Sat; MOutram Park) You need to book ahead to visit Baba House, but the guided tour of this faithfully restored Peranakan heritage home is well worth the effort. Furnished as it was in the 1920s, its knowledgeable tour guides weave tales of affluent Peranakan life with every detail, including the secret peepholes through which shy Nonya ladies could spy on guests in the central hall.

Built in the 1890s, the property once housed shipping tycoon Wee Bin.

Chinatown & the CBD

◎ **Top Sights**
Baba House A4

◎ **Sights**
1 Buddha Tooth Relic Temple D2
2 Chinatown Heritage Centre................... D1
3 Singapore City Gallery D3
4 Sri Mariamman Temple D2
5 Thian Hock Keng Temple...................... E2

◎ **Activities, Courses & Tours**
6 Kenko Wellness Spa E1
Mr Lim Foot Reflexology .... (see 7)
7 People's Park Complex C1

◎ **Sleeping**
8 Club.. D3
9 Fernloft.. D2
10 Hotel 1929.. C2
11 Klapsons... C6
12 New Majestic Hotel.............................. B3
13 Pillows & Toast D1
14 Scarlet... D3
15 Wink Hostel.. D1

◎ **Eating**
16 Blue Ginger D4
17 Chinatown Complex C2
18 Ci Yan Organic Vegetarian
Health Food D2

19 Cumi Bali C4
20 Da Dong Restaurant............................. D2
21 Esquina C3
22 Latteria Mozzarella Bar C3
23 Maxwell Rd Hawker Centre D3
Tong Heng .... (see 36)
24 Ya Kun Kaya Toast E1

◎ **Drinking**
25 1 Altitude G1
26 Backstage Bar D2
27 Beaujolais Wine Bar D2
La Terrazza .... (see 33)
28 Plain... C4
29 Tantric Bar C3
30 Tea Chapter C3
31 Yixing Xuan Teahouse D3

◎ **Entertainment**
32 Chinese Theatre Circle D2
33 Screening Room D2
34 Singapore Chinese Orchestra E4
35 Taboo C3

◎ **Shopping**
36 Eu Yan Sang D2
37 Far East Legend D2
38 Utterly Art... D1
39 Yue Hwa Chinese Products.................... C1

Chinatown Heritage Centre MUSEUM
(Map p482; www.chinatownheritagecentre.sg; 48 Pagoda St; adult/child S$10/6; ⊙9am-8pm, last entry 7pm; ⓜChinatown) Spread across three adjoining shophouses, the Chinatown Heritage Centre lifts the lid on Chinatown's chaotic, colourful and often scandalous past. While its production values can't match those of the city's blockbuster museums, its endearing jumble of old photographs, personal anecdotes and recreated interiors deliver a moving journey through the neighbourhood's highs and lows.

Buddha Tooth Relic Temple BUDDHIST TEMPLE
(Map p482; www.btrts.org.sg; 288 South Bridge Rd; ⊙7am-7pm, relic viewing 9am-6pm; ⓜChinatown) Consecrated in 2008, this huge, five-storey Buddhist temple houses what is reputedly the left canine tooth of the Buddha, recovered from his funeral pyre in Kushinagar, northern India. While its authenticity is contested, the relic enjoys VIP status inside a 420kg solid-gold stupa (BYO binoculars) in a dazzlingly ornate 4th-floor room.

More religious relics await at the 3rd-floor museum, while the peaceful rooftop garden features a huge prayer wheel inside a 10,000 Buddha Pavilion.

Sri Mariamman Temple HINDU TEMPLE
(Map p482; 244 South Bridge Rd; ⊙7am-noon, 6-9pm; ⓜChinatown) Originally built in 1823, then rebuilt in 1843, Singapore's oldest Hindu temple is most famous for its explosively colourful *gopuram* (entrance tower), built in the 1930s and featuring deliciously kitsch statues of Brahma the creator, Vishnu the preserver and Shiva the destroyer. Every October, the temple hosts the Thimithi Festival, during which devotees hot foot it over burning coals. Ouch.

Thian Hock Keng Temple HINDU TEMPLE
(Map p482; 158 Telok Ayer St; ⊙7.30am-5.30pm; ⓜChinatown, Tanjong Pagar, Raffles Place) While

Chinatown's most famous Hindu temple is swamped, its oldest and most important Hokkien temple is often a haven of tranquillity. Built between 1839 and 1842, it was once the favourite landing point of Chinese sailors, before land reclamation pushed the sea far down the road. Curiously, the gates are Scottish and the tiles Dutch.

Singapore City Gallery   GALLERY
(Map p482; www.ura.gov.sg/gallery; URA Bldg, 45 Maxwell Rd; ☺9am-5pm Mon-Sat; MTanjong Pagar) This city-planning exhibition gallery provides a compelling insight into the government's resolute policies of high-rise housing and land reclamation. The highlight is an 11m-by-11m scale model of the city, which shows how Singapore should look once the projects currently under development are finished.

LITTLE INDIA

Riotous Little India slaps you across the face with its teeming five-foot ways, blaring Bollywood tunes and crayon-hued shophouses. Originally a European enclave, the district bloomed into an Indian hub after a Jewish-Indian businessman started farming buffalo here. Today, the area is packed with men on two-year contracts from India, Bangladesh and Sri Lanka doing the dirty construction jobs that Singaporeans won't stoop to. For the full 'Mumbai' effect, head in on a crowded Sunday afternoon.

Sri Veeramakaliamman Temple   HINDU TEMPLE
(Map p486; 141 Serangoon Rd; ☺5.15am-12.15pm & 4pm-9.15pm; MLittle India) Little India's most colourful, bustling temple is dedicated to the goddess Kali, usually depicted wearing a necklace of skulls and disembowelling unfortunate humans. The bloodthirsty consort of Shiva has always been popular in Bengal, the birthplace of the labourers who built the structure in 1881. The temple is at its most evocative during each of the four daily *puja* (prayer) sessions.

Abdul Gafoor Mosque   MOSQUE
(Map p486; 41 Dunlop St; MLittle India) Completed in 1910, the Abdul Gafoor mosque serves up a storybook fusion of Moorish, southern Indian and Victorian architectural styles. Look out for the elaborate sundial crowning its main entrance, each of its 25 rays decorated with Arabic calligraphy denoting the names of 25 prophets. The sundial is the only one of its kind in the world. Only worshippers can enter the prayer hall.

Sri Srinivasa Perumal Temple   HINDU TEMPLE
(Map p486; 397 Serangoon Rd; ☺5.45am-noon & 5-9pm; MFarrer Park) Dedicated to Vishnu, this temple dates from 1855 but the striking, 20m-tall *gopuram* is a S$300,000 1966 addition. Inside is a statue of Vishnu, his sidekicks Lakshmi and Andal, and his bird-mount Garuda. If you're here in February for the Thaipusam Festival, the procession of devotees, with spikes and skewers driven through their bodies, begins under the temple's *gopuram*.

Sakya Muni Buddha Gaya Temple   BUDDHIST TEMPLE
(Temple of 1000 Lights; Map p486; 366 Race Course Rd; ☺8am-4.45pm; MFarrer Park) This 1927 temple's 15m-tall, 300-tonne Buddha has some

SINGAPORE SIGHTS

STREET SCULPTURE

Singapore is spiked with a healthy collection of public sculpture by acclaimed local and international artists. Check out these babies:

» **Abundance** (Map p478; Millenia Walk, 9 Raffles Blvd; MEsplanade) Sun Yu Li

» **Between Sea & Sky** (Map p478; Marina Mandarin Hotel, 6 Raffles Blvd; MEsplanade) Olivier Strehelle

» **Bird** (Map p478; UOB Plaza) Fernando Botero

» **First Generation** (Map p478; Cavenagh Bridge; MRaffles Place) Chong Fat Cheong

» **Homage to Newton** (Map p478; UOB Plaza) Salvador Dalí

» **Love** (Map p490; Penang Rd; MDhoby Ghaut) Robert Indiana

» **Millennium** (Map p478; Empress Pl; MRaffles Place) Victor Tan

» **Reclining Figures** (Map p478; OCBC Bldg, Chulia St) Henry Moore

» **Seed** (Map p478; Esplanade waterfront garden) Han Sai Por

» **Six Brushstrokes** (Map p478; Millenia Walk, 9 Raffles Blvd) Roy Lichtenstein

Little India & Kampong Glam

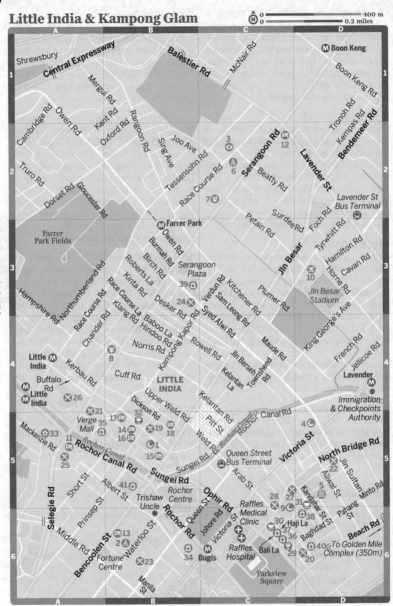

very heterogeneous housemates, including Kuan Yin (Guanyin), the Chinese goddess of mercy, and the Hindu deities Brahma and Ganesh. While the yellow tigers at the entrance symbolise protection and vitality, the temple's huge mother-of-pearl Buddha footprint is reputedly a replica of the one on top of Adam's Peak in Sri Lanka.

Leong San See Temple   CHINESE TEMPLE
(Map p486; 371 Race Course Rd; ⊗6am-6pm; MFar-rer Park) This Taoist temple's name translates

Little India & Kampong Glam

⊙ Sights
1 Abdul Gafoor Mosque B5
2 Kuan Im Thong Hood Cho Temple B6
3 Leong San See Temple C2
4 Malabar Muslim Jama-Ath Mosque D5
5 Malay Heritage Centre D5
6 Sakya Muni Buddha Gaya Temple C2
7 Sri Srinivasa Perumal Temple C2
8 Sri Veeramakaliamman Temple B4
9 Sultan Mosque C6

⊕ Activities, Courses & Tours
10 Jalan Besar Swimming Complex D3

⊟ Sleeping
11 Albert Court Village Hotel A5
12 Hive C2
13 Ibis Singapore on Bencoolen B6
14 InnCrowd B5
15 Mayo Inn B5
16 Perak Hotel B5
17 Prince of Wales B5
18 Wanderlust B5

⊗ Eating
Ah-Rahman Royal Prata .... (see 26)
Ananda Bhavan .... (see 26)
19 Bismillah Biryani B5
20 Café Le Caire D6

21 Moghul Sweet Shop A4
22 Nan Hwa Chong Fish-Head
   Steamboat Corner D5
23 QS269 Food House B6
24 Sankranti B3
25 Shish Mahal A5
26 Tekka Centre A4
27 Warong Nasi Pariaman C5
28 Zam Zam C5

⊙ Drinking
29 BluJaz Cafe C6
30 Going Om C6
31 Maison Ikkoku D5
32 Zsofi Tapas Bar B5

⊙ Entertainment
Prince of Wales .... (see 17)
33 Rex Cinemas A5

⊙ Shopping
34 Bugis Street Market B6
35 Celebration of Arts A5
36 Dulcetfig C6
37 K.I.N. C6
38 Little Shophouse D6
39 Mustafa Centre B3
40 Sifr Aromatics D6
41 Sim Lim Square B5

SINGAPORE SIGHTS

as Dragon Mountain Temple. It dates from 1917 and is dedicated to Kuan Yin (Guanyin). The temple features timber beams beautifully carved with chimera, dragons, flowers and human figures, and sees more religious fervour than other, larger Taoist temples in Singapore. To get here, walk north up Serangoon Rd. The temple is opposite the intersection with Beatty Rd.

KAMPONG GLAM

Compact Kampong Glam is as intriguing as it is incongruous. Not only is it Singapore's Muslim heartland – sprinkled with mosques, sheesha-scented cafes, perfume traders, and fabric and rug shops – it's also home to Haji Lane, a hipster hangout lined with fashion-forward boutiques. Roughly bounded by Victoria St, Jln Sultan and Beach Rd – all immediately northeast of Bugis MRT – the district's name derives from *kampung* (the Malay word for village) and *gelam*, a type of tree that once grew here.

Sultan Mosque   MOSQUE
(Map p486; www.sultanmosque.org.sg; 3 Muscat St; ☺9am-noon & 2-4pm Sat-Thu, 2.30-4pm Fri; MBugis) Singapore's largest mosque is the golden-domed focal point of Kampong Glam. It was originally built in 1825 with the aid of a grant from Raffles and the East India Company, as a result of Raffles' treaty with the Sultan of Singapore that allowed him to retain sovereignty over the area. A hundred years later in 1928, the original mosque was replaced by the present magnificent building.

Interestingly, the building was designed by an Irish architect who worked for the same company that designed the Raffles Hotel. Bear in mind that this is a functioning mosque and only go inside if there isn't a prayer session going on. Non-Muslims are asked to refrain from entering the prayer hall at any time.

Malabar Muslim Jama-Ath Mosque   MOSQUE
(Map p486; 471 Victoria St; 11am-9pm; MLavender) The blue-tiled Malabar Muslim Jama-Ath

TIONG BAHRU

Those with finely tuned hipster radars will most likely end up in Singapore's Tiong Bahru neighbourhood. Yet Singapore's latest epicentre of cool is more than just idiosyncratic boutiques, bars and cafes – it's also a rare heritage gem. Distinctly low-rise, the area was Singapore's first public housing estate and its streetscapes of whitewashed, 'walk-up' art deco apartments are an unexpected architectural treat.

For a taste of pre-gentrification, dive into the **Tiong Bahru Market & Food Centre** (83 Seng Poh Rd; MTiong Bahru), old school right down to its orange exterior, the neighbourhood's original hue. The upstairs hawker centre is home to cultish **Tiong Bahru Roasted Pig** (02-38, Tiong Bahru Market & Food Centre; ⊘7.30am-7.30pm) and **Jan Bo Shui Kueh** (02-05, Tiong Bahru Market & Food Centre; ⊘6.30am-10.30pm), the latter famous for its amazing *chwee kueh* (steamed rice cake topped with diced preserved radish).

For new-school cool, hit Yong Siak St. It's here that you'll find coffee geek mecca **40 Hands** (www.40handscoffee.com; 78 Yong Siak St; ⊘8.30am-6.30pm Tue & Sun, 8.30am-10pm Wed & Thu, 8.30am-11pm Fri & Sat; MTiong Bahru), fantastic independent bookshop **BooksActually** (www.booksactually.com; 9 Yong Siak St; ⊘11am-6pm Mon, 11am-9pm Tue-Fri, 10am-9pm Sat, 10am-6pm Sun; MTiong Bahru), and worldly design store **Strangelets** (www.strangelets.sg; 7 Yong Siak St; MTiong Bahru). Around the corner from Strangelets, **Nana & Bird** (www.nanaandbird.com; 01-02, 79 Chay Yan St; ⊘noon-7pm Wed-Fri, 11am-7pm Sat & Sun; MTiong Bahru) stocks forward fashion, accessories and art, including local labels Aijek and By Invite Only.

A few blocks away, **Fleas & Trees** (01-10, 68 Seng Poh Lane; £01-10; ⊘6-10pm Tue-Fri, 10am-10pm Sat & Sun; MTiong Bahru) offers hand-picked men's and women's vintage threads, decorative objects, eclectic plants and backcopies of *Wallpaper*, *Vanity Fair* and *Vogue*. To reach Tiong Bahru, catch the MRT to Tiong Bahru station, walk east along Tiong Bahru Rd for 350m, then turn right onto Kim Pong Rd.

Mosque, the only one on the island dedicated to Malabar Muslims from the South Indian state of Kerala, is one of the most distinctive in Singapore, but it didn't always look this way. Work on the building started in 1956, but it wasn't officially opened until 1963 due to cash-flow problems. The magnificent tiling on the mosque was only finished in 1995.

If you are appropriately attired and do not come in during prayer sessions, you can now visit the mosque. Simply approach the imam (available at the ground floor resource room).

Malay Heritage Centre   MUSEUM
(Map p486; www.malayheritage.org.sg; 85 Sultan Gate; adult/under 6yr S\$4/free; ⊘10am-6pm Tue-Sun; Ⓟ; MBugis) The Kampong Glam area is the historic seat of the Malay royalty, resident here before the arrival of Raffles, and the *istana* (palace) on this site was built for the last sultan of Singapore, Ali Iskandar Shah, between 1836 and 1843. It's now a museum, offering an interesting account of Singapore's Malay people.

ORCHARD ROAD & SURROUNDS

What was once a dusty road lined with spice plantations and orchards is now a 2.2km torrent of blockbuster malls, department stores, and speciality shops; enough to burn out the toughest shopaholics. But wait, there's more, including drool-inducing food courts, a heritage-listed side street rocking with bars, and a somewhat off-the-radar film museum.

TOP CHOICE **Singapore Botanic Gardens**   GARDENS
(Map p490; ☎6471 7361; www.sbg.org.sg; 1 Cluny Rd; Garden admission free, National Orchid Garden adult/senior/child S\$5/1/free; ⊘5am-midnight, National Orchid Garden 8.30am-7pm, last entry 6pm; ☐7, 105, 123, MBotanic Gardens) Located 2km west of Orchard Rd, Singapore's 52-hectare Botanic Gardens are an urban Xanax, complete with lakes, rare rainforest, symphony stage and themed gardens (including the National Orchid Garden). A late-afternoon stroll along its myriad paths, followed by a drink or dinner at **Halia** (☎6476 6711; www.halia.com.sg; Singapore Botanic Gardens; mains S\$30-60; ⊘noon-3pm & 6-10pm) or Au

Jardin Les Amis (p523) is one of the city's most memorable experiences.

The **National Orchid Garden** is home to over 1000 species and 2000 hybrids of orchids, around 600 of which are on display – the largest showcase of tropical orchids on earth. Look out for the *Vanda Miss Joaquim*, Singapore's national flower, which Agnes Joaquim discovered in her garden in 1893. Free classical music concerts are held regularly in the Botanic Gardens. Check the website for upcoming events.

Emerald Hill Road   HISTORIC NEIGHBOURHOOD
(Map p490; Ⓜ Somerset) Take refuge from retail on Emerald Hill Road, a heritage-lauded street lined with some of Singapore's finest terrace houses. Special mentions go out to No 56 (built in 1902, and one of the earliest buildings here), Nos 39 to 45 (with unusually wide frontages and a grand Chinese-style entrance gate) and Nos 120 to 130 (with art deco features dating from around 1925).

At the Orchard Rd end of the hill is a cluster of buzzing bars housed in beautiful shophouse renovations, among them handsome Latino Que Pasa (p529).

Cathay Gallery   MUSEUM
(Map p490; www.thecathaygallery.com.sg; 2nd fl, 2-16 The Cathay, 2 Handy Rd; ⊙11am-7pm Mon-Sat; Ⓜ Dhoby Ghaut) A cinematic museum housed in Singapore's first high-rise building, the Cathay Gallery traces the history of the Loke family, early pioneers in film production and distribution in Singapore and founders of the Cathay Organisation. Pore over movie posters, cameras and programs that capture the golden age of local cinema.

EASTERN SINGAPORE

They're oft overshadowed by Singapore's tourist-trampled central districts, but the vibrant eastern neighbourhoods offer an altogether more authentic slice of daily Singaporean life. Bipolar Geylang serves up brothel-pimped laneways, righteous temples and mosques, and cultish street-food strip Geylang Rd. Further east, Katong (also known as Joo Chiat) offers ornate Peranakan terrace houses, craft shops and (more) fabulous nosheries, while neighbouring East Coast Park is a leafy seafront strip laced with cycling paths, picnic areas, bars and good seafood restaurants. The island's far east is where you'll find Pasir Ris, the moving Changi Museum and Chapel, and sleepy Changi Village, the jumping-off point for bucolic Pulau Ubin.

EAST COAST PARK

East Coast Park   PARK
(Map p492) Starting at the end of Tanjong Katong Rd in Katong and ending at the National Sailing Centre in Bedok, this 11km stretch of seafront park is where Singaporeans come to swim, windsurf, kayak, picnic, bicycle, rollerblade and, of course, eat and drink. The whole park has been superbly designed so that the many leisure facilities don't crowd the green space.

On weekends only, bus 401 from Bedok Bus Interchange, outside Bedok MRT, takes you directly to East Coast Park. On weekdays, take bus 197 from Bedok and stop along Marine Pde Rd (ask the bus driver where to get off). Walk 250m south to an underpass, which will take you into East Coast Park.

GEYLANG

Amitabha Buddhist Centre   BUDDHIST CENTRE
(Map p492; ☑6745 8547; www.fpmtabc.org; 44 Lorong 25A; ⊙10.30am-6pm Tue-Sat, 10am-6pm Sun; Ⓜ Aljunied) Take a class on dharma and meditation at the seven-floor Amitabha Buddhist Centre, whose upstairs meditation hall, swathed in red-and-gold cloth, is open to the public and filled with beautiful devotional objects. The in-house store stocks religious and spiritual items, including prayer flags and spinning wheels. Check the website for class schedules.

Tan Swie Hian Museum   GALLERY
(Map p492; ☑6744 0716; www.tomlinson-collection.com/museum1.html; 460 Sims Ave; ⊙Mon-Fri, by appt only; Ⓜ Aljunied) The under-the-radar Tan Swie Hian Museum is dedicated to the work of prolific Singaporean artist Tan Swie Hian, whose works span vibrant paintings and contemporary sculpture, to Chinese calligraphy and poetry. Tan was the first person to translate the works of Samuel Beckett and Marin Sorescu into Chinese.

KATONG

Peranakan Terrace Houses   NOTABLE BUILDINGS
(Map p492; Koon Seng Rd & Joo Chiat Pl; ☐16, Ⓜ Eunos) These two streets just off Joo Chiat Rd are where you'll find some of the finest Peranakan terrace houses in Singapore. They're a fantastical sight, lavished with stucco dragons, birds, crabs and brilliantly glazed tiles imported from Europe. *Pintu pagar* (swinging doors) at the front of the houses are another typical feature, allowing in breezes while retaining privacy.

SINGAPORE SIGHTS

Orchard Road

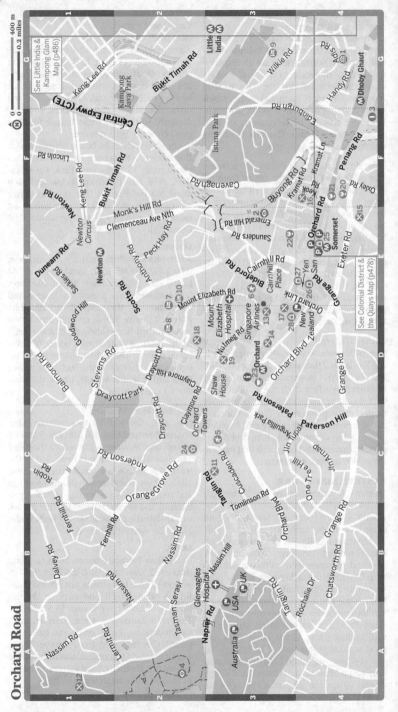

See Little India &
Kampong Glam
Map (p486)

See Colonial District &
the Quays Map (p478)

400 m
0.2 miles

Little India

Bukit Timah Rd

Central Expwy (CTE)

Dhoby Ghaut

Penang Rd

Oxley Rd

Orchard Rd

Somerset

Grange Rd

Exeter Rd

Newton Rd

Dunearn Rd

Bukit Timah Rd

Keng Lee Rd

Lincoln Rd

Newton Circus

Scotts Rd

Clemenceau Ave Nth

Monk's Hill Rd

Anthony Rd

Peck Hay Rd

Mount Elizabeth Rd

Bideford Rd

Cairnhill Rd

Cairnhill Place

Emerald Hill Rd

Saunders Rd

Orchard Link

San

Yen

Grange Rd

New Zealand

Orchard Blvd

Paterson Rd

Paterson Hill

Nutmeg Rd

Claymore Rd

Shaw House

Claymore Dr

Draycott Dr

Draycott Hill

Draycott Park

Stevens Rd

Balmoral Rd

Goodwood Hill

Sarkies Rd

Anderson Rd

Orange Grove Rd

Robin Rd

Tanglin Rd

Cuscaden Rd

Tomlinson Rd

Angullia Park

Jln Tupai

One Tr

Jln Arnap

Orchard Blvd

Grange Rd

Chatsworth Rd

Rochalie Dr

Tanglin Rd

Napier Rd

USA

UK

Australia

Gleneagles Hospital

Nassim Hill

Nassim Rd

Tasman Serasi

Lermit Rd

Nassim Rd

Dalvey Rd

Fernhill Rd

Fernhill Rd

Keng Lee Rd

Kampong Java Park

Istana Park

Cavenagh Rd

Buyong Rd

Neok

Kramat Rd

Kramat Ln

Handy Rd

Edinburgh Rd

Wilkie Rd

Adis Rd

Mount Elizabeth Hospital

Singapore Airlines

Mount Elizabeth

Orchard Towers

Napier Rd

Nassim Hill

Orchard Road

⊙ Sights
1	Cathay Gallery	G4
2	Emerald Hill Road	E3
3	Love	F4
4	Singapore Botanic Gardens	A2

⊙ Activities, Courses & Tours
5	Como Shambhala Urban Escape	C3
6	Fitness First	E3

⊑ Sleeping
7	Elizabeth Hotel	E2
8	Goodwood Park Hotel	D2
9	hangout@mt.emily	G3
10	Quincy	E2

⊗ Eating
11	Bombay Woodlands	C3
12	Casa Verde	A1
13	Din Tai Fung	D3
14	Food Republic	D3
	Iggy's	(see 5)
15	Killiney Kopitiam	E4
16	Nagomi	F4
17	Takashimaya Food Village	D3
18	Wasabi Tei	D2
19	Wild Honey	D3

⊙ Drinking
20	Dubliners	F4
21	KPO	F4
22	Que Pasa	E3
23	TWG Tea	D3

⊙ Entertainment
24	Tab	C2

⊙ Shopping
25	313 Somerset	E4
	Antiques of the Orient	(see 11)
26	Cathay Cineleisure Orchard	E4
	ION Orchard Mall	(see 23)
	Kinokuniya	(see 28)
27	Mandarin Gallery	E4
28	Ngee Ann City	D3
	Paragon	(see 6)
	Select Books	(see 11)
	Tanglin Shopping Centre	(see 11)

SINGAPORE SIGHTS

The terrace houses on Joo Chiat Place are on the north side of the street, between Everett and Mangis Rds.

Geylang Serai Market MARKET
(Map p492; 1 Geylang Serai; ⓂPaya Lebar) A hub for Singapore's Malay community, Geylang Serai Market packs a lively wet market, a hawker food centre, and stalls selling everything from spices and fabrics, to skull caps and Malay CDs. If you're feeling peckish, hunt down some *goreng pisang* (banana fritters) and wash them down with a glass of *bandung* (milk with rose cordial syrup).

Sri Senpaga Vinayagar Temple HINDU TEMPLE
(Map p492; 19 Ceylon Rd; ⊙7am-noon & 6-9pm; 🚌10, 12, 14, 32) One of Singapore's most beautiful Hindu temples, Sri Senpaga Vinayagar Temple stuns visitors with its interior of colourful devotional art. One of its star features is the *kamalapaatham*, a specially sculptured granite foot-stone found in certain ancient Hindu temples. The roof of the inner sanctum is covered in gold.

Katong Antique House MUSEUM
(Map p492; ☏6345 8544; 208 East Coast Rd) This tiny shop-cum-museum is the domain of Peter Wee, a noted expert on Peranakan culture. Peter will happily regale you with tales as you browse his collection of books, antiques and cultural artefacts. By appointment only, though it's sometimes open to the public.

CHANGI & PASIR RIS

Changi Museum & Chapel MUSEUM
(☏6214 2451; www.changimuseum.com; 1000 Upper Changi Rd Nth; admission free, guided tour adult/child S$8/4; ⊙9.30am-5pm, last entry 4.30pm) Although no longer at the original Changi prison location, this memorial site remains a moving tribute to the Allied POWs captured and subject to horrific treatment by the invading Japanese forces during WWII. Stories are told through photographs, letters, and drawings, with tales of heroism and peace tempering the mood. Its centrepiece chapel is a replica of the original Changi Chapel built by inmates.

Another highlight are the full-sized replicas of the famous Changi Murals painted by POW Stanley Warren in the old POW hospital. The originals are off limits in what is now Block 151 of the nearby Changi Army Camp. Bus 2, from Victoria St or Tanah Merah MRT, passes by the entrance.

Changi Village NEIGHBOURHOOD
Clinging to Singapore's far northeast coast, Changi Village delivers a chilled-out, village vibe far removed from Singapore's high-rise

Eastern Singapore

SINGAPORE SIGHTS

N

1 km
0.5 miles

G

New Upper Changi Rd
Bedok
Bedok South Ave
8
Siglap Rd
East Coast Rd
16
11 East Coast Park
East Coast Parkway

F

Siglap Rd
Frankel Ave
Kembangan
22
Siglap Canal
Telok Kurau Rd
Marine Vista
Marine Parade Rd
East Coast Rd
15
Strait of Singapore

E

Jalan Eunos
KATONG (JOO CHIAT)
Still Rd
Dunman Rd
4
13
Sims Ave
Eunos
Changi Rd
Joo Chiat Tce
Joo Chiat Pl
18
17
Koon Seng Rd
Tembeling Rd
26
5
12 25
19
2

D

Pan-Island Expressway
3
Joo Chiat Rd
14
Onan Rd
Ceylon Rd
Carpmael Rd
Marshall Rd
6
Brooke Rd
Marine Parade Rd
Amber Rd
24

C

Paya Lebar Rd
GEYLANG SERAI
21
Paya Lebar
Geylang Rd
7
Guillemard Rd
Haig Rd
Dunman Rd
Tanjong Katong Rd
Goodman Rd
Broadrick Rd
Arthur Rd
Mountbatten Rd
East Coast Park

B

Aljunied
1
Aljunied Rd
Geylang Rd
Sims Ave
23
20
Mountbatten
Mountbatten Rd
Fort Rd
9
Katong Park
Geylang River
East Coast Parkway
East Coast Park

A

Express Car
KALLANG
Lor 1
Lor 3
Kallang
Sims Ave
Mountbatten Rd
Stadium Blvd
Stadium Rd
10
Kallang River
East Coast Park

1 2 3 4

Eastern Singapore

◎ **Sights**
1 Amitabha Buddhist Centre B2
2 East Coast Park E3
3 Geylang Serai Market D2
4 Katong Antique House E3
5 Peranakan Terrace Houses D2
6 Sri Senpaga Vinayagar Temple D3
7 Tan Swie Hian Museum C2

✪ **Activities, Courses & Tours**
8 Cookery Magic F1
9 Katong Swimming Complex B3
10 Paddle Lodge A3
11 SKI360° G3

✖ **Eating**
12 328 Katong Laksa D3
13 Chin Mee Chin Confectionery E3

14 Djanoer Koening D2
15 East Coast Lagoon Food Village F3
16 East Coast Seafood Centre G3
17 Guan Hoe Soon D2
18 Kim's Place Seafood D2
19 Maeda D3
20 Old Airport Rd Food Centre B2
21 Rochor Beancurd C2
22 Seng Kee Black Chicken Herbal
      Soup E1
23 Sik Wai Sin Eating House B2

◒ **Drinking**
24 1-TwentySix D4

◔ **Shopping**
25 112 Katong D3
26 Kim Choo Kueh Chang D3

norm. At its heart is a lively hawker centre, while the polluted waters of Changi Beach (where thousands of Singaporean civilians were executed during WWII) are best for looking, not touching. Opposite the hawker centre, bumboats go to Pulau Ubin.

To get here, catch bus 2 from Tanah Merah MRT or from Victoria St.

Pasir Ris Park   PARK
(Ⓜ Pasir Ris) Waterside Pasir Ris Park is packed with family-friendly activties. You can rent a bike or in-line skates, or explore the 6-hectare **mangrove boardwalk** – go during low tide to see little crabs scurrying in the mud. Little darlings will love the pony rides at **Gallop Stables** (☏ 6583 9665; 61 Pasir Ris Green; rides S$10; ⊙ 8am-noon, 2-7pm Tue-Sun). Make it over to Downtown East to grab a bite or look out for the park's handful of bars.

Downtown East   MALL, THEME PARK
(www.downtowneast.com.sg; cnr Pasir Ris Dr 3 & Pasir Ris Close; Ⓜ Pasir Ris) Yes, it's the building with the indoor Ferris wheel (rides S$6.50), not to mention a popular **cinema** and **bowling complex**, but the real highlight here is **Wild Wild Wet** (www.wildwildwet.com; adult/child/family S$16/11/44; ⊙ 1-7pm Mon & Wed-Fri, 10am-7pm Sat & Sun). Set to expand, this family-friendly outdoor water theme park has enough waterslide, wave pool and rafting action to keep you soaked, squealing and sunburnt.

NORTHERN & CENTRAL SINGAPORE

Major sights aside, you'll also probably find yourself lingering in **Dempsey Hill** (Dempsey Rd), a once-crumbling army barracks now packed with trendy eateries, cafes, bars, up-market antique and furniture stores, and the odd art gallery. More buzzing eateries, bars and chi-chi locals await in the nearby expat enclave of **Holland Village**.

TOP CHOICE **Singapore Zoo**   ZOO
(☏ 6269 3411; www.zoo.com.sg; 80 Mandai Lake Rd; adult/child S$20/13; ⊙ 8.30am-6pm; ☐ 138, Ⓜ Ang Mo Kio) Even if you're not a zoo fan, Singapore Zoo should leave you purring. Set on a peninsula jutting into the Upper Seletar Reservoir, its 28 lushly landscaped hectares feel like an oasis. Cages are ditched for 'open concept' enclosures, and there is a range of engaging child-friendly shows and feeding sessions.

In fact, there are more than 2800 residents here and most of them seem pretty happy. Attractions such as the 'The Great Rift Valley of Ethiopia' enclosure convey entire ecosystems: animal, mineral, vegetable and human. Visitors can stand behind a window in 'Ethiopia' and watch 50 shameless red-bummed baboons doing things that Singaporeans get arrested for. Get around the zoo on foot or by tram (adult/child S$5/2.50); the zoo's 15-minute reservoir boat ride offers a relaxing interlude. Save money by buying a three-in-one ticket (adult/child S$58/38) for the zoo, the Night Safari (p494) and Jurong Bird Park (p498), and book online to avoid the queues.

WORTH A TRIP

PULAU UBIN

It may be a quick 10-minute bumboat ride from Changi Village, but Pulau Ubin feels worlds apart from mainland Singapore and its jungle of tower blocks. Indeed, it's the perfect day-trip getaway, coloured with unkempt expanses of jungle and tin-roofed buildings that ooze a sleepy *kampung* (village) vibe.

Bumboats (one-way S$2.50, bicycle surcharge S$2; ⊙varies, usually 6am-9pm) to Pulau Ubin depart from Changi Point Ferry Terminal in Changi Village. There's no timetable: boats depart when 12 people are ready to go, dropping passengers off at **Pulau Ubin Village**. Food outlets aside (expect to pay between S$20 and S$40 for chilli crab), Pulau Ubin Village is the place to rent bikes (around S$5-10 per day for adults and S$2 for kids). For the sake of your booty, opt for a mountain bike. While you can't get maps of the island, there are signboards dotted around the place, though it's fun to simply trundle off on your bike and see where the road takes you.

For those keen on scraping their knees, there's **Ketam Mountain Bike Park**, with a series of trails of varying difficulty. This is also where you'll find the quirky **German Girl Shrine**, housed in a yellow hut beside an Assam tree. According to legend, the young German daughter of a coffee plantation manager was running away from British troops who had come to arrest her parents during WWI when she fell fatally into the quarry behind her house. Somewhere along the way, the Roman Catholic child became a Taoist deity, bestowing good health and fortune.

If you only have time for one part of Pulau Ubin, make it the **Chek Jawa Wetlands** (⊙8.30am-6pm). Located on the eastern end of the island, its 1km coastal boardwalk takes you out over the sea before looping back through the mangrove swamp to the 20m-high **Jejawi Tower** and its stunning views. You can't bring your bike into the reserve so make sure the one you've rented comes with a bike lock so you can lock it securely to the bike stands at the entrance.

TOP CHOICE **Night Safari**   WILDLIFE RESERVE
(www.nightsafari.com.sg; 80 Mandai Lake Rd; adult/child S$32/21; ⊙7.30pm-midnight, restaurants and shops from 6pm; 🚌138, Ⓜ️Ang Mo Kio) Night Safari offers a very different type of after-dark thrill. The park's moats and barriers seem to melt away in the darkness, giving you the feeling of travelling through a mysterious jungle filled with over 120 species of animals, including lions and leopards. While you can walk around the three trails, the best experience is on the tram tour (adult/child S$10/5).

Consider coming early, when the animals have just been fed and are happy to come out to play, and never use the flash on your camera (it unsettles the animals).

Also, don't miss the impressive, humorous 'Creatures of the Night' show (7.30pm, 8.30pm, 9.30pm, plus 10.30pm Friday and Saturday), which will make you wonder why we ever bothered to evolve. To save money, consider buying a combined Zoo (p493) and Night Safari ticket (adult/child S$42/28). After the Night Safari catch a return bus by 10.45pm to ensure you make the last train from Ang Mo Kio (11.30pm). Otherwise,

there's a taxi rank out the front. Expect to pay around S$20 for a taxi ride back to central Singapore.

FREE **Bukit Timah Nature Reserve**   PARK
(📞1800-468 5736; www.nparks.gov.sg; 177 Hindhede Dr; ⊙6am-7pm, visitors centre 8.30am-5pm; 🚌171, or 75 to Bukit Timah Shopping Centre) Singapore's steamy heart of darkness is Bukit Timah Nature Reserve, a 164-hectare tract of undeveloped primary rainforest clinging to Singapore's highest peak, Bukit Timah (163.63m). Five walking trails weave through the reserve, taking anywhere from 35 minutes to two-hours return, while cyclists can peddle over 6km of bike trails circumnavigating the forest – pick up a trail map from the visitors centre.

The most popular and easiest of the walking trails is the concrete-paved route straight to the summit, though you should leave time to explore the less busy side trails too. The steep paths are sweaty work, so take plenty of water, embalm yourself in mosquito repellent, and don't feed the monkeys no matter how politely they ask.

Monkeys aside, the reserve's unbroken forest canopy shelters numerous surviving species of Singapore's native wildlife, including pythons and dozens of bird species. To get here catch bus 171 from Orchard MRT or bus 75 from the CBD. Get off at the Bukit Timah Shopping Centre; the park's entrance is about 1km north along Hindhede Dr.

MacRitchie Reservoir　　　　　PARK

(☏1800 4717300; www.nparks.gov.sg; Lornie Rd; ⏱7am-7pm, Treetop Walk 9am-5pm Tue-Fri, 8.30am-5pm Sat & Sun, closed Mon; 🚌157, MToa Payoh) While not quite as wonderfully wild as Bukit Timah, MacRitchie Reservoir does boast much longer walking trails skirting the water's edge and snaking through parts of the surrounding forest. You can rent kayaks at the Paddle Lodge (p513), but most people come here for the excellent 10km walking trail – and its various well-signposted offshoots – that circumnavigates the reservoir.

The most popular place to aim for is Treetop Walk, the highlight of which is traversing a 250m-long suspension bridge, perched 25m up in the forest canopy. Trails then continue through the forest and around the reservoir, sometimes on dirt tracks, sometimes on wooden boardwalks. It takes three to four hours to complete the main circuit. Whichever trail you choose, you'll almost certainly encounter monkeys (long-tailed macaques) in the forest. If you're really lucky, you may even spot one of the huge monitor lizards that dart around the shallows of the reservoir with frightening speed.

FREE Kranji War Memorial　　　MEMORIAL

(☏6269 6158; www.cwgc.com; 9 Woodlands Rd; ⏱7am-6pm ; 🚌170, MKranji) The austere white structures and rolling manicured lawns of the Kranji War Memorial contain the WWII graves of thousands of Allied troops. Walls are inscribed with the names of 24,346 men and women who lost their lives in Southeast Asia, while more than a few of the headstones are simply engraved with 'A Soldier of the 1939-1945 War'.

Row 262 has the name of a suspected (but never convicted) Japanese spy, Patrick Balcombe Heenan, while the bodies of Singapore's first two presidents are interred at the front.

The memorial is near the Causeway, off Woodlands Rd. To get here catch the MRT to Kranji, then walk 10 minutes, or take bus 170 two stops west.

SOUTHERN & WESTERN SINGAPORE
This vast area is home to a handful of lesser-known museums and historic sites, as well as the soothing Southern Ridges walking trail.

TOP CHOICE **Southern Ridges**　　　　PARK

(www.nparks.gov.sg; admission free; MPasir Panjang, then 15min walk to Reflections at Bukit Chandu) Made up of a series of parks and hills connecting West Coast Park to Mt Faber, the Southern Ridges will have you trekking through the jungle without ever really leaving the city. While the whole route spans 9km, the best stretch is from Kent Ridge Park to Mt Faber. Not only is it relatively easy, it delivers lofty vistas, treetop boardwalks and the one-of-a-kind Henderson Waves walkway.

Consider starting your saunter at Reflections at Bukit Chandu (www.s1942.org.sg; 31K Pepys Rd; adult/child S\$2/1; ⏱9am-5.30pm Tue-Sun; MPasir Panjang), an absorbing WWII interpretive centre commemorateing the last stand of the Malay Regiment against the Japanese in 1942. Kent Ridge Park and its short-but-satisfying canopy walk are a few steps away. When done, stroll downhill to HortPark (⏱7.45am-8pm), home to a small children's playground, cute herb and flower gardens, and prototype glasshouses. From HortPark, the leaf-like Alexander Arch

---

EIGHT RIVERS, ONE ADDRESS

Due to open in the first quarter of 2013, River Safari (www.riversafari.com.sg) is set to become Singapore's latest blockbuster attraction. Flanking Singapore Zoo and Night Safari, the S\$160 million, 12-hectare wildlife park ambitiously recreates the ecosystems of eight iconic world rivers: the Amazon, Congo, Ganges, Mississippi, Murray, Mekong, Nile and Yangtze. Not only will it showcase 150 types of plants, it plans to house 300 animal species, among them giant pandas, critically endangered Mekong giant catfish, giant river otter, salamander, and shamelessly cute manatee. For updates on River Safari's debut, opening times and admission prices, check the River Safari website.

WORTH A TRIP

BUKIT BROWN CEMETERY

In a country obsessed with all things shiny and new, **Bukit Brown Cemetery Complex** is a precious heritage jewel. Incorporating three adjoining cemeteries – Lau Sua (Old Hill), Kopi Sua (Coffee Hill) and Seh Ong Sua (Ong Clan Hill) – not only is Bukit Brown the world's largest Chinese cemetery outside of China, but the site also offers an unexpected glimpse into Singapore's eclectic history.

Originally owned by British ship-owner, trader and broker George Henry Brown, the area was bought in 1872 by Ong Kew Ho, Ong Ewe Hai and Ong Chong Chew, three wealthy Hokkien entrepreneurs set on establishing a self-sufficient village for poorer members of their clan. Mysteriously, the land came to be used solely as a burial ground before being turned into a municipal Chinese cemetery in 1922. As a municipal cemetery, it was open to Chinese people from all dialect groups, a radical departure from their relative segregation in both life and death.

With burials ceasing here in 1973, Bukit Brown is now a history buffs' dream, its thick, rambling swathes of jungle regularly revealing beautiful, long-forgotten tombs. Among these is the sprawling double tomb of entrepreneur Ong Sam Leong (1857–1918) and his wife, perched atop Seh Ong Sua. Built in 1918 and reputedly the largest tomb in Singapore, it's adorned with delicate carvings depicting scenes of filial piety, beautiful Minton floor tiles, and carved Sikh guards.

Many of the cemetery's Peranakan tombs are adorned with brightly coloured ceramic tiles (including sumptuous art nouveau majolica from England), while numerous tombs are engraved with death poems reflecting on the deceased's migration to Nanyang (Southeast Asia) from China. Those adorned with Sikh statues often belong to former police force members. These funerary guards are reputedly so rare that only one other cemetery in Shanghai lays claim to them. Within Bukit Brown itself, you'll find a great number of them in Block 4. Interestingly, tombs carved with Japanese calendar dates span back to the dark days of Singapore's Japanese occupation; the area itself was a battleground during WWII.

Ironically, Bukit Brown is once more a battleground, this time between the government, which plans to build a highway and subsequent housing here, and Bukit Brown supporters, who demand a reassessment of the government's plans and guaranteed protection of the area's heritage.

While you can download a site map on the excellent volunteer-run website www.bukitbrown.com, the best way to explore this threatened slice of Singaporean history is on one of the regular, free volunteer tours (upcoming dates are posted on the website). Information on Bukit Brown's history and individual tombs can also be found at www.bukitbrown.org, a blog written by Bukit Brown expert Raymond Goh. To reach the cemetery, catch the MRT to Botanic Gardens, then walk north up Adam Rd to the bus stop outside Singapore Bible College. From here, catch bus 74, 93, 157, 165, 852 or 855 and alight two stops later (just before Singapore Island Country Club). Cross the bridge over Adam Rd and continue walking north. Turn right into Sime Rd and left into Lorong Halwa.

bridge leads to a stunning, elevated walkway that offers eye-level views of the jungle canopy covering Telok Blangah Hill. Further along you'll hit the remarkable **Henderson Waves**, an undulating sculptural walkway suspended 36m above the forest floor. The wavelike towers that seem to rise straight out of the jungle are part of **Reflections at Keppel Bay** – a residential development designed by world-renowned architect Daniel Libeskind.

Further on await the restaurants and bars of Mt Faber (p496), Singapore's highest point and a perfect spot for a post-walk sip or nibble.

Mt Faber Park & Cable Car PARK
(www.mountfaber.com.sg; cable car one-way adult/child S$24/14; ⏰park 8.30am-2am, cable car 8.30am-9.30pm; ⓂHarbourFront) Standing proud (if not tall) at 116m on the southern fringe of the city, Mt Faber forms the centrepiece of Mt Faber Park, and the climax to the

bracing, 4km-long walk along the Southern Ridges (p495). The most spectacular way to reach the top is on the cable car, which connects Sentosa and HarbourFront to a cluster of slick hilltop bars and restaurants. Alternatively, take bus 409 (weekends only, midday to 9pm) or walk. It's a short but steep climb through secondary rainforest, dotted with strategically placed benches, pavilions and lookout posts, as well as some splendid colonial-era black-and-white bungalows.

NUS Museums
MUSEUMS

(www.nus.edu.sg/museum; 50 Kent Ridge Cres, University Cultural Centre; admission free; ⊙10am-7.30pm Tue-Sat, 10am-6pm Sun; 🚌A2 (university shuttle bus), MKent Ridge) Located on the campus of the National University of Singapore (NUS), these three beautifully curated galleries hold some remarkable collections. The **Lee Kong Chian Art Museum** houses ancient Chinese ceramics, bronzes and porcelain, while the **South & Southeast Asian Gallery** focuses on mixed media regional art. Above them, the **Ng Eng Teng Gallery** showcases the paintings, drawings and sculptures by prolific Singaporean artist Ng Eng Teng (1934–2001).

Departing regularly from Kent Ridge MRT station, the free A2 university shuttle bus stops right outside the gallery building.

Labrador Nature Reserve & Labrador Secret Tunnels
HISTORIC SITE

(www.nparks.gov.sg; Labrador Villa Rd; MLabrador Park) Combining historic sites, walking trails through forest inhabited by over 70 bird species, and great views from Singapore's only sea cliffs, Labrador Park is well worth spending an afternoon at. Examine the old British guns, hike through the jungle, and visit the **Labrador Secret Tunnels**.

A series of storage and armament bunkers built by the British in the 1880s, the Secret Tunnels remained undiscovered for 50 years after WWII. Small, but fascinating, you'll find displays of artefacts left behind when the British abandoned the tunnels in 1942, as well as the buckled walls from a direct hit from a Japanese bomb. At the time of research, the tunnels were closed indefinitely for repairs.

Haw Par Villa
MUSEUM

(262 Pasir Panjang Rd; theme park free, museum adult/child S$4/2.50; ⊙9am-7pm, museum to 5pm; MHaw Par Villa) For a free freak out, head to this mythological theme park. Formerly the Tiger Balm Gardens (co-founder

JUNGLE BREAKFAST WITH WILDLIFE

If you like your buffets in the company of cheeky primates, don't miss Singapore Zoo's **Jungle Breakfast with Wildlife** (📞6360 8560; es.szgadmin@wrs.com.sg; Ah Meng Restaurant (Terrace), Singapore Zoo; adult/child S$$31/20.30; ⊙9-10.30am), best booked ahead. Your breakfast companions will include the zoo's obscenely adorable orang-utans. If you miss out (the orang-utans are out until 10am), you can still get that happy snap shot with them at the zoo's **Free-Ranging Orang-utan Island** (11am and 3.30pm) and **Free-Ranging Orang-utan Boardwalk** (4.30pm).

Aw Boon Haw also created the medicinal salve Tiger Balm), its psychedelic statues and dioramas capture some rather bizarre scenes from Chinese mythology. Also onsite is the **Hua Song Museum**, which offers a glimpse into the lives, enterprises and adventures of Chinese migrants around the world.

Singapore Science Centre
MUSEUM

(www.sci-ctr.edu.sg; 15 Science Centre Rd; adult/child S$9/5; ⊙10am-6pm daily; MJurong East) Packed with enough push-pull-twist-and-turn gadgets to keep kids enthralled for hours, this absorbing museum covers subjects like the human body, ecosystems and robotics.

To reach it, alight at Jurong East MRT station, turn left along the covered walkway, cross the road and continue past a covered row of stalls before crossing Jurong Town Hall Rd.

The centre is also home to **Snow City** (www.snowcity.com.sg; 21 Jurong Town Hall Rd; adult/child per 2hr S$27/22, combined 1hr snow access & Science Centre ticket S$16/14; ⊙9.45am-5.15pm daily), a hangar-sized deep freeze complete with a three-storey high, 70m-long slope. Each session gives you one or two hours to throw yourself at high speed down the slope on a black inner tube and throw snowballs. All visitors must be wearing long trousers (which can be rented) and socks (which can be bought). Visitors are provided with a ski jacket and warm boots. Ski and snowboarding lessons also available.

Jurong Bird Park
BIRD PARK

(www.birdpark.com.sg; 2 Jurong Hill; adult/child S$18/12, tram adult/child S$5/3, combined ticket incl Singapore Zoo & Night Safari adult/child S$58/38; ◷8.30am-6pm; ▢194 or 251, Ⓜ Boon Lay) Run by the same company that operates the excellent Singapore Zoo (p493) and Night Safari (p494), the somewhat neglected Jurong Bird Park houses around 600 species of birds.

SENTOSA ISLAND

Epitomised by its star attraction, Universal Studios, Sentosa is essentially one giant Pleasure Island. The choices are truly head-spinning, from duelling roller coasters and indoor skydiving, to stunt shows, luge racing, Ibiza-style beach bars and a casino. Many of the attractions cost extra, making it easy for a family to rack up a hefty bill in one day. The beaches, however, are completely free and a hit with locals and tourists alike.

Universal Studios
AMUSEMENT PARK

(Map p499; www.rwsentosa.com; Resorts World; adult/child/senior S$74/54/36; ◷10am-7pm) The top-draw attraction at Resorts World, Universal Studios' booty of rides, roller coasters, shows, shops and restaurants are neatly packaged into fantasy-world themes based on your favourite Hollywood films. One of the highlights is the pair of 'duelling roller coasters' in Sci-fi City, said to be the tallest of their kind in the world.

Maritime Experiential Museum
MUSEUM

(Map p499; www.rwsentosa.com; Resorts World; adult/child museum S$5/2, theatre S$6/4; ◷10am-7pm Mon-Thu, 10am-9pm Fri-Sun, Typhoon Theatre closes 1hr earlier) Explore the intriguing history of the maritime Silk Route at this interactive, state-of-the-art museum. While the 360-degree Typhoon Theatre is a slight let down (think 10 minutes of computer-generated wizardry, wind machines and bad acting), the Maritime Archaeology in Southeast Asia exhibition is genuinely engrossing, with fascinating information on the conservation of shipwreck artefacts. Many of these artefacts are on display, including beautiful 15th-century Thai earthenware.

Underwater World
AQUARIUM

(Map p499; ☑6275 0030; www.underwaterworld.com.sg; behind Siloso Beach; adult/child S$25.90/17.60; ◷10am-7pm) Seadragons and wobbling medusa jellyfish are mesmeric, while stingrays and 10ft sharks cruise inches from your face as the travelator transports you through the Ocean Colony's submerged glass tubes. If you're brave, book a 30-minute Dive with the Sharks experience (S$120 per person, bookings essential). Entry includes admission to next-door Dolphin Lagoon, where Indo-Pacific humpbacked dolphins perform with seals several times daily (check times online).

For S$170 you can swim with the dolphins. Call or book through the Underwater World website.

Songs of the Sea
SHOW

(Map p499; www.sentosa.com.sg; Siloso Beach; admission S$10; ◷shows 7.40pm & 8.40pm daily, additional show 9.40pm Sat) Set around a replica Malay fishing village, this ambitious show fuses Lloyd Webber-esque theatricality

---

DON'T MISS

GILLMAN BARRACKS

Singapore's hot new cultural trump card is Gillman Barracks (www.gillmanbarracks.com; 9 Lock Rd; ◷11am-8pm Tue-Sat, 10am-6pm Sun; Ⓜ Labrador Park), a military camp-turned-contemporary art hub. The S$10 million project includes no less than 13 international galleries, including Berlin's Michael Janssen Gallery (02-21, 9 Lock Rd), Tokyo's Mizuma Gallery (01-34, 22 Lock Rd) and Manila's The Drawing Room (01-06, 5 Lock Rd). Expectantly, the list of represented artists reads like a who's who of established and emerging talent, from Alfredo and Isabel Aquilizan and Heman Chong, to Yayoi Kusama and Sebastião Salgado. And it's only the beginning, with another five galleries in the pipeline, as well as a dedicated Centre for Contemporary Art (CCA) featuring international artist residencies, research facilities and exhibition programmes. Peckish art fiends are covered too, with French flavours at Masons (01-17, 8 Lock Road; ◷noon-11pm), regionally flavoured seafood at The Naked Finn (01-13, 41 Malan Road; ◷dinner Mon-Sat), or a mix of international bistro grub (including pizza) and live tunes at Timbre @ Gillman (01-05, 9A Lock Road; ◷dinner Mon-Sat). Gillman Barracks is an easy 10-minute walk north of Labrador Park MRT station.

Sentosa Island

Sentosa Island

◎ Sights

1 Fort Siloso	A1
2 Images of Singapore	B2
3 Maritime Experiential Museum	B1
4 Palawan Beach	B2
5 Siloso Beach	A2
6 Songs of the Sea	B2
7 Tanjong Beach	C3
8 Underwater World	A1
9 Universal Studios	B2

⚡ Activities, Courses & Tours

10 Gogreen Segway Eco Adventure	B2
11 iFly	B2
12 Sentosa Golf Club	C3
13 Spa Botanica	C3

🛏 Sleeping

14 Capella Singapore	B2
15 Siloso Beach Resort	A2
The Sentosa	(see 13)

✗ Eating

Cliff	(see 13)
16 Coastes	A2
17 Malaysian Food Street	B1

🍸 Drinking

18 Azzura Beach Club	A2
19 Tanjong Beach Club	C3
20 Wave House	A2

✪ Entertainment

21 Boiler Room	B1
Movida	(see 21)
St James Power Station	(see 21)

🛍 Shopping

22 Vivocity	B1

with an awe-inspiring sound, light and laser extravaganza worth a hefty S$4 million. Prepare to gasp, swoon and (occasionally) cringe.

Fort Siloso   MUSEUM
(Map p499; www.sentosa.com.sg; Siloso Point; adult/child S$8/5; ⏰10am-6pm; free guided tours 12.40pm & 3.40pm Fri-Sun) Designed to repel a maritime assault from the south, Siloso's

heavy guns had to be turned around when the Japanese invaded from the Malaya mainland in WWII. The British surrender soon followed, and later the fort was used by the Japanese as a prisoner-of-war camp. Documentaries, artefacts, animatronics and re-created historical scenes will absorb history buffs, while the **underground tunnels** are especially fun to explore.

Images of Singapore
MUSEUM

(Map p499; www.sentosa.com.sg; Imbiah Lookout; adult/child S$10/7; ⊘9am-7pm) Time-travel through seven centuries of Singapore history at this genuinely insightful, interactive museum. Kicking off with Singapore as a Malay sultanate, it takes you through its consolidation as a port and trading centre, WWII, and the subsequent Japanese surrender. Scenes are recreated using lifelike wax dummies, film footage and dramatic light-and-sound effects.

Beaches
BEACHES

Sentosa's three southern beaches – **Siloso** (Map p499) to the west, **Palawan** (Map p499) in the middle and **Tanjong** (Map p499) to the east – will never match the beaches in Malaysia or Indonesia, but that doesn't seem to matter to the Singaporeans who flock here. The sandy coconut vibe is soporific, even if the muddy Straits of Singapore are a little uninviting.

🏃 Activities

Adventure Sport

G-Max Reverse Bungy & GX-5 Extreme Swing
THRILL RIDE

(Map p478; www.gmax.com.sg; 3E River Valley Rd; per ride S$49; ⊘2pm-late; ⓜClarke Quay) Fancy being flung 60m skywards at over 200km/h?

If so, get yourself strapped inside the G-Max metal cage and prepare for a breathless view (both figuratively and literally). A few Clarke Quay beers might improve your courage, but your stomach mightn't agree. Less terrifying is the neighbouring GX5, which will have you swinging over the Singapore River at a (slightly) more merciful speed.

iFly
THRILL RIDE

(Map p499; www.iflysingapore.com; Cable Car Rd; adult/child from S$69/59; ⊘10.30am-10pm Thu-Tue, noon-10pm Wed) Indoor skydiving in a vertical wind chamber, and exceptionally popular. The price includes an hour's instruction then two short skydives. They say the time you spend on one skydive here is like free-falling from 12,000ft to 3,000ft. Gulp!

Cycling

You can hire a bike and trundle along the foreshore at East Coast Park, at Pasir Ris Park or on Pulau Ubin for between S$5 and S$10 per hour, depending on the quality of the bike. There are also tandem bikes.

There's a 5.7km bicycle track looping around Sentosa Island that takes in most of its attractions. Hire a bike at Siloso or Palawan Beaches.

For a more challenging workout tackle the mountain-bike trails around Bukit Timah Nature Reserve and at Pulau Ubin.

Two Wheel Action
CYCLING

(✆6471 2775; www.twa.com.sg) Organises Sunday rides in collaboration with the Singapore chapter of the Hash House Harriers. You bring your own bike, meet at a prearranged point, then propel yourself into it. It costs S$10 per session.

SENTOSA'S ENTRANCE FEE & TRANSPORT

There is a small entrance fee to enter Sentosa Island, but it varies depending on which form of transport you choose. If you walk across from the VivoCity shopping mall, the fee is S$1. If you catch the Sentosa Express monorail (which leaves from Level 3 of VicoCity), it's S$3.50. If you ride the cable car, the fee is included in the cable car ticket price.

Once on the island, it's easy to get around, either by walking, taking the Sentosa Express (7am–midnight), riding the free 'beach tram' (shuttling the length of all three beaches, 9am–11pm, to midnight Friday and Saturday) or by using the free three colour-coded bus routes that link the main attractions (7am–11pm, to 12.30am Friday and Saturday).

Alternatively, if you fancy a more novel way to get around, there's **Gogreen Segway Eco Adventure** (Map p499; www.segway-sentosa.com; one circuit S$12, 30/60min guided tour S$38/80, night tour S$78-88; ⊘10am-9.30pm). Get perpendicular on these two-wheeled vehicles and scoot around a 10-minute circuit, or opt for the longer guided trips along the beachfront. The adults-only Gogreen After Dark tour offers an atmospheric night tour of the island. The company also rents electric bikes (per hour S$12).

START SINGAPORE ART MUSEUM
FINISH SINGAPORE RIVER
DISTANCE 2KM
DURATION TWO HOURS

Walking Tour
Colonial Singapore

> In a city-state firmly fixed on tomorrow, the Colonial District offers a nostalgic glimpse of a Singapore of far-flung missionaries, Palladian architecture and high-society cricket clubs. Finish your walk with a well-deserved lunch or dinner at riverside Jumbo Seafood (p520).

Start at the **1 Singapore Art Museum**, which occupies the former St Joseph's Institution, a Catholic boys' school. Original architectural features include the shuttered windows and ceramic floor tiles. The central dome and sweeping arcade portico were early 20th-century additions.

Heading southeast along Bras Basah Rd, you'll pass the Renaissance-inspired **2 Cathedral of the Good Shepherd** and the English Gothic-style **3 Chijmes**, a convent-cum-restaurant complex. Diagonally opposite Chijmes is **4 Raffles Hotel**. Past guest Somerset Maugham described it as a symbol for 'all the fables of the Exotic East', and it remains one of Singapore's most beautiful heritage sites. Relive its golden era at the Raffles Museum before heading south on North Bridge Rd to **5 St Andrew's Cathedral**, one of Singapore's few surviving examples of English Gothic-style architecture.

Across the street, **6 City Hall** is where Lord Louis Mountbatten announced Japanese surrender in 1945 and where Lee Kwan Yew declared Singapore's independence in 1965. City Hall and the neighbouring Supreme Court will reopen as the National Art Gallery of Singapore in 2015. Opposite the building is the open field of the **7 Padang**, home to the Singapore Cricket Club and Singapore Recreation Club. During WWII, the invading Japanese herded the European community together here before marching them off to Changi Prison.

Continue south along St Andrew's Rd – where the road curves to the left stand a cluster of colonial-era buildings, including the **8 Victoria Theatre & Concert Hall**. Completed in 1862, the Victoria Theatre was one of Singapore's first Victorian Revivalist buildings, inspired by the Italian Renaissance. Hang a right to hit the **9 Singapore River**, where towering skyscrapers pull you back into the future.

The Mega-Diversity Region

Home to thousands of natural species (with still more being discovered), Malaysia, Singapore and Brunei are a dream come true for budding David Attenboroughs. The festival of tropical flora and fauna is so abundant that this region is considered to be one of the world's 'mega-diversity' hotspots. Although vast areas of old growth forest have been cleared, a few magnificent stands remain, mostly protected within reserves and parks. You don't need to venture deep into the jungle to see wildlife, either. Botanical gardens, zoos and wildlife sanctuaries are features of each country.

Large parts of Peninsular Malaysia (132,090 sq km) are covered by dense jungle, particularly the mountainous, thinly populated northern half, although it's dominated by palm oil and rubber plantations. On the western side of the peninsula there is a long, fertile plain running down to the sea, while on the eastern side the mountains descend more steeply and the coast is fringed with sandy beaches. Jungle features heavily in Malaysian Borneo, along with many large river systems, particularly in Sarawak. Mt Kinabalu (4095m) in Sabah is Malaysia's highest mountain.

Singapore, consisting of the main, low-lying Singapore island and 63 much smaller islands within its territorial waters, is a mere 137km north of the equator. The central area is an igneous outcrop, containing most of Singapore's remaining forest and open areas.

The western part of the island is a sedimentary area of low-lying hills and valleys, while the southeast is mostly fla and sandy. The undeveloped northern coast and the offshore islands are home some mangrove forest.

The sultanate of Brunei covers just 576 sq km (the Brunei government–owned cattle farm in Australia is larger than this!). The capital, Bandar Seri Begawan, overlooks the estuary of the mangrove-fringed Sungai Brunei (Brunei River), wh opens onto Brunei Bay and the separate, eastern part of the country, Temburong, a sparsely populated area of largely unspoil rainforest. Approximately 75% of Brunei retains its original forest cover.

Clockwise from top left
1 Deer Cave (p440), Gunung Mulu National Park, Borneo
2 Danum Valley (p354), Sabah, Borneo 3 Red lionfish

Jungle Life

The region's lush natural habitats, from steamy rainforests to tidal mangroves, teem with mammals, birds, amphibians, reptiles and insects, many of them found nowhere else on earth. Although vast areas of old-growth forest have been cleared, a few magnificent stands remain, mostly protected within reserves and parks.

Primates, Cats & Elephants

Orang-utans, Asia's only great apes, are at the top of many visitors' list. It's thought that around 11,300 live in the Bornean jungle, while they can be viewed in captivity at Sabah's Sepilok Orang-Utan Rehabilitation Centre, Sarawak's Semenggoh Wildlife Rehabilitation Centre and Singapore Zoo.

Among the many species of apes and monkey you may spot are **proboscis monkeys**. The male is an improbable-looking creature with a pendulous nose and bulbous belly; females and youngsters are more daintily built, with quaint upturned noses. Another langur (leaf monkey) is the **silvered leaf monkey**, whose fur is frosted with grey tips. **Macaques** are the stocky, aggressive monkeys that solicit snacks from tourists at temples and nature reserves. If you are carrying food, watch out for daring raids and be wary of bites – remember that rabies is a potential hazard.

Shy, tailless **gibbons** live in the trees and feed on fruits like figs. Their raucous hooting – one of the most distinctive sounds of the Malaysian jungle – helps them establish territories and find mates.

Around 2000 **pygmy elephants** live in northeastern Borneo, the largest group roams the forests around Sungai Kinabatangan. It's thought that they've lived on the island for at least 18,000 years.

Species of leopard including the **black panther** and the rare **clouded leopard** are found in Malaysia, as well as smaller species of wild cats, for example the **bay cat**, a specialised fish-eater, and the **leopard cat**, which is a bit larger than a domestic cat but with spotted fur.

Clockwise from top left
1 Macaques 2 Elephants by Sungai Kinabatangan (p348), Sabah, Borneo 3 Malayan tiger 4 Orang-utan at Sepilok Orang-Utan Rehabilitation Centre (p343), Sabah, Borneo

Birds & Bats

Well over 1000 species of birds flutter across the skies of this part of the world. Among the 742 species that call Malaysia home, the most easily recognisable are the various types of hornbill – the rhinoceros hornbill is the most flashy. Other birds on the twitchers' spotting lists include the brightly coloured kingfishers, pitas and trogons as well as the spectacularly named racket-tailed drongo.

The region has more than 100 species of bat, most of which are tiny, insectivorous (insect-eating) species that live in caves and under eaves and bark. Fruit bats (flying foxes) are only distantly related to insectivorous bats; unlike them they have well-developed eyes and do not navigate by echolocation.

LAST CHANCE TO SEE...

Habitat loss and hunting has placed several of the region's animals in serious danger of extinction.

» Orang-utan The WWF estimate that 12,300 live in the dwindling forests of Sabah and Sarawak, 40% less than the population 20 years ago.

» Malayan tiger The exact population is unknown but considered by WWF to be around 490, the vast majority of which are found in the jungles of Pahang, Perak, Terengganu and Kelantan.

» Asian elephant In 2009 a herd of 631 elephants was found living in Taman Negara; in 2012 two elephants were also spotted breakfasting in the grounds of the park's main resort. Across the wider region, however, the population is thought to be between 30,000 and 50,000.

» Sumatran rhinoceros These are found mainly in isolated areas of Sabah and Endau-Rompin National Park on the peninsula. Since they need at least 10 sq km of rainforest in which to roam, their chance of survival is slim, especially given the rate at which this forest is disappearing.

Clockwise from top left
1 Great hornbill 2 Malayan flying fox 3 Sumatran rhinoceros

Aquatic Life

Just as on land, in the region's waters – rivers, lakes and oceans – you'll also find a mind-boggling variety of corals, fish and aquatic life. The seas around islands and atolls like Sipadan, the Perhentians and Tioman offer some of the finest scuba diving in the world. Experienced divers will not want to miss the tiny islands off the northeast coast of Sabah in particular. Amid thriving coral – **sea fans** can grow to 3km – and a wealth of **sponges**, divers often encounter shimmering schools of **jacks**, **bumphead parrotfish** and **barracudas**, and may find themselves making the acquaintance of **green turtles**, **dolphins**, **manta rays** and several species of **shark**.

Of the world's seven types of turtle, four are native to Malaysia. The **hawksbill** and the **green turtle** both have nesting areas within Sabah's Turtle Islands National Park. Both these species, along with the **olive ridley** and **giant leatherback**, also swim in the waters off Peninsular Malaysia's east coast. There are established turtle rookeries on several beaches, where you may chance upon mother turtles dragging themselves above the high-tide line to bury their eggs.

TOP DIVE SITES

» **Sipadan** Legendary for its deep wall dives, Sipadan is a favoured hang-out of turtles, sharks and open-ocean fish.

» **Layang Layang** A deep-ocean island famed for its pristine coral and 2000m drop-off.

» **Pulau Perhentian** Coral reefs surround both islands – you can even wade out to some of them.

» **Pulau Redang** Corals, green and hawksbill turtles and a rainbow of tropical fish.

» **Pulau Tioman** One of the few places where you stand a good chance of seeing pods of dolphins.

Clockwise from top left
1 Coral reef, Sipadan (p359), Sabah 2 Sea turtle, Sipadan (p359), Sabah 3 Diving in Sabah (p304)

Natural Wonders

Rafflesia A parasite without roots, stems or leaves, this botanical wonder astonishes not only for of its world-record size (up to 1m in diameter), but also for its mysterious lifestyle. They bloom for just three to five days before turning into a ring of black slime. Taman Negara and the parks of East Malaysia are the places to view these extraordinary specimens.

Deer Cave The world's largest cave passage open to the public, in Gunung Mulu National Park, is over 2km in length and 174m in height. It's home to anything between two and three million bats belonging to more than 12 species, who cling to the roof in a seething black mass as they gear up for the evening prowl.

Mt Kinabalu Formed some nine million years ago, Malaysia's highest mountain is botanical paradise. Over half the species growing above 900m are unique to the area and include oaks, laurels, chestnuts and a dense rhododendron forest. Elsewhere in the park are many varieties of orchids and insect-eating pitcher plants.

Mangroves These remarkable coastal trees have developed extraordinary ways to deal with an ever-changing mix of salt and fresh water. Uncounted marine organisms and nearly every commercially important seafood species find sanctuary and nursery sites among the mangrove's muddy roots. They also fix loose coastal soil, protecting against erosion and tsunamis. You'll see them on Pulau Langkawi, Bako National Park, Kuching Wetland National Park and Brunei's Temburong District.

Kerangas These heath forests, whose name in Iban means 'land that cannot grow rice', are composed of small, densely packed trees. They also support the world's greatest variety of pitcher plants (nepenthes), which trap insects in chambers full of enzyme-rich fluid and then digest them. There are patches in Sarawak's Bako National Park and Sabah's Maliau Basin Conservation Area.

Clockwise from top left
1 Rafflesia, Sarawak (p379) 2 Deer Cave (p440), Gunung Mulu National Park, Sarawak 3 Mt Kinabalu (p322), Sabah

(Continued from page 500)

Golf

Sentosa Golf Club
GOLF

(Map p499; ☑6275 0022; www.sentosagolf.com; 27 Bukit Manis Rd; green fees per round S$280-450, club rental per set S$80, buggy fee per person S$25, shoe rental S$10) Luxury golf club with two of the best championship courses in Asia.

Jurong Country Club
GOLF

(☑6560 5655; www.jcc.org.sg; 9 Science Centre Rd; green fees per round 9/18 holes S$95-160/140-260, buggy fee 9/18 holes S$12/20; ☺7am-7:30pm Mon-Fri, 7am-7pm Sat & Sun, night golf Tue, Thu & Fri; ⒨Jurong East) Recently redesigned 18 hole, par 72 course and driving range.

Gyms

Fitness First
GYM

(Map p490; ☑6737 7889; www.fitnessfirst.com.sg; 08-13 Paragon, 290 Orchard Rd; ☺6.30am-10.30pm Mon-Sat, 8am-10pm Sun; ⒨Orchard, Somerset) One of several Fitness First branches across Singapore, with state-of-the-art equipment and group fitness classes.

True Fitness
GYM

(Map p478; ☑6820 9000; www.truefitness.com.sg; 07-0011 Suntec City Mall, 3 Temasek Blvd; ☺6am-11pm Mon-Thu, to 10pm Fri, to 9pm Sat, 8am-8pm Sun; ⒨Esplanade) Another popular, multi-branch gym with extensive equipment and group classes.

Spas & Massage

Massage, beauty treatments and reflexology are regulation Singaporean indulgences. Every mall seems to have a spa or massage joint of some sort, so you're never too far from an overhaul.

Willow Stream
SPA

(Map p478; ☑6339 7777; www.willowstream.com/ singapore; Level 6, Fairmont Hotel, 80 Bras Basah Rd; massage treatments from S$149; ⒨City Hall) Plunge pools, jacuzzis, and aromatic steam rooms await at this luxe oasis. Top-of-the-range treatments include herbal, algae and thermal mineral baths, body wraps, and 11 types of massage (including 'travel recovery' and 'shoppers' relief' options).

People's Park Complex
MASSAGE

(Map p482; 101 Upper Cross St; reflexology from S$15; ⒨Chinatown) This no-frills Chinatown mall is packed with cheap massage places ready to vie for your body parts (opt for the busier ones). Our favourite is **Mr Lim Foot Reflexology** (Map p482; 03-53 & 03-78).

Feeling adventurous? Try out one of the fish-pond foot spas on Level 3, where schools of fish nibble the dead skin right off your feet.

Kenko Wellness Spa
SPA

(Map p482; www.kenko.com.sg; 199 South Bridge Rd; reflexology per 30min S$36, body massage per 60min S$91; ☺10am-10pm; ⒨Chinatown) Kenko is the McDonalds of Singapore spas, with branches throughout the city, but there's nothing drive-through about its foot reflexology, romantic couples' sessions (S$328 per 2.5 hour session) or Chinese and Swedish massage (if you're after something forceful, go Chinese).

Spa Botanica
SPA

(Map p499; ☑6371 1318; www.spabotanica.sg; The Sentosa, 2 Bukit Manis Rd; treatments from S$80; ☺10am-10pm) For the ultimate Sentosa treat, book a treatment at this spa nirvana, complete with cascading waterfalls, mud pools and lush, landscaped grounds. The signature treatment is the galaxy steam bath, a 45-minute wallow in medicinal chakra mud in a specially designed steam room. A free shuttle connects the spa to VivoCity, as well as to Paragon Shopping Centre on Orchard Rd.

Swimming

Given the polluted waters, Singapore's beaches aren't particularly swim-friendly, although there are safe swimming areas at East Coast Park and on Sentosa and the southern islands. Alternatively, Singapore's 50m public swimming pools (per adult S$1 to S$1.30, child 50¢ to70¢) are winners.

Delta Swimming Complex
SWIMMING

(☑6474 7573; 900 Tiong Bahru Rd; ☺8am-9.30pm Wed-Mon, 2.30-9.30pm Tue; ⒨Redhill)

Jalan Besar Swimming Complex
SWIMMING

(Map p486; ☑6293 9058; 100 Tyrwhitt Rd; ☺8am-9.30pm Thu-Tue, 2.30-9.30pm Wed; ⒨Lavender)

Katong Swimming Complex
SWIMMING

(Map p492; ☑6344 9609; 111 Wilkinson Rd; ☺8am-9.30pm Wed-Mon, 2.30-9.30pm Tue; ⒨Mountbatten)

Water Sports

Aquabikes, canoes, kayaks and sailboards are available for hire on Sentosa's beaches for around S$15 per hour.

SKI360°
WATER SPORTS

(Map p492; www.ski360degree.com; 1206A East Coast Parkway; first hr weekdays/weekends S$32/

42, each subsequent hr S$16/22; ⊘10am-7pm Mon-Fri, 9am-10pm Sat & Sun) Forget swimming. Cool off by strapping on some waterskis, a kneeboard or a wakeboard and getting dragged around a lagoon on the end of a cable. If possible, head in on weekday mornings, when there's usually hardly anyone there. On weekdays, take bus 197, stop along Marine Pde Rd and head through an underpass. On weekends, take bus 401 from Bedok MRT.

Paddle Lodge BOATING
(Map p492; ☑6344 6337; www.scf.org.sg; per 2hr S$15-20; ⊘9am-6pm Tue-Sun; MStadium) The Singapore Canoe Federation rents out kayaks from this place locateed at MacRitchie Reservoir.

Yoga

Como Shambhala Urban Escape YOGA
(Map p490; ☑6304 3552; www.singapore.como shambhala.bz; 06-05 Forum, 583 Orchard Rd; 90min class S$37; ⊘9am-8.30pm Mon-Fri, 8.45am-5pm Sat, 9am-4pm Sun; MOrchard) This smart yoga and massage centre offers Hatha, Iyengar, and Ashtanga classes, Pilates, as well as oil and deep tissue massage. No booking required.

Absolute Yoga YOGA
(☑6732 6007; www.absoluteyogasingapore.com; 02-01 Valley Point, 491 River Valley Rd; drop-in class S$40.66; ⊘7am-9pm Mon-Fri, 8.30am-6pm Sat & Sun; ☐970) Absolute Yoga offers 'Hot Yoga', Hatha and Vinyasa classes along with Pilates.

Courses

Cooking

You've eaten the food, now learn how to cook it yourself, Singapore-style! Cooking classes generally run from two to four hours. Many are hands-on; some are instruction only. We advise checking websites or calling first for bookings and schedules.

 Cookery Magic COOKING COURSE
(Map p492; ☑6348 9667; www.cookerymagic. com; 117 Fidelio St; 3hr classes from S$100; ☐28, MEunos) Ruqxana conducts standout Asian-cooking classes in her own home. She also conducts classes in an old *kampung* home on the island of Pulau Ubin. Optional market trips before a class are organised for an extra S$50.

Palate Sensations
Cooking School COOKING COURSE
(☑6478 9746; www.palatesensations.com; 10 Biopolis Road, Chromos 01-03; 3hr courses from S$100; MBuona Vista) Both novices and serious foodies head here to hone their skills with top-notch chefs. Standard courses run for three hours and are wonderfully hands-on, with themes spanning anything from Malay festival foods, to classic Punjab cuisine and German Yuletide treats.

Shermay's Cooking School COOKING COURSE
(☑6479 8442; www.shermay.com; Block 43, Jalan Merah Saga 01-76; classes from S$60; MHolland Village) Singaporean, Thai, Peranakan, chocolate and guest chefs are Shermay's specialities! Hands-on classes cost more.

Tours

The Singapore Tourism Board books a range of tours and publishes a handful of free, self-guided walking-tour brochures.

Harbour Cruises

Imperial Cheng Ho
Dinner Cruise BOAT TOUR
(☑6533 9811; www.watertours.com.sg; adult/child daytime cruises S$29/16, dinner cruises $57/31; MMarina Bay) Three daily tours from Marina South to Sentosa or Kusu Island on a hulking old replica of the *Cheng Ho* junk. The food may not be spectacular, but the views are.

Duck Tour TOUR
(Map p478; ☑6338 6877; www.ducktours.com.sg; adult/child S$33/23; MEsplanade) A one-hour romp in the 'Wacky Duck', a Vietnam War amphibious curio, departing from Suntec City. Check out the city's sites from the road then hit the water for a harbour cruise. A good one for the kids.

River Cruises

A fabulous way to get a feel for central Singapore and its history is to take a river cruise. Bumboat cruises depart from various jetties along the Singapore River including Clarke Quay, Raffles Landing and Boat Quay, as well as Merlion Park and the Esplanade Jetty on Marina Bay, generally running between 9am and 11pm.

Hippo River Cruise BOAT TOUR
(Map p478; ☑6338 6877; www.ducktours.com.sg; adult/child S$18/13, day pass S$23/17; MClarke Quay) This is a 30-minute open-top boat ride departing from Clarke Quay every 25

minutes. You can opt for a day pass, which allows ticket holders to hop on/off at nine stops along the Singapore River.

Singapore River Cruise BOAT TOUR
(Map p478; ☑6336 6111; www.rivercruise.com.sg; adult/child from S$17/10; ⓜClarke Quay) Jump on a traditional bumboat and sail up and down the Singapore River on these 40- and 60-minute tours from the Merlion at the river mouth upstream to the city's famous quays.

Special Interest Tours

Original Singapore Walks WALKING TOUR
(☑6325 1631; www.singaporewalks.com; adult/child from S$30/15) Engaging, themed walking tours through Chinatown, Little India, Kampong Glam, the Colonial District and war-related sites. Tours last from two to three and a half hours; check the website for meeting places and times.

Charlotte Chu Tours WALKING TOUR
(☑8101 1003.; charlottechutours@gmail.com; 3hr tour S$240) Protégé of veteran tour guide Geraldene Lowe-Ahmad, Charlotte Chu conducts lively, specialised walking tours. Themes include heritage and culinary Singapore, as well as off-the-beaten-track and festival-related tours. While not obligatory, tours are best booked one week ahead.

Geraldene Lowe-Ahmad WALKING TOUR
(geraldenestours@hotmail.com; private tour from S$100 per hr, group tours from S$40) Although her colleague Charlotte Chu now runs most of her famous specialised walking tours, veteran tour guide Geraldene does still organise tours, though mostly for established clients and professional researchers. Her various private tours lend a unique insight into Singapore's history, architecture, religions, botany and culture. Subject to availability, individuals can sometimes join her group tours. Email for details.

Food Safari Tours FOOD TOUR
(☑6438 4038; www.makansutra.com; tours from S$160) Runs four-hour foodie tours, usually including three pit-stops. Options include the North-South-East-West Tour (street food), Multicultural Tour (Little India, Chinatown, Geylang and Katong), Uniquely Singapore Tour (*bak kut teh*, fish-head curry, chicken-rice) and Midnight Tour (duh!).

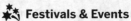 Festivals & Events

With so many cultures and religions, there are an astounding number of colourful celebrations in Singapore. Some have fixed dates, but Hindus, Muslims and Chinese follow a lunar calendar that varies annually. Check out www.yoursingapore.com for exact dates and full event listings.

Thaipusam HINDU
Usually held in February, this dramatic Hindu festival sees devotees pierced with *kavadis* (heavy metal frames decorated with peacock feathers, fruit and flowers) walk from from Sri Srinivasa Perumal Temple to Chettiar Hindu Temple.

Chingay CULTURE
(www.chingay.org.sg) Singapore's biggest street party, held on the 22nd day after Chinese New Year.

Mosaic Music Festival MUSIC
(www.mosaicmusicfestival.com) A 10-day feast of music in March showcasing world music, jazz and indie acts, and numerous free events.

World Gourmet Summit FOOD
(www.worldgourmetsummit.com) A lip-smacking gathering of top chefs for ten days of masterclasses, workshops and lavish dinners in late April or early May.

Singapore Arts Festival CULTURE
(www.singaporeartsfest.com) Held in May or June, the National Arts Council's premier arts festival delivers world-class music, dance, drama, and art.

Great Singapore Sale SHOPPING
(www.greatsingaporesale.com.sg) Eight credit-crunching weeks of sales starting in late May. For the best bargains, dive in during the first two weeks.

Singapore Food Festival FOOD
(www.singaporefoodfestival.com) A month-long feast of food stalls, tours, special events, and cooking demos held each July.

Singapore National Day PARADE
(www.ndp.org.sg) Patriotic revelry, with extravagant processions, military parades and fireworks on 9 August.

Hungry Ghost Festival CHINESE
Fires, food offerings and Chinese opera honour roaming spirits at this traditional August festival.

Formula One Grand Prix GRAND PRIX

(www.f1singapore.com) Singapore has bragging rights for hosting the world's first after-dark Formula 1, held in late September.

🛏 Sleeping

Sleeping in Singapore is expensive. Budget travellers have it best, as hostel rooms can be had for as little as S$20 a night. Most mid-range hotels are more about location than quality, while at the other end of the scale, many of Singapore's luxury digs offer history, cutting-edge design, or resort-style lushness.

Solid midrange options line the Singapore River, while Orchard Rd and the Colonial District groan under the weight of high-end chain hotels. Boutique midrange hotels convene around Chinatown. Both Chinatown and Little India offer solid budget options. If you want to be close to the beach, head to Sentosa Island.

For more information on sleeping in Singapore see p537.

COLONIAL DISTRICT & THE QUAYS

TOP CHOICE ✦ Raffles Hotel HOTEL $$$

(Map p478; ☑6337 1886; www.raffleshotel.com; 1 Beach Rd; ste from S$1400; ❄@🛜🏊; MCity Hall) For colonial-era luxury, it's hard to beat this 125-year-old icon. Rooms feature spacious parlours, verandahs, lazily swirling ceiling fans and a Singapore Sling from the Long Bar, while the rooftop pool, rambling gardens and historic bars offer perfect backdrops for languid posing. A dress code is in effect, so ditch those sleeveless shirts, sandals or grubby backpacker threads.

TOP CHOICE ✦ Naumi BOUTIQUE HOTEL $$$

(Map p478; ☑6403 6000; www.naumihotel.com; 41 Seah Street; S$340-400; ❄@🛜🏊; MEsplanade, City Hall) Naumi is dressed so sharply in glass and steel you could get cut just by looking. It balances cool looks with lots of silk, leather and fluffy pillows. The small rooftop infinity pool offers jaw-dropping views across to neighbouring Raffles Hotel.

Fullerton Hotel HOTEL $$$

(Map p478; ☑6733 8388; www.fullertonhotel.com; 1 Fullerton Sq; r incl breakfast from S$515; ❄@🛜🏊; MRaffles Place) Occupying what was once Singapore's magnificent, Palladian-style general post office, the lavish Fullerton offers elegant, conservative rooms, with muted tones and views of the inner atrium, waterfront or skyline. Pool aficionados will swoon

ℹ BOOKING ON THE FLY

If you arrive in Singapore without a hotel booking, the efficient **Singapore Hotel Association** (www.stayin singapore.com.sg) has desks at Changi Airport Terminals 1, 2 and 3. There are dozens of hotels on its lists, starting from S$33 a night. There's no charge for the service, and promotional or discounted rates, when available, are passed on to you. You can also book the hotels on their website.

over the 25m showpiece pool, complete with river and skyline views. Close by, sister property **Fullerton Bay Hotel** (Map p478; ☑6333 8388; www.fullertonbayhotel.com; 80 Collyer Quay; MRaffles Place) serves up flashy bay-facing rooms at similar rates.

Ritz-Carlton Millenia Singapore HOTEL $$$

(Map p478; ☑6337 8888; www.ritzcarlton.com/singapore; 7 Raffles Ave; r from S$912; ❄@🛜🏊; MPromenade) Not every hotel boasts an art collection with works by Warhol, Chihuly and Hockney, but then few hotels match the sophistication of this one. Live it up with obscenely comfortable feather beds and pillows, and marbled bathrooms with skyline views. Service is near-faultless, and culture vultures can enjoy a self-guided audio tour of the superlative in-house art. Check online for discounts of up to 50%.

Fort Canning Hotel BOUTIQUE HOTEL $$$

(Map p478; ☑6559 6770; www.hfcsingapore.com; 11 Canning Walk; s/d incl breakfast from S$350/375; ❄@🛜🏊; MDhoby Ghaut) An absolutely drop-dead gorgeous refit of a colonial complex at the top of Fort Canning Park. Rooms here are the epitome of modern chic, though the open bathroom in some means you'll need to be more than 'just friends' if sharing a room. Deluxe garden rooms have a small but cosy outdoor deck for lounging, and all guests are treated to complimentary drinks between 6pm and 8pm.

Gallery Hotel BOUTIQUE HOTEL $$$

(Map p478; ☑6849 8686; www.galleryhotel.com.sg; 1 Nanson Rd; d incl breakfast from S$320; ❄@🛜🏊; MClarke Quay) The Gallery remains one of Singapore's truly boutique hotels. Sure, guests have to switch elevators on the 4th floor to get to the rooms but knock-down online deals bring you top-end rooms at midrange prices. Its grey fascia is studded with primary-coloured window boxes and rooms feature retro furnishings, steel beams and frosted-glass bathroom walls. The glass rooftop pool and free internet access are bonuses.

Five Stones Hostel HOSTEL $
(Map p478; ☎6535 5607; www.fivestoneshostel.com; 61 South Bridge Rd; dm incl breakfast S$30-37, r incl breakfast S$105-110; ❄@📶; MClarke Quay) Five Stones is an old-school Singaporean game, and it's local cultural references that inspire the bright, funky murals at this upbeat hostel. Perks include comfy orthopedic mattresses in both the dorms and private rooms, modern bathrooms, free breakfast and wi-fi, and an enviable location within walking distance of the Quays, Chinatown, the CBD and the Colonial District.

Marina Bay Sands HOTEL $$$
(☎6688 8897; www.marinabaysands.com; 10 Bayfront Avenue; r S$525; ❄@📶🏊; MBayfront) Part of the ambitious Marina Bay Sands casino/retail complex, the Sands hotel is famed for its amazing rooftop infinity pool, which straddles across the roofs of the three hotel buildings. Hotel rooms are spacious, modern and comfortable, though admittedly cookie-cutter in style. A good choice for casino and mall fans; check online for the best deals. Marina Bay Sands is directly east of the CBD, on the opposite side of Marina Bay.

Robertson Quay Hotel HOTEL $$
(Map p478; ☎6735 3333; www.robertsonquayhotel.com.sg; 15 Merbau Rd; r S$200; ❄@📶🏊; MFort Canning) Probably the best-value hotel along the river, this medieval-castle-like circular tower has immaculate albeit unadventurous rooms with cheesy wallpaper and throwaway wall art, and a surprisingly pretty palm-fringed rooftop swimming pool. Internet discounts of up to 35% are often available.

Ibis Singapore on Bencoolen HOTEL $$
(Map p486; ☎6593 2888; www.ibishotel.com; 170 Bencoolen St; r from S$200; ❄@📶; MBugis) With their clean rooms decked out in pine and orangey hues, LCD TVs, comfy beds and great city views, the Ibis group probably hopes visitors extend their stay to match the length of the hotel's name.

CHINATOWN

TOP CHOICE Wangz BOUTIQUE HOTEL $$$
(☎6595 1388; www.wangzhotel.com; 231 Outram Rd; r S$228-408; ❄@📶; MOutram Park) Another boutique newcomer, curvaceous Wangz sits just west of Chinatown. Its 41 rooms are smart and modern, sexed up with contemporary local art, sublimely comfortable beds, iPod docking stations and sleek bathrooms. Further perks include an in-house gym and a rooftop lounge serving well-mixed drinks.

TOP CHOICE Klapsons BOUTIQUE HOTEL $$$
(Map p482; ☎6521 9000; www.klapsons.com; 15 Hoe Chiang Rd; r from S$290; ❄@📶; MTanjong Pagar) New-kid Klapsons delivers Modernist-inspired luxury and stunning design features (reception is in a steel sphere suspended above a pool of water). Rooms are beautifully textured and individually designed, each with soft goose-down bedding, showpiece showers and a personal Nespresso machine. Refreshingly for an upscale hotel, both the minibar and wi-fi are complimentary.

New Majestic Hotel BOUTIQUE HOTEL $$$
(Map p482; ☎6347 1927; www.newmajestichotel.com; 31-37 Bukit Pasoh Rd; r incl breakfast from S$468; ❄@📶🏊; MOutram Park) Even within Chinatown's burgeoning boutique hotel market, the New Majestic continues to impress. Vintage and designer furniture define the 30 rooms – top choices include the private garden suite, attic rooms with loft beds and 6m-high ceilings, and the fabulous aquarium room with a glass-encased bathtub as its central feature. Discounts can bring rates down to less than S$315.

Club BOUTIQUE HOTEL $$$
(Map p482; ☎6808 2188; www.theclub.com.sg; 28 Ann Siang Rd; r from S$276; ❄@📶; MOutram Park) Behind its crisp colonial-era facade, the Club keeps things svelte and light with 28 spacious, minimalist, white-and-black rooms spiked with coloured mood lighting. A-list in-house hangouts include rooftop bar Ying Yang and designer whiskey bar B28, though most punters seem to prefer mingling at nearby La Terrazza.

Scarlet BOUTIQUE HOTEL $$$
(Map p482; ☎6511 3333; www.thescarlethotel.com; 33 Erskine Rd; r from S$374; ❄@📶; MOutram Park) Despite the sexy marketing, Scarlet's rooms are actually pretty homely – think cottage chic – decorated with soothing wooden furniture, thick drapes and tasteful artwork. Many of them are windowless, but the interiors are far from gloomy thanks to the cheerful decor. The wi-fi in the lobby only reaches some rooms. Discounts of 30% are common.

Hotel 1929
BOUTIQUE HOTEL **$$$**

(Map p482; ☑6347 1929; www.hotel1929.com; 50 Keong Saik Rd; s/d incl breakfast from S$197/290; ✳@⌂; ⓂOutram Park) It's slick, but not quite in the same class as its big brother, the New Majestic. Rooms are tight, but good use is made of limited space, and interiors are cheerily festooned with vintage designer furniture (look out for reproduction Eames and Jacobson) and technicolor mosaics. Terrace suites feature terrace bathtubs, and discounts mean you can snag some rooms for under S$200.

Wink Hostel
HOSTEL **$**

(Map p482; ☑6222 2940; www.winkhostel.com; 8 Mosque Street; s/d pod S$50/90; ✳@⌂; ⓂChinatown) Centrally located in a restored Chinatown shophouse, flashbacker favourite Wink combines hostel and capsule-hotel concepts. Instead of bunks, dorms feature private, soundproof 'pods', each with a comfortable mattress, coloured mood lighting, adjacent locker and enough room to sit up in. Communal bathrooms come with rainforest showerheads, while the in-house kitchenette, laundry and lounge areas crank up the homely factor.

Fernloft
HOSTEL **$**

(Map p482; ☑6323 3221; www.fernloft.com; 2nd fl, 5 Banda St 02-92; dm S$22, r from S$65; ✳@⌂; ⓂChinatown) In a housing block overlooking the Buddha Tooth Relic Temple, this compact branch of the excellent Fernloft hostel chain offers only two private rooms, but they are large and pleasant. The dorm room is clean and tidy, with comfortable wooden-framed beds. Although rooms are windowless, the corner-terrace seating overlooking the green is a lovely spot to hang out.

Pillows & Toast
HOSTEL **$**

(Map p482; ☑6220 4653; 40 Mosque St; dm incl breakfast S$28-39; ✳@⌂; ⓂChinatown) It's dorm beds only at this super friendly, centrally located hostel, but the rooms are bright and clean and come with comfy wooden-framed bunk beds. Common areas are small but treated with TLC.

LITTLE INDIA

TOP CHOICE **Wanderlust**
BOUTIQUE HOTEL **$$**

(Map p486; ☑6396 3322; www.wanderlusthotel.com; 2 Dickson Rd; r incl breakfast from S$232; ✳@⌂; ⓂBugis) Wanderlust is genuinely boutique, with highly imaginative, individually designed rooms – think monochromatic

'Pantone' rooms, comic-book 'Mono' rooms', and 'Whimsical' rooms with themes like 'tree' and 'space'. Extra perks include excellent service, a funky French noshery, not to mention free wi-fi.

Albert Court Village Hotel
HOTEL **$$**

(Map p486; ☑6339 3939; www.stayvillage.com; 180 Albert St; r from S$200; ✳@⌂; ⓂLittle India) This splendid, colonial-era hotel, a short walk south of Little India, offers top-notch service and rooms with all the standard mod cons, including a choice of fan or air-con. The promotional rates go as low as S$150, with the best deals to be had online.

Perak Hotel
HOTEL **$$**

(Map p486; ☑6299 7733; www.peraklodge.net; 12 Perak Rd; r incl breakfast S$150-185; ✳@⌂; ⓂLittle India) Located on a quiet side street in the heart of Little India, this long-time favourite fuses a handsome colonial exterior with a soothing Eastern interior, complete with meditation spaces. Rooms are comfortable and well furnished, staff members are welcoming and helpful, and the rates include free wi-fi.

hangout@mt.emily
HOSTEL **$$**

(Map p490; ☑6438 5588; www.hangouthotels.com; 10A Upper Wilkie Rd; dm/d from S$40/115; ✳@⌂; ⓂLittle India, Dhoby Ghaut) You'll find some of Sinapore's swankiest dorms atop leafy Mount Emily, making this a quiet retreat rather than a central hangout. Pimped with murals by local art students, the vibrant dorms and private rooms are immaculate, as are the bathrooms. It also has a lovely rooftop terrace, free internet and cosy lounging areas. Book online – it's cheaper.

Hive
HOSTEL **$**

(Map p486; ☑6341 5041; www.thehivebackpackers.com; 269A Lavender St; dm incl breakfast S$22-24, s/d/tr incl breakfast from S$40/60/105; ✳@⌂; ⓂBoon Keng) The Hive's friendliness and cleanliness go a long way towards making up for a slightly inconvenient location. Although the dorms lack natural light, they're comfy, and offer a female-only option. The bright, colourful private rooms are excellent value, and there's a pleasant lounge/dining area to boot.

InnCrowd
HOSTEL **$**

(Map p486; ☑6296 9169; www.the-inncrowd.com; 73 Dunlop St; dm/d/tr incl breakfast S$20/59/79; ✳@⌂; ⓂLittle India) As close to a typical backpacker hostel as you'd find in Singapore. Clean accommodation, living areas

STUCK AT THE AIRPORT?

If you're only in Singapore for a short time or have an endless wait between connections, try the **Ambassador Transit Hotel** (☑Terminal 1 6542 5538, Terminal 2 6542 8122, Terminal 3 6507 9788; www.airport-hotel.com.sg; s/d S$76.51/91.81; ☒). Rates quoted are for the first six hours and each additional hour block thereafter is S$16.48; rooms don't have windows and there are budget singles (S$47.08 for 6 hours) with shared bathrooms. The Terminal 1 branch has a sauna, gym and outdoor pool.

The only swish option at Changi Airport is Terminal 3's **Crowne Plaza Hotel** (☑6823 5300; www.cpchangiairport.com; r from S$250; @☎☒). The business-oriented focus shows through its sleek lines, geometric-patterned carpets and (over)use of wood panels.

where travellers like to hang and sweet staff. The atmosphere's decidedly convivial, with free lockers and internet, discounted tickets to sights and cheap Tiger draft beer on tap.

Mayo Inn
HOTEL $$

(Map p486; ☑6295 6631; www.mayoinn.com; 9 Jln Besar; r from S$110; ☒@☎; ⓂBugis) New, spotlessly clean midrange hotel with good-sized, IKEA-fitted rooms and sparkling bathrooms. More expensive rooms come with their own small roof terrace.

Prince of Wales
HOSTEL $

(Map p486; ☑6299 0130; www.pow.com.sg; 101 Dunlop St; dm/d S$20/60; ☒@☎; ⓂLittle India) Australian-style pub and hostel, featuring a spit-and-sawdust live-music pub downstairs and clean, brightly painted dorms and private rooms upstairs. The noise won't suit everyone, but it's a fun place to stay, is very well run and is deservedly popular. The free breakfast includes fresh coffee and fruit as well as the usual buttered toast.

ORCHARD ROAD

Goodwood Park Hotel
HOTEL $$$

(Map p490; ☑6737 7411; www.goodwoodparkhotel. com; 22 Scotts Rd; r from S$328; ☒@☎☒; ⓂOrchard) A venerable slumber spot dating back to 1900, the Goodwood Park is both classic and elegant. Rooms include artful black-and-white photos of Singapore, plush furnishings and tastefully hidden TVs and minibars. While we adore the choice of two swimming pools, we're less than impressed by the S$30 wi-fi fee.

Quincy
BOUTIQUE HOTEL $$$

(Map p490; ☑6738 5888; www.quincy.com.sg; 22 Mount Elizabeth; s/d from S$295/355; ☒@☎☒; ⓂOrchard) Swish, ultramodern rooms come with large double beds and plenty of space. Everything here is included in the price – wi-fi, use of the gym and the glass-enclosed

balcony pool, happy-hour drinks and even a slightly gimmicky three meals a day. (In food-crazy Singapore, who wants to eat three meals a day in a hotel?)

Elizabeth Hotel
HOTEL $$

(Map p490; ☑6885 7888; www.theelizabeth.com. sg; 24 Mt Elizabeth Rd; r from S$160; ☒@☎☒; ⓂOrchard) One of a cluster of three hotels located in a quiet nook off Orchard Rd, the Elizabeth is old but has aged gracefully. Rooms are warm and welcoming, with lots of wooden furniture and soft lighting. Guests can chomp on excellent wood-fired pizzas at in-house Modesto's.

SENTOSA ISLAND

TOP CHOICE / Capella Singapore
RESORT $$$

(Map p499; ☑6591 5000; www.capellahotels.com/ singapore; 1 The Knolls; d S$700; ☒@☎) The Capella Singapore resort is arguably the crème de la crème of Sentosa's, possibly even Singapore's, accommodation options, with majestic whitewashed colonial architecture, lavish pools and gardens, and beautifully appointed rooms, villas and manors.

The Sentosa
RESORT $$$

(Map p499; ☑6275 0331; www.thesentosa.com; 2 Bukit Manis Rd; r S$285-S$525 (breakfast not included); ☒@☎☒) The salubrious five-star Sentosa resort and spa is a low-rise cliff-top belle, replete with contemporary furnishings, the romantic restaurant Cliff (p527), Singapore's only garden spa – Spa Botanica (p512) – and peacocks wandering aimlessly underneath frangipani trees. Check the website for promo deals.

Siloso Beach Resort
RESORT $$$

(Map p499; ☑6722 3333; www.silosobeachresort. com; 51 Imbiah Walk; r incl breakfast from S$230, ste from S$450, villa from S$1000; ☒@☎☒) A sanctuary unto itself, Siloso Beach Resort is designed with lots of ecofriendly touches (the natural spring-fed pool has its own filtration system, gardens on top of buildings lower ambient temperatures and some rooms are built around trees). Rooms are comfortable enough to tempt you into staying in, but the landscaped grounds, 95m-long pool and nearby Siloso Beach will ensure you get your fix of the sun.

✗ Eating

Singapore is an international culinary hotspot. The locals' obsession with all things edible borders on the maniacal and everyone is a self-proclaimed expert on where to find the best *nasi lemak,* chicken-rice or *murtabak.* While cuisines span everything from classic French to Modern Australian, it's the Chinese, Indian, Malay and unique Peranakan (Malay-style sauces with Chinese ingredients) dishes you're really here for. Picky local palates have set high standards across the board, from Michelin-chef hotspots, to dirt-cheap hawker centres and food courts, where memorable bites cost as little as S$3. So be adventurous, join the longest queues, and read what the locals are saying at www.hungrygowhere.com, www.makansutra.com and www.ladyironchef.com.

COLONIAL DISTRICT

TOP CHOICE Jaan FRENCH $$$
(Map p478; ☑9199 9008; www.jaan.com.sg; 2 Stamford Rd, Swissôtel The Stamford; S$238, with wine parings S$398; ☺lunch Mon-Sat, dinner daily; MCity Hall) Perched 70 floors above Singapore, chic, intimate Jaan is home to young-gun French chef Julien Royer and his showstopping Gallic creations; think wild langoustine with fregola sarda, grey chanterelle, rosemary-smoked organic egg and black Périgord truffle. The set 7-course menu is a revelation. Always book ahead, and request a window seat overlooking Marina Bay Sands for a bird's-eye view of the nightly lightshow.

Flutes at the Fort INTERNATIONAL $$$
(Map p478; ☑6338 8770; www.flutes.com.sg; Fort Canning Park, entrance via 23B Coleman St; mains S$38-48; ☺lunch & dinner Mon-Sat, 10am-5pm Sun; MCity Hall) In a 1908 bungalow on the edge of Fort Canning Park, fine-dining Flutes seduces with its lush setting, attentive service and imaginative mod-Oz flavours. If the budget permits, opt for the Chef's Table menu (S$108), whose showstoppers might include melt-in-the-mouth sea scallops with

kataifi prawn roll, micro celery, nori cracker and chill-lime dressing. Book ahead.

Chef Chan's Restaurant CHINESE $$$
(Map p478; www.chefchanrestaurant.com.sg; 93 Stamford Rd, 01-06 National Museum; set menus from S$38; ☺lunch & dinner; MDhoby Ghaut) Eponymous chef, sick of cooking for over 200 people in his large restaurant, closes shop and opens tiny restaurant with nine tables and a daily changing set menu. While we love the antique furnishings, even they pale in comparison to dishes like sauteed scallops with mango and fresh milk, or steamed garoupa fish with black fungus and red dates.

My Humble House CHINESE $$$
(Map p478; ☑6423 1881; www.myhumblehouse.com.sg; 8 Raffles Ave, 02-27, Esplanade Mall; lunch/dinner set menu S$60-80/$100-120; ☑; MCity Hall) Humble is not the first word that comes to mind when you clap eyes on the outlandish decor (designed by Chinese artist Zhang Jin Jie) and set menus with names like 'Someone is Singing Behind the Mountain'. If you're longing for bold dishes like steamed Boston lobster with Hua Diao wine topped with steamed dried scallop and egg, book a table and dress up. There is a dedicated vegetarian menu for herbivore foodies.

Saveur FRENCH $$
(Map p478; www.saveur.sg; 5 Purvis St; mains S$10-24; MEsplanade) It may have sexed up since its *kopitiam* (old-style Chinese coffee shop) days in Katong, but Saveur remains true to democratic prices and contemporary French-inspired brilliance. Snack on the likes of duck rillette with butter bread, then fill up on dishes such as angel-hair pasta with sherry minced pork and sakura ebi, or crispy barramundi with crab potato and French bean. No bookings.

Raffles City INTERNATIONAL $$
(Map p478; www.rafflescity.com.sg; 252 North Bridge Rd; MCity Hall) You'll find several excellent eating options in this mall, most located in the confusing basement warren. **Hand Burger** flips gourmet (albeit small) burgers, **Skinny Pizza** is popular for its gourmet-topped pizzas made with flat cracker bread, punters queue out the door at **Din Tai Fung** for divine *xiao long bao* (soup dumplings), or guzzle German beer and munch on sausages at **Brotzeit**.

Wah Lok CHINESE $$$
(Map p478; ☑6311 8188; 2nd fl, Carlton Hotel, 76 Bras Basah Rd; mains from S$20; MCity Hall, Bras Basah)

A hit with families, long-running Wah Lok peddles seriously fine Peking duck and dim sum. Just leave room for the sublimely flaky *char siew soh* (roast pork pastry) and flavour-packed tofu with broccoli.

Yet Con
CHINESE $

(Map p478; 25 Purvis St; chicken-rice S$5.50; ☺10am-10pm; ⓜCity Hall) There's no designer decor or charm at this septuagenarian restaurant, just unbeatable Hainanese chicken-rice, packed with flavour and served to faithful suits, old-timers and 20-something food nerds. Don't be put off by the crowds – turn over is usually fast.

YY Kafei Dian
CHINESE $

(Map p478; 37 Beach Rd; meals from S$3; ☺7.30am-10.30pm; ⓜEsplanade) Channeling old-school Hainanese eateries with its ceiling fans, linoleum floors, round marble-top tables and wooden chairs, the coffee shop is an all-day staple. Start the day with soft *kaya* (coconut jam) buns, half-boiled eggs (go nuts with the condiments) and a thick, sweet *kopi* (coffee).

Kopitiam
COFFEE SHOP $

(Map p478; www.kopitiam.biz; cnr Bras Basah Rd & Bencoolen St; ☺24hr; ⓜCity Hall, Bras Basah) A top spot in the district for a late-night feed, this branch of the Kopitiam chain is brisk and blindingly bright, so if it's a late, boozy night grab a table outside where the light is more friendly. The food is uniformly good and you won't pay much more than S$6 for a meal.

THE QUAYS

TOP CHOICE Jumbo Seafood
SEAFOOD $$$

(Map p478; ☏6532 3435; www.jumboseafood.com.sg; 30 Merchant Rd, at 01-01/02 Riverside Point; dishes from S$8, chilli crab around S$48 per kg; ⓜClarke Quay) If you're lusting for chilli crab, indulge right here. The gravy is sublimely sweet and nutty, with just the right amount of chilli. Make sure to order some yeasty, fried *man-tou* buns to dip with. While all of Jumbo's outlets have the dish down to an art, this one has the best riverside location. One kilo of crab is enough for two.

Coriander Leaf
FUSION $$$

(Map p478; ☏6732 3354; www.corianderleaf.com; River Valley Rd, 02-03, 3A Merchant Court; mains S$25-40; ☺lunch Mon-Fri, dinner Mon-Sat; ☏; ⓜClarke Quay) Well-executed, cross-cultural experimentation is what you get at this highly regarded bistro. Celebrate world harmony with the likes of lentil tagliatelle with coriander-chilli pesto, pita chips and eggplant ratatouille, or grain-fed Angus ribeye steak with kimchi rice and spicy Asian eggplant.

MARINA BAY

TOP CHOICE Din Tai Fung
TAIWANESE $

(Map p478; www.dintaifung.com.sg; 2 Bayfront Ave, The Shoppes at Marina Bay Sands; ☺buns from S$3.80, dumplings from S$6.80; ⓜBayfront, Marina Bay) Even hype-resistant luminaries such as chef Anthony Bourdain have declared that this chain produces the world's best dumplings (though some insist that only applies to the Taiwanese original on Orchard Rd). The signature *xiao long bao* are nevertheless sublime, the shrimp-pork wanton soup delectable, and the free-flowing jasmine tea appreciated.

DB Bistro Moderne
FRENCH, MEDITERRANEAN $$$

(Map p478; ☏6688 8525; 2 Bayfront Ave, The Shoppes at Marina Bay Sands; 2/3-course set lunch S$42/52, dinner mains S$22-46; ⓜBayfront, Marina Bay) Singaporean outpost of French chef Daniel Boulud, this smart yet relaxed hotspot is the best of Marina Bay Sands' celeb chef eateries. Comfort grub standouts include succulent seafood risotto and a decadent, foie-gras stuffed DB burger. Choose from almost 30 wines by glass, including drops from lesser-known boutique wineries. Book ahead if dining Thursday to Sunday.

Pizzeria Mozza
ITALIAN $$$

(Map p478; www.pizzeriamozza.com; 2 Bayfront Ave, The Shoppes at Marina Bay Sands; pizzas S$18-37, mains S$25-36; ⓜBayfront, Marina Bay) This dough-kneading winner is co-owned by New York culinary superstar Mario Batali. It's also one of the few celebrity eateries at Marina Bay Sands that won't have you mortgaging your house. While both the antipasti and pasta dishes are solid, the star turn is the wood-fired pizzas, famed for their addictive, crispy crust.

CHINATOWN & THE CBD

TOP CHOICE Blue Ginger
PERANAKAN $$

(Map p482; ☏6222 3928; www.theblueginger.com; 97 Tanjong Pagar Rd; mains S$10-30; ⓜTanjong Pagar) A perennial favourite, famed for its beautifully cooked Peranakan food, a unique cuisine fusing Chinese and Malay influences. Savour rich, spicy, sour flavours in Blue Ginger's signature *ayam panggang* (grilled chicken in coconut and spices). Other winners include the soulful *bakwan kepiting* (minced pork and crabmeat ball soup) and *sambal terong goreng* (spicy fried eggplant). Bookings recommended.

TOP CHOICE **Maxwell Rd Hawker Centre** HAWKER $
(Map p482; cnr Maxwell Rd & South Bridge Rd; ⊙individual stalls vary; ⊘; MChinatown) One of Chinatown's most accessible hawker centres, Maxwell Rd is a user-friendly spot to chomp and slurp on Singapore street-food classics. While stalls slip in and out of favour with fickle Singaporeans, enduring favourites include **Tian Tian Hainanese Chicken Rice** (Stall 10; chicken rice S$3; ⊙11am-8pm Tue-Sun), **Maxwell Fuzhou Oyster Cake** (Stall 5; oyster cake S$1.50; ⊙9.30am-8.30pm Mon-Sat), and **Fried Sweet Potato Dumpling** (Stall 76; snacks from S$0.50; ⊙1-8pm Wed-Mon).

Esquina TAPAS $$
(Map p482; www.esquina.com.sg; 16 Jiak Chuan Rd; dishes S$12-24.50; ⊙lunch Mon-Fri, dinner Mon-Sat; MOutram Park) Co-owned by UK Michelin-starred chef Jason Atherton, Esquina has tongues wagging with its classic-with-a-twist Spanish morsels. Scan the paper placemat menu for standouts like the palate-shaking, wasabi-spiked scallops with ceviche and radish salsa, or melt-in-your-mouth Iberico pork and foie gras sliders, best devoured at the stainless steel bar while swilling a sherry and chatting to the chefs. No reservations.

Chinatown Complex HAWKER $
(Map p482; 11 New Bridge Rd; ⊙individual stalls vary; MChinatown) Standouts at this labyrinthine hawker centre include **Lian He Ben Ji Claypot** (Stall 02-082; claypot dishes from S$5; ⊙4-10.30pm Fri-Wed) and **Xiu Ji Ikan Bilis Yong Tau Foo** (Stall 02-87/88; dishes S$2-4; ⊙5.45am-3pm). The latter is famed for its dry *bee hoon* (vermicelli noodles), topped with *ikan bilis* (dried anchovies) and accompanied by a bowl of *yong taufoo* (consomme). Optional add-ins include homemade fishcakes and tofu.

Latteria Mozzarella Bar ITALIAN $$
(Map p482; ⊘6866 1988; www.latteriamb.com; 40 Duxton Hill; mains S$25-35; MTanjong Pagar) While we adore the leafy alfresco deck, the draw here is the silky mozzarella. From *burrata* (cream-filled mozzarella) to *affumicata* (smoked), its many variations are flown in from Italy twice weekly to star in modern classic dishes like *stracciatella* with eggplant caponata and pine nuts.

Cumi Bali INDONESIAN $$
(Map p482; www.cumibali.com; 66 Tanjong Pagar Rd; dishes S$6.50-28; ⊙closed Sun; MTanjong Pagar) Lo-fi decor meets mouthwatering Indonesian grub at this unsung gem. Tuck into delicate nasi goreng (opt for the lamb, not the chicken), grilled-to-perfection *sate madura* (a Javanese-style chicken satay), and the restaurant's namesake dish, consisting of grilled squid in a luscious spicy paste.

Peach Garden CHINESE $$$
(Map p478; ⊘6535 7833; www.peachgarden.com.sg; Level 33, OCBC Centre, 65 Chulia St; set menu from S$38; MRaffles Place) For a Chinese restaurant with a view, it's tough to beat this one. The food and service are immaculate too. Try to reserve a window table well in advance and tuck into superb dim sum, or equally sublime dishes like double-boiled chicken soup with sea whelk and fish maw, or stewed noodle with shredded pork, black fungus and bean paste.

Ya Kun Kaya Toast COFFEE SHOP $
(Map p482; www.yakun.com; 01-01 Far East Sq, 18 China St; kaya toast set S$4; ⊙7.30am-6.30pm Mon-Fri, 8.30am-5pm Sat & Sun; MChinatown, Raffles Place) A chain of Ya Kun outlets has mushroomed across Singapore, but this one, with terrace seating alongside it, is the most atmospheric and the closest geographically to the 1944 original. Perfect for breakfast, the speciality is *kaya* toast served with runny eggs (sprinkle them with black pepper like the locals do) and strong coffee.

Ci Yan Organic Vegetarian Health Food VEGETARIAN $
(Map p482; 2 Smith St; mains S$5-8; ⊙noon-10pm; ⊘; MChinatown) Friendly Ci Yan peddles organic, flesh-free dishes in the heart of Chinatown. Scan the blackboard for the day's small selection of offerings, which might include golden curry puffs, durian swiss rolls, or wholemeal hamburgers. Our favourite is the brown-rice set menu, which comes with soul-coaxing Chinese vegetables and stew.

Da Dong Restaurant CHINESE $$
(Map p482; ⊘6221 3822; 39 Smith St; yum cha S$2.80-4.80, mains from S$12; ⊙11am-11pm Mon-Fri, 9am-11pm Sat & Sun; MChinatown) One of Chinatown's longest lasting restaurants first opened its doors in 1928. These days, it still serves up some of the best dim sum in town. Longevity hasn't equated to great service, but *char siew* (barbecue pork) buns this good, who cares?

Tong Heng BAKERY $
(Map p482; 285 South Bridge Rd; snacks from S$1; ⊙9am-10pm; MChinatown) Hit the spot at this veteran pastry shop, locally revered for its melt-in-your-mouth egg tarts. Just leave

WORTH A TRIP

OFF THE RADAR HAWKER HIGHS

Chicken-rice and oyster cake at Maxwell Rd Hawker Centre: check. *Bee hoon* at Chinatown Complex: check. *Murtabak* at Tekka Centre: check. Once you've ploughed through Singapore's central hawker centres, head further out to where the real street-food geeks click their sticks.

Chomp Chomp Food Centre (20 Kensington Park Rd; ⊙stalls vary; ☐73, ☑Toa Payoh) Despite its privileged status as (arguably) Singapore's best hawker centre, this evening option in Serangoon Gardens gives off a chilled, convivial vibe, with packs of young Singaporeans gossiping happily over giant jugs of sugar cane juice each night. Eavesdrop over tender, juicy barbecue stingray from **Chomp Chomp Hai Wei Yuan Seafood BBQ** (Stall 1; stingray from S$10; ⊙5pm-midnight Tue-Sun), where stock-standard sweet chilli sauce is ditched for a zestier Melakan-style chinchalok sauce, made with fermented shrimp or krill. Leave room for moreish carrot cake from the **Carrot Cake Stall** (Stall 36; cakes from S$2; ⊙5.30pm-midnight, closed alternative Tues), and prawn Hokkien noodles from **Ah Hock Fried Hokkien Noodle** (Stall 27; dishes from S$3; ⊙5-11pm daily).

Old Airport Rd Food Centre (Map p492; Block 51 Old Airport Rd; ⊙10am-late; ☑Mountbatten) You'll find a few more out-of-towners here than at Chomp Chomp, but the grub is no less authentic. The Hokkien fried mee (noodles) at **Na Sing Hokkien Fried Mee** (Stall 01-32; dishes from S$3; ⊙11am-7pm) are obligatory, while other winners include sweet'n'savoury rojak (salad of pineapple, cucumber, you tiao, turnip, crushed peanuts and homemade Rojak sauce) from **Toa Payoh Rojak** (Stall 01-108; dishes from S$3; ⊙noon-8pm Mon-Sat), and cooked-on-the-spot sweet potato porridge from **Lau Pa Sat Taiwan Porridge** (Stall 01-167; dishes from S$4; ⊙4.30-11.30pm Tue-Sun).

room for the slightly charred perfection of the *char siew su* (barbecue pork puff). Oh, and did we mention the sublime coconut tarts?

EAST COAST

TOP CHOICE **Maeda** JAPANESE **$$$**
(Map p492; ☑6345 0745; 467 Joo Chiat Rd; dishes from S$10; ⊙dinner Tue-Sun; ☐16) Superlatives fail to describe the authentic Osaka-style cuisine served up by owner and chef Maeda Hiroaki. Sweet, fresh sashimi is dotted with chrysanthemum flowers, and the menu features rare dishes like squid guts. Maeda works the sushi counter and is more than happy to down some sake with you. Can't decide what to order? Opt for the *omakase* menu (S$90 to S$150). Bookings recommended.

TOP CHOICE **Kim's Place Seafood** SEAFOOD **$$**
(Map p492; www.kims.com.sg; 37 Joo Chiat Place; mains S$4-30; ⊙11am-2.30am; ☐16, 33, ☑Eunos) Make time for a little feasting at heirloom Kim's Place Seafood. Must-trys include the insanely flavoursome, sticky-sweet black pepper crab in claypot, the Hokkien mee, and the refreshing lemongrass jelly with lemon sorbet. Tip: go for the Sri Lankan crabs, which are fleshier than their Indonesian counterparts.

East Coast Seafood Centre SEAFOOD **$$$**
(Map p492; 1202 East Coast Parkway; mains S$15-75; ⊙dinner; ☐48, 196) Overlooking the Straits of Singapore in the salty breeze, this renowned seafood centre boasts several excellent restaurants, all with outdoor seating. Don't miss the chilli crab, black-pepper crab and the intoxicating 'drunken' prawns. Best of the lot is **Long Beach** (www.longbeachseafood.com.sg; dishes S$26-80; ⊙lunch & dinner).

Sik Wai Sin Eating House CHINESE **$$**
(Map p492; 287 Geylang Rd; mains S$17-25; ⊙lunch & dinner daily; ☑Kallang) Geylang is famous for its gut-rumbling food peddlers, and hot, loud, Cantonese Sik Wai Sin Eating House is living proof. Cult favourites include homemade tofu fried with giant prawns in egg sauce, double-boiled herbal soup, pork ribs with bitter gourd and the signature steamed grass carp head in bean sauce.

East Coast Lagoon Food Village HAWKER **$**
(Map p492; 1220 East Coast Parkway; dishes from S$3; ⊙8am-9pm; ☐48, 196) There are few hawker centres with a better location. Tramp barefoot off the beach and order up some satay, seafood, or the uniquely Singaporean satay *bee hoon* from Meng Kee at stall 17. Expect to queue. Cheap beer and wine (!) are available.

328 Katong Laksa
PERANAKAN $

(Map p492; 53 East Coast Rd; laksa from S$4; ⊙8am-10pm; ☐10, 14) Several laksa stalls along this stretch have long been bickering over who was first and best. They're all delicious, but this one is the most loved. The namesake dish is a bowl of rice noodles in a light curry broth made with coconut milk and Vietnamese coriander, and topped with shrimp and cockles. Order a side of *otah-otah* (spiced mackerel cake grilled in a banana leaf).

Guan Hoe Soon
PERANAKAN $$

(Map p492; 38 Joo Chiat Pl; mains from $12; ☐16, 33, ⓂEunos) Famously, this is Singapore's oldest Peranakan restaurant (established 1953) and Lee Kuan Yew's favourite, but even boasts like that don't cut much ice with picky Singaporeans if the food doesn't match up. Fortunately, its fame hasn't inspired complacency and the Nonya food here is top notch. The definitive Peranakan *ayam buah keluak* (chicken with black nut) is a standout.

Seng Kee Black Chicken Herbal Soup
CHINESE $

(Map p492; 467 Changi Rd; dishes from S$6; ⊙5pm-4am; ⓂKembangan) Hot tropical nights, buzzing crowds and oh-so-good Chinese-Malay street food collide at Seng Kee, the best of a row of alfresco street-food joints just east of Katong. Hunt down a plastic table and get dirty over fruity Penang-style rojak; homemade bean curd with chicken floss; signature sesame oil chicken and their equally famous *qi*-soothing black chicken herbal soup.

Djanoer Koening
INDONESIAN $

(Map p492; 191 Joo Chiat Rd; mains S$6-9.50; ⊙11am-9.30pm; ☐16) Simply decorated with Javanese water puppets, this casual, lo-fi nosh spot cooks up homely, soulful Javanese dishes. Gems include a wonderfully fragrant *bakso urat* (Indonesian soup with beef balls, noodles, spinach and fried bean curd) and a smoky, sticky bebek goreng/bakar sambal dewa (fried/grilled duck with chilli). Service is friendly and casual.

Changi Village Hawker Centre
HAWKER CENTRE $

(2 Changi Village Rd; dishes from S$3; ⊙10.30am-11.30pm; ☐2, Tanah Merah) Row after row of stalls offering a plethora of food might bewilder most. But there's only one thing the locals come here for – the *nasi lemak*. Fragrant coconut rice is topped with fried chicken or fish, *ikan bilis* (fried anchovies) and sambal chilli. The original stall at 01-57 has spawned neighbouring imitators if you can't be bothered queuing.

Rochor Beancurd
SWEETS $

(Map p492; 745 Geylang Rd; ⊙24hr; ⓂPaya Lebar) End on a sweet note at Rochor Beancurd, a tiny bolthole with an epic reputation. People head here from all over the city for a bowl of their obscenely fresh, silky beancurd (opt for it warm). Order a side of dough sticks and dip to your heart's content. Oh, did we mention the delicious egg tarts?

Chin Mee Chin Confectionery
BREAKFAST, BAKERY $

(Map p492; 204 East Coast Rd; dishes from S$4; ⊙8am-4pm Tue-Sun; ☐10, 14, 16) *Kaya* (jam made from coconut and egg) toast like grandma used to make. A nostalgia trip for many older Singaporeans, old-style bakeries like Chin Mee Chin are a dying breed, with their mosaic floors, wooden chairs and strong coffee. One of the few Singaporean breakfast joints that still makes its own *kaya*, apparently.

DEMPSEY ROAD & HOLLAND VILLAGE

ⓉOP CHOICE Au Jardin Les Amis
FRENCH $$$

(☑6466 8812; www.lesamis.com.sg; Cluny Rd, EJH Corner House, Singapore Botanic Gardens; set dinner menus from S$200; ⊙dinner daily, lunch Fri, brunch 11.30am-1.30pm Sun; ⓂBotanic Gardens) If you plan on seducing someone, look no further – think romantic colonial-era bungalow, Botanic Gardens backdrop, and decadent French fare. Style up, forget the bill and steal a kiss from your sweetheart in the gardens afterwards. Daily dinner aside, there's a lunchtime sitting on Fridays (2/3 courses S$58/70) and a Sunday brunch (S$88). Book ahead.

Halia
FUSION $$$

(☑6476 6711; www.halia.com.sg; Singapore Botanic Gardens, 1 Cluny Rd; mains S$40-86; ☑; ⓂBotanic Gardens) Beautifully nestled among ginger plants in the botanic gardens, Halia serves inspired fusion fare like pan-seared and crème brulee foie gras, caramelised fig and ice-wine jelly. Book a table on the verandah for a perfect romantic dinner, or savour and save with the good value set lunch (2/3 courses S$28/32) Monday to Friday.

Miao Yi Vegetarian Restaurant
VEGETARIAN $$

(☑6467 1331; 03-01/02, Coronation Shopping Plaza, 587 Bukit Timah Rd; dishes S$5-15; 🛜☑;

Botanic Gardens) Even carnivores can expect a little finger licking at this hidden gem, tucked away inside a dated suburban mall. The dishes practically sing with flavour, from the wonderfully textured spicy 'prawn' (crumbed soy with basil leaves, chilli and cashew nuts) to the legendary suckling 'pig', served with a moreish sweet soy sauce. Book ahead on weekends.

Da Paolo Pizza Bar   ITALIAN $$

(www.dapaolo.com.sg; 44 Jln Merah Saga; pizzas S$18-29; ⊙lunch & dinner Mon-Fri, 9am-10.30pm Sat & Sun; ✐; ⓂHolland Village) One of three Da Paolo outlets on the street – the fine-dining restaurant is next door and the gourmet deli at No 43 – this svelte bistro peddles bubbly, thin-crust pizzas that would make Italy proud. Dough aside, offerings include salads, salumi, cheeses, and an Italo-centric wine list. Weekend breakfast options include piadinas, eggs and pancakes.

Jones the Grocer   CAFE, DELI $$

(www.jonesthegrocer.com; Dempsey Rd, Block 9; breakfast S$6.50-20, mains S$13.50-28; ⊙9am-11pm Sun-Thu, to midnight Fri & Sat; ☎; ☐7, 75, 77, 106, 123, 174) Posh-nosh grocer Jones is the darling of the expat set. Scan the shelves for gourmet foodstuffs and wine, raid the fromagerie for artisan cheeses, or kick back with A-grade coffee, breakfast, salads, sandwiches, tapas, or heartier fare like organic beef burgers with Australian Tarago River blue cheese. Head in before 9.30am on weekends to avoid the breakfast queues.

Casa Verde   INTERNATIONAL $$

(Map p490; www.lesamis.com.sg; Singapore Botanic Gardens, 1 Cluny Road; lunch $9-18, dinner mains $25-30, pizzas S$21-25; ⊙7.30am-9.30pm; ✎; ⓂBotanic Gardens) The most accessible and family-friendly restaurant in the Botanic Gardens, 'Green House' serves up satisfying Western grub – pasta, salads, sandwiches – plus scrumptious wood-fired pizzas and a smattering of local dishes. Mercifully, the alfresco dining area comes with cooling fans for sweat-free noshing.

Samy's Curry Restaurant   INDIAN $

(www.samyscurry.com; Civil Service Club, Block 25, Dempsey Rd; mains S$6-10; ⊙closed Tue; ✐; ☐7, 77, 106, 123, 174) For over 30 years, the ceiling fans spun above the banana leaves in this leafy, open-walled, timber-shuttered colonial throwback. Alas the timber shutters have gone, but the food remains magnificent and the vibe one of the least pretentious in the

neighbourhood. Do not go past the fragrant fish head curry.

Daily Scoop   ICE CREAM $

(www.thedailyscoop.com.sg; 43 Jln Merah Saga; ice cream from S$2; ⊙11am-10pm Mon-Thu, to 10.30pm Fri & Sat, 2-10pm Sun; ⓂHolland Village) Daily Scoop keeps the magic alive with over 40 creative flavours of hand-churned ice cream. Lickable options include brandied figs and honey, strawberry shortcake, and lychee martini (that's right, vodka-infused ice cream). And it doesn't end there, with milkshakes, waffles and there-goes-the-diet brownies.

Holland Village Market & Food Centre   HAWKER $

(Lor Mambong; dishes from S$2; ⊙10am-late; ⓂHolland Village) Despite the signboard outside telling foreigners how to navigate hawker centres and describing different dishes, few venture from the pricier restaurants across the road. Break free and sample some street food classics, from barbecue seafood and Katong laksa to fried *kway teow* (rice noodles).

KAMPONG GLAM

⭐ Warong Nasi Pariaman   MALAY, INDONESIAN $

(Map p486; ☎6292 2374; 738 North Bridge Rd; dishes S$2.60-4.60; ⊙7.30am-2.30pm Mon-Sat; ⓂBugis) With fans including former Malaysian prime minister Dr Mahathir Mohamad, this threadbare nasi padang stall is the stuff of legends. Don't miss the *belado* (fried mackerel in a slow-cooked chilli, onion and vinegar sauce), delicate beef rendang or *ayam bakar* (grilled chicken with coconut sauce). Get here by 11am to avoid the hordes, and be warned... it mostly sells out by 1pm.

Nan Hwa Chong Fish-Head Steamboat Corner   CHINESE $$

(Map p486; 812-816 North Bridge Rd; fish-head steamboats from S$18; ⊙4.30pm-12.30am; ⓂLavender) If you only try fish-head steamboat once, you'd do well to make it at this hawker-style legend. The fish head is brought to you in the steaming broth of a large conical-shaped pot and is then shared by everyone at the table. One is enough for three or four people, and can stretch to more with rice and side dishes. There are four types of fish to choose from – go for the fleshier red snapper (S$20).

Zam Zam   MALAY $

(Map p486; 699 North Bridge Rd; dishes S$5-8; ⊙8am-11pm; ⓂBugis) Mention Zam Zam to any verified Singaporean foodie and watch their eyes light up: here since 1908, this unadorned, tout-fronted dive serves up incredibly good *murtabak* (stuffed savoury pancake). Filled with succulent mutton, beef, chicken or venison, they're crisp and golden, yet never greasy. Servings are epic, so opt for one between two people if you're not especially hungry.

Kilo   FUSION $$$
(☑6467 3987; www.kilokitchen.com; 66 Kampong Bugis; mains $21-38; ☺dinner Mon-Sat; MLavender) While its location might be slightly off the radar – the second floor of an industrial riverside building – gastro geeks know exactly how to reach this 'it kid'. Radiating a simple, contemporary, dinner-club vibe, it's famed for brilliant, Italo-Japanese creations like unagi and teriyaki linguine. Simplify life by taking a taxi to the restaurant.

QS269 Food House   HAWKER $
(Map p486; Block 269b Queen St; ☺8am-5pm Sat-Thu; MBugis) This 'food house' is actually an undercover laneway jammed with superlative street-food stalls. Work up a sweat with award-winning coconut curry noodle soup from **Ah Heng Curry Chicken Bee Hoon Mee** (dishes from S$3.50; ☺8am-5pm Sat-Thu), or join the queue for succulent roast duck at the equally revered **New Rong Liang Ge Cantonese Roast Duck Boiled Soup** (dishes from S$3; ☺9am-8pm).

Café Le Caire   MIDDLE EASTERN $$
(Map p486; www.cafelecaire.com; 33 Arab St; dishes S$4-22; ☺10am-3.30am; ☑; MBugis) Join lounging shisha-smokers and eager diners for creamy hummus, olives, felafel, pita, salads and succulent kebabs, served as mains or side-dish snacks. To soak up the vibe at its best, head in on a weekend evening.

LITTLE INDIA

Shish Mahal   INDIAN $$
(Map p486; www.shishmahal.com.sg; 01-20, Albert Court Hotel & Mall, 180 Albert St; mains S$7-17.90; ☺11.30am-11.30pm; ☑; MLittle India) Although just south of Little India, Shish Mahal channels the flavours of northern India and Nepal like few others. From the delicate *momo* (chicken- or vegetable-filled dumplings with coriander) to the slightly smoky, cardamom-spiked *mahal ka makhanwala* chicken, dishes are lively and complex, but never overbearing.

Tekka Centre   HAWKER $
(Map p486; cnr Serangoon & Buffalo Rds; dishes S$3-5; ☺7am-11pm; ☑; MLittle India) Queue up for biryani, mutton curries, roti prata and *teh tarik* (pulled tea) at Little India's most famous hawker hangout. Foodies flock to the legendary **Ah-Rahman Royal Prata** (Map p486; stall 01-248; murtabak S$4-5; ☺7am-10pm), whose *murtabak* are so incredibly good that even Singapore's president is a fan. If you're undecided, go for the chicken *murtabak* with cheese.

Bismillah Biryani   INDIAN $
(Map p486; 50 Dunlop St; kebabs from S$4, biryani from S$6; ☺noon-8pm; MLittle India) Head here for Singapore's best biryani. While the mutton biryani is the speciality – and it *is* special – even that is surpassed by the mutton sheekh kebab, which is a melt-in-the-mouth revelation. Just don't leave it too late in the day to get here. Most of the best stuff is history before 8pm.

Sankranti   INDIAN $
(Map p486; 100 Sayed Alwi Rd; mains from S$8; ☺11.30am-4pm & 6pm-midnight; MLittle India) Specialising in food from the south Indian state of Andhra Pradesh, this is arguably the best of a cluster of good restaurants in and around Little India's 24-hour shopping hub, the Mustafa Centre. The extensive menu includes a number of north Indian dishes too, and has a lip-smacking choice of set-meal thalis, the pick of the bunch being the Sankranti Special, a 10-piece culinary extravaganza.

Ananda Bhavan   INDIAN, VEGETARIAN $
(Map p486; Block 663, 01-10 Buffalo Rd; dishes S$3-5; ☺6.30am-10.30pm; ☑; MLittle India) This super-cheap chain restaurant is a top spot to sample south Indian breakfast staples like *idly* and *dosa* (spelt 'thosai' on the menu). It also does great-value thali, some of which are served on banana leaves. You'll find other Little India outlets at 58 Serangoon Rd and 95 Syed Alwi Rd; there's also an outlet at Changi Airport's Terminal 2.

Moghul Sweet Shop   SWEETS $
(Map p486; 48 Serangoon Rd; sweets from S$1; ☺11am-11pm; MLittle India) If you're after a sub-continental sugar rush, tiny Moghul is the place to get it. Sink your teeth into luscious *gulab jamun* (syrup-soaked fried dough balls), harder-to-find *rasmalai* (paneer cheese soaked in cardamom-infused clotted cream) and *barfi* (condensed milk and sugar slice) in flavours including pistachio, chocolate...and carrot.

ORCHARD ROAD

Burrow into most Orchard Rd malls and you'll find great-value food courts.

TOP CHOICE Iggy's
INTERNATIONAL $$$

(Map p490; ☑6732 2234; www.iggys.com.sg; 581 Orchard Rd, Level 3, Hilton Hotel; lunch S$85, dinner S$195-275; ☺lunch Mon-Fri, dinner Mon-Sat; ☑; MOrchard) What is arguably Singapore's best restaurant is now housed at the Hilton Hotel after a long run at the Regent. The setting is swankier here, and the food as incredible as it always was: Japanese and European sensibilities meshed together in a tasting menu of epic proportions (eight courses for dinner!). The wine list is as impressive as it is extensive and there is a dedicated vegetarian tasting menu. Book ahead.

Takashimaya Food Village
FOOD COURT $

(Map p490; B2, Takashimaya Department Store, Ngee Ann City, 391 Orchard Rd; snacks from S$1; ☺10am-9.30pm; MOrchard) Roam and salivate at Takashimaya's basement food hall, a slick, sprawling sea of stalls serving up Japanese, Korean and other Asian culinary classics. Look out for *soon kueh* – steamed dumplings stuffed with bamboo shoots, bangkwang (a root vegetable), dried mushroom, carrot and dried prawn – and do *not* pass on a fragrant bowl of noodles from the Tsurukoshi stand.

Food Republic
FOOD COURT $

(Map p490; Level 4, Wisma Atria Shopping Centre, 435 Orchard Rd; dishes from S$3; ☺8am-10pm Mon-Thu, to 11pm Fri-Sun; MOrchard) It's survival of the quickest when it comes to grabbing a table at peak times, but the mix of hawker classics, Thai, Japanese and Indian grub is well worth it. Stake a seat before joining the longest queues. Roving 'aunties' push around trolleys filled with drinks and dim sum, while the Waan Waan Thai stall does a seriously fine chilli-laced mango salad.

Din Tai Fung
TAIWANESE $

(Map p490; www.dintaifung.com.sg; B1-03/06, Paragon Shopping Centre, 290 Orchard Rd; buns from S$3.80, dumplings from S$6.80; MOrchard) This is one of three Din Tai Fung outlets on Orchard Rd; you'll find the other two inside the Wisma Atria and 313 Somerset shopping malls. The chain is famous for its exquisite *xiao long bao* (soup dumplings),

Bombay Woodlands
INDIAN, VEGETARIAN $$

(Map p490; B1-01/02, Tanglin Shopping Centre, 19 Tanglin Rd; mains from S$9; ☺10am-3pm & 6-10pm Mon-Fri, 10am-10pm Sat & Sun; ☑; MOrchard) You'll find Bombay Woodlands – still one of the hidden gems of the Orchard area – below street level in the Tanglin Shopping Centre. The food is magnificent and cheap for this end of town: opt for the bottomless lunchtime buffet or order à la carte for south Indian classics like *idly* (spongy, fermented rice cake) or dosa (paper-thin lentil-flour pancake), washed down with a cooling *lassi* (icy yoghurt drink).

Wasabi Tei
JAPANESE $$

(Map p490; 05-70 Far East Plaza, 14 Scotts Rd; meals S$10-30; ☺closed Sun; MOrchard) Channelling 1972 with its Laminex countertop and Brady Bunch wall panels, this pocked-sized sushi joint feels like a secret hideout. Stake a spot at the counter and watch the Chinese chef prove that you don't have to be Japanese to make raw fish sing with flavour. Choose carefully as post-order amendments are a no no.

Killiney Kopitiam
COFFEE SHOP $

(Map p490; 67 Killiney Rd; mains S$4-6; ☺6am-11pm Mon & Wed-Sat, to 9pm Tue & Sun; MSomerset) This old school coffee joint, decked out in white wall tiles, fluorescent lights and endearingly lame laminated jokes, is a solid spot to tuck into a Singaporean breakfast of toast, soft-boiled eggs and sucker-punch coffee. Post-breakfast, devour 'just-like-auntie's' chicken curry, laksa and *nasi lemak* (coconut rice, dried anchovies and spices wrapped in banana leaf), topped off with a sweet-dumpling dessert.

Nagomi
JAPANESE $$$

(Map p490; ☑6732 4300; www.nagomirestaurant.com.sg; 02-22 Cuppage Plaza, 5 Keok Rd; meals S$40-80; ☺dinner Mon-Sat; MSomerset) Plush, elegant Nagomi pairs sublime sakes with obscenely fresh, delicate Japanese nosh. Ingredients are flown in from Japan four times a week, and meals are prepared *omakase*, meaning that menus are ditched for the chef's seasonal specialities. Prepare to be transported.

Wild Honey
CAFE $$

(Map p490; www.wildhoney.com.sg; Lvl 3, Scotts Sq, 6 Scotts Rd; breakfast S$12-24; ☺9am-9pm; ☑; MOrchard) Located in the fashion-conscious Scotts Square shopping centre, trendy Wild Honey peddles scrumptious, all-day breakfast from around the world, from the tofu-laced (Californian) to the shaksouka-spiced (Tunisian). Other options include fresh muffins and cakes, gourmet sandwiches and rich roasted coffee. The smaller, original branch is in the Mandarin Gallery shopping centre on nearby Orchard Rd.

SENTOSA ISLAND

TOP CHOICE **Cliff** SEAFOOD $$$
(Map p499; ☎6371 1425; www.thecliff.sg; Sentosa Resort, 2 Bukit Manis Rd; mains S$56-125; ☼dinner) Perched high above Palawan Beach (although tree cover obscures some of the view), chi-chi Cliff serves up sublime seafood to a soundtrack of jazz, crickets and rustling leaves. Expect scallops to be paired with apples, tartare with watermelon, and barramundi with prosciutto 'floss'. If you're indecisive, opt for the four-course set menu (S$130).

Malaysian Food Street HAWKER $
(Map p499; www.rwsentosa.com; Resorts World; dishes from S$4; ☼11am-10pm) With its faux Malaysian streetscape, this indoor hawker centre does feel a bit Disney. Thankfully, there's nothing fake about the food itself, cooked by some of Malaysia's best hawker vendors. Taste-test Singapore's northern neighbour with classics like *char koay teow* (stir-fried flat rice noodles with chilli, belachan, prawns and cockles) and *yong tau foo* (consomme with fried tofu, bitter gourd and vegetables).

Coastes INTERNATIONAL $$
(Map p499; www.coastes.com; Siloso Beach; sandwiches & burgers S$16-20; ☼10am-10pm Mon-Thu, 11am-1am Fri & Sat, 9am-10pm Sun) Coastes is the best of the Sentosa Beach eateries, serving up excellent pizzas, pasta and curries to a relaxed crowd. Grab a rustic table under the pergola, or look louche on the sun loungers. It's not exclusively for the hip, tanned and beautiful, as the thumping music suggests.

Drinking

Singapore's bar scene is a kicking mix of designer rooftop lounges and cocktail dens, Euro-centric wine bars, microbreweries and hipster-approved coffee roasters. Popular drinking hubs include Boat Quay and Clarke Quay, Chinatown's trendy Club St, Ann Siang Hill and Duxton Hill precincts, sheesha-scented Kampong Glam, heritage-listed Emerald Hill Rd, and ex-pat hangouts Dempsey Hill and Holland Village.

Despite Singapore's high-priced drinks (expect to pay S$10 to S$18 for a beer in most city bars), there are ways to sip and save. Hit the bars early to cash in on happy hours, typically stretching from 5pm to 8pm and offering two-for-one drinks. On Wednesday or Thursday nights, some bars offer cheap (sometimes free) drinks for women – a common practice in Singapore, without the stench of sleaze. If you really need to scrimp and don't mind plastic tables and fluoro lights, bottles of Tiger will set you back S$6 at hawker centres and coffee shops.

Unless otherwise stated, bars open around 5pm until at least midnight Sunday to Thursday, and through to 2am or 3am on Friday and Saturday.

COLONIAL DISTRICT

New Asia BAR
(Map p478; Swissôtel The Stamford, 2 Stamford Rd; ☼3pm-1am Sun-Tue, to 2am Wed & Thu, to 3am Fri & Sat; ⓜCity Hall) Martinis demand dizzying skyline views and few deliver like this sleek bar-club hybrid, perched 71 floors above street level. Style up and head in early to watch the sun sink, then strike a pose on the dance floor. The S$25 cover charge on Friday and Saturday includes one drink... but with views like these, who's counting?

Loof BAR
(Map p478; www.loof.com.sg; 03-07 Odeon Towers Building, 331 North Bridge Rd; ⓜCity Hall) Rooftop Loof cheekily gets its name from the Singlish mangling of the word 'roof'. Up here, City Hall district views are paired with smooth tunes, retro-Asian bar snacks, and regionally inspired libations - think Ho Chi Mint (pear juice, vodka, mint and cucumber) and Java Ginger Crush (ginger beer, fresh ginger and Canton ginger liqueur).

Raffles Hotel BAR
(Map p478; www.raffles.com; 1 Beach Rd; ⓜCity Hall) Yup, it's a cliché, but still, few visit Singapore without at least stopping off for drinks at one of the bars in the famous Raffles Hotel. Ditch the **Long Bar** (☼11-12.30am Sun-Thu, 11-1.30am-1am Fri & Sat) and its overpriced Singapore Slings and chill out Raj-style at the much more appealing **Bar & Billiard Room** (☎6412 1816; ☼11am-midnight Tue-Sat). Alternatively, rehydrate below rattling palms at the **Raffles Courtyard bar** (☼11am-10.30pm).

Paulaner Bräuhaus BREWERY
(Map p478; www.paulaner.com.sg; 01-01 Times Square, Millenia Walk, 9 Raffles Blvd; ☼noon-1am Sun-Thu, to 2am Fri & Sat; ⓜCity Hall, Promenade) Join business types for brothy tankards of Munich lager, Munich dark brews and

platters of sausage and cheese 'knacker' at this three-level, wood-and-brass microbrewery. Beers are served in 300mL, 500mL and 1L steins, with seasonal brews like Salvator Beer, Mailbock Beer and Oktoberfest Beer adding to the temptation.

THE QUAYS

Lantern Bar
BAR

(Map p478; ☑6597 5299; Fullerton Bay Hotel, 80 Collyer Quay; ⊙8am-1am Sun-Thu, 8am-2am Fri & Sat; ⓂRaffles Place) Fifth-floor Lantern may be height challenged, but it has no shortage of X-factor. Surrounding a glittering mosaic pool, it's a seductive melange of frangipani trees, skyscraper views, DJ-spun house and well-mixed libations. Call three days ahead if you fancy your own cabana.

Brewerkz
BREWERY

(Map p478; www.brewerkz.com; 01-05 Riverside Point Centre, 30 Merchant Rd; ⊙noon-midnight Sun-Thu, noon-1am Fri & Sat; ⓂClarke Quay) The first among Singapore's crop of microbreweries and still the biggest and arguably the best. The beers are uniformly superb, from the hugely popular India Pale Ale to the quirkier seasonal fruit beers, with a solid choice of American comfort grub to soak it all up. Best (or worst) of all, the earlier you arrive, the cheaper the drinks.

Penny Black
PUB

(Map p478; www.pennyblack.com.sg; 26/27 Boat Quay; ⊙11.30am-1am Mon-Thu, 11.30am-2am Fri & Sat, 11.30am-midnight Sun; ⓂRaffles Place) Fitted out like a Victorian London pub (without the tuberculosis and dodgy gin), the Penny Black's interior was actually built in London and shipped to Singapore, so it has some claim to authenticity. Specialises in hard-to-find English ales for the swaths of expat Brits who work in the area. The upstairs bar is especially inviting.

Harry's
BAR

(Map p478; www.harrys.com.sg; 28 Boat Quay; ⊙11.30am-1am Sun-Thu, 11.30am-2am Fri & Sat; ⓂRaffles Place) The original and best of the 31 Harry's branches, this classic city-slicker hangout gained moderate infamy as the haunt of Barings-buster Nick Leeson. Loosen your tie and toast to happy hour (till 8pm), the occasional live band, or the free pool table.

Molly Malone's
IRISH PUB

(Map p478; www.molly-malone.com; 56 Circular Rd; ⊙11am-midnight Mon & Sun, 11am-2am Tue-Sat; ⓂRaffles Place) Well-travelled drinkers will have seen the mock-Irish interior and the genuine Irish stew and fish-and-chip menu a hundred times before, but that doesn't make it any less cosy or welcoming. It's just behind Boat Quay on Circular Rd. Make it a pint or three of Guinness, please.

Brussels Sprouts Belgian Beer & Mussels
BEER HALL

(Map p478; www.brusselssprouts.com.sg; 01-12 Robertson Quay, 80 Mohamed Sultan Rd; ⊙5pm-midnight Mon-Thu, 5pm-1am Fri, noon-1am Sat, noon-midnight Sun; ⓂClarke Quay) This cute and popular restaurant/bar lays the Belgian theme on heavily with mussels, Trappist ales galore and Tintin murals on the wall (the whole gang's there, down to Thomson and Thompson). Choose between the hundred-plus beers on the menu.

Next Page
BAR

(Map p478; ☑6235 6967; 17 Mohamed Sultan Rd; ⊙3pm-3am; ⓂFort Canning) This is where Hunter S Thompson would have hung out if he'd been a journo in Singapore. Dark timber bar, red lanterns, exposed brickwork, booths, pool table, Carlsberg on tap and quirky bartenders – sit down and write the next page of your novel.

Cuba Libre
BAR

(Map p478; www.cubalibre.com.sg; 3B River Valley Rd, Block B, 01-03 Clarke Quay; ⊙6pm-2am Sun-Thu, 6pm-3am Fri & Sat; ⓂClarke Quay) The live Cuban music (Tuesday to Sunday) surges with energy and will compel even the most wooden of legs to start moving. If you can resist the siren of salsa, nurse a Caipirinha and watch students shake their *culo* on the dance floor. Pop tarts will appreciate Monday night's Top 40 tunes.

CHINATOWN & THE CBD

1 Altitude
BAR

(Map p482; www.1-altitude.com; Lvl 63, 1 Raffles Place; admission S$25 (S$30 after 9pm), incl one drink; ⓂRaffles Place) Fancy sipping cocktails perched on a cloud? This is the next best thing. Occupying the 63rd floor of the soaring 1 Raffles Place skyscraper, this bar is a seductive combo of smooth lounge tunes, swaying palms and the twinkling sprawl of Singapore and beyond. Dress up (no shorts or flip-flops) and don't forget your camera.

Level 33
BREWERY

(www.level33.com.sg; Level 33, Marina Bay Financial Tower 1, 8 Marina Blvd; ⊙noon-midnight Sun-Thu, noon-2am Fri & Sat; ⓂRaffles Place) Brews with a view is what you get at the world's highest 'urban craft-brewery'. While the food doesn't quite match the loftiness of its locale, the house-brewed blonde lager, pale ale, porter and stout go down as smoothly as the view over Marina Bay.

La Terrazza
BAR

(Map p482; ☑6221 1694; www.screeningroom.com.sg; Level 4, 12 Ann Siang Rd; ⓜChinatown) The Chinatown-meets-CBD panorama from this very popular rooftop bar, part of the Screening Room film complex (p531), are superb. Hunt down a comfy couch, kick off your shoes and have a shouting-into-each-other's-ears conversation over nostalgic 80s and 90s tunes. To reserve a bar table, call or email three days ahead.

Tantric Bar
GAY

(Map p482; 78 Neil Rd; ⓧ8pm-3am Sun-Fri, 8pm-4am Sat; ⓜOutram Park, Chinatown) Complete with a palm-fringed courtyard, Tantric is Singapore's hottest gay drinking hole. Especially heaving on Friday and Saturday nights, it's a hit with preened locals and eager expats, who schmooze and cruise to Gaga, Kylie and K-pop. Lushes shouldn't miss Wednesday nights, where S$20 gets you two martinis.

Beaujolais Wine Bar
WINE BAR

(Map p482; 1 Ann Siang Hill; ⓧnoon-1am; ⓜChinatown) A tiny, raffish bar perched on the corner of two trendy, bar-filled streets, Beaujolais is *très bon* for people-watching sessions. While we love the upstairs lounge; head in early for a terrace table and toast to the tropics over a glass of well-priced wine.

Plain
CAFE

(Map p482; www.theplain.com.sg; 50 Craig Rd; ⓧ7.30am-7.30pm; ⓜTanjong Pagar) A hipster-approved mix of stark interiors, neatly piled design magazines and a Scandi-style communal table, the Plain gets it right with Australian Genovese coffee, decent all-day breakfasts and sweet treats like lemon and lime tarts. Service is friendly and the vibe refreshingly relaxed.

Backstage Bar
GAY

(Map p482; www.backstagebar.moonfruit.com; 13A Trengganu St; ⓜChinatown) While most of the look-at-me pretty boys head to Tantric Bar and Taboo (p532), less pretentious types gravitate here. Sit on the balcony to chat and flirt with local lads, or just sit back and watch the Chinatown action below. Entrance on Temple St.

KAMPONG GLAM & LITTLE INDIA

Maison Ikkoku
CAFE, COCKTAIL BAR

(Map p486; www.maison-ikkoku.net; 20 Kandahar St; ⓧcafe 9am-9pm Mon-Thu, to 11pm Fri & Sat, to 7pm Sun, bar 6pm-late Mon-Sat; ⊚; ⓜBugis) Pimped with Chesterfield banquettes and suspended wooden dressers, Maison Ikkoku keeps coffee snobs satisfied with speciality brewing methods like syphon and pourover, as well as old-school espresso. Edibles include decent salads and cakes – and *musubi*, a sushi-like Hawaiian snack topped with seasoned spam. Two floors up is the slinky cocktail bar, complete with alfresco terrace.

Zsofi Tapas Bar
BAR

(Map p486; www.tapasbar.com.sg; 68 Dunlop St; ⓜLittle India) It's all about the rooftop here, a wonderful and highly unusual space for this part of town, and big enough to (nearly) always find a seat on. Drinks are anything but cheap – expect to pay at least S$12 for a beer – but every one of them comes with free tapas, which goes some way to softening the blow when you get the bill.

Going Om
CAFE, BAR

(Map p486; www.going-om.com; 63 Haji Lane; ⓧclosed Tue; ⓜBugis) Part cafe, part chill-out space. The seating area downstairs offers shisha, cocktails, coffees, teas and even 'chakra drinks' of seven colours (one for each chakra). Upstairs has a flexible space for yoga, tarot-card readings and group meditation. There's a house magician on Thursday nights, and live music gigs on Mondays, Wednesdays, Thursdays and Sundays after 8.30pm.

ORCHARD ROAD

Que Pasa
WINE BAR

(Map p490; 7 Emerald Hill Rd; ⓜSomerset) This wine bar channels old España with its tin lamps, strung chilli lights and *El Pais* wallpaper. It also boasts an astute wine list – the perfect match for succulent bites like anchovy bread. Que Pasa's location on buzzing, heritage-handsome Emerald Hill Rd is nothing short of *fabuloso*.

KPO
BAR

(Map p490; www.imaginings.com.sg; 1 Killiney Rd; ⓧ3pm-1am Mon-Thu, 3pm-2am Fri & Sat; ⓜSomerset) Stamps, cocktails and Lamborghinis: welcome to one of Singapore's quirkiest cocktail spots. Housed in a renovated postmaster's house, trendy KPO is as well known for its philatelic pedigree as it is for the luxury wheels of its see-and-be-seen evening

TEA CULTURE

For soothing cultural enlightenment, slip into one of Chinatown's atmospheric teahouses. Start at **Yixing Yuan Teahouse** (Map p482; www.yixingxuan-teahouse.com; 30/32 Tanjong Pagar Rd; 45min demonstration S$20; ☺10am-9pm Mon-Sat, 10am-7pm Sun; ⓜTanjong Pagar), where reformed corporate banker Vincent Low explains everything you need to know about sampling different types of tea. Demonstrations with tastings last around 45 minutes to two hours (S$20 to S$40).

Once you know your green tea from your oolong, duck around the corner to **Tea Chapter** (Map p482; www.tea-chapter.com.sg; 9-11 Neil Rd; tea from $5; ☺11am-10.30pm Sun-Thu, 11am-11pm Fri & Sat; ⓜChinatown), where Queen Elizabeth dropped by for a cuppa in 1989. If you don't know the tea-making drill, the server will give you a brief demonstration. Downstairs, all manner of tea paraphernalia are precariously balanced on display shelves and can be purchased.

If you're on Orchard Rd, drop into upmarket tea purveyor **TWG Tea** (Map p490; www.twgtea.com; 02-20 ION Orchard, 2 Orchard Rd; ☺10am-10pm; ⓜOrchard), which peddles over 800 varieties of tea from around the world, including Rolls Royce varieties like Da Hong Pao from Fujian. Savour the flavour with a few tea-infused macaroons (the bain de roses is divine). You'll find other outlets at Ngee Ann City's Takashimaya (p535) and the Shoppes at Marina Bay Sands (p533) mall.

clientele. Style up, order a cocktail, and scan the gorgeous rooftop terrace for your prospective ride home.

Dubliners IRISH PUB
(Map p490; www.dublinersingapore.com; 165 Penang Rd; ☺11.30am-1am Sun-Thu, to 2am Fri & Sat; ⓜSomerset) Lousy Irish pubs filled with bellowing, beer-bellied execs are omnipresent in Singapore. Thankfully, this colonial beauty isn't one of them. Nurse your Guinness in the cosy gloom inside, or embrace the tropics on the alfresco verandah. The pub grub is well-priced and tasty, and the service worth a little toast.

DEMPSEY ROAD & HOLLAND VILLAGE

TOP CHOICE **Da Paolo Bistro Bar** BAR, RESTAURANT
(www.dapaolo.com.sg; 3 Rochester Park; ☺bar 5.30-11.30pm Mon-Fri, 2-11.30pm Sat & Sun, restaurant lunch & dinner daily; ⃤74, 91, 92, 95, 191, 196, 198, 200, ⓜBuona Vista) Looking straight off the pages of *Vogue Living*, this tropical-chic gem sits on a lush, secluded street 2km southwest of Holland Village. Settle in on the patio and taste test the speciality tea-based cocktails – we love the Oo Lá Lá (oolong ginseng tea–infused gin, Campari, sweet Vermouth and lemon juice). If you can't pull yourself away, Italian bites will sustain you throughout the evening.

Tippling Club COCKTAIL BAR
(www.tipplingclub.com; 8D Dempsey Rd; ☺6pm-late Mon-Fri, noon-3pm & 6pm-late Sat; ⃤7, 77, 106, 123, 174) Forest-fringed Tippling Club takes

mixology to new heights. Savour the brilliance in cocktails like 'Wake Me Up, F*ck Me Up' (VSOP cognac, fresh espresso and mole bitters), or 'Smoky Old Bastard' (a large whisky served in a glass tube filled with smoke made from dried orange powder and flavoured with maple syrup and banana). Not cheap (cocktails from S$21), but worth it.

RedDot Brewhouse BREWERY
(wwwreddotbrewhouse.com.sg; 25A Dempsey Rd; ☺noon-midnight Mon-Thu, noon-2am Fri & Sat, 10am-midnight Sun; ⃤7, 77, 106, 123, 174) This microbrewery, tucked away in a quiet part of Dempsey Hill, is Valhalla for beer fiends. Seven brews on tap include a green pilsner, its alien tinge coming from the spirulina used in the brewing process. Food options are generally mediocre, so kick back on the deck and focus on the liquid gold.

Wala Wala Café Bar BAR
(www.imaginings.com.sg; 31 Lorong Mambong; ☺4pm-1am Mon-Thu, 4pm-2am Fri, 3pm-2am Fri, 3pm-1am Sat; ⓜHolland Village) Large, raucous and friendly, Wala Wala has been a long-standing favourite with the young expat crowd for its breezy vibe and its live-music bar upstairs. Downstairs it pulls in football fans with its large sports screens. Beers start at $10, a relative bargain in this part of town.

SENTOSA ISLAND

Azzura Beach Club BAR
(Map p499; ☎6270 8003; www.azzura.sg; 46 Siloso Beach Walk; ☺10am-10pm Mon-Thu, to 2am Fri-Sun)

Body beautifuls head here to nibble, sip and flirt over tasting plates and cooling cocktails. Flaunt it in the Harem-inspired lounge/club or catch a breeze under sinuous palms.

Tanjong Beach Club BAR
(Map p499; www.tanjongbeachclub.com; Tanjong Beach; ⊙11am-11pm Tue-Thu, 10am-11pm Fri & Sat) Don't fancy swimming at the beach? Cool down in the infinity pool at this stylish beach bar/restaurant. Aside from Sundays, this place is remarkably quiet, making it an ideal getaway from the madding Sentosa crowds.

Wave House BAR
(Map p499; www.wavehousesentosa.com; Siloso Beach; ⊙10am-11pm) Surfer-friendly beach bar with its own ordinary pool plus two 'flowriders': wave pools that you can pay to surf in.

EAST COAST
1-TwentySix BAR
(Map p492; www.1-twentysix.com; 902 East Coast Parkway; ☎; ⎙401) Palms, gurgling fountains and cocktails with names like 7 Desirable Sins await at this chic, beachside bar. Sip on old and new world vino, and line your stomach with decadent (and admittedly pricey) nibbles like French fries with truffle oil. For the best value, head in during happy hour (5pm to 8pm).

☆ Entertainment

Dance, theatre, Chinese opera, live rock, symphony concerts, A-list DJs: Singapore gives you no excuse for an early night. While the city's performing arts hub is Esplanade – Theatres on the Bay, many visiting Broadway musicals hit the stage at Marina Bay Sands. Clubs, which generally close at 3am and are strictly drug-free, often feature top local and visiting DJs, while Singapore's small but kicking local music scene counters the dominance of cover bands. Tickets for most events are available through Sistic (☑6348 5555; www.sistic.com.sg). Check the website for the nearest outlets. The *Straits Times, I-S Magazine* and *Time Out* have listings for movies, theatre and music. For nightlife, pick up the free street mags *I-S Magazine* and *Juice* at cafes, hotels and music stores.

Chinese Opera
Chinese Theatre Circle CHINESE OPERA
(Map p482; ☑6323 4862; 5 Smith St; ⓂChinatown) Every Friday and Saturday at 8pm, this not-for-profit opera group delivers a brief talk (in English; S$20) on Chinese opera, followed by a 45-minute performance from an opera classic. Lychee tea and tea cakes are included in the price and bookings are recommended. For S$35, turn up at 7pm and you can enjoy a Chinese meal beforehand. Search for Chinese Theatre Circle on Facebook.

Cinema
Singaporeans love to watch movies, and at around S$10 per ticket, it's great value. Multiplex cinemas abound, and most are clustered around the city area, on or near Orchard Rd. Non-English films are subtitled. Dress warmly – Singaporean cinemas are notoriously chilly.

Golden Village Gold Class CINEMA
(www.gv.com.sg) With locations at VivoCity (Map p499; www.vivocity.com.sg; 1 HarbourFront Walk; ⓂHarbourFront), 112 Katong (Map p492; 112 East Coast Road; ⎙10, 10E, 14, 14E, 16, 32, 40), and Great World City (www.greatworldcity.com.sg; 1 Kim Seng Promenade; ⎙16, 32, 54, 139, 195, 75, 970, ⎙free shuttle from City Hall MRT), these swanky cinemas feature plush carpeting and single and double reclining seats complete with footrests, table service and a reasonable menu. On the second and fourth Wednesday evening of every month, Golden Village at Great World City showcases independent Asian cinema curated by Sinema (www.sinema.sg).

Screening Room CINEMA
(Map p482; www.screeningroom.com.sg; 12 Ann Siang Rd; ⓂChinatown) Get your ticket, order some food and drinks and sink into a comfy sofa to watch a film projected onto the pull-down screen. After the performance, head upstairs to the rooftop bar for some post-show drinks with a view.

Rex Cinemas CINEMA
(Map p486; 2 Mackenzie Rd; ⓂLittle India) Where can you catch the Bollywood blockbusters advertised all over Little India? Why at the Rex, of course. This beautifully renovated historic three-screen theatre shows films from around the subcontinent, most subtitled in English.

Clubs
Most clubs have cover charges of around S$15 to S$40, often including at least one drink; women usually pay less (or even nothing!).

Zouk CLUB
(www.zoukclub.com; 17 Jiak Kim St; ⊙Zouk 10pm-late Wed, Fri & Sat, Phuture & Velvet Underground

9pm-late Wed, Fri & Sat, Wine Bar 6pm-2am Tue, to 3am Wed & Thu, to 4am Fri & Sat) Singapore's hottest club is well known for its prolific DJs, massive dance floor and five bars. While weekends are reserved for fresh dance, hip-hop and electro, Wednesdays are a retro affair of 70s, 80s and 90s tunes. The complex is also home to alfresco Zouk Wine Bar, avant-garde Phuture, and boudoir-inspired Velvet Underground, hung with Andy Warhol and Keith Haring originals. Take a taxi.

Home Club
CLUB

(Map p478; www.homeclub.com.sg; B1-1/06 The Riverwalk, 20 Upper Circular Rd; ⊘7pm-3am Tue-Fri, 7pm-4am Sat; MClarke Quay) Home Club enjoys serious cred with music buffs. The resident nights kick some serious 'A', with playlists spanning house, electro, and retro, to drum and bass and psy-trance. The venue is also known for its credible live pop and rock acts, and its Tuesday comedy night.

Butter Factory
CLUB

(Map p478; www.thebutterfactory.com; 02-02 One Fullerton, 1 Fullerton Rd; ⊘10pm-4am Wed, Fri & Sat; MClarke Quay) At 8000 sq ft, Butter Factory is as huge as it is slick. Street art on the walls of Bump, the hip hop, rhythm and blues room, betrays its young and overdressed crowd. Fash is its chilled-out 'art' bar, and walls are plastered with colourful pop art reminiscent of underground comics (yes, the ones you hid from mum).

Taboo
GAY

(Map p482; www.taboo.sg; 65/67 Neil Rd; ⊘8pm-2am Wed & Thu, 10pm-3am Fri, 10pm-4am Sat; MOutram Park, Chinatown) After drinks at Tantric, cross the street and hit the dance floor at what remains the hottest gay dance club on the scene. Expect the requisite line-up of shirtless gyrators, dance-happy straight women and regular racy themed nights.

St James Power Station
CLUB, LIVE MUSIC

(Map p499; www.stjamespowerstation.com; 3 Sentosa Gateway; MHarbourFront) This reformed 1920s coal-fired power station boasts a booty of interconnected venues, including live rock/pop club Boiler Room (Map p499; ⊘6pm-3am Mon-Thu, 6pm-4am Fri & Sat) and Latin club Movida (Map p499; ⊘8pm-3am Tue-Thu, 8pm-5am Fri & Sat, 6pm-3am Sun). All venues are interconnected and included in the one cover charge (men S$20 Fridays and Saturdays, women free daily). Some bars have no cover charge at all. Wednesday's Ladies Night offers women a room-spinning five free drinks from 11pm.

Live Music
CLASSICAL
Singapore Symphony Orchestra
CLASSICAL MUSIC

(Map p478; ☑6348 5555; www.sso.org.sg; MEsplanade) The 1800-seater state-of-the-art concert hall at the Esplanade – Theatres on the Bay is home to this respected orchestra. It plays frequently each month; check the website for details and book in advance. Student and senior (55-plus) discounts are available; kids under six years old are unceremoniously banned.

Singapore Chinese Orchestra
CLASSICAL MUSIC

(Map p482; ☑6557 4034; www.sco.com.sg; Singapore Conference Hall, 7 Shenton Way; MTanjong Pagar) The orchestra performs classical Chinese concerts throughout the year, with traditional instruments including the *liuqin, ruan* and *sanxian,* and occasionally collaborates with Japanese, jazz and Malay musicians.

ROCK
Crazy Elephant
LIVE MUSIC, BLUES

(Map p478; www.crazyelephant.com; 01-03/04, Clarke Quay; MClarke Quay) If the remodelled Clarke Quay is a collection of eager-faced college kids, then this beery, blokey, graffiti-strewn rock dive is the crusty old-timer shaking his head. One of Singapore's oldest, trustiest live-music venues, it's the place to ditch all that electronic nonsense and surrender yourself to some serious, loud, grunting rock and blues.

Prince of Wales
LIVE MUSIC

(Map p486; ☑6299 0130; www.pow.com.sg; 101 Dunlop St; MLittle India) This Aussie-hewn pub has backpacker accommodation upstairs. Rub shoulders with resident surfy beer-boffins effusing over acoustic rock, indie and folk. Entry is free and music is from 7.30pm most nights, though it's a good idea to check the website for details.

Tab
LIVE MUSIC

(Map p490; www.tab.com.sg; 442 Orchard Rd, 02-29 Orchard Hotel; ⊘9pm-5am Sun-Tue, 7pm-5am Wed & Thu, 7pm-6am Fri & Sat; MOrchard) Head in before 10.30pm on Wednesday, Friday or Saturday to see local bands belt out their stuff, or on any night after that for Asian bands, dancers and DJs.

JAZZ & BLUES
BluJaz Cafe
PUB

(Map p486; www.blujaz.net; 11 Bali Ln; ⊘noon-1am Mon-Thu, noon-2am Fri, 4pm-2am Sat; 🛜; MBugis)

Brightly coloured and eccentrically decorated, this boho hangout keeps punters happy with its well-priced beers (from S$6), live jazz or blues on Friday and Saturday (and the first Monday of the month), and funky upstairs lounge. Best seats in the house, however, line the side alley linking Bali and Haji Lanes.

Spectator Sports

Singapore Turf Club   HORSE RACING
(www.turfclub.com.sg; 1 Turf Club Ave; **M**Kranji) Watch Singaporeans get hot under the collar as their four-legged bets roar to the finish line. Seats range from lower grandstand (S$3-4) up to the Gold Card Room (S$15). Dress code is collared shirt and pants for men; closed shoes for women. Betting is government controlled; check the website for race schedules (usually Friday nights and all day on weekends). Kranji MRT station is right outside.

Theatre & Dance

Singapore Repertory Theatre   THEATRE
(Map p478; ✆6733 8166; www.srt.com.sg; DBS Arts Centre, 20 Merbau Rd; **M**Clarke Quay) The bigwig of the Singapore theatre scene has a repertoire spanning Shakespeare, modern Western classics and contemporary works from Singapore, Asia-Pacific and beyond. Recent coups include a season of Sam Mendes' *Richard III* starring Kevin Spacey. Although based at the DBS Arts Centre, productions are also held at Esplanade – Theatres on the Bay and Fort Canning Park.

Singapore Dance Theatre   DANCE
(Map p478; ✆6338 0611; www.singaporedance theatre.com; 2nd fl, Fort Canning Centre, Cox Tce; **M**Dhoby Ghaut) Traditional ballet and contemporary works is what you'll get from Singapore's world-class dance company. The group's Ballet under the Stars season at Fort Canning Park is justifiably popular, and their regular, on-site ballet classes are just the ticket for budding Fonteyns and Nureyevs.

🔒 Shopping

Bangkok and Hong Kong might upstage it on the bargain front, but when it comes to choice, few cities match Singapore. Mall-heavy, chain-centric **Orchard Rd** is Singapore's retail queen, though it's only one of several retail hubs. For computers and electronics, hit specialist malls such as Funan DigitaLife Mall, Sim Lim Square and Mustafa Centre. Good places for antiques

include Tanglin Shopping Centre (p536) **Dempsey Hill**, and **Chinatown**. For fabrics and textiles, scour **Little India** and **Kampong Glam**. Kampong Glam is also famous for its perfume traders, as well as for the booty of hip, independent fashion boutiques on **Haji Lane**.

COLONIAL DISTRICT, THE QUAYS & MARINA BAY

Funan DigitaLife Mall   ELECTRONICS
(Map p478; www.funan.com.sg; 109 North Bridge Rd; **M**City Hall) Tech mall of choice for people who prefer to pay a bit more for branded products and cast-iron guarantees, rather than brave the aisles of Sim Lim Square. **Challenger Superstore** (www.challenger.com. sg; ⊙10am-10pm) is the best one-stop shop for all IT desires. For cameras, visit family-run **John 3:16** (Map p478; ⊙12.30-9.30pm Mon-Sat).

Shoppes at Marina Bay Sands   MALL
(Map p478; www.marinabaysands.com; 10 Bayfront Ave; **M**Bayfront, Marina Bay, Promenade) You'll find all the 'It' brands at this giant, glossy mall, including runway royalty Prada and Miu Miu. Clued-up fashionistas shop at unisex **Society of Black Sheep** (Map p478; www. societyofblacksheep.com), whose adventurous labels include Sydney's cyber punk-inspired Injury, Singapore's geometric Yumumu, as well as artisan jewellery from local talent Carrie K. You'll also find an ice-free skating rink, celebrity nosh spots, and a floating Louis Vuitton store.

Peninsula Plaza   MALL
(Map p478; 111 North Bridge Rd; **M**City Hall) The shopping centre that props up the Peninsula Excelsior Hotel has seen better days, but it's one of the city's best hunting grounds for sporting goods and second-hand camera gear. Shutter fiends shouldn't miss **Cathay Photo** (Map p478; www.cathayphoto.com. sg; ⊙10am-7pm Mon-Sat), Singapore's best-stocked (though not necessarily cheapest) camera store.

Raffles City   MALL
(Map p478; www.rafflescity.com.sg; 252 North Bridge Rd; **M**City Hall) One of Singapore's best shopping malls, buzzing Raffles' includes a three-level branch of the excellent Robinsons department store, global fashion brands such as Topshop, agnès b, Kate Spade, a good selection of children's clothes and toys, the Ode to Art gallery, as well as a satisfying booty of food court stalls and restaurants for flagging shopaholics.

TOP SHOPPING TIPS

» Prices are usually fixed except at markets and in tourist areas; don't start bargaining if you have no interest in purchasing.

» Shop around when buying electronics like computers, tablets and cameras. Researching prices means less chance of getting overcharged.

» Especially in smaller shops, ensure international guarantees are filled out correctly, including the shop's name and the item's serial number. When buying antiques, ask for a certificate of antiquity, required by many countries to avoid paying customs duty.

» If buying a Bluray, DVD player or a gaming system, check that it will play your home country's discs. Also, check the voltage and cycle of electrical goods. Most shops will attach the correct plug for your country if you ask.

» Although the annual **Great Singapore Sale** (www.greatsingaporesale.com.sg) spans late May to late July, the best bargains are had during the first week.

» In the unlikely case you're ripped off or taken for a ride, contact the Singapore Tourism Board (p541) or the **Small Claims Tribunal** (☑6435 5994; www.smallclaims.gov. sg; Subordinate Courts, 1 Havelock Sq; ⊙8.30am-6pm Mon-Thu, 8.30am-5.30pm Fri, 8.30am-1pm Sat; ⓜChinatown).

Raffles Hotel Arcade
MALL

(Map p478; www.raffles.com; 328 North Bridge Rd; ⓜCity Hall) Part of the hotel complex, stylish Raffles Hotel Arcade is firmly upmarket, with designer clothes and accessories, watchmakers, galleries, wine sellers and similarly refined places gently tempting you into credit-card wantonness. You can shop for fashion-forward local threads and accessories at **Front Row** (www.frontrowsingapore.com; ⊙noon-8pm Mon-Sat, noon-5pm Sun) and find contemporary Singaporean art at **Chan Hampe Galleries** (www.chanhampegalleries.com; ⊙11am-7pm).

Suntec City
MALL

(Map p478; www.sunteccity.com.sg; 3 Temasek Blvd; ⓜPromenade, Esplanade) Vast Suntec has every-thing under the sun, plus 60 restaurants, cafes and several food courts. Its crowd-pulling Fountain of Wealth was once accorded the status of World's Largest Fountain in the *Guinness Book of Records*. Scan the media for one of Suntec's regular themed 'fairs', where you can pick up substantially discounted items such as cameras, electronics and computer gear.

MICA Building
ART

(Map p478; 140 Hill St) This rainbow-shuttered colonial building houses a clutch of quality galleries, including **Art-2 Gallery** (Map p478; www.art2.com.sg; ⊙11am-7pm Mon-Sat), **Cape of Good Hope Art Gallery** (Map p478; www.capeof goodhope.com.sg) and **Gajah Gallery** (Map p478; www.gajahgallery.com), which showcases the best of Asia's vibrant contemporary art scene.

CHINATOWN

TOP CHOICE Utterly Art
ART

(Map p482; www.utterlyart.com.sg; Level 3, 20B Mosque St; ⊙noon-8pm Mon-Sat, noon-5.30pm Sun; ⓜChinatown) This small, welcoming art gallery is an excellent introduction to Singapore's contemporary art scene. It's mostly paintings, although they exhibit sculpture and ceramics on occasion, and roughly half of the stuff on show is the work of Singaporean artists. They exhibit a lot of Filipino work, too. Call or check the website for what's on when you're in town.

Far East Legend
ANTIQUES, HANDICRAFTS

(Map p482; 233 South Bridge Rd; ⊙11.30am-6.30pm; ⓜChinatown) Squeeze inside this cluttered bolthole for an excellent collection of furniture, lamps, handicrafts, statues and other *objets d'art* from all over Asia. Expect anything from dainty porcelain snuff boxes to ceramic busts of Chairman Mao. The owner is usually willing to 'discuss the price'.

Eu Yan Sang
CHINESE MEDICINE

(Map p482; www.euyansang.com; 269 South Bridge Rd; ⊙8.30am-7pm Mon-Sat; ⓜChinatown) Get your *qi* back at this venerable peddler of Chinese medicines and tonics. You can consult a herbalist (from S$12), or get off-the-shelf remedies such as instant bird's nest (to tone the lung) or deer's tail pills (to invigorate the kidneys). Most remedies also come with English instructions.

Yue Hwa Chinese Products
DEPARTMENT STORE

(Map p482; www.yuehwa.com.sg; 70 Eu Tong Sen St; MChinatown) Five floors of everything Chinese, from porcelain teapots and jade jewellery to slinky silk cheongsams, dried fish and medicinal herbs, fungi and spices. Pick up some ginseng, a snakeskin drum or a jar full of seahorses for the road.

LITTLE INDIA, BUGIS & KAMPONG GLAM

TOP CHOICE Sifr Aromatics
PERFUME

(Map p486; www.sifr.sg; 42 Arab St; ⊙11am-8pm Sun-Thu, 11am-9pm Fri & Sat; MBugis) This Zen-like perfume laboratory belongs to thirdgeneration perfume maker Johari Kazura, whose exquisite concoctions include the heady East (50ml S$140), a blend of oud, rose absolute, amber and neroli. Perfumes range from S$80 to S$300 for 50ml, while vintage perfume bottles range from S$60 to S$2000. Those after a custom-made fragrance should call a day before their visit.

Sim Lim Square
ELECTRONICS, MALL

(Map p486; www.simlimsquare.com.sg; 1 Rochor Canal Rd; ⊙11am-8pm; MBugis) If you know what you're doing, there are real bargains to be had at this computer and electronics mega mall. The untutored, however, are more likely to be taken for a ride, so check the price at three vendors before bargaining hard. If it all sounds too difficult, opt for the cool 'n' cheap mobile phone and tablet covers.

Little Shophouse
HANDICRAFTS

(Map p486; 43 Bussorah St; ⊙10am-6pm; MBugis) In his little workshop-cum-store, craftsman Robert Sng handbeads riotously colourful Peranakan slippers. Starting at around S$300, each pair takes two months to complete, with many admirers simply framing the shoe covers as works of art in themselves. Beadwork aside, you can also stock up on Peranakan-style tea sets, crockery, vases, handbags and jewellery.

Celebration of Arts
HANDICRAFTS

(Map p486; 2 Dalhousie Lane; ⊙9am-9.30pm; MLittle India) Dive into this treasure trove for beautiful Indian ornaments, statues, lampshades, cushions, bedspreads, furniture and pashmina shawls. Several larger items aren't displayed, so if you're looking for something in particular, ask the friendly owner.

Mustafa Centre
DEPARTMENT STORE

(Map p486; www.mustafa.com.sg; 145 Syed Alwi Rd; ⊙24hr; MFarrer Park) As much cultural rite of passage as shopping experience, Mustafa's narrow aisles and tiny nooks have everything from electronics, clothing, toiletries, tacky clothes (lurid Bollywood shirts always make great presents), cheap DVDs, gold, moneychangers, a supermarket packed with Indian spices and pickles, and – on Sundays – half the population of Singapore.

Bugis Street Market
MARKET

(Map p486; www.bugis-street.com; Victoria St; ⊙11am-10pm; MBugis) Singapore's once infamous sleaze pit – packed with foreign servicemen on R&R, gambling dens and 'sisters' (transvestites) – is now its largest street market, crammed with cheap clothes, shoes, accessories, manicurists, food stalls and, in a nod to its past, a sex shop. Tiny **The Good Old Days** (Shop CSL/D4, Level 2; ⊙noon-10pm) is famed for its 70s to 90s vintage frocks, handbags, jewellery, and vintage-inspired heels.

ORCHARD ROAD

ION Orchard Mall
MALL

(Map p490; www.ionorchard.com; 430 Orchard Rd; MOrchard) Curvaceous, high-tech and striking, Ion is Singapore's hottest (and most photogenic) mall, packed with both high-end couture and more affordable 'It' labels like Paul Frank, G-Star, and True Religion. Shopped out? Recharge in the brilliant basement food court. The adjoining 56-storey tower comes with a top-floor observation deck, **ION Sky** (www.ionsky.com.sg; observation deck ticket counter level 4; observation deck adult/child S$16/8; ⊙10am-noon & 2-8pm).

Ngee Ann City
MALL

(Map p490; www.ngeeanncity.com.sg; 391 Orchard Rd; MOrchard) Housed in a downright ugly, brown-hued marble and granite building, Ngee Ann City redeems itself with seven floors of retail pleasure, where can't-afford luxury brands compete for space with the likes of **Kinokuniya** (Map p490; www.kinokuniya.com.sg; 03-09/10/15), Southeast Asia's largest bookstore, and Japanese department store Takashimaya, home to the mouthwatering Takashimaya Food Village (p526).

Blackmarket No. 2
FASHION

(www.theblackmarket.sg/blog; 181 Orchard Rd, 02-10, Orchard Central; MSomerset) Hip, emerging Asian designers rule the racks at guys-and-gals Blackmarket No 2, among them Singapore's WanderWonder and Feist, the

HAJI LANE

Fashion fiends in search of fresher, lesser-known labels flock to Haji Lane, a pastel-hued strip in Kampong Glam lined with hipster-approved, one-off boutiques. **Dulcetfig** (Map p486; www. dulcetfig.wordpress.com; 41 Haji Lane; ⏱12.30-9pm Mon-Thu, 12.30-10pm Fri & Sat, 1-8pm Sun; Ⓜ Bugis) sets female fashion bloggers into overdrive with its cool local and foreign frocks and accessories, which includes high-end vintage bags and jewellery. Fashion-literate guys should check out minimalist **K.I.N** (Map p486; 51 Haji Lane; ⏱1-8pm Mon-Sat, 3-7pm Sun; Ⓜ Bugis), where vintage-inspired shirts from Gitman Bros and design-centric bags from Makr sit beside K.I.N's own street-chic, preppy-cool threads and shoes.

Philippines' Gian Romano, Black Heart and Anthology, and Indonesia's Rebirth. Pick up anything from graphic tees and whimsically detailed shirts, to handcrafted shoes and jewellery. The store's centrepiece 'wooden shack' showcases a different designer every month.

313 Somerset
MALL

(Map p490; www.313somerset.com.sg; 313 Orchard Rd; Ⓜ Somerset) Hugely popular 313 has a great location above Somerset MRT Station and houses a cool, youthful mix of High St favourites like Zara, Uniqlo, Mango, GUESS and much-loved local women's label M)phosis. You'll also find music stores, restaurants, cafes, and the always-busy Apple shop EpiCentre. Coffee lovers can get a decent fix at Oriole Café & Bar, just outside the west entrance.

Paragon
MALL

(Map p490; www.paragon.com.sg; 290 Orchard Rd; Ⓜ Somerset) Even if you don't have a Gold Amex, strike a pose inside the Maserati of Orchard Rd malls. The Shop Directory reads like a Vogue index: Burberry, Bulgari, Gucci, Hermès, Jimmy Choo. Thankfully, mere mortals with a passion for fashion have a string of options, including Miss Selfridges, Calvin Klein Jeans, Banana Republic and Diesel.

Tanglin Shopping Centre
MALL

(Map p490; www.tanglinsc.com; 19 Tanglin Rd; ⏱9.30-9pm; Ⓜ Orchard) This retro mall is *the* place for rugs, carvings, ornaments, jewellery,

paintings, furniture and the like. The fascinating **Antiques of the Orient** (Map p490; www.aoto.com.sg; ⏱10am-6pm Mon-Sat, 11am-4pm Sun) is housed here, with its wonderful old books, photographs and genuinely ancient maps from all parts of Asia. You'll also find **Select Books** (Map p490; www.selectbooks. com.sg; ⏱9.30am-6.30pm Mon-Sat, 10am-4pm Sun), an Asian book specialist, as well as some decent Asian-food options.

Mandarin Gallery
MALL

(Map p490; www.mandaringallery.com.sg; 333a Orchard Rd; ☎; Ⓜ Somerset, Orchard) Rehabilitate your wardrobe at this high-end, fashion-obsessed mall. Standout stores include Tokyo-based, boys-only **Bape Store** (www. bape.com; 02-02/03), which is famed for its pop-meets-hip hop-meets-preppy threads, sneakers and accessories in bold prints, luscious fabrics and playful detailing (think hoodies with 'monster' motifs). Female fashionistas shouldn't miss **Hansel** (www.ilovehan sel.com; 02-14), domain of local designer Jo Soh and her chic, playful, vintage-inspired creations.

Cathay Cineleisure Orchard
MALL

(Map p490; www.cineleisure.com.sg; 8 Grange Rd; Ⓜ Somerset) Packed with enough candy, bubble tea and *kawaii* (cuteness) to pop a pimple, this Technicolor mall is home to a few edgy local designers. Unisex **Depression** (www.depression.com.sg; 03-05A; ⏱noon-10pm Sun-Thu, noon-midnight Fri & Sat) stocks playful, androgynous street-smart threads melding influences as diverse as Goth culture and kids' books. Guys should also check out the selection of bold tees, shirts and knits at neighbouring **Frederic Sai** (www.fredericsai. com; 03-04B; ⏱noon-10pm Sun-Thu, noon-11pm Fri & Sat).

DEMPSEY ROAD & HOLLAND VILLAGE
Dempsey Road, a former British Army barracks, is now a shopping precinct specialising in Kashmiri carpets, teak furniture and antiques.

Shang Antique
ANTIQUES

(www.shangantique.com.sg; 16 Dempsey Rd; ⏱10.30am-7pm; 🚍7, 77, 106, 123, 174) Shang specialises in antique religious artefacts from Cambodia, Laos, Thailand, India and Burma, as well as reproductions; there are items in here dating back nearly 2000 years. Those with more style than savings can pick up beautifully embroidered silk shawls and table runners from S$35. Don't be afraid to ask for a 'good price'.

Antipodean — FASHION

(www.antipodeanshop.com; 27A Lorong Mambong; Ⓜ Holland Village) Cult Singaporean and Australian fashion labels rule at this sneaky boutique, hidden away above Harry's Bar. While men are limited to cool tees and jerseys from local outfitter Sundays, women are spoiled with a mix of flirtatious, sculptural threads from the likes of AL&ALICA, Fleur Wood, Rodeo Show and Hansel. Striking heels, creative handbags and artisan jewellery complete the picture.

Holland Village Shopping Centre — MALL

(211 Holland Ave; ⊙10am-8pm; Ⓜ Holland Village) It might look stuck in 1986, but Holland Village Shopping Centre remains a magnet for expats and fashionable Singaporeans looking for art, handicrafts, homewares and offbeat fashion. Top billing goes to **Lim's Arts & Living** (02-01), packed with carvings, furnishings, stationary and Asian textiles. Shopped out? Hit the massage and reflexology peddlers on Level 3.

EAST COAST

Kim Choo Kueh Chang — FOOD, HANDICRAFTS

(Map p492; 109 East Coast Rd; ☐10, 14, 16) Joo Chiat is stuffed with bakeries and dessert shops, but Kim Choo retains that old-world atmosphere, selling its traditional pineapple tarts and other brightly coloured Peranakan *kueh* (bite-sized snacks) from a wooden counter that looks more like an apothecary's shop. Head upstairs to catch artisans making traditional handicrafts and bag some Peranakan souvenirs.

SINGAPORE SURVIVAL GUIDE

Directory A–Z

ACCOMMODATION

Accommodation listings in this chapter quote the published hotel rates. This said, daily rates can fluctuate significantly at most midrange and top end hotels, where room rates are about supply and demand. Weekend rates and occupancy levels are higher than midweek. Rates are also higher during holidays and during major events such as the Formula One night race (book way ahead!).

Be aware that top hotels usually add a 'plus plus' (++) after the rate they quote you. The two pluses denote service charge and GST, which together amounts to an extra 17% on your room rate. Prices quoted are net prices ('net' includes taxes and the service charge).

Apart from booking directly on the hotel's website listed in our reviews, you can also book rooms on the following websites.

Agoda (www.agoda.com)

Asiarooms (www.asiarooms.com)

Booking (www.booking.com)

Kayak (www.kayak.com)

Lonely Planet (hotels.lonelyplanet.com)

BUSINESS HOURS

BUSINESS	STANDARD HOURS
Banks	9.30am-4pm Mon-Fri, 9am-noon Sat
Bars	5pm-1am or 2am
Department Stores & Shopping Malls	10am or 11am-10pm
Hawker Centres	11am-10pm or 1am (sometimes 24hr)
Restaurants	11.30am-2.30pm & 6-10.30pm
Shops	10am-6pm

Many small shops, except those in Little India, close on Sunday. Any exception to these standard hours are noted in specific listings.

CUSTOMS REGULATIONS

» It is illegal to bring in the following items: chewing gum, firecrackers, drugs, pornography, gun-shaped cigarette lighters, endangered species or their byproducts, pirated recordings and publications, and toy currency and coins. Drug trafficking carries the death penalty.

» It is illegal to bring in tobacco unless you pay duty.

» The total limit on alcohol is 1L of wine, 1L beer and 1L spirits duty-free, or 2L of wine and 1L of beer (or 2L of beer and 1L of wine). There is no duty-free concession if you're arriving from Malaysia or have been out of Singapore for less than 48 hours.

» Take a letter from your doctor if you carry prescription medication.

PRICE RANGES

Accommodation listings in this chapter are given one of the following price symbols:

$ less than S$100

$$ S$100–250

$$$ more than S$250

DISCOUNTS

» Travellers arriving on Singapore Airlines or SilkAir are entitled to discounts at selected hotels, shops, restaurants, and attractions by presenting their boarding pass. See www.singaporeair.com/boardingpass for details.

» Children receive up to 50% discount at many tourist attractions, and children six and under are sometimes admitted free. Discounts are often available to visitors over 60. Present your passport or ID with your date of birth on it.

» The National Heritage Board's **3 Day Museum Pass** (www.nhb.gov.sg/WWW/3daymuseumpass.html; adult/family S$20/50) offers unlimited admission to eight city museums, including the Asian Civilisations Museum, National Museum of Singapore and Singapore Art Museum. Passes can be purchased at the museums.

ELECTRICITY

Plugs are of the three-pronged, square-pin type used in Malaysia and the UK (see p594 for an illustration). Electricity runs at 230V and 50 cycles.

EMBASSIES & CONSULATES

For a full list of foreign embassies and consulates in Singapore, go to http://embassy.goabroad.com/embassies-in/Singapore.

Australia (6836 4100; www.australia.org.sg; 25 Napier Rd)

Canada (6854 5900; www.singapore.gc.ca; #11-01, 1 George St)

France (6880 7800; www.ambafrance-sg.org; 101-103 Cluny Park Rd)

Germany (6533 6002, emergency 9817 0414; www.singapur.diplo.de; #12-00 Singapore Land Tower, 50 Raffles Pl)

Indonesia (6737 7422; www.kemlu.go.id/singapore; 7 Chatsworth Rd)

Ireland (6238 7616; www.embassyofireland.sg; #08-00 Liat Towers, 541 Orchard Rd)

Malaysia (6235 0111; www.kln.gov.my/web/sgp_singapore; 301 Jervois Rd)

Netherlands (6737 1155; http://singapore.nlambassade.org; #13-01 Liat Towers, 541 Orchard Rd)

New Zealand (6235 9966; www.nzembassy.com/singapore; Tower A, 15-06/10 Ngee Ann City, 391A Orchard Rd)

Thailand (6737 2475; www.thaiembassy.sg; 370 Orchard Rd)

UK (6424 4200; http://ukinsingapore.fco.gov.uk; 100 Tanglin Rd)

USA (6476 9100; http://singapore.usembassy.gov; 27 Napier Rd)

EMERGENCY

Useful emergency numbers:

Ambulance/Fire (995)

Police (999)

FOOD

The following price ranges – used throughout this chapter – refer to the cost of a standard starter, main course and soft drink.

» **$** less than S$10

» **$$** S$10–30

» **$$$** more than S$30

For in-depth information about the region's food culture, turn to p579.

GAY & LESBIAN TRAVELLERS

Sex between males is illegal in Singapore, carrying a minimum sentence of 10 years. In reality, nobody is ever likely to be prosecuted and LGBT Singaporeans celebrate their pride each August with the multifaceted festival **IndigNation** (www.facebook.com/IndigNationSG). There are also numerous LGBT bars and clubs, several of which are located in Chinatown.

A good place to start looking for information is on the websites of **Utopia** (www.utopia-asia.com) or **Fridae** (www.fridae.com), both of which provide excellent coverage of venues and events across Asia. Singaporeans are fairly conservative about public affection, though it's more common to see displays of familiarity among lesbian couples these days. A gay male couple doing the same would definitely draw negative attention.

INTERNET ACCESS

» In this guide, the internet symbol (@) is used where hotels have business centres or dedicated computers for guest use. The wi-fi symbol (🛜) is used for places where wireless internet is available.

» Every top hotel has internet access and will help get you set up if you bring your own laptop. The backpacker hostels all offer free internet access and wi-fi.

» Changi Airport has numerous free internet terminals.

» You will find free wi-fi hotspots in many of Singapore's shopping malls.

» SingTel (www.singtel.com.sg), StarHub (www.starhub.com) and M1 (www.m1.com) are local providers of broadband internet via USB modem dongles. Bring your own or buy one from them. You can get prepaid data SIM cards if you have your own dongle.

» Internet cafes are increasingly rare in Singapore. Most double as gaming centres and charge around S$3 to S$5 per hour.

LEGAL MATTERS

Singapore's reputation for harsh laws is not undeserved: don't expect any special treatment for being a foreigner. Police have broad powers and you would be unwise to refuse any requests they make of you. If you are arrested, you will be entitled to legal counsel and contact with your embassy. Don't even think about importing or exporting drugs. At best, you'll get long jail terms; at worse, you'll get the death penalty.

Smoking is banned in most public places, including shopping and entertainment centres, restaurants, hawker centres and food courts, public tranport, taxis, and within a 5m radius of most building entrances. The maximum fine for first time offenders is S$1000. You can smoke on the street (as long as you put your butt in the bin).

Jaywalking (crossing the road within 50m of a designated crossing) could cost you S$50, while littering could set you back S$1000.

MEDICAL SERVICES

Singapore's medical institutions are world class and generally cheaper than private healthcare in the West. This said, travel insurance cover is advisable. Check with insurance providers what treatments and procedures are covered before you leave home. Note that local GPs also dispense medication on premises, saving you a trip to the pharmacy.

Your hotel or hostel should be able to direct you to a local GP; there are plenty around.

Raffles Medical Clinic MEDICAL
(☑6311 1111; www.raffleshospital.com; 585 North Bridge Rd; ⊘24hr; Ⓜ Bugis) A walk-in clinic at the Raffles Hospital.

Singapore General Hospital Accident & Emergency Department HOSPITAL
(☑6321 4311; www.sgh.com.sg; Level 2, Block 1, Outram Rd; Ⓜ Outram Park) Located in Block 1 of this big compound.

EMERGENCY ROOMS

The following operate 24-hour emergency rooms:

Gleneagles Hospital (☑6735 5000; www.gleneagles.com.sg; 6A Napier Rd; 🚍7, 75, 77, 105, 106, 123, 174)

Mount Elizabeth Hospital (☑6735 5000; www.mountelizabeth.com.sg; 3 Mt Elizabeth Rd; Ⓜ Orchard)

Raffles Hospital (☑6311 1111; www.raffleshospital.com; 585 North Bridge Rd; Ⓜ Bugis)

MONEY

The unit of currency is the Singapore dollar (comprising 100¢). There are 5¢, 10¢, 20¢, 50¢ and S$1 coins, while notes come in S$2, S$5, S$10, S$50, S$100, S$500 and S$1000 denominations.

ATMS

Cirrus-enabled machines are widely available throughout Singapore, including shopping malls and MRT stations.

CREDIT CARDS

Credit cards are widely accepted, except at local hawkers and food courts. Note that smaller stores might charge you an extra 2% to 3% for credit card payments. For card cancellations or assistance, contact the following:

American Express (☑6396 6000, local calls only 1800 299 1997; www.americanexpress.com/sg)

Diners Club (☑6571 0128; www.dinersclub.com.sg)

MasterCard (☑1800-110 0113; www.mastercard.com)

Visa (☑1800-448 1250; www.visa.com.sg)

CHANGING MONEY

Banks change money, but virtually nobody uses them for currency conversion because the rates are better at the moneychangers dotted all over the city. These tiny stalls can be found in just about every shopping centre (though not necessarily in the more

PRACTICALITIES

» English dailies in Singapore include the broadsheet *Straits Times* (which includes the *Sunday Times*), the *Business Times*, and the afternoon tabloid *New Paper*.

» Singapore has seven free-to-air channels, including the English-language Channel 5 and okto. English-language radio stations include the BBC World Service (88.9FM), Gold (90.5FM), Symphony (92.4FM), 938LIVE (93.8FM), Class (95FM) and 987FM (98.7FM).

» Singapore uses the metric system.

modern malls). Rates can be haggled a little if you're changing amounts of S$500 or more.

TAXES & REFUNDS

A 7% goods-and-services tax (GST) is applied to all goods and services. There are tax and service charges that apply to room rates. Restaurants charge 17% extra on top of listed prices (7% GST, 10% service charge and a 1% CESS charge).

Visitors purchasing goods worth S$300 or more through a shop participating in the GST Tourist Refund Scheme (look for the 'Tax-Free Shopping' logo) can apply for a GST refund. When you purchase an item, fill in a claim form and show your passport. You'll receive a global refund cheque – present it with your passport and goods at the Customs GST inspection counter in the departure hall at Changi *before* you check in. You can then cash your cheque at counters inside the airport, or have credited to your credit card or bank account. Pick up a *How to Shop Tax-free in Singapore* brochure at the airport or visitors centres for more information.

TIPPING

Tipping is largely unnecessary and unexpected in restaurants due to the 10% service charge automatically added to your bill. Some restaurants voluntarily omit the charge, leaving a tip to your discretion. Tipping in taxis and hawker centres is not expected. Elsewhere a thank-you tip for good service is discretionary.

TELEPHONE

Country code	☑65
International access code	☑001
Directory Assistance	☑100
Flight information	☑1800-542 4422
STB Tourist Line	☑1800-736 2000

There are no area codes within Singapore; telephone numbers are eight digits unless you are calling toll-free (1800).

You can make local and international calls from public phone booths. Most phone booths take phonecards. Singapore also has credit card phones that can be used by running your card through the slot.

Calls to Malaysia (from Singapore) are considered to be STD (long-distance or trunk) calls. Dial the access code 020, followed by the area code of the town in Malaysia that you wish to call (minus the leading zero) and then your party's number. Thus, for a call to 346 7890 in Kuala Lumpur (area code 03) you dial 02 3346 7890. Call 109 for assistance with Malaysian area codes.

MOBILE PHONES

In Singapore, mobile phone numbers start with 9 or 8. You can buy a local SIM card for around S$18 (including credit) from post offices, convenience stores and local telco stores – by law you must show your passport to get one. The main local telcos:

SingTel (www.singtel.com.sg)

StarHub (www.starhub.com)

M1 (www.m1.com)

PHONECARDS

Local phonecards are widely available from 7-Eleven stores, post offices, SingTel centres, stationers and bookshops. There's also a small thriving phonecard stall outside the Centrepoint shopping centre on Orchard Rd, but check which countries they service before you buy.

POST

Postal delivery in Singapore is very efficient. Call 1605 to find the nearest branch or check www.singpost.com.sg.

PUBLIC HOLIDAYS

New Year's Day 1 January

Chinese New Year January/February (two days)

Good Friday April (variable)

Labour Day 1 May

Vesak Day May (variable)

National Day 9 August

Deepavali October/November (variable)

Hari Raya Puasa (variable)

Christmas Day 25 December

Hari Raya Haji (variable)

SCHOOL HOLIDAYS

In Singapore there's a week's holiday towards the end of March, four weeks in June, one week in early September, and a long break from the end of November until the beginning of January.

TIME

Singapore is eight hours ahead of GMT/UTC (London).

When it is noon in Singapore, it is 4am in London, 5am in Paris, 2pm in Sydney, 8pm (previous day) in Los Angeles and 11pm (previous day) in New York. Note that these times may vary during daylight savings periods. Singapore itself does not observe daylight savings.

TOILETS

Toilets in Singapore are Western-style. Public toilets are usually very clean and readily available at shopping malls, hotel lobbies and at tourist attractions.

TOURIST INFORMATION

The **Singapore Tourism Board** (STB; ☑1800-736 2000, 6736 2000; www.yoursingapore.com) provides the widest range of services, including tour bookings, event ticketing and a list of Singapore Tourism offices around the world. It has visitor centres at **Changi Airport** (⊙Terminals 1 & 2 6am-midnight, Terminal 3 6am-2am) and **ION Orchard** (Level 1, ION Orchard Mall, 2 Orchard Turn; ⊙10am-10pm; ⓂOrchard).

TRAVELLERS WITH DISABILITIES

In recent years, a major government campaign has seen ramps, lifts and other facilities progressively installed around Singapore. The pavements in the city are nearly all immaculate, although the crowded narrow footpaths of Little India and Chinatown can prove challenging to anyone with mobility, sight or hearing issues. MRT stations all have lifts and some buses and taxis are equipped with wheelchair-friendly equipment.

The **Disabled People's Association** (☑6899 1220; www.dpa.org.sg) offers information on accessibility in Singapore, as well as links to the country's numerous disability organisations.

VISAS

Citizens of most countries are granted 30-day visas on arrival by air or overland (though the latter may get 14-day visas). The exceptions are the Commonwealth of Independent States, Myanmar, India, Pakistan, and most Middle Eastern countries. Visitors must have a valid passport or internationally recognised travel document valid for at least six months beyond the date of entry into Singapore. Extensions can be applied for, in person or online, through the **Immigration & Checkpoints Authority** (☑6391 6100; www.ica.gov.sg; 10 Kallang Rd; ⓂLavender). Keep in mind that applications take at least a day to process.

WOMEN TRAVELLERS

Singaporean women enjoy a high degree of autonomy and respect, and the city is one of the safest destinations in Southeast Asia – though women might be a little uncomfortable in Little India during the weekends, when tens of thousands of male migrant workers throng the area. Tampons, over-the-counter medications and contraceptive pills are readily available.

Transport

GETTING THERE & AWAY

Singapore is a major air hub, serviced by both full-service and budget airlines. The city-state has excellent and extensive regional and international flight connections, making it an ideal stopover city. You can also catch trains to Malaysia and Thailand. A slew of comfortable, privately run buses also run through Malaysia up to Thailand. Book flights, tours and rail tickets online at lonelyplanet.com/bookings.

AIR

Singapore's location and excellent facilities have made it a natural choice as a major Southeast Asian aviation hub, with direct services all over the world.

AIRPORTS & AIRLINES

Most planes will land at one of the three main terminals or the Budget Terminal at **Changi Airport** (☑6595 6868, flight information 1800-542 4422; www.changiairport.com), located around 20km east of the city centre. Regularly voted the world's best airport, Changi

SINGAPORE TRANSPORT CONNECTIONS

DESTINATION	AIR	BUS	TRAIN
Kuala Lumpur	1hr /from $S30	4-5hr/from S$20	6-7hr/from S$34
Penang	1hr 20min/from S$40	9-10hr/from S$45	9hr/from S$60

Airport is vast, efficient and amazingly well organised. Among its many facilities you'll find free internet, courtesy phones for local calls, foreign-exchange booths, medical centres, left luggage, hotels, showers, a gym, swimming pool and of course, plenty of shops.

Changi Airport is the home base of Singapore's highly esteemed national carrier, **Singapore Airlines** (✉6223 8888; www.singaporeair. com; 04-05 ION Orchard Mall, 2 Orchard Turn) and its subsidiary regional carrier **SilkAir** (✉6223 8888; www.silkair.com; 17-08, 371 Beach Road).

It is also serviced by the following six budget airlines, which often offer extremely cheap deals within the region if booked well in advance. Routes change all the time, so check the websites.

Air Asia (✉6307 7688; www.airasia.com)

Berjaya Air (✉6227 3688; www.berjaya-air. com)

Cebu Pacific (✉3158 0808; www.cebupacific air.com)

Firefly (✉Malaysia +603 7845 4543; www. fireflyz.com.my)

Jetstar (✉1800-852 9507; www.jetstar.com)

Tiger Airways (✉6808 4437; www.tigerair ways.com)

LAND

The Causeway linking Johor Bahru (JB) with Singapore handles most traffic between the countries. Trains and buses run from all over Malaysia straight through to Singapore, or you can get a taxi or bus to/from JB. There's also a crossing called the Second Link linking Tuas, in western Singapore, with Geylang Patah in Malaysia – some buses to Melaka and Malaysia's west coast head this way. If you have a car, tolls on the Second Link are much higher than the Causeway.

BUSES

Buses run frequently from Singapore into Malaysia, some continuing to Thailand. If you are travelling beyond Johor Bahru (JB) in Malaysia, the simplest option is to catch a bus straight from Singapore, though there are more options and lower fares travelling from JB.

While long-distance bus terminals include **Queen Street Bus Terminal** (cnr Queen & Arab Sts) and **Lavender St Bus Terminal** (cnr Lavender St & Kallang Bahru), a large number of buses depart from the **Golden Mile Complex** (5001 Beach Road), where you'll also find a plethora of bus agencies selling tickets (shop around). You can also book online at www.busonlineticket.com. You can check the latest prices and book tickets with the following companies:

Aeroline   BUS
(✉6258 8800; www.aeroline.com.sg; 02-52 HarbourFront Centre, 1 Maritime Square) Coaches to Kuala Lumpur and Penang departing from HarbourFront Centre.

First Coach   BUS
(✉6822 2111; www.firstcoach.com.my; 03-33 Novena Square, 238 Thompson Rd) Daily buses to Kuala Lumpur departing from Novena Square. Some services depart from The Plaza and West Coast Plaza.

Grassland Express   BUS
(✉6293 1166; www.grassland.com.sg; 01-26 Golden Mile Complex, 5001 Beach Rd) Daily buses to Kuala Lumpur, Penang, Meleka, Perak and numerous other destinations.

Transtar Travel   BUS
(✉6299 9009; www.transtar.travel; 5001 Beach Rd, 01-12 Golden Mile Complex) Luxury coaches to Kuala Lumpur, Genting, Ipoh and Penang.

TRAIN

Singapore is the southern terminus for the Malaysian railway system, **Keretapi Tanah Malayu** (KTM; www.ktmb.com.my).

Malaysia has two main rail lines: the primary line goes from Singapore to Kuala Lumpur (KL), Butterworth, Alor Setar and then into Hat Yai, Thailand; the second branches off at Gemas and continues through the centre of the country to Tumpat, near Kota Bharu on the east coast.

Note that the art deco railway station in Singapore was closed for private redevelopment in 2011. The KTM train to Malaysia now runs out of the **Woodlands Train Checkpoint** (11 Woodlands Crossing; ☐170, Causeway Link from Queen St).

Three express trains depart every day to Kuala Lumpur roughly around 8am, 1pm and 10.30pm, and take six and seven hours; check the website for connecting train timings. You can book tickets either at the station or via the KTM website (www.ktmb.com.my).

Finally, the luxurious **Eastern & Oriental Express** (✆6395 0678; www.orient-express.com) departs Singapore on the 42-hour, 1943km journey to Bangkok before heading onwards to Chiang Mai and Nong Khai (for Laos). Don your linen suit, sip a gin and tonic, and dig deep for the fare: from S$3737 per person in a double compartment to S$7462 in the presidential suite. You can go as far as KL or Butterworth for a lower fare.

SEA

The following main ferry terminals run services to Malaysia and/or Indonesia:

Changi Point Ferry Terminal (✆6546 8518; Ⓜ Tanah Merah, then ☐2) Located 200m north of the bus terminal.

Harbourfront Cruise & Ferry Terminal (✆6513 2200; www.singaporecruise.com; Ⓜ HarbourFront)

Tanah Merah Ferry Terminal (✆6513 2200; www.singaporecruise.com; ☐35, Ⓜ Tanah Merah)

FERRIES TO RIAU ARCHIPELAGO (INDONESIA)

Direct ferries run between Singapore and the Indonesian islands of Pulau Batam, Pulau Bintan and Pulau Karimun Besar in the Riau Archipelago. The ferries are modern, fast and air-conditioned. The main companies include these ones:

BatamFast FERRY
(✆6270 0311; www.batamfast.com) Ferries to Batam Centre, Sekupang, and Waterfront City depart from Harbourfront Ferry Terminal. Ferries to Nongsapura depart from the Tanah Merah Ferry Terminal.

Berlian Ferries FERRY
(✆6546 8830) Ferries to Pulau Batam depart from Harbourfront Ferry Terminal.

Bintan Resort Ferries FERRY
(✆6542 4369; www.brf.com.sg) Ferries to Bandar Bintan Telani depart from Tanah Merah Ferry Terminal.

Indo Falcon FERRY
(✆6542 6786, 6278 3167; www.indofalcon.com.sg) Ferries to Pulau Batam depart from HarbourFront Ferry Terminal. Ferries to Tanjung Pinang in Bintan depart from Tanah Merah Ferry Terminal.

Sindo Ferries FERRY
(✆6271 4866; www.sindoferry.com.sg) Ferries going to Batam Centre and Sekupang, Tanjung Balai and Waterfront City depart from HarbourFront Ferry Terminal. Ferries to Tanjung Pinang depart from the Tanah Merah Ferry Terminal.

SINGAPORE TRANSPORT

GETTING TO MALAYSIA: SINGAPORE TO JOHOR BAHRU

Getting to the border The easiest way to reach the border is on the 'Singapore–Johore Express' bus (S$2.40; one hour, every 15 minutes from 6.30am to 11pm), which departs from the Queen Street Bus Terminal in Little India. The quickest way is to catch the MRT to Kranji, then bus 160 to the border. The cheapest (and slowest) way is on bus 170 (S$1.90, every 10-15 minutes from 5.20am to 12.10am), which also leaves from Queen Street Bus Terminal. Try to avoid crossing back into Singapore on Sunday nights, when traffic is hellish. Shared taxis also depart for Johor Bahru (JB) from the Queen Street Bus Terminal.

At the border At the Singapore checkpoint, disembark from the bus with your luggage, go through immigration, and reboard the next bus (keep your ticket). After repeating the process on the Malaysian side, it's a quick walk into central JB. Alternatively, bus 160 terminates at JB's Kotaraya Bus Terminal. Both Bus 170 and the 'Singapore–Johore Express' bus terminate at Larkin Bus Terminal, inconveniently located 5km north of the Causeway.

Moving on From Larkin Bus Terminal, long-distance buses depart to numerous Malaysian destinations, including Melaka, KL and Ipoh.

See p232 for details on doing the trip in the opposite direction.

Destination	Singapore Ferry Terminal	Journey Time	Cost
Bandar Bintan Telani (Pulau Bintan)	Tanah Merah	55min	S$25.45
Batam Centre (Pulau Batam)	Harbour-Front	1hr	S$31
Nongsapara (Pulau Batam)	Tanah Merah	45min	S$31
Sekupang (Pulau Batam)	Harbour-Front	45min	S$29
Tanjung Balai (Karimun Besar)	Harbour-Front	1hr 35min	S$40
Tanjung Pinang (Pulau Bintan)	Tanah Merah	1hr 50min	S$31

GETTING AROUND

Singapore is the easiest city in Asia to get around. The TransitLink Guide – S$2.80 from MRT ticket booths and Kinokuniya book store (p535) – lists all MRT and bus routes and includes maps showing the surrounding area of all MRT stations. For online bus information, which includes the useful IRIS service (which offers live next-bus departure times), see www.sbstransit.com.sg or download the 'SBS Transit iris' Smartphone app. For train information, see www.smrt.com.sg.

BICYCLE

Singapore's roads are not for the faint-hearted. It's furiously hot, and drivers tend to be fast, aggressive and not particularly sympathetic to the needs of cyclists. Fortunately, there's a large network of parks and park connectors and a few exceptional dedicated mountain-biking areas – at Bukit Timah Nature Reserve, Tampines and Pulau Ubin. Cycling up to Changi Village and then taking the bike over to Pulau Ubin is an excellent adventure. Other great places for cycling include East Coast Park, Sentosa Island, Pasir Ris Park and the route linking Mt Faber Park, Telok Blangah Hill Park and Kent Ridge Park.

If you have your own bike, be aware that it's not allowed on public transport unless it's a fold-up bike. You can take fold-up bikes on trains and buses during these hours: Monday to Friday 9.30am-4pm & 8pm onwards; all-day Saturday and Sunday and public holidays. Note that only ONE fold-up bike is allowed on buses at all times, so you might as well ride if you have to.

If you haven't brought your own, pick up some wheels at **Treknology Bikes 3** (6732 7119; www.treknology3.com; 01-02, 91 Tanglin Place; 24hr hire S$35-50; 11am-7.30pm Mon-Sat, 11.30am-3pm Sun). Bikes can also be rented at several places along East Coast Parkway, on Sentosa Island and Pulau Ubin, with adult prices ranging from S$5 on Pulau Ubin to S$12 on Sentosa.

BOAT & FERRY

There are regular ferry services from **Marina South Pier** (6275 03888; 31 Marina Coastal Dr; Marina Bay, then 402) to other southern islands (p543) and from Changi Point Ferry Terminal (p543) to Pulau Ubin.

BUS

Singapore's extensive bus service is clean, efficient and regular, reaching every corner of the island.

The two main operators are **SBS Transit** (1800-287 2727; www.sbstransit.com.sg) and **SMRT** (www.smrt.com.sg). Both offer similar service. For information and routes, check the websites. Bus fares range from S$1 to S$2.10 (less with an EZ-Link card). When you board the bus, drop the exact money into the fare box (no change is given), or tap your EZ-Link card or Tourist Pass on the reader as you board, then again when you get off.

MRT also runs seven NightRider bus routes between the city and various suburbs on Friday and Saturday nights from 11.45pm to 3.45am. SBS runs six Nite Owl weekend routes between midnight and 2am. See the websites for route details.

TOURIST BUSES

SIA Hop-On (9457 2896; www.siahopon.com; 1-day ticket for SIA passengers adult/child S$6/3, non-passengers S$12/6) Singapore Airlines' tourist bus traverses the main tourist arteries every 30 minutes daily, starting opposite Marina Square on Raffles Blvd at 9am, with the last bus leaving at 7.35pm and terminating at Raffles Hotel at 8.55pm. Buy tickets from the driver and see the website for route details.

City Hippo (✆6338 6877; www.ducktours.com.sg; 24hr Singapore Sightseeing Pass (incl river cruise) adult/child S$33/23) offers a confusing array of tour options round all the major sites. There are numerous pick-up points around town. See the website for tour options.

CAR & MOTORCYCLE

Singaporeans drive on the left-hand side of the road and the wearing of seat belts is compulsory. Traffic is orderly though aggressive driving, tailgating, speeding and lane-changing without signalling is very common. The profusion of one-way streets and streets that change names (sometimes several times) can also make driving stressful. The *Mighty Minds Singapore Street Directory* is essential for negotiating the city.

Motorcycles are held in very low esteem. Some drivers display almost no regard for bike safety. Be alert when riding.

DRIVING LICENCE

If you plan on driving in Singapore, bring your current home driver's licence. Some car hire companies may also require you to have an international driving permit.

HIRE

If you want a car for local driving only, it's worth checking smaller operators, whose rates are often cheaper than the big global rental firms.

If you're going into Malaysia, you're better off renting in Johor Bahru, where the rates are significantly lower (besides, Malaysian police are renowned for targeting Singapore licence plates).

Rates start from around S$60 a day. Special deals may be available, especially for longer-term rental. Most rental companies also require that drivers are at least 23 years old.

All major car-hire companies have hire booths at Changi Airport. There are other offices around Singapore:

Avis (✆6737 1668; www.avis.com.sg; 01-07 Waterfront Plaza, 390A Havelock Rd)

Express Car (✆6748 9963; www.expresscar.com.sg; 1 Sims Lane)

Hawk (✆6469 4468; www.hawkrentacar.com.sg; 32A Hillview Terrace)

Hertz (✆6542 5300, 6542 5300; www.hertz.com.sg; Singapore Changi Airport Terminal 2 & 3)

Premier (www-singapore.com/premier; 03-05 Balmoral Plaza, 271 Bukit Timah Rd)

RESTRICTED ZONES & CAR PARKING

Between 7.30am and 7pm weekdays, and from 10.15am to 2pm Saturdays, the area encompassing the CBD, Chinatown and Orchard Rd becomes a restricted zone. Cars may enter but they must pay a toll. Vehicles are automatically tracked by sensors on overhanging gantries that prompt drivers to insert a cashcard (available from 7-Elevens and petrol stations) into their in-vehicle unit. The toll is extracted from the card. The

AIRPORT-CITY CONNECTIONS

MODE	AIRPORT TERMINALS	DESTINATION	COST	FREQUENCY
Train (MRT)	2 & 3	Extensive island coverage (interchange at Tanah Merah station)	varies, Orchard Rd S$2.10	every 12 mins, 5.30am-11.18pm
Taxi	All terminals	Anywhere	varies, around $18 to $35 (most expensive between 5pm and 6am)	
Bus 36	All terminals	Orchard Rd & Colonial District	S$1.80	every 5-15 mins, 6.09am-midnight
Airport Shuttle	All terminals	Any hotel (Sentosa and Changi Village hotels excluded)	adult/child S$9/6	every 15-30 mins, 24hrs

TRISHAWS

Trishaws peaked just after WWII when motorised transport was practically nonexistent and trishaw drivers could make a tidy income. Today there are only around 250 trishaws left in Singapore, mainly plying the tourist routes. Trishaws have banded together and are now managed in a queue system by **Trishaw Uncle** (☑9012 1233; www.trishawuncle.com.sg; Queen St btwn Fu Lu Shou Complex & Albert Centre Market; rides from S$39).

You can also find freelance trishaw riders outside Raffles Hotel and outside the Chinatown Complex.

same system is also in operation on certain expressways. Rental cars are subject to the same rules.

Parking in the city centre is expensive, but relatively easy to find – almost every major mall has a car park. Outdoor car parks and street parking spaces are usually operated by the government – you can buy booklets of parking coupons, which must be displayed in the window, from post offices and convenience stores. Many car parks are now run using the same in-vehicle unit and cashcard and ERP gantries instead of the coupon system.

MASS RAPID TRANSIT (MRT)

The ultraclean, safe and efficient Singapore **MRT** (☑1800-336 8900; www.smrt.com.sg) subway and light-rail system is the most comfortable and hassle-free way to get around Singapore. Trains run from around 5.30am to midnight, departing every three to four minutes at peak times and every six to eight off-peak. It consists of four lines: North–South, North–East and East–West, and the Circle Line. More lines are set to open between now and 2020. MRT map and trip planner available online: www.smrt.com.sg.

FARES & FARE CARDS

Single-trip tickets cost from S$1.20 to S$2.20 (plus a S$1 refundable deposit), but if you're using the MRT a lot it can become a hassle buying and refunding tickets for every journey.

Much more convenient is the **EZ-link card** (www.ezlink.com.sg). Costing S$12 (which includes a S$5 nonrefundable deposit) and available from the customer service windows at MRT stations, it's valid on all buses and trains and will save you up to 30% on fares. The card can also be bought from 7-Eleven stores for S$10 (which includes a S$5 nonrefundable deposit). Cards can be topped up with cash or ATM cards at station ticket machines.

Alternatively, a **Singapore Tourist Pass** (www.thesingaporetouristpass.com) offers unlimited train and bus travel (S$8 plus a S$10 refundable deposit) for one day.

TAXI

You can flag down a taxi any time, but in the city centre taxis are not allowed to stop anywhere except at designated taxi stands. Finding a taxi during peak hours, at night, or in the rain is harder than it should be.

The fare system is also complicated, but thankfully it's all metered, so there's no haggling over fares. The basic flagfall is S$3 to S$3.40, then 22¢ for every 400m. There are a raft of surcharges to note, among them:
» 50% of the metered fare from midnight to 6am.
» 25% of the metered fare between 6am and 9.30am Monday to Friday, and 6pm to midnight daily.
» S$3 city area surcharge from 5pm to midnight.
» S$2.30 to S$8 for telephone bookings.
» S$3 on all trips from the CBD between 5pm and midnight, Monday to Saturday.

You may also have to pay another surcharge if you take the taxi into the CBD during restricted hours (S$5 from 5pm to midnight Friday to Sunday; S$3 all other times for journeys from the airport) and credit card payments incur a 10% surcharge.

Confused? We are too. Just follow the meter and ask for a receipt to check charges.

If you need a taxi, contact one of the following companies:

Comfort Taxi and CityCab (☑6552 1111)

Premier Taxis (☑6363 6888)

SMRT Taxis (☑6555 8888)

Understand
Malaysia,
❭Singapore & Brunei

MALAYSIA, SINGAPORE & BRUNEI TODAY.....548

The lowdown on the political, economic and social issues facing Malaysians, Singaporeans and Bruneians.

HISTORY.....................................551

How these three countries emerged from and were forged by the lucrative trade in spices, rubber and oil around the Malay Peninsula.

PEOPLE, CULTURE & POLITICS...............562

Malays, Chinese and Indians mingle in these multicultural nations. There are also scores of indigenous people, particularly in Borneo.

RELIGION...................................569

Islam is the region's main religion but it is predated by Hinduism. Christianity and various Chinese beliefs are also present.

ARTS & MEDIA..............................574

Alongside traditional arts and crafts there's a thriving contemporary art scene, particularly in Malaysia and Singapore. The internet is also bringing greater media freedom.

FOOD & DRINK..............................579

In Malaysia it's not 'How are you?' but 'Sundah makan?' (Have you eaten yet?). Your entrée to the region's best eats and drinks.

THE REGION'S ENVIRONMENT...............585

Find out how these countries are balancing conservation of their mega-diverse environments with economic development.

MALAYSIA   SINGAPORE   BRUNEI

≈ 70 people

Malaysia, Singapore & Brunei Today

Malaysia's 2013 Election

At the time of research, Malaysia's Prime Minister Najib Razak has until April 2013 to call the country's next general election – all indications are that he will leave it until the last minute to do so. Ever since the previous elections in 2008 – in which the United Malays National Organisation (UMNO) and its coalition partner, Barisan Nasional (BN), saw their parliamentary dominance slashed to less than the customary two-thirds majority – the ruling coalition has been looking nervously at the increasing popularity of Pakatan Rakyat (PR), the opposition People's Alliance, led by Anwar Ibrahim. PR already are in control of three of Malaysia's 13 state governments.

In July 2011 and April 2012 rallies by Bersih (www.bersih.org), a civil rights organisation seeking fairer elections, brought tens of thousands of people onto the streets of central Kuala Lumpur (KL). Both ended up being broken up by police with tear gas and water cannons. Such is the suspicion of the government that Anwar admitted to being surprised when sodomy charges against him were thrown out in January 2012 because of unreliable evidence; the trial had dragged on for two years by that point. Information Minister Rais Yatim said that the verdict showed that judges were free to rule as they saw fit. See (p559) for more details about Anwar's trial and political career.

Winning Policies?

Malaysia saw strong economic growth in 2012, partly linked to the government's $444 billion Economic Transformation Program (ETP), which aims to lift the country to high-income status by 2020. To tackle public concerns about rampant graft, Najib also set up the independent

The Malaysian national oil and gas company Petronas (www. petronas.com. my) is one of the most profitable in the world. It accounted for about a third of the Malaysian government's estimated RM183 billion revenue in 2011.

Top Fiction

The Garden of Evening Mists (Tan Twan Eng) Horticultural intrigue in the Malaysian highlands.
Little Ironies: Stories of Singapore (Catherine Lim) A collection by the doyenne of Singaporean fiction.

Urban Odysseys (Janet Tay & Eric Forbes, eds) Short stories set in KL that capture the city's multifaceted, multicultural flavour.

Top Websites

www.thenutgraph.com Features on Malaysian politics and popular culture.
www.theedgemalaysia.com Business news and more general features.
www.themalaysianinsder.com The people shaping Malaysia.

if Malaysia were 100 people

50 would be Malay
24 would be Chinese
11 would be Orang Asli
7 would be Indian
8 would be other

if Singapore were 100 people

14 would be Malay
76 would be Chinese
8 would be Indian
2 would be other

Malaysian Anti-Corruption Agency (MACC), which in 2011 resulted in 900 individuals being arrested on corruption charges.

While the hope is that such policies will persuade voters to stick with the ruling coalition rather than take a chance with PR when the election comes around, other government actions have played into the oppositions hands. The government's decision to replace the draconian *Internal Security Act* (ISA) with the *Security Offences (Special Measures) Act 2012* has been criticised by many, including Human Rights Watch, who believe the new legislation doesn't go far enough to protect the fundamental rights and freedoms of Malaysians.

Uneven Society in Singapore

With a per capita GDP of S$63,000 in 2011, Singaporeans enjoy one of the world's highest standards of living. However, modern Singapore is grappling with several social and lifestyle issues. Features in the newspapers and the talk at local coffee shops invariably revolve around the soaring cost of living and the growing gap between the haves and have nots: a study in 2009 by the United Nations Development Programme found that Singapore has the most uneven distribution of wealth in the developed world, after Hong Kong.

There are also worries about the impact of gambling now that the island has two casinos and the ethnic tension created by an ever-increasing foreign population versus a declining citizen base. Singapore's birthrate is among the lowest in the world (7.7 births per 1000 people). The government offers plenty of incentives convincing couples to procreate, ranging from baby bonuses to government-subsidised salsa classes and amusing viral video campaigns advising couples to 'do their civic duty' to help increase the city-state's birthrate. Even so,

Majulah Singapura (Onward Singapore), the Singaporean national anthem, was composed by Zubir Said in 1958. Its lyrics are in Bahasa Malaysia, even though English is now the national language.

Playlist

Ghostbird (Zee Avi; www.zeeavi. com) Second album from the folksy pop diva who was once a KL art student.
Yuna (Yuna; www.yunamusic. com) First all-English album by another Malaysian beauty with

a soulful voice to match her sultry looks.
Harapan (Reshmonu; www. reshmonu.com) Dance master Reshmonu's latest album.

Top Non-Fiction

Singapore: A Biography (Mark Ravinder Frost & Yu-Mei Balasingam-chow; 2010) A well-written and handsomely illustrated history of Singapore.
Malaysia at Random (Editions Didier Millet; 2010) Quirky compendium of facts and anecdotes.

Singapore's population doubled from 1980 to 2010 because of the influx of foreign workers, who now make up 27% of the population. To diffuse tensions, the government has put the breaks on the intake of migrants.

The use of social media is increasing, and it is now a viable voice alongside mainstream media, which is often accused of being a goverment mouthpiece. Prime Minister Lee Hsien Loong participated in an online chat for the 2011 election. However, on his Facebook page in October 2012 Lee posted, 'Let us be mindful of what we say, online and in person', following community anger sparked when a Singaporean resident's racially abusive Facebook rant went viral.

Brunei: An Islamic Monarchy

Brunei finds itself in an odd position these days. Its population is becoming more connected to the outside world via the internet, MASwings flights and the physical upgrading of Bandar Seri Begawan's (BSB) airport, but on the other hand the Sultanate's vice laws are being expanded, and the existing ones now come with harsher penalties. The big question continues to be: what will happen when the oil runs out? For the average Brunei citizen, who is practically guaranteed work and a comfortable lifestyle by the government, that question feels too much like rocking the boat.

Many economists believe Brunei has focused heavily on a few segments of its National Development Plan – namely increasing GDP and employment – and ignored the bits on economic diversification. Tourism potential is always discussed, but a lack of alcohol will be a serious issue to overcome. In the meantime the Sultan continues to steer his nation towards Islamic fundamentalism, adopting a national ideology known as Melayu Islam Beraja (Malay Islamic Monarchy; MIB).

A 2012 report by the UN Refugee Agency noted 100,000 migrant workers in Brunei, some of whom face debt bondage, nonpayment of wages, passport confiscation, abusive employers and confinement to the home – conditions widely recognised as indicators of human trafficking.

Dos and Don'ts

» Do cover your head, arms and legs when visiting a mosque.

» Do use your right hand only if eating with your fingers.

» Don't embrace or kiss in public.

» Don't point with your forefinger: use the thumb of your right hand with fingers folded under.

Greetings

» A *salam* involves both parties briefly clasping each other's hand then bringing the same hand to touch their heart.

» Malay women don't shake hands with men – smile and nod or bow slightly instead.

Malaysia Bagus! (Sharon Cheah; 2012) Engaging travelogue with stories from all of Malaysia's states plus Singapore.

History

As the countries we know today, Malaysia, Singapore and Brunei have been around since 1963, 1965 and 1984 respectively. The region's history, of course, stretches back much further, although pinning down exactly how far back is a moot point due to a lack of archaeological evidence and early written records.

Earliest evidence of human life in the region is a 40,000-year-old skull found in Sarawak's Niah Caves, a period when Borneo was still connected to the Southeast Asian mainland. Discovered in 1991, the complete 11,000-year-old skeleton, 'Perak Man', has genetic similarities to the Negrito who now live in the mountainous rainforests of northern Malaysia.

The Negrito were joined by Malaysia's first immigrants, the Senoi, from southern Thailand, and later by the Proto-Malay, ancestors of to-day's Malays, who came by sea from Indonesia between 1500BC and 500 BC. Early civilisation here was shaped by the ebb and flow of the convergent sea trade from China and India. For example, it's thought that the word Malay (or Melayu) is based on the ancient Tamil word *malia,* meaning 'hill'. Other Malay words like *bahasa* (language), *raja* (ruler) and *jaya* (success) are Sanskrit terms imported to the area by Indian visitors as early as the 2nd century.

Events from the rise of the Melaka Sultanate in the 16th century were well documented locally and by the nations which came to trade with, and later rule over, the peninsula and Borneo, including the Portuguese, the Dutch and, finally, the British. It is during these centuries that re-nown colonial figures such as Sir Stamford Raffles and James Brookes made their mark on the region. Post WWII, as Britain shed its Empire, the three proto-countries carved out independent identities resulting in the distinct but historically entwined nations of today.

A History of Malaya by Barbara and Leonard Andaya brilliantly explores the evolution of 'Malayness' in Malaysia's history and the challenges of building a multiracial, post-independence nation.

TIMELINE

c 150AD	200	600
European knowledge of the Malay peninsula is confirmed in Ptolemy's book *Geographia*. It's likely that Romans visited the region during trading expeditions to India and China.	Langkasuka, one of the first Hindu-Malay kingdoms, is established on the peninsula around the area now known as Kedah. It lasted in one form or another until the 15th century.	From their base in southern Sumatra, most likely around modern-day Palembang, the Buddhist Srivijaya Empire dominates Malaya, Singapore, Indonesia and Borneo for another six centuries.

Early Trade & Empires

By the 2nd century Malaya was known as far away as Europe. Ptolemy, the Greek geographer, labelled it Aurea Chersonesus (Golden Chersonese); Indian traders, who came in search of precious metals, tin and aromatic jungle woods, referred to the land as Savarnadvipa (Land of Gold). The first formalised religions on the peninsula – Hinduism and Buddhism – arrived with those Indian traders, giving rise to the first recorded Hindu kingdom on the peninsula, Langkasuka (from the Sanskrit for 'resplendent land').

From the 7th century to the 13th century, the area fell under the sway of the Srivijaya Empire, based in southern Sumatra. This Buddhist empire controlled the entire Malacca Straits, Java and southern Borneo and became fabulously rich through trade with India and China. Under the protection of the Srivijayans, a significant Malay trading state grew up in the Bujang Valley area in the far northwest of the Thai–Malay peninsula. The growing power of the southern Thai kingdom of Ligor and the Hindu Majapahit Empire of Java finally led to the demise of the Srivijayans in the 14th century.

The Melaka Empire

The history of the Malay state begins in earnest in the late 14th century when Parameswara, a renegade Hindu prince/pirate from a little kingdom in southern Sumatra, washed up around 1401 in the tiny fishing village that would become Melaka. As a seafarer, Parameswara recognised a good port when he saw it and he immediately lobbied the Ming emperor of China for protection from the Thais in exchange for generous trade deals. Thus the Chinese came to Malaysia.

Equidistant between India and China, Melaka became a major stop for freighters from India loaded with pepper and cloth, and junks from

---

THE ADOPTION OF ISLAM

Peninsular Malaysia was Buddhist and Hindu for a thousand years before the local rulers adopted Islam. The religion is believed to have spread through contact with Indian Muslim traders; in 1136 the Kedah Annals record that Hindu ruler Phra Ong Mahawangsa converted to Islam and founded the sultanate of Kedah, the oldest on Peninsular Malaysia.

The first sultan of Brunei, Muhammad Shah, converted to Islam in 1363 upon his marriage to a princess from Johor-Temasik. Maharaja Mohammed Shah of Melaka, who reigned between 1424 and 1444, also converted. The maharaja's son, Mudzaffar Shah, later took the title of sultan and made Islam the state religion. With its global trade links, Melaka became a regional hub for the dissemination of Islam and the Malay language.

1402	1446	1509	1511
Hindu prince and pirate Parameswara (1344–1414) founds the great trading port and sultanate of Melaka; seven years later he marries a Muslim princess and adopts the Persian title Iskandar Shah.	A naval force from Siam (Thailand) attacks Melaka. Warded off, the Siamese return in 1456 but are again rebuffed. Such attacks encourage Melaka's rulers to develop closer relations with China.	Portuguese traders sail into Melaka. Although at first greeted warmly, acting on the advice of his Indian Muslim councillors, the Melakan sultan later attacks the Portuguese ships, taking 19 prisoners.	Following the Portuguese conquest of Melaka, the sultan and his court flee, establishing two new sultanates on the peninsula: Perak to the north and Johor to the south.

China loaded with porcelain and silks, which were traded for local metal and spices. Business boomed as regional ships and *perahu* (Malay-style sampans) arrived to take advantage of trading opportunities. The Melakan sultans soon ruled over the greatest empire in Malaysia's history.

The Portuguese Era

By the 15th century, Europe had developed an insatiable appetite for spices, which were conveyed there via a convoluted trade route through India and Arabia. The Portuguese decided to cut out the middle man and go directly to the source: Melaka. Reaching the Malay coast in 1509, the Portuguese were greeted warmly by the local sultan, but relations soon soured. The invaders laid siege to Melaka in 1511, capturing the city and driving the sultan and his forces back to Johor.

The Portuguese secured Melaka by building the robust Porta de Santiago (A'Famosa fortress) and their domination lasted 130 years, though the entire period was marked by skirmishes with local sultans. Compared with Indian Muslim traders, the Portuguese contributed little to Malay culture; attempts to introduce Christianity and the Portuguese language were never a big success, though a dialect of Portuguese, Kristang, is still spoken in Melaka.

The Dutch Period

Vying with the Portuguese for control of the spice trade, the Dutch formed an allegiance with the sultans of Johor to oust the Portuguese from Melaka. A joint force of Dutch and Johor soldiers and sailors besieged Melaka in 1641 and wrested the city from the Portuguese. In return for its cooperation, Johor was made exempt from most of the tariffs and trade restrictions imposed on other vassal states. Despite maintaining control of Melaka for about 150 years, the Dutch never really realised the full potential of the city. High taxes forced merchants to seek out other ports and the Dutch focused their main attention on Batavia (now Jakarta) as their regional headquarters.

East India Company

British interest in the region began with the need for a halfway base for East India Company (EIC) ships plying the India–China maritime route. The first base was established on the island of Penang in 1786.

Meanwhile, events in Europe were conspiring to consolidate British interests on the Malay peninsula. When Napoleon overran the Netherlands in 1795, the British, fearing French influence in the region, took over Dutch Java and Melaka. When Napoleon was defeated in 1818, the

Sabri Zain's colourful website *Sejarah Melayu: A History of the Malay Peninsula* (www.sabrizain.org/malaya) contains a wealth of historical info including a virtual library of nearly 500 books and academic papers.

HISTORY THE PORTUGUESE ERA

Sejarah Melayu (Malay Annals), a literary work covering the establishment of the Melaka sultanate and 600 years of Malay history, is believed to have been compiled by Tun Sri Lanang, the *bendahara* (chief minister) of the Johor Royal Court in the early 17th century.

1629	1641	1786
The Portuguese in Melaka and the sultanate of Johor unite to successfully defend themselves against the navy of Iskandar Muda, the sultan of Aceh in Sumatra, who had already conquered Kedah.	After a siege lasting several months the Dutch, with the help of the Johor sultanate, wrest Melaka from the Portuguese. Melaka starts to decline as a major trading port.	Francis Light cuts a deal with the sultan of Kedah to establish a settlement on the largely uninhabited island of Penang. Under a free-trade policy the island's new economy thrives.

» Francis Light, Penang

STUART DEE/GETTY IMAGES ©

THE NAVEL OF THE MALAY COUNTRIES

'It is impossible to conceive a place combining more advantages...it is the Navel of the Malay countries', wrote a delighted Raffles soon after landing in Singapore in 1819. The statement proves his foresight because at the time the island was an inhospitable swamp surrounded by dense jungle, with a population of 150 fishermen and a small number of Chinese farmers. Raffles returned to his post in Bencoolen, Sumatra, but left instructions on Singapore's development as a free port with the new British Resident, Colonel William Farquhar.

In 1822 Raffles returned to Singapore and governed it for one more year. He initiated a town plan that included levelling a hill to form a new commercial district (now Raffles Place) and erecting government buildings around Forbidden Hill (now Fort Canning Hill). Wide streets of shophouses with covered walkways, shipyards, churches and a botanical garden were all built to achieve his vision of a Singapore that would one day be 'a place of considerable magnitude and importance'.

Raffles' blueprint also embraced the colonial practice of administering the population according to neat racial categories, with the Europeans, Indians, Chinese and Malays living and working in their own distinct quarters.

British handed the Dutch colonies back – but not before leaving the fortress of A'Famosa beyond use.

The British lieutenant-governor of Java, Stamford Raffles – yes, *that* Stamford Raffles – soon persuaded the EIC that a settlement south of the Malay peninsula was crucial to the India–China maritime route. In 1819, he landed in Singapore and negotiated a trade deal with Johor that saw the island ceded to Britain in perpetuity, in exchange for a significant cash tribute.

In 1824, Britain and the Netherlands signed the Anglo-Dutch Treaty, dividing the region into two distinct spheres of influence. The Dutch controlled what is now Indonesia, and the British controlled Penang, Melaka, Dinding and Singapore, which were soon combined to create the 'Straits Settlements'.

F Spencer Chapman's *The Jungle is Neutral* follows a British guerrilla force based in the Malaysian jungles during the Japanese occupation of Malaya and Singapore.

Borneo Developments

Britain did not include Borneo in the Anglo-Dutch treaty, preferring that the EIC concentrate its efforts on consolidating their power on the peninsula rather than furthering their geographical scope. Into the breach jumped opportunistic British adventurer James Brooke. In 1841, having helped the local viceroy quell a rebellion, Brooke was installed as raja of Sarawak, with the fishing village of Kuching as his capital.

1790	1819	1823	1826
The sultan of Kedah's attempt to retake Penang from the British fails. He is forced to cede the island to the British East India Company for 6000 Spanish dollars per annum.	By backing the elder brother in a succession dispute in Johor, Stamford Raffles gains sole rights to build a trading base on the island of Singapore.	The Johor sultan fully cedes Singapore to Britain. A year later the Dutch and British carve up the region into what eventually becomes Malaya and Indonesia.	Having swapped Bencoolen on Sumatra for the Dutch-controlled Melaka, the British East India Company combines this with Penang and Singapore to create the Straits Settlements.

Through brutal naval force and skilful negotiation, Brooke extracted further territory from the Brunei sultan and eventually brought peace to a land where piracy, headhunting and violent tribal rivalry had been the norm. The 'White Raja' dynasty of the Brookes was to rule Sarawak until 1941 and the arrival of the Japanese.

Unlike the British, the White Rajas included tribal leaders in their ruling council. They also discouraged large European companies from destroying native jungle to plant massive rubber plantations. They encouraged Chinese migration, which meant that the Chinese, without European competition, came to dominate the economy.

Meanwhile, the once-mighty empire of Brunei, which had held sway over all the islands of Borneo and much of present-day Philippines, continued to shrink. In 1865 the American consul to Brunei persuaded the ailing sultan to grant him what is now Sabah in return for an annual payment. The rights eventually passed to an Englishman, Alfred Dent. In 1881, with the support of the British government, Dent formed the British North Borneo Company to administer the new settlement. To prevent a scramble for Brunei's remains, in 1888 the British government acceded to a request by the sultan to declare his territory a British protectorate.

Noel Barber's *The War of the Running Dogs* is a classic account of the 12-year Malayan Emergency. The title refers to what the communist fighters called the opposition who were loyal to the British.

British Malaya

In Peninsular Malaya, Britain's policy of 'trade, not territory' was challenged when trade was disrupted by civil wars within the Malay sultanates of Negeri Sembilan, Selangor, Pahang and Perak. In 1874 the British started to take political control by appointing the first colonial governor of Perak. In 1896 Perak, Selangor, Negeri Sembilan and Pahang were united under the banner of the Federated Malay States, each governed by a British Resident.

CREATING A MULTICULTURAL NATION

British rule radically altered the ethnic composition of Malaya. Chinese and Indian migrant workers were brought into the country as they shared a similar economic agenda and had less nationalist grievances against the colonial administration than the native Malays. The Chinese were encouraged to work the mines and the Indians to tap the rubber trees and build the railways. The Ceylonese were clerks in the civil service, and the Sikhs manned the police force.

Even though the 'better-bred' Malays were encouraged to join a separate arm of the civil service, there was growing resentment among the vast majority of Malays that they were being marginalised in their own country. A 1931 census revealed that the Chinese numbered 1.7 million and the Malays 1.6 million. Malaya's economy was revolutionised, but the impact of this liberal immigration policy continues to reverberate today.

1839	1874	1888	1896
British buccaneer James Brooke lands in Sarawak and helps quell a local rebellion. In gratitude, the Brunei sultanate installs him as the first White Raja of Sarawak two years later.	The British start to take control of Peninsular Malaysia after Pankor Treaty with the sultan of Perak; Sir James Birch is installed as the Perak's first British Resident.	Having lost much territory to the British Empire, Brunei's sultan signs a treaty to make his country a British protectorate. A British Resident is installed in 1906.	Perak, Selangor, Negeri Sembilan and Pahang join as Federated Malay States; the sultans concede political power to British Residents but keep control of matters relating to Malay traditions and Islam.

Covering events up to 2001, the second edition of Graham Saunder's *History of Brunei* is the only full-length study of how this tiny country came to be formed.

Amir Muhammad's *Malaysian Politicians Say the Darndest Things Vols 1 & 2* (see www.kinibooks.com) gathers together jaw-dropping statements uttered by the local pollies over the last three decades – including 'If you come across a snake and a man from a certain ethnic community, you should hit the man first'.

Kelantan, Terengganu, Perlis and Kedah were then purchased from the Thais, in exchange for the construction of the southern Thai railway, much to the dismay of local sultans. The 'Unfederated Malay States' eventually accepted British 'advisers', though the sultan of Terengganu held out till 1919 – to this day, the states of the northeast peninsula form the heartland of the fundamentalist Malay Muslim nationalist movement.

By the eve of WWII Malays from all states were pushing for independence.

WWII Period

A few hours before the bombing of Pearl Harbor in December 1941, Japanese forces landed on the northeast coast of Malaya. Within a few months they had taken over the entire peninsula and Singapore. The poorly defended Borneo states fell even more rapidly.

Singapore's new governor, General Yamashita, slung the Europeans into the infamous Changi Prison, and Chinese communists and intellectuals, who had vociferously opposed the Japanese invasion of China, were targeted for Japanese brutality. Thousands were executed in a single week. In Borneo, early resistance by the Chinese was also brutally put down.

The Japanese achieved very little in Malaya. The British had destroyed most of the tin-mining equipment before their retreat, and the rubber plantations were neglected. The Malayan People's Anti-Japanese Army (MPAJA), comprising remnants of the British army and Chinese from the fledgling Malayan Communist Party, waged a weak jungle-based guerrilla struggle throughout the war.

The Japanese surrendered to the British in Singapore in 1945. Despite the eventual Allied victory, Britain had been humiliated by the easy loss of Malaya and Singapore to the Japanese, and it was clear that their days of controlling the region were now numbered.

Federation of Malaya

In 1946 the British persuaded the sultans to agree to the Malayan Union, which amalgamated all the peninsular Malayan states into a central authority and offered citizenship to all residents regardless of race. In the process, the sultans were reduced to the level of paid advisers, the system of special privileges for Malays was abandoned and ultimate sovereignty passed to the king of England.

The normally acquiescent Malay population were less enthusiastic about the venture than the sultans. Rowdy protest meetings were held throughout the country, and the first Malay political party, the United Malays National Organisation (UMNO), was formed, leading to the dissolution of the Malayan Union and, in 1948, the creation of the Federation

1909	1941	1942	1946
Britain does a deal with Thailand to gain control of Kelantan, Terengganu, Perlis and Kedah. Johor succumbs to a British Resident in 1914, completing the set of 'Unfederated Malay States'.	The Japanese land on Malaya's northeast coast. Within a month they've taken Kuala Lumpur, and a month later they are at Singapore's doorstep.	The British suffer a humiliating defeat in February as Singapore capitulates to the Japanese. The occupiers rename it Syonan (Light of the South).	The United Malays National Organisation (UMNO) is formed on 1 March, signalling the rise of Malay nationalism and a desire for political independence from Britain.

THE EMERGENCY

While the creation of the Federation of Malaya appeased Malays, the Chinese felt betrayed, particularly given their massive contribution to the war effort. Many joined the Malayan Communist Party (MCP), which promised an equitable and just society. In 1948 the MCP took to the jungles and embarked on a 12-year guerrilla war against the British. Even though the insurrection was on par with the Malay civil wars of the 19th century, it was classified as an 'Emergency' for insurance purposes.

The effects of the Emergency were felt most strongly in the countryside, where villages and plantation owners were repeatedly targeted by rebels. In 1951 the British high commissioner was assassinated on the road to Fraser's Hill. His successor, General Sir Gerald Templer, set out to 'win the hearts and minds of the people'. Almost 500,000 rural Chinese were forcibly resettled into protected *kampung baru* (new villages), restrictions were lifted on guerrilla-free areas, and the jungle-dwelling Orang Asli were bought into the fight to help the police track down the insurgents.

In 1960 the Emergency was declared over, although sporadic fighting continued and the formal surrender was signed only in 1989.

of Malaya, which reinstated the sovereignty of the sultans and the special privileges of the Malays.

Merdeka & Malaysia

Malaysia's march to independence from British rule was led by UMNO, which formed a strategic alliance with the Malayan Chinese Association (MCA; www.mca.org.my) and the Malayan Indian Congress (MIC; www.mic.org.my). The new Alliance Party led by Tunku Abdul Rahman won a landslide victory in the 1955 election and, on 31 August 1957, Merdeka (Independence) was declared. Sarawak, Sabah (then North Borneo) and Brunei remained under British rule.

In 1961 Tunku Abdul Rahman proposed a merger of Singapore, Malaya, Sabah, Sarawak and Brunei, which the British agreed to the following year. At the eleventh hour Brunei pulled out of the deal, as Sultan Sri Muda Omar Ali Saifuddien III (and, one suspects, Shell Oil) didn't want to see the revenue from its vast oil reserves channelled to the peninsula.

When modern Malaysia was born in July 1963 it immediately faced a diplomatic crisis. The Philippines broke off relations, claiming that Sabah was part of its territory (a claim upheld to this day), while Indonesia laid claim to the whole of Borneo, invading parts of Sabah and Sarawak before finally giving up its claim in 1966.

The marriage between Singapore and Malaya was also doomed from the start. Ethnic Chinese outnumbered Malays in both Malaysia and

Revolusi 48 (http://revolusi48.blogspot.co.uk, in Bahasa Malaysia), the sequel to Fahmi Reza's doco 10 Tahun Sebelum Merdeka (10 Years Before Merdeka), chronicles the largely forgotten armed revolution for national liberation launched against British colonial rule in Malaya.

1948	1951	1953
The Malayan Communist Party (MCP) take to the jungles and begins fighting a guerrilla war against the British, known as the 'Emergency', that will last 12 years.	Sir Henry Gurney, British high commissioner to Malaya, is assassinated by MCP rebels on the road to Fraser's Hill, a terrorist act that alienates many of the party's moderate Chinese members.	The Parti Perikatan (Alliance Party) is formed, an alliance between UNMO, the Malayan Chinese Association (MCA) and Malayan Indian Congress (MIC). Two years later the party wins Malaya's first national elections.

POPPERFOTO/GETTY IMAGES ©

» Sir Henry Gurney

Singapore and the new ruler of the island-state, Lee Kuan Yew, refused to extend constitutional privileges to the Malays in Singapore. Riots broke out in Singapore in 1964; in August 1965 Tunku Abdul Rahman was forced to boot Singapore out of the federation.

Ethnic Tensions

1957–2007 Chronicle of Malaysia, edited by Philip Mathews, is a beautifully designed book showcasing 50 years of the country's history in news stories and pictures.

Impoverished Malays became increasingly resentful of the economic success of Chinese Malaysians, while the Chinese grew resentful of the political privileges granted to Malays. Things reached breaking point when the Malay-dominated government attempted to suppress all languages except Malay and introduced a national policy of education that ignored Chinese and Indian history, language and culture.

In the 1969 general elections, the Alliance Party lost its two-thirds majority in parliament and a celebration march by the opposition Democratic Action Party (DAP) and Gerakan (The People's Movement) in KL led to a full-scale riot, which Malay gangs used as a pretext to loot Chinese businesses, killing hundreds of Chinese in the process.

Stunned by the savageness of the riots, the government decided that if there was ever going to be harmony between the races then the Malay community needed to achieve economic parity. To this end the New Economic Policy (NEP), a socioeconomic affirmative action plan, was introduced. The Alliance Party also invited opposition parties to join them and work from within, and the expanded coalition was renamed the Barisan Nasional (BN; National Front).

The Era of Mahathir

Dr Mahathir Mohamad's first book, *The Malay Dilemma*, in which he postulated that Malay backwardness was due to hereditary and cultural factors, was banned in 1970.

In 1981 former UMNO member Mahathir Mohamad became prime minister. Malaysia's economy went into overdrive, growing from one based on commodities such as rubber to one firmly rooted in industry and manufacturing. Government monopolies were privatised, and heavy industries like steel manufacturing (a failure) and the Malaysian car (successful but heavily protected) were encouraged. Multinationals were successfully wooed to set up in Malaysia, and manufactured exports began to dominate the trade figures.

One notable criticism of Mahathir's premiership was that the main media outlets became little more than government mouthpieces. The sultans lost their right to give final assent on legislation, and the once proudly independent judiciary appeared to become subservient to government wishes, the most notorious case being that of Anwar Ibrahim. Mahathir also permitted widespread use of the Internal Security Act (ISA) to silence opposition leaders and social activists, most famously in 1987's Operation Lalang, when 106 people were arrested and the publishing licences of several newspapers were revoked.

1957	1963	1965	1967
On 31 August Merdeka (independence) is declared in Malaya; Tunku Abdul Rahman becomes first prime minister and the nine sultans agree to take turns as the nation's king.	In July the British Borneo territories of Sabah and Sarawak are combined with Singapore and Malaya to form Malaysia – a move that sparks confrontations with Indonesia and the Philippines.	In August, following Singapore's refusal to extend constitutional privileges to the Malays on the island and subsequent riots, Singapore is booted out of Malaysia. Lee Kuan Yew becomes Singapore's first prime minister.	Sultan Sri Muda Omar Ali Saifuddien III voluntarily abdicates in favour of his eldest son and the current ruler, the 29th in the unbroken royal Brunei line, Sultan Hassanal Bolkiah.

BUMIPUTRA PRIVELEGES

When introduced in 1971, the aim of the New Economic Policy (NEP) was that 30% of Malaysia's corporate wealth be in the hands of indigenous Malays, or *bumiputra* (princes of the land), within 20 years. A massive campaign of positive discrimination began which handed majority control over the army, police, civil service and government to Malays. The rules extended to education, scholarships, share deals, corporate management and even the right to import a car.

By 1990 *bumiputra* corporate wealth had risen to 19%, but was still 11% short of the original target. Poverty in general fell dramatically, a new Malay middle class emerged and nationalist violence by Malay extremists receded. However, cronyism and discrimination against Indians and Chinese increased, while Malays still accounted for three in four of the poorest people in the country.

Affirmative action in favour of *bumiputra* continues today but there is a growing recognition that it is hampering rather than helping Malaysia. Former law minister Zaid Ibrahim was reported in the *New York Times* as saying that Malaysia had 'sacrificed democracy for the supremacy of one race', because of the economic privileges given to *bumiputra*. In September 2010 Prime Minister Najib advocated a fundamental reform of the pro-Malay policies, but fell short of calling for outright scrapping of the system.

In the opposite corner are those, like former prime minister Mahathir, who believe that *bumiputra* would suffer the most if the administration were to implement a 100 per cent meritocracy-based system. A July 2010 poll by the independent Merdeka Centre shows that Malays in general are split on the matter: 45% believing the policies only benefit the rich and well-connected, 48% thinking they are good for the general public.

Economic & Political Crisis

In 1997, after a decade of near constant 10% growth, Malaysia was hit by the regional currency crisis. Mahathir blamed it all on unscrupulous Western speculators deliberately undermining the economies of the developing world for their personal gain. He pegged the Malaysian ringgit to the US dollar, bailed out what were seen as crony companies, forced banks to merge and made it difficult for foreign investors to remove their money from Malaysia's stock exchange. Malaysia's subsequent recovery from the economic crisis, which was more rapid than that of many other Southeast Asian nations, further bolstered Mahathir's prestige.

Anwar Ibrahim, Mahathir's deputy prime minister and heir apparent, was at odds with Mahathir over how to deal with the economic crisis. Their falling out was so severe that in September 1998 Anwar was sacked and soon after charged with corruption and sodomy. Many Malaysians, feeling that Anwar had been falsely arrested, took to the streets chanting Anwar's call for *'reformasi'*. The demonstrations were harshly quelled

Amir Muhammad's 2009 documentary *Malaysian Gods* commemorates the decade after the Reformasi movement began with the sacking of Anwar Ibrahim as deputy PM in 1998.

1969	1974	1981	1984
Following the general election, on 13 March race riots erupt in KL, killing 198. In response the government devises the New Economic Policy of positive discrimination for Malays.	Following the formation of the Barisan Nasional (BN) in 1973, this new coalition led by Tun Abdul Razak wins the Malaysian general election by a landslide.	Dr Mahathir Mohamad becomes prime minister of Malaysia and introduces policies of 'Buy British Last' and 'Look East' to encourage the country to emulate Japan, South Korea and Taiwan.	A somewhat reluctant Sultan Hassanal Bolkiah leads Brunei to complete independence from Britain. The country subsequently veers towards Islamic fundamentalism, introducing full Islamic law in 1991.

and, in trials that were widely criticised as unfair, Anwar was sentenced to a total of 15 years' imprisonment. The international community rallied around Anwar, with Amnesty International proclaiming him a prisoner of conscience.

In the following year's general elections BN suffered huge losses, particularly in the rural Malay areas. The big winners were the fundamentalist Islamic party, PAS (Parti Islam se-Malaysia), which had vociferously supported Anwar, and a new political party, Keadilan (People's Justice Party), headed by Anwar's wife Wan Azizah.

BN on the Ropes

Prime Minister Mahathir's successor, Abdullah Badawi, was sworn into office in 2003 and went on to lead BN to a landslide victory in the following year's election. In stark contrast to his feisty predecessor, the pious Abdullah immediately impressed voters by taking a nonconfrontational, consensus-seeking approach. He set up a royal commission to investigate corruption in the police force (its recommendations have yet to be implemented) and called time on several of the massively expensive mega projects that had been the hallmark of the Mahathir era, including a new bridge across the Straits of Johor to Singapore.

Released from jail in 2004, Anwar returned to national politics in August 2008 on winning the bi-election for the seat vacated by his wife. However, sodomy charges were again laid against the politician in June and he was arrested in July.

In the March 2008 election, UMNO and its coalition partners in Barisan Nasional (BN) saw their parliamentary dominance slashed to less than the customary two-thirds majority. Pakatan Rakyat (PR), the opposition People's Alliance, led by Anwar Ibrahim, not only bagged 82 of parliament's 222 seats but also took control of four out of Malaysia's 13 states, including the key economic bases of Selangor and Penang. PR subsequently lost Perak following a complex powerplay between various defecting MPs.

Abdullah Badawi resigned in favour of his urbane deputy, Mohd Najib bin Tun Abdul Razak (typically refered to as Najib Razak), in April 2008. Son of Abdul Razak, Malaysia's second prime minister after independence and nephew of Razak's successor Hussein Onn, Najib has been groomed for this role ever since he first entered national politics at the age of 23 in 1976. However, the change of guard may be too late to resurrect the fortunes of UMNO, a party seen as corrupt and out of touch with the people, according a survey by the Merdeka Centre (www.merdeka.org).

Brunei's ties with its former colonial master remain strong: UK judges sit in the High Court and Court of Appeal and a British Army Gurkha battalion is permanently stationed in Seria.

1998	2003	2007	2008
Anwar Ibrahim is sacked, arrested, sent for trial and jailed following disagreements with Dr Mahathir over how to deal with the Asian currency crisis and tackle government corruption.	Having announced his resignation the previous year, Dr Mahathir steps down as prime minister in favour of Abdullah Badawi. He remains very outspoken on national politics.	As the country celebrates 50 years since independence it is also shaken by two anti-government rallies in November in which tens of thousands take to the streets of KL to protest.	In the March election BN retains power but suffers heavy defeats to the revitalised opposition coalition Pakatan Rakyat (PR); in August Anwar Ibrahim becomes PR leader following his re-election to parliament.

Improving International Relations

Ever since Malaysia booted Singapore out of the federation in 1965, leaving Lee Kuan Yew sobbing on camera, the two countries have acted like squabbling siblings. Singapore, the over-achieving youngster with few natural resources beyond its hard working population, has managed to claw its way from obscurity to world admiration for its rapid and successful industrialisation. Across the causeway big brother Malaysia has achieved a no less impressive economic transformation, albeit one built on prodigious resources, in particular the profits from oil and gas.

Relations between the two reached the heights of touchiness in the 1990s. Malaysian Prime Minister Dr Mahathir and Singapore's 'Minister Mentor' Lee Kuan Yew parried insults back and forth across the Causeway, the former accusing Singaporeans of being the sort of people who 'urinate in lifts' and the latter retorting that the Malaysian town of Johor Bahru was 'notorious for shootings, muggings and car-jackings'.

Recently however, relations seem to be improving. Persistent squabbles over water (under a 1962 accord, Malaysia supplies Singapore with 250 million gallons of raw water daily) are becoming moot as Singapore develops alternative sources of supply. The 2011 land swap deal that ended a long running dispute over the KTM railway line in Singapore was also heralded as a historic breakthrough in attitudes between the two countries.

Relations between Malaysia and Brunei also became a lot more cordial in 2009, when the two signed a deal that ended a 20-year territorial dispute between the neighbouring countries over the land border around Limbang and ownership of offshore gas and oil exploration sites. Malaysian company Petronas is now working with Brunei to develop the the sites.

Lee's Law: How Singapore Crushes Dissent, by Chris Lydgate, is a disturbing and sad account of the rise and systematic destruction of Singapore's most successful opposition politician lawyer, JB Jeyaretnam.

2009
In April, Najib Tun Razak succeeds Abdullah Badawi as prime minister; the 1Malaysia policy is introduced to build respect and trust between the country's different races.

2011
Elections in Sarawak return a BN state government but with a reduced majority; tens of thousands rally in KL in support of fairer elections.

» Mural of previous prime ministers, Kuala Lumpur (p46)

AFP/GETTY IMAGES ©

HISTORY IMPROVING INTERNATIONAL RELATIONS

People, Culture & Politics

Travelling in this region you will invariably meet friendly, welcoming Malaysians, Singaporeans and Bruneians who hold a strong sense of shared experience and national identity. However, none of these multicultural nations is the perfect melting pot – underlying religious and ethnic tensions are a fact of life, particularly in Malaysia.

Status-conscious Malaysians love their honourable titles which include, in order of importance, Tun, Tan Sri, Datuk and Dato.

There are distinct cultural differences between the region's three main ethnic communities – Malays, Chinese and Indians. There's also the Peranakan (Straits Chinese) and other mixed race communities to take into account, alongside older aboriginal nations – the Orang Asli of Peninsula Malaysia and Borneo's indigenous community – comprising scores of different tribal groups and speaking around well over 100 languages and dialects.

All three countries have dabbled, to different degrees, with social and economic policies to shape the lives of their citizens. In Malaysia, the New Economic Policy (NEP) was designed to promote the position of Malays – it's only been partially successful. In Singapore the government encouraged birth control in the 1970s and 1980s (to stem a booming population), but that plan worked too well and it now provides much encouragement, financial and otherwise (in particular, to educated Chinese Singaporeans) to have more children. In Brunei the Sultan has steered his nation towards Islamic fundamentalism, adopting a national ideology known as *Melayu Islam Beraja* (MIB).

The Region's Peoples

The Malays

All Malays, Muslims by birth, are supposed to follow Islam, but many also adhere to older spiritual beliefs and *adat*. With its roots in the Hindu period, *adat* places great emphasis on collective responsibility and maintaining harmony within the community – almost certainly a factor in the general goodwill between the different ethnic groups in Malaysia.

The Malay surname is the child's father's first name. This is why Malaysians will use your given name after the Mr or Miss; to use your surname would be to address your father.

The enduring appeal of the communal *kampung* (village) spirit shouldn't be underestimated – many an urban Malay hankers after it, despite the affluent Western-style living conditions they enjoy at home. In principle, villagers are of equal status, though a headman is appointed on the basis of his wealth, greater experience or spiritual knowledge. Traditionally the founder of the village was appointed village leader (*penghulu* or *ketua kampung*) and often members of the same family would also become leaders. A *penghulu* is usually a haji, one who has made the pilgrimage to Mecca.

The Muslim religious leader, the imam, holds a position of great importance in the community as the keeper of Islamic knowledge and the leader of prayer, but even educated urban Malaysians periodically turn to *pawang* (shamans who possess a supernatural knowledge of harvests and nature) or *bomoh* (spiritual healers with knowledge of curative plants and the ability to harness the power of the spirit world), for advice before making any life-changing decisions.

The Chinese

Religious customs govern much of the Chinese community's home life, from the moment of birth, which is carefully recorded for astrological consultations later in life, to funerals which also have many rites and rituals. The Chinese who started arriving in the region in early 15th century came mostly from the southern Chinese province of Fujian and eventually formed one half of the group known as Peranakans. They developed their own distinct hybrid culture whereas later settlers, from Guangdong and Hainan provinces stuck more closely to the culture of their homelands, including keeping their dialects.

If there's one cultural aspect that all Chinese in the region agree on it's the importance of education. It has been a very sensitive subject amongst the Malaysian Chinese community since the attempt in the 1960s to phase out secondary schools where Chinese was the medium of teaching, and the introduction of government policies that favour Malays in the early 1970s. The constraining of educational opportunities within Malaysia for the ethnic Chinese has resulted in many families working doubly hard to afford the tuition fees needed to send their offspring to private schools within the country and to overseas institutions.

Kiasu, a Hokkien word describing Singaporeans, literally means 'afraid to lose', but embraces a range of selfish and pushy behaviour in which the individual must not lose out at all cost.

The Indians

Like the Chinese settler, Indians in the region hail from many parts of the subcontinent and have different cultures depending on their religions - mainly Hinduism, Islam, Sikhism and Christianity. Most are Tamils, originally coming from the area now known as Tamil Nadu in southern India where Hindu traditions are strong. Later Muslim Indians from northern India followed along with Sikhs. These religious affiliations dictate many of the home life customs and practices of Malaysian Indians, although one celebration that all Hindus and much of the rest of the region takes part in is Deepavali.

A small, English-educated Indian elite has always played a prominent role in Malaysian and Singaporean society, and a significant merchant class exists. However, a large percentage of Indians - imported as indentured labourers by the British - remain a poor working class in both countries.

The Orang Asli

The indigenous people of Malaysia - known collectively as Orang Asli - played an important role in early trade, teaching the colonialists about forest products and guiding prospectors to outcrops of tin and precious metals. They also acted as scouts and guides for anti-insurgent forces during the communist Emergency in the 1950s.

Despite this, the Orang Asli remain marginalised in Malaysia. According to the most recent data published by the Department of Orang Asli Affairs (JHEOA; www.jheoa.gov.my), in December 2004 Peninsular Malaysia had just under 150,000 Orang Asli (Original People); 80% live below the poverty line, compared with an 8.5% national average. The tribes are generally classified into three groups: the Negrito; the Senoi; and the Proto-Malays, who are subdivided into 18 tribes, the smallest being the Orang Kanak with just 87 members. There are dozens of different tribal languages and most Orang Asli follow animist beliefs, though there are vigorous attempts to convert them to Islam.

PEOPLE, CULTURE & POLITICS THE REGION'S PEOPLES

563

THE PERANAKANS

Peranakan means 'half-caste' in Malay, which is exactly what the Peranakans are: descendants of Chinese immigrants who from the 16th century onwards settled principally in Singapore, Melaka and Penang and married Malay women.

The culture and language of the Peranakans is a fascinating melange of Chinese and Malay traditions. The Peranakans took the name and religion of their Chinese fathers, but the customs, language and dress of their Malay mothers. They also used the terms Straits-born or Straits Chinese to distinguish themselves from later arrivals from China.

Another name you may hear for these people is Baba-Nonyas, after the Peranakan words for men (baba) and women (nonya). The Peranakans were often wealthy traders who could afford to indulge their passion for sumptuous furnishings, jewellery and brocades. Their terrace houses were brightly painted, with patterned tiles embedded in the walls for extra decoration. When it came to the interior, Peranakan tastes favoured heavily carved and inlaid furniture.

Peranakan dress was similarly ornate. Women wore fabulously embroidered kasot manek (beaded slippers) and kebaya (blouses worn over a sarong), tied with beautiful kerasong (brooches), usually of fine filigree gold or silver. Men – who assumed Western dress in the 19th century, reflecting their wealth and contacts with the British – saved their finery for important occasions such as the wedding ceremony, a highly stylised and intricate ritual dictated by adat (Malay customary law).

The Peranakan patois is a Malay dialect but one containing many Hokkien words – so much so that it is largely unintelligible to a Malay speaker. The Peranakans also included words and expressions of English and French, and occasionally practised a form of backward Malay by reversing the syllables.

Although the JHEOA was originally set up to represent Orang Asli concerns to the government (ie land rights), the department has evolved into a conduit for government decisions. Asli land rights are not recognised, and when logging, agricultural or infrastructure projects require their land, their claims are generally regarded as illegal.

In 2010 the government put forward plans to corporatise JHEOA so it could take charge of Orang Asli lands (currently the Orang Asli manage their own small holdings). The Centre for Orang Asli Concerns (www.coac.org.my) has criticised the plan saying it will further impoverish an already poor group of people.

Famous Singaporeans of Peranakan descent include Lee Kuan Yew (Singapore's first prime minister) and Dick Lee (singer, composer).

Dayaks & the People of Borneo

Not all of Borneo's indigenous tribes refer to themselves as Dayaks, but the term usefully groups together peoples who have a great deal in common – and not just from an outsider's point of view.

SARAWAK

Dayak culture and lifestyles are probably easiest to observe and experience in Sarawak, where Dayaks make up about 48% of the population.

About 29% of Sarawakians are Iban, a group that migrated from West Kalimantan's Kapuas River starting five to eight centuries ago. Also known as Sea Dayaks for their exploits as pirates, the Iban are traditionally rice growers and longhouse dwellers. A reluctance to renounce headhunting enhanced the Iban's ferocious reputation.

The Bidayuh (8% of the population), many of whom also trace their roots to what is now West Kalimantan, are concentrated in the hills south and southwest of Kuching. Few Bidayuh still live in longhouses and adjacent villages sometimes speak different dialects.

Upland groups such as the Kelabit, Kayan and Kenyah (ie everyone except the Bidayuh, Iban and coastal dwelling Melenau) are often grouped under the term Orang Ulu ('upriver people'). There are also the Penan (see p447), originally a nomadic hunter-gatherer group living in northern Sarawak.

SABAH
None of Sabah's 30 odd indigenous ethnicities are particularly keen on the term Dayak. The state's largest ethnic group, the Kadazan-Dusun, make up 18% of the population. Mainly Roman Catholic, the Kadazan and the Dusun share a common language and have similar customs; the former originally lived mainly in the state's western coastal areas and river deltas, while the latter inhabited the interior highlands.

The Murut (3.2% of the population) traditionally lived in the south-western hills bordering Kalimantan and Brunei, growing hill-rice and hunting with spears and blowpipes. They were soldiers for Brunei's sultans, and the last group in Sabah to abandon head-hunting.

BRUNEI
Indigenous non-Malays, mainly Iban and Kelabit, account for less than 10% of Brunei's population.

Multiculturalism
From the ashes of Malaysia's interracial riots of 1969, when distrust between the Malays and Chinese peaked, the country has managed to forge a more tolerant multicultural society. Though ethnic loyalties remain strong, the emergence of a single 'Malaysian' identity is now a much-discussed and lauded concept, even if it is far from being actually realised.

The government's *bumiputra* policy (see p559) has increased Malay involvement in the economy, albeit largely for an elite. This has helped defuse Malay fears and resentment of Chinese economic dominance, but at the expense of Chinese or Indian Malaysians being discriminated against by government policy. The reality is that the different communities coexist rather than mingle, intermarriage being rare and education still largely split along ethnic lines.

The term 'Dayak' was first used by colonial authorities in about 1840; it means upriver or interior in some local languages, human being in others.

Some Dayak societies, like the Iban and Bidayuh, are remarkably egalitarian, while others, including the Kayan, have a strict social hierarchy – now somewhat blurred – with classes of nobles (*maren*), aristocrats (*hipuy*), commoners (*panyin*) and slaves (*dipen*).

LONGHOUSE LIFE

One of the most distinctive features of Dayak life is the longhouse (*rumah batang* or *rumah panjai*), which is essentially an entire village under one seemingly interminable roof. Longhouses take a variety of shapes and styles, but all are raised above the damp jungle floor on hardwood stilts and most are built on or near river banks.

The focus of longhouse life is the covered verandah, known as a *ruai* to the Iban, an *awah* to the Bidayuh and a *dapur* to the Kelabits (other groups use other terms). Residents use this communal space to socialise, engage in economic activities, cook and eat meals, and hold communal celebrations.

One wall of the verandah, which can be up to 250m long, is pierced by doors to individual families' *bilik* (apartments), where there's space for sleeping and storage. If you ask about the size of a longhouse, you will usually be told how many doors – ie family units – it has.

Like the rest of us, Dayaks love their mod cons, so longhouses where people actually live fuse age-old forms with contemporary conveniences – the resulting mash-up can see traditional bamboo-slat floors mixed with corrugated iron, linoleum, satellite dishes, and a car park out the front.

Most young Dayaks move away from the longhouse to seek higher education and jobs in the cities, but almost all keep close ties with home, returning for major family and community celebrations.

A poll by the independent Merdeka Centre, published in July 2010, showed that only 39% of non-Malays believed the government's 1Malaysia policy was a sincere effort to unite Malaysians of all ethnicities. That such a policy is needed at all speaks volumes about the underlying tensions and suspicions that continue to simmer beneath the apparent harmony.

Singaporean government policy has always promoted Singapore as a multicultural nation in which Chinese, Indians and Malays can live in equality and harmony while maintaining their distinct cultural identities. There are imbalances in the distribution of wealth and power among the racial groups, but on the whole multiculturalism seems to work much better in small-scale Singapore than it does in Malaysia.

Similarly, Brunei's small scale (not to mention great wealth) has allowed all its citizens, 30% of whom are not Muslim, to find common goals and live together harmoniously in a state run according to Islamic laws.

Malaysian politicians have been known to call in a *bomoh* – a traditional spiritual healer and spirit medium – during election campaigns to assist in their strategy and provide some foresight.

The Region's Polticial Systems
Malaysia

Malaysia is made up of 13 states and three federal territories (Kuala Lumpur, Pulau Labuan and Putrajaya). Each state has an assembly and government headed by a *menteri besar* (chief minister). Nine of the 13 states have hereditary rulers (sultans), while the remaining four have appointed governors as do the federal territories. In a pre-established order, every five years one of the sultans takes his turn in the ceremonial position of Yang di-Pertuan Agong (king). Since December 2011 the king, who is also the head of state and leader of the Islamic faith, has been Sultan Abdul Halim of Kedah. This is the second time the 83-year-old has held the position, the first being from 1970 to 1975.

At the time of writing Malaysia's prime minister is Najib Razak, who heads up the BN, a coalition of the United Malays National Organisation (UMNO) and 13 other parties. The official opposition is Pakatan Rakyat (PR), led by Anwar Ibrahim; it's a coalition between Parti Keadilan Rakyat (PKR), the (DAP) and Parti Islam se-Malaysia (PAS). They all sit in a two-house parliament, comprising a 70-member Senate (*Dewan Negara*; 26 members elected by the 13 state assemblies, 44 appointed by the king on the prime minister's recommendation) and a 222-member House of Representatives (*Dewan Rakyat;* elected from single-member districts). National and state elections are held every five years.

TALKING THE TALK: THE REGION'S MANY LANGUAGES

As former British colonies, Malaysia, Singapore and Brunei are all fantastic countries to visit for English speakers, but linguists will be pleased to tackle the region's multitude of other languages. Malaysia's national language is Bahasa Malaysia. This is often a cause of confusion for travellers, who logically give a literal translation to the two words and call it the 'Malaysian language'. In fact you cannot speak 'Malaysian'; the language is Malay.

Other languages commonly spoken in the region include Tamil, Hokkien, Cantonese and Mandarin, but there are also Chinese dialects, various other Indian and Orang Asli languages and even, in Melaka, a form of 16th-century Portuguese known as Cristang. All Malaysians speak Malay, and many are fluent in at least two other languages – a humbling thought for those of us who only speak English!

One final thing: you may be slightly confused by the English you do hear – both Malaysia and Singapore have developed their own unique way with the language, known respectively as Manglish and Singlish.

WOMEN IN MALAYSIA, SINGAPORE & BRUNEI

Women had great influence in pre-Islamic Malay society; there were female leaders and the descendants of the Sumatran Minangkabau in Negeri Sembilan still have a matriarchal society. The arrival of Islam weakened the position of women in the region. Nonetheless, women were not cloistered or forced to wear full purdah as in the Middle East, and Malay women today still enjoy more freedom than their counterparts in many other Muslim societies.

As you travel throughout the region you'll see women taking part in all aspects of society: politics, big business, academia and family life. However, no less a figure than Marina Mahathir, prominent women's rights campaigner and daughter of the former prime minister, in 2006 compared the lot of Malaysia's Muslim women to that of blacks under apartheid in South Africa. In Mahathir's view her Muslim sisters are treated as second-class citizens held back by rules that don't apply to non-Muslim women.

Mahathir's outburst followed changes to Malaysia's Islamic family law that make it easier for Muslim men to take multiple wives, to divorce them and to take a share of their wives' property (similar laws already exist in Brunei, where the Sultan has two wives).

In Chinese-dominated Singapore women traditionally played a small role in public life. However, in recent years women have started to take up key positions in government and industry.

In Islamic Brunei more women wear the *tudong* (headscarf) than in Malaysia. Many work and there are even one or two female politicians. Since 2002 female Bruneians have been able to legally transfer their nationality to their children if the father is not Bruneian.

An anti-democratic hangover from the 1960s is the lack of local government elections – KL, Georgetown and Melaka's city councillors have all been government appointees since 1964. The DAP made reintroducing these elections part of their 2008 election campaign manifesto, but since taking power in Penang they have been unable to deliver through lack of the necessary federal approval.

Singapore

Singapore is a parliamentary republic modelled on the United Kingdom's Westminster System. There are numerous political parties in Singapore, but one party, the People's Action Party (PAP), has dominated the political landscape since independence. The President of Singapore (since 2011, Tony Tan Keng Yam) is the democratically elected head of state, a traditionally ceremonial role that has since 1991 included powers to veto a small number of decisions, largely related to security and the armed service. The president appoints a prime minister (currently Lee Hsien Loong) as the head of government. Legislative power is vested in both the government and the Parliament of Singapore.

Some critics say the electoral system makes it difficult for opposition parties to gain seats, entrenching the dominance of the PAP. This position is backed up by the strict (by Western standards) controls the government places on political assembly, freedom of expression and behaviours deemed antisocial.

However, the most recent election in 2011 would seem to indicate that things are changing: there was a decline in the popularity of the PAP, whose votes fell by 8.69%. Moreover, the number of contented seats was the highest it's been since Singapore achieved its independence in 1965. The biggest gains went to the Worker's Party (WP) whose political agenda

ISLAM & POLITICS

Islam has always played a key role in Malaysian politics. The fundamentalist Islamic party PAS (Parti Islam se-Malaysia) has a policy aim to install an Islamic government in Malaysia. However, since it has teamed up with the PKR and DAP in the PR opposition alliance it has toned down this message and made a greater effort to reach out to non-Malays.

In an effort to outflank PAS's religious credentials, UMNO has from its dominant position with the BN been inching Malaysia closer to becoming more of a conservative Islamic state. Some local authorities have tried to ban or restrict dog ownership (conservative Muslims see dogs as unclean) and prosecute couples for holding hands or kissing in public. There was a move for policewomen, regardless of their religion, to wear the *tudong* (headscarf) at official parades and the controversy over the banning, then unbanning, of the Bible in Iban (see p572). There have also been several high-profile demolitions of non-Muslim religious buildings (including a couple of 19th-century Hindu temples) for allegedly not having proper planning permission.

focuses on everyday concerns of Singaporeans (wages, cost of living and healthcare, public transport, affordability of housing, and the disproportionately high salaries of ministers).

Local media, often accused of being mouthpieces of the government, gave fair and equal coverage to both the PAP and opposition parties. Social media, once banned in campaigning, played a huge part in the dissemination of information. Even Prime Minister Lee Hsien Loong participated in an online chat (his first).

Post-election, it seems as though the PAP has realised that its position has gone from unshakable to slightly tenuous. A review of ministerial salaries was immediately mooted, and Senior Minister Goh Chok Tong and Minister Mentor Lee Kuan Yew both tendered their resignations. Senior Minister Goh perhaps put it best, describing the results as, 'a sea change in the political landscape'.

Brunei

Although internationally classified as a constitutional monarchy, Brunei officially deems itself a *Melayu Islam Beraja* (MIB; Malay Islamic Monarchy) and is, in many ways, an absolute monarchy. Sultan Hassanal Bolkiah has been in power since 1967; he appoints his advisory cabinet, privy council and council of succession. There is a 33-member legislative council, but those members are also appointed by the sultan; in 2004 there was talk of holding elections for 15 more seats, but those elections have never materialised.

Religion

Freedom of religion is guaranteed throughout this mainly Islamic region, although in Brunei the Baha'i faith is banned you are and unlikely to encounter practising Jews. Hinduism's roots in the region long pre-date Islam, and the various Chinese religions are also strongly entrenched. Christianity has a presence, more so in Singapore than Peninsula Malaysia where it has never been strong. In Malaysian Borneo many of the indigenous people have converted to Christianity, yet others still follow their animist traditions.

Islam

Islam most likely came to the region in the 14th century with south Indian traders; it was not one of Arabia's more orthodox Islamic traditions. It absorbed rather than conquered existing beliefs, and was adopted peacefully by Malaysia's coastal trading ports. Islamic sultanates replaced Hindu kingdoms – though the Hindu concept of kings remained – and the Hindu traditions of *adat* continued despite Islamic law dominating.

Malay ceremonies and beliefs still exhibit pre-Islamic traditions, but most Malays are ardent Muslims – to suggest otherwise would cause great offence. With the rise of Islamic fundamentalism, the calls to introduce Islamic law and purify the practices of Islam have increased; yet, while the federal government of Malaysia is keen to espouse Muslim ideals, it is wary of religious extremism.

Key Beliefs & Practices

Most Malaysian Muslims are Sunnis, but all Muslims share a common belief in the Five Pillars of Islam:

Shahadah (the declaration of faith) 'There is no God but Allah; Mohammed is his Prophet.'

Salat (prayer) Ideally five times a day, in which the muezzin (prayer leader) calls the faithful to prayer from the minarets of every mosque.

Zakat (tax) Usually taking the form of a charitable donation.

Sawm (fasting) Includes observing the fasting month of Ramadan.

Hajj (pilgrimage to Mecca) Every Muslim aspires to do the hajj at least once in their lifetime.

Muslim dietary laws forbid alcohol, pork and all pork-based products. Restaurants where it's OK for Muslims to dine will be clearly labelled halal; this is a stricter definition than places that label themselves simply 'pork-free'.

A radical Islamic movement has not taken serious root in Malaysia but religious conservatism has grown over recent years. For foreign visitors, the most obvious sign of this is the national obsession with propriety, which extends to newspaper polemics on female modesty and raids by the police on 'immoral' public establishments, which can include clubs and bars where Muslims may be drinking.

Adat, with its roots in the region's Hindu period and earlier, is customary law that places great emphasis on collective rather than individual responsibility and on maintaining harmony.

Islam in Malaysia: Perceptions & Facts by Dr Mohd Asri Zainul Abidin, the former Mufti of Perlis, is a collection of articles on aspects of the faith as practised in Malaysia.

ISLAMIC FESTIVALS

The highpoint of the Islamic festival calendar is Ramadan, when Muslims fast from sunrise to sunset. Ramadan always occurs in the ninth month of the Muslim calendar and lasts between 29 and 30 days, based on sightings of the moon. Fifteen days before the start of Ramadan, on Nisfu Night, it is believed the souls of the dead visit their homes. On Laylatul Qadr (Night of Grandeur), during Ramadan, Muslims celebrate the arrival of the Quran on earth, before its revelation by the Prophet Mohammed.

Hari Raya Puasa (also known as Hari Raya Aidilfitri) marks the end of the month-long fast, with two days of joyful celebration and feasting. Hari Raya Puasa is the major holiday of the Muslim calendar and it can be difficult to find accommodation, particularly on the coast. The start of Ramadan moves forward 11 days every year in line with the Muslim lunar calendar.

The other major Islamic festivals celebrated across the region are:

Hari Raya Haji A two-day festival usually in November marking the successful completion of the hajj – the pilgrimage to Mecca – and commemorating the willingness of the Prophet Ibrahim (the biblical Abraham) to sacrifice his son. Many shops, offices and tourist attractions close and locals consume large amounts of cakes and sweets.

Mawlid al-Nabi Usually in March and celebrating the birth of the prophet Mohammed.

Awal Muharram The Muslim New Year which falls in November or December.

Sisters in Islam (www.sistersin islam.org.my) is a website run by and for Malaysian Muslim women who refuse to be bullied by patriarchal interpretations of Islam.

More Muslim women wear the hijab (a head covering also known regionally as the *tudong*) today than, say, 20 years ago. In 2011, a young Muslim filmmaker Norhayati Kaprawi made the documentary *Siapa Aku?* (Who Am I?), which examines some of the reason behind this interviewing a spectrum of Malaysian women from across the country. Shamsul Amri Bahruddin, director of the Institute of Ethnic Studies at the National University of Malaysia, is is quoted within the film as saying that 'conformity is the most dominating factor on why women in Malaysia wear a *tudung*'.

On the other hand, the *New York Times* in 2011 reported that Malaysia was leading the way in the Islamic world with regard to embracing women as preachers and teachers of the Muslim faith, an area traditionally dominated by men, citing Zaleha Kamaruddin, the first female rector appointed to head the country's International Islamic University. However, women preachers still are not allowed to lead prayers at mosques.

Chinese Religions

The Chinese in the region usually follow a mix of Buddhism, Confucianism and Taoism. Buddhism takes care of the afterlife, Confucianism looks after the political and moral aspects of life, and Taoism contributes animistic beliefs to teach people to maintain harmony with the universe. But to say that the Chinese have three religions is too simplistic a view of their traditional religious life. At the first level Chinese religion is animistic, with a belief in the innate vital energy in rocks, trees, rivers and springs. At the second level people from the distant past, both real and mythological, are worshipped as gods. Overlaid on this are popular Taoist, Mahayana Buddhist and Confucian beliefs.

The most popular Chinese gods and local deities, or *shen*, are Kuan Yin, the goddess of mercy; Kuan Ti, the god of war and wealth; and Toh Peh Kong, a local deity representing the spirit of the pioneers and found only outside China.

On a day-to-day level most Chinese are much less concerned with the high-minded philosophies and asceticism of the Buddha, Confucius or Lao Zi than they are with the pursuit of worldly success, the appeasement of the dead and the spirits, and seeking knowledge about the future. Chinese religion incorporates elements of what Westerners might call 'superstition' – if you want your fortune told, for instance, you go to a temple. The other thing to remember is that Chinese religion is polytheistic. Apart from the Buddha, Lao Zi and Confucius there are many divinities, such as house gods, and gods and goddesses for particular professions.

Hinduism

Hinduism in the region dates back at least 1500 years and there are Hindu influences in cultural traditions, such as *wayang kulit* (shadow-puppet theatre) and the wedding ceremony. However, it is only in the last 100 years or so, following the influx of Indian contract labourers and settlers, that it has again become widely practised.

Hinduism has three basic practices: puja (worship), the cremation of the dead, and the rules and regulations of the caste system. Although still very strong in India, the caste system was never significant in Malaysia, mainly because the labourers brought here from India were mostly from the lower classes.

Hinduism has a vast pantheon of deities, although the one omnipresent god usually has three physical representations: Brahma, the creator; Vishnu, the preserver; and Shiva, the destroyer or reproducer. All three gods are usually shown with four arms, but Brahma has the added advantage of four heads to represent his all-seeing presence.

Animism

The animist religions of Malaysia's indigenous peoples are as diverse as the peoples themselves. While animism does not have a rigid system of tenets or codified beliefs, it can be said that animists perceive natural phenomena to be animated by various spirits or deities, and a complex system of practices is used to propitiate these spirits.

Ancestor worship is also a common feature of animist societies; departed souls are considered to be intermediaries between this world and the next. Examples of elaborate burial rituals can still be found in some parts of Sarawak, where the remains of monolithic burial markers and funerary objects still dot the jungle around longhouses in the Kelabit

Dayak animism considers the hornbill a powerful spirit – the bird is honoured in dance and ceremony and its feathers treasured.

THAIPUSAM

The most spectacular Hindu festival in Malaysia and Singapore is Thaipusam, a wild parade of confrontingly invasive body piercings. The festival, which originated in Tamil Nadu (but is now banned in India), happens every year in the Hindu month of Thai (January/February) and is celebrated with the most gusto at the Batu Caves, just outside Kuala Lumpur.

The greatest spectacle is the devotees who subject themselves to seemingly masochistic acts as fulfilment for answered prayers. Many carry offerings of milk in *paal kudam* (milk pots), often connected to the skin by hooks. Even more striking are the *vel kavadi* – great cages of spikes that pierce the skin of the carrier and are decorated with peacock feathers, pictures of deities and flowers. Some penitents go as far as piercing their tongues and cheeks with hooks, skewers and tridents.

The festival is the culmination of around a month of prayer, a vegetarian diet and other ritual preparations, such as abstinence from sex or sleeping on a hard floor. While it looks excruciating, a trance-like state stops participants from feeling pain; later the wounds are treated with lemon juice and holy ash to prevent scarring. As with the practice of firewalking, only the truly faithful should attempt the ritual. It is said that insufficiently prepared devotees keep doctors especially busy over the Thaipusam festival period with skin lacerations, or by collapsing after the strenuous activities.

Thaipusam is also celebrated in Penang at the Nattukotai Chettiar Temple and the Waterfall Hilltop Temple, and in Johor Bahru at the Sri Thandayuthabani Temple. Ipoh attracts a large number of devotees, who follow the procession from the Sri Mariamar Temple in Buntong to the Sri Subramaniar Temple in Gunung Cheroh. In Singapore, Hindus march from the Sri Srinivasa Perumal Temple on Serangoon Rd to the Chettiar Hindu Temple.

Highlands. However, most of these are no longer maintained and they're being rapidly swallowed up by the fast-growing jungle.

In Malaysian Borneo, Dayak animism is known collectively as Kaharingan. Carvings, totems, tattoos and other objects (including, in earlier times, head-hunting skulls) are used to repel bad spirits, attract good spirits and soothe spirits that may be upset. Totems at entrances to villages and longhouses are markers for the spirits.

Religious Issues

Freedom of Religon?

Islam is Malaysia's state religion, which has an impact on the cultural and social life of the country at several levels. Government institutions and banks, for example, are closed for two hours at lunchtime on Friday to allow Muslims to attend Friday prayers.

Government censors, with Islamic sensitivities in mind, dictate what can be performed on public stages or screened in cinemas. This has led to Beyoncé cancelling her shows when asked to adhere to strict guidelines on dress and her performance style, and to the banning of movies like *Schindler's List* and *Babe* – the themes of Jews being saved from the Holocaust and a cute pig star are not to Muslim tastes. In 2008, Malaysia's leading Islamic council issued an edict against yoga, fearing the exercises could corrupt Muslims.

Syariah (Islamic law) is the preserve of state governments, as is the establishment of Muslim courts of law, which since 1988 cannot be overruled by secular courts. This has had a negative impact on Muslims wishing to change their religion and divorced parents who cannot agree on which religion to raise their children by. The end result is that Malaysian Muslims who change their religion or practise no faith at all rarely make their choice official.

In theory Brunei's constitution also allows for the practice of religions other than the official Sunni Islam. However, as Freedom House (www.freedomhouse.org) reports, proselytizing by non-Muslims is prohibited and other forms of Islam are actively discouraged. Christianity suffers censorship. Marriage between Muslims and non-Muslims is not allowed. With permission from the Ministry of Religious Affairs Muslims can convert their faith, but in reality conversion is practically impossible.

Inter-Religious Relations

Muslim-Christian relations in Malaysia were clouded in 2010 as the result of a campaign by Muslim fundamentalists to forbid Christians from referring to God as 'Allah' in Bahasa Malaysia. The Home Ministry seized 35,000 Bahasa Malaysia Bibles at Kuching's port, prompting the Christian Federation of Malaysia to lodge a formal complaint with PM Najib Razak; the Bibles were later released.

Anecdotal evidence from across the region indicates that whereas in the past the various religion communities participated in each other's communal festivities (Hari Raya, Chinese New Year), such easy mingling is becoming less frequent these days, especially among younger people.

Intra-religious relations in Sabah and Sarawak are less fraught than on the mainland, but Christians and Chinese (the groups overlap to a certain degree) and Muslim moderates often express concern that the island – especially Sabah – is not immune to the Islamist winds blowing in from other parts of the country.

Anti-Semitism

The only part of the region where you'll find a community of practising Jews is in Singapore. Penang once had a Jewish community large enough to support a synagogue (closed in 1976) and there's been a Jewish cemetery in George Town since 1805. Elsewhere in Malaysia and Brunei, Jewish life is practically unknown.

Sadly, anti-Semitism, ostensibly tied to criticism of Israel, is a feature of Malaysia and Brunei. In the region's bookshops it's not difficult to find anti-Semetic publications like *The Protocols of the Elders of Zion*. Former prime minister Mahathir is the most infamously outspoken Malaysian anti-Semite: in 2003 he made a speech to an Islamic leadership conference claiming the USA is a tool of Jewish overlords, and he once cancelled a planned tour of Malaysia by the New York Philharmonic because the program included work by a Jewish composer.

More recently, after the July 2011 Bersih rally in KL to demand greater transparency in electoral law, the UMNO-owned Malay newspaper *Utusan Malaysia* claimed such demonstrations would make the country vulnerable to interference by Jews and Israel. The Malaysian government later distanced itself from the newspaper's comments.

Israeli passport holders are not permitted to enter Malaysia without clearance from the Ministry of Home Affairs, and very few local Muslims differentiate between Israelis and Jews generally – something worth noting if you're Jewish and travelling in the region.

The Jewish Community of Singapore website (www.singaporejews.com) contains information about the history of Jews on the island and the current community.

RELIGION RELIGIOUS ISSUES

Arts & Media

Malaysia, Singapore and Brunei are not widely known for their arts, which is a shame as there is much creativity here, particularly in Malaysia and Singapore. Traditional art forms like *wayang kulit* (shadow puppetry) and *mak yong* (dance and music performances) continue alongside contemporary art, drama and filmmaking. There's a distinctive look to Malaysia's vernacular architecture as well as a daring and originality in modern constructions. The region also produces authors who are gaining attention in the wider world.

Singapore has boosted spending on arts across the board with the aim of making the island state the arts hub of the region, in stark contrast to Malaysia, where very little public money is assigned to the arts. Even private sponsors like Petronas are pulling back their support; in June 2012, the Petronas Performing Art Group took their final bows after 22 years.

Literature

Writers W Somerset Maugham, Joseph Conrad and Noel Coward were inspired by the region in the early 20th century. The classic colonial expat experience is recounted by Anthony Burgess in *The Malayan Trilogy* written in the 1950s. In the late 1960s Paul Theroux lived in Singapore, which, together with Malaysia, forms the backdrop to his novel *Saint Jack* and his short-story collection *The Consul's Wife*.

Leading lights of the contemporary Malaysian literary scene include Tash Aw (www.tash-aw.com), whose debut novel, *The Harmony Silk Factory,* won the 2005 Whitbread First Novel Award; the Man Booker Prize nominated author Tan Twan Eng (www.tantwaneng.com), whose literature fuses a fascination with Malaysia's past and the impact of Japanese culture; and Preeta Samarasan (http://preetasamarasan.com), whose novel *Evening is the Whole Day* shines a light on the experiences of an Indian immigrant family living on the outskirts of Ipoh in the early 1980s.

Foreign Bodies and *Mammon Inc* by Hwee Hwee Tan (www.geocities.com/hweehwee_tan) are among the best of contemporary Singaporean fiction. Tan pinpoints the peculiar dilemmas and contradictions facing Singaporean youth. Other celebrated novels by Singaporean writers include *Tigers in Paradise* by Philip Jeyaretnam, *Juniper Loa* by Lin Yutang, *Tangerine* by Colin Cheong and *Playing Madame Mao* by Lau Siew Mai.

Several small-press publishers have released works of poetry, fiction and even children's books. Of note, Booksactually (p488), an independent book store in Singapore, publishes up-and-coming authors via its Maths Paper Press imprint. Encouragingly, the National Arts Council of Singapore has beefed up its program with competitions and events like the Singapore Children's Literature Festival.

Contemporary Malaysian Fiction

» *The Harmony Silk Factory* (Tash Aw)

» *The Gift of Rain* (Tan Twan Eng)

» *Evening is the Whole Day* (Preeta Samarasan)

» *Body 2 Body: A Malaysian Queer Anthology* (Jerome Kugan & Pang Khee Teik, eds)

Architecture

Malaysia and Singapore have both made their mark in the world of modern architecture with iconic buildings like KL's Petronas Towers and the Marina Bay Sands complex in Singapore. Other interesting skyscrapers and civic buildings in the cities take inspiration from both local culture and the environment – for example the Tabung Haji and Menara Maybank buildings in KL, both designed by Hijjas Kasturi.

Vividly painted and handsomely proportioned, traditional wooden Malay houses are also perfectly adapted to the hot, humid conditions of the region. Built on stilts, with high, peaked roofs, they take advantage of even the slightest cooling breeze. Further ventilation is achieved by full-length windows, no internal partitions, and latticelike grilles in the walls. The layout of a traditional Malay house reflects Muslim sensibilities. There are separate areas for men and women, as well as distinct areas where guests of either sex may be entertained.

Although their numbers are dwindling, this type of house has not disappeared altogether. The best places to see examples are in the *kampung* of Peninsular Malaysia, particularly along the east coast in the states of Kelantan and Terengganu. Here you'll see that roofs are often tiled, showing a Thai and Cambodian influence.

In Melaka, the Malay house has a distinctive tiled front stairway leading up to the front verandah – examples can be seen around Kampung Morten. The Minangkabau-style houses found in Negeri Sembilan are the most distinctive of the *kampung* houses, with curved roofs resembling buffalo horns; the design is imported from Sumatra.

Few Malay-style houses have survived Singapore's rapid modernisation – the main place they remain is on Pulau Ubin. Instead, the island state has some truly magnificent examples of Chinese shophouse architecture, particularly in Chinatown, Emerald Hill (off Orchard Rd) and around Katong. There are also the distinctive 'black and white' bungalows built during colonial times; find survivors lurking in the residential areas off Orchard Rd. Most noticeable of all, though, will be the rank upon rank of Housing Development Board (HDB) flats that the vast majority of Singaporeans call home.

Despite its oil wealth, there's little that's flashy in the architecture of Brunei's modest capital, Bandar Seri Begawan, where the city's skyline is dominated by the striking Omar Ali Saifuddien Mosque. It's quite a different story, however, out at Jerudong, home to the Sultan's opulent palace and the eye-boggling Empire Hotel.

Drama & Dance

Traditional Malay dances include *menora,* a dance-drama of Thai origin performed by an all-male cast dressed in grotesque masks; and the similar *mak yong,* where the participants are female. These performances often take place at Puja Ketek, Buddhist festivals held at temples near

> The cartoonist and artist Lat is a national institution in Malaysia. His witty sketches turn up in the *New Straits Times* newspaper, advertisements, and books including *Kampung Boy*.

ARTS & MEDIA ARCHITECTURE

Online Arts Resources

» Arts.com.my (www.arts.com.my)

» Malaysia Design Archive (www.malaysiadesignarchive.org)

» National Arts Council Singapore (www.nac.gov.sg)

SHADOW PUPPETERY

It's in east coast Peninsula Malaysian towns like Kota Bharu and Kuala Terengganu that you're most likely to see *wayang kulit* – shadow-puppet performances, similar to those of Java in Indonesia, which retell tales from Hindu epic the Ramayana. It's a feat of endurance both for performer and audience since the shadow plays, which often take place at weddings or after the harvest, can last for many hours.

In November 2008 Malaysian composer Yii Kah Hoe collaborated with the Singapore Chinese Orchestra and the *wayang kulit* troupe Istamuzika to perform the modern *wayang kulit* piece *Bayang*.

CHINESE OPERA

In Malaysia and Singapore *wayang*, Chinese opera, is derived from the Cantonese variety. The performances mix dialogue, music, song and dance; what they lack in literary nuance they make up for with garish costumes and the crashing music that follows the action. Scenery and props are minimal; it's the action that is important, and even for the uninitiated it's usually easy to get the gist of the plot.

Performances can go for an entire evening. Even though the acting is very stylised, and the music can be discordant to Western ears, they are worth seeing. Free street performances are held in the Chinatown areas of KL and Singapore, Melaka and Penang's George Town during important festivals like Chinese New Year (January/February), the Festival of the Hungry Ghosts (August/September) and the Festival of the Nine Emperor Gods (September/October).

the Thai border in Kelantan. There's also the *rodat*, a dance from Terengganu, and the *joget*, an upbeat dance with Portuguese origins, often performed at Malay weddings by professional dancers; in Melaka it's better known as *chakunchak*.

When it comes to contemporary drama and dance, Singapore tends to have the edge. There's a lot of interesting work by local theatre companies like Action Theatre (www.action.org.sg), W!ld Rice (www.wildrice.com.sg), Toy Factory Ensemble (www.toyfactory.com.sg) and the Singapore Repertory Theatre (www.srt.com.sg). Singapore's leading dance company, Singapore Dance Theatre (www.singaporedancetheatre.com), puts on performances ranging from classical ballet to contemporary dance.

Silat, or *bersilat*, is a Malay martial art that originated in 15th-century Melaka. Today it is a highly refined and stylised activity, more akin to dance than self-defence.

Music

Traditional & Classical

Traditional Malay music is based largely on *gendang* (drums), but other percussion instruments include the gong and various tribal instruments made from seashells, coconut shells and bamboo. The Indonesian-style *gamelan* (a traditional orchestra of drums, gongs and wooden xylophones) also crops up on ceremonial occasions. The Malay *nobat* uses a mixture of percussion and wind instruments to create formal court music. For Western-style orchestration, attend a performance at the Dewan Filharmonik Petronas at the base of the Petronas Towers.

Islamic and Chinese influences are felt in the music of *dondang sayang* (Chinese-influenced romantic songs), and *hadrah* (Islamic chants, sometimes accompanied by dance and music). The KL-based Dama Orchestra (www.damaorchestra.com) combines modern and traditional Chinese instruments and play songs that conjure up the mood of 1920s and 1930s Malaysia.

In Singapore, catch the Singapore Symphony Orchestra (SSO, at the Esplanade – Theatres on the Bay) and the well-respected Singapore Chinese Orchestra which plays not only traditional and symphonic Chinese music but also Indian, Malay and Western pieces.

Popular Music

Snapping at the high heels of demure Malaysian pop songstress Siti Nurhaliza (http://sitizone.com) are Zee Avi (www.zeeavi.com), who was signed by the US label Brushfire Records for her eponymous debut CD; and the sultry Yuna (www.yunamusic.com), who has also cut a US record deal.

Winner of three AIM awards – the Malaysian equivalent of the Grammies – in 2004 for his debut album *Monumental*, singer-songwriter

Reshmonu (www.reshmonu.com) blends local rhythmns and instruments into r'n'b and latin grooves like samba and bossanova.

Singapore's pop music scene creates only a small blip internationally; visitors should look out for local festivals, like the annual Baybeats (www.baybeats.com), showcasing alternative singers and bands.

Cinema

The heyday of Malaysia's film industry was the 1950s, when P Ramlee took to the silver screen. This Malaysian icon acted in 66 films, recorded 300 songs and was also a successful film director – his directorial debut *Penarik Becha* (The Trishaw Man; 1955) is a classic of Malay cinema.

Yasmin Ahamad is considered to be the most culturally important Malaysian filmmaker since Ramlee. Her film *Sepet* (2005), about a Chinese boy and Malay girl falling in love, cut across the country's race and language barriers upsetting many devout Malays, as did her follow up, *Gubra* (2006), which dared to take a sympathetic approach to prostitutes. Causing less of stir were *Mukshin* (2007), a romantic tale about Malay village life, and *Talentime* (2009), about an inter-school performing arts contest, and what would be Yasmin's final film before her death from a stroke the same year. Find out more about her work from Amir Muhammad's tribute book *Yasmin Ahamad's Films* (www.mataharibooks.com).

TRADITIONAL CRAFTS

The region's crafts have much rustic beauty and incorporate traditional designs. Check out the online shop **Gerai OA** (www.elevyn.com/shop/geraioa), which sells crafts by Malaysia's indigenous minorities.

» **Batik** Batik is made across Malaysia, but Kelantan and Terengganu are its true homes. Produced by drawing or printing a pattern on fabric with wax and then dyeing the material, batik can be made into clothes, homewares, or simply be created as works of art.

» **Basketry & Weaving** The baskets of the Iban, Kayan, Kenyah and Penan are highly regarded. Weaving material include rattan, bamboo, swamp nipah grass and pandanus palms. Related weaving techniques produce sleeping mats, seats and materials for shelters. While each ethnic group has certain distinctive patterns, hundreds or even thousands of years of trade and interaction has led to an intermixing of patterns.

» **Kain Songket** This hand-woven fabric with gold and silver threads through the material is a speciality of Kelantan and Terengganu. Clothes made from it are usually reserved for important festivals and occasions. You can also buy pieces of the fabric for decorative purposes.

» **Kites & Puppets** The *wau bulan* (moon kite) of Kelantan is a traditional paper and bamboo crescent-shaped kite as large as 3m in length and breadth, while kite makers in Terengganu specialise in the *wau kucing* (cat kite). *Wayang kulit* (shadow puppets) are made from buffalo hide in the shape of characters from epic Hindu legends.

» **Metalwork** Kelantan is famed for its silversmiths, who work in a variety of ways and specialise in filigree and repoussé work. In the latter, designs are hammered through the silver from the underside. Brasswork is an equally traditional skill in Kuala Terengganu. Objects crafted out of pewter (an alloy of tin) are synonymous with Selangor, where you'll find the Royal Selangor Pewter Factory as well as other pewter manufacturers.

» **Woodcarving** The Orang Asli tribe of Hma' Meri, who live in a village on Pulau Carey, off the coast of Selangor, are renowned woodcarving craftsmen. In Malaysian Borneo the Kenyah and Kayan peoples are also skilled woodcarvers, producing hunting-charms and ornate knife-hilts known as *parang ilang*.

Amir Muhammad's movies also push the boundaries on issues that the government prefers not be discussed in the public arena. His movie *Lelaki Komunis Terakhir* (The Last Communist Man; 2006) was banned, along with his follow-up movie *Apa Khabar Orang Kampung* (Village People Radio Show; 2007).

Singapore has never been a leading light in film production, but during the 1990s some local movies began to gain international attention, in particular Yonfan's *Bugis Street* and Eric Khoo's *Mee Pok Man*, both released in 1995. Khoo's *12 Storeys* (1997) and more recent *Be with Me* (2005) and *My Magic* (2008) have since featured in competition at Cannes.

Royston Tan continues his love/hate relationship with Singapore's censors. His first feature, *15,* had 27 scenes snipped. In response, he produced the hilarious short music video *Cut* (available on YouTube). His last two films, *881* and *12 Lotus,* were Chinese-language features.

Visual Arts

The Brunei Art Forum in Bandar Seri Begawan promotes local contemporary artists (mostly painters) including Zakaria Bin Omar, Haji Padzil Haji Ahmad, Pengiran Mohd Roslan Pg Haji Bakar and Teck Kwang Swee, and fosters international links.

Among the most interesting and internationally successful contemporary Malaysian artists are Jalaini Abu Hassan ('Jai'), Wong Hoy Cheong, landscape painter Wong Perng Fey, and Australian-trained multimedia artist Yee I-Lann. Amron Omar has focused for nearly 30 years on *silat* (a Malay martial art) as a source of inspiration for his paintings – several are in the National Visual Art Gallery in KL. A young contemporary sculptor who's making a name for himself internationally is Abdul Multhalib Musa. His work has won awards and he created several pieces in Beijing for the 2008 Olympics.

In Singapore the visual-arts scene is also vibrant, with painting, sculpture and multimedia the vehicles of choice for dynamic explorations into the tensions between Western art practices and the perceived erosion of traditional values. Highly regarded local artists include Da Wu Tang, Vincent Leow, Jason Lim and Zulkifle Mahmod, all of whom took part in the 2007 Venice Biennale.

Media

For the last decade, since Mahathir's retirement as prime minister in 2003, there has been noticeably more freedom in what the media covers in Malaysia. The stringent laws haven't changed, but the mind-set of journalists has and there's less self-censorship than in the past. Malaysia has one of the liveliest blogospheres of the region, with the practically unfettered expansion of politically linked websites and blogs proof of a more liberal attitude.

The Singaporean government restricts freedom of speech and freedom of the press, as well as other civil and political rights. Censorship of sexual, political and racially or religiously sensitive content is extensive. However, the government's attitude towards online media has been relaxed since 2006. Once banned during elections, blogs and social media are now allowed as part of the media coverage. Social media increasingly plays a part in the Singapore mediascape, with local newspapers often quoting bloggers and reporting on issues generated in the blogosphere.

Freedom House has listed Brunei as 'not free' when it comes to the media. The government can arbitrarily shut down media outlets and bar distribution of foreign publications. Journalists can be jailed for up to three years for reporting 'false and malicious' news. This said, there have been no reports of attacks on or harassment of journalists in recent years. Both the country's main newspapers, the *Borneo Bulletin* (owned by members of the Sultan's family) and the *Borneo Times,* are believed to practise self-censorship.

Food & Drink

Centuries of trade, colonisation, and immigration have left their culinary mark on Malaysia, Singapore and Brunei in the form of cuisines so multifaceted it would take months of nonstop grazing to truly grasp their breadth. Nowhere else in Asia are the elements of three great culinary traditions – those of China, India and the Malay archipelago – so intertwined. The result is dishes both starkly monocultural (think Chinese wonton noodles and the southern Indian rolled 'pancakes' called *dosa*) and confusingly – but delightfully – multicultural *(debal,* a Melakan Eurasian stew, marries European-originated red wine vinegar, Indian blackmustard seeds, Chinese soy sauce and Malay candlenuts).

Flavours

Malaysia, Brunei and Singapore have similar populations, share a tropical climate and were all at one time home to important trading ports along the spice route. As a result, their cuisines are characterised by comparable flavours and are built on a shared foundation of basic ingredients.

Chillies *(cili),* both fresh and dried, are a kitchen staple. (Chilli-phobes need not worry; the region boasts plenty of mild dishes too.) Capsicum stars in *sambal,* a dip cum relish; its many varieties incorporate ingredients ranging from dried shrimp to fruit and are served alongside humble soup noodles, lavish rice spreads and every meal in between. Chillies are the base of *rempah* (called *bumbu* in Brunei), a pounded paste also containing, at its most basic, garlic and shallots, which forms the foundation of curries, soups and stews.

Herbs and aromatics like coriander, mint, *daun kesom* (polygonum, a peppery, slightly astringent leaf also known as laksa leaf), celery leaves (from the slender, jade-green Asian variety rather than thick-stemmed, mild-flavoured Western celery) *daun kunyit* (turmeric leaves), curry leaves, lemongrass and wild lime leaves impart a fresh liveliness to curries and noodle dishes. Fragrant pandan leaves are often called 'Southeast Asian vanilla' for the light, slightly sweet essence they lend to sweets. (Pandan is also a natural deodoriser, so don't be surprised to see a bundle of leaves stashed beneath the rear window of your taxi).

Sourness is also an important facet of the region's cuisines. *Asam* (sour) curries and noodle dishes derive piquancy primarily from tamarind and *asam keping,* the flesh of a tart fruit related to the mangosteen that's sliced into thin coins and dried. Malay cooks also make sour soups and sambals with a tiny green fruit called *belimbing,* a relative of the star fruit. Both limes and calamansi, a cross between lime and Mandarin orange, are juiced for salads; slices are served with laksa and other noodle dishes.

Grated coconut is dry-fried, sometimes with dried chillies and other

Recommended Websites & Blogs

» Chubby Hubby (www.chubby-hubby.net/blog)

» Eating Asia (www.eatingasia.typepad.com)

» Fried Chillies (www.friedchillies.com)

» ieatishootipost (www.ieatishootipost.sg)

» Makansutra (www.makansutra.com)

» Masak-masak (www.masak-masak.blogspot.com)

» Rasa Malaysia (www.rasamalaysia.com)

» What2See: The Best of Penang Food! (www.what2seeonline.com)

When the Portuguese conquered Melaka with a fleet launched from Goa they brought along vindaloo, which morphed into the Cristang-inspired dish *debal.*

FOR THE LOVE OF SAMBAL

There are as many variations of *sambal* as there are Malay cooks. Mild to fiery, made with fresh or dried chillies, and incorporating ingredients from dried fish to fruit, this cross between a dip and a relish accompanies simple soup noodles, lavish feasts and every meal in between. The most common variation is *sambal belacan*, made from fresh or dried red chillies pounded with dried *belacan* (fermented prawn paste). If its pungent punch puts you off initially, try, try again – *sambal belacan* is rarely loved at first bite but often proves addictive in the long run.

flavourings, to make *kerisik,* a garnish for rice, and is an ingredient in many *kuih* (sweets), where it's often paired with *gula Melaka,* a distinctive dark brown sugar made by boiling the sap collected from cut flower stalks of the coconut palm.

Belacan (dried shrimp paste) embodies the Malaysian, Singaporean and Bruneian love of fishy flavours. A black, sticky-sweet version native to Penang, called *hae ko,* dresses vegetable and fruit salad *(rojak)* and is stirred into *asam* laksa, a sour fishy noodle dish, right before serving. Other well-loved condiments made from the fruits of the sea include *cincalok (cencalu* in Brunei), krill mixed with salt and sugar and left to ferment (it's often eaten with rice and eggs) and *budu,* a sludgy long-fermented anchovy sauce favoured by Malay cooks. These piscine condiments lend umami to many a *sambal,* dipping sauce and curry and, though certainly odoriferous, can be addictive; after a few weeks of sampling you may find yourself wishing you could sneak a block of *belacan* past your home country's custom agents.

No local kitchen is complete without sauces that were originally introduced to the region by the Chinese: soy sauce (and its sweetened cousin *kecap manis),* fermented salted bean paste *(taucu),* oyster sauce and hoisin sauce.

> Many upscale restaurants add a 10% service charge. If you see '++' at the bottom of your menu, add 15% for government taxes and service charge.

Staples

Curries

Though chillies are a mainstay of Malaysian cuisine, few dishes are prohibitively spicy. Curries start with *rempah* – a pounded paste of chillies and aromatics like garlic, shallots, *serai* (lemongrass), *kunyit* (turmeric) and *lengkuas* (galangal). Dried spices – coriander seeds, fennel seeds, cumin, fenugreek – might also be included, especially if the dish is Indian-influenced. Curries and sweets are made *lemak* (fatty and rich) with coconut milk.

Rice & Noodles

> 'Ketchup' is thought to be derived from the Hokkien word *ke-tsiap,* which describes a fermented fish sauce brought by Chinese traders to Melaka, where it was encountered by Europeans.

The locals would be hard-pressed to choose between *nasi* (rice) and *mee* (noodles) – one or the other features in almost every meal. Rice is boiled in water or stock to make porridge *(congee* or *bubur),* fried with chillies and shallots for *nasi goreng,* and packed into banana leaf-lined bamboo tubes, cooked, then sliced and doused with coconut-and-vegetable gravy for the Malay dish *lontong.* Glutinous (sticky) rice – both white and black – is a common *kuih* ingredient; Malays mix glutinous rice with sugar and allow it to ferment for sweet-and-sour, slightly alcoholic *tapai,* which goes nicely with ice cream.

Rice flour, mixed with water and allowed to ferment, becomes the batter for Indian *idli,* steamed cakes to eat with dhal (stewed lentils*),* and *apam,* crispy-chewy pancakes cooked in special concave pans. Rice flour–based dough is transformed into sweet dumplings like *onde-onde,* coconut flake-dusted, pandan-hued balls hiding a filling of semi-liquid *gula Melaka* (palm sugar).

Many varieties of noodle are made from rice flour, both the wide, flat *kway teow* and *mee hoon* (or *bee hoon,* rice vermicelli). *Chee cheong fun –* steamed rice flour sheets – are sliced into strips and topped with sweet brown and red chilli sauces; stubby *loh see fun* (literally 'rat-tail noodles') are stewed in a claypot with dark soy sauce.

Round yellow noodles form the basis of the Muslim Indian dish *mee mamak*. The Chinese favourite *won ton mee*, found anywhere in the region, comprises wheat-and-egg vermicelli, a clear meat broth and silky-skinned dumplings.

A primary starch for Bruneians and some indigenous communities in the eastern Malaysian states of Sabah and Sarawak is sago flour, laboriously extracted from the trunk of a variety of palm tree. In Brunei, it's mixed with water and cooked to make *ambuyat* (or *ambulung*), a sticky whitish paste. It was popularised during WWII, when the Japanese invaded Borneo and cut off the rice supply.

Meat & Seafood

In Malaysia, religion often dictates a diner's choice of protein. *Haram* (forbidden) to Muslims, *babi* (pork) is the king of meats for Chinese; some hawkers even drizzle noodles with melted lard. Whether roasted till crispy-skinned *(char yoke)* or marinated and barbecued till sweetly charred *(char siew),* the meat is eaten with rice, added to noodles, and stuffed into steamed and baked buns. Malaysian Hakka (a Chinese ethnic group) are renowned for succulent, long-cooked pork dishes like *khaw yoke,* sliced belly seasoned with five spice, layered with sliced taro and steamed.

Chicken *(ayam)* is tremendously popular in Malaysia and Singapore, but more of a special occasion meat in Brunei (as is beef or buffalo). Malay eateries offer a variety of chicken curries, and the meat regularly turns up on skewers, grilled and served with peanut sauce for satay. Another oft-enjoyed fowl is *itik* (duck), roasted and served over rice, simmered in star anise–scented broth and eaten with yellow *mee,* or stewed with aromatics for a spicy Indian Muslim curry.

Tough local beef *(daging)* is best cooked long and slowly, for dishes like coconut milk–based *rendang*. Chinese-style beef noodles feature tender chunks of beef and springy meatballs in a rich, mildly spiced broth lightened with pickled mustard. Indian Muslims do amazing things with mutton; it's worth searching out *sup kambing,* stewed mutton riblets (and other parts, if you wish) in a thick soup, flavoured with loads of aromatics and chillies that's eaten with sliced white bread.

The word laksa is thought to derive from the Persian word for noodle, *lakhsha* (slippery). The *Oxford Companion to Food* speculates that pasta was introduced to Indonesia (from where it migrated to Malaysia) by Arab traders or Indian Muslims in the 13th century.

Geragau, the tiny prawn found in the seas off the Strait of Melaka and the waters around Penang, are used to make *belacan* and *cincaluk,* extremely salty fermented pastes.

FOOD & DRINK STAPLES

CHOP TO IT!

Dine at enough *kopi tiam* (coffee shops) and you're bound to run into lamb chops and mushroom soup. Though these may seem out of place on a menu that also features *belacan* (fermented prawn paste), fried rice and fish in sour curry, these dishes are as much a part of the Malaysian culinary universe as laksa *lemak* (curry laksa). Western classics like chops (pork and chicken, in addition to lamb) and fish and chips are Malaysia's intergenerational comfort foods. They were introduced by the British but popularised in the early decades of the 20th century by the Hainanese immigrants who served as their private cooks – and later became known throughout the country for their prowess in the kitchen. The best versions, found in old-time *kopi tiam* sporting original floor tiles and peeling paint, are astoundingly authentic. Seek them out when a break from local fare is in order, and eat a bit of history.

Lengthy coastlines and abundant rivers and estuaries mean that seafood forms much of the diet for many of the region's residents. The region's wet markets devote whole sections to dried seafood, with some stalls specialising in *ikan bilis* – tiny dried anchovies that are deep-fried till crispy and incorporated into sambal or sprinkled atop noodle and rice dishes – and others displaying an array of salted dried fish.

Vegetables

Vegetable lovers will have a field day. Every rice-based Malay meal includes *ulam,* a selection of fresh and blanched vegetables – wing beans, cucumbers, okra, eggplant and the fresh legume *petai* (or stink bean, so-named for its strong garlicky taste) – and fresh herbs to eat on their own or dip into *sambal.* Indians cook cauliflower and leafy vegetables like cabbage, spinach and roselle (sturdy leaves with an appealing sourness) with coconut milk and turmeric. Other greens – *daun ubi* (sweet potato leaves), *kangkong* (water spinach), Chinese broccoli and yellow-flowered mustard – are stir-fried with *sambal belacan* or garlic. The humble jicama is particularly versatile; it's sliced and added raw to *rojak;* grated, steamed, and rolled into *popiah* (soft spring rolls) and mashed, formed into a cake and topped with deep-fried shallots and chillies for Chinese *oh kuih.* Sweet corn is plentiful, sold by vendors grilled or off-the-cob and steamed, at almost every night market.

Tahu (soy beans) are consumed in many forms. Soy-milk lovers can indulge in the freshest of the fresh at Chinese wet markets, where a vendor selling deep-fried *crullers* (long fried-doughnut sticks) for dipping is never far away. *Dou fu* (soft fresh bean curd), eaten plain or doused with syrup, makes a great light snack. *Yong tauhu* is a healthy Hakka favourite of firm bean curd and vegetables like okra and eggplant stuffed with ground fish paste and served with chilli sauce. *Fucuk,* which is the chewy skin that forms on the surface of boiling soy milk, is fried golden or eaten fresh in noodle dishes, and absorbent deep-fried *tauhu pok* (bean curd 'puffs') are added to noodles and stews. Malays often cook with *tempeh,* a fermented soy bean cake with a nutty flavour, stir-frying it with *kecap manis,* lemongrass and chillies, and stewing it with vegetables in mild coconut gravy.

Sweets

The locals are passionate about sweets; vendors of cakes and pastries lie in wait on street corners, footpaths and in markets. Many *kuih* incorporate coconut, grated or in the form of milk, and palm sugar; among the tastiest are *ketayap,* rice flour 'pancakes' rolled around a mix of the two, and *putu piring* (steamed rice flour 'flapjacks' filled with palm sugar and topped with coconut). Some *kuih* – *pulut panggang* (banana leaf–wrapped and grilled glutinous rice-and-coconut tubes filled with grated coconut, chopped dried chillies and dried shrimp), for example – combine sweet and savoury flavours to fantastic effect.

Tong sui (the Chinese name for 'sweet soups'), like sweet potato and sago pearls in a coconut milk-based broth, are reviving snacks. Perhaps the region's most beloved dessert is *cendol,* a heat-beating mound of shaved ice and chewy mung-bean-flour 'pasta' doused with fresh coconut milk and palm sugar syrup. ABC (for *ais batu campur* or 'mixed ice'), its more flamboyant cousin, is a hillock of shaved ice garnished with fluorescent-coloured (and mostly artificial-tasting) syrups, jellies, red beans, palm seeds and sweet corn. Don't leave the region without investigating the colourful sub-continental *mithai* (sweets) stacked in

Practising Muslims can relax in Malaysia, which is a world leader in offering halal food; even fast food outlets sport halal certification. Look for window stickers and on menus to check an outlet's accreditation.

When is a fruit not a fruit? When it's a young jackfruit *(nangka muda),* which Malay cooks treat as a vegetable, stirring it into coconut milk-based curries.

FRUIT FOR THOUGHT

Those who have overindulged in *kuih* might repent with a dose of healthy tropical fruits. *Nenas* (pineapple), watermelon, *jambu* (rose apple), papaya and green guava are year-round choices, with more unusual fruits available seasonally. The dull brown skin of the *ciku* (sopadilla) hides supersweet flesh that tastes a bit like a date. Strip away the yellowish peel of the *duku* (also known as *dokong* and *langsat*) to find segmented, perfumed pearlescent flesh with a lychee-like flavour.

April and May are mango months, and come December to January and June to July, follow your nose to sample notoriously odoriferous love-it-or-hate-it durian. Should the king of fruits prove too repellent, consider the slightly smelly but wonderfully sweet yellow flesh of the young *nangka* (jackfruit).

Other tropical fruits you may come across at markets and street stalls:

» **Buah nona** The custard apple; a knobbly green skin conceals hard, black seeds and sweet, gloopy flesh with a granular texture.

» **Buah salak** Known as the snakeskin fruit because of its scaly skin; the exterior looks like a mutant strawberry and the soft flesh tastes like unripe bananas.

» **Cempedak** The Malaysian breadfruit; a huge green fruit with skin like the Thing from the *Fantastic Four*; the seeds and flesh are often curried or fried.

» **Dragon fruit** An alien-looking red pod with tongue-like flanges hiding fragrant, kiwi fruit-like flesh with lots of tiny edible seeds.

» **Guava** A green, apple-like ball containing sweet pink or white flesh.

» **Jambu merah** Rose apple; elongated pink or red fruit with a smooth, shiny skin and pale, watery flesh; a good thirst quencher on a hot day.

» **Longan** A tiny, hard ball like a mini lychee with sweet, perfumed flesh; peel it, eat the flesh and spit out the hard seeds.

» **Mangosteen** A hard, purple shell conceals delightfully fragrant white segments, some containing a tough seed that you can spit out or swallow.

» **Pomelo** Like a grapefruit on steroids, with a thick pithy green skin hiding sweet, tangy segments; cut into the skin, peel off the pith then break open the segments and munch on the flesh inside.

» **Rambutan** People have different theories about what rambutans look like, not all repeatable in polite company; the hairy shell contains sweet, translucent flesh, which you scrape off the seed with your teeth.

» **Soursop** A sack-like fruit with tasty but tart granular flesh and hard, black seeds; it's only ripe when soft and it goes off within days so eat it quickly.

» **Starfruit** The star-shaped cross-section is the giveaway; the yellow flesh is sweet and tangy and believed by many to lower blood pressure.

» **Tamarind** Fresh tamarind comes in a curved, brown pod; the hard seeds are hidden inside the delicious, tart flesh.

Little India shop windows; our favourite is creamy, buttery – and, yes, tooth-achingly sweet – milk halva.

Drinks

Half the fun of taking breakfast in one of Singapore's or Malaysia's Little Indias is watching the tea *wallah* toss-pour an order of *teh tarik* ('pulled' tea) from one cup to the other. Locals love their leaves; tea is also brewed with ginger for *teh halia,* drunk hot or iced, with or without milk *(teh ais* or *teh-o ais),* and soured with lime juice *(teh limau).* For an especially rich cuppa head to an Indian cafe and ask for *teh susu kerabu,* hot tea with boiled fresh cow's milk. *Kopi* (coffee) is also extremely popular, and the inky, thick brew owes its distinctive colour and flavour to the fact that its beans are roasted with sugar. *Kopi* is served in Chinese coffee shops (ask for *kopi-o* if you don't want sweetened condensed milk in yours, *kopi gao* if you want it especially strong, and *kopi bing* if you want it milky and iced) and is an excellent antidote to jet lag.

Caffeine-free alternatives include freshly squeezed or blended vegetable and fruit juices, sticky-sweet fresh sugar-cane juice (nice with a squeeze of calamansi), and *kelapa muda,* or young coconut water, drunk straight from the fruit with a straw. Other more-unusual drinks are *ee bee chui* (barley boiled with water, pandan leaf and rock sugar), *air mata kucing* (made with dried longan), and *cincau* or herbal grass jelly. Chinese salted plums add an oddly refreshing dimension to sweetened lime juice, in *asam boi*.

Thanks to sky-high duties, alcohol is pricey in Singapore and Malaysia (and banned or, more accurately, limited to hotels and high-end restaurants in Brunei); for a cheap, boozy night out stick to locally brewed beers like Tiger, Carlsberg and Guinness. Chinese stores stock a variety of less expensive and sometimes surprisingly palatable hard liquors.

Habits & Customs

Fork and spoon are the cutlery of choice, except in Western-oriented establishments or *kopitiam* (coffee shops) serving chops and fish and chips, where you might get a knife, too. Don't put the fork in your mouth, but use it to gently nudge food onto your spoon. Chinese noodles and dishes served in Chinese restaurants are usually eaten with chopsticks (though forks and spoons are available on request). Malays and Indians eat rice-based meals with their right hand only, using thumb to manoeuvre rice onto the balls of the fingers and then into the mouth. (This is easier done if you moisten your rice with curries and side dishes and mash the lot together.) Wash your hands before and after with water from the teapot-like container on the table (Malay eateries) or at a communal sink at the side or rear of the room. Napkins are a rarity so it's always a good idea to carry a pack of tissues.

In some Chinese eateries you'll be given a basin of hot water containing saucers, chopsticks, bowls and cutlery. This is meant to allow for hygiene concerns; remove the items and dry them off or shake them dry.

Ever wondered why many durian stalls also sell mangosteens? The latter is thought to be a 'cooling fruit' that, eaten on the heels of 'heaty' durian, brings the body back into balance.

The Region's Environment

Malaysia's federal government maintains that it is doing its best to balance out the benefits of economic development with environmental protection and conservation. Others, including a long list of wildlife and environmental-protection agencies and pressure groups, beg to differ, pointing out how big business continues to have the ear of government when decision time rolls around.

It's far from a clear-cut situation: Malaysia's logging and oil palm businesses provide hundreds of thousands of jobs, yet they also wreak untold ecological damage and have caused the displacement of many tribal people and the consequent erosion of these unique cultures.

In Singapore strict laws control littering and waste emissions are policed vigilantly. Though little of the island's original wilderness is left, growing interest in ecology has seen bird sanctuaries and parkland areas created, with new parks in the Marina Bay development as well as a series of connectors that link up numerous existing parks and gardens around the island.

With few roads and much of its tiny area covered by forest, car emissions are the least of Brunei's problems. However, like much of the region, it suffers the effects of smoke haze from Indonesia.

Deforestation

There's a disparity between government figures and those of environmental groups, but it's probable that more than 60% of Peninsular Malaysia's rainforests have been logged, with similar figures applying to Malaysian Borneo. Government initiatives like the National Forestry Policy have led to deforestation being cut to 900 sq km a year, a third slower than previously. The aim is to reduce the timber harvest by 10% each year, but even this isn't sufficient to calm the many critics who remain alarmed at the rate at which Malaysia's primary forests are disappearing.

At the United Nations Framework Convention on Climate Change in 2008, Malaysia committed to maintaining 50% of its land with forest cover. However, as the Malaysian Nature Society and others have pointed out, the problem is how the government defines 'forest cover' – currently the description includes rubber plantations. In many states old-growth forests are being cut down to plant rubber.

Environmental groups like TREES (http://trees.org.my) have also been campaigning for the protection of the rainforests and water catchment areas along the eastern flank of Selangor. In 2010, 93,000 hectares of these uplands were gazetted as the Selangor State Park making it the peninsula's third largest protected area of forest after

Online Resources

» Sahabat Alam Malaysia (SAM; www.foe-malaysia.org)

» Orangutan Foundation (www.orangutan.org.uk)

» Wild Singapore (www.wildsingapore.com)

» Malaysian Conversation Alliance for Tigers (MYCAT; http://malayantiger.net/v4)

Taman Negara and Royal Belum State Park. Find out more at http://selangorstatepark.blogspot.com.

In Sarawak and Sabah several national parks and reserves have recently been created or extended, like the Maliau Basin Conservation Area and the Pulong Tau National Park. However, the effects of logging are still clearly being felt in the region, which now suffers unusually long floods during the wet season.

The Heart of Borneo Project (www.heartofborneo.org) is a hugely ambitious initiative led by WWF (www.panda.org) to safeguard the island's biodiversity for future generations and ensure indigenous people's cultural survival by protecting 24,000 sq km of interconnected forest land in Sabah, Sarawak, Brunei and Kalimantan – altogether almost a third of Borneo.

Another ray of light comes from the Kuching-based Sarawak Biodiversity Centre (www.sbc.org.my), an organisation that aims to assist drug companies in their search for valuable medical compounds from the rainforest. If the cure for cancer or AIDS can be found in these forests, it might just be their partial saviour.

For more on what the government is doing in relation to forest management, see the websites of the forestry departments of Peninsular Malaysia (www.forestry.gov.my), Sarawak (www.forestry.sarawak.gov.my) and Sabah (www.forest.sabah.gov.my). For the alternative point of view, read William W Bevis's award-winning *Borneo Log: The Struggle for Sarawak's Forests,* an evocative narrative that starkly outlines the environmental and human impacts of the logging in Sarawak.

The Clouded Leopard Project (http://cloudedleopard.org) has funded several conservation efforts on Malaysian Borneo for this beautiful animal that may be rarer than the Malayan tiger.

Improving Wildlife Conservation

At the end of 2010 Malaysia started to enforce its new Wildlife Conservation Act, which includes fines of up to RM100,000 and long prison sentences for poaching, smuggling of animals and other wildlife-related crimes. This first revision of such laws in over 30 years has been welcomed by local pressure groups including Traffic Southeast Asia (www.traffic.org/southeast-asia) and the Malaysian Nature Society.

Smuggling of live animals and animal parts is a particular problem in the region. Pangolins, also known as scaly anteaters, are the most traded species even though they are protected under Malaysian law; their scales, believed to have medicinal properties, can fetch up to RM800 per kg. In July 2010 police looking for stolen cars also uncovered an illegal 'mini zoo' in a KL warehouse containing 20 species of protected wildlife, including a pair of rare birds of paradise worth RM1 million.

A month later, the notorious animal smuggler Alvin Wong was nabbed at Kuala Lumpur International Airport after his bag burst open revealing 95 boa constrictors, two rhinoceros vipers and a mata mata turtle. He was sentenced to five years in prison. Wong is described as 'the Pablo Escobar of wildlife trafficking' in Bryan Christy's *The Lizard King* (http://thelizardkingbook.com), a fascinating account of international animal and reptile smuggling.

There's an ongoing environmental threat in the region from 'haze' – smoke from fires set by Indonesian farmers and plantation companies to clear land for agricultural purposes. The haze is usually at its worst in Singapore and parts of Malaysia around March and just before September and October's rainy season.

Palm Oil Plantations

The oil palm, a native of West Africa that was introduced into Malaysia in the 1870s, is probably now the most common tree in Malaysia. The country's first palm-oil plantation was established in 1917; today, according to the Malaysian Palm Oil Council (www.mpoc.org.my), Malaysia is the world's leading producer of palm oil, accounting for over 40% of global production. The oil is extracted from the orange-coloured fruit, which grows in bunches just below the fronds. It is used primarily for cooking, although it can also be refined into biodiesel – an alternative to fossil fuels.

For all the crops' benefits, there have been huge environmental consequences to the creation of vast plantations that have replaced the native jungle and previously logged forests; in 2003 Friends of the Earth reported that palm-oil production was responsible for 87% of deforestation in Malaysia. The use of polluting pesticides and fertilisers in palm-oil production also undermines the crop's eco credentials. Palm-oil plantations convert land into permanent monoculture, reducing the number of plant species by up to 90%. Oil palms require large quantities of herbicides and pesticides that can seep into rivers; drainage may lower water tables, drying out nearby peat forests (and releasing huge quantities of greenhouse gases in the process). Plantations also fragment the natural habitats that are especially important to large mammals.

The Palm Oil Action Group (www.palmoilaction.org.au) is an Australian pressure group raising awareness about palm oil and the need to use alternatives. Roundtable on Sustainable Palm Oil tries to look at the issue from all sides while seeking to develop and implement global standards. Proforest (www.proforest.net) has also been working with Wild Asia (www.wildasia.org) on the Stepwise Support Programme, designed to promote sustainability within the palm-oil industry.

Hydroelectric Dams

Hydoelectric dams are touted as sources of carbon-free energy, but these huge projects often have serious environmental impacts. In addition, indigenous people are often forcibly relocated to areas where they have a difficulty earning a living or maintaining their traditions. Such was the case with the controversial Bakun Dam (www.bakundam.com) in Sarawak.

In October 2010 the 207m high structure began flooding a reservoir that will eventually submerge an area of once-virgin rainforest about the size of Singapore (690 sq km). According to the Malaysian government, 'the second-highest concrete-faced rockfill dam in the world' will produce 2400MW of 'emission-free clean energy,' giving a much needed boost to Sarawak's economy.

However, Malaysian and international watchdogs claim the whole project – including contracts to clear the site of biomass, which involves logging old-growth jungle – has been shot through with corrupt

Environmental Reads

» *The Encyclopaedia of Malaysia: The Environment* (Sham Sani, ed.)

» *A Field Guide to the Mammals of Borneo* (Junaidi Payne, Charles M Francis & Karen Phillipps)

» *Wild Malaysia: The Wildlife & Scenery of Peninsular Malaysia* (Junaidi Payne & Gerald Cubitt)

For up-to-date news and information on environmental issues affecting Malaysian Borneo check out the website of Rengah Sarawak (Sarawak News; www.rengah.c2o.org).

CUTTING CARBON EMISSIONS

At the 2009 climate change conference in Copenhagen, Prime Minister Najib pledged to slash Malaysia's carbon emissions by 40% by 2020. According to the International Energy Agency the country emitted 6.68 tonnes of carbon dioxide per capita in 2007 – more than twice the world's average – and the fourth highest amount in the region after Brunei, Taipei and Singapore. Compared to these three countries, Malaysia's emission per capita percentage change between 1990 and 2007 was the highest, growing by 143%.

To reach its stated goal the federal government has added green technology to the portfolio of the Ministry of Energy and Water and announced the launch of a national green technology policy. The details remain sketchy, however, and the overall aim sits awkwardly with the nation's poor record on public transport and the continuing expansion of local budget airlines like AirAsia.

dealings designed to benefit the business associates of local politicians. Transparency International (www.transparency.org) has declared the dam a 'monument of corruption.'

Borneo does not need the power that the dam will produce; the original plan was to send 70% of the energy to Peninsular Malaysia along a 670km undersea cable. That part of the project has been shelved, however, leaving Sarawak with a huge over-capacity (when all turbines are operating, the dam will produce 2.5 times as many watts as Sarawak's current peak demand). Some of the slack may be taken up by a massive aluminium smelter being built near Mukah.

Despite this, a dozen more dams in highland Sarawak are in various stages of planning and execution, including the 944MW Murum Dam, located in a Penan area 60km upriver from Bakun.

Rivers

There has been some success in both Penang and Melaka when it comes to cleaning up polluted waterways. The Sungai Pinang that flows through the heart of George Town was once so filthy that it had a Class V classification, meaning it was unable to sustain life and contact with the water was dangerous. The state's clean-up program resulted in the waterway's pollution rating dropping to Class III in 2010. By 2015 it's hoped that the river will be waste free.

According to the Malayisan Nature Society, the revival of the once sludgy Sungei Melaka flowing through Melaka is also a model of how a river can be cleaned. Starting in 2005 the city invested about RM100 million in the project, which also included building grassy areas and walking paths along the river banks. A catamaran designed to clean up oil slicks was employed to remove rubbish then compress it into a material that could be used to reinforce the banks. The next step was

Regional Environmental Awareness Cameron Highlands (REACH; www. reach.org.my) has been working since 2001 to preserve, restore and maintain this region as an environmentally sustainable agricultural area and tourist resort within a permanent nature reserve.

THE PLIGHT OF TASIK CHINI

Part of the Pahang river basin and with a catchment size of 45 sq km, Tasik Chini is Malaysia's sole Unesco Biosphere Reserve. As late as 10 years ago the lake was a major tourist draw for the lotus flowers that practically carpeted its surface. Today pollution of the lake (which is actually a freshwater swamp) has resulted in murky waters and the near extinction of the lotuses.

Problems began in the mid-1980s, when the state government began approving land development schemes around the lake, and got worse when the federal government built a weir at the end of Sungai Chini in 1995 to facilitate navigation of tourist boats, despite protests by the Orang Asli who live in six villages around Tasik Chini.

The weir raised the lake by at least 2m, submerging thousands of trees and many stands of rattan by the water's edge, as well endangering the survival of the lotus plants, which grow best in shallow water. The water, already spoiled by run-off from open-cut iron ore mines as close as 50m from the lake's edge, was further polluted by the methane and hydrogen sulphide the dead vegetation in the lake produced as it rotted.

In August 2012 Transparency International-Malaysia (TI-M) and environmental agencies including WWF-Malaysia and Malaysian Nature Society launched a Save Tasik Chini campaign. Citing a Universiti Kebangsaan Malaysia report, TI-M claimed that Tasik Chini's eco-system is in a 'critical situation' and if nothing was done the lake would perish by 2030 – a view strongly refuted by Pahang's Chief Minister Adnan Yaakob. The Star reported that Orang Asli are furious at Adnan's denials of the problem, quoting local leaders who says they can no longer fish in the polluted lake or harvest roots and herbs from areas now off limits because of mining operations.

WHAT CAN YOU DO?

» Tread lightly and buy locally, avoiding (and reporting) instances where you see parts of or products made from endangered species for sale. On Peninsular Malaysia there's a 24-hour Wildlife Crime Hotline (☏019-356 4194) you can call to report illegal activities.

» Visit nature sites, hire local trekking guides and provide custom for ecotourism initiatives. By doing so you're putting cash in local pockets and casting a vote for the economic (as opposed to the purely ecological) value of sustainability and habitat conservation.

» Sign up to be a voluntary forest monitor at Forest Watch (www.timalaysia-forest watch.org.my), a project by Transparency International Malaysia.

» Check out Wild Asia's website (www.wildasia.org) to learn more about responsible tourism in the region.

» Keep abreast of and support local campaigns by checking out the websites of organisations like WWF Malaysia (www.wwfmalaysia.org) and the Malaysian Nature Society (www.mns.org.my).

the beautification of the banks, followed by domestic wastewater and cesspool treatment; reservoirs were built to trap scum, oil and refuse.

The focus has now turned to KL and the Klang Valley. The literal translation of Kuala Lumpur is 'muddy estuary'; anyone gazing on any of the milk-coffee-coloured waterways that flow through the city would still find that name highly appropriate. Following moves in 2010 by the Selangor state government to clean up a 21km stretch of the Sungei Klang around Klang, the much larger River of Life program now focuses anti-pollution efforts on the river's upper reaches. The government has allocated RM3 billion for the task of raising the river water quality from the current Class III and Class IV (not suitable for body contact) to Class IIb (suitable for body contact and recreational usage) by 2020.

Overdevelopment

On hillsides in Peninsular Malaysia, overdevelopment married to poor construction standards has caused several disastrous landslides, one of the most recent being in December 2008 in Bukit Antarabangsar, when four people died as 14 luxury homes tumbled down the slope. The collapse of a 12-storey building in Selangor in December 1993 killed 49 people. The government has toughened up construction codes, but development of such precariously sited facilities continues apace in the cooler highland areas within easy reach of KL, for example in the Cameron Highlands.

The marina being constructed in Tekek on Pulau Tioman has aggravated environmentalists who argue it will damage coral reefs in the area. It has already forced a few hotel operations to close and, as of recently, was an ugly construction site. The proposed second (offshore) airstrip at Pulau Tioman has also drawn fire for similar reasons, although it appears this project may have been postponed.

Some 75% of Kelantan's coast is also under attack from erosion; in the worst cases the shoreline is retreating by up to 10m a year.

Green, Clean Singapore

Singapore's reputation as an efficiently run, squeaky clean place is well justified. Visitors will no doubt notice the absence of trash on the streets: this is a result of a vast network of street cleaners and garbage

Ian Buchanan spent eight years creating the exquisite illustrations and text for *Fatimah's Kampung* (http://en.cap.org.my), a parable about how Malaysia is in the process of sacrificing nature and traditional values for economic development.

collection trucks. At the Housing Development Board flat complexes that the vast majority of Singaporeans live in there are seven types of formal and informal recycling schemes.

Waste is shipped off to Pulau Semakau, an island 8km south of the mainland. This landfill was planned and built by the National Environment Agency in 1999 and has been projected to meet the country's waste needs till 2040. More interestingly, the island itself has been much promoted by the government as an 'eco' hotspot (there isn't a stench, as waste buried has been processed or incinerated prior). Rehabilitated mangrove swamps sit next to a coral nursery. In 2005, the island was also opened for recreation activities such as nature walks and fishing.

Survival
Guide

DIRECTORY A–Z....592

Business Hours 593
Children 593
Climate................ 594
Customs Regulations ... 594
Electricity 594
Embassies &
Consulates 594
Food 594
Gay & Lesbian
Travellers 595
Insurance............. 595
Internet Access........ 595
Legal Matters 595
Maps................. 595
Money................ 595
Photography 596
Post.................. 596
Public Holidays........ 596
Safe Travel 596
Telephone 597
Time 597
Toilets................597
Tourist Information 597
Travellers with
Disabilities............ 598
Visas................. 598
Volunteering 598
Women Travellers....... 599
Work 599

TRANSPORT 600

GETTING THERE &
AWAY 600
Entering Malaysia....... 600
Air................... 600
Land 600
Sea 601
GETTING AROUND.......601
Air...................601
Bicycle 601
Boat 602
Bus 602
Car & Motorcycle 602
Hitching 603
Local Transport........ 604
Long-Distance Taxi...... 604
Tours................. 604
Train 604

HEALTH 606

LANGUAGE 611

Directory A–Z

Accommodation

Malaysia's accommodation possibilities range from rock-bottom flophouses to luxurious five-star resorts. Outside the peak holiday seasons (around major festivals such as Chinese New Year in January/February) big discounts are frequently available – it's always worth asking about special offers.

Budget listings in this guide (denoted with a '$') are those offering a double room with attached bathroom or dorm bed for under RM100; midrange properties ($$) have double rooms with attached baths for RM100 to RM400; top-end places ($$$) charge over RM400 including 10% service and 5% tax (expressed as ++).

Promotional rates can bring rooms at many top-end hotels into the midrange category. A 6% government tax applies to all hotel rooms (including at cheaper hotels where it is invariably included in the quoted rate) and almost all top-end hotels levy an additional 10% service charge. Credit cards are widely accepted at midrange and top-end hotels; cash payment is expected at cheaper places.

Warning: bed bug infestations are common in Malaysia's hotels and are a particular problem at the budget end of the market.

Camping

Many of Malaysia's national parks have official camping grounds and will permit camping in nondesignated sites once you are deep in the jungle. There are also many lonely stretches of beach that are ideal for camping. Likewise, it is possible to camp on uninhabited bays on many of Malaysia's islands. A two-season tent with mosquito netting is ideal. A summer-weight sleeping bag is OK, but the best choice is a lightweight bag-liner, since even the nights are warm.

Homestays

Staying with a Malaysian family will give you a unique experience many times removed from the fast-paced and largely recognisable life of the cities and towns. It's worth enquiring with **Tourism Malaysia** (www.tourism malaysia.gov.my) and each of the state tourism bodies about the homestay programs operating throughout the country in off-the-beaten-track *kampung* (villages).

Hostels & Guesthouses

At beach resorts and in the main tourist cities you will find a variety of cheap hostels and guesthouses. Dormitory accommodation is usually available. Rooms may be spartan (with flimsy walls and sometimes no window) and have shared bathrooms, but this is the cheapest accommodation option around and a great place to meet fellow travellers. These places offer their customers lots of little extras to outdo the competition, such as free wi-fi, tea and coffee, bicycles and transport. You'll normally pay around RM10 to RM30 for a dorm bed or RM15 to RM70 for a hotel-style room with air-con.

Hotels

Standard rooms at top-end hotels are often called 'superior' in the local parlance. Most hotels have slightly more expensive 'deluxe' or 'club' rooms, which tend to be larger, have a better view and include extras such as breakfast or free internet access. Many also have suites.

At the low end of the price scale are the traditional

BOOK YOUR STAY ONLINE

For more accommodation reviews by Lonely Planet authors, check out http://hotels.lonelyplanet.com. You'll find independent reviews, as well as recommendations on the best places to stay. Best of all, you can book online.

PRACTICALITIES

Connect to the reliable electricity supply (220V to 240V, 50 cycles) with a UK-type three-square-pin plug.

Read English-language newspapers the *New Straits Times*, the *Star* and the *Malay Mail*. In Malaysian Borneo you'll also find the *Borneo Post*, the *New Sarawak Tribune* and the *New Sabah Times*.

Listen to Traxx FM (www.traxxfm.net; 90.3FM), HITZ FM (www.hitz.fm; 92.9FM) and MIX FM (www.mix.fm; 94.5FM) for pop music and BFM (www.bfm.my; 89.9FM) or Fly FM (www.flyfm.com.my; 95.8FM) for news (these frequencies are for the KL area). In Sabah, listen to Traxx FM (90.7FM) or Muzik FM (88.9FM); in Sarawak tune in to Traxx FM (89.9FM), or Wai FM (101.3FM) for tribal music.

Watch Malaysia's two government TV channels (TV1 and TV2), four commercial stations (TV3, NTV7, 8TV and TV9) as well as a host of satellite channels.

Use the metric system for weights and measures.

Chinese-run hotels usually offering little more than simple rooms with a bed, a table and chair, and a sink. The showers and toilets (which will sometimes be Asian squat-style) may be down the corridor. Note couples can sometimes economise by asking for a single, since in Chinese-hotel language 'single' means one double bed, and 'double' means two beds. Don't think of this as being tight; in Chinese hotels you can pack as many into one room as you wish.

The main catch with these hotels is that they can sometimes be terribly noisy. They're often on main streets, and the cheapest ones often have flimsy walls that stop short of the ceiling – great for ventilation but terrible for acoustics and privacy.

Longhouses

A distinctive feature of indigenous Dayak life in Malaysian Borneo is the longhouse – essentially an entire village under one seemingly interminable roof. Contemporary longhouses fuse age-old forms with highly functional features such as corrugated iron roofs and satellite dishes.

According to longstanding Dayak tradition, anyone who shows up at a longhouse must be welcomed and given accommodation. However, these days turning up at a longhouse unannounced may be an unwelcome imposition on the residents – in short, bad manners. The way to avoid these pitfalls is to hire a locally-savvy guide or tour company that can co-ordinate your visit and make introductions.

Resthouses

A few of the old British-developed resthouses, set up during the colonial era to provide accommodation for travelling officials, are still operating. Many are still government owned but are privately operated. Some have been turned into modern midrange resorts, others retain old colonial decor. The average price for a room in a resthouse is between RM70 and RM100, and this usually includes air-con and attached bathroom.

Business Hours

Reviews won't list operating hours unless they deviate from the following:

» **Banks** 10am to 3pm Monday to Friday, 9.30am to 11.30am Saturday
» **Restaurants** noon to 2.30pm and 6pm to 10.30pm
» **Shops** 9.30am to 7pm, malls 10am to 10pm

Children

Practicalities

Travelling with the kids in Malaysia is generally a breeze. For the most part, parents needn't be overly concerned, but it pays to lay down a few ground rules – such as regular hand-washing – to head off potential problems. Children should especially be warned not to play with animals, as rabies occurs in Malaysia.

Lonely Planet's *Travel with Children* contains useful advice on how to cope with kids on the road and what to bring along to make things go more smoothly, with special attention paid to travelling in developing countries. Also useful for general advice is www.travelwithyourkids.com.

There are discounts for children for most attractions and for most transport. Many beach resorts have special family chalets. Cots, however, are not widely available in cheaper accommodation. Public transport is comfortable and relatively well organised. Pushing a stroller around isn't likely to be easy given there are often no footpaths and kerbs are high.

Baby formula, baby food and nappies (diapers) are widely available. However, it makes sense to stock up on these items before heading to remote destinations or islands.

Sights & Activities

Some beach destinations suitable for families with younger children include Pulau Perhentian, Pulau Kapas and Tunku Abdul Rahman National Park. Those with older children might enjoy some of the jungle parks of the country, including Taman Negara and, over in Sarawak, the Bako and Gunung Mulu national parks. For more animal encounters also consider the Sepilok Orang-Utan Rehabilitation Centre in Sabah.

There are several ways to entertain the kids in Kuala Lumpur.

Climate

Lying just 2° to 7° north of the equator, Peninsular Malaysia is hot and steamy year-round, with temperatures rarely dropping below 20°C, even at night.

Although Malaysia is monsoonal, only the east coast of the peninsula has a real rainy season – elsewhere there is just a little more rain than usual. Rain tends to arrive in brief torrential downpours, providing a welcome relief from the heat. During the monsoon it may rain every day, but it rarely rains all day. Humidity tends to hover around the 90% mark; escape the clammy heat by retreating to the cooler hills.

For current weather forecasts check the website of the **Malaysian Meteorological Department** (www.kjc.gov.my/english/weather/weather.html).

Customs Regulations

The following can be brought into Malaysia duty free:

» 1L of alcohol

» 225g of tobacco (200 cigarettes or 50 cigars)

» souvenirs and gifts not exceeding RM200 (RM500 when coming from Labuan or Langkawi).

Cameras, portable radios, perfume, cosmetics and watches do not incur duty. Prohibited items include weapons (including imitations), fireworks and 'obscene and prejudicial articles' (pornography, for example, and items that may be considered inflammatory, or religiously offensive) and drugs. Drug smuggling carries the death penalty in Malaysia.

Visitors can carry only RM1000 in and out of Malaysia; there's no limit on foreign currency.

Electricity

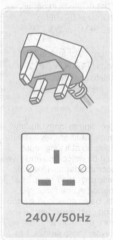

240V/50Hz

Embassies & Consulates

For a full list of Malaysian embassies and consulates outside the country check out www.kln.gov.my. The following foreign embassies are in Kuala Lumpur and are generally open 8am to 12.30pm and 1.30pm to 4.30pm Monday to Friday:

Australia (☑03-2146 5555; www.malaysia.embassy.gov.au; 6 Jln Yap Kwan Seng)

Brunei (☑03-2161 2800; www.mofat.gov.bn; 19-01, 19th fl, Menara Tan & Tan, Jln Tun Razak)

Canada (☑03-2718 3333; www.canadainternational.gc.ca/malaysia-malaisie; 17th fl, Menara Tan & Tan, 207 Jln Tun Razak)

France (☑03-2053 5500; www.ambafrance-my.org; 196 Jln Ampang)

Germany (☑03-2170 9666; www.kuala-lumpur.diplo.de; 26th fl, Menara Tan & Tan, 207 Jln Tun Razak)

Ireland (☑03-2161 2963; www.embassyofireland.my; 218 Jln Ampang)

Netherlands (☑03-2168 6200; www.netherlands.org.my; 7th fl, South Block, The Amp Walk, 218 Jln Ampang)

New Zealand (☑03-2078 2533; www.nzembassy.com/malaysia; Level 21, Menara IMC, 8 Jln Sultan Ismail)

Singapore (☑03-2161 6277; www.mfa.gov.sg/content/mfa/overseasmission/kuala_lumpur.html; 209 Jln Tun Razak)

UK (☑03-2170 2200; http://ukinmalaysia.fco.gov.uk; 185 Jln Ampang)

USA (☑03-2168 5000; http://malaysia.usembassy.gov; 376 Jln Tun Razak)

Food

The following price ranges refer to a two-course meal including a soft drink.

» $ less than RM10

» $$ RM10-50

» $$$ more than RM50

Gay & Lesbian Travellers

Malaysia is a predominantly Muslim country and the level of tolerance for homosexuality is vastly different from its neighbours. It's illegal for men of any age to have sex with other men. In addition, the Islamic *syariah* laws (which apply only to Muslims) forbid sodomy and cross-dressing. Fortunately, outright persecution of gays and lesbians is rare.

Nonetheless, gay and lesbian travellers should avoid behaviour that attracts unwanted attention. Malaysians are conservative about displays of public affection. Although same-sex hand-holding is quite common for men and women, this is rarely an indication of sexuality; an overtly gay couple doing the same would attract attention, though there is little risk of vocal or aggressive homophobia.

There's actually a fairly active gay scene in KL. The lesbian scene is more discreet, but it exists for those willing to seek it out. Start looking for information on www.utopia-asia.com or www.fridae.com, both of which provide good coverage of gay and lesbian events and activities across Asia.

The **PT Foundation** (www. ptfmalaysia.org) is a voluntary nonprofit organisation providing sexuality and HIV/AIDS education, care and support programs for marginalised communities.

Insurance

It's always a good idea to take out travel insurance. Check the small print to see if the policy covers potentially dangerous sporting activities such as caving, diving or trekking, and make sure that it adequately covers your valuables. Health-wise, you may prefer a policy that pays doctors or hospitals directly rather than your having to pay on the spot and claim later. If you have to claim later, make sure that you keep all documentation. Check that the policy covers ambulances, an emergency flight home and, if you plan trekking in remote areas, a helicopter evacuation.

A few credit cards offer limited, sometimes full, travel insurance to the holder.

Internet Access

You'll have to be deep in the jungle to be off-line in Malaysia. Urban centres have ubiquitous hot spots for wi-fi connections (often free) and internet cafes typically charging RM3 per hour for broadband access. You can also use a smartphone to access the internet via wi-fi. In the remote reaches of the peninsula and Malaysian Borneo don't expect the internet to be fast, though.

Among the internet providers in Malaysia are **Jaring** (www.jaring.my) and **Telekom Malaysia** (www.tm. com.my).

Legal Matters

In any dealings with the local police it will pay to be deferential. You're most likely to come into contact with them either through reporting a crime (some of the big cities in Malaysia have tourist police stations for this purpose) or while driving. Minor misdemeanours may be overlooked, but don't count on it.

Drug trafficking carries a mandatory death penalty. A number of foreigners have been executed in Malaysia, some of them for possession of amazingly small quantities of heroin. Even possession of tiny amounts can bring down a lengthy jail sentence and a beating with the *rotan* (cane). Just don't do it.

Maps

Periplus (peripluspublishing group.com) has maps covering Malaysia, Peninsular Malaysia and KL. Tourism Malaysia's free *Map of Malaysia* has useful distance charts, facts about the country and inset maps of many major cities.

For accurate maps of rural areas contact the **National Survey & Mapping Department** (Ibu Pejabat Ukur & Pemetaan Malaysia; ☏03-2617 0800; www.jupem.gov.my; Jln Semarak, Kuala Lumpur; ⊙7.30am-5.30pm Mon-Fri).

Money

ATMs & Credit Cards

MasterCard and Visa are the most widely accepted brands of credit card. You can make ATM withdrawals with your PIN, or banks such as Maybank (Malaysia's biggest bank), HSBC and Standard Chartered will accept credit cards for over-the-counter cash advances. Many banks are also linked to international banking networks such as Cirrus (the most common), Maestro and Plus, allowing withdrawals from overseas savings or cheque accounts.

If you have any questions about whether your cards will be accepted in Malaysia, ask your home bank about its reciprocal relationships with Malaysian banks.

Contact details for credit card companies in Malaysia:
American Express (☏2050 0000; www.americanexpress. com/malaysia)
Diners Card (☏2161 1055; www.diners.com.my)
MasterCard (☏1800 804 594; www.mastercard.com/sea)
Visa (☏1800 802 997; www. visa-asia.com)

Currency

The ringgit (RM) is made up of 100 sen. Coins in use are

1 sen, 5 sen, 10 sen, 20 sen and 50 sen; notes come in RM1, RM2 (rare), RM5, RM10, RM20, RM50 and RM100.

Malaysians sometimes refer to ringgit as 'dollars', the old name used for the country's currency – if in doubt ask if people mean US dollars or 'Malaysian dollars' (ie ringgit).

Be sure to carry plenty of small bills with you when venturing outside cities – in some cases people cannot change bills larger than RM10.

Taxes & Refunds

There is no general sales tax but there is a government tax of 6% at some midrange and all top-end hotels and many larger restaurants (in addition to an establishment's 10% service fee).

Travellers Cheques & Cash

Banks in the region are efficient and there are plenty of moneychangers. For changing cash or travellers cheques, banks usually charge a commission (around RM10 per transaction, with a possible small fee per cheque), whereas moneychangers have no charges but their rates vary more. Compared with a bank, you'll generally get a better rate for cash at a moneychanger – it's usually quicker too. Away from the tourist centres, moneychangers' rates are often poorer and they may not change travellers cheques.

All major brands of travellers cheques are accepted across the region. Cash in major currencies is also readily exchanged, though like everywhere else in the world the US dollar has a slight edge.

Photography

Malaysians usually have no antipathy to being photographed, although of course it's polite to ask permission before photographing people and taking pictures in mosques or temples. For advice on taking better photos, Lonely Planet's *Travel Photography: A Guide to Taking Better Pictures* is written by travel photographer Richard I'Anson.

Burning digital photos to a disk can easily be arranged at photo development shops across the country; it will cost around RM10 per disk. In bigger cities like KL, you'll find photo shops with a decent range of equipment at reasonable prices.

Post

Pos Malaysia Berhad (☎1300 300 300; www.pos.com.my) runs an efficient postal system. Post offices are open 8am to 5pm from Monday to Saturday, but closed on the first Saturday of the month and public holidays.

Aerograms and postcards cost 50 sen to send to any destination. Letters weighing 20g or less cost 90 sen to Asia, RM1.40 to Australia or New Zealand, RM1.50 to the UK and Europe, and RM1.80 to North America. Parcel rates range around RM20 to RM60 for a 1kg parcel, depending on the destination. Main post offices in larger cities sell packaging materials and stationery.

Public Holidays

As well as fixed secular holidays, various religious festivals (which change dates annually) are national holidays. These include Chinese New Year (in January/February), the Hindu festival of Deepavali (in October/November), the Buddhist festival of Wesak (April/May) and the Muslim festivals of Hari Raya Haji, Hari Raya Puasa, Mawlid al-Nabi and Awal Muharram (Muslim New Year); see p22 for dates.

Fixed annual holidays include the following:

» **New Year's Day** 1 January
» **Federal Territory Day** 1 February (in Kuala Lumpur and Putrajaya only)
» **Good Friday** March or April (in Sarawak & Sabah only)
» **Labour Day** 1 May
» **Yang di-Pertuan Agong's (King's) Birthday** 1st Saturday in June
» **Governor of Penang's Birthday** 2nd Saturday in July (in Penang only)
» **National Day** (Hari Kebangsaan) 31 August
» **Malaysia Day** 16 September
» **Christmas Day** 25 December

School Holidays

Schools break for holidays five times a year. The actual dates vary from state to state but are generally in January (one week), March (two weeks), May (three weeks), August (one week) and October (four weeks).

Safe Travel

Operators mentioned in this book have been personally checked by the authors and should be reliable. However, you should always check terms and conditions carefully.

Animal Hazards

Rabies occurs in Malaysia, so any bite from an animal should be treated very seriously. In the jungles and mangrove forests, living hazards include leeches (annoying but harmless), snakes (some kinds are highly venomous), macaques (prone to bag-snatching in some locales), orang-utans (occasionally aggressive) and, in muddy estuaries, saltwater crocodiles (deadly if they drag you under).

Theft & Violence

Theft and violence are not particularly common in Malaysia and compared with Indonesia or Thailand it's extremely safe. Nevertheless, it pays to keep a close eye on your belongings, especially your travel documents (passport, travellers cheques etc), which should be kept with you at all times.

Muggings do happen, particularly in KL and Penang, and physical attacks have been known to occur, particularly after hours and in the poorer, run-down areas of cities. We've been told that thieves on motorbikes particularly target women for grab raids on their handbags. Also keep a watch out for sleazy local 'beach boys' in Langkawi and the Perhentians.

Credit-card fraud is a growing problem in Malaysia. Use your cards only at established businesses and guard your credit-card numbers closely.

A small, sturdy padlock is well worth carrying, especially if you are going to be staying at any of the cheap chalets found on Malaysia's beaches, where flimsy padlocks are the norm.

Telephone

Landline services are provided by the national monopoly **Telekom Malaysia** (TM; www.tm.com.my).

Fax

Fax facilities are available at TM offices in larger cities and at some main post offices. If you can't find one of these try a travel agency or large hotel.

International Calls

The easiest and cheapest way to make international calls is to buy a local SIM card for your mobile (cell) phone. Only certain payphones permit international calls. You can make operator-assisted international calls from local TM offices. To save money on landline calls, buy a prepaid international calling card (available from convenience stores).

Local Calls

Local calls cost 10 sen for three minutes. Payphones take coins or prepaid cards which are available from TM offices and convenience stores. Some also take international credit cards. You'll also find a range of discount calling cards at convenience stores and mobile-phone counters.

Mobile (Cell) Phones

If you have arranged global roaming with your home provider, your GSM digital phone will automatically tune into one of the region's digital networks. If not, cheap prepaid SIM cards (RM8.50; passport required) are available almost everywhere from mobile-phone shops and kiosks (including at airports). If you bring along your own phone, make sure it can handle 900/1800MHz and is not locked. In Borneo, the cheapest mobile phones start at about US$40.

Local calls cost RM0.12 to RM0.15 per minute; international direct dialling costs just RM0.18 per minute to North America and to landline numbers in Australia and the UK (mobile lines cost RM0.88 per minute). SMSs (text messages; RM0.06 or less each) are hugely popular and a great way to communicate with locals and expats.

There are three mobile-phone companies, all with similar call rates and prepaid packages:

» **Celcom** (www.celcom. com.my; numbers beginning with 013 or 019) This is the best company to use if you'll be spending time in remote regions of Sabah & Sarawak.
» **DiGi** (www.digi.com.my; numbers beginning with 016)
» **Maxis** (www.maxis.com. my; numbers beginning with 012 or 017).

Time

Malaysia is eight hours ahead of GMT/UTC (London). Noon in Kuala Lumpur is:

» 8pm in Los Angeles
» 11pm in New York
» 4am in London
» 2pm in Sydney and Melbourne

Toilets

Although there are still some places with Asian squat-style toilets, you'll most often find Western-style ones these days. At public facilities toilet paper is not usually provided. Instead, you will find a hose which you are supposed to use as a bidet or, in cheaper places, a bucket of water and a tap. If you're not comfortable with this, remember to take packets of tissues or toilet paper wherever you go.

Tourist Information

Tourism Malaysia has an efficient network of overseas offices, which are useful for predeparture planning. Unfortunately, its domestic offices are less helpful and are often unable to give specific information about destinations and transport. Nonetheless, they do stock some decent brochures as well as the excellent *Map of Malaysia*.

Within Malaysia there are also a number of state tourist-promotion organisations, which often have more detailed information about specific areas. These include:

» **Johor Tourism** (www.johortourism.com.my)
» **Sabah Tourism** (www.sabahtourism.com)
» **Pahang Tourism** (www.pahangtourism.com.my)
» **Perak Tourism** (www.peraktourism.com)
» **Sarawak Tourism** (www.sarawaktourism.com)

Tourism Penang
(www.tourismpenang.gov.my)
Tourism Selangor
(www.tourismselangor.org)
Tourism Terengganu
(http://tourism.terengganu.
gov.my)

Travellers with Disabilities

For the mobility impaired, Malaysia can be a nightmare. In most cities and towns there are often no footpaths, kerbs are very high, construction sites are everywhere, and crossings are few and far between. On the upside, taxis are cheap and both Malaysia Airlines and KTM (the national rail service) offer 50% discounts on travel for travellers with disabilities.

Before setting off get in touch with your national support organisation (preferably with the travel officer, if there is one). Also try:

» **Accessible Journeys** (☏800-846 4537; www.disability travel.com) in the US.

» **Mobility International USA** (☏541-343 1284; www. miusa.org) in the US.

» **Nican** (☏02-6241 1220; www.nican.com.au) in Australia

» **Tourism For All** (☏08-45 124 9971; www.tourismforall. org.uk) in the UK.

Visas

Visitors must have a passport valid for at least six months beyond the date of entry into Malaysia. The following gives a brief overview of other requirements – full details of visa regulations are available on the website www.kln.gov.my.

Nationals of most countries are given a 30- or 60-day visa on arrival, depending on the expected length of stay. As a general rule, if you arrive by air you will be given 60 days automatically, though coming overland you may be given 30 days

unless you specifically ask for a 60-day permit. It's possible to get an extension at an immigration office in Malaysia for a total stay of up to three months. This is a straightforward procedure that is easily done in major Malaysian cities.

Only under special circumstances can Israeli citizens enter Malaysia.

Both Sabah and Sarawak retain a certain degree of state-level control of their borders. Malaysian citizens from Peninsular Malaysia (West Malaysia) cannot work in Malaysian Borneo (East Malaysia) without special permits, and tourists must go through passport control and have their passports stamped whenever they:

» arrive in Sabah or Sarawak from Peninsular Malaysia or the federal district of Pulau Labuan

» exit Sabah or Sarawak on their way to Peninsular Malaysia or Pulau Labuan

» travel between Sabah and Sarawak.

When entering Sabah or Sarawak from another part of Malaysia, your new visa stamp will be valid only for the remainder of the period left on your original Malaysian visa. In Sarawak, an easy way to extend your visa is to make a 'visa run' to Brunei or Indonesia (through the Tebedu–Entikong land crossing).

Volunteering

Opportunities include the following:

All Women's Action Society Malaysia (www.awam. org.my) Aims to improve the lives of women in Malaysia by lobbying for a just, democratic and equitable society with respect and equality for both genders.

Ecoteer (www.ecoteer responsibletravel.com)

Eden Handicap Service Centre (www.edenhandicap. org) Christian-run

organisation caring for the handicapped of Penang – volunteers are needed to help with a variety of activities.

Great Orangutan Project (www.orangutanproject.com) Places paying volunteers at the Matang Wildlife Centre in Sarawak.

LASSie (www.langkawilassie. org.my) Dog and cat lovers can help out at the Langkawi Animal Shelter & Sanctuary Foundation, next to Bon Ton Resort.

Malaysian AIDS Council (www.mac.org.my) Seeks volunteers and interns to assist in their campaigning work.

Malaysian Nature Society (www.mns.org.my) Check their website or drop them a line to find out ways you can get involved in helping preserve Malaysia's natural environment.

Miso Walai Homestay Program (www.misow alaihomestay.com) Gets travellers involved with local wetlands restoration projects.

Nur Salaam (www.nursalam. bbnow.org) This charity works with street kids in the Chow Kit area of KL.

PAWS (www.paws.org.my) Animal rescue shelter in Subang, about 30 minutes from central KL.

Real Gap (www.realgap.co.uk) Arranges trips that involve environmental project and community work in Sabah, or work as an assistant at Zoo Negara near KL.

Regional Environmental Awareness Cameron Highlands (Reach; www. reach.org.my) Take part in reforestation and recycling programs in the Cameron Highlands.

Sepilok Orang-Utan Rehabilitation Centre Has one of the best established volunteer programs for animal lovers.

Travellers Worldwide (www.travellersworldwide.com) Offers a range of programs including working on wildlife reserves, working with disabled children, teaching English and scuba-diving work experience.

Trekforce (www.trekforce.org.uk) Offers a 10-week course working with the Kelabit people on community projects in Sarawak's Kelabit Highlands.

Wild Asia (www.wildasia.org) A variety of volunteer options generally connected with the environment and sustainable tourism in the region.

World Challenge (www.world-challenge.co.uk) Brings a lot of (mainly UK) volunteers to Malaysia for conservation and other projects.

Zoo Negara Help the zookeepers feed and care for their charges.

Women Travellers

The key to travelling with minimum hassle in Malaysia is to blend in with the locals, which means dressing modestly and being respectful, especially in areas of stronger Muslim religious sensibilities such as the northeastern states of Peninsula Malaysia.

Regardless of what local non-Muslim women wear, it's better to be safe than sorry – we've had reports of attacks on women ranging from minor verbal aggravation to physical assault. Hard as it is to say, the truth is that women are much more likely to have problems in Malay-dominated areas, where attitudes are more conservative.

In Malay-dominated areas, you can halve your hassles just by tying a bandanna over your hair (a minimal concession to the headscarf worn by most Muslim women). When visiting mosques, cover your head and limbs with a headscarf and sarong (many mosques lend these out at the entrance). At the beach, most Malaysian women swim fully clothed in T-shirts and shorts, so don't even think about going topless.

Be proactive about your own safety. Treat overly friendly strangers, both male and female, with a good deal of caution. In cheap hotels check for small peepholes in the walls and doors; when you have a choice, stay in a Chinese-operated hotel. On island resorts, stick to crowded beaches, and choose a chalet close to reception and other travellers. Take taxis after dark and avoid walking alone at night in quiet or seedy parts of town.

Work

There are possibilities for those who seek them out, from professional-level jobs in finance, journalism and the oil industry to temporary jobs at some guesthouses and dive centres in popular resort areas. Those with teaching credentials can find English-teaching jobs in Malaysia, though pickings are slim compared to Japan and Korea. Teachers can check some of the many TEFL sites, including **Edufind Jobs** (www.jobs.edufind.com).

Depending on the nature of your job, you'll need either an Expatriate Personnel Visa or a Temporary Employment Visa. For details and requirements, check the website of the **Immigration Department of Malaysia** (www.imi.gov.my/index.php/ms).

Transport

GETTING THERE & AWAY

Entering Malaysia

The main requirements are a passport that's valid for travel for at least six months, proof of an onward ticket and adequate funds for your stay, although you will rarely be asked to prove this.

Flights, tours and rail tickets can be booked online at www.lonelyplanet.com/travel_services.

Air

Airports & Airlines

Kuala Lumpur International Airport (☑8777 8888; www.klia.com.my), 75km south of Kuala Lumpur (KL), is the main gateway. Near KLIA, the Low Cost Carrier Terminal (LCCT), from which AirAsia currently operates, will be replaced in 2013 by a new terminal, KLIA2. These terminals handle the bulk of international flights, with the exception of a few flights from Asia and Australia, which come via Penang,

Kuching, Kota Kinabalu and a few other cities.

Airlines Flying To/From Malaysia

AirAsia (☑600 85 8888; www.airasia.com)

Batavia Air (☑0804 1 222 888; www.batavia-air.com)

Berjaya Air (☑03-2119 6616; www.berjaya-air.com)

Cathay Pacific (www.cathaypacific.com)

Emirates (www.emirates.com)

Eva Air (www.evaair.com)

Firefly (☑03-7845 4543; www.fireflyz.com.my)

Jetstar (www.jetstar.com)

Malaysia Airlines (MAS; ☑1300-883 000, outside Malaysia 03-2161 0555; www.malaysia-airlines.com.my)

Royal Brunei Airlines (www.bruneiair.com)

Silk Air (www.silkair.com)

Singapore Airlines (☑2692 3122; www.singaporeair.com)

Tiger Airways (www.tigerairways.com)

Tickets

When shopping for a ticket, compare the cost of flying into Malaysia versus the cost of flying into Singapore. From Singapore you can travel overland to almost any place in Peninsular Malaysia in less than a day, and Singapore also has direct flights to Malaysian Borneo and Brunei. KL and Singapore are also good places to buy tickets for onward travel.

Land

See also Visas.

Brunei

Border crossings are possible into Brunei from Sarawak.

Indonesia

Several express buses run between Pontianak in Kalimantan and Kuching and Miri in Sarawak, and Kota Kinabulu in Sabah. The bus crosses at the Tebedu–Entikong border.

Singapore

The Causeway linking Johor Bahru with Singapore handles most traffic between the countries. Trains and buses run from all over Malaysia straight through to Singapore terminating at Woodlands, or you can take a bus to JB and get a taxi or one of the frequent buses from JB to Singapore.

Trains linking Singapore and KL cost between S$30/RM34 and S$130/RM130 depending on what class of ticket you buy and whether you go for a berth or not. The journey takes about seven hours.

A good website with details of express buses between Singapore, Malaysia and Thailand is the **Express Bus Travel Guide** (www.singaporemalaysiabus.com).

There is also a causeway linking Tuas, in western Singapore, with Geylang Patah in JB. This is known as the Second Link, and some bus services to Melaka and up the west coast head this way. If you have a car, tolls on the Second Link are much higher than those on the main Causeway.

Thailand

BUS & CAR

You can cross the border by road into Thailand at Padang Besar, Bukit Kayu Hitam, Rantau Panjang (Sungai Golok on the Thai side) and Pengkalan Kubor.

TRAIN

The rail route into Thailand is on the Butterworth–Alor Setar–Hat Yai route, which crosses into Thailand at Padang Besar. You can take the International Express from Butterworth all the way to Bangkok. Trains from KL and Singapore are timed to connect with this service.

From Butterworth to Hat Yai the 2nd-class fare is upper/lower berth RM65/73, to Bangkok RM95/103, from Alor Setar to Hat Yai RM58.40/66.40 and to Bangkok RM88.40/96.40.

From Alor Setar there is an additional daily northbound train to Hat Yai (from RM12, three hours). And from KL there is one through service daily (the Senandung Langkawi) to Hat Yai (seat/upper berth/lower berth RM44/52/57).

From Hat Yai there are frequent train and bus connections to other parts of Thailand.

The opulent **Eastern & Oriental Express** (www. orient-express.com) also connects Singapore and Bangkok making stops in KL and Butterworth (for Penang).

Sea

Brunei

Boats connect Brunei to Pulau Labuan, from where boats go to Sabah. All international boats depart from Muara, 25km northeast of Bandar Seri Begawan, where Brunei immigration formalities are also handled.

Indonesia

The following are the main ferry routes between Indonesia and Malaysia:

» Bengkalis (Sumatra) to Melaka
» Pulau Batam to Johor Bahru
» Dumai (Sumatra) to Melaka
» Medan (Sumatra) to Penang
» Pekanbaru (Sumatra) to Melaka
» Tanjung Pinang Bintan to Johor Bahru
» Tanjung Balai (Sumatra) to Pelabuhan Klang and Kukup
» Tarakan (Kalimantan) to Tawau

Philippines

Ferries link Sandakan with Zamboanga, on the Philippine island of Mindanao, twice a week.

Singapore

Singapore has a number of regular ferry connections to Malaysia. Cruise trips in the region are also very popular with locals.

Thailand

Ferries connect Kuah on Pulau Langkawi with Satun on the Thai coast, and from November to mid-May, with Ko Lipe; make sure you get your passport stamped going in either direction.

GETTING AROUND

Air

Airlines in Malaysia

The two main domestic operators are **Malaysia Airlines** (MAS; ☑1300-883 000, outside Malaysia 03-2161 0555; www.malaysia-airlines. com.my) and **AirAsia** (☑600 85 8888; www.airasia.com).

The MAS subsidiary **Firefly** (☑03-7845 4543; www.fireflyz. com.my) has flights from KL (SkyPark Subang Terminal) to Penang, Kota Bharu, Kuala Terengganu, Kerteh, Langkawi, Johor Bahru, Alor Setar and Kuantan, and from Penang to KL, Johor Bahru and Langkawi.

Berjaya Air (☑03-7847 8228; www.berjaya-air.com) flies between KL (SkyPark Subang Terminal), Pulau Tioman, Pulau Pangkor and Pulau Redang in Peninsular Malaysia, as well as Singapore and Koh Samui in Thailand.

In Malaysian Borneo, Malaysia Airlines' subsidiary **MASwings** (www.maswings. com.my) offers local flights within and between Sarawak and Sabah; it's main hub is Miri. These services, especially those handled by 18-seat Twin Otters, are very much reliant on the vagaries of the weather. In the wet season (October to March in Sarawak and on Sabah's northeast coast; May to November on Sabah's west coast), places like Bario in Sarawak can be isolated for days at a time, so don't venture into this area if you have a very tight schedule. These flights are completely booked during school holidays. At other times it's easier to get a seat at a few days' notice, but always book as far in advance as possible.

Discounts

All the airlines offer discounts tickets on the internet, depending on how far in advance you book – in some cases you might only pay for the airport taxes. A variety of other discounts (typically between 25% and 50%) are available for flights around Malaysia on Malaysia Airlines, including for families and groups of three or more (it's worth inquiring when you book tickets in Malaysia). Student discounts are available, but only for students enrolled in institutions that are in Malaysia.

Bicycle

Bicycle touring around Malaysia and neighbouring countries is an increasingly popular activity. The main road system is well engineered and has good surfaces, but the secondary road system is limited. Road conditions are good enough for touring bikes in most places, but mountain bikes are recommended for forays off the beaten track.

Top-quality bicycles and components can be bought in major cities, but generally 10-speed (or higher) bikes and fittings are hard to find. Bringing your own is the best bet. Bicycles can be transported on most international flights; check with the airline about extra charges and shipment specifications.

Useful websites include:

» **KL Bike Hash** (www.klmbh. org) Details of the monthly bike ride out of KL and links to other cycling-connected sites in Malaysia.

» **Bicycle Touring Malaysia** (www.bicycletouring malaysia.com) A mine of information about cycling around the region, run by Dave, a local who also offers homestays at his home in the state of Perak.

» **Malaysia Cycling Events & Blogs** (www.malaysia cycling.blogspot.co.uk) Includes listings of cycle shops around the country.

» **MTB Asia** (www.mtbasia. com) A portal with links to several mountain-biking related sites covering Malaysia.

Boat

There are no services connecting Peninsular Malaysia with Malaysian Borneo. On a local level, there are boats and ferries between the peninsula and offshore islands, and along the rivers of Sabah and Sarawak. Note that some ferry operators are notoriously lax about observing safety rules, and local authorities are often nonexistent. If a boat looks overloaded or otherwise unsafe, *do not board it* – no-one else will look out for your safety.

Bus

Bus travel in Malaysia is economical and generally comfortable, and seats can be reserved. It's also fast – sometimes too fast. In a bid to pack in as many trips as possible, some bus drivers speed recklessly, resulting in frequent, often fatal, accidents.

Konsortium Transnasional Berhad (www. ktb.com.my) is Malaysia's largest bus operator running services under the **Transnasional** (☎1300-888 582; www.transnasional.com. my), **Nice** (☎2272 1586; www.nice-coaches.com.my), **Plusliner** (www.plusliner. com) and **Cityliner** (www. cityliner.com.my) brands. Its services tend to be slower than rivals, but its buses have also been involved in several major accidents. They have competition from a variety of privately operated buses on the longer domestic routes including **Aeroline** (www.aeroline.com. my) and **Supernice** (www. supernice.com.my). There are so many buses on major runs that you can often turn up and get a seat on the next bus.

On main routes most private buses have air-con (often turned to frigid so bring a sweater!) and cost only a few ringgit more than regular buses.

In larger towns there may be a number of bus stations; local/regional buses often operate from one station and long-distance buses from another; in other cases, KL for example, bus stations are differentiated by the destinations they serve.

Bus travel off the beaten track is relatively straightforward. Small towns and *kampung* (villages) all over the country are serviced by public buses, usually nonair-conditioned rattlers. Unfortunately, they are often poorly signed and sometimes the only way for you to find your bus is to ask a local. These buses are invariably dirt cheap and provide a great sample of rural life. In most towns there are no ticket offices, so buy your ticket from the conductor after you board.

Car & Motorcycle

Driving in Malaysia is fantastic compared with most Asian countries. There has been a lot of investment in the country's roads, which are generally of a high quality. New cars for hire are commonly available and fuel is inexpensive (RM1.85 per litre).

It's not all good news, though. Driving in the cities, particularly KL, can be a nightmare, due to traffic and confusing one-way systems. Malaysian drivers aren't always the safest when it comes to obeying road rules – they mightn't be as reckless as those you might see elsewhere in Southeast Asia, but they still take risks. For example, hardly any of the drivers keep to the official 110km/h speed limit on the main highways and tailgating is a common problem.

The Lebuhraya (North–South Hwy) is a six-lane expressway that runs for 966km along the length of the peninsula from the Thai border in the north to JB in the south. There are quite steep toll charges for using the expressway and these vary according to the distance travelled. As a result the normal highways remain crowded while traffic on the expressway is light. Many other highways are in excellent condition and many are under construction.

Bringing Your Own Vehicle

It's technically possible to bring your vehicle into Malaysia, but there are reams of red tape and the costs are prohibitively expensive – a hire car is a much better proposition.

CLIMATE CHANGE & TRAVEL

Every form of transport that relies on carbon-based fuel generates CO_2, the main cause of human-induced climate change. Modern travel is dependent on aeroplanes, which might use less fuel per kilometre per person than most cars but travel much greater distances. The altitude at which aircraft emit gases (including CO_2) and particles also contributes to their climate change impact. Many websites offer 'carbon calculators' that allow people to estimate the carbon emissions generated by their journey and, for those who wish to do so, to offset the impact of the greenhouse gases emitted with contributions to portfolios of climate-friendly initiatives throughout the world. Lonely Planet offsets the carbon footprint of all staff and author travel.

Driving Licence

A valid overseas licence is needed to rent a car. An International Driving Permit (a translation of your state or national driver's license and its vehicle categories) is usually not required by local car-hire companies, but it is recommended that you bring one. Most rental companies also require that drivers are at least 23 years old (and less than 65) with at least one year of driving experience.

Hire

Major rent-a-car operations include **Avis** (www.avis.com. my), **Hertz** (www.simedarby carrental.com), **Mayflower** (www.mayflowercarrental.com) and **Orix** (www.orixcarrentals. com.my); there are many others, though, including local operators only found in one city. Unlimited distance rates for a 1.3L Proton Saga, one of the cheapest and most popular cars in Malaysia, are posted at around RM190/1320 per day/week, including insurance and collision-damage waiver. The Proton is basically a Mitsubishi assembled under licence in Malaysia.

You can often get better prices, either through smaller local companies or when the major companies offer special deals. Rates drop substantially for longer rentals, and if you shop around by phone, you can get wheels for as little as RM2500 per month, including unlimited kilometres and insurance.

The advantage of dealing with a large company is that it has offices all over the country, giving better backup if something goes wrong and allowing you to pick up in one city and drop off in another (typically for a RM50 surcharge). Mayflower is one local company with offices all over and some competitive rates.

The best place to look for car hire is KL, though Penang is also good. In Sabah and Sarawak there is less competition and rates are higher, partly because of road conditions; there's also likely to be a surcharge if you drop your car off in a different city from the one you rented it in.

Insurance

Rental companies will provide insurance when you hire a car, but always check what the extent of your coverage will be, particularly if you're involved in an accident. You might want to take out your own insurance or pay the rental company an extra premium for an insurance excess reduction.

Road Rules

Driving in Malaysia broadly follows the same rules as in Britain and Australia – cars are right-hand drive, and you drive on the left side of the road. The only additional precaution you need to take is to be aware of possible road hazards: stray animals, wandering pedestrians and the large number of motorcyclists. The speed limit is 110km per hour on expressways slowing down to 50km per hour on *kampung* (village) back roads, so take it easy.

Wearing safety belts is compulsory. Malaysia drivers show remarkable common sense compared to other countries in the region. However, there are still plenty of drivers who take dangerous risks. Lane-drift is a big problem and signalling, when used at all, is often unclear. Giving a quick blast of the horn when you're overtaking a slower vehicle is common practice and helps alert otherwise sleepy drivers to your presence.

Hitching

Keep in mind hitching is never entirely safe in any country in the world, and we don't recommend it. Travellers who decide to hitch, particularly single women, should understand that they are taking a small but potentially serious risk. People who do choose to hitch will be safer if they travel in pairs and let someone know where they are planning to go.

This said, Malaysia has long had a reputation for being a great place for hitch-hiking, and it's generally still true, though with inexpensive bus travel most travellers don't bother. Note that hitchers are banned from the Lebuhraya expressway.

Local Transport

Local transport varies widely from place to place. Taxis are found in all large cities, and most have meters. Fares in KL and other cities on the peninsula are as follows: flagfall (first 2km) is RM3, with an additional 20 sen for each 200m or 45 seconds thereafter; 20 sen for each additional passenger over two passengers; RM1 for each piece of luggage in the boot (trunk); plus 50% on each of these charges between midnight and 6am. Drivers are legally required to use meters if they exist – you can try insisting that they do so, but sometimes you'll just have to negotiate the fare before you get in.

Bicycle rickshaws (trishaws) supplement the taxi service in George Town and Melaka and are definitely handy ways of getting around the older parts of town, which have convoluted and narrow streets.

In major cities there are also buses, which are extremely cheap and convenient, provided you can figure out which one is going your way. KL also has commuter trains, a Light Rail Transit (LRT) and a monorail system.

In the bigger cities across Malaysian Borneo, such as Kuching and Kota Kinabalu, you will find taxis, buses and minibuses. Once you're out of the big cities, though, you're basically on your own and must either walk or hitch. If you're really in the bush, of course, riverboats and aeroplanes are the only alternatives to lengthy jungle treks.

Long-Distance Taxi

Long-distance taxis make Malaysian travel – already easy and convenient even by the best Asian standards – a real breeze. In almost every town there will be a *teksi* stand where the cars are lined up and ready to go to their various destinations.

Taxis are ideal for groups of four, and are also available on a share basis. As soon as a full complement of four passengers turns up, off you go.

If you're travelling between major towns, you have a reasonable chance of finding other passengers to share without having to wait too long, but otherwise you will have to charter a whole taxi, which is four times the single-fare rate.

As Malaysia becomes increasingly wealthy, and people can afford to hire a whole taxi, the share system is becoming less reliable. Early morning is generally the best time to find people to share a taxi, but you can inquire at the taxi stand the day before as to the best time.

Taxi rates to specific destinations are fixed by the government and are posted at the taxi stands. Air-con taxis cost a few more ringgit than nonair-con, and fares are generally about twice the comparable bus fares. If you want to charter a taxi to an obscure destination, or by the hour, you'll probably have to do some negotiating. On the peninsula you're likely to pay around 50 sen per kilometre. In Sarawak, the taxi meter price (for kilometres beyond the first 3km which is RM10) is RM1.20 per km.

Taxi drivers often drive at frighteningly high speeds. They don't have as many head-on collisions as you might expect, but closing your eyes at times of high stress certainly helps! You also have the option of demanding that the driver slow down, but this can be met with varying degrees of hostility. Another tactic is to look for ageing taxis and taxi drivers – they must be doing something right to have made it this far!

Tours

Reliable tours of both Peninsular Malaysia and Malaysian Borneo are run regularly by international operators, including **Exodus** (www.exodus.co.uk), **Explore** (www.explore.co.uk) **Peregrine Adventures** (www.peregrineadventures.com) and **Intrepid Travel** (www.intrepidtravel.com) as well as local specialist outfits. Such tours are often a good way to see the best of Malaysian Borneo in a short period of time and without having to worry about possibly problematic transport connections.

In contrast, getting around the peninsula under your own steam is rarely difficult, making a tour less necessary.

Train

Malaysia's privatised national railway company is **Keretapi Tanah Melayu** (KTM; ☎1300 885 862; www.ktmb.com.my). It runs a modern, comfortable and economical railway service, although there are basically only two lines and for the most part services are slow.

One line runs up the west coast from Singapore, through KL, Butterworth and on into Thailand. The other branches off from this line at Gemas and runs through Kuala Lipis up to the northeastern corner of the country near Kota Bharu in Kelantan. Often referred to as the 'jungle train', this line is properly known as the 'East-coast line'.

In Sabah the **North Borneo Railway** (www.suteraharbour.com), a small narrow-gauge line running through the Sungai Padas gorge from Tenom to Beaufort, offers tourist trips lasting four hours on Wednesday and Saturday.

Services & Classes

There are two main types of rail services: express and local trains. Express trains are air-conditioned and have 'premier' (1st class), 'superior' (2nd class) and sometimes 'economy' (3rd class) seats. Similarly, on overnight trains you'll find 'premier night deluxe' cabins (upper/lower berth RM50/70 extra), 'premier night standard' cabins (upper/lower berth RM18/26 extra), and 'standard night' cabins (upper/lower berth RM12/17 extra). Local trains are usually economy-class only, but some have superior seats.

Express trains stop only at main stations, while local services, which operate mostly on the east-coast line, stop everywhere, including the middle of the jungle, to let passengers and their goods on and off. Consequently local services take more than twice as long as the express trains and run to erratic schedules, but if you're in no hurry they provide a colourful experience and are good for short journeys.

Train schedules are reviewed biannually, so check the KTM website, where you can make bookings and buy tickets.

Health

BEFORE YOU GO

» Take out health insurance.
» Pack medications in their original, clearly labelled containers.
» Carry a signed and dated letter from your physician describing your medical conditions and medications, including their generic names.
» If you have a heart condition bring a copy of your ECG taken just prior to travelling.
» Bring a double supply of any regular medication in case of loss or theft.

Recommended Vaccinations

Proof of yellow fever vaccination will be required if you have visited a country in the yellow-fever zone (Africa or South America) within the six days prior to entering the region. Otherwise the World Health Organization (WHO) recommends the following vaccinations:

» **Adult diphtheria and tetanus** Single booster recommended if none in the previous 10 years.

» **Hepatitis A** Provides almost 100% protection for up to a year. A booster after 12 months provides at least another 20 years' protection.

» **Hepatitis B** Now considered routine for most travellers. Given as three shots over six months. A rapid schedule is also available, as is a combined vaccination with Hepatitis A.

» **Measles, mumps and rubella (MMR)** Two doses of MMR are required unless you have had the diseases. Many young adults require a booster.

» **Polio** There have been no reported cases of polio in recent years. Only one booster is required as an adult for lifetime protection.

» **Typhoid** Recommended unless your trip is less than a week and is only to developed cities. The vaccine offers around 70% protection, lasts for two to three years and comes as a single shot. Tablets are also available; however the injection is usually recommended as it has fewer side effects.

» **Varicella** If you haven't had chickenpox, discuss this vaccination with your doctor.

Internet Resources & Further Reading

Lonely Planet's *Asia & India: Healthy Travel* is packed with useful information. Other recommended references include *Traveller's Health* by Dr Richard Dawood and *Travelling Well* by Dr Deborah Mills. Online resources include:

» **Centres for Disease Control and Prevention** (CDC; www.cdc.gov)
» **MD Travel Health** (www.mdtravelhealth.com)
» **World Health Organization** (www.who.int/ith)

IN MALAYSIA, SINGAPORE & BRUNEI

Availability & Cost of Health Care

In Malaysia the standard of medical care in the major centres is good, and most problems can be adequately dealt with in Kuala Lumpur.

Singapore has excellent medical facilities. You cannot buy medication over the counter without a doctor's prescription in Singapore.

In Brunei, general care is reasonable. There is no local medical university, so expats and foreign-trained locals run the health-care system. Serious or complex cases are better managed in Singapore, but adequate primary health care and stabilisation are available.

Infectious Diseases

The following are the most common for travellers:

» **Dengue Fever** Becoming increasingly common in cities. The mosquito that carries dengue bites day and night, so use insect

HEALTH ADVISORIES

It's usually a good idea to consult your government's travel-health website, if one is available, before departure:

» **Australia** (www.smartraveller.gov.au)
» **Canada** (www.phac-aspc.gc.ca)
» **New Zealand** (www.safetravel.govt.nz)
» **UK** (www.dh.gov.uk)
» **USA** (wwwnc.cdc.gov/travel)

avoidance measures at all times. Symptoms can include high fever, severe headache, body ache, a rash and diarrhoea. There is no specific treatment, just rest and paracetamol – don't take aspirin as it increases the likelihood of hemorrhaging.

» **Hepatitis A** This food- and water-borne virus infects the liver, causing jaundice (yellow skin and eyes), nausea and lethargy. All travellers to to region should be vaccinated against it.

» **Hepatitis B** The only sexually transmitted disease (STD) that can be prevented by vaccination, hepatitis B is spread by body fluids, including sexual contact.

» **Hepatitis E** Transmitted through contaminated food and water and has similar symptoms to hepatitis A, but is far less common. It is a severe problem in pregnant women and can result in the death of both mother and baby. There is currently no vaccine, and prevention is by following safe eating and drinking guidelines.

» **HIV** Unprotected heterosexual sex is the main method of transmission.

» **Influenza** Can be very severe in people over the age of 65 or in those with underlying medical conditions such as heart disease

or diabetes; vaccination is recommended for these individuals. There is no specific treatment, just rest and paracetamol.

» **Malaria** Uncommon in the region and antimalarial drugs are rarely recommended for travellers. However, there may be a small risk in rural areas. Remember that malaria can be fatal. Before you travel, seek medical advice on the right medication and dosage for you.

» **Rabies** A potential risk, and invariably fatal if untreated, rabies is spread by the bite or lick of an infected animal – most commonly a dog or monkey. Pretravel vaccination means the post-bite treatment is greatly simplified. If an animal bites you, gently wash the wound with soap and water, and apply iodine based antiseptic. If you are not prevaccinated you will need to receive rabies immunoglobulin as soon as possible.

» **Typhoid** This serious bacterial infection is spread via food and water. Symptoms include high and slowly progressive fever, headache, a dry cough and stomach pain. Vaccination, recommended for all travellers spending more than a week in Malaysia, is not 100% effective so you must still be careful with what you eat and drink.

Traveller's Diarrhoea

By far the most common problem affecting travellers and commonly caused by a bacteria. Treatment consists of staying well hydrated; use a solution such as Gastrolyte. Antibiotics such as Norfloxacin, Ciprofloxacin or Azithromycin will kill the bacteria quickly.

Loperamide is just a 'stopper', but it can be helpful in certain situtations, eg if you have to go on a long bus ride. Seek medical attention quickly if you do not respond to an appropriate antibiotic.

Giardiasis is relatively common. Symptoms include nausea, bloating, excess gas, fatigue and intermittent diarrhoea. The treatment of choice is Tinidazole, with Metroniadzole being a second option.

DRINKING WATER

» Never drink tap water unless you've verified that it's safe (many parts of Malaysia, Singapore and Brunei have modern treatment plants).

» Bottled water is generally safe – check the seal is intact at purchase.

» Avoid ice in places that look dubious.

» Avoid fruit juices if they have not been freshly squeezed or you suspect they may have been watered down.

» Boiling water is the most efficient method of purifying it.

» The best chemical purifier is iodine. It should not be used by pregnant women or those with thyroid problems.

» Water filters should also filter out viruses. Ensure your filter has a chemical barrier such as iodine and a small pore size, ie less than 4 microns.

LEECHES

You may not encounter any of these slimy little vampires while walking through the region's jungle, but if the trail is leafy and it's been raining, chances are you'll be preyed upon.

The local leeches are so small they can squeeze through tight-knit socks. They don't stay tiny for long, however, since once a leech has attached to your skin, it won't let go until it has sucked as much blood as it can hold.

Two species are common: the brown leech and the tiger leech. The tiger leech is recognisable by its cream and black stripes, but you'll probably feel one before you see it. Unlike the brown leech, whose suction is painless, tiger leeches sting a bit. Brown leeches hang around on, or near, the forest floor, waiting to grab onto passing boots or pants. Tiger leeches lurk on the leaves of small trees and tend to attack between the waist and neck, and that can mean any orifice there and around. Keep your shirt tucked in.

Leeches are harmless, but bites can become infected. Prevention is better than the cure and opinion varies on what works best. Insect repellent on feet, shoes and socks works temporarily; loose tobacco in your shoes and socks also helps – Kelabit hunters swear by it. Better yet, invest in some leech-proof socks, which are a kind of tropical gaiter that covers the foot and boot heel and fastens below the knees.

Safe and effective ways to dislodge leeches include flicking them off sideways (pulling a leech off by the tail might make it dig in harder) or sprinkling salt on them. Tiger balm, iodine or medicated menthol oil will also get leeches off. High-pitched screaming doesn't seem to affect them much. Succumb to your fate as a reluctant blood donor and they will eventually drop off.

Environmental Hazards

Air Pollution

If you have severe respiratory problems, speak with your doctor before travelling to any heavily polluted urban centres. If troubled by the pollution, leave the city for a few days to get some fresh air.

Diving & Surfing

If planning on diving or surfing, seek specialised advice before you travel to ensure your medical kit also contains treatment for coral cuts and tropical ear infections. Have a dive medical before you leave your home country – there are certain medical conditions that are incompatible with diving, and economic considerations may override health considerations at some dive operations in Asia.

Heat

It can take up to two weeks to adapt to the region's hot climate. Swelling of the feet and ankles is common, as are muscle cramps caused by excessive sweating. Prevent these by avoiding dehydration and excessive activity in the heat.

Dehydration is the main contributor to heat exhaustion. Symptoms include feeling weak; headache; irritability; nausea or vomiting; sweaty skin; a fast, weak pulse; and a normal or slightly elevated body temperature. Treat by getting out of the heat; applying cool, wet cloths to the skin; laying flat with legs raised; and re-hydrating with water containing a quarter of a teaspoon of salt per litre.

Heat stroke is a serious medical emergency. Symptoms come on suddenly and include weakness; nausea; a hot, dry body with a body temperature of over 41°C; dizziness; confusion; loss of coordination; fits; and, eventually, collapse and loss of consciousness. Seek medical help and commence cooling by getting out of the heat, removing clothes, and applying cool, wet cloths or ice to the body, especially to the groin and armpits.

Prickly heat – an itchy rash of tiny lumps – is caused by sweat being trapped under the skin. Treat by moving out of the heat and into an air-conditioned area for a few hours and by having cool showers. Creams and ointments clog the skin so they should be avoided.

Insect Bites & Stings

» **Lice** Most commonly inhabit your head and pubic area. Transmission is via close contact with an infected person. Treat with numerous applications of an antilice shampoo such as Permethrin.

» **Ticks** Contracted after walking in rural areas. If you are bitten and experience symptoms – such as a rash at the site of the bite or elsewhere, fever, or muscle aches – see a doctor. Doxycycline prevents tick-borne diseases.

» **Leeches** Found in humid rainforest areas. Don't transmit any disease but their bites can be itchy for weeks afterwards and can easily become infected. Apply an iodine-based antiseptic to any leech bite to help prevent infection.

» **Bees or wasps** If allergic to their stings, carry an injection of adrenaline (eg an Epipen) for emergency treatment.

» **Jellyfish** Most are not dangerous. If stung, pour vinegar onto the affected area to neutralise the poison. Take painkillers, and seek medical advice if your condition worsens.

Skin Problems

There are two common fungal rashes that affect travellers in humid countries such as Malaysia, Singapore and Brunei. The first occurs in moist areas that get less air, such as the groin, armpits and between the toes. It starts as a red patch that slowly spreads and is usually itchy. Treatment involves keeping the skin dry, avoiding chafing and using an antifungal cream such as Clotrimazole or Lamisil. Tinea versicolour is also common – this fungus causes small, light-coloured patches, most commonly on the back, chest and shoulders. Consult a doctor.

Cuts and scratches become easily infected in humid climates. Take meticulous care of any cuts and scratches to prevent complications such as abscesses. Immediately wash all wounds in clean water and apply antiseptic. If you develop signs of infection (increasing pain and redness), see a doctor. Divers and surfers should be particularly careful with coral cuts as they become easily infected.

Snakes

Southeast Asia is home to many species of poisonous and harmless snakes. Assume all snakes are poisonous and never try to catch one. Always wear boots and long pants if walking in an area that may have snakes.

First aid in the event of a snake bite involves pressure immobilisation via an elastic bandage firmly wrapped around the affected limb, starting at the bite site and working up towards the chest. The bandage should not be so tight that the circulation is cut off; the fingers or toes should be kept free so the circulation can be checked. Immobilise the limb with a splint and carry the victim to medical attention. Don't use tourniquets or try to suck out the venom. Antivenin is available for most species.

Sunburn

Even on a cloudy day, sunburn can occur rapidly. Always use a strong sunscreen (at least SPF 30), making sure to reapply after a swim, and always wear a wide-brimmed hat and sunglasses outdoors. Avoid lying in the sun during the hottest part of the day (10am to 2pm). If

you're sunburnt, stay out of the sun until you've recovered, apply cool compresses and take painkillers for the discomfort. Applied twice daily, 1% hydrocortisone cream is also helpful.

Travelling with Children

There are specific issues you should consider before travelling with your child:

» All routine vaccinations should be up to date, as many of the common childhood diseases that have been eliminated in the West are still present in parts of Southeast Asia. A travel-health clinic can advise on specific vaccines, but think seriously about rabies vaccination if you're visiting rural areas or travelling for more than a month, as children are more vulnerable to severe animal bites.

DON'T LET THE BEDBUGS BITE

Bedbugs live in the cracks of furniture and walls and migrate to the bed at night to feed on you. They are a particular problem in the region and are more likely to strike in high-turnover accommodation, especially backpacker hostels, though they can be found anywhere. The room may look very clean but they can still be there. Protect yourself with the following strategies:

» Ask the hotel or hostel what they do to avoid bed bugs. It's a common problem and reputable establishments should have a pest-control procedure in place.

» Keep your luggage elevated off the floor to avoid having the critters latch on – this is one of the common ways bedbugs are spread from place to place.

» Check the room carefully for signs of bugs – you may find their translucent light brown skins or poppy seed–like excrement. Pay particular attention to places less likely to have seen a dusting from cleaning staff.

If you do get bitten:

» Treat the itch with antihistamine.

» Thoroughly clean your luggage and launder all your clothes, sealing them after in plastic bags to further protect them.

» Be sure to tell the management – if they seem unconcerned or refuse to do anything about it complain to the local tourist office and write to us.

» Children are more prone to getting serious forms of mosquito-borne diseases such as malaria, Japanese B encephalitis and dengue fever. In particular, malaria is very serious in children and can rapidly lead to death – you should think seriously before taking your child into a malaria-risk area. Permethrin-impregnated clothing is safe to use, and insect repellents should contain between 10% and 20% DEET.

» Diarrhoea can cause rapid dehydration and you should pay particular attention to keeping your child well hydrated. The best antibiotic for children with diarrhoea is Azithromycin.

» Children can get very sick very quickly so locate good medical facilities at your destination and make contact if you are worried – it's always better to get a medical opinion than to try to treat your own children.

Women's Health

Pregnant women should receive specialised advice before travelling. The ideal time to travel is in the second trimester (between 16 and 28 weeks), when the risk of pregnancy-related problems is at its lowest and pregnant women generally feel at their best. During the first trimester there's a risk of miscarriage and in the third trimester complications such as premature labour and high blood pressure are possible. It's wise to travel with a companion. Always carry a list of quality medical facilities available at your destination and ensure you continue your standard antenatal care at these facilities. Avoid travel in rural areas with poor transport and medical facilities. Most of all, ensure travel insurance covers all pregnancy-related possibilities, including premature labour.

» Malaria is a high-risk disease in pregnancy. The World Health Organization recommends that pregnant women do not travel to areas with malaria resistant to chloroquine. None of the more effective antimalarial drugs is completely safe in pregnancy.

» Traveller's diarrhoea can quickly lead to dehydration and result in inadequate blood flow to the placenta. Many of the drugs used to treat various diarrhoea bugs are not recommended in pregnancy. Azithromycin is considered safe.

» In urban areas, supplies of sanitary products are readily available. Birth-control options may be limited so bring adequate supplies of your own form of contraception. Heat, humidity and antibiotics can all contribute to thrush. Treatment is with antifungal creams and pessaries such as clotrimazole. A practical alternative is a single tablet of Fluconazole (Diflucan). Urinary-tract infections can be precipitated by dehydration or long bus journeys without toilet stops; bring suitable antibiotics.

Traditional & Folk Medicine

Throughout Asia, traditional medical systems are widely practised. There is a big difference between these traditional healing systems and 'folk' medicine. Folk remedies should be avoided, as they often involve rather dubious procedures with potential complications. In comparison, traditional healing systems, such as traditional Chinese medicine, are well respected, and aspects of them are being increasingly utilised by Western medical practitioners.

All traditional Asian medical systems identify a vital life force, and see blockage or imbalance as causing disease. Techniques such as herbal medicines, massage and acupuncture bring this vital force back into balance or maintain balance. These therapies are best used for treating chronic disease such as chronic fatigue, arthritis, irritable bowel syndrome and some chronic skin conditions. Traditional medicines should be avoided for treating serious acute infections such as malaria.

Be aware that 'natural' doesn't always mean 'safe', and there can be drug interactions between herbal medicines and Western medicines. If you are using both systems, ensure you inform both practitioners as to what the other has prescribed.

Language

The national language of Malaysia is Malay, also known as Bahasa Malaysia. It's spoken with slight variations throughout Malaysia, Singapore and Brunei, although it's by no means the only language. Various dialects of Chinese are spoken by those of Chinese ancestry, and Mandarin is fairly widely used. Indian Malaysians also speak Tamil, Malayalam and other languages. In Singapore, the official languages alongside Malay (which is mostly restricted to the Malay community) are Tamil, Mandarin and English.

You'll find it easy to get by with English not only in Singapore and on mainland Malaysia, but also in Malaysian Borneo (Sabah and Sarawak) and Brunei. English is the most common second language for Borneo's ethnic groups and is often used by people of different backgrounds, like ethnic Chinese and ethnic Malays, to communicate with one another.

In Bahasa Malaysia, most letters are pronounced more or less the same as their English counterparts, except for the letter c which is always pronounced as the 'ch' in 'chair'. Nearly all syllables carry equal emphasis, but a good approximation is to lightly stress the second-last syllable.

Pronouns, particularly 'you', are rarely used in Bahasa Malaysia. *Kamu* is the egalitarian form designed to overcome the plethora of terms relating to a person's age and gender that are used for the second person.

BASICS

Hello.	*Helo.*
Goodbye.	*Selamat tinggal/jalan.* (said by person leaving/ staying)

WANT MORE?

For in-depth language information and handy phrases, check out Lonely Planet's *Malay Phrasebook*. You'll find it at **shop .lonelyplanet.com**, or you can buy Lonely Planet's iPhone phrasebooks at the Apple App Store.

How are you?	*Apa kabar?*
I'm fine.	*Kabar baik.*
Excuse me.	*Maaf.*
Sorry.	*Maaf.*
Yes./No.	*Ya./Tidak.*
Please.	*Silakan.*
Thank you.	*Terima kasih.*
You're welcome.	*Sama-sama.*
What's your name?	*Siapa nama kamu?*
My name is ...	*Nama saya ...*
Do you speak English?	*Adakah anda berbahasa Inggeris?*
I don't understand.	*Saya tidak faham.*

ACCOMMODATION

Do you have any rooms available?	*Ada bilik kosong?*
How much is it per day/person?	*Berapa harga satu malam/orang?*
Is breakfast included?	*Makan pagi termasukkah?*

Question Words	
How?	*Berapa?*
What?	*Apa?*
When?	*Bilakah?*
Where?	*Di mana?*
Who?	*Siapakah?*
Why?	*Mengapa?*

KEY PATTERNS

To get by in Malay, mix and match these simple patterns with words of your choice:

When's (the next bus)?
Jam berapa (bis yang berikutnya)?

Where's (the station)?
Di mana (stasiun)?

I'm looking for (a hotel).
Saya cari (hotel).

Do you have (a local map)?
Ada (peta daerah)?

Is there a (lift)?
Ada (lift)?

Can I (enter)?
Boleh saya (masuk)?

Do I need (a visa)?
Saya harus pakai (visa)?

I'd like (the menu).
Saya minta (daftar makanan).

I'd like (to hire a car).
Saya mau (sewa mobil).

Could you (help me)?
Bisa Anda (bantu) saya?

campsite	*tempat perkhemahan*
guesthouse	*rumah tetamu*
hotel	*hotel*
youth hostel	*asrama belia*
single room	*bilik untuk seorang*
room with a double bed	*bilik untuk dua orang*
room with two beds	*bilik yang ada dua katil*
air-con	*pendingin udara*
bathroom	*bilik air*
mosquito coil	*obat nyamuk*
window	*tingkap*

DIRECTIONS

Where is ...?	*Di mana ...?*
What's the address?	*Apa alamatnya?*
Could you write it down, please?	*Tolong tuliskan alamat itu?*
Can you show me (on the map)?	*Tolong tunjukkan (di peta)?*
Turn left/right.	*Belok kiri/kanan.*
Go straight ahead.	*Jalan terus.*

at the corner	*di simpang*
at the traffic lights	*di tempat lampu isyarat*
behind	*di belakang*
far (from)	*jauh (dari)*
in front of	*di depan*
near (to)	*dekat (dengan)*
opposite	*berhadapan dengan*

EATING & DRINKING

A table for (two), please.	*Meja untuk (dua) orang.*
What's in that dish?	*Ada apa dalam masakan itu?*
Bring the bill, please.	*Tolong bawa bil.*
I don't eat ...	*Saya tak suka makan ...*
chicken	*ayam*
fish	*ikan*
(red) meat	*daging (merah)*
nuts	*kacang*

Key Words

bottle	*botol*
breakfast	*sarapan pagi*
cold	*sejuk*
cup	*cawan*
dinner	*makan malam*
food	*makanan*
fork	*garfu*
glass	*gelas*
hot	*panas*
knife	*pisau*
lunch	*makan tengahari*
market	*pasar*
menu	*menu*
plate	*pinggan*
restaurant	*restoran*
spicy	*pedas*
spoon	*sedu*
vegetarian	*sayuran saja*
with	*dengan*
without	*tanpa*

Meat & Fish

beef	*daging lembu*
chicken	*ayam*
crab	*ketam*

fish	ikan
lamb	anak biri-biri
mussels	kepah
pork	babi
shrimp	udang

Fruit & Vegetables

apple	epal
banana	pisang
carrot	lobak
cucumber	timun
jackfruit	nangka
mango	mangga
orange	jeruk oren
peanut	kacang
starfruit	belimbing
tomato	tomato
watermelon	tembikai

Other

bread	roti
cheese	keju
egg	telur
ice	ais
rice	nasi
salt	garam
sugar	gula

Drinks

beer	bir
bottled water	air botol
citrus juice	air limau
coffee	kopi
milk	susu
tea	teh
water	air
wine	wain

EMERGENCIES

Help!	Tolong!
Stop!	Berhenti!
I'm lost.	Saya sesat.
Go away!	Pergi!
There's been an accident.	Ada kemalangan.

Call the doctor!	Panggil doktor!
Call the police!	Panggil polis!
I'm ill.	Saya sakit.
It hurts here.	Sini sakit.
I'm allergic to (nuts).	Saya alergik kepada (kacang).

SHOPPING & SERVICES

I'd like to buy ...	Saya nak beli ...
I'm just looking.	Saya nak tengok saja.
Can I look at it?	Boleh saya tengok barang itu?
How much is it?	Berapa harganya?
It's too expensive.	Mahalnya.
Can you lower the price?	Boleh kurang?
There's a mistake in the bill.	Bil ini salah.

ATM	ATM ('a-te-em')
credit card	kad kredit
internet cafe	cyber cafe
post office	pejabat pos
public phone	telpon awam
tourist office	pejabat pelancong

TIME & DATES

What time is it?	Pukul berapa?
It's (seven) o'clock.	Pukul (tujuh).
It's half past (one).	Pukul (satu) setengah.

in the morning	pagi
in the afternoon	tengahari
in the evening	petang

yesterday	semalam
today	hari ini
tomorrow	esok

Signs

Buka	Open
Dilarang	Prohibited
Keluar	Exit
Lelaki	Men
Masuk	Entrance
Perempuan	Women
Tandas	Toilets
Tutup	Closed

Monday	hari Isnin
Tuesday	hari Selasa
Wednesday	hari Rabu
Thursday	hari Kamis
Friday	hari Jumaat
Saturday	hari Sabtu
Sunday	hari Minggu
January	Januari
February	Februari
March	Mac
April	April
May	Mei
June	Jun
July	Julai
August	Ogos
September	September
October	Oktober
November	November
December	Disember

Numbers

1	satu
2	dua
3	tiga
4	empat
5	lima
6	enam
7	tujuh
8	lapan
9	sembilan
10	sepuluh
11	sebelas
12	dua belas
20	dua puluh
21	dua puluh satu
22	dua puluh dua
30	tiga puluh
40	empat puluh
50	lima puluh
60	enam puluh
70	tujuh puluh
80	lapan puluh
90	sembilan puluh
100	seratus
200	dua ratus
1000	seribu
2000	dua ribu

TRANSPORT

At what time does the ... leave?	Pukul berapa ... berangkat?
boat	kapal
bus	bas
plane	kapal terbang
train	kereta api
I want to go to ...	Saya nak ke ...
Does it stop at ... ?	Berhenti di ...?
How long will it be delayed?	Berapa lambatnya?
I'd like to get off at ...	Saya nak turun di ...
Please put the meter on.	Tolong pakai meter.
Please stop here.	Tolong berhenti di sini.
I'd like a ... ticket.	Saya nak tiket ...
1st-class	kelas pertama
2nd-class	kelas kedua
one-way	sehala
return	pergi balik
the first	pertama
the last	terakhir
the next	berikutnya
bus station	stesen bas
bus stop	perhentian bas
cancelled	dibatalkan
delayed	lambat
platform	landasan
ticket office	pejabat tiket
ticket window	tempat/kaunter tikit
timetable	jadual waktu
train station	stesen keretapi
I'd like to hire a ...	Saya nak menyewa ...
bicycle	basikal
car	kereta
jeep	jip
motorbike	motosikal
diesel	disel
helmet	topi keledar
leaded petrol	petrol plumbum
unleaded petrol	tanpa plumbum
petrol	petrol
pump	pam

SINGLISH

One of the most intriguing things the visitor to Singapore will notice is the strange patois spoken by the locals. Nominally English, it contains borrowed words from Hokkien and Malay, such as *shiok* (delicious) and *kasar* (rough). Unnecessary prepositions and pronouns are dropped, word order is flipped, phrases are clipped short, and stress and intonation are unconventional, to say the least. The result is known locally as Singlish. Singlish is frowned upon in official use, though you'll get a good idea of its pervasive characteristics of pronunciation if you listen to the news bulletins on TV or the radio.

There are a number of interesting characteristics that differentiate Singlish from standard English. First off, there's the reverse stress pattern of double-barrelled words. For example, in standard English the stress would be '*fire*-fighter' or '*theatre* company' but in Singlish it's 'fire-*fighter*' and 'theatre *company*'. Word-final consonants – particularly *l* or *k* – are often dropped, and vowels are often distorted; a Chinese-speaking taxi driver might not understand 'Perak Road' since they pronounce it 'Pera Roh'. The particle -*lah* is often tagged on to the end of sentences as in, 'No good, *lah*', which could mean (among other things) 'I don't think that's such a good idea'. Requests or questions will often be marked with a tag ending, since direct questioning is considered rude. So a question such as 'Would you like a beer?' might be rendered as 'You want beer or not?', which, ironically, might come across to speakers of standard English as being rude. Verb tenses tend to be nonexistent – future, present or past actions are all indicated by time phrases, so in Singlish it's 'I go tomorrow' or 'I go yesterday'.

The following are some frequently heard Singlishisms:

ah beng – unsophisticated person with no fashion sense or style; redneck

Aiyah! – 'Oh, dear!'

Alamak! – exclamation of disbelief, frustration or dismay, like 'Oh my God!'

ayam – Malay word for chicken; adjective for something inferior or weak

blur – a slow or uninformed person

buaya – womaniser, from the Malay for 'crocodile'

Can? – 'Is that OK?'

Can! – 'Yes! That's fine.'

char bor – babe, woman

cheena – old-fashioned Chinese in dress or thinking (derogatory)

go stan – to reverse, as in 'Go stan the car' (from the naval expression 'go astern'; pronounced 'go stun')

heng – luck, good fortune (from Hokkien)

hiao – vain

inggrish – English

kambing – foolish person, literally 'goat' (from Malay)

kena ketuk – ripped off, literally 'get knocked'

kiasee – scared, literally 'afraid to die'; a coward

kiasu – selfish, pushy, always on the lookout for a bargain, literally 'afraid to lose'

lah – generally an ending for any phrase or sentence; can translate as 'OK', but has no real meaning; added for emphasis to just about everything

looksee – take a look

malu – embarrassed

minah – girlfriend

Or not? – general tag for questions, as in 'Can or not?' (Can you or can't you?)

see first – wait and see what happens

shack – tired

shiok – good, great, delicious

steady lah – well done, excellent; expression of praise

Wah! – general exclamation of surprise or distress

ya ya – boastful, as in 'He always *ya ya*'

Is this the road to ...?	*Ini jalan ke ...?*	**The car has broken down at ...**	*Kereta saya telah rosak di ...*
Where's a petrol station?	*Stesen minyak di mana?*	**I have a flat tyre.**	*Tayarnya kempis.*
(How long) Can I park here?	*(Beberapa lama) Boleh saya letak kereta di sini?*	**I've run out of petrol.**	*Minyak sudah habis.*
I need a mechanic.	*Kami memerlukan mekanik.*	**I've had an accident.**	*Saya terlibat dalam kemalangan.*

GLOSSARY

adat – Malay customary law

adat temenggong – Malay law with Indian modifications, governing the customs and ceremonies of the sultans

air – water

air terjun – waterfall

alor – groove; furrow; main channel of a river

ampang – dam

ang pow – red packets of money used as offerings, payment or gifts

APEC – Asia-Pacific Economic Cooperation

arak – Malay local alcohol

arrack – see arak

Asean – Association of Southeast Asian Nations

atap – roof thatching

Baba-Nonya – descendants of Chinese immigrants to the Straits Settlements (namely Melaka, Singapore and Penang) who intermarried with Malays and adopted many Malay customs; also known as Peranakan, or Straits Chinese; sometimes spelt Nyonya

Bahasa Malaysia – Malay language; also known as Bahasa Melayu

bandar – seaport; town

Bangsawan – Malay opera

batang – stem; tree trunk; the main branch of a river

batik – technique of imprinting cloth with dye to produce multicoloured patterns

batu – stone; rock; milepost

belukar – secondary forest

bendahara – chief minister

bendang – irrigated land

bomoh – spiritual healer

British Resident – chief British representative during the colonial era

bukit – hill

bumboat – motorised sampan

bumiputra – literally, sons of the soil; indigenous Malays

bunga raya – hibiscus flower (national flower of Malaysia)

dadah – drugs

dato', datuk – literally, grandfather; general male nonroyal title of distinction

dipterocarp – family of trees, native to Malaysia, that have two-winged fruits

dusun – small town; orchard; fruit grove

genting – mountain pass

godown – river warehouse

gua – cave

gunung – mountain

hilir – lower reaches of a river

hutan – jungle; forest

imam – keeper of Islamic knowledge and leader of prayer

istana – palace

jalan – road

kain songket – traditional Malay handwoven fabric with gold threads

kampung – village; also spelt kampong

kangkar – Chinese village

karst – characteristic scenery of a limestone region, including features such as underground streams and caverns

kedai kopi – coffee shop

kerangas – distinctive vegetation zone of Borneo, usually found on sandstone, containing pitcher plants and other unusual flora

khalwat – literally, close proximity; exhibition of

public affection between the sexes, which is prohibited for unmarried Muslim couples

kongsi – Chinese clan organisations, also known as ritual brotherhoods, heaven-man-earth societies, triads or secret societies; meeting house for Chinese of the same clan

kopitiam – coffee shop

kota – fort; city

kramat – Malay shrine

KTM – Keretapi Tanah Melayu; Malaysian Railways System

kuala – river mouth; place where a tributary joins a larger river

laksamana – admiral

langur – small, usually tree-dwelling monkey

laut – sea

lebuh – street

Lebuhraya – expressway or freeway; usually refers to the North–South Highway, which runs from Johor Bahru to Bukit Kayu Hitam at the Thai border

lorong – narrow street; alley

LRT – Light Rail Transit (Kuala Lumpur)

lubuk – deep pool

macaque – any of several small species of monkey

mandi – bathe; Southeast Asian wash basin

masjid – mosque

MCP – Malayan Communist Party

Melayu Islam Beraja – MIB; Brunei's national ideology

merdeka – independence

Merlion – half-lion, half-fish animal; symbol of Singapore

MRT – Mass Rapid Transit (Singapore)

muara – river mouth

muezzin – mosque official who calls the faithful to prayer

negara – country

negeri – state

nonya – see Baba-Nonya

orang asing – foreigner

Orang Asli – literally, Original People; Malaysian aborigines

Orang Laut – literally, Coastal People; Sea Gypsies

Orang Ulu – literally, Up-river People

padang – grassy area; field; also the city square

pantai – beach

PAP – People's Action Party

parang – long jungle knife

PAS – Parti Islam se-Malaysia

pasar – market

pasar malam – night market

Pejabat Residen – Resident's Office

pekan – market place; town

pelabuhan – port

pencak silat – martial-arts dance form

penghulu – chief or village head

pengkalan – quay

Peranakan – literally, half-caste; refers to the Baba-Nonya or Straits Chinese

PIE – Pan-Island Expressway, one of Singapore's main road arteries

pua kumbu – traditional finely woven cloth

pulau – island

puteri – princess

raja – prince; ruler

rakyat – common people

rantau – straight coastline

rattan – stems from climbing palms used for wickerwork and canes

rimba – jungle

rotan – cane used to punish miscreants

roti – bread

sampan – small boat

samsu – Malay alcohol

sarong – all-purpose cloth, often sewn into a tube, and worn by women, men and children

seberang – opposite side of road; far bank of a river

selat – strait

semenanjung – peninsula

silat – see pencak silat

simpang – crossing; junction

songkok – traditional Malay headdress worn by males

Straits Chinese – see Baba-Nonya

sungai – river

syariah – Islamic system of law

tambang – river ferry; fare

tamu – weekly market

tanah – land

tanjung – headland

tasik – lake

teluk – bay; sometimes spelt telok

temenggong – Malay administrator

towkang – Chinese junk

tuai rumah – longhouse chief (Sarawak)

tuak – local 'firewater' alcohol (Malaysian Borneo)

tunku – prince

ujung – cape

UMNO – United Malays National Organisation

warung – small eating stalls

wayang – Chinese opera

wayang kulit – shadow-puppet theatre

wisma – office block or shopping centre

yang di-pertuan agong – Malaysia's head of state, or 'king'

yang di-pertuan besar – head of state in Negeri Sembilan

yang di-pertuan muda – under-king

yang di-pertuan negeri – governor

Behind the Scenes

SEND US YOUR FEEDBACK

We love to hear from travellers – your comments keep us on our toes and help make our books better. Our well-travelled team reads every word on what you loved or loathed about this book. Although we cannot reply individually to postal submissions, we always guarantee that your feedback goes straight to the appropriate authors, in time for the next edition. Each person who sends us information is thanked in the next edition – the most useful submissions are rewarded with a selection of digital PDF chapters.

Visit **lonelyplanet.com/contact** to submit your updates and suggestions or to ask for help. Our award-winning website also features inspirational travel stories, news and discussions.

Note: We may edit, reproduce and incorporate your comments in Lonely Planet products such as guidebooks, websites and digital products, so let us know if you don't want your comments reproduced or your name acknowledged. For a copy of our privacy policy visit lonelyplanet.com/privacy.

OUR READERS

Many thanks to the travellers who used the last edition and wrote to us with helpful hints, useful advice and interesting anecdotes:

A Akke Albada, Pascal Amez-Droz, Jack Arnold, Caroline Atkins **B** Ralph Bain, Caroline Baroud, Stephan Bauer, Adrian Beadles, Wendy Bell, Peter Berende, Jaimeson Bilodeau, Louise Blais, Gert Blockx, Stephen Bonsall, Patricia Bosch, Andrea Brimelow, Colin Bussey **C** Benjamin Carson, Kathryn Clarkson, Russell Clegg, Lucy Crane **D** Thu Danh, Lola Danlos, Owen Davies, Russell Donald, Alynda de Fluiter, Niels de Fluiter, Merijn de Veer, Bradley Draper **E** Michael Joseph Edwards, Michelle Elphinstone, Caroline Evans, Linda Evans **F** Wibo Feenstra, Paul Ferris, David Fletcher **G** Marc Glaudemans, Noel Gokel, Pilar Alvarez Gonzalez, Dan Gosser, Denise Groeneweg **H** Anna Hames, Janette Hartwig, Christian Hochleitner, Serge Hoffmann, Marjolein Hofman-Jonkers, Alan Holden, Wouter Hoogenraad, Van Havere Johnno **J** Sinead Joyce **K** Denis Kearney, Mohanan Kesavan, Ken Khor, Giel Klanker, Annerieke Kroon, Reto Krummenacher, Diana Kuan, Suzanne Kuiper **L** Tim Laslavic, Cher Chua Lassalvy, Jenny Leak, Si Poh Liang, Maud Loonen **M** Bevis Man, Emily Mannes, Jean-Paul Marchetti, Andrena McNabb, Ursa Mekis, Vijay Anand Mohan, Heather Monell, Daniel Moore, Willemijn Mors, Sahane Muftuoglu, Nerissa Murphy **N** Klemen Naversnik, Anthony Ng **O** Petra O'Neill, Steve Oxlade **P** Alan Pails, Juan Pinto, Yuri Ponjee, Havana Poole, Florian Poppe, Patrick Post, Ian Prescott, Torben Prokscha **R** Cindy Rimmington, Andrée-anne Roberge, David Robertson, Ian Ross, Rick Ross, Helen Rudd, Shyam Rupani **S** Meg Satterthwaite, Ray Sinniger, Hari Sriskantha, Bob Simon, Eric Sivignon, Bettina Schömig, Barney Smith, Larry Stagg, Bart Steegmans, Maartje Sterk, Klaus Suemmerer **T** Mary Tan, Rachael Tan, Isla Tasker, Chris Sonja Thurnherr, Tranter, Bjorn Trompet, Kay Turner **U** Mark Uleman **V** Patricia Vacano, Paco van de Ven, Claudia van Dongen, Martijn van Tol, Lennart van Vliet, Maurice Varkevisser, Erik Vermeulen, Yvonne Verburgh-Laurense, Peter Voelger, Sabina Vogt **W** Catherine Waters, Carl Wagner, Esther Wapstra, Michael Weilguni, Katie Wenigmann, Jonas Wernli, Katrien Wuyts **Y** Kim Chan Yap, Peter Young **Z** Adrienne Zinn, Elie Zwiebel

AUTHOR THANKS

Simon Richmond

Terima kasih to the great team of coauthors and to Ilaria for support from LP HQ. In Malaysia, many thanks to Alex Yong, Nani Kahar,

Peter Kiernan, Andrew Sebastian, Claudia Low, David Hogan Jr, Narelle McMurtrie, Chris Bauer, Eddy Chew, Adly Rizal, Karl Steinberg, Chris Ong. And to Neil for blissful company and encouraging me to capture the Malaysia I love through art as well as words.

Cristian Bonetto

A heartfelt *xièxie* to Jasmine Chai, Ally Wong, Walter Cheng Eng Teck, Mark Chng, Wayne Soon and Ian Chong for their incredible generosity and insight. Many thanks also to Ilaria Walker, Alvin Jin Tan, Yu Ying Cheng and Mary-Ann Gardner.

Celeste Brash

Thanks to Shannon Bryant for staying with me throughout and at the hospital. To Peck Choo Ho and Brandon Tan for beyond-wonderful help, support and friendship; Richard Abraham for Johor stuff; Maryanne Netto for contacts and *sob* no chicken rice; Mani and Raymond; Dr Wan and the Endau-Rompin office. Ilaria and Simon, *terima kasih* for being awesome. As always, huge thanks to my family for letting me be me.

Joshua Samuel Brown

Thanks to my old chum Astrid P for being a most excellent travel companion for part of the research phase, Lauren Q for being half the team that steered us in circles around Pulau Kapas, and motorcycle guide extraordinaire Ronnie V for not getting me killed in Pahang. As always, thanks to Phil and Tammy at Pristine (Taiwan), and special thanks to Marina at Kibbutz Bardo in Taipei for giving me a space to call home before and after the journey.

Austin Bush

Thanks to talented LPers Ilaria Walker and Bruce Evans, my ever-roving coauthors, and the kind folks on the ground in Malaysia including Ahmad, Zac Chan, Robyn Eckhardt, Nazlina Hussin, Teong Ong Jin, Joann Khaw, Steve Khong, Mark Lay, Djohan Lee, Bee Yinn and CK Low, Narelle McMurtrie, Chris Ong, Wanida Razali, Khoo Salma, Simon and Rachel Tan, Stan and Pat Woolliscroft, and Jek Yap.

Adam Karlin

Terima kasih: Katie King, rock-star contact who redefines break dancing; the people who gave me insight, Charlie Ryan, Jessica Yew, Tom, Joel, Silas and Howard (I'm greatly privileged to have met you, and to have had the opportunity to explore your island with you); Angelica, the baddest-ass bartender in Oakland, thanks for the laughs; Alex Zawadzki, Daniele Cohen, Serge, Johnny and the rest, your company was always hilarious; Mom and Dad, thanks for your constant support; and Rachel, for your love, and your voice every morning and evening when I'm away.

Daniel Robinson

Scores of people went out of their way to make this a better book, but I'm especially indebted to Amélie Blanc; Borbala Nyiri; Donald and Marina Tan; Eric and Annie Yap; Jacqueline Fong; Jo-Lynn Liao; Kelvin Egay; Polycarp; Mathew Ngau Jau; Philip Yong; Thomas Ulrich and Vernon Kedit (Kuching); Jessie, Noriza and Peter Tiong (Sibu); Paul Chuo; Sandra Kromdijk; Vincent Tiong and Wouter Mullink (Kapit); Camille de Kerchove; Captain David (Bennet); Elyn Chan and family, and Mrs Lee (Miri); Amy McGoldrick; Antonella Mori; Helen van Lindere; Jeremy Clark; Peter Hogge and my guides Bian Rumai, Esther Abu, Jeffry Simun, Susan Pulut and Syria Lejau (Gunung Mulu National Park); Apoi Ngimat; Jaman Riboh; Joanna Joy; Rebita Lupong; Rian John Pasan Lamulun; Stephen and Tine, and Stu Roach (Bario); Mr Lim (Chong Teah); Mr Chua (Eng Hin) and Ferdinand Gibson (Limbang); the dedicated staff of Sarawak's national parks; Glenn van Zutphen; Leonard Koh; Michelle Elias Solomon and Seng Beng Yeo and their families (Singapore); and, finally, my beloved wife Rachel Safman, our son Yair Lev and my mother-in-law Edie Safman (Los Angeles).

ACKNOWLEDGMENTS

Climate map data adapted from Peel MC, Finlayson BL & McMahon TA (2007) 'Updated World Map of the Köppen-Geiger Climate Classification', Hydrology and Earth System Sciences, 11, 1633–44.

Integrated Transit Network of Kuala Lumpur Map © 2012 Tourism Malaysia

Cover photograph:
View over the Bharat Tea Estate, Cameron Highlands, Perak, Ross Barnett/Getty/Lonely Planet Images

THIS BOOK

Tony and Maureen Wheeler first researched Malaysia in 1973 when writing the book that started it all, *Across Asia on the Cheap*. Since then, many Lonely Planet authors have followed in their sandalled footsteps to make sure travellers get the most out of this wild region's idyllic beaches, spicy fusion cuisine and stunning colonial architecture. This 12th edition of *Malaysia, Singapore & Brunei* was researched and written by some of Lonely Planet's finest. Malaysia guru and veteran coordinating author Simon Richmond researched Kuala Lumpur, Selangor and Negeri Sembilan and led a star-studded team of travel writers: Cristian Bonetto, Celeste Brash, Austin Bush,

Joshua Samuel Brown, Adam Karlin and Daniel Robinson. The Health chapter was based on research supplied by Dr Trish Batchelor. This guidebook was commissioned in Lonely Planet's Melbourne office, and produced by the following:

Commissioning Editor Ilaria Walker

Coordinating Editor Mardi O'Connor

Coordinating Cartographer Alex Leung

Coordinating Layout Designer Lauren Egan

Managing Editors Barbara Delissen, Bruce Evans

Senior Editor Andi Jones

Managing Cartographers Adrian Persoglia, Anthony Phelan, Diana von Holdt

Managing Layout Designer Chris Girdler

Assisting Editors Jenna Myers, Karyn Noble, Ross Taylor, Gina Tsarouhas, Fionnuala Twomey, Jeanette Wall

Assisting Cartographers Mick Garrett, Jolyn Philcox, Samantha Tyson

Assisting Layout Designers Yvonne Bischofberger, Nicholas Colicchia, Kerrianne Southway

Cover Research Naomi Parker

Internal Image Research Aude Vauconsant

Language Content Branislava Vladisavljevic

Thanks to Dan Austin, Sasha Baskett, Laura Crawford, Ryan Evans, Larissa Frost, Jane Hart, Jouve India, Asha Ioculari, Tobias Gattineau, Kate McDonell, Catherine Naghten, Trent Paton, Raphael Richards, Dianne Schallmeiner, Laura Stansfeld, Gerard Walker

Index

1Malaysia policy 566
8 Heeren Street 213
8Q SAM 477

A
Abu Bakar Mosque 252
accommodation, *see
  also individual locations*
  Brunei 454, 471
  language 611
  Malaysia 592-3
  Singapore 473, 515-19,
    537, 538
Acheen St Mosque 155
activities 28-34, *see also
  individual activities*
A'Famosa 209, 212
A'Famosa Resort 225-6
Agnes Keith House 339
Air Batang (ABC) 247-8
Air Hangat 188-9
air travel
  airfares 600
  airlines 600
  airports 600
  to/from Brunei 465-6
  to/from Malaysia 600
  to/from Singapore 541-2
  within Malaysia 601
alcoholic drinks 584
Alor Gajah 225-6
Alor Setar 200-4, **201**
ambuyat 36, 82, 463, 581
amusement parks, *see*
  theme parks
animals, *see individual species,* wildlife sanctuaries
  & reserves, zoos
animism 571-2
Annah Rais Longhouse
  408-9
apes, *see* orang-utans

Aquaria KLCC 47
aquariums
  Aquaria KLCC 47
  Lagenda Langkawi Dalam
    Taman 185
  Underwater World (Pulau
    Langkawi) 185-6
  Underwater World
    (Sentosa Island) 498
architecture 20, 575
  Ipoh 118
  itineraries 144, 501, **144**,
    501
  Penang 156
  Putrajaya 104
  Seremban 109-10
Architecture Museum 209
area codes 19
art galleries, *see* galleries,
  museums
arts 21, 574-8, *see also
  individual arts*
  contemporary
    sculpture 485
Asah Waterfall 246
Asian Civilisations Museum
  477
Atkinson Clock Tower 306
ATMs 595
Aur, Pulau 239
Ayor Keroh 225

B
Ba Kelalan 448
Baba House 483
Baba-Nonya, *see* Peranakan
  people
Baba-Nonya Heritage
  Museum 214
Badan Warisan Malaysia 51
Badawi, Abdullah 560
Bahasa Malaysia (Malay),
  see language
bak kut teh 38
Bako National Park 400-4
Bakun Dam Project 587-8
Balai Besar 202

Balai Nobat 202
Bandar Labuan 375-8, **376**
Bandar Seri Begawan
  456-67, **458**
  accommodation 461-2
  activities 456-60
  drinking 464
  emergencies 465
  entertainment 464
  food 462-4
  internet access 465
  macaques 461
  medical services 465
  money 465
  postal services 465
  road safety 457
  shopping 464
  sights 456-60
  tourist information 465
  tours 460-1
  travel to/from 465-6
  travel within 466-7
Bangar 468-9
Banggi, Pulau 336
Bangsar Baru 65-6, 83-4,
  86, 89-90, **84**
Bank Kerapu 273
Bank Negara Malaysia Mu-
  seum & Art Gallery 57
Bario 444-8
Barisan Nasional (National
  Front) 548, 558, 560
basketry 577
Batang Ai 416-17
Batang Duri 470
Batang Rejang 421-6
bathrooms 541, 597
batik 577
  courses & classes 59, 89,
    250, 258, 276-7
  galleries 58
  shopping 59, 89, 172, 250
Batu Caves 16, 99-100, **17**
Batu Ferringhi 176-9
Batu Maung 181
Batu Punggol 371-2

Bau 411-13
Bawang Assan Longhouse
  Village 417-18
Bazaar Baru Chow Kit 67, **73**
beaches
  Air Batang (ABC) 247-8
  Batu Ferringhi 176-9
  Brunei 460
  Cherating 257-60, **259**
  Genting 250
  Juara 249-50
  Kampung Paya 250
  Mukut 251
  Nipah 251
  Port Dickson 113-15
  Pulau Besar (Johor) 237-8
  Pulau Besar (Melaka)
    225-6
  Pulau Lang Tengah 291-2
  Pulau Langkawi 10, 189,
    186-7, **11**
  Pulau Manukan 320
  Pulau Pangkor 134-40,
    135, **137**
  Pulau Perhentian 9, 286,
    284, **9**
  Pulau Rawa 238-9
  Pulau Redang 292-3
  Pulau Sibu 238
  Pulau Tinggi 238
  Salang 248-9
  Singapore 500
Beaufort 372-3
Beaufort Division 372-4
bedbugs 609
bedil (cannons) 460
Bee Yinn Low 169
belacan 580
Belaga 425
Belait District 467-8
bersilat (Malaysian martial
  art) 576
Besar, Pulau (Johor) 237-8
Besar, Pulau (Melaka) 225-6
bicycling, *see* cycling
Bidayuh people 564

Bidong Island 301
Bilit 351-2
Bintulu 426-7, **428**
binturong (bear cat) 245
bird-singing contest 277
birdwatching 34
  Cape Rachado Forest Reserve 113, 114
  Danum Valley Conversation Area 355
  Endau-Rompin National Park 239
  Fraser's Hill (Bukit Fraser) 102
  Gomantong Caves 348, 350
  Jurong Bird Park 498
  Kenong Rimba State Park 268-9
  Kinabalu National Park 328
  KL Bird Park 53
  Mt Kinabalu 328
  Taman Negara Perlis 205
  Tawau Hills Park 367
Boat Quay 477
boat travel 602
  to/from Brunei 465, 601
  to/from Indonesia 601
  to/from Singapore 601
  to/from Thailand 601
  to/from the Philippines 601
boat trips 34
  Kuantan 254
  Melaka River Cruise 216
  Pulau Langkawi 190, 191
  Sungai Kinabatangan 349-50
  Taman Negara 263
Boh Sungei Palas Tea Estate 127, **13**
Bolkiah, Sultan Hassanal 568
books 548, 549-50, 574
  environment 587, 589
  history 552, 553, 554, 555, 556, 558
  religion 569
border crossings 600-1, see also boat travel
  Brunei to Sabah 465
  Brunei to Sarawak 466
  Johor Bahru to Indonesia (Riau Islands) 234

Johor Bahru to Singapore 232
  Kedah to Thailand 203, 206
  Kota Bharu to Thailand 280
  Kuching to Indonesia 409
  Malaysia to Indonesia 224
  Sabah to Indonesia 366
  Sabah to the Philippines 343
  Sarawak to Brunei 439
  Sarawak to Indonesia 451
  Singapore to Johor Bahru 543, 544
Borneo, see Brunei, Sabah, Sarawak
Borneo Sun Bear Conservation Centre 344-5
Botanical Gardens 158
Brickfields 53-5, 65-6, 83, 89-90, **54**
Brunei 43, 454-72, **455**
  accommodation 454, 471
  budget 471
  climate 454
  currency 471
  drugs & alcohol 471
  economy 550
  emergencies 471
  food 454
  highlights 455
  history 555
  holidays 471
  legal matters 471
  medical services 471
  money 465, 471
  politics 550, 568
  postal services 465
  public holidays 471
  tourist information 465, 471
  travel seasons 454
  travel to/from 465-6
  travel within 466-7
  visas 471
  women travellers 471
Brunei Museum 460
Buddha Tooth Relic Temple 484
Buddhism 160, 570-1
budgeting 18, 471, 538, 592, 594
Bukit Brown Cemetery 496
Bukit China 215
Bukit Fraser (Fraser's Hill) 102-4, **103**

Bukit Gemok Forest Reserve 364
Bukit Larut 146
Bukit Malawati 108
Bukit Nanas Forest Reserve 47
Bukit Timah Nature Reserve 494
bumiputra (indigenous Malaysians) 559, 565
bus travel
  within Malaysia 602
  within Singapore 544-5
business hours
  Malaysia 593
  Singapore 537
butterflies 331
  Butterfly Park 55
  Cameron Highlands Butterfly Farm 129
  Penang Butterfly Farm 180
  Zoo Negara (National Zoo) 100

C

cable cars 101
Cameron Bharat Tea Plantation 127
Cameron Highlands 13, 126-33, **128**, **131**, **13**
  accommodation 129-32
  food 132-3
  sights 127-9
  tea 127, 133
  tours 129
  travel to/from 133
  travel within 133
  trekking 130
camping 592
canopy walkways
  Danum Valley Conservation Area 355
  Forestry Research Institute of Malaysia (FRIM) 100
  Gunung Mulu National Park 440
  Hutan Rekreasi Air Keroh 225
  MacRitchie Reservoir 495
  Maliau Basin Conservation Area 368
  Pulau Langkawi 192
  Sabah 331
  Taman Negara 261-2
  Ulu Temburong National Park 471-2
Cape Rachado Forest Reserve 113, 114

car travel
  within Malaysia 602-3
  within Singapore 545-6
Carey, Pulau 107
casinos 101
Cat Musuem 389
Cathay Gallery 408
Cave Villa 99-100
caves
  Batu Caves 16, 99-100, **17**
  Batu Tulug 348-9
  Dark Cave 99
  Deer Cave 440, **502-3**, **511**
  Fairy Cave 412
  Gomantong Caves 348, 350
  Gua Charas 258
  Ipoh's temple caves 119
  Lang's Cave 440
  Mulu's adventure caves 441-2
  Mulu's show caves 440-1
  Niah National Park 429-31
  Sleeping Buddha Cave 258
  Taman Negara Perlis 205
  Tasik Chini 252, 588
  Tasik Kenyir 302
caving 33, 412
cell phones 19
  in Malaysia 597
  in Singapore 540
cemeteries
  Bukit Brown Cemetery 496
  Bukit China 215
  Commonwealth Allied War Cemetery 142
  Kranji War Memorial 495
  Protestant Cemetery 156
cendol 36-8, 582
Central Market (Kota Bharu) 279, **75**, **78-9**
Central Market (Kota Kinabalu) 306
Changi 491-3
Changi Museum & Chapel 491
Changi Village 491-3
char kway teow 38
Cheah Kongsi 158
Cheng Ho Cultural Museum 214
Cheng Hoon Teng Temple 214
Cheong Fatt Tze Mansion 159

Cherating 257-60, **259**
children, travel with 61, 593-4, 609-10
Chiling Waterfall 101
Chinatown (George Town) 151-5, 163, 165, 167-8
Chinatown (Kuala Lumpur) 16, 51-3, 61-2, 72, 86, 89, **50-1, 16, 80**
Chinatown (Melaka City) 213-14, 217-19, 220-1
Chinatown (Singapore) 483-5, 516-17, 520-2, 528-9, 534-5, **482-3**
Chinatown Wet Market 67
Chinese Heritage Museum 229
Chinese New Year 22, 35
Chinese opera 576
Chinese people 563
Chingay 22
Chow Kit 55-7, **56-7**
churches
    Changi Museum & Chapel 491
    Church of the Visitation 111
    St Andrew's Cathedral 483
    St Michael's & All Angels Church 339
    St Paul's Church 212
    St Peter's Church 215
    Wesley Church 111
cinema 577-8
civets 268
Clan Jetties 156
clanhouses 151-3, 158
Clarke Quay 477
classes, see courses & classes
climate 18, 22-3, see also individual regions
    Brunei 454
    Malaysia 594
    Singapore 473
Clock Tower 202
coffee (kopi) 583
coffee shops (kopi tiams) 39, 581
Colonial District 476-83, 515-16, 519-20, 527-8, 533-4, **478-9**
Commonwealth Allied War Cemetery 142
Confucianism 570-1
consulates
    Malaysia 594
    Singapore 538
contemporary art 21, 578
costs 18, 471, 538, 592, 594

courses & classes
    batik 59, 89, 250, 258, 276-7
    cooking 36, 59, 159, 177, 215-16, 273-6, 389, 513
    gamelan 59
    horse-riding 258
    language 59
    meditation 59
    music & dance 59-60
    pewtersmithing 59
    surfing 249, 257
    yoga 58, 159, 513
crafts 21, 577, see also markets, shopping
credit cards 595
cruises, see boat trips
culture 562-8
currency 18
    Brunei 471
    Malaysia 595-6
    Singapore 539-40
curries 580
customs regulations
    Malaysia 594
    Singapore 537
cycling, see also mountain biking
    Melaka City 216
    Malaysia 601-2

D
dance 59-60, 88, 533, 575-6
dangers 596-7, 603
Danum Valley Conservation Area 9, 354-6, **8**
Dark Cave 99
Dayak people 564-5
Dayang, Pulau 239
Deepavali 23, 35
deer 271
Deer Park 55
Deerland 271
Dempsey Hill 493
dengue fever 606-7
desserts 395, 582
diarrhoea, traveller's 607
Din Tai Fung 520
disabilities, travellers with
    Malaysia 598
    Singapore 541
diving 6, 28, **508**, see also snorkelling
    Bandar Labuan 375
    costs 34
    health 608
    Layang Layang 336-7
    Mabul 361-2

planning 33-4
    Pulau Aur 239
    Pulau Dayang 239
    Pulau Kapas 293-4
    Pulau Langkawi 190-1
    Pulau Lankayan 347-8
    Pulau Mantanani 336
    Pulau Pemanggil 239
    Pulau Perhentian 283-5, 287
    Pulau Redang 292-3
    Pulau Sibu 238
    Pulau Tinggi 238
    Pulau Tioman 244-5
    Semporna Archipelago 359-61
    Sipadan 6, 359-61, **3, 7**
    Tunku Abdul Rahman National Park 320-2
dolphins 405, 407, 498
Dr Ho Eng Hui 222
Dr Sun Yat Sen's Penang Base 154
Dragon Boat Festival 22-3
drama 575-6
drinking water 607
drinks 584
driving, see car travel
drugs 471, 595
Durian Perangin 188
durians 583

E
East Coast Park 489
East India Company 553-4
Eastern & Oriental Hotel 163, 166
economy 550, 559-60
ecotourism
    accommodation 300, 335, 351, 356, 436
    food 314
    sights 343-4
    tour operators 295, 311
electricity 538, 593, 594
elephants 239, 270-1, **505**
embassies
    Malaysia 594
    Singapore 538
emergencies 19, 471, 613
Emergency, the 555, 557
endangered species 344, 415, 586, 589
Endau 252
Endau-Rompin National Park 239-41, **240**
environmental issues 270, 585-90

Esplanade – Theatres on the Bay 481
events 22-3
exchange rates 19
Expedition Robinson 237
EZ-Link card 546

F
fax services 597
festivals 22-3, 514
    food 390
    Hindu 16, 571
    Islamic 570
film 577-8
fireflies 108, 257, 300
Fish Cave (Gua Ikan) 282
fish heads, steamed 38
fishing
    Cherating 257
    Taman Negara 262
    Tasik Kenyir 302
folk medicine 610
food 35-9, 579-84, 594, see also individual foods & regions
    cooking courses 36, 59, 159, 177, 215-16, 273-6, 389, 513
    desserts 395, 582
    language 612-13
    street 6
    tours 60
Forestry Research Institute of Malaysia (FRIM) 100
forts
    Fort Canning Park 481
    Fort Cornwallis 156
    Fort Siloso 498-9
    Fort Sylvia 422
Fraser's Hill (Bukit Fraser) 102-4, **103**
FRIM (Forestry Research Institute of Malaysia) 100
fruit 583

G
Galeri Pengangkutan Air 253
Galeri Petronas 47
Galeri Sultan Abdul Halim 202
Galeria Perdana 190
galleries, see also museums
    Bank Negara Malaysia Museum & Art Gallery 57
    Cathay Gallery 489
    Galeri Petronas 47

galleries *continued*
Gillman Barracks 498
KL City Gallery 52
Melaka City 214
National Visual Art
Gallery 58
State Art Gallery 202
gardens, *see also* parks &
reserves
Botanical Gardens 158
Lake Gardens Park (Tun
Abdul Razak Heritage
Park) 54-5
Lake Gardens
(Seremban) 109
National Orchid Garden
489
Singapore Botanic
Gardens 488-9
Taman Botani 104
Tun Abdul Razak
Heritage Park (Lake
Gardens Park) 54-5
Gardens by the Bay 477-81
gay travellers 538-9, 595
Brunei 471
Kuala Lumpur 87
Melaka City 223
Singapore 532
Gaya, Pulau 320
Genting 250
Genting Highlands 101
Genting Skyway 101
George Town 10, 151-76,
152-3, 10, 21
accommodation 162-7
Chinatown 151-5, 163,
165, 167-8
courses 159
drinking 171-2
entertainment 171-2
festivals & events 160,
162
food 167-71
internet access 174
internet resources 174-5
Little India 155-7, 166,
168-9
medical services 174
money 174
postal services 174
shopping 172-4
sights 151-9
tourist information 174-5
tours 159-60, 161, **161**
travel agencies 174

travel to/from 175-6
travel within 176
walking tours 161, **161**
George Town World
Heritage Inc.
Headquarters 156
Geylang 489
Geylang Serai Wet Market
491
giardiasis 607
gibbons, white-handed 205
Gillman Barracks 498
golf
Alor Gajah 225-6
Gopeng 125
Kemasik 301
Santubong Peninsula
406
Singapore 512
Tioman 247
Gomantong Caves 348,
350
Gombak 100-1
Gopeng 125-6
Gua Charas 258
Gua Ikan (Fish Cave) 282
Gua Kelam 205
Gua Wang Burma 205
guesthouses 592
Gunung Bengoh 412-13
Gunung Gading National
Park 413-14
Gunung Kinabalu, *see* Kina-
balu National Park
Gunung Ledong National
Park 235
Gunung Mulu National Park
438-44, **32, 503**
Gunung Raya 189
Gunung Stong State Park
282

H
Hainan Temple 155
Hainanese chicken-rice
38, **81**
handicrafts, 21, 577, *see
also individual crafts*
hantu jarang gigi (snaggle-
toothed ghost) 241
Haw Par Villa 497
hawker stalls
George Town 170, **37**
Johor Bahru 232
Kota Kinabalu 316
Kuala Lumpur 66, 71,
72, 83
Melaka City 220
Singapore 522
Tawau 365

health 606-10
diving 608
environmental hazards
608-9
infectious diseases
606-7
language 613
malaria 607
traditional medicine 610
vaccinations 606
heat stroke 608
helicopter flights 191
Heritage District 229
Hidden Valley (Lost World)
412-13
hiking, *see* trekking,
walking
hill stations
Bukit Larut 146
Cameron Highlands 13,
126-33, **128, 13**
Fraser's Hill (Bukit
Fraser) 102-4, **103**
Genting Highlands 101
Hinduism 571
history 551-61
Asian financial crisis
559-60
Badawi, Abdullah 560
Borneo 554-6
British rule 555-6
Dutch rule 553
East India Company
553-4
Emergency, the 555, 557
Ibrahim, Anwar 558, 559
Mahathir, Mohamad 558
Malay independence 557
Malaya, Federation of
556-7
Melaka empire 552-3
Napoleon 553-4
Portuguese rule 553
WWII 556
hitching 603
holidays
Brunei 471
Malaysia 596
Singapore 540-1
Holland Village 493
home stays 592
George Town 166
Kelantan 282
Kota Bharu 277
Penang 181
Semporna Archipelago
359
Sungai Kinabatangan
352
Temerloh 271

hostels 592
hot springs, *see also* spas
Air Hangat 188-9
Sabah 331
Tawau Hills Park 367
hotels 592-3
House of Yeap Chor Ee 156
Hui, Dr Ho Eng 222
Hulu Klang 100
Hungry Ghost Festival 23
Hutan Rekreasi Air Keroh
225

I
Iban (Sea Dayak) people
564
Ibrahim, Anwar 558, 559
Images of Singapore 500
Imbi Market 66
immigration 600
Indian people 563
indigenous peoples
Bidayuh 564
Iban (Sea Dayak) 564
Minangkabau 109
Orang Asli 240, 252, 261,
269, 563-4
Penan 447
insurance
car 603
health 539
travel 595
internet access 595,
*see also individual
locations*
internet resources 19, 548,
*see also individual
locations*
food & drink 575
health 606, 607
Ipoh 118-25, **120-1**
Iskandar Development
Region 229
Islam 552, 568, 569-70
Islamic Arts Museum 53
Islamic Museum 209
Istana Abu Bakar 252
Istana Lama 112
Istana Permai 252
itineraries 24-7, **24-7**
Kuala Lumpur 53
Singapore 481

J
Jaan 519
jackfruit 583
Jalan Alor 71
Jalan Labi 467
Jalan Petaling 51

Jek Yap 129
Jerantut 265-7, **266**
Jerejak, Pulau 180
Johor 41, 227-41, **228**
　accommodation 227
　activities 227
　climate 227
　highlights 228
　travel seasons 227
Johor Bahru 228-34, **230**
Johor National Parks
　Corporation 239
Jonker's Walk Night Market
　15, 222, 223, **15**
Juara 249-50
Jurong Bird Park 498

K

Kadazan-Dusun people 565
kain songket (fabric with
　gold thread) 577
Kampong Glam 487-8,
　524-5, 529, 535, **486**
Kampung Ayer 9, 456, **8**
Kampung Baru 55-7, **56-7**
Kampung Baru Mosque 57
Kampung Baru Night
　Market 83
Kampung Benuk 408
Kampung Chitty 215
kampung houses 575
Kampung Kling Mosque
　214
Kampung Paya 250
Kampung Pulau Betong
　181-2
Kangar 204-5
Kapalai 363
Kapas, Pulau 293-4
Kapit 422-5, **424**
Katong 489-91
kayaking 34
　Cherating 257
　Pulau Tioman 249
Kedah 41, 183-206, **184**
　accommodation 183
　climate 183
　food 183
　highlights 184
　travel seasons 183
kek lapis (striped layer
　cakes) 395
Kek Lok Si Temple 157-8
Kelabit Highlands 12,
　444-51
Kelantan 273-82, **274-5**
　accommodation 272
　climate 272
　food 272

highlights 274-5
travel seasons 272
Kemasik 301
Kenong Rimba State Park
　268-9
kerabu beromak 38
Khoo Kongsi 151-3
Kinabalu National Park
　13, 322-30, **323**, **329**,
　13, **511**
　accommodation 328-30
　climbing trails 325-7
　food 330
　permits 323-4
　planning 323-5
　travel to/from 330
　via ferrata 327
　walking 327-8
Kinabatangan Orang-utan
　Conservation Project
　(KOCP) 349
Kinabatangan River 348-53
Kinta Heritage 129
Kinta Valley Heritage
　Loop 126
kite festival 277
kites 577
KL Bird Park 53
KL City Gallery 52
KL Festival 60
KL Train Station 55
Klang 106-7
Klang Valley 105-7
KLIA (Kuala Lumpur
　International Airport)
　19, 91, 600
kongsi (Chinese
　clanhouses) 151-3, 158
kopi (coffee) 583
kopi tiams (coffee shops)
　39, 581
Kota Belud 333-4
Kota Bharu 14, 273-81,
　276, **281**, **14**
Kota Kinabalu 306-20,
　308
　accommodation 312-14
　activities 306-11
　drinking 316-17
　emergencies 317
　entertainment 316-17
　food 314-16
　internet access 317
　medical services 317
　money 317-18
　postal services 318
　shopping 317
　sights 306-11
　tourist information 313
　tours 311-12

travel to/from 318-19
travel within 319-20
Kota Kuala Kedah 204
Kota Mahsuri 189-90
Kranji War Memorial 495
Kris Cave 282
Kuah 185, 192-3, 196
Kuala Belait 468
Kuala Gandah Elephant
　Conservation Centre
　270-1
Kuala Kangsar 140-2, **141**
Kuala Kedah 204
Kuala Kubu Bharu 101
Kuala Lipis 267-8
Kuala Lumpur 40, 46-96,
　48-9, **56-7**, **63**
　accommodation 46,
　60-6
　activities 58
　Bangsar Baru 65-6, 83-4,
　86, 89-90, **84**
　Brickfields 53-5, 65-6,
　83, 89-90, **54**
　children, travel with 61
　Chinatown 16, 51-3,
　61-2, 72, 86, 89, **50-1**,
　16, **80**
　climate 46
　courses 59-60
　drinking 84-6
　entertainment 86-8
　festivals & events 60
　food 46, 66-7, 70-2, 83-4
　Golden Triangle 47, 51,
　62-4, 66-7, 70-1, 85-6,
　88-9, **68-9**
　highlights 48-9
　history 47
　internet access 90
　internet recources 91
　itineraries 53
　Little India 55, 57, 64, 72
　medical services 91
　money 91
　postal services 91
　shopping 88-90
　sights 47, 51-8
　Titiwangsa 58, **59**
　tourist information 91
　tours 60
　travel seasons 46
　travel to/from 91-3
　travel within 93-6, **95**
Kuala Lumpur International
　Airport (KLIA) 19,
　91, 600
Kuala Pilah 112-13
Kuala Selangor 107-9
Kuala Terengganu
　295-9, **296**

Kuan Yin Teng 154
Kuantan 254-7, **255**
Kubah National Park
　409-11
Kuching 11, 382-400,
　384-5, **401**, **11**
　accommodation 390-2
　activities 389
　climate 379
　courses 389
　drinking 394-5
　emergencies 397
　entertainment 395-6
　festivals & events 390
　food 392-4
　internet access 397
　medical services 397
　money 397
　postal services 397
　shopping 396
　sights 382-9
　tourist information 397-8
　tours 389-90
　travel to/from 398-9
　travel within 399-400
Kuching Wetlands National
　Park 406-7
Kudat 335-6

L

Labrador Nature Reserve
　497
Labrador Secret Tunnels
　497
Labuk Bay Proboscis
　Monkey Sanctuary
　345-6
Lagenda Langkawi Dalam
　Taman 185
Lahad Datu 353-4
Lake Gardens Park (Tun
　Abdul Razak Heritage
　Park) 54-5
Lake Titiwangsa 58, **59**
laksa 394, **77**, **80**
Lambir Hills National Park
　431-2
Lang Tengah, Pulau 291-2
Langkawi 10, 41, 185-200,
　184, **186-7**, **11**
　accommodation 183,
　192-6
　activities 185-90, 190-2
　climate 183
　drinking 198-9
　festivals & events 192
　food 183, 196-8
　highlights 184
　internet access 199
　internet resources 199

Langkawi *continued*
medical services 199
money 199
shopping 199
sights 185-90
tourist information 199
tours 190-2
travel seasons 183
travel to/from 199-200
travel within 200
Langkawi Bird Paradise 185
Langkawi Crocodile Farm 188
Lankayan, Pulau 347-8
language 18, 59, 566, 611-15
Layang Layang 336-7
leeches 262, 608
legal matters
Brunei 471
Malaysia 595
Singapore 539
Legoland 231
Lei Shen Gong Buddhist Temple 252
lesbian travellers 538-9, 595
Brunei 471
Kuala Lumpur 87
Melaka City 223
Singapore 532
Limbang 451-3
literature 574, *see also* books
Little India (George Town) 155-7, 166, 168-9
Little India (Kuala Lumpur) 55, 57, 64, 72
Little India (Melaka City) 215
Little India (Singapore) 485-7, 517-18, 525, 529, 535, **486**
Little Penang Street Market 173
lizards, monitor 248, 257, 320, 321
Loke Mansion 57
longhouses 15, 565, 593
Annah Rais Longhouse 408-9
Batang Rejang 421, 423, 425
Bawang Assan Longhouse Village 417-18
Pulau Kapas 294

Map Pages **000**
Photo Pages **000**

Sarawak Cultural Village 404, **15**
Lundu 413

M
Mabul 361-2
macaques 205, 245, 402, 461, **504**
MacRitchie Reservoir 495
Mahathir, Marina 567
Mahathir, Mohamad 558
Mahathir's Birthplace 200-1
Malabar Muslim Jama-Ath Mosque 487-8
malaria 607
Malay people 562-3
Malaya, Federation of 556-7
Malayan Railway Administration Building 55
Malaysia 46-453
accommodation 592-3
business hours 593
camping 592
climate 594
consulate 594
customs regulations 594
disabilities, travellers with 598
embassies 594
food 579-85
history 556-7, 560
holidays 596
home stays 592
legal matters 595
maps 595
money 595-6
politics 548-9, 566-7
population 548
postal services 596
tourist information 597-8
tours 604
travel to/from 600-1
travel within 601-5
visas 598
volunteering 598
women travellers 599
work 599
Maliau Basin Conservation Area 367-9
Malihom 182
malls
George Town 173-4
Johor Bahru 232-3
Kuala Lumpur 88-90
Melaka City 223
Singapore 533-4, 535-7
Mantanani, Pulau 336

Manukan, Pulau 320
maps 595
Marang 300-1
Mariamnan Hindu Temple 252
Marina Bay 476-83, 520, 533-4
Maritime Experiential Museum 498
Maritime Museum & Naval Museum 213
markets 6-7, **14**
Bazaar Baru Chow Kit 67, **73**
Central Market (Kota Bharu) 279, **75**, **78-9**
Central Market (Kota Kinabalu) 306
Central Market (Kuala Lumpur) 89
Imbi Market 66
Jalan Petaling 51
Jonker's Walk Night Market **15**, 222, 223, **15**
Kampung Baru Night Market 83
Kuala Lumpur 67
Little Penang Street Market 173
Pulau Langkawi night market 197
Sibu Central Market 419
Masjid Jamek 51
Masjid Kampung Hulu 214
Masjid Kapitan Keling 157
Masjid Negara 55
Masjid Negeri 254
Masjid Zahir 202
Mass Rapid Transit (MRT) 546
massage
Batu Ferringhi 177
Kuala Lumpur 58
Melaka City 216
Ranau 331
Singapore 512
Mataking 363
Matang Mangrove Forest Reserve 146-7
Matang Wildlife Centre 410-11
Maxwell Rd Hawker Centre 521
McMurtrie, Narelle 194
measures
Malaysia 593
Singapore 540
media 578
medical services 606, *see also individual locations*

medicine, traditional & folk 610
Melaka 41, 207-26, **208**
accommodation 207
climate 207
food 207
highlights 208
travel seasons 207
Melaka City 209-25, **210-11**
accommodation 217-20
activities 215-16
Chinatown 213-14, 217-19, 220-1
drinking 222
emergencies 223
entertainment 222-3
festivals & events 216
food 220-2
internet access 224
medical services 224
money 224
postal services 224
shopping 223
sights 209, 212-15
tourist information 223-4
tours 216
travel to/from 224
travel within 224-5
Melaka Zoo 225
Menara Alor Star 201-2
Menara Taming Sari 216
Merang 299-300
Merdeka Square 52
Mersing 234-7, **236**
Mesilau Nature Resort 330-1
metalwork 577
Minangkabau people 109
Miri 432-8, **434**
mobile phones 19
Malaysia 597
Singapore 540
money 18, 19
Brunei 465, 471
Malaysia 595-6
Singapore 539-40
moneychangers 596
monkeys 257, 268, 345-6, *see also individual species*
mosques
Abu Bakar Mosque 252
Acheen St Mosque 155
Kampung Baru Mosque 57
Kampung Kling Mosque 214

Malabar Muslim Jama-Ath Mosque 487-8
Masjid Jamek 51
Masjid Kampung Hulu 214
Masjid Kapitan Keling 157
Masjid Negara 55
Masjid Negeri 254
Masjid Zahir 202
Sultan Abdullah Mosque 252
Sultan Abu Bakar Mosque 229
Sultan Mosque 487
motorcycle travel 602-3
mountain biking 311, 494, 544, see also cycling
mountain climbing
costs 28, 31
Gunung Mulu Summit 442
Mt Kinabalu 13, 322-30, **323**, **329**, **13**, **511**
planning 31-3
Pulau Berhala 349
Mr Raja 119
MRT (Mass Rapid Transit) 546
Mt Kinabalu, see Kinabalu National Park
Muar 234
Mukut 251
museums 21, see also galleries
Architecture Museum 209
Asian Civilisations Museum 477
Baba House 483
Baba-Nonya Heritage Museum 214
Bank Negara Malaysia Museum & Art Gallery 57
Brunei Museum 460
Cat Museum 389
Changi Museum & Chapel 491
Cheng Ho Cultural Museum 214
Cheong Fatt Tze Mansion 159
Chinese Heritage Museum 229
Chinese History Museum 382
Dr Sun Yat Sen's Penang Base 154
Galeri Pengangkutan Air 253
Galeri Sultan Abdul Halim 202

Galeria Perdana 190
House of Yeap Chor Ee 156
Images of Singapore 500
Islamic Arts Museum 53
Islamic Museum 209
Laman Padi 186-7
Mahathir's Birthplace 200-1
Maritime Experiential Museum 498
Maritime Museum & Naval Museum 213
Museum Sultan Abu Bakar 253
Muzium Diraja 202
Muzium Kota Kayang 204-5
Muzium Negeri (Alor Setar) 200
Muzium Negeri Perlis 205
Muzium Negeri (Seremban) 109-10
Muzium Perak 142
Muzium Rakyat 209
National Museum 53-4
National Museum of Singapore 476-7
National Textiles Museum 52-3
NUS Museums 497
Orang Asli Museum 100-1
P Ramlee House 158-9
Paddy Museum 204
Penang Museum 155-6
Peranakan Museum 477
Petrosains 57
Pinang Peranakan Mansion 155
Royal Abu Bakar Museum 229
Sultanate Palace 212

N
nasi lemak 39, 74, 122
National Front (Barisan Nasional) 548, 558, 560
National Monument 54
National Museum 53-4

National Museum of Singapore 476-7
National Orchid Garden 489
national parks, see parks & reserves
National Planetarium 55
National Textiles Museum 52-3
National Visual Art Gallery 58
Negeri Sembilan 40, 97-115, **98**
accommodation 97
climate 97
food 97
highlights 98
history 99
travel seasons 97
newspapers
Malaysia 593
Singapore 540
Niah National Park 429-31
Night Market (Kota Bharu) 278
Night Safari 17, 494
Nipah 251
noodles 580, **76**

O
opening hours
Malaysia 593
Singapore 537
opera, Chinese 576
Orang Asli people 240, 252, 261, 269, 563-4
Orang Asli Museum 100-1
orang-utans 10, 333, 343-4, 345, 349, 407-8, **10**, **504**
Orchard Road 488-9, 518, 526-7, 529-30, 535-6, **490**
Oriental Village 187-8

P
P Ramlee House 158-9
Paddy Museum 204
Pahang 42, 242-71, **243**, **14**
accommodation 242
climate 242
food 242
highlights 243
travel seasons 242
palaces
Ampang Tinggi Palace 109
Istana Abu Bakar 252

Istana Alam Shah 106
Istana Iskandanah 140
Istana Lama 112
Istana Maziah 295
Istana Nurul Iman 459
Istana Permai 252
palm oil 586-7
Pangkor, Pulau 134-40, **135**, **137**
Pantai Tengah 190-1, **190**
parks & reserves 31, see also gardens
Bako National Park 400-4
Batang Ai National Park 416-17
Bukit Gemok Forest Reserve 364
Bukit Nanas Forest Reserve 47
Bukit Timah Nature Reserve 494
Cape Rachado Forest Reserve 113, 114
Danum Valley Conservation Area 9, 354-6, **8**
East Coast Park 489
Endau-Rompin National Park 239-41, **240**
Forestry Research Institute of Malaysia (FRIM) 100
Fort Canning Park 481
Gunung Gading National Park 413-14
Gunung Legan National Park 235
Gunung Mulu National Park 438-44, **32**, **503**
Gunung Stong State Park 282
Kenong Rimba State Park 268-9
Kinabalu National Park 13, 322-30, **323**, **329**, **13**, **511**
Kubah National Park 409-11
Kuching Wetlands National Park 406-7
Lambir Hills National Park 431-2
MacRitchie Reservoir 495
Matang Mangrove Forest Reserve 146-7
Mesilau Nature Resort 330-1
Niah National Park 429-31
Penang National Park 179-80

parks & reserves *continued*
　Royal Belum State Park 147-8
　Similajau National Park 427-9
　Southern Ridges 495-6
　Tabin Wildlife Reserve 356-7
　Talang-Satang National Park 415-17
　Taman Negara 12, 260-5, **261**, 12
　Taman Negara Perlis 205-6
　Taman Wetland 104
　Tanjung Datu National Park 415
　Tawau Hills Park 367
　Tunku Abdul Rahman National Park 320-2
　Wind Cave Nature Reserve 411-12
Pasir Ris 491-3
passports 600
Pavilion KL 88
Pekan 252-4, **253**
Pelabuhan Klang 106-7
Pemanggil, Pulau 239
Penan people 447
Penan villages 452
Penang 41, 149-82, **150**, *see also* George Town
　accommodation 149
　architecture 156
　climate 149
　food 149, **76**, **77**
　highlights 150
　history 150-1
　travel seasons 149
Penang Butterfly Farm 180
Penang Hill 157
Penang Museum 155-6
Penang National Park 179-80
Penarik 300
Penarik Firefly Sanctuary 300
Peradayan Forest Reserve 470
Perak 40, 116-48, **117**
　accommodation 116
　climate 116
　food 116
　highlights 117
　history 118
　travel seasons 116

Map Pages **000**
Photo Pages **000**

Peranakan Museum 477
Peranakan people 564
Perhentian, Pulau 9, 283-91, **284**, 9
Perhentian Museum 477
Perlis 41, 204-6, **184**
　accommodation 183
　climate 183
　food 183
　highlights 184
　travel seasons 183
permits
　Kenong Rimba State Park 269
　Kinabalu National Park 323-4
　Taman Negara 260
　Upper Rejang 422
Petaling Jaya 105-6
Petronas Towers 55, 57, **81**
Petrosains 57
pewtersmithing 59
photography 596
Pinang, Pulau, *see* Penang
Pinang Peranakan Mansion 155
Ping Anchorage 295
planning, *see also individual regions*
　budget 18, 471, 538, 592, 594
　calendar of events 22-3
　caving 33
　children, travel with 61, 593-4, 609-10
　diving 33-4
　food & dining 35-9
　internet resources 19
　itineraries 24-7, 53, 481, **24-7**
　Malaysia, Singapore & Brunei basics 18-19
　Malaysia, Singapore & Brunei's regions 40-3
　mountain climbing 31-3
　rock climbing 31-3
　snorkelling 33-4
　surfing 34
　travel seasons 18, 22-3
　trekking 29-30
politics 548-9, 550, 562-8, 566-7
Pom Pom 363
population 548, 549-50
Port Dickson 113-15
Porta de Santiago 209, 212
postal services, *see also individual locations*
　Brunei 465
　Malaysia 596

Singapore 540
proboscis monkeys 345-6
Protestant Cemetery 156
public holidays
　Brunei 471
　Malaysia 596
　Singapore 540-1
Publika 90
Pudu Market 67
Pulau Aur 239
Pulau Banggi 336
Pulau Besar (Johor) 237-8
Pulau Besar (Melaka) 225-6
Pulau Carey 107
Pulau Dayang 239
Pulau Gaya 320
Pulau Jerejak 180
Pulau Kapas 293-4
Pulau Lang Tengah 291-2
Pulau Langkawi 10, 41, 185-200, **184**, **186-7**, 11
　accommodation 183, 192-6
　activities 185-90, 190-2
　climate 183
　drinking 198-9
　festivals & events 192
　food 183, 196-8
　highlights 184
　internet access 199
　internet resources 199
　medical services 199
　money 199
　shopping 199
　sights 185-90
　tourist information 199
　tours 190-2
　travel seasons 183
　travel to/from 199-200
　travel within 200
Pulau Lankayan 347-8
Pulau Mantanani 336
Pulau Manukan 320
Pulau Pangkor 134-40, **135**, **137**
Pulau Pemanggil 239
Pulau Perhentian 9, 283-91, **284**, 9
Pulau Rawa 238-9
Pulau Redang 292-3
Pulau Sapi 320
Pulau Satang 416
Pulau Selirong 470
Pulau Sibu 238
Pulau Sipadan 6, 359-61, **3**, **7**
Pulau Sulug 321
Pulau Talang-Talang 416

Pulau Tinggi 238
Pulau Tioman 14, 243-51, **244**, 14
　accommodation 246-51
　diving & snorkelling 244-5
　drinking 246-51
　food 246-51
　walking 245-6
Pulau Ubin 494
puppetry, shadow 575, 577
Putrajaya 104-5

Q
Quays, the 477, 515-16, 520, 528, 533-4, **478-9**

R
rabies 596, 607
radio
　Malaysia 593
　Singapore 540
Raffles, Stamford 554
rafflesias 413-14, **510**
rafting 34, **32**
Rainforest World Music Festival 23
Raja, Mr 119
Ramadan 36, 457
Raptor Watch Festival 114
Raub 269-70
Rawa, Pulau 238-9
Razak, Najib 560
Redang, Pulau 292-3
refunds 596
Regatta Lepa 360
religion 549, 552, 569-73
reptiles, *see individual species*
reserves, *see* parks & reserves, wildlife sanctuaries & reserves
resthouses 593
rhinoceros, Sumatran 239, **506-7**
rice 580
river cruises, *see* boat trips
River Safari 495
Robertson Quay 477
rock climbing 31-3, 349
roti canai 38, **37**
Royal Abu Bakar Museum 229
Royal Belum State Park 147-8
Royal Pahang Polo Club 252
rubber trees 140

S

Sabah 42, 304-78, **305**
  accommodation 304
  climate 304
  food 304
  highlights 305
  history 554-5
  travel seasons 304
safety 596-7, 603
sailing 34
Salang 248-9
salt licks 448
sambal 580
Sandakan 337-43, **338**
Sandakan Archipelago 347-8
Santubong Peninsula 404-6
Sapi, Pulau 320
Sapulot 371-2
Sarawak 42, 379-453, **380-1**
  accommodation 379
  climate 379
  food 379
  highlights 380-1
  history 382, 554-5
  travel seasons 379
Sarawak Cultural Village 404-5, **15**
Satang, Pulau 416
sculpture 485
Sea Dayak (Iban) people 564
Sekayu Falls 302
Selangor 40, 97-115, **98**
  accommodation 97
  climate 97
  food 97
  highlights 98
  history 99
  travel seasons 97
Selirong, Pulau 470
Sematan 414-15
Semenggoh Nature Reserve 407-8
Semporna 357-9, **358**
Semporna Archipelago 359-63
Sentosa Island 498-500, 518-19, 527, 530-1, **499**
Sepilok 343-7, **344**
Sepilok Orang-Utan Rehabilitation Centre (SORC) 10, 343-4, **10**, **504**
Seremban 109-112, **110**
Seria 467-8
Seribuat Archipelago 237-9

shadow puppetry 575, 577
Shah Alam 106
shopping 21, see also malls, markets
  arts & crafts 89, 90, 172-3
  batik 59, 89, 172, 250
  electronics 89
  fine art 90
  language 613
  shrines 189-90
siat 38
Sibu, Pulau 238
Sibu 417-21, **418**
Sibu Central Market 419
silat (Malaysian martial art) 576
Similajau National Park 427-9
Singamata 361
Singapore 43, 473-546, **474-5**, **492**
  accommodation 473, 515-19, 537, 538
  activities 500, 512-13
  addresses 476
  budget 538
  business hours 537
  CBD 483-5, 520-2, 528-9, **482-3**
  Chinatown 483-5, 516-17, 520-2, 528-9, 534-5, **482-3**
  climate 473
  Colonial District 476-83, 515-16, 519-20, 527-8, 533-4, **478-9**
  consulates 538
  courses 513
  culture 549-50
  customs regulations 537
  disabilities, travellers with 541
  drinking 527-31
  electricity 538
  embassies 538
  emergencies 538
  entertainment 531-3
  festivals & events 514-15
  food 473, 488, 519-27, 538
  Geylang 489
  highlights 474-5
  history 476
  holidays 540-1
  internet access 538-9
  internet resources 537
  itineraries 481
  Kampong Glam 487-8, 524-5, 529, 535, **486**

Katong 489-91
  language 615
  legal matters 539
  Little India 485-7, 517-18, 525, 529, 535, **486**
  Marina Bay 476-83, 520, 533-4
  medical services 539
  money 539-40
  Mass Rapid Transit (MRT) 546
  Orchard Road 488-9, 518, 526-7, 529-30, 535-6, **490**
  politics 567-8
  postal services 540
  Pulau Ubin 494
  Quays, the 477, 515-16, 520, 528, 533-4, **478-9**
  Sentosa Island 498-500, 518-19, 527, 530-1, **495**
  shopping 533-7
  sights 476-500
  teahouses 530
  telephone services 540
  Tiong Bahru 488
  tipping 540
  tourist information 541
  tours 513-14
  travel seasons 473
  travel to/from 541-4
  travel within 544-6
  visas 541
  walking tours 501, **501**
Singapore Botanic Gardens 488-9
Singapore Hotel Association 515
Singapore Science Centre 497
Singapore Tourist Pass 546
Singapore Zoo 17, 493, **17**
Singlish 615
Sipadan, Pulau 6, 359-61, **3**, **7**
Sleeping Buddha Cave 258
Snake Temple 181
snakes 609, **12**
snorkelling 9, 28, see also diving
  Layang Layang 336-7
  planning 33-4
  Pulau Kapas 293-4
  Pulau Langkawi 190-1
  Pulau Mantanani 336
  Pulau Manukan 320
  Pulau Pangkor 136
  Pulau Perhentian 9, 283-5

Pulau Redang 292-3
Pulau Tioman 244-5
Semporna Archipelago 359-61
Sipadan 359-61
Songs of the Sea 498-9
spas, see also hot springs
  Kuala Lumpur 58, 60
  Melaka City 216
  Pulau Langkawi 187, 188-9
  Singapore 512
spelunking, see caving
squirrels 245, 328
Sri Mahamariamman Temple 51
Sri Mariamman Temple (George Town) 156-7
Sri Mariamman Temple (Singapore) 484, **2-3**
Sri Menanti 112
Sri Poyatha Venayagar Moorthi Temple 214
Sri Raja Mariamman Devasthanam 229
Sri Veeramakaliamman Temple 485
St Paul's Church 212
St Peter's Church 215
Stadthuys 209
State Art Gallery 202
state parks, see parks & reserves
Stepping Stone Cave 282
Suffolk House 159
Sultan Abdul Samad Building 52
Sultan Abdullah Mosque 252
Sultan Abu Bakar Mosque 229
Sultan Mosque 487
Sultanate Palace 212
Sulug, Pulau 321
Sumatran rhinoceros 239, **506-7**
Sungai Kinabatangan 348-53
sup torpedo 38
surfing 34
  Cherating 257
  Juara 249
  Teluk Chempedak 257
sustainable travel
  accommodation 300, 335, 351, 356, 436
  food 314
  sights 343-4
  tour operators 295, 311
swans 419

sweets 395, 582
swimming holes
  Endau-Rompin National Park 240
  Pulau Tioman 246
  Taman Negara 262
Sze Ya Temple 52, **16**

T

Tabin Wildlife Reserve 356-7
Taiping 142-6, **143**, **144**
Talang-Satang National Park 415-17
Talang-Talang, Pulau 416
Taman Alam Kuala Selangor Nature Park 108
Taman Mini Malaysia/ Asean 225
Taman Negara 12, 260-5, **261**, **12**
Taman Negara Perlis 205-6
Tanah Rata 129-33, **131**
Tanjung Bidara 226
Tanjung Datu National Park 415
Tanjung Tuan Forest Reserve 113
Taoism 570-1
tapir 269
Tarawe, John 446
Tasik Chini 252, 588
Tasik Kenyir 301-3
Tatt Khalsa Diwan Gurdwara 57
Tawau 363-7, **364**
Tawau Hills Park 367
taxes 596
taxis, long-distance 604
tea drinking 583
tea plantations
  Boh Sungei Palas Tea Estate 127, **13**
  Cameron Bharat Tea Plantation 127
teahouses 530
Tekek 246-7
Telaga Tujuh 193
telephone services 19
  Malaysia 597
  Singapore 540
Teluk Bahang 179-80
Teluk Chempedak 257
Teluk Kumbar 182
Teluk Nipah 136-7, **137**

Temburong District 468-72
Temerloh 270, 271
temples
  Buddha Tooth Relic Temple 484
  Cheng Hoon Teng Temple 214
  Hainan Temple 155
  Kek Lok Si Temple 157-8
  Kuan Yin Teng 154
  Lei Shen Gong Buddhist Temple 252
  Liesheng Temple 110-11
  Mariamnan Hindu Temple 252
  Sam Poh Temple 127
  Sri Mahamariamman Temple 51
  Sri Mariamman Temple (George Town) 156-7
  Sri Mariamman Temple (Singapore) 484, **2-3**
  Sri Poyatha Venayagar Moorthi Temple 214
  Sri Raja Mariamman Devasthanam 229
  Sri Tehndayuthapany Swamy 129
  Sri Veeramakaliamman Temple 485
  Sze Ya Temple 52, **16**
  Tatt Khalsa Diwan Gurdwara 57
  Thean Hou Temple 58
  Thian Hock Keng Temple 484-5
  Tumpat temple district 281-2
  Wat Siam Nikrodharam 202
Temurun Waterfall 188
Teochew Temple 158
Terengganu 294-303, **274-5**
  accommodation 272
  climate 272
  food 272
  highlights 274-5
  travel seasons 272
Terrapuri Heritage Village 300
Thaipusam 22, 99, 571, **17**
Thean Hou Temple 58
theatre 575-6
theme parks
  A'Famosa Resort 225-6
  Genting Highlands 101
  Taman Mini Malaysia/ Asean 225
  Underwater World (Pulau Langkawi) 185-6

Underwater World (Sentosa Island) 498
Universal Studios 498
Thian Hock Keng Temple 484-5
tigers 239, **17**, **505**
time 541, 597
Tinggi, Pulau 238
Tioman, Pulau 14, 243-51, **244**, **14**
  accommodation 246-51
  diving & snorkelling 244-5
  drinking 246-51
  food 246-51
  walking 245-6
Tiong Bahru 488
Titiwangsa 58, **59**
toilets 541, 597
tourist information, see also individual destinations
  Malaysia 597-8
  Singapore 541
tours 604
  adventure 60
  Cameron Highlands 129
  fishing 257
  food 60
  George Town 159-60
  Kuala Lumpur 60
  Singapore 513-14
  walking 144, 161, **144**, **161**
train travel
  Malaysia 604-5
  Singapore 542-3
travel to/from Brunei 465-6
travel to/from Malaysia 600-1
travel to/from Singapore 541-4
travel with children 61, 593-4, 609-10
travel within Malaysia 601-5
travel within Singapore 544-6
travellers cheques 596
TreeTops Lodge 436
trekking 12, 28, see also walking
  Cameron Highlands 130
  Cape Rachado Forest Reserve 113
  Danum Valley Conservation Area 9, 355
  Endau-Rompin National Park 239-41, **240**

Gunung Bengoh 412-13
Gunung Mulu Summit 442
Gunung Santubong 405
Hidden Valley (Lost World) 412-13
Kelabit Highlands 12, 448-51
Kinabalu National Park 325-7, 327-8
Maliau Basin Conservation Area 367-8
Penan villages 452
planning 29-30
Pulau Perhentian 285
Sungai Kinabatangan 350
Taman Negara 261-2
Tasik Chini 252, 588
Tringgus Bong 412-13
Tringgus 412-13
trishaws 225, 546
Tuaran 333
Tumpat temple district 281-2
Tun Abdul Razak Heritage Park (Lake Gardens Park) 54-5
Tunku Abdul Rahman National Park 320-2
turtles 257-8, 347, 359, **3**, **509**
Tutong 467
Tutong District 467-8
TV
  Malaysia 593
  Singapore 540
typhoid 607

U

Ubin, Pulau 494
Ulu Temburong National Park 470-2
Underwater World (Pulau Langkawi) 185-6
Underwater World (Sentosa Island) 498
Unesco World Heritage Site (Penang) 156
United Malays National Organisation (UMNO) 556-7
Universal Studios 498
Urban Village 55

V

vacations
  Brunei 471
  Malaysia 596
  Singpore 540-1

vaccinations 606
vegetarian & vegan travellers 39
Villa Sentosa 215
visas 19, *see also* passports
  Brunei 471
  Malaysia 598
  Singapore 541
volunteering 411, 416, 598

W

walking, *see also* trekking
  Bako National Park 402
  Kinabalu National Park 327-8
  Pulau Perhentian 285
  Pulau Tioman 245-6
  Southern Ridges 495-6
  Taman Negara 261-2
  Teluk Chempedak 257
walking tours
  George Town 161, **161**
  Singapore 501
  Taiping 144, **144**
Wat Siam Nikrodharam 202
water, drinking 607
waterfalls
  Asah Waterfall 246
  Chiling Waterfall 101

  Durian Perangin 188
  Endau-Rompin National Park 240
  Maliau Basin Conservation Area 367-8
  Sekayu Falls 302
  Tasik Chini 252, 588
  Temurun Waterfall 188
wayang kulit (shadow-puppet performances) 575
weather 18, 22-3, 594, *see also individual regions*
  Brunei 454
  Malaysia 594
  Singapore 473
weaving 577
Weber, Birgit 287
websites, *see* internet resources
weights
  Malaysia 593
  Singapore 540
Western Sarawak 400-17
white-water rafting 34, **32**
wildlife, *see individual species*, wildlife sanctuaries & reserves, zoos
wildlife sanctuaries & reserves
  Borneo Sun Bear Conservation Centre 344-5

  Butterfly Park 55
  Cherating Turtle Sanctuary 258
  Deer Park 55
  KL Bird Park 53
  Kuala Gandah Elephant Conservation Centre 270-1
  Labuk Bay Proboscis Monkey Sanctuary 345-6
  Matang Wildlife Centre 410-11
  Penarik Firefly Sanctuary 300
  Sepilok Orang-Utan Rehabilitation Centre (SORC) 10, 343-4, **10**, **504**
  Tabin Wildlife Reserve 356-7
  Taman Alam Kuala Selangor Nature Park 108
wildlife watching 29, 401-2, 407-8, *see also* birdwatching
Wind Cave Nature Reserve 411-12
women travellers
  Brunei 471
  Malaysia 599
  Singapore 541

women's health 610
women's rights 567
woodcarving 577
work 599
WWII 556
WWII Kranji War Memorial 495

Y

yachting 34
Yap Kongsi 158
yoga
  George Town 159
  Kuala Lumpur 58
  Singapore 513

Z

Zoo Negara (National Zoo) 100
zoos, *see also* wildlife sanctuaries & reserves
  Deerland 271
  Melaka Zoo 225
  Singapore Zoo 17, 493, **17**
  Zoo Negara (National Zoo) 100
  Zoo Taiping & Night Safari 142

NOTES

how to use this book

These symbols will help you find the listings you want:

◉ Sights	☞ Tours	🍷 Drinking
🏊 Beaches	🎊 Festivals & Events	☆ Entertainment
🏃 Activities	🛏 Sleeping	🛍 Shopping
🎓 Courses	✖ Eating	ℹ Information/Transport

These symbols give you the vital information for each listing:

☑ Telephone Numbers	📶 Wi-Fi Access	🚌 Bus
⊘ Opening Hours	🏊 Swimming Pool	⛴ Ferry
P Parking	🌱 Vegetarian Selection	M Metro
⊖ Nonsmoking	📋 English-Language Menu	S Subway
❄ Air-Conditioning	👪 Family-Friendly	⊖ London Tube
@ Internet Access	🐾 Pet-Friendly	🚊 Tram
		🚆 Train

Reviews are organised by author preference.

Look out for these icons:

TOP CHOICE	Our author's recommendation
FREE	No payment required
🌱	A green or sustainable option

Our authors have nominated these places as demonstrating a strong commitment to sustainability – for example by supporting local communities and producers, operating in an environmentally friendly way, or supporting conservation projects.

Map Legend

Sights
- ● Beach
- ● Buddhist
- ● Castle
- ● Christian
- ● Hindu
- ● Islamic
- ● Jewish
- ● Monument
- ● Museum/Gallery
- ● Ruin
- ● Winery/Vineyard
- ● Zoo
- ● Other Sight

Activities, Courses & Tours
- ● Diving/Snorkelling
- ● Canoeing/Kayaking
- ● Skiing
- ● Surfing
- ● Swimming/Pool
- ● Walking
- ● Windsurfing
- ● Other Activity/Course/Tour

Sleeping
- ● Sleeping
- ● Camping

Eating
- ● Eating

Drinking
- ● Drinking
- ● Cafe

Entertainment
- ● Entertainment

Shopping
- ● Shopping

Information
- ● Bank
- ● Embassy/Consulate
- ● Hospital/Medical
- @ Internet
- ● Police
- ● Post Office
- ● Telephone
- ● Toilet
- ● Tourist Information
- ● Other Information

Transport
- ● Airport
- ● Border Crossing
- ● Bus
- ●+ Cable Car/Funicular
- ● Cycling
- ● Ferry
- ● Monorail
- P Parking
- ● Petrol Station
- ● Taxi
- ● Train/Railway
- ● Tram
- M Underground Train Station
- ● Other Transport

Routes
- Tollway
- Freeway
- Primary
- Secondary
- Tertiary
- Lane
- Unsealed Road
- Plaza/Mall
- Steps
-)=(Tunnel
- Pedestrian Overpass
- Walking Tour
- Walking Tour Detour
- Path

Geographic
- ● Hut/Shelter
- ● Lighthouse
- ● Lookout
- ▲ Mountain/Volcano
- ● Oasis
- ● Park
-)(Pass
- ● Picnic Area
- ● Waterfall

Population
- ✪ Capital (National)
- ◉ Capital (State/Province)
- ● City/Large Town
- ● Town/Village

Boundaries
- ――― International
- ------ State/Province
- --- Disputed
- --- Regional/Suburb
- Marine Park
- Cliff
- Wall

Hydrography
- River, Creek
- Intermittent River
- Swamp/Mangrove
- Reef
- Canal
- Water
- Dry/Salt/Intermittent Lake
- Glacier

Areas
- Beach/Desert
- +++ Cemetery (Christian)
- ××× Cemetery (Other)
- Park/Forest
- Sportsground
- Sight (Building)
- Top Sight (Building)

Austin Bush
Eat Like a Local; Regional Specialities; Perak; Penang; Langkawi, Kedah & Perlis; Food & Drink Austin Bush came to Thailand in 1998 on a language scholarship and has remained in Southeast Asia ever since. This is his first time contributing to *Malaysia, Singapore & Brunei*, a gig he soon came to realise is quite possibly Lonely Planet's most delicious. Austin is a native of Oregon and a freelance writer and photographer who often focuses on food. Samples of his work can be seen at www.austinbushphotography.com.

Adam Karlin
Sabah, Brunei Adam thinks Borneo is like a savage garden, which may explain why he loves it truly, madly, deeply. On this trip, his second exploring Sabah (and third exploring Malaysia) for Lonely Planet, he glimpsed primates, hiked jungle mountains, held his own in expat drinking games and floated on his back down a river through virgin rainforest – a pretty good moment, that. He has written or contributed to some 30 titles for Lonely Planet.

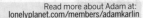

Read more about Adam at:
lonelyplanet.com/members/adamkarlin

Daniel Robinson
Sarawak Daniel has been covering Southeast Asia and its rainforests since 1989, when he researched Lonely Planet's first award-winning guides to Vietnam and Cambodia. On his many visits to Sarawak, he has developed a fondness for travelling *ulu-ulu* (way upriver) by longboat, tramping through the jungle in search of gargantuan rafflesia flowers, and slurping Sarawak laksa. Daniel, who holds a BA in Near Eastern Studies from Princeton University, writes on travel for a variety of magazines and newspapers, including *The New York Times*.

Read more about Daniel at:
lonelyplanet.com/members/daniel_robinson

OUR STORY

A beat-up old car, a few dollars in the pocket and a sense of adventure. In 1972 that's all Tony and Maureen Wheeler needed for the trip of a lifetime – across Europe and Asia overland to Australia. It took several months, and at the end – broke but inspired – they sat at their kitchen table writing and stapling together their first travel guide, *Across Asia on the Cheap*. Within a week they'd sold 1500 copies. Lonely Planet was born.

Today, Lonely Planet has offices in Melbourne, London and Oakland, with more than 600 staff and writers. We share Tony's belief that 'a great guidebook should do three things: inform, educate and amuse'.

OUR WRITERS

Simon Richmond

Coordinating Author, Plan Your Trip, Kuala Lumpur & Around, Selangor & Negeri Sembilan, Understand, Survival Guide Simon first started travelling in the region back in the early 1990s. A lot has changed since, but both Malaysia and Singapore remain among Simon's favourite destinations for their easily accessible blend of cultures, landscapes, adventure and, crucially, lip-smacking range of cuisines. This is the fourth time the award-winning travel writer and photographer has helmed Lonely Planet's *Malaysia, Singapore & Brunei* guide. He's also the coordinating author of Lonely Planet's *Kuala Lumpur, Melaka & Penang* guide as well as a shelf-load of other titles for this and other publishers.

Read more about Simon at:
lonelyplanet.com/members/simonrichmond

Cristian Bonetto

Singapore Cristian's voracious appetite was custom made for Singapore, and you'll often find him chomping his way across the island in search of edible thrills. Throw in a passion for contemporary architecture and postcolonial politics, and his soft spot for Singapore makes perfect sense. Cristian graduated from the University of Melbourne with a degree in politics and cultural studies, and his musings on food, culture and design have appeared in publications worldwide. To date, his Lonely Planet titles include *New York*, *Italy* and *Denmark*.

Celeste Brash

Melaka, Johor Celeste first visited Malaysia while she was studying at Chiang Mai University, Thailand, in 1993; she later moved to Singapore to teach English. The more of Malaysia she's visited over the years, the more she's fallen in love with it – especially the food. When not desensitising her taste buds with *sambal*, Celeste lives in Portland, Oregon with her husband and two children. She's contributed to around 40 Lonely Planet titles. Find out more about her at www.celestebrash.com.

Read more about Celeste at:
lonelyplanet.com/members/celestebrash

Joshua Samuel Brown

Pahang & Tioman Island; East Coast Islands, Kelantan & Terengganu Writer, raconteur and lifestyle gypsy Joshua Samuel Brown has been on the road semi-constantly since the last century and writing for Lonely Planet since 2006; he's also a regular contributor to www.lonelyplanet.com. His blog Snarky Tofu (josam bro.blogspot.com) contains regular updates, photos and the occasional rant.

Read more about Joshua at:
lonelyplanet.com/members/josambro

OVER PAGE MORE WRITERS

Published by Lonely Planet Publications Pty Ltd
ABN 36 005 607 983
12th edition – May 2013
ISBN 978 1 74179 847 0
© Lonely Planet 2013   Photographs © as indicated 2013
10 9 8 7 6 5 4 3 2
Printed in China

Although the authors and Lonely Planet have taken all reasonable care in preparing this book, we make no warranty about the accuracy or completeness of its content and, to the maximum extent permitted, disclaim all liability arising from its use.